# Inside the e-Pages for *The Bedford Guide*



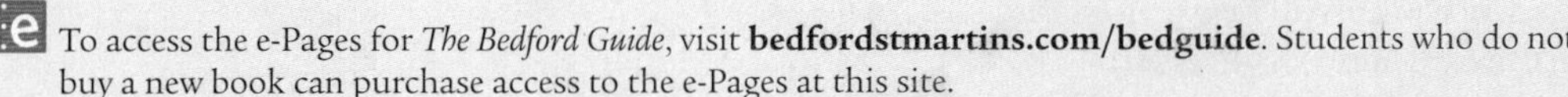
To access the e-Pages for *The Bedford Guide*, visit **bedfordstmartins.com/bedguide**. Students who do not buy a new book can purchase access to the e-Pages at this site.

TENTH EDITION

# THE Bedford Guide *for* College Writers

## *with* Reader, Research Manual, and Handbook

X. J. Kennedy | Dorothy M. Kennedy | Marcia F. Muth

BEDFORD/ST. MARTIN'S
Boston ♦ New York

**For Bedford/St. Martin's**

*Publisher:* Leasa Burton
*Senior Developmental Editor:* Martha Bustin
*Senior Production Editor:* Gregory Erb
*Senior Production Supervisor:* Steven Cestaro
*Executive Marketing Manager:* Molly Parke
*Associate Editor:* Regina Tavani
*Editorial Assistant:* Brenna Cleeland
*Copy Editor:* Hilly van Loon
*Indexer:* Constance A. Angelo
*Photo Researcher:* Naomi Kornhauser
*Senior Art Director:* Anna Palchik
*Text Design:* Lisa Buckley
*Cover Design:* Mariné Miller
*Cover Photo:* By Fuse courtesy of gettyimages®
*Composition:* Graphic World, Inc.
*Printing and Binding:* RR Donnelley and Sons

*President, Bedford/St. Martin's:* Denise B. Wydra
*Editorial Director, English and Music:* Karen S. Henry
*Director of Marketing:* Karen R. Soeltz
*Production Director:* Susan W. Brown
*Director of Rights and Permissions:* Hilary Newman



Manufactured in the United States of America.

8 7 6 5 4
f e d c

*For information, write:* Bedford/St. Martin's, 75 Arlington Street, Boston, MA 02116 (617-399-4000)

ISBN 978-1-4576-3076-7 (paperback Student Edition)
ISBN 978-1-4576-3104-7 (hardcover Student Edition)
ISBN 978-1-4576-4904-2 (loose-leaf Student Edition)

**Acknowledgments**

Acknowledgments and copyrights are continued at the back of the book on pages A-59–A-62, which constitute an extension of the copyright page. It is a violation of the law to reproduce these selections by any means whatsoever without the written permission of the copyright holder.

# Preface

## TO THE INSTRUCTOR

The tenth edition of *The Bedford Guide for College Writers* gives students all the tools they need to succeed as writers, especially in the rapidly changing times in which we now live and write. Whether their writing class meets on campus or online, students benefit from qualities integral to *The Bedford Guide*'s enduring success—clear and succinct instruction, thorough coverage with a flexible organization, and frequent opportunities for active learning, engaging students with what is presented. The tenth edition extends active learning into the online environment, offering assignable e-Pages. These videos, audio segments, and photo essays take advantage of what the Web can do. All aspects of this new edition of *The Bedford Guide*—from its updated research manual to its new student and professional readings and visuals—are designed with one overarching goal: to help students to become the confident, resourceful, and *independent* writers they will need to be.

Several key interrelated ideas have shaped this book from the beginning. First, *students learn best by doing. The Bedford Guide* therefore includes an exceptional number of opportunities for practice and self-assessment. Throughout the book, we intersperse class-tested "Learning by Doing" activities and assignments in a helpful rhythm with concise instruction and models of writing. Students have frequent opportunities to apply what they have learned and become comfortable with each step in the process as they go along.

Second, we intend *The Bedford Guide for College Writers* to be an effective, engaging text that gives students *everything they need to write well—all in one flexible book.* Written and developed as four books in one, it offers a process-oriented rhetoric, a provocative thematic reader, an up-to-date research manual, and a comprehensive handbook. *The Bedford Guide* gives students all the tools they need to succeed as writers.

Most important, the focus of the book is *building transferable skills.* Recognizing that the college composition course may be one of a student's last classes with in-depth writing instruction, we have made every effort to ensure that *The Bedford Guide* develops writers able to meet future challenges. It offers supportive, step-by-step guidance; "Why

Writing Matters" features; a full chapter on "Strategies for Future Writing"; and varied, end-of-chapter "Additional Writing Assignments." These and other features prepare students to apply what they have learned in other courses and in the workplace, meeting whatever rhetorical challenges lie ahead, in college and in life.

Built on these cornerstone concepts, the tremendous success of *The Bedford Guide* has been gratifying. And especially gratifying has been the way that this book has continued to evolve over time. New ideas on teaching and writing and excellent suggestions from users of the book improve and enrich each edition of the book. Now the tenth edition includes many thought-provoking new readings, revised chapters on analyzing visuals and conducting research, recurring options for a Source Activity or Source Assignment, a new series of reflective "Learning by Doing" activities, and a new APA sample paper. It also expands popular features, offering new "Take Action" charts on literary analysis and APA style as well as many more "Why Writing Matters" chapter openers for both writing and research chapters. These changes and others throughout the book do even more to involve students in their own development as writers.

## Everything You Need

The tenth edition continues to offer four coordinated composition books integrated into one convenient text—all of them now even better resources for students. *The Bedford Guide* is also available in a brief version, containing the rhetoric and reader, in a new concise edition, and in e-book versions. (For more details on the e-book versions and other exciting new resources accompanying *The Bedford Guide,* see pp. xiii–xvii. For more information on what is new in the tenth edition, see p. viii.)

### BOOK 1 A Writer's Guide

This uniquely accessible—yet thorough—process-oriented rhetoric helps students become better writers, regardless of their skill level. Addressing all the assignments and topics typically covered in a first-year writing course, it is divided into four parts.

Part One, "A College Writer's Processes," introduces students to the interconnected processes of writing (Chapter 1), reading (Chapter 2), and critical thinking (Chapter 3). In the tenth edition, the student writing in these chapters now includes a new critical reading response in Chapter 2, "Reading Processes."

In Part Two, "A Writer's Situations," nine core chapters—each including two sample readings (one by a student)—guide students step-by-step through a full range of common first-year writing assignments. The rhetorical situations in Part Two include recalling an experience (Chapter 4), observing a scene (Chapter 5), interviewing a subject (Chapter 6), comparing and contrasting (Chapter 7), explaining causes and effects (Chapter 8), taking a stand (Chapter 9), proposing a solution (Chapter 10), evaluating and reviewing (Chapter 11), and supporting a position with sources (Chapter 12). "Why Writing Matters" features, readings, visuals, "Responding to an Image" chapter openers for class discussion and journal writing, and "Additional Writing Assignments" – now including both visual and source-based options – make these chapters both useful and interesting for students. If followed sequentially, these chapters lead students gradually into the rigorous analytical writing that will comprise most of their college writing. Rearranged and selected chapters readily support a course emphasizing argument, source-based writing, or other rhetorical or thematic approaches.

Part Three, "Other Writing Situations," offers helpful strategies and examples to focus students' efforts in five special rhetorical situations: responding to literature (Chapter 13), responding to visual representations (Chapter 14), writing online (Chapter 15), writing and presenting under pressure (Chapter 16), and writing in the workplace (Chapter 17). The more sharply focused Chapter 15, "Writing Online," and revised sections on visual analysis in Chapter 14 succinctly address rhetorical situations that college students now encounter.

Part Four, "A Writer's Strategies," is a convenient resource for approaching different writing processes. The first chapter, "Strategies: A Case Study" (Chapter 18), follows a student as she develops and revises her "Recalling an Experience" paper through multiple drafts. It also includes her self-reflective portfolio letter. The next five chapters explain and further illustrate stages of common writing processes: generating ideas (Chapter 19), stating a thesis and planning (Chapter 20), drafting (Chapter 21), developing (Chapter 22), and revising and editing (Chapter 23), each now concluding with a "Learning by Doing" process reflection. Marginal annotations in the earlier parts of the book guide students to these chapters, which collectively serve as a writer's toolbox. The part ends with "Strategies for Future Writing" (Chapter 24), helping students apply what they have learned to other rhetorical situations. It includes two new student samples, one from a multigenre history assignment and one from a philosophy of teaching portfolio.

## BOOK 2 A Writer's Reader

*A Writer's Reader* is a thematic reader, unique in a book of this kind. In this edition, ten new e-Pages readings add a rich array of integrated, assignable, multimodal content. The reader offers forty selections in all – twenty-three of them new – arranged around five themes that provide a meaningful context for students, giving them something to write about. The themes are families (Chapter 25), men and women (Chapter 26), popular culture (Chapter 27), digital living (Chapter 28), and explorations on living well (Chapter 29). This last distinctive theme considers what different people value as components of a life well lived. Apparatus that encourages critical thinking and writing accompanies each reading. A rhetorical table of contents (p. xl) shows how the selections are coordinated with *A Writer's Guide* and illustrate writing situations assigned there. A biographical headnote and a brief prereading tip or question introduce each reading. Each selection is followed by questions on meaning, writing strategies, critical reading, vocabulary, and connections to other selections; journal prompts; and suggested writing assignments, one personal and the other analytical. These questions lead students from reading carefully for both thematic and rhetorical elements to applying new strategies and insights in their own writing.

BOOK 3

### A Writer's Research Manual

*A Writer's Research Manual* is a remarkably comprehensive guide to source-based writing, detailing all the essential steps for print, electronic, and field research. Updated to reflect current text practices gathered from a survey of academic librarians, this manual covers planning a research project (Chapter 30), working with sources (Chapter 31), finding sources (Chapter 32), evaluating sources (Chapter 33), integrating sources (Chapter 34), and writing the research paper (Chapter 35). Each chapter now opens with a "Why Research Matters" feature. Chapters 36 and 37 include extensive coverage of MLA and APA documentation, with ninety-eight MLA-style models and over seventy APA-style models, along with a new example of an APA research paper and a new APA "Take Action" chart. In the appendices, a "Quick Research Guide" conveniently—and briefly—reviews how to find, evaluate, integrate, cite, and document sources. Here also, a "Quick Format Guide" illustrates academic document design.

BOOK 4

### A Writer's Handbook

A most complete handbook, with superior ESL coverage (in "ESL Guidelines"), this useful reference clearly explains grammar, style, and usage topics. It also includes nearly fifty exercise sets for practice in and out of class. Answers to half of the questions in most sets are provided in the back of the book so that students can check their understanding. Beyond the coverage in the handbook, a "Quick Editing Guide" in the appendices gives special attention to the most troublesome grammar and editing problems.

## New to the Tenth Edition

The tenth edition gives students even more opportunities for learning by doing and developing transferable skills. Through innovative e-Pages, activities, assignments, visuals, readings, and examples of students' work, this new edition prepares students for writing challenges in college and beyond. New activities reflect classroom experiences, advances from the always-developing field of composition, and the insightful suggestions of many helpful reviewers.

## Now with Bedford Integrated Media

### e e-Pages connect with students and build writing and critical thinking skills

*The Bedford Guide* now comes with Bedford Integrated Media: e-Pages that give the book a rich array of assignable, multimodal content. These materials extend the book's focus on active learning and transferable skills into the online environment. They also expand alternatives for class-specific activities, such as using the e-Pages research cluster on celebrity culture (Chapter 12) to improve source handling. Two types of e-Pages accompany the book and take advantage of all the Web can do:

- **Readings.** Multimodal readings in e-Pages include videos, audio segments, interviews, infographics, and visual essays. Each is contextualized by a headnote and accompanied by critical reading and thinking questions. Students type their answers into response boxes that report to their instructor's gradebook. The e-Pages reading topics include a humorous look at the subject of texting while walking (video), athletes interviewed on the role of superstitions in sports (video), *Hurricane Katrina Pictures: Then & Now, Ruin & Rebirth* (visual essay), the physiological effects of drinking with a closer look at why drinking and driving don't mix (infographic), and from NPR's *This American Life*, a story of school, relationships, and mistaken perceptions (audio segment).

  In Part Two (Chapters 4–12), the e-Pages readings are part of the "Learning from Other Writers" feature, with one e-Pages reading available for each of the nine main assignment chapters (Recalling an Experience through Supporting a Position with Sources). In Book 2, *A Writer's Reader* (Chapters 25 to 29), two e-Pages readings in each chapter explore this section's five themes: Families, Men and Women, Popular Culture, Digital Living, and Explorations on Living Well.

- **Assignments and activities.** Assignments in e-Pages include the critical reading and thinking questions that accompany each reading. In addition, online e-Pages "Learning by Doing" activities encourage students to explore topics such as Analyzing Audience, Reading Online, Recalling from Photographs, and Analyzing Surprising Interviews. For a complete list of e-Pages content, turn to the front of the book.

Students access e-Pages materials through the Bedford Integrated Media page for *The Bedford Guide for College Writers* at **bedfordstmartins.com/bedguide**. They receive automatic access to e-Pages with the purchase of a new book. (Students who do not buy a new book can purchase access at this same site.) The e-Pages format makes it easy for instructors to see and evaluate what students are doing and gives new options for readings and assignments.

Instructors receive log-in information in a separate e-mail with access to all of the resources in Bedford Integrated Media. You can also log in or request access information at the book's media page.

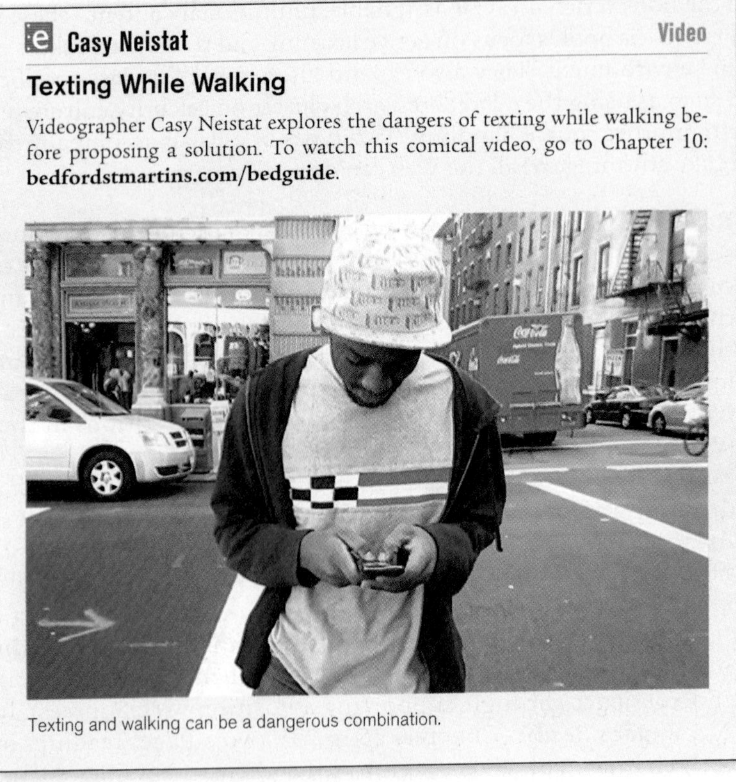

**Casy Neistat** — Video

**Texting While Walking**

Videographer Casy Neistat explores the dangers of texting while walking before proposing a solution. To watch this comical video, go to Chapter 10: **bedfordstmartins.com/bedguide**.

Texting and walking can be a dangerous combination.

# Focus on Active Learning and Transferable Skills

## More "Learning by Doing" Activities

"Learning by Doing" activities, many drawn from instructors' suggestions, encourage active learning and the development of transferable skills. A new Learning by Doing on Analyzing Interview Questions, for example, helps develop critical thinking and awareness of genre. Other additions help students reflect on their own writing processes. With some Learning by Doing activities available in the print book and some in e-Pages, students have different ways to practice and apply what they are learning.

**Learning by Doing** Analyzing Interview Questions

Listen to several radio interviews on a local station or National Public Radio (which archives many types of interviews, including programs such as *Fresh Air*). As you listen, jot down the names of the interviewer and interviewee, the topic, and any particularly fruitful or useless questions. Working with others in person or online, discuss your conclusions about the success of the interviews you heard. Develop a collaborative set of guidelines for preparing good questions and dodging bad ones.

## New "Take Action" charts

The unique "Take Action" charts guide students through assessing and revising challenging aspects of writing. In the tenth edition, new "Take Action" charts help students improve their use of APA documentation style and understand the basics of literary analysis. These self-assessment charts are designed to help students of varying skill levels become stronger and more independent writers by reflecting on their own writing, identifying its weaknesses, and then using concrete and relevant strategies for strengthening their papers. Other "Take Action" charts address such important issues as supporting a stand, integrating sources, and strengthening thesis statements.

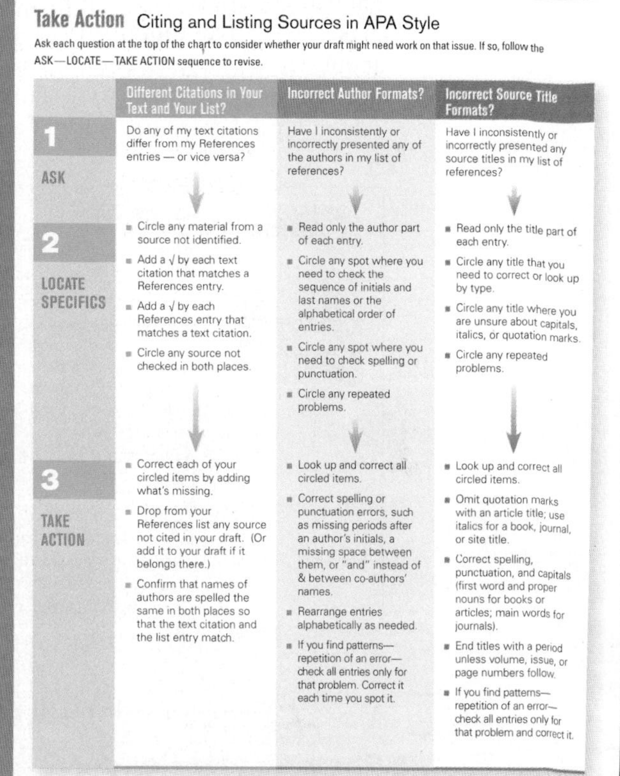

**Take Action** Citing and Listing Sources in APA Style

Ask each question at the top of the chart to consider whether your draft might need work on that issue. If so, follow the ASK—LOCATE—TAKE ACTION sequence to revise.

| | Different Citations in Your Text and Your List? | Incorrect Author Formats? | Incorrect Source Title Formats? |
|---|---|---|---|
| 1 ASK | Do any of my text citations differ from my References entries — or vice versa? | Have I inconsistently or incorrectly presented any of the authors in my list of references? | Have I inconsistently or incorrectly presented any source titles in my list of references? |
| 2 LOCATE SPECIFICS | ▪ Circle any material from a source not identified.<br>▪ Add a √ by each text citation that matches a References entry.<br>▪ Add a √ by each References entry that matches a text citation.<br>▪ Circle any source not checked in both places. | ▪ Read only the author part of each entry.<br>▪ Circle any spot where you need to check the sequence of initials and last names or the alphabetical order of entries.<br>▪ Circle any spot where you need to check spelling or punctuation.<br>▪ Circle any repeated problems. | ▪ Read only the title part of each entry.<br>▪ Circle any title that you need to correct or look up by type.<br>▪ Circle any title where you are unsure about capitals, italics, or quotation marks.<br>▪ Circle any repeated problems. |
| 3 TAKE ACTION | ▪ Correct each of your circled items by adding what's missing.<br>▪ Drop from your References list any source not cited in your draft. (Or add it to your draft if it belongs there.)<br>▪ Confirm that names of authors are spelled the same in both places so that the text citation and the list entry match. | ▪ Look up and correct all circled items.<br>▪ Correct spelling or punctuation errors, such as missing periods after an author's initials, a missing space between them, or "and" instead of & between co-authors' names.<br>▪ Rearrange entries alphabetically as needed.<br>▪ If you find patterns—repetition of an error—check all entries only for that problem. Correct it each time you spot it. | ▪ Look up and correct all circled items.<br>▪ Omit quotation marks with an article title; use italics for a book, journal, or site title.<br>▪ Correct spelling, punctuation, and capitals (first word and proper nouns for books or articles; main words for journals).<br>▪ End titles with a period unless volume, issue, or page numbers follow.<br>▪ If you find patterns—repetition of an error—check all entries only for that problem and correct it. |

## Updated Research Manual

As they continue in college, students will most likely investigate research topics and write papers in which they will need to cite sources. Book 3 of *The Bedford Guide, A Writer's Research Manual*, and the "Quick Research Guide" now give students more practice and support to prepare them for source-based academic writing. Revised with the input of research librarians from around the country who shared their "best practices," these sections now more sharply focus on effectively searching for and organizing sources, as well as relating them to one's thesis. A new APA research paper and updated APA examples prepare students who might find that this style is the one required in future classes.

# New Readings

## Readings from a Wide Range of Perspectives

A third of the readings are new in the tenth edition, including essays by well-known authors such as Anna Quindlen, Sandra Cisneros, Dagoberto Gilb, Katha Pollitt, David Brooks, and Jhumpa Lahiri. The readings also reflect a wide range of experience, since students come to the composition class varying in age, work background, comfort with technology, life situations, and other factors. Terrell Jermaine Starr, for example, writes about his grandmother, a strong woman who raised him and saw that he got a good education, despite not having had one herself. Libby Copeland examines how Facebook can sometimes make people feel more isolated and depressed, not less. Mike Haynie writes about PTSD, veterans, and the media. Throughout *The Bedford Guide*, the readings encourage students to see familiar topics from new angles and to use critical thinking skills to gain insight and understanding.

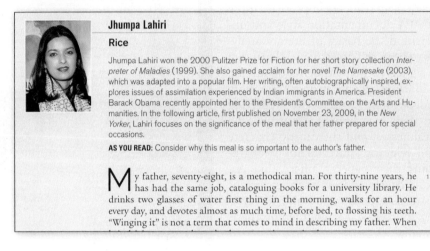

**Jhumpa Lahiri**

**Rice**

Jhumpa Lahiri won the 2000 Pulitzer Prize for Fiction for her short story collection *Interpreter of Maladies* (1999). She also gained acclaim for her novel *The Namesake* (2003), which was adapted into a popular film. Her writing, often autobiographically inspired, explores issues of assimilation experienced by Indian immigrants in America. President Barack Obama recently appointed her to the President's Committee on the Arts and Humanities. In the following article, first published on November 23, 2009, in the *New Yorker*, Lahiri focuses on the significance of the meal that her father prepared for special occasions.

**AS YOU READ:** Consider why this meal is so important to the author's father.

My father, seventy-eight, is a methodical man. For thirty-nine years, he 1
has had the same job, cataloguing books for a university library. He drinks two glasses of water first thing in the morning, walks for an hour every day, and devotes almost as much time, before bed, to flossing his teeth. "Winging it" is not a term that comes to mind in describing my father. When

## More Connections between *The Bedford Guide*'s Rhetoric and Reader

Throughout the tenth edition, new connections and references have been added to make it easier for instructors and students to use *A Writer's Guide* (Chapters 1–24) with *A Writer's Reader* (Chapters 25–29) and vice versa. Many new internal cross-references, marginal notes, thematic correspondences, interlinked excerpts, and complementary assignments improve the way these two sections of the book can work in tandem. All serve to integrate the different parts of the book into a more useful whole. Instructors and students can now more easily find relevant examples and support for the writing skills and strategies presented.

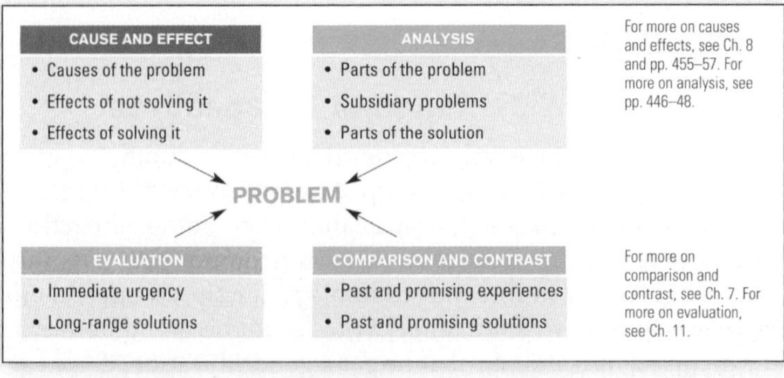

CAUSE AND EFFECT
• Causes of the problem
• Effects of not solving it
• Effects of solving it
ANALYSIS
• Parts of the problem
• Subsidiary problems
• Parts of the solution
For more on causes and effects, see Ch. 8 and pp. 455–57. For more on analysis, see pp. 446–48.
PROBLEM
EVALUATION
• Immediate urgency
• Long-range solutions
COMPARISON AND CONTRAST
• Past and promising experiences
• Past and promising solutions
For more on comparison and contrast, see Ch. 7. For more on evaluation, see Ch. 11.

## New Examples of Student Writing

**Jacob Griffin** **Student Essay**

**Karate Kid vs. Kung Fu Panda: A Race to the Olympics**

Student Jacob Griffin compares and contrasts karate and kung fu, asking which of the two deserves to be the first declared an Olympic sport.

About three de[…] into the American […] like Jackie Chan be[…]

Karate Kung fu

Throughout the tenth edition, interesting new examples of student writing provide helpful models. Four of nine student essays are new in Part Two, such as an observation on arrival in Stockholm (Chapter 5) and an essay comparing and contrasting karate and kung fu (Chapter 7). Other new student work includes a critical reading response to "The New Literacy" in "Reading Processes" (Chapter 2), selections from a history paper and a portfolio (Chapter 24), entries from an annotated bibliography (Chapter 30), and a full APA research paper (Chapter 37).

## Many New Photographs and Multimodal Genres

Thought-provoking visuals begin and conclude each Part Two assignment chapter, supporting the goals of the chapter with skills-building apparatus. Chapter 14, "Responding to Visual Representations," contains new examples and a new visual essay. More public announcements, news photos, visuals from Web sites, movie critiques, and videos appear throughout this edition of *The Bedford Guide*. All give engaging opportunities for discussion, critical thinking, and written analysis.

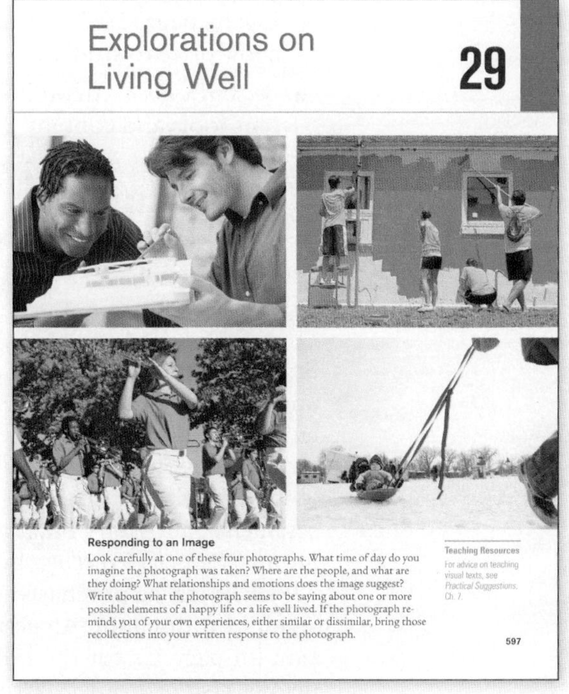

Explorations on Living Well 29

**Responding to an Image**

Look carefully at one of these four photographs. What time of day do you imagine the photograph was taken? Where are the people, and what are they doing? What relationships and emotions does the image suggest? Write about what the photograph seems to be saying about one or more possible elements of a happy life or a life well lived. If the photograph reminds you of your own experiences, either similar or dissimilar, bring those recollections into your written response to the photograph.

**Teaching Resources**

For advice on teaching visual texts, see *Practical Suggestions*, Ch. 7.

597

# You Get More Choices for *The Bedford Guide for College Writers*, Tenth Edition

Bedford/St. Martin's offers resources and format choices that help you and your students get even more out of the book and your course. To learn more about or order any of the following products, contact your Bedford/St. Martin's sales representative, e-mail sales support (sales_support@bfwpub.com), or visit the Web site at bedfordstmartins .com/bedguide/catalog.

## Turn Reading into Learning with the *Bedford x-Book for The Bedford Guide*

Bedford x-Books reimagine what a text can do online. Pages come alive with multimodal readings, video, animation, audio, and interactive elements. Students can read, watch, reflect, and share—right in the pages of the text. A smarter search understands what students are really looking for and suggests targeted results. In one click, instructors can assign a chapter or page, pull together different sections of the book into one assignment, or begin to compose their own. With a Bedford x-Book, you can create exactly the text that you need for your class and track progress as it happens.

## Choose from Alternative Formats of *The Bedford Guide*

Bedford/St. Martin's offers a range of affordable formats, allowing students to choose the one that works for them. For details, visit bedfordstmartins .com/bedguide/catalog/formats.

- *Hardcover or paperback*
- *Loose-leaf edition* The loose-leaf edition does not have a traditional binding; its pages are loose and two-hole punched to provide flexibility and a low price to students.
- *Bedford x-Book* An online e-book format that integrates interactive content tools and content
- *Bedford e-Book to Go* A portable, downloadable e-book at about half the price of the print book
- *Other popular e-book formats* For details, visit bedfordstmartins.com/ebooks

## Choose the Flexible *Bedford e-Portfolio*

Students can collect, select, and reflect on their coursework and personalize and share their e-Portfolio for any audience—instructors, peers, potential employers, or family and friends. Instructors can provide as much or as little structure as they see fit. Rubrics and learning outcomes can be aligned to student work, so instructors and programs can gather reliable and useful assessment data. Every *Bedford e-Portfolio* comes pre-loaded with *Portfolio Keeping* and *Portfolio Teaching*, by Nedra Reynolds and Elizabeth Davis. *Bedford e-Portfolio* can be purchased separately or packaged with the print book at a significant discount. An activation code is required. See Ordering Information on page xix for the ISBN to order *e-Portfolio* with the print book. For details, visit bedfordstmartins.com/eportfolio.

## Watch Peer Review Work

*Eli Review* lets instructors scaffold their assignments in a clearer, more effective way for students—making peer review more visible and teachable.

Because teachers get real-time analytics about how well students have met criteria in a writing task *and* about how helpful peer comments have been, they can intervene in real time to teach how to give good feedback and how to shape writing to meet criteria. When students can instantly see which comments are endorsed by their teacher and how their feedback has been rated by their peers, they're motivated to give the best reviews, get the best ratings, think like writers and revise with a plan. *Eli Review* can be purchased separately or packaged with the print book at a significant discount. An activation code is required. See Ordering Information on page xix for the ISBN to order *Eli Review* with the print book. For details, visit bedfordstmartins .com/eli.

## Upgrade Your Composition Space with *LaunchPad for The Bedford Guide for College Writers*

*LaunchPad for The Bedford Guide* takes advantage of everything Bedford/St. Martin's knows about composition. *LaunchPad* combines the new *x-Book* with robust writing tools that help you start conversations around content, build regular writing practice into every assignment, and create peer review groups as your students work toward larger projects. Diagnostics and LearningCurve, our adaptive quizzing engine, offer remediation and practice as students build skills in reading, writing, and grammar. For more information, please contact your sales representative or visit bedfordstmartins.com.

## Select Value Packages

Add value to your text by packaging one of the following resources with *The Bedford Guide*. To learn more about package options for any of the following products, contact your Bedford/St. Martin's sales representative or visit bedfordstmartins.com/bedguide/catalog.

***LearningCurve for Readers and Writers,*** Bedford/St. Martin's adaptive quizzing program, quickly learns what students already know and helps them practice what they don't yet understand. Game-like quizzing motivates students to engage with their course, and reporting tools help teachers discern their students' needs. *LearningCurve for Readers and Writers* can be packaged with *The Bedford Guide* at a significant discount. An activation code is required. See Ordering Information on page xviii for the ISBN to order *LearningCurve* packaged with the print book. For details, visit bedfordstmartins .com/englishlearningcurve.

***VideoCentral: English*** is a growing collection of videos for the writing class that captures real-world, academic, and student writers talking about how and why they write. Writer and teacher Peter Berkow interviewed hundreds of people – from Michael Moore to Cynthia Selfe – to produce 50 brief videos about topics such as revising and getting feedback. *VideoCentral: English* can be packaged with *The Bedford Guide* at a significant discount. An activation code is required. See Ordering Information on page xix for the ISBN to order *VideoCentral: English* packaged with the print book.

***i-series*** is a popular series presenting multimedia tutorials in a flexible format—because there are things you cannot do in a book.

- *ix visual exercises* helps students put into practice key rhetorical and visual concepts. See Ordering Information on page xviii for the ISBN to order *ix visual exercises* packaged with the print book.
- *i-claim: visualizing argument* offers a new way to see argument—with 6 tutorials, an illustrated glossary, and over 70 multimedia arguments. See Ordering Information on page xviii for the ISBN to order *i-claim: visualizing argument* packaged with the print book.

***Portfolio Keeping*, Third Edition,** by Nedra Reynolds and Elizabeth Davis, provides all the information students need to use the portfolio method successfully in a writing course. *Portfolio Teaching*, a companion guide for instructors, provides the practical information instructors and writing program administrators need to use the portfolio method successfully in a writing course. See Ordering Information on page xix for the ISBN to order *Portfolio Keeping* packaged with the print book.

***Oral Presentations in the Composition Course: A Brief Guide*,** by Matthew Duncan and Gustav W. Friedrich, offers students the advice they need to plan, prepare, and present their work effectively. With sections on analyzing audiences, choosing effective language, using visual aids, collaborating on group presentations, and dealing with the fear of public speaking, this booklet helps students develop strong oral presentations. See Ordering Information on page xviii for the ISBN to order *Oral Presentations in the Composition Course* packaged with the print book.

## Try *Re:Writing 2* at bedfordstmartins.com/rewriting

Part of the enjoyment of teaching writing is trying something new. The best collection of free writing resources on the Web, *Re:Writing 2* gives you and your students even more ways to think, watch, practice, and learn about writing concepts. Listen to Nancy Sommers on using a teacher's comments to revise. Try a logic puzzle. Consult our resources for writing centers. For details, visit bedfordstmartins.com/rewriting.

## Instructor Resources

## bedfordstmartins.com/bedguide/catalog

You have a lot to do in your course. Bedford/St. Martin's wants to make it easy for you to find the support you need—and to get it quickly.

***Instructor's Annotated Edition of The Bedford Guide for College Writers*** puts information right where busy instructors need it: on the pages of the book itself. The marginal annotations offer teaching tips, analysis tips with readings, last-minute in-class activities, vocabulary glosses, additional assignments, and cross-references to other ancillaries.

***Practical Suggestions for Teaching with The Bedford Guide for College Writers,*** by Dana Waters of Dodge City Community College, Shirley Morahan, and Sylvia A. Holladay, is available in PDF that can be downloaded from the Bedford/St. Martin's online catalog. *Practical Suggestions* helps instructors plan and teach their composition course. In addition to chapter overviews and practical tips on designing an effective course, the Instructor's Manual includes sample syllabi, suggested answers to questions, notes on assignments, classroom activities, and suggestions for using the electronic media package.

***Teaching Composition: Background Readings,* Third Edition,** edited by T. R. Johnson of Tulane University, addresses the concerns of both new and veteran writing instructors. This collection includes thirty professional readings on composition and rhetoric written by leaders in the field. Selections are accompanied by helpful introductions, activities, and practical insights for inside and outside the classroom. This edition offers up-to-date advice on avoiding plagiarism, classroom blogging, and more.

***TeachingCentral*** offers the entire list of Bedford/St. Martin's print and online professional resources in one place. You will find landmark reference works, sourcebooks on pedagogical issues, award-winning collections, and practical advice for the classroom—all free for instructors at bedfordstmartins.com/teachingcentral.

***Bits*** collects creative ideas for teaching a range of composition topics in an easily searchable blog format. A community of teachers—leading scholars, authors, and editors—discuss revision, research, grammar and style, technology, peer review, and much more. Take, use, adapt, and pass the ideas around. Then, come back to the site to comment or share your own suggestion. Visit bedfordbits.com.

**Bedford Coursepacks** for the most common course management systems—Blackboard, Angel, Desire2Learn, Web CT, Moodle, or Sakai—allow you to easily download digital materials from Bedford/St. Martin's for your course. To see what's available for *The Bedford Guide for College Writers*, Tenth Edition, visit bedfordstmartins.com/coursepacks.

**Testing Tool Kit: A Writing and Grammar Test Bank.** This CD-ROM allows instructors to create secure, customized tests and quizzes. The pre-built diagnostic tests are also included.

## Ordering Information

To order any of the ancillaries, please contact your Bedford/St. Martin's sales representative, e-mail sales support at sales_support@bfwpub.com, or visit our Web site at bedfordstmartins.com. Note that activation codes are required for *LearningCurve*, *ix visualizing composition*, *i-claim*, *VideoCentral: English*, *Eli*, and *Bedford ePortfolio*. Codes can be purchased separately or packaged with the print book at a significant discount.

To order the ***LearningCurve*** **access card** with the print book, use these ISBNs:

- with *Reader, Research Manual, and Handbook* (hardcover): 978-1-4576-7770-0
- with *Reader, Research Manual, and Handbook* (paperback): 978-1-4576-7838-7
- with *Reader, Research Manual, and Handbook* (loose-leaf): 978-1-4576-7808-0
- with *Reader* (paperback only): 978-1-4576-7742-7

To order the ***ix visualizing composition*** **access card** with the print book, use these ISBNs:

- with *Reader, Research Manual, and Handbook* (hardcover): 978-1-4576-7766-3
- with *Reader, Research Manual, and Handbook* (paperback): 978-1-4576-7837-0
- with *Reader, Research Manual, and Handbook* (loose-leaf): 978-1-4576-7802-8
- with *Reader* (paperback only): 978-1-4576-7741-0

To order the ***i-claim 2.0*** **access card** with the print book, use these ISBNs:

- with *Reader, Research Manual, and Handbook* (hardcover): 978-1-4576-7762-5
- with *Reader, Research Manual, and Handbook* (paperback): 978-1-4576-7836-3
- with *Reader, Research Manual, and Handbook* (loose-leaf): 978-1-4576-7801-1
- with *Reader* (paperback only): 978-1-4576-7691-8

To order ***Oral Presentations in the Composition Course*** with the print book, use these ISBNs:

- with *Reader, Research Manual, and Handbook* (hardcover): 978-1-4576-7777-9
- with *Reader, Research Manual, and Handbook* (paperback): 978-1-4576-7840-0

- with *Reader, Research Manual, and Handbook* (loose-leaf): 978-1-4576-7810-3
- with *Reader* (paperback only): 978-1-4576-7745-8

To order the ***VideoCentral: English* access card** with the print book, use these ISBNs:

- with *Reader, Research Manual, and Handbook* (hardcover): 978-1-4576-7775-5
- with *Reader, Research Manual, and Handbook* (paperback): 978-1-4576-7839-4
- with *Reader, Research Manual, and Handbook* (loose-leaf): 978-1-4576-7809-7
- with *Reader* (paperback only): 978-1-4576-7743-4

To order ***Portfolio Keeping*, Third Edition**, with the print book, use these ISBNs:

- with *Reader, Research Manual, and Handbook* (hardcover): 978-1-4576-7778-6
- with *Reader, Research Manual, and Handbook* (paperback): 978-1-4576-7841-7
- with *Reader, Research Manual, and Handbook* (loose-leaf): 978-1-4576-7812-7
- with *Reader* (paperback only): 978-1-4576-7754-0

To order the ***Eli Review* 6-month access card** with the print book, use these ISBNs:

- with *Reader, Research Manual, and Handbook* (hardcover): 978-1-4576-7756-4
- with *Reader, Research Manual, and Handbook* (paperback): 978-1-4576-7832-5
- with *Reader, Research Manual, and Handbook* (loose-leaf): 978-1-4576-7798-4
- with *Reader* (paperback only): 978-1-4576-7567-6

To order the ***Bedford e-Portfolio* access card** with the print book, use these ISBNs:

- with *Reader, Research Manual, and Handbook* (hardcover): 978-1-4576-7759-5
- with *Reader, Research Manual, and Handbook* (paperback): 978-1-4576-7834-9
- with *Reader, Research Manual, and Handbook* (loose-leaf): 978-1-4576-7799-1
- with *Reader* (paperback only): 987-1-4576-7583-6

## Thanks and Appreciation

Many individuals contributed significantly to the tenth edition of *The Bedford Guide for College Writers*, and we extend our sincerest thanks to all of them.

### Editorial Advisory Board

As we began to prepare the tenth edition, we assembled an editorial advisory board to respond to the many significant changes we planned and to share ideas about how to make the book more useful to both students and teachers. These dedicated instructors responded thoroughly and insightfully to new features of the text, answered innumerable questions, and suggested many ideas, activities, and assignments. They also submitted student papers and in ways large and small helped to shape the new and revised sections of the tenth edition. We are extremely grateful to each one of them:

- Kathleen Beauchene, Community College of Rhode Island
- Vicki Besaw, College of Menominee Nation
- Thomas Eaton, Southeast Missouri State University
- Sonia Feder-Lewis, Saint Mary's University of Minnesota
- Audrey Hillyer, University of Southern Indiana
- Beth Koruna, Columbus State Community College
- Tracy Kristo, Anoka-Ramsey Community College
- Kathryn Lane, Northwestern Oklahoma State University
- Leigh Martin, Community College of Rhode Island
- Anna McKennon, Fullerton College
- Terry Novak, Johnson and Wales University
- Arthur L. Schuhart, Northern Virginia Community College–Annandale
- Dana Waters, Dodge City Community College

### Other Colleagues

We also extend our gratitude to instructors across the country who took time and care to review this edition, to participate in a focus group, to send us their students' work, and to share excellent suggestions gleaned from their experience. For this we thank

- Jacob Agatucci, Central Oregon Community College
- Jennifer Aly, University of Hawaii Maui College
- Laura Ballard, Mesa Community College
- Norman Bates, Cochise College
- Sean Bernard, University of La Verne
- Laura Caudill, Sullivan University
- Donna Craine, Front Range Community College

- Andrea Deacon, University of Wisconsin-Stout
- Sharon Derry, Sierra College
- Marcia Dinneen, Bridgewater State College
- Kimberly Fangman, Southeast Community College
- Dwedor Ford, Winston-Salem State University
- Anissa Graham, University of North Alabama
- Letizia Guglielmo, Kennesaw State University
- Russell Hall, Penn State Behrend
- Alexis Hart, Virginia Military Institute
- Jane Holwerda, Dodge City Community College
- Peter Huk, University of California Santa Barbara
- Sarah Hutton, University of Massachusetts-Amherst
- Diane Jakacki, Georgia Institute of Technology
- Saiyeda Khatun, Johnson & Wales University
- Karla Saari Kitalong, Michigan Technological University
- Lynn Lampert, California State University-Northridge
- Ellen Leonard, Springfield Technical Community College
- John Lusk, St. Clair County Community College
- Todd McCann, Bay College
- Linda McHenry, Fort Hays State University
- Lanell Mogab, Clinton Community College
- Susan Perry, Greenville Technical College
- Sheryl Ruszkiewicz, Baker College of Allen Park
- Laura Saunders, Simmons College
- Laurie Sherman, Community College of Rhode Island
- Tammy Sugarman, Georgia State University
- Anthony Vannella, San Antonio College
- Laura Wind, Northeastern University

We also want to acknowledge the tremendous and enduring help provided by reviewers of previous editions. Their expert ideas and suggestions live on in the pages of this edition.

Mary Ellen Ackerman, Alice B. Adams, Rosemary R. Adams, Ted Allder, Patricia Allen, Steve Amidon, David Auchter, Mary Baken, Renee Bangerter, Stuart Barbier, Marci Bartolotta, Barry Batorsky, Shannon Beasley, Randolph A. Beckham, Pamela J. Behrens, Carmine J. Bell, Kay Berg, Tanya Boler, Jan Bone, Jeannie Boniecki, Debbie Boyd, Crystal Brothe, Barbara Brown, Karen Davis Brown, Ty Buckman, Rita Buscher-Weeks, Joan Campbell, Sarah Canfield-Fuller, Terri Carine, Tom Casey, Sandra L. Cavender, Steve Cirrone, Susan

Romayne Clark, Laurie Lopez Coleman, Ted Contreras, Nancy Cook, Connie Corbett-Whittier, Jane Corbly, Monica Cox, Carolyn Craft, Sheilah Craft, Mary Cullen, P. R. Dansby, Fred D'Astoli, Ed Davis, Patricia Ann Delamar, John Dethloff, Dale Dittmer, Helen Duclos, Irene Duprey-Gutierrez, Corinna Evett, Carol Luers Eyman, Rosary Fazende-Jones, Patrick Finn, Leora Freedman, Julie Freeman, Lisa J. Friedrich-Harris, LaDonna Friesen, Sandy Fuhr, Jan Fulwiler, Pamela Garvey, Mary Ann Gauthier, Michael Gavin, Caroline Gebhard, Olga Geissler, Barbara Gleason, Robert Gmerlin, Aaron Goldweber, Daniel Gonzales, Sherry F. Gott, Daniel V. Gribbin, Robert Grindy, Joyce Hall, Jefferson Hancock, Alyssa Harad, Johnnie Hargrove, M. Suzanne Harper, Judy Hatcher, Elaine Hays, Stephen B. Heller, Virginia Scott Hendrickson, Marlene Hess, Diana Hicks, Marita Hinton, Tom Hodges, Susanna Hoeness-Krupsaw, Jane Holwerda, Patricia Hunt, Karen Keaton Jackson, Elizabeth Jarok, Barbara Jensen, Greg Jewell, Jean L. Johnson, Ted Johnston, Andrew Jones, Anne D. Jordan, M. L. Kayser, Cynthia Kellogg, Dimitri Keriotis, Kate Kiefer, Yoon Sik Kim, Kaye Kolkmann, Fred A. Koslowski III, Brandy Kreisler, Sandra Lakey, Norman Lanquist, Colleen Lloyd, Denise Longsworth, Stephen Ma, Susan Peck MacDonald, Jennifer Madej, Janice Mandile, Phil Martin, Gerald McCarthy, Miles S. McCrimmon, Jackie McGrath, Eileen Medeiros, Jenna Merritt, Elizabeth Metzger, Eric Meyer, Mike Michaud, Heather Michael, Libby Miles, Anthony C. Miller Sr., Sandra Moore, Cleatta Morris, Robert Morse, Julie A. Myatt, Sheryl A. Mylan, Clement Ndulute, Jerry Nelson, Annie Nguyen, Kimme Nuckles, Peggy J. Oliver, Laura Osborne, Brit Osgood-Treston, Roy Kenneth Pace II, Mike Palmquist, Geraldine C. Pelegano, Zachary Perkinson, Laurel S. Peterson, Mary F. Pflugshaupt, Marianne G. Pindar, John F. Pleimann, Kenneth E. Poitras, Michael Punches, Patrice Quarg, Jeanie Page Randall, Betty Ray, Joan Reteshka, Mark Reynolds, Kira Roark, Peggy Roche, Dawn Rodrigues, Amy Rosenbluth, Samantha Ruckman, Ann Westmoreland Runsick, Karin Russell, Joyce Russo, Wendy Schmidt, Nancy J. Schneider, Janis Schulte, Susan Schurman, Patricia C. Schwindt, Sara E. Selby, Herbert Shapiro, Andrea Shaw, Candice Simmons, Suzanne Skipper, Elizabeth Smart, Ognjen Smiljanic, Allison Smith, Patrick Smith, David Sorrells, Ann Spencer-Livingstone, Lori Spillane, Scott R. Stankey, Leroy Sterling, Dean Stover, Ellen Straw, Monnette Sturgill, Ronald Sudol, Darlene Summers, David Tammer, William G. Thomas, Daphne Thompson, Janice M. Vierk, Dave Waddell, Christopher Walker, Laurie Walker, Lori Weber, Bridgette Weir, Carol Westcamp, Patricia South White, Susan Whitlow, Jim Wilcox, Carmiele Wilkerson, Mary Zacharias, and Valerie P. Zimbaro.

## Contributors

The tenth edition could not have been completed without the help of numerous individuals. Special thanks go to Dana Waters (Dodge City Community College) for once again revising *Practical Suggestions.* Jennifer Krisuk (Dodge City Community College) contributed an insightful new section, "Teaching with Tablets," to *Practical Suggestions.* We thank her for the care she took in sharing her knowledge on this topic. Text from two faculty members—Kathleen Beauchene at Community College of Rhode Island and Pamela Laird at University of Colorado Denver—appears in and enhances Chapter 15, "Writing Online," and Chapter 24, "Strategies for Future Writing," respectively. Stefanie Wortman and Wendy Perkins were excellent resources in developing apparatus for the new reading selections. Art researcher Naomi Kornhauser helped us by finding eye-catching and thought-provoking photographs and other images. She also cleared permissions for the art. Caryn Burtt efficiently cleared text permissions under the able guidance of Kalina Ingham. Shannon Walsh contributed tremendously to the Reader and e-Pages. Kate Mayhew helped us with expert e-Pages research. Candace Rardon was our special student consultant on many matters concerning student writing and brought her great energy and valuable perspective to the project.

For the functional and attractive design adjustments that grace the tenth edition, we thank the very talented and patient graphic designer Lisa Buckley. Anna Palchik, senior art director, also played a crucial role in the design, from the first imagining to the late fine-tuning stages.

We gratefully acknowledge the contribution of photographer David L. Ryan. His beautiful and unusual photographs of urban bathers, boats, commuters, and playing fields appear at the beginnings of Parts One through Four and on pages A-63–A-64. We are honored to feature these works, and we thank the artist for letting us include them.

## Student Writers

We offer sincere thanks to all the students who have challenged us over the years to find better ways to help them learn. In particular, we would like to thank those who granted us permission to use their essays in the tenth edition. Focused as this textbook is on student writing, we consider it essential to provide effective sample essays by students. Earlier editions, as well as this one, included the writings of Richard Anson, Cristina Berrios, Linn Bourgeau, Betsy Buffo, Jonathan Burns, Andrew Dillon Bustin, Anne Cahill, Yun Yung Choi, Heather Church, David Ian Cohn, Heather Colbenson, Olof Eriksson, Marjorie Lee Garretson, Sarah E. Goers, Stephanie Hawkins, Cindy Keeler, Heidi Kessler, Melissa Lamberth, Emily Lavery, Daniel Matthews, Angela Mendy, Jennifer Miller, Susanna Olsen, Shari O'Malley, Candace Rardon, Lorena A. Ryan-Hines, Lindsey Schendel, Erin Schmitt, Robert G. Schreiner, Rachel Steinhaus, Lacey Taylor, Joshua Tefft, Leah Threats, Joel Torres, Lillian Tsu, Donna Waite, Arthur Wasilewski, Christopher Williams, and Carrie Williamson.

New to the tenth edition are the writings of Joseph Cauteruccio Jr., Elizabeth Erion, Alea Eyre, Jacob Griffin, Alley Julseth, Shannon Kintner, Jenny Lidington, Abigail Marchand, Schyler Martin, Benjamin Reitz, and Maria Thompson.

## Editorial

At Bedford/St. Martin's two individuals merit special recognition. President of Bedford/St. Martin's Denise B. Wydra (also a former editor of *The Bedford Guide*) continues to contribute invaluable suggestions for improving the book for both students and instructors. We also greatly value the guidance of editor in chief Karen S. Henry, who has helped sustain the direction of the book throughout many editions and who has provided perceptive advice at crucial points in the development of the current edition.

The editorial effort behind this edition was truly a team endeavor. Marcia F. Muth assumed a major authorial role in the seventh edition, answering needs expressed by users with many exciting new features. She has continued in that role through the tenth edition, bringing innovation to every part of the book and making it an even stronger resource for all students, regardless of their skill level. Senior editor Martha Bustin brought fresh eyes and great insight to this edition, encouraging lively innovation while patiently coordinating text, design, and images. Associate editor Regina Tavani skillfully and thoughtfully developed the e-Pages and the new *Concise* edition. She was a key team member, tackling many crucial and time-sensitive jobs, large and small. Editorial assistant Brenna Cleeland joined the team when the book was in its final stages and lent her efficient help to ongoing work on the print and electronic ancillaries. Kimberly Hampton guided the production of the electronic resources, bringing creativity and energy to the development of the e-book and other parts of the book's ancillary package.

Other members of the Bedford/St. Martin's staff contributed greatly to the tenth edition. Many thanks and heartfelt appreciation go to Gregory Erb, who, with an exacting eye, great patience, and good humor, shepherded the book through production. Under Greg's care, the production process could not have gone more smoothly. Sue Brown, Elise Kaiser, and Elizabeth Schaaf helped immensely with production's "big picture" issues. Marine Bouvier Miller created the lovely redesign of the book's cover. Molly Parke skillfully coordinated the marketing of the book and offered much good advice based on feedback from the field. Karen Melton Soeltz and Jane Helms also offered valuable marketing advice. The book's promotion was ably handled by Mike Paparisto. Pelle Cass generously contributed to the pages (located after the appendices) about the book's four part-opening photographs and about key correspondences between the work of writers and photographers.

Marcia Muth is especially grateful to the School of Education and Human Development at the University of Colorado Denver for sponsoring her writing workshops. She also thanks CU Online for its many creative suggestions about online instruction, especially those presented at Web Camp and in *The CU Online Handbook: Teach Differently: Create and Collaborate.* Special appreciation also goes to Mary Finley, University Library at California State University Northridge, and Rodney Muth, University of Colorado Denver, for ongoing expert advice. Finally, we once again thank our friends and families for their unwavering patience, understanding, and encouragement.

# Contents

e For readings that go beyond the printed page, see **bedfordstmartins.com/bedguide**

e bedfordstmartins.com/bedguide

# BOOK 2 A WRITER'S READER

Internet and by e-mails and texts that just keep coming at us.

■ **Brad Shoup,** "Harlem Shake" vs. History: Is the YouTube Novelty Hits Era That Novel? *[Multimodal Essay]* e and 570
To the dismay of music purists, *Billboard* now factors YouTube streams into its Hot 100 list, but the list has always contained plenty of goofy songs.

## 28. Digital Living 571

■ **Emily Yoffe,** Seeking 572
Our tendency toward compulsive browsing stems from our innate impulse to forage — to explore our environment with eager, expectant curiosity.

■ **Nicholas A. Christakis and James H. Fowler,** Hyperconnected 576
When a virtual contagion spread in the computer game *World of Warcraft*, scholars saw how people might react to a real bioterror attack.

■ **David Gelernter,** Computers Cannot Teach Children Basic Skills 580
A prominent computer scientist challenges the widely held view that computers are always a "godsend" in the classroom.

■ **Clive Thompson,** The New Literacy 584
The author points to research findings that suggest technology is increasing literacy and improving students' writing.

PAIRED ESSAYS

■ **Elizabeth Stone,** Grief in the Age of Facebook 587
Reactions to the tragic death of a talented young woman lead the author to consider the emerging practices of online mourning.

■ **Libby Copeland,** Is Facebook Making Us Sad? 591
Facebook can lead to depression and "presentation anxiety," if we compare ourselves unfavorably with friends who appear to have perfect, fun-filled lives.

E-PAGES SELECTIONS

■ **Sherry Turkle,** How Computers Change the Way We Think *[Text]* e and 595
A psychologist explores the effect of online chat, PowerPoint slides, word processors, and simulation games on our "habits of mind."

■ **Off Book Editors,** Generative Art – Computers, Data, and Humanity *[Video]* e and 596
Three innovative creators discuss how they allow computers to make some key decisions about their creations.

## 29. Explorations on Living Well 597

■ **Jhumpa Lahiri,** Rice 598
The author honors her father by describing how he makes a special rice dish for festive occasions and improvises as necessary.

■ **William Zinsser,** The Right to Fail 601
As much as many in society do not want to admit it, failure is vitally important, the author argues.

■ **Gareth Cook,** Getting It All Done 605
For those stressed from too much to do and too little time, helping others can generate a productive sense of efficiency.

■ **Mihaly Csikszentmihalyi,** Happiness Revisited 608
Happiness is often "an unintended side effect" when we push ourselves to accomplish or master something difficult and worthwhile.

PAIRED ESSAYS

■ **Juliet Schor,** The Creation of Discontent 611
The author questions whether luxury and consumerism lead to happiness, as promised, or whether the opposite is true.

■ **Llewellyn H. Rockwell Jr.,** In Defense of Consumerism 615
The author sees consumerism as beneficial and argues that it has many positive effects.

## BOOK 3 A WRITER'S RESEARCH MANUAL

## APPENDICES AND OTHER RESOURCES

# RHETORICAL CONTENTS

*(Essays listed in order of appearance; * indicates student essays)*

### Analyzing a Subject



### Analyzing Processes



e For readings that go beyond the printed page, see **bedfordstmartins.com/bedguide**

### Analyzing Visuals



### Arguing



### Comparing and Contrasting

### Defining



### Describing



### Dividing and Classifying



### Evaluating and Reviewing



### Explaining Causes and Effects

## Supporting a Position with Sources



## Taking a Stand

# SELECTED VISUAL CONTENTS

For names of photographers, artists, and illustrators, see pages A-59–A-62.

## Other Images



## Pairs, Series, and Collages



## Representations of Data and Processes



## Workplace Documents



* Indicates an accompanying "Responding to an Image" activity

# FEATURES OF *THE BEDFORD GUIDE*, TENTH EDITION, AND ANCILLARIES

## Correlated to the Writing Program Administrators (WPA) Outcomes Statement

| WPA Goals and Learning Outcomes | Support in *The Bedford Guide*, Tenth Edition |
|---|---|
| **Rhetorical Knowledge: Student Outcomes** | |
| **Focus on a purpose** | ▪ Purpose and Audience (pp. 11–15)<br>▪ Chs. 4–14, including thesis development and revision<br>▪ Ch. 20: Strategies for Stating a Thesis and Planning (pp. 398–99)<br>▪ Ch. 23: Strategies for Revising and Editing with revision for purpose, thesis, and audience (pp. 459–60)<br>▪ Re:Writing: Visualizing Purpose tutorial<br>▪ *VideoCentral**: videos on rhetorical purpose<br><br>*For instructors*<br>The following ancillaries contain helpful tips, strategies, and resources for teaching purpose, as well as for the other topics considered throughout this chart.<br>▪ *Instructor's Annotated Edition of The Bedford Guide for College Writers,* Tenth Edition<br>▪ *Practical Suggestions for Teaching with The Bedford Guide for College Writers,* Tenth Edition |
| **Respond to the needs of different audiences** | ▪ Writing for Your Audience and Targeting a College Audience (pp. 12–16)<br>▪ Using Evidence to Appeal to Your Audience (pp. 44–45)<br>▪ Chs. 4–12, with situational consideration of audience and Peer Response questions<br>▪ Attention to writing for specific audiences such as Messages to Your Instructor (pp. 320–23), Online Threaded Discussions (pp. 324–27), workplace (p. 353), and research (p. 628)<br>▪ Ch. 24: Strategies for Future Writing (pp. 476–81)<br>▪ Shaping Your Topic for Your Purpose and Audience (pp. 398–99)<br>▪ Revising for Audience (pp. 460–61),Working with a Peer Editor (pp. 462–64), and Meeting with Your Instructor (p. 464)<br>▪ Re:Writing: Visualizing Audience tutorial |
| **Respond appropriately to different kinds of rhetorical situations** | ▪ Part Two: A Writer's Situations (pp. 56–255) with detailed advice on responding to varied rhetorical situations from recalling an experience to supporting a position with sources<br>▪ Chs. 4–17 with opening "Why Writing Matters" and Chs. 30–35 with "Why Research Matters" feature illustrating college, workplace, and community situations (e.g., pp. 59 and 223)<br>▪ Part Three: Other Writing Situations (pp. 256–369): responding to literature and visuals; writing online, under pressure, and at work<br>▪ Ch. 24: Strategies for Future Writing (pp. 476–87)<br>▪ Re:Writing: Visualizing Context tutorial<br>▪ e-Pages: Learning by Doing activities for Part Two |

** This resource is available packaged with the print book. See the preface for details.*

| WPA Goals and Learning Outcomes | Support in *The Bedford Guide*, Tenth Edition |
|---|---|
| **Rhetorical Knowledge: Student Outcomes** | |
| **Use conventions of format and structure appropriate to the rhetorical situation** | ▪ Examples of effective structure in Part Two (see sample annotations, pp. 158–61)<br>▪ Ch. 15 on file management and templates (pp. 327–30)<br>▪ Chs. 36 and 37 with sample MLA and APA papers<br>▪ Quick Format Guide<br>▪ Quick Research Guide<br>▪ Re:Writing: Sample student writing |
| **Adopt appropriate voice, tone, and level of formality** | ▪ Ch. 40: Word Choice (pp. 834–38)<br>▪ Purpose and audience coverage (pp. 11–15 and throughout)<br>▪ Facing the Challenge: Finding Your Voice (pp. 231–32) and Join the Academic Exchange (pp. 236 and 238–42) |
| **Understand how genres shape reading and writing** | ▪ Part Two: A Writer's Situations (pp. 56–255) with professional and student essays, guided writing advice, and opening and closing images for analysis for a variety of rhetorical situations<br>▪ Why Writing Matters sections opening Chs. 4–17 and 30–35 with applications in college, at work, in the community (e.g., p. 157).<br>▪ Part Three: Other Writing Situations (pp. 256–369) with responding to literature and visuals and writing online, under pressure, and at work<br>▪ Ch. 24: Strategies for Future Writing, including genre analysis<br>▪ *A Writer's Reader* with 40 readings in five thematic groups<br>▪ *A Writer's Research Manual* (Chs. 30–37) and Quick Research Guide (pp. A-20–A-38)<br>▪ Re:Writing: Sample student writing |
| **Write in several genres** | ▪ Rhetorical strategies for varied situations in Part Two, including student and professional examples, Why Writing Matters, Facing the Challenge, and Discovery, Revision, and Editing checklists (e.g., pp. 136–55)<br>▪ Part Three: Other Writing Situations (pp. 256–369) with responding to literature and visuals and writing online, under pressure, and at work<br>▪ Ch. 24: Strategies for Future Writing, including disciplinary assumptions, genre analysis, and a Genre Checklist (pp. 479–83)<br>▪ *A Writer's Research Manual* (Chs. 30–37) and Quick Research Guide (pp. A-20–A-38) |

** This resource is available packaged with the print book. See the preface for details.*

| WPA Goals and Learning Outcomes | Support in *The Bedford Guide*, Tenth Edition |
|---|---|
| **Critical Thinking, Reading, and Writing: Student Outcomes** | |
| **Use writing and reading for inquiry, learning, thinking, and communicating** | ▪ Part One: writing, reading, and critical thinking processes<br>▪ Parts Two, Three, and Four emphasizing the connection between reading and writing<br>▪ *A Writer's Reader* with 40 readings grouped thematically<br>▪ Critical reading apparatus in Part Two: A Writer's Situations (e.g., pp. 60, 63) and in *A Writer's Reader* (e.g., pp. 572, 575)<br>▪ Re:Writing: Reading Critically video<br><br>*For instructors:*<br>▪ *Practical Suggestions for Teaching with The Bedford Guide for College Writers,* Ch. 3, Teaching Critical Thinking and Writing<br>▪ *Teaching Composition: Background Readings:* Ch. 1, Teaching Writing: Key Concepts, Philosophies, Frameworks, and Experiences |
| **Understand a writing assignment as a series of tasks, including finding, evaluating, analyzing, and synthesizing appropriate primary and secondary sources** | ▪ Chs. 4–14 breaking writing assignments into guided tasks<br>▪ Ch. 18: Strategies: A Case Study showing one student's stages writing an essay<br>▪ Ch. 12: Supporting a Position with Sources<br>▪ Ch. 30: Planning Your Research Project<br>▪ Ch. 31: Working with Sources, including capturing information and developing an annotated bibliography<br>▪ Chs. 32–34 on finding, evaluating, integrating, and synthesizing sources (pp. 657–99)<br>▪ Quick Research Guide<br>▪ e-Pages: Additional Learning by Doing activity on finding and evaluating credible sources<br>▪ *VideoCentral**: Videos on integrating sources<br>▪ Visual and Source Activity options in Part 1; Visual and Source Assignment options in Parts 2 and 3. |
| **Integrate students' own ideas with those of others** | ▪ *A Writer's Reader* with journal prompts, writing suggestions, and paired essays<br>▪ Ch. 12: Supporting a Position with Sources (pp. 222–55)<br>▪ Chs. 32–34 on finding, evaluating, integrating and synthesizing sources (pp. 657–99)<br>▪ Quick Research Guide<br>▪ Re:Writing: Research and documentation advice and models |
| **Understand the relationships among language, knowledge, and power** | ▪ Ch. 40: Appropriateness (pp. 834–38) and Bias (pp. 842–45)<br>▪ Purpose and Audience (pp. 11–15) and audience analysis throughout<br>▪ Selections in *A Writer's Reader* on language and literacy by Tan, Rodriguez, Tannen, and others<br>▪ Re:Writing: Why Writing Matters video<br><br>*For instructors:*<br>▪ *Teaching Composition: Background Readings:* Ch. 4, Issues in Writing Pedagogy: Institutional Politics and the Other |

| WPA Goals and Learning Outcomes | Support in *The Bedford Guide*, Tenth Edition |
|---|---|
| **Processes: Student Outcomes** | |
| **Be aware that it usually takes multiple drafts to create and complete a successful text** | ▪ Ch. 1: Writing Processes (pp. 6–16) with process overview<br>▪ Chs. 4–14 with situation-specific process guidance<br>▪ Part Four writing processes in detail, including Ch. 18: Strategies: A Case Study (pp. 372–83) showing one student's stages<br>▪ *Portfolio Keeping,* Third Edition,* discussing portfolio keeping as a reflection of writing processes<br><br>*For instructors:*<br>▪ *Teaching Composition: Background Readings:* Ch. 2, Thinking about the Writing Process |
| **Develop flexible strategies for generating ideas, revising, editing, and proofreading** | ▪ Ch. 1: A Writer's Processes with an overview of generating ideas, planning, drafting, developing, revising, editing, and proofreading (pp. 6–16)<br>▪ Parts Two and Three with situation-specific process strategies<br>▪ Part Four: A Writer's Strategies with detailed coverage of writing processes (pp. 370–487)<br>▪ Re:Writing: Getting Started video<br><br>*For instructors:*<br>▪ *Teaching Composition: Background Readings:* Revising a Draft (pp. 195–246); Ch. 3, Responding to and Evaluating Student Writing |
| **Understand writing as an open process that permits writers to use later invention and rethinking to revise their work** | ▪ Ch. 20: Strategies for Revising and Editing<br>▪ Revision coverage with examples in every Part Two chapter<br>▪ Recurring presentation of a flexible and recursive process of writing (pp. 7–11)<br>▪ Re:Writing: Revising video<br>▪ *Portfolio Keeping,* Third Edition*, discussing portfolio keeping as a reflection of writing processes<br><br>*For instructors:*<br>▪ *Teaching Composition: Background Readings:* Ch. 2, Thinking about the Writing Process |
| **Understand the collaborative and social aspects of writing processes** | ▪ Learning by Doing features including collaborative activities (e.g., pp. 111, 150, 173) and Peer Response guidelines (Part Two and pp. 462–64)<br>▪ Part Two: Additional Writing Assignments with collaborative options (e.g., pp. 133–34)<br>▪ Ch. 18: Strategies: A Case Study including Rough Draft with Peer and Instructor Responses (pp. 375–77) and Reflective Portfolio Letter (p. 383)<br>▪ Ch. 30 advice, Planning Collaborative Research (p. 638)<br>▪ *Portfolio Keeping,* Third Edition*, Ch. 5, Keeping Company and Working with Others, addressing community and peer response<br>▪ *Oral Presentations in the Composition Course: A Brief Guide**: Ch. 9, Presenting as a Group<br><br>*For instructors:*<br>▪ *Practical Suggestions for Teaching with* The Bedford Guide for College Writers, Ch. 2, Creating a Writing Community |

** This resource is available packaged with the print book. See the preface for details.*

| WPA Goals and Learning Outcomes | Support in *The Bedford Guide,* Tenth Edition |
|---|---|
| **Processes: Student Outcomes** | |
| **Learn to critique their own and others' works** | ■ Ch. 23: Strategies for Revising and Editing with peer-editing advice (pp. 462–64)<br>■ Peer Response sections for each chapter in Part Two<br>■ Self-assessment Take Action charts (e.g., p. 179)<br>■ Ch. 18: Strategies: A Case Study including Rough Draft with Peer and Instructor Responses (pp. 375–77) and Reflective Portfolio Letter (p. 383)<br>■ Ch. 24: Strategies for Future Writing with Connecting Expectations and Assessments (pp. 478–79)<br>■ *Portfolio Keeping,* Third Edition*, Ch. 5, Keeping Company and Working with Others, addressing community and peer response<br>■ *Oral Presentations in the Composition Course: A Brief Guide**: Ch. 10, Evaluating Presentations<br><br>*For instructors:*<br>■ *Practical Suggestions for Teaching with The Bedford Guide for College Writers,* Ch. 2, Creating a Writing Community |
| **Learn to balance the advantages of relying on others with the responsibility of doing their part** | ■ Face-to-face and online individual, paired, small-group, and whole-class "Learning by Doing" activities throughout<br>■ Ch. 30 advice, Planning Collaborative Research (p. 638)<br>■ Ethical explorations in Ch. 3: Critical Thinking Processes, Ch. 12: Supporting a Position with Sources, Ch. 15: Writing Online, Ch. 34: Integrating Sources, and the Quick Research Guide<br>■ *Portfolio Keeping,* Third Edition*, Ch. 5, Keeping Company and Working with Others, addressing community and peer response<br><br>*For instructors:*<br>■ *Practical Suggestions for Teaching with The Bedford Guide for College Writers,* Ch. 2, Creating a Writing Community |
| **Use a variety of technologies to address a range of audiences** | ■ Visual Activities in Part 1, which also includes Reading Online and Multimodal Texts in Ch. 2<br>■ Visual Assignment options in Parts 2 and 3 (Chs. 4–17)<br>■ Ch. 14: Responding to Visual Representations<br>■ Ch. 15: Writing Online<br>■ Ch. 16, including oral presentations with visuals<br>■ *A Writer's Research Manual* with online strategies throughout (Chs. 30–37)<br>■ Quick Research Guide, including Searching for Recommended Sources (pp. A-24–A-26)<br>■ Quick Format Guide, including a section on integrating and crediting visuals (pp. A-8–A-12)<br>■ *ix visualizing composition**: Interactive assignments and guided analysis offer practice with multimedia texts<br>■ e-Pages: Multimodal readings that integrate audio, video, visuals, and text<br><br>*For instructors:*<br>■ *Practical Suggestions for Teaching with The Bedford Guide for College Writers,* Part One, Writing Online<br>■ *Teaching Composition: Background Readings:* Teaching Writing with Computers (pp. 305–37); Teaching Visual Literacy (pp. 337–76) |

| WPA Goals and Learning Outcomes | Support in *The Bedford Guide*, Tenth Edition |
|---|---|
| **Knowledge of Conventions** | |
| **Learn common formats for different kinds of texts** | ▪ Advice on various types of assignments in Part Two and Part Three<br>▪ Quick Format Guide with MLA and APA paper and table formats<br>▪ Examples of varied formats for online course (pp. 320–27) and business (pp. 355–65) communication, portfolio letters (pp. 344–47 and 382–83), résumés and application letters (pp. 356–61 and A-18–A-19), presentation visuals (pp. 366–68), and questionnaires (pp. 675–77)<br>▪ *ix visualizing composition**: Interactive assignments and guided analysis for practice with multimedia texts<br><br>*For instructors:*<br>▪ *Teaching Composition: Background Readings:* Teaching Visual Literacy (pp. 337–76) |
| **Develop knowledge of genre conventions ranging from structure and paragraphing to tone and mechanics** | ▪ Part Two: A Writer's Situations and Part Three, Other Writing Situations<br>▪ Ch. 24: Strategies for the Future, including Genre Checklist and Learning by Doing genre analysis (pp. 479–83)<br>▪ Part Four: A Writer's Strategies, including chapters on planning, drafting, and developing<br>▪ Chs. 40: Word Choice, 41: Punctuation, and 42: Mechanics<br>▪ Re:Writing: Why Proofreading Matters video |
| **Practice appropriate means of documenting their work** | ▪ Options for source-based activities (Chs. 1–3) and assignments (Chs. 4–17) concluding each chapter<br>▪ Ch. 12: Supporting a Position with Sources (pp. 222–55), including The Academic Exchange (pp. 238–39)<br>▪ Take Action self-assessment and revision charts on Integrating Source Information Effectively (p. 250), Integrating and Synthesizing Sources (p. 697), MLA style (p. 710), and APA style (p. 738)<br>▪ Chs. 31–34 on working with, finding, evaluating, integrating, and synthesizing sources, including annotated bibliographies (pp. 655–56)<br>▪ Source Navigators (pp. 642–49)<br>▪ Ch. 36 (MLA) and Ch. 37 (APA) with sample entries and full papers<br>▪ Quick Research Guide (pp. A-20–A-38)<br>▪ Re:Writing: *The Bedford Bibliographer* for help in collecting sources and creating bibliography; exercises on MLA and APA style |
| **Control such surface features as syntax, grammar, punctuation, and spelling** | ▪ *A Writer's Handbook* (pp. 761–908) with exercises<br>▪ Quick Editing Guide with Editing Checklist (pp. A-39–A-40) and two Take Action charts (pp. A-50–A-51)<br>▪ Part Two revising and editing advice, including cross-references to relevant topics in the Quick Editing Guide<br>▪ Ch. 20: Strategies for Revising and Editing<br>▪ Re:Writing: Take Action charts<br>▪ LearningCurve exercises on grammar and usage<br><br>*For instructors:*<br>▪ *Practical Suggestions for Teaching with The Bedford Guide for College Writers,* Ch. 4, Providing Support for Underprepared Students |

* *This resource is available packaged with the print book. See the preface for details.*

| WPA Goals and Learning Outcomes | Support in *The Bedford Guide*, Tenth Edition |
|---|---|
| **Composing in Electronic Environments** | |
| **Use electronic environments for drafting, reviewing, revising, editing, and sharing texts** | ▪ Ch. 15: Writing Online, including course or learning management systems<br>▪ Additional Writing Assignments in Parts Two and Three with online options<br>▪ Ch. 20: Strategies for Revising and Editing<br>▪ Learning by Doing activities with many online options<br>▪ *Portfolio Keeping,* Third Edition*, discussion of electronic presentation of portfolios<br>▪ e-Pages: Learning by Doing: Becoming Familiar with Your Course Management System<br>▪ e-Pages: Questions with each essay that students can answer online<br>*For instructors:*<br>▪ *Practical Suggestions for Teaching with The Bedford Guide for College Writers:* Chs. 5 and 6, Teaching Writing Online and Assessing Student Writing<br>▪ *Teaching Composition: Background Readings:* Teaching Writing with Computers (pp. 305–37) |
| **Locate, evaluate, organize, and use research material collected from electronic sources** | ▪ Reading Online and Multimodal Texts, pp. 33–35<br>▪ Ch. 12: Supporting a Position with Sources including e-Pages Research Cluster<br>▪ Chs. 31–34 on working with, finding, evaluating, and integrating sources, including annotated bibliographies (pp. 655–56)<br>▪ Quick Research Guide<br>▪ Re:Writing: *The Bedford Bibliographer* for help in collecting sources and creating bibliography; research checklists<br>*For instructors:*<br>▪ *Practical Suggestions for Teaching with The Bedford Guide for College Writers:* Chs. 5 and 6, Teaching Writing Online, and Assessing Student Writing<br>▪ *Teaching Composition: Background Readings:* Teaching Writing with Computers (pp. 305–37) |
| **Understand and exploit the differences in the rhetorical strategies and in the affordances available for both print and electronic composing processes and texts** | ▪ Ch. 15: Writing Online<br>▪ Part Four: A Writer's Strategies<br>▪ Reading Online and Multimodal Texts, pp. 33–35<br>▪ *A Writer's Reader,* Ch. 28: Digital Living, including eight provocative essays<br>▪ Re:Writing: tutorial on Web design<br>▪ e-Pages: Multimodal readings that integrate audio, video, and visuals<br>*For instructors:*<br>▪ *Practical Suggestions for Teaching with The Bedford Guide for College Writers,* Part One, Using Technology in Your Composition Course and Teaching Writing Online<br>▪ *Teaching Composition: Background Readings:* Teaching Writing with Computers (pp. 305–37) |

# How to Use *The Bedford Guide for College Writers*

Just as you may be unsure of what to expect from your writing course, you may be unsure of what to expect from your writing textbook. You may even be wondering how any textbook can improve your writing. In fact, a book alone can't make you a better writer, but practice can, and *The Bedford Guide for College Writers* is designed to make your writing practice effective and productive. This text offers help – easy to find and easy to use – for writing essays most commonly assigned in college.

Underlying *The Bedford Guide* is the idea that writing is a necessary and useful skill beyond the writing course. The skills you will learn throughout this book are transferable to other areas of your life – future courses, jobs, and community activities – making *The Bedford Guide* both a time-saver and a money-saver. The following sections describe how you can get the most out of this text.

## Finding Information in *The Bedford Guide*

In *The Bedford Guide,* it is easy to find what you need when you need it. Each of the tools described here directs you to useful information – fast.

**Brief List of Contents.** Open the book to the inside front cover. At a glance you can see a list of the topics in *The Bedford Guide.* If you are looking for a specific chapter, this brief list of contents is the quickest way to find it.

e **List of e-Pages Contents.** Facing the inside front cover you will find a list of readings and writing activities available online at **bedfordstmartins.com/bedguide**. This list is a guide to the book's multimodal readings (such as videos, audio segments, interviews, infographics, and visual essays) and online assignments (such as "Learning by Doing" activities as well as critical reading and thinking questions about the e-Pages readings). The e-Pages extend this book into the online environment, giving you a rich array of integrated multimodal content.

# Contents



For readings that go beyond the printed page, see **bedfordstmartins.com/bedguide** xxv

**Detailed List of Contents.** Beginning on p. xxv, the longer, more detailed list of contents breaks down the topics covered within each chapter of the book. Use this list to find a specific part of a chapter. For example, if you have been asked to read Olof Eriksson's paper, "The Problems with Masculinity," a quick scan of the detailed contents will show you that it begins on page 24.

**Rhetorical List of Contents.** This list, beginning on page xl, includes all the readings in *The Bedford Guide,* organized by writing strategy or situation, such as "Explaining Causes and Effects," or "Evaluating and Reviewing." Use this list to locate examples of the kind of writing you are doing and to see how other writers have approached their material.

**Selected List of Visuals.** On page xlv is a list of many of the photographs or other visual images in *The Bedford Guide,* arranged by type, genre, or purpose. This list can help you locate photographs, such as an advertisement or visual essay, to analyze or compare in your writing. In our increasingly visual age, knowing how to read and analyze visuals and then to write about them is a particularly valuable skill.

**Locator Guide.** If you find yourself stuck at any stage of the writing process, open the book to the page facing the inside back cover. There you will find the page numbers of Learning by Doing activities, self-assessment flowcharts, and other resources. If you are having trouble writing an opening to your paper, for example, this Locator Guide makes it easy for you to turn to the right place at the right time.

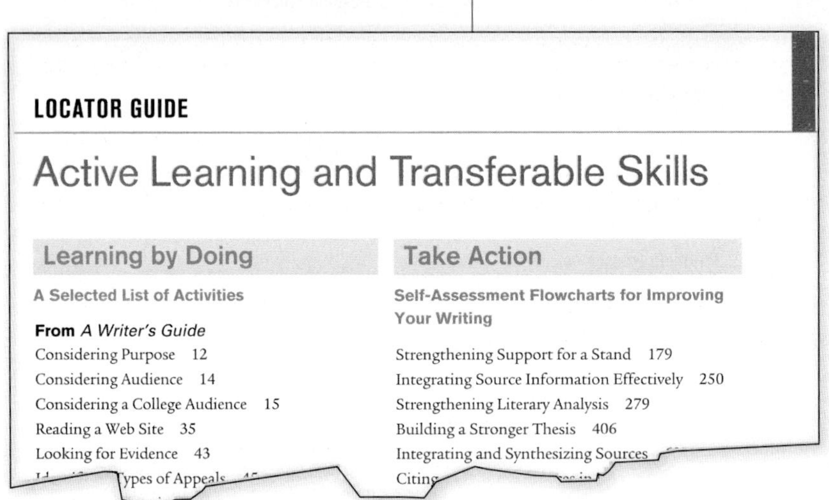

**LOCATOR GUIDE**

Active Learning and Transferable Skills

**Learning by Doing**

A Selected List of Activities

**From** *A Writer's Guide*



**Take Action**

Self-Assessment Flowcharts for Improving Your Writing





**Index.** *The Bedford Guide*'s index is an in-depth list of the book's contents in alphabetical order. Turn to page I-1 when you want to find the information available in the book for a particular topic. This example shows you all the places to look for help with analyzing material, a common assignment in college.

**Guide to the Handbook.** After the index, you will find a guide that shows you at a glance the entire contents of *A Writer's Handbook.* Turn to this guide when you need help editing your essays. It gives page numbers for each handbook topic, such as "sentence fragments." If English is not your native language, this guide notes all of the "ESL Guidelines" included in the handbook, such as "Cumulative Adjectives."

**Marginal Cross-References.** You can find additional information quickly by using the references in the margins – notes on the sides of each page that tell you where to turn in the book or on the book's companion Web site. For online resources, visit **bedfordstmartins.com/bedguide** for more help or for other activities related to what you are reading.

**Color-Coded Pages.** Several sections of *The Bedford Guide* are color-coded to make them easy to find.

- "MLA Style" (pp. 708–734). If you need help using MLA guidelines to document the sources you have used in your paper, turn to the green-edged pages.
- "APA Style" (pp. 736–759). If you need help using APA guidelines to document the sources you have used in your paper, turn to the turquoise-edged pages.
- "Quick Format Guide" (pp. A-1–A-19). If you need help formatting your paper, turn to this section at the back of the book, which is designated with yellow-edged pages.
- "Quick Research Guide" (pp. A-20–A-38). If you need fast help with research processes, sources, or the basics of MLA or APA style, turn to this section at the back of the book, which is designated with orange-edged pages.
- "Quick Editing Guide" (pp. A-39–A-58). If you need help as you edit your writing, turn to this section at the back of the book, which is designated with blue-edged pages.

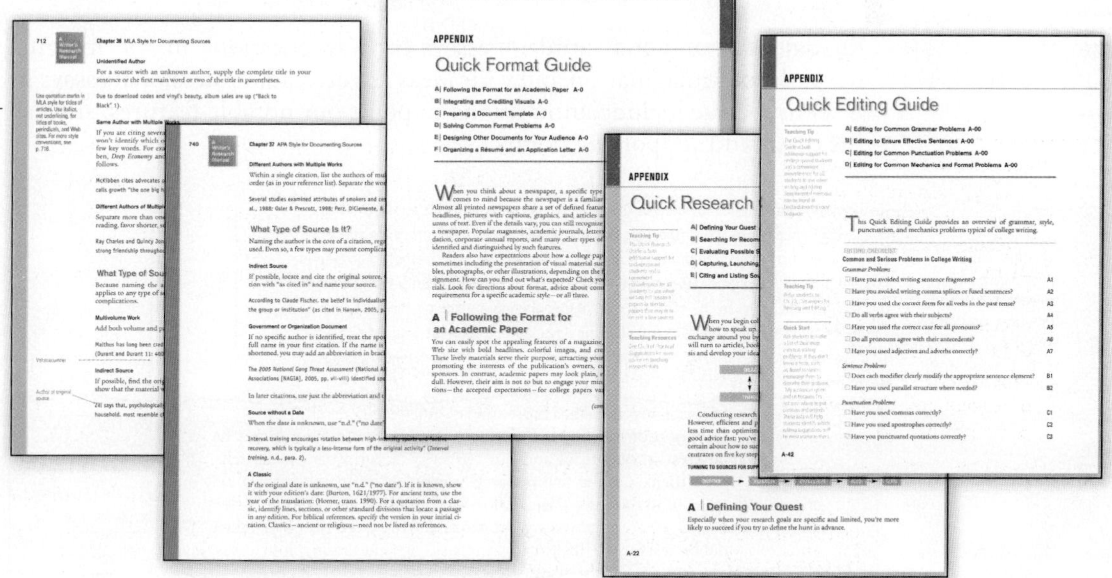

**Color-Coded Tabs.** Your instructor may use correction symbols, such as "agr" for subject-verb agreement, to indicate areas in your draft that need editing. Tabs at the top of each page in *A Writer's Handbook* link these common correction symbols with explanations, examples, and exercises related to the particular editing problem. The example below shows a page from the handbook.

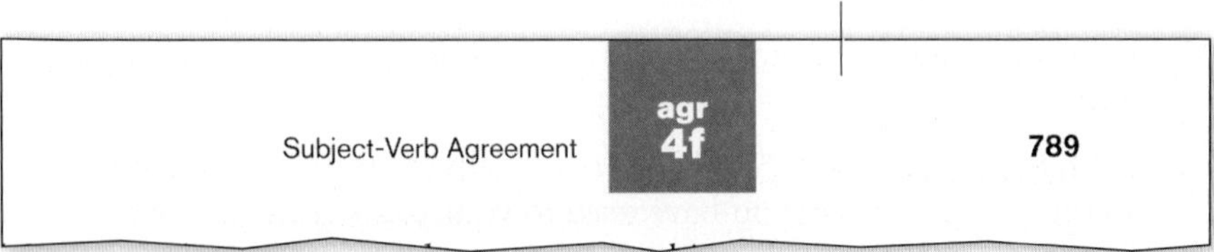


**Answers to Exercises.** As you complete the exercises in the handbook, you will want to know if you are learning what is expected. Turn to pages 900–907 in the back of the book to find the correct answers to the lettered exercises.

# Becoming a Better Writer by Using *The Bedford Guide*

*The Bedford Guide* includes readings, checklists, activities, and other features that will help you to improve your writing and to do well in college and on the job.

**Model Readings and e-Pages.** *The Bedford Guide* is filled with examples of both professional and student essays, located on the beige pages in *A Writer's Guide* and in *A Writer's Reader*. All these essays are accompanied by informative notes about the author, prereading questions, definitions of difficult words, questions for thinking more deeply about the reading, and suggestions for writing.

**Reading Annotations.** Student essays include questions in the margins to spark your imagination and your ideas as you read. Professional essays in *A Writer's Guide* include annotations to point out notable features, such as the thesis and supporting points.

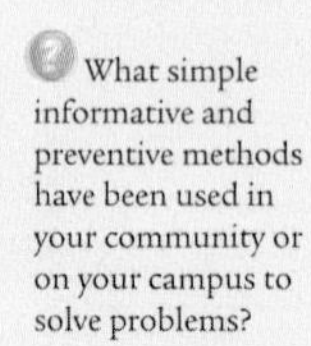
What simple informative and preventive methods have been used in your community or on your campus to solve problems?

... students about bicycle ... happens all the time and that it could happen to them. The program also would need to tell students about certain steps that they could take to avoid becoming victims of bike theft. For example, it could provide information about different methods of bicycle security such as keeping the serial number in case the bike is stolen and engraving a name on the bike so that it can be easily identified. The program also should tell students what to do if a bicycle is actually stolen such as calling the police and filing a report. This awareness program would prevent many students from ending up with stolen bicycles.

five to thirty-four) living alone has more than quadrupled (Russell).

The combination of loneliness and our innate° desire to belong may be fueling our interest in celebrities and our tendency to form para-social relationships° with them. Only a few research psychologists have seriously explored this possibility, among them Lynn McCutcheon and Dianne Ashe. McCutcheon and Ashe compared results from 150 subjects who had taken three personality tests—one measuring shyness, one measuring loneliness, ...

2 THESIS presenting position

Supporting evidence, including description of psychological study

*The Bedford Guide* also includes e-Pages, which are multimodal readings (such as videos, audio segments, and infographics) and online assignments (such as critical thinking and reading questions and "Learning by Doing" activities). The e-Pages are marked in the main Contents and in the book pages with this icon: To access them, visit **bedfordstmartins.com/bedguide**.

**Tiana Chavez** — Video

### ASU Athletes Discuss Superstitions

Tiana Chavez interviews athletes from Arizona State University about what pregame superstitions they engage in. To watch the video, go to Chapter 6: **bedfordstmartins.com/bedguide**.

**Clear Assignments.** In Chapters 4 to 14, the "Learning by Writing" section presents the assignment for the chapter and guides you through the process of writing that type of essay. The "Facing the Challenge" section in each of these chapters helps you through the most complicated step in the assignment.

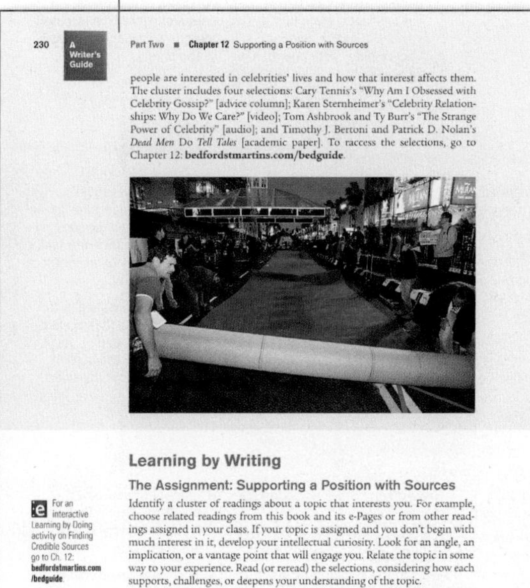

230 A Writer's Guide — Part Two ■ **Chapter 12** Supporting a Position with Sources

people are interested in celebrities' lives and how that interest affects them. The cluster includes four selections: Cary Tennis's "Why Am I Obsessed with Celebrity Gossip?" [advice column]; Karen Sternheimer's "Celebrity Relationships: Why Do We Care?" [video]; Tom Ashbrook and Ty Burr's "The Strange Power of Celebrity" [audio]; and Timothy J. Bertoni and Patrick D. Nolan's *Dead Men* Do *Tell Tales* [academic paper]. To raccess the selections, go to Chapter 12: **bedfordstmartins.com/bedguide**.

**Learning by Writing**

**The Assignment: Supporting a Position with Sources**

Identify a cluster of readings about a topic that interests you. For example, choose related readings from this book and its e-Pages or from other readings assigned in your class. If your topic is assigned and you don't begin with much interest in it, develop your intellectual curiosity. Look for an angle, an implication, or a vantage point that will engage you. Relate the topic in some way to your experience. Read (or reread) the selections, considering how each supports, challenges, or deepens your understanding of the topic.

Based on the information in your cluster of readings, develop an enlightening position about the topic that you'd like to share with an audience of college readers. Support this position—your working thesis—using quotations, paraphrases, summaries, and syntheses of the information in the readings as evidence. Present your information from sources clearly, and credit your sources appropriately.

For an interactive Learning by Doing activity on Finding Credible Sources go to Ch. 12: **bedfordstmartins.com/bedguide**.

See the contents of *A Writer's Reader* on pp. 490–91.

Learning by Writing 231

Three students investigated topics of great variety:

One student examined local language usage that combined words from English and Spanish, drawing on essays about language diversity to analyze the patterns and implications of such usage.

Another writer used a cluster of readings about technology to evaluate the privacy issues on a popular Web site for student profiles.

A third, using personal experience with a blended family and several essays on families, challenged misconceptions about today's families.

**Facing the Challenge** Finding Your Voice

The major challenge that writers face when using sources to support a position is finding their own voice. You create your voice as a college writer through your choice of language and angle of vision. You probably want to present yourself as a thoughtful writer with credible insights, someone a reader will want to hear from.

Finding your own voice may be difficult in a source-based paper. After all, you need to read carefully and then capture information to strengthen your discussion by quoting, paraphrasing, or summarizing. You need to introduce it, feed it into your draft, and credit it. By this time, you may worry that your sources have taken over your paper. You may feel there's no room left for your own voice and, even if there were, it's too quiet to jostle past the powerful words of your sources. That, however, is your challenge.

As you develop your voice as a college writer and use it to guide your readers' understanding, you'll restrict sources to their proper role as supporting evidence. Don't let them get pushy or dominate your writing. Use these questions to help you strengthen your voice:

For more on evidence, see pp. 40–44 and pp. 170–74.

- Can you write a list or passage explaining what you'd like readers to hear from your voice? Where could you add more of this in your draft?
- Have you used your own voice, not quotations or paraphrases from sources, to introduce your topic, state your thesis, and draw conclusions?
- Have you generally relied on your own voice to open and conclude paragraphs and to reinforce your main ideas in every passage?
- Have you alternated between your voice and the voices of sources? Can you strengthen your voice if it gets trampled by a herd of sources?
- Have you used your voice to identify and introduce source material before you present it? Have you used your voice to explain or interpret source material after you include it?
- Have you used your voice to tell readers why your sources are relevant, how they support your points, and what their limits might be?
- Have you carefully created your voice as a college writer, balancing passion and personality with rock-solid reasoning?

**Learning by Doing** Selecting Reliable Sources

When you choose your own sources, evaluate them to be sure they are reliable choices that your audience will respect. When your sources are assigned, assess their strengths, weaknesses, and limitations to use them effectively. Bring your articles, essays, and other sources to a small-group evaluation session. Using the checklist in C3 in the Quick Research Guide (pp. A-27–A-28), discuss your common sources or a key source selected by each writer in the group. Look for points that you might mention in a paper to bolster a source's credibility with readers (for example, the author's professional affiliation). Look as well for limitations that might restrict what a source can support.

**"Learning by Doing."** These activities are designed to let you practice and apply what you are learning to your own writing. They encourage you to make key concepts your own so that you will be able to take what you have learned and apply it in other writing situations and contexts in college and in the workplace.

**"Take Action" Charts.** These flowcharts focus on common writing challenges. They help you to ask the right questions of your draft and to take active steps to revise effectively. They are a powerful tool in helping you become an independent writer, able to assess what you have written and improve it on your own.

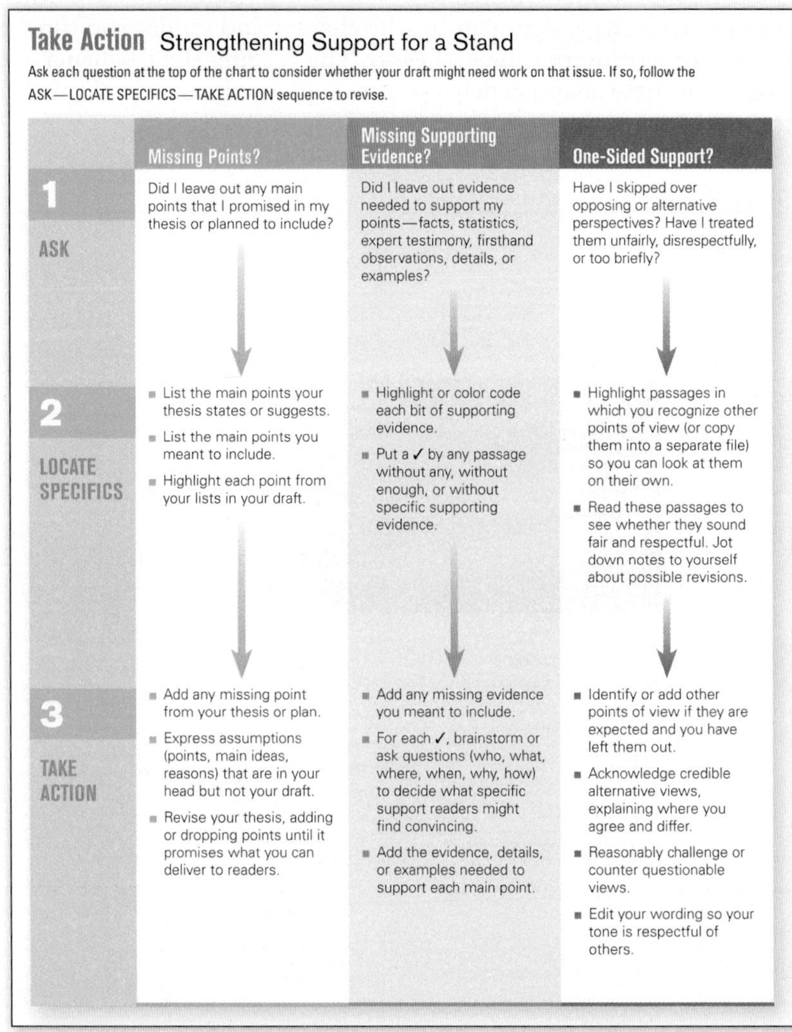
Take Action Strengthening Support for a Stand
Ask each question at the top of the chart to consider whether your draft might need work on that issue. If so, follow the ASK—LOCATE SPECIFICS—TAKE ACTION sequence to revise.
Missing Points?
Missing Supporting Evidence?
One-Sided Support?
1 ASK
Did I leave out any main points that I promised in my thesis or planned to include?
Did I leave out evidence needed to support my points—facts, statistics, expert testimony, firsthand observations, details, or examples?
Have I skipped over opposing or alternative perspectives? Have I treated them unfairly, disrespectfully, or too briefly?
2 LOCATE SPECIFICS
■ List the main points your thesis states or suggests.
■ List the main points you meant to include.
■ Highlight each point from your lists in your draft.
■ Highlight or color code each bit of supporting evidence.
■ Put a ✓ by any passage without any, without enough, or without specific supporting evidence.
■ Highlight passages in which you recognize other points of view (or copy them into a separate file) so you can look at them on their own.
■ Read these passages to see whether they sound fair and respectful. Jot down notes to yourself about possible revisions.
3 TAKE ACTION
■ Add any missing point from your thesis or plan.
■ Express assumptions (points, main ideas, reasons) that are in your head but not your draft.
■ Revise your thesis, adding or dropping points until it promises what you can deliver to readers.
■ Add any missing evidence you meant to include.
■ For each ✓, brainstorm or ask questions (who, what, where, when, why, how) to decide what specific support readers might find convincing.
■ Add the evidence, details, or examples needed to support each main point.
■ Identify or add other points of view if they are expected and you have left them out.
■ Acknowledge credible alternative views, explaining where you agree and differ.
■ Reasonably challenge or counter questionable views.
■ Edit your wording so your tone is respectful of others.

**Source Navigator**

Article in a Print Magazine

**Record this information in your notes about each source:**

1 The complete name of the author
2 The title and any subtitle of the article
3 The title and any subtitle of the magazine
4 The full date of the issue
5 The article's page numbers
6 The periodical's volume number and issue number if available (for APA), sometimes found on title or contents page
7 The medium of publication (for MLA)

CITIES

SCIENTIFIC AMERICAN

6 Volume 305, Number 3

Cynthia Rosenzweig is a senior research scientist at the NASA Goddard Institute for Space Studies and at Columbia University's Earth Institute.

2 All Climate Is Local

Mayors are often better equipped than presidents to cut greenhouse gases

1 By Cynthia Rosenzweig

For years scientists have urged national leaders to tackle climate change, based on the assumption that prevention efforts would require the coordinated actions of entire nations to be effective. But as anyone who has watched the past 15 years of international climate negotiations can attest, most countries are still reluctant to take meaningful steps to lower their production of greenhouse gases, much less address issues such as how to help developing countries protect themselves from the extreme effects of climate change. Frustrated by the ongoing diplomatic stalemate, a number of urban leaders have decided to take mat- severe. Most of the world's major metropolises were originally built on rivers or coastlines and are therefore subject to flooding from rising seas and instances of heavier rainfall.

Many civic leaders point to Hurricane Katrina and the devastation it visited on New Orleans in 2005 as their moment of awakening. They saw how the multiple failures of an aging and inadequate infrastructure, plus indifferent planning, sharply increased the death toll of a catastrophe that had long been predicted. Indeed, two major alliances of city mayors to combat climate change formed within months after Hurricane Katrina's landfall. The organization now known as the C40 Cities Climate Leadership Group launched in London in October

5 70 Scientific American, September 2011 (3) (4)

Photograph by Dan Saelinger

642

**Create a source entry out of the information you collect:**

MLA

Source entry in MLA style: (1) Rosenzweig, Cynthia. (2) "All Climate Is Local." (3) *Scientific American* (4) Sept. 2011: (5) 70-73. (7) Print.

Source note with a general summary of the article: Discusses the benefits of tackling climate change at the local level as opposed to the national level.

APA

Source entry in APA style: (1) Rosenzweig, C. (4) (2011, September). (2) All climate is local. (3) *Scientific American,* (6) *305*(3), (5) 70-73.

Source note with a technical summary of the article: Reviews climate-change research and conferences on temperature shifts, weather events, emission rates, and other issues that help mayors and urban planners develop innovative responses.

643

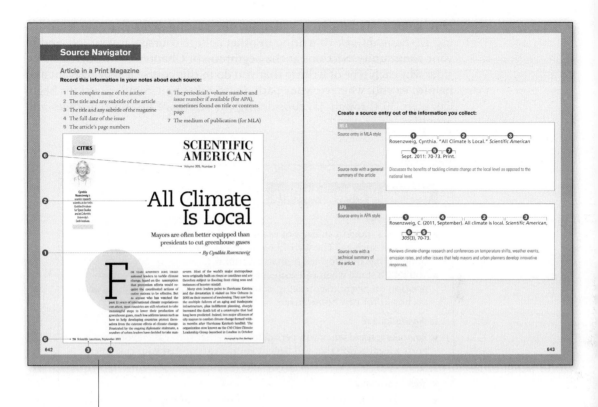

**Resources for Crediting Sources.** Source Navigators, on pages 642–49, show you where to look in several major types of sources so that you can quickly find the details needed to credit these sources correctly.

**Helpful Checklists.** Easy-to-use checklists help you to consider your purpose and audience, discover something to write about, get feedback from a peer, revise your draft, and edit for grammatical correctness, using references to the "Quick Editing Guide" (pages A-39–A-58).

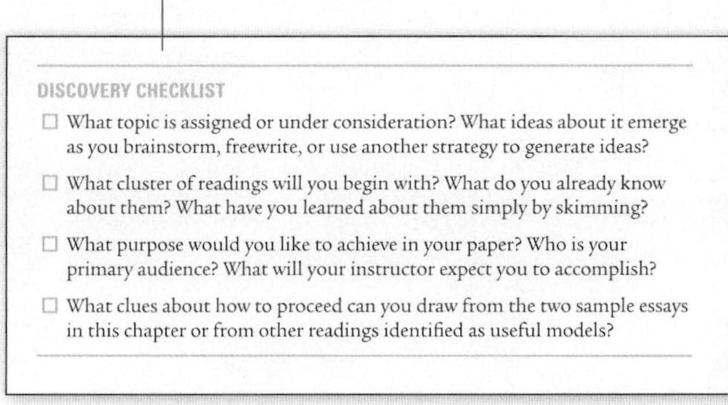

DISCOVERY CHECKLIST

- ☐ What topic is assigned or under consideration? What ideas about it emerge as you brainstorm, freewrite, or use another strategy to generate ideas?
- ☐ What cluster of readings will you begin with? What do you already know about them? What have you learned about them simply by skimming?
- ☐ What purpose would you like to achieve in your paper? Who is your primary audience? What will your instructor expect you to accomplish?
- ☐ What clues about how to proceed can you draw from the two sample essays in this chapter or from other readings identified as useful models?

**Why Writing Matters.** You will apply the writing skills that you learn using *The Bedford Guide* to writing in other college courses, at your job, and in your community. Sections at the beginning of Chapters 4 through 17 consider why each type of writing that you do in this course will be relevant and helpful to you, wherever your path ahead takes you. Similar sections begin Chapters 30 through 35, considering the relevance of research stages and activities.

### Why Taking a Stand Matters

**In a College Course**

- You take a stand in an essay or exam when you respond, pro or con, to a statement such as "The Web, like movable type for printing, is an invention that has transformed human communication."
- You take a stand when you write research papers that support your position on juvenile sentencing, state support for higher education, or tax breaks for new home buyers.

**In the Workplace**

- You take a stand when you persuade others that your case report supports a legal action that will benefit your clients or that your customer-service initiative will attract new business.

**In Your Community**

- You take a stand when you write a letter to the editor appealing to voters to support a local bond issue.

When have you taken a stand in your writing? In what circumstances are you likely to do so again?

# A WRITER'S GUIDE

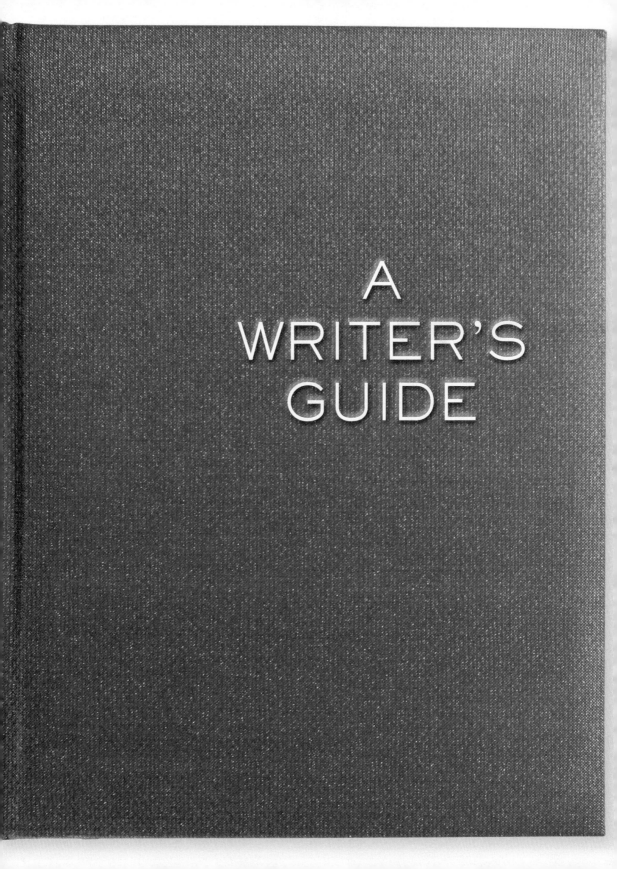

# A Writer's Guide Contents

## Part One A College Writer's Processes

## Part Two A Writer's Situations



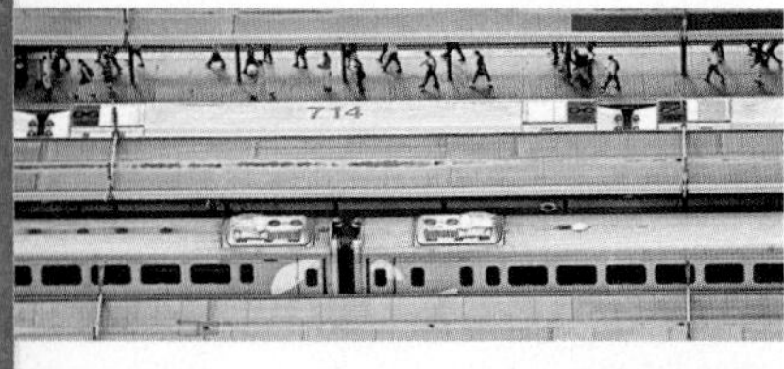


## Part Three Other Writing Situations

## Part Four A Writer's Strategies

# Introduction: Writing in College

As a college writer you probably wrestle with the question, What should I write? You may feel you have nothing to say or nothing worth saying. Maybe your difficulty lies in understanding the requirements of your writing situation, finding a topic, or uncovering information about it. Perhaps you, like many other college writers, have convinced yourself that professional writers have some special way of discovering ideas for writing. But they have no magic. In reality, what they have is experience and confidence, the products of lots of practice writing.

In *The Bedford Guide for College Writers,* we want you to become a better writer by actually writing. To help you do so, we'll give you a lot of practice as well as useful advice to help you build your skills and confidence. Because writing and learning to write are many-faceted tasks, each part of *A Writer's Guide* is devoted to a different aspect of writing. Together, these four parts contribute to a seamless whole, much like the writing process itself.

**Part One, "A College Writer's Processes."** This part introduces writing, reading, and thinking critically—essential processes for meeting college expectations.

**Part Two, "A Writer's Situations."** The nine chapters in Part Two form the core of *The Bedford Guide*. Each presents a writing situation and then guides you as you write a paper in response. You'll develop skills in recalling, observing, interviewing, comparing and contrasting, explaining causes and effects, taking a stand, proposing a solution, evaluating and reviewing, and supporting a position with sources.

**Part Three, "Other Writing Situations."** This part leads you through five special situations that most students encounter at some point—writing about literature or visuals and writing online, under pressure, or at work.

**Part Four, "A Writer's Strategies."** Part Four opens with one student's strategies, showing how a paper evolves from idea to final form. The rest is packed with tips and activities that you can use to generate ideas, plan, draft, develop, revise, edit, and carry to the future what you have learned as a writer.

# A COLLEGE WRITER'S PROCESSES

PART ONE

# 1 Writing Processes

You are already a writer with long experience. In school you have taken notes, written book reports and term papers, answered exam questions, perhaps kept a journal. In the community or on the job you've composed letters and e-mails. You've sent text messages or tweets to friends, made lists, maybe even written songs or poetry. All this experience is about to pay off as you tackle college writing, learning by doing.

In this book our purpose is to help you to write better, deeper, clearer, and more satisfying papers than you have ever written before and to learn to do so by actually writing. Throughout the book we'll give you a lot of practice—in writing processes, patterns, and strategies—to build confidence. And we'll pose various writing situations and say, "Go for it!"

## Writing, Reading, and Critical Thinking

In college you will expand what you already know about writing. You may be asked not only to recall an experience but also to reflect upon its significance. Or you may go beyond summarizing positions about an issue to present your own position or propose a solution. Above all, you will read and think critically—not just stacking up facts but analyzing what you discover, deciding what it means, and weighing its value. As you read—and write—actively, you will engage with the ideas of others, analyzing and judging those ideas. You will use criteria—models, conventions, principles, standards—to assess or evaluate what you are doing.

For more on reading critically, see Ch. 2. For more on thinking critically, see Ch. 3.

**WRITER'S CHECKLIST**

- ☐ Have you achieved your purpose?
- ☐ Have you considered your audience?
- ☐ Have you clearly stated your point as a thesis or unmistakably implied it?
- ☐ Have you supported your point with enough reliable evidence to persuade your audience?

- ☐ Have you arranged your ideas logically so that each follows from, supports, or adds to the one before it?
- ☐ Have you made the connections among ideas clear to a reader?
- ☐ Have you established an appropriate tone?

In large measure, learning to write well is learning what questions to ask as you write. For that reason, we include questions, suggestions, and activities to help you accomplish your writing tasks and reflect on your own processes as you write, read, and think critically.

For information and journal questions about the Part One photograph, see the last two pages of the Appendices.

## A Process of Writing

Writing can seem at times an overwhelming drudgery, worse than scrubbing floors; at other moments, it's a sport full of thrills—like whizzing downhill on skis, not knowing what you'll meet around a bend. Unpredictable as the process may seem, nearly all writers do similar things:

- They generate ideas.
- They plan, draft, and develop their papers.
- They revise and edit.

These three activities form the basis of most effective writing processes, and they lie at the heart of each writing situation in this book.

For full chapters on stages of the writing process, see Chs. 18–24.

e For an interactive Learning by Doing activity on Analyzing Audience, go to Ch. 1: **bedfordstmartins .com/bedguide**.

### Getting Started

Two considerations—what you want to accomplish as a writer and how you want to appeal to your audience—will shape the direction of your writing. Clarifying your purpose and considering your audience are likely to increase your confidence as a writer. Even so, your writing process may take you in unexpected directions, not necessarily in a straight line. You can skip around, work on several parts at a time, test a fresh approach, circle back over what's already done, or stop to play with a sentence until it clicks.

### Generating Ideas

The first activity in writing—finding a topic and something to say about it—is often the most challenging and least predictable. The chapter section called "Generating Ideas" is filled with examples, questions, checklists, and visuals designed to trigger ideas that will help you begin the writing assignment.

**Discovering What to Write About.** You may get an idea while texting friends, riding your bike, or staring out the window. Sometimes a topic lies near home, in a conversation or an everyday event. Often, your reading will

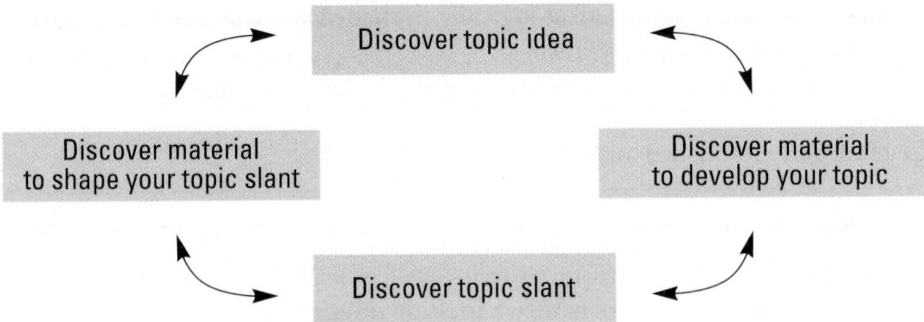


raise questions that call for investigation. Even if an assignment doesn't appeal to you, your challenge is to find a slant that does. Find it, and words will flow—words to engage readers and accomplish your purpose.

**Discovering Material.** To shape and support your ideas, you'll need facts and figures, reports and opinions, examples and illustrations. How do you find supporting material that makes your slant on a topic clear and convincing? Luckily you have many sources at your fingertips. You can recall your experience and knowledge, observe things around you, talk with others who are knowledgeable, read enlightening materials that draw you to new approaches, and think critically about all these sources.

For an online class discussion of writing processes, see pp. 324–26.

### Learning by Doing Reflecting on Ideas

Think over past writing experiences at school or work. How do you get ideas? Where do they come from? Where do you turn for related material? What are your most reliable sources of inspiration and information? Share your experiences with others in class or online, noting any new approaches you would like to try.

## Planning, Drafting, and Developing

Next you will plan your paper, write a draft, and develop your ideas further. The sections titled "Planning, Drafting, and Developing" will help you through these stages for the assignment in that chapter.

**Planning.** Having discovered a burning idea to write about (or at least a smoldering one) and some supporting material (but maybe not enough yet), you will sort out what matters most. If you see one main point, or thesis, test various ways of stating it, given your purpose and audience:

| | |
|---|---|
| MAYBE | Parking in the morning before class is annoying. |
| OR | Campus parking is a big problem. |

Next arrange your ideas and material in a sensible order that will clarify your point. For example, you might group and label your ideas, make an outline, or analyze the main point, breaking it down into parts:

> Parking on campus is a problem for students because of the long lines, inefficient entrances, and poorly marked spaces.

But if no clear thesis emerges quickly, don't worry. You may find one while you draft—that is, while you write an early version of your paper.

For practice developing a main point, go to the interactive "Take Action" charts in Re:Writing at **bedfordstmartins.com/bedguide**.

**Drafting.** As your ideas begin to appear, welcome them and lure them forth so they don't go back into hiding. When you take risks at this stage, you'll probably be surprised and pleased at what happens, even though your first version will be rough. Writing takes time; a paper usually needs several drafts and maybe a clearer introduction, stronger conclusion, more convincing evidence, or even a fresh start.

**Developing.** Weave in explanations, definitions, examples, details, and varied evidence to make your ideas clear and persuasive. For example, you may define an at-risk student, illustrate the problems of single parents, or

For advice on using a few sources, see the Quick Research Guide, pp. A-20–A-38.

PLAN
• Identify your purpose and audience
• Decide on one main point
• State a thesis
• Organize ideas by grouping or outlining
• Explain and support
• Add definitions, examples, and details
• Supply evidence such as facts, statistics, expert testimony, and observations
• Start and restart
• Build paragraphs
• Open and conclude
• Create coherence
DEVELOP
DRAFT

Processes for Planning, Drafting, and Developing

supply statistics about hit-and-run accidents. If you need specific support for your point, use strategies for developing ideas—or return to those for generating ideas. Work in your insights if they fit.

### Learning by Doing Reflecting on Drafts

Reflect on your past writing experiences. How do you usually plan, draft, and develop your writing? How well do your methods work? How do you adjust them to the situation or type of writing you're doing? Which part of producing a draft do you most dread, enjoy, or wish to change? Why? Write down your reflections, and then share your experiences with others in class or online.

## Revising and Editing

You might be tempted to relax once you have a draft, but for most writers, revising begins the work in earnest. Each "Revising and Editing" section provides checklists as well as suggestions for working with a peer.

**Revising.** Revising means both reseeing and rewriting, making major changes so your paper does what you want it to. You may revise what you know and what you think while you write or when you reread. You might reconsider your purpose and audience, rework your thesis, decide what to put in or leave out, move paragraphs around, and connect ideas better. Perhaps you'll add costs to a paper on parking problems or switch attention from mothers to fathers as you consider teen parents.

If you put aside your draft for a few hours or a day, you can reread it with fresh eyes and a clear mind. Other students can also help you—sometimes more than a textbook or an instructor can—by responding to your drafts as engaged readers.

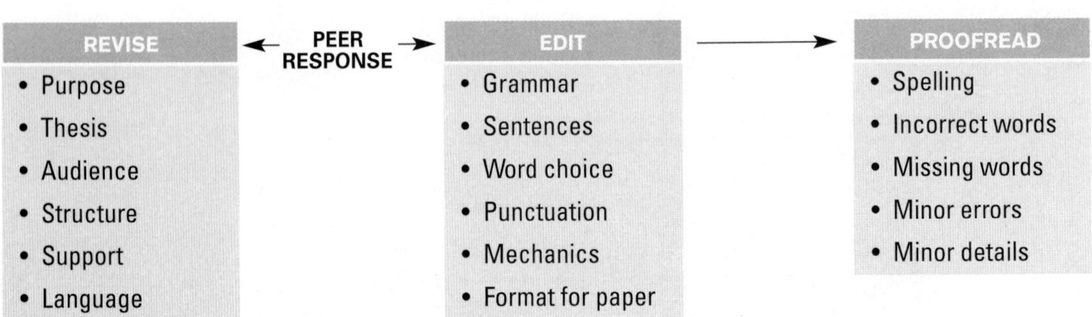

**Editing.** Editing means refining details, improving wording, and correcting flaws that may stand in the way of your readers' understanding and enjoyment. Don't edit too early, though, because you may waste time on parts that you later revise out. In editing, you usually make these repairs:

For editing advice, see the Quick Editing Guide, pp. A-39–A-58. For format advice, see the Quick Format Guide, pp. A-1–A-19.

- Drop unnecessary words; choose lively and precise words.
- Replace incorrect or inappropriate wording.
- Rearrange words in a clearer, more emphatic order.
- Combine short, choppy sentences, or break up long, confusing ones.
- Refine transitions for continuity of thought.
- Check grammar, usage, punctuation, and mechanics.

**Proofreading.** Finally you'll proofread, taking a last look, checking correctness, and catching doubtful spellings or word-processing errors.

### Learning by Doing Reflecting on Finishing

Think over past high-pressure writing experiences: major papers at school, reports at work, or personal projects such as a blog or Web site. What steps do you take to rethink and refine your writing before submitting or posting it? What prompts you to make major changes? How do you try to satisfy concerns or quirks of your main reader or a broader audience? Work with others in class or online to collect and share your best ideas about wrapping up writing projects.

## Purpose and Audience

At any moment in the writing process, two questions are worth asking:

WHY AM I WRITING? WHO IS MY AUDIENCE?

### Writing for a Reason

Like most college writing assignments, every assignment in this book asks you to write for a definite reason. For example, you'll recall a memorable experience in order to explain its importance for you; you'll take a stand on a controversy in order to convey your position and persuade readers to respect it. Be careful not to confuse the sources and strategies

For more on using your purpose for planning, see pp. 398–99, and for revising, see pp. 459–60.

you apply in these assignments with your ultimate purpose for writing. "To compare and contrast two things" is not a very interesting purpose; "to compare and contrast two Web sites *in order to explain which is more reliable*" implies a real reason for writing. In most college writing, your purpose will be to explain something to your readers or to convince them of something.

To sharpen your concentration on your purpose, ask yourself from the start: What do I want to do? And, in revising, Did I do what I meant to do? These practical questions will help you slice out irrelevant information and remove other barriers to getting your paper where you want it to go.

### Learning by Doing Considering Purpose

Imagine that you are in the following writing situations. For each, write a sentence or two summing up your purpose as a writer.

1. The instructor in your psychology course has assigned a paragraph about the meanings of three essential terms in your readings.
2. You're upset about a change in financial aid procedures and plan to write a letter asking the financial aid director to remedy the problem.
3. You're starting a blog about your first year at college so your extended family can envision the environment and share your experiences.
4. Your supervisor wants you to write an article about the benefits of a new company service for the customer newsletter.
5. Your Facebook profile seemed appropriate last year, but you want to revise it now that you're attending college and have a job with future prospects.

## Writing for Your Audience

For more on planning for your readers, see pp. 398–99. For more on revising for them, see pp. 460–61.

Your audience, or your readers, may or may not be defined in your assignment. Consider the following examples:

ASSIGNMENT 1 — Discuss the advantages and disadvantages of homeschooling.

ASSIGNMENT 2 — In a letter to parents of school-aged children, discuss the advantages and disadvantages of homeschooling.

If your assignment defines an audience, as the second example does, you need to think about how to approach those readers and what to assume about their views. For example, what points would you include in a discussion aimed at parents? How would you organize your ideas? Would you discuss advantages or disadvantages first? On the other hand, how might your approach differ if the assignment read this way?

ASSIGNMENT 3 — In a newsletter article for teachers, discuss the advantages and disadvantages of homeschooling.

## Audience Characteristics and Expectations

| | General Audience | College Instructor | Work Supervisor | Campus Friend |
|---|---|---|---|---|
| **Relationship to You** | Imagined but not known personally | Known briefly in a class context | Known for some time in a job context | Known in campus and social contexts |
| **Reason for Reading Your Writing** | Curious attitude and interest in your topic assumed | Professional responsibility for your knowledge and skills | Managerial interest in and reliance on your job performance | Personal interest based on shared circumstances |
| **Knowledge About Your Topic** | Level of awareness assumed and gaps addressed with logical presentation | Well informed about college topics but wants to see what you know | Informed about the business and expects reliable information from you | Friendly but may or may not be informed beyond social interests |
| **Forms and Formats Expected** | Essay, article, letter, report, or other format | Essay, report, research paper, or other academic format | Memo, report, Web page, e-mail, or letter using company format | Notes, blog entries, social networking, or other informal messages |
| **Language and Style Expected** | Formal, using clear words and sentences | Formal, following academic conventions | Appropriate for advancing you and the company | Informal, using abbreviations, phrases, and slang |
| **Attitude and Tone Expected** | Interested and thoughtful about the topic | Serious and thoughtful about the topic and course | Respectful, showing reliability and work ethic | Friendly and interested in shared experiences |
| **Amount of Detail Expected** | Sufficient detail to inform or persuade the reader you envision | Enough sound or research-based evidence to support your thesis | General or technical information as needed | Much detail or little, depending on the topic |

Audiences may be identified by characteristics, such as role (parents) or occupation (teachers), that suggest values to which a writer might appeal. As the chart above suggests, you can analyze preferences, biases, and concerns of readers to engage and influence them more successfully. When you consider what readers know, believe, and value, you can aim your writing toward them with a better chance of hitting your mark.

**AUDIENCE CHECKLIST**

- ☐ Who are your readers? What is their relationship to you?
- ☐ What do they know about this topic? What do you want them to learn?
- ☐ How much detail will they want to read about this topic?

- ☐ What objections are they likely to raise as they read? How can you anticipate and overcome their objections?
- ☐ What is likely to convince them? What's likely to offend them?
- ☐ What tone and style would most effectively influence them?

## Learning by Doing — Considering Audience

Read the following notices directed to subscribers of two magazines, *Zapped!* and *works & conversations*. Examine the style, tone, language, sequence of topics, or other features of each appeal. Write two short paragraphs—one about each notice—explaining what you can conclude about the letter's target audience and its appeal to that audience.

**_Zapped!_ misses you.**

Dear Dan Morrison,

All last year, *Zapped!* magazine made the trek to 5 Snowden Lane and it was always a great experience. You took great care of *Zapped!*, and *Zapped!* gave you hours of entertainment, with news and interviews from the latest indie bands, honest-as-your-momma reviews of musical equipment, and your first glimpse of some of the finest graphic serials being published today.

But, Dan, we haven't heard from you and are starting to wonder what's up. Don't you miss *Zapped!*? One thing's for sure: *Zapped!* misses you.

We'd like to re-establish the relationship: if you renew your subscription by March 1, you'll get 20% off last year's subscription price. That's only $24 for another year of great entertainment. Just fill out the other side of this card and send it back to us; we'll bill you later.

Come on, Dan. Why wait?

Thanks,

*Carly Bevins*

Carly Bevins
Director of Sales

**Figure 1.1** Renewal Letter from *Zapped!*

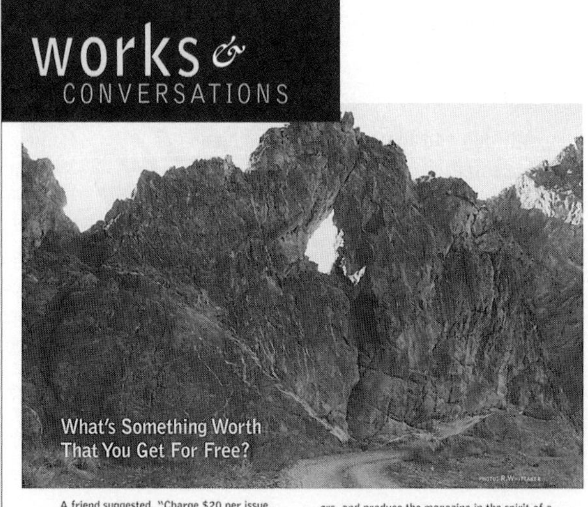

works & CONVERSATIONS
What's Something Worth
That You Get For Free?
PHOTO: R.WHITTAKER


A friend suggested, "Charge $20 per issue. People will value it more." There's something true about that. So how can what we do be valued if no money is charged? Of course, the magazine is not really free. What you're receiving has been paid for by others—both in dollars and effort.

We don't sell ads, either. We found something refreshing about creating an ad-free space.

We live in a transactional time, in an if-then culture deeply accustomed to the conditional. The gift economy then, is a whisper in the ear of the collective, a whisper insisting against the odds that there is another way of encountering this world and each other: through generosity.

We participate in a quiet, no-strings revolution where each act serves as its own catalyst—and as a movement from isolation to community, from scarcity to abundance. That's the spirit in which *works & conversations* is offered. We count on support from like-minded and like-hearted readers, and produce the magazine in the spirit of a gift. It comes to you through an invisible circle of giving. We are grateful to, and much encouraged by, the generosity that has been shown by readers.

If you are paying this forward in some way other than with a financial contribution, we'd love to hear about it. Please send us a note at the address below or by email to rwhit@jps.net.

Thank you for your readership.

—servicespace.org volunteers

If you wish to help pay-it-forward with a financial contribution you can...

•Donate online at:
http://www.conversations.org/?op=donate

•Or send a check payable to "*works & conversations*" at: works & conversations
P. O. Box 5008
Berkeley, CA 94705

70 works & conversations

**Figure 1.2** Appeal to Readers of *works & conversations*

## Targeting a College Audience

Many of your college assignments, like Assignment 1 on page 12, may assume that you are addressing general college readers, represented by your instructor and possibly your classmates. Such readers typically expect clear, logical writing with supporting evidence to explain or persuade. Of course, the format, approach, or evidence may differ by field. For example, biologists might expect the findings from your experiment while literature specialists might look for relevant quotations from the novel you're analyzing.

### COLLEGE AUDIENCE CHECKLIST

- ☐ How has your instructor advised you to write for readers? What criteria related to audience will be used for grading your papers?
- ☐ What do the assigned readings in your course assume about an audience? Has your instructor recommended models or sample readings?
- ☐ What topics, issues, and problems intrigue readers in the course area? What puzzles do they want to solve? How do they want to solve them?
- ☐ How is writing in the course area commonly organized? For example, do writers tend to follow a persuasive pattern – introducing the issue, stating an assertion or a claim, backing the claim with logical points and supporting evidence, acknowledging other views, and concluding? Or do they use conventional headings – perhaps *Abstract, Introduction, Methodology, Findings,* and *Discussion*?
- ☐ What evidence typically supports ideas or interpretations – facts and statistics, quotations from texts, summaries of research, references to authorities or prior studies, experimental findings, observations, or interviews?
- ☐ What style, tone, and level of formality do writers in the field use?

For more strategies for future college writing, see Ch. 24.

### Learning by Doing Considering a College Audience

Use the checklist above to examine reading or writing assignments for another course. What are some prominent features of writing in the area? Which of these might be expected in student papers? How would your college paper differ from writing on the same topic for another audience (perhaps a letter to the editor, newspaper article, consumer brochure, summary for young students, or Web page)?

## Additional Writing Activities

1. Write a few paragraphs or an online posting about your personal goals as a writer during this class. What do you already do well as a writer? What do you need to improve? What do you hope to accomplish? How might you benefit, in college or elsewhere, from improving your writing?
2. **Source Activity.** Select a passage from a textbook or reading assigned in a course. Rewrite the passage for a nonacademic audience (such as readers of a specific magazine or newspaper, visitors to a certain Web site, or interested amateurs).
3. **Source Activity.** Find a nonacademic article, pamphlet, or Web page. Try your hand at rewriting a passage as a college textbook or reading in the field might present the material. Then write an informal paragraph explaining why this task was easy, challenging, or impossible.
4. **Visual Activity.** Working with classmates, examine an academic and a nonacademic resource (such as those for questions 2 and 3 above). Compare and contrast physical features such as page layout, arrangement of text and space, images, color, type size and font, section divisions, and source credits. Write a paragraph about each resource, explaining how its features serve its purpose and appeal to its audience.

# Reading Processes 2

What's so special about college reading? Don't you just pick up the book, start on the first page, and keep going as you have ever since you met *The Cat in the Hat*? Reading from beginning to end works especially well when you are eager to find out what happens next, as in a thriller, or what to do next, as in a cookbook. On the other hand, much of your college reading is complicated. Dense, challenging material often requires closer, slower reading and deeper thinking – in short, a process for reading critically.

## A Process of Critical Reading

Reading critically means approaching whatever you read in an active, questioning manner. This essential college-level skill changes reading from a spectator sport to a contact sport. You no longer sit in the stands, watching graceful skaters glide by. Instead, you charge right into a rough-and-tumble hockey game, gripping your stick and watching out for your teeth.

Critical reading, like critical thinking, is not an activity reserved for college courses. It is a continuum of strategies that thoughtful people use every day to grapple with new information, to integrate it with existing knowledge, and to apply it to problems in daily life:

For more on critical thinking, see Ch. 3.

- They get ready to do their reading.
- They respond as they read.
- They read on literal and analytical levels.

Building your critical reading skills can bring many benefits, especially if you aren't a regular reader. You'll open the door to information you've never encountered and to ideas unlikely to come up with friends. For this course alone, you will be prepared to evaluate strengths and weaknesses of essays by professionals, students, and classmates. If you research a topic, you will be ready to figure out what your sources say, what they assume and imply, whether they are sound, and how you might use them to help make your point. In addition, you can apply your expanded skills in other courses, your job, and your community.

Many instructors help you develop your skills, especially once you realize that they want to improve your critical reading, not complicate your life. Some prepare you by previewing a reading so you learn its background or structure. Others supply reading questions so you know what to look for or give motivational credit for reading responses. Still others may share their own reading processes with you, revealing what they read first (maybe the opening and conclusion) or how they might decide to skip a section (such as Methods in a report whose conclusions they want first).

In the end, however, making the transition to college reading requires your time and energy—and both will be well spent. Once you build your skills as a critical reader, you'll save time by reading more effectively, and you'll save energy by improving both your reading and your writing.

### Learning by Doing Describing Your Reading Strategies

Briefly describe your reading strategies in different situations. For example, how do you read a magazine, newspaper, or popular novel? What's different about reading the material assigned in college? What techniques do you use for reading assignments? Working with others in class or online, collect your best ideas about how to cope effectively, especially in classes with lots of reading.

Scene from *Hansel and Gretel*, a Grimm's fairy tale.

## Getting Started

College reading is active reading. Your instructors expect you to do far more than recognize the words on the page. They want you to read their assignments critically and then to think and write critically about what you have read. Many offer pointers about readings: they want to help you find a trail through the text so you won't get lost as you read.

- If you know the old tale of Hansel and Gretel, you'll recall those resourceful children who dropped crumbs as they walked so that they could retrace their steps through the deep, dark woods. If so, you are interacting with this book, bringing to it your memories and experience. You won't stop to puzzle over woods, trails, and crumbs. You'll just keep reading.

- If you have never met Hansel and Gretel, you may have to stop and puzzle out how they might connect to the reading process.

Many readers – even college professors – feel lost when they begin complex texts about something new. However, experienced critical readers hike through the intellectual woods with confidence because they know how to use many reading strategies. You can learn and practice such strategies, too, following the trail of bread crumbs left by other writers and dropping them for your readers as well.

## Preparing to Read

Before you read, think ahead about how to approach the reading process – how to make the most of the time you spend reading.

**Thinking about Your Purpose.** When you begin to read, ask questions like these about your immediate purpose:

- What are you reading?
- Why are you reading? What do you want to do with the reading?
- What does your instructor expect you to learn from the reading?
- Do you need to memorize details, find main points, or connect ideas?
- How does this reading build on, add to, contrast with, or otherwise relate to other reading assignments in the course?

**Planning Your Follow-Up.** When you are required to read or to select a reading, ask yourself what your instructor expects to follow it:

- Do you need to be ready to discuss the reading during class?
- Will you need to mention it or analyze it during an examination?
- Will you need to write about it or its topic?
- Do you need to find its main points? Sum it up? Compare it? Question it? Spot its strengths and weaknesses? Draw useful details from it?

**Gaining Background.** Knowing a reading's context, approach, or frame of reference can help you predict where the reading is likely to go and how it relates to other readings. Begin with your available resources:

- Do the syllabus, schedule, and class notes reveal why your instructor assigned the reading? What can you learn from reading questions, tips about what to watch for, or connections with other readings?
- Does your reading have a book jacket or preface, an introduction or abstract that sums it up, or reading pointers or questions?
- Does any enlightening biographical or professional information about the author accompany the reading?
- Can you identify or speculate about the reading's original audience based on its content, style, tone, or publication history?

**Skimming the Text.** Before you actively read a text, skim it—quickly read only enough to introduce yourself to it. If it has a table of contents or subheadings, read those first to figure out what it covers and how it is organized. Read the first paragraph and then the first (or first and last) sentence of each paragraph that follows. Read the captions of any visuals.

### Learning by Doing — Preparing to Read

Select a reading from this book or its e-Pages, and try out a few strategies for preparing to read. Then sum up which strategies worked, which didn't, and whether you feel prepared to read the selection critically. Discuss your experience with others in class or online.

## Responding to Reading

You may be accustomed to reading simply for facts or main ideas. However, critical reading is far more active than fact hunting. It requires responding, questioning, and challenging as you read.

**Reading Deeply.** College assignments often require more concentration than other readings do. Use these questions to dive below the surface:

- How does the writer begin? What does the opening paragraph or section reveal about the writer's purpose and point? How does the writer prepare readers for what follows?
- How might you trace the progression of ideas in the reading? How do headings, previews of what's coming up, summaries of what's gone before, and transitions signal the organization?
- Are difficult or technical terms defined in specific ways? How might you highlight, list, or record such terms so that you master them?
- How might you record or recall the details in the reading? How could you track or diagram interrelated ideas to grasp their connections?

- How do word choice, tone, and style alert you to the complex purpose of a reading that is layered or indirect rather than straightforward?
- Does the reading include figurative or descriptive language, references to other works, or recurring themes? How do these enrich the reading?
- Can you answer any reading questions in your textbook, assignment, study guide, or syllabus? Can you restate headings in question form to create your own questions and then supply the answers? For example, change "Major Types of X" to "What are the major types of X?"

For more on figurative language, see p. 270.

For more on evaluating what you read, see section C in the Quick Research Guide, pp. A-26–A-28.

For a Critical Reading Checklist, see pp. 28–29.

**Annotating the Text.** Writing notes on the page (or on a copy if the material is not your own) is a useful way to trace the author's points, question them, and add your own comments as they pop up. The following passage ends the introduction of "The New Science of Siblings," written by Jeffrey Kluger (with reporting by Jessica Carsen, Wendy Cole, and Sonja Steptoe) and featured as the cover story in the July 10, 2006, *Time* (pp. 47–48). Notice how one writer annotated this passage:

*Key point — both ...us and surprising*

*...ood quote — from ...C Davis authority*

*Scary — I never thought of my sister this way!*

Our spouses arrive comparatively late in our lives; our parents eventually leave us. Our siblings may be the only people we'll ever know who truly qualify as partners for life. "Siblings," says family sociologist Katherine Conger of the University of California, Davis, "are with us for the whole journey."

*...s up past studies but new to me*

*...Not exactly! My ...sister's definitely ...a striver, but I'm ...no rebel*

Within the scientific community, siblings have not been wholly ignored, but research has been limited mostly to discussions of birth order. Older sibs were said to be strivers; younger ones rebels; middle kids the lost souls. The stereotypes were broad, if not entirely untrue, and there the discussion mostly ended.

*Wow — global research!*

*Cousins= example — pulled together when parents split*

*...to go for the ...a — competition ...favorites!!*

But all that's changing. At research centers in the United States, Canada, Europe, and elsewhere, investigators are launching a wealth of new studies into the sibling dynamic, looking at ways brothers and sisters steer one another into—or away from—risky behavior; how they form a protective buffer against family upheaval; how they educate one another about the opposite sex; how all siblings compete for family recognition and come to terms—or blows—over such impossibly charged issues as parental favoritism.

When you annotate a reading, don't passively highlight big chunks of text. Instead, respond actively using pen or pencil or adding a comment to a file. Next, read slowly and carefully so that you can follow what the reading says and how it supports its point. Record your own reactions, not what you think you are supposed to say:

- Jot down things you already know or have experienced to build your own connection to the reading.
- Circle key words, star or check ideas when you agree or disagree, add arrows to mark connections, or underline key points, ideas, or definitions to learn the reading's vocabulary.
- Add question marks or questions about meaning or implications.
- Separate main points from supporting evidence and detail. Then you can question a conclusion, or challenge the evidence that supports it. (Main points often open a section or paragraph, followed by supporting detail, but sometimes this pattern is reversed.)
- React to quotable sentences or key passages. If they are hard to understand, restate them in your own words.
- Talk to the writer – maybe even talk back. Challenge weak points, respond with your own thoughts, draw in other views, or boost the writer's persuasive ideas.
- Sum up the writer's main point, supporting ideas, and notable evidence or examples.
- Consider how the reading appeals to your head, heart, or conscience.

## Learning by Doing Annotating a Passage

For a sample annotated passage, see p. 21.

Annotate the following passage. It opens the summary of findings for the survey "How Mobile Devices Are Changing Community Information Environments" (Pew Internet & American Life Project, *2011 State of the News Media Report*).

Local news is going mobile. Nearly half of all American adults (47%) report that they get at least some local news and information on their cellphone or tablet computer. 1

What they seek out most on mobile platforms is information that is practical and in real time: 42% of mobile device owners report getting weather updates on their phones or tablets; 37% say they get material about restaurants or other local businesses. These consumers are less likely to use their mobile devices for news about local traffic, public transportation, general news alerts or to access retail coupons or discounts. 2

One of the newest forms of on-the-go local news consumption, mobile applications are just beginning to take hold among mobile device owners. 3

Compared with other adults, these mobile local news consumers are younger, live in higher income households, are newer residents of their communities, live in nonrural areas, and tend to be parents of minor children. Adults who get local news and information on mobile devices are more likely than others to feel they can have an impact on their communities, more likely to use a variety of media platforms, feel more plugged into the media 4 environment than they did a few years ago, and are more likely to use social media:

- 35% of mobile local news consumers feel they can have a big impact on their community (vs. 27% of other adults)
- 65% feel it is easier today than five years ago to keep up with information about their community (vs. 47% of nonmobile connectors)
- 51% use six or more different sources or platforms monthly to get local news and information (vs. 21%)
- 75% use social network sites (vs. 42%)
- 15% use Twitter (vs. 4%)

Tablets and smartphones have also brought with them news applications or 5
"apps." One-quarter (24%) of mobile local news consumers report having an app that helps them get information or news about their local community. That equates to 13% of all device owners and 11% of the total American adult population. Thus while nearly 5 in 10 get local news on mobile devices, just 1 in 10 use apps to do so. Call it the app gap.

**Keeping a Reading Journal.** A reading journal is an excellent place to record not just what you read but how you respond to it. As you read actively, you will build a reservoir of ideas for follow-up writing. Use a special notebook or an easy-to-sort research file to address questions like these:

For advice on keeping a writer's journal, see Ch. 19.

- What is the subject of the reading? What is the writer's stand?
- What does the writer take for granted? What assumptions does he or she begin with? Where are these stated or suggested?
- What are the writer's main points? What evidence supports them?
- Do you agree with what the writer has said? Do his or her ideas clash with your ideas or question something you take for granted?
- Has the writer told you more than you wanted to know or failed to tell you something you wish you knew?
- What conclusions can you draw from the reading?
- Has the reading opened your eyes to new ways of viewing the subject?

## Learning by Doing Responding in a Reading Journal

Return to the passage that you annotated on pages 22–23. Write a brief journal entry about this passage. Concentrate on two points: what the passage says and how you respond.

## Learning from Another Writer: Reading Summary and Response

For another reading response on both literal and analytical levels, see pp. 29–31.

Olof Eriksson's instructor asked students to write a one-page reading response, including a summary and a personal response, before writing each assigned essay. Your instructor may also ask you to keep a reading journal or to submit or post online your responses to readings. Your assignment might require brief features such as these:

- Summary: a short statement in your own words of the reading's main points (without your opinion, evaluation, or judgment).
- Paraphrase: a restatement of a passage using your own words and sentences.
- Quotation: a noteworthy expression or statement in the author's exact words, presented in quotation marks and correctly cited.
- Personal response: a statement and explanation of your reaction to the reading.
- Critique: your evaluation of the strengths or weaknesses of the reading.
- Application: a connection between the reading and your experience.
- Question: a point of curiosity or uncertainty that you wish the writer had covered.

For more on citing sources, see E1–E2 in the Quick Research Guide, pp. A-32–A-38.

**Olof Eriksson** — **Student Summary and Response**

For Jensen's essay, see pp. 534–38.

### The Problems with Masculinity

Robert Jensen writes in his essay "The High Cost of Manliness" about masculinity and how our culture creates expectations of certain traits from the males in our society. He strongly opposes this view of masculinity and would prefer that sociological constructs like masculinity and femininity were abolished. As examples of expected traits, he mentions strength and competition. Males are supposed to take what they want and avoid showing weaknesses. Then Jensen points out negative consequences of enforcing masculinity, things like rape and men having trouble showing vulnerability. He counters the argument of differences in biology between males and females by pointing out that we do not know how much comes from biology and how much comes from culture, but that both certainly matter and we should do what we can. He is also concerned about giving positive attributes to masculinity, as that effectively tells us they only belong with males. He ends by observing that we are facing challenges now that cannot be met with the current view of masculinity. 1

I agree with what Jensen says, and I find it a problem today that the definition of masculinity is so closely connected to competition and aggression. Even so, I 2 find that my own definition of masculinity is very close to the general one. I would say it is to be strong and determined, always winning. I'm sure most people have a similar idea of what it is, even as most people would disagree logically. That is why we need to make an effort to change our culture, just as Jensen argues. If we can either abolish masculinity and femininity or simply change them into a lot more neutral and closely related terms, then we will be a lot closer to real equality between the genders. This change will not only help remove most of the negative impacts Jensen brought up but also help pave a better way for future generations, reducing their problems.

Works Cited

Jensen, Robert. "The High Cost of Manliness." *The Bedford Guide for College Writers.* 10th ed. Ed. X. J. Kennedy, Dorothy M. Kennedy, and Marcia F. Muth. Boston: Bedford, 2014. 534–38. Print.

### Questions to Start You Thinking

Meaning

1. According to Eriksson, what is Jensen's topic and Jensen's position on this topic? Where does Eriksson present this information?
2. What is Eriksson's personal response to the essay? Where does he present his views?

Writing Strategies

3. How does Eriksson consider his audience as he organizes and develops his summary and response?
4. What kinds of material from the essay does Eriksson use to develop his summary?

## Reading on Literal and Analytical Levels

Educational expert Benjamin S. Bloom identified six levels of cognitive activity: knowledge, comprehension, application, analysis, synthesis, and evaluation.[1] (A recent update recasts *synthesis* as *creating* and moves it above evaluation to the highest level.) Each level acts as a foundation for the next. Each also demands higher thinking skills than the previous one. Experienced readers, however, jump among these levels, gathering information and insight as they occur.

[1]Benjamin S. Bloom et al., *Taxonomy of Educational Objectives, Handbook 1: Cognitive Domain* (New York: McKay, 1956). See also the update in David R. Krathwohl, "A Revision of Bloom's Taxonomy: An Overview," *Theory into Practice* 41.4 (2002): 212–218.

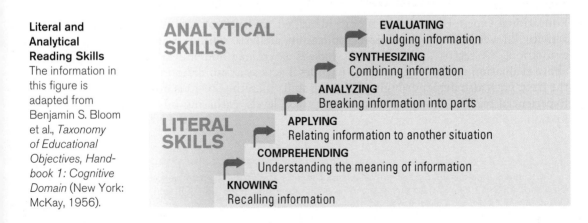

The first three levels are literal skills, building blocks of thought. The last three levels—analysis, synthesis, and evaluation—are analytical skills that your instructors especially want you to develop. To read critically, you must engage with a reading on both literal and analytical levels. Suppose you read in your history book a passage about Franklin Delano Roosevelt (FDR), the only American president elected to four consecutive terms.

**Knowing.** Once you read the passage, even if you have little background in American history, you can decode and recall the information it presents about FDR and his four terms in office.

**Comprehending.** To understand the passage, you need to know that a term for a U.S. president is four years and that *consecutive* means "continuous." Thus FDR was elected to serve for sixteen years.

**Applying.** To connect this knowledge to what you already know, you think of other presidents—George Washington, who served two terms; Grover Cleveland, who served two terms but not consecutively; Jimmy Carter, who served one term; the second George Bush, who served two terms. Then you realize that four terms are quite unusual. In fact, the Twenty-second Amendment to the Constitution, ratified in 1951, now limits a president to two terms.

**Analyzing.** You can scrutinize FDR's four terms from various angles, selecting a principle for analysis that suits your purpose. Then you can use this principle to break the information into its components or parts. For example, you might analyze FDR's tenure in relation to that of other presidents. Why has FDR been the only president elected to serve four terms? What circumstances contributed to three reelections?

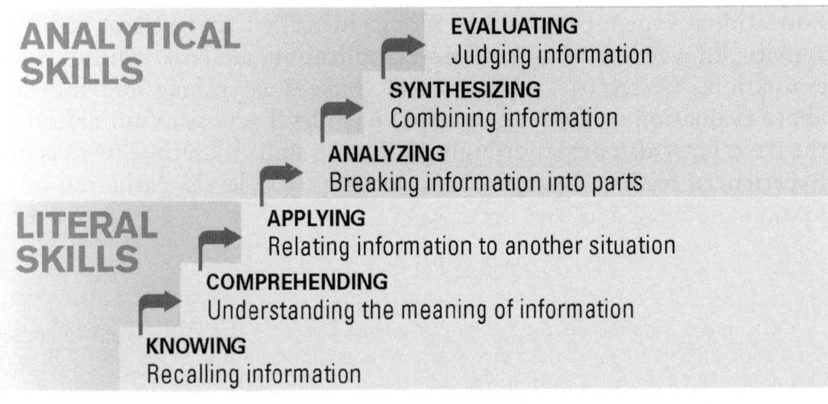


**Literal and Analytical Reading Skills**
The information in this figure is adapted from Benjamin S. Bloom et al., *Taxonomy of Educational Objectives, Handbook 1: Cognitive Domain* (New York: McKay, 1956).

**Synthesizing.** To answer your questions, you may read more or review past readings. Then you begin synthesizing—creating a new approach or combination by pulling together facts and opinions, identifying evidence accepted by all or most sources, examining any controversial evidence, and drawing conclusions that reliable evidence seems to support. For example, you might logically conclude that the special circumstances of the Great Depression and World War II contributed to FDR's four terms, not that Americans reelected him out of pity because he had polio.

**Evaluating.** Finally, you evaluate the significance of your new knowledge for understanding Depression-era politics and assessing your history book's approach. You might ask yourself, Why has the book's author chosen to make this point? How does it affect the rest of the discussion? And you may also have concluded that FDR's four-term presidency is understandable in light of the events of the 1930s and 1940s, that the author has mentioned this fact to highlight the era's unique political atmosphere, and that, in your opinion, it is evidence neither for nor against FDR's excellence as a president.

### Learning by Doing — Reading Analytically

Think back to something you have read recently that helped you make a decision, perhaps a newspaper or magazine article, an electronic posting, or a college brochure. How did you analyze what you read, breaking the information into parts? How did you synthesize it, combining it with what you already knew? How did you evaluate it, judging its significance for your decision?

e For an interactive Learning by Doing activity on Reading Online, go to Ch. 2: **bedfordstmartins.com/bedguide**.

## Generating Ideas from Reading

For more on generating ideas, see Ch. 19.

Like flints that strike each other and cause sparks, readers and writers provoke one another. For example, when your class discusses an essay, you may be surprised by the range of insights your classmates report. Of course, they may be equally surprised by what you see. Above all, reading is a dynamic process. It may change your ideas instead of support them. Here are suggestions for unlocking the potential of a good text.

**Looking for Meaty Pieces.** Spur your thinking about current topics by browsing through essay collections or magazines in the library or online. Try *Atlantic, Harper's, New Republic, Commentary,* or special-interest magazines such as *Architectural Digest* or *Scientific American.* Check editorials and op-ed columns in your local newspaper, the *New York Times,* or the *Wall Street Journal.* Search the Internet on intriguing topics (such as silent-film technology) or issues (such as homeless children). Look for meaty, not superficial, articles written to inform and convince, not entertain or amuse.

**Logging Your Reading.** For several days keep a log of the articles that you find. Record the author, title, and source for each promising piece so that you can easily find it again. Briefly note the subject and point of view as well, so you can identify a range of possibilities.

**Recalling Something You Have Already Read.** What have you read lately that started you thinking? Return to a reading—a chapter in a history book, an article for sociology, a research report for biology.

**Paraphrasing and Summarizing Complex Ideas.** Do you feel overwhelmed by challenging reading? If so, read slowly and carefully. Try two common methods of recording and integrating ideas from sources into papers.

For more on paraphrase and summary, see Ch. 12 and D4–D5 in the Quick Research Guide, pp. A-29–A-30.

- Paraphrase: restate an author's complicated ideas fully but in your own language, using different wording and different sentence patterns.
- Summarize: reduce an author's main point to essentials, using your own clear, concise, and accurate language.

Accurately recording what a reading says can help you grasp its ideas, especially on literal levels. Once you understand what it says, you can agree, disagree, or question.

**Reading Critically.** Instead of just soaking up what a reading says, try a conversation with the writer. Criticize. Wonder. Argue back. Demand convincing evidence. Use the following checklist to get started.

---

## CRITICAL READING CHECKLIST

- ☐ What problems and issues does the author raise?
- ☐ What is the author's purpose? Is it to explain or inform? To persuade? To amuse? In addition to this overall purpose, is the author trying to accomplish some other agenda?
- ☐ How does the author appeal to you as a reader? Where do you agree and disagree? Where do you want to say "Yeah, right!" or "I don't think so!"?
- ☐ How does this piece relate to your own experiences or thoughts? Have you encountered anything similar? Does the topic or approach engage you?

- ☐ Are there any important words or ideas that you don't understand? If so, do you need to reread or turn to a dictionary or reference book?
- ☐ What is the author's point of view? What does the author assume or take for granted? Where does the author reveal these assumptions? Do they make the selection seem weak or biased?
- ☐ Which statements are facts, verifiable by observation, firsthand testimony, or research? Which are opinions? Does one or the other dominate?
- ☐ Is the writer's evidence accurate, relevant, and sufficient? Is it persuasive?

For more on facts and opinions, see pp. 40–42.

For more on evaluating evidence, see C1–C3 in the Quick Research Guide, pp. A-26–A-28.

**Analyzing Writing Strategies.** Reading widely and deeply can reveal what others say and how they shape and state it. For some readings in this book, notes in the margin identify key features such as the introduction, thesis statement or main idea, major points, and supporting evidence. Ask questions such as these to help you identify writing strategies:

### WRITING STRATEGIES CHECKLIST

- ☐ How does the author introduce the reading and try to engage the audience?
- ☐ Where does the author state or imply the main idea or thesis?
- ☐ How is the text organized? What main points develop the thesis?
- ☐ How does the author supply support—facts, data, statistics, expert opinions, experiences, observations, explanations, examples, other information?
- ☐ How does the author connect or emphasize ideas for readers?
- ☐ How does the author conclude the reading?
- ☐ What is the author's tone? How do the words and examples reveal the author's attitude, biases, or assumptions?

## Learning from Another Writer: Critical Reading and Response

Alley Julseth was asked to read an essay on both literal and analytical levels. Her critical reading analysis presents a thoughtful personal response to Clive Thompson's "The New Literacy."

For Thompson's essay, see pp. 584–587.

**Alley Julseth** **Student Critical Reading Response**

## Analyzing "The New Literacy"

For another reading response, see pp. 24–25.

Being part of a generation that spends an immense amount of time online, I find 1
it rather annoying to hear that youth today are slowly diminishing the art of writing. Because Facebook and Twitter have limited character space, I do use abbreviations such as s.m.h. (shaking my head), "abt" (about), and "u" (you). However, my simplistic way of writing informally for online media has no correlation with my formal writing. In "The New Literacy" essay, Clive Thompson indicates that this lack of correlation seems to be the case with many more students.

Thompson explores the idea that the advancing media is changing the way 2
students write. After citing Professor Sutherland blaming technology for "bleak, bald, sad shorthand" (qtd. in Thompson 584), he goes on to describe the Stanford Study of Writing, conducted by writing professor Andrea Lunsford. She studied over 14,000 examples of student writing from academic essays to e-mails and chats. From these samples, she learned that "young people today write far more than any generation before them" (585). I completely agree with this point based on the large volume I write socializing on the Internet. I believe that the time I spend online writing one-dimensional phrases does not weaken my formal writing as a student.

Thompson goes on to explain that the new way of writing on the Internet is 3
actually more similar to the Greek tradition of argument than to the essay and letter-writing tradition of the last half century. Lunsford concluded that "the students were remarkably adept at what rhetoricians call *kairos* — assessing their audience and adapting their tone and technique to get their point across" (585). Their Internet writing is like a conversation with another person.

I find this conclusion interesting. As I advance in my writing as a student, I 4
remember being taught as a child that there is a distinct line between writing an essay that is due to a teacher and writing a letter to a friend. Although the two are different, there are similarities as well. The nice thing about writing on the Internet is that I can choose what I write about and how I say it. When I'm writing to a friend, sticking to the point isn't exactly the goal, but I do get my main point across. However, I never write a formal essay unless it is assigned. Like the Stanford students, I do not look forward to writing an essay simply for the grade. Writing for a prompt I did not choose does not allow me to put my full-hearted passion into the essay. When I was younger, I wrote essays that were more bland and straight to the point. As I write now, I try to think as though I am reading to a room full of people, keeping my essay as interesting as I can.

Thompson ends his piece on the importance of good teaching. This importance is 5
true; teaching is the way students learn how to draw that line between formal and

informal writing and how to write depending on audience. I appreciate and completely agree with Thompson's essay. I feel that he describes the younger generation very well. He is pushing away what high-brow critics say, and he is saying we are almost inventing a new way of writing.

Works Cited

Thompson, Clive. "The New Literacy." *The Bedford Guide for College Writers.* 10th ed. Ed. X. J. Kennedy, Dorothy M. Kennedy, and Marcia F. Muth. Boston: Bedford, 2014. 584–87. Print.

## Questions to Start You Thinking

Meaning

1. According to Julseth, what is the issue that Thompson raises, and what is his position on this topic? Where does Julseth present this information?
2. What are Julseth's main points in her analysis?
3. How does Julseth apply this reading to her own life?

Writing Strategies

4. How has Julseth demonstrated both literal and critical reading responses?
5. How does Julseth develop her analysis? What kinds of material does she draw from the essay?

## Learning by Doing Reading Critically

Using the advice in this chapter, critically read the following *Scientific American* essay, written by the author of *The Believing Brain.* First, add your own notes and comments in the margin, responding on both literal and analytical levels. Second, add notes about writing strategies. (Sample annotations are supplied to help you get started.) Finally, write a brief summary of the reading and your own well-reasoned conclusions about it.

For a sample annotated passage, see p. 21.

## Michael Shermer

### The Science of Righteousness

Which of these two narratives most closely matches your political perspective? 1

*Once upon a time people lived in societies that were unequal and oppressive, where the rich got richer and the poor got exploited. Chattel slavery, child labor, economic inequality, racism, sexism and discriminations of all types abounded until the liberal tradition of fairness, justice, care and equality brought about a free and fair society. And now conservatives want to turn back the clock in the name of greed and God.* 2

Sounds like Grandpa!

*Once upon a time people lived in societies that embraced values and tradition, where people took personal responsibility, worked hard, enjoyed the fruits of their labor and through charity helped those in need. Marriage, family, faith, honor, loyalty, sanctity, and respect for authority and the rule of law brought about a free and fair society. But then liberals came along and destroyed everything in the name of "progress" and utopian social engineering.* 3

And this sounds like Uncle Bill!

Stories lead to thesis

Although we may quibble over the details, political science research shows that the great majority of people fall on a left-right spectrum with these two grand narratives as bookends. And the story we tell about ourselves reflects the ancient tradition of "once upon a time things were bad, and now they're good thanks to our party" or "once upon a time things were good, but now they're bad thanks to the other party." So consistent are we in our beliefs that if you hew to the first narrative, I predict you read the *New York Times*, listen to progressive talk radio, watch CNN, are pro-choice and anti-gun, adhere to separation of church and state, are in favor of universal health care, and vote for measures to redistribute wealth and tax the rich. If you lean toward the second narrative, I predict you read the *Wall Street Journal*, listen to conservative talk radio, watch Fox News, are pro-life and anti-gun control, believe America is a Christian nation that should not ban religious expressions in the public sphere, are against universal health care, and vote against measures to redistribute wealth and tax the rich. 4

Writer cites source →

Quote + summary

Why are we so predictable and tribal in our politics? In his remarkably enlightening book, *The Righteous Mind: Why Good People Are Divided by Politics and Religion* (Pantheon, 2012), University of Virginia psychologist Jonathan Haidt argues that to both liberals and conservatives, members of the other party are not just wrong; they are righteously wrong—morally suspect and even dangerous. "Our righteous minds made it possible for human beings," Haidt argues, "to produce large cooperative groups, tribes, and nations without the glue of kinship. But at the same time, our righteous minds guarantee that our cooperative groups will always be cursed by moralistic strife." Thus, he shows, morality binds us together into cohesive groups but blinds us to the ideas and motives of those in other groups. 5

6 The evolutionary Rubicon that our species crossed hundreds of thousands of years ago that led to the moral hive mind was a result of "shared intentionality," which is "the ability to share mental representations of tasks that two or more of [our ancestors] were pursuing together. For example, while foraging, one person pulls down a branch while the other plucks the fruit, and they both share the meal." Chimps tend not to display this behavior, Haidt says, but "when early humans began to share intentions, their ability to hunt, gather, raise children, and raid their neighbors increased exponentially. Everyone on the team now had a mental representation of the task, knew that his or her partners shared the same representation, knew when a partner had acted in a way that impeded success or that hogged the spoils, and reacted negatively to such violations." Examples of modern political violations include Democrat John Kerry being accused of being a "flip-flopper" for changing his mind and Republican Mitt Romney declaring himself "severely conservative" when it was suggested he was wishy-washy in his party affiliation.

*Rubicon??*

7 Our dual moral nature leads Haidt to conclude that we need both liberals and conservatives in competition to reach a livable middle ground. As philosopher John Stuart Mill noted a century and a half ago: "A party of order or stability, and a party of progress or reform, are both necessary elements of a healthy state of political life."

## Reading Online and Multimodal Texts

Traditionally, a literate person was someone who could read and write. That definition remains current, but online technologies have vastly increased the complexity of reading and writing. Multimodal texts now combine written materials with images, sounds, and motions. Such texts cannot be confined to the fixed form of a printed page and may be randomly or routinely updated. They also may be accessed flexibly as a reader wanders through sites and follows links rather than paging through the defined sequence of a bound book. More innovations, unimaginable now, might well emerge even before you graduate from college.

For more on responding to images, see Ch. 14.

Learning to read and write effectively has likewise increased in complexity. Many people simply assume that a reader's eye routinely moves from left to right, from one letter or word to the next. However, eye-movement studies show that readers actually jump back and forth, skip letters and words, and guess at words the eye skips. Online readers also may jump

from line to line or chunk to chunk, scanning the page (see heat maps below). In addition, multimodal texts may draw the eye to, or from, the typical left-to-right, top-to-bottom path with an image. Analyzing the meaning or impact of an image may require "reading" its placement and arrangement.

What might these changes mean for you as a reader and writer? Your critical reading skills are likely to be increasingly useful. The essential challenge of deep, thoughtful reading applies to graphic novels, blogs, photo essays, and YouTube videos just as it applies to printed books, articles, and essays. In fact, some might argue that texts using multiple components and appealing to multiple senses require even more thorough scrutiny to grasp what they are saying and how they are saying it. Here are some suggestions about how you might apply your critical skills in these new contexts:

- Concentrate on your purpose to stay focused when you read online or multimodal texts, especially if those texts tug you further and further away from your original search or material.
- Create an online file, reading journal, research journal, or writer's blog so that you have a handy location for responding to new materials.

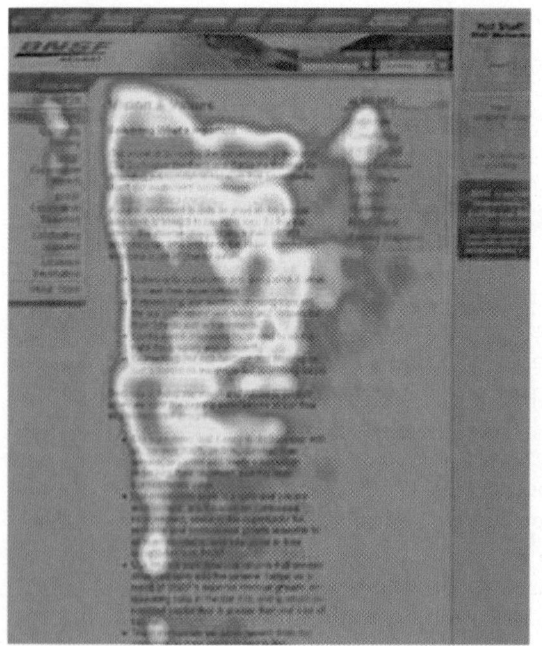

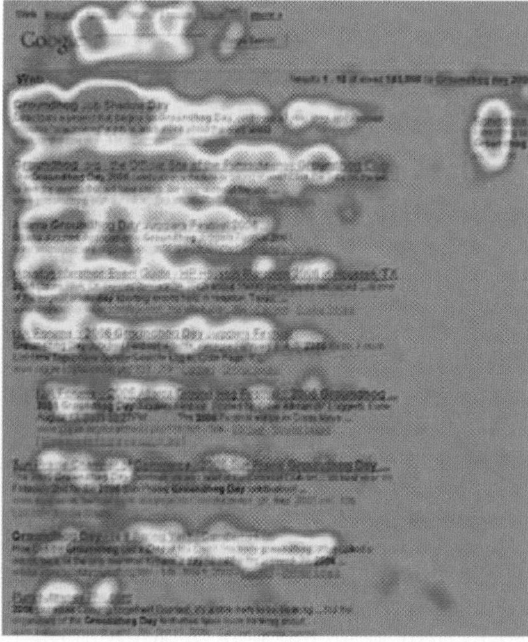

Heat maps from eye-tracking studies showing how people scan online pages in an F-shaped pattern.

- Bookmark meaty online readings, sites, or multimodal texts so you can easily return to examine their details. Consider what you see or hear, what the material suggests, and how it appeals to you.
- Read features and effects of visual or multimodal texts as carefully as you read words in print texts. Observe composition, symmetry, sequence, shape, color, texture, brightness, and other visual components.
- Listen for the presence and impact of audio characteristics such as sound effects (accuracy, clarity, volume, timing, emotional power), speech (pitch, tone, dialect, accent, pace), and music (instrumentation, vocals, melody, rhythm, harmony, musical roots, cuts, remix decisions).
- Examine visual or multimodal materials critically—analyzing components, synthesizing varied information, and evaluating effects.
- Evaluate research material that presents evidence to support your points or to challenge other views so that you rely on trustworthy sources.
- Secure any necessary permission to add someone else's visual or other material to your text and to credit your source appropriately.
- Generate even more ideas by rereading this chapter and thinking about how you could apply the skills presented here in new situations.

### Learning by Doing: Reading a Web Site

Working with a small group — on a laptop in class, at the computer lab, or online — examine a Web site about a topic you might want to investigate. Critically "read" and discuss the site's text, images, organization, and other features that might persuade you that it would or would not be a reliable source.

## Additional Writing Activities

1. **Source Activity.** Select a print or e-Pages essay from this book. Annotate the reading, marking both its key ideas and your own reactions to it. Review the text and your annotations, and then write two paragraphs, one summarizing the reading and the other explaining your personal response to it.

For the contents of *A Writer's Reader*, see pp. 490–91.

2. **Source Activity.** Follow up on Activity 1, working with others who have responded to the same essay. Share your summaries, noting the strengths of each. Then develop a collaborative summary that briefly and fairly presents the main points of the reading. (You can merge your existing summaries or

make a fresh start.) When you finish the group summary, decide which methods of summarizing work best.

3. **Source Activity.** Follow up on Activity 1 by adding a critical reading analysis and response.
4. **Source Activity.** Select a passage from the textbook or readings for another course you are taking or have taken. Annotate the passage, and make some notes using the Critical Reading Checklist and the Writing Strategies Checklist (pp. 28–29) as guides. Pay special attention to the reading's purpose and its assumptions about its audience. Write a paragraph or two about your critical examination of the passage.
5. **Visual Activity.** Select a multimodal e-Pages selection, Web page, blog entry, YouTube video, photo from an online gallery, or another brief online text. "Read" this text critically, adapting reading processes and skills from this chapter. Write a short summary and response, including a link or a printout of the page or section to which you have responded.

# Critical Thinking Processes

# 3

*Critic,* from the Greek word *kritikos,* means "one who can judge and discern"—in short, someone who thinks critically. College will have given you your money's worth if it leaves you better able to judge and discern—to determine what is more and less important, to make distinctions and recognize differences, to generalize from specifics, to draw conclusions from evidence, to grasp complex concepts, to choose wisely. The effective thinking that you will need in college, on the job, and in daily life is active and purposeful, not passive and ambling. It is critical thinking.

## A Process of Critical Thinking

Critical thinking, like critical reading, draws on a cluster of intellectual strategies and skills.

For more on critical reading, see Ch. 2.

| Critical Thinking Skill | Definition | Applications for Readers | Applications for Writers |
|---|---|---|---|
| Analysis | Breaking down information into its parts and elements | Analyzing the information in articles, reports, and books to grasp the facts and concepts they contain | Analyzing events, ideas, processes, and structures to understand them and explain them to readers |
| Synthesis | Putting together elements and parts to form new wholes | Synthesizing information from several sources, examining implications, and drawing conclusions supported by reliable evidence | Synthesizing source materials with your own thoughts in order to convey the unique combination to others |
| Evaluation | Judging according to standards or criteria | Evaluating a reading by determining standards for judging, applying them to the reading, and arriving at a conclusion about its value, significance, or credibility | Evaluating something in writing by convincing readers that your standards are reasonable and that the subject either does or does not meet those standards |

These three activities—analysis, synthesis, and evaluation—are the core of critical thinking. They are not new to you, but applying them rigorously in college-level reading and writing may be. When you approach college reading and writing tasks, instructors will expect you (and you should expect yourself) to think, read, write, and think some more.

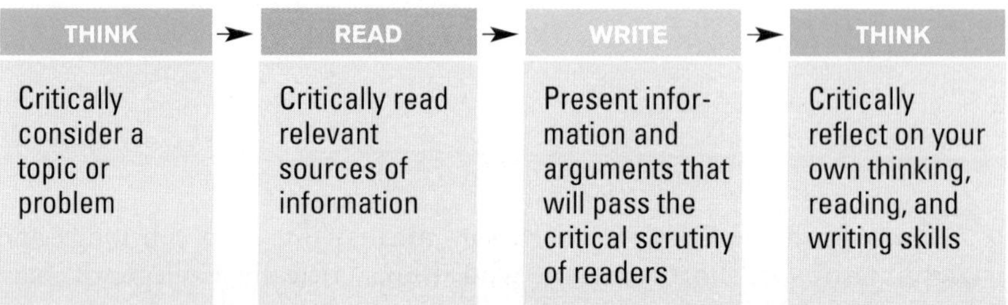
THINK
Critically consider a topic or problem
READ
Critically read relevant sources of information
WRITE
Present information and arguments that will pass the critical scrutiny of readers
THINK
Critically reflect on your own thinking, reading, and writing skills

## Getting Started

You use critical thinking every day to explore problems step by step and reach solutions. Suppose you don't have enough money both to pay your tuition and to buy the car you need. First, you might pin down the causes of your financial problem. Next, you might examine your options to find the best solution, as shown in the graphic on page 39.

### Learning by Doing: Thinking Critically to Solve a Campus Problem

With classmates, identify a common problem for students at your college—juggling a busy schedule, parking on campus, making a class change, joining a social group, or some other issue. Working together, use critical thinking to explore the problem and identify possible solutions.

You can follow the same steps to examine many types of issues, helping you analyze a situation or dilemma, creatively synthesize to develop alternatives, and evaluate a possible course of action.

### Learning by Doing: Thinking Critically to Explore an Issue

You have worked hard on a group presentation that will be a major part of your grade—and each member of the group will get the same grade. Two days before the project is due, you discover that one group member has plagiarized heavily from sources well known to your instructor. Working together with classmates, use critical thinking to explore your problem and determine what you might do.

## PROBLEM

*You can't afford both your college tuition and the car you need.*

## SOLUTION

**1 IDENTIFY CAUSES**

***Causes in your control:***
Expensive vacation?
Credit-card debt?

***Causes out of your control:***
Medical emergency?
Job loss?
Tuition increase?
Financial aid policy change?

**2 ANALYZE, SYNTHESIZE, AND EVALUATE OPTIONS**

| | | |
|---|---|---|
| Do without a car | (*how?*) | • Get rides with family or friends?<br>• Take public transportation? |
| Decrease your tuition | (*how?*) | • Take fewer courses? |
| Get more money | (*how?*) | • Get a college loan?<br>• Get a loan from a family member?<br>• Get another job? |

**3 REACH A LOGICAL CONCLUSION**

Apply for a short-term loan through the college for tuition.

Critical Thinking in Action

## Applying Critical Thinking to Academic Problems

As you grapple with academic problems and papers, you'll be expected to use your critical thinking skills—analyzing, synthesizing, and evaluating—as you read and write. You may simply dive in, using each skill as needed. However, the very wording of an assignment or examination question may alert you to a skill that your instructor expects you to use, as the first sample assignment in each set illustrates in the chart below.

### Learning by Doing  Thinking Critically to Respond to an Academic Problem

Working with a classmate or small group, select a sample assignment (not already explained) from the table above or from one of your classes. Explain how you would approach the assignment to demonstrate your critical thinking. Share your strategies for tackling college assignments.

## Using Critical Thinking for College Assignments

| Critical Thinking Skill | Sample College Writing Assignments |
|---|---|
| *Analysis:* breaking into parts and elements based on a principle | ■ Describe the immediate causes of the 1929 stock market crash. (Analyze by using the principle of immediate causes to identify and explain the reasons for the 1929 crash.)<br>■ Trace the stages through which a bill becomes federal law.<br>■ Explain and illustrate the three dominant styles of parenting.<br>■ Define *romanticism,* identifying and illustrating its major characteristics. |
| *Synthesis:* combining parts and elements to form new wholes | ■ Discuss the following statement: High-minded opposition to slavery was only one cause, and not a very important one, of the animosity between North and South that in 1861 escalated into civil war. (Synthesize by combining the causes or elements of the North-South animosity, going beyond the opposition to slavery, to form a new whole: your conclusion that accounts for the escalation into civil war.)<br>■ Imagine that you are a trial lawyer in 1921, charged with defending Nicola Sacco and Bartolomeo Vanzetti, two anarchists accused of murder. Argue for their acquittal on whatever grounds you can justify. |
| *Evaluation:* judging according to standards or criteria | ■ Present and evaluate the most widely accepted theories that account for the disappearance of the dinosaurs. (Evaluate, based on standards such as scientific merit, the credibility of each theory.)<br>■ Defend or challenge the idea that houses and public buildings should be constructed to last no longer than twenty years.<br>■ Contrast the models of the solar system advanced by Copernicus and by Kepler, showing how the latter improved on the former. |

## Supporting Critical Thinking with Evidence

As you write a college paper, you try to figure out your purpose, position, and strategies for getting readers to follow your logic and accept your points. Your challenge, of course, is not just to think clearly but to demonstrate your thinking to others, to persuade them to pay attention to what you say. And sound evidence is what critical readers want to see.

For advice on using a few sources, see the Quick Research Guide, pp. A-20–A-38.

Sound evidence supports your main idea or thesis, convincing readers by substantiating your points. It also bolsters your credibility as a writer, demonstrating the merit of your position. When you write, you need to marshal enough appropriate evidence to clarify, explain, and support your ideas. Then you need to weave claims, evidence, and your own interpretations together into a clearly reasoned explanation or argument.

## Types of Evidence

What is evidence? It is anything that demonstrates the soundness of a claim. Facts, statistics, expert testimony, and firsthand observations are four reliable forms of evidence. Other evidence might include examples, illustrations, details, and opinions. Depending on the purpose of your assignment, some kinds of evidence weigh more heavily than others. For example, readers might appreciate your memories of livestock care on the farm in an essay recalling your childhood summers. However, they would probably discount your memories in an argumentative paper about ethical agricultural methods unless you could show that your memories are representative or that you are an expert on the subject. Personal experience may strengthen an argument but generally is not sufficient as its sole support. If you are in doubt about the type of evidence an assignment requires, ask your instructor whether you should use sources or rely on personal experience and examples.

For more on using evidence in a paper that takes a stand, see pp. 170–74.

**Facts.** Facts are statements that can be verified objectively, by observation or by reading a reliable account. They are usually stated dispassionately: "If you pump the air out of a five-gallon varnish can, it will collapse." Of course, we accept many of our facts based on the testimony of others. For example, we believe that the Great Wall of China exists, although we may never have seen it with our own eyes.

Sometimes people say facts are true statements, but truth and sound evidence may be confused. Consider the truth of these statements:

| | |
|---|---|
| The tree in my yard is an oak. | *True* because it can be verified |
| A kilometer is 1,000 meters. | *True* using the metric system |
| The speed limit on the highway is 65 miles per hour. | *True* according to law |
| Fewer fatal highway accidents have occurred since the new exit ramp was built. | *True* according to research studies |
| My favorite food is pizza. | *True* as an opinion |
| More violent criminals should receive the death penalty. | *True* as a belief |
| Murder is wrong. | *True* as a value judgment |

Some would claim that each statement is true, but when you think critically, you should avoid treating opinions, beliefs, judgments, or personal experience as true in the same sense that verifiable facts and events are true.

**Statistics.** Statistics are facts expressed in numbers. What portion of American children are poor? According to statistics from the U.S. Census Bureau, 13.2 million children (or 18.2 percent of all children) lived in poverty in 2008 compared with 16.4 million (or 22.5 percent) in 2011. Clear as such figures seem, they may raise complex questions. For example, how

significant is the increase in the poverty rate over three years? Has the percentage fluctuated or steadily increased? What percentage of children were poor over longer terms such as fifteen years or twenty?

Few people save some of a candy bar to eat later.

Most writers, without trying to be dishonest, interpret statistics to help their causes. The statement "Fifty percent of the populace have incomes above the poverty level" might substantiate the fine job done by the government of a developing nation. Putting the statement another way—"Fifty percent of the populace have incomes below the poverty level"—might use the same statistic to show the inadequacy of the government's efforts.

Even though a writer is free to interpret a statistic, statistics should not be used to mislead. On the wrapper of a peanut candy bar, we read that a one-ounce serving contains only 150 calories. The claim is true, but the bar weighs 1.6 ounces. Gobble it all—more likely than eating 62 percent of it—and you'll ingest 240 calories, a heftier snack than the innocent statistic on the wrapper suggests. Because abuses make some readers automatically distrustful, use figures fairly when you write, and make sure they are accurate. If you doubt a statistic, compare it with figures reported by several other sources. Distrust a statistical report that differs from every other report unless it is backed by further evidence.

Should you want to contact a campus expert, turn to Ch. 6 for advice about interviews.

**Expert Testimony.** By "experts," we mean people with knowledge gained from study and experience in a particular field. The test of an expert is whether his or her expertise stands up to the scrutiny of others who are knowledgeable in that field. The views of Peyton Manning on how to play offense in football carry authority. So do the views of economist and former Federal Reserve chairman Alan Greenspan on what causes inflation. However, Manning's take on the economy or Greenspan's thoughts on football might not be authoritative. Also consider whether the expert has any bias or special interest that would affect reliability. Statistics on cases of lung cancer attributed to smoking might be better taken from government sources than from the tobacco industry.

**Firsthand Observation.** Firsthand observation is persuasive. It can add concrete reality to abstract or complex points. You might support the claim "The Meadowfield waste recycling plant fails to meet state guidelines" by recalling your own observations: "When I visited the plant last January, I was struck by the number of open waste canisters and by the lack of protective gear for the workers who handle these toxic materials daily."

For more on observation, see Ch. 5.

As readers, most of us tend to trust the writer who declares, "I was there. This is what I saw." Sometimes that trust is misplaced, however, so always be wary of a writer's claim to have seen something that no other evidence supports. Ask yourself, Is this writer biased? Might the writer have (intentionally or unintentionally) misinterpreted what he or she saw? Of course, your readers will scrutinize your firsthand observations, too; take care to reassure them that your observations are unbiased and accurate.

### Learning by Doing — Looking for Evidence

Using the issue you explored for the activity on page 38, what would you need to support your identification, explanation, or solution of the problem? Working with classmates, identify the kinds of evidence that would be most useful. Where or how might you find such evidence?

For more on selecting evidence to persuade readers, see pp. 173–74.

## Testing Evidence

As both a reader and a writer, always critically test and question evidence to see whether it is strong enough to carry the weight of the writer's claims.

For advice on evaluating sources of evidence, see C in the Quick Research Guide, pp. A-26–A-28.

**EVIDENCE CHECKLIST**

- ☐ Is it accurate?
  - Do the facts and figures seem accurate based on what you have found in published sources, reports by others, or reference works?
  - Are figures or quoted facts copied correctly?
- ☐ Is it reliable?
  - Is the source trustworthy and well regarded?
  - Does the source acknowledge any commercial, political, advocacy, or other bias that might affect the quality of its information?
  - Does the writer supplying the evidence have appropriate credentials or experience? Is the writer respected as an expert in the field?
  - Do other sources agree with the information?
- ☐ Is it up-to-date?
  - Are facts and statistics – such as population figures – current?
  - Is the information from the latest sources?
- ☐ Is it to the point?
  - Does the evidence back the exact claim made?
  - Is the evidence all pertinent? Does any of it drift from the point to interesting but irrelevant evidence?
- ☐ Is it representative?
  - Are examples typical of all the things included in the writer's position?
  - Are examples balanced? Do they present the topic or issue fairly?
  - Are contrary examples acknowledged?
- ☐ Is it appropriately complex?
  - Is the evidence sufficient to account for the claim made?
  - Does it avoid treating complex things superficially?
  - Does it avoid needlessly complicating simple things?

For information on mistakes in thinking, see pp. 50–52 and pp. 180–81.

☐ Is it sufficient and strong enough to back the claim and persuade readers?
- Are the amount and quality of the evidence appropriate for the claim and for the readers?
- Is the evidence aligned with the existing knowledge of readers?
- Does the evidence answer the questions readers are likely to ask?
- Is the evidence vivid and significant?

---

## Using Evidence to Appeal to Your Audience

For more on appeals, see pp. 175–77.

One way to select evidence and to judge whether it is appropriate and sufficient is to consider the types of appeals—logical, emotional, and ethical. Most effective arguments work on all three levels, using all three types of appeals with evidence that supports all three.

### Logical Appeal (Logos)

When writers use a logical appeal (*logos,* or "word" in Greek), they appeal to the reader's mind or intellect. This appeal relies on evidence that is factual, objective, clear, and relevant. Critical readers expect to find logical evidence that supports major claims and statements.

> Example: If a writer were arguing for term limits for legislators, she wouldn't want to base her argument on the evidence that some long-term legislators were or weren't reelected (irrelevant) or that the current system is unfair to young people who want to get into politics (illogical). Instead, she might argue that the absence of term limits encourages corruption, using evidence of legislators who repaid lobbyists for campaign contributions with key votes.

### Emotional Appeal (Pathos)

When writers use an emotional appeal (*pathos,* or "suffering" in Greek), they appeal to the reader's heart. They choose language, facts, quotations, examples, and images that evoke emotional responses. Of course, convincing writing does touch readers' hearts as well as their minds. Without this heartfelt tug, a strict logical appeal may seem cold and dehumanized.

> Example: If a writer opposed hunting seals for their fur, he might combine statistics about the number of seals killed each year and the overall population decrease with a vivid description of baby seals being slaughtered.

Some writers use emotional words and sentimental examples to manipulate readers—to arouse their sympathy, pity, or anger in order to convert them without much logical evidence—but dishonest emotional appeals may alienate readers.

> Example: Instead of basing an argument against a political candidate on pitiful images of scrawny children living in roach-infested squalor, a good writer would report the candidate's voting record on issues that affect children.

### Ethical Appeal (Ethos)

When writers use an ethical appeal (*ethos,* or "character" in Greek), they call on the reader's sense of fairness and trust. They select and present evidence in a way that will make the audience trust them, respect their judgment, and believe what they have to say. The best logical argument in the world falls flat when readers don't take the writer seriously. How can you use an ethical appeal to establish your credibility as a writer? First you need to establish your credentials in the field through experience, reading, or interviews that helped you learn about the subject.

> Example: If you are writing about water quality, tell your readers about the odor, taste, and color of your local water. Identify medical or environmental experts you contacted or whose reports you read.

Demonstrate your knowledge through the information you present, the experts and sources you cite, and the depth of understanding you convey. Establish a rapport with readers by indicating values and attitudes that you share with them and by responding seriously to opposing arguments. Finally, use language that is precise, clear, and appropriate in tone.

#### Learning by Doing Identifying Types of Appeals

Bring to class or post links for the editorial or opinion page from a newspaper, newsmagazine, or blog with a strong point of view. Read some of the pieces, and identify the types of appeals used by each author to support his or her point. With classmates, evaluate the effectiveness of these appeals.

## Learning from Another Writer: Rhetorical Analysis

Richard Anson was asked to read an outside selection critically and then write a brief rhetorical analysis to identify the reading's audience and its writer's logical, emotional, and ethical appeals to that audience. Because his class was analyzing the 2012 presidential election campaign, Anson found an essay with a historical perspective on the involvement of young adults in current events.

**Richard Anson** **Student Rhetorical Analysis**

## Young Americans and Media News

In a world where young adults may be more interested in *American Idol* than in who is running for president, it is critical to take a step back and look at the factors involved prior to the presidential elections of 2008 and 2012. Stephen Earl Bennett has done just that in "Young Americans' Indifference to Media Coverage of Public Affairs," an essay that appeared in *PS: Political Science & Politics*, a journal that focuses on contemporary politics and the teaching thereof. Being featured in this journal, as well as being a Fellow of the Center for the Study of Democratic Citizenship at the University of Cincinnati, easily establishes Bennett's trustworthy character or ethos. 1

Given where the article was published, it is safe to say that he is trying to reach an audience of professors in the field of political science and possibly policy makers as well. With this assumption, however, Bennett makes an error. His essay focuses solely on facts and numbers and not at all on the audience's emotions. A reader would be hard-pressed to find any appeals to emotion (pathos) in his essay at all and could liken it to an instruction manual on American youth's indifference to current events. Professors may be more likely to respond to the logical appeal (logos) of facts and numbers than some other readers, but they are still human, and few humans enjoy reading instruction manuals for fun. For example, Bennett starts off with "Although young Americans are normally less engaged in politics than their elders (Converse with Niemi 1971), today's youth are more withdrawn from public affairs than earlier birth cohorts were when they were young (Bennett 1997)" (Bennett 1). In this first sentence alone, Bennett is citing from two other sources, one of which happens to be his own. There is nothing wrong with jumping right in, but this is a little over the top and very dry for an introduction. 2

The idea that more people vote for *American Idol* than their own president in the leading democratic nation in the world is just pathetic. There's no other way to describe it. On this point, Bennett agrees with other readings discussed in class. He also agrees that current affairs and news need to be more widely taught in schools across the nation and that something needs to be done to attract American youth to the news. The Bennett article was published in 1998, and maybe the interest of young voters in the 2008 and 2012 presidential elections shows that Americans have started listening. 3

Works Cited

Bennett, Stephen Earl. "Young Americans' Indifference to Media Coverage of Public Affairs." *PS: Political Science & Politics* 31.3 (1998): 535–41. *General OneFile.* Web. 15 Nov. 2012.

### Questions to Start You Thinking

Meaning

1. According to Anson, what position about the political engagement of young people does Bennett take?
2. What is Anson's position about Bennett's article?

Writing Strategies

3. Why do you think that Anson begins with information about the article and its author instead of a summary of Bennett's main points?
4. Why do you think that Anson decided to arrange his discussion of the three appeals – ethos, pathos, and logos – in that order?

## Presenting Your Critical Thinking

Why do you have to worry about critical thinking? Isn't it enough just to tell everybody else what you think? That tactic probably works fine when you casually debate with your friends. After all, they already know you, your opinions, and your typical ways of thinking. They may even find your occasional rant entertaining. Whether they agree or disagree, they probably tolerate your ideas because they are your friends.

For more on taking a stand, see Ch. 9; on proposals, see Ch. 10; on evaluation, see Ch. 11; and on supporting a position, see Ch. 12.

When you write a paper in college, however, you face a different type of audience, one that expects you to explain what you assume, what you advocate, and why you hold that position. That audience wants to learn the specifics – reasons you find compelling, evidence that supports your view, and connections that relate each point to your position. Because approaches and answers to complex problems may differ, your college audience expects reasoning, not emotional pleading or bullying or preaching.

How you reason and how you present your reasoning are important parts of gaining the confidence of college readers. College papers typically develop their points based on logic, not personal opinions or beliefs. Most are organized logically, often as a series of reasons, each making a claim, a statement, or an assertion that is backed up with persuasive supporting evidence. Your assignment or your instructor may recommend ways such as the following for showing your critical thinking.

**Reasoning Deductively or Inductively.** When you state a *generalization,* you present your broad general point, viewpoint, or conclusion.

For more about the statement-support pattern, see A in the Quick Research Guide, pp. A-21–A-24.

The admissions requirements at Gerard College are unfair.

On the other hand, when you supply a *particular,* you present an instance, a detail, an example, an item, a case, or other specific evidence to demonstrate that a general statement is reasonable.

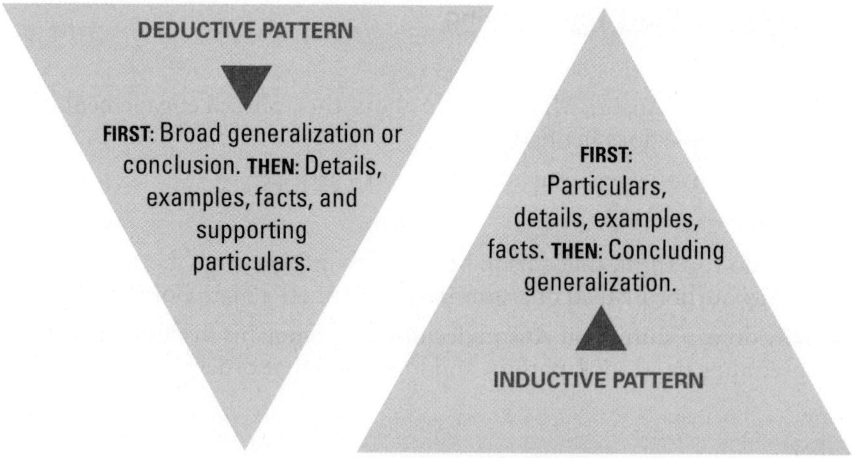

DEDUCTIVE PATTERN

**FIRST:** Broad generalization or conclusion. **THEN:** Details, examples, facts, and supporting particulars.

**FIRST:** Particulars, details, examples, facts. **THEN:** Concluding generalization.

INDUCTIVE PATTERN

> A Gerard College application form shows the information collected by the admissions office. Under current policies, standardized test scores are weighted more heavily than better predictors of performance, such as high school grades. Qualified students who do not test well often face a frustrating admissions process, as Irma Lang's situation illustrates.

Your particulars consist of details that back up your broader point; your generalizations connect the particulars so that you can move beyond isolated, individual cases.

Most college papers are organized *deductively*. They begin with a general statement (often a thesis) and then present particular cases to support or apply it. Readers like this pattern because it reduces mystery; they learn right away what the writer wants to show. Writers like this pattern because it helps them state up front what they want to accomplish (even if they have to figure some of that out as they write and state it more directly as they revise). Papers organized deductively sacrifice suspense but gain directness and clarity.

For more about thesis statements, see Ch. 20.

On the other hand, some papers are organized *inductively*. They begin with the particulars – a persuasive number of instances, examples, or details – and lead up to the larger generalization that they support. Because readers have to wait for the generalization, this pattern allows them time to adjust to an unexpected conclusion that they might initially reject. For this reason, writers favor this pattern when they anticipate resistance from their audience and want to move gradually toward the broader point.

For more on inductive and deductive reasoning, see pp. 443–45.

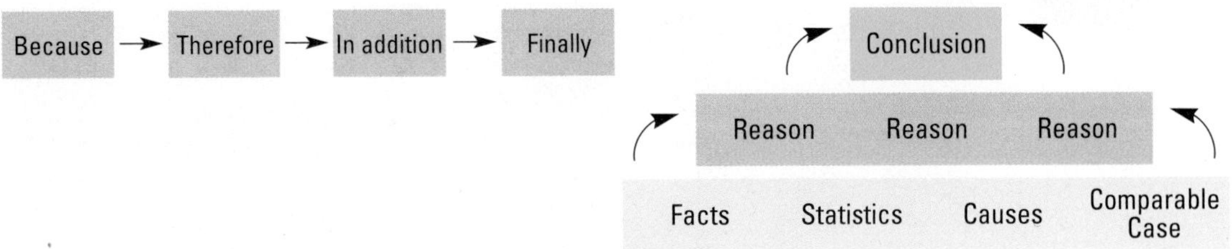


**Building Sequences and Scaffolds.** You may use several strategies for presenting your reasoning, depending on what you want to show and how you think you can show it most persuasively. You may develop a line of reasoning, a series of points and evidence, running one after another in a sequence or building on one another to support a persuasive scaffold.

**Developing Logical Patterns.** The following patterns are often used to organize reasoning in college papers. They can help show relationships but don't automatically prove them. In fact, each has advantages but may also have disadvantages, as the sample strengths and weaknesses illustrate.

For more strategies for developing, see Ch. 22.

*Pattern:* Least to Most
*Advantage:* Building up to the best points can produce a strong finish.
*Disadvantage:* Holding back on strong points makes readers wait.

*Pattern:* Most to Least
*Advantage:* Beginning with the strongest point can create a forceful opening.
*Disadvantage:* Tapering off with weaker points may cause readers to lose interest.

LEAST TO MOST PATTERN

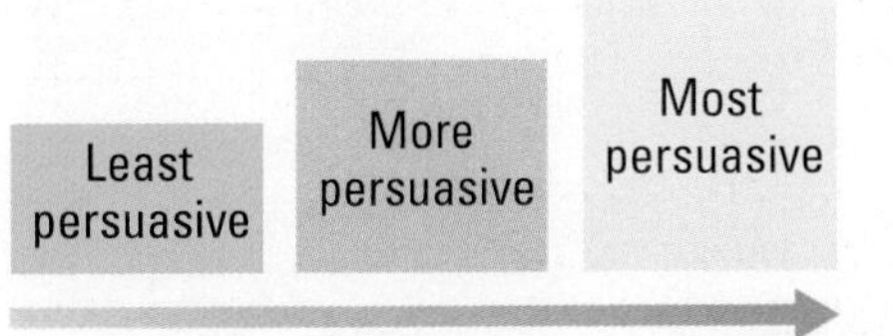


MOST TO LEAST PATTERN

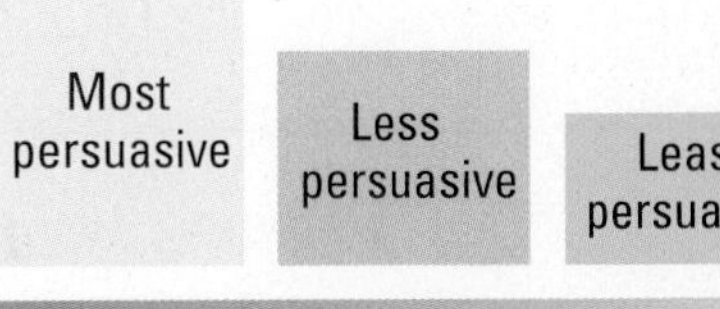


*Pattern:* Comparison and Contrast
*Advantage:* Readers can easily relate comparable points about things of like kind.
*Disadvantage:* Some similarities or differences don't guarantee or prove others.

For more on comparison and contrast, see Ch. 7.

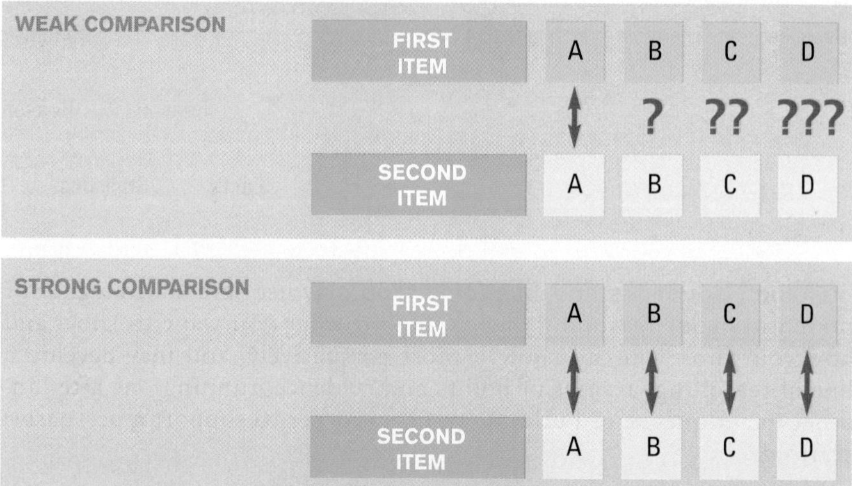


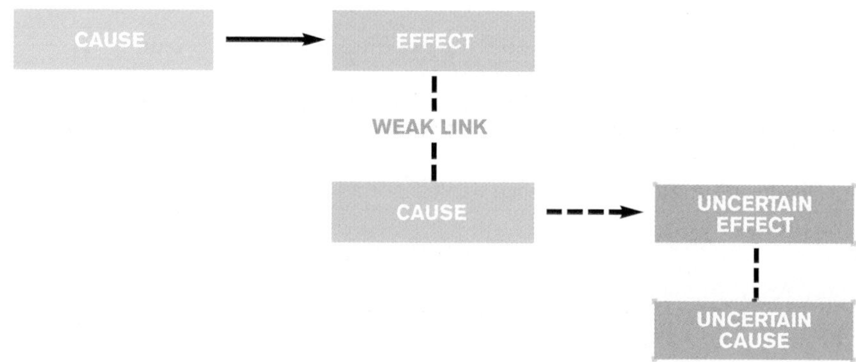


For more on cause and effect, see Ch. 8.

*Pattern:* Cause and Effect
*Advantage:* Tracing causes or effects can tightly relate and perhaps predict events.
*Disadvantage:* Weak links can call into question all relationships in a series of events.



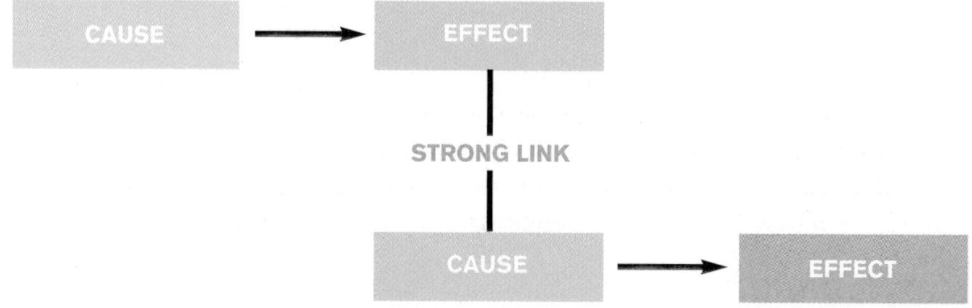

| | Sound Reasoning | Weak Reasoning |
|---|---|---|
| **Comparisons** | Comparison that uses substantial likeness to project other similarities:<br><br>Like the third graders in the innovative reading programs just described, the children in this town also could become better readers. | Inaccurate comparison that relies on slight or superficial likenesses to project other similarities:<br><br>Like kittens eagerly stalking mice in the fields, young readers should gobble up the tasty tales that were the favorites of their grandparents. |
| **Causes and Effects** | Causal analysis that relies on well-substantiated and specific connections relating events and outcomes:<br><br>City water reserves have suffered from below-average rainfall, above-average heat, and steadily increasing consumer demand. | Faulty reasoning that oversimplifies causes, confuses them with coincidences, or assumes a first event must cause a second:<br><br>One cause—and one alone—accounts for the ten-year drought that has dried up local water supplies. |
| **Reasons** | Logical reasons that are supported by relevant evidence and presented with fair and thoughtful consideration:<br><br>As the recent audit indicates, all campus groups that spend student activity fees should prepare budgets, keep clear financial records, and substantiate expenses. | Faulty reasons that rely on bias, emotion, or unrelated personal traits or that accuse, flatter, threaten, or inspire fear:<br><br>All campus groups, especially the arrogant social groups, must stop ripping off the average student's fees and threatening to run college costs sky high. |
| **Evidence** | Evidence that is accurate, reliable, current, relevant, fair, and sufficient to persuade readers:<br><br>Both the statistics from international agencies and the accounts of Sudanese refugees summarized earlier suggest that, while a fair immigration policy needs to account for many complexities, it should not lose sight of compassion. | Weak evidence that is insufficient, dated, unreliable, slanted, or emotional:<br><br>As five-year-old Lannie's frantic flight across the Canadian border in 1988 proves, refugees from all the war-torn regions around the world should be welcomed here because this is America, land of the free. |
| **Conclusions** | Solid conclusions that are based on factual evidence and recognize multiple options or complications:<br><br>As the recent campus wellness study has demonstrated, college students need education about healthy food and activity choices. | Hasty conclusions that rely on insufficient evidence, assumptions, or simplistic two-option choices:<br><br>The campus health facility should refuse to treat students who don't eat healthy foods and exercise daily. |

## Learning by Doing Testing Logical Patterns

Continuing with the issue and possible evidence you explored for the activities on pages 38 and 43, work with classmates to figure out several patterns you could use to present your evidence to an audience of people who could help to solve the problem or address the issue. What would be the advantages or disadvantages of each pattern, given your issue, audience, and possible evidence?

For an interactive Learning by Doing activity on Analyzing Logic, go to Ch. 3: **bedfordstmartins .com/bedguide**.

For specific logical fallacies, see pp. 180–81.

## Avoiding Faulty Thinking

Common mistakes in thinking can distort evidence or lead to wrong conclusions. How can you avoid such mistakes as you write or spot them as you read? A good strategy is to look carefully at the ways in which you (or the author of a reading) describe events, relate ideas, identify reasons, supply evidence, and draw conclusions.

Use the following questions to help you refine your reasoning as you plan, draft, or revise a college paper:

---

### LOGICAL REASONING CHECKLIST

- ☐ Have you reviewed your assignment or syllabus, looking for advice or requirements about the kind of reasoning or evidence expected?
- ☐ Have you developed your reasoning on a solid foundation? Are your initial assumptions sound? Do you need to identify, explain, or justify them?
- ☐ Is your thesis or position stated clearly? Are its terms explained or defined?
- ☐ Have you presented your reasons for thinking your thesis is sound? Have you arranged them in a sequence that will make sense to your audience? Have you used transitions to introduce and connect them so readers can't miss them?
- ☐ Have you used evidence that your audience will respect to support each reason you present? Have you favored objective, research-based evidence (facts, statistics, and expert testimony that others can substantiate) rather than personal experiences or beliefs that others cannot or may not share?
- ☐ Have you explained your evidence so that your audience can see how it supports your points and applies to your thesis? Have you used transitions to specify relationships for readers?
- ☐ Have you enhanced your own credibility by acknowledging, rather than ignoring, other points of view? Have you integrated or countered these views?
- ☐ Have you adjusted your tone and style so you come across as reasonable and fair-minded? Have you avoided arrogant claims about proving (rather than showing) points?
- ☐ Have you credited any sources as expected by academic readers?

---

### Learning by Doing Analyzing Reasoning

Analyze the following newspaper column, which uses irony to make its case. Identify its stated and actual position, its sequence of reasons or points, its supporting evidence, and its methods of appealing to readers. The column by David Rothkopf, author of *Power, Inc.*, appeared in the *Denver Post* on August 23, 2012.

## David Rothkopf

### A Proposal to Draft America's Elderly

It is sadly apparent to those who travel this great country—when they see along the highways aging bikers with long grey ponytails or on the beaches men who are long past the age when they should be seen in Speedos or at political rallies, where they quake in fear over competing claims about retirement benefits—that the elderly are not only an eyesore but also a growing threat to our society because of their cost, the speed at which they drive, and because, absent real work to do or support from their impoverished government, they could easily turn to crime or worse, turn to us, their relatives, and seek to move into our basement or family rooms. 1

What tone does the writer use to introduce his argument?

2 I think it is agreed by all Americans that this prodigious number of burdensome old folks visible to all as they conduct their morning mall walks or take up valuable bench space in public parks are—given the present deplorable state of the nation—a source of great unease, debate and public dissension and therefore whoever could find a fair, cheap, and easy method of making these chronologically challenged Americans sound and useful members of the commonwealth would earn the gratitude of the public to such a degree that he would have a statue erected in his honor.

Do all Americans agree with the writer? Why does the writer claim that they do?

3 The great advantage to my program is instantly apparent to anyone who hears it, even those with profound intellectual deficits like reality-show contestants and members of Congress: It solves not only the greatest problem the country faces—that of ensuring care for the elderly—but it also does so instantly and in such a sweeping nature that it might once again reknit the rent fabric of our polity and restore unity to a fractured, hurting society.

4 The aforementioned program is the draft, nationwide conscription, and my proposal is that we institute mandatory military service for all Americans over 65.

Is this a serious proposal? How do you know that?

5 Can you think of a single proposal that so directly addresses the shared concerns of an aging nation for its oldest citizens while at the same time guaranteeing the public care for those seniors sought by Democrats and providing for the strengthened national defense so important to all Republicans? One that helps trim our fiscal deficit and eliminate the retirement health-care deficit altogether?

6 This approach would immediately place our elderly into the care of the government via an institution, the military, which is accustomed to providing for every need of its members and has a long history of putting into productive use those whom age also renders nearly impossible to deal with: teenagers.

How persuasive are the benefits that the writer identifies?

Second, because every older American would be in the military, we would actually have no need at all for Medicare. 7

Third, because the nature of modern warfare is increasingly limited to electronic, cyber, drone-based or other joystick-driven activities, the physical limitations of many older Americans should not be a problem. 8

Fourth, because it is unavoidable that conflicts do occur, were we to field an army of the elderly, we would eliminate war's greatest tragedy: the untimely death of the young who have historically been called upon to fight. This would have the added benefit of significantly reducing the health-care and Social Security costs these honored dead might otherwise have incurred, especially those associated with the last six months of life. 9

The program would get aging drivers off the roads. Similarly, programs like "Don't Ask, Don't Tell" would be unnecessary, as most members of the military won't remember what the question was in the first place. 10

Supposing that there are 40 million Americans over the age of 65, and 48 million on Medicare, this would clearly both largely remove the problems associated with that failing program and, at the same time, provide a large pool of people for military service. While there are currently 73 million people between the ages of 18 and 49 and thus eligible for military service, it must be remembered that a draft would bring far more people into service than the approximately 2.25 million Americans in active or reserve service today. 11

? What other ideas might be proposed?

Given the obvious merits of such a program, I think it is fair to ask that no man or woman take issue with it unless he or she has a superior idea. 12

## Additional Writing Activities

1. List your main reasons (and some supporting details) for and against doing something: going somewhere, joining something, buying something, or the like. Then outline one presentation directed to someone who would agree with you and another directed to someone who would disagree. Do your two plans differ? If so, how and why?
2. Working with a group, survey several opinion pieces. Refer to Presenting Your Critical Thinking (pp. 47–51) to help you identify the patterns the writers use to present their views. Then speculate about why they chose to organize as they did.
3. Divide a page into three columns, or create a table in a file. Label each column with a type of appeal: logical, emotional, ethical. Pick a specific local issue about which you have a definite view, and identify a specific

audience that you might be able to persuade to agree with, or at least consider, your position. Start filling in the columns with persuasive evidence that supports your view. Discuss your table with one or two classmates to decide what evidence would most effectively appeal to your audience.

4. **Source Activity.** Select an editorial, opinion column, or brief blog entry that takes a clear stand on an issue. Analyze its stand, main points, evidence, and appeals to readers. Write a paragraph explaining how it makes its case. Then write a second paragraph stating and justifying your judgment about how well it succeeds.
5. If you disagree with the opinion piece that you analyzed in Activity 4, write a paragraph or two explaining and supporting your own point of view.
6. **Visual Activity.** Select a Web page, a powerful photo, a cartoon, a graphical display of information, or another text that uses an image to help make its point about an issue. Adapt the critical thinking skills in this chapter to analyze this visual text, examining its evidence and its appeals to viewers. Write a paragraph or two explaining how it makes its case, including a link to the item or a printout.

# A WRITER'S SITUATIONS

PART TWO

# 4 Recalling an Experience

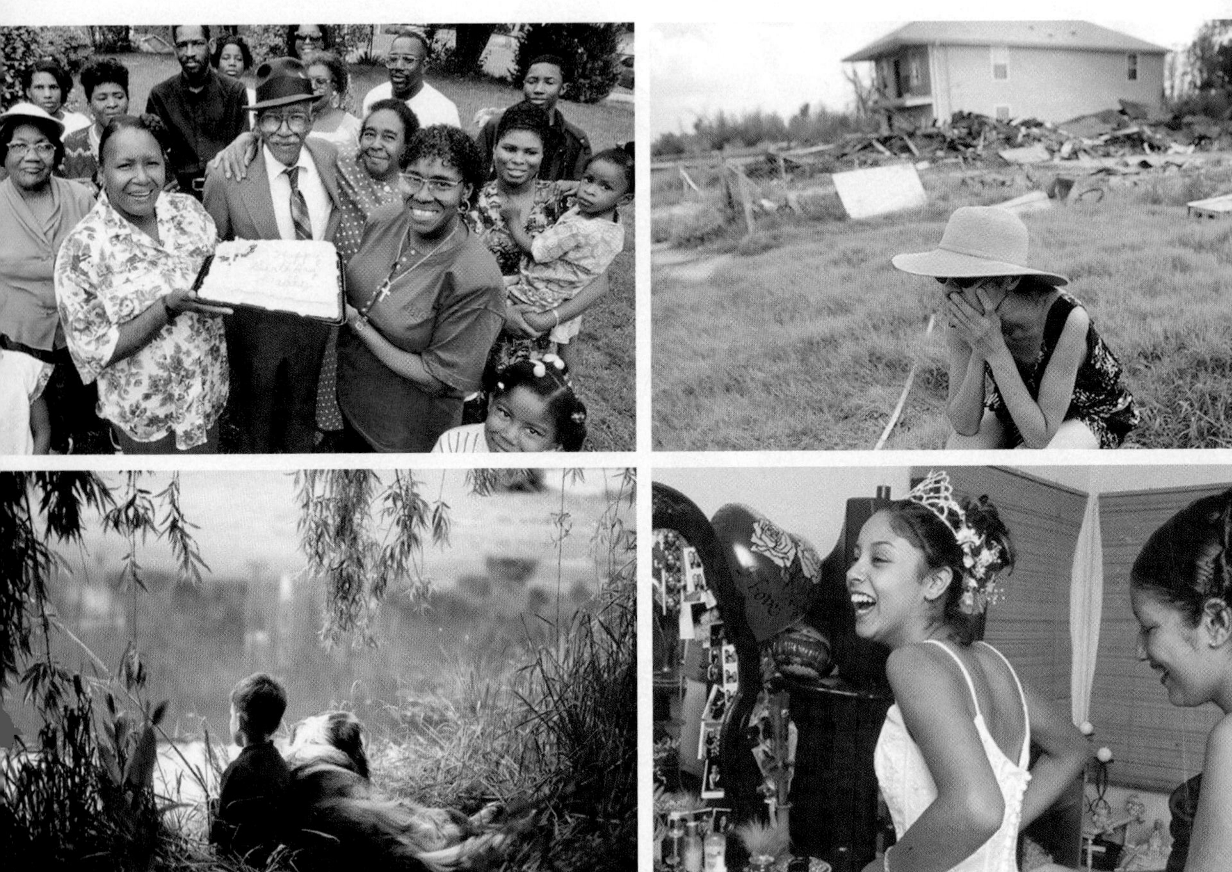

## Responding to an Image

Look carefully at one of the photographs in the grid. In your view, when was this photograph taken? Who might the person or people be? Where are they, and why are they there? What are they doing? What relationships and emotions does the picture suggest with its focal point and arrangement? Write about an experience the image helps you recall or about a possible explanation of events in this picture. Use vivid detail to convey what happened to you or what might have happened to the people in the picture.

Writing from recall is writing from memory, a writer's richest—and handiest—resource. Recall is clearly necessary when you write of a personal experience, a favorite place, a memorable person. Recall also helps you probe your memories of specific events. For example, in a literacy narrative you might examine the significance of your experiences learning to read or write. On the other hand, in a reflection you might begin with an incident that you recall and then explore the ideas that evolve from it.

Even when an instructor hands you a subject that seems to have nothing to do with you, your memory is the first place to look. Suppose you have to write a psychology paper about how advertisers prey on consumers' fears. Begin with what you remember. What ads have sent chills down your back? What ads have suggested that their products could save you from a painful social blunder, a lonely night, or a deadly accident? All by itself, memory may not give you enough to write about, but you will rarely go wrong if you start by jotting down something remembered.

For information and journal questions about the Part Two photograph, see the last two pages of the Appendices.

## Why Recalling an Experience Matters

**In a College Course**

- You recall your experiences of visiting or living in another region or country to add authority to your sociology paper on cultural differences.
- You recall and record both routine and unusual events in the reflective journal you keep during your internship or clinical experience.

**In the Workplace**

- You recall past successes, failures, or customer comments to provide compelling reasons for adopting your proposals for changing a product or service.

**In Your Community**

- You recall your own experiences taking standardized tests to add impact to your appeal to the local school board to change the testing program at your child's school.

? When have you recalled experiences in your writing? What did these recollections add to your writing? In what situations might you rely on recollection again in future writing?

## Learning from Other Writers

Here are two samples of good writing from recall – one by a professional writer, one by a college student. To help you begin to analyze the first reading, look at the notes in the margin. They identify features such as the main idea, or thesis, and the first of the main events that support it in a paper written from recall.

### As You Read These Recollections

As you read these essays, ask yourself the following questions:

1. Is the perspective of the essay primarily that of a child or an adult? Why do you think so?
2. What does the author realize after reflecting on the events recalled? Does the realization come soon after the experience or later, when the writer examines the events from a more mature perspective?
3. How does the realization change the individual?

### Russell Baker

### The Art of Eating Spaghetti

In this essay from his autobiography *Growing Up* (1982), columnist Russell Baker recalls being sixteen in urban Baltimore and wondering what to do with his life.

Introduction

The only thing that truly interested me was writing, and I knew that 1
sixteen-year-olds did not come out of high school and become writers. I thought of writing as something to be done only by the rich. It was so obviously not real work, not a job at which you could earn a living. Still, I had begun to think of myself as a writer. It was the only thing for which I seemed to have the smallest talent, and, silly though it sounded when I told people I'd like to be a writer, it gave me a way of thinking about myself which satisfied my need to have an identity.

THESIS stating main idea

The notion of becoming a writer had flickered off and on in my head 2
since the Belleville days, but it wasn't until my third year in high school that the possibility took hold. Until then I'd been bored by everything associated with English courses. I found English grammar dull and baffling. I hated the assignments to turn out "compositions," and went at them like heavy labor, turning out leaden, lackluster paragraphs that were agonies for teachers to read and for me to write. The classics thrust on me to read seemed as deadening as chloroform.

Major event 1

When our class was assigned to Mr. Fleagle for third-year English I antici- 3
pated another grim year in that dreariest of subjects. Mr. Fleagle was notorious among City students for dullness and inability to inspire. He was said to be stuffy, dull, and hopelessly out of date. To me he looked to be sixty or sev-

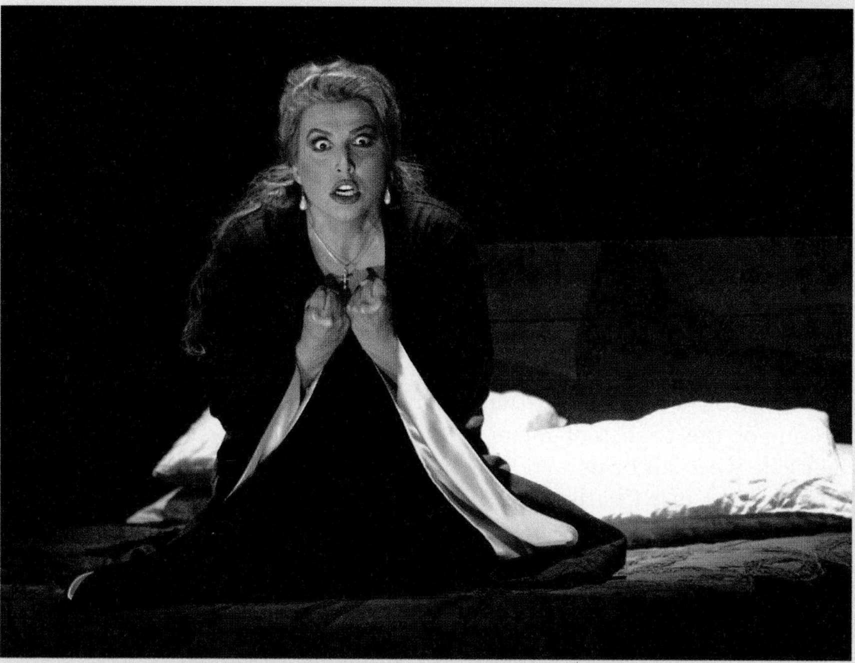

Lady Macbeth, played by Maria Guleghina, Royal Opera House, London.

enty and prim to a fault. He wore primly severe eyeglasses, his wavy hair was primly cut and primly combed. He wore prim vested suits with neckties blocked primly against the collar buttons of his primly starched white shirts. He had a primly pointed jaw, a primly straight nose, and a prim manner of speaking that was so correct, so gentlemanly, that he seemed a comic antique.

4 I anticipated a listless,° unfruitful year with Mr. Fleagle and for a long time was not disappointed. We read *Macbeth*. Mr. Fleagle loved *Macbeth* and wanted us to love it too, but he lacked the gift of infecting others with his own passion. He tried to convey the murderous ferocity of Lady Macbeth one day by reading aloud the passage that concludes

Support for major event 1

> . . . I have given suck, and know
> How tender 'tis to love the babe that milks me.
> I would, while it was smiling in my face,
> Have plucked my nipple from his boneless gums. . . .

The idea of prim Mr. Fleagle plucking his nipple from boneless gums was too much for the class. We burst into gasps of irrepressible snickering. Mr. Fleagle stopped.

5 "There is nothing funny, boys, about giving suck to a babe. It is the—the very essence of motherhood, don't you see."

6 He constantly sprinkled his sentences with "don't you see." It wasn't a question but an exclamation of mild surprise at our ignorance. "Your

**listless:** Lacking energy or enthusiasm.

pronoun needs an antecedent, don't you see," he would say, very primly. "The purpose of the Porter's scene, boys, is to provide comic relief from the horror, don't you see."

Late in the year we tackled the informal essay. "The essay, don't you see, is the . . ." My mind went numb. Of all forms of writing, none seemed so boring as the essay. Naturally we would have to write informal essays. Mr. Fleagle distributed a homework sheet offering us a choice of topics. None was quite so simpleminded as "What I Did on My Summer Vacation," but most seemed to be almost as dull. I took the list home and dawdled until the night before the essay was due. Sprawled on the sofa, I finally faced up to the grim task, took the list out of my notebook, and scanned it. The topic on which my eye stopped was "The Art of Eating Spaghetti." 7

This title produced an extraordinary sequence of mental images. Surging up out of the depths of memory came a vivid recollection of a night in Belleville when all of us were seated around the supper table—Uncle Allen, my mother, Uncle Charlie, Doris, Uncle Hal—and Aunt Pat served spaghetti for supper. Spaghetti was an exotic treat in those days. Neither Doris nor I had ever eaten spaghetti, and none of the adults had enough experience to be good at it. All the good humor of Uncle Allen's house reawoke in my mind as I recalled the laughing arguments we had that night about the socially respectable method for moving spaghetti from plate to mouth. 8

For an essay about family and food, see Jhumpa Lahiri's "Rice," pp. 598–601.

Suddenly I wanted to write about that, about the warmth and good feeling of it, but I wanted to put it down simply for my own joy, not for Mr. Fleagle. It was a moment I wanted to recapture and hold for myself. I wanted to relive the pleasure of an evening at New Street. To write it as I wanted, however, would violate all the rules of formal composition I'd learned in school, and Mr. Fleagle would surely give it a failing grade. Never mind. I would write something else for Mr. Fleagle after I had written this thing for myself. 9

When I finished it the night was half gone and there was no time left to compose a proper, respectable essay for Mr. Fleagle. There was no choice next morning but to turn in my private reminiscence° of Belleville. Two days passed before Mr. Fleagle returned the graded papers, and he returned everyone's but mine. I was bracing myself for a command to report to Mr. Fleagle immediately after school for discipline when I saw him lift my paper from his desk and rap for the class's attention. 10

"Now, boys," he said, "I want to read you an essay. This is titled 'The Art of Eating Spaghetti.'" 11

And he started to read. My words! He was reading *my words* out loud to the entire class. What's more, the entire class was listening. Listening attentively. Then somebody laughed, then the entire class was laughing, and not in contempt and ridicule, but with openhearted enjoyment. Even Mr. Fleagle stopped two or three times to repress a small prim smile. 12

I did my best to avoid showing pleasure, but what I was feeling was pure ecstasy at this startling demonstration that my words had the power to make 13

**reminiscence:** Memory.

people laugh. In the eleventh grade, at the eleventh hour as it were, I had discovered a calling. It was the happiest moment of my entire school career. When Mr. Fleagle finished he put the final seal on my happiness by saying, "Now that, boys, is an essay, don't you see. It's—don't you see—it's of the very essence of the essay, don't you see. Congratulations, Mr. Baker."

For the first time, light shone on a possibility. It wasn't a very heartening possibility, to be sure. Writing couldn't lead to a job after high school, and it was hardly honest work, but Mr. Fleagle had opened a door for me. After that I ranked Mr. Fleagle among the finest teachers in the school. 14

Conclusion restating thesis

## Questions to Start You Thinking

Meaning

1. In your own words, state what Baker believes he learned in the eleventh grade about the art of writing. What incidents or statements help identify this lesson for readers? What lesson, if any, did you learn from the essay?
2. Why do you think Baker included this event in his autobiography?
3. Have you ever changed your mind about something you had to do, as Baker did about writing? Or about a person, as he did about Mr. Fleagle?

Writing Strategies

4. What is the effect, in paragraph 3, of Baker's repetitions of the words *prim* and *primly*? What other devices does he use to characterize Mr. Fleagle vividly? Why do you think Baker uses so much space to portray his teacher?
5. What does the quotation from *Macbeth* add to Baker's account? Had the quotation been omitted, what would have been lost?
6. How does Baker organize the essay? Why does he use this order?

**Robert G. Schreiner** **Student Essay**

## What Is a Hunter?

In this college essay, Robert G. Schreiner uses vivid details to bring to life a significant childhood event.

What is a hunter? This is a simple question with a relatively straightforward answer. A hunter is, according to *Webster's New Collegiate Dictionary*, a person who hunts game (game being various types of animals hunted or pursued for various reasons). However, a second question is just as simple but without such a straightforward answer: What characteristics make up a hunter? As a child, I had always considered the most important aspect of the hunter's person to be his ability 1 to use a rifle, bow, or whatever weapon was appropriate to the type of hunting being done. Having many relatives in rural areas of Virginia and Kansas, I had been exposed to rifles a great deal. I had done extensive target shooting and considered myself to be quite proficient in the use of firearms. I had never been hunting, but I had always thought that since I could fire a rifle accurately I would make a good hunter.

One Christmas holiday, while we were visiting our grandparents in Kansas, my grandfather asked me if I wanted to go jackrabbit hunting with him. I eagerly accepted, anxious to show off my prowess° with a rifle. A younger cousin of mine also wanted to come, so we all went out into the garage, loaded two .22 caliber rifles and a 20-gauge shotgun, hopped into the pickup truck, and drove out of town. It had snowed the night before, and to either side of the narrow road swept six-foot-deep powdery drifts. The wind twirled the fine crystalline snow into whirling vortexes° that bounced along the icy road and sprayed snow into the open windows of the pickup. As we drove, my grandfather gave us some pointers about both spotting and shooting jackrabbits. He told us that when it snows, jackrabbits like to dig out a hollow in the top of a snowdrift, usually near a fencepost, and lie there soaking up the sunshine. He told us that even though jackrabbits are a grayish brown, this coloration is excellent camouflage in the snow, for the curled-up rabbits resemble rocks. He then pointed out a few rabbits in such positions as we drove along, showing us how to distinguish them from exposed rocks and dirt. He then explained that the only way to be sure that we killed the rabbit was to shoot for the head and, in particular, the eye, for this was on a direct line with the rabbit's brain. Since we were using solid point bullets, which deform into a ball upon impact, a hit anywhere but the head would most likely only wound the rabbit. 2

? How does the writer convey his grandfather's definition of hunting?

My grandfather then slowed down the pickup and told us to look out for the rabbits hidden in the snowdrifts. We eventually spotted one about thirty feet from the road in a snow-filled gully. My cousin wished to shoot the first one, so he hopped out of the truck, balanced the .22 on the hood, and fired. A spray of snow erupted about a foot to the left of the rabbit's hollow. My cousin fired again, and again, and again, the shots pockmarking the slope of the drift. He fired once more and the rabbit bounced out of its hollow, its head rocking from side to side. He was hit. My cousin eagerly gamboled into the snow to claim his quarry.° He brought it back holding it by the hind legs, proudly displaying it as would a warrior the severed head of his enemy. The bullet had entered the rabbit's right shoulder and exited through the neck. In both places a thin trickle of crimson marred the gray sheen of the rabbit's pelt. It quivered slightly and its rib cage pulsed with its labored breathing. My cousin was about to toss it into the back of the pickup when 3

**prowess:** Superior skill. **vortex:** Rotation around an axis, as in a whirlwind.
**quarry:** Prey.

my grandfather pointed out that it would be cruel to allow the rabbit to bleed slowly to death and instructed my cousin to bang its head against the side of the pickup to kill it. My cousin then proceeded to bang the rabbit's head against the yellow metal. Thump, thump, thump, thump; after a minute or so my cousin loudly proclaimed that it was dead and hopped back into the truck.

The whole episode sickened me to some degree, and at the time I did not know 4
why. We continued to hunt throughout the afternoon, and feigning boredom, I allowed my cousin and grandfather to shoot all of the rabbits. Often, the shots didn't kill the rabbits outright so they had to be killed against the pickup. The thump, thump, thump of the rabbits' skulls against the metal began to irritate me, and I was strangely glad when we turned around and headed back toward home. We were a few miles from the city limits when my grandfather slowed the truck to a stop, then backed up a few yards. My grandfather said he spotted two huge "jacks" sitting in the sun in a field just off the road. He pointed them out and handed me the .22, saying that if I didn't shoot something the whole afternoon would have been a wasted trip for me. I hesitated and then reluctantly accepted the rifle. I stepped out onto the road, my feet crunching on the ice. The two rabbits were about seventy feet away, both sitting upright in the sun. I cocked and leveled the rifle, my elbow held almost horizontal in the military fashion I had learned to employ. I brought the sights to bear on the right eye of the first rabbit, compensated° for distance, and fired. There was a harsh snap like the crack of a whip and a small jolt to my shoulder. The first rabbit was gone, presumably knocked over the side of the snowdrift. The second rabbit hadn't moved a muscle; it just sat there staring with that black eye. I cocked the rifle once more and sighted a second time, the bead of the rifle just barely above the glassy black orb that regarded me so passively. I squeezed the trigger. Again the crack, again the jolt, and again the rabbit disappeared over the top of the drift. I handed the rifle to my cousin and began making my way toward the rabbits. I sank into powdery snow up to my waist as I clambered to the top of the drift and looked over.

? Why do you think that the writer reacts as he does?

On the other side of the drift was a sight that I doubt I will ever forget. There was 5
a shallow, snow-covered ditch on the leeward side of the drift and it was into this ditch that the rabbits had fallen, at least what was left of the rabbits. The entire ditch, in an area about ten feet wide, was spattered with splashes of crimson blood, pink gobbets of brain, and splintered fragments of bone. The twisted corpses of the rabbits lay in the bottom of the ditch in small pools of streaming blood. Of both the rabbits, only the bodies remained, the heads being completely gone. Stumps of vertebrae protruded obscenely from the mangled bodies, and one rabbit's hind legs twitched spasmodically. I realized that my cousin must have made a mistake and loaded the rifle with hollowpoint explosive bullets instead of solid ones.

**compensate:** Counterbalance.

I shouted back to the pickup, explaining the situation, and asked if I should bring them back anyway. My grandfather shouted back, "No, don't worry about it, just leave them there. I'm gonna toss these jacks by the side of the road anyway; jackrabbits aren't any good for eatin'." 6

Why do you think the writer returns in silence?

Looking at the dead, twitching bodies I thought only of the incredible waste of life that the afternoon had been, and I realized that there was much more to being a hunter than knowing how to use a rifle. I turned and walked back to the pickup, riding the rest of the way home in silence. 7

## Questions to Start You Thinking

### Meaning

1. Where in the essay do you first begin to suspect the writer's feelings about hunting? What in the essay or in your experience led you to this perception?
2. How would you characterize the writer's grandfather? How would you characterize his cousin?
3. How did the writer's understanding of himself change as a result of this hunting experience?

### Writing Strategies

4. How might the essay be strengthened or weakened if the opening paragraph were cut out? Without this paragraph, how would your understanding of the author and his change be different?
5. Would Schreiner's essay be more or less effective if he explained in the last paragraph what he means by "much more to being a hunter"?
6. What are some of Schreiner's memorable images?
7. Using highlighters or marginal notes, identify the essay's introduction, thesis, major events, support for each event, and conclusion. How effective is the organization of this essay?

**e Howie Chackowicz** **Audio**

## The Game Ain't Over 'til the Fatso Man Sings

In this audio piece, recorded for Chicago Public Media's popular radio program *This American Life*, Howie Chackowicz recalls the irrational and amusing methods he unsuccessfully employed as a child to win girls' hearts. To listen to the selection, go to Chapter 4: **bedfordstmartins.com/bedguide**.

# Learning by Writing

## The Assignment: Recalling a Personal Experience

Write about one specific experience that changed how you acted, thought, or felt. Use your experience as a springboard for reflection. Your purpose is not merely to tell an interesting story but to show your readers—your instructor and your classmates—the importance of that experience for you.

We suggest you pick an event that is not too personal, too subjective, or too big to convey effectively to others. Something that happened to you or that you observed, an encounter with a person who greatly influenced you, a decision that you made, or a challenge or an obstacle that you faced will be easier to recall (and to make vivid for your readers) than an interior experience like a religious conversion or falling in love.

For an interactive Learning by Doing activity on Recalling from Photographs, go to Ch. 4: **bedfordstmartins.com/bedguide**.

These students recalled experiences heavy and light:

One writer recalled guitar lessons with a teacher who at first seemed harsh but who turned out to be a true friend.

Another student recalled a childhood trip when everything went wrong and she discovered the complexities of change.

Another recalled competing with a classmate who taught him a deeper understanding of success.

### Facing the Challenge Writing from Recall

The major challenge writers confront when writing from recall is to focus their essays on a main idea. When writing about a familiar—and often powerful—experience, it is tempting to include every detail that comes to mind and equally easy to overlook familiar details that would make the story's relevance clearer to the reader.

When you are certain of your purpose in writing about a particular event—what you want to show readers about your experience—you can transform a laundry list of details into a narrative that connects events clearly around a main idea. You can select details that work together to convey the significance of your experience. To help you decide what to show your readers, respond to each of these questions in a few sentences:

- What was important to you about the experience?
- What did you learn from it?
- How did it change you?
- How would you reply to a reader who asked "So what?"

Once you have decided on your main point about the experience, you should select the details that best illustrate that point and show readers why the experience was important to you.

For more on each strategy for generating ideas in this section or for additional strategies, see Ch. 19.

## Generating Ideas

You may find that the minute you are asked to write about a significant experience, the very incident will flash to mind. Most writers, though, will need a little time for their memories to surface. Often, when you are busy doing something else – observing the scene around you, talking with someone, reading about someone else's experience – the activity can trigger a recollection. When a promising one emerges, write it down. Perhaps, like Russell Baker, you found success when you ignored what you thought you were supposed to do in favor of what you really wanted to do. Perhaps, like Robert Schreiner, you learned from a painful experience.

**Try Brainstorming.** When you brainstorm, you just jot down as many ideas as you can. You can start with a suggestive idea – *disobedience, painful lesson, childhood, peer pressure* – and list whatever occurs through free association. You can also use the questions in the following checklist:

---

**DISCOVERY CHECKLIST**

- ☐ Did you ever break an important rule or rebel against authority? What did you learn from your actions?
- ☐ Did you ever succumb to peer pressure? What were the results of going along with the crowd? What did you learn?
- ☐ Did you ever regard a person in a certain way and then have to change your opinion of him or her? What produced this change?
- ☐ Did you ever have to choose between two equally attractive alternatives? How might your life have been different if you had chosen differently?
- ☐ Have you ever been appalled by witnessing an act of prejudice or insensitivity? What did you do? Do you wish you had done something different?

---

**Try Freewriting.** Devote ten minutes to freewriting – simply writing without stopping. If you get stuck, write "I have nothing to say" over and over, until ideas come. They will come. After you finish, you can circle or draw lines between related items, considering what main idea connects events.

**Try Doodling or Sketching.** As you recall an experience such as breaking your arm during a soccer tournament, try sketching whatever helps you recollect the event and its significance. Turn doodles into words by adding comments on main events, notable details, and their impact on you.

**Try Mapping Your Recollections.** Identify a specific time period such as your birthday last year, the week when you decided to enroll in college, or a time when you changed in some way. On a blank page, on movable sticky notes, or

in a computer file, record all the details you can recall about that time—people, statements, events, locations, and related physical descriptions.

**Try a Reporter's Questions.** Once you recall an experience you want to write about, ask "the five **W**'s and an **H**" that journalists find useful.

- **W**ho was involved?
- **W**hat happened?
- **W**here did it take place?
- **W**hen did it happen?
- **W**hy did it happen?
- **H**ow did the events unfold?

Any question might lead to further questions—and to further discovery.

- **Who** was involved? → What did the others look like?
  → What did they say or do?
  → Would their words supply any lively quotations?
- **What** happened? → What did you think as the event unfolded?
  → When did you see its importance?

**Consider Sources of Support.** Because your memory both retains and drops details, you may want to check your recollections of an experience. Did you keep a journal at the time? Do your memories match those of a friend or relative who was there? Was the experience (big game, new home, birth of a child) a turning point that you or your family would have photographed? Was it sufficiently public (such as a community catastrophe) or universal (such as a campus event) to have been recorded in a newspaper? If so, these resources can remind you of forgotten details or angles.

### Learning by Doing — Creating Your Writing Space

If you are online, in a computer lab, or on your laptop, begin your first writing assignment right now by creating your electronic writing space. Open, label, and save a file for generating ideas. Systematically label your writing files for submission as directed or with your name, course, assignment, and writing stage, draft number, or date so that their sequence is clear: Marcus Recall Ideas 9-14-13 or Chung W110 Recall 1. Store the first file to a course folder or a subfolder for each assignment. If you are in a face-to-face class, label a new page in your notebook so that your ideas are easy to find. Now use your new file or your notebook to brainstorm, freewrite, or try another strategy for generating ideas.

## Planning, Drafting, and Developing

For more strategies for planning, drafting, and developing papers, see Chs. 20, 21, and 22.

Now, how will you tell your story? If the experience is still fresh in your mind, you may be able simply to write a draft, following the order of events. If you want to plan before you write, here are some suggestions.

For more on stating a thesis, see pp. 399–408.

For practice developing effective thesis statements, go to the interactive "Take Action" charts in Re:Writing at **bedfordstmartins .com/bedguide**.

**Start with a Main Idea, or Thesis.** Jot down a few words that identify the experience and express its importance to you. Next, begin to shape these words into a sentence that states its significance—the main idea that you want to convey to a reader. If you aren't certain yet about what that idea is, just begin writing. You can work on your thesis as you revise.

| | |
|---|---|
| TOPIC IDEA + SLANT | reunion in Georgia + really liked meeting family |
| WORKING THESIS | When I went to Georgia for a family reunion, I enjoyed meeting many relatives. |

### Learning by Doing — Stating the Importance of Your Experience

Work up to stating your thesis by completing these two sentences: The most important thing about my experience is ____________. I want to share this so that my readers ____________. Exchange sentences with a classmate or a small group, either in person or online. Ask each other questions to sharpen ideas about the experience and express them in a working thesis.

For examples of time markers and other transitions, see pp. 431–35.

**Establish Your Chronology.** Retelling an experience is called *narration,* and the simplest way to organize is chronologically—relating the essential events in the order in which they occurred. On the other hand, sometimes you can start an account of an experience in the middle and then, through *flashback,* fill in whatever background a reader needs to know.

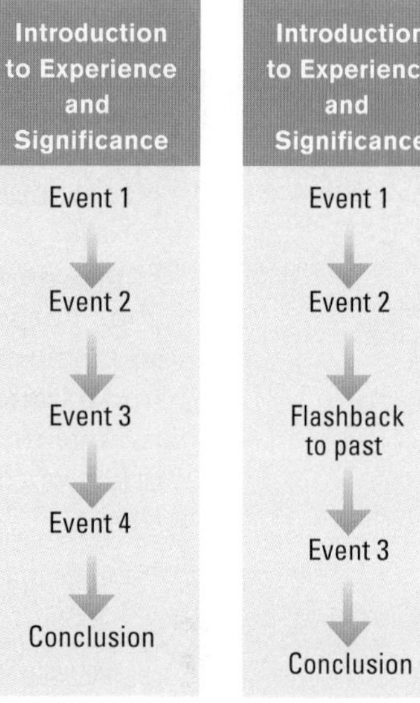


Richard Rodriguez, for instance, begins *Hunger of Memory* (Boston: David R. Godine, 1982), a memoir of his bilingual childhood, with an arresting sentence:

> I remember, to start with, that day in Sacramento, in a California now nearly thirty years past—when I first entered a classroom, able to understand about fifty stray English words.

The opening hooks our attention. In the rest of his essay, Rodriguez fills us in on his family history, on the gulf he came to perceive between the public language (English) and the language of his home (Spanish).

## Learning by Doing — Selecting and Arranging Events

Open a new file, or start a new page in your notebook. List the main events in the order in which they occurred during the experience you plan to write about. Next, sum up the main idea you want to convey to readers. Then decide whether each event in your list supports that main idea. Drop unrelated events, or refine your main idea to reflect the importance of the events more accurately. Exchange files or pages with a classmate, and test each other's sequence of events against the main idea. Note clear connections and engaging events. Add question marks and comments if you notice shifts, gaps, irrelevant events, or missing connections. Use these comments to improve your selection of events and the clarity of your main idea.

**Show Your Audience What Happened.** How can you make your recollections come alive for your readers? Return to Baker's account of Mr. Fleagle teaching *Macbeth,* Schreiner's depiction of his cousin putting the wounded rabbits out of their misery, or Chackowicz's experiences. These writers have not merely told us what happened; they have *shown* us, by creating scenes that we can see in our mind's eye.

For more on providing details, see pp. 439–41.

As you tell your story, zoom in on at least two or three specific scenes. Show your readers exactly what happened, where it occurred, what was said, who said it. Use details and words that appeal to all five senses—sight, sound, touch, taste, smell. Carefully position any images you include to clarify visual details for readers. (Be sure that your instructor approves such additions.)

For practice supporting a thesis, go to the interactive "Take Action" charts in Re:Writing at **bedfordstmartins .com/bedguide**.

## Revising and Editing

For more on adding visuals, see the Quick Format Guide, pp. A-1–A-19.

After you have written an early draft, put it aside for a few days – or hours if your deadline is looming. Then read it over carefully. Try to see it through the eyes of a reader, noting both pleasing and confusing spots. Revise to express your thoughts and feelings clearly and strongly to your readers.

For more revising and editing strategies, see Ch. 23.

**Focus on a Main Idea, or Thesis.** As you read over the essay, return to your purpose: What was so important about this experience? Why is it so memorable? Will readers see why it was crucial in your life? Will they understand how your life has been different ever since? Be sure to specify a genuine difference, reflecting the incident's real impact on you. In other words, revise to keep your essay focused on a single main idea or thesis.

| | |
|---|---|
| WORKING THESIS | When I went to Georgia for a family reunion, I enjoyed meeting many relatives. |
| REVISED THESIS | Meeting my Georgia relatives showed me how powerfully two values – generosity and resilience – unite my family. |

### Peer Response Recalling an Experience

Have a classmate or friend read your draft and suggest how you might present the main idea about your experience more clearly and vividly. Ask your peer editor questions such as these about writing from recall:

For general questions for a peer editor, see p. 463.

- What do you think the writer's main idea or thesis is? Where is it stated or clearly implied? Why was this experience significant?
- What emotions do people in the essay feel? How did *you* feel as a reader?
- Where does the essay come alive? Underline images, descriptions, and dialogue that seem especially vivid.
- If this paper were yours, what is the one thing you would be sure to work on before handing it in?

**Add Concrete Detail.** Ask whether you have made events come alive for your audience by recalling them in sufficient concrete detail. Be specific enough that your readers can see, smell, taste, hear, and feel what you experienced. Make sure that all your details support your main idea or thesis. Notice again Robert Schreiner's focus in his second paragraph on the world outside his own skin: his close recall of the snow, of his grandfather's pointers about the habits of jackrabbits and the way to shoot them.

## Learning by Doing Appealing to the Senses

Working online or in person with a classmate, exchange short passages from your drafts. As you read each other's paragraphs, highlight the sensory details—sights, sounds, tastes, sensations, and smells that bring a description to life. Then jot down the sense to which each detail appeals in the margin or in a file comment. Return each passage to the writer, review the notes about yours, and decide whether to strengthen your description with more—or more varied—details.

**Follow a Clear Sequence.** Reconsider the order of events, looking for changes that make your essay easier for readers to follow. For example, if a classmate seems puzzled about the sequence of your draft, make a rough outline or list of main events to check the clarity of your arrangement. Or add more transitions to connect events and clarify where your account is going.

For more on outlining, see pp. 411–19.

For more on transitions, see pp. 431–35.

Revise and rewrite until you've related your experience and its impact as well as you can. Here are some useful questions about revising your paper:

### REVISION CHECKLIST

- ☐ Where have you shown why this experience was important and how it changed your life?
- ☐ How have you engaged readers so they will keep reading? Will they find your paper dramatic, instructive, or revealing? Will they see and feel your experience?
- ☐ Why do you begin your narration as you do? Is there another place in the draft that would make a better beginning?
- ☐ If the events are not in chronological order, how have you made the organization easy for readers to follow?
- ☐ In what ways does the ending provide a sense of finality?
- ☐ Do you stick to a point? Is everything relevant to your main idea or thesis?
- ☐ If you portray any people, how have you made their importance clear? Which details make them seem real, not just shadowy figures?
- ☐ Does any dialogue sound like real speech? Read it aloud. Try it on a friend.

After you have revised your recall essay, edit and proofread it. Carefully check the grammar, word choice, punctuation, and mechanics—and then correct any problems you find. Here are some questions to get you started:

For more editing and proofreading strategies, see pp. 471–75.

For more help, find the relevant checklist sections in the Quick Editing Guide on p. A-39. Turn also to the Quick Format Guide beginning on p. A-1.

### EDITING CHECKLIST

- ☐ Is your sentence structure correct? Have you avoided writing fragments, comma splices, or fused sentences? A1, A2
- ☐ Have you used correct verb tenses and forms throughout? When you present a sequence of past events, is it clear what happened first and what happened next? A3
- ☐ When you use transitions and other introductory elements to connect events, have you placed any needed commas after them? C1
- ☐ In your dialogue, have you placed commas and periods before (inside) the closing quotation mark? C3
- ☐ Have you spelled everything correctly, especially the names of people and places? Have you capitalized names correctly? D1, D2

Also check your paper's format using the Quick Format Guide. Follow the style expected by your instructor for features such as the heading, title, running head, page numbers, margins, and paragraph indentation.

When you have made all the changes you need to make, save your file, print out a clean copy of your paper or attach the file—and submit it.

## Additional Writing Assignments

1. Choose a person outside your immediate family who had a marked effect on your life, either good or bad. Jot down ten details that might show what that person was like: physical appearance, way of talking, habits, or memorable incidents. Then look back at "The Art of Eating Spaghetti" to identify the kinds of detail Baker uses to portray Mr. Fleagle, noting any you might add to your list. Write your paper, including details to help readers experience the person's impact on you.
2. Recall a place you were fond of—your grandma's kitchen, a tree house, a library, a locker room, a vacation retreat. What made it different from other places? Why was it important? What do you feel when you remember it? Write a paper that uses specific, concrete details to explain to your audience why this place was memorable. If you have a photograph of the place, look at it to jog your memory, and consider adding it to your paper.
3. Write a paper or a podcast text to recall a familiar ceremony, ritual, or observation, perhaps a holiday, a rite of passage (confirmation, bar or bat

mitzvah, college orientation, graduation), a sporting event, a family custom. How did the tradition originate? Who takes part? How has it changed over the years? What does it add to the lives of those who observe it? Share with your audience the importance of the tradition to you.

4. Recall how you learned to read, write, or see how literacy could shape or change your life. What early experiences with reading or writing do you recall? How did these experiences affect you? Were they turning points for you? Write an essay about the major events in your literacy story—your personal account of your experiences learning to read or write—so that your audience understands the impact of those events on you. If you wish, address a specific audience—such as students or a teacher at your old school, a younger relative, your own children (real or future), or a person involved in your experience.
5. **Source Assignment.** Respond to one of the preceding assignments by supplementing your recollections with information from a source. You might turn to a personal source (family record, photograph, relative's account) or a published account (newspaper story reporting an event, article about a tradition, essay recalling an experience). Jot down relevant details from your source, or write a brief summary of it. Integrate this information in your essay, and be sure to cite your source.
6. **Visual Assignment.** Examine the images on the next two pages. What do you recall about an experience in a similar social, natural, or urban environment? What events took place there? How did you react to those events? What was their importance to you? How did the experience change you, your ideas, or your decisions? Write an essay that briefly recalls your experience and then reflects on its importance or consequences for you. Add your own photo to your text, if you wish.

YOU'VE MADE IT HERE. BUT WILL YOU BE ABLE TO RETIRE ANYWHERE?
Kodak
Kodak

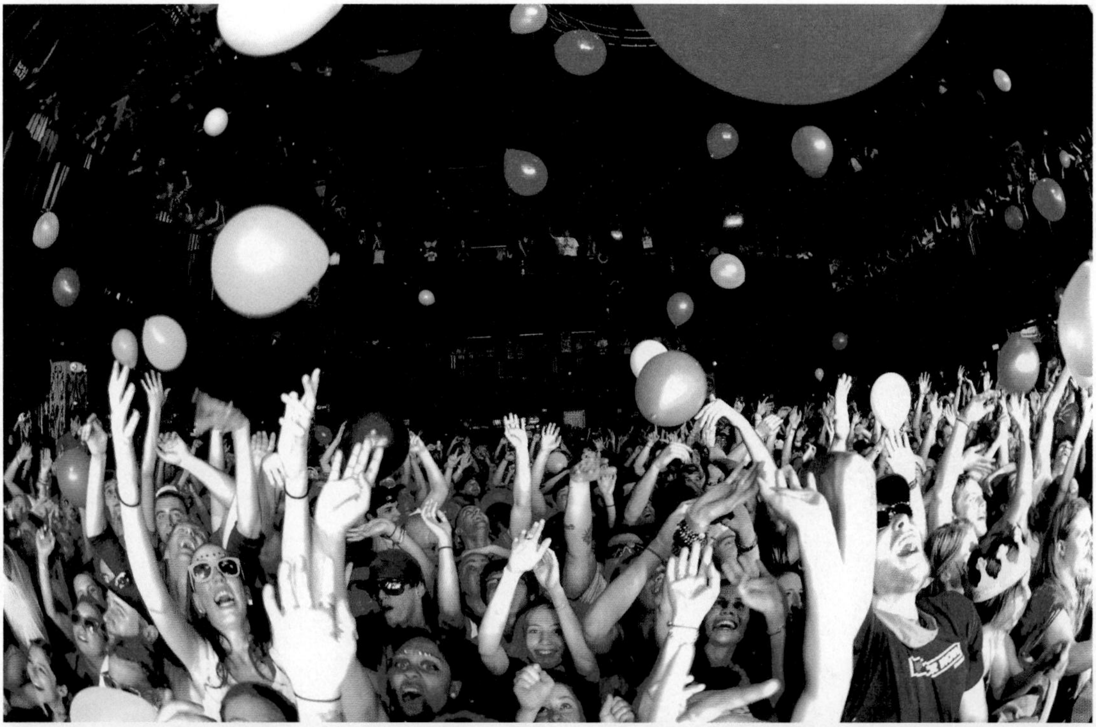

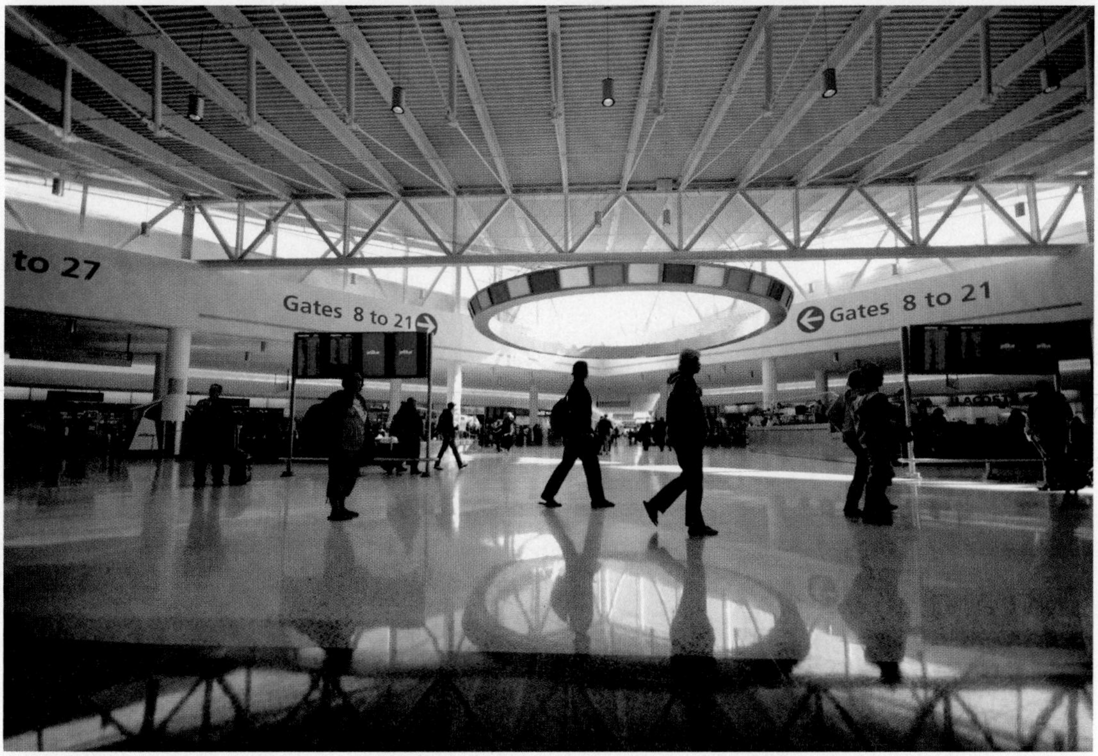
to 27
Gates 8 to 21
Gates 8 to 21

# 5 Observing a Scene

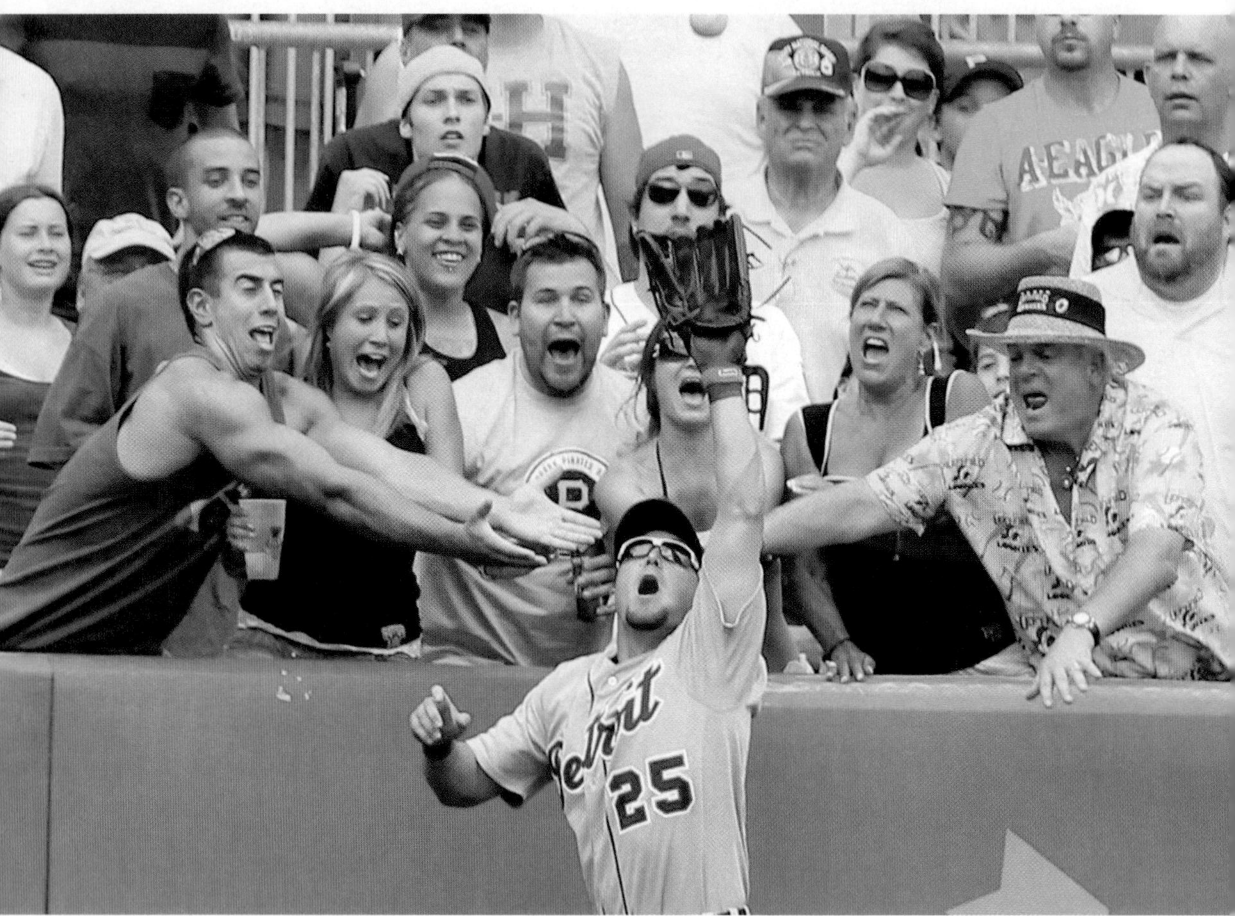


Ryan Raburn of the Detroit Tigers saves a home run by catching a fly ball in the eighth inning against the Pittsburgh Pirates on June 24, 2012, at PNC Park in Pittsburgh, Pennsylvania.

### Responding to an Image

This scene might look and feel quite different to different observers, depending on their vantage points, emotions, and experiences. In this image, what prominent element attracts your attention? Who are the observers? Which details might be important for them? Although visual details are central, what other senses and emotions might come into play?

Most writers begin to write by recalling what they know. Then they look around and add what they observe. Some writing consists almost entirely of observation—a reporter's eyewitness account of a fire, a clinical report by a nurse detailing a patient's condition, a scientist's account of a laboratory experiment, a traveler's blog or photo essay. In fact, observation plays a large role in any writing that describes a person, place, or thing. Observation also provides support, details to make a point clear or convincing. For example, a case study might report information from interviews and analyze artifacts—whether ancient bowls, new playground equipment, or decades of airport records. However, to make its abstractions and statistics more vivid, it also might integrate compelling observation.

If you need more to write about, open your eyes—and your other senses. Take in what you can see, hear, smell, touch, and taste. As you write, report your observations in concrete detail. Of course, you can't record everything your senses bring you. You must be selective based on what's important and relevant for your purpose and audience. To make a football game come alive for readers of your college newspaper, you might mention the overcast cold weather and the spicy smell of bratwurst. But if your purpose is primarily to explain which team won and why, you might stress the muddy playing field, the most spectacular plays, and the players who scored.

## Why Observing a Scene Matters

### In a College Course

- You observe and report compelling information from field trips in sociology, criminal justice, or anthropology as well as impressions of a play, a concert, an exhibit, or a historical site for a humanities class.
- You observe clinical practices in health or education, habitats for plants and animals, the changing night sky, or lab experiments to report accurate information and to improve your own future practice.

### In the Workplace

- You observe and analyze to lend credibility to your case study as a nurse, teacher, or social worker or to your site report as an engineer or architect.

### In Your Community

- You observe, photograph, and report on hazards (a dangerous intersection, a poorly lighted park, a run-down building), needs (a soccer arena, a performing arts center), or disasters (an accident, a crime scene, a flood) to motivate action by authorities or fellow citizens.

? When have you included observations in your writing? How did these observations contribute to your writing? In what situations might you use observation in future writing?

# Learning from Other Writers

Here are two essays by writers who observe their surroundings and reflect on their observations. As you begin to analyze the first reading, look at the notes in the margin. They identify features such as the main impression created in the observation and stated in the thesis, the first of the locations observed, and the supporting details that describe the location.

## As You Read These Observations

As you read these essays, ask yourself the following questions:

1. What does the writer observe? Places? People? Behavior? Things?
2. What senses does each writer rely on? What sensory images does each develop? Find some striking passages in which the writer reports observations. What makes these passages memorable to you?
3. Why does the writer use observation? What conclusion does the writer draw from reflecting on the observations?

### Eric Liu

## The Chinatown Idea

Eric Liu is an educator, lecturer, and author of *Guiding Lights* (2004), a book about mentorship. In this selection from *The Accidental Asian* (1998), he describes a childhood visit to Chinatown in New York City.

Introduction

Another family outing, one of our occasional excursions to the city. It was a Saturday. I was twelve. I remember only vaguely what we did during the day—Fifth Avenue, perhaps, the museums, Central Park, Carnegie Hall. But I recall with precision going to Chinatown as night fell. 1

Vantage point 1

Supporting detail

We parked on a side street, a dim, winding way cluttered with Chinese placards° and congested with slumbering Buicks and Chevys. The license plates—NEW YORK, EMPIRE STATE—seemed incongruous here, foreign. We walked a few blocks to East Broadway. Soon we were wading through thick crowds on the sidewalk, passing through belts of aroma: sweat and breath, old perfume, spareribs. It was late autumn and chilly enough to numb my cheeks, but the bustle all around gave the place an electric warmth. Though it was evening, the scene was lit like a stage, thanks to the aluminum lamps hanging from every produce stand. Peddlers lined the street, selling steamed buns and chicken feet and imitation Gucci bags. Some shoppers moved along slowly. Others stopped at each stall, inspecting the greens, negotiating the price of fish, talking loudly. I strained to make sense of the chopped-off twangs of 2

**placards:** Posters, signs.

Cantonese coming from every direction, but there were more tones than I knew: my ear was inadequate; nothing was intelligible.

3 This was the first time I had been in Chinatown after dark. Mom held Andrea's hand as we walked and asked me to stay close. People bumped us, brushed past, as if we were invisible. I felt on guard, alert. I craned my neck as we walked past a kiosk° carrying a Chinese edition of *Playboy*. I glanced sidelong at the teenage ruffians on the corner. They affected an air of menace with their smokes and leather jackets, but their feathery almost-mustaches and overpermed hair made them look a bit ridiculous. Nevertheless, I kept my distance. I kept an eye on the sidewalk, too, so that I wouldn't soil my shoes in the streams of putrid° water that trickled down from the alleyways and into the parapet° of trash bags piled up on the curb.

Supporting detail

4 I remember going into two stores that night. One was the Far Eastern Bookstore. It was on the second floor of an old building. As we entered, the sounds of the street fell away. The room was spare and fluorescent. It looked like an earnest community library, crowded with rows of chest-high shelves. In the narrow aisles between shelves, patrons sat cross-legged on the floor, reading intently. If they spoke at all it was in a murmur. Mom and Dad each found an absorbing book. They read standing up. My sister and I, meanwhile, wandered restlessly through the stacks, scanning the spines for stray English words or Chinese phrases we might recognize. I ended up in children's books and leafed through an illustrated story about the three tigers. I couldn't read it. Before long, I was tugging on Dad's coat to take us somewhere else.

5 The other shop, a market called Golden Gate, I liked much more. It was noisy. The shoppers swarmed about in a frenzy. On the ground level was an emporium° of Chinese nonperishables: dried mushrooms, spiced beef, seaweed, shredded pork. Open crates of hoisin sauce° and sesame chili paste. Sweets, like milky White Rabbit chews, coconut candies, rolls of sour "haw flakes." Bags of Chinese peanuts, watermelon seeds. Down a narrow flight of stairs was a storehouse of rice cookers, ivory chopsticks, crockery, woks that hung from the wall. My mother carefully picked out a set of rice bowls and serving platters. I followed her to the long checkout line, carrying a basket full of groceries we wouldn't find in Poughkeepsie. I watched with wonder as the cashier tallied up totals with an abacus.

6 We had come to this store, and to Chinatown itself, to replenish our supply of things Chinese: food and wares, and something else as well. We had ventured here from the colorless outer suburbs to touch the source, to dip into a pool of undiluted Chineseness. It was easier for my parents, of course, since they could decode the signs and communicate. But even I, whose bond to his ancestral culture had frayed down to the inner cord of *appetite*—even I could feel somehow fortified by a trip to Chinatown.

THESIS stating main impression

**kiosk:** Booth. **putrid:** Rotten; decaying. **parapet:** Wall, as on a castle. **emporium:** Marketplace. **hoisin sauce:** A sweet brown sauce that is a popular Chinese condiment.

Yet we knew that we couldn't stay long—and that we didn't really want 7
to. We were Chinese, but we were still outsiders. When any peddler addressed us in Cantonese, that became obvious enough. They seemed so familiar and so different, these Chinatown Chinese. Like a reflection distorted just so. Their faces were another brand of Chinese, rougher-hewn. I was fascinated by them. I liked being connected to them. But was it because of what we shared—or what we did not? I began that night to distinguish between my world and theirs.

Conclusion drawn from observation

It was that night, too, as we were making our way down East Broadway, 8
that out of the blur of Chinese faces emerged one that we knew. It was Po-Po's° face. We saw her just an instant before she saw us. There was surprise in her eyes, then hurt, when she peered up from her parka. Everyone hugged and smiled, but this was embarrassing. Mom began to explain: we'd been up-town, had come to Chinatown on a whim, hadn't wanted to barge in on her unannounced. Po-Po nodded. We made some small talk. But the realization that her daily routine was our tourist's jaunt,° that there was more than just a hundred miles between us, consumed the backs of our minds like a flame to paper. We lingered for a minute, standing still as the human current flowed past, and then we went our separate ways.

Afterward, during the endless drive home, we didn't talk about bumping 9
into Po-Po. We didn't talk about much of anything. I looked intently through the window as we drove out of Chinatown and sped up the FDR Drive, then over the bridge. Manhattan turned into the Bronx, the Bronx into Yonkers, and the seams of the parkway clicked along in soothing intervals as we cruised northward to Dutchess County. I slipped into a deep, open-mouthed slumber,

**Po-Po:** The narrator's grandmother. **jaunt:** Trip, outing.

not awakening until we were back in Merrywood, our development, our own safe enclave. I remember the comforting sensation of being home: the sky was clear and starry, the lawn a moon-bathed carpet. We pulled into our smooth blacktop driveway. Silence. It was late, perhaps later than I'd ever stayed up. Still, before I went to bed, I made myself take a shower.

## Questions to Start You Thinking

Meaning

1. Why do Liu and his family go to Chinatown?
2. How do Liu and his family feel when they encounter Po-Po? What observations and descriptions lead you to that conclusion?
3. What is the significance of the last sentence? How does it capture the essence of Liu's Chinatown experience?

Writing Strategies

4. In which paragraphs or sections does the writer's use of sensory details capture the look, feel, or smell of Chinatown? In general, how successfully has Liu included various types of observations and details?
5. How does Liu organize his observations? Is this organization effective? Why or why not?
6. Which of the observations and events in this essay most clearly reveal that Liu considers himself to be a "tourist"?

For another observation of an unfamiliar place, see James McBride's "Full Circle," pp. 558–61.

**Alea Eyre** **Student Essay**

## Stockholm

For her first-year composition class, Alea Eyre records her introduction to an unfamiliar location.

When have you had similar surprises in a new environment?

The amount of noise and movement bustling around me was almost electrifying. As soon as I stepped off the plane ramp, I was enveloped into a brand new world. I let all my heightened senses work together to take in this new experience. Fear and elation collided in my head as I navigated this new adventure by myself. I was thirteen years old and just taking the final steps of a lonely twenty-six-hour journey across the world from Hawaii to Sweden. 1

I had never seen so many white folks in one place. Hundreds crowded and rushed to be somewhere. The busy airport felt like a culture shock but not in a bad way. Blonde hair whipped past me, snuggled in caps and scarves. Skin tucked in coats and jeans appeared so shockingly white it almost blinded me. Delicate yet tall and sturdy people zipped around me as if they had to attend to an emergency. 2

A music-like language danced around my ears, exciting me as I drew closer to the baggage claim. The sound was so familiar yet seemed so distant. I had heard it 3 inconsistently since childhood with the coming and going of my three half sisters. It unfurled off native speakers' tongues, rising and falling in artistic tones. For the past few months, I had studied my Swedish language book diligently, attempting to match my untrained tongue to the rolling R's and foreign sounds. On paper, the language looked silly, complicated, and unpronounceable. When spoken correctly, it sounded magical and delighted the ears. As I walked swiftly, trying to keep up with the general pace of this international airport, my ears stayed perked up, catching bits and pieces of conversations.

? What kinds of places does this building bring to mind?

The building was cavernous and had modern wooden architecture that accentuated every corner. Floor to ceiling windows brightened each area, letting in ample light and a view of the dreary early spring surroundings. I felt my eyes widen as I viewed the melting, slushy brown snow and bright green grass peeking up beneath it. Endless birch trees spread before me, and vibrant flowers dotted their roots. Everything inside and out felt so clean and new; even all of the people looked fresh and well dressed. The true Europeans that I had read about for so long were now displayed up close. Pale as they were, none of them looked as if they were sick, overweight, or druggies. I was taken aback, used to the vivid rainbow of shapes, colors, sizes, and overall variety of my Honolulu neighborhood. Every race and social class crammed into the concrete blocks of apartments in my hometown. Everything there felt dirty and unpredictable, but here in Stockholm, everything felt like a lily-white world. 4

? When have you been observed as well as observer?

As I neared the head of the line at customs, sets of eyes from every direction lingered on me. I was still a child, traveling by myself and sticking out against the array of white with my thick dark hair and almond-colored skin. I figured that my features kept them guessing. I was obviously not white, black, or Middle Eastern, but a mix of many different races and cultures that were completely foreign to them. Even back home, people could never guess what my blood combination was. I soon learned that Sweden has extremely strict immigration rules, and hardly anybody can get in. The country took in some Middle Eastern refugees during past wars, but other than that, blonde-haired blue-eyed Swedes turn up around every corner. 5

With my passport stamped and luggage in tow, I descended down a steep escalator, sandwiched in among a family of five. Listening intently to the lilt of their language, I tried to pick up on what they were discussing. Only able to translate a few simple words, I felt discouraged. Exhaustion was creeping up on me both mentally and physically as the initial adrenaline started to wear off. The flights to get here were lengthy and cramped, while the layovers were stressful and rushed. Jet lag settled in and clouded my already foggy head. I needed the luxury of rejuvenating sleep as soon as possible. 6

Finally, the escalator neared the ground floor. I surveyed the crowd anxiously, winding my way through the masses of people. My sister was supposed to be here somewhere, ready to begin a five-month-long period of dealing with my adolescent 7 hormones. I came here to live and learn, go to a Swedish school, and be immersed in a foreign culture. I spotted her, all the way at the end of the floor, near the sets of doors that led to this new world. She stood there, completely still and silent, but smiling and relieved that I actually made it. Her belly filled out the coat she wore, blossoming with her first child. Her hair was long and silky, and her eyes bright and earnest. She glowed with happiness, now looking like a mother. I fell into her arms, feeling ecstatic after not seeing her for years. We left the airport together, beaming as we walked through the crisp, freezing air. As we neared the car, I reached down and touched the melting snow. My virgin hands explored this new texture, and my nerves tingled. Feeling content, I slid into the car and prepared myself for the exciting journey ahead of me.

? How have you responded to the sights, sounds, and emotions that the writer has described?

### Questions to Start You Thinking

Meaning

1. What is Eyre's response to the scene at the Stockholm airport?
2. What is the point of the overall impression Eyre creates? What does that impression reveal about her?
3. In paragraph 7, what does Eyre mean when she says she prepared herself "for the exciting journey ahead"?

Writing Strategies

4. How does contrasting Honolulu and Stockholm contribute to the vivid impression of the scene Eyre observes?
5. Which sense does Eyre use most effectively? Point to a few examples that support your choice.
6. How does Eyre convey motion and movement? What does this activity contribute to her observation?
7. Using highlighters or marginal notes, identify the essay's introduction, thesis, major vantage points for observation, details supporting each part of the observation, and conclusion. How effective is this organization?

**e Multiple Photographers** **Visual Essay**

## Observing the *Titanic*: Past and Present

On its maiden voyage in 1912, the *Titanic* hit an iceberg and sank within three hours, killing more than 1,500 people on board. The wreck was discovered in 1985 by Robert Ballard, at a depth of two miles beneath the Atlantic's surface, and has been visited by many, including filmmaker James

Cameron. To click through a series of photos that contrasts images of the ship when it was first built with images of its remains, go to Chapter 5: **bedfordstmartins.com/bedguide**.

The *Titanic*, 1912.

# Learning by Writing

## The Assignment: Observing a Scene

For an interactive Learning by Doing activity on Scenes from the News, go to Ch. 5: **bedfordstmartins .com/bedguide**.

Observe a place near your campus, home, or job and the people who frequent it. Then write a paper that describes the place, the people, and their actions so as to convey the spirit of the place and offer some insight into its impact on the people.

This assignment is meant to start you observing closely enough that you go beyond the obvious. Go somewhere nearby, and station yourself where you can mingle with the people there. Open all your senses so that you see, smell, taste, hear, and feel. Jot down what you immediately notice, especially the atmosphere and its effect on the people there. Take notes describing the location, people, actions, and events you see. Then use your observations to convey the spirit of the scene. What is your main impression of the place? Of the people there? Of the relationship between people and

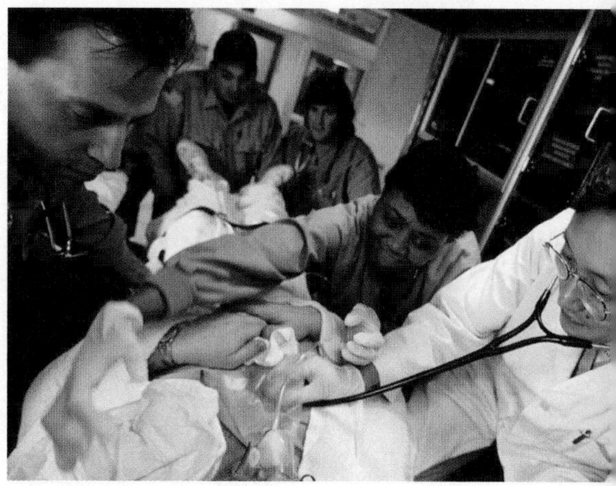

place? Your purpose is not only to describe the scene but also to express thoughts and feelings connected with what you observe.

Three student writers wrote about these observations:

> One student, who works nights in the emergency room, observed the scene and the community that abruptly forms when an accident victim arrives: medical staff, patient, friends, and relatives.
>
> Another observed a bar mitzvah celebration that reunited a family for the first time in many years.
>
> Another observed the activity in the bleachers in a baseball stadium before, during, and after a game.

When you select the scene you wish to observe, find out from the person in charge whether you'll need to request permission to observe there, as you might at a school, business, or other restricted or privately owned site.

## Facing the Challenge Observing a Scene

The major challenge writers face when writing from observation is to select compelling details that convey an engaging main impression of a scene. As we experience the world, we are bombarded by sensory details, but our task as writers is to choose those that bring a subject alive for readers. For example, describing an oak as "a big tree with green leaves" is too vague to help readers envision the tree or grasp its unique qualities. Consider:

- What colors, shapes, and sizes do you see?
- What tones, pitches, and rhythms do you hear?
- What textures, grains, and physical features do you feel?
- What fragrances and odors do you smell?
- What sweet, spicy, or other flavors do you taste?

After recording the details that define the scene, ask two more questions:

- What overall main impression do these details establish?
- Which specific details will best show the spirit of this scene to a reader?

Your answers will help you decide which details to include in your paper.

## Generating Ideas

For more on each strategy for generating ideas in this section or for additional strategies, see Ch. 19.

Although setting down observations might seem cut-and-dried, to many writers it is true discovery. Here are some ways to generate such observations.

**Brainstorm.** First, you need to find a scene to observe. What places interest you? Which are memorable? Start brainstorming—listing rapidly any ideas that come to mind. Here are a few questions to help you start your list:

---

**DISCOVERY CHECKLIST**

- ☐ Where do people gather for some event or performance (a stadium, a church, a theater, an auditorium)?
- ☐ Where do people meet for some activity (a gym, a classroom)?
- ☐ Where do crowds form while people are getting things or services (a shopping mall, a dining hall or student union, a dentist's waiting room)?
- ☐ Where do people pause on their way to yet another destination (a light-rail station, a bus or subway station, an airport, a restaurant on the toll road)?
- ☐ Where do people go for recreation or relaxation (an arcade, a ballpark)?
- ☐ Where do people gather (a fire, a party, a wedding, a graduation, an audition)?

---

**Get Out and Look.** If nothing on your list strikes you as compelling, plunge into the world to see what you see. Visit a city street or country hillside, a campus building or practice field, a contest, a lively scene—a mall, an airport, a fast-food restaurant, a student hangout—or a scene with only a few people sunbathing, walking dogs, or tossing Frisbees. Observe for a while, and then mix and move to gain different views.

**Record Your Observations.** Alea Eyre's essay "Stockholm" began with some notes about her vivid memories of her trip. She was able to mine those memories for details to bring her subject to life.

Your notes on a subject—or tentative subject—can be taken in any order or methodically. To draw up an "observation sheet," fold a sheet of paper in half lengthwise. Label the left column "Objective," and impartially list what you see, like a zoologist looking at a new species of moth. Label the right column "Subjective," and list your thoughts and feelings about what you observe. The quality of your paper will depend in large part on the truthfulness and accuracy of your observations. Your objective notes will trigger more subjective ones.

Elvis impersonators gather to audition in a Las Vegas contest.

| *Objective* | *Subjective* |
| --- | --- |
| The ticket holders form a line on the weathered sidewalk outside the old brick hall, standing two or three deep all the way down the block. | This place has seen concerts of all kinds — you can feel the history as you wait, as if the hall protects the crowds and the music. |
| Groups of friends talk, a few couples hug, and some guys burst out in staccato laughter as they joke. | The crowd seems relaxed and friendly, all waiting to hear their favorite group. |
| Everyone shuffles forward when the doors open, looking around at the crowd and edging toward the entrance. | The excitement and energy grow with the wait, but it's the concert ritual — the prelude to a perfect night. |

**Include a Range of Images.** Have you captured not just sights but sounds, textures, odors? Have you observed from several vantage points or on several occasions to deepen your impressions? Have you added sketches or doodles to your notes, perhaps drawing the features or shape of the place? Can you begin writing as you continue to observe? Have you noticed how other writers use *images,* evoking sensory experience, to record what they sense? In the memoir *Northern Farm* (New York: Rinehart, 1948), naturalist Henry Beston describes a remarkable sound: "the voice of ice," the midwinter sound of a whole frozen pond settling and expanding in its bed.

> Sometimes there was a sort of hollow oboe sound, and sometimes a groan with a delicate undertone of thunder. . . . Just as I turned to go, there came from below one curious and sinister crack which ran off into a sound like the whine of a giant whip of steel lashed through the moonlit air.

### Learning by Doing Enriching Sensory Detail

Review the detail in your observation notes. Because observers often note first what they see, mark references to other senses by underlining sounds, circling smells, and boxing textures or by adding different color highlights to your file. (Mark taste, too, if appropriate.) Compare your coverage with that of a classmate or small group, either in class or online. Add more variety from memory, or list what you want to observe when you return to the scene to listen, sniff, taste, or touch. (You can also use this activity to analyze sensory details in paragraphs from the two essays opening this chapter.)

## Planning, Drafting, and Developing

For more strategies for planning, drafting, and developing, see Chs. 20, 21, and 22.

For more on stating a thesis, see pp. 399–408.

For practice developing effective thesis statements, go to the interactive "Take Action" charts in Re:Writing at **bedfordstmartins .com/bedguide**.

After recording your observations, look over your notes, circling whatever looks useful. Maybe you can rewrite your notes into a draft, throwing out details that don't matter, leaving those that do. Maybe you'll need a plan to help you organize all the observations, laying them out graphically or in a simple scratch outline.

**Start with a Main Impression or Thesis.** What main insight or impression do you want to convey? Answering this question will help you decide which details to include, which to omit, and how to avoid a dry list of facts.

| | |
|---|---|
| PLACE OBSERVED | Smalley Green after lunch |
| MAIN IMPRESSION | relaxing activity is good after a morning of classes |
| WORKING THESIS | After their morning classes, students have fun relaxing on Smalley Green with their dogs and Frisbees. |

**Organize to Show Your Audience Your Point.** How do you map out a series of observations? Your choice depends on your purpose and the main impression you want to create. Whatever your choice, add transitions—words or phrases to guide the reader from one vantage point, location, or idea to the next. Consider options such as those shown on the next page.

For more organization strategies, see pp. 408–11.

For transitions that mark place or direction, see p. 433.

As you create your "picture," you bring a place to life using the details that capture its spirit. If your instructor approves, consider whether adding a photograph, sketch, diagram, or other illustration—with a caption—would enhance your written observation.

## Learning by Doing Experimenting with Organization

Take a second look at the arrangement of the details in your observation. Select a different yet promising sequence, and test it by outlining your draft (or reorganizing another file) in that order. Ask classmates for reactions as you consider which sequence most effectively conveys your main impression.

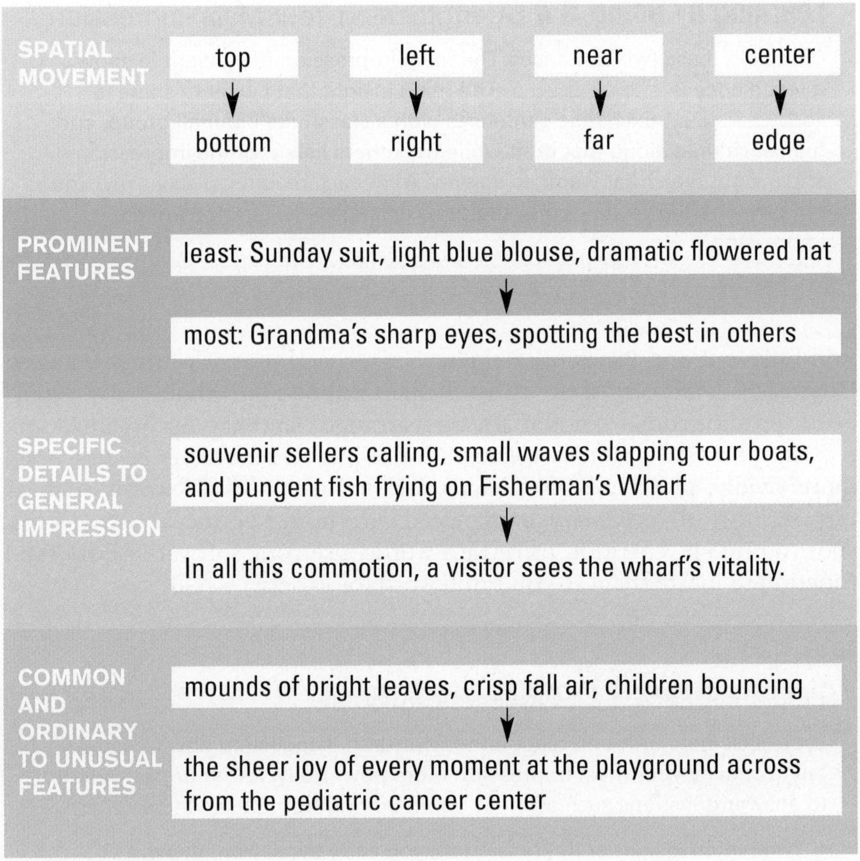

| | | | | |
|---|---|---|---|---|
| SPATIAL MOVEMENT | top ↓ bottom | left ↓ right | near ↓ far | center ↓ edge |
| PROMINENT FEATURES | least: Sunday suit, light blue blouse, dramatic flowered hat ↓ most: Grandma's sharp eyes, spotting the best in others | | | |
| SPECIFIC DETAILS TO GENERAL IMPRESSION | souvenir sellers calling, small waves slapping tour boats, and pungent fish frying on Fisherman's Wharf ↓ In all this commotion, a visitor sees the wharf's vitality. | | | |
| COMMON AND ORDINARY TO UNUSUAL FEATURES | mounds of bright leaves, crisp fall air, children bouncing ↓ the sheer joy of every moment at the playground across from the pediatric cancer center | | | |

Sequential Organization of Details

## Revising and Editing

For more revising and editing strategies, see Ch. 23.

Your revising, editing, and proofreading will be easier if you have accurate notes on your observations. But what if you don't have enough detail for your draft? If you have doubts, go back to the scene to take more notes.

**Focus on a Main Impression or Thesis.** As you begin to revise, have a friend read your observation, or read it yourself as if you had never seen the place you observed. Note gaps that would puzzle a reader, restate the spirit of the place, or sharpen the description of the main impression you want to convey in your thesis.

| | |
|---|---|
| WORKING THESIS | After morning classes, students have fun relaxing on Smalley Green with their dogs and Frisbees. |
| REVISED THESIS | When students, dogs, and Frisbees accumulate on Smalley Green after lunch, they show how much campus learning takes place outside of class. |

### Learning by Doing — Strengthening Your Main Impression

Complete these two sentences: The main impression that I want to show my audience is ______________. The main insight that I want to share is ______________. Exchange sentences with a classmate or small group, and then each read aloud that draft while the others listen for the impression and insight the writer wants to convey. After each reading, discuss revision options with the writer—cuts, additions, changes—to strengthen that impression.

For practice supporting a thesis, go to the interactive "Take Action" charts in Re:Writing at **bedfordstmartins .com/bedguide**.

**Add Relevant and Powerful Details.** Next, check your selection of details. Does each detail contribute to your main impression? Should any details be dropped or added? Should any be rearranged so that your organization, moving point to point, is clearer? Could any observations be described more vividly, powerfully, or concretely? Could any vague words such as *very, really, great,* or *beautiful* be replaced with more specific words? (As you spot too much repetition of certain words, use your software's Edit-Find function to locate them so you can reword for variety.)

### Peer Response — Observing a Scene

For general questions for a peer editor, see p. 463.

Let a classmate or friend respond to your draft, suggesting how to use detail to convey your main impression more powerfully. Ask your peer editor to answer questions such as these about writing from observation:

- What main insight or impression do you carry away from this draft?
- Which sense does the writer use particularly well? Are any senses neglected?

- Can you see and feel what the writer experienced? Would more detail be more compelling? Put check marks wherever you want more details.
- How well has the writer used evidence from the senses to build a main impression? Which sensory impressions contribute most strongly to the overall picture? Which seem superfluous?
- If this paper were yours, what is the one thing you would be sure to work on before handing it in?

To see where your draft could need work, consider these questions:

**REVISION CHECKLIST**

- ☐ Have you accomplished your purpose – to convey to readers your overall impression of your subject and to share some telling insight about it?
- ☐ What can you assume your readers know? What do they need to be told?
- ☐ Have you gathered enough observations to describe your subject? Have you observed with *all* your senses when possible – even smell and taste?
- ☐ Have you been selective, including details that effectively support your overall impression?
- ☐ Which observations might need to be checked for accuracy? Which might need to be checked for richness or fullness?
- ☐ Is your organizational pattern the most effective for your subject? Is it easy for readers to follow? Would another pattern work better?

After you have revised your essay, edit and proofread it. Carefully check the grammar, word choice, punctuation, and mechanics – and then correct any problems. If you have added details while revising, consider whether they have been sufficiently blended with the ideas already there. Here are some questions to get you started:

For more editing and proofreading strategies, see pp. 471–75.

**EDITING CHECKLIST**

- ☐ Is your sentence structure correct? Have you avoided writing fragments, comma splices, and fused sentences? A1, A2
- ☐ Have you used an adjective when you describe a noun or pronoun? Have you used an adverb when you describe a verb, adjective, or adverb? Have you used the correct form to compare two or more things? A7

For more help, find the relevant checklist sections in the Quick Editing Guide on p. A-39. Turn also to the Quick Format Guide beginning on p. A-1.

- ☐ Is it clear what each modifier in a sentence modifies? Have you created any dangling or misplaced modifiers? B1
- ☐ Have you used parallel structure wherever needed, especially in lists or comparisons? B2

## Additional Writing Assignments

1. To develop your powers of observation, go for a walk through either an unfamiliar scene or a familiar scene worth a closer look (such as a supermarket, a city street, an open field). Avoid a subject so familiar that you would struggle to take a fresh look (such as a dormitory corridor or a parking lot). Record your observations in two or three detailed paragraphs. Sum up your impression of the place, including any opinion you form through close observation.
2. The perspective of a tourist, an outsider alert to details, often reveals the distinctive character of places and people. Think of a place you've recently visited as an outsider, and jot down details you recall. Or spend a few minutes as a tourist right now. Go to a busy spot on or off campus, and record what you find amusing, surprising, puzzling, or intriguing. Then write an essay on the unique character of the place.
3. Select an observation site that relates to your current or possible career plans. For example, you might choose a medical facility (for nursing or medical school), a school or playground (for education), or an office complex or work site (for business). Observe carefully at this location, noting details that contribute to your main impression of the place and your insight about the site or the work done there. Write an essay to convey these points to an audience interested in the same career path.
4. Observe the details of a specific place on campus as if you were seeing it for the first time. Write about your main impression and insight about it in an essay for campus readers, a letter to a prospective student (who will want to know the relevance of the place), or an entry on your travel blog for foreign tourists (who will want to know why they should stop at this spot). If you wish, include your own photograph of the scene or a standard campus shot; add a caption that expresses its essence.
5. **Source Assignment.** Locate a community tourist guide, a town history or architectural survey, a campus guidebook, or a similar resource; select one of its attractions or locations to visit. Put aside the guide while you inde-

pendently observe and record details about the location. Then present your main impression of the character or significance of the place, supplementing your detailed observations with historical, technical, or other information from your source. Clearly and accurately credit your source so that a reader can easily tell what you observed, what you learned, and where you learned it.

6. **Visual Assignment.** Use one of the photographs below and on page 96 to explore the importance of the observer's point of view. After a preliminary look at the scene, select your vantage point as an observer, and identify the audience your essay will address (for example, readers who would or would not share your perspective). Observe the image carefully, and use its details to support your main impression of the scene from your perspective. Direct your specific insight about it to your audience.

For advice on analyzing an image, refer to Ch. 14, "Responding to Visual Representations."

# Interviewing a Subject 6

## Responding to an Image

Suppose that you had an opportunity to interview one of the people shown here. Business leader Indra Nooyi (top left) is CEO of PepsiCo, the international beverage and food company. Stephen Colbert (top right) entertains as a comedian, satirist, and television host. Harvard Law School graduate Lobsang Sangay (bottom right) is the leader-in-exile of Tibet, elected in 2011 but not recognized by China, which rules Tibet. Author Toni Morrison (bottom left) is the recipient of a Pulitzer Prize, Nobel Prize, and Presidential Medal of Freedom. What questions would you most like to ask the interviewee? Based on the person's public image and personality as revealed in these photos, what kind of response would you expect to receive? How do you think the photographer has tried to suggest something about the person?

Don't know what to write about? Go talk with someone. Meet for half an hour with an anthropology professor, and you probably will have plenty of material for a paper. Just as likely, you can get a paper's worth of information from a ten-minute exchange with a mechanic who relines brakes. Both the mechanic and the professor are experts. But even people who aren't usually considered experts may provide you with material.

As this chapter suggests, you can direct a conversation by asking questions to elicit what you want to find out. You do so in an *interview*—a conversation with a purpose—usually to help you understand the other person or to find out what that person knows. You may use what you learn to profile the individual interviewed. However, interviews also provide expert information about a topic, intriguing firsthand accounts of an event or an era, or systematic research samples of selected or representative people.

## Why Interviewing a Subject Matters

### In a College Course

- You interview people for your American Studies course, talking in person, by telephone, or online. You seek firsthand knowledge about a moment in history that engages you from a veteran, a civil rights activist, a disaster survivor, or a person who experienced a local event.
- You interview a person who mentors students or sponsors internships to gain career advice (perhaps from an early childhood educator, public safety officer, health care provider, artist, catering manager).

### In the Workplace

- You interview an "informed source" for a news site, a benefits specialist for a profile in your company newsletter, or your customers or clients for feedback on company products and services.

### In Your Community

- You contact experts to learn about composting food waste through the new city program or about installing a ramp to make your home accessible for your child who uses a wheelchair.

? Who would you like to interview as an intriguing personality? Who would you like to interview for answers or advice about some of your questions? In what situations might you conduct interviews in the future?

# Learning from Other Writers

Here are two essays whose writers talked to someone and reported the conversations, using direct quotations and telling details to reveal engaging personalities. To help you begin to analyze the first reading, look at the notes in the margin. They identify features such as the main idea, or thesis, and the quotations providing support.

### As You Read These Interview Essays

As you read these essays, ask yourself the following questions:

1. Was the conversation reported from an informal talk or planned as an interview? Does the writer report the conversation directly or indirectly?
2. What does the interview show about the character and personality of the speaker? What does it show about the author who is listening?
3. Why do you think the writer draws on conversation?

## Farhad Manjoo

### You Will Want Google Goggles

Farhad Manjoo, the author of *True Enough: Learning to Live in a Post-Fact Society* (2008), is a technology contributor to National Public Radio, the *New York Times*, and *Slate*. The following selections from his July/August 2012 *Technology Review* article capture his interview of Thad Starner, a Google project manager and technology designer.

At first glance, Thad Starner does not look out of place at Google. A pio- 1
neering researcher in the field of wearable computing, Starner is a big, charming man with unruly° hair. But everyone who meets him does a double take, because mounted over the left lens of his eyeglasses is a small rectangle. It looks like a car's side-view mirror made for a human face. The device is actually a minuscule° computer monitor aimed at Starner's eye; he sees its display—pictures, e-mails, anything—superimposed° on top of the world, Terminator-style.

Opening description bringing subject to life

Starner's heads-up display is his own system, not a prototype° of Project 2
Glass, Google's recently announced effort to build augmented-reality° goggles. . . . Google says the project is still in its early phases; Google employees have been testing the technology in public, but the company has declined to show prototypes to most journalists, including myself. Instead, Google let me speak to Starner, a technical lead for the project, who is one of the world's

Background

**unruly:** Hard to manage or control. **minuscule:** Very small. **superimposed:** Positioned or placed over. **prototype:** The first or standard type. **augmented reality:** Increased or intensified experience.

Elaboration of dominant impression

Challenge of interview

leading experts on what it's like to live a cyborg's life.° He has been wearing various kinds of augmented-reality goggles full time since the early 1990s, which once meant he walked around with video displays that obscured much of his face and required seven pounds of batteries. Even in computer science circles, then, Starner has long been an oddity. I went to Google headquarters not only to find out how he gets by in the world but also to challenge him. Project Glass—and the whole idea of machines that directly augment your senses—seemed to me to be a nerd's fantasy, not a potential mainstream technology.

3 But as soon as Starner walked into the colorful Google conference room where we met, I began to question my skepticism.° I'd come to the meeting laden with gadgets—I'd compiled my questions on an iPad, I was recording audio using a digital smart pen, and in my pocket my phone buzzed with updates. As we chatted, my attention wandered from device to device in the distracted dance of a tech-addled° madman.

Details and quotation respond to challenge

4 Starner, meanwhile, was the picture of concentration. His tiny display is connected to a computer he carries in a messenger bag, a machine he controls with a small, one-handed keyboard that he's always gripping in his left hand. He owns an Android phone, too, but he says he never uses it other than for calls (though it would be possible to route calls through his eyeglass system). The spectacles take the place of his desktop computer, his mobile computer, and his all-knowing digital assistant. For all its utility, though, Starner's machine is less distracting than any other computer I've ever seen. This was a revelation. Here was a guy *wearing a computer*, but because he could use it without becoming lost in it—as we all do when we consult our many devices—he appeared less in thrall° to the digital world than you and I are every day. "One of the key points here," Starner says, "is that we're trying to

**cyborg's life:** The life of an engineered or electronic human. **skepticism:** Doubt or uncertainty. **tech-addled:** Confused or mixed up by technology. **in thrall:** Bound in service or slavery.

make mobile systems that help the user pay *more* attention to the real world as opposed to retreating from it."

5 By the end of my meeting with Starner, I decided that if Google manages to pull off anything like the machine he uses, wearable computers seem certain to conquer the world. It simply will be better to have a machine that's hooked onto your body than one that responds to it relatively slowly and clumsily. . . .

THESIS

6 This wasn't possible 20 years ago, when the technology behind Starner's cyborg life was ridiculously awkward. But Starner points out that since he first began wearing his goggles, wearable computing has followed the same path as all digital technology—devices keep getting smaller and better, and as they do, they become ever more difficult to resist. "Back in 1993, the question I would always get was, 'Why would I want a mobile computer?'" he says. "Then the Newton came out and people were still like, 'Why do I want a mobile computer?' But then the Palm Pilot came out, and then when MP3 players and smart phones came out, people started saying, 'Hey, there's something really useful here.'" Today, Starner's device is as small as a Bluetooth headset, and as researchers figure out ways to miniaturize displays—or even embed them into glasses and contact lenses—they'll get still less obtrusive. . . .

Quotations showing subject's personality

7 You could argue that the glasses would open up all kinds of problems: would people be concerned that you were constantly recording them? And what about the potential for deeper distraction—goofing off by watching YouTube during a meeting, say? But Starner counters that most of these problems exist today. Your cell phone can record video and audio of everything around you, and your iPad is an ever-present invitation to goof off. Starner says we'll create social and design norms for digital goggles the way we have with all new technologies. For instance, you'll probably need to do something obvious—like put your hand to your frames—to take a photo, and perhaps a light will come on to signal that you're recording or that you're watching a video. It seems likely that once we get over the initial shock, goggles could go far in mitigating° many of the social annoyances that other gadgets have caused.

8 I know this because during my hour-long conversation with Starner, he was constantly pulling up notes and conducting Web searches on his glasses, but I didn't notice anything amiss. To an outside observer, he would have seemed far less distracted than I was. "One of the coolest things is that this makes me more socially graceful," he says.

9 I got to see this firsthand when Starner let me try on his glasses. It took my eye a few seconds to adjust to the display, but after that, things began to look clearer. I could see the room around me, except now, hovering off to the side, was a computer screen. Suddenly I noticed something on the screen: Starner had left some notes that a Google public-relations rep had sent him. The notes were about me and what Starner should and should

**mitigating:** Relieving or reducing.

not say during the interview, including "Try to steer the conversation away from the specifics of Project Glass." In other words, Starner was being coached, invisibly, right there in his glasses. And you know what? He'd totally won me over.

Resolution of the challenge of the interview

## Questions to Start You Thinking

Meaning

1. In what ways is Starner "one of the world's leading experts on what it's like to live a cyborg's life" (paragraph 2)?
2. What issue motivates Manjoo to challenge Starner (and Google's Project Glass)?
3. What does Manjoo conclude about the possible future of wearable computer goggles?

Writing Strategies

4. What different kinds of evidence does Manjoo use to show readers the advantages of wearable computers?
5. How does Manjoo seem to feel about his dominant impression of Starner? What observations and details does he include to affect your impression of him?
6. How does Manjoo combine physical description and direct quotation of Starner? Would the essay be as effective if he focused more on one or the other? Why or why not?

**Lorena A. Ryan-Hines** **Student Essay**

## Looking Backwards, Moving Forward

Lorena Ryan-Hines, a student in a nursing program, wrote this essay after interviewing an experienced professional in her field.

Someone once said, "You cannot truly know where you are going unless you know where you have come from." I don't think I understood this statement until I got the opportunity to sit down with Joan Gilmore, assistant director of nursing at Smithville Health Care Center. With the blur of everyday activities going on during the change of third shift to first shift at the nursing home, I had never recognized what value Joan could bring to the younger nurses. Once we started to talk, I began to realize that, although I am a nurse, I don't know much about how nursing has evolved over the years. During our conversation, I discovered how much history, wisdom, and advice Joan has to share. 1

Joan tries to stay as active as she can working on the floor so she does not use an office. We decided just to sit down in one of the multi-purpose conference rooms. Joan looks very good for a woman of her age. In fact, no one would ever suspect by looking at her that she is a young sixty-four years old. She is approximately 5′2″ tall and dressed in white scrub pants with a flowered scrub top. Although her hair is dyed, the color is a nice natural tone for her. She is not flashy or outspoken, but she knows what she is doing. However, if she has a question, she does not have a problem asking someone else. 2

? Can you identify with Ryan-Hines's work environment and relationship with Joan? In what ways?

When we first sat down, we started talking about how she grew up. She was the third child of seven children. Her father worked in a factory and also farmed over one hundred acres. Her mom stayed home to take care of the children. As I watched her talk about her upbringing, a glaze seemed to roll across her face. I could see a slight twinkle in her eyes. She almost appeared to be back in that time and space of childhood. She went on to explain to me that she decided to go to nursing school because it was one of the few jobs, forty-five years ago, that could be productive for a woman. 3

She decided to enter the three-year program at St. Elizabeth Hospital's School for Nursing in Dayton, Ohio. Students were not allowed to be married and had to live in the nursing school's brick dormitory. Whenever they were in class and on the floors of the hospital, they were required to wear their uniforms, light blue dresses with white pin stripes. The student nursing cap, the "dignity cap" as Joan called it, was all white. When students graduated, they earned their black stripe which distinguished them as registered nurses. Joan said that she did not think we should continue to wear the all-white uniforms or nursing caps. However, she conveyed a sense of sadness when she said, "I think we have gone too far to the left these days because everyone dresses and looks the same. I think as a nurse you have worked hard and earned the right to stand out somehow." 4

? Why do you think that the "dignity cap" was so important for Joan?

I asked Joan about the pros and cons of being a registered nurse and whether she ever regretted her decision. Her philosophy is that being a nurse is a calling. Although nursing pay is generally considered a decent living wage, sometimes dealing with management, long hours, and the grief of tough cases is hard. Through experience and commitment, a nurse learns to take each day as it comes and grow with it. Even though life-and-death situations can be very stressful and the fast-paced nursing world can be draining, nurses can never forget that patients are people. For Joan, when patients are demanding and short fused, they are not really angry at the nurses but at the situation they are in. She believes that a nurse is always able to help her patients in some way, be it physical or emotional. 5

The advice Joan gave me about becoming a new registered nurse may be some of the best advice of my life. Each registered nurse specialty has its demands. She recommended working for a while in a medical surgery area. This area is a great place to gain knowledge and experience about multiple acute illnesses and disease 6 processes. From there, nurses can move forward and find the specialty areas that best suit them. This fit is important because nurses need to be knowledgeable and confident, leaders who are not afraid to ask questions when they do not know the answers. To gain the respect of others, nurses also must be willing to help and to let others help them because no one can be a nurse all alone. Joan recommended being courteous, saying "please" and "thank you" when asking someone to do something as well as encouraging others with different talents. Lastly, she urged me always to do my best and be proud of my accomplishments.

Have you ever received valuable advice from someone like Joan? How has that advice affected you and your decisions?

Afterwards, I thanked her for the advice and her time. She got up smiling and simply walked out of the room and back to the job she has loved for so many years. I found myself sitting back down for a few minutes to reflect on everything she had just told me. Nursing from yesterday to today has changed not only with the technological advances but even the simplest things. Uniforms are nothing like they were forty years ago. The rules back then could never be enforced today. Some things will never change though, like the simple respect a nurse gives another human being. The profound advice Joan gave me is something I will carry with me for the rest of my personal and professional career. 7

Works Cited

Gilmore, Joan. Personal interview. 4 June 2009.

## Questions to Start You Thinking

### Meaning

1. What is the main point of Ryan-Hines's essay?
2. What kind of person is Joan Gilmore? How does Ryan-Hines feel about her?
3. How is Gilmore's history the history of nursing during the last few decades? Is an interview an effective method of relating the history of a profession? Why or why not?

### Writing Strategies

4. Why does Ryan-Hines begin her essay with a quotation and an impression of the nursing home? How does this opening serve as a frame for her conversation with Joan?
5. What details does Ryan-Hines use to describe Joan? What senses does she draw on? Does she provide enough detail for you to form a clear image of Joan?
6. How much of the interview does Ryan-Hines quote directly? Why does she choose to quote directly rather than paraphrase in these places? Would her essay be stronger if she used more of Joan's own words?
7. Using highlighters or marginal notes, identify the essay's introduction, thesis, major emphases, supporting details for each emphasis, and conclusion. How effective is the organization of this essay?

**Tiana Chavez** — **Video**

## ASU Athletes Discuss Superstitions

Tiana Chavez interviews athletes from Arizona State University about what pregame superstitions they engage in. To watch the video, go to Chapter 6: **bedfordstmartins.com/bedguide**.

ASU tennis player Jacqueline Cako switches visors when losing.

# Learning by Writing

## The Assignment: Interviewing

Write a paper about someone who interests you and base the paper primarily on a conversation with that person. Select any acquaintance, relative, or person you have heard about whose traits, interests, activities, background, or outlook on life might intrigue your readers. Your purpose is to show this person's character and personality – to bring your subject to life for your readers – through his or her conversation.

For an interactive Learning by Doing activity on Analyzing Surprising Interviews, go to Ch. 6: **bedfordstmartins .com/bedguide**.

These students found notable people to interview:

One student wrote about a high school science teacher who had left teaching for a higher-paying job in the computer industry, only to return three years later to the classroom.

One writer recorded the thoughts and feelings of a discouraged farmer she had known since childhood.

Another learned about adjustment to life in a new country by talking to his neighbor from Somalia.

To interview someone for information about something, see Additional Writing Assignments on pp. 113–14.

## Facing the Challenge Writing from an Interview

The major challenge writers face when writing from an interview is to find a clear focus. They must first sift through the huge amount of information generated in an interview and then decide what dominant impression of the subject to present in an essay. Distilling the material you have gathered into a focused, overall impression may seem overwhelming. As a writer, however, you have the responsibility to select and organize your material for your readers, not simply transcribe your notes.

To identify possible angles, jot down answers to these questions:

- What did you find most interesting about the interview?
- What topics did your subject talk about the most?
- What did he or she become most excited or animated about?
- What topics generated the most interesting quotations?

Your answers should help you to determine a dominant impression—the aspect of your interviewee's character or personality that you want to emphasize for your readers. Once you have this focus, you can pick the details from the interview that best illustrate the points you want to make. Make sure that all quotations—long or short—are accurate. Use them strategically and sparingly to reveal the character traits that you wish to emphasize. Select colorful quotations that allow readers to "hear" your subject's distinctive voice. To capture the dynamic of conversation, include your own observations as well as actual quotations.

## Generating Ideas

For more on each strategy for generating ideas in this section or for additional strategies, see Ch. 19.

If an image of the perfect subject has flashed into your mind, consider yourself lucky, and set up an appointment with that person at once. If you have drawn a blank, you'll need to cast about for a likely interview subject.

**Brainstorm for Possible Subjects.** Try brainstorming for a few minutes to see what pops into your mind. Your subject need not be spectacular or unusual; ordinary lives can make fascinating reading.

### DISCOVERY CHECKLIST

- ☐ Are you acquainted with anyone whose life has been unusually eventful, stressful, or successful?
- ☐ Are you curious about why someone you know made a certain decision or how that person got to his or her current point in life?

- ☐ Is there an expert or a leader whom you admire or are puzzled by?
- ☐ Do you know someone whose job or hobby interests you?
- ☐ What older person could tell you about life thirty or even fifty years ago?
- ☐ Who has passionate convictions about society, politics, sex, or childrearing?
- ☐ Whose background and life history would you like to know more about?
- ☐ Whose lifestyle, values, or attitudes are utterly different from your own and from those of most people you know?

**Tap Local Interview Resources.** Investigate campus resources such as departmental or faculty Web pages, student activity officers and sponsors, recent yearbook photographs, stories from the newspaper archives, or facilities such as the theater, media, or sports centers. Look on campus, at work, or in your community for people with intriguing backgrounds or experiences. Campuses and libraries often maintain databases of local authorities, researchers, and authors available for press contacts or expert advice. Identify several prospects in case your first choice isn't available.

Former President Richard Nixon, right, is interviewed by David Frost, May 5, 1977. Their exchanges later inspired an award-winning play and the movie *Frost/Nixon*.

**Set Up an Interview.** Find out whether your prospect will grant an interview, talk at length—an hour, say—and agree to appear in your paper. If you sense reluctance, find another subject.

Don't be timid about asking for an interview. After all, your request is flattering, acknowledging that person as someone with valuable things to say. Try to schedule the interview on your subject's own ground—his or her home or workplace. The details you observe in those surroundings can make your essay more vivid.

**Prepare Questions.** The interview will go better if you are an informed interviewer with prepared questions. Find out a bit about your subject's life history, experience, affiliations, and interests, and then work on your questions.

Ask about the person's background, everyday tasks, favorite activities, and hopes to encourage your subject to open up. Asking for a little imagining may elicit a revealing response. (If your house were on fire, what would you try to save? If you had your life to live over, what would you do differently?) Focus on whatever aspects best reveal your subject's personality. Good questions will help you lead the conversation where you want it to go, get it back on track when it strays, and avoid awkward silences. For example, to interview someone with an unusual job or hobby, try questions like these:

- How long have you been a park ranger?
- How did you get involved in this work?
- How have you learned about the physical features and ecological balance in your park?
- What happens in a typical day? What do you like most or least?
- How has this job changed your life or your concerns?
- What are your plans and hopes for the future?

One good question can get some people talking for hours, and four or five may be enough for any interview, but it's better to prepare too many than too few. You can easily skip any that seem irrelevant during the interview. Simply listening and responding may encourage genuine communication.

## Learning by Doing — Analyzing Interview Questions

Listen to several radio interviews on a local station or National Public Radio (which archives many types of interviews, including programs such as *Fresh Air*). As you listen, jot down the names of the interviewer and interviewee, the topic, and any particularly fruitful or useless questions. Working with others in person or online, discuss your conclusions about the success of the interviews you heard. Develop a collaborative set of guidelines for preparing good questions and dodging bad ones.

**Be Flexible and Observant.** Sometimes a question won't interest your subject. Or the person may seem reluctant to answer, especially if you're unwittingly trespassing into private territory, such as someone's love life. Don't badger. If you wait silently for a bit, you might be rewarded. If not, just go on to the next question. Should the conversation drift, steer it back: "But to get back to what you were saying about . . ."

For more on using observation, see Ch. 5.

Sometimes the most rewarding question simply grows out of what the subject says or an item you note in the environment. Observing your subject's clothing, expressions, mannerisms, or equipment may also suggest unexpected facets of personality. For example, Ryan-Hines describes Joan Gilmore's appearance as she introduces her character.

### Peer Response — Preparing Questions for an Interview

Ask a classmate to read the questions you plan to use in your interview. Then interview your classmate, asking the following:

- Are the questions appropriate for the person who will be interviewed?
- Will the questions help gather the information I am seeking?
- Are any of the questions unclear? How could I rephrase them?
- Do any of the questions seem redundant? Irrelevant?
- What additional questions would you suggest that I ask?

**Decide How to Record the Interview.** Many interviewers use only paper and pen to take notes unobtrusively. Even though they can't write down everything the person says, they want to look the subject in the eye and keep the conversation lively. As you take notes, be sure to record or sketch details on the scene—names and dates, numbers, addresses, surroundings, physical appearance. Also jot down memorable words exactly as the speaker says them, and put quotation marks around them. When you transcribe your notes, you will know that they are quoted directly.

A telephone or an e-mail interview sounds easy but lacks the interplay you can achieve face-to-face. You'll miss observing possessions that reveal personality or seeing smiles, frowns, or other body language. Meet in person if possible, or set up an online video chat.

Many professionals advise against using a recorder because it may inhibit the subject and make the interviewer lazy about concentrating on the subject's responses. Too often, the objections go, it tempts the interviewer simply to quote rambling conversation without shaping it into good writing. If you do bring a recorder to your interview, be sure that the person you're talking with has no objections. Arm yourself with paper and pen in case the recorder malfunctions. Perhaps the best practice is to combine both methods. Write down the main points, and use your recording to check quotations for accuracy or add more words from the interview.

As soon as the interview ends, rush to the nearest desk, and write down everything you recall but couldn't record. The questions you prepared for the interview will guide your memory, as will notes you took while talking.

### Learning by Doing — Transcribing Your Interview Notes

After your interview, follow the lead of reporters and other interviewers who routinely store digital conversations. If you recorded the interview, type out the exact conversation. If you took notes, type as much of the interview as possible from them. If you have both, combine them in one file, but use bold for your notes so you don't confuse them with direct quotations from the recording. If you use voice recognition software such as Dragon Naturally Speaking, you may save typing time by reading aloud your notes and by restating each of your subject's recorded comments if the software does not recognize the second voice. Save the record of your original research—the complete, unedited transcript and your notes—with a descriptive name. Begin your draft in a new file so that you do not change or lose any of your interview record. Check your record for accuracy when you summarize; copy and paste from it when you quote, adding quotation marks to show exact words from the interview.

## Planning, Drafting, and Developing

For more strategies for planning, drafting, and developing, see Chs. 20, 21, and 22.

After your interview, you may have a good notion of what to include in your first draft, what to emphasize, what to quote directly, what to summarize. But if your notes seem a confused jumble, what should you do?

**Evaluate Your Material.** Remember your purpose: to reveal your subject's character and personality through conversation. Start by listing details you're likely to include. Photographs, sketches, or your doodles also may help you find a focus. As you sift your material, try these questions:

What part of the conversation gave you the most insight into your subject's character and circumstances?

Which direct quotations reveal the most about your subject? Which are the most amusing, pithy, witty, surprising, or outrageous?

Which objects in the subject's environment provide you with valuable clues about his or her interests?

What, if anything, did your subject's body language reveal? Did it suggest discomfort, pride, self-confidence, shyness, pomposity?

What did tone or gestures tell you about the person's state of mind?

How can you summarize your subject's character or personality?

Does one theme run through your material? If so, what is it?

For more on stating a thesis, see pp. 399–408.

**Focus Your Thesis on a Dominant Impression.** Most successful portraits focus on a single dominant impression of the interview subject.

For exercises on choosing effective thesis statements, visit **bedfordstmartins .com/bedguide**.

| | |
|---|---|
| DOMINANT IMPRESSION | Del talked a lot about freedom of the press. |
| WORKING THESIS | Del Sampat is a true believer in freedom of the press. |

If you have lots of material and if, as often happens, your conversation rambled, you may want to develop the dominant impression by emphasizing just a few things about your subject – personality traits, views on particular topics, or shaping influences. To find such a focus, try grouping your details in three layers of notes, following the pattern below:

1. Dominant Impression ☐
2. Main Emphases ☐ ☐
   points about traits, views, influences
3. Supporting Details ☐ ☐ ☐ ☐ ☐
   quotations, reported words, description

## Learning by Doing Stating a Dominant Impression

How would you characterize in one sentence the person you interviewed? What single main impression do you want to convey? Specify your ideas by completing this sentence: My dominant impression of ____________ is ____________. Share your sentence with a classmate or small group, either in person or online. Respond to each other's sentences to help each writer achieve a sentence that is both thoughtful and clear.

**Bring Your Subject to Life.** To begin your paper, can you immediately frame the person you interviewed? A quotation, a physical description, a portrait of your subject at home or at work can bring the person instantly to life in your reader's mind. If your instructor approves adding an image, place it so that it supplements but does not overshadow your essay.

For more on selecting and presenting quotations, see D3 (p. A-29) and D6 (p. A-31) in the Quick Research Guide. For more on using visuals, see pp. 367–68.

When you quote directly, be as accurate as possible, and don't put into quotation marks anything your subject didn't say. Sometimes you may quote a whole sentence or more, sometimes just a phrase. Keep evaluating your quotations until they convey the essence of your subject.

**Double-Check Important Information.** Maybe you can't read your hasty handwriting or some crucial information escaped your notes. In such a case, telephone or e-mail the person you interviewed to ask specific questions without taking much time. You might also read back any direct quotations you plan to use so your subject can confirm their accuracy.

## Revising and Editing

For more revising and editing strategies, see Ch. 23.

As you read over your first draft, keep in mind that your purpose was to make the person you interviewed come alive for your reader.

## Peer Response: Interviewing a Subject

For general questions for a peer editor, see p. 463.

Have a classmate or friend read your draft and suggest how to make the portrait more vivid, complete, and clear. Ask your peer editor to answer questions such as these about writing from an interview:

- Does the opening make you want to know the person portrayed? If so, how has the writer interested you? If not, what gets in your way?
- What makes the interviewee interesting to the writer?
- What is the writer's dominant impression of the person interviewed?
- Does the writer include any quotations or details that contradict or are unrelated to the dominant impression or insight?
- Do the quoted words or reported speech "sound" real to you? Would you drop any conversation the writer used? If so, mark it.
- Do you have questions about the subject that aren't answered?
- If this paper were yours, what is the one thing you would be sure to work on before handing it in?

**Focus on Your Main Idea or Thesis.** Once you have finished a draft, you may still feel swamped by too much information. Will readers find your essay overloaded? Will they understand the dominant impression you want to convey? To be certain that they will, first polish and refine your thesis.

| | |
|---|---|
| WORKING THESIS | Del Sampat is a true believer in freedom of the press. |
| REVISED THESIS | Del Sampat, news editor for the *Campus Times,* sees every story he writes as an opportunity to exercise and defend the freedom of the press. |

For exercises on supporting a thesis, visit **bedfordstmartins.com/bedguide**.

## Learning by Doing: Screening Your Details

Using your revised thesis as a guide, look again at the quotations and other details in your draft. Keep only those that support your thesis and enhance the dominant impression. Drop the others, even if they are vivid or catchy. Then select a passage from your draft—perhaps one that still seems slightly off track—and ask for a classmate's opinion as you decide whether all the details in the passage strengthen the dominant impression expressed in your thesis.

### REVISION CHECKLIST

- ☐ Are the details focused on a dominant impression you want to emphasize? Are all of them relevant? How do you convey the impression to readers?

- ☐ How do the parts of the conversation you've reported reveal the subject's unique personality, character, mood, or concerns?
- ☐ Does your paper need a stronger beginning? Is your ending satisfactory?
- ☐ Should some quotations be summarized or indirectly quoted? Should some explanation be enlivened by adding specific quotations?
- ☐ When the direct quotations are read out loud, do they sound as if they're from the mouth of the person you're portraying?
- ☐ Where might you need to add revealing details about the person's surroundings, personal appearance, or mannerisms?
- ☐ Have you included your own pertinent observations and insights?
- ☐ Does any of your material strike you now as irrelevant or dull?

For more editing and proofreading strategies, see pp. 471–75.

After you have revised your essay, edit and proofread it. Carefully check the grammar, word choice, punctuation, and mechanics—and then correct any problems you find.

For more help, find the relevant checklist sections in the Quick Editing Guide on p. A-39. Turn also to the Quick Format Guide beginning on p. A-1.

**EDITING CHECKLIST**

- ☐ Is it clear what each *he*, *she*, *they*, or other pronoun refers to? Does each pronoun agree with (match) its antecedent? A6
- ☐ Have you used the correct case (*he* or *him*) for all your pronouns? A5
- ☐ Is your sentence structure correct? Have you avoided writing fragments, comma splices, or fused sentences? A1, A2
- ☐ Have you used quotation marks, ellipses (to show the omission of words), and other punctuation correctly in all quotations? C3

## Additional Writing Assignments

1. Interview someone from whom you can learn, possibly someone whose profession interests you or whose advice can help you solve a problem or make a decision. Your purpose will be to communicate what you have learned, not to characterize the person you interview.
2. Write a paper based on an interview with at least two members of your extended family about some incident that is part of your family lore. Direct your paper to younger relatives. If accounts of the event don't always agree,

combine them into one vivid account, noting that some details may be more trustworthy than others. Give credit to your sources.

3. Briefly talk with fifteen or twenty students on your campus to find out their career goals and their reasons for their choices. Are they feeling uncertain about a career, pursuing the one they have always wanted, or changing careers for better employment options? Are most looking for security, income, or personal satisfaction? Write a short essay summing up what you find out. Provide some quotations to flesh out your survey and perhaps characterize your classmates. Are they materialists? Idealists? Practical people? (Ask your instructor if any campus permission is needed before you begin these interviews.)
4. With the approval of your instructor, plan an individual or collaborative interview project with a possible public outcome—an article for the campus newspaper or alumni magazine, a page for the course Web site, a podcast for the campus radio station, a multimodal presentation for future students (combining written text with audio clips or photographs), or some other option that you or your group have the expertise to prepare. Analyze the purpose of the proposed outlet; select a campus interviewee whose knowledge or experience might assist or intrigue its audience. Develop your questions, conduct your interview, and present it.
5. **Source Assignment.** With your whole class or a small group, collaborate to interview someone from campus or the local community with special knowledge about a matter that concerns the group. Prepare by turning to background sources: your interviewee's Web page or résumé, any campus or local news coverage, public-meeting or presentation records, or relevant statistics. Plan the interview by working together on these questions:

   > What do you want to find out? What lines of questioning will you pursue? What topic will each student ask about? How much time will each have to ask a series of questions? Who will record the interview (if your subject agrees)? Who will take notes (as your record or backup)?

   Preview each other's questions to avoid duplication. Ask open-ended, not yes/no, questions to encourage discussion. Your group's product can be many individual papers or one collaborative effort (such as a paper, an online threaded discussion, or a blog), as your instructor directs. Be sure to credit all of your sources.
6. **Visual Assignment.** Select a photograph of a person from this chapter (pp. 107 or 115) or elsewhere in the book or its e-Pages. Use that image to explore the experience of an interview from the standpoint of what is communicated through expression, body language, clothing, environment, and other nonverbal cues. Use your analysis of the image to support your thesis about the interview relationship it portrays.

For advice on analyzing an image, refer to Ch. 14, "Responding to Visual Representations."

Disaster Assistance
1-800-462-9029
FEMA

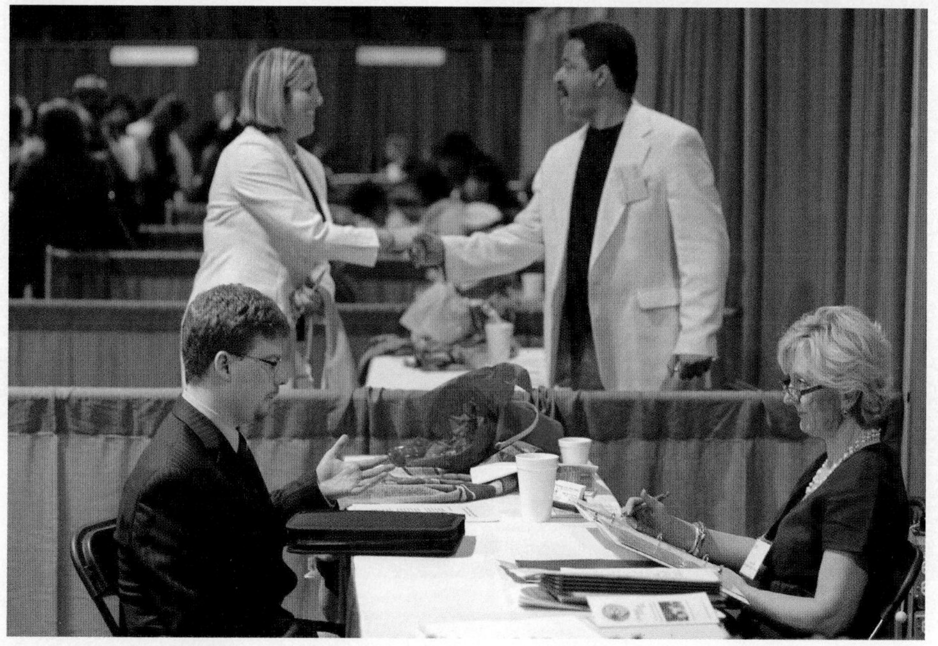

# 7 Comparing and Contrasting

## Responding to an Image

The large photograph of the young couple was taken at Woodstock in August 1969 and then featured on the cover for the album and the poster for the movie that recorded the event. The smaller insert, taken before the event's fortieth anniversary, shows the same couple, Nick and Bobbi Ercoline, now married for decades. Examine the two photographs carefully, noting similarities and differences. What does each image convey about its era? What does each convey about the couple, whether age twenty or sixty? What qualities made the original image iconic? What similar or different qualities are captured in the more recent image?

Which city—Dallas or Atlanta—has more advantages or drawbacks for a young single person thinking of settling down to a career? Which of two ads for the same toy appeals more effectively to parents who want to get durability as well as educational value for their money? As singers and songwriters, how are Beyoncé Knowles and Taylor Swift similar and dissimilar? Such questions invite answers that set two subjects side by side.

When you compare, you point out similarities; when you contrast, you discuss differences. When you write about two complicated subjects, usually you need to do both. Considering Mozart and Bach, you might find that each has traits the other has—or lacks. Instead of concluding that one is great and the other inferior, you might conclude that they're two distinct composers, each with an individual style. On the other hand, if your main purpose is to judge between two subjects (such as moving either to Dallas or to Atlanta), you would look especially for positive and negative features, weigh the attractions and faults of each city, and then stick your neck out and make your choice.

## Why Comparing and Contrasting Matter

### In a College Course

- You compare and contrast to "evaluate" the relative merits of Norman Rockwell and N. C. Wyeth in an art history course or the relative accuracy of two Civil War Web sites for a history course.
- You compare and contrast to "describe" a little-known subject, such as medieval funeral customs, by setting it next to a similar yet familiar subject, such as modern funeral traditions.

### In the Workplace

- You compare and contrast your company's products or services with those of competitors, just as your experience, education, and personal attributes were compared and contrasted with those of others before you were hired.

### In Your Community

- You compare and contrast your options in choosing a financial aid package, cell phone contract, childcare provider, bike helmet, or new mayor.

? What are some instances when you compare or contrast products, services, opportunities, options, solutions, or other things? When might you use comparison, contrast, or both in your writing? What would you expect them to contribute?

# Learning from Other Writers

In this chapter you will be asked to write a paper setting two subjects side by side, comparing and contrasting them. Let's see how two other writers have used these familiar habits of thought in writing. To help you begin to analyze the first reading, look at the notes in the margin. They identify features such as the thesis, or main idea, the sequence of the broad subjects considered, and the specific points of comparison and contrast.

## As You Read These Comparisons and Contrasts

As you read these essays, ask yourself the following questions:

1. What two (or more) items are compared and contrasted? Does the writer use comparison only? Contrast only? A combination of the two? Why?
2. What is the purpose of the comparison and contrast? What idea does the information support or refute?
3. How does the writer organize the essay? Why?

### David Brooks

## The Opportunity Gap

In this column from the *New York Times*, David Brooks takes a look at some of the social and political issues that engage him as a commentator and an author of books such as *The Social Animal* (2011).

Introduction to issue

Over the past few months, writers from Charles Murray° to Timothy Noah° have produced alarming work on the growing bifurcation° of American society. Now the eminent Harvard political scientist Robert Putnam° and his team are coming out with research that's more horrifying. While most studies look at inequality of outcomes among adults and help us understand how America is coming apart, Putnam's group looked at inequality of opportunities among children. They help us understand what the country will look like decades ahead. The quick answer? More divided than ever. 1

**Charles Murray:** Conservative author of *Coming Apart: The State of White America, 1960–2010* (2012). **Timothy Noah:** Liberal author of *The Great Divergence: America's Growing Inequality Crisis and What We Can Do about It* (2012). **bifurcation:** Division into two parts. **Robert Putnam:** Political scientist, author of *Bowling Alone: The Collapse and Revival of American Community* (2000), and authority on class differences and social mobility.

2 Putnam's data verifies what many of us have seen anecdotally, that the children of the more affluent and less affluent are raised in starkly different ways and have different opportunities. Decades ago, college-graduate parents and high-school-graduate parents invested similarly in their children. Recently, more affluent parents have invested much more in their children's futures while less affluent parents have not.

THESIS

Subjects A and B over time

Point 1

3 They've invested more time. Over the past decades, college-educated parents have quadrupled the amount of time they spend reading "Goodnight Moon," talking to their kids about their day and cheering them on from the sidelines. High-school-educated parents have increased child-care time, but only slightly. A generation ago, working-class parents spent slightly more time with their kids than college-educated parents. Now college-educated parents spend an hour more every day. This attention gap is largest in the first three years of life when it is most important.

Alternating Subjects A and B

Point 2

4 Affluent parents also invest more money in their children. Over the last 40 years upper-income parents have increased the amount they spend on their kids' enrichment activities, like tutoring and extracurriculars, by $5,300 a year. The financially stressed lower classes have only been able to increase their investment by $480, adjusted for inflation.

Subject A

Subject B

5 As a result, behavior gaps are opening up. In 1972, kids from the bottom quartile° of earners participated in roughly the same number of activities as kids from the top quartile. Today, it's a chasm.° Richer kids are roughly twice as likely to play after-school sports. They are more than twice as likely to be the captains of their sports teams. They are much more likely to do nonsporting activities, like theater, yearbook and scouting. They are much more likely to attend religious services.

Point 3

6 It's not only that richer kids have become more active. Poorer kids have become more pessimistic and detached. Social trust has fallen among all income groups, but, between 1975 and 1995, it plummeted among the poorest third of young Americans and has remained low ever since. As Putnam writes in notes prepared for the Aspen Ideas Festival: "It's perfectly understandable that kids from working-class backgrounds have become cynical and even paranoid, for virtually all our major social institutions have failed them—family, friends, church, school and community." As a result, poorer kids are less likely to participate in voluntary service work that might give them a sense of purpose and responsibility. Their test scores are lagging. Their opportunities are more limited.

7 A long series of cultural, economic and social trends have merged to create this sad state of affairs. Traditional social norms were abandoned, meaning more children are born out of wedlock. Their single parents simply have less time and resources to prepare them for a more competitive world. Working-class jobs were decimated,° meaning that many parents are too

**quartile:** A one-quarter group (1/4 or 25%) in a statistical study. **chasm:** A deep divide, like a canyon. **decimated:** Dramatically reduced (originally meaning by a tenth).

stressed to have the energy, time or money to devote to their children. Affluent, intelligent people are now more likely to marry other energetic, intelligent people. They raise energetic, intelligent kids in self-segregated, cultural ghettoes where they know little about and have less influence upon people who do not share their blessings. The political system directs more money to health care for the elderly while spending on child welfare slides.

Conclusion

Equal opportunity, once core to the nation's identity, is now a tertiary° concern. If America really wants to change that, if the country wants to take advantage of all its human capital rather than just the most privileged two-thirds of it, then people are going to have to make some pretty uncomfortable decisions. Liberals are going to have to be willing to champion norms that say marriage should come before childrearing and be morally tough about it. Conservatives are going to have to be willing to accept tax increases or benefit cuts so that more can be spent on the earned-income tax credit and other programs that benefit the working class. Political candidates will have to spend less time trying to exploit class divisions and more time trying to remedy them — less time calling their opponents out of touch elitists, and more time coming up with agendas that comprehensively address the problem. It's politically tough to do that, but the alternative is national suicide. 8

## Questions to Start You Thinking

### Meaning

1. Does Brooks favor one group of parents and children over the other? Which details or statements support your response?
2. Based on the details presented here, why do the groups differ? What has changed over time?
3. What is Brooks's purpose in contrasting the two groups? Is his goal to explain or to convince? Or is it something else?

### Writing Strategies

4. In the introduction, Brooks refers to several studies. Is that technique effective? How else might he have begun the essay?
5. Which method of organization does Brooks use to arrange his essay? How effectively does he switch between his two subjects?
6. From reading this essay, what are readers to assume that affluent and less affluent parents and children have in common? Why?

**tertiary:** Third.

**Jacob Griffin** **Student Essay**

## Karate Kid vs. Kung Fu Panda: A Race to the Olympics

Student Jacob Griffin compares and contrasts karate and kung fu, asking which of the two deserves to be the first declared an Olympic sport.

About three decades ago, the first Karate Kid waxed on and off, kicking his way into the American sports scene. During the same era, martial arts movies with stars like Jackie Chan began to popularize kung fu with American audiences. Films such as the *Karate Kid* trilogy were instant classics, while kung fu has appeared in *Kill Bill*, the *Matrix* movies, and even the animated *Kung Fu Panda*. Despite the worldwide popularity of both fighting styles, neither has yet been approved for Olympic competition. The International Olympic Committee should consider which of these styles first deserves to be declared an official Olympic sport. 1

? Why do you think the writer raises this issue here?

Besides their shared status in movies and popular culture, these two fighting styles are similar because each is an umbrella term for several different variations. The World Karate Federation includes four styles on its official list, while hundreds of kung fu categories are based on types of movement, locations of origin, and specific characteristics. Additionally, both fighting styles promote more than just the physical development of those who practice the art. Neither has combat as its only end. Humility, virtue, and courtesy are all important values in the philosophy of karate, just as the kung fu idea of *qi*, or *ch'i*, expresses the life energy inside practitioners. Each emphasizes spiritual growth as well as physical strength and stamina. 2

Although both fighting styles have found success in Western pop culture and have encouraged the inner growth of practitioners, karate is the younger of the two. Karate developed on the island chain between China and Japan, where Okinawa, Japan, is today. Given the regional politics, geography, and trade routes, Chinese martial arts probably traveled to Okinawa in the 14th century and then merged with the local fighting system known as *te*. In contrast, kung fu is a popular term for many Chinese martial arts, including hand-to-hand combat and wrestling that date back to the 5th century BC. But, despite this long history, it wasn't until the founding of the People's Republic of China in 1949 that kung fu became a national activity with training manuals, academies, and exams. Given kung fu's ancient roots, karate could be considered an offshoot of Chinese martial arts. 3

The techniques for each fighting style are also different. Although both use linear and circular movements, karate is usually considered to be more linear than kung fu. This difference means that karate tends to have more straight lines and more direct punches, strikes, and kicks in its sequences. Daniel's crane kick in the first *Karate Kid* film, in which his leg shoots right out in front of him, is the perfect example of karate's directness. This characteristic style might have been developed by the king's bodyguards in Okinawa so that they could take quick control of a contest and fend off 4 multiple attackers. Now the style remains most evident in the short, distinct sets of moves that practitioners must learn and then apply in competition.

What other differences between martial arts come to mind? Which matter most?

In contrast, kung fu is better known for being circular, rather than linear, especially in its hand movements. While just as powerful as karate movements, kung fu's more fluid motions draw their strength from centrifugal° force, as opposed to a direct hit. The movements learned by kung fu practitioners also have more of a flow to them than those in karate, and they tend to be longer, more complicated sets of moves. For these reasons, karate is often considered "hard" and kung fu "soft," although the many kung fu variations have both hard and soft qualities, blurring such distinctions. 5

Finally, karate and kung fu practitioners wear different uniforms and use different weapons. The traditional karate uniform is white with a white kimono top over which a belt is tied. The color of the belt changes with the practitioner's rank, from white, yellow, and orange in the beginning stages, all the way up to purple, 6

**centrifugal:** Moving away from the center.

Karate

Kung fu

brown, and the famous black belt given to instructors. Karate is also practiced barefoot. When weapons are used in karate, they include the bo staff, a long stick up to six feet, and the *nunchaku*, two shorter sticks connected by a chain.

In contrast, kung fu practitioners may wear a greater variety of uniforms. Their outfits can be black or bold colors (like blue, red, or gold) and made of fabrics such as silk or satin. The tops of kung fu uniforms feature Chinese "frog" buttons, unlike karate's overlapping kimono-style jacket. Colored sashes may be worn as belts are in karate, but this practice of showing rank appears mainly in North American kung fu schools. Kung fu practitioners wear shoes and may use hook swords, butterfly swords, or nine section whips as well as many other weapons. 7

Because both karate and kung fu are now well established in Western pop culture, which of the two fighting styles deserves to be the first approved as an Olympic sport? Although karate has a rich heritage in Okinawa and Japan, the origins of kung fu stretch back even further and point to the influence of Chinese martial arts on karate as it developed. Furthermore, many more variations gather under the umbrella of kung fu than of karate. Kung fu's movements are usually more connected and complex than karate's shorter, more distinct sequences. Thus, if karate is actually an off-shoot of Chinese martial arts, perhaps kung fu deserves to claim Olympic status before karate does. And yet karate's simplified approach—forever memorialized by Mr. Miyagi's wax on, wax off teachings—might be more fit for an international stage. 8

? How do you think this question should be decided?

## Questions to Start You Thinking

### Meaning

1. In what specific ways does Griffin claim that karate and kung fu are similar? In what ways are these two different? Do the similarities outweigh the differences, or vice versa?
2. Can you think of other types of similarities and differences that Griffin might have included?
3. Would you nominate another sport for Olympic status? If so, why?

### Writing Strategies

4. Is Griffin's support for his comparison and contrast sufficient and balanced? Explain.
5. What transitional devices does Griffin use to indicate when he is comparing and when he is contrasting?
6. What is Griffin's thesis? Why does Griffin state it where he does?
7. Using highlighters or marginal notes, identify the essay's introduction, thesis, contrasting subjects, points of comparison and contrast, and conclusion. How effective is the organization of this essay?

## e *National Geographic* Editors

Visual Essay

# Hurricane Katrina Pictures: Then & Now, Ruin & Rebirth

National Geographic compiled a series of images showing how New Orleans has recovered since the immediate aftermath of Hurricane Katrina, which hit the area in 2005. To view the photos, go to Chapter 7: **bedfordstmartins .com/bedguide**.

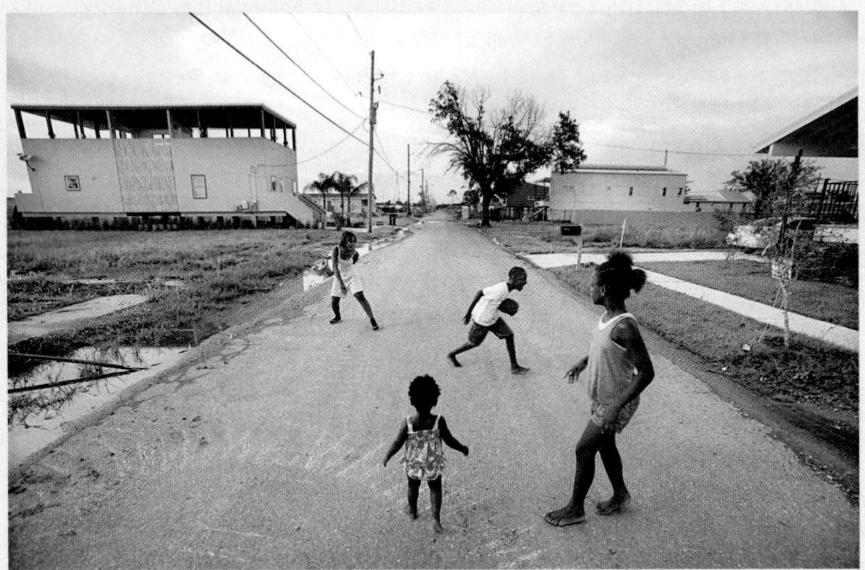

Top, children playing on a street in the Ninth Ward in 2010. Below, Amish student volunteers walking down the same street shortly after Hurricane Katrina.

# Learning by Writing

## The Assignment: Comparing and Contrasting

Write a paper in which you compare and contrast two items to enlighten readers about both subjects. The specific points of similarity and difference will be important, but you will go beyond them to draw a conclusion from your analysis. This conclusion, your thesis, needs to be more than "point A is different from point B" or "I prefer subject B to subject A." You will need to explain why you have drawn your conclusion. You'll also need to provide specific supporting evidence to explain your position and to convince your readers of its soundness. You may choose two people, two kinds of people, two places, two objects, two activities, or two ideas, but be sure to choose two you care about. You might write an impartial paper that distinctly portrays both subjects, or you might show why you favor one over the other.

e For an interactive Learning by Doing activity on Comparing and Contrasting Experience of a Major Event, go to Ch. 7: **bedfordstmartins.com/bedguide**.

These students found a clear reason for comparison and contrast:

An American student compared and contrasted her home life with that of her roommate, a student from Nigeria. Her goal was to deepen her understanding of Nigerian society and her own.

A student who was interested in history compared and contrasted civilian responses to the Vietnam and Iraq wars, considering how popular attitudes about military service had changed.

Another writer compared and contrasted facilities at two city parks, making a case for a revised funding formula.

### Facing the Challenge Comparing and Contrasting

The major challenge that writers face when comparing and contrasting two subjects is to determine their purpose. Writers who skip this step run the risk of having readers ask, "So, what's the point?" Suppose you develop brilliant points of similarity and difference between the films of Oliver Stone and those of Stanley Kubrick. Do you want to argue that one director is more skilled than the other? Or perhaps you want to show how they treat love or war differently in their films? Consider the following questions as you determine your primary purpose for comparing and contrasting:

- Do you want to inform your readers about these two subjects in order to provide a better understanding of the two?
- Do you want to persuade your readers that one of the two subjects is preferable to the other?

Ask what you want to demonstrate, discover, or prove *before* you begin to draft so you can write a more effective comparison-and-contrast essay.

## Generating Ideas

For strategies for generating ideas, see Ch. 19.

**Find Two Subjects.** Pick subjects you can compare and contrast purposefully. An examination question may give them to you, ready-made: "Compare and contrast ancient Roman sculpture with that of the ancient Greeks." But suppose you have to find your subjects for yourself. You'll need to choose things that have a sensible basis for comparison, a common element.

> moon rocks + stars = no common element
>
> Dallas + Atlanta = cities to consider settling in
>
> Jimmy Fallon + Jimmy Kimmel = television talk-show personalities

Besides having a common element, the subjects should share enough to compare but differ enough to throw each other into sharp relief.

> sports cars + racing cars = common element + telling differences
>
> sports cars + oil tankers = limited common element + unpromising differences

Try generating a list or brainstorming. Recall what you've recently read, discussed, or spotted on the Web. Let your mind skitter around in search of pairs that go together, or play the game of *free association,* jotting down a word and whatever it brings to mind: *Democrats? Republicans. New York? Los Angeles. Facebook? LinkedIn.* Or try the following questions:

---

**DISCOVERY CHECKLIST**

- ☐ Do you know two people who are strikingly different in attitude or behavior (perhaps your parents or two brothers, two friends, two teachers)?
- ☐ Can you think of two groups that are both alike and different (perhaps two teams, two clubs, two sets of relatives)?
- ☐ Have you taken two courses that were quite different but both valuable?
- ☐ Do you prefer one of two places where you have lived or visited?
- ☐ Can you recall two events in your life that shared similar aspects but turned out to be quite different (perhaps two sporting events, two romances, two vacations, the births of two children, an event then and now)?
- ☐ Can you compare and contrast two holidays or two family customs?
- ☐ Are you familiar with two writers, two artists, or two musicians who seem to have similar goals but quite different accomplishments?

---

Once you have a list of pairs, put a star by those that seem promising. Ask yourself what similarities immediately come to mind. What differences?

Can you jot down several of each? Are these striking, significant similarities and differences? If not, move on until you discover a workable pair.

**Limit Your Scope.** If you want to compare and contrast Japanese literature and American literature in 750 words, your task is probably impossible. But to cut down the size of your subject, you might compare and contrast, say, a haiku of Bashō about a snake with a short poem about a snake by Emily Dickinson. This topic you could cover in 750 words.

**Develop Your Pair to Build Support.** As you examine your two subjects, your goal is twofold. First, analyze each using a similar approach so you have a reasonable basis for comparison and contrast. Then find the details and examples that will support your points. Consider these sources of support:

- Two events, processes, procedures — Ask a reporter's questions—5 *W*'s (who, what, where, when, why) and an *H* (how).
- Two events from the past — Using the same questions, interview someone present at each event, or read news or other accounts.
- Two perceptions (public and private) — Interview someone behind the scenes; read or listen to contrasting views.
- Two approaches or viewpoints — Browse online for Web sites or pages that supply different examples.
- Two policies or options — Look for articles reporting studies or government statistics.

For more on interviewing, see Ch. 6.

For advice on finding a few useful sources, turn to B1–B2 in the Quick Research Guide, pp. A-25–A-26. For more on using sources for support, see Ch. 12.

## Learning by Doing: Making a Comparison-and-Contrast Table

After deciding what to compare, write down what you know about subject A and then subject B. Next, divide a page or use your software to create a table with three columns (up and down) and at least half a dozen rows (across). Use the first row to label the columns:

| Categories | Subject A | Subject B |
|---|---|---|
| | | |
| | | |

Now read over your notes on subject A. When you spot related details, identify a logical category for them. Enter that category name in the left column of the second row. Then add related details for subject A in the middle column. Repeat this process, labeling more rows as categories and filling in corresponding details for subject A. (Draw more lines, or use the menu to add new rows as needed.)

Next, review your notes on subject B. If some details fall into categories already listed in your table, add those details in the subject B column for each category. If new categories emerge, add them in new rows along with the subject B details. After you finish with your notes, round out the table—adding details to fill in empty cells, combining or adding categories. Select the most promising categories from your table as common features for logical comparison and contrast.

## Planning, Drafting, and Developing

For more on planning, drafting, and developing, see Chs. 20, 21, and 22. For more about informal outlines, see pp. 412–15.

As you start planning your paper, be prepared to cover both subjects in a similar fashion. Return to your table or make a scratch outline so that you can refine your points of comparison or contrast, consolidate supporting details, and spot gaps in your information. Remind yourself of your goal. What is it you want to show, argue, or find out?

For more on stating a thesis, see pp. 399–408.

**State Your Purpose in a Thesis.** You need a reason to place two subjects side by side—a reason that you and your audience will find compelling and worthwhile. If you prefer one subject over the other, what reasons can you give for your preference? If you don't have a preference, try instead to understand them more clearly, making a point about each or both. Comparing and contrasting need not be a meaningless exercise. Instead, think clearly and pointedly in order to explain an idea you care about.

For practice developing and supporting effective thesis statements, go to the interactive "Take Action" charts in Re:Writing at **bedfordstmartins .com/bedguide**.

| | |
|---|---|
| TWO SUBJECTS | two teaching styles in required biology courses |
| REASON | to show why one style is better |
| WORKING THESIS | Although students learn a lot in both of the required introductory biology courses, one class teaches information and the other teaches how to be a good learner. |

### Learning by Doing Pinpointing Your Purpose

Following the model above on teaching styles, specify your two subjects, identify your reason for comparing, and state your working thesis, making it as pointed as you can. To learn how others react to your purpose, exchange statements with a classmate or small group in person or online. Discuss possibilities for increasing clarity and purposefulness.

**Select a Pattern to Help Your Audience.** Besides understanding your purpose and thesis, readers also need to follow your supporting evidence — the clusters of details that reveal the nature of each subject you consider. They're likely to expect you to follow one of two ways to organize a comparison-and-contrast essay. Both patterns present the same information, but each has its own advantages and disadvantages.

| OPPOSING PATTERN, SUBJECT BY SUBJECT | ALTERNATING PATTERN, POINT BY POINT |
|---|---|
| Subject A | Point 1 |
| Point 1 | Subject A |
| Point 2 | Subject B |
| Point 3 | |
| | Point 2 |
| Subject B | Subject A |
| Point 1 | Subject B |
| Point 2 | |
| Point 3 | Point 3 |
| | Subject A |
| | Subject B |

**Use the Opposing Pattern of Organization.** When you use the opposing pattern of subject by subject, you state all your observations about subject A and then do the same for subject B. In the following paragraph from *Whole-Brain Thinking* (New York: William Morrow, 1984), Jacquelyn Wonder and Priscilla Donovan use the opposing pattern of organization to explain the differences in the brains of females and males.

> At birth there are basic differences between male and female brains. The female cortex is more fully developed. The sound of the human voice elicits more left-brain activity in infant girls than in infant boys, accounting in part for the earlier development in females of language. Baby girls have larger connectors between the brain's hemispheres and thus integrate information more skillfully. This flexibility bestows greater verbal and intuitive skills. Male infants lack this ready communication between the brain's lobes; therefore, messages are routed and rerouted to the right brain, producing larger right hemispheres. The size advantage accounts for males having greater spatial and physical abilities and explains why they may become more highly lateralized and skilled in specific areas.

*Subject A: Female brain*

*Point 1: Development*

*Point 2: Consequences*

*Shift to subject B: Male brain*

*Point 1: Development*

*Point 2: Consequences*

For a single paragraph or a short essay, the opposing pattern can effectively unify all the details about each subject. For a long essay or a complicated subject, it has a drawback: readers might find it difficult to remember all the separate information about subject A while reading about subject B.

For Griffin's complete essay, see pp. 121–23. For more on outlines, see pp. 411–19.

**Use the Alternating Pattern of Organization.** There's a better way to organize most long papers: the *alternating pattern* of *point by point*. Using this method you take up one point at a time, applying it first to one subject and then to the other. Jacob Griffin uses this pattern to lead the reader along clearly and carefully, looking at each subject before moving on to the next point.

THESIS: The International Olympic Committee should consider which of these styles first deserves to be declared an official Olympic sport.

I. Similarities of styles
   A. American popularity through movies
      1. Karate
      2. Kung fu
   B. Variety within styles
      1. Karate
      2. Kung fu
   C. Emphasis on internal values
      1. Karate
      2. Kung fu

II. Differences between styles
   A. Age and origins
      1. Karate
      2. Kung fu
   B. Techniques
      1. Karate's linear movement
      2. Kung fu's circular movement
   C. Uniforms and weapons
      1. Karate
      2. Kung fu

For more on transitions, see pp. 431–35.

**Add Transitions.** Once your essay is organized, you can bring cohesion to it through effective transitional words and phrases—*on the other hand, in contrast, also, both, yet, although, finally, unlike*. Your choice of wording will depend on the content, but keep it varied and smooth. Jarring, choppy transitions distract attention instead of contributing to a unified essay, each part working to support a meaningful thesis.

### Learning by Doing Building Cohesion with Transitions

Working on paper or in a file, add color highlights to mark each transitional expression already in your draft. Then check any passages without much highlighting to decide whether your audience will need more cues to see how your ideas connect. Next, check each spot where you switch from one subject or point to another to be sure that readers can easily make the shift. Finally, smooth out the wording of your transitions so that they are clear and helpful, not repetitious or mechanical. Test your changes on a reader by exchanging drafts with a classmate.

## Revising and Editing

For more on revising and editing strategies, see Ch. 23.

**Focus on Your Thesis.** Reconsider your purpose when you review your draft. If your purpose is to illuminate two subjects impartially, ask whether you have given readers a balanced view. Obviously it would be unfair to set forth all the advantages of Oklahoma City and all the disadvantages of Honolulu and then conclude that Oklahoma City is superior on every count.

Of course, if you love Oklahoma City and can't stand Honolulu, or vice versa, go ahead: don't be balanced; take a stand. Even so, you will want to include the same points about each city and to admit, in all honesty, that Oklahoma City has its faults. One useful way to check for balance or thoroughness is to outline your draft and give the outline a critical look.

### Peer Response Comparing and Contrasting

For general questions for a peer editor, see p. 463.

You may want a classmate or friend to respond to your draft, suggesting how to present your two subjects more clearly. Ask your peer editor to answer questions like these about comparison and contrast:

- How does the introduction motivate you to read the entire essay?
- What is the point of the comparison and contrast of the two subjects? Is the thesis stated in the essay, or is it implied?
- Is the essay organized by the opposing pattern or by the alternating pattern? Is the pattern appropriate, or would the other one work better?
- Are the same categories discussed for each item? If not, should they be?
- Are there enough details for you to understand the comparison and contrast? Put a check where more details or examples would be useful.
- If this paper were yours, what is the one thing you would be sure to work on before handing it in?

If classmates have made suggestions, perhaps about clearer wording to sharpen distinctions, use their ideas as you rework your thesis.

WORKING THESIS Although students learn a lot in both of the required introductory biology courses, one class teaches information and the other teaches how to be a good learner.

REVISED THESIS Although students learn the basics of biology in both of the required introductory courses, one class teaches how to memorize information and the other teaches an invaluable lesson: how to be an active learner.

**Vary Your Wording.** Make sure, as you go over your draft, that you have escaped a monotonous drone: A does this, B does that; A has these advantages, B has those. Comparison and contrast needn't result in a paper as symmetrical as a pair of sneakers. Revising and editing give you a chance to add lively details, transitions, dashes of color, and especially variety:

> The menu is another major difference between the Cozy Cafe and the Wilton Inn. For lunch, the Cozy Cafe offers sandwiches, hamburgers, and chili. ~~For lunch,~~ *(L) (at)* the Wilton Inn ~~offers~~ *features* dishes such as fajitas, shrimp salads, and onion soup topped with Swiss cheese. ~~For dinner, the Cozy Cafe continues to serve the lunch menu and~~ *adding* adds home-style comfort foods such as meatloaf, stew, macaroni and cheese, and barbecued ribs. By dinner, *after five o'clock* the Wilton's specialties for the day are posted—perhaps marinated buffalo steak or orange-pecan salmon.

---

**REVISION CHECKLIST**

- ☐ Does your introduction present your topic and main point clearly? Is it interesting enough to make a reader want to read the whole essay?
- ☐ Is your reason for doing all the comparing and contrasting unmistakably clear? What do you want to demonstrate, argue for, or find out? Do you need to reexamine your goal?
- ☐ Have you used the same categories for each item so that you treat them fairly? In discussing each feature, do you always look at the same thing?
- ☐ Have you selected points of comparison and supporting details that will intrigue, enlighten, and persuade your audience?
- ☐ What have you concluded about the two? Do you prefer one to the other? If so, is this preference (and your rationale for it) clear?
- ☐ Does your draft look thin at any point for lack of evidence? If so, how might you develop your ideas?
- ☐ Have you used the best arrangement, given your subjects and your point?
- ☐ Are there any spots where you need to revise a boringly mechanical, monotonous style ("On one hand, . . . now on the other hand")?

---

For more editing and proofreading strategies, see pp. 471–75.

After you have revised your comparison-and-contrast essay, edit and proofread it. Carefully check the grammar, word choice, punctuation, and mechanics – and then correct any problems you may find.

### EDITING CHECKLIST

- ☐ Have you used the correct comparative forms (for two things) and superlative forms (for three or more) for adjectives and adverbs? A7
- ☐ Is your sentence structure correct? Have you avoided writing fragments, comma splices, or fused sentences? A1, A2
- ☐ Have you used parallel structure in your comparisons and contrasts? Are your sentences as balanced as your ideas? B2
- ☐ Have you used commas correctly after introductory phrases and other transitions? C1

For more help, find the relevant checklist sections in the Quick Editing Guide on p. A-39. Turn also to the Quick Format Guide beginning on p. A-1.

## Additional Writing Assignments

1. Listen to two different recordings of the same piece of music as performed by two different groups, orchestras, or singers. What elements of the music does each stress? What contrasting attitudes toward the music do you detect? In an essay, compare and contrast these versions.
2. In a serious or nonserious way, introduce yourself to your class by comparing and contrasting yourself with someone else. You might choose either a real person or a character in a film, a TV series, a novel, or a comic strip, but you and this other person should have much in common. Choose a few points of comparison (an attitude, a habit, or a way of life), and deal with each in an essay or, if your instructor approves, a mixed-media format.
3. With a classmate or small group, choose a topic, problem, or campus issue about which your views differ to some extent. Agree on several main points of contrast that you want each writer to consider. Then have each person write a paragraph summing up his or her point of view, concentrating on those main points. After your passages are written, collaboratively develop an introduction that outlines the issue, identifies the main points, and previews the contrasting views. Arrange the paragraphs effectively, add transitions, and write a collaborative conclusion. Revise and edit as needed to produce an orderly, coherent collaborative essay.
4. Compare and contrast yourself with a classmate in a collaborative essay. Decide together what your focus will be: Your backgrounds? Your paths to college? Your career goals? Your lives outside class? Your study habits? Your taste in music or clothes? Your politics? Have each writer use this focus to work on a detailed analysis of himself or herself. Then compare analyses, clarify the purpose and thesis of your comparison, and decide how to shape the essay. If your instructor approves, you might prepare a mixed-media presentation or post your essay to introduce yourselves to the class.

For more on using sources to support a position, see Ch. 12 and the Quick Research Guide beginning on p. A-20.

5. **Source Assignment.** Write an essay in which you compare and contrast the subjects in any of the following pairs for the purpose of throwing light on both. Turn to readings or essay pairs or e-Pages for this book, a source from the library, an interview with a friendly expert, news coverage, a Web page or image, or another relevant source for details and support. Be sure to credit your sources.

   The coverage of a world event on television and in a newspaper
   The experience of watching a film on a DVD and in a theater
   The styles of two athletes playing in the same position (two pitchers, two quarterbacks, two goalies)
   English and another language
   Two differing views of a current controversy
   Northern and southern California (or two other regions)
   Two similar works of architecture (two churches, two skyscrapers, two city halls, two museums, two campus buildings)
   Two articles, essays, or Web sites about the same topic
   Two short stories, two poems, or two literary works about the same theme
   Two articles or other types of sources for an upcoming research paper

For other contrasting images of families, see pp. 58, 183, 311, and 492.

6. **Visual Assignment.** The following images are selected from *What the World Eats,* a book that shows families around the world with their food for a week. Compare and contrast two of the images here in an essay, following the advice in this chapter. Be sure that you identify the purpose of your comparison, organize your subjects and points effectively, and support your points with details that you observe in the images.

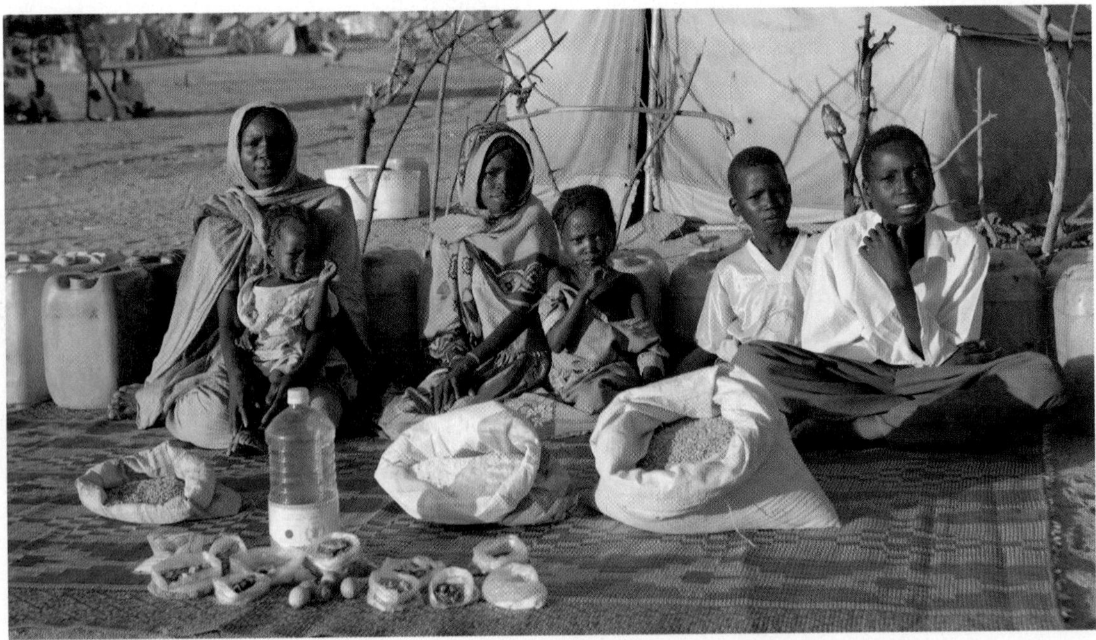

The Aboubakar family of Darfur province, Sudan, in a refugee camp in Chad with a week's worth of food (cost: $1.22 USD).

The Mendoza family and a servant in their courtyard in Guatemala, with a week's worth of food (cost: $75.70 USD).

The Revis family at home in Raleigh, North Carolina, with a week's worth of food (cost: $341.98 USD).

# 8 Explaining Causes and Effects

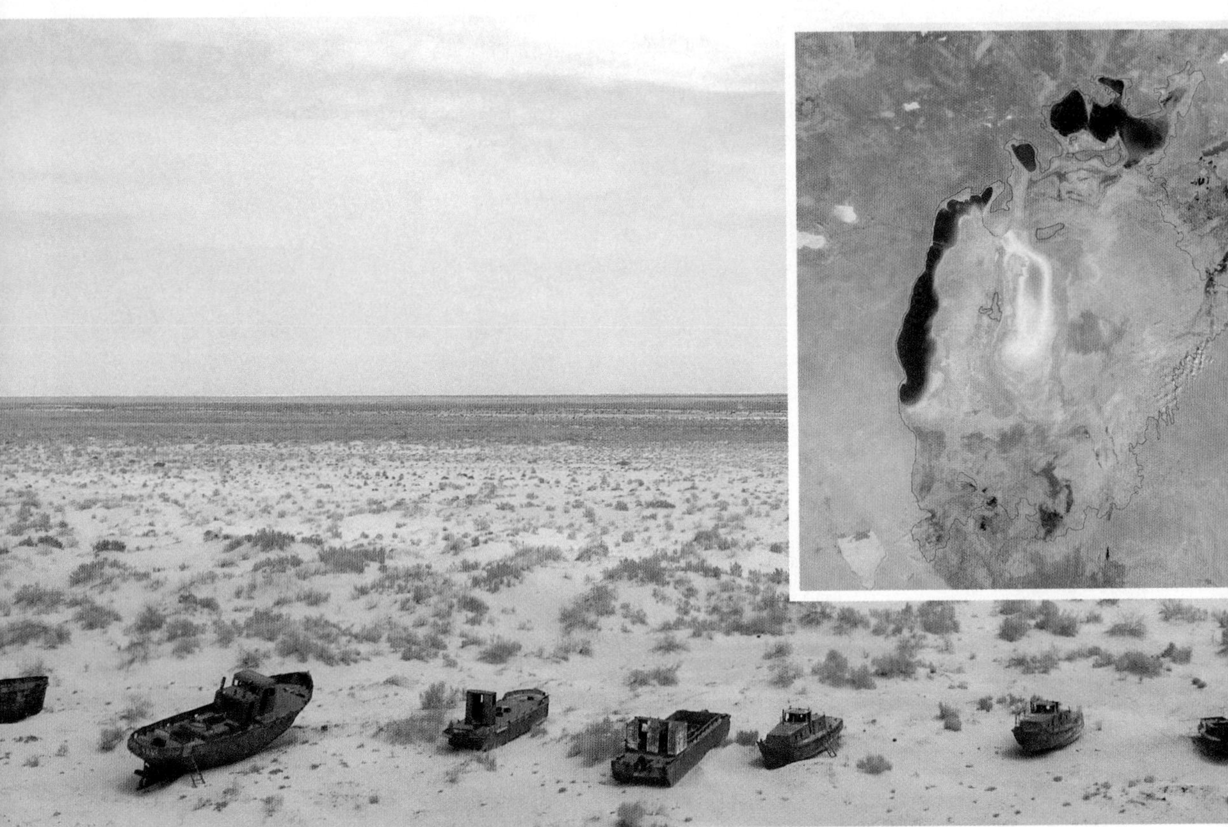

Since the 1960s, the size of the Aral Sea in Uzbekistan has greatly decreased (see satellite image from 2009, *inset*, with thin black line indicating original size). The decreased area is due largely to short-sighted irrigation projects that diverted the rivers that fed this body of water. The resulting environmental disaster left formerly prosperous fishing villages marooned many miles from any shoreline and brought pollution, hardship, and a more extreme climate to the area.

## Responding to an Image

These two images suggest both causes and effects. What causes can you identify? What effects? Also consider artistic choice – the selection of each scene and the vantage point from which it was photographed. What mood does each photograph create? How does each affect you?

When a house burns down, an insurance company assigns a claims adjuster to look into the disaster and ask, Why? He or she investigates to find the answer—the *cause* of the fire, whether lightning, a cooking mishap, or a match that someone deliberately struck—and presents it in a written report. The adjuster also details the *effects* of the fire—what was destroyed or damaged, what replacement or restoration will be necessary, what repairs will be required, how much they will cost, and how long the family may need temporary housing.

Often in college you are asked to investigate and think like the insurance adjuster, tracing causes or identifying effects. To do so, you have to gather information to marshal evidence. Effects are usually easier to identify than causes. Results of a fire are apparent to an onlooker the next day, although its cause may be obscure. For this reason, seeking causes and effects may be an uncertain pursuit, and you are unlikely to set forth definitive explanations with absolute certainty. Despite these uncertainties, causes and effects intrigue investigative journalists, stock market analysts, historians, and geographers, as well as families who look for one generation's impact on another.

## Why Explaining Causes and Effects Matters

### In a College Course

- You explore causes or effects to add depth to your papers whether you are investigating teen parenthood in sociology, romanticism in American fiction, or head traumas in speech pathology.
- You identify causes (such as those for the decline or the revival of the U.S. auto industry) or effects (such as those of widespread unemployment in Detroit) in essay exams.

### In the Workplace

- You consider causes and effects when you recommend changing from one advertising campaign to another to improve sales or from an old procedure to a new one to improve quality, efficiency, or safety.

### In Your Community

- You use causal analysis to help you advocate for more rigorous standards for the fuel efficiency of new vehicles or for stronger school board support for early childhood programs.

When have you explained causes, effects, or both in your writing? What situations are likely to require this kind of analysis?

## Learning from Other Writers

The following essays explore causes and effects, each examining a different environment. To help you begin to analyze the first reading, look at the notes in the margin. They identify features such as the thesis, or main idea, and the first of the causes or effects that the paper analyzes.

### As You Read These Cause-and-Effect Essays

As you read these essays, ask yourself the following questions:

1. Does the writer explain causes? Or effects? Or both? Why?
2. Does the writer perceive and explain a chain or series of causal relationships? If so, how are the various causes and effects connected?
3. What evidence does the writer supply? Is the evidence sufficient to clarify the causal relationships and to provide credibility to the essay?

**Jeffrey Pfeffer**

### Lay Off the Layoffs

Jeffrey Pfeffer, a professor at Stanford University's Graduate School of Business, examines the common business practice of laying off workers in an economic downturn. In this essay, originally published in *Newsweek* in February 2010, he considers the effects of layoffs — for both workers and businesses.

Introduction to situation

On Sept. 12, 2001, there were no commercial flights in the United States. It was uncertain when airlines would be permitted to start flying again — or how many customers would be on them. Airlines faced not only the tragedy of 9/11 but the fact that [the] economy was entering a recession.° So almost immediately, all the U.S. airlines, save one, did what so many U.S. corporations are particularly skilled at doing: they began announcing tens of thousands of layoffs. Today the one airline that didn't cut staff, Southwest, still has never had an involuntary layoff in its almost 40-year history. It's now the largest domestic U.S. airline and has a market capitalization° bigger than all its domestic competitors combined. As its former head of human resources once told me: "If people are your most important assets,° why would you get rid of them?" . . . 1

**recession:** A long period of widespread economic decline. **market capitalization:** The estimated value of a company or stock. **assets:** Resources.

It's difficult to study the causal effect of layoffs—you can't do double- 2
blind,° placebo-controlled° studies as you can for drugs by randomly assigning some companies to shed workers and others not, with people unaware of what "treatment" they are receiving. Companies that downsize are undoubtedly different in many ways (the quality of their management, for one) from those that don't. But you can attempt to control for differences in industry, size, financial condition, and past performance, and then look at a large number of studies to see if they reach the same conclusion.

Question raised about effects

THESIS

That research paints a fairly consistent picture: layoffs don't work. And for 3
good reason. In *Responsible Restructuring,* University of Colorado professor Wayne Cascio lists the direct and indirect costs of layoffs: severance pay; paying out accrued vacation and sick pay; outplacement costs; higher unemployment-insurance taxes; the cost of rehiring employees when business improves; low morale and risk-averse survivors; potential lawsuits, sabotage, or even workplace violence from aggrieved employees or former employees; loss of institutional memory and knowledge; diminished trust in management; and reduced productivity. . . .

Effects specified

Some managers compare layoffs to amputation: that sometimes you have 4
to cut off a body part to save the whole. As metaphors go, this one is particularly misplaced. Layoffs are more like bloodletting, weakening the entire organism. That's because of the vicious cycle that typically unfolds. A company cuts people. Customer service, innovation, and productivity fall in the face of a smaller and demoralized workforce. The company loses more ground, does more layoffs, and the cycle continues. That's part of the story of now-defunct Circuit City, the electronics retailer that decided it needed to get rid of its 3,400 highest-paid (and almost certainly most effective) sales associates to cut its costs. Fewer people with fewer skills in the Circuit City stores permitted competitors such as Best Buy to gain ground, and once the death spiral started, it was hard to stop. Circuit City filed for bankruptcy in 2008 and closed its doors last March.

Causal chain traced

Beyond the companies where layoffs take place, widespread downsizing 5
can have a big impact on the economy—a phenomenon that John Maynard Keynes° taught us about decades ago, but one that's almost certainly going on now. The people who lose jobs also lose incomes, so they spend less. Even workers who don't lose their jobs but are simply fearful of layoffs are likely to cut back on spending too. With less aggregate° demand in the economy, sales fall. With smaller sales, companies lay off more people, and the cycle continues. That's why places where it is harder to shed workers—such as (can

**double-blind:** A testing procedure in which neither participants nor experimenters know what treatment participants are receiving, used to eliminate accidental bias. **placebo-controlled:** A testing procedure in which one group of participants receives an accepted or experimental treatment and another group receives an inactive or false treatment (the *placebo*). **John Maynard Keynes** (1883–1946): British economist who introduced new ideas about economics during the 1930s. **aggregate:** Overall.

I dare say it?) France—have held up comparatively better during the global economic meltdown. Workers there are confident that they'll remain employed, so they needn't pull back on spending so dramatically.

The airline industry provides a case study of the downside of retrenchment.° After the layoffs following 9/11, airline service deteriorated and flying became a truly unpleasant experience. That carried predictable consequences: the number of "premium" passenger trips, defined as full-fare coach, first-, or business-class fares (where airlines make their biggest margins), declined by 47 percent between 2000 and 2007. According to an industry survey published in 2008, in the preceding 12 months airlines had lost $9.6 billion in revenue as people voluntarily flew less because they found the experience so noxious.° In a fixed-cost industry like airlines, that was the difference between an industrywide loss and profitability. . . . 6

As bad as the effects of layoffs are on companies and the economy, perhaps the biggest damage is done to the people themselves. . . . When people lose their jobs, they get angry and depressed—not a big surprise. Angry and depressed people who believe they have been treated unfairly can lose psychological control and exact vengeance on those they deem responsible. We have all seen too-frequent cable-news coverage of the fired employee who returns to the workplace with a gun and wounds or kills people. It's not just the occasional anecdote. Research shows that people who had no history of violent behavior were six times more likely to exhibit violent behavior after a layoff than similar people who remained employed. 7

And some research has looked directly at the health consequences of losing one's job or being unemployed on mortality. A study in New Zealand found that for people 25 to 64 years old, being unemployed increased the likelihood of committing suicide by 2.5 times. When two meat-processing plants closed in New Zealand, epidemiologists° followed what happened to their employees over an eight-year period. The odds of self-harm and the rate of admission to hospitals for mental-health problems increased significantly compared with people who remained employed. A recent National Bureau of Economic Research working paper reported that in the United States, job displacement led to a 12 to 20 percent increase in death rates during the following 20 years, implying a loss of life expectancy of 1.5 years for an employee who loses his job at the age of 40. Even in societies with strong social-welfare provisions, job loss is traumatic. A study of plant closures in Sweden reported a 44 percent increase in the mortality risk among men during the first four years following the loss of work. 8

Anyone who's suffered a layoff or watched a loved one lose a job can understand why downsizees exhibit increased rates of alcoholism, smoking, drug abuse, and depression. In economic terms, we should think of these as 9

**retrenchment:** Cutting back. **noxious:** Unpleasant and harmful. **epidemiologists:** People who study health and illness in large populations.

"externalities",° just like air and water pollution, since many of the costs of these behaviors and ailments are borne by the larger society.

10 Despite all the research suggesting downsizing hurts companies, managers everywhere continue to do it. That raises an obvious question: why? Part of the answer lies in the immense pressure corporate leaders feel—from the media, from analysts, from peers—to follow the crowd no matter what. When SAS Institute, the $2 billion software company, considered going public about a decade ago, its potential underwriter° told the company to do things that would make it look more like other software companies: pay sales people on commission, offer stock options, and cut back on the lavish benefits that landed SAS at No. 1 on *Fortune*'s annual Best Places to Work list. (SAS stayed private.) It's an example of how managerial behavior can be contagious, spreading like the flu across companies. One study of downsizing over a 15-year period found a strong "adoption effect"—companies copied the behavior of other firms to which they had social ties.

11 The facts seem clear. Layoffs are mostly bad for companies, harmful for the economy, and devastating for employees. This is not news, or should not be. There is substantial research literature in fields from epidemiology to organizational behavior documenting these effects. The damage from overzealous downsizing will linger even as the economy recovers—and as it does, perhaps managers will learn from their mistakes.

Conclusion restating thesis

## Questions to Start You Thinking

Meaning

1. Why is the comparison of layoffs to amputations misguided, according to Pfeffer (paragraph 4)?
2. How does widespread downsizing affect the wider economy?
3. Pfeffer discusses how layoffs can make workers angry and depressed. What are the wider effects of this anger and depression?

Writing Strategies

4. Pfeffer begins the essay with the story of Southwest Airlines after 9/11. Is this an effective beginning? Why or why not? In what other ways might he have begun his essay?
5. Pfeffer uses a mixture of anecdotal evidence and scientific studies to discuss the causes and effects of layoffs. How effective is this mix? Does he depend too strongly on one or the other? Why or why not?
6. Does Pfeffer's essay deal predominantly with causes or effects? Where and to what degree does he examine each of these? How would his essay change if he changed his focus?

**externalities:** Hidden or indirect costs of economic activities. **underwriter:** Financial backer.

**Yun Yung Choi** **Student Essay**

## Invisible Women

Yun Yung Choi examines the adoption of a new state religion in her native Korea and the effects of that adoption on Korean women.

How would you have answered this question?

1 For me, growing up in a small suburb on the outskirts of Seoul, the adults' preference for boys seemed quite natural. All the important people that I knew—doctors, lawyers, policemen, and soldiers—were men. On the other hand, most of the women that I knew were either housekeepers or housewives whose duty seemed to be to obey and please the men of the family. When my teachers at school asked me what I wanted to be when I grew up, I would answer, "I want to be the wife of the president." Because all women must become wives and mothers, I thought, becoming the wife of the president would be the highest achievement for a woman. I knew that the birth of a boy was a greatly desired and celebrated event, whereas the birth of a girl was a disappointing one, accompanied by the frequent words of consolation for the sad parents: "A daughter is her mother's chief help in keeping house."

2 These attitudes toward women, widely considered the continuation of an unbroken chain of tradition, are, in fact, only a few hundred years old, a relatively short period considering Korea's long history. During the first half of the Yi dynasty, which lasted from 1392 to 1910, and during the Koryo period, which preceded the Yi dynasty, women were treated almost as equals with many privileges that were denied them during the latter half of the Yi dynasty. This turnabout in women's place in Korean society was brought about by one of the greatest influences that shaped the government, literature, and thoughts of the Korean people—Confucianism.°

3 Throughout the Koryo period, which lasted from 918 to 1392, and throughout the first half of the Yi dynasty, according to Laurel Kendall in her book *View from the Inner Room*, women were important and contributing members of the society and not marginal and dependent as they later became. Women were, to a large extent, in command of their own lives. They were permitted to own property and receive inheritances from their fathers. Wedding ceremonies were held in the bride's house, where the couple lived, and the wife retained her surname. Women were also allowed freedom of movement—that is, they were able to go outside the house without any feelings of shame or embarrassment.

4 With the introduction of Confucianism, however, the rights and privileges that women enjoyed were confiscated. The government of the Yi dynasty made great efforts to incorporate into society the Confucian ideologies, including the principle of *agnation*. This principle, according to Kendall, made men the important members of society and relegated° women to a dependent position. The government succeeded in Confucianizing the country and encouraging the acceptance of Confucian proverbs such as the following: "Men are honored, but women are abased."

**Confucianism:** Ethical system based on the teachings of Chinese philosopher Confucius (551–479 B.C.). **relegated:** Reduced to a less important position.

"A daughter is a 'robber woman' who carries household wealth away when she marries."

How do you respond to this historical background?

5 The unfortunate effects of this Confucianization in the lives of women were numerous. The most noticeable was the virtual confinement of women. They were forced to remain unseen in the *anbang*, the inner room of the house. This room was the women's domain, or, rather, the women's prison. Outside, a woman was carried through the streets in a closed sedan chair. Walking outside, she had to wear a veil that covered her face and could travel abroad only after nightfall. Thus, it is no wonder that Westerners traveling through Korea in the late nineteenth century expressed surprise at the apparent absence of women in the country.

6 Women received no formal education. Their only schooling came from government textbooks. By giving instruction on the virtuous° conduct of women, these books attempted to fit women into the Confucian stereotype—meek, quiet, and obedient. Thus, this Confucian society acclaimed particular women not for their talent or achievement but for the degree of perfection with which they were able to mimic the stereotype.

7 A woman even lost her identity in such a society. Once married, she became a stranger to her natal° family, becoming a member of her husband's family. Her name was omitted from the family *chokpo*, or genealogy book, and was entered in the *chokpo* of her in-laws as a mere "wife" next to her husband's name.

8 Even a desirable marriage, the ultimate hope for a woman, failed to provide financial and emotional security for her. Failure to produce a son was legal grounds for sending the wife back to her natal home, thereby subjecting the woman to the greatest humiliation and to a life of continued shame. And because the Confucian ideology stressed a wife's devotion to her husband as the greatest of womanly virtues, widows were forced to avoid social disgrace by remaining faithfully unmarried, no matter how young they were. As women lost their rights to own or inherit property, these widows, with no means to support themselves, suffered great hardships. Thus, as Sandra Martielle says in *Virtues in Conflict*, what the government considered "the ugly custom of remarriage" was slowly eliminated at the expense of women's happiness.

9 This male-dominated system of Confucianism is one of the surviving traditions from the Yi dynasty. Although the Constitution of the Republic of Korea proclaimed on July 17, 1948, guarantees individual freedom and sexual equality, these ideals failed to have any immediate effect on the Korean mentality that stubbornly adheres to its belief in the superiority of men. Women still regard marriage as their prime objective in life, and little girls still wish to become the doctor's wife, the lawyer's wife, and even the president's wife. But as the system of Confucianism is slowly being forced out of existence by new legal and social standards, perhaps a day will come, after all, when a little girl will stand up in class and answer, "I want to be the president."

Why do you think the writer ends with this quotation?

**virtuous:** Moral, honorable. **natal:** Relating to one's birth.

## Questions to Start You Thinking

### Meaning

1. What effect does Choi observe? What cause does she attribute it to?
2. What specific changes in Korean culture does Choi attribute to the introduction of Confucianism?
3. What evidence do you find of the writer's critically rethinking an earlier belief and then revising it? What do you think may have influenced her to change her belief?

### Writing Strategies

4. What does Choi gain by beginning and ending with her personal experience?
5. Where does Choi use the strategy of comparing and contrasting?
6. How does Choi consider readers for whom her culture might be foreign?
7. Using highlighters or marginal notes, identify the essay's introduction, thesis, major causes or effects, supporting explanations and details for each of these, and conclusion. How effective is the organization?

**e Total DUI Editors** **Infographic**

## The Scientific Effects of Drunk Driving

Drawing on information from the National Institute on Alcohol Abuse and Alcoholism and other sources, this infographic uses science to explain how alcohol impairs driving abilities. To view the infographic, go to Chapter 8: **bedfordstmartins.com/bedguide**.

# Learning by Writing

## The Assignment: Explaining Causes and Effects

Pick a disturbing fact or situation that you have observed, and seek out its causes and effects to help you and your readers understand the issue better. You may limit your essay to the causes *or* the effects, or you may include both but emphasize one more than the other. Yun Yung Choi uses the last approach when she identifies the cause of the status of Korean women (Confucianism) but spends most of her essay detailing effects of this cause.

For an interactive Learning by Doing activity on Analyzing Causes and Effects, go to Ch. 8: **bedfordstmartins .com/bedguide**.

The situation you choose may have affected you and people you know well, such as student loan policies, the difficulty of working while going to school, or a challenge facing your family. It might have affected people in your city or region—a small voter turnout in an election, decaying bridge supports, or pet owners not using pooper-scoopers. It may affect society at large—identity theft, immigration laws, or the high cost of health care. It might be gender or racial stereotypes on television, binge drinking at parties, spouse abuse, teenage suicide, global warming, student debt, or the use of dragnets for ocean fishing. Don't think you must choose an earthshaking topic to write a good paper. On the contrary, you will do a better job if you are personally familiar with the situation you choose.

These students selected topics of personal concern for causal analysis:

One student cited her observations of the hardships faced by Indians in rural Mexico as one cause of rebellions there.

Another analyzed the negative attitudes of men toward women at her workplace and the resulting tension, inefficiency, and low production.

A third contended that buildings in Miami are not constructed to withstand hurricanes due, in part, to an inadequate inspection system.

### Facing the Challenge Causes and Effects

The major challenge writers face when exploring causal relationships is how to limit the subject. When you explore a given phenomenon—whether local unemployment or the success of your favorite band—devoting equal space to all possible causes and effects will either overwhelm your readers or put them to sleep. Instead, you need to decide what you want to show your readers—and then emphasize the causal relationships that help achieve this purpose.

Rely on your purpose to help you decide which part of the relationship—cause or effect—to stress and how to limit your ideas to strengthen your overall point. If you are writing about your family's transportation problems, for example, you may be tempted to discuss all the possible *causes* and then analyze all the *effects* it has had on you. Your readers, however, won't want to know about every single complication. Both you and your readers will have a much easier time if you make some decisions about your focus:

- Do you want to concentrate on *causes* or *effects*?
- Which of your explanations are most and least compelling?
- How can you emphasize the points that are most important to you?
- Which relatively insignificant or irrelevant ideas can you omit?

## Generating Ideas

For more strategies for generating ideas, see Ch. 19.

**Find a Topic.** What familiar situation would be informative or instructive to explore? This assignment leaves you the option of writing from what you know, what you can find out, or a combination of the two. Begin by letting your thoughts wander over the results of a particular situation. Has the situation always been this way? Or has it changed in the last few years? Have things gotten better or worse?

When your thoughts begin to percolate, jot down likely topics. Then choose the idea that you care most about and that promises to be neither too large nor too small. A paper confined to the causes of a family's move from New Jersey to Montana might be a single sentence: "My father's company transferred him." But the subsequent effects of the move on the family might become an interesting essay. On the other hand, you might need hundreds of pages to study all the effects of gangs in urban high schools. Instead, you might select just one unusual effect, such as gang members staking out territory in the parking lot of a local school.

### DISCOVERY CHECKLIST

- ☐ Has a difficult situation resulted from a change in your life (a lost job or a new one; a fluctuation in income; personal or family upheaval following death, divorce, accident, illness, or good fortune; a new school)?
- ☐ Has the environment changed (due to a drought, a flood or a storm, a fire, a new industry, the collapse of an old industry)?
- ☐ Has a disturbing situation been caused by an invention (the laptop, the e-reader, the DVD player, the 3-D television, the ATM, the smartphone)?
- ☐ Do certain employment trends cause you concern (for women in management, for young people in rural areas, for men in nursing)?
- ☐ Is a situation on campus or in your neighborhood, city, or state causing problems for you (traffic, housing, access to healthy food, health care)?

## Learning by Doing — Visualizing the Situation

Working by yourself or with a group, try mapping to investigate likely causes and effects in the situation you have selected. Use a blank page with movable sticky notes, note cards, a computer file where you can position chunks or boxes of text, or software for clustering ideas. Identify causes and effects, and then arrange them to show their relationships or their relative importance.

**List Causes and Effects.** After noting causes and effects, consider which are immediate (evident and close at hand), which are remote (underlying, more basic, or earlier), and how you might arrange them in a logical sequence or causal chain.

Causes and effects during a mishap in Connemara, Ireland.

FOCUS ON CAUSAL CHAIN

| **Remote Causes** | → | **Immediate Causes** | → | **Situation** | → | **Immediate Effects** | → | **Remote Effects** |
|---|---|---|---|---|---|---|---|---|
| Foreign competition | → | Sales, profits drop | → | Clothing factory closing | → | Jobs vanish | → | Town flounders |

For more on thinking critically, see Ch. 3.

Once you figure out the basic causal relationships, focus on complexities or implications. Probe for contributing, related, or even hidden factors. As you draft, these ideas will be a rich resource, allowing you to focus on the most important causes or effects and to skip any that are minor.

| FOCUS ON IMMEDIATE EFFECTS | | | FOCUS ON REMOTE EFFECTS |
|---|---|---|---|
| Factory workers lose jobs | → | Households curtail spending | Town economy undermined |
| Grocery and other stores suffer | → | Businesses fold | Food pantry, social services overwhelmed |
| Workers lose health coverage | → | Health needs ignored | Hospital limits services and doctors leave |
| Retirees fear benefits lost | → | Confidence erodes | Unemployed and young people leave |

## Learning by Doing Making a Cause-and-Effect Table

Use the Table menu in your word processor or draw on paper a four-column table to help you assess the importance of causes and effects. Divide up your causes and effects, making entries under each heading. Refine your table as you relate, order, or limit your points.

| Major Cause | Minor Cause | Major Effect | Minor Effect |
|---|---|---|---|
| | | | |
| | | | |

For advice on finding a few pertinent sources, turn to the Quick Research Guide, beginning on p. A-20.

**Consider Sources of Support.** After identifying causes and effects, note your evidence next to each item. You can then see at a glance exactly where you need more material. Star or underline any causes and effects that stand out as major ones. Ask, How significant is this cause? Would the situation not exist without it? (This major cause deserves a big star.) Or would the situation have arisen without it, for some other reason? (This minor cause might still matter but be less important.) Has this effect had a resounding impact? Is it necessary to explain the results adequately?

As you set priorities – identifying major causes or effects and noting missing information – you may wish to talk with others, use a search engine, or browse the library Web site for sources of supporting ideas, details, and statistics. You might look for illustrations of the problem, accounts of comparable situations, or charts showing current data and projections.

## Planning, Drafting, and Developing

**Start with a Scratch Outline and Thesis.** Yun Yung Choi's "Invisible Women" follows a clear plan based on a brief scratch outline that simply lists the effects of the change:

For Choi's complete essay, see pp. 142–44. For more about informal outlines, see pp. 412–15.

Intro — Personal anecdote
- Tie with Korean history
- Then add working thesis: The turnabout for women resulted from the influence of Confucianism in all aspects of society.

Comparison and contrast of status of women before and after Confucianism
Effects of Confucianism on women
1. Confinement
2. Little education
3. Loss of identity in marriage
4. No property rights

Conclusion: Impact still evident in Korea today but some hints of change

For exercises on choosing effective thesis statements, visit **bedfordstmartins .com/bedguide**.

The paper makes its point: it identifies Confucianism as the reason for the status of Korean women and details four specific effects of Confucianism on women in Korean society. And it shows that cause and effect are closely related: Confucianism is the cause of the change in the status of Korean women, and Confucianism has had specific effects on Korean women.

For more about stating your main point in a thesis, see pp. 399–408.

**Organize to Show Causes and Effects to Your Audience.** Your paper's core – showing how the situation came about (the causes), what followed as a result (the effects), or both – likely will follow one of these patterns:

| | | |
|---|---|---|
| I. The situation | I. The situation | I. The situation |
| II. Its causes | II. Its effects | II. Its causes |
| | | III. Its effects |

Try planning by grouping causes and effects, then classifying them as major or minor. If you are writing about why more students accumulate credit-card debt now than a generation ago, you might list the following:

1. available credit for students
2. high credit limits and interest
3. reduced or uncertain income
4. excessive buying

On reflection you might decide that available credit, credit limits, and interest rates are determined by the credit card industry, government regulation, and current economic conditions. These factors certainly affect students, but you are more interested in causes and effects that individual students might be able to influence in order to minimize their debt. You consider whether your own growing debt is due to too little income or too many expenses. You could then organize the causes from least to most important, giving the major one more space and the final place. When your plan seems logical, discuss it or share a draft with a classmate, a friend, or your instructor. Ask whether your organization will make sense to someone else.

**Introduce the Situation.** Begin your draft by describing the situation you want to explain in no more than two or three paragraphs. Tell readers your task – explaining causes, effects, or both. Instead of doing this in a flat, mechanical fashion ("Now I am going to explain the causes"), announce your task casually, as if you were talking to someone: "At first, I didn't realize that keeping six pet cheetahs in our backyard would bother the neighbors." Or tantalize your readers as one writer did in a paper about her father's sudden move to a Trappist monastery: "The real reason for Father's decision didn't become clear to me for a long while."

### Learning by Doing — Focusing Your Introduction

Read aloud the draft of your introduction for a classmate or small group, or post it for online discussion. Ask your readers first to identify where you state the main point of your essay—why you are explaining causes or effects. Then ask them to share their helpful observations about the clarity of that statement or about any spots where your introduction bogs down in detail or skips over essentials.

For more on using sources for support, see Ch. 12 or the Quick Research Guide beginning on p. A-20.

**Work in Your Evidence.** Some writers want to rough out a cause-and-effect draft, positioning all the major points first and then circling back to pull in supporting explanations and details. Others want to plunge deeply into each section – stating the main point, elaborating, and working in the evidence all at once. Tables, charts, and graphs can often consolidate information that substantiates or illustrates causes or effects. Place any graphics near the related text discussion, supporting but not duplicating it.

For exercises on supporting a thesis, visit **bedfordstmartins.com/bedguide**.

## Revising and Editing

For more revising and editing strategies, see Ch. 23.

Because explaining causes and effects takes hard thought, set aside plenty of time for rewriting. As Yun Yung Choi approached her paper's final version, she wanted to rework her thesis for greater precision with more detail.

| | |
|---|---|
| WORKING THESIS | The turnabout for women resulted from the influence of Confucianism in all aspects of society. |
| REVISED THESIS | This turnabout in women's place in Korean society was brought about by one of the greatest influences that shaped the government, literature, and thoughts of the Korean people – Confucianism. |

She also faced a problem pointed out by classmates: how to make a smooth transition from recalling her own experience to probing causes.

*(emphasize that everyone thinks that) → widely*

These attitudes toward women, ~~which I once~~ believed to be the continuation of an unbroken chain of tradition, are, in fact, only a few hundred years old*, a relatively short time, considering Korea's long history*. During the first half of the Yi dynasty, which lasted from 1392 to 1910, and during [the Koryo period,] *[tell when]* women were treated almost as equals, with many privileges that were denied them during the latter half of the Yi dynasty. This upheaval in women's place in Korean society was brought about by one of the greatest influences that shaped the government, literature, and thoughts of the Korean people: Confucianism. Because of Confucianism, my birth was not greeted with joy and celebration but rather with these words of consolation: "A daughter is her mother's chief help in keeping house."

*(belongs in opening paragraph)*

## Peer Response Explaining Causes and Effects

Have a classmate or friend read your draft, considering how you've analyzed causes or effects. Ask your peer editor to answer questions such as the following:

For an explanation of causes:

- Does the writer explain, rather than merely list, causes?
- Do the causes seem logical and possible?
- Are there other causes that the writer might consider? If so, list them.

For an explanation of effects:

- Do all the effects seem to be results of the situation the writer describes?
- Are there other effects that the writer might consider? If so, list them.

For general questions for a peer editor, see p. 463.

For all cause-and-effect papers:

- What is the writer's thesis? Does the explanation of causes or effects help the writer accomplish the purpose of the essay?

- Is the order of supporting ideas clear? Can you suggest a better organization?
- Are you convinced by the writer's logic? Do you see any logical fallacies?
- Are any causes or effects hard to accept?
- Do the writer's evidence and detail convince you? Put stars where more or better evidence is needed.
- If this paper were yours, what is the one thing you would be sure to work on before handing it in?

### REVISION CHECKLIST

☐ Have you shown your readers your purpose in presenting causes or effects?

☐ Is your explanation thoughtful, searching, and reasonable?

☐ Where might you need to reorganize or add transitions so your paper is easy for readers to follow?

If you are tracing causes,

☐ Have you made it clear that you are explaining causes?

☐ Do you need to add any significant causes?

For more on evidence, see pp. 40–44. For more on mistakes in thinking called logical fallacies, see pp. 100–01.

☐ At what points might you need to add more evidence to convince readers that the causal relationships are valid, not just guesses?

☐ Do you need to drop any remote causes you can't begin to prove? Or any assertions made without proof?

☐ Have you oversimplified by assuming that only one small cause accounts for a large outcome or that one thing caused another just by preceding it?

If you are determining effects,

☐ Have you made it clear that you are explaining effects?

☐ What possible effects have you left out? Are any of them worth adding?

☐ At what points might you need more evidence that the effects occurred?

☐ Could any effect have resulted not from the cause you describe but from some other cause?

For more editing and proofreading strategies, see pp. 471–75.

After you have revised your cause-and-effect essay, edit and proofread it. Carefully check the grammar, word choice, punctuation, and mechanics – and then correct any problems you find.

EDITING CHECKLIST

- ☐ Have you used correct verb tenses and forms throughout? When you describe events in the past, is it clear what happened first and what happened next? A3
- ☐ Have you avoided creating fragments when adding causes or effects? (Check revisions carefully, especially those beginning "*Because* . . ." or "*Causing* . . .") Have you avoided comma splices or fused sentences when integrating ideas? A1, A2
- ☐ Do your transitions and other introductory elements have commas after them, if these are needed? C1

For more help, find the relevant checklist sections in the Quick Editing Guide on p. A-39. Turn also to the Quick Format Guide beginning on p. A-1.

## Additional Writing Assignments

1. Pick a change that has taken place during your lifetime—a noticeable, lasting transformation produced by an event or a series of events. Write an essay exploring its causes, effects, or both to help you and your audience understand that change better. The change might have affected only you, such as a move, a decision, or an alteration in a strong personal opinion or belief. It might have also affected others in your community (a new zoning law), in a region (the growth of a new industry), or in society at large (general access to the Internet). Or it might be a new invention, medical breakthrough, or deep-down shift in the structure or attitudes of society.
2. Reflect on your background and experience to identify a major event, person, circumstance, habit, routine, or other factor that significantly shaped you as a person. In your journal, write informally about the nature of this cause and its effects on you. Use this entry to develop a cause-and-effect essay about yourself that will enlighten a reader about how you came to be the person that you are now or are now becoming.
3. Write a formal letter or memo addressed to someone who could make a change that you advocate. Support this change by explaining causes, effects, or both. For example, address a college official to support a change in a campus event or policy, the principal to advocate for a change at your child's school, your work supervisor to encourage a change in procedures, or an official to promote a change in services or rules.
4. **Source Assignment.** Read a newspaper or magazine article that probes the causes of some contemporary problem: the shortage of certain types of jobs, for instance, or tuition increases in your state. Can you suggest causes that the article writer ignored? Write an essay in which you argue that the author has or has not done a good job of explaining the causes of this problem. Be sure to credit the article correctly.

5. **Visual Assignment.** Write an essay explaining the causes, effects, or both captured or implied in the visuals below and on the next page. Follow the advice in this chapter as you establish the purpose of your explanation, effectively identify and organize the causes or effects, and support your points with details that you observe in the images.

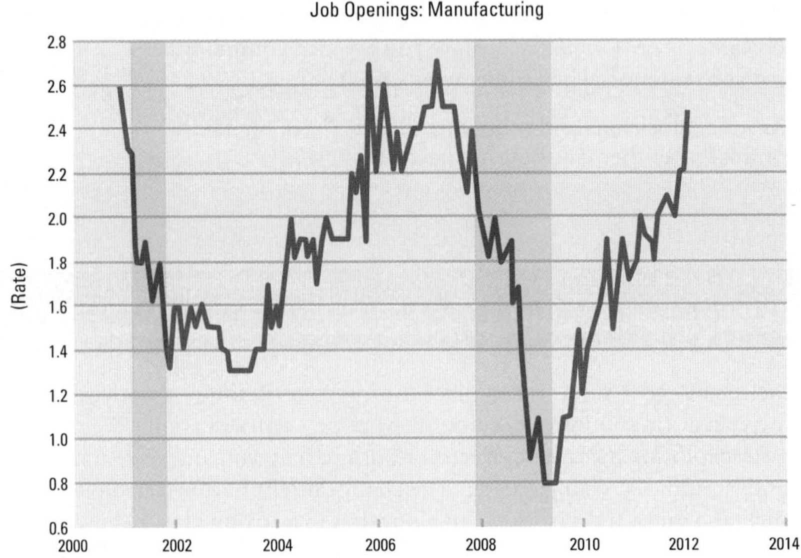


This chart shows an increase in U.S. manufacturing job openings. The shaded areas indicate periods of recession. *Source*: U.S. Department of Labor: Bureau of Labor Statistics

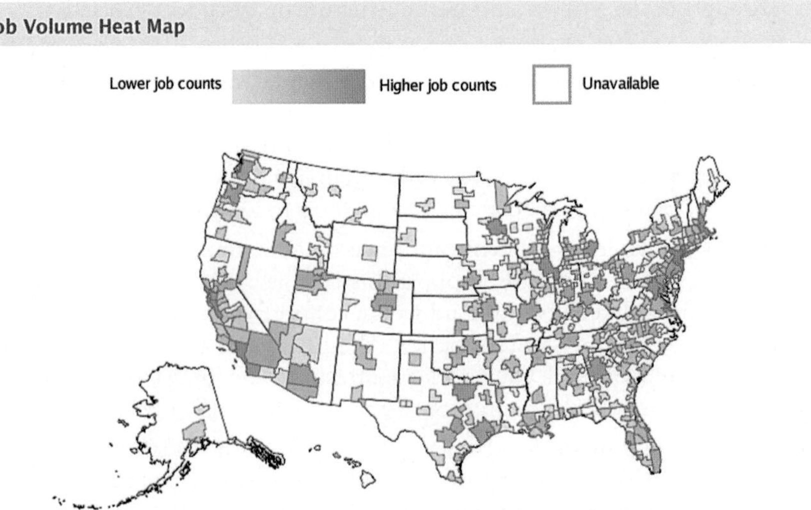


The number of U.S. manufacturing jobs increased in 2013, particularly in areas such as New York, San Jose, and Los Angeles (shown in dark blue). To track industry hiring trends, WANTED, Analytics gathers data on help-wanted ads posted online by manufacturers. *Source*: WANTED, Analytics

A factory closed during recession in 2009.

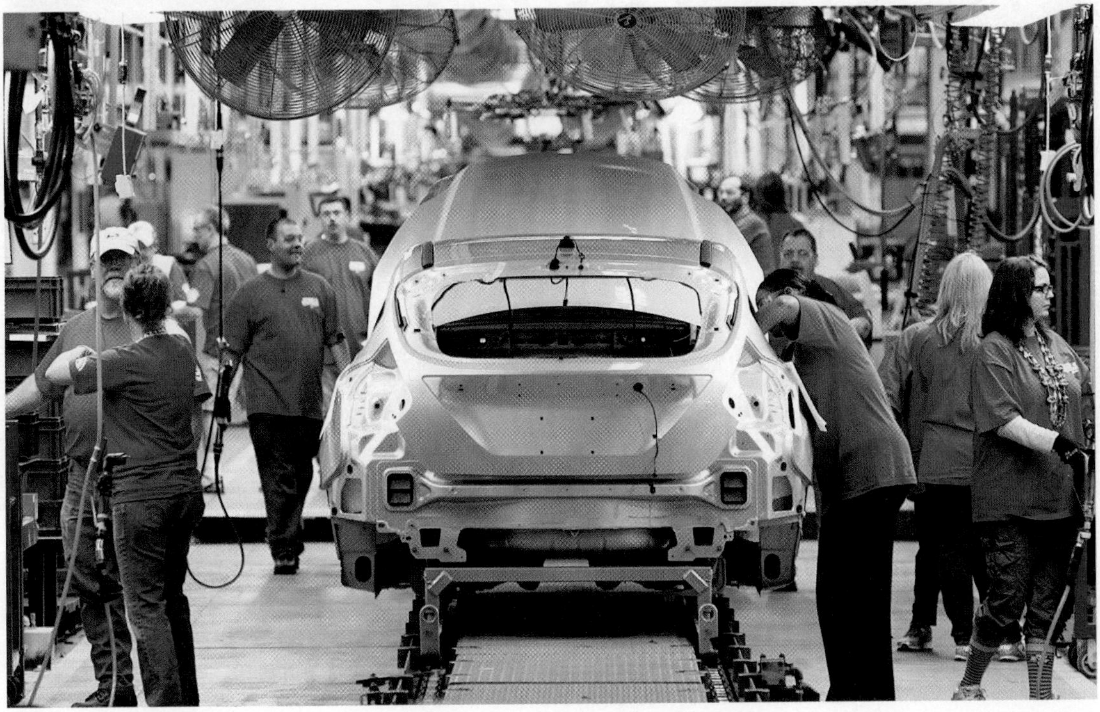

Workers assembling Ford Focus vehicles in a plant in Wayne, Michigan in 2011.

# 9 Taking a Stand

### Responding to an Image

The signs in this image identify a group and its position. What issue motivates this group? What concerns might have led to this position? Based on the image, what event do you think it portrays? What might the photographer have wanted to convey?

Both in and outside of class, you'll hear controversial issues discussed — health care costs, immigration policy, bullying, gun legislation, disaster responses, global outsourcing of jobs, copyright issues. Such controversies may be national, regional, or local. Even in academic fields, experts don't always agree, and issues may remain controversies for years. Taking a stand in response to such issues will help you understand the controversy and clarify what you believe. Such writing is common in editorials, letters to the editor, or columns on the op-ed page in print and online news outlets. It is also the foundation of persuasive brochures, partisan blogs, and Web pages that take a stand.

Writing of this kind has a twofold purpose — to state, and to win your readers' respect for, an opinion. What you say might or might not change a reader's opinion. But if you fulfill your purpose, a reader at least will see good reasons for your views. In taking a stand, you do these things:

- You state your opinion or stand.
- You give reasons with evidence to support your position.
- You enlist your readers' trust.
- You consider and respect what your readers probably think and feel.

## Why Taking a Stand Matters

### In a College Course

- You take a stand in an essay or exam when you respond, pro or con, to a statement such as "The Web, like movable type for printing, is an invention that has transformed human communication."
- You take a stand when you write research papers that support your position on juvenile sentencing, state support for higher education, or tax breaks for new home buyers.

### In the Workplace

- You take a stand when you persuade others that your case report supports a legal action that will benefit your clients or that your customer-service initiative will attract new business.

### In Your Community

- You take a stand when you write a letter to the editor appealing to voters to support a local bond issue.

? When have you taken a stand in your writing? In what circumstances are you likely to do so again?

## Learning from Other Writers

In the following two essays, the writers take a stand on issues of importance to them. To help you begin to analyze the first reading, look at the notes in the margin. They identify features such as the thesis, or main idea, and the first of the points that support it in a paper that takes a stand.

### As You Read These Essays That Take a Stand

As you read these essays, ask yourself the following questions:

1. What stand does the writer take? Is it a popular opinion, or does it break from commonly accepted beliefs?
2. How does the writer appeal to readers?
3. How does the writer support his or her position? Is the evidence sufficient to gain your respect? Why or why not?

### Suzan Shown Harjo

### Last Rites for Indian Dead

As a result of persuasive efforts such as Suzan Shown Harjo's essay, the Native American Graves Protection and Repatriation Act was passed in 1990.

Introduction appeals to readers

What if museums, universities, and government agencies could put your dead relatives on display or keep them in boxes to be cut up and otherwise studied? What if you believed that the spirits of the dead could not rest until their human remains were placed in a sacred area? 1

THESIS taking a stand

The ordinary American would say there ought to be a law—and there is, for ordinary Americans. The problem for American Indians is that there are too many laws of the kind that make us the archaeological property of the United States and too few of the kind that protect us from such insults. 2

Point 1

Supporting evidence

Some of my own Cheyenne relatives' skulls are in the Smithsonian Institution today, along with those of at least 4,500 other Indian people who were violated in the 1800s by the U.S. Army for an "Indian Crania Study." It wasn't enough that these unarmed Cheyenne people were mowed down by the cavalry at the infamous Sand Creek massacre; many were decapitated and their heads shipped to Washington as freight. (The Army Medical Museum's collection is now in the Smithsonian.) Some had been exhumed° only hours after being buried. Imagine their grieving families' reaction on finding their loved ones disinterred° and headless. 3

**exhumed:** Dug up out of the earth. **disinterred:** Taken out of a place of burial.

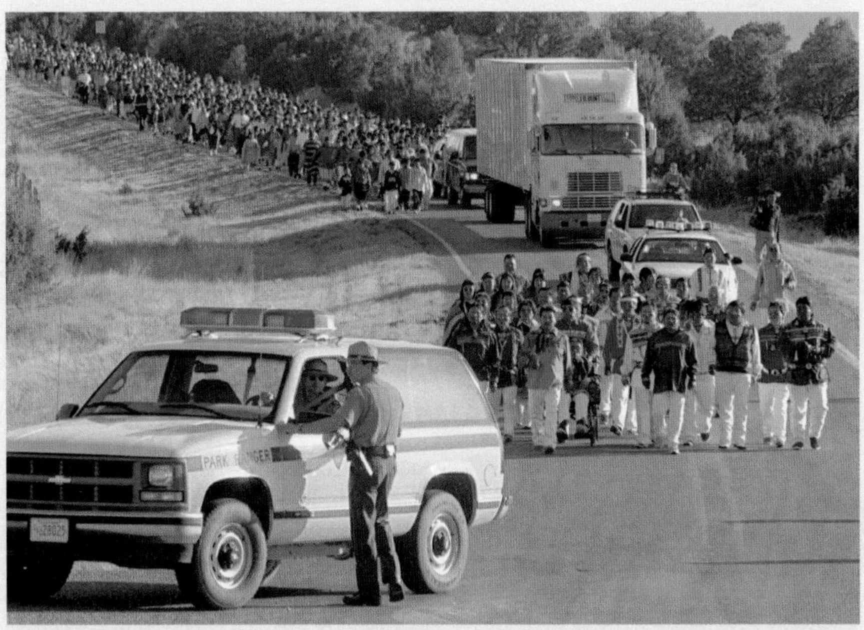


Native Americans march with a truck returning 2,000 skeletal remains of Jemez Pueblo Indian ancestors for reburial in New Mexico. The remains had been in the collections of Harvard University.

Some targets of the army's study were killed in noncombat situations and beheaded immediately. The officer's account of the decapitation of the Apache chief Mangas Coloradas in 1863 shows the pseudoscientific nature of the exercise. "I weighed the brain and measured the skull," the good doctor wrote, "and found that while the skull was smaller, the brain was larger than that of Daniel Webster." 4 — Supporting evidence

These journal accounts exist in excruciating detail, yet missing are any records of overall comparisons, conclusions, or final reports of the army study. Since it is unlike the army not to leave a paper trail, one must wonder about the motive for its collection. 5

The total Indian body count in the Smithsonian collection is more than 19,000, and it is not the largest in the country. It is not inconceivable that the 1.5 million of us living today are outnumbered by our dead stored in museums, educational institutions, federal agencies, state historical societies, and private collections. The Indian people are further dehumanized by being exhibited alongside the mastodons and dinosaurs and other extinct creatures. 6

Where we have buried our dead in peace, more often than not the sites have been desecrated. For more than two hundred years, relic-hunting has been a popular pursuit. Lately, the market in Indian artifacts has brought this abhorrent activity to a fever pitch in some areas. And when scavengers 7 come upon Indian burial sites, everything found becomes fair game, including sacred burial offerings, teeth, and skeletal remains.

One unusually well-publicized example of Indian grave desecration oc- 8
curred two years ago in a western Kentucky field known as Slack Farm, the site of an Indian village five centuries ago. Ten men—one with a business card stating "Have Shovel, Will Travel"—paid the landowner $10,000 to lease digging rights between planting seasons. They dug extensively on the forty-acre farm, rummaging through an estimated 650 graves, collecting burial goods, tools, and ceremonial items. Skeletons were strewn about like litter.

Question used as transition

What motivates people to do something like this? Financial gain is the 9
first answer. Indian relic-collecting has become a multimillion-dollar industry. The price tag on a bead necklace can easily top $1,000; rare pieces fetch tens of thousands.

And it is not just collectors of the macabre° who pay for skeletal re- 10
mains. Scientists say that these deceased Indians are needed for research that someday could benefit the health and welfare of living Indians. But just how many dead Indians must they examine? Nineteen thousand?

There is doubt as to whether permanent curation of our dead really 11
benefits Indians. Dr. Emery A. Johnson, former assistant Surgeon General, recently observed, "I am not aware of any current medical diagnostic or treatment procedure that has been derived from research on such skeletal remains. Nor am I aware of any during the thirty-four years that I have been involved in American Indian . . . health care."

Indian remains are still being collected for racial biological studies. 12
While the intentions may be honorable, the ethics of using human remains this way without the full consent of relatives must be questioned.

Some relief for Indian people has come on the state level. Almost half of 13
the states, including California, have passed laws protecting Indian burial sites and restricting the sale of Indian bones, burial offerings, and other sacred items. Representative Charles E. Bennett (D-Fla.) and Senator John McCain (R-Ariz.) have introduced bills that are a good start in invoking the federal government's protection. However, no legislation has attacked the problem head-on by imposing stiff penalties at the marketplace, or by changing laws that make dead Indians the nation's property.

Some universities—notably Stanford, Nebraska, Minnesota, and Seattle— 14
have returned, or agreed to return, Indian human remains; it is fitting that institutions of higher education should lead the way.

Congress is now deciding what to do with the government's extensive 15
collection of Indian human remains and associated funerary objects. The secretary of the Smithsonian, Robert McC. Adams, has been valiantly° attempting to apply modern ethics to yesterday's excesses. This week, he announced that the Smithsonian would conduct an inventory and return all Indian skeletal remains that could be identified with specific tribes or living kin.

**macabre:** Gruesome, ghastly. **valiantly:** Bravely.

But there remains a reluctance generally among collectors of Indian remains to take action of a scope that would have a quantitative impact and a healing quality. If they will not act on their own – and it is highly unlikely that they will – then Congress must act. 16

Transition to concluding proposal

The country must recognize that the bodies of dead American Indian people are not artifacts to be bought and sold as collector's items. It is not appropriate to store tens of thousands of our ancestors for possible future research. They are our family. They deserve to be returned to their sacred burial grounds and given a chance to rest. 17

The plunder of our people's graves has gone on too long. Let us rebury our dead and remove this shameful past from America's future. 18

Conclusion proposes action

## Questions to Start You Thinking

Meaning

1. What is the issue Harjo identifies? How extensive does she show it to be?
2. What is Harjo's position on this issue? Where does she first state it?
3. What evidence does Harjo present to refute the claim that housing skeletal remains of Native Americans in museums is necessary for medical research and may benefit living Indians?

Writing Strategies

4. What assumptions do you think Harjo makes about her audience?
5. What types of evidence does Harjo use to support her argument? How convincing is the evidence to you?
6. How does Harjo use her status as a Native American to enhance her position? Would her argument be as credible if it were written by someone of another background?
7. How does she appeal to the emotions of the readers in the essay? In what ways do these strategies strengthen or detract from her logical reasons?
8. Why does Harjo discuss what legislatures and universities are doing in response to the situation?

**Marjorie Lee Garretson** **Student Essay**

## More Pros Than Cons in a Meat-Free Life

Marjorie Lee Garretson's opinion piece originally appeared in *The Daily Mississippian*, the student newspaper of the University of Mississippi, in April 2010.

What would you say if I told you there was a way to improve your overall health, decrease environmental waste, and save animals from inhumane treatment at the same time? You would probably ask how this is possible. The answer is quite simple: 1

go vegetarian. Vegetarians are often labeled as different or odd, but if you take a closer look at their actions, vegetarians reap multiple benefits meat eaters often overlook or choose to ignore for convenience.

Do you find Garretson's discussion of the health benefits of vegetarianism convincing? Why or why not?

The health benefits vegetarians acquire lead us to wonder why more people are not jumping on the meat-free bandwagon. On average, vegetarians have a lower body mass index,° significantly decreased cancer rates, and longer life expectancies. In addition, Alzheimer's disease° and osteoporosis° were linked to diets containing dairy, eggs, and meat. 2

Is it possible to decrease damage to the environment from factory farms without becoming a vegetarian? What other options might there be?

The environment also encounters benefits from vegetarians. It takes less energy and waste to produce vegetables and grains than the energy required to produce meat. Producing one pound of meat is estimated to require 16 pounds of grain and up to 5,000 gallons of water, which comes from adding the water used to grow the grain crop as well as the animal's personal water consumption. Also, according to the Environmental Protection Agency, the runoff of fecal matter from meat factories is the single most detrimental° pollutant to our water supply. In fact, it is said to be the most significant pollutant in comparison to sources of all other industries combined. 3

The inhumane treatment of animals is common at most animal factories. The living conditions chickens, cows, pigs, and other livestock are forced into are far removed from their natural habitats. The goal of animal agriculture nowadays seems to be minimizing costs without attention to the sacrifices being made to do so. Animals are crammed into small cages where they often cannot even turn around. Exercise is denied to the animals to increase energy toward the production of meat. Female cows are pumped with hormones to allow their bodies to produce triple the amount of milk they are naturally capable of. Chickens are stuffed tightly into wire cages, and conditions are manipulated to increase egg production cycles. When chickens no longer lay eggs and cows cannot produce milk, they are transported to slaughterhouses where their lives are taken from them—often piece by piece. 4

Do you agree that Americans are hypocritical about the different treatment of household pets and farm animals? Why or why not?

Animal factory farms do a great job convincing Americans that their industry is vital to our health because of the protein, calcium, and other nutrients available in chicken, beef, and milk. We are bombarded with "Got Milk?" ads featuring various celebrities with white milk mustaches. We are told the egg is a healthy breakfast choice and lean protein is the basis of many good weight loss diets. What all of the ads and campaigns for animal products leave out are all the hormones injected into the animals to maximize production. Also, the tight living conditions allow for feces to contaminate the animals, their environment, and the potential meat they are 5

**body mass index:** A measurement of body fat, based on height and weight. **Alzheimer's disease:** An incurable brain disorder causing memory loss and dementia. **osteoporosis:** A disease that increases risk of bone fractures. **detrimental:** Harmful.

growing. It is ironic how irate° Americans react to puppy mills and the inhumane treatment of household pets, but for our meat and dairy products we look the other way. We pretend it is fine to confine cows, pigs, and chickens to tiny spaces and give them hormones and treat them inhumanely in their life and often in the way they are killed. We then cook and consume them at our dinner tables with our families and friends.

Therefore, I encourage you to consider a meat-free lifestyle not only for the sake of the animals and the environment, but most importantly your personal health. All of your daily nutrients can be found in plant-based sources, and oftentimes when you make the switch to being a vegetarian, your food choices expand because you are willing to use vegetables and grains in innovative ways at the dinner table. Going vegetarian is a life-changing decision and one you can be proud of because you know it is for your own health as well as the greater good. 6

## Questions to Start You Thinking

### Meaning

1. What points does Garretson make to support her position that vegetarianism has multiple benefits?
2. What, according to Garretson, are the environmental consequences of meat-eating?
3. In the author's view, why is it especially troubling that we are willing to "look the other way" (paragraph 5) on the inhumane treatment of farm animals?

### Writing Strategies

4. What kind of support does Garretson use to back up her claims about the benefits of vegetarianism? Do you find her argument effective? Why or why not?
5. To what extent does Garretson account for other points of view? How does the inclusion (or absence) of opposing views affect your opinion on the issue?
6. This article was written as an editorial for a student newspaper. How might Garretson change the article if she were submitting it as an essay or research paper?
7. Using highlighters or marginal notes, identify the essay's introduction, thesis, major points or reasons, supporting evidence for each point, and conclusion. How effective is the organization of this essay?

**irate:** Angry.

## UNICEF Editors — Video

### Dirty Water Campaign

In 2009, UNICEF's Tap Project bottled the water that millions of people drink worldwide and "sold" it from a Dirty Water vending machine. This campaign garnered media attention and raised money to help people access clean, safe water. To watch a video that documents the project, go to Chapter 9: **bedfordstmartins.com/bedguide**.

The Dirty Water vending machine collected donations for the TAP Project.

# Learning by Writing

## The Assignment: Taking a Stand

For an interactive Learning by Doing activity on Writing Your Representative, go to Ch. 9: **bedfordstmartins .com/bedguide**.

Find a controversy that rouses your interest. It might be a current issue, a long-standing one, or a matter of personal concern: military benefits for national guard troops sent to war zones, the contribution of sports to a school's educational mission, or the need for menu changes at the cafeteria to accommodate ethnic, religious, and personal preferences. Your purpose isn't to solve a social or moral problem but to make clear exactly where you stand on an issue and to persuade your readers to respect your position, perhaps even to accept it. As you reflect on your topic, you may change your position, but don't shift positions in the middle of your essay.

Assume that your readers are people who may or may not be familiar with the controversy, so provide relevant background or an overview to help them understand the situation. They also may not have taken sides yet or may hold a position different from yours. You'll need to consider their views and choose strategies to enlist their support.

Each of these students took a clear stand:

> A writer who pays her own college costs disputed the opinion that working during the school year provides a student with valuable knowledge. Citing her painful experience, she maintained that devoting full time to studies is far better than juggling school and work.
>
> Another writer challenged his history textbook's portrayal of Joan of Arc as "an ignorant farm girl subject to religious hysteria."
>
> A member of the wrestling team argued that the number of weight categories in the sport should be increased because athletes who overtrain to qualify for the existing categories often damage their health.

For essays taking different stands on consumer culture, see the pair on pp. 611–20.

## Facing the Challenge Taking a Stand

The major challenge writers face when taking a stand is to gather enough relevant evidence to support their position. Without such evidence, you'll convince only those who agreed with you in the first place. You also won't persuade readers by ranting emotionally about an issue or insulting as ignorant those who hold different opinions. Moreover, few readers respect an evasive writer who avoids taking a stand.

What does work is respect—yours for the views of readers who will, in turn, respect your opinion, even if they don't agree with it. You convey—and gain—respect when you anticipate readers' objections or counterarguments, demonstrate knowledge of these alternate views, and present evidence that addresses others' concerns as it strengthens your argument.

To anticipate and find evidence that acknowledges other views, list groups that might have strong opinions on your topic. Then try putting

Joan of Arc (1412–1431), heroine, martyr, saint, and cultural icon who boldly led French forces against the English.

yourself in the shoes of a member of each group by writing a paragraph on the issue from that point of view.

- What would that person's opinion be?
- On what grounds might he or she object to your argument?
- How can you best address these concerns and overcome objections?

Your paragraph will suggest additional evidence to support your claims.

---

## Generating Ideas

For this assignment, you will need to select an issue, take a stand, develop a clear position, and assemble evidence that supports your view.

For more strategies for generating ideas, see Ch. 19.

**Find an Issue.** The topic for this paper should be an issue or controversy that interests both you and your audience. Try brainstorming a list of possible topics. Start with the headlines of a newspaper or newsmagazine, review the letters to the editor, check the political cartoons on the opinion page, or watch for stories on demonstrations or protests. You might also consult the library index to *CQ Researcher*, browse news or opinion Web sites, talk with friends, or consider topics raised in class. If you keep a journal, look over your entries to see what has perplexed or angered you. If you need to understand the issue better or aren't sure you want to take a stand on it, investigate by freewriting, reading, or turning to other sources.

Once you have a list of possible topics, drop those that seem too broad or complex or that you don't know much about. Weed out anything that might not hold your—or your readers'—interest. From your new list, pick the issue or controversy for which you can make the strongest argument.

**Start with a Question and a Thesis.** At this stage, many writers try to pose the issue as a question—one that will be answered through the position they take. Skip vague questions that most readers wouldn't debate, or convert them to questions that allow different stands.

| | |
|---|---|
| VAGUE QUESTION | Is stereotyping bad? |
| CLEARLY DEBATABLE | Should we fight gender stereotypes in advertising? |

You can help focus your position by stating it in a sentence—a thesis, or statement of your stand. Your statement can answer your question:

For more on stating a thesis, see pp. 399–408.

| | |
|---|---|
| WORKING THESIS | We should expect advertisers to fight rather than reinforce gender stereotypes. |
| OR | Most people who object to gender stereotypes in advertising need to get a sense of humor. |

Your thesis should invite continued debate by taking a strong position that can be argued rather than stating a fact.

| | |
|---|---|
| FACT | Hispanics constitute 16 percent of the community but only 3 percent of our school population. |
| WORKING THESIS | Our school should increase outreach to the Hispanic community, which is underrepresented on campus. |

## Learning by Doing Asking Your Question

Using your list of possible topics, start writing down questions you might want to answer. Then work with a classmate or small group, in person or chatting online, to review everyone's list. Weed out questions that seem vague or difficult to debate. For questions with potential, write out some working thesis statements until you settle on a statement you want to support.

**Use Formal Reasoning to Refine Your Position.** As you take a stand on a debatable matter, you are likely to use reasoning as well as specific evidence to support your position. A *syllogism* is a series of statements, or premises, used in traditional formal logic to lead deductively to a logical conclusion.

| | |
|---|---|
| MAJOR STATEMENT | All students must pay tuition. |
| MINOR STATEMENT | You are a student. |
| CONCLUSION | Therefore, you must pay tuition. |

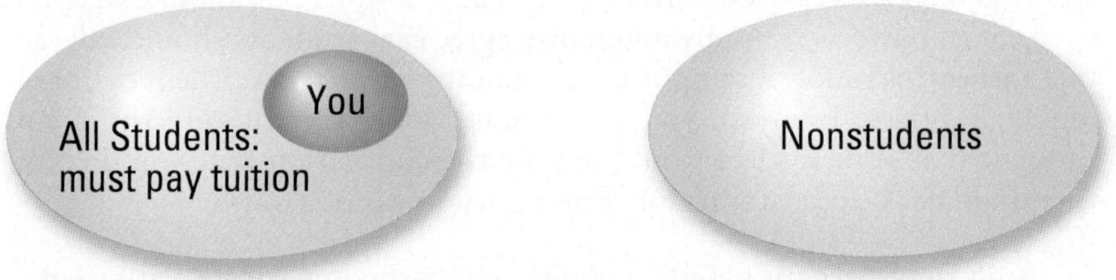

For a syllogism to be logical, ensuring that its conclusion always applies, its major and minor statements must be true, its definitions of terms must remain stable, and its classification of specific persons or items must be accurate. In real-life arguments, such tidiness may be hard to achieve.

For example, maybe we all agree with the major statement above that all students must pay tuition. However, some students' tuition is paid for them through a loan or scholarship. Others are admitted under special programs, such as a free-tuition benefit for families of college employees or a back-to-college program for retirees. Further, the word *student* is general; it might apply to students at public high schools who pay no tuition. Next, everyone might agree that you are a student, but maybe you haven't completed registration or the computer has mysteriously dropped you from the class list. Such complications can threaten the success of your conclusion, especially if your audience doesn't accept it. In fact, many civic and social arguments revolve around questions such as these: What—exactly—is the category or group affected? Is its definition or consequence stable—or does it vary? Who falls in or out of the category?

**Use Informal Toulmin Reasoning to Refine Your Position.** A contemporary approach to logic is presented by the philosopher Stephen Toulmin (1922–2009) in *The Uses of Argument* (2nd ed., 2003). He describes an informal way of arguing that acknowledges the power of assumptions in our day-to-day reasoning. This approach starts with a concise statement—the essence of an argument—that makes a claim and supplies a reason to support it.

CLAIM | REASON

Students should boycott the café because the food costs too much.

You develop a claim by supporting your reasons with evidence—your *data* or grounds. For example, your evidence might include facts about the cost of lunches on campus, especially in contrast to local fast-food options, and statistics about the limited resources of most students at your campus.

However, most practical arguments rely on a *warrant,* your thinking about the connection or relationship between your claim and your supporting data. Because you accept this connection and assume that it applies, you generally assume that others also take it for granted. For instance, nearly all students might accept your assumption that a campus café should serve the needs of its customers. Many might also agree that students should take action rather than allow a campus facility to take advantage of them by charging high prices. Even so, you could state your warrant directly if you thought that your readers would not see the connection that you do. You also could back up your warrant, if necessary, in various ways:

- using facts, perhaps based on quality and cost comparisons with food service operations on other campuses
- using logic, perhaps based on research findings about the relationship between cost and nutrition for institutional food as well as the importance of good nutrition for brain function and learning
- making emotional appeals, perhaps based on happy memories of the café or irritation with its options
- making ethical appeals, perhaps based on the college mission statement or other expressions of the school's commitment to students

As you develop your reasoning, you might adjust your claim or your data to suit your audience, your issue, or your refined thinking. For instance, you might *qualify* your argument (perhaps limiting your objections to most, but not all, of the lunch prices). You might also add a *rebuttal* by identifying an *exception* to it (perhaps excluding the fortunate, but few, students without financial worries due to good jobs or family support). Or you might simply reconsider your claim, concluding that the campus café is, after all, convenient for students and that the manager might be willing to offer more inexpensive options without a student boycott.

REVISED CLAIM — REASON

The café should offer less expensive options because most students can't afford a balanced meal at current prices.

Toulmin reasoning is especially effective for making claims like these:

- Fact — *Loss of polar ice can accelerate ocean warming.*
- Cause — *The software company went bankrupt because of its excessive borrowing and poor management.*
- Value — *Cell phone plan A is a better deal than cell phone plan B.*
- Policy — *Admissions policies at Triborough University should be less restrictive.*

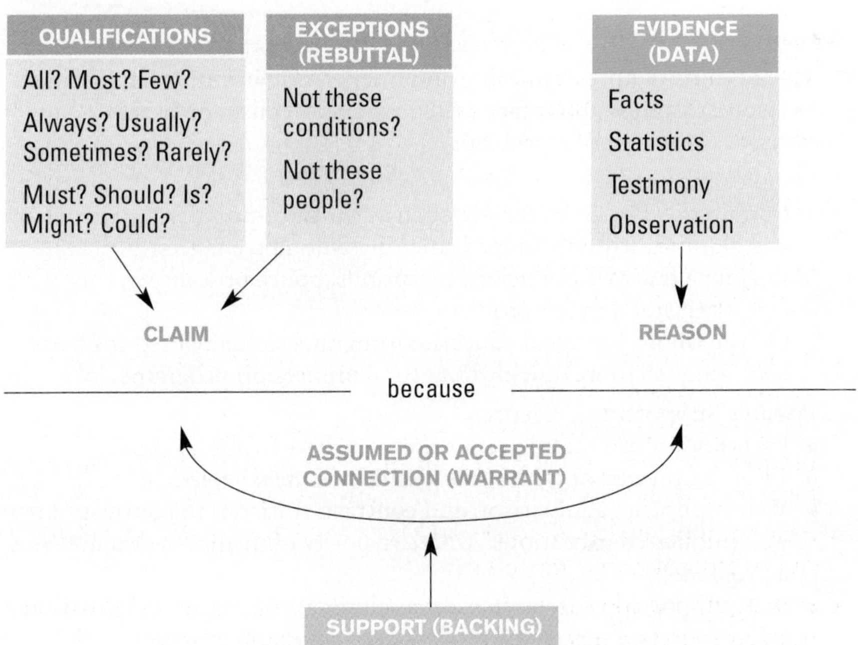

**DISCOVERY CHECKLIST**

- ☐ What issue or controversy concerns you? What current debate engages you?
- ☐ What position do you want to take? How can you state your stand? What evidence might you need to support it?
- ☐ How might you refine your working thesis? How could you make statements more accurate, definitions clearer, or categories more exact?
- ☐ What assumptions are you making? What clarification of or support for these assumptions might your audience need?
- ☐ How might you qualify your thesis? What exceptions should you note? What other views might you want to recognize?

**Select Evidence to Support Your Position.** When you state your claim, you state your overall position. You also may state supporting claims as topic sentences that establish your supporting points, introduce supporting evidence, and help your reader follow your reasoning. To decide how to support a claim, try to reduce it to its core question. Then figure out what reliable and persuasive evidence might answer the question.

As you begin to look for supporting evidence, consider the issue in terms of the three general types of claims—claims that require substantiation, provide evaluation, and endorse policy.

1. Claims of Substantiation: What Happened?

   These claims require examining and interpreting information in order to resolve disputes about facts, circumstances, causes or effects, definitions, or the extent of a problem.

   Sample Claims:

   a. Certain types of cigarette ads, such as the once-popular Joe Camel ads, significantly encouraged smoking among teenagers.
   b. Despite a few well-publicized exceptions, police brutality in this country is not a major problem.
   c. On the whole, bilingual education programs actually help students learn English more quickly than total immersion programs do.

   Possible Supporting Evidence:

   - Facts and information: parties involved, dates, times, places
   - Clear definitions of terms: *police brutality* or *total immersion*
   - Well-supported comparison and contrast: statistics to contrast "a few well-publicized exceptions" with a majority of instances that are "not a problem"
   - Well-supported cause-and-effect analysis: authoritative information to demonstrate how actions of tobacco companies "significantly encouraged smoking" or bilingual programs "help students learn English faster"

2. Claims of Evaluation: What Is Right?

   These claims consider right or wrong, appropriateness or inappropriateness, and worth or lack of worth involved in an issue.

   Sample Claims:

   a. Research using fetal tissue is unethical in a civilized society.
   b. English-only legislation promotes cultural intolerance in our society.
   c. Keeping children in foster care for years, instead of releasing them for adoption, is wrong.

   Possible Supporting Evidence:

   - Explanations or definitions of appropriate criteria for judging: deciding what's "unethical in a civilized society"
   - Corresponding details and reasons showing how the topic does or does not meet the criteria: details or applications of English-only legislation that meet the criteria for "cultural intolerance" or reasons with supporting details that show why years of foster care meet the criteria for being "wrong"

3. Claims of Policy: What Should Be Done?

   These claims challenge or defend approaches for achieving generally accepted goals.

   Sample Claims:

   a. The federal government should support the distribution of clean needles to reduce the rate of HIV infection among intravenous drug users.
   b. Denying children of undocumented workers enrollment in public schools will reduce the problem of illegal immigration.
   c. All teenagers accused of murder should be tried as adults.

   Possible Supporting Evidence:

   - Explanation and definition of the policy goal: assuming that most in your audience agree that it is desirable to reduce "the rate of HIV infection" or "the problem of illegal immigration" or to try murderers in the same way regardless of age
   - Corresponding details and reasons showing how your policy recommendation would meet the goal: results of "clean needle" trials or examples of crime statistics and cases involving teen murderers
   - Explanations or definitions of the policy's limits or applications, if needed: why some teens should not be tried as adults because of their situations

**Consider Your Audience as You Develop Your Claim.** The nature of your audience might influence the type of claim you choose to make. For example, suppose that the nurse or social worker at the high school you attended or that your children now attend proposed distributing free condoms to students. The following table illustrates how the responses of different audiences to this proposal might vary with the claim. As you develop your claims, try to put yourself in the place of your audience. For example, if you are a former student, what claim would most effectively persuade you? If you are the parent of a teenager, what claim would best address both your general views and your specific concerns about your own child?

| Audience | Type of Claim | Possible Effect on Audience |
|---|---|---|
| Conservative parents who believe that free condoms would promote immoral sexual behavior | *Evaluation:* In order to save lives and prevent unwanted pregnancies, distributing free condoms in high school is our moral duty. | Counterproductive if the parents feel that they are being accused of immorality for not agreeing with the proposal |
| Conservative parents who believe that free condoms would promote immoral sexual behavior | *Substantiation:* Distributing free condoms in high school can effectively reduce pregnancy rates and the spread of STDs, especially AIDS, without substantially increasing the rate of sexual activity among teenagers. | Possibly persuasive, based on effectiveness, if parents feel that their desire to protect their children from harm, no matter what, is recognized and the evidence deflates their main fear (promoting sexual activity) |
| School administrators who want to do what's right but don't want hordes of angry parents pounding down the school doors | *Policy:* Distributing free condoms in high school to prevent unwanted pregnancies and the spread of STDs, including AIDS, is best accomplished as part of a voluntary sex education program that strongly emphasizes abstinence as the primary preventative. | Possibly persuasive if administrators see that the proposal addresses health and pregnancy issues without setting off parental outrage (by proposing a voluntary program that would promote abstinence, thus addressing concerns of parents) |

For more about forms of evidence, see pp. 40–44.

For more about using sources, see Ch. 12 and the Quick Research Guide beginning on p. A-20.

**Assemble Supporting Evidence.** Your claim stated, you'll need evidence to support it. That evidence can be anything that demonstrates the soundness of your position and the points you make—facts, statistics, observations, expert testimony, illustrations, examples, and case studies.

The three most important sources of evidence are these:

1. *Facts, including statistics.* Facts are statements that can be verified by objective means; statistics are facts expressed in numbers. Facts usually form the basis of a successful argument.
2. *Expert testimony.* Experts are people with knowledge of a particular field gained from study and experience.
3. *Firsthand observation.* Your own observations can be persuasive if you can assure your readers that your account is accurate.

For more on logical fallacies, see pp. 180–81.

Of course, evidence must be used carefully to avoid defending logical fallacies—common mistakes in thinking—and making statements that lead to wrong conclusions. Examples are easy to misuse (claiming proof by example or too few examples). Because two professors you know are dissatisfied with state-mandated testing programs, you can't claim that all—or even most—professors are. Even if you surveyed more professors at your school, you could speak only generally of "many professors." To claim more, you might need to conduct scientific surveys, access reliable statistics from the library or Internet, or solicit the views of a respected expert in the area.

### Learning by Doing Supporting a Claim

Write out, in one complete sentence, the core claim or position you plan to support. Working in a small group, drop all these "position statements" into a hat, with no names attached. Then draw and read each aloud in turn, inviting the group to suggest useful supporting evidence and possible sources for it. Ask someone in the group to act as a recorder, listing suggestions on a separate page for each claim. Finally, match up writers with claims, and share reactions. (If you are working online, follow your instructor's directions, possibly sending your statement privately to your instructor for anonymous posting for a threaded discussion.) If this activity causes you to alter your stand, be thankful: it will be easier to revise now rather than later.

**Record Evidence.** For this assignment, you will need to record your evidence in written form in a notebook or a computer file. Note exactly where each piece of information comes from. Keep the form of your notes flexible so that you can easily rearrange them as you plan your draft.

**Test and Select Evidence to Persuade Your Audience.** Now that you've collected some evidence, sift through it to decide which information to use. Evidence is useful and trustworthy when it is accurate, reliable, up-to-date, to the point, representative, appropriately complex, and sufficient and strong enough to back the claim and persuade readers. You may find that your evidence supports a different stand than you intended to take. Might you find facts, testimony, and observations to support your original position after all? Or should you rethink your position? If so, revise your working thesis. Does your evidence cluster around several points or reasons? If so, use your evidence to plan the sequence of your essay.

For more on testing evidence, see pp. A-21–A-24.

In addition, consider whether information presented visually would strengthen your case or make your evidence easier for readers to grasp.

For more on the use of visuals and their placement, see section B in the Quick Format Guide, pp. A-8–A-12.

- Graphs can effectively show facts or figures.
- Tables can convey terms or comparisons.
- Photographs or other illustrations can substantiate situations.

Test each visual as you would test other evidence for accuracy, reliability, and relevance. Mention each visual in your text, and place the visual close to that reference. Cite the source of any visual you use and of any data you consolidate in your own graph or table.

Most effective arguments take opposing viewpoints into consideration whenever possible. Use these questions to help you assess your evidence from this standpoint.

ANALYZE YOUR READERS' POINTS OF VIEW

- What are their attitudes? Interests? Priorities?
- What do they already know about the issue?
- What do they expect you to say?
- Do you have enough appropriate evidence that they'll find convincing?

FOCUS ON THOSE WITH DIFFERENT OR OPPOSING OPINIONS

- What are their opinions or claims?
- What is their evidence?
- Who supports their positions?
- Do you have enough appropriate evidence to show why their claims are weak, only partially true, misguided, or just plain wrong?

ACKNOWLEDGE AND REBUT THE COUNTERARGUMENTS

- What are the strengths of other positions? What might you want to concede or grant to be accurate or relevant?
- What are the limitations of other positions? What might you want to question or challenge?
- What facts, statistics, testimony, observations, or other evidence supports questioning, qualifying, challenging, or countering other views?

## Planning, Drafting, and Developing

**Reassess Your Position and Your Thesis.** Now that you have looked into the issue, what is your current position? If necessary, revise the thesis that you formulated earlier. Then summarize your reasons for holding this view, and list your supporting evidence.

For practice developing and supporting effective thesis statements, go to the interactive "Take Action" charts in Re:Writing at **bedfordstmartins .com/bedguide**.

| | |
|---|---|
| WORKING THESIS | We should expect advertisers to fight rather than reinforce gender stereotypes. |
| REFINED THESIS | Consumers should spend their shopping dollars thoughtfully in order to hold advertisers accountable for reinforcing rather than resisting gender stereotypes. |

## Learning by Doing Refining Your Plans

Follow the steps outlined in the previous section: update your thesis to match your current view, summarize the reasons behind that position, and list your supporting evidence. Ask a classmate for a second opinion on these plans, and continue reworking them if your exchange generates significant questions or ideas.

**Organize Your Material to Persuade Your Audience.** Arrange your notes into the order you think you'll follow, perhaps making an outline. One useful pattern is the classical form of argument:

For more on outlines, see pp. 411–19.

1. Introduce the subject to gain the readers' interest.
2. State your main point or thesis.
3. If useful, supply historical background or an overview of the situation.
4. Present your points or reasons, and provide evidence to support them.
5. Refute the opposition.
6. Reaffirm your main point.

When you expect readers to be hostile to your position, stating your position too early might alienate resistant readers or make them defensive. Instead, you may want to refute the opposition first, then replace those views by building a logical chain of evidence that leads to your main point, and finally state your position. Of course, you can always try both approaches to see which one works better. Note also that some papers will be mostly based on refutation (countering opposing views) and some mostly on confirmation (directly supporting your position). Others might even alternate refutation and confirmation rather than separate them.

**Define Your Terms.** To prevent misunderstanding, make clear any unfamiliar or questionable terms used in your thesis. If your position is "Humanists are dangerous," you will want to give a short definition of what you mean by *humanists* and by *dangerous* early in the paper.

**Attend to Logical, Emotional, and Ethical Appeals.** The logical appeal engages readers' intellect; the emotional appeal touches their hearts; the ethical appeal draws on their sense of fairness and reasonableness. A persuasive argument usually operates on all three levels. For example, you might use all three appeals to support a thesis about the need to curb accidental gunshot deaths, as the following table illustrates.

For more on appeals, see pp. 44–45.

| Type of Appeal | Ways of Making the Appeal | Possible Supporting Evidence |
|---|---|---|
| Logical (logos) | ■ Rely on clear reasoning and sound evidence to influence a reader's thinking.<br>■ Demonstrate what you claim, and don't claim what you can't demonstrate.<br>■ Test and select your evidence. | ■ Supply current and reliable statistics about gun ownership and accidental shootings.<br>■ Prepare a bar graph that shows the number of incidents each year in Lion Valley during the past ten years, using data from the county records.<br>■ Describe the immediate and long-term consequences of a typical shooting accident. |
| Emotional (pathos) | ■ Choose examples and language that will influence a reader's feelings.<br>■ Include effective images, but don't overdo them.<br>■ Complement logical appeals, but don't replace them. | ■ Describe the wrenching scenario of a father whose college-age son unexpectedly returns home at 3 A.M. The father mistakes his son for an intruder and shoots him, throwing the family into turmoil.<br>■ Use quotations and descriptions from newspaper accounts to show reactions of family and friends. |
| Ethical (ethos) | ■ Use a tone and approach that appeal to your reader's sense of fairness and reasonableness.<br>■ Spell out your values and beliefs, and acknowledge values and beliefs of others with different opinions.<br>■ Establish your credentials, if any, and the credentials of experts you cite.<br>■ Instill confidence in your readers so that they see you as a caring, trustworthy person with reliable views. | ■ Establish your reasonable approach by acknowledging the views of hunters and others who store guns at home and follow recommended safety procedures.<br>■ Supply the credentials or affiliation of experts ("Ray Fontaine, public safety director for the town of Lion Valley").<br>■ Note ways in which experts have established their authority ("During my interview with Ms. Dutton, she related recent incidents involving gun accidents in the home, testifying to her extensive knowledge of this issue in our community.") |

## Learning by Doing Making Columns of Appeals

Use columns to help you write about your logical, emotional, and ethical appeals. Go to the Format menu in your word processor, select Columns, and click on the preset three-column pattern. (Or draw three columns on paper.) Under "Logical Appeals," write the claims and support that rely on reasoning and sound evidence. Under "Emotional Appeals," note the claims and support that may affect readers' emotions. Under "Ethical Appeals," add your claims and support based on values, both your values and those of opposing points of view as you understand them. As you reread each column, consider how to relate your claims and support across columns, how to organize your ideas persuasively, and how best to merge or separate your logical, emotional, and ethical appeals. Add color coding if you want to identify related ideas.

| Logical Appeals | Emotional Appeals | Ethical Appeals |
|---|---|---|
| | | |
| | | |

**Credit Your Sources.** As you write, make your sources of evidence clear. One simple way to do so is to incorporate your source into the text: "As analyzed in an article in the October 15, 2012, issue of *Time*" or "According to my history professor, Dr. Harry Cleghorn . . ."

For pointers on integrating and documenting sources, see Ch. 12 and D6 (p. A-31) and E1–E2 (pp. A-32–A-38) in the Quick Research Guide.

## Revising and Editing

When you're writing a paper that takes a stand, you may fall in love with the evidence you've gone to such trouble to collect. Taking out information is hard to do, but if it is irrelevant, redundant, or weak, the evidence won't help your case. Play the crusty critic as you reread your paper. Consider outlining what it actually includes so that you can check for missing or unnecessary points or evidence. Pay special attention to the suggestions of friends or classmates who read your draft for you. Apply their advice by ruthlessly cutting unneeded material, as in the following passage:

For more revising and editing strategies, see Ch. 23.

> The school boundary system requires children who are homeless or whose families move frequently to change schools repeatedly. ~~They often lack clean clothes, winter coats, and required school supplies.~~ As a result, these children struggle to establish strong relationships with teachers, to find caring advocates at school, and even to make friends to join for recess or lunch.

### Peer Response Taking a Stand

Enlist several other students to read your draft critically and tell you whether they accept your arguments. For a paper in which you take a stand, ask your peer editors to answer questions such as these:

For general questions for a peer editor, see p. 463.

- Can you state the writer's claim?
- Do you have any problems following or accepting the reasons for the writer's position? Would you make any changes in the reasoning?

- How persuasive is the writer's evidence? What questions do you have about it? Can you suggest good evidence the writer has overlooked?
- Has the writer provided enough transitions to guide you through the argument?
- Has the writer made a strong case? Are you persuaded to his or her point of view? If not, is there any point or objection that the writer could address to make the argument more compelling?
- If this paper were yours, what is the one thing you would be sure to work on before handing it in?

For online Take Action help, visit **bedfordstmartins .com/bedguide** and go to Re:Writing.

Use the Take Action chart (p. 179) to help you figure out how to improve your draft. Skim across the top to identify questions you might ask about strengthening support for your stand. When you answer a question with "Yes" or "Maybe," move straight down the column to Locate Specifics under that question. Use the activities there to pinpoint gaps, problems, or weaknesses. Then move straight down the column to Take Action. Use the advice that suits your problem as you revise.

**REVISION CHECKLIST**

- ☐ Is your main point, or thesis, clear? Do you stick to it rather than drifting into contradictions?
- ☐ Where might you need better reasons or more evidence?
- ☐ Have you tried to keep in mind your readers and what would appeal to them? Where have you answered their likely objections?
- ☐ Have you defined all necessary terms and explained your points clearly?
- ☐ Is your tone suitable for your readers? Would any wording alienate them, or, at the other extreme, sound weak or apologetic?
- ☐ Might your points seem stronger if arranged in a different sequence?
- ☐ Have you unfairly omitted any evidence that would hurt your case?
- ☐ In rereading your paper, do you have any excellent, fresh thoughts? If so, where might you make room for them?

For more editing and proofreading strategies, see pp. 471–75.

After you have revised your argument, edit and proofread it. Carefully check the grammar, word choice, punctuation, and mechanics—and then correct any problems you find. Wherever you have given facts and figures as evidence, check for errors in names and numbers.

## Take Action Strengthening Support for a Stand

Ask each question at the top of the chart to consider whether your draft might need work on that issue. If so, follow the ASK—LOCATE SPECIFICS—TAKE ACTION sequence to revise.

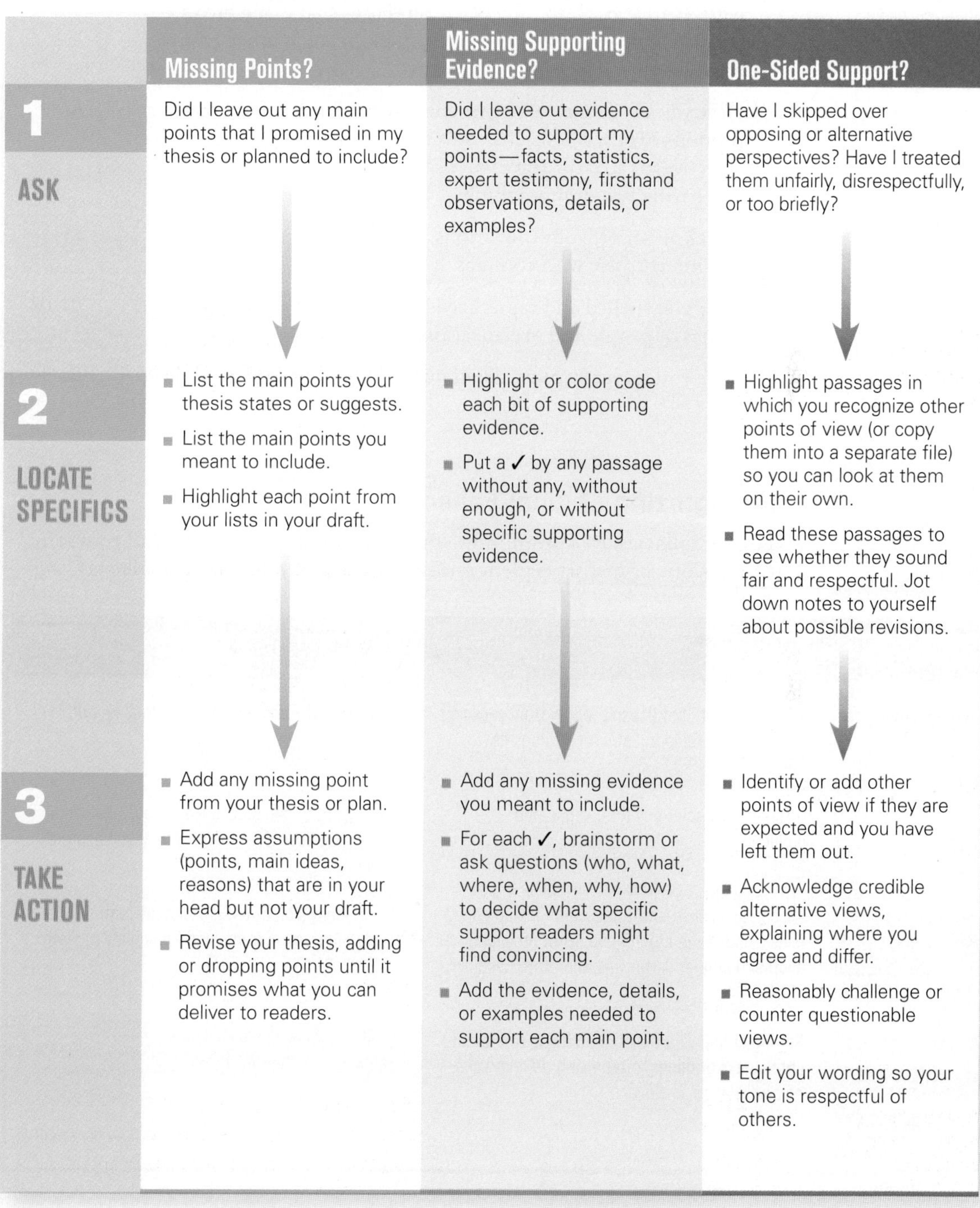

| | Missing Points? | Missing Supporting Evidence? | One-Sided Support? |
|---|---|---|---|
| 1 ASK | Did I leave out any main points that I promised in my thesis or planned to include? | Did I leave out evidence needed to support my points—facts, statistics, expert testimony, firsthand observations, details, or examples? | Have I skipped over opposing or alternative perspectives? Have I treated them unfairly, disrespectfully, or too briefly? |
| 2 LOCATE SPECIFICS | ■ List the main points your thesis states or suggests.<br>■ List the main points you meant to include.<br>■ Highlight each point from your lists in your draft. | ■ Highlight or color code each bit of supporting evidence.<br>■ Put a ✓ by any passage without any, without enough, or without specific supporting evidence. | ■ Highlight passages in which you recognize other points of view (or copy them into a separate file) so you can look at them on their own.<br>■ Read these passages to see whether they sound fair and respectful. Jot down notes to yourself about possible revisions. |
| 3 TAKE ACTION | ■ Add any missing point from your thesis or plan.<br>■ Express assumptions (points, main ideas, reasons) that are in your head but not your draft.<br>■ Revise your thesis, adding or dropping points until it promises what you can deliver to readers. | ■ Add any missing evidence you meant to include.<br>■ For each ✓, brainstorm or ask questions (who, what, where, when, why, how) to decide what specific support readers might find convincing.<br>■ Add the evidence, details, or examples needed to support each main point. | ■ Identify or add other points of view if they are expected and you have left them out.<br>■ Acknowledge credible alternative views, explaining where you agree and differ.<br>■ Reasonably challenge or counter questionable views.<br>■ Edit your wording so your tone is respectful of others. |

For more help, find the relevant checklist sections in the Quick Editing Guide on p. A-39. Turn also to the Quick Format Guide beginning on p. A-1.

**EDITING CHECKLIST**

- ☐ Is it clear what each pronoun refers to? Does each pronoun agree with (match) its antecedent? Do pronouns used as subjects agree with their verbs? Carefully check sentences that make broad claims about *everyone, no one, some, a few,* or some other group identified by an indefinite pronoun. A6
- ☐ Have you used an adjective whenever describing a noun or pronoun? Have you used an adverb whenever describing a verb, adjective, or adverb? Have you used the correct form when comparing two or more things? A7
- ☐ Have you set off your transitions, other introductory elements, and interrupters with commas, if these are needed? C1
- ☐ Have you spelled and capitalized everything correctly, especially names of people and organizations? D1, D2
- ☐ Have you correctly punctuated quotations from sources and experts? C3

## Recognizing Logical Fallacies

For more on faulty thinking, see pp. 51–52.

Logical fallacies are common mistakes in thinking that may lead to wrong conclusions or distort evidence. Here are a few familiar logical fallacies.

| Term | Explanation | Example |
|---|---|---|
| Non Sequitur | Stating a claim that doesn't follow from your first premise or statement; Latin for "It does not follow" | Jenn should marry Mateo. In college he got all A's. |
| Oversimplification | Offering easy solutions for complicated problems | If we want to end substance abuse, let's send every drug user to prison for life. (Even aspirin users?) |
| *Post Hoc Ergo Propter Hoc* | Assuming a cause-and-effect relationship where none exists, even though one event preceded another; Latin for "after this, therefore because of this" | After Jenny's black cat crossed my path, everything went wrong, and I failed my midterm. |
| Allness | Stating or implying that something is true of an entire class of things, often using *all, everyone, no one, always,* or *never* | Students enjoy studying. (All students? All subjects? All the time?) |

*(continued on next page)*

| Term | Explanation | Example |
|---|---|---|
| Proof by Example or Too Few Examples | Presenting an example as proof rather than as illustration or clarification; overgeneralizing (the basis of much prejudice) | Armenians are great chefs. My neighbor is Armenian, and can he cook! |
| Begging the Question | Proving a statement already taken for granted, often by repeating it in different words or by defining a word in terms of itself | Rapists are dangerous because they are menaces.<br>Happiness is the state of being happy. |
| Circular Reasoning | Supporting a statement with itself; a form of begging the question | He is a liar because he simply isn't telling the truth. |
| Either/Or Reasoning | Oversimplifying by assuming that an issue has only two sides, a statement must be true or false, a question demands a yes or no answer, or a problem has only two possible solutions (and one that's acceptable) | What are we going to do about global warming? Either we stop using all of the energy-consuming vehicles and products that cause it, or we just learn to live with it. |
| Argument from Dubious Authority | Using an unidentified authority to shore up a weak argument or an authority whose expertise lies outside the issue, such as a television personality selling insurance | According to some of the most knowing scientists in America, smoking two packs a day is as harmless as eating oatmeal cookies. |
| Argument *ad Hominem* | Attacking an individual's opinion by attacking his or her character, thus deflecting attention from the merit of a proposal; Latin for "against the man" | Diaz may argue that we need to save the polar bears, but he's the type who gets emotional over nothing. |
| Argument from Ignorance | Maintaining that a claim has to be accepted because it hasn't been disproved or that it has to be rejected because it has not been proved | Despite years of effort, no one has proved that ghosts don't exist; therefore, we should expect to see them at any time.<br>No one has ever shown that life exists on any other planet; clearly the notion of other living things in the universe is absurd. |
| Argument by Analogy | Treating an extended comparison between familiar and unfamiliar items, based on similarities and ignoring differences, as evidence rather than as a useful way of explaining | People were born free as the birds; it's cruel to expect them to work. |
| Bandwagon Argument | Suggesting that everyone is joining the group and that readers who don't may miss out on happiness, success, or a reward | Purchasing the new Global Glimmer admits you to the nation's most elite group of smartphone users. |

## Additional Writing Assignments

1. Write a letter to the editor of your newspaper or a newsmagazine in which you agree or disagree with the publication's editorial stand on a current question. Make clear your reasons for holding your view.
2. Write one claim each of substantiation, evaluation, and policy for or against a specific policy or proposal. Indicate an audience each claim might address effectively. Then list reasons and types of evidence you might need to support one of these claims. For the same claim, indicate what opposing viewpoints you would need to consider and how you could best do so.
3. Write a short paper, blog entry, or class posting expressing your view on one of these topics or another that comes to mind. Make clear your reasons for thinking as you do.

   Bilingual education
   Nonsmokers' rights
   Dealing with date rape
   Salaries of professional athletes
   Raising the minimum wage
   Protecting the gray wolf
   Controlling terrorism
   Prayer in public schools

For more on supporting a position with sources, see Ch. 12.

4. Working with a classmate or a small group online, develop a discussion or collaborative blog to inform your audience about multiple points of view on an issue. Present the most compelling reasons and evidence to support each view. Counter other views as appropriate with reasons and evidence, but avoid emotional outbursts attacking them. Before you begin posting, decide which view each person will present. Considering your purpose and audience, also decide whether the discussion or blog should cover certain points or be organized in a particular way. Before you post your contribution, write it in a location or file where you can save and return to it. Take some time to revise and edit before you send it or paste it in.
5. **Source Assignment.** Find a letter to the editor, opinion piece, or blog that takes a stand that you disagree with. Write a response to that piece, countering its points, presenting your points, and supporting them with evidence. Be sure to cite the other piece, and identify any quotations or summaries from it. Decide which audience to address: The writer? Readers likely to support the other selection? Readers with interest in the issue but without loyalty to the original publication? Some other group?
6. **Visual Assignment.** Select one of the images on the next two pages. Analyze its argument, noting its persuasive visual elements. Write an essay that first explains its argument, including its topic and its visual appeals to viewers, and then agrees, disagrees, or qualifies that argument.

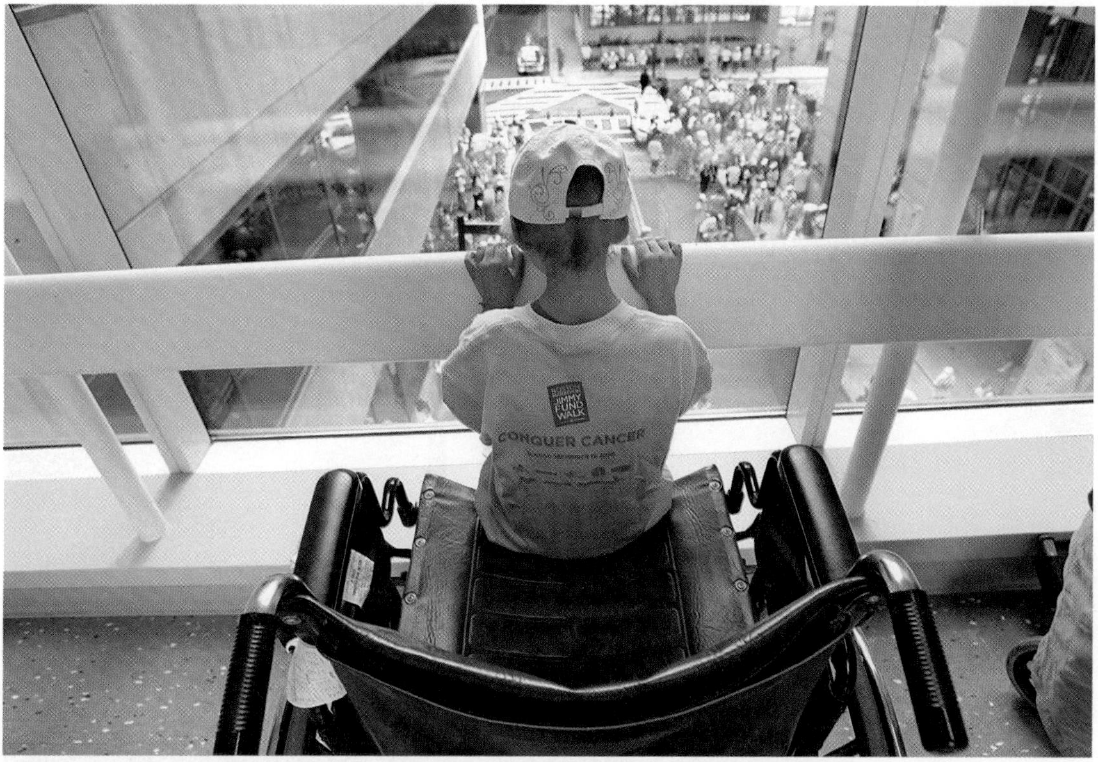

A young person hospitalized with cancer watches a fundraising walkathon.

A family in Connecticut reads after dinner.

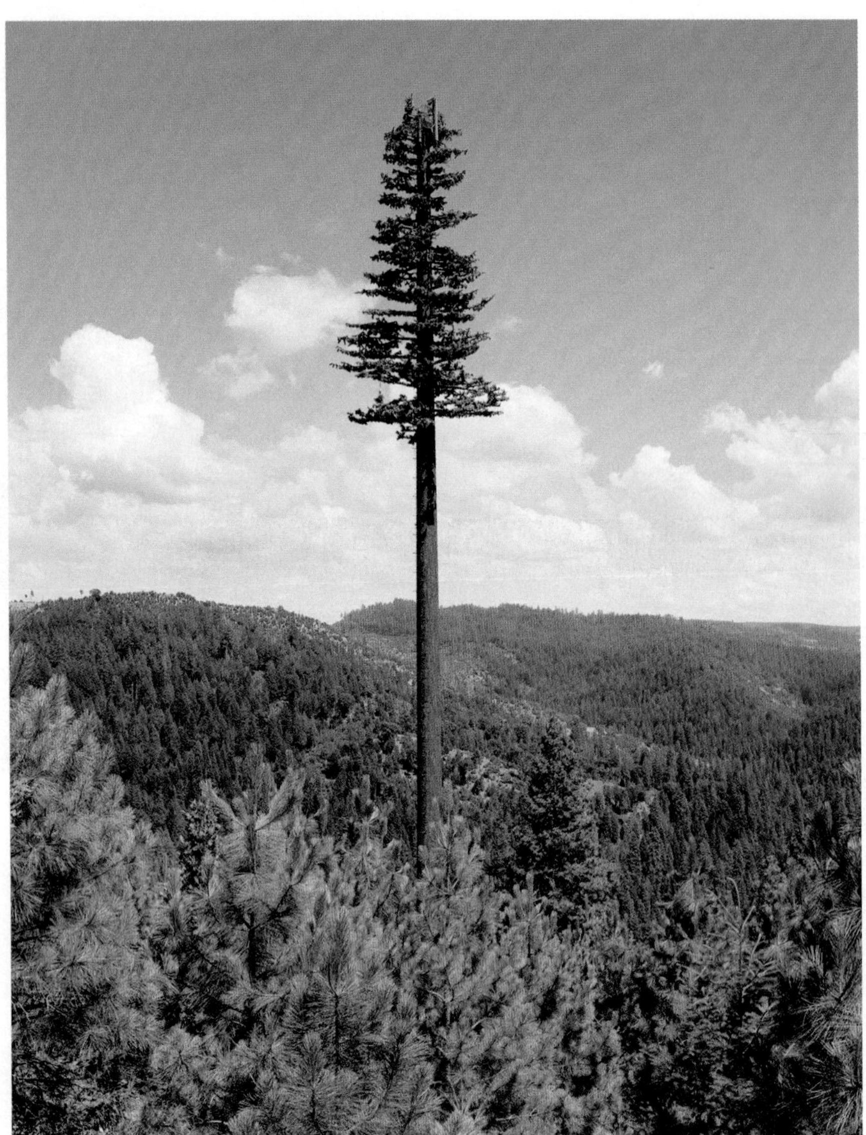

A cell phone tower in Mono Lake, California, from photographer Robert Voit's series, "New Trees."

# Proposing a Solution 10

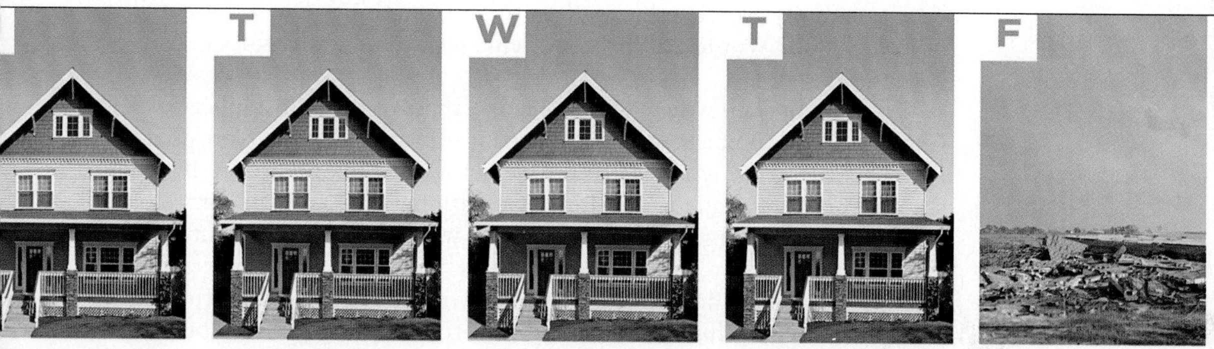


**What does the day before a natural disaster look like?**
**Any other day.**

Prepare for tomorrow. Ready.gov/today

Ready.

### Responding to an Image

This image from the public service campaign of FEMA, the Federal Emergency Management Agency, proposes a solution to a problem that affects hundreds of thousands of Americans every year. What is the problem that the image identifies? Why is the problem presented as it is? How might the presentation help viewers understand the problem? What solution does the image suggest or imply? For FEMA's proposals, visit fema.gov. Look for advice that might apply to you – preparing for many stages (before, during, after) of many disasters (floods, hurricanes, earthquakes, fires) with citizen action plans (for community responders, families, individuals, pet owners, and students who want to sign up for emergency training).

Sometimes when you learn of a problem such as the destruction caused by a natural disaster, homelessness, or famine, you say to yourself, "Something should be done about that." You can do something constructive yourself—through the powerful and persuasive activity of writing.

Your purpose in such writing, as political leaders and advertisers well know, is to rouse your audience to action. Even in your daily life at college, you can write a letter to your college newspaper or to someone in authority and try to stir your readers to so something. Does some college policy irk you? Would you urge students to attend a rally for a cause or a charity?

The uses of such writing go far beyond these immediate applications. In Chapter 9, you took a stand and backed it up with evidence. Now go a step further, writing a *proposal*—a recommendation for taking action. If, for instance, you have made the claim "Our national parks are in sorry condition," you might urge readers to act—to write to their representatives in Congress or to visit a national park and pick up trash. This paper would be a call to immediate action on the part of your readers. On the other hand, you might suggest that the Department of the Interior be given a budget increase to hire more park rangers, purchase additional park land to accommodate more visitors, and buy more cleanup equipment. You might also suggest that the department raise funds through sales of park DVDs, which might, in turn, attract more visitors. This second paper would attempt to forge a consensus about what needs to be done.

## Why Proposing a Solution Matters

### In a College Course

- You identify a problem and propose a solution, tackling issues such as sealed adoption records, rising costs of prescriptions, overcrowded prisons, and hungry children whose families cannot afford both food and housing.
- You propose a field research study, explaining and justifying your purposes and methods, in order to gain faculty and institutional approval for your capstone project.

### In the Workplace

- You propose developing services for a new market to avoid layoffs during an economic downturn.

### In Your Community

- You propose starting a tutoring program at the library for the many adults in your region with limited literacy skills.

What solutions have you proposed? What others might you propose? What situations have encouraged you to write proposals?

## Learning from Other Writers

The writers of the following two essays propose sensible solutions for pressing problems. To help you begin to analyze the first reading, look at the notes in the margin. They identify features such as the introduction of the problem, the thesis, or main idea, and the introduction of the proposed solution.

### As You Read These Proposals

As you read these essays, ask yourself the following questions:

1. What problem does the writer identify? Does the writer rouse you to want to do something about the problem?
2. What solution does the writer propose? What evidence supports the solution? Does the writer convince you to agree with this solution?
3. How is the writer qualified to write on this subject?

**Wilbert Rideau**

### Why Prisons Don't Work

Wilbert Rideau, editor of the *Angolite,* the Louisiana State Penitentiary newsmagazine and author of his memoir *In the Place of Justice* (2010), offers a voice seldom heard in the debate over crime control—that of the criminal.

I was among thirty-one murderers sent to the Louisiana State Penitentiary in 1962 to be executed or imprisoned for life. We weren't much different from those we found here, or those who had preceded us. We were unskilled, impulsive, and uneducated misfits, mostly black, who had done dumb, impulsive things—failures, rejects from the larger society. Now a generation has come of age and gone since I've been here, and everything is much the same as I found it. The faces of the prisoners are different, but behind them are the same impulsive, uneducated, unskilled minds that made dumb, impulsive choices that got them into more trouble than they ever thought existed. The vast majority of us are consigned to suffer and die here so politicians can sell the illusion that permanently exiling people to prison will make society safe. 1

Introduction of the problem

THESIS stating the problem

2 Getting tough has always been a "silver bullet," a quick fix for the crime and violence that society fears. Each year in Louisiana—where excess is a way of life—lawmakers have tried to outdo each other in legislating harsher mandatory penalties and in reducing avenues of release. The only thing to do with criminals, they say, is get tougher. They have. In the process, the purpose of prison began to change. The state boasts one of the highest lockup rates in the country, imposes the most severe penalties in the nation, and vies to execute more criminals per capita than anywhere else. This state is so tough that last year, when prison authorities here wanted to punish an

inmate in solitary confinement for an infraction,° the most they could inflict on him was to deprive him of his underwear. It was all he had left.

If getting tough resulted in public safety, Louisiana citizens would be the safest in the nation. They're not. Louisiana has the highest murder rate among states. Prison, like the police and the courts, has a minimal impact on crime because it is a response after the fact, a mop-up operation. It doesn't work. The idea of punishing the few to deter the many is counterfeit because potential criminals either think they're not going to get caught or they're so emotionally desperate or psychologically distressed that they don't care about the consequences of their actions. The threatened punishment, regardless of its severity, is never a factor in the equation. But society, like the incorrigible° criminal it abhors, is unable to learn from its mistakes. 3

Prison has a role in public safety, but it is not a cure-all. Its value is limited, and its use should also be limited to what it does best: isolating young criminals long enough to give them a chance to grow up and get a grip on their impulses. It is a traumatic experience, certainly, but it should be only a temporary one, not a way of life. Prisoners kept too long tend to embrace the criminal culture, its distorted values and beliefs; they have little choice—prison is their life. There are some prisoners who cannot be returned to society—serial killers, serial rapists, professional hit men, and the like—but the monsters who need to die in prison are rare exceptions in the criminal landscape. 4

Introduction of the proposed solution

Crime is a young man's game. Most of the nation's random violence is committed by young urban terrorists. But because of long, mandatory sentences, most prisoners here are much older, having spent fifteen, twenty, thirty, or more years behind bars, long past necessity. Rather than pay for new prisons, society would be well served by releasing some of its older prisoners who pose no threat and using the money to catch young street thugs. Warden John Whitley agrees that many older prisoners here could be freed tomorrow with little or no danger to society. Release, however, is governed by law or by politicians, not by penal professionals. Even murderers, those most feared by society, pose little risk. Historically, for example, the domestic staff at Louisiana's Governor's mansion has been made up of murderers, handpicked to work among the chief-of-state and his family. Penologists° have long known that murder is almost always a once-in-a-lifetime act. The most dangerous criminal is the one who has not yet killed but has a history of escalating offenses. He's the one to watch. 5

Transitions (underlined) for coherence

Rehabilitation can work. Everyone changes in time. The trick is to influence the direction that change takes. The problem with prisons is that they don't do more to rehabilitate those confined in them. The convict who enters prison illiterate will probably leave the same way. Most convicts want to be better than they are, but education is not a priority. This prison houses 6

**infraction:** Violation. **incorrigible:** Incapable of reform. **penologists:** Those who study prison management and criminal justice.

4,600 men and offers academic training to 240, vocational training to a like number. Perhaps it doesn't matter. About 90 percent of the men here may never leave this prison alive.

7 The only effective way to curb crime is for society to work to prevent the criminal act in the first place, to come between the perpetrator° and crime. Our youngsters must be taught to respect the humanity of others and to handle disputes without violence. It is essential to educate and equip them with the skills to pursue their life ambitions in a meaningful way. As a community, we must address the adverse life circumstances that spawn criminality. These things are not quick, and they're not easy, but they're effective. Politicians think that's too hard a sell. They want to be on record for doing something now, something they can point to at reelection time. So the drumbeat goes on for more police, more prisons, more of the same failed policies.

Conclusion summing up solution

8 Ever see a dog chase its tail?

## Questions to Start You Thinking

### Meaning

1. Does Rideau convince you that the belief that "permanently exiling people to prison will make society safe" is an "illusion" (paragraph 1)?
2. According to Rideau, why don't prisons work?
3. What does he propose as solutions to the problem of escalating crime? What other solutions can you think of?

### Writing Strategies

4. What justifications, if any, for the prison system has Rideau left out of his essay? Do these omissions help or hurt his essay? Why or why not?
5. What evidence does the author provide to support his assertion that Louisiana's "getting tough" policy has not worked? Does he provide sufficient evidence to convince you? Does he persuade you that action is necessary?
6. What would make Rideau's argument for his proposals more persuasive?
7. Other than himself, what authorities does Rideau cite? Why do you think he does this?
8. Does the fact that the author is a convicted criminal strengthen or weaken his argument? Why do you think he mentions this in his first sentence?
9. How do you interpret the last line, "Ever see a dog chase its tail?" Is this line an effective way for Rideau to end his essay? Explain.

**perpetrator:** One who is responsible for an action or a crime.

**Lacey Taylor** **Student Essay**

## It's Not Just a Bike

Lacey Taylor drew on personal experience in her essay to identify a problem on her campus and to propose solutions for it.

Imagine one day waking up to find that your car had been stolen. To many students, a bicycle is just like a car. They depend on their bicycles for all their transportation needs, getting to and from classes and work. Too many bicycles are being stolen on campus, and this situation has become a major problem for students who depend on them. In the past year, one friend has had two new bicycles stolen. Just three months ago, I went home for the weekend, and when I got back, my bicycle was gone. I could not believe that anyone would do such a horrible thing, but I was wrong, and someone did do it. This theft was a major blow to me because my bicycle was my only transportation to work. I am not the only person and will not be the last to have my bicycle taken, so something should be done and should be done soon. The campus community should use methods such as posting warning signs, starting an awareness program, and investing in new technology like cameras, chain alarms, and tracking devices to help solve this problem. 1

What comparable local problems have you experienced or observed?

Although many solutions are available to help alleviate this problem, some may be as simple as posting signs. Signs are a cheap and easy way to alleviate bike theft. The signs should read that bicycle theft is a crime, punishable by law, and they should explain the consequences that go along with stealing bicycles. The signs would need to be posted at all the bicycle racks just like the signs posted at every parking spot warning about being a tow-away zone. These signs would not completely solve the problem, but they would discourage some potential bicycle thieves. 2

The school also needs to begin a bicycle-theft awareness program. The program should inform students about bicycle theft, warning that it happens all the time and that it could happen to them. The program also would need to tell students about certain steps that they could take to avoid becoming victims of bike theft. For example, it could provide information about different methods of bicycle security such as keeping the serial number in case the bike is stolen and engraving a name on the bike so that it can be easily identified. The program also should tell students what to do if a bicycle is actually stolen such as calling the police and filing a report. This awareness program would prevent many students from ending up with stolen bicycles. 3

What simple informative and preventive methods have been used in your community or on your campus to solve problems?

A more advanced method for solving this problem would be to install security cameras all around campus. The cameras would keep track of all the activity going on at the bicycle racks and let the person watching the camera know if someone is stealing a bicycle. If no one sees the illegal act take place, then the camera tape could be pulled, watched, and used as evidence against the bike thief. For this solution to succeed, the cameras should be placed a certain way, all facing the bike racks and close enough for a viewer to tell what is going on at the racks. The cameras also need to be in plain sight for everyone to see so that anyone considering stealing a bicycle would think twice 4 before acting. After all, no one wants to be caught doing something illegal on camera. Finally, these cameras should be linked to a TV in the lobby of each dorm. Keeping an eye on the TV, watching for any strange activity, should be part of the job of the resident assistant on duty. The resident assistant then could report a bicycle being stolen to the campus police. These cameras would not only ward off some potential criminals but also help to catch the ones who were not scared off.

5 A creative solution would be to invest in chain alarms. These chains contain small wires; if the chains are cut, an alarm in the lock goes off just like a car alarm. This alarm would alert people nearby that someone was stealing a bicycle. The sound also might scare the thief into dropping the bike and running off. These chains could be rented out to students by the transportation department. If the rental cost around ten dollars a semester, the chains would pay for themselves over a short period of time and eventually make a profit for the transportation department. If someone never returned the chain at the end of the semester, the student should be fined, and a hold should be placed on his or her account just as the library does with book fines that must be paid before graduation. These chains would help to catch the bike thieves and also, just like the signs and cameras, help to scare off potential thieves.

6 Finally tracking devices could be placed on all campus bicycles. This would be the most effective solution to the bicycle theft problem because these tracking devices would come into play if all the other solutions failed to do the job. These devices should be small and placed in a hard-to-find spot on the bicycle. If a bike is stolen, then the bike could be traced on a campus police computer and its location identified. Then the police could go through the proper procedure to catch the thief. These tracking devices could be rented out just like the bicycle chains. Even though this method would not stop bicycles from being stolen, it would make it easy to find the bikes and catch the thieves.

? Would students on your campus welcome technological solutions to problems like bike theft, or would they worry about privacy, costs, or other issues?

7 Bicycle theft is a major problem that deserves attention. Too many bicycles are being stolen, and bikes are too important to everyday campus life to let this problem go unnoticed. The campus should use simple methods such as posting warning signs or sponsoring an awareness program and also invest in new technology like cameras, chain alarms, and tracking devices to help solve this problem. Bicycle riders should be aware that theft is a problem that could happen to them at any time, but bicycle thieves should not be able to take whatever they like with no action being taken against them. Bicycles, like cars, provide essential transportation, and no one wants to have that necessity stolen.

## Questions to Start You Thinking

Meaning

1. What problem does Taylor identify? Does she convince you that this is an important problem? Why, or why not?
2. What solutions does she propose? Why does she arrange them as she does? Which is her strongest solution? Her least convincing? Can you think of other ideas that she might have included?

3. How effectively would Taylor's proposal persuade various members of a campus audience? Which people would she easily persuade? Which might need more convincing? Can you think of other arguments that would appeal to specific readers?

### Writing Strategies

4. Is Taylor's argument easy to follow? Why or why not? What kinds of transitions does she use to lead readers through her points? How effective do you find them?
5. Is Taylor's evidence specific and sufficient? Explain.
6. What qualifies Taylor to write about this topic? How do these qualifications contribute to her ability to persuade?
7. Using highlighters or marginal notes, identify the essay's introduction, explanation of the problem, thesis, proposal to solve the problem, and conclusion. How effective is the organization of this essay?

**e Casey Neistat** **Video**

## Texting While Walking

Videographer Casey Neistat explores the dangers of texting while walking before proposing a solution. To watch this comical video, go to Chapter 10: **bedfordstmartins.com/bedguide**.

Texting and walking can be a dangerous combination.

# Learning by Writing

## The Assignment: Proposing a Solution

In this essay you'll first carefully analyze and explain a specific social, economic, political, civic, or environmental problem—a problem you care about and strongly wish to see resolved. The problem may be large or small, but it shouldn't be trivial. It may affect the whole country or mainly people from your city, campus, or classroom. Show your readers that this problem really exists and that it matters to you and to them. After setting it forth, you also may want to explain why it exists. Write for an audience who, once aware of the problem, may be expected to help do something about it.

For an interactive Learning by Doing activity on Proposing a Solution to a Local Problem, go to Ch. 10: **bedfordstmartins.com/bedguide**.

The second thing you are to accomplish in the essay is to propose one or more ways to solve the problem or at least alleviate it. In making a proposal, you urge action by using words like *should, ought,* and *must*: "This city ought to have a Bureau of Missing Persons"; "Small private aircraft should be banned from flying close to a major commercial airport." Lay out the reasons why your proposal deserves to be implemented; supply evidence that your solution is reasonable and can work. Remember that your purpose is to convince readers that something should be done about the problem.

These students cogently argued for action in their papers:

Based on research studies and statistics, one student argued that using standardized test scores from the SAT or the ACT as criteria for college admissions is a problem because it favors aggressive students from affluent families. His proposal was to abolish this use of the scores.

Another argued that speeders racing past an elementary school might be slowed by a combination of more warning signs, surveillance equipment, police patrols, and fines.

A third argued that cities should consider constructing public buildings with "living walls" in order to reduce energy consumption, improve air quality, and allow for urban agriculture.

A "living wall" or "green wall" is a wall that is completely or partially covered with plants.

## Facing the Challenge Proposing a Solution

The major challenge writers face when writing a proposal is to develop a detailed and convincing solution. Finding solutions is much harder than finding problems. Convincing readers that you have found a reasonable, workable solution is harder still. For example, suppose you propose the combination of a rigorous exercise program and a low-carb diet as a solution for obesity. While these solutions seem reasonable and workable to you, readers who have lost weight and then gained it back might point out that their main problem is not losing weight but maintaining weight loss over time. To account for their concerns and enhance your credibility, you might revise your solution to focus on realistic long-term goals and strategies for sticking to an exercise program. For instance, you might recommend that friends walk together two or three times a week or that employees lobby for a fitness center at work.

To develop a realistic solution that fully addresses a problem and satisfies the concerns of readers, consider questions such as these:

- How might the problem affect different groups of people?
- What range of concerns are your readers likely to have?
- What realistic solution addresses the concerns of readers about *all* aspects of the problem?

## Generating Ideas

**Identify a Problem.** Brainstorm by writing down all the topics that come to mind. Observe events around you to identify irritating campus or community problems you would like to solve. Watch for ideas in the news. Browse through issue-oriented Web sites. Look for sites sponsored by large nonprofit foundations that accept grant proposals and fund innovative solutions to societal issues. Although a controversy or current issue might start you thinking, be sure to stick to problems that you want to solve as you consider options. Star the ideas that seem to have the most potential.

### DISCOVERY CHECKLIST

- ☐ Can you recall any problem that needs a solution? What problems do you meet every day or occasionally? What problems concern people near you?
- ☐ What conditions in need of improvement have you observed on television, on the Web, or in your daily activities? What action is called for?
- ☐ What problems have been discussed recently on campus or in class?
- ☐ What problems are discussed in blogs, online or print newspapers, or newsmagazines such as *Time, The Week,* or *U.S. News & World Report*?

**Consider Your Audience.** Readers need to believe that your problem is real and your solution is feasible. If you are addressing classmates, maybe they haven't thought about the problem before. Look for ways to make it personal for them, to show that it affects them and deserves their attention.

- Who are your readers? How would you describe them?
- Why should your readers care about this problem? Does it affect their health, welfare, conscience, or pocketbook?
- Have they ever expressed any interest in the problem? If so, what has triggered their interest?
- Do they belong to any organization or segment of society that makes them especially susceptible to — or uninterested in — this problem?
- What attitudes about the problem do you share with your readers? Which of their assumptions or values that differ from yours will affect how they view your proposal?

## Learning by Doing Describing Your Audience

Write a paragraph or so describing the audience you intend to address. Who are they? Which of their circumstances, interests, traits, social circles, attitudes, and values best prepare them to grasp the problem? Which make them most (or least) receptive to your solution? If aspects of the problem or the solution especially appeal (or do not appeal) to them, consider how to present your ideas most persuasively. (Save these notes for the next activity on p. 197.) If you want a second opinion, share your analysis in person or online with a classmate.

**Think about Solutions.** Once you've chosen a problem, brainstorm — alone or with classmates — for possible solutions, or use your imagination. Some problems, such as reducing international tensions, present no easy solu-

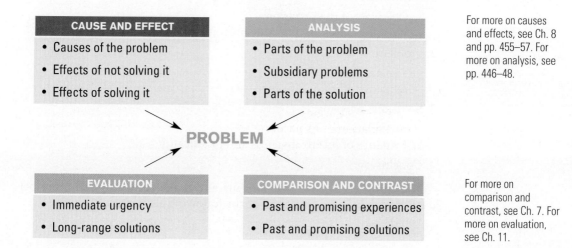

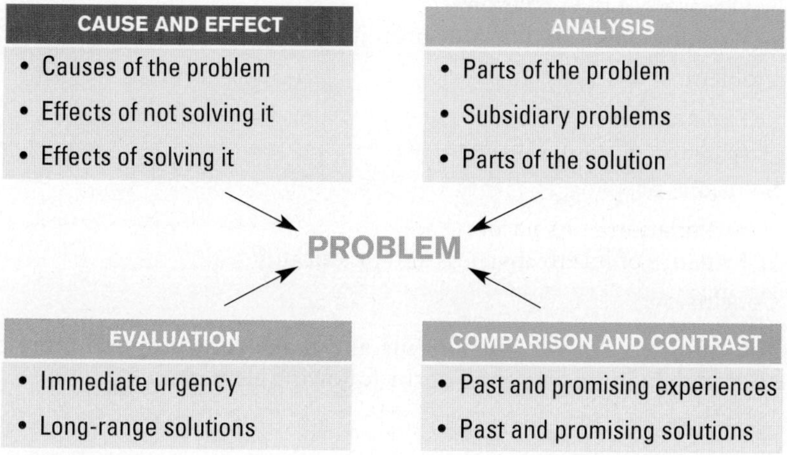

**CAUSE AND EFFECT**
- Causes of the problem
- Effects of not solving it
- Effects of solving it

**ANALYSIS**
- Parts of the problem
- Subsidiary problems
- Parts of the solution

**PROBLEM**

**EVALUATION**
- Immediate urgency
- Long-range solutions

**COMPARISON AND CONTRAST**
- Past and promising experiences
- Past and promising solutions

For more on causes and effects, see Ch. 8 and pp. 455–57. For more on analysis, see pp. 446–48.

For more on comparison and contrast, see Ch. 7. For more on evaluation, see Ch. 11.

tions. Still, give some strategic thought to any problem that seriously concerns you, even if it has stumped experts. Sometimes a solution reveals itself to a novice thinker, and even a partial solution is worth offering.

For more on evidence, see Ch. 3. For more on using evidence to support an argument, see pp. 170–74.

**Consider Sources of Support.** To show that the problem really exists, you'll need evidence and examples. If further library research will help you justify the problem, now is the time to do it. Consider whether local history archives, newspaper stories, accounts of public meetings, interviews, or relevant Web sites might identify concerns of readers, practical limits of solutions, or previous efforts that help you develop your solution.

For advice on finding a few sources, see sections A and B in the Quick Research Guide, pp. A-21–A-26.

## Planning, Drafting, and Developing

**Start with Your Proposal and Your Thesis.** A basic approach is to state your proposal in a sentence that can act as your thesis.

For more on stating a thesis, see pp. 399–408.

| | |
|---|---|
| PROPOSAL | Let people get divorced without having to go to court. |
| WORKING THESIS | The legislature should pass a law allowing couples to divorce without the problem of going to court. |

From such a statement, the rest of the argument may start to unfold, often falling naturally into a simple two-part shape:

For practice developing and supporting effective thesis statements, visit **bedfordstmartins.com/bedguide**.

1. *A claim that a problem exists.* This part explains the problem and supplies evidence of its significance – for example, the costs, adversarial process, and stress of divorce court for a couple and their family.
2. *A claim that something ought to be done about it.* This part proposes a solution to the problem – for example, legislative action to authorize other options such as mediation.

These two parts can grow naturally into an informal outline.

For more on outlines, see pp. 411–19.

1. Introduction
   - Overview of the situation
   - Working thesis stating your proposal
2. Problem
   - Explanation of its nature
   - Evidence of its significance
3. Solution
   - Explanation of its nature
   - Evidence of its effectiveness and practicality
4. Conclusion

You can then expand your outline and make your proposal more persuasive by including some or all of the following elements:

- Knowledge or experience that qualifies you to propose a solution (your experience as a player or a coach, for example, that establishes your credibility as an authority on Little League or soccer clubs)
- Values, beliefs, or assumptions that have caused you to feel strongly about the need for action
- An estimate of the resources—money, people, skills, material—and the time required to implement the solution (perhaps including what is available now and what needs to be obtained)
- Step-by-step actions needed to achieve your solution
- Controls or quality checks to monitor implementation

A sign from part of a popular and successful anti-littering campaign.

- Possible obstacles or difficulties that may need to be overcome
- Reasons your solution is better than others proposed or tried already
- Any other evidence that shows that your suggestion is practical, reasonable in cost, and likely to be effective

**Imagine Possible Objections of Your Audience.** You can increase the likelihood that readers will accept your proposal in two ways. First, start your proposal by showing that a problem exists. Then, when you turn to your claim that something should be done, begin with a simple and inviting suggestion. For example, a claim that national parks need better care might suggest that readers head for a park and personally size up the situation. Besides drawing readers into the problem and the solution, you may think of objections they might raise—reservations about the high cost, complexity, or workability of your plan, for instance. Persuade readers by anticipating and laying to rest their likely objections.

### Learning by Doing Making Problem–Solution Columns

A persuasive proposal should show that you understand a problem well enough to suggest solutions while addressing specific audience needs. Considering these ideas in columns can help you see them differently than you do as you write. Open a new file, go to the Format menu, choose Columns, select the three-column format, and label the columns. Use your audience description (p. 195), notes, plan, and working draft to copy and paste ideas into the appropriate columns. Add points as needed so that you can move logically from problem to solution to answering readers' objections point by point. If you can't see how to make solid connections, ask your classmates for advice.

| Problems | Solutions | Reader Objections |
|---|---|---|
| | | |

For pointers on integrating and documenting sources, see Ch. 12 and D6 and E1–E2 (pp. A-31–A-38) in the Quick Research Guide.

**Cite Sources Carefully.** When you collect ideas and evidence from outside sources, you need to document your evidence—that is, tell where you found everything. Follow the documentation method your instructor wants you to use. You may also want to identify sources as you introduce them to assure a reader that they are authoritative.

According to *Newsweek* correspondent Josie Fair, . . .

In his biography *FDR: The New Deal Years*, Davis reports . . .

While working as a Senate page in the summer of 2013, I observed . . .

For more about integrating visuals, see section B (pp. A-8–A-12) in the Quick Format Guide.

Introduce visual evidence (table, graph, drawing, map, photo), too.

As the 2010 census figures in Table 1 indicate, . . .

The photograph showing the run-down condition of the dog park (see Fig. 2) . . .

For more revising and editing strategies, see Ch. 23.

## Revising and Editing

As you revise, concentrate on a clear explanation of the problem and solid supporting evidence for the solution. Make your essay coherent and its parts clear to help achieve your purpose of convincing your readers.

**Clarify Your Thesis.** Your readers are likely to rely on your thesis to identify the problem and possibly to preview your solution. Look again at your thesis from a reader's point of view.

WORKING THESIS The legislature should pass a law allowing couples to divorce without the problem of going to court.

REVISED THESIS Because divorce court can be expensive, adversarial, and stressful, passing a law that allows couples to divorce without a trip to court would encourage simpler, more harmonious ways to end a marriage.

**Reorganize for Unity and Coherence.** When Heather Colbenson revised her first draft, she wanted to clarify the presentation of her problem.

Why would high schools in farming communities drop agriculture classes and the FFA program? *The main reason that* ~~S~~*s*mall schools are *is that* cutting ag programs because the state has not provided significant funding for the schools to operate. The small schools have to make cuts, and some small schools are deciding that the agriculture classes are not as important as other courses. Some small schools are consolidating to receive more aid. Many of these schools have been able to save their ag programs.

*Move main reason last for emphasis*

*Why did I put a solution here? Move to end!*

*One reason is that m* ~~M~~any colleges are demanding that students have two years of foreign language. In small schools, like my own, the students could take either foreign language or ag classes. Therefore, students choose language classes to fill the college requirement. When the students leave the ag classes to take foreign language, the number of students declines, which makes it easier for school administrators to cut ag classes.

*Rewrite this! Not really college requirements but college-prep courses vs. others when budget is tight*

Her revised paper was more forcefully organized and more coherent, making it easier for readers to follow. The bridges between ideas were now on paper, not just in her mind.

For strategies for achieving coherence, see pp. 431–35.

## Learning by Doing Revising for Clear Organization

Check the actual organization of your draft against your plans and the two-part structure commonly used in proposals (see p. 196). Outline what you've actually done, not what you intended, to see your organization as readers will. Does your draft open with a sufficient overview for your audience? Do you state your actual proposal clearly? Does your draft progress from problem to solution without mixing ideas together? Have you included elements appropriate for your audience? Reorganize and revise as needed. Exchange drafts with a classmate if you want a second opinion on organization.

**Be Reasonable.** Exaggerated claims for a solution will not persuade readers. Neither will oversimplifying the problem so the solution seems more workable. Don't be afraid to express reasonable doubts about the completeness of your solution. If necessary, rethink both problem and solution.

## Peer Response — Proposing a Solution

Ask several classmates or friends to review your proposal and solution, answering questions such as these:

For general questions for a peer editor, see p. 463.

- What is your overall reaction to this proposal? Does it make you want to go out and do something about the problem?
- Are you convinced that the problem is of concern to you? If not, why not?
- Are you persuaded that the writer's solution is workable? Why, or why not?
- Has the writer paid enough attention to readers and their concerns?
- Restate what you understand to be the proposal's major points:

    Problem
    Explanation of problem and why it matters
    Proposed solution
    Explanation of proposal and its practicality
    Reasons and procedure to implement proposal
    Proposal's advantages, disadvantages, and responses to other solutions
    Final recommendation

- If this paper were yours, what is the one thing you would be sure to work on before handing it in?

### REVISION CHECKLIST

- ☐ Does your introduction invite the reader into the discussion?
- ☐ Is your problem clear? How have you made it relevant to readers?
- ☐ Have you clearly outlined the steps necessary to solve the problem?
- ☐ Where have you demonstrated the benefits of your solution?
- ☐ Have you considered other solutions before rejecting them for your own?
- ☐ Have you anticipated the doubts readers may have about your solution?
- ☐ Do you sound reasonable, willing to admit that you don't know everything? If you sound preachy, have you overused *should* and *must*?
- ☐ Have you avoided promising that your solution will do more than it can possibly do? Have you made believable predictions for its success?

After you have revised your proposal, edit and proofread it. Carefully check the grammar, word choice, punctuation, and mechanics—and then correct any problems you find. If you have used sources, be sure that you have cited them correctly in your text and added a list of works cited.

For more editing and proofreading strategies, see pp. 471–75. For more on documenting sources, see E1–E2 in the Quick Research Guide, pp. A-32–A-38.

Make sure your sentence structure helps you make your points clearly and directly. Don't let yourself slip into the passive voice, a grammatical construction that represents things as happening without any obvious agent: "The problem should be remedied by spending money on prevention." Instead, every sentence should specify who should act: "The dean of students should remedy the problem by spending money on prevention."

**EDITING CHECKLIST**

| | |
|---|---|
| ☐ Is it clear what each pronoun refers to? Is any *this* or *that* ambiguous? Does each pronoun agree with (match) its antecedent? | A6 |
| ☐ Is your sentence structure correct? Have you avoided writing fragments, comma splices, or fused sentences? | A1, A2 |
| ☐ Do your transitions and other introductory elements have commas after them, if these are needed? | C1 |
| ☐ Have you spelled and capitalized everything correctly, especially names of people and organizations? | D1, D2 |

For more help, find the relevant checklist sections in the Quick Editing Guide on p. A-39. Turn also to the Quick Format Guide beginning on p. A-1.

## Additional Writing Assignments

1. If you followed the assignment in Chapter 9 and took a stand, now write a few paragraphs extending that paper to propose a solution that argues for action. To gather ideas, brainstorm with classmates first.
2. Brainstorm with classmates to develop a list of campus problems that irritate students or complicate their lives. Write an essay that tackles one of these problems by explaining it and proposing a practical, workable solution. (If you can't identify a workable solution, select a different problem.) Address an audience on your campus or in your college system that could implement a solution. Present your ideas tactfully. After all, they may also be the ones responsible for creating or at least not solving the problem earlier. (If appropriate, investigate any campus history that might help you overcome resistance based on tradition.)

3. Write a memo to your supervisor at work in which you propose an innovation (related to procedures, schedules, policies, or similar matters) that could benefit your department or company.
4. As part of a problem-solution blog, thread, or discussion area for your class, post a concise passage identifying and explaining a problem. (Your instructor may limit the problems to relevant campus, community, student, educational, technology, or topical issues.) Then post a second passage identifying and explaining a solution to the problem you identified. Respond to each other's problem-solution statements with questions, comments, connections, or suggestions to develop a focused exchange about the class proposals.
5. **Source Assignment.** Choose from the following list a practice that you find inefficient, unethical, unfair, or morally wrong as a solution to a problem. In a few paragraphs, give reasons for your objections. Then narrow the issue as needed to propose a better solution in a persuasive essay. Locate, use, and cite some statistics or other data to help raise readers' awareness.

   Censorship
   Goods made with child labor
   Laboratory experiments on animals
   Genetic engineering
   Outsourcing jobs
   Dumping wastes in the ocean

6. **Visual Assignment.** Select one of the following images. Write an essay that analyzes the problem that it identifies, noting how elements of the image draw the viewer into the problem. Include any solution suggested or implied by the image or your own solution to the problem.

EAST 241 ST
CONSIDERED
A CRIME. WHY?
SUCH AS
CANNOT SEE THAT
BEAUTIFUL
TRUE...
ART!
FOR:
WANDA

# 11 Evaluating and Reviewing

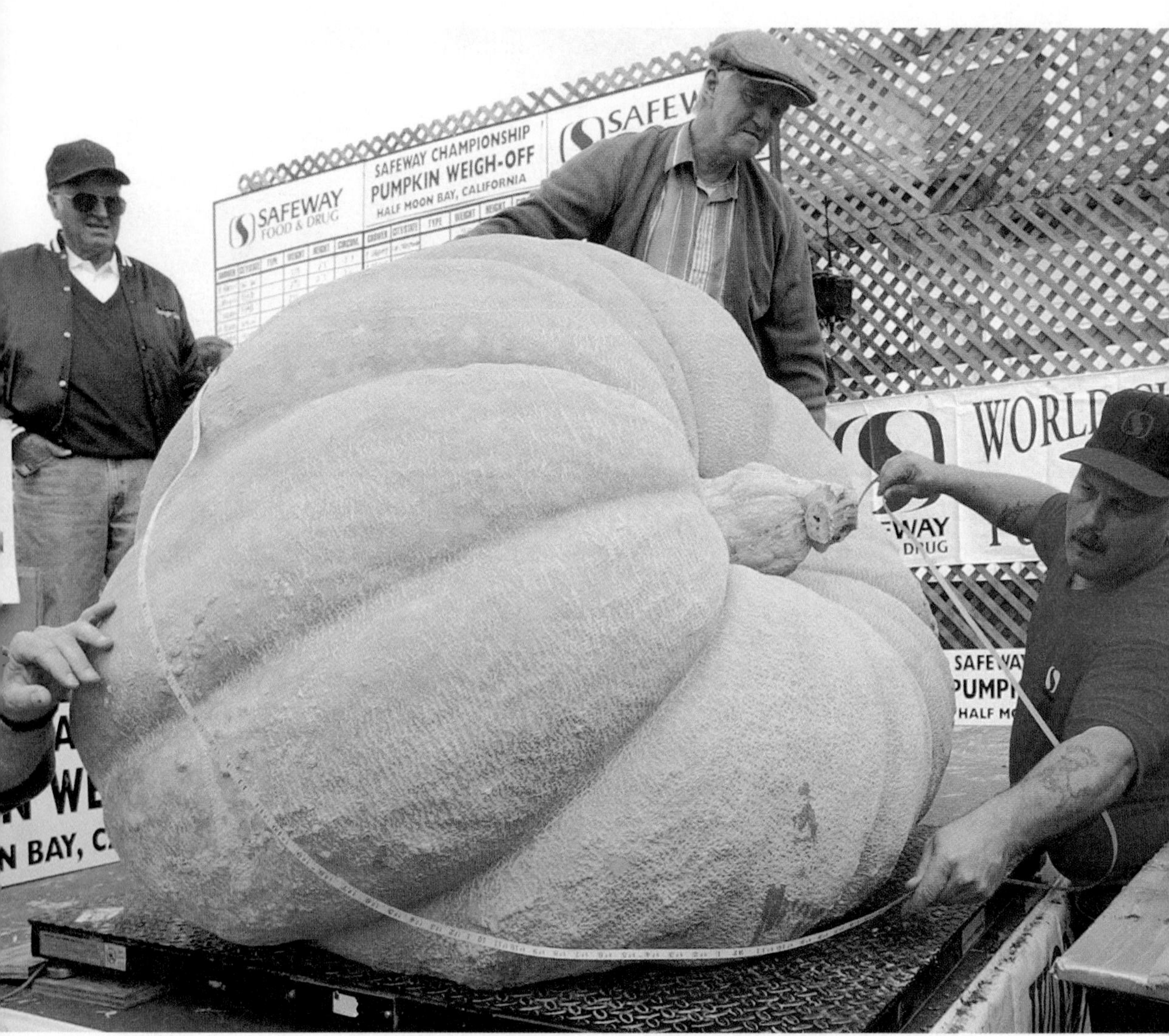


## Responding to an Image

In what respects does this photograph of a giant-pumpkin weigh-in capture the essence of such competitions? What overall impression does the image convey? What details contribute to this impression? How does the photograph direct the viewer's eye? In what ways does this image suggest, represent, or comment on a particular set of criteria and process of evaluation?

Evaluating means judging. You do it when you decide what candidate to vote for, pick which camera to buy, or recommend a new restaurant to your friends. All of us pass judgments—often snap judgments—as we move through a day's routine. A friend asks, "How was that movie you saw last night?" and you reply, "Terrific—don't miss it" or maybe "Pretty good, but it had too much blood and gore for me."

But to *write* an evaluation calls for you to think more critically. As a writer you first decide on *criteria,* or standards for judging, and then come up with evidence to back up your judgment. Your evaluation zeroes in on a definite subject that you inspect carefully in order to reach a considered opinion. The subject might be a film, a book, or a performance that you review. Or it might be a sports team, a product, or a body of research that you evaluate. The possibilities are endless.

## Why Evaluating and Reviewing Matter

### In a College Course

- You evaluate theories and methods in the fields you study, including long-standing controversies such as the dispute about teaching methods raging in education for the deaf.
- You evaluate instructors, courses, and sometimes campus facilities and services to participate in the process of monitoring and improving your college.

### In the Workplace

- You evaluate people, projects, goals, and results, just as your potential was evaluated as a job applicant and your performance is evaluated as an employee.

### In Your Community

- You evaluate video games for yourself or your children and review films, music, shows, and restaurants as you decide how to spend your money and time.

? What have you evaluated within the last few weeks? How have evaluations and reviews been useful for you? How have you incorporated evaluations and reviews into your writing?

## Learning from Other Writers

Here are evaluations by a professional and a student. To help you analyze the first reading, look at the notes in the margin. They identify features such as the thesis, or main idea, the criteria for evaluation, and the evidence supporting the writer's judgment, all typical of essays that evaluate.

### As You Read These Evaluations

As you read these essays, ask yourself the following questions:

1. Do you consider the writer qualified to evaluate the subject he or she chose? What biases and prejudices might the writer bring to the task?
2. What criteria for evaluation does the writer establish? Are these reasonable standards for evaluating the subject?
3. What is the writer's assessment of the subject? Does the writer provide sufficient evidence to convince you of his or her evaluation?

### Scott Tobias

### The Hunger Games

Film critic Scott Tobias has reviewed movies for NPR.org, the *Village Voice*, and the *Hollywood Reporter*. As the film editor for the A.V. Club section of the *Onion*, where this review appeared, he evaluates the film version of the popular book, *The Hunger Games*.

If Suzanne Collins's novel *The Hunger Games* turns up on school curricula 50 years from now—and as accessible dystopian° science fiction with allusions° to early-21st-century strife, that isn't out of the question—the lazy students of the future can be assured that they can watch the movie version and still get better than a passing grade. But that's a dubious triumph: A book is a book and a movie is a movie, and whenever the latter merely sets about illustrating the former, it's a failure of adaptation, to say nothing of imagination. When the goal is simply to be as faithful as possible to the material—as if a movie were a marriage, and a rights contract the vow—the best result is a skillful abridgment, one that hits all the important marks without losing anything egregious.° And as abridgments go, they don't get much more skillful than this one. 1

THESIS

Introduction to criterion 1: adaptation of situation

That such a safe adaptation could come of *The Hunger Games* speaks more to the trilogy's commercial ascent than the book's actual content, which is audacious and savvy in its dark calculations. The opening crawl (and a stirring propaganda movie) informs us that "The Hunger Games" are an annual event 2

**dystopian:** Presenting miserable places (as opposed to utopias or perfect places) in fiction. **allusions:** Indirect or casual references. **egregious:** Glaring or outrageous.

in Panem, a North American nation divided into 12 different districts, each in service to the Capitol, a wealthy metropolis that owes its creature comforts to an oppressive dictatorship. For the 75 years since a district rebellion was put down, the Games have existed as an assertion of the Capitol's power, a winner-take-all contest that touts heroism and sacrifice—participants are called "tributes"—while pitting the districts against each other. At "The Reaping," a boy and a girl between the ages of 12 and 18 are taken from each district—with odds determined by age and the number of rations they accept throughout the year—and thrown into a controlled arena, where they're forced to kill each other until only one survives.

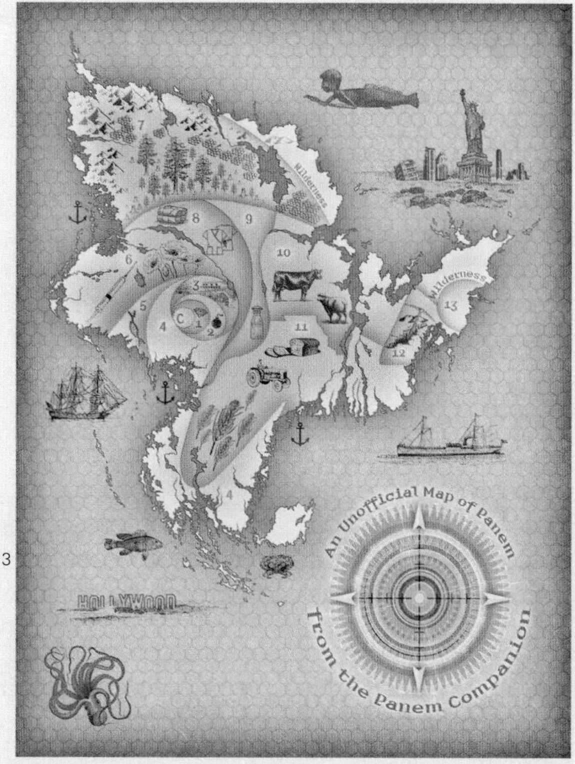


*Source: The Panem Companion,* Smart Pop Books, 2012. © V. Arrow.

3 In District 12, a dirt-poor coal-mining community that looks like a Dorothea Lange° photograph, Katniss Everdeen (Jennifer Lawrence) quietly rebels against the system by hunting game in a forbidden area with her friend Gale (Liam Hemsworth) and trading it on the black market. Katniss prepares her meek younger sister Prim (Willow Shields) for her first Reaping, but the odds of a single entry being selected among teenagers with many entries apiece are long. In the film's most affecting scene, those long odds turn against Prim in a shock that Ross renders in agonizing silence, punctuated only by Katniss screaming that she'll volunteer in her sister's place. She's joined, on the boys' side, by Peeta (Josh Hutcherson), a baker's son whose earnestness masks a gift for strategy that Katniss lacks. Together, with the help of the drunkard Haymitch (Woody Harrelson), the only District 12 citizen ever to win the Games, they challenge tributes that range from sadistic volunteers to crafty kids like the pint-sized Rue (Amandla Stenberg) to the truly helpless and soon-to-be-dead.

Introduction to criterion 2: adaptation of characters

Director Gary Ross and his screenwriters do well with the unenviable task of setting the table for the series, but with so many characters and subplots to service, they have to ration as stingily as the Capitol. The Reaping is one of the few sequences that's given time to breathe a little, and it makes all the difference—the hushed crowd, neither roused by propaganda nor open in resistance, says everything about the fear and shimmering resentment that stirs in the

4 Introduction to criterion 3: adaptation of plot

**Dorothea Lange:** Documentary photographer whose images captured the Depression and the Dust Bowl migration.

districts. Once Katniss volunteers, *The Hunger Games* jets from one plot point to another without emphasizing any to great effect. Ross and company deliver on the franchise more effectively than, say, the first *Harry Potter* movie, but there's little evidence that they had any other agenda in mind.

Limitations of adaptation

The primary strength of Collins's book is Katniss herself, a model of 5
steel-spined resourcefulness and power whose internal monologue° roils with daft naiveté and self-doubt, especially when it comes to reading her supposed allies. Absent that monologue, Ross's film mostly has the book's action, and that's enough for a rousing two hours through the surreality of the Capitol—which looks like Dubai meets Nuremberg—and the excitement of the Games themselves, which are sanitized by the PG-13 rating, but nonetheless suspenseful and dread-soaked. And beyond the mayhem are the periodic reminders that the Games are as rigged as any reality show; as with a casino, it's important that the house always wins, even if that means shaking up the rules as it goes along.

Conclusion, returning to thesis

*The Hunger Games* has its share of standalone payoffs, though some are 6
too sketchily developed to have much of an impact, like Katniss's motherly connection to Rue. Nonetheless, it's the first act in a three-act story, and characters who seem thin now may resonate more down the line. With all the dirty work out of the way, perhaps the sequels will come closer to channeling the revolutionary fervor of Collins's books, and perhaps given the current focus on income inequality, find a populist° edge in the process. Whether the films will take on a life of their own is another matter: As of the first installment, it's stenography° in light.

For another review of *The Hunger Games*, see Katha Pollitt's essay on pp. 554–57.

## Questions to Start You Thinking

### Meaning

1. How does Tobias categorize *The Hunger Games* film? How does this category influence his review?
2. What does Tobias show in paragraphs 2, 3, and 4? How do the topics of these paragraphs support his overall evaluation?
3. What does Tobias mean when he wonders how well the sequels will convey "the revolutionary fervor of Collins's books" (paragraph 6)? To what extent does he feel that the first film showed met his expectations?

### Writing Strategies

4. What is Tobias's overall judgment of the film? What evidence does he use to support this judgment?
5. In your view, how well does he support his judgment? Point to some specific examples in making your case.

**monologue:** One-person speech. **populist:** Advocating for ordinary people. **stenography:** Shorthand notes for a copy.

6. Why does Tobias refer to "dystopian science fiction" (paragraph 1) as well as reality shows and casinos (5)? What do such references add to his review?
7. How would you describe Tobias's tone, the quality of his writing that reveals his attitude toward his topic and his readers? Does the tone seem appropriate for his purpose and audience?

**Elizabeth Erion** **Student Essay**

## Internship Program Falls Short

Elizabeth Erion drew on two valuable resources for her evaluation: her investigation of the campus internship program and her own experience as an intern. An earlier version of her essay appeared as an editorial in the campus student newspaper.

1 Since its creation in 1978, the Coram Internship Program has been a mainstay of the Career Development Center. The program matches interested students—usually those entering their junior year—with companies offering paid summer employment. Participating companies vary by year but range from The Guggenheim Museum in New York to the Keck School of Medicine in Los Angeles. In 2011, the program placed thirteen students from the class of 2012 at eleven companies or organizations. While this statistic may at first sound impressive, it accounts for only 2.8% of the class of 2012. Given the popularity of summer internships to lead into one's junior year, it is surprising that a higher percentage of the student body didn't make use of such a seemingly excellent, paid opportunity. But the program's low participation rate may be explained by one of its biggest flaws: its inherently restrictive nature.

What would you want to gain from an internship program?

2 By offering funded opportunities at only a certain set of companies, the Coram program limits its utility to a certain set of students—those whose career interests match the industries and whose geographical options match the locations of companies participating during a particular summer. What's more, certain locations and industries are heavily privileged over others. In 2012, nine of the fourteen companies were located in the Boston area. This regionalism is understandable given the college's location in Maine and the high percentage of students and alumni from the Boston area, but it still represents a concerning lack of geographic diversity.

3 Massachusetts natives probably would find this location far more doable than would students who hail from elsewhere. Local students might have the opportunity to live at home and save significant money (the program stipend does not cover living or travel expenses) or might have an easier time finding roommates or an apartment to sublet due to a strong network of friends and family in the area. They would incur no significant travel costs for a flight, a long train ride, or long-distance

What advice would you give a nonlocal student?

gas mileage to arrive and depart from their summer destination. A student from elsewhere who could not afford such expenses or who could not relocate for a personal reason—perhaps a family member who is ill—is at a disadvantage. If students were able to select the locations of their internships, they would be much more likely to participate in the program.

Similarly, students are restricted to opportunities in a certain set of industries. Four of the participating programs in 2012 were in the financial services sector. Five were in science and medicine. Only one opportunity was available for students interested in museum work. The aspiring journalist is out of luck, as the program offers no journalism internships. So too is the student wishing to gain exposure to law firm work. These students are forced to look elsewhere, at both paid and unpaid opportunities. In many sectors—especially the arts—unpaid internships abound, usually located in prohibitively expensive metropolitan areas. Students who cannot afford to take unpaid internships are then left with no options, which jeopardizes their entry into the job market after graduating. Had the Coram program offered internships in the desired fields of such students, those students could have spent the summer attaining the experience they needed. 4

What kinds of internship opportunities would students on your campus want?

The Coram Internship Program offers an excellent opportunity for the fortunate student who finds a good employment fit with a geographically convenient company. Unfortunately, the percentage of students who are able to find such a fit is prohibitively small, as illustrated by the program's low participation rate. The program's structure denies the chance of obtaining rewarding, paid opportunities to the majority of the college's students, which is problematic given the importance of internships in gaining entry-level employment. Ultimately, the Coram Internship Program proves itself an ineffective career resource for a geographically and professionally diverse student community. 5

## Questions to Start You Thinking

### Meaning

1. Why does Erion feel that evaluating the internship program is important? Who might belong to the audience that she would like to influence?
2. What does Erion mean when she refers to the internship program's major flaw as "its inherently restrictive nature" (paragraph 1)?
3. Based on her evaluation, what changes do you think Erion would want the Career Development Center or the internship program to make?

### Writing Strategies

4. What criteria does Erion use to judge the internship program? To what extent has the program met these criteria, according to Erion?

5. Does Erion provide enough evidence to support her judgment? Why or why not?
6. Do you find Erion's use of statistics effective? Why or why not?
7. Using highlighters or marginal notes, identify the essay's introduction, thesis, criteria for evaluation, supporting evidence, and conclusion. How effective is the organization of the essay?

### e *Consumer Reports* Editors — Video

## Best Buttermilk Pancakes

Consumer Reports is a nonprofit organization dedicated to reviewing products ranging from cars to pancakes. To watch this video review, go to Chapter 11: **bedfordstmartins.com/bedguide**.

Source: "Best Buttermilk Pancakes" Copyright 2012 Consumers Union of U.S., Inc. Yonkers, NY 10703-1057, a nonprofit organization. Reprinted with permission from *ConsumerReports.org* for educational purposes only. www.ConsumerReports.org.

# Learning by Writing

## The Assignment: Writing an Evaluation

Pick a subject to evaluate—one you have personal experience with and feel competent to evaluate. This subject might be a movie, a TV program, a piece of music, an artwork, a new product, a government agency, a campus facility or policy, an essay or reading, or anything else you can think of.

e For an interactive Learning by Doing activity on Evaluating Film, go to Ch. 11: **bedfordstmartins.com /bedguide**.

Composer and pianist George Gershwin (1898–1937), known for *Rhapsody in Blue, An American in Paris,* and many songs for musical shows and movies.

Then in a thoughtful essay, analyze your subject and evaluate it. You will need to determine specific criteria for evaluation and make them clear to your readers. In writing your evaluation, you will have a twofold purpose: (1) to set forth your assessment of the quality of your subject and (2) to convince your readers that your judgment is reasonable.

These three students wrote lively evaluations:

A music major evaluated works by American composer Aaron Copland, finding him trivial and imitative, "without a tenth of the talent or inventiveness that George Gershwin or Duke Ellington had in his little finger."

A student planning a career in business management evaluated a computer firm in which he had worked one summer. His criteria were efficiency, productivity, appeal to new customers, and employee satisfaction.

A student from Brazil, who had seen firsthand the effects of industrial development in the Amazon rain forest, evaluated the efforts of the U.S. government to protect forests and wetlands, comparing them with the efforts in her own country.

## Facing the Challenge Evaluating and Reviewing

The major challenge writers face when writing evaluations is to make clear to their readers the criteria they have used to arrive at an opinion. While you may not be an expert in any field, you should never underestimate your powers of discrimination. When reviewing a movie, for example, you may begin by simply summarizing its story and saying whether you like it or not. However, for readers who wonder whether to see the movie, you need to go further. For example, you might find its special effects, exotic sets, and unpredictable plot effective but wish that the characters had seemed more believable. Based on these criteria, your thesis might maintain that the movie is not realistic but is entertaining and well worth seeing.

Once you've chosen a topic, clarify your standards for evaluating it:

- What features or aspects will you use as criteria for evaluating?
- How could you briefly explain each of the criteria for a reader?

- What judgment or evaluation about your topic do the criteria support?

After identifying your criteria, you can examine each in turn. Explaining your criteria will ensure that you move beyond a summary to an opinion or judgment that you can justify to your readers.

## Generating Ideas

**Find Something to Evaluate.** Try *brainstorming* or *mapping* to identify as many possible topics as you can. Test your mastery of each option with potential by concisely describing or summarizing it. Spend enough time investigating possibilities that you can comfortably choose your subject.

For more strategies for generating ideas, see Ch. 19.

**Consider Sources of Support.** You'll want to spend time finding material to help you develop a judgment. You may recall a program on television or browse for an article to read. You might observe a performance or a sports team. Perhaps you'll want to review several examples of your subject: watching several films or campus plays, listening to several CDs, examining several works of art, testing several products, or interviewing several spectators.

**Establish Your Criteria.** Jot down criteria, standards to apply to your subject based on the features of the subject worth considering. How well, for example, does a popular entertainer score on musicianship, rapport with the audience, selection of material, originality? In evaluating Portland as a home for a young careerist, you might ask: Does it offer ample entry-level positions in growth firms? Any criterion for evaluation has to fit your subject, audience, and purpose. After all, ample entry-level jobs might not matter to an audience of retirees.

For more on comparing and contrasting, see Ch. 7.

**Try Comparing and Contrasting.** Often you can readily size up the worth of a thing by setting it next to another of its kind. (When you *compare,* you point to similarities; when you *contrast,* you note differences.) To be comparable, of course, your two subjects need to have plenty in common. The quality of a Harley-Davidson motorcycle might be judged by contrasting it with a Honda but not with a school bus.

Impressionistic set for *The Cabinet of Dr. Caligari* (1920), in which a man investigates the murder of his friend in a mountain village.

For example, if you are writing a paper for a film history course, you might compare and contrast the classic German horror movie *The Cabinet of Dr. Caligari* with the classic Hollywood movie *Frankenstein,* concluding that *Caligari* is more artistic. Then try listing characteristics of each film, point by point:

| | *CALIGARI* | *FRANKENSTEIN* |
|---|---|---|
| SETS | Dreamlike and impressionistic | Realistic, but with heavy Gothic atmosphere |
| | Sets deliberately angular and distorted | Gothic sets |
| LIGHTING | Deep shadows that throw figures into relief | Torches highlighting monster's face in night scene |

By jotting down each point and each bit of evidence side by side, you can outline your comparison and contrast with great efficiency. Once you have listed them, decide on a possible order for the points.

For more on defining, see pp. 441–43.

**Try Defining Your Subject.** Another technique for evaluating is to define your subject, indicating its nature so clearly that your readers can easily distinguish it from others of its kind. Defining helps readers understand your subject—its structure, habitat, functions. In evaluating a classic television show such as *Roseanne,* you might want to include an *extended* definition of sitcoms over the years, their techniques, views of women, effects on the audience. Unlike a *short definition,* as in a dictionary, an extended definition is intended not simply to explain but to judge: What is the nature of my subject? What qualities make it unique, unlike others of its sort?

**Develop a Judgment That You Can Explain to Your Audience.** In the end, you will have to come to a decision: Is your subject good, worthwhile, significant, exemplary, preferable—or not? Most writers come to a judgment gradually as they explore their subjects and develop criteria.

---

**DISCOVERY CHECKLIST**

- ☐ What criteria do you plan to use in making your evaluation? Are they clear and reasonably easy to apply?
- ☐ What evidence can back up your judgments?
- ☐ Would comparing or contrasting help in evaluating your subject? If so, with what might you compare or contrast your subject?
- ☐ What qualities define your subject, setting it apart from the rest of its class?

---

## Learning by Doing Developing Criteria

With a small group of classmates, meeting in person or online, discuss the subjects each of you plan to evaluate. Make a detailed report about what you're evaluating. If possible, pass around a product, show a photograph of artwork, play a song, or read aloud a short literary work or an idea expressed in a reading. Ask your classmates to explain the reasons for their own evaluations. Maybe they'll suggest criteria or evidence that hadn't occurred to you.

## Planning, Drafting, and Developing

**Start with a Thesis.** Reflect a moment: What is your purpose? What is your main point? Try writing a paragraph that sums up the purpose of your evaluation or stating a thesis that summarizes your main point.

For more on stating a thesis, see pp. 399–408.

For practice developing and supporting effective thesis statements, go to the interactive "Take Action" charts in Re:Writing at **bedfordstmartins.com/bedguide**.

TOPIC + JUDGMENT — Campus revival of *South Pacific*—liked the performers featured in it plus the problems the revival raised

WORKING THESIS — Chosen to showcase the achievements of graduating seniors, the campus revival of *South Pacific* also brings up societal problems.

## Learning by Doing Stating Your Overall Judgment

Build your criteria into your working thesis statement by filling in this sentence:

This subject is ____________ because it ____________.
(your judgment) (your criteria)

With a classmate or small group, compare sentences and share ideas about improving your statement of your judgment and criteria. Use this advice to rework and sharpen your working thesis.

**Consider Your Criteria.** Many writers find that a list of specific criteria gives them confidence and provokes ideas. Consider filling in a chart with three columns—criteria, evidence, judgment—to focus your thinking.

**Develop an Organization.** You may want to begin with a direct statement of your judgment: Based on durability, cost, and comfort, the Classic 7 is an ideal campus backpack. On the other hand, you may want to reserve judgment by opening with a question about your subject: How good a film is *Argo*? Each approach suggests a different organization:

Thesis or main point → Supporting evidence → Return to thesis
Opening question → Supporting evidence → Overall judgment

Either way, you'll supply lots of evidence—details, examples, maybe comparisons or contrasts—to make your case compelling. You'll also cluster your evidence around your points or criteria for judgment so that readers know how and why you reach your judgment. You might try both patterns of organization to see which works better for your subject and purpose.

Most writers find that an outline—even a rough list—helps them keep track of points to make. If you compare and contrast your subject with something else, one way to arrange the points is *subject by subject:* discuss subject A, and then discuss subject B. For a longer comparison, a better way to organize is *point by point,* applying each point first to one subject and then the other. If approved by your instructor, you also might include a sketch, photograph, or other illustration of your subject or develop a comparative table summarizing the features of similar items you have compared.

### Learning by Doing Supporting Your Judgments

Consider how well you have linked specific support to your judgments to make your draft interesting and persuasive. Scroll through the file for your draft, and highlight each judgment or opinion in one color. (Look under Format to find Font choices, including color, or use your highlighting options.) Then go back to the beginning, and this time highlight all the facts and evidence in a different color. (If you work on a printed copy, use two highlighters.)

Now observe the flow of color in your draft. Are your judgments followed by evidence that supports them? Do you need to add more support at any points? Should you move sentences around to link support more closely to judgments? Once you have connected judgments and evidence, reread to confirm how well they match. Do you need to modify any judgments or revise any support?

## Revising and Editing

For more revising and editing strategies, see Ch. 23.

**Focus on Your Thesis.** Make your thesis as precise and clear as possible.

WORKING THESIS Chosen to showcase the graduating seniors, the campus revival of *South Pacific* also brings up societal problems.

REVISED THESIS The senior showcase, the musical *South Pacific,* spotlights outstanding performers and raises timely societal issues such as prejudice.

**Be Fair.** Make your judgments reasonable, not extreme. A reviewer can find fault with a film and still conclude that it is worth seeing. There's nothing wrong, of course, with a fervent judgment ("This play is the trashiest excuse for a drama I have ever suffered through"), but consider your readers and their likely reactions. Read some reviews in your local newspaper or online, or watch some movie critics on television to see how they balance their judgments. Because readers will have more confidence in your opinions if you seem fair and reasonable, revise your tone where needed. For example, one writer revised his opening after he realized that he was criticizing the audience rather than evaluating the performance.

> The most recent performance by a favorite campus group—Rock Mountain—
>
> *disappointing concert* *Although t*
>
> was a~~n~~ ~~incredibly revolting~~ experience. ~~T~~he ~~outlandish~~ crowd ignored the DJ who
>
> *people*
>
> introduced the group~~.~~ and a few ~~nameless members of one social group spent~~
>
> *ed*
>
> ~~their time~~ toss~~ing~~ around trash cans in front of the stage~~.~~*, the opening number still announced the group's powerful musical presence.*

## Peer Response Evaluating and Reviewing

Enlist the advice of a classmate or friend as you determine your criteria for evaluation and your judgment. Ask your peer editor to answer questions like these about your evaluation:

- What is your overall reaction to this essay? Does the writer persuade you to agree with his or her evaluation?
- When you finish the essay, can you tell exactly what the writer thinks of the subject? Where does the writer express this opinion?
- How do you know what criteria the writer is using for evaluation?
- Does the writer give you sufficient evidence for his or her judgment? Put stars wherever more or better evidence is needed.
- What audience does the writer seem to have in mind?
- Would you recommend any changes in the essay's organization?
- If this paper were yours, what is the one thing you would be sure to work on before handing it in?

For general questions for a peer editor, see p. 463.

### REVISION CHECKLIST

- ☐ Is the judgment you pass on your subject unmistakably clear?
- ☐ Have you given your readers evidence to support each point you make?

- ☐ Have you been fair? If you are championing something, have you deliberately skipped over its disadvantages or faults? If you are condemning your subject, have you omitted its admirable traits?
- ☐ Have you anticipated and answered readers' possible objections?
- ☐ If you compare two things, do you look at the same points in both?

For more on comparison and contrast, see Ch. 7.

For more editing and proofreading strategies, see pp. 471–75.

After you have revised your evaluation, edit and proofread it. Carefully check grammar, word choice, punctuation, and mechanics—and then correct any problems you find. Make sentences in which you describe the subject of your evaluation as precise and useful as possible. If you have used comparisons or contrasts, make sure these are clear: don't lose your readers in a fog of vague pronouns or confusing references.

For more help, find the relevant checklist sections in the Quick Editing Guide on p. A-39. Turn also to the Quick Format Guide beginning on p. A-1.

**EDITING CHECKLIST**

- ☐ Is it clear what each pronoun refers to? Does each pronoun agree with (match) its antecedent? A6
- ☐ Is it clear what each modifier in a sentence modifies? Have you created any dangling or misplaced modifiers, especially in descriptions of your subject? B1
- ☐ Have you used parallel structure wherever needed, especially in lists or comparisons? B2

## Additional Writing Assignments

1. Write an evaluation of a college course you have taken or are now taking. Analyze its strengths and weaknesses. Does the instructor present the material clearly, understandably, and engagingly? Are the assignments pointed and purposeful? Is the textbook helpful, readable, and easy to use? Does this course give you your money's worth?
2. Evaluate an unfamiliar magazine, an essay in this textbook, a proposal being considered at work, a source you have read for a college class, an academic Web site about an area that interests you, or a possible source for a

research project. Specify your criteria for evaluation, and identify the evidence that supports your judgments.

3. Evaluate a product that you might want to purchase. Establish criteria that matter to you – and to the other prospective purchasers who might turn to you for a recommendation. Consider, for example, the product's features, construction, utility, beauty, color, cost, or other criteria that matter to purchasers. Make a clear recommendation to your audience: buy or not.

4. Visit a restaurant, museum, or tourist attraction, and evaluate it for others who might consider a visit. Present your evaluation as an essay, an article for a travel or lifestyle magazine, or a travel blog that informs about local sites and evaluates what they offer. Specify your criteria, and include plenty of detail to create the local color your audience will expect.

5. **Source Assignment.** Read these two poems on a similar theme, and decide which seems to you the better poem. In a brief essay, set forth your evaluation. Some criteria to apply might be the poet's choice of concrete, specific words that appeal to the senses and his awareness of his audience. Quote, paraphrase, summarize, and accurately credit supporting evidence from the poems.

For more on responding to literature, see Ch. 13.

**Putting in the Seed**

Robert Frost (1874–1963)

You come to fetch me from my work tonight
When supper's on the table, and we'll see
If I can leave off burying the white
Soft petals fallen from the apple tree
(Soft petals, yes, but not so barren quite,
Mingled with these, smooth bean and wrinkled pea),
And go along with you ere you lose sight
Of what you came for and become like me,
Slave to a springtime passion for the earth.
How Love burns through the Putting in the Seed
On through the watching for that early birth
When, just as the soil tarnishes with weed,
The sturdy seedling with arched body comes
Shouldering its way and shedding the earth crumbs.

**Between Our Folding Lips**

T. E. Brown (1830–1897)

Between our folding lips
God slips
An embryon life, and goes;
And this becomes your rose.
We love, God makes: in our sweet mirth
God spies occasion for a birth.
*Then is it His, or is it ours?*
I know not – He is fond of flowers.

6. **Visual Assignment.** Select one pair of the following images, and examine their features carefully. Write an essay that evaluates the items portrayed in the images or the images themselves. Specify for your audience your criteria for judging. Observe carefully to identify enough visual detail to support your judgments.

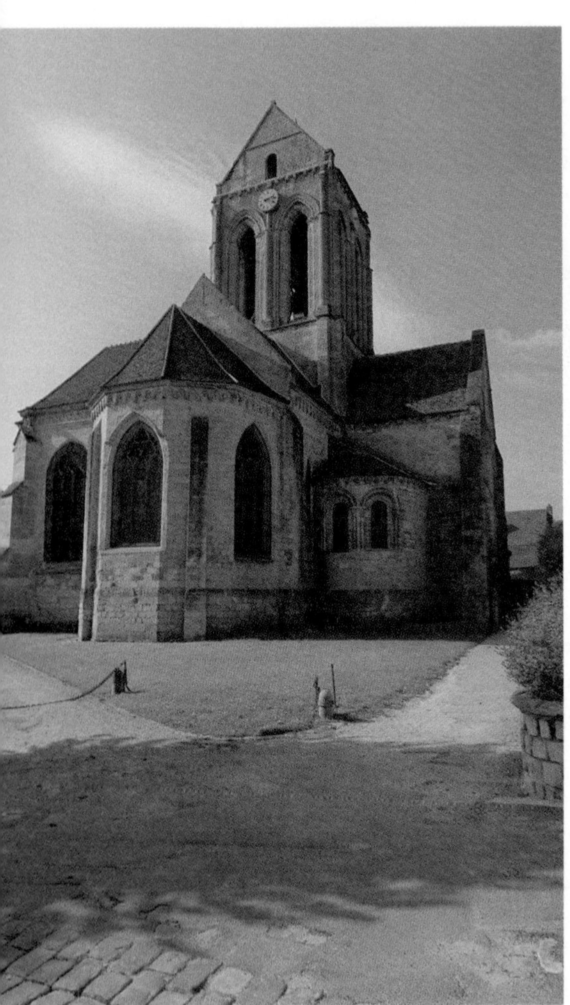

Church at Auvers-sur-Oise, France (2002)

"Church at Auvers-sur-Oise" painted by Vincent van Gogh (1853–1890)

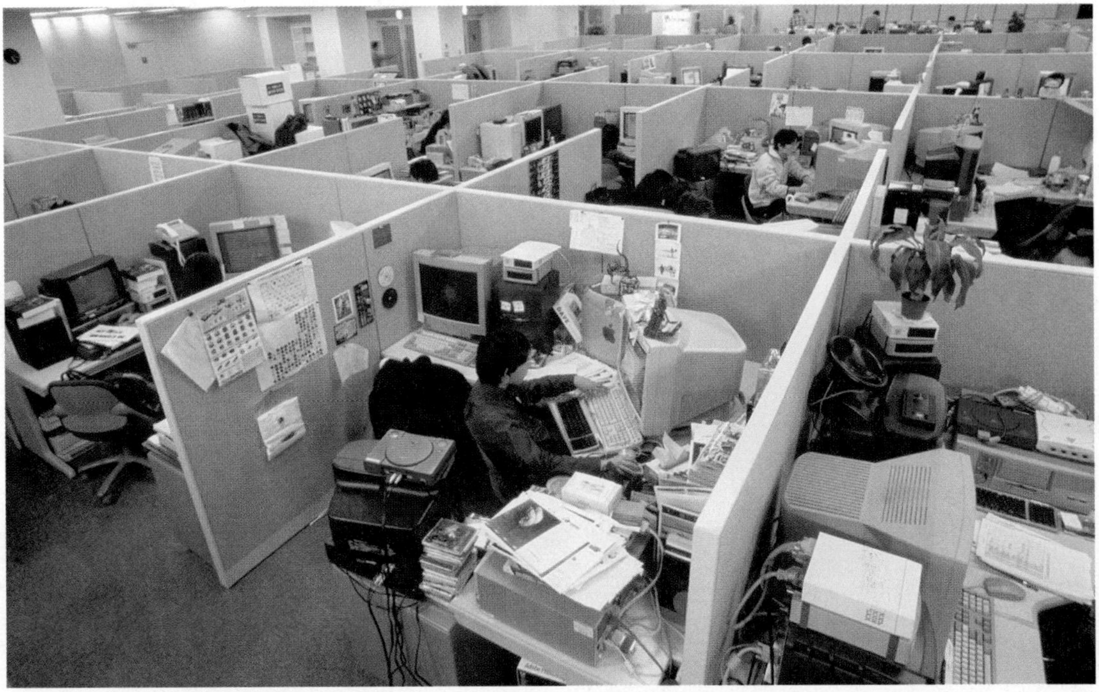

Designers and software engineers at work in a division of Sony Computer Entertainment, 1999.

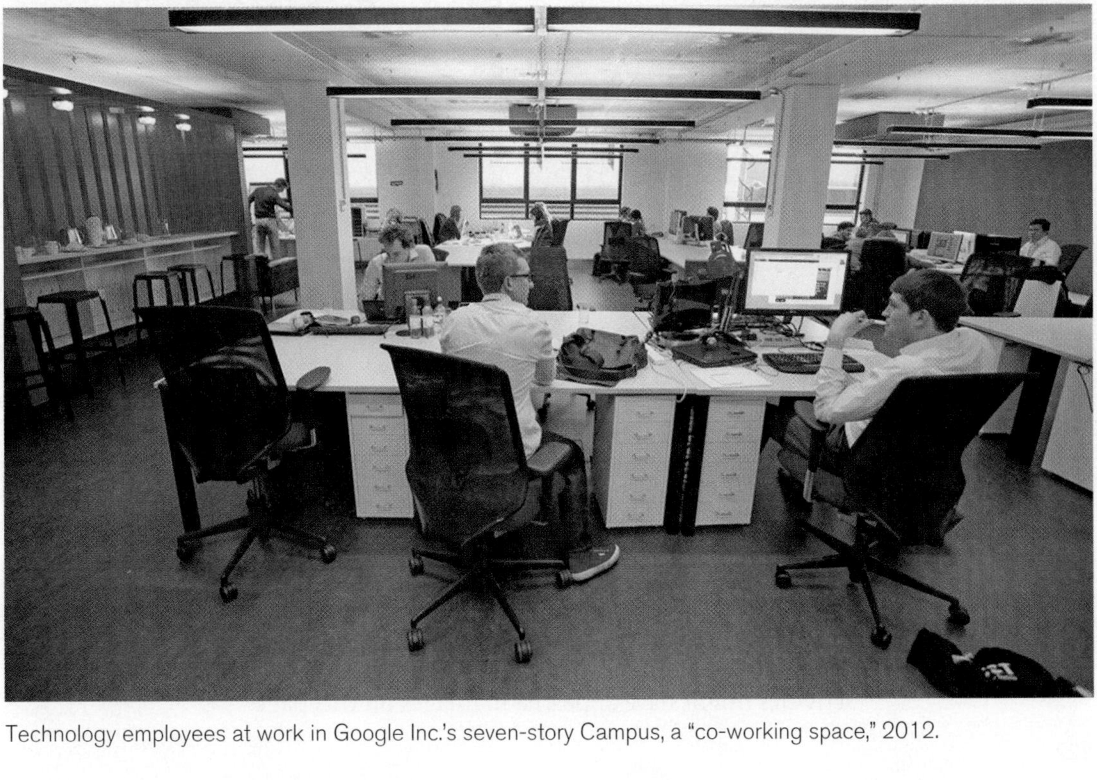

Technology employees at work in Google Inc.'s seven-story Campus, a "co-working space," 2012.

# 12 Supporting a Position with Sources

### Responding to an Image

These images show activities that might help a student gather evidence from sources to support a position in a college paper. What does each image suggest about possible sources? What do the images suggest about the process of inquiry? Which activities look most intriguing? What other activities might have appeared in images on this page?

Suppose you surveyed a random group of graduating students about the typical college writing assignment. The odds are good that this assignment might boil down to reading a few texts and writing a paper about them. Simple as this description sounds, it suggests what you probably expect from a college education: an opportunity to absorb and think seriously about provocative ideas. It also suggests the values that lie behind college expectations—a deep respect for the process of inquiry (the academic method of asking and investigating intriguing questions) and for the products of inquiry (the analyses, interpretations, and studies in each academic field).

When you first tackle such assignments, you may wonder "How do I figure out what my instructor really wants?" or "How could I possibly do that?" In response, you may turn to peripheral questions such as "How long does my paper have to be?" or "How many sources do I have to use?" Instead, try to face the central question: "How can I learn the skills I need to use a few sources to develop and support a position in a college paper?"

Unlike a debate or a Super Bowl game, a paper that takes a position generally doesn't have two sides or a single winner. Instead, the writer typically joins the ongoing exchange of ideas about an intriguing topic in the field. Each paper builds on the exchanges of the past—the articles, essays, reports, and books that convey the perspectives, research findings, and conclusions of others. Although reading such sources may seem daunting, you are not expected to know everything yourself but simply to work hard at learning what others know. Your paper, in turn, advances the exchange to convey your well-grounded point of view or to defend your well-reasoned interpretation.

## Why Supporting with Sources Matters

### In a College Course

- You support a position with sources when you write a history paper about an event, synthesizing a first-person account, contemporary newspaper story, and scholarly article.
- You support a position with sources when you write an analysis after reading a short story along with several critical essays about it.

### In the Workplace

- You support a position with sources when you write a report pulling together multiple accounts and records to support your recommendation.

### In Your Community

- You support a position with sources when you write a well-substantiated letter to the editor.

When have you used sources to support a position in your writing? What source-based writing might you do at work or in your community?

## Learning from Other Writers

The selections here illustrate how two different writers draw on evidence from sources to substantiate their points. The notes in the margin of the first reading will help you begin to analyze features such as the thesis, or main idea, and the variety of methods used to introduce and integrate information from sources.

### As You Read These Essays That Support a Position with Sources

As you read these essays, ask yourself the following questions:

1. What thesis, or main idea, expresses the position supported by the essay? How does the writer try to help readers appreciate the importance of this position?
2. How does the writer use information from sources to support a thesis? Do you find this information relevant and persuasive?
3. How does the writer vary the way each source is introduced and the way information is drawn from it?

### Jake Halpern

### The Popular Crowd

Works by author and radio producer Jake Halpern include *Braving Home* (2003), a study of people who live in extreme places, and *Dormia* (2009), a fantasy novel. The selection here comes from *Fame Junkies* (2007), Halpern's analysis of celebrity worship. Its references to sources have been adapted to illustrate MLA style.

1 Americans now appear to be lonelier than ever. In his book *The Loss of Happiness in Market Democracies,* the Yale political scientist Robert Lane notes that the number of people who described themselves as lonely more than quadrupled in the past few decades (85). We have increasingly become a nation of loners—traveling salesmen, Web designers, phone-bank operators, and online day traders who live and work in isolation. According to the U.S. Census Bureau, we also marry later in life. In 1956 the median age for marriage was 22.5 for men and 20.1 for women; by 2004 it was 27.4 for men and 25.8 for women (Russell). This helps to explain something else the Census Bureau has noted: Americans are increasingly living alone. The share of American households including seven or more people dropped from 35.9 percent in 1790, 5.8 percent in 1950, and 1.2 percent in 2004. Meanwhile, the number of households consisting of just one person rose from 3.7 percent in 1790 to 9.3 percent in 1950 and 26.4 percent in 2004. Nowadays, one out of four

Background information including facts and statistics

American households consists of a single person. In recent years this trend has been especially discernible° among young people (Cushman 599; U.S. Census Bureau). Since 1970 the number of youths (ages fifteen to twenty-five) living alone has almost tripled, and the number of young adults (ages twenty-five to thirty-four) living alone has more than quadrupled (Russell).

The combination of loneliness and our innate° desire to belong may be 2
fueling our interest in celebrities and our tendency to form para-social relationships° with them. Only a few research psychologists have seriously explored this possibility, among them Lynn McCutcheon and Dianne Ashe. McCutcheon and Ashe compared results from 150 subjects who had taken three personality tests—one measuring shyness, one measuring loneliness, and one measuring celebrity obsession, on something called the Celebrity Attitudes Scale, or CAS. The CAS asks subjects to rate the veracity° of statements such as "I am obsessed by details of my favorite celebrity's life" and "If I were lucky enough to meet my favorite celebrity, and he/she asked me to do something illegal as a favor, I would probably do it." McCutcheon and Ashe found a correlation among scores on loneliness, shyness, and the CAS (Ashe and McCutcheon 129). Their results led McCutcheon to observe in a subsequent paper, "Perhaps one of the ways [we] cope with shyness and loneliness is to cultivate a 'safe,' non-threatening relationship with a celebrity" (McCutcheon et al. 503).

THESIS presenting position

Supporting evidence, including description of psychological study

Examples quoted from survey

Point 1

Direct quotation

Et al. ("and others") used for source with four or more authors

Another investigation, led by Jacki Fitzpatrick, of Texas Tech University, 3
looked at the correlation° between para-social relationships and actual romantic relationships. Fitzpatrick asked forty-five college students to complete a questionnaire containing several psychological measures, including one that gauged para-social relationships (the Para-social Interaction Scale) and another that gauged romantic relationships (the Multiple Determinants of Relationship Commitment Inventory). She and her colleague, Andrea McCourt, discovered that subjects who were less invested in their romantic relationships were more involved in para-social relationships. They concluded, "It makes sense that individuals may use para-social relationships as one way to fulfill desires or address needs (e.g., for attention, companionship) that are unmet in their romances" (Fitzpatrick and McCourt).

Paraphrase

Point 2

The Rochester survey,* too, provides evidence that lonely teenagers are 4
especially susceptible to forming para-social relationships with celebrities. Boys who described themselves as lonely were almost twice as likely as others to endorse the statement "My favorite celebrity just helps me feel good and forget about all of my troubles." Girls who described themselves as lonely were almost three times as likely as others to endorse that statement.

Author's position based on study

**discernible:** Distinguishable, noticeable. **innate:** Inborn from birth. **para-social relationships:** One-sided friendships, based on the illusion of interaction and mutual knowledge. **veracity:** Truthfulness. **correlation:** Agreement, parallelism.

*The Rochester, NY, survey of 653 fifth to eighth grade students, conducted by Jake Halpern and Carol M. Liebler, is discussed in full in *Fame Junkies* (New York: Houghton Mifflin 2007). [Editor's note]

Another survey question asked teens whom they would most like to meet for dinner: Jesus Christ, Albert Einstein, Shaquille O'Neal, Jennifer Lopez, 50 Cent, Paris Hilton, or the President. Among boys who said they were not lonely, the clear winner was Jesus Christ; but among those who described themselves as lonely, Jesus finished last and 50 Cent was the clear winner. Similarly, girls who felt appreciated by their parents, friends, and teachers tended to choose dinner with Jesus, whereas those who felt underappreciated were likely to choose Paris Hilton. One possible interpretation of these results is that lonely and underappreciated teens particularly want to befriend the ultimate popular guy or girl. Regardless of who exactly this figure is at a given time, it's clear that many of us—lonely people in particular—yearn to belong to the popular crowd. 5

Paraphrase

Analysis

Conclusion synthesizing sources

## Works Cited


Ashe, D. D., and Lynn McCutcheon. "Shyness, Loneliness, and Attitude Toward Celebrities." *Current Research in Social Psychology* 6.9 (2001): 124–33. Print.

Cushman, Philip. "Why the Self Is Empty: Toward a Historically Situated Psychology." *American Psychologist* 45.5 (1990): 599–612. Print.

Fitzpatrick, Jacki, and Andrea McCourt. "The Role of Personal Characteristics and Romantic Characteristics in Para-social Relationships: A Pilot Study." *Journal of Mundane Behavior* 2.1 (2001): n. pag. Web. [Author's date of access not known.]

Lane, Robert E. *The Loss of Happiness in Market Democracies*. New Haven: Yale UP, 2000. Print.

McCutcheon, Lynn, Mara Aruguete, Vann B. Scott, Jr., and Kristen L. VonWaldner. "Preference for Solitude and Attitude Toward One's Favorite Celebrity." *North American Journal of Psychology* 6.3 (2004): 499–505. Print.

Russell, Cheryl. *newstrategist.com*. New Strategist Publications, n.d. Web. [Author's date of access not known.]

United States Census Bureau. Fertility and Family Branch. *HH-4: Households by Size: 1960 to Present*. 15 Sept. 2004. *U.S. Census Bureau*. Web. [Author's date of access not known.]


Each source cited in Halpern's essay listed alphabetically by author, with full publication information

First line of entry placed at left margin; with subsequent lines indented ½″

## Questions to Start You Thinking

Meaning

1. What position does Halpern take in this essay?
2. In paragraph 1, Halpern refers to America as "a nation of loners." What does he mean by this statement, and how does he see the problem changing in recent decades?
3. How does Halpern suggest that following and watching a celebrity could help people cope with shyness?
4. How has Halpern arranged the main points of his essay? How do these points develop his thesis in paragraph 2 and lead up to paragraph 5?

Writing Strategies

5. What types of evidence does Halpern use to support his position? How convincing is this evidence to you?
6. Halpern alternates between stating some source information in his own words and quoting some directly. What are the advantages and disadvantages of these two approaches?
7. How would you describe Halpern's tone, the quality of his writing that reveals his attitude toward his topic and his readers? What specific words, phrases, or sentences contribute to his tone? Does the tone seem appropriate for his purpose and audience?
8. Compare this selection, excerpted from a book, with an article written for a newspaper (see, for example, "The Opportunity Gap," p. 118). What differences in formatting, style, and presentation do you notice between the two selections?

**Abigail Marchand** **Student Essay**

## The Family Dynamic

Abigail Marchand wrote this essay in response to a reading assigned in her composition class. She used MLA style to cite and list sources.

Children are resilient creatures, and often adults underestimate their vast emotional capabilities, their compassion, and their ability to find the good in everything. When babies are brought home from the hospital, they don't care if their parents are same sex or not. They only want to feel safe, to be held, and most of all to be loved. It is unfortunate that we as a human race allow our own petty ideals to interfere with these simple needs. 1

The notion that a child can thrive only in a "nuclear" family has long been dispelled. With the increase in the divorce rate and the number of children born to single mothers, many children are not raised in that traditional family. Thus, the idea of a child being raised by a same-sex couple really shouldn't seem that foreign. According to a 2011 U.S. Census Bureau report, only about 1% of couples are of the same sex (1), but over 115,000 of their households include children (3). Anna Quindlen very directly sums up this situation: "Evan has two moms. This is no big thing" (501). 2

What does a "nuclear" family mean to you?

For a variety of reasons, many children today are growing up in a completely different environment than that of their grandparents of the 1950s and 1960s. However, as Quindlen says, "the linchpin of family has commonly been a loving commitment between two adults" (501). Even though a family might have two mothers or two fathers or even one single parent, what should matter is not the quantity of love a child receives but the quality of that love. 3

A child's development will neither be hurt nor helped by a same-sex family. Frankly, the makeup of the family and specifically the absence of an opposite-sex partner have 4 little impact on the day-to-day lives of most children. As two sociologists who reviewed past research studies on parenting concluded, "The gender of parents correlates in novel ways with parent-child relationships but has minor significance for children's psychological adjustment and social success" (Biblarz and Stacey 3). Many same-sex households involve members of the opposite sex in some capacity, whether as friend, aunt, uncle, or cousin. In addition, as children from same-sex families attend schools, they encounter any number of people, both male and female. The argument that the child would interact only with one gender is ludicrous.

How do you view parenting responsibilities — as your parents' child or as your children's parent?

The advantages of a same-sex household would be similar to those of a standard father-and-mother household: Two people are there to help raise the children. Compared to a single mother raising a child alone, the same-sex household would benefit from having another person to shoulder some of the responsibilities. As a parent of four sons, I know the benefits of having a second person to help with transportation to various events, dinner preparation, or homework. Navigating the treacherous landscape of child rearing is far easier with an ally. 5

On a developmental level, a same-sex household would not affect the child's ability to grow and become a productive member of society. Certainly most children can adapt to any situation, and in the case of same-sex relationships, a child usually is brought into the home as a baby, so that environment is all he or she would know. The absence of an opposite-sex parent would never come into question since most children don't concern themselves with the gender of their family members. Instead, they view their caregivers as any other child would—as mommy or daddy. 6

The only disadvantage to same-sex households rests with the concerned citizens bent on "explaining" to the children how their parental unit is somehow doing something wrong. These naysayers pose the greatest risk to the children because they cannot look beyond the surface of the same-sex partners to see that most of these households function better than many "normal" ones. In a recent collection of interviews, seventeen-year-old Chris echoes this sentiment: "The hardest part about having a gay dad is that no matter how okay you are with it, there's always going to be someone who will dislike you because of it" (Snow 3). Garner's interviews with grown-up children of gay parents also raise the same theme, "the personal impact of a public issue" (15). 7

In fact, most people are unlikely to recognize a child being raised in a same sex household unless they specifically know the child's parents. My son attends daycare with two brothers who have two mothers. I never would have known this if I hadn't personally met both mothers. Their children are well-adjusted little boys who are fortunate to have two caring women in their lives. 8

What do you think that children need from parents and from society?

The real focus should be on whether all of the child's needs are met. It shouldn't matter if those needs are met by a mother and father, two mothers, or two fathers. Children should feel loved and cared for above all else. Unfortunately, in the case of same-sex households, external pressures can potentially shatter a child's well-being when "well-meaning" people attempt to interfere with something they know nothing about. It is amazing that people are more focused on the bedroom activities, 9 activities that never enter a child's consciousness anyway, than on the run-of-the-mill activities that most same-sex couples encounter in the rearing of a child. The only real disadvantage to these households lies solely with the closed minds of intolerance.

Works Cited

Biblarz, Timothy J., and Judith Stacey. "How Does the Gender of Parents Matter?" *Journal of Marriage and Family* 72.1 (2010): 3–22. Print.

Garner, Abigail. *Families Like Mine: Children of Gay Parents Tell It Like It Is*. New York: Harper Perennial, 2005. Print.

Quindlen, Anna. "Evan's Two Moms." *The Bedford Guide for College Writers*. 10th ed. Ed. X. J. Kennedy, Dorothy M. Kennedy, and Marcia F. Muth. Boston: Bedford/St. Martin's, 2014. 501–02. Print.

Snow, Judith E. *How It Feels to Have a Gay or Lesbian Parent: A Book by Kids for Kids of All Ages*. New York: Harrington Park, 2004. 1–3. Print.

United States. Dept. of Commerce. Census Bureau. *Same-Sex Couple Households*. 2011. *American Community Survey Briefs*. Web. 27 Sept. 2012.

For more on MLA citation style, see E1–E2 in the Quick Research Guide, pp. A-32–A-38.

## Questions to Start You Thinking

### Meaning

1. What position does Marchand support in this essay?
2. What reasons for her view does Marchand supply?
3. How does Marchand see children? What does she expect of families?

### Writing Strategies

4. What types of evidence does Marchand use to support her position? How convincing is this evidence to you?
5. Has Marchand considered alternative views? How does the inclusion (or lack) of these views contribute to or detract from the essay?
6. Marchand uses specific examples in several places. Which of these seem most effective to you? Why?
7. Using highlighters or marginal notes, identify the essay's introduction, thesis, major points, supporting evidence for each point, and conclusion. How effective is the organization of this essay?

**e Research Cluster** — **Text, Audio, and Video**

## Celebrity Culture

Most of us interact with celebrity culture, whether hunting for photos of a favorite actor's wedding or scanning headlines at the cash register, but few of us question this interaction. This cluster offers varying viewpoints on why people are interested in celebrities' lives and how that interest affects them. The cluster includes four selections: Cary Tennis's "Why Am I Obsessed with Celebrity Gossip?" [advice column]; Karen Sternheimer's "Celebrity Relationships: Why Do We Care?" [video]; Tom Ashbrook and Ty Burr's "The Strange Power of Celebrity" [audio]; and Timothy J. Bertoni and Patrick D. Nolan's "Dead Men *Do* Tell Tales" [academic paper]. To access the selections, go to Chapter 12: **bedfordstmartins.com/bedguide**.

# Learning by Writing

## The Assignment: Supporting a Position with Sources

For an interactive Learning by Doing activity on Finding Credible Sources, go to Ch. 12: **bedfordstmartins.com/bedguide**.

See the contents of *A Writer's Reader* on pp. 490–91.

Identify a cluster of readings about a topic that interests you. For example, choose related readings from this book and its e-Pages or from other readings assigned in your class. If your topic is assigned and you don't begin with much interest in it, develop your intellectual curiosity. Look for an angle, an implication, or a vantage point that will engage you. Relate the topic in some way to your experience. Read (or reread) the selections, considering how each supports, challenges, or deepens your understanding of the topic.

Based on the information in your cluster of readings, develop an enlightening position about the topic that you'd like to share with an audience of college readers. Support this position—your working thesis—using quotations, paraphrases, summaries, and syntheses of the information in the readings as evidence. Present your information from sources clearly, and credit your sources appropriately.

Three students investigated topics of great variety:

One student examined local language usage that combined words from English and Spanish, drawing on essays about language diversity to analyze the patterns and implications of such usage.

Another writer used a cluster of readings about technology to evaluate the privacy issues on a popular Web site for student profiles.

A third, using personal experience with a blended family and several essays on families, challenged misconceptions about today's families.

## Facing the Challenge Finding Your Voice

The major challenge that writers face when using sources to support a position is finding their own voice. You create your voice as a college writer through your choice of language and angle of vision. You probably want to present yourself as a thoughtful writer with credible insights, someone a reader will want to hear from.

Finding your own voice may be difficult in a source-based paper. After all, you need to read carefully and then capture information to strengthen your discussion by quoting, paraphrasing, or summarizing. You need to introduce it, feed it into your draft, and credit it. By this time, you may worry that your sources have taken over your paper. You may feel there's no room left for your own voice and, even if there were, it's too quiet to jostle past the powerful words of your sources. That, however, is your challenge.

As you develop your voice as a college writer and use it to guide your readers' understanding, you'll restrict sources to their proper role as supporting evidence. Don't let them get pushy or dominate your writing. Use these questions to help you strengthen your voice:

For more on evidence, see pp. 40–44 and pp. 170–74.

- Can you write a list or passage explaining what you'd like readers to hear from your voice? Where could you add more of this in your draft?
- Have you used your own voice, not quotations or paraphrases from sources, to introduce your topic, state your thesis, and draw conclusions?
- Have you generally relied on your own voice to open and conclude paragraphs and to reinforce your main ideas in every passage?
- Have you alternated between your voice and the voices of sources? Can you strengthen your voice if it gets trampled by a herd of sources?
- Have you used your voice to identify and introduce source material before you present it? Have you used your voice to explain or interpret source material after you include it?
- Have you used your voice to tell readers why your sources are relevant, how they support your points, and what their limits might be?
- Have you carefully created your voice as a college writer, balancing passion and personality with rock-solid reasoning?

Whenever you are uncertain about the answers to these questions, make an electronic copy of your file or print it out. Highlight all of the wording in your own voice in a bright, visible color. Check for the presence and prominence of this highlighting, and then revise the white patches (the material drawn from sources) as needed to strengthen your voice.

---

## Generating Ideas

For more strategies for generating ideas, see Ch. 19.

**Pin Down Your Working Topic and Your Cluster of Readings.** Specify what you're going to work on. This task is relatively easy if your instructor has assigned the topic and the required set of readings. If not, figure out what limits your instructor has set and which decisions are yours.

- Carefully follow any directions about the number or types of sources that you are expected to use.
- Instead of hunting only for sources that share your initial views about the topic, look for a variety of reliable and relevant sources so that you can broaden, even challenge, your perspective.

For advice about finding and evaluating academic sources, turn to sections B and C in the Quick Research Guide, pp. A-24–A-28.

**Consider Your Audience.** You are writing for an academic community that is intrigued by your topic (unless your instructor specifies another group). Your instructor's broad goal probably includes making sure that you are prepared to succeed when you write future assignments, including full research papers. For this reason, you'll be expected to quote, paraphrase, and summarize information from sources. You'll also need to introduce—or launch—such material and credit its source, thus demonstrating that you have mastered the essential skills for source-based writing.

In addition, your instructor will want to see your own position emerge from the swamp of information that you are reading. You may feel that your ideas are like a prehistoric creature, dripping as it struggles out of the bog. If so, encourage your creature to wade toward dry land. Jot down your own ideas whenever they pop into mind. Highlight them in color on the page or on the screen. Store them in your writing notebook or a special file so that you can find them, watch them accumulate, and give them well-deserved prominence in your paper.

For clusters of readings on this topic and others, see the contents of *A Writer's Reader* (pp. 490–91) and this book's e-Pages.

### One Student Thinking through a Topic

*General Subject:* Men and Women

*Assigned topic:* State and support a position about differences in the behavior of men and women.

What do I know about?
What do I care about?

RECALL PERSONAL EXPERIENCES: Friends at school? Competition for jobs? Pressure on parents to be good role models?

CONSIDER READINGS: Razdan? Jensen? Zeilinger? Staples? Brady?

• Stereotypes of women—emotional and caring
• Stereotypes of men—tough and aggressive
• What aboout me? I'm a woman in training to be a police officer—and I'm a mother. I'm emotional, caring, aggressive, and tough.

I bet that men and women are more alike than different. What do the readings say? What evidence do they present?

- RETURN TO THE READINGS.
- TEST AND REFINE YOUR WORKING THESIS.
- LOOK FOR EVIDENCE.

**Take an Academic Approach.** Your experience and imagination remain your own deep well, an endless reservoir from which you can draw ideas whenever you need them. For an academic paper, this deep well may help you identify an intriguing topic, raise a compelling question about it, or pursue an unusual slant. For example, you might recall talking with your cousin about her expensive prescriptions and decide to investigate the controversy about importing low-cost medications from other countries.

For more on generating ideas, see Ch. 19.

You'll also be expected to investigate your topic using authoritative sources. These sources—articles, essays, reports, books, Web pages, and other reliable materials—are your second deep well. When one well runs dry for the moment, start pumping the other. As you read critically to tap your second reservoir, you join the academic exchange. This exchange is the flow of knowledge from one credible source to the next as writers and researchers raise questions, seek answers, evaluate information, and advance knowledge. As you inquire, you'll move from what you already know to deeper knowledge. Welcome sources that shed light on your inquiry from varied perspectives rather than simply agree with a view you already hold.

For more on reading critically, see Ch. 2.

To see how the academic exchange works, turn to pp. 238–39.

## Learning by Doing Selecting Reliable Sources

When you choose your own sources, evaluate them to be sure they are reliable choices that your audience will respect. When your sources are assigned, assess their strengths, weaknesses, and limitations to use them effectively. Bring your articles, essays, and other sources to a small-group evaluation session. Using the checklist in C3 in the Quick Research Guide (pp. A-27–A-28), discuss your common sources or a key source selected by each writer in the group. Look for points that you might mention in a paper to bolster a source's credibility with readers (for example, the author's professional affiliation). Look as well for limitations that might restrict what a source can support.

**Skim Your Sources.** When you work with a cluster of readings, you'll probably need to read them repeatedly. Start out, however, by skimming—quickly reading only enough to find out what direction a selection takes.

- Leaf through the reading; glance at any headings or figure labels.
- Return to the first paragraph; read it in full. Then read only the first sentence of each paragraph. At the end, read the final paragraph in full.
- Stop to consider what you've already learned.

Do the same with your other selections, classifying or comparing them as you begin to think about what they might contribute to your paper.

### DISCOVERY CHECKLIST

- ☐ What topic is assigned or under consideration? What ideas about it emerge as you brainstorm, freewrite, or use another strategy to generate ideas?
- ☐ What cluster of readings will you begin with? What do you already know about them? What have you learned about them simply by skimming?
- ☐ What purpose would you like to achieve in your paper? Who is your primary audience? What will your instructor expect you to accomplish?
- ☐ What clues about how to proceed can you draw from the two sample essays in this chapter or from other readings identified as useful models?

For more on stating a thesis, see pp. 399–408.

For practice developing effective thesis statements, go to the interactive "Take Action" charts in Re:Writing at **bedfordstmartins .com/bedguide**.

## Planning, Drafting, and Developing

**Start with a Working Thesis.** Sometimes you start reading for a source-based paper with a clear position in mind; other times, you begin simply with your initial response to your sources. Either way, try to state your main idea as a working thesis even if you expect to rewrite it—or replace it—later on. Once your thesis takes shape in words, you can assess the richness and relevance of your reading based on a clear main idea.

| | |
|---|---|
| FIRST RESPONSE TO SOURCES | Joe Robinson, author of "Four Weeks Vacation," and others say that workers need more vacation time, but I can't see my boss agreeing to this. |
| WORKING THESIS | Although most workers would like longer vacations, many employers do not believe that they would benefit, too. |

Once your thesis takes shape in words, you can analyze its parts and use them to guide your search for reliable information. Of course you'll want to support your view, but often material that questions it proves more valuable, prompting you to rethink your thesis, refine it, or counter more effectively whatever challenges it. For example, the working thesis above breaks into two parts: workers and employers. Each might benefit from, or suffer from, longer vacations. Instead of looking for a perfect source to prove your thesis, you're now ready to look for the light each source can shed on either view (benefit or suffer) held by either party (worker or employer) you've identified.

## Learning by Doing Connecting Evidence and Thesis

State your working thesis, no matter how shaky it seems. List the parties or components it mentions, the views they might hold, or whatever else your evidence from sources might support, qualify, or challenge. Keep your working thesis and your evidence list handy as you read.

**Read Each Source Thoughtfully.** Before you begin copying quotations, scribbling notes, or highlighting a source, simply read, slowly and carefully. After you have figured out what the source says, you are ready to decide how you might use its information to support your ideas. Read again, this time sifting and selecting what's relevant to your thesis.

- How does the source use its own sources to support its position?
- Does it review major sources chronologically (by date), thematically (by topic), or by some other method?
- Does it use sources to supply background for its own position? Does it compare its position or research findings with those of other studies?
- What audience does the source address? What was its author's purpose?
- How might you want to use the source?

**Join the Academic Exchange.** A well-researched article that follows academic conventions will identify its sources for several reasons. It gives honest credit to the work on which it relies—work done by other researchers and writers. They deserve credit because their information contributes to the article's credibility and substantiates its points. The article also informs you about its sources so you, or any other reader, could find them yourself.

The visual on pages 238–39 illustrates how this exchange of ideas and information works and how you join this exchange from the moment you begin to use sources in your college writing. The middle of the visual shows the opening of a sample article about a global health problem: obesity. Because this article appears online, it credits its sources by providing a link to each one. A comparable printed article might identify its sources by supplying brief in-text citations (in parentheses in MLA or APA style), footnotes, numbers keyed to its references, or source identifications in the text itself. To the left of and below the source article are several of its sources. (They, in turn, also supply information about their sources.) The column to the right of the source article illustrates ways that you might capture information from the source.

For more on plagiarism, see D1 in the Quick Research Guide, pp. A-28–A-29.

For practice avoiding plagiarism, go to the interactive "Take Action" charts in Re:Writing at **bedfordstmartins.com/bedguide**.

For more on citing and listing sources, see E1 and E2 in the Quick Research Guide, pp. A-32–A-38.

**Capture Information and Record Source Details.** Consider how you might eventually want to capture each significant passage or point from a source in your paper—by quoting the exact words of the source, by paraphrasing its ideas in your own words, or by summarizing its essential point. Keeping accurate notes and records as you work with your sources will help you avoid accidental plagiarism (using someone else's words or ideas without giving the credit due). Accurate notes also help to reduce errors or missing information when you add the source material to your draft.

As you capture information, plan ahead so that you can acknowledge each source following academic conventions. Record the details necessary to identify the source in your discussion and to list it with other sources at the end of your paper. The next sections illustrate how to capture and credit your sources, using examples for a paper that connects land use and threats to wildlife. Compare the examples with the original passage from the source.

**Identify Significant Quotations.** When an author expresses an idea so memorably that you want to reproduce those words exactly, quote them word for word. Direct quotations can add life, color, and authority; too many can drown your voice and overshadow your point.

ORIGINAL The tortoise is a creature that has survived virtually unchanged since it first appeared in the geologic record more than 150 million years ago. The species became threatened, however, when ranchers began driving their herds onto Mojave Desert lands for spring grazing, at the very time that the tortoise awakens from hibernation and emerges from its burrows to graze on the greening desert shrubs and grasses. As livestock trampled the burrows and monopolized the scarce desert vegetation, tortoise populations plummeted. (page 152)

Babbitt, Bruce. *Cities in the Wilderness: A New Vision of Land Use in America*. Washington: Island Press-Shearwater, 2005. Print.

TOO MUCH QUOTATION When "tortoise populations plummeted," a species "that has survived virtually unchanged since it first appeared in the geologic record more than 150 million years ago" (Babbitt 152) had losses that helped to justify setting workable boundaries for the future expansion of Las Vegas.

MEMORABLE QUOTATION When "tortoise populations plummeted" (Babbitt 152), an unlikely species that has endured for millions of years helped to establish workable boundaries for the future expansion of Las Vegas.

The Mojave Desert

Writers often begin by highlighting or copying too many quotations as they struggle to master the ideas in the source. The better you understand the reading and your own thesis, the more effectively you'll choose quotations. After all, a quotation in itself is not necessarily effective evidence; too many quotations suggest that your writing is padded or lacks originality.

HOW TO QUOTE

- Select a quotation that is both notable and pertinent to your thesis.
- Record it accurately, writing out exactly what it says. Include its punctuation and capitalization. Avoid abbreviations that might later be ambiguous.
- Mark both its beginning and ending with quotation marks.
- Note the page or other location (such as an electronic paragraph) where the quotation appears. If the quotation begins on one page but ends on another, mark where the switch occurs so that the credit in your draft will be accurate no matter how much of the quotation you eventually use.
- Double-check the accuracy of each quotation as you record it.

For more on quotations, see D3 in the Quick Research Guide, p. A-29.

Use an ellipsis mark – three spaced dots (. . .) within a sentence or four dots (. . . .), a period and three spaced dots, concluding a sentence – to show where you leave out any original wording. You may omit wording that doesn't relate to your point, but don't distort the original meaning. For example, if a

For more on punctuating quotations and using ellipsis marks, see C3 in the Quick Editing Guide, pp. A-55–A-56.

**THE ACADEMIC EXCHANGE** Suppose that you used the center article to support a position. In turn, your source drew on other writings, some of which are shown to the left of and below the center article. The various ways you might use this source are shown on the right-hand page.

## Sources Cited in Your Source

### Source: U.S. Department of Agriculture

<www.usda.gov>

**AREI Chapter 3.5: Global Resources and Productivity**

Keith Wiebe

**Abstract**—*Global food production has grown faster than population in recent decades, due largely to improved seeds and increased use of fertilizer and irrigation. Soil degradation which has slowed yield growth in some areas, depends on farmers' incentives to adopt conservation practices, but does not threaten food security at the global level.*

**Introduction**

Increased resource use and improvements in technology and efficiency have increased global food production more rapidly than population in recent decades, but 800 million people remain food insecure (fig. 3.5.1). . . .

### Source: World Bank

<web.worldbank.org>

**Poverty Analysis: Overview**

**Trends in poverty over time: Living Standards have improved...**

Living standards have risen dramatically over the last decades. The proportion of the developing world's population living in extreme economic poverty -- defined as living on less than $1 per day ($1.08 in 1993 dollars, adjusted to account for differences in purchasing power across countries) -- has fallen from 28 percent in 1990 to 21 percent in 2001.

Substantial improvements in social indicators have accompanied growth in average incomes. Infant mortality rates in low- and middle-income countries have fallen from 86 per 1,000 live births in 1980 to 60 in 2002. Life expectancy in these countries has risen from 60 to 65 between 1980 and 2002. For more health, nutrition and population statistics, see the HNPStats database. . . .

## Your Source <www.slate.com>

# Please Do Not Feed the Humans

THE GLOBAL EXPLOSION OF FAT.

*By William Saletan*

Posted Saturday, Sept. 2, 2006, at 8:22 AM ET

In 1894, Congress established Labor Day to honor those who "from rude nature have delved and carved all the grandeur we behold." In the century since, the grandeur of human achievement has multiplied. Over the past four decades, global population has doubled, but food output, driven by increases in productivity, has outpaced it. Poverty, infant mortality, and hunger are receding. For the first time in our planet's history, a species no longer lives at the mercy of scarcity. We have learned to feed ourselves.

We've learned so well, in fact, that we're getting fat. Not just the United States or Europe, but the whole world. Egyptian, Mexican, and South African women are now as fat as Americans. Far more Filipino adults are now overweight than underweight. In China, one in five adults is too heavy, and the rate of overweight in children is 28 times higher than it was two decades ago. In Thailand, Kuwait, and Tunisia, obesity, diabetes, and heart disease are soaring.

Hunger is far from conquered. But since 1990, the global rate of malnutrition has declined an average of 1.7 percent a year. Based on data from the World Health Organization and the U.N. Food and Agriculture Organization, for every two people who are malnourished, three are now overweight or obese. Among women, even in most African countries, overweight has surpassed underweight. The balance of peril is shifting.

### Indirect Source: U.S. Department of Labor

**<www.dol.gov/opa/aboutdol/laborday.htm>**

**The History of Labor Day**

**Labor Day: How it Came About; What it Means**

"Labor Day differs in every essential way from the other holidays of the year in any country," said Samuel Gompers, founder and longtime president of the American Federation of Labor. "All other holidays are in a more or less degree connected with conflicts and battles of man's prowess over man, of strife and discord for greed and power, of glories achieved by one nation over another. Labor Day...is devoted to no man, living or dead, to no sect, race, or nation."

Labor Day, the first Monday in September, is a creation of the labor movement and is dedicated to the social and economic achievements of American workers. It constitutes a yearly national tribute to the contributions workers have made to the strength, prosperity, and well-being of our country.

**Founder of Labor Day**

More than 100 years after the first Labor Day observance, there is still some doubt as to who first proposed the holiday for workers.

Some records show that Peter J. McGuire, general secretary of the Brotherhood of Carpenters and Joiners and a cofounder of the American Federation of Labor, was first in suggesting a day to honor those "who from rude nature have delved and carved all the grandeur we behold."

### Sample Working Thesis

A clear thesis statement establishes a framework for selecting source material as useful evidence and for explaining its relevance to readers.

WORKING THESIS In order to counter national and worldwide trends toward obesity, agricultural communities like Grand Junction need to apply their expertise as food producers to the promotion of healthy food products.

### Quotation from an Indirect Source

A quotation from an indirect source captures the exact words of an author quoted within the source.

> An 1894 action by Congress created a holiday to recognize workers who "delved and carved" to produce what Americans enjoy (qtd. in Saletan).

If possible, go to the original source to be sure that the quotation is accurate and that you are using it appropriately. (See the bottom of the left-hand page.)

> Credit, though disputed, has gone to labor leader Peter McGuire for promoting the recognition of those who "delved and carved all the grandeur we behold" (US Dept. of Labor).

### Quotation from a Source

A quotation captures the author's exact words directly from the source.

> As Saletan observes, "We have learned to feed ourselves," but the success of agricultural enterprise and technology does not guarantee that well-fed people are healthy.

### Paraphrase of a Source

A paraphrase captures an author's specific ideas fully and accurately, restating them in your own words and sentences.

> Though the number of hungry people drops nearly 2 percent annually, more people, including African women, are now overfed by a ratio of 3 to 2 and thus have traded the health risks of malnutrition for those of obesity (Saletan).

### Summary of a Source

A summary reduces an author's main point to essentials, using your own words and sentences.

> Given that a worldwide shift in food security has led to an obesity epidemic (Saletan), consumers need lighter, healthier food options, a goal that the Grand Junction agricultural community can actively support.

### MLA Works Cited Entry

AUTHOR'S NAME — TITLE OF ARTICLE — TITLE OF MAGAZINE

Saletan, William. "Please Do Not Feed the Humans: The Global Explosion of Fat." *Slate*. Slate Group, Washington Post, 2 Sept. 2006. Web. 20 Sept. 2012.

SPONSOR/PUBLISHER — PUBLICATION DATE — MEDIUM — ACCESS DATE

reviewer calls a movie "a perfect example of poor directing and inept acting," don't quote this comment as "perfect . . . directing and . . . acting."

**Paraphrase Specific Information.** Paraphrasing involves restating an author's ideas in your own language. A paraphrase is generally about the same length as the original. It conveys the ideas and emphasis of the original in your words and sentences, thus bringing your own voice to the fore. A fresh and creative paraphrase expresses your style without awkwardly jumping between it and your source's style. Be sure to name the source so that your reader knows exactly where you move from one to the other.

Here, again, is the original passage by Bruce Babbitt, followed by a sloppy paraphrase. The paraphrase suffers from a common fault, slipping in too many words from the original. (The borrowed words are underlined in the paraphrase.) Those words need to be expressed in the writer's own language or identified as direct quotations with quotation marks.

ORIGINAL

The tortoise is a creature that has survived virtually unchanged since it first appeared in the geologic record more than 150 million years ago. The species became threatened, however, when ranchers began driving their herds onto Mojave Desert lands for spring grazing, at the very time that the tortoise awakens from hibernation and emerges from its burrows to graze on the greening desert shrubs and grasses. As livestock trampled the burrows and monopolized the scarce desert vegetation, tortoise populations plummeted. (page 152)

Babbitt, Bruce. *Cities in the Wilderness: A New Vision of Land Use in America*. Washington: Island Press-Shearwater, 2005. Print.

SLOPPY PARAPHRASE

Babbitt says that the tortoise is a creature in the Mojave that is virtually unchanged over 150 million years. Over the millennia, the tortoise would awaken from hibernation just in time for spring grazing on the new growth of the region's shrubs and grasses. In recent years the species became threatened. When cattle started to compete for the same food, the livestock trampled the tortoise burrows and monopolized the desert vegetation while the tortoise populations plummeted (152).

To avoid picking up language from the original as you paraphrase, state each sentence afresh instead of just changing a few words in the original. If possible, take a short break, and then check each sentence against the original. Highlight any identical words or sentence patterns, and rework your paraphrase again. Proper nouns or exact terms for the topic (such as *tortoise*) do not need to be rephrased.

The next example avoids parroting the original by making different word choices while reversing or varying sentence patterns.

PARAPHRASE As Babbitt explains, a tenacious survivor in the Mojave is the 150-million-year-old desert tortoise. Over the millennia, the hibernating tortoise would rouse itself each spring just in time to enjoy the new growth of the limited regional plants. In recent years, as cattle became rivals for this desert territory, the larger animals destroyed tortoise homes, ate tortoise food, and thus eliminated many of the tortoises themselves (152).

A common option is to blend paraphrase with brief quotation, carefully using quotation marks to identify any exact words drawn from the source.

BLENDED Babbitt describes a tenacious survivor in the Mojave, the 150-million-year-old desert tortoise. Over the millennia, the hibernating tortoise would rouse itself each spring just in time to munch on the new growth of the sparse regional plants. As cattle became rivals for the desert food supply and destroyed the tortoise homes, the "tortoise populations plummeted" (152).

Even in a brief paraphrase, be careful to avoid slipping in the author's words or closely shadowing the original sentence structure. If a source says, "President Obama called an emergency meeting of his cabinet to discuss the crisis," and you write, "The president called his cabinet to hold an emergency meeting to discuss the crisis," your words are too close to those of the source. One option is to quote the original, though it doesn't seem worth quoting word for word. Or, better, you could write, "Summoning his cabinet to an immediate session, Obama laid out the challenge before them."

HOW TO PARAPHRASE

- Select a passage with detailed information relevant to your thesis.
- Reword the passage: represent it accurately but use your own language.
- Change both its words and its sentence patterns. Replace its words with different expressions. Begin and end sentences differently, simplify long sentences, and reorder information.
- Note the page or other location (such as an electronic paragraph) where the original appears in your source. If the passage runs from one page

For more on paraphrases, see D4 in the Quick Research Guide, pp. A-29–A-30.

onto the next, record where the page changes so that your credit will be accurate no matter how much of the paraphrase you use.

- After a break, recheck your paraphrase against the original to be certain that it does not repeat the same words or merely replace a few with synonyms. Revise as needed, placing fresh words in fresh arrangements.

For advice on writing a synopsis of a literary work, see pp. 281–83.

**Summarize an Overall Point.** Summarizing is a useful way of incorporating the general point of a whole paragraph, section, or work. You briefly state the main sense of the original in your own words and also identify the source. Like a paraphrase, a summary uses your own language. However, a summary is shorter than the original; it expresses only the most important ideas – the essence – of the original. This example summarizes the section of Babbitt's book containing the passage quoted on pages 236–37 and 240.

SUMMARY According to Bruce Babbitt, former Secretary of the Interior and governor of Arizona, the isolated federal land in the West traditionally has been open to cattle and sheep ranching. These animals have damaged the arid land by grazing too aggressively, and the ranchers have battled wildlife grazers and predators alike to reduce competition with their stock. Protecting species such as the gray wolf and the desert tortoise has meant limiting grazing, an action supported by the public in order to conserve the character and beauty of the public land.

HOW TO SUMMARIZE

For more on summaries, see D5 in the Quick Research Guide, p. A-30.

- Select a passage, an article, a chapter, or an entire book whose main idea bears on your thesis.
- Read the selection carefully until you have mastered its overall point.
- Write a sentence or a series of sentences that states its essence in your own words.
- Revise your summary until it is as concise, clear, and accurate as possible. Replace any vague generalizations with precise words.
- Name your source as you begin your summary, or identify it in parentheses.

For more on plagiarism, see D1 in the Quick Research Guide, pp. A-28–A-29.

For practice avoiding plagiarism, go to the interactive "Take Action" charts in Re:Writing at **bedfordstmartins .com/bedguide**.

**Credit Your Sources Fairly.** As you quote, paraphrase, or summarize, be certain to note which source you are using and exactly where the material appears in the original. Carefully citing and listing your sources will give credit where it's due as it enhances your credibility as a careful writer.

Although academic fields prefer specific formats for their papers, MLA style is widely used in composition, English, and other humanities courses.

## Methods of Capturing Information from Sources

| | Quotation | Paraphrase | Summary |
|---|---|---|---|
| **Format for Wording** | Use exact words from the source, and identify any additions, deletions, or other changes | Use your words and sentence structures, translating the content of the original passage | Use your words and sentence structures, reducing the original passage to its core |
| **Common Use** | Capture lively and authoritative wording | Capture specific information while conserving its detail | Capture the overall essence of an entire source or a passage in brief form |
| **Advantages** | Catch a reader's attention<br>Emphasize the authority of the source | Treat specifics fully without shifting from your voice to the source's | Make a broad but clear point without shifting from your voice to the source's |
| **Common Problems** | Quoting too much<br>Quoting inaccurately | Slipping in the original wording<br>Following the original sentence patterns too closely | Losing impact by bogging down in too much detail<br>Drifting into vague generalities |
| **Markers** | Identify source in launch statement or text citation and in final list of sources<br>Add quotation marks to show the source's exact words<br>Use ellipses and brackets to mark any changes | Identify source in launch statement or text citation and in final list of sources | Identify source in launch statement or text citation and in final list of sources |

In MLA style, you credit your source twice. First, identify the author's last name (and the page number in the original) in the text as you quote, paraphrase, summarize, or refer to the source. Often you will simply mention the author's name (or a short version of the title if the author is not identified) as you introduce the information from the source. If not, note the name and page number of the original in parentheses after you present the material: (Walton 88). Next, fully identify the source in an alphabetical list at the end of your paper.

For sample source citations and lists, see the readings on pp. 224–29 and the MLA and APA examples in E in the Quick Research Guide, pp. A-32–A-38, and in A in the Quick Format Guide, pp. A-1–A-7.

Right now, the methods for capturing information and crediting sources may seem complicated. However, the more you use them, the easier they become. Experienced writers also know some time-tested secrets. For example, how can you save time, improve accuracy, and avoid last-minute stress about sources? The answer is easy. Include in your draft, even your very first one, both the source identification and the location. Add them at the very moment when you first add the material, even if you are just dropping it in so you don't forget it. Later on, you won't have to hunt for the details.

For practice supporting a thesis, go to the interactive "Take Action" charts in Re:Writing at **bedfordstmartins .com/bedguide**.

**Let Your Draft Evolve.** No matter how many quotations, paraphrases, and summaries you assemble, chunks of evidence captured from sources do not—on their own—constitute a solid paper. You need to interpret and explain that evidence for your readers, helping them to see exactly why, how, and to what extent it supports your position.

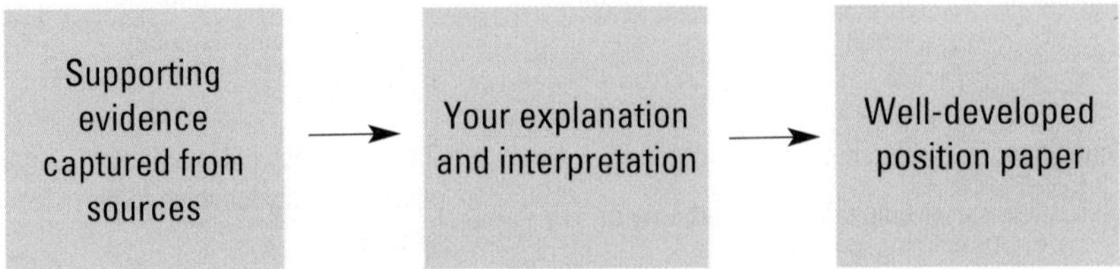


To develop a solid draft, many writers rely on one of two methods, beginning either with the evidence or with the position they wish to support.

METHOD 1 Start with your evidence. Use one of these strategies to arrange quotations, paraphrases, and summaries in a logical, compelling order.

- Cut and paste the chunks of evidence, moving them around in a file until they fall into a logical order.
- Print each chunk on a separate page, and arrange the pages on a flat surface like a table, floor, or bed until you reach a workable sequence.
- Label each chunk with a key word, and use the key words to work out an informal outline.

Once your evidence is organized logically, add commentary to connect the chunks for your readers: introduce, conclude, and link pieces of evidence with your explanations and interpretations. (Ignore any leftovers from sources unless they cover key points that you still need to integrate.) Let your draft expand as you alternate evidence and interpretation.

METHOD 2 Start with your position or your conclusion, selecting a way to focus on how you want your paper to present it.

- You can state your case boldly and directly, explaining your thesis and supporting points in your own words.
- If you feel too uncertain to take that step, you can write out directions, telling yourself what to do in each part of the draft (in preparation for actually doing it).

Either way, use this working structure to identify where to embed the evidence from your sources. Let your draft grow as you pull in your sources and expand your comments.

For more on quotations, paraphrases, and summaries, see D3, D4, and D5 in the Quick Research Guide, pp. A-29–A-30.

**DEVELOPMENT CHECKLIST**

☐ Have you quoted only notable passages that add support and authority?

☐ Have you checked your quotations for accuracy and marked where each begins and ends with quotation marks?

- ☐ Have you paraphrased accurately, reflecting both the main points and the supporting details in the original?
- ☐ Does each paraphrase use your own words without repeating or echoing the words or the sentence structure of the original?
- ☐ Have you briefly stated supporting ideas that you wish to summarize, sticking to the overall point without bogging down in details or examples?
- ☐ Has each summary remained respectful of the ideas and opinions of others, even if you disagree with them?
- ☐ Have you identified the source of every quotation, paraphrase, summary, or source reference by noting in parentheses the last name of the writer and the page number (if available) where the passage appears in the source?
- ☐ Have you ordered your evidence logically and effectively?
- ☐ Have you interpreted and explained your evidence from sources with your own comments in your own voice?

## Revising and Editing

As you read over the draft of your paper, remember what you wanted to accomplish: to develop an enlightening position about your topic and to share this position with a college audience, using sources to support your ideas.

For more on revising and editing strategies, see Ch. 23.

**Strengthen Your Thesis.** As you begin revising, you may decide that your working thesis is ambiguous, poorly worded, hard to support, or simply off the mark. Revise it so that it clearly alerts readers to your main idea.

| | |
|---|---|
| WORKING THESIS | Although most workers would like longer vacations, many employers do not believe that they would benefit, too. |
| REVISED THESIS | Despite assumptions to the contrary, employers who increase vacation time for workers also are likely to increase creativity, productivity, and the bottom line. |

**Launch Each Source.** Whenever you quote, paraphrase, summarize, or refer to a source, launch it with a suitable introduction. An effective launch sets the scene for your source material, prepares your reader to accept it, and marks the transition from your words and ideas to those of the source. As you revise, confirm that you launch all of your source material well.

For more about launching sources, see D6 in the Quick Research Guide, p. A-31.

In a launch statement, often you will first identify the source – by the author's last name or by a short version of the title when the author isn't named – in your introductory sentence. If not, identify the source in parentheses, typically to end the sentence. Then try to suggest why you've mentioned this source at this point, perhaps noting its contribution, its credibility, its vantage point, or its relationship to other sources. Vary your launch statements to avoid tedium and to add emphasis. Boost your credibility as a writer by establishing the credibility of your sources.

Here are some typical patterns for launch statements:

As Yung demonstrates, . . .

Although Zeffir maintains . . . , Matson suggests . . .

Many schools educated the young but also unified the community (Hill 22). . . .

In *Forward March*, Smith's study of the children of military personnel, . . .

Another common recommendation is . . . ("Safety Manual").

Making good use of her experience as a travel consultant, Lee explains . . .

These examples follow MLA style. For more about how to capture, launch, and cite sources in your text using either MLA or APA style, see D6 and E in the Quick Research Guide, pp. A-31–A-38.

When you quote or paraphrase from a specific page (or other location, such as a paragraph numbered on a Web page), include that exact location.

The classic definition of . . . (Bagette 18) is updated to . . . (Zoe par. 4).

Benton distinguishes four typical steps in this process (248–51).

## Learning by Doing: Launching Your Sources

Make a duplicate file of your draft or print it. Add highlights in one color to mark all your source identifications; use another color to mark source material:

> The problem of unintended consequences is well illustrated by many environmental changes over recent decades. For instance, if using the Mojave Desert for cattle grazing seemed efficient to ranchers, it also turned out to be destructive for long-time desert residents such as tortoises (Babbitt 152).

Now examine your draft. How do the colors alternate? Do you find color globs where you simply list sources without explaining their contributions? Do you find material without source identification (typically the author's name) or without a location in the original (typically a page number)? Fill in whatever gaps you discover.

**Synthesize Several Sources.** Often you will compare, contrast, or relate two or three sources to deepen your discussion or to illustrate a range of views. When you synthesize, you pull together several sources in the same passage to build a new interpretation or reach a new conclusion. You go beyond the separate contributions of the individual sources to relate the sources to each other and to connect them to your thesis. A synthesis should be easy to follow and use your own wording.

HOW TO SYNTHESIZE

- Summarize (see pp. 242–43) each of the sources you want to synthesize. Boil down each summary to its essence.
- Write a few sentences that state in your own words how the sources are linked. For example, are they similar, different, or related? Do they share assumptions and conclusions, or do they represent alternatives, opposites, or opponents? Do they speak to chronology, influence, logical progression, or diversity of opinion?
- Write a few more sentences stating what the source relationships mean for your thesis and the position you develop in your paper.
- Refine your synthesis statements until they are clear and illuminating for your audience. Embed them as you move from one source summary to the next and as you reach new interpretations or conclusions that go beyond the separate sources.

**Use Your Own Voice to Interpret and Connect.** By the time your draft is finished, you may feel that you have found relevant evidence in your sources but that they now dominate your draft. As you reread, you may discover passages that simply string together ideas from sources.

DRAFT

Easterbrook says in "In Search of the Cause of Autism: How about Television?" that television may injure children who are susceptible to autism. The Centers for Disease Control and Prevention says that autism trails only mental retardation among disabilities that affect children's development. The Kaiser Family Foundation study says that parents use television and other electronic entertainment "to help them manage their household and keep their kids entertained" (Rideout, Hamel, and Kaiser Family Foundation 4).

*Whole passage repeats "says"*

*Repeats sentence pattern opening with author*

*Jumps from one source to the next without transitions*

When your sources overshadow your thesis, your explanations, and your writing style, revise to restore balance. Try strategies such as these to regain control of your draft:

- Add your explanation and interpretation of the source information so that your ideas are clear.
- Add transitions, and state the connections that you assume are obvious.
- Arrange information in a logical sequence, not in the order in which you read it or recorded notes about it.

- Clarify definitions, justify a topic's importance, and recognize alternative views to help your audience appreciate your position.
- Reword to vary your sentence openings, and avoid repetitive wording.

Thoughtful revision can help readers grasp what you want to say, why you have included each source, and how you think that it supports your thesis.

REVISION

*Connects two sources*

*Adds transitions*

*Identifies author's experience to add credibility*

*Defines issue and justifies concern*

Two major studies take very different looks at the development of children in our society. First, a research study sponsored by the Kaiser Family Foundation examines how parents use television and other electronic options "to help them manage their household and keep their kids entertained" (Rideout, Hamel, and Kaiser Family Foundation 4). Next, based on statistics about how often major developmental disabilities occur in children, the Centers for Disease Control and Prevention reports that autism currently trails only mental retardation among disabilities that affect children's development. Journalist and book author Gregg Easterbrook pulls together these two views, using the title of his article to raise his unusual question: "In Search of the Cause of Autism: How about Television?" He urges study of his speculation that television may injure children who are vulnerable to autism and joins an ongoing debate about what causes autism, a challenging disability that interferes with children's ability to communicate and interact with other people.

**List Your Sources as College Readers Expect.** When you use sources in a college paper, you'll be expected to identify them twice: briefly when you draw information from them and fully when you list them at the end of your paper, following a conventional system. The list of sources for the draft and revision in the previous section would include these entries.

Centers for Disease Control and Prevention. "Frequently Asked Questions—Prevalence." *Autism Information Center*. CDC, 30 Jan. 2006. Web. 12 Sept. 2006.

Easterbrook, Gregg. "In Search of the Cause of Autism: How about Television?" *Slate*. Washington Post, 5 Sept. 2006. Web. 12 Sept. 2006.

Rideout, Victoria, Elizabeth Hamel, and Kaiser Family Foundation. *The Media Family: Electronic Media in the Lives of Infants, Toddlers, Preschoolers and Their Parents*. Menlo Park: Henry J. Kaiser Family Foundation, 2006. *Kaiser Family Foundation*. Web. 12 Sept. 2006.

## Learning by Doing Checking Your Presentation of Sources

Use your software to help you improve the presentation of source materials in your draft. For example, search for all the quotation marks in your paper. Make sure that each is one of a pair surrounding every quotation in your paper. At the same time, be sure that the source and location are identified for each quotation. Try color highlighting in your final list of sources to help you spot and refine details, especially any common personal errors. For instance, if you forget periods after names of authors or mix up semicolons and colons, highlight those marks in color so you slow down and focus on them. Then correct or add marks as needed. After you check your entries, restore the passage to the usual black color.

Use the Take Action chart (p. 250) to help you figure out how to improve your draft. Skim across the top to identify questions you might ask about integrating sources in your draft. When you answer a question with "Yes" or "Maybe," move straight down the column to Locate Specifics under that question. Use the activities there to pinpoint gaps, problems, or weaknesses. Then move straight down the column to Take Action. Use the advice that suits your problem as you revise.

For online Take Action help, visit **bedfordstmartins.com/bedguide** and go to Re:Writing.

## Peer Response Supporting a Position with Sources

Have several classmates read your draft critically, considering how effectively you have used your sources to support a position. Ask your peer editors to answer questions such as these:

- Can you state the writer's position on the topic?
- Do you have any trouble seeing how the writer's points and the supporting evidence from sources connect? How might the writer make the connections clearer?
- How effectively does the writer capture the information from sources? Would you recommend that any of the quotations, paraphrases, or summaries be presented differently?

For general questions for a peer editor, see p. 463.

## Take Action Integrating Source Information Effectively

Ask each question at the top of the chart to consider whether your draft might need work on that issue. If so, follow the ASK—LOCATE SPECIFICS—TAKE ACTION sequence to revise.

| | Weak Launch Statements? | Too Little Voice? | Too Few Source Credits? |
|---|---|---|---|
| **1 ASK** | Have I tossed in source material without preparing my audience for it? Do I repeat the same words in my launch statements? | Have I lost my own voice? Have I allowed my sources to take over my draft? Have I strung together too many quotations? | Have I identified any source only once or twice even though I use it throughout a section? |
| **2 LOCATE SPECIFICS** | ■ Underline each launch statement (the sentence or its part that introduces source material). Decide if it assures readers that the source is credible, logical, and relevant to your thesis.<br>■ Highlight any repeated words (*says, states*) or transitions (*also, then*). | ■ Highlight the material from sources in one color and your own commentary in another.<br>■ Check the color balance in each paragraph. If the source color dominates, consider how to restore your own voice. | ■ Select a passage that relies on sources. Highlight your ideas in one color and those from sources in a different color.<br>■ Add a slash to mark each switch between two sources or between your ideas and a source. |
| **3 TAKE ACTION** | ■ Sharpen underlined launch statements, perhaps noting (a) an author's credentials significant to readers, (b) a source's historical or current contributions, or (c) its relationship to other sources.<br>■ Edit the highlighted words (and any other repeated expressions) for variety and precision. For *says*, try *emphasizes, suggests, reviews, presents*, or *explains*. For *also*, try *in addition, furthermore*, or *similarly*. | ■ Restore your voice in each paragraph by adding a topic sentence in your own words that links to your thesis and a conclusion that sums up.<br>■ Add transitions (*further, in contrast, as a result*) and explanations where you move point to point or source to source.<br>■ Reduce what you quote to focus on striking words. Sum up, or drop the rest.<br>■ Weave in your ideas until they, not your sources, dominate. | ■ At each slash marking a source switch, add a launch statement for the second source.<br>■ At each slash (or color change) marking a switch to your ideas, phrase your comment so that it does not sound like more of the source.<br>■ At each slash (or color change) marking a switch from your ideas, identify the source again.<br>■ When you quote and then continue with the same source, identify it again. |

- Are any of the source citations unclear? Can you tell where source information came from and where quotations and paraphrases appear in a source?
- Is the writer's voice clear? Do the sources drown it out in any spots?
- If this paper were yours, what is the one thing you would be sure to work on before handing it in?

### REVISION CHECKLIST

- ☐ Is your thesis, or main idea, clear? Is it distinguished from the points made by your sources?
- ☐ Do you speak in your own voice, interpreting and explaining your sources instead of allowing them to dominate your draft?
- ☐ Have you moved smoothly back and forth between your explanations and your source material?
- ☐ Have you credited every source in the text and in a list at the end of your paper? Have you added each detail expected in the format for listing sources?
- ☐ Have you been careful to quote, paraphrase, summarize, and credit sources accurately and ethically? Have you hunted up missing details, double-checked quotations, and rechecked the accuracy of anything prepared hastily?

After you have revised your paper, edit and proofread it. Carefully check the grammar, word choice, punctuation, and mechanics—and then correct any problems you find. Be certain to check the punctuation with your quotations, making sure that each quotation mark is correctly placed and that you have used other punctuation, such as commas, correctly.

For more help, find the relevant checklist sections in the Quick Editing Guide on p. A-39. Turn also to the Quick Format Guide beginning on p. A-1.

### EDITING CHECKLIST

- ☐ Do all the verbs agree with their subjects, especially when you switch from your words to those of a source? A4
- ☐ Do all the pronouns agree with their antecedents, especially when you use your words with a quotation from a source? A6
- ☐ Have you used commas correctly, especially where you integrate material from sources? C1
- ☐ Have you punctuated all your quotations correctly? C3

## Additional Writing Assignments

1. **Source Assignment.** Read several sources about the same topic. Instead of using them as evidence to support your ideas on the topic, analyze how well they function as sources. State your thesis about them, and evaluate their strengths and weaknesses, using clear criteria. (See, for example, the criteria in C3 in the Quick Research Guide, pp. A-27–A-28.)
2. **Source Assignment.** Locate several different accounts of a notable event in newspapers, magazines, published letters or journals, books, blogs, or other sources, depending on the time when the event occurred. State and support a thesis that explains the differences among the accounts. Use the accounts as evidence to support your position.
3. **Source Assignment.** Browse in your library's new book and periodical areas (on site or online) or in specialty search engines to identify a current topic of interest to you. (Adding the current or previous year's date to a search is one way to find recent publications or acquisitions.) Gather and evaluate a cluster of resources on your topic. Write an essay using those readings to support your position about the new development.

For more on interviewing, see Ch. 6. For more on reviewing and evaluating, see Ch. 11.

4. **Source Assignment.** Following the directions of your instructor, use several types of sources to support your position in an essay. One option might be to select paired or related readings (from this book or its e-Pages), and also to interview someone with the background or experience to act as another valuable source of information. A second option might be to view and evaluate a film, television program, radio show, blog, Web site, art exhibit, performance, or other event. Then supplement your review by reading several articles that review the same event, evaluate a different or related production, or discuss criteria for similar types of items or events.
5. **Source Assignment.** Create a concise Web site that addresses a question of interest to you. Select and read a few reliable sources about that question, and then create several screens or short pages to explain what you have learned. For example, you might want to define or explain aspects of the question, justify the conclusion you have reached, or evaluate alternative answers as well as your own. Credit all of your sources, and supply links when appropriate.
6. **Visual Assignment.** Examine the following images, and analyze one (or more) of them. Use the image to support your position in an essay, perhaps a conclusion about the image or about what it portrays. Point out relevant detail to persuade your audience of your view. Cite the images correctly, using the style your instructor specifies.

WARNING
RECENT SHARK SIGHTINGS
• Swim Close to Shore
• Don't Swim With Seals
• Don't Swim Alone
USE AREA AT OWN RISK
NO DOGS ALLOWED ANYWHERE ON BEACH

714
3313
acela

# PART THREE

# OTHER WRITING SITUATIONS

# 13 Responding to Literature

As countless readers know, reading fiction gives pleasure and delight. Whether you read Stephen King or Stephen Crane, you can be swept up into an imaginative world where you journey to distant lands and meet exotic people. You may also meet characters like yourself with familiar as well as new ways of viewing life. By sharing the experiences of literary characters, you gain insight into your own problems and tolerance of others.

## Why Responding to Literature Matters

### In a College Course

- You apply methods of literary analysis to spot themes, images, symbols, and figures of speech in history speeches, political essays, or business case studies.
- You respond to plays in your theater class, novels in cultural studies, essays in philosophy, or poetry in Literature 2.

### In the Workplace

- You use literary analysis as you critique the characters, plot, setting, point of view, and theme for your company's advertising campaign.

### In Your Community

- You support the library's story hour for your children, the community theater's plays, and the hospital's journal project for wounded veterans.

When have you responded to a short story, novel, poem, or play? In what situations might you respond to literature in future writing?

## Using Strategies for Literary Analysis

More often than not, a writing assignment in a literature or humanities course requires you to read closely a literary work (short story, novel, play, or poem) and then to divide it into elements, explain its meaning, and support your interpretation with evidence from the work. You might also be asked to evaluate a selection or to compare and contrast several readings. Such analysis is not an end in itself; its purpose is to illuminate the meaning of the work, to help you and others understand it better.

This way of writing about literature, called *literary analysis,* requires you to analyze, interpret, and evaluate what you read. Because literary analysis has its own vocabulary—as do fields as diverse as scuba diving, gourmet cooking, and engineering—a handy glossary presents terms used to discuss the elements of fiction, poetry, and drama (see pp. 270–71). The chapter concludes with two writing activities—synopsis (summarizing the events in a narrative) and paraphrase (expressing the content of a work in your own words)—that can help you prepare to write a literary analysis or to integrate essentials about the literary work into your analysis.

For a sample literary analysis, see pp. 268–69. For a sample synopsis, see pp. 281–82; for a sample paraphrase, see p. 285.

To begin your analysis, first read closely and mark key points in the text to comprehend its meaning. Next reread the work, *at least* twice more, each time checking your interpretations and identifying possible evidence to back up your claims as you analyze and evaluate. Use this checklist to structure several close readings, each for a different reason.

---

**READING CHECKLIST**

*Reading to Comprehend*

For more on literal and critical reading, see Ch. 2.

- ☐ What is the literal meaning? Write a few sentences explaining the overall situation—what happens to whom, where, when, why, and how.
- ☐ What are the facts of the situation—the events of the plot, the aspects of the setting, and the major attributes, words, and actions of the characters?
- ☐ What does the vocabulary mean, especially in titles or poems? Look up both unfamiliar words and words whose familiar meanings don't fit the context.

For information and journal questions about the Part Three photograph, see the last two pages of the Appendices.

*Reading to Analyze*

- ☐ What are the main parts or elements of the work? Read, read aloud, mark, or make notes on theme, character, language, style, symbol, or form.
- ☐ What does the literary work mean? What does it imply?
- ☐ What does it suggest about the human condition? How does it expand your understanding? What insights can you apply to your own life?

*Reading to Evaluate*

- ☐ How do you assess the work's soundness and plausibility?
- ☐ Are the words and tone appropriate for the purpose and audience?
- ☐ Does the author achieve his or her purpose? Is it a worthwhile purpose?

---

## Learning from Other Writers

Jonathan Burns was assigned to write a literary analysis of "The Lottery," a provocative short story by Shirley Jackson. Read this story yourself to understand its meaning. Then read on to see what Burns made of it.

**Shirley Jackson**

### The Lottery

The morning of June 27th was clear and sunny, with the fresh warmth of a full-summer day; the flowers were blossoming profusely and the grass was richly green. The people of the village began to gather in the square, between the post office and the bank, around ten o'clock; in some towns there were so many people that the lottery took two days and had to be started on June 26th, but in this village, where there were only about three hundred people, the whole lottery took less than two hours, so it could begin at ten o'clock in the morning and still be through in time to allow the villagers to get home for noon dinner. 1

The children assembled first, of course. School was recently over for the summer, and the feeling of liberty sat uneasily on most of them; they tended to gather together quietly for a while before they broke into boisterous play, and their talk was still of the classroom and the teacher, of books and reprimands. Bobby Martin had already stuffed his pockets full of stones, and the other boys soon followed his example, selecting the smoothest and roundest stones; Bobby and Harry Jones and Dickie Delacroix—the villagers pronounced his name "Dellacroy"—eventually made a great pile of stones in one corner of the square and guarded it against the raids of the other boys. The girls stood aside, talking among themselves, looking over their shoulders at the boys, and the very small children rolled in the dust or clung to the hands of their older brothers or sisters. 2

Soon the men began to gather, surveying their own children, speaking of planting and rain, tractors and taxes. They stood together, away from the pile of stones in the corner, and their jokes were quiet and they smiled rather than laughed. The women, wearing faded house dresses and sweaters, came shortly after their menfolk. They greeted one another and exchanged bits of gossip as they went to join their husbands. Soon the women, standing by their husbands, began to call to their children, and the children came reluctantly, having to be called four or five times. Bobby Martin ducked under his mother's grasping hand and ran, laughing, back to the pile of stones. His father spoke up sharply, and Bobby came quickly and took his place between his father and his oldest brother. 3

The lottery was conducted—as were the square dances, the teenage club, the Halloween program—by Mr. Summers, who had time and energy to devote to civic activities. He was a round-faced, jovial man and he ran the coal 4 business, and people were sorry for him, because he had no children and his wife was a scold. When he arrived in the square, carrying the black wooden box, there was a murmur of conversation among the villagers, and he waved and called, "Little late today, folks." The postmaster, Mr. Graves, followed him, carrying a three-legged stool, and the stool was put in the center of the square and Mr. Summers set the black box down on it. The villagers kept their distance, leaving a space between themselves and the stool, and when Mr. Summers said, "Some of you fellows want to give me a hand?" there was a hesitation before two men, Mr. Martin and his oldest son, Baxter, came forward to hold the box steady on the stool while Mr. Summers stirred up the papers inside it.

The original paraphernalia for the lottery had been lost long ago, and the 5
black box now resting on the stool had been put into use even before Old Man Warner, the oldest man in town, was born. Mr. Summers spoke frequently to the villagers about making a new box, but no one liked to upset even as much tradition as was represented by the black box. There was a story that the present box had been made with some pieces of the box that had preceded it, the one that had been constructed when the first people settled down to make a village here. Every year, after the lottery, Mr. Summers began talking again about a new box, but every year the subject was allowed to fade off without anything's being done. The black box grew shabbier each year; by now it was no longer completely black but splintered badly along one side to show the original wood color, and in some places faded or stained.

Mr. Martin and his oldest son, Baxter, held the black box securely on the 6
stool until Mr. Summers had stirred the papers thoroughly with his hand. Because so much of the ritual had been forgotten or discarded, Mr. Summers had been successful in having slips of paper substituted for the chips of wood that had been used for generations. Chips of wood, Mr. Summers had argued, had been all very well when the village was tiny, but now that the population was more than three hundred and likely to keep on growing, it was necessary to use something that would fit more easily into the black box. The night before the lottery, Mr. Summers and Mr. Graves made up the slips of paper and put them in the box, and it was then taken to the safe of Mr. Summers's coal company and locked up until Mr. Summers was ready to take it to the square the next morning. The rest of the year, the box was put away, sometimes one place, sometimes another; it had spent one year in Mr. Graves's barn and another year underfoot in the post office, and sometimes it was set on a shelf in the Martin grocery and left there.

There was a great deal of fussing to be done before Mr. Summers declared 7
the lottery open. There were the lists to make up—of heads of families, heads of households in each family, members of each household in each family. There was the proper swearing-in of Mr. Summers by the postmaster, as the official of the lottery; at one time, some people remembered, there had been a recital of some sort, performed by the official of the lottery, a perfunctory, tuneless chant that had been rattled off duly each year; some people believed that the official of the lottery used to stand just so when he said or sang it,

others believed that he was supposed to walk among the people, but years and years ago this part of the ritual had been allowed to lapse. There had been, also, a ritual salute, which the official of the lottery had had to use in addressing each person who came up to draw from the box, but this also had changed with time, until now it was felt necessary only for the official to speak to each person approaching. Mr. Summers was very good at all this; in his clean white shirt and blue jeans, with one hand resting carelessly on the black box, he seemed very proper and important as he talked interminably to Mr. Graves and the Martins.

Just as Mr. Summers finally left off talking and turned to the assembled 8
villagers, Mrs. Hutchinson came hurriedly along the path to the square, her sweater thrown over her shoulders, and slid into place in the back of the crowd. "Clean forgot what day it was," she said to Mrs. Delacroix, who stood next to her, and they both laughed softly. "Thought my old man was out back stacking wood," Mrs. Hutchinson went on, "and then I looked out the window and the kids was gone, and then I remembered it was the twenty-seventh and came a-running." She dried her hands on her apron, and Mrs. Delacroix said, "You're in time, though. They're still talking away up there."

Mrs. Hutchinson craned her neck to see through the crowd and found her 9
husband and children standing near the front. She tapped Mrs. Delacroix on the arm as a farewell and began to make her way through the crowd. The people separated good-humoredly to let her through; two or three people said, in voices just loud enough to be heard across the crowd, "Here comes your Missus, Hutchinson," and "Bill, she made it after all." Mrs. Hutchinson reached her husband, and Mr. Summers, who had been waiting, said cheerfully, "Thought we were going to have to get on without you, Tessie." Mrs. Hutchinson said, grinning, "Wouldn't have me leave m'dishes in the sink, now, would you, Joe?" and soft laughter ran through the crowd as the people stirred back into position after Mrs. Hutchinson's arrival.

"Well, now," Mr. Summers said soberly, "guess we better get started, get 10
this over with, so's we can go back to work. Anybody ain't here?"

"Dunbar," several people said. "Dunbar, Dunbar." 11

Mr. Summers consulted his list. "Clyde Dunbar," he said. "That's right. 12
He's broke his leg, hasn't he? Who's drawing for him?"

"Me, I guess," a woman said, and Mr. Summers turned to look at her. 13
"Wife draws for her husband," Mr. Summers said. "Don't you have a grown boy to do it for you, Janey?" Although Mr. Summers and everyone else in the village knew the answer perfectly well, it was the business of the official of the lottery to ask such questions formally. Mr. Summers waited with an expression of polite interest while Mrs. Dunbar answered.

"Horace's not but sixteen yet," Mrs. Dunbar said regretfully. "Guess I 14
gotta fill in for the old man this year."

"Right," Mr. Summers said. He made a note on the list he was holding. 15
Then he asked, "Watson boy drawing this year?"

A tall boy in the crowd raised his hand. "Here," he said. "I'm drawing for 16
m'mother and me." He blinked his eyes nervously and ducked his head as several voices in the crowd said things like "Good fellow, Jack," and "Glad to see your mother's got a man to do it."

"Well," Mr. Summers said, "guess that's everyone. Old Man Warner 17
make it?"

"Here," a voice said, and Mr. Summers nodded. 18

A sudden hush fell on the crowd as Mr. Summers cleared his throat and 19
looked at the list. "All ready?" he called. "Now, I'll read the names—heads of families first—and the men come up and take a paper out of the box. Keep the paper folded in your hand without looking at it until everyone has had a turn. Everything clear?"

The people had done it so many times that they only half listened to the 20
directions; most of them were quiet, wetting their lips, not looking around. Then Mr. Summers raised one hand high and said, "Adams." A man disengaged himself from the crowd and came forward. "Hi, Steve," Mr. Summers said, and Mr. Adams said, "Hi, Joe." They grinned at one another humorlessly and nervously. Then Mr. Adams reached into the black box and took out a folded paper. He held it firmly by one corner as he turned and went hastily back to his place in the crowd, where he stood a little apart from his family, not looking down at his hand.

"Allen," Mr. Summers said. "Anderson. . . . Bentham." 21

"Seems like there's no time at all between lotteries anymore," Mrs. Dela- 22
croix said to Mrs. Graves in the back row. "Seems like we got through with the last one only last week."

"Time sure goes fast," Mrs. Graves said. 23

"Clark. . . . Delacroix." 24

"There goes my old man," Mrs. Delacroix said. She held her breath while 25
her husband went forward.

"Dunbar," Mr. Summers said, and Mrs. Dunbar went steadily to the box 26
while one of the women said, "Go on, Janey," and another said, "There she goes."

"We're next," Mrs. Graves said. She watched while Mr. Graves came 27
around from the side of the box, greeted Mr. Summers gravely, and selected a slip of paper from the box. By now, all through the crowd there were men holding the small folded papers in their large hands, turning them over and over nervously. Mrs. Dunbar and her two sons stood together, Mrs. Dunbar holding the slip of paper.

"Harburt. . . . Hutchinson." 28

"Get up there, Bill," Mrs. Hutchinson said, and the people near her laughed. 29

"Jones." 30

"They do say," Mr. Adams said to Old Man Warner, who stood next to 31
him, "that over in the north village they're talking of giving up the lottery."

Old Man Warner snorted. "Pack of crazy fools," he said. "Listening to the 32
young folks, nothing's good enough for *them*. Next thing you know, they'll be

wanting to go back to living in caves, nobody work anymore, live *that* way for a while. Used to be a saying about 'Lottery in June, corn be heavy soon.' First thing you know, we'd all be eating stewed chickweed and acorns. There's *always* been a lottery," he added petulantly. "Bad enough to see young Joe Summers up there joking with everybody."

33 "Some places have already quit lotteries," Mrs. Adams said.

34 "Nothing but trouble in *that,*" Old Man Warner said stoutly. "Pack of young fools."

35 "Martin." And Bobby Martin watched his father go forward. "Overdyke. . . . Percy."

36 "I wish they'd hurry," Mrs. Dunbar said to her older son. "I wish they'd hurry."

37 "They're almost through," her son said.

38 "You get ready to run tell Dad," Mrs. Dunbar said.

39 Mr. Summers called his own name and then stepped forward precisely and selected a slip from the box. Then he called, "Warner."

40 "Seventy-seventh year I been in the lottery," Old Man Warner said as he went through the crowd. "Seventy-seventh time."

41 "Watson." The tall boy came awkwardly through the crowd. Someone said, "Don't be nervous, Jack," and Mr. Summers said, "Take your time, son."

42 "Zanini."

43 After that, there was a long pause, a breathless pause, until Mr. Summers, holding his slip of paper in the air, said, "All right, fellows." For a minute, no one moved, and then all the slips of paper were opened. Suddenly, all the women began to speak at once, saying, "Who is it?" "Who's got it?" "Is it the Dunbars?" "Is it the Watsons?" Then the voices began to say, "It's Hutchinson. It's Bill." "Bill Hutchinson's got it."

44 "Go tell your father," Mrs. Dunbar said to her older son.

45 People began to look around to see the Hutchinsons. Bill Hutchinson was standing quiet, staring down at the paper in his hand. Suddenly, Tessie Hutchinson shouted to Mr. Summers, "You didn't give him time enough to take any paper he wanted. I saw you. It wasn't fair!"

46 "Be a good sport, Tessie," Mrs. Delacroix called, and Mrs. Graves said, "All of us took the same chance."

47 "Shut up, Tessie," Bill Hutchinson said.

48 "Well, everyone," Mr. Summers said, "that was done pretty fast, and now we've got to be hurrying a little more to get done in time." He consulted his next list. "Bill," he said, "you draw for the Hutchinson family. You got any other households in the Hutchinsons?"

49 "There's Don and Eva," Mrs. Hutchinson yelled. "Make *them* take their chance!"

50 "Daughters draw with their husbands' families, Tessie," Mr. Summers said gently. "You know that as well as anyone else."

51 "It wasn't *fair,*" Tessie said.

"I guess not, Joe," Bill Hutchinson said regretfully. "My daughter draws 52
with her husband's family, that's only fair. And I've got no other family except the kids."

"Then, as far as drawing for families is concerned, it's you," Mr. Summers 53
said in explanation, "and as far as drawing for households is concerned, that's you, too. Right?"

"Right," Bill Hutchinson said. 54

"How many kids, Bill?" Mr. Summers asked formally. 55

"Three," Bill Hutchinson said. "There's Bill, Jr., and Nancy, and little 56
Dave. And Tessie and me."

"All right, then," Mr. Summers said. "Harry, you got their tickets back?" 57

Mr. Graves nodded and held up the slips of paper. "Put them in the box, 58
then," Mr. Summers directed. "Take Bill's and put it in."

"I think we ought to start over," Mrs. Hutchinson said, as quietly as she 59
could. "I tell you it wasn't *fair*. You didn't give him time enough to choose. *Every*body saw that."

Mr. Graves had selected the five slips and put them in the box, and he 60
dropped all the papers but those onto the ground, where the breeze caught them and lifted them off.

"Listen, everybody," Mrs. Hutchinson was saying to the people around her. 61

"Ready, Bill?" Mr. Summers asked, and Bill Hutchinson, with one quick 62
glance around at his wife and children, nodded.

"Remember," Mr. Summers said, "take the slips and keep them folded 63
until each person has taken one. Harry, you help little Dave." Mr. Graves took the hand of the little boy, who came willingly with him up to the box. "Take a paper out of the box, Davy," Mr. Summers said. Davy put his hand into the box and laughed. "Take just *one* paper," Mr. Summers said. "Harry, you hold it for him." Mr. Graves took the child's hand and removed the folded paper from the tight fist and held it while little Dave stood next to him and looked up at him wonderingly.

"Nancy next," Mr. Summers said. Nancy was twelve, and her school 64
friends breathed heavily as she went forward, switching her skirt, and took a slip daintily from the box. "Bill, Jr.," Mr. Summers said, and Billy, his face red and his feet overlarge, nearly knocked the box over as he got a paper out. "Tessie," Mr. Summers said. She hesitated for a minute, looking around defiantly, and then set her lips and went up to the box. She snatched a paper out and held it behind her.

"Bill," Mr. Summers said, and Bill Hutchinson reached into the box and 65
felt around, bringing his hand out at last with the slip of paper in it.

The crowd was quiet. A girl whispered, "I hope it's not Nancy," and the 66
sound of the whisper reached the edges of the crowd.

"It's not the way it used to be," Old Man Warner said clearly. "People ain't 67
the way they used to be."

"All right," Mr. Summers said. "Open the papers. Harry, you open little 68
Dave's."

Mr. Graves opened the slip of paper and there was a general sigh through 69
the crowd as he held it up and everyone could see that it was blank. Nancy and Bill, Jr., opened theirs at the same time, and both beamed and laughed, turning around to the crowd and holding their slips of paper above their heads.

"Tessie," Mr. Summers said. There was a pause, and then Mr. Summers 70
looked at Bill Hutchinson, and Bill unfolded his paper and showed it. It was blank.

"It's Tessie," Mr. Summers said, and his voice was hushed. "Show us her 71
paper, Bill."

Bill Hutchinson went over to his wife and forced the slip of paper out of 72
her hand. It had a black spot on it, the black spot Mr. Summers had made the night before with the heavy pencil in the coal-company office. Bill Hutchinson held it up, and there was a stir in the crowd.

"All right, folks," Mr. Summers said. "Let's finish quickly." 73

Although the villagers had forgotten the ritual and lost the original black 74
box, they still remembered to use stones. The pile of stones the boys had made earlier was ready; there were stones on the ground with the blowing scraps of paper that had come out of the box. Mrs. Delacroix selected a stone so large she had to pick it up with both hands and turned to Mrs. Dunbar. "Come on," she said. "Hurry up."

Mrs. Dunbar had small stones in both hands, and she said, gasping for 75
breath, "I can't run at all. You'll have to go ahead and I'll catch up with you."

The children had stones already, and someone gave little Davy Hutchin- 76
son a few pebbles.

Tessie Hutchinson was in the center of a cleared space by now, and she 77
held her hands out desperately as the villagers moved in on her. "It isn't fair," she said. A stone hit her on the side of the head.

For essays about *The Hunger Games*, a novel and film that also comments on societal traditions, see pp. 206 and 554.

Old Man Warner was saying, "Come on, come on, everyone." Steve Adams 78
was in the front of the crowd of villagers, with Mrs. Graves beside him.

"It isn't fair, it isn't right," Mrs. Hutchinson screamed, and then they were 79
upon her.

## Questions to Start You Thinking

Meaning

1. Where does this story take place? When?
2. How does this lottery differ from what we usually think of as a lottery? Why would people conduct a lottery such as this?
3. What does this story mean to you?

Writing Strategies

4. Can you see and hear the people in the story? Do they seem to be real or based on fantasy? Who is the most memorable character to you?
5. Are the events believable? Does the ending shock you? Is it believable?
6. Is the story realistic, or is Jackson using it to represent something else?

## Preparing to Write a Literary Analysis

As Jonathan Burns first read "The Lottery," he was carried along to the startling ending. Then he reread to understand the story well enough to identify and analyze elements such as setting, character, or tone. He began turning understanding into text by writing a synopsis to clarify the literal events in the story. Summing up events immediately suggested writing about the story's undertone of violence, but he decided that it would be hard to write about something so subtle.

Then he considered the characters in the story, especially Mr. Summers, Tessie Hutchinson, or the memorable Old Man Warner. Burns experimented by paraphrasing Old Man Warner's comments from one paragraph. But he decided not to focus on the characters because he couldn't think of more than the vague statement that they were memorable. He considered other elements—language, symbols, ambiguity, foreshadowing—and dismissed each in turn. All of a sudden, he hit on the surprise ending. How did Jackson manipulate all the details to generate such a shock?

For Burns's synopsis, see pp. 281–82; for his paraphrase, see p. 285.

To focus his thinking, he brainstormed for possible essay titles about the ending: Death Comes as a Surprise, The Unsuspected Finish, and his straightforward choice "The Hidden Truth." After reviewing his notes, Burns realized that Jackson uses characterization, symbolism, and ambiguous description to build up to the ending. He listed details under those three headings to plan his paper informally:

For more on seeking motives of characters, see pp. 393–95.

For more on stating a thesis, organizing ideas, and outlining, see Ch. 20.

Title: The Hidden Truth

Working Thesis: In "The Lottery" Jackson effectively crafts a shock ending.

1. Characterization that contributes to the shock ending
   - –The children of the village
   - –The adults of the village
   - –Conversations among the villagers
2. Symbols that contribute to the shock ending
   - –The stones
   - –The black box
3. Ambiguous description that contributes to the shock ending
   - –The word "lottery"
   - –Comments: "clean forgot," "wish they'd hurry," "It isn't fair."
   - –Actions: relief, suspense

Then he drafted the following introduction:

For more on introductions, see pp. 426–28.

Unsuspecting, the reader follows Shirley Jackson's softly flowing tale of a rural community's timeless ritual, the lottery. Awareness of what is at stake—the savage murder of one random member—comes slowly. No sooner does the realization set in than the story is over. It is a shock ending.

What creates the shock that the reader experiences reading "The Lottery"? Jackson carefully produces this effect, using elements such as language, symbolism, and characterization to lure the reader into not anticipating what is to come.

With his synopsis, his paraphrase, his plan, his copy of the story, and this starting point, Burns revised the introduction and wrote his essay.

**Jonathan Burns** **Student Literary Analysis**

## The Hidden Truth: An Analysis of Shirley Jackson's "The Lottery"

It is as if the first stone thrown strikes the reader as well as Mrs. Hutchinson. And even though there were signs of the stoning to come, somehow the reader is taken by surprise at Tessie's violent death. What factors contribute to the shock ending to "The Lottery"? On closer examination of the story, the reader finds that through all the events leading up to the ending, Shirley Jackson has used unsuspicious characterizations, unobtrusive symbolism, and ambiguous descriptions to achieve so sudden an impact. 1

By all appearances, the village is a normal place with normal people. Children arrive at the scene first, with school just over for the summer, talking of teachers and books, not of the fact that someone will die today (260). And as the adults show up, their actions are just as stereotypical: the men talk of farming and taxes, while the women gossip (260). The scene conveys no trace of hostility, no sense of dread in anyone: death seems very far away here. 2

The numbers in parentheses are page-number citations following MLA style. For more on citing and listing sources, see D6 and E (pp. A-31–A-38) in the Quick Research Guide.

The conversations between the villagers are no more ominous. As the husbands draw slips of paper for their families, the villagers make apparently everyday comments about the seemingly ordinary event of the lottery. Mr. Summers is regarded as a competent and respected figure, despite his wife being "a scold" (261). Old Man Warner criticizes other towns that have given up their lottery tradition and brags about how many lotteries he's seen (263–64). The characters' comments show the crowd to be more a close-knit community than a murderous mob. 3

The symbols of "The Lottery" seem equally ordinary. The stones collected by the boys (260) are unnoticed by the adults and thus seem a trivial detail. The reader thinks of the "great pile" (260) as children's entertainment, like a stack of imaginary coins, rather than an arsenal. Ironically, no stones are ever thrown during the children's play, and no violence is seen in the pile of stones. 4

Similarly, Jackson describes the box and its history in great detail, but nothing seems unusual about it. It is just another everyday object, stored away in the post office or on a shelf in the grocery (261). Every other day of the year, the box is in plain view but goes virtually unnoticed. The only indication that the box has lethal consequences is that it is painted black (261), yet this is an ambiguous detail, as a black box can also signify mystery or magic, mystical forces that are sometimes thought to exist in any lottery. 5

In her ambiguous descriptions, Jackson refers regularly to the village's lottery and emphasizes it as a central ritual for the people. The word *lottery* itself is ironic, as it typically implies a winning of some kind, like a raffle or sweepstakes. It is paralleled 6 to square dances and to the teenage club, all activities people anticipate under the direction of Mr. Summers (260). There is no implied difference between the occurrences of this day and the festivities of Halloween: according to Jackson, they are all merely "civic activities" (260). Equally ambiguous are the people's emotions: some of the villagers are casual, such as Mrs. Hutchinson, who arrives late because she "'clean forgot'" what day it is (262), and some are anxious, such as Mrs. Dunbar, who repeats to her son, "'I wish they'd hurry,'" without any sign of the cause of her anxiety (264). With these descriptive details, the reader finds no threat or malice in the villagers, only vague expectation and congeniality.

Even when it becomes clear that the lottery is something no one wants to win, Jackson presents only a vague sense of sadness and mild protest. The crowd is relieved that the youngest of the Hutchinsons, Davy, doesn't draw the fatal slip of paper (266). One girl whispers that she hopes it isn't Nancy (265), and when the Hutchinson children discover they aren't the winners, they beam with joy and proudly display their blank slips (266). Suspense and excitement grow only when the victim is close to being identified. And when Tessie is revealed as the winner of the lottery (266), she merely holds her hands out "desperately" and repeats, "'It isn't fair'" (266). 7

With a blend of character, symbolism, and description, Jackson paints an overall portrait of a gentle-seeming rural community, apparently no different from any other. The tragic end is sudden only because there is no recognition of violence beforehand, despite the fact that Jackson provides the reader with plenty of clues in the ample details about the lottery and the people. It is a haunting discovery that the story ends in death, even though such is the truth in the everyday life of all people. 8

## Questions to Start You Thinking

### Meaning

1. What is Burns's thesis?
2. What main points does he use to support the interpretation in his thesis? What specific elements of the story does he include as evidence?

### Writing Strategies

3. How does this essay differ from a synopsis, a summary of the events of the plot? (For a synopsis of "The Lottery," see pp. 281–82.)
4. Does Burns focus on the technique of the short story or on its theme?
5. Is his introduction effective? Compare and contrast it with his first draft (p. 267). What did he change? Which version do you prefer?
6. Why does he explain characterization first, symbolism second, and description last? How effective is this organization? Would discussing these elements in a different order have made much difference?
7. Is his conclusion effective?
8. How does he tie ideas together as he moves from paragraph to paragraph? How does he keep the focus on ideas and technique instead of plot?

## A Glossary of Terms for Literary Analysis

**Characters.** Characters are imagined people. The author shows you what they are like through their actions, speech, thoughts, attitudes, and background. Sometimes a writer also includes physical characteristics or names or relationships with other people. For example, in "The Lottery," the description of Mr. Summers introduces the lottery official as someone with civic interests who wants to avoid slip-ups (paragraphs 4, 9, and 10).

**Figures of Speech.** Figures of speech are lively or fresh expressions that vary the expected sequence or sense of words. Some common types of figurative language are the *simile*, a comparison using *like* or *as*; the *metaphor*, an implied comparison; and *personification*, the attribution of human qualities to inanimate or nonhuman creatures or things. In "The Lottery," three boys *guard* their pile of stones "against the *raids*" of others (paragraph 2).

**Imagery.** Images are words or groups of words that refer to any sense experience: seeing, hearing, smelling, tasting, touching, or feeling. The images in "The Lottery" help readers envision the "richly green" grass (paragraph 1), the smooth and round stones the children gather (paragraph 2), the "hush" that comes over the crowd (paragraph 19), and Mrs. Dunbar "gasping for breath" (paragraph 75).

**Irony.** Irony results from readers' sense of discrepancy. A simple kind of irony, *sarcasm*, occurs when you say one thing but mean the opposite: "I just love scrubbing the floor." In literature, an *ironic situation* sets up a contrast or incongruity. In "The Lottery," cruel and horrifying actions take place on a sunny June day in an ordinary village. *Ironic dialogue* occurs when a character says one thing, but the audience or reader is aware of another meaning. When Old Man Warner reacts to giving up the lottery as "wanting to go back to living in caves" (paragraph 32), he implies that such a change would return the villages to a more primitive life. His comment is ironic because the reader is aware that this lottery is a primitive ritual. A story has an *ironic point of view* when readers sense a difference between the author and the narrator or the character who perceives the story; Jackson, for instance, clearly does not condone the actions of the villagers.

**Plot.** Plot is the arrangement of the events of the story—what happens to whom, where, when, and why. If the events follow each other logically and are in keeping with the characters, the plot is *plausible*, or believable. Although the ending of "The Lottery" at first may shock readers, the author uses *foreshadowing*, hints or clues such as the villagers' nervousness about the lottery, to help readers understand future events or twists in the plot.

Most plots place the *protagonist*, or main character, in a *conflict* with the *antagonist*, some other person or group. In "The Lottery," a reader might see Tessie as the protagonist and the villagers as the antagonist. *Conflict* consists of two forces trying to conquer each other or resist being conquered—not merely vaguely defined turmoil. *External conflicts* occur outside an individual—between two people, a person and a group (Tessie versus the villagers), two groups (lottery supporters and opponents), or even a character and the environment. *Internal conflicts* between two opposing forces or desires occur within an individual (such as fear versus hope as the lottery slips are drawn). The *central conflict* is the primary conflict for the protagonist that propels the action of the story. Events of the plot *complicate* the conflict (Tessie arrives late, Bill draws the slip) and lead to the *climax*, the moment when the outcome is inevitable (Tessie draws the black dot). This outcome is the *resolution*, or conclusion (the villagers stone Tessie). Some stories let events unfold without any apparent plot—action and change occur inside the characters.

**Point of View.** The point of view, the angle from which a story is told, might be the author's or a character's. The *narrator* is the one who tells the story and perceives the events, perhaps with limited knowledge or a part to play. Two common points of view are those of a *first-person narrator* (*I*), the *speaker* who tells the story, and a *third-person narrator* (*he, she*) who tells the story from an all-knowing perspective, from the perspective of a single character, or from numerous, shifting perspectives. The point of view may be *omniscient* (the speaker knows all and has access to every character's thoughts and feelings); *limited omniscient* (the speaker knows the thoughts and feelings of one or more characters, but not all); or *objective* (the speaker observes the characters but cannot share their thoughts or feelings). In "The Lottery," a third-person objective narrator seemingly looks on and reports what occurs without knowing what the characters think.

**Setting.** Setting refers to the time and place of events and may include the season, the weather, and the people in the background. The setting often helps establish a literary work's *mood* or *atmosphere*, the emotional climate that a reader senses. For example, the first sentence of "The Lottery" establishes its setting (paragraph 1).

**Symbols.** Symbols are tangible objects, visible actions, or characters that hint at meanings beyond themselves. In "The Lottery," the black box suggests outdated tradition, resistance to change, evil, cruelty, and more.

**Theme.** A theme is a work's main idea or insight—the author's observation about life, society, or human nature. Sometimes you can sum up a theme in a sentence ("Human beings cannot live without illusion"); other times, a theme may be implied, hard to discern, or one of several in a work.

To state a theme, go beyond a work's topic or subject by asking yourself, What does the author say about this subject? Details from the story should support your statement of theme, and your theme should account for the details. "The Lottery" treats subjects such as the unexpected, scapegoating, outmoded rituals, and violence; one of its themes might be stated as "People are selfish, always looking out for number one."

For an interactive Learning by Doing activity on Recommending Fiction to a Friend, go to Ch. 13: **bedfordstmartins.com/bedguide**.

# Learning by Writing: Literary Analysis

## The Assignment: Analyzing a Literary Work

For this assignment, you are to be a literary critic – analyzing, interpreting, and evaluating a literary selection for your classmates. Your purpose is to deepen their understanding because you will have devoted time and effort to digging out the work's meaning. Even if they too have studied the work carefully, you will try to convince them that your interpretation is valid.

Choose a literary work that intrigues you or expresses a worthwhile meaning. Your selection might be a short story, a poem, a play, or a novel. (Follow directions if your instructor wants to approve your choice, assign the literary work, or limit your options to several works read by your class.) After careful analysis of the work, write an essay as the expert critic, explaining the meaning you discern, supporting your interpretation with evidence from the work, and evaluating the effectiveness of literary elements used by the author and the significance of the theme.

You cannot include everything about the work in your paper, so you should focus on one element (such as character, setting, or theme) or the interrelationship of two or three elements (such as characterization and symbolism). Although a summary, or *synopsis,* of the plot is a good beginning point, retelling the story is not a satisfactory literary analysis.

These college writers successfully responded to such an assignment:

> One showed how the rhythm, rhymes, and images of Adrienne Rich's poem "Aunt Jennifer's Tigers" mesh to convey the poem's theme of tension between a woman's artistic urge and societal constraints.
>
> Another, a drummer, read James Baldwin's "Sonny's Blues" and established Sonny's credibility as a musician – based on attitudes, actions, struggles, and his relationship with his instrument and with other musicians.
>
> A psychology major concluded that the relationship between Hamlet and Claudius in Shakespeare's *Hamlet* represents tension, jealousy, and misunderstanding between stepsons and stepfathers.

## Facing the Challenge Analyzing Literature

The major challenge that writers face when analyzing a literary work is to state and support a thesis that takes a stand. If you simply explain the literal meaning of the work – retelling the story or summing up the topic of an essay or a poem – your readers will be disappointed. Instead, they expect a clear thesis that presents your specific interpretation. They want to see how you analyze the work and which features of the work you use to support your position about it. For instance, your thesis might identify a theme—an insight, main idea, or observation about life—developed in the work. Then your essay would show how selected features of the work express, develop, or illustrate this theme. On the other hand, your thesis might present your analysis of how a story, poem, or play works. Then your essay might discuss how several elements—such as the mood established by the setting, the figurative language used to describe events, and the arc of the plot—work together to develop its meaning. Whatever the case that you argue, your thesis needs to be clearly focused and your supporting evidence needs to come from the words and expressions of the work itself.

## Generating Ideas

Read several literary works from the course options to find two or three you like. Next, reread those that interest you. Select one that strikes you as especially significant—realistic or universal, moving or disturbing, believable or shocking—with a meaning you wish to share with classmates.

Analyzing a literary work is the first step in interpreting meaning and evaluating literary quality. As you read the work, identify its elements and analyze them. Then focus on *one* significant element or a cluster of related elements. As you write, restrict your discussion to that focus.

For more on analysis, see pp. 446–50.

We provide three checklists to guide you in analyzing different types of literature. Each of these is an aid to understanding, *not* an organizational outline for writing about literature. The first checklist focuses on short stories and novels, but some of its questions can help you analyze setting, character, theme, or your reactions as a reader for almost any kind of literary work.

**DISCOVERY CHECKLIST**

### Analyzing a Short Story or a Novel

For a glossary of literary terms, see pp. 270–71.

- ☐ What is your reaction to the story? Jot it down.
- ☐ Who is the *narrator*—not the author, but the one who tells the story?
- ☐ What is the *point of view*?
- ☐ What is the *setting* (time and place)? What is the *atmosphere* or *mood*?
- ☐ How does the *plot* unfold? Write a synopsis, or summary, of the events in time order, including relationships among those events (see pp. 281–82).
- ☐ What are the *characters* like? Describe their personalities, traits, and motivations based on their actions, speech, habits, and so on. What strategies does the author use to develop the characters? Who is the *protagonist*? The *antagonist*? Do any characters change? Are the changes believable?
- ☐ How would you describe the story's *style*, or use of language? Is it informal, conversational, or formal? Does the story use dialect or foreign words?

- ☐ What are the *external conflicts* and the *internal conflicts*? What is the *central conflict*? Express the conflicts using the word *versus,* such as "dreams versus reality" or "the individual versus society."
- ☐ What is the *climax* of the story? Is there any *resolution*?
- ☐ Are there important *symbols*? What might they mean?
- ☐ What does the *title* of the story mean?
- ☐ What are the *themes* of the story? Are they universal (applicable to all people everywhere at all times)? Write down your interpretation of the main theme. How is this theme related to your own life?
- ☐ What other literary works or life experiences does the story remind you of?

When looking at a poem, consider the elements specific to poetry and those shared with other genres, as the following checklist suggests.

### DISCOVERY CHECKLIST
**Analyzing a Poem**

- ☐ What is your reaction to the poem? Jot it down.
- ☐ Who is the *speaker*—not the author, but the one who narrates?
- ☐ Is there a *setting*? What *mood* or emotional *atmosphere* does it suggest?
- ☐ Can you put the poem into your own words—paraphrase it?
- ☐ What is striking about the poem's language? Is it informal or formal? Does it use irony or figurative language: *imagery, metaphor, personification*? Identify repetition or words that are unusual, used in an unusual way, or *archaic* (no longer commonly used). Consider *connotations*, the suggestions conjured by the words: *house* versus *home,* though both refer to the same place.
- ☐ Is the poem *lyric* (expressing emotion) or *narrative* (telling a story)?
- ☐ How is the poem structured or divided? Does it use *couplets* (two consecutive rhyming lines), *quatrains* (units of four lines), or other units? How do the beginning and end relate to each other and to the poem as a whole?
- ☐ Does the poem use *rhyme* (words that sound alike)? If so, how does the rhyme contribute to the meaning?
- ☐ Does the poem have *rhythm* (regular meter or beat, patterns of accented and unaccented syllables)? How does the rhythm contribute to the meaning?
- ☐ What does the *title* of the poem mean?

- ☐ What is the major *theme* of the poem? How does this underlying idea unify the poem? How is it related to your own life?
- ☐ What other literary works or life experiences does the poem remind you of?

A play is written to be seen and heard, not read. You may analyze what kind it is and how it would appear onstage, as this checklist suggests.

**DISCOVERY CHECKLIST**

**Analyzing a Play**

- ☐ What is your reaction to the play? Jot it down.
- ☐ Is the play a serious *tragedy* (which arouses pity and fear in the audience and usually ends unhappily with the death or downfall of the *tragic hero*)? Or is it a *comedy* (which aims to amuse and usually ends happily)?
- ☐ What is the *setting* of the play? What is its *mood*?
- ☐ In brief, what happens? Summarize each act of the play.
- ☐ What are the characters like? Who is the *protagonist*? Who is the *antagonist*? Are there *foil characters* who contrast with the main character and reveal his or her traits? Which characters are in conflict? Which change?
- ☐ Which speeches seem especially significant?
- ☐ What is the plot? Identify the *exposition* or background information needed to understand the story. Determine the main *external* and *internal* conflicts. What is the *central conflict*? What events *complicate* the central conflict? How are these elements of the plot spread throughout the play?
- ☐ What is the *climax* of the play? Is there a *resolution* to the action?
- ☐ What does the *title* mean?
- ☐ Can you identify any *dramatic irony*, words or actions of a character that carry meaning unperceived by the character but evident to the audience?
- ☐ What is the major *theme*? Is it universal? How is it related to your life?
- ☐ What other literary works or life experiences does the play remind you of?

**Learning by Doing** Developing Your Literary Analysis

Once you have chosen and read the work you want to write about, also select an appropriate checklist from the preceding section. Then concentrate on a few questions that seem interesting and potentially fruitful to you. Answer them, jotting notes in a file, on the work itself, or on a separate card or page for each question. If you find a good idea, highlight or underline relevant evidence in the work. If not, try a few more questions until an idea starts to take shape.

## Planning, Drafting, and Developing

For more on planning, drafting, and developing, see Chs. 20, 21, and 22.

When you write your analysis, your purpose is to explain the work's deeper meaning. Don't try to impress readers with your brilliance. Instead, regard them as friends in whose company you are discussing something familiar to all, though they may not have studied the work as carefully as you have. This assumption will help you decide how much evidence from the work to include and will reduce summarizing.

**Identify Your Support.** After you have determined the major element or cluster of elements that you intend to focus on, go through the work again to find all the passages that relate to your main point. Mark them as you find them, or put them on note cards or in a computer file, along with the page references. If you use any quotations, quote exactly.

For more on stating a thesis, see pp. 399–408.

**Develop Your Main Idea or Thesis.** Begin by trying to express your point in a thesis statement that identifies the literary work and the author.

WORKING THESIS — In "The Lottery," Shirley Jackson reveals the theme.

But this statement is too vague, so you rewrite it to be more precise:

IMPROVED — In "The Lottery" by Shirley Jackson, the theme is tradition.

This thesis is better but still doesn't state the theme clearly or precisely. You try other ways of expressing what Jackson implies about tradition:

IMPROVED — In "The Lottery" by Shirley Jackson, one of the major themes is that outmoded traditions can be harmful.

Adding *one of* shows that this is not the story's only theme, but the rest is vague. What does *outmoded* mean? How are traditions harmful?

MORE PRECISE — In "The Lottery" by Shirley Jackson, one of the major themes is that traditions that have lost their meaning can still move people to act abnormally without thinking.

This thesis is better but may change as you write. For instance, you might go beyond interpretation of Jackson's ideas by adding *tragic* to convey your evaluation of her observation of the human condition:

EVALUATION ADDED — In "The Lottery," Jackson reveals the tragic theme that traditions that have lost their meaning can still move people to abnormal and thoughtless action.

Or you might say this, alerting readers to your main points:

PREVIEW ADDED — In "The Lottery," Jackson effectively uses symbolism and irony to reveal the theme that traditions that have lost their meaning can still move people to abnormal action.

Focus on analyzing ideas, not retelling events. Maintain that focus by analyzing your thesis: divide it into parts, and then develop each part in turn. The thesis just presented could be divided into (1) use of symbolism to reveal theme and (2) use of irony to reveal theme. Similarly, you might divide a thesis about character change into the character's original traits, the events that cause change, and the character's new traits.

## Learning by Doing Developing Your Thesis

Follow the preceding pattern for developing a thesis statement. Start with your working thesis. Then improve it, make it more precise, and consider adding an evaluation or preview. Present your thesis drafts to a classmate or small group, perhaps asking questions like these: What wording needs to be clearer? What idea could I narrow down? What point sounds intriguing? What might a reader want me to emphasize? Continue to refine your thesis as you work on your essay.

**Introduce Your Essay.** Tie your beginning to your main idea, or thesis. If you are uncertain how to begin, try one of these openings:

For more on introductions, see pp. 426–28.

- Focus on a character's universality (pointing out that most people might feel as Tessie in "The Lottery" did if their names were drawn).
- Focus on a theme's universality (discussing briefly how traditions seem to be losing their meaning in modern society).
- Quote a striking line from the work ("and then they were upon her" or "'Lottery in June, corn be heavy soon'").
- Make a statement about the work's point, your reaction when you read it, a parallel personal experience, or the writer's technique.
- Ask a "Have you ever?" question to draw readers into your interpretation.

For general questions for a peer editor, see p. 463. For peer response worksheets, visit **bedfordstmartins.com/bedguide**.

## Peer Response Responding to Literature

Ask a classmate to read your draft and to consider how effectively you have analyzed the literary work and presented your analysis. Ask your peer editor to answer specific questions such as these:

- What is your first reaction to the literary analysis?
- In what ways does the analysis add to your understanding of the literary work? In what ways does it add to your insights into life?
- Does the introduction make you want to read the rest of the analysis? What changes would you suggest to strengthen the opening?
- Is the main idea clear? Is there sufficient relevant evidence from the work to support that point? Put stars wherever additional evidence is needed. Put a check mark by any irrelevant information.
- Does the essay go beyond plot summary to analyze elements, interpret meaning, and evaluate literary merit? If not, how might the writer revise?
- Is the analysis organized by ideas instead of events? What changes in organization would you suggest?
- Do the transitions guide you smoothly from one point to the next? Do the transitions focus on ideas, not on time or position in the story? Note any places where you would suggest adding transitions.
- If this paper were yours, what is the one thing you would be sure to work on before handing it in?

For more on citing and listing literary works, see MLA style in E (pp. A-32–A-38) in the Quick Research Guide.

**Support Your Interpretation.** As you develop your analysis, include supporting evidence—descriptions of setting and character, summaries of events, quotations of dialogue, and other specifics. Cite page numbers (for prose) or line numbers (for poetry) where the details can be found in the work. Integrate evidence from the story with your comments and ideas.

For a list of transitions showing logical connections, see p. 433.

Keep the focus on ideas, not events, by using transition markers that refer to character traits and personality change, not to time. Say "Although Mr. Summers was . . ." instead of "At the beginning of the story Mr. Summers was. . . ." Write "Tessie became . . ." instead of "After that Tessie was . . ." State "The villagers in 'The Lottery' changed . . . ," not "On the next page. . . ."

For more on conclusions, see pp. 428–30.

**Conclude Your Essay.** When you reach the end, don't just stop. Close as you might open—with a personal experience, a comment on technique, a quotation—to provide a sense of finality. Refer to or reaffirm your thesis. Often an effective conclusion ties in directly with the introduction.

Use the Take Action chart (p. 279) to help you figure out how to improve your draft. Skim across the top to identify questions you might ask about your literary analysis. When you answer a question with "Yes" or "Maybe," move straight down the column to Locate Specifics under that

## Take Action Strengthening Literary Analysis

Ask each question at the top of the chart to consider whether your draft might need work on that issue. If so, follow the ASK—LOCATE—TAKE ACTION sequence to revise.

| | Broad Thesis? | Vague Main Points? | Weak Evidence? |
|---|---|---|---|
| 1 ASK | Could I state my overall thesis or main idea more clearly? | Could I present my main points more specifically? | Could I add more or better evidence from the literary work? |
| 2 LOCATE SPECIFICS | ■ Write out your current thesis.<br>■ Highlight key words that pin down your main idea about the literary work.<br>■ Circle any words that seem vague or general. | ■ Underline or list the main points you want to present.<br>■ Confirm the relevance of each point for your stated thesis (not just your general idea).<br>■ Read the passage about each point and use an X to mark any gap in development. | ■ Color-code each bit of supporting evidence in your draft.<br>■ Put a ✓ by any passages with little, no, or irrelevant support.<br>■ Jot down ideas about compelling examples and details to add support. |
| 3 TAKE ACTION | ■ Replace circled words with clear, concrete, exact words.<br>■ Narrow down any broad terms or claims.<br>■ Reveal your analysis of significant elements instead of telling what happened.<br>■ Decide whether to add an evaluation or a preview of your main points. | ■ If any points do not connect to your thesis, rework the thesis or replace the points.<br>■ If any points lack development, add explanation, examples, or details to clarify your analysis.<br>■ Read your draft aloud, listening for logical jumps or weak connections. Use specifics to fill in gaps or spell out connections. | ■ Return to each ✓ to work in strong, persuasive support based on analysis.<br>■ Figure out how to fit in more examples and details.<br>■ Smooth out each paragraph, making sure each main point is clear for a reader and that transitions link your ideas and evidence. |

question. Use the activities there to pinpoint gaps, problems, or weaknesses. Then move straight down the column to Take Action. Use the advice that suits your problem as you revise.

## Revising and Editing

For more revising and editing strategies, see Ch. 25.

As you read over your draft, keep in mind your thesis and the evidence that supports it.

### REVISION CHECKLIST

- ☐ Have you clearly identified the literary work and the author near the beginning of the analysis?
- ☐ Is your main idea or thesis clear? Does everything else relate to it?
- ☐ Have you focused on one element or a cluster of related elements in your analysis? Have you organized around these ideas rather than events?
- ☐ Do your transitions focus on ideas, not on plot or time sequence? Do they guide readers easily from one section or sentence to the next?
- ☐ Are your interpretations supported by evidence from the literary work? Do you need to add examples of dialogue, action, or description? Have you selected details relevant to the points of analysis, not interesting sidelights?
- ☐ Have you woven the details from the work smoothly into your text? Have you cited their correct page or line numbers? Have you quoted and cited carefully instead of lifting language without proper attribution?
- ☐ Do you understand all the words and literary terms you use?
- ☐ Have you tried to share your insights into the meaning of the work with your readers, or have you slipped into trying to impress them?

For more editing and proofreading strategies, see pp. 471–75.

After you have revised your literary analysis, check the grammar, word choice, punctuation, and mechanics—and then correct any problems you find. Make sure that you smoothly introduce all of your quotations and references to the work and weave them into your own discussion.

For more help, find the relevant checklist sections in the Quick Editing Guide on p. A-39. Turn also to the Quick Format Guide beginning on p. A-1.

### EDITING CHECKLIST

- ☐ Have you used the present tense for events in the literary work and for comments about the author's presentation? A3
- ☐ Have you used quotation marks correctly whenever you give the exact words of the literary work? C3
- ☐ Have you used correct manuscript format for your paper?

# Learning from Another Writer: Synopsis

You may write synopses of literary works to help you prepare to write about them or to sum up information about them for an essay or exam. A synopsis can help you get the chronology straight, pick out significant events and details, and relate parts of a work to each other. Condensing a story to a few hundred words forces you to focus on what's most important, often leading to a statement of theme.

A *synopsis* is a summary of the plot of a narrative — a short story, a novel, a play, or a narrative poem. It describes the literal meaning, condensing the story to the major events and most significant details. Do not include your interpretation, but summarize the work in your own words, taking care not to lift language or sentence structure from the work itself. To prepare for writing his literary analysis of "The Lottery" (pp. 260–66) — making sure he had the sequence of events clear — Jonathan Burns wrote a synopsis of the story.

For more on summarizing and paraphrasing, see Ch. 12 and D (pp. A-28–A-31) in the Quick Research Guide.

**Jonathan Burns** **Student Synopsis**

## A Synopsis of "The Lottery"

Around ten o'clock on a sunny June 27, the villagers gathered in the square for a lottery, expecting to be home in time for lunch. The children came first, gathering stones and talking as they enjoyed the summer vacation. Then came the men, followed by the women. When parents called, the children joined their families. 1

Mr. Summers, who always conducted the town lottery, arrived with the traditional black wooden box and placed it on the three-legged stool that Mr. Graves had brought out. The villagers remained apart from these men, but Mr. Martin and his son reluctantly helped hold the shabby black box as Mr. Summers mixed the paper slips in it, now substituted for the original wooden chips. To prepare for the drawing, they listed the members of every household and swore in Mr. Summers. Although they had dropped much of the original ritual, the official still greeted each person individually. 2

Tessie Hutchinson rushed into the square, telling her friend Mrs. Delacroix she had almost forgotten the day. Then she joined her husband and children. When Mr. Summers asked if everyone was present, he was told that Clyde Dunbar was absent because of a broken leg but that his wife would draw for the family. Summers noted that the Watson boy was drawing for his mother and checked to see if Old Man Warner was present. 3

The crowd got quiet. Mr. Summers reminded everybody of the procedure and began to call the family names in alphabetical order. People in the group joked and talked nervously until Mr. Summers finished calling the roll. After a pause, the heads 4

of households opened their slips. Everybody wondered who had the special slip of paper, who had won the lottery. They discovered it was Bill Hutchinson. When Tessie complained that the drawing hadn't been done fairly, the others told her to "Be a good sport" (264).

Mr. Graves put five slips into the box, one for each member of the Hutchinson 5
family, although Tessie kept charging unfairness. The children drew first, then Tessie, then Bill. The children opened their slips and held up blank pieces of paper. Bill opened his, also blank. Tessie wouldn't open hers; Bill had to do it for her, revealing its black spot.

Mr. Summers urged everyone to complete the process right away. They picked up 6
stones, even young Davy Hutchinson, and started throwing them at Tessie, as she kept screaming, "It isn't fair, it isn't right" (266). Then the villagers stoned her.

### Questions to Start You Thinking

Meaning

1. In what ways does this synopsis help you understand the story better?
2. Why isn't a synopsis as interesting as a short story?
3. Can you tell from this synopsis whether Burns understands Jackson's story beyond the literal level? How can you tell?

Writing Strategies

4. Does Burns retell the story accurately and clearly? Does he get the events in correct time order? How does he show the relationships of the events to each other and to the whole?
5. Does Burns select the details necessary to indicate what happened in "The Lottery"? Why do you think he omits certain details?
6. Are there any details, comments, or events that you would add to his synopsis? Why or why not?
7. How does this synopsis differ from Burns's literary analysis (pp. 268–69)?

## Learning by Writing: Synopsis

### The Assignment: Writing a Synopsis of a Story by Kate Chopin

Kate Chopin was a nineteenth-century American writer whose female characters search for identity and freedom from oppression. Write a synopsis of two to three hundred words of Chopin's "The Story of an Hour." Keep your synopsis of the plot true to the original, noting accurate details in time order.

**DISCOVERY CHECKLIST**

- ☐ What are the major events and details of the story?
- ☐ In what time order do events take place?
- ☐ How are the story's parts related (without adding interpretations)?
- ☐ Which of the author's words might you want to quote?

## Kate Chopin

### The Story of an Hour

Knowing that Mrs. Mallard was afflicted with a heart trouble, great care was taken to break to her as gently as possible the news of her husband's death. 1

It was her sister Josephine who told her, in broken sentences, veiled hints that revealed in half concealing. Her husband's friend Richards was there, too, near her. It was he who had been in the newspaper office when intelligence of the railroad disaster was received, with Brently Mallard's name leading the list of "killed." He had only taken the time to assure himself of its truth by a second telegram, and had hastened to forestall any less careful, less tender friend in bearing the sad message. 2

She did not hear the story as many women have heard the same, with a paralyzed inability to accept its significance. She wept at once, with sudden, wild abandonment, in her sister's arms. When the storm of grief had spent itself she went away to her room alone. She would have no one follow her. 3

There stood, facing the open window, a comfortable, roomy armchair. Into this she sank, pressed down by a physical exhaustion that haunted her body and seemed to reach into her soul. 4

She could see in the open square before her house the tops of trees that were all aquiver with the new spring life. The delicious breath of rain was in the air. In the street below a peddler was crying his wares. The notes of a distant song which someone was singing reached her faintly, and countless sparrows were twittering in the eaves. 5

There were patches of blue sky showing here and there through the clouds that had met and piled one above the other in the west facing her window. 6

She sat with her head thrown back upon the cushion of the chair, quite motionless, except when a sob came up into her throat and shook her, as a child who has cried itself to sleep continues to sob in its dreams. 7

She was young, with a fair, calm face, whose lines bespoke repression and even a certain strength. But now there was a dull stare in her eyes, whose gaze was fixed away off yonder on one of those patches of blue sky. It 8 was not a glance of reflection, but rather indicated a suspension of intelligent thought.

There was something coming to her and she was waiting for it, fearfully. 9
What was it? She did not know; it was too subtle and elusive to name. But she felt it, creeping out of the sky, reaching toward her through the sounds, the scents, the color that filled the air.

Now her bosom rose and fell tumultuously. She was beginning to recog- 10
nize this thing that was approaching to possess her, and she was striving to beat it back with her will—as powerless as her two white slender hands would have been.

When she abandoned herself a little whispered word escaped her slightly 11
parted lips. She said it over and over under her breath: "Free, free, free!" The vacant stare and the look of terror that had followed it went from her eyes. They stayed keen and bright. Her pulses beat fast, and the coursing blood warmed and relaxed every inch of her body.

She did not stop to ask if it were not a monstrous joy that held her. 12
A clear and exalted perception enabled her to dismiss the suggestion as trivial.

She knew that she would weep again when she saw the kind, tender 13
hands folded in death; the face that had never looked save with love upon her, fixed and gray and dead. But she saw beyond that bitter moment a long procession of years to come that would belong to her absolutely. And she opened and spread her arms out to them in welcome.

There would be no one to live for during those coming years; she would 14
live for herself. There would be no powerful will bending her in that blind persistence with which men and women believe they have a right to impose a private will upon a fellow creature. A kind intention or a cruel intention made the act seem no less a crime as she looked upon it in that brief moment of illumination.

And yet she had loved him—sometimes. Often she had not. What did it 15
matter! What could love, the unsolved mystery, count for in face of this possession of self-assertion which she suddenly recognized as the strongest impulse of her being.

"Free! Body and soul free!" she kept whispering. 16

Josephine was kneeling before the closed door with her lips to the 17
keyhole, imploring for admission. "Louise, open the door! I beg; open the door—you will make yourself ill. What are you doing, Louise? For heaven's sake open the door."

"Go away. I am not making myself ill." No; she was drinking in a very 18
elixir of life through that open window.

Her fancy was running riot along those days ahead of her. Spring days, 19
and summer days, and all sorts of days that would be her own. She breathed a quick prayer that life might be long. It was only yesterday she had thought with a shudder that life might be long.

She arose at length and opened the door to her sister's importunities. 20
There was a feverish triumph in her eyes, and she carried herself unwittingly

like a goddess of Victory. She clasped her sister's waist, and together they descended the stairs. Richards stood waiting for them at the bottom.

Someone was opening the front door with a latchkey. It was Brently Mallard who entered, a little travel-stained, composedly carrying his gripsack and umbrella. He had been far from the scene of the accident, and did not even know there had been one. He stood amazed at Josephine's piercing cry; at Richards's quick motion to screen him from the view of his wife. 21

But Richards was too late. 22

When the doctors came they said she had died of heart disease—of joy that kills. 23

## Learning from Another Writer: Paraphrase

Like a synopsis, a *paraphrase* conveys the meaning of the original piece of literature and the relationships of its parts in your own words. A paraphrase, however, converts the original poetry to your own prose or the original prose to your own words in a passage about as long as the original.

As Jonathan Burns read through "The Lottery" preparing to write his analysis, he paid close attention to several of the characters that he planned to mention. To sharpen his understanding of Old Man Warner, he wrote a paraphrase of that character's comments in paragraph 32.

**Jonathan Burns** **Student Paraphrase**

### A Paraphrase from "The Lottery"

Old Man Warner criticized people who were willing to give up the lottery as stupid idiots or uppity young people who were not satisfied with anything. He claimed that such people would be content to quit work and move to caves. Then he repeated an old folk expression about a good corn crop following the June lottery and claimed that without it the villagers would end up living on weeds and nuts. Finally, he maintained that the lottery had been a tradition forever. He even criticized Mr. Summers as a youngster, faulting him for not being serious enough about the lottery (263–64).

### Questions to Start You Thinking

Meaning

1. In what ways do you think this paraphrase helped Jonathan Burns understand Old Man Warner better?
2. Why isn't a paraphrase as interesting as the original passage in a story?

Writing Strategies

3. To what extent does Burns paraphrase clearly and accurately? Would you add or drop any details or comments from his paraphrase?
4. How does this paraphrase differ from Burns's synopsis (pp. 281–82)?

### Learning by Doing Collaborating on a Paraphrase

Working with a classmate or small group, select from "The Lottery" a short paragraph that describes or reveals a character in the story. Either (1) collaboratively compose a paraphrase, line by line, of that paragraph, or (2) separately write a paraphrase, then exchange and comment as peer editors on each of your drafts. Either way, present the meaning of the passage, but stick to your own words and sentence structures.

## Learning by Writing: Paraphrase

### The Assignment: Writing a Paraphrase of a Poem

See p. 219 and the Additional Writing Assignments section below for poems you might paraphrase.

You can benefit from paraphrasing poetry—expressing the content of a poem in your own words without adding opinions or interpretations. A paraphrase forces you to divide the poem into logical sections, then to figure out what the poet says in each section and how the parts relate. It also prepares you to state its theme—its main idea or insight—in a sentence or two.

**DISCOVERY CHECKLIST**

- ☐ What are the poem's major sections? What does the poet say in each one?
- ☐ How are the sections of the poem related?
- ☐ Are any words unfamiliar or used in a special sense, different from the usual meanings? What do those words mean in the context of the poem?
- ☐ Does the poet use images to create sensory pictures or figurative language (see p. 270) to create comparisons? How do these contribute to the meaning?

## Additional Writing Assignments

1. **Source Assignment.** Analyze the themes of "The Story of an Hour" or another literary work from an earlier era and assigned by your instructor. Which themes are relevant now? How do they relate to twenty-first-century readers and their issues?
2. **Source Assignment.** Write an essay comparing and contrasting a literary element in two or three assigned or optional short stories or poems.
3. **Source Assignment.** Write an essay comparing and contrasting a literary element in a short story and another type of narrative such as a novel or film that tells a story. For example, for "The Lottery" (a short story) and *The Hunger Games* (either the novel or the film), you might compare themes (such as the power of traditions like the lottery and the reaping), settings (such as the village and the Seam), or characters (such as Tessie Hutchinson and Katniss Everdeen or Mr. Summers and District 12's escort Effie Trinket). Use specific evidence from each narrative to support your conclusions.

For more on writing a comparison and contrast essay, see Ch. 7.

4. **Source Assignment.** Read the poem below by Robert Frost (1874–1963). Write an essay using a paraphrase of the poem as a springboard for your thoughts on a fork in the road of your life – a decision that made a difference for you.

For another poem by Robert Frost, see p. 219.

**The Road Not Taken**

Two roads diverged in a yellow wood,
And sorry I could not travel both
And be one traveler, long I stood
And looked down one as far as I could
To where it bent in the undergrowth;

Then took the other, as just as fair,
And having perhaps the better claim,
Because it was grassy and wanted wear;
Though as for that the passing there
Had worn them really about the same,

And both that morning equally lay
In leaves no step had trodden black.
Oh, I kept the first for another day!
Yet knowing how way leads on to way,
I doubted if I should ever come back.

I shall be telling this with a sigh
Somewhere ages and ages hence:
Two roads diverged in a wood, and I –
I took the one less traveled by,
And that has made all the difference.

For more on writing a comparison and contrast essay, see Ch. 7.

5. **Source Assignment.** Read the poem below by Edwin Arlington Robinson (1869–1935). Have you known and envied someone like Richard Cory, a person everyone thought had it all? What happened to him or her? What did you discover about your impression of the person? Analyze the poem and draw on experience as you write a personal response essay to compare and contrast the person you knew with Richard Cory.

**Richard Cory**

Whenever Richard Cory went down town,
We people on the pavement looked at him:
He was a gentleman from sole to crown,
Clean favored, and imperially slim.

And he was always quietly arrayed,
And he was always human when he talked;
But still he fluttered pulses when he said,
"Good-morning," and he glittered when he walked.

And he was rich—yes, richer than a king—
And admirably schooled in every grace:
In fine, we thought that he was everything
To make us wish that we were in his place.

So on we worked, and waited for the light,
And went without the meat, and cursed the bread;
And Richard Cory, one calm summer night,
Went home and put a bullet through his head.

For more about analyzing visuals, see Ch. 14. For more on analysis in general, see pp. 446–50.

6. **Source Assignment.** Write a critical analysis of a song, a movie, or a television show. Play or view it several times to pull out specific evidence to support your interpretation. If your instructor approves, present your analysis in a podcast, a multimedia format, or a series of Web pages.

# Responding to Visual Representations

# 14

Images are a constant and persistent presence in our lives. The sign atop a taxi invites us to try the new ride at a local tourist attraction. A celebrity sporting a milk mustache smiles from the side of a city bus, accompanied by the familiar question, "Got milk?" The lettering on a pickup truck urges us to call for a free landscaping estimate. During campaign season, politicians beam at us from brochures, billboards, and screens. On television, video, and the Web, advertising images surround us, trying to shape our opinions about everything from personal hygiene products to snack foods to political issues.

Besides ads, all sorts of cartoons, photos, drawings, paintings, logos, graphics, and other two-dimensional media work to evoke responses. The critical skills you develop for analyzing these still images also apply to other visual representations, including television commercials, films, and stage productions. Whether visual images provoke a smile or a frown, one thing is certain: visuals help to structure our views of reality.

## Why Responding to Visuals Matters

### In a College Course

- You respond to images of people and places in class discussions and papers for sociology, foreign language, and international business classes.
- You write reports on digital images during your health-sciences lab or clinical experience.

### In the Workplace

- You evaluate the values conveyed by proposed images for a new Web page.

### In Your Community

- You gather recent newspaper images of local teens to document the need for a community sports program.

When have you responded to visuals in your writing? In what situations might you analyze images in future writing?

## Using Strategies for Visual Analysis

For an interactive Learning by Doing activity on Analyzing the Web Site for Your Campus, go to Ch. 14: **bedfordstmartins.com/bedguide**.

Just as you annotate or respond to a written text, do the same to record your observations and interpretations of images. Include a copy of the image, if available, when you solicit peer review or submit your essay. Begin your visual analysis by conducting a *close reading* of the image. Like a literal and critical reading of a written text, a close reading of an image involves careful, in-depth examination of the advertisement, photograph, cartoon, artwork, or other visual on three levels:

- **What is the big picture?** What is the source of the image? What is its purpose? What audience does it address? What prominent element in the image stands out? What focal point draws the eye?
- **What characteristics of the image can you observe?** What story does the image tell? What people or animals appear in the image? What are the major elements of the image? How are they arranged?
- **How can you interpret what the image suggests?** What feeling or mood does it create? What is its cultural meaning? What are the roles of any signs, symbols, or language that it includes? What is its theme?

For more on literal and critical reading of texts, see Ch. 2. For checklists for analyzing images, see pp. 293, 299–300, and 304–5.

As you analyze visuals, you may discover that your classmates respond differently than you do to some images, just as they might to a written text. Your personal cultural background and your experiences may influence how you see the meaning of an image. As a result, your thesis interpreting the meaning of an image or analyzing its effectiveness will be your own – shaped by your responses and supported by your observations.

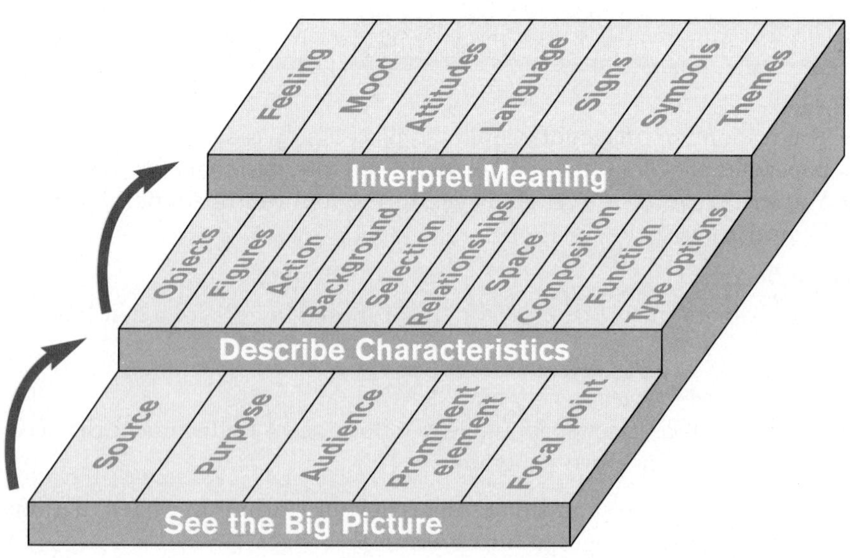

# Level One: Seeing the Big Picture

Begin your close reading of an image by discovering what you can about its origins and overall composition. If you include the image in a paper, you will need to cite the source and its "author" or artist, just as you would if you were including text from a reading, an article, or a literary work.

For more on crediting sources of visuals, see section B in the Quick Format Guide, pp. A-8–A-12.

## Source, Purpose, and Audience

Identifying the background of an image is sometimes complicated. For example, an image may appear in its original context or in a different situation, used seriously, humorously, or allusively.

- What is the context for the image? If it is an ad, when and where did it run? If it is a photograph, painting, or other work of art, who is the artist? Where and how has it been published, circulated, or exhibited?
- What is the purpose of the image?
- What audience does it aim to attract? How does it appeal to viewers?

## Prominent Element

Next, examine the overall composition of the image. Ask yourself, "Is there one prominent element—object, person, background, writing—in the image that immediately attracts my attention?"

Answering that question is easy for a visual that showcases a single object or person, as in Figure 14.1. There, the child is the obvious prominent element. Her dark eyes, framed by her dark hair, draw the viewer to her alert, intent expression. That expression suggests her capacity to learn from all she observes. The text above and below her image reinforces this message as it cautions adults to be careful what they teach children through their own conduct.

Identifying the prominent element can be more complicated for a visual showing a whole scene or inviting many interpretations. For example, what draws your eye in Figure 14.2? Many people would first notice the neon sign on the left. The sign is bright, colorful (in a photo otherwise dominated by black and white tones), and framed neatly by the first window panel. People who read from left to right and top to bottom—including most Americans and Europeans—typically read photographs in the same way. For this reason, artists and photographers often position key elements—those they want viewers to see right away—somewhere in the upper left quadrant, drawing the viewer's eye into the image at the upper left corner. (See Figure 14.3.)

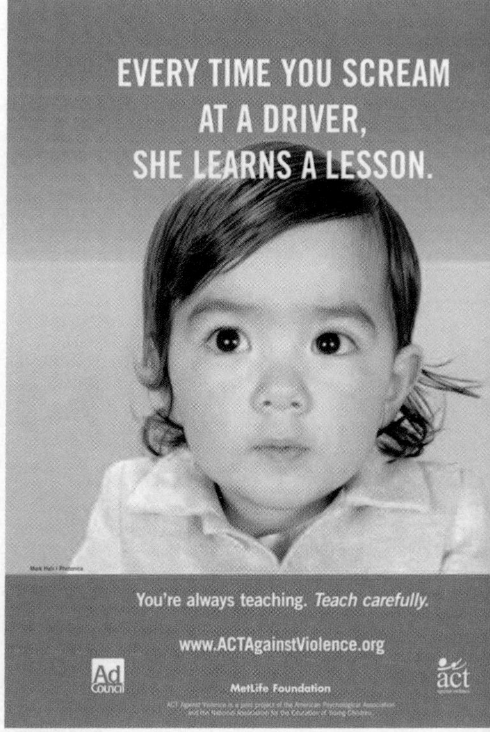

EVERY TIME YOU SCREAM
AT A DRIVER,
SHE LEARNS A LESSON.
You're always teaching. Teach carefully.
www.ACTAgainstViolence.org
Ad Council
MetLife Foundation
act


**Figure 14.1** Public Service Announcement with One Prominent Element. *Source:* Act Against Violence.org/Ad Council

**Figure 14.2 (top)** Photograph by Ian Pool

**Figure 14.3 (above left)** Photograph Divided into Quarters

**Figure 14.4 (above right)** Z Pattern Often Used to Read Images

**Figure 14.5 (right)** Close-Up Detail of Photograph

## Focal Point

There is another reason the reader's eye might be drawn first to the neon sign on the left in Figure 14.2. This simple yet bold sign communicates much about the place as a whole, announcing it to be an inexpensive, down-to-earth restaurant, offering simple fare. It probably opens early and stays open late, maybe even all night, serving average people of modest means. As a focal point, therefore, this sign sets up an important point of contrast with the unusual customer seated at the right. Because of the left-to-right and top-to-bottom reading pattern, most of us view photographs in a *Z* pattern, as shown in Figure 14.4. Thus, the bottom right corner of an image is a second important position that a skilled photographer can use to hold viewers' attention. When you look at the "big picture," you can see an image's overall composition, identify its prominent element, and determine its focal point.

**VISUAL ANALYSIS CHECKLIST**

**Seeing the Big Picture**

- ☐ What is the source of the image? What is its purpose and audience?
- ☐ What prominent element in the image immediately attracts your attention? How and why does it draw you into the image?
- ☐ What is the focal point of the image? How does the image direct your attention to this point? What path does your eye follow as you observe the image?

### Learning by Doing: Seeing the Big Picture

Working with a classmate or a small group, select another image in this book such as one that opens or closes a chapter. Consider the image's purpose and audience (in its original context or in this book), but concentrate on its prominent element, which draws the viewer's eye, and its focal point, which suggests the center of its action or moment. Share analyses in a class discussion, or report or post yours for another group.

# Level Two: Observing the Characteristics of an Image

As you read a written text literally, you become aware of what it presents, what it means, and how it applies in other situations. Similarly, your close reading of an image includes observing its *denotative* or literal characteristics. At this stage, you focus on exactly what the image depicts – observing it objectively – rather than probing what it means or signifies.

## Cast of Characters

**Objects.** Examine the condition, colors, sizes, functions, and positions of the objects included in the image. In Figure 14.2, for example, the main object outside is a luxurious black car, parked at the far right. Though little of the car is visible, its sleek design, wide tire, and position near the Batman figure mark it as the iconic Batmobile. In contrast, the objects inside the restaurant are mundane and predictable: a trash can, three potted plants, a narrow blue cash machine, tables and chairs, stainless steel food-service machines, a napkin dispenser, and stacks of empty cups.

**Figures.** Look closely at any figures (people, animals) in the image. Consider facial expressions, poses, hairstyles and colors, ages, sexes, ethnicity, possible education or occupation, apparent relationships, and so on.

Figure 14.2 shows a lone, seated man, framed by the window panel and silhouetted against the white floor-to-ceiling blinds. The man wears a black cape, a close-fitting, rubberized suit, wide gold belt, gloves, and boots, an outfit that accentuates his muscled physique. A mask hides all but the lower part of his face. Like no other detail, the mask's large, pointy ears identify the figure as the comic-book superhero Batman.

## Story of the Image

**Action.** The action shown in an image suggests its "plot" or story, the events surrounding the moment it captures. Figure 14.2 shows Batman eating a quick dinner or late-night snack. It suggests his earlier actions driving to the place, parking outside, ordering his food, and taking a seat at a small corner table.

**Background.** The background in an image shows where and when the action takes place. In Figure 14.2, the background is a bagel and donut shop on a winter night. This eatery—well lit and ordinary—sharply contrasts with its only customer, the figure of Batman, who is dark and mysterious, both in costume and mission. Because he is usually engaged in dangerous and high-minded crime-fighting crusades, the background seems designed to surprise viewers, who might ask, "What is the Dark Knight doing in a place like this?" Beyond the physical details of the photograph's background, fans will know that Batman is the secret disguise of the billionaire industrialist-playboy Bruce Wayne, a man traumatically orphaned who has vowed to devote his life to bringing criminals to justice. For anonymity, he does his crime-fighting and detective work clothed in the mystique and costume of Batman, a creature of the night. Throughout all his comic-book exploits, he is known for his intelligence, athleticism, command of technology, sense of justice—and damaged psyche.

## Design and Arrangement

**Selection of Elements.** When you look at the design of an image, reflect on both the elements included and their organization.

- What are the major colors and shapes? How are they arranged?
- Does the image look balanced? Are light and dark areas symmetrical?
- Does the image appear organized or chaotic?
- Is one area darker (heavier) or brighter (lighter) than other areas?
- What emotion, historical period, or memory does the image evoke?

In Figure 14.2, the shapes and colors are arranged so that the building's interior looks like daytime—bright, safe, warm, and cozy—which accentuates the cold, dark, and dangerous night outside. The bright areas in the middle of the photograph are surrounded by shadowy spaces with Batman sitting on the edge between the two. In this way, the image balances light and dark. Batman has come in for a few moments, but the photo's organization still connects him with the inhospitable world outside.

**Relationship of Elements.** Visual elements may be related to one another or to written text that appears with them. In Figure 14.2, for instance, the sign identifies a familiar, everyday location. However, the four big plate glass window panels, stretching across the front of the shop, suggest the way that drawings in a comic book march across a page, separated into neat rectangular frames. But here, no "thought balloon" emerges from Batman's head, allowing viewers to share his thoughts and learn why he is out of context. The photograph is arranged to raise, not answer, the question of what Batman is doing here. It invites viewers to interpret what is happening, to insert their own thought balloons over Batman's head. At the same time, it makes the point that we rarely know other people's stories, thoughts, and interior lives. When we see strangers in public settings, they are essentially unknowable, as this figure is.

**Use of Space.** An image may be surrounded by "white space"—empty space without text or graphics—or it may be "busy," filled with visual and written elements. Effective white space provides relief from a busy layout or directs the reader's eye to key elements. The image in Figure 14.2 uses the white-tiled wall above the counter and the white blinds to set off the shadowy darkness. Figure 14.6 specifically uses empty white space to call attention to the Volkswagen's small size. When this advertisement was produced back in 1959, many American cars were large and heavy. The VW, a German import, provided consumers with an alternative, and the advertising emphasized this contrast.

## Artistic Choices

Whatever the form of an image, the person who composes it considers its artistic effect, function, and connection to related text.

**Composition Decisions.** Aesthetic or artistic choices may vary with the designer's preferences and the characteristics of the medium. A photographer might use a close-up, medium, or wide-angle shot—and also determine the

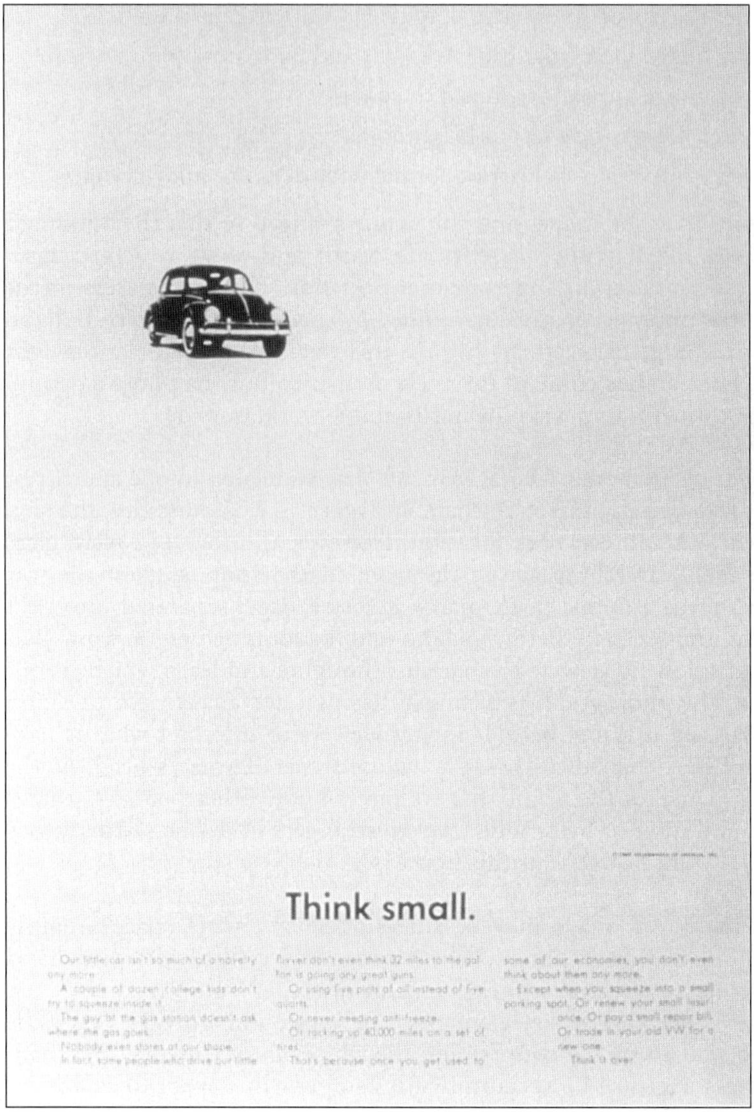

**Figure 14.6** Volkswagen Advertisement, about 1959

angle of the shot, the lighting, and the use of color. Compare Figures 14.2 and 14.5 to see how a close-up may leave out context but accent detail, such as Batman's white cup. On the other hand, in the Volkswagen ad (Figure 14.6), the white space creates the effect of a long shot taken from below with a telephoto lens. We see the car as it might appear through the wrong end of a pair of binoculars. This vantage point shrinks the car so that the small vehicle looks even smaller.

**Which one of these Chevrolet sport models would you rather have fun with?**

Are you the type that likes to breeze along the open road on a bright summer day with nothing above between you and the blue? Do you like the sound of rain against a snug fabric top? If so, that Chevrolet Convertible in our picture is for you! No question about it. For here's a car that's as young in spirit as you are—and looks it! Even the smart all-vinyl interior is made to live outdoors.

But maybe you like a car that can carry anything from small fry to outboard motors with equal ease. That would be the "Two-Ten" Handyman Station Wagon you see over there (one of five Chevrolet station wagons). Here's one car that's so versatile it practically makes you a two-car family all by itself. So low it sets a new height of fashion for station wagons! Practical? If the kids track sand inside, you can wash it out in a jiffy.

On the other hand, if you go for hardtops—and like 'em long, low and dashing—that Bel Air Sport Coupe in the background is just your dish. It's a "show car" from the word go!

Whichever Chevrolet you choose, you're bound to have the driving time of your life! You can't miss with Chevrolet's new 162-h.p. "Turbo-Fire V8" under the hood (180 h.p. is an extra-cost option in *all* V8 models), or with one of the two highest powered 6's in the low-price field. Your Chevrolet dealer is the man to see. . . . Chevrolet Division of General Motors, Detroit 2, Michigan.

STEALING THE THUNDER FROM THE HIGH-PRICED CARS! . . . *motoramic*

**Figure 14.7** Chevrolet Advertisement, 1955

For sample presentation visuals, see pp. 349 and 367–68. For a sample brochure, see pp. 366–67. For sample tables and figures, see B (pp. A-8–A-12) in the Quick Format Guide. For sample photographs, turn to the images opening Chs. 4–12 and 25–29, as well as the e-Pages.

**Function Decisions.** An image that illustrates a point needs to serve the overall purpose of the document. In other words, form should follow function. Of the many illustrations available—photographs, drawings, charts, graphs, tables—certain types are especially suited to certain functions. For example, the 1955 Chevrolet ad, Figure 14.7, shows people having a good time enjoying a summer day near the shore. This illustration suggests that Chevrolet purchasers will enjoy life, a notion that undoubtedly suits the advertiser's goals. Likewise, a pie chart effectively conveys parts of a whole, while a photograph captures the drama and intensity of the moment—a child's rescue, a family's grief, an earthquake's toll. When you look at visuals in publications, consider how they function and why the writer might have chosen them.

**Typeface Options.** Many images, especially advertisements, combine image and text, using the typeface to set a mood and convey an impression. For example, Times New Roman is a common typeface, easy to read and somewhat conservative, whereas Comic Sans MS is considered informal—almost playful—and looks handwritten. Any printed element in an image may be trendy or conservative, large or small, in relation to the image as a whole. Further, it may inform, evoke emotion, or decorate the page.

Look back at Figure 14.6, the 1959 Volkswagen ad. The words "Think small" are printed in a sans serif typeface, one "without serifs," the small tails at the ends of the letters. This type is spare and unadorned, just like the VW itself. The ad also includes significant text across the bottom of the page. While this text is difficult to read in the reproduction in this book, it humorously points out the benefits of driving a small imported vehicle instead of one of the large, roomy cars common at the time.

In contrast to the VW ad campaign, the 1955 Chevrolet marketing strategy promoted big vehicles, as Figure 14.7 illustrates. Here the cars are shown in medium to close-up view to call attention to their length. Happy human figures in and beside the cars emphasize their size, and the cars are painted in bright colors, unlike the VW's serviceable black. The primary text below the scene is large enough to be read in the reproduction here. It asks which sporty Chevy would be most fun for the reader—the Bel Air convertible, the Handyman Station Wagon, or the stylish Sport Coupe. Then some "fine print"—difficult to read in the reproduction—notes other features of each car, such as its top, interior, and power.

Other images besides ads use type to set a mood or convey feelings and ideas. Figure 14.8 is a design student's response to an assignment that called for using letters to create an image. The simple typeface and stairlike arrangement help viewers "experience" the word *stairway*. Figure 14.9 illustrates how certain typefaces have become associated with countries—even to the point of becoming clichés. In fact, designers of travel posters and brochures often draw on

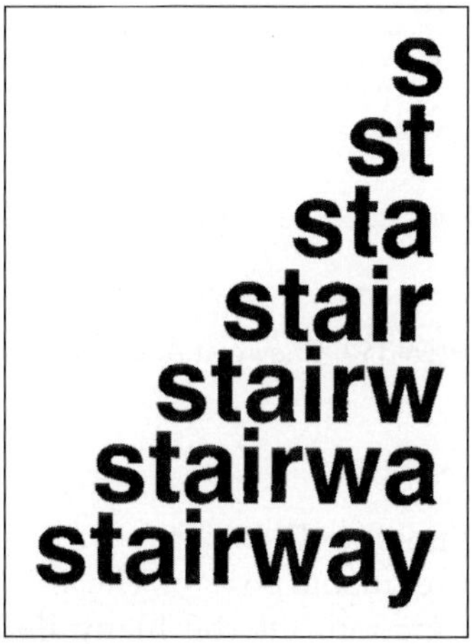

**Figure 14.8** Stairway.
*Source:* Design for Communication: Conceptual Graphic Design Basics

GREECE
JAMAICA
Ceylon
China
MEXICO
Tahiti
Canada
Ireland
Scotland
Denmark
Japan
PORTUGAL
BRITAIN

**Figure 14.9** Type as Cultural Cliché. *Source:* From *Publication Design*, 3/e, by Roy Paul Nelson, © 1983 McGraw-Hill Education.

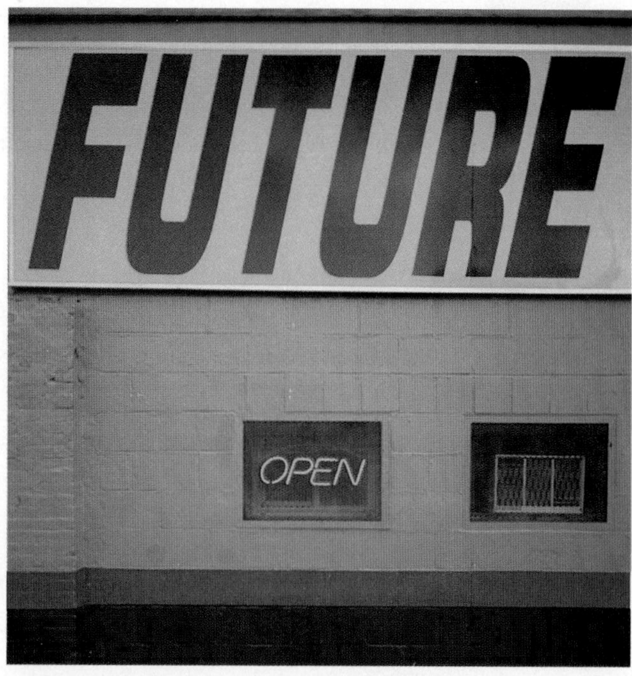


**Figure 14.10** Type that Contributes to Meaning. *Source:* Andrew Dillon Bustin, Boston, Massachusetts, 2011

predictable choices like these to suggest a mood—for example, boldness, tradition adventure, history. Similarly, the plain, slanted type in Figure 14.10 suggests movement toward the future, reinforcing the message of the words.

---

### VISUAL ANALYSIS CHECKLIST

#### Observing the Characteristics of an Image

- ☐ What objects are included in the image?
- ☐ What figures (people or animals) appear in the image?
- ☐ What action takes place in the image? What is its "plot" or story?
- ☐ What is in the background? In what place does the action take place?
- ☐ What elements, colors, and shapes contribute to the design? How are they arranged or balanced? What feeling, memory, or association is evoked?
- ☐ How are the pictorial elements related to one another? How are they related to any written material? What do these relationships tell you as a viewer?
- ☐ Does the image include white space, fill its space, or seem busy?

- ☐ What composition decisions has the designer or artist made? What type of shot, shot angle, lighting, or color is used?
- ☐ What is the function of the image? How does form support function?
- ☐ What typefaces are used? What impressions do they convey?

### Learning by Doing Observing Characteristics

Working with a classmate or small group, continue analyzing the image you selected for the activity on page 293. Examine a major characteristic—such as characters, story, design, or artistic choices—to determine exactly what it shows. Report or post your conclusions for your class or another group.

## Level Three: Interpreting the Meaning of an Image

When you read a written text analytically, you examine its parts from different angles, synthesize the material by combining it with related information, and finally evaluate or judge its significance. When you interpret an image, you do much the same, actively examining what the image *connotes* or suggests, speculating about what it means.

Because interpretation is more personal than observation, this process can reveal deep-seated individual and cultural values. In fact, interpreting an image is sometimes emotional or difficult because it may require you to examine beliefs that you are unaware of holding. You may even feel that too much is being read into the image because the process takes patience.

Like learning to read critically, learning to interpret images is a valuable skill. When you give an image a close, patient, in-depth examination, you can often deepen your understanding of its creator's artistic, political, economic, or other motives. You can also become more aware of the cultural values and personal views you bring to an image and gain a better sense of why you respond to it as you do.

### General Feeling or Mood

To begin interpreting an image, consider what feeling or mood it creates and how it does so. In Figure 14.2, the mood created by the photo of Batman is one of loneliness and isolation without even the companionship of someone working behind the counter. Yet the campy humor in the photo leads one to wonder whether the figure is an actor, a guest from a costume party, or somehow, improbably, the Caped Crusader himself. Is he waiting to meet someone? Has he stopped to relax after battling evildoers all night? Is he a regular or a one-time visitor?

Whatever the story, the image shrinks a superhero down to human size, simply having a snack. From the perspective of the photograph, the Batman figure looks relatively small and vulnerable, despite his imposing costume. He looks like someone who is resting and recharging his energy level but will soon go back out into the night. He suggests a policeman taking a break from his beat, or a worker or student on a coffee break. The image might be suggesting that in the real world, the superheroes are regular people, like us. Indeed, we all might be on heroic missions, just by going about our daily work, getting an education, raising children, and participating in community life.

Another image might capture or represent a different version of this feeling or mood. As Figure 14.11 illustrates, people take many kinds of breaks, finding carefree moments of escape in various ways. Perhaps Batman unwinds at a late-night donut shop while the silhouetted people in Figure 14.11 ride a Ferris wheel at an amusement park, lifted up on a short, circular detour from their normal routine. Here, a lighthearted mood of family fun or romance predominates. The seated figures are not alone; they are paired off on the ride's gondola benches, with sneakered or sandaled feet dangling. The fiery reds and oranges of the sunset infuse the scene with warmth although the ride's heavy triangular shapes, octopus arms, and burned out

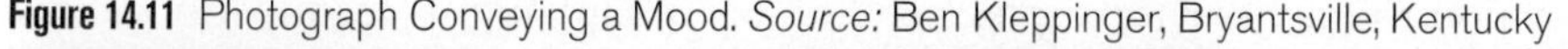

**Figure 14.11** Photograph Conveying a Mood. *Source:* Ben Kleppinger, Bryantsville, Kentucky

bulbs might suggest a slightly menacing mechanical contraption. Although the mood of Figure 14.2 is wintery, and the mood of this photo is summery, both invite reflection on what it means to take a break.

## Sociological, Political, Economic, or Cultural Attitudes

On the surface, the Volkswagen ad in Figure 14.6 (p. 296) is simply an attempt to sell a car. But its message might be interpreted to mean "scale down"—lead a less consumer-oriented lifestyle. If Volkswagen had distributed this ad in the 1970s, it would have been unremarkable—faced with the first energy crisis that adversely affected American gasoline prices, many advertisers used ecological consciousness to sell cars. In 1959, however, energy conservation was not really a concern. Contrasted with other automobile ads of its time, the Volkswagen ad seems somewhat eccentric, making the novel suggestion that larger cars are excessively extravagant.

Whereas the Volkswagen ad suggests that "small" refers to both size and affordability, the Chevrolet ad in Figure 14.7 (p. 297) depicts a large vehicle, "stealing the thunder from the high-priced cars." Without a large price tag, the Chevrolet still offers a large lifestyle, cruising in a convertible or vacationing at the shore. Figure 14.12 deliberately contrasts presence and absence, projecting a possible future scene—without the bear—to bring home its message about the need to protect our national parks and their residents. What's missing also may be more subtle, especially for viewers who wear the blinders of their own times, circumstances, or expectations. For example, viewers of today might readily notice the absence of people of color in the 1955 Chevrolet ad. An interesting

**Figure 14.12** Photograph Using a Missing Element to Convey a Message.
*Source:* Public Service Announcement, Americans for National Parks

study might investigate what types of magazines originally carried this ad, whether their readers recognized what was missing, and whether (and how) Chevrolets were also advertised in publications aimed at Asian, African, or Spanish-speaking Americans.

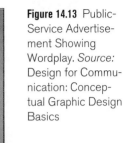

**Figure 14.13** Public-Service Advertisement Showing Wordplay. *Source:* Design for Communication: Conceptual Graphic Design Basics

## Language

Just as you examine figures, colors, and shapes in an image, so you need to examine its words, phrases, and sentences to interpret what it suggests. Does its language provide information, generate an emotional response, or do both? Do its words repeat a sound or concept, signal a comparison (such as a "new, improved" product), carry sexual overtones, issue a challenge, or offer a philosophy of life? The words in the center of the Chevolet ad in Figure 14.7 (p. 297) associate the car with a sporty, fun-filled lifestyle. On the other hand, VW's "Think small" ad in Figure 14.6 turns compactness into a goal, a desirable quality in a car and, by extension, in life.

Frequently advertisements employ wordplay—lighthearted or serious—to get their messages across. Consider the public-service advertisement in Figure 14.13, created by a graphic-design student. This ad features a play on the word *tolerance,* which is scrambled on the chalkboard so that the letters in the center read *learn.* The chalkboard, a typical classroom feature, suggests that tolerance is a basic lesson to be learned. Also, the definition of tolerance at the bottom of the ad is much like other definitions students might look up in a dictionary. (It reads, "The capacity for, or practice of, recognizing or respecting the behavior, beliefs, opinions, practices, or rights of others, whether agreeing with them or not.")

**Figure 14.14** Billboard Showing Wordplay. *Source:* Photograph by Bill Aron, PhotoEdit

Wordplay can also challenge viewers' preconceptions about an image. The billboard in Figure 14.14 shows a romantic—indeed, a seductive—scene. The sophisticated couple gaze deeply into each other's eyes as the man kisses the woman's hand. However, the verbal exchange undermines that intimate scene and viewers' expectations about what happens next. Instead of a similar compliment in response to "Your scent is intoxicating," the billboard makes plain its antismoking position with the reply: "Yours is carcinogenic." In just seven words, the billboard counters the suave, romantic image of smoking with the reality of smelly, cancer-causing tobacco smoke.

## Signs and Symbols

Signs and symbols, such as product logos, are images or words that communicate key messages. In the Chevrolet ad in Figure 14.7 (p. 297), the product logo concludes the ad, promoting "motoramic" fun and power. Sometimes a product logo alone may be enough, as in the Hershey chocolate company's holiday ads with little more than a single Hershey's Kiss.

## Themes

The theme of an image is not the same as its plot. When you identify the plot, you identify the story that is told by the image. When you identify the theme, you explain what the image is about. An ad for a diamond ring may tell the story of a man surprising his wife with a ring on their twenty-fifth wedding anniversary, but the advertisement's theme could be sex, romance, commitment, or another concept. Similarly, the theme of a soft-drink ad might be competition, community, compassion, or individualism.

Through close reading, you can unearth details to support your interpretation of the theme and convince others of its merit. For example, the image in Figure 14.15, appears to illustrate a recipe for a tasty margarita. However, the list of ingredients suggests a tale of too many drinks and a drunk-driving accident after running a red light. Instead of promoting an alcoholic beverage or promising relaxing fun, this public-service announcement challenges the assumption that risky behavior won't carry consequences. Its text reminds viewers of its theme: well-being comes not from alcohol-fueled confidence but from responsible choices.

**Figure 14.15** Poster Conveying a Theme. *Source:* U.S. Department of Transportation/Ad Council

### VISUAL ANALYSIS CHECKLIST
**Interpreting the Meaning of an Image**

- ☐ What general feeling do you get from looking at the image? What mood does it create? How does it do so?
- ☐ What sociological, political, economic, or cultural attitudes are reflected?
- ☐ What language is included in the image? How does the language function?

- ☐ What signs and symbols can you identify? What role do these play?
- ☐ What theme or themes can you identify in the image?

### Learning by Doing — Interpreting Meaning

Working with a classmate or small group, continue analyzing the image you selected for the activity on page 293. Examine one of its major characteristics—feeling or mood, attitude, language, signs or symbols, or theme—to interpret what the image might mean. Share your conclusions with your class or another group in a brief oral report or an online posting.

## Learning from Another Writer: Visual Analysis

Because visual images surround us, you may be asked to respond to them and to analyze them, concentrating on persuasive, cultural, historical, sociological, or other qualities. Rachel Steinhaus analyzed a television commercial to investigate how advertisements persuade us to buy.

**Rachel Steinhaus** — **Student Analysis of an Advertisement**

### "Life, Liberty, and the Pursuit"

The television commercial for the 2008 Cadillac CTS, featuring the star Kate Walsh, epitomizes a car advertisement that focuses not on the vehicle itself, but on the ideas that the company wants to associate with its product. Rather than focusing on the power and features of the car, the commercial emphasizes the ideas of sex, social status, freedom, and Americanism, wrapping the car in a shroud of social contradictions and ideals. Viewers are enticed to see the car as more than a means of transportation. This other image of the car as a sexual object is what resonates most clearly with viewers as it illustrates how the ad manipulates their emotions and ideas in order to sell the product. 1

This commercial begins with the word *Cadillac* scrawled across a view of a city with the lights creating long stretches across the screen, as though the viewer is in a car traveling quickly down the street. This effect, the illusion of fast motion, is maintained throughout the commercial. Kate Walsh, star of the television shows *Private Practice* and *Grey's Anatomy*, then lists a number of the car's optional features, from a pop-up navigation system to sunroofs and 40G hard drives, saying that those 2

opportunities are not what are important "in today's luxury game" (Cadillac). The ad continues to show different aspects of the car as Kate Walsh reveals what she presumably believes is the most important quality in a car: "When you turn your car on, does it return the favor?" (Cadillac). A few more images show the sleek car driving through the city and a tunnel, and then the name of the car, the phrase "Life, Liberty, and the Pursuit," and the Cadillac logo appear on the screen sequentially.

The most prominent aspect of this ad is its focus on the automobile as a sex symbol, which is most blatantly expressed by the line in the commercial, "When you turn it on, does it return the favor?" (Cadillac). This colloquial phrase clearly sends the message that cars that are not sexy are inferior to the 2008 CTS. The phrase also personifies the vehicle itself, giving it the capability to turn someone on, which is generally a human action. This use of personification fits with the idea presented in "The New Citroen," where Barthes describes the automobile as "humanized art" (89). The car may be a product with a particular function, but it is designed to look appealing while also having human qualities that allow people to be more emotionally attached to their car than the average product. 3

Kate Walsh reinforces the sexual ideas connected to the car in this commercial. Her attire, a dress and heels, is clearly chosen to provide sex appeal. The camera shots, angled to show her looking over the steering wheel as she delivers the end of the line and to show her foot as she hits the accelerator in her strappy heels, objectify her as a source of sex appeal (Garfield). Her celebrity status also influences the viewer's idea of what it would mean to own the car. Although the car's available features are casually listed, making Cadillac appear modest about its technology and luxury embellishments, Kate Walsh places the focus on the prospective owner's status. Simply attaching the name of a celebrity to a car is enough to raise interest for some viewers as they imagine themselves owning something that a rich and successful star also enjoys. The combination of Walsh's stardom and her sex appeal becomes the main focus of this advertisement. 4

In addition to these strong sexual and status connotations, the commercial emphasizes the idea that this car is a solid American product. The tagline at the end of the commercial, "Life, Liberty, and the Pursuit" (Cadillac) is a reference to the well-known line of the Declaration of Independence, automatically connecting the Cadillac CTS to patriotism. Even without finishing the phrase, this added plug connects supporting one's country to buying an American-made Cadillac 2008 CTS. The ad assumes that the typical American viewer will automatically insert the words "of happiness" to complete the phrase and also connect buying a CTS with furthering their own "pursuit of happiness." The context of the phrase within the Declaration of Independence is also important because it describes our inalienable rights, therefore connecting the thought that buying this car is the right of an American. 5

The open-ended phrase, however, also lends itself to interpretation as a literal statement, alluding to the idea that the Cadillac CTS will give one the freedom to 6 pursue whatever one wishes. In a physical sense, the driver can use the CTS horsepower to pursue other, "lesser" cars. On the other hand, the emotional message is that the driver can pursue different dreams and lifestyles because of the reputation and self-image that the CTS affords. This second interpretation relates well to the celebrity power that Kate Walsh brings to the ad.

The freedom to follow one's dreams goes hand in hand with the freedom of the road that this advertisement conveys. As Walsh goes speeding down a tunnel, nothing inhibits her progress. However, Böhm and the other authors of "Impossibilities of Automobility" see things in a much more realistic light. Both the congestion created by the infrastructure required to support automobiles and our reliance on cars make driving far from pleasurable, according to the article. Driving is often marked by frustration and danger, rather than absolute freedom. Cadillac's commercial, however, ignores these facts, instead showing off speed by the blurred lights as the car flies by and giving Kate Walsh the freedom to go wherever she wishes. 7

Cadillac's commercial promotes the 2008 CTS without much focus on the car's actual features. Instead, the ad uses appeals to sex, celebrity, freedom, and Americanism. Cadillac is proud to attach its name to a car that could mean so much to the life of the viewer, and the Cadillac logo appears in the commercial no less than six times. Even this constant repetition of the brand name takes away from the car itself, as its name, CTS, is mentioned only once. Despite a lack of focus on the actual vehicle, the advertiser assumes that our culture responds well to the appeals to sex, status, freedom, and patriotism that the automobile industry chooses to show in ads like this one. 8

Works Cited

Barthes, Roland. "The New Citroen." *Mythologies*. Trans. Annette Lavers. 1957. New York: Hill-Farrar, 2001. 88–90. Print.

Böhm, Steffen, Campbell Jones, Chris Land, and Matthew Paterson. "Impossibilities of Automobility." *Against Automobility*. Ed. Böhm, Jones, Land, and Paterson. Oxford: Wiley-Blackwell, 2006. 1–16. Print.

Cadillac. Advertisement. Web. 8 Mar. 2009. http://www.youtube.com/watch?v=jkEw1rsBUak.

Garfield, Bob. "Taking Cadillac from Stodgy to Sexy: Kate Walsh." *Advertising Age* 1 Oct. 2007. Web. 8 Mar. 2009.

## Questions to Start You Thinking

Meaning

1. How does Steinhaus say that the Cadillac ad sells cars?
2. What selling points does Kate Walsh add to the commercial? What does the wording from the Declaration of Independence add?

Writing Strategies

3. Where does Steinhaus introduce her thesis and her major supporting points?
4. How does Steinhaus ensure that readers know enough about the advertisement to follow her discussion?
5. How does Steinhaus help her audience follow her paper?
6. What different kinds of support does Steinhaus draw from her sources?

# Learning by Writing

## The Assignment: Analyzing a Visual Representation

Find a print or online advertisement that uses an image to promote a product, service, or nonprofit group. Study the ad carefully, using the three Visual Analysis checklists (pp. 293, 299–300, and 304–5) to observe the characteristics of the image and interpret meaning. Write an essay analyzing how the ad uses visual elements to persuade viewers to accept its message. Include a copy of the ad with your essay or supply a link to it. If your instructor approves, you may select a brochure, flyer, graphic, photo essay, art work, sculpture, campus landmark, or other visual option for analysis.

### Facing the Challenge Analyzing an Image

The major challenge that writers face when analyzing an image is to state a clear thesis about how the image creates its impact and then to support that thesis with relevant detail. Although you may analyze the many details that an image includes, you need to select and group those that support your thesis in order to develop a successful essay. If you try to pack in too many details, you are likely to distract your audience and bury your main point. On the other hand, if you include too few, your case may seem weak. In addition, you need to select and describe your details carefully so that they persuasively, yet fairly, confirm your points about the image.

## Generating Ideas

Browse through print or online publications to gather several possibilities—ads that make clear appeals to viewers. Look for ads that catch your eye and promise rich detail for analysis.

As you consider how an ad tries to attract a viewer's attention, try several approaches. For example, think about the purpose of the ad and the audience likely to view it where it is published or circulated. Consider the same appeals you might identify in written or spoken texts: its logical appeal to the mind, its emotional appeal to the heart, and its ethical appeal, perhaps to trust the product or sponsor. Look also for the specific visual components analyzed in this chapter – elements that guide a viewer's attention, develop the ad's persuasive potential, and convey its meaning.

---

**DISCOVERY CHECKLIST**

- ☐ What is the overall meaning and impact of the ad?
- ☐ What main points about the ad seem most important? Which details support each point most clearly and fairly?
- ☐ How do the ad's visual elements contribute to its persuasiveness? Which elements appeal most strongly to viewers?

---

## Planning, Drafting, and Developing

Begin working on a thesis that states how the advertisement tries to attract and influence viewers. For example, you might identify a consistent persuasive appeal used in major components of the ad, or you might show how several components work together to persuade particular viewers.

| | |
|---|---|
| WORKING THESIS | The dog food ad has photos of puppies to interest animal lovers. |
| IMPROVED | The Precious Pooch dog food advertisement uses photos of cuddly puppies to appeal to dog owners. |
| MORE PRECISE | The Precious Pooch dog food advertisement shows carefully designed photos of cuddly puppies to soften the hearts and wallets of devoted dog owners. |

**Point Out the Details.** Identify details – and explain their significance – to guide readers through your supporting evidence. Help them see exactly which visual elements create an impression, solidify an appeal, or connect with a viewer as you say that they do. Avoid general description for its own sake, but supply enough relevant description to make your points clear.

**Organize Support for Your Thesis.** As you state your thesis more precisely, break down the position it expresses into main points. Then list the relevant supporting detail from the ad that can clarify and develop each point.

**Open and Conclude Effectively.** Begin by introducing to your audience both the ad and your thesis about it. Describe the ad briefly but clearly so that your readers start off with an overall understanding of its structure and primary features. State your thesis equally clearly so that your readers know how you view the ad's persuasive strategy. Use your conclusion to pull together your main points and confirm your thesis.

## Revising and Editing

Exchange drafts with your peers to learn what is—or isn't—clear to someone else who is not immersed in your ad. Then revise as needed.

---

### REVISION CHECKLIST

- ☐ Have you briefly described the ad as you open your essay?
- ☐ Have you stated your thesis about how the ad persuades its audience?
- ☐ Have you identified visual features and details that support your view?
- ☐ Do you need more detail about the ad's figures, action, or design?
- ☐ Do you need more on the feeling, attitude, theme, or meaning conveyed?
- ☐ Have you moved smoothly between each main point about the effectiveness of the ad and the detail from the ad that demonstrates the point?

---

After you have revised your visual analysis, check the grammar, word choice, punctuation, and mechanics—then correct any problems you find.

For more help, find the relevant checklist sections in the Quick Editing Guide on p. A-39. Turn also to the Quick Format Guide beginning on p. A-1.

---

### EDITING CHECKLIST

- ☐ Have you used adjectives and adverbs correctly to present the ad? A7
- ☐ Have you placed modifiers correctly so that your descriptions are clear? B1
- ☐ Have you used correct manuscript format for your paper?

---

# Learning from Another Writer: Visual Essay

Besides responding to visual representations designed by others, you might have opportunities to create your own series of images and text. Visual essays can record an event or situation, or they can support an observation, interpretation, or position, usually through a combination of image and text or a multimedia text incorporating sound or video.

## Shannon Kintner

Student Visual Essay

### Charlie Living with Autism

In this excerpt from a photo essay, we are given a glimpse into the life of Charlie, a five-year-old boy diagnosed with nonsevere autism. Shannon Kintner took this series while a student at the University of Texas, though not for a class nor as part of her job at *The Daily Texan*. She did the project on her own to learn more about autism, to gain experience, and to develop her portfolio, a collection of work that demonstrates one's interests and abilities. To view the rest of the slideshow, read a brief article about Charlie, and complete more activities, go to Chapter 14: **bedfordstmartins.com/bedguide**.

Mindy Minto, Charlie's mother, wipes pizza sauce off Charlie's shoulder during dinner one night. Charlie has echolalia, which means he repeats certain phrases to apply to all scenarios; he often says "popcorn, please" to indicate that he is hungry.

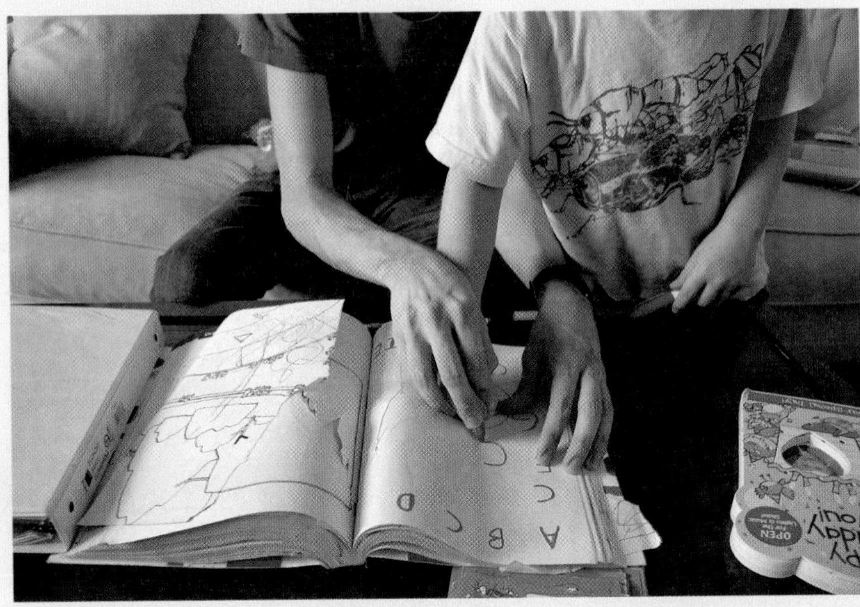


A behavioral therapist guides Charlie's hand while writing his name. Charlie just wrote his name by himself for the first time in mid-April.

Charlie plays with his dog, Lola, before dinner. Both of Charlie's parents have described the two as best friends.

Kari Hughes, a behavioral therapist, asks Charlie to point out certain objects pictured on flashcards. His at-home therapy balances between a few minutes of playtime for every five achievements he makes, such as identifying flashcards or completing a puzzle.

## Questions to Start You Thinking

Meaning

1. What story does the selection of images tell?
2. The photographer shows Charlie eating with his family, learning with his teacher, and playing with his dog. How does this variety enhance the viewer's experience?
3. Autism is a complex condition that can affect language ability, intellectual functioning, and behavioral patterns. Some symptoms often generally linked to autism include repetitive behavior, restricted interests, trouble having easy-flowing, "back-and-forth"-style communications, and difficulty with social interactions, which depend on the ability to read facial expressions and other cues. However, autism, as expressed in individuals, varies a great deal from person to person and from setting to setting, and it changes as a person with autism grows and develops. How does this photo essay help us to better understand – and to put a human face on – a word one often hears: "autism"?

e For more Questions to Start You Thinking, go to Ch. 14: **bedfordstmartins.com/bedguide**.

Writing Strategies

4. How would you describe the nature of Kintner's written text? Why do you think that she uses this approach?
5. What is the effect of Kintner's title for her photo essay?

## Additional Writing Assignments

For criteria for visual analysis, review this chapter. For more on comparison and contrast (Ch. 7), evaluation (Ch. 11), or other relevant situations, turn to Part 2.

1. **Visual Activity.** Select an image such as an advertisement, a visual from a magazine or image database, or a CD or album cover. Make notes on its "literal" characteristics (see pp. 293–300). Then, bring your image and notes to class. In small groups of three to five students, share your images and discuss your literal readings.
2. **Visual Activity.** In a small group, pick one or two of the images analyzed for activity 1. Ask each group member, in turn, to suggest possible interpretations of the images. (For guidance, see pp. 300–05.) What different interpretations do group members suggest? How do you account for the differences? Share your findings with the rest of the class.
3. **Visual Assignment.** Find a Web page that draws a strong emotional response. Study the page closely, observing its characteristics and interpreting its meaning. Write an essay in which you explain the techniques by which the page evokes your emotional response. If appropriate, you also may want to define a standard for its type of Web page and evaluate the site in terms of that standard. Include a link to the page with your essay.
4. **Visual Assignment.** Volkswagen continues to produce thought-provoking advertisements like the one shown in Figure 14.6 on page 296. Search online for some of the company's recent ads (try VW or Volkswagen commercials). View one or two ads, considering such features as their stories or "plots"; the choice of figures, settings, and images; the angles from which subjects are filmed; and any text messages included. Based on your analysis, decide what message you think that the company wants to communicate about its cars. In your essay, describe this message, the audience that Volkswagen seems to aim for, and the artistic choices in the ads that appeal to this audience.
5. **Visual Assignment.** Compile a design notebook. Over several weeks, collect ten or twelve images that appeal to you. Your teacher may assign a genre or theme, or you may wish to choose examples of a genre such as snack food ads, portraits, photos of campus landmarks, or landscape paintings. On the other hand, your collection might revolve around a theme, such as friendship, competition, community, or romance. "Read" each image closely, and write short responses explaining your reactions. At the end of the collection period, choose two or three images. Write an essay to compare or contrast them, perhaps analyzing how they illustrate the same genre, convey a theme, or appeal to different audiences.
6. **Visual Assignment.** Prepare your own visual essay on a topic that engages or concerns you. Decide on the purpose and audience for your essay. Take, select, and arrange photographs that will help to achieve this purpose. (Use the guidelines in this chapter to help you evaluate your own photos.) Add concise complementary text to the photos. Ask your classmates to review your essay to help you reach the clearest and most effective final form.

7. **Visual Assignment.** Find a CD cover whose design interests you. Make notes about design choices such as its prominent element and focal point and its use of color, imagery, and typography. Based on the design, try to predict what kind of music is on the CD, and then listen to a track or two. Did the music match your expectations based on the CD design? If you had been the CD designer, would you have made any different artistic choices? Write a brief essay discussing your observations, and try to attach a copy of the CD cover (perhaps printed from the Web). As an alternative assignment, listen to some music that's new to you, and design a CD cover for it, applying the elements discussed in this chapter. Describe in a brief paper the visual elements you would include on your CD cover. If you wish, sketch your cover design.
8. **Visual Assignment.** Using the advice in this chapter, analyze an episode in a television series, a film, a multimodal blog, a YouTube or other video, a television or video commercial, or a campus theater, dance, or other production. Analyze the visual elements of your selection, and also evaluate it in terms of criteria that you explain to your audience.

For sample essays responding to films, see Chs. 11 and 27.

# 15 Writing Online

Perhaps you are an experienced online writer — texting friends, chatting with family, updating your social-network page, and commenting on YouTube videos. On the other hand, perhaps you need help from co-workers or from younger or more experienced classmates to master new online tasks. Either way, you — like most college students — are increasingly likely to be an online academic writer. Many college classes are now offered in three formats, all likely to expect online writing:

- **face-to-face classes,** meeting at a set time and place but possibly with online communication and paper submissions
- **online classes** with synchronous (scheduled at the same time) or asynchronous (unscheduled, but available when convenient) virtual meetings, discussions, activities, paper exchanges, and submissions
- **hybrid (or blended) classes** with both in-person and online meetings, discussions, activities, paper exchanges, and submissions

In addition, any of these three class formats may rely on the campus course or learning management system (CMS or LMS), a Web-accessible environment where class participants can access information, communicate with each other, and post papers or other assignments. This chapter will review likely online activities in your current course, whatever its format.

## Why Writing Online Matters

### In a College Course

- You need to take a course offered only online, so you want to be ready to meet deadlines, manage files, and contribute to online discussions.
- You want to improve your online discussion contributions so that they sound more academic and professional.

### In the Workplace

- You need to help online customers in a friendly yet efficient manner.

**In Your Community**

- You design an online tenant newsletter to unify your neighbors and help motivate your apartment manager.

When have you done academic or professional writing online? How effective was this writing? In what situations might you need to do such writing in the future?

## Getting Started

Many schools provide an orientation program for new or returning students as well as directions for using online campus resources. Whatever the format of your course, you are expected to have or to gain technical skills sufficient to meet course requirements. Find out how to tap campus resources for immediate crises, self-help tutorials, and technology consultation. In addition, your instructors will supply a syllabus, course policies, assignments, assessment criteria, and other information for each course. Especially for online work, remember these two essential survival skills: read first, and then ask questions.

**Learning by Doing** Identifying Online Writing Expectations

Review your course syllabus and assignments. List each type of online writing that you will need to do. Write down any problems or questions you can anticipate. Then map out a plan to begin solving or answering those issues.

For interactive Learning by Doing activities on Tracking Your Time Online and Exploring Your CMS or LMS, go to Ch. 15: **bedfordstmartins.com /bedguide**.

### Class Courtesy

All of your classes – face-to-face, online, or hybrid – have expectations for conduct and procedures. Some rules, such as keeping food and beverages out of a computer lab or laptop-cart classroom, obviously protect the equipment for everyone's benefit. Although explicit rules may vary by campus or instructor, conduct yourself in ways that demonstrate your attentiveness, courtesy, and consideration for others. During a face-to-face class, avoid texting or taking mobile phone calls. When technology problems inevitably arise, ask about solutions instead of blaming the online environment for snags. Online, consider both your tone and level of formality. Use the relative anonymity of online participation to advance your intellectual growth, not to make negative comments at the expense of others. Think twice before you post each message so you don't regret a hasty attack, a bad joke, a personal revelation, or an emotional rant. If you are uncertain about what is appropriate, ask your instructor for guidelines, and observe the conventions of professional communication. Strive to be

**Common Interactive CMS or LMS Options**

| CMS or LMS Options | Typical Functions | Components Your Class Might Use |
|---|---|---|
| **Course Materials** | Handy essential information, available online for reference anytime during the course | Course syllabus and calendar, required and background readings, online reserve readings coordinated with the library, optional sources and links, reading or writing assignments, directions for activities, class and lecture notes, study guides, assessment criteria, online tutorials, podcasts, videos, and Webliographies |
| **Course Communication** | Convenient and varied systems for course messages and discussions, limited to class members | Convenient e-mail (to the whole class, a small group, or an individual), notices about changes or cancellations, text messaging, social networking, chats, threaded discussions, paper exchanges, a comment system, and a whiteboard for graphics or drawings |
| **Class Profiles** | Individual introductions posted for all the class to read, establishing each person's online personality and presence | Descriptions of the individual's background, interests, or expectations of the class, possibly with a photo or other personal representation; possibly CMS or LMS reports on whole-class patterns to allow for timely improvements |
| **Threaded Discussions** | Series of related exchanges focused on a specific course topic, question, or issue (open to all classmates or only to a group) | Questions and comments exploring and thinking critically about a topic along with any subthreads that evolve during discussion |
| **Text Exchanges and Responses** | Drafts and final papers posted for response from other students or for assessment by the instructor | Overall responses to the strengths, weaknesses, and effectiveness of the paper as well as detailed comments noted in the file; possibly options for feedback requests |

a thoughtful learner who treats others respectfully as colleagues in a learning community.

## Online Ethics

Respect class or campus guidelines for online text exchanges with other students. Treat each other courteously and respectfully, address others in an appropriate classroom manner, and follow directions designed to protect each other's privacy and hard work. Your instructor may provide cautions about sharing personal or confessional information, especially because your CMS, LMS, or campus may retain indefinite access to class materials.

In addition, find out whether your papers might be routinely or randomly submitted to a plagiarism-detection site. Be certain that you understand your campus rules about plagiarism and your instructor's directions about online group exchanges so that you do not confuse individual and collaborative work. Further, use sources carefully as you do online research:

## Common Interactive Online Options

| Online Options | Typical Functions | Applications Your Class Might Use |
|---|---|---|
| **Class Blogs** | Individual or collaborative Web logs or journals for a sequence of public (whole class) or private (small group or instructor) comments on a topic or theme | Regular comments to encourage writing, reflecting, exploring, analyzing, and sharing ideas that could evolve into more fully developed written pieces |
| **Class Wiki** | An encyclopedia of collaborative entries explaining terms relevant to a course topic or issue | An existing or evolving set of essential key terms, activities, concepts, issues, or events |
| **Class Ning** | Private social network for class members (as a whole or in special-interest groups) to share information and exchange ideas | List of relevant campus or community events, participant profiles, and a forum or blog to comment on key topics |
| **Text Exchanges** | Texts submitted for response from others through messages with attached files (to use software to add comments) or a real-time document-sharing Web site (to use its comment system) | Overall comments on strengths, weaknesses, and effectiveness; suggestions noted in the file (perhaps color coded by respondent); one-on-one exchanges, such as questions and answers, about a draft |
| **Audio Applications** | Recorded spoken comments, including responses to drafts, in-person group discussions, presentation or podcast practices, podcasts, course lectures, or interviews | Verbal comments to strengthen personal connections, recorded by the instructor or peers for one student or a group; class interviews of content or research experts (authors, librarians, faculty) |
| **Visual Applications** | Organized and archived photos, videos, Web shots, or other images | Visual materials to prompt, inform, illustrate texts, or add to presentation software |
| **Course Resources** | Public social-network page, department Web page, program resources, library Web site, open-source materials, online writing lab (OWL), Web pages | Opportunities for building a supportive online academic group and accessing recommended course resources |

- Distinguish your writing and your ideas from those of sources so that you avoid blurring or confusing the two.
- Keep track of sources so that you can credit their words and ideas accurately, following the style expected by your instructor.
- Respect intellectual property rights by asking permission and crediting sources if you integrate someone else's images or media in your paper.

For more about using sources, see the Quick Research Guide beginning on p. A-20.

### Learning by Doing Making Personal Rules

Using brainstorming or mapping, develop the list of rules only you know that you need—rules to bring out your best as an online student or writer. For example, do you need a personal "rule" about checking for your USB drive, card, or portable hard drive after every computer session on campus so you don't lose your work? Or do you need a "rule" about backing up files? List your rules in an e-mail message to yourself. Then sum up the most important points, using your software's word count tool to limit this statement to the 140 characters allowed by Twitter for a "tweet." If you wish, also note your "rules" in your cell phone notepad for quick reference along with your online course PIN number, if needed. Return to standard English—correct grammar, punctuation, capitalization, and complete words, not abbreviations—for material submitted to your instructor.

## Common Online Writing Situations

The expectations for your college writing may be the same whether you hand in a printed paper during class, send the file to your instructor, or post your work in a CMS or LMS. Some assignments might specify required, encouraged, or accepted online features such as links for references or multimedia components. For other online writing, consider the conventions—accepted practices readers are likely to expect—and the class directions.

### Messages to Your Instructor

Learning online requires a lot of communication. Because you aren't meeting—and communicating—face-to-face, you need to engage actively in other types of exchanges. First, welcome available communication by reading posted assignments and directions that advise you about how to meet expectations successfully. Next, initiate communication, asking specific questions online about what to do and how to do it.

When you e-mail your instructor with a question, practice respectful professional communication. Think about your audience—a hard-working teacher who probably posts many class materials and responds to many questions from students in different courses. You can guess that a busy instructor appreciates a direct question from a motivated student who wants help. Ask specific questions well before deadlines, and give your instructor plenty of time to reply. Consider your tone so that you sound polite, interested, and clear about what you need to know.

VAGUE — I don't know how to start this assignment.

SPECIFIC — I've listed my ideas in a scratch outline, but I'm not sure what you mean by . . .

If your class uses a CMS or LMS, send your message through that system (unless your instructor asks you to use his or her campus e-mail address). Right away your instructor will know which class you're in and, in a small composition class, recognize you by your first name. If you e-mail outside the CMS, send the message from your campus account, and use the subject line to identify the course name or number and your problem: Deadline for Comp 101 Reading or Question about Math 110 Study Guide.

If you are unsure how to address your instructor, begin with "Hello, Professor Welton" or "Hi, Ms. Welton," following the instructor's preference if known. Avoid too much informality, such as greeting your instructor with "Yo, Prof" or "Hiya, Chief," asking "Whatzup with the paper?" or closing with "Later." Conclude with your name (including your last name and a section number if the class is large).

Proofread and spell-check your message before you send it so that your writing does not look hasty or careless. Consider setting it to return an automatic "read" confirmation when the recipient opens it so that you do not need to e-mail again to check its arrival. Avoid e-mailing from a personal account that might be mistaken for spam and blocked from the campus system. Remember that your instructor's relationship with you is professional, not social; do not send social-networking invitations or forward humorous stories or messages about politics, religion, or other personal topics.

### Learning by Doing Finding a College Voice

Working with a small group in person or online, list at least a dozen popular greetings, closings, and other expressions currently part of your (or your friends') informal voice in text messaging, social networking, or other informal electronic communication. Translate each expression into a clear, polite version without abbreviations, shortcuts, or unconventional grammar—in short, a version appropriate for a message to an instructor in your "college" voice.

## Learning from Other Writers: Messages to Your Instructor

Here are two requests sent to the students' instructor in an online composition class, one asking about how to cite an assigned reading and the other about the instructor's comments on a draft.

STUDENT QUESTION ABOUT AN ASSIGNMENT

From: Heather Church

Subject: Reading Response

Hi, Ms. Beauchene,

I want to make sure I am doing this assignment correctly. Is the source an online newspaper article? Also, I can't find out how to cite part of a sentence included in my response. If I quote "binge drinking," for example, do I have to say the page number next to it? I thought that I would cite this as if it is an article with no author. Is that correct?

Thank you.

Heather

STUDENT QUESTION ABOUT COMMENTS ON A DRAFT

From: Arthur Wasilewski

Subject: Comments on Last Paper

Hello, Professor Beauchene,

I would like to ask you a question about your corrections. You changed the last sentence of the last paragraph. I was wondering if you could explain the change. Is it something structural or grammatical? Or was it changed for the sake of style or flow?

Arthur

## Questions to Start You Thinking

Meaning

1. Why is Heather Church contacting the instructor? What does she want to know?
2. Why is Arthur Wasilewski contacting the instructor? What does he want to know?

Writing Strategies

3. What impression on their instructor do you think that the students wanted to make? What features of their messages indicate this?

**e Portland State University Writing Center** Video Tutorial

## Sample E-mail to an Instructor

The Portland State University Writing Center created an online tutorial about how to use the appropriate tone and language when e-mailing an instructor. To watch the video, go to Chapter 15: **bedfordstmartins/bedguide**.

Subject: my grade

yo prentice!!!

i just got my paper back and i'm a little upset about my grade. ☹ i worked really hard on it, i went to the writing center, i didn't miss the workshop, and still i got a B. i feel that i deserved a better grade because of the reasons i listed above. i worked harder on this than on any of my other classes. i have to get an A in this class for my financial aid. also, i may not have told you this, but i have been sort of sick this month and had a hard time writing the paper, so if it's not very good, that's why. ☺

## Learning by Doing Contacting Your Instructor

Write an e-mail to your instructor requesting information. For example, you might have a question about requirements, assessment criteria for your first essay, procedures for activities such as timed quizzes, or policies such as penalties for late work. Clearly and briefly specify what you want to know. As you ask your question, also try to show your instructor that you are a thoughtful, hard-working learner. Exchange drafts with classmates to learn what they would suggest to make your question clearer or your tone more appropriate.

## Online Profile

Because you may never meet your online classmates in person, you may be asked to post a brief online profile introducing yourself to the class. You also might be asked to interview a classmate so that each of you can post an introduction of the other. Such assignments are intended to increase online camaraderie. However, if you feel shy or wish to retain anonymity, cover suggested topics such as academic interests or writing experiences, but stick to general background with limited personal detail. If you prefer not to post a photograph of yourself, consider an image or icon of a pet, possession, or favorite place. If the class already has much in common—for example, all in the same discipline or program—you might include your career plans. Avoid overly personal revelations, gushing enthusiasm, and clipped brevity.

The following profiles, illustrating a personal post and an interview, combine some personal background with academic and career interests.

From: LaTanya Nash

Subject: My Profile as a Future Nurse

After almost a month in the hospital when I was six, I knew that I wanted to be a nurse. That's when I found out how important nurses are to patients and how much they can add to a patient's recovery. I've had after-school and summer jobs in an assisted living center for seniors and a center for children with disabilities. Now that I'm starting college, I'm ready to work on my nursing degree. I'm glad to have this writing class because I've learned from my jobs how important it is for nurses to write clearly.

## Learning by Doing Posting a Personal Profile

Write a brief personal profile introducing yourself to your instructor and classmates. Provide enough information about your college interests, background, or goals to give your audience a clear impression about you as a member of the class online learning community. (Avoid any confessional or overly personal revelations.) Consider adding a photo or an image representing you or your interests.

From: Lainie Costas

Subject: Interview of Tomas

After interviewing Tomas online, I want to introduce a classmate who has just started college this semester. He has been working since high school—doing everything from washing dishes to making pizzas. Now he's planning on getting a business degree to help him start his own restaurant. He already knows what employees need to do, but he wants to learn about things like business plans, finances, and advertising. Like me, he's a little worried about starting with a writing class, but I know from his messages that he has plenty of interesting things to say.

### Learning by Doing  Introducing a Classmate

E-mail, chat, schedule an online video call, or talk in person with a classmate to learn about each other's background, interests, and expectations of the course. (If your instructor assigns pairs or topics, follow those directions.) Using what you learn, write and post a professional message to introduce your classmate.

## Online Threaded Discussions or Responses

When you add your response to a topic in a threaded discussion, an interactive forum, or a class reading blog, follow your instructor's directions, and also read responses from classmates to clarify how to meet the assignment. Because everyone participating already understands the writing situation, you don't need to write a full introduction as you would in an essay. Instead, simply dive in as requested – for example, add your thoughtful comments on a reading, identify and explain a key quotation from it, or reflect on your own reading or writing processes. If you comment on a previous post, do so politely; clarify how your ideas differ without any personal criticism. Follow length guidelines, and be sure to proofread and spell-check your post.

### Learning from Other Writers: Threaded Discussion

The following string of messages begins with the instructor's explanation of the assignment – responding to an assigned reading in one of two specific ways – followed by a few responses of students. Notice how each writer responds personally but sticks to the focus by extending the "thread." Directions for other discussions might emphasize different ways to extend the thread—for example, responding specifically to a preceding comment, summarizing several comments and adding to them, synthesizing and then advancing ideas, raising a different but relevant line of consideration, comparing or contrasting possible responses, tracing possible causes and effects, or other paths that apply your critical thinking skills.

STUDENT ONLINE THREADED DISCUSSION

Instructor Kathleen Beauchene and Students Cristina Berrios, Joshua Tefft, Leah Threats, Arthur Wasilewski, and Joel Torres

Discussion of Writing Processes

**Message no. 2706**

**Author:** Kathleen Beauchene (ENGL1010_600_Beauchene)

**Date:** Saturday, October 10, 2:37pm

In the attached file, you will read about one author's writing process. In your post, you may either comment on a point he makes or share your own writing process, what works or doesn't work for you.

**Message no. 2707**

**Author:** Cristina Berrios

**Date:** Saturday, October 10, 4:02pm

I find that the author's writing process is similar in many ways to how most write, but I do not always have time to write and rewrite and organize and write and so on. . . . Of course I can see if you are a professional writer rewriting and making sure that your work can be produced to sell, but in my eyes I only need to make sure that my story is interesting, consecutive and progressive, and grammatically correct to the best of my ability. . . . Luckily I work in an office where I can interact closely with colleagues who are willing to listen to my "draft" (some of them are college students as well) and give me feedback.

**Message no. 2708**

**Author:** Joshua Tefft

**Date:** Saturday, October 10, 4:43pm

My writing process, like most people's, is similar to what the author does, given I have a lot of time anyway. I really have trouble with not erasing initial drafts, that is, incomplete drafts. I always find myself too critical of my work before it is anywhere near the final stages. But I've begun to learn to receive outside criticism before I put my own on it; this usually gives me a more open-minded perspective on my writing. But I've realized it's a long process to get the results one wants.

**Message no. 2709**

**Author:** Leah Threats

**Date:** Saturday, October 10, 11:49pm

My writing process includes a lot of thought process before I go anywhere near writing a first draft. Then I begin to write and reread it a few times while in the first paragraph, change wording, cut and paste all over the paper. Then I will move on to the middle of the paper, make sure my introduction has enough to it, and the mid section is full of "beef." Then in the ending, I try to make sure I don't leave the writer thinking, What else? . . . I do take the time to make sure I am not shortchanging my reader. As a person who LOVES to read, I want to be able to draw the reader into whatever it is I am writing to them.

**Message no. 2711**

**Author:** Arthur Wasilewski

**Date:** Sunday, October 11, 1:41pm

I approach the writing process with a shoot-from-the hip mentality. Whatever comes to my head first is usually the right idea. I'll think about the idea throughout the whole day or week, and transcribe it to paper after I've gone through a few mental iterations of my original idea.

**Message no. 2713**

**Author:** Joel Torres

**Date:** Sunday, October 11, 8:21pm

After reading this attachment I realize there are some things I sort of start to do in my own writing process, but stop halfway or do not go through thoroughly. I have used the outline idea from time to time. I should go into more depth and organize the ideas in my papers better in the future though. The whole concept of sleeping between drafts does not sit well with me. I find that when I sit down and write a paper, it is best when I dedicate a couple of hours and get into the "zone" and let the ideas flow through me. If the paper is a research paper, I usually do best when I type it directly onto a word processor. When the assignment is an essay or something along the lines of a written argument or a literary work, I like to handwrite and then go back and type it after. Distractions for me are a huge issue; TV, other Web sites, and just lack of focus definitely hurt my writing and are obstacles I must overcome every time a written assignment is due.

## Questions to Start You Thinking

### Meaning

1. What did the instructor ask the class to do in the discussion?
2. Highlight or jot down a few key words to sum up the approach of each student in the threaded discussion.

Writing Strategies

3. In what ways do the students show that they are focused on the "thread" that connects their contributions to the discussion?

**Learning by Doing** Joining a Threaded Discussion

Read the preceding sample online discussion of writing processes. Write your addition to the string, explaining your process—what works or doesn't work.

## File Management

Electronic submission of papers is convenient, saving trees as well as time. Writing online has immediacy—potentially a 24/7 audience, ready to read and respond to your writing. On the other hand, online college writing requires longer-term planning, especially to organize and manage files in classes that encourage revising drafts or developing a portfolio.

For sample pages, see the Quick Format Guide (pp. A-1–A-19). For sample source citations in MLA and APA style, see the Quick Research Guide, pp. A-20–A-38.

**Using File Templates.** No matter how you submit an essay or research paper, instructors generally expect you to use MLA, APA, or another academic style accepted in the field. These styles specify page layout, font style and size, paragraph indentations, formats for citations, and many other details that determine both the look and the approach of the paper.

Instead of treating each paper as a separate item, set up a template for any style you are required to use in a specific class or field of study. Check your software menu for Tools, File, or Format, or go to Help for directions on making a template, a basic paper format with built-in design features. Refine the details, using samples and checklists in this book as well as your instructor's directions and comments on the format of your drafts. When you begin a new draft, call up your template, and start writing. The template will automatically format the features you have customized. If you need several templates, keep them clearly labeled in a template folder.

**Learning by Doing** Preparing a Template

Set up a template for your papers for your composition class or your portfolio. Follow your instructor's directions about the academic style to follow and any special features to add. Turn to the campus computer lab or writing center if you need help preparing the template or figuring out what it should include.

**Naming and Organizing Files.** Check your syllabus or assignments to find out whether you need to follow a certain system or pattern for naming your files. Such systems help an instructor to see at a glance who wrote which assignment for which class: Lopez Recall 101Sec2. If you are expected to save or submit your drafts or build a portfolio, you will want to add a draft number, draft code (noting a first draft or a later revision), or a date: Lopez Recall 3, Lopez Recall Dft, Lopez Recall Rev, or Lopez Recall 9-14-13. Remember that your downloaded essay will be separated from your e-mail message; be certain that the file label alone will be clear.

Even if you are not required to submit your drafts, it's a good idea to save each major stage as you develop the paper instead of always reworking the same file. If you set up a folder for your course, perhaps with subfolders for each assignment, your writing records will be organized in a central location. Then you can easily go back to an earlier draft and restore something you cut or show your development to your instructor if asked to do so. You also have a handy backup if you lose a draft or forget to save it to your flash drive (or forget the flash drive itself).

## Learning by Doing Organizing Your Files

Outline the principles behind your system for managing files. If your system is random or disorganized, figure out a system that makes sense to you and keeps your writing for several courses well organized. Compare your ideas with those of a few classmates, and help each other to improve your plans. Then move your existing files into your new or refined system. Maintain your system by storing files where they belong and sticking to the pattern for naming and dating them.

**Inserting Comments.** When you need to exchange files with other students for peer responses, use your software menu (Tools, Options, or Inserts), try its Help feature, or find a tutorial on the class comment system – track-and-comment word-processing tools, CMS or LMS posts, or a document-sharing site with comment options. If the directions seem complicated, print the Help page, and refer to it as you learn the system.

A comment system typically allows you to use color to show cross-outs and additions or to add initials or color to identify comments in "balloons" in the margin. Less formal options include adding comments or a note at the end of a paragraph, highlighted in yellow. Be sure to send your peer response file on time with helpful suggestions.

### COMMENT CHECKLIST

- ☐ How do you post or send a draft for peer or instructor review?
- ☐ How do you access Help or a tutorial about adding comments?

- ☐ What do you do to turn the Comment function on and off?
- ☐ How do you add comments in the text and in balloons or boxes in the margins using the color that identifies you as a reader?
- ☐ What do you need to do to read, print, save, or delete comments?
- ☐ How do you access the file-exchange site your class uses?
- ☐ How do you record and identify your comments on other writers' papers?
- ☐ How do you retrieve your own draft with the comments of others?

**Polishing Electronically.** As you revise and edit a draft, use all your resources, online and off. Call up the assignment or syllabus. Review what is required and how it will be assessed. Reread any comments from your peers or instructor. Use the Find or Search menu to hunt for repeated errors or too many repetitions of a favorite word or transition. Use the spelling and grammar checkers in your software, CMS, or LMS, even for short messages, so that you always present careful work. If your concentration slips, go offline: print out your draft and read it aloud.

**Submitting Papers Online.** It's usually easy to walk into a face-to-face class and hand in a printed paper. Online, you might hit snags – problems with a transmittal message if your CMS, LMS, or e-mail system is down; problems with a drop box or forum that closes early due to an error or power outage; problems with a file, attaching or remembering to attach yours or opening someone else's. Try to avoid sending an assignment two minutes before the deadline because a time crunch may increase problems.

Many instructors will see "the computer ate my homework" as a problem you should have solved, not an acceptable excuse for late work. If you have trouble transmitting a file, send a short separate message to your instructor to explain how you are solving the problem, or ask your instructor to confirm the file's safe arrival. (Instructors are likely to prefer that you keep explanations to a minimum, concentrate on solutions, and use an automatic "read" reply to confirm receipt.) If your computer has a problem, you are responsible for going to the lab or using another computer to submit your work on time. If your campus system is temporarily down, you are responsible for submitting your work as soon as access is restored.

No matter what software you use, "translate" your file to the required format – maybe Word (.doc or .docx) but often Rich Text Format (.rtf), a general format most word-processing software can read. Check your File menu for two different commands: Save (to save the file to the location where you routinely store class files) and Save As (to save the file in a different format, to a different location, or with a different name). If you consistently add the date at the end of the file name, you will simplify finding and sending the most current version. If you use the same name or same date for duplicate files in different formats, you also will know that they correspond. Once the correct file is properly formatted, attach it to your message. If your file is returned with comments from your instructor or classmates, give it a new name and date so it does not replace your original.

**Backing Up Your Files.** No matter how tired or rushed you are, always save and back up your work, preferably using several methods. Use a backup card, portable drive, flash drive, smart stick, file storage site, or whatever is available and efficient for you. Label or identify your equipment with your name so that you could pull your drive out of the lost-and-found basket at the library or someone could arrange to return it to you.

If you are working on a campus computer, carry your drive with you on a neck strap or clipped to your backpack so that your current work is always with you. If you are working on a major project with a tight deadline, attach major drafts to an e-mail to yourself. If you back up your files at home or in your room, do so every day. Then, if a file is damaged or lost, your hard drive fails during finals week, or you leave your drive at the library, you can still finish your writing assignments on time.

---

### FILE CHECKLIST

- ☐ What academic style and paper format is expected in your class? Have you prepared a template or file format in this style?
- ☐ Have you saved the files that show your paper's development during several drafts? Have you named or dated them so that the sequence is clear?
- ☐ Have you named a file you are submitting as directed? Have you used Save As to convert it to the required file format?
- ☐ Have you developed a file storage system so that you have a folder for each course and a subfolder for all related files for a specific paper?
- ☐ Do you carry a flash drive or other storage device with you so that you can work on your papers in the computer lab or library whenever you have time?
- ☐ Do you consistently back up your files every time you write using a flash drive, portable drive, or other device?
- ☐ If a CMS or LMS is new to you, do you know—exactly—when your assignment is due? Do you know how to submit the file, confirm its arrival, and download your paper when it is returned with comments?

---

## Additional Writing Assignments

1. Begin a reflective electronic journal. Add entries daily or several times each week to record ideas, observations, thoughts, and reactions that might enrich your writing. Use your file as a resource as you write assigned essays. Post selections, if you wish, for class or small-group discussion.
2. Write a comparison-and-contrast essay based on your experiences with face-to-face, online, or hybrid courses. Consider starting with a table with columns to help you systematically compare features of the class formats, the learning requirements or priorities they encourage, any changes in your priorities or activities as a student, or other possible points of comparison.
3. Keep a blog about your writing experience. (If this will be your first blog, begin by looking for tips or tutorials on the CMS, LMS, or site where your class will establish their blogs.) Post regular entries as you work on a specific essay or writing project, commenting on the successes, challenges, and surprises that the college writer meets.
4. Establish a collaborative blog with others in your class about a key course topic or possible sources or ideas for your writing or research projects. Decide on a daily or weekly schedule for blogging.
5. Start a threaded discussion about resources for your course topic, current assignment, research project, or other class project. Ask contributors to identify a resource, explain how to locate or access it, evaluate its strengths, and describe any limitations.
6. Set up a small-group or class Wiki, encouraging everyone to identify terms, concepts, strategies, activities, or events of significance to the course, a common academic program, or a shared writing interest. Write and edit collaboratively to arrive at clear, accurate, and useful explanations of these items to help everyone master the course (or program) material.
7. Set up a class Help Board on your CMS or LMS, a place where a student can post an immediate problem while working on the course reading or writing. Ask participants to respond to at least two or three questions for each that they post. Ask your instructor to add advice as needed.
8. Working with a small group, use a document-sharing system to draft an essay or other project, giving all group members and your instructor access to the process. Work collaboratively through simultaneous or sequential drafting, using chat or other electronic messaging to discuss your work. When your draft is complete, have all participants (including your instructor, if possible) share reflections about both the process and the outcome.
9. Use an available communication system (for example, for a Web-based telephone call, conference call, or video call; for a real-time online meeting; or for an audio chat) for a conversation with a classmate or small group. Set a specific time for the meeting, and circulate any materials ahead of time. The purpose of the conversation might be discussing a reading, responding

to each other's current draft, reviewing material before an exam, or a similar group activity. After the conversation, write an evaluation of the experience, including recommendations for the next time you use the technology.

10. **Source Assignment.** Conduct some research using your college's online catalog. Look up several courses that you must or might take during the next few terms. What formats – face-to-face, online, or hybrid – are available for these courses? In what ways would the courses differ, based on the catalog or a linked description? How might each format appeal to your strengths, learning preferences, and educational circumstances? Write a short report that summarizes what you learn and then uses that information to explain which choices might best suit you.
11. **Visual Assignment.** Prepare graphics, take photographs, or identify images (credited appropriately) that contribute to one of the other assignments for this chapter.

# Writing and Presenting Under Pressure

# 16

Most college writing is done for assessment – that is, most of the papers you hand in are eventually evaluated and graded. But some college writing tasks exist *only* as methods of assessment, designed to allow you to demonstrate what you have mastered. You often need to do such writing on the spot – a quiz to finish in twenty minutes, a final exam to complete in a few hours, an impromptu essay to dash off in one class period. How do you discover and shape your ideas in a limited time?

This chapter provides tips for three types of in-class writing – the essay exam, the short-answer exam, and the timed writing assignment. It also covers online assessments, the writing portfolio, and the oral presentation, which may include software slides.

e For an interactive Learning by Doing activity on Using Visuals, go to Ch. 16: **bedfordstmartins.com/bedguide**.

## Why Writing and Presenting under Pressure Matters

### In a College Course

- You write under pressure when you take reading quizzes in biology or annotate bibliography entries in history.
- You work under pressure as you prepare an oral presentation about your internship.

### In the Workplace

- You meet frequent deadlines as you justify your productivity and report on customer service problems.

### In Your Community

- You learn that the school board is about to vote on closing your child's school, so you need to alert other parents right away.

? When have you most often needed to write or speak under pressure? How might you reduce stress in such situations in the future?

# Essay Examinations

In many courses an essay exam is the most important kind of in-class writing. Instructors believe that such writing shows that you have examined material critically and can clearly communicate your thoughts about it.

## Preparing for the Exam

Some instructors favor an open-book exam in which you bring your books and perhaps your notes to class for reference. For this exam, memory and recall are less important than reasoning and selecting what matters. On the other hand, for a closed-book exam, you need to fix in your memory vital names, dates, and definitions. Either way, prepare by imagining likely questions and then planning answers. If your instructor supplies sample questions, pattern new ones after them. Look for main ideas and questions in relevant textbook chapters. Ask yourself: How do ideas relate? How might they be combined? What can I conclude?

# Learning from Another Writer: Essay Exam

To look at techniques for answering *any* exam question, let's take one example. A final exam in developmental psychology posed this question:

> What evidence indicates innate factors in perceptual organization? You might find it useful to recall any research that shows how infants perceive depth and forms.

David Ian Cohn sat back and thought over the course reading. What perception research had used babies for subjects? He jotted down an informal outline, took a deep breath, and wrote a straightforward answer.

**David Ian Cohn** **Student Essay Answer**

## Response to Psychology Question

Research on infants is probably the best way to demonstrate that some factors in perceptual organization are innate. As the cliff box experiment shows, an infant will avoid what looks like a drop-off, even though its mother calls it and even though it can feel glass covering the drop-off area. The same infant will crawl to the other end of the box, which appears (and is) safe. Apparently, infants do not have to be taught what a cliff looks like.

Psychologists have also observed that infants are aware of size constancy. They recognize a difference in size between a 10 cm box at a distance of one meter and a 20 cm box at a distance of two meters. If this phenomenon is not innate, it is at least learned early, for the subjects of the experiment were infants of sixteen to eighteen months.

When shown various patterns, infants tend to respond more noticeably to patterns that resemble the human face than to those that appear random. This seemingly innate recognition helps the infant distinguish people (such as its mother) from less important inanimate objects.

Infants also seem to have an innate ability to match sight with sound. When simultaneously shown two television screens, each depicting a different subject, while being played a tape that sometimes matched one screen and sometimes the other, infants looked at whichever screen matched what they heard — not always, but at least twice as often.

### Questions to Start You Thinking

Meaning

1. What is the main idea of Cohn's answer?
2. If you were the psychology instructor, how could you immediately see that Cohn had thoroughly dealt with – and only with – the question?

Writing Strategies

3. In what places is Cohn's answer concrete and specific, not general?
4. Suppose Cohn had tacked on a conclusion: "Thus I have conclusively proved that there are innate factors in perceptual organization, by citing much evidence showing that infants definitely can perceive depth and forms." Would that sentence strengthen his answer? Why, or why not?

## Generating Ideas

When the clock is ticking away, generating ideas right on the exam sheet saves time. First read over all the questions carefully. If you don't understand what a question calls for, ask your instructor right away. If you are offered a choice, cross out questions you are *not* going to answer so you don't waste time on them by mistake. Annotate questions, underline important points, and scribble short definitions. Write reminders that you will notice while you work: TWO PARTS! or EXAMPLE OF ABORIGINES.

**Outline a Concrete Answer.** Instructors prefer concrete and specific answers to those that wander in the clouds of generality. David Cohn's informal outline helped him cite evidence – particular experiments with infants – all the way through.

Thesis: Research on infants is probably the best way to demonstrate that some factors in perceptual organization are innate.
Cliff box — kid fears drop despite glass, mother; knows shallow side safe
Size constancy — learned early if not intrinsic
Shapes — infants respond more/better to face shape than nonformed
Match sound w/ sight — 2 TVs, look twice as much at right one

**Focus on the Question.** Instructors prefer answers that are organized and coherent rather than rambling. Check the question for directive words that define your task: *evaluate, compare, discuss, explain, describe, summarize, trace the development of.* To put yourself on the right track, incorporate a form of such a word in your first sentence.

| | |
|---|---|
| QUESTION | Define socialism, and give examples of its main types. |
| ANSWER | Socialism is defined as . . . |
| ANSWER | Socialism is an economic and political concept, difficult to define because it takes many forms. It . . . |

## Planning for Typical Exam Questions

For examples of many methods of development, see Ch. 22.

Most exam questions fall into types. If you can recognize them, you will know how to organize and begin to write.

**The cause and effect question** asks for *causes, effects,* or both.

> What were the immediate causes of the Dust Bowl in the 1930s?
>
> Describe the main economic effects of a low prime interest rate.

**The compare or contrast question** asks you to point out similarities (*compare*), differences (*contrast*), or both. Directions to *show similarities* or *identify likenesses* ask for comparisons, while those to *distinguish, differentiate,* or *show differences* ask for contrasts, perhaps to evaluate in what respects one thing is better than the other. You explain not one subject but two, paralleling your points and giving both equal space.

> Compare and contrast *iconic memory* and *eidetic imagery,* defining the terms and indicating how they differ and are related or alike.

After supplying a one-sentence definition of each term, a student proceeded first to contrast and then to compare, for full credit.

> Iconic memory is a picturelike impression that lasts for only a fraction of a second in short-term memory. Eidetic imagery is the ability to take a mental photograph, exact in detail, as though its subject were still present. But iconic memory soon disappears. Unlike an eidetic image, it does not last long enough to enter long-term memory. IM is common; EI is unusual: very few people have it. Iconic memory and eidetic imagery are similar, however: both record visual images, and every sighted person of normal intelligence has both abilities to some degree.

**The definition question** requests explanation in many forms, short and extended.

> Explain three common approaches to parenting—*permissive, authoritarian-restrictive,* and *authoritative*. [Supply a trio of definitions.]
>
> Define the Stanislavsky method of acting, citing outstanding actors who followed it. [Explain a single method and give examples.]

**The demonstration question** asks you to back up a statement.

> Demonstrate the truth of Freud's contention that laughter may contain elements of aggression. [Explain Freud's claim and supply evidence to support it, maybe crowd scenes, a joke, or examples from reading.]

**The discussion question** isn't an invitation to ramble.

> Discuss three events that precipitated Lyndon B. Johnson's withdrawal from the 1968 presidential race.

Try rewording the question to help you focus your discussion.

> Why did President Johnson decide not to seek another term? Analyze and briefly explain three causes.

A discussion question may announce itself with *describe, explain,* or *explore.*

> Describe the national experience following passage of the Eighteenth Amendment. What did most Americans learn from it?

Provided you know that this amendment banned the sale, manufacture, and transportation of alcoholic drinks and that it was finally repealed, you can discuss its effects – or perhaps the reasons for its repeal.

**The divide or classify question** asks you to slice a subject into sections, sort things into kinds, or break the idea, person, or process into parts.

> Identify the ways in which each resident of the United States uses, on average, 1,595 gallons of water a day. How and to what degree might a person reduce this amount?

First, divide up water uses – drinking, cooking, bathing, washing cars, and so on. Then give tips for conservation and tell how effective each is.

> What different genres of film did Robert Altman direct? Name at least one outstanding example of each kind.

Sort films into categories – possibly comedy, war, drama, mystery, western – and give examples.

**The evaluation question** asks you to think critically and present a judgment based on criteria.

> Evaluate this idea, giving reasons for your judgments: cities should stop building highways to the suburbs and instead build public lightrail.

Other argument questions might begin "Defend the idea of..." or "Show weaknesses in the concept of..." or otherwise call on you to take a stand.

**The process analysis question** often begins with *trace.*

> Trace the stages through which a bill becomes a state law.
>
> Trace the development of the medieval Italian city-state.

Both questions ask you to tell how something occurs or occurred, dividing the process into steps and detailing each step. The next question calls for the other type of process analysis, the "how-to" variety:

> An employee, late for work daily by fifteen to thirty minutes, has been on the job only five months but shows promise of learning skills that your firm needs badly. How would you deal with this situation?

**The response question** might supply a statement, a comment, or a quotation, asking you to test the writer's opinion against what you know. Carefully read the statement, and jot down contrary or supporting evidence.

> Was the following passage written by Gertrude Stein, Kate Chopin, or Tillie Olsen? On what evidence do you base your answer?
>
> > She waited for the material pictures which she thought would gather and blaze before her imagination. She waited in vain. She saw no pictures of solitude, of hope, of longing, or of despair. But the very passions themselves were aroused within her soul, swaying it, lashing it, as the waves daily beat upon her splendid body. She trembled, she was choking, and the tears blinded her.

If you were familiar with the stories of Kate Chopin, who specializes in physical and emotional descriptions of impassioned women, you would point to language (*swaying, lashing*) that marks the passage as hers.

### Learning by Doing Asking Questions

Working by yourself or with a study group, review your study guide, class notes, textbook, or other material for an exam. Make your own list of likely questions, or review your instructor's list of sample questions. Consider each question, and identify its type, using the preceding list or adding categories. Then underline, circle, or highlight the key words that tell you what your answer needs to do.

## Drafting: The Only Version

When you have two or more essay questions to answer, block out your time roughly based on the points or minutes your instructor allots to each. Give extra minutes to a complicated question with several parts. Then pace yourself as you write. For example, wrap up question 2 at 10:30 and move on.

As you draft, give yourself room for second thoughts by writing on only one side of the page in your exam booklet and skipping every other line. Should you wish to add material later, you can do so with ease.

**Begin with the Easy Questions.** Many students find that it boosts their morale to start with the question they feel best able to answer. Unless your instructor specifies otherwise, why not skip around? Clearly number or label each answer as your instructor does. Then begin in such a way that the instructor will immediately recognize which question you're answering.

QUESTION

Compare and contrast the 1930s depression with the recession of 2008 on.

ANSWER

Compared to the paralyzing depression that began in 1929, the recession that began in 2008 seems like . . .

**State Your Thesis at the Start.** Try making your opening sentence a thesis statement that immediately makes clear the main point. Then the rest of your answer can back up that statement. Get started by turning the question into a statement and using it to begin an answer.

QUESTION

What reasons for leasing cars and office equipment, instead of purchasing them, can be cited for a two-person partnership?

ANSWER

I can cite at least four reasons for a two-person partnership to lease cars and office equipment. First, under present tax laws, the entire cost of a regular payment under a leasing agreement may be deducted. . . .

**Stick to the Question.** Throwing into your answer everything you have learned in the course defeats the purpose of the exam – to use your knowledge, not to parade it. Answer by selecting and shaping *what matters.* On the other hand, if a question has two parts, answer both.

Name three styles of contemporary architecture. Evaluate one of them.

**Stay Specific.** Pressed for time, some exam takers think, "I haven't got time to get specific here. I'll just sum this up in general." That's a mistake. Every time you throw in a broad statement ("The Industrial Revolution was beneficial for the peasant"), take time to add specific examples ("In Dusseldorf, as Taine notes, deaths from starvation among displaced Prussian farmworkers dropped from a peak of almost 10 percent a year").

## Revising: Rereading and Proofing

If you pace yourself, you'll have a few minutes left to look over your work. Check that your ideas are clear and hang together. Add sentences where new ones are needed. If you recall a key point, add a paragraph on a blank left-hand page. Just draw an arrow to show where it goes. Naturally, more errors occur when you write under pressure than when you have time to proofread carefully. Simply add words with carets (^) or neatly strike them out.

When your paper or blue book is returned, consider these questions as you look it over so that you improve your essay-exam skills:

---

**ESSAY EXAM CHECKLIST**

- ☐ Did you answer the whole question, not just part of it?
- ☐ Did you stick to the point, not throw in unrequested information?
- ☐ Did you make your general statements clear by citing evidence or examples?
- ☐ Did you proofread for omissions and lack of clarity?
- ☐ On what questions do you feel you did a good job, whatever your grade?
- ☐ If you had to write this exam over again, how would you now go about it?

---

## Short-Answer Examinations

The *short-answer exam* may call on you to identify names or phrases from your reading, in a sentence or a few words.

> Identify the following: Clemenceau, Treaty of Versailles, Maginot line.
>
> Georges Clemenceau — This French premier, nicknamed The Tiger, headed a popular coalition cabinet during World War I and at the Paris Peace Conference demanded stronger penalties against Germany.

Writing a short identification is much like writing a short definition. Mention the general class to which a thing belongs to make clear its nature.

For more about defining, see pp. 441–43.

> Treaty of Versailles — pact between Germany and the Allies that . . .
> Maginot line — fortifications that . . .

## Timed Writings

Many instructors give you experience in writing on demand by assigning impromptu in-class essays. Their purpose is to test writing skills, not recall. Although time is limited, the setting controlled, and the subject assigned, your usual methods of writing can still serve you well.

**Budget Your Time.** For an in-class essay with forty-five minutes to write, try to spend ten minutes preparing, thirty minutes writing, and five minutes rereading and making last-minute changes. Plan quickly to leave time to get ideas on paper in an essay — the part you will be graded on.

**Consider Types of Topics.** Often you can expect the same types of questions for in-class writings as for essay exams. Do what the key words say.

For common types of exam questions, see pp. 336–38.

> What were the *causes* of World War I?
>
> *Compare and contrast* the theories of capitalism and socialism.
>
> *Define* civil rights.

Add your personal twist to a general subject, but note the key words.

> *Analyze* a problem in education that is *difficult to solve.*
>
> *Discuss ways to cope* with stress.

Standardized tests often ask you to respond to a short passage, testing not only your writing ability but also your reading comprehension.

> Thomas Jefferson stated, "If a nation expects to be ignorant and free, in a state of civilization, it expects what never was and never will be." *How* is his comment *relevant* to education today?

**Choose Your Topic Wisely.** For on-the-spot writing, the trick is to make the topic your own. If you have a choice, pick the one you know about, not one to impress your readers. They'll be most impressed by logical argument and solid evidence. Bring a broad subject down to something you have experienced. Have you seen traffic jams, power outages, or condos ruining beaches? Then write about increased population, using these examples.

**Think before You Write.** Despite your limited time, read the instructions or questions carefully, restrict your topic to something you know about, focus on a main idea, and jot down main points for development. If a good hook to open or conclude occurs to you, use it, too.

**Don't Try to Be Perfect.** No one expects in-class essays to read as smoothly as reports written over several weeks. You can't polish every sentence or remember the exact word for every spot. And never waste time recopying.

**Save Time to Proofread.** Your best-spent minutes may be the last few when you read over your work. Cross out errors and make neat corrections using asterisks (*), arrows, and carets (^). Watch for the following:

- letters omitted (*-ed* or *-s*), added (develop*e*), or inverted (rec*ie*ve)
- wrong punctuation (a comma instead of a period)
- omitted apostrophes (*dont* instead of *don't*)
- omitted words ("She going" instead of "She *is* going")
- wrong (*except* instead of *accept*) or misspelled words (*mispelled*)

### Learning by Doing Thinking Fast

Practice planning quickly for timed writing or tests as a class. Brainstorm to explore approaches to sample topics provided in this chapter. Select one class member (or three, in turn) to record ideas on the board. Devote exactly ten minutes of discussion per topic. Focus on these key parts of a successful response:

- possible thesis sentences
- possible patterns of organization
- possible kinds and sources of evidence

Expect a wide range of ideas. Spend the last part of class evaluating them.

## Online Assessment

For more on writing online, see Ch. 15.

The outcomes or standards for assessing the qualities and effectiveness of a specific essay for a composition class are probably the same whether a course is face-to-face, hybrid, or online. On the other hand, online activities can significantly expand the options for class participation. If your class uses a learning or course management system (LMS or CMS) or has other online components, find out which activities are required and which recommended. Class sites or systems may track and report detailed data on participation such as the following:

- time spent online and active
- time and activity (even keystrokes) within class units and tools
- completion of tasks by the deadline or within the allotted time
- number of attempts to complete tasks
- quantity and quality of contributions to threaded discussions (sorted alphabetically to group each individual's contributions)
- number of correct multiple-choice or other objective answers

Also consider nonstatistical measures of your performance and your engagement. For example, suppose your instructor asks you to post a question about a challenging reading and also to respond to two questions from other students. You might receive credit simply for making a conscientious effort to do both, whether your answers were correct or not. After all, the purpose of the assignment is to generate discussion. On the other hand, if you are asked to submit your final, revised version of an essay, posting it before the deadline would be only the first step, followed by your instructor's assessment based on the criteria for the assignment.

Once you know the many ways that your online participation can be measured, you are prepared to view time online as a possible limitation or deadline, as well as a measure of effort and attention. You also are prepared to read assignment prompts more critically. For example, suppose you are asked to write a short answer to a question, perhaps with thirty minutes allowed and about 250 words (one double-spaced page) expected. How is your instructor likely to assess your 174 words written in nine minutes? How will your response compare with someone else's 249 words and twenty-nine minutes of attention? Will your instructor think that you felt pressured and rushed, ignored the implications of the directions, didn't care enough to use the time allowed, or simply said what you had to say?

## Portfolio Assessment

Portfolio courses typically emphasize revision and reflection – your ability to identify and discuss your decisions, strengths, or learning processes. To build your portfolio, save all your drafts and notes, keep track of your choices and changes, and eventually select and submit your best writing.

The portfolio, printed or electronic, collects pieces of writing that represent the writer's best work. Compiled over time and across projects, it showcases a writer's talent, hard work, and ability to make thoughtful choices. A course portfolio is usually due as the term ends and includes pieces written and revised for that class. Portfolios may include an introduction (often a self-assessment or rationale) for readers, who might be teachers, supervisors, evaluators, parents, or classmates.

### Understanding Portfolio Assessment

The portfolio method of evaluation and teaching shapes the whole course, beginning to end. Your course will probably emphasize responses to your writing – from your classmates and instructor – but not necessarily grades on separate papers. This method shifts attention to the writing process – to discovery, planning, drafting, peer response, revision, editing – allowing time for your skills to develop before the portfolio is graded. Because this method is flexible, read your assignments carefully, and listen well to determine the kind of portfolio you'll need to keep, such as the following types.

**A Writing Folder.** Students submit all drafts, notes, outlines, doodles, and messy pages – all writing for the course, finished or unfinished. Students may also revise two or three promising pieces for a "presentation portfolio." The folder usually does not have a reflective cover letter.

**A Learning (or Open) Portfolio.** Students submit a variety of materials that have contributed to their learning. They may even determine the contents, organization, and presentation of the portfolio, which might include photos, other images, or nonprint objects that demonstrate learning.

**A Closed Portfolio.** Students must turn in assignments that are specified by the instructor, or their options for what to include may be limited.

**A Midterm Portfolio.** The portfolio is given a trial run at midterm, or the midterm grade is determined by one or two papers that are submitted for evaluation, perhaps with a brief self-assessment.

**A Final or Presentation Portfolio.** The portfolio is evaluated at the end of the course after being revised, edited, and polished for presentation.

**A Modified or Combination Portfolio.** The student has some, but not unlimited, choice in what to include. For example, the instructor may ask for three entries that show certain features or parts of the course.

Find out what your instructor has in mind. For example, your combination portfolio might contain three revised papers (out of five or six required). You decide, late in the term, which three to revise and edit. You also may reflect on how those choices define you as a writer, show your learning, or explain your decisions while writing. Here are some questions your instructor, syllabus, or assignment sheets may answer:

- Is the portfolio paper or electronic?
- How many papers should you include in the portfolio?
- Do all the papers need to be revised? If so, what level of revision is expected? What criteria will be used to assess them?
- How much of the course grade is determined by the portfolio? Are entries graded separately, or does the portfolio receive one grade?
- May you include papers written for other courses or entries other than texts—such as photos, videos, maps, Web pages, or other visuals?
- Do you need an introduction or a cover letter? What approach is expected: Description? Explanation? Exploration? Reflection? Self-assessment?
- Does each entry need its own cover sheet? Should descriptions of your processes or choices appear before or after each entry?

## Tips for Keeping a Portfolio

**Keep Everything, and Stay Organized.** Don't throw anything away! Keep all your notes, lists, drafts, outlines, clusters, responses from readers, photocopied articles, and source references. On your own computer, *back up everything*. At the computer lab, save your work to a portable drive or card. Organize your files, and invest in a good folder with pockets. Label and store drafts, notes, outlines, and peer review forms for each assignment.

**Manage Your Time.** The portfolio isn't due until midterm or the end of the course, but plan ahead to save time and frustration. As your instructor returns each assignment with comments, make changes in response while the ideas are fresh. If you don't understand or know how to approach those comments, ask right away. Make notes about what you want to do. Then, even if you want to let a paper simmer, you will have both a plan and fresh insight ready when you work on it again.

**Practice Self-Assessment.** For complex activities, learn to step back and evaluate your own performance. Maybe you have great ideas but find it hard to organize them. Maybe you write powerful thesis statements but run out of ideas to support them. Don't wait until the portfolio cover letter is due to begin assessing your strengths, weaknesses, or preferences.

For more help with self-assessment, see the Peer Response questions, the Revision Checklists, and the Take Action sections throughout *The Bedford Guide*.

Practice self-assessment from the start. After reviewing the syllabus, write a paragraph or two about how you expect to do in this course. What might you do well? Why? What may be hard? Why? For each paper you share with peers or hand in, write a journal entry about what the paper does well and what it still needs. Keep track of your process as you plan, research, or draft each paper—where you get stuck and where things click.

**Choose the Entries Carefully.** If you can select what to include, consider the course emphasis. Of course, you want to select pieces your evaluator will think are "the best," but also consider which show the most promise or potential. Which drafts show creativity, insight, or an unusual approach? Which show variety—different purposes, audiences, or voices? Which show depth—your ability to do thorough research or stay with a topic for several weeks? Also consider the order of the entries—which piece might work best first or last, and how each placement affects the whole.

For a sample reflective portfolio letter, see p. 383.

**Write a Strong Reflective Introduction or Cover Letter.** Your introduction—usually a self-assessment in the form of a cover letter, a statement, or a description for each of your entries—could be the most important text you write all semester. Besides introducing your collection and portraying you as a writer, it explains your choices in putting the portfolio together. It shows that you can evaluate your work and your writing process. Like a "final exam," your reflective introduction tests what you've learned about good writing, readers' needs, and the details of a careful self-presentation.

### DISCOVERY CHECKLIST

- ☐ Who will read this reflection?
- ☐ What qualities of writing will your reader value?
- ☐ Will the reader suggest changes or evaluate your work?
- ☐ What will the outcome of the reading be? How much can you influence it?
- ☐ What do you want to emphasize about your writing? What are you proud of? What have you learned? What did you have trouble with?
- ☐ How can you present your writing ability in the best light?

If your reader is your instructor, look back over responses on your returned papers. Review the course syllabus and assignment sheets. What patterns do you see in the comments or directions? What could you tell a friend about this reader's expectations—or pet peeves? Use what you've learned to develop a convincing introduction or cover letter.

For more on appeals, see pp. 44–45.

If your readers are unknown, ask your instructor for as much information as possible so you can decide which logical, ethical, or emotional appeals might be most effective. Although you won't know your readers personally, it's safe to assume that they will be trained in portfolio assessment and will share many of your instructor's ideas about good writing. If your college writing program has guidelines, consult them, too.

For more on the format for business letters, see pp. 361–64.

How long should your introduction or cover letter be? Check with your instructor, but regardless of length, develop your ideas or support your claims as in any effective writing. If you are asked to write a letter, follow the format for a business letter: include the date, a salutation, and a closing.

In the reflective introduction, you might try some of the following (but don't try to use all of them):

- Discuss your best entry, and explain why it is your best.
- Detail your revisions—the improvements you want readers to notice.
- Review everything included, touching on the strengths of each.
- Outline your writing and revising process for one or more entries.
- State what the portfolio illustrates about you as a writer, student, researcher, or critical thinker.
- Acknowledge your weaknesses, but show how you've worked to overcome them.
- Acknowledge the influence of your readers on your entries.
- Reflect on what you've learned about writing and reading.
- Lay the groundwork for a positive evaluation of your work.

**Polishing the Final Portfolio.** From the first page to the last, printed or electronic, your portfolio should be ready for public presentation. Take pride in it. Think about creative ways to give it a final distinctive feature, such as adding a colorful cover, illustrations, a table of contents, or a running head. Although a cheerful cover will not make up for weak writing or careless editing, readers will value your extra effort.

## Oral Presentations

In many courses students make oral presentations. Individuals might summarize final essays, research reports, or capstone projects. Groups or teams might organize pro-and-con debates, roundtable presentations of viewpoints, organized analyses, problem-solution proposals, or field reports. Such presentations require thoughtful written materials and confident oral delivery, perhaps using visuals prepared with PowerPoint or other software.

Because presentations draw on multiple skills, you may feel anxious or uncertain about how to prepare. You need to write under pressure, preparing a speaking script or notes as well as text for any presentation slides. You need to speak under pressure, making your presentation and possibly fielding questions. You may be assessed on both your prepared content and your actual presentation. Nevertheless, each presentation provides valuable experience, preparing you for future classes, job interviews, workplace reports, professional talks, and community appearances.

**Start Early.** Get organized, don't procrastinate, and draw on your writing strategies when a presentation looms. Review your assignment and any assessment criteria; be sure you understand what is expected. If you are reporting on a paper or project, finish it well ahead of the deadline. If your presentation requires separate reading or research, get it done early. If you are working with a group, establish a timetable with regular face-to-face meetings or online checkpoints so everyone is prepared. This advance work is necessary to leave time to plan the presentation as a separate activity—and avoid just walking in, looking disorganized or ill-prepared.

For sample readings written for oral presentation, turn to the radio broadcasts by Frank Deford, "Mind Games: Football and Head Injuries" (p. 350 and e-Pages); Tom Ashbrook and Ty Burr, from *The Strange Power of Celebrity* (p. 229 and e-Pages); and Sarah Adams, "Be Cool to the Pizza Dude" (p. 621 and e-Pages).

**Develop Your Oral Presentation.** As you work on the presentation itself, consider your audience and purpose, the time allotted, and the formality expected. Think hard about an engaging start—something surprising, intriguing, or notable to help your audience focus. Map out the main points appropriate for your audience and situation. Preview them so your words tell listeners what's major, what's minor, and what's coming up. Be selective: listeners can absorb only limited detail.

Instead of writing out a speech like an essay, record your main points on cards or on a page using easy-to-read type. Then practice—speaking out loud, timing yourself, revising your notes, testing your talk on a friend, or maybe recording yourself so you can catch rough spots. If you feel nervous, practice taking a deep breath or counting to five before you begin. Also practice looking around the room, making eye contact. Connecting with your audience turns anonymous faces into sympathetic people.

**Align Your Visuals.** As your talk takes shape, work on any slides or images for projection or distribution. Listeners appreciate concise visuals that support—not repeat—your words. If possible, project a few in the room where you will speak. Sit there, as your audience will, to see how large the type needs to be for easy reading. Try to align your slides with your main points so they appear steadily and appropriately. Aim for a simple, professional look without exotic designs or dramatic colors. All this preparation will improve your presentation and reduce any fears about public speaking.

---

### PRESENTATION CHECKLIST

- ☐ Have you developed your presentation as effectively as possible?
- ☐ Do you begin and end with an engaging flair?
- ☐ Have you stated your points clearly in an order easy to follow?
- ☐ Are your words, tone, and level of formality well chosen for the situation?
- ☐ Have you practiced enough to look relaxed and avoid getting lost?
- ☐ Have you taken a deep breath and looked around at your audience before speaking? Have you continued to make eye contact as you present?
- ☐ Have you projected your voice and spoken slowly so everyone could hear?
- ☐ Does your appearance—posture, dress, hand motions—increase your credibility?
- ☐ Do you stick to the expected time, format, procedure, or other guidelines?
- ☐ Are your visuals clear, spacious, and easy to read?
- ☐ Do the design, text, and presentation of your visuals complement your talk?

---

### Learning by Doing  Pairing Up to Practice

Pair up, and present your talks to each other, ideally in the room where you will make the final presentation. Using the Presentation Checklist or the class assessment rubric, identify and discuss the most important improvements each classmate might make. Practice your talks until you're at ease with the changes.

# Learning from Other Writers: Visuals for Oral Presentations

This series of images on urban design was prepared by a student for a face-to-face presentation in his geography class. As this student reported on urbanization, he showed slides with images of the ten most populous cities in the world as well as summaries of key points from sources on this topic. Traditional Urban Design, the example here, combines text and images.

**Andrew Dillon Bustin** **Face-to-Face Class Presentation**

### Traditional Urban Design

***TRADITIONAL URBAN DESIGN***

- ❖High residential densities
- ❖Mixed land uses
- ❖Gridded street patterns
- ❖Land use plans that maximize social contact, spatial efficiency, and local economy

### Questions to Start You Thinking

Meaning

1. What information does the slide present?
2. How do the images relate to the words?

Writing Strategies

3. How does the slide try to appeal to an audience of classmates?
4. If the presenter were your classmate, what helpful comments would you make about his slide?

 **Frank Deford** **Audio**

## Mind Games: Football and Head Injuries

Frank Deford has been an award-winning journalist at *Sports Illustrated* for over fifty years and also a regular contributor to National Public Radio. In this audio presentation, he explores our culpability at the intersection of football and head injuries. To listen to the selection, go to Chapter 16: **bedfordstmartins.com/bedguide**.

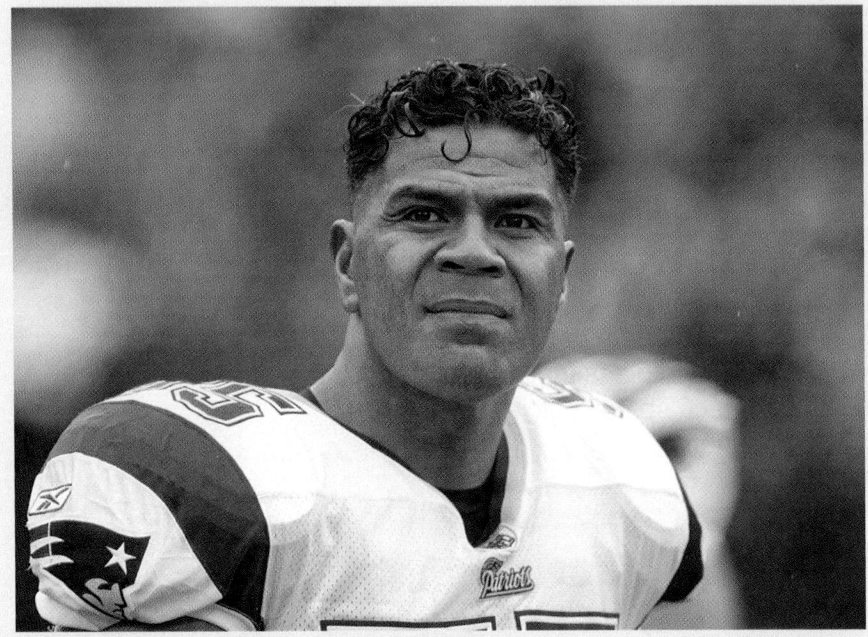

Junior Seau, a former NFL player who committed suicide in 2012, suffered concussion-related brain damage.

## Additional Writing Assignments

1. Review available information about an upcoming exam as well as advice about such exams in this chapter. Write a set of directions for yourself, explaining the process for preparing for your exam. (Follow your directions.)
2. Prepare for an examination by writing sample questions about major issues in the course. Then outline possible answers to these questions.
3. Begin to organize your writing portfolio. First, sum up the type of portfolio assigned, and list the components you need to supply. Then outline your current ideas about how to introduce and organize your portfolio.
4. Imagine a professional portfolio that would effectively present you and your talents to a prospective employer or an advanced academic program. Write up your plan for this portfolio, including what it would contain, how you would introduce it, and how you would design it to try to persuade readers to hire or admit you.
5. **Source Assignment.** Prepare an oral presentation on a topic approved by your instructor. Consider reporting on a reading, expanding on a recent essay, exploring a campus issue, identifying effects on students of physical features of your campus, proposing a change for your campus or workplace, or interpreting a distinctive community feature.
6. **Visual Assignment.** Prepare presentation slides or other visuals to project or distribute as part of an oral presentation such as assignment 5.

# 17 Writing in the Workplace

Most of the world's workplace communication takes place in writing. Although a conversation or voice mail may be forgotten or ignored, a written message provides a permanent record of a business exchange, often calling for action. This chapter first outlines some general guidelines for workplace writing and then shows you types likely to prove useful.

## Why Writing in the Workplace Matters

**In a College Course**

- You write job applications, memos, and letters in your business communications course.
- You prepare a compelling application – letter, résumé, and memo of understanding about your goals – for the summer internship program.

**In the Workplace**

- You personalize letters and e-mails to clients every day, providing company services.

**In Your Community**

- You write a letter of support for a grant proposal to open a high school health clinic.

When have you already prepared workplace writing? In what situations might you do so in the future?

## Guidelines for Writing in the Workplace

Good workplace writing succeeds in achieving a clear purpose. When you write to a business, your writing represents you; when you write as part of your job, your writing represents your company as well.

## Know Your Purpose

Your purpose, or reason for writing, helps you select and arrange information; it sets a standard for measuring your final draft. Most likely you will want to create a certain response in your readers.

---

**DISCOVERY CHECKLIST**

- ☐ Do you want to inform – announce something, update others, explain some specialized knowledge, or reply to a request?
- ☐ Do you want to motivate some action – get a question answered, a wrong corrected, a decision made, or a personnel director to hire you?
- ☐ When your readers are finished reading what you've written, what do you want them to think? What do you want them to do?

---

## Keep Your Audience in Mind

For an interactive Learning by Doing activity on Considering Job Advertisements, go to Ch. 17: **bedfordstmartins.com/bedguide**.

Consider all your workplace writing from your audience's point of view. If you don't know the person to whom you are writing, make educated guesses based on what you know about the position or company. Your purpose is not to express your ideas but to have readers act on them, even if the action is simply to notice your grasp of the situation. To motivate, focus on how "you, the reader" will benefit instead of what "I, the writer" would like.

| | |
|---|---|
| "I" ATTITUDE | Please send me the form so I can process your order. |
| "YOU" ATTITUDE | To make sure that you receive your shipment promptly, please send me the order form. |

---

**DISCOVERY CHECKLIST**

- ☐ What do your readers already know about the subject? Are they experts in the field? Have they been kept up to date on the situation?
- ☐ What do your readers need to know? What information do they expect you to provide? What do they need before they can take action?
- ☐ What can you assume about your readers' priorities and expectations? Will they expect a clear, efficient overview or detailed background?
- ☐ What is most likely to motivate readers to take the action you want?

---

## Use an Appropriate Tone

Tone is the quality of writing that reveals your attitude toward your topic and your readers. If you show readers that you respect them, they are far more likely to view you and your message favorably. Most workplace writing today ranges from the informal to the slightly formal. Gone are extremely formal phrases such as *enclosed herewith*, or *pursuant to the stated request*. At the other extreme, slang, or a casual, overly friendly style might cast doubts on your credibility. Strive for a relaxed and conversational style, using simple sentences and familiar words.

Observe business etiquette in courteous writing. If you have a complaint, recall that your reader may not have caused the problem—and courtesy is more likely than sarcasm or insults to motivate help. When delivering bad news, remember that your reader may interpret a bureaucratic response as unsympathetic. And if you have made a mistake, acknowledge it.

**REVISION CHECKLIST**

- ☐ Have you avoided slang terms and extremely casual language?
- ☐ Have you avoided unnecessarily formal or sophisticated words?
- ☐ Are your sentences of a manageable length?
- ☐ Have you used the active voice ("I am sending it") rather than the passive voice ("It is being sent")?
- ☐ Does anything you've written sound blaming or accusatory?
- ☐ Do you hear a friendly, considerate, competent person behind your words?
- ☐ Have you asked someone else to read your writing to check for tone?

## Present Information Carefully

For sample business documents, see the figures later in this chapter. For more on adding visuals and formatting job applications, see the Quick Format Guide beginning on p. A-1.

In business, time is money: time wasted reading poorly written material is money wasted. Organize so that readers can move through your writing quickly and easily. Make the topic absolutely clear from the beginning, usually in the first paragraph of a letter or the subject line of a memo or e-mail message. Use the conventional format that readers expect (see Figures 17.4 and 17.6 later in this chapter). Break information into easily processed chunks; order these chunks logically and consistently. Finally, use topic sentences and headings (when appropriate) to label each chunk of information and to give readers an overview of your document.

**REVISION CHECKLIST**

For more revising and editing strategies, see Ch. 23.

- ☐ Have you kept your letter, memo, or résumé to a page or two?
- ☐ Have you cut all unnecessary or wordy explanations?

- ☐ Have you scrutinized every word to ensure that it can't be misinterpreted? Have you supplied all the background information readers need?
- ☐ Have you emphasized the most important part of your message? Will readers know what you want them to do?
- ☐ Have you followed a consistent, logical order and a conventional format?
- ☐ If appropriate, have you included labels and headings?

# E-mail

Because *e-mail* is so easy, speedy, and convenient, it dominates business communication. Communication advances—such as texting and tweeting—may simplify quick exchanges and arrangements. On the other hand, traditional letters and memos may still be preferred for formal, official correspondence. However, e-mail messages easily meet traditional needs because they can be (1) transmitted within organizations (like memos) or between them and other parties (like letters), (2) printed or stored electronically (like permanent file copies), (3) written with standard components and length (like traditional memos or letters), or (4) used to cover transmittals (with formal reports, memos, or other documents attached).

E-mail's conversational quality also necessitates professional caution. Although regular correspondents may write informally and overlook each other's quirks, your e-mail messages are part of your company's official record and have no guarantee of privacy. Without warning, your confidential exchange can be intercepted, reviewed by others, forwarded to other computers, distributed electronically, or printed.

## Format for E-mail

E-mail headings are predetermined by your system and typically follow memo format: *To:*, *cc:*, *Subject:*, and an automatic *From:* line with your name as sender. Write messages that readers find helpful, efficient, and courteous.

- Use a clear subject line to simplify replying and archiving.
- Move promptly to your purpose: state what you need and when.
- Be concise, adding headings and space between sections if needed.
- Follow company practice as you include or delete a trail of replies.
- Observe company etiquette in copying messages to others.
- Avoid personal statements, humor, or informality that might undermine your professional credibility.

# Résumés and Application Letters

The most important business correspondence you write may be the résumé and letter you use to apply for a job. In any economic climate – but especially in a weak one with reduced job prospects – your materials need to be carefully developed and crafted. They need to reflect as many applicable skills and experiences as possible, including your summer, campus, part-time, or full-time employment as you attend college. First, prepare for job prospects by developing opportunities systematically, well before graduation:

- Turn to campus career services as well as local library or community resources to investigate job opportunities and career strategies.
- Consider internships or volunteer posts relevant to your goals.
- Attend preprofessional or career-oriented workshops or gatherings.
- Network with workplace and professional contacts to learn about your future options and prospects.

Remain flexible, too. Instead of looking only for the single job title you want, consider what other experiences might build your skills on your way to that job. For example, if you are in a public health program and want to join a major city health department, by all means gain expertise so you can pursue that job despite the city's recent budget cutbacks. But also consider rural or statewide positions, hospital outreach, companies with employee health programs, or the growing field of senior care. Take advantage of serendipity – the surprise that offers a new or unexpected option.

Finally, as opportunities arise, apply your college writing experience to the workplace in order to draft and revise effectively. Direct, persuasive, correct prose can help you stand out from the crowd.

## Résumés

For more on résumé format and another student sample, see the Quick Format Guide beginning on p. A-1.

In a résumé, you present yourself as someone qualified to excel at a job and be an asset to the organization. Job seekers often have copies of a single résumé on hand, but you may want to customize yours for each application if you can easily print attractive copies. Either way, keep it to one page unless you have extensive relevant work experience.

A résumé is highly formatted but allows many decisions about style, organization, and appearance. A typical résumé consists of a heading and labeled sections that detail experience and qualifications. Highlight labels with underlining, boldface, or larger type. Within a section, use brief, pointed phrases and clauses, not complete sentences. Use action verbs (*supervised, ordered, maintained*) and active voice whenever possible. Arrange information to please the eye; use the best paper and clearest printer you can. (See Figure 17.1.)

For electronic applications, you may need a résumé in several forms: a text file for attaching to an e-mail, an electronically readable version for a company to scan into its database, or a Web version for posting on your

**Figure 17.1**
Conventional Résumé

Centers heading with contact information

**Anne Cahill**
402 Pigeon Hill Road
Windsor, CT 06095
(860) 555-5763
acahill783@yahoo.com

---

Labels sections

**Objective** Position as Registered Nurse in pediatric hospital setting

**Education**

**University of Connecticut**, Storrs, CT. Bachelor of Science, Major in nursing, May 2013. GPA: 3.5; licensed as Registered Nurse by the State of Connecticut in June 2013

**Manchester Community Technical College**, Manchester, CT. Associate degree in occupational therapy, May 2007. GPA: 3.3.

Specifies background and experience

**Work Experience**

*9/08–present* **Certified Occupational Therapy Assistant**, Johnson Memorial Hospital, Stafford Springs, CT
- Assist children with delayed motor development and cerebral palsy to develop skills for the activities of daily life

*9/06–9/08* **Nursing Assistant**, Woodlake Healthcare Center, Tolland, CT
- Helped geriatric residents with activities of daily living
- Assisted nursing staff in treating acute care patients

Places current information first

*9/04–9/06* **Cashier**, Stop and Shop Supermarket, Vernon, CT
- Trained newly hired cashiers

**Clinical Internships**

**St. Francis Hospital**, Hartford, CT
- Student Nurse, Maternity and Postpartum, spring 2013

**Hartford Hospital**, Hartford, CT
- Student Nurse, Pediatrics, fall 2012

**Visiting Nurse and Community Health**, Mansfield, CT
- Student Nurse, Community, spring 2012

**Manchester General Hospital**, Manchester, CT
- Student Nurse, Medical-Surgical, fall 2011

**Computer Skills**
- Proficient with Microsoft Office, Database, and Windows applications and electronic records
- Experienced with Internet research

Adds relevant skills for health-care record keeping

**Activities**
- Student Union Board of Governors, University of Connecticut, class representative
- Intramural soccer

**References** Available upon request

**Figure 17.2** Résumé for the Web

Uses clear and direct heading

Organizes menu of available information

Creates professional Web design using bullets, color, and white space

# Anne Cahill

**Objective:** **Position as a Registered Nurse in pediatric hospital setting**

- Education
- Experience
- Other Activities
- References
- Contact Me

## Profile

New nursing graduate combines proficiency in the latest nursing techniques with significant clinical experience

- Experienced in providing professional, compassionate health-care services to children, others
- Able to work proficiently and productively in hospital settings
- Accustomed to working in a team with a broad range of health professionals and administrators
- Proficient with Microsoft Office, Database, and Windows applications, with electronic records, and with Internet research

site or a job site (see Figure 17.2). Format these versions carefully so that recipients can easily read what you supply. Turn to your campus career center for résumé samples and advice about alternate formats.

**Heading.** The heading is generally centered (or otherwise pleasingly aligned) on the page with separate lines for your name; street address, city, state, and zip code; phone number; and e-mail address.

**Employment Objective.** This optional section allows personnel officers to see at a glance your priorities and goals. Try to sound confident and eager but not pompous or presumptuous.

**Education.** This section is almost always included, often first. Specify each postsecondary school you've attended, your major, your date of graduation (or expected graduation), and your grade point average (if it reflects well on you). You can also add any awards, honors, or relevant course work.

**Experience.** In this key section, list each job, most recent first. You can include full- and part-time jobs. For each, name the organization, your position, your responsibilities, and the dates you held the job. Describe any involvement in unusual projects or responsibility for major developments. Highlight details that show relevant work experience and leadership ability. Minimize information unrelated to the job you're seeking.

**Skills.** List any special skills (data processing, technical drawing, multiple languages) that aren't obvious from your education and work experience.

**Activities.** You can specify either professional interests and activities (*Member of Birmingham Bricklayers Association*) or personal pursuits (*skiing, hiking, needlepoint*) showing that you are dedicated and well-rounded.

**References.** If a job advertisement requests references, provide them. Always contact your references in advance to make sure they are willing to give you a good recommendation. For each person, list the name, his or her organization and position, and the organization's address and phone number. If references have not been requested, you can simply note "Available on request."

As you prepare your résumé, and possibly your professional Web site, also consider your electronic trail and workplace etiquette. A future employer may well assume that anything you write at work is company correspondence, without personal rights to privacy, and that anywhere you travel online at work will represent or be subsidized by the company. That same employer is unlikely to be amused by your confessional Facebook page or your party photos. Though you might consider social-networking materials personal, they may seem very public to an employer who checks your background and your credibility. Your electronic presence should correspond with the reliable-future-employee presence you wish to project.

## Application Letters

When writing a letter applying for a job, follow all the guidelines for other business letters. As you compete against others, your letter and résumé are all the employer has to judge you on. Your immediate objective is to obtain an interview, so read any advertisement critically.

For general guidelines for business letters, see pp. 361–64. For more on letter format and another sample, see the Quick Format Guide beginning on p. A-1.

- What qualifications are listed? Ideally, you should have them all. If you lack one, try to find something in your background that compensates, some similar experience in a different form.
- What else can you tell about the organization or position from the ad? How does the organization represent itself? (Check its Web site.)
- How does the ad describe the ideal candidate? As a team player? A dynamic individual? If you feel that you are the person this organization is seeking, portray yourself this way in your letter.

**Figure 17.3**
Application Letter

Follows standard letter format

Addresses specific person

Identifies job sought and describes interest

Explains qualifications

Confirms interest and supplies contact information

Encloses résumé and proof of certification

402 Pigeon Hill Road
Windsor, CT 06095
July 8, 2013

Sheryl Sullivan
Director of Nursing
Center for Children's Health and Development
St. Francis Hospital and Medical Center
114 Woodland Street
Hartford, CT 06105

Dear Ms. Sullivan:

I am writing to apply for the full-time position as a pediatric nurse at the Center for Children's Health and Development at St. Francis Hospital, which was advertised on the Eastern Connecticut Health Network Web site. I feel that my varied clinical experiences and my desire to work with children ideally suit me for the job. In addition, I am highly motivated to grow and succeed in the field of health care.

For the past five years, I have worked as a certified occupational therapy assistant. In this capacity, I help children with delayed motor function acquire the skills necessary to achieve as high a level of independence as possible. While working as a COTA, I attended nursing school with the ultimate goal of becoming a pediatric nurse. My varied clinical experiences as a student nurse and my previous experience as a nurse's aide in a geriatric center have exposed me to many types of care. I feel that these experiences have helped me to become a well-rounded caregiver.

I believe that I would be a strong addition to the medical team at the Children's Center. My clinical experiences have prepared me to deal with a wide range of situations. In addition, I am dedicated to maintaining and enhancing the well-being of children. I am enclosing proof of my recent certification as a Registered Nurse in the state of Connecticut. Please write to me at the address above, e-mail me at acahill783@yahoo.com, or call me at (860) 555-5763. Thank you for your consideration. I look forward to hearing from you.

Sincerely,

*Anne Cahill*

Anne Cahill

Enclosures

Your letter should spark your readers' interest, convince them you're qualified, and motivate them to interview you. If possible, address your letter to the person who screens applicants and sets up interviews; you may need to call the organization to find out this person's name. In the first paragraph, identify the job, indicate how you heard about it, and summarize your qualifications. In the second paragraph, expand on your qualifications, highlighting key information on your résumé. Add details if necessary to show that you're a better candidate than others. In the third paragraph, restate your interest in the job, ask for an interview, and let your prospective employer know how to reach you. (See Figure 17.3.) If you get an interview, follow up with a thank-you note. The note may reemphasize your qualifications and strong interest in the position.

### Learning by Doing Planning a Job Application

Look for a job advertisement for a position or in a field that might interest you. Check the newspaper, a professional publication, or an organization's Web site. First, analyze the ad to identify what type of applicant it seeks, noting qualifications, experience, ambitions, or other expectations. Then list the kind of information an applicant might supply in response. Discuss your analysis with a classmate or small group to see whether your interpretations match.

## Business Letters

To correspond with outside individuals or groups, organizations use business letters to request and provide information, motivate action, respond to requests, and sell goods and services. Because letters become part of a permanent record, they can be checked later to determine exactly who said what and when. Keep a copy and back up every letter you write.

A good business letter is brief—limited to one page if possible. It supplies what the reader needs, no more. A letter of inquiry might simply request a booklet, sample, or promotional piece. A special request might add why you are writing, what you need, and when you need it. On the other hand, a letter of complaint focuses on your problem—what product is involved, when and where you purchased it, why you are unhappy, and how you'd like the problem solved. Include specifics such as product numbers and dates, and maintain a courteous tone. Because they are so brief, business letters are often judged on details—format, appearance, openings, closings.

### Format for Business Letters

The format of business letters (see Figure 17.4) is established by convention.

- Use 8½-by-11-inch bond paper, with matching envelopes. Write on only one side of the page.
- Single-space and use an extra line of space to separate paragraphs and the different elements of the letter. In very short letters, it's acceptable to leave additional space before the inside address.

- Leave margins of at least one inch on both sides; try to make the top and bottom margins fairly even, although you may have a larger bottom margin if your letter is very short.
- Pay attention to grammar, punctuation, spelling, and mechanics. Your readers will.

**Return Address.** This is your address or the address of the company for which you are writing. Abbreviate only the state using its two-letter postal abbreviation. Omit a return address on preprinted letterhead stationery.

**Date.** Supply this on the line right after the return address. Spell out the month; follow it by the day, a comma, and the year.

**Inside Address.** This is the address of the person to whom you are writing. Begin with the person's full name and title (*Mr.*, *Ms.*, *Dr.*, *Professor*); when addressing a woman without a professional title, use *Ms.* unless you know that she prefers *Miss* or *Mrs.* The second line should identify the position the person holds, and the third line should name the organization. If you don't know your reader, start with the name of the position, department, or organization. Avoid abbreviations except for the state.

**Salutation.** Skip a line. Then type *Dear* followed by the person's title and last name (*Dear Dr. Diaz*). If you don't know who will read your letter, use that person's position (*Dear Editor*) or organization (*Dear Angell's Bakery*) in place of a name. End with a colon.

**Body.** Present your message. Leave one line of space between paragraphs; begin each paragraph even with the left margin (no indentations). Paragraphs should generally be no longer than seven or eight typed lines.

**Closing.** Leave one line of space after the last paragraph, and then use a conventional closing followed by a comma: *Sincerely, Sincerely yours, Respectfully yours, Yours truly.*

**Typed Name with Position.** Leave four lines of space after the closing, and type your name in full, even if you will sign only your first name. Do not include a title before your name. If you are writing on behalf of an organization, you can include your position on the next line. You may add your e-mail address or telephone number here unless already supplied.

**Signature.** Print the letter, and sign your name in the space above the typed name. Unless you have a personal relationship with the recipient, use both your first and last names. Do not include a title before your name.

**Abbreviations at End.** Leave at least two lines of space between your typed name and any abbreviations used to communicate more about the letter. Put each abbreviation on a separate line. If you send a copy to someone other than the recipient, use *cc:* followed by the name of the person or organization receiving a copy. If the letter is accompanied by another document in the same envelope, use *Enc.* or *Enclosure*. If the letter has been typed by someone else, the writer's initials are capitalized, followed by a slash and the typist's initials in lowercase format: *VW/dbw*.

**Modified and Full Block Style.** To format a letter using *modified block style* (see Figure 17.4), imagine a line running down the center of the page from

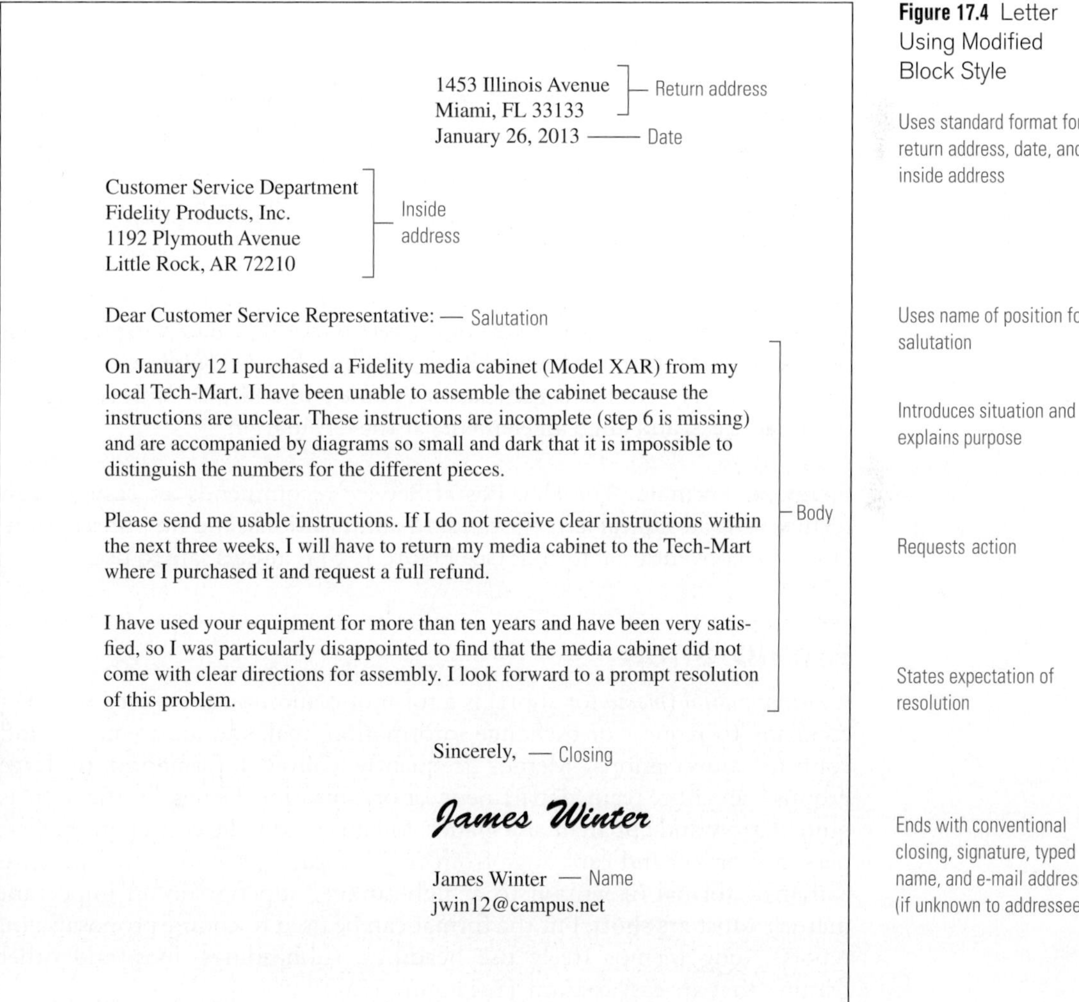
1453 Illinois Avenue
Miami, FL 33133
January 26, 2013

Customer Service Department
Fidelity Products, Inc.
1192 Plymouth Avenue
Little Rock, AR 72210

Dear Customer Service Representative:

On January 12 I purchased a Fidelity media cabinet (Model XAR) from my local Tech-Mart. I have been unable to assemble the cabinet because the instructions are unclear. These instructions are incomplete (step 6 is missing) and are accompanied by diagrams so small and dark that it is impossible to distinguish the numbers for the different pieces.

Please send me usable instructions. If I do not receive clear instructions within the next three weeks, I will have to return my media cabinet to the Tech-Mart where I purchased it and request a full refund.

I have used your equipment for more than ten years and have been very satisfied, so I was particularly disappointed to find that the media cabinet did not come with clear directions for assembly. I look forward to a prompt resolution of this problem.

Sincerely,

James Winter

James Winter
jwin12@campus.net



**Figure 17.4** Letter Using Modified Block Style

Uses standard format for return address, date, and inside address

Uses name of position for salutation

Introduces situation and explains purpose

Requests action

States expectation of resolution

Ends with conventional closing, signature, typed name, and e-mail address (if unknown to addressee)

**Figure 17.5** Envelope Formats

U.S. Postal Service format

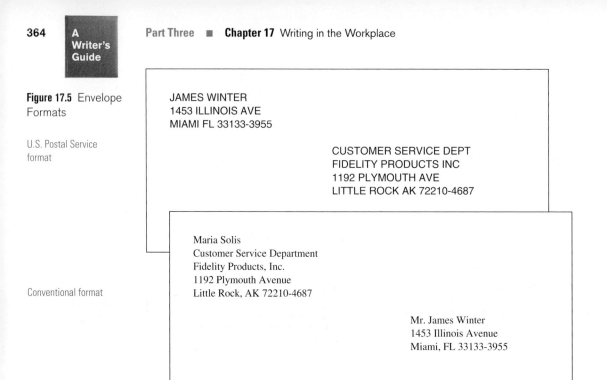

JAMES WINTER
1453 ILLINOIS AVE
MIAMI FL 33133-3955

CUSTOMER SERVICE DEPT
FIDELITY PRODUCTS INC
1192 PLYMOUTH AVE
LITTLE ROCK AK 72210-4687

Conventional format

Maria Solis
Customer Service Department
Fidelity Products, Inc.
1192 Plymouth Avenue
Little Rock, AK 72210-4687

Mr. James Winter
1453 Illinois Avenue
Miami, FL 33133-3955

top to bottom. Align the left side of the return address, date, closing, signature, and your typed name with this center line. Use *full block style* on letterhead stationery with the organization's name and address. Omit typing the return address, and align all elements at the left margin.

**Envelope Formats.** The U.S. Postal Service recommends an easy-to-scan format with all capital letters, standard abbreviations, and no punctuation. However, conventional format (see Figure 17.5) is always safe to use.

## Memoranda

A *memorandum* (*memo* for short) is a form of communication used within a company to request or exchange information, make announcements, and confirm conversations. Memos frequently convey information to large groups—an entire team, department, or organization. Generally, the topic is quite narrow and apparent at a glance. Memos tend to be written in the first person (*I* or *we*) and can range from very informal (if written to a peer) to extremely formal (if written to a high-ranking superior on an important matter). Most are short, but the format can be used to convey proposals and reports; long memos freely use headings, subheadings, lists, and other features that are easy to skim. (See Figure 17.6.)

**Figure 17.6**
Memorandum

INTERLINK SYSTEMS, INC.

To: All Employees
From: Erica Xiang *EX*
Subject: Changes in employee benefits
Date: October 26, 2013

*Uses standard format to identify readers, writer, topic, and date*

Each fall the Human Resources group looks closely at the company's health insurance benefits to make certain that we are providing an excellent level of coverage in a way that makes economic sense. To that end, we have made some changes to our plan, effective January 1, 2014. Let me outline the three major changes.

*Explains purpose, noting reader's priorities*

*Previews clear organization in blocks*

1. We are pleased to be able to offer employees the opportunity, through a **Flexible Spending Account**, to pay for dependent care and unreimbursed health expenses on a pre-tax basis, a feature that can result in considerable savings. I have attached a summary and will provide more information on this benefit at our staff meeting tomorrow, October 27, at 10:30 A.M. I will be available immediately after the meeting to answer any specific questions.

*Uses friendly tone to note new benefit for employees*

*Offers assistance*

2. Those of you who have taken advantage of our **vision care benefit** in the past know that it offers significant help in paying for eye exams, eyeglasses, and contact lenses. The current plan will change slightly on January 1. Employees and covered dependents will be eligible to receive up to $50 each year toward the cost of a routine eye exam and up to $100 every two years toward the cost of eyeglasses or contact lenses. If you see a provider within our health insurance network, you will pay only $10 per office visit.

*Introduces benefit change with positive background*

3. We at Interlink Systems feel strongly that our health insurance benefits are excellent, but as you know, the cost of such plans continues to rise every year. In the interest of maintaining excellent coverage for our employees, we will raise our **employee contribution**. Starting January 1, we are asking employees with single coverage to contribute $12.50 more per pay period toward the cost of medical insurance, and employees who cover dependents to contribute $40 more per pay period. Even with this increase, the amount the company asks its employees to contribute towards the premiums (about 8%) is significantly less than the nationwide average of 30%.

*Presents increased cost carefully, noting coverage quality and high employer contribution*

Please contact me if you have questions or concerns about the changes that I have outlined in this memo. You can reach me at x462 or at exiang@interlink.net.

*Offers more help and supplies contact information*

Enclosure

*Notes enclosure*

### Format for Memoranda

Although every organization has its own format for memos, the heading generally consists of a series of lines with clear labels (followed by colons).

| | |
|---|---|
| Date: | (date on which memo is sent) |
| To: | (person or persons to whom it is primarily addressed) |
| cc: | (names of anyone else who receives a copy) |
| From: | (name of the writer) |
| Subject: *or* Re: | (concise, accurate statement of the memo's topic) |

The subject line often determines whether a memo is read. (The old-fashioned abbreviation *Re:* for *regarding* is still used, but we recommend the more common *Subject.*) Accurately sum up the topic in a few words ("Agenda for 12/10 meeting," "Sales estimates for new product line").

## Brochures and Presentation Visuals

For more on understanding visuals, see Ch. 14.

When you design a workplace brochure, presentation slide, or other visual document, you write the text and also direct a reader's attention using tools such as type options, lists, white space, headings, repetition, and color.

### Format for Brochures

Although workplace brochures do not follow a specific format, artists and designers aim to attract readers' attention by making important elements prominent. Consider Figure 17.7, for example, which shows two of six panels of a student-designed brochure. The image of the mannequin on the brochure's cover immediately draws the eye, but the pattern of light guides readers to the central question: "Is your life out of control?" Other words on the left panel (such as "broken," "stuck," "lost," and "depressed") serve as a suggestive backdrop, but there is no mistaking the main message.

Providing a prominent element helps your readers focus on what you or your organization thinks is most important. First ask, "What is the main message I want to get across?" Then think of ways to give that message prominence. For example, you might want to surround one large headline by significant space, as in the left panel of the brochure. Note in the right panel how the headings—all questions, parallel in form—appear in color, separated by white space so the breaks between topics are clear. The inside panels of the brochure respond to these questions, pointing readers toward helpful resources.

For more on parallel structure, see B2 (p. A-52) in the Quick Editing Guide.

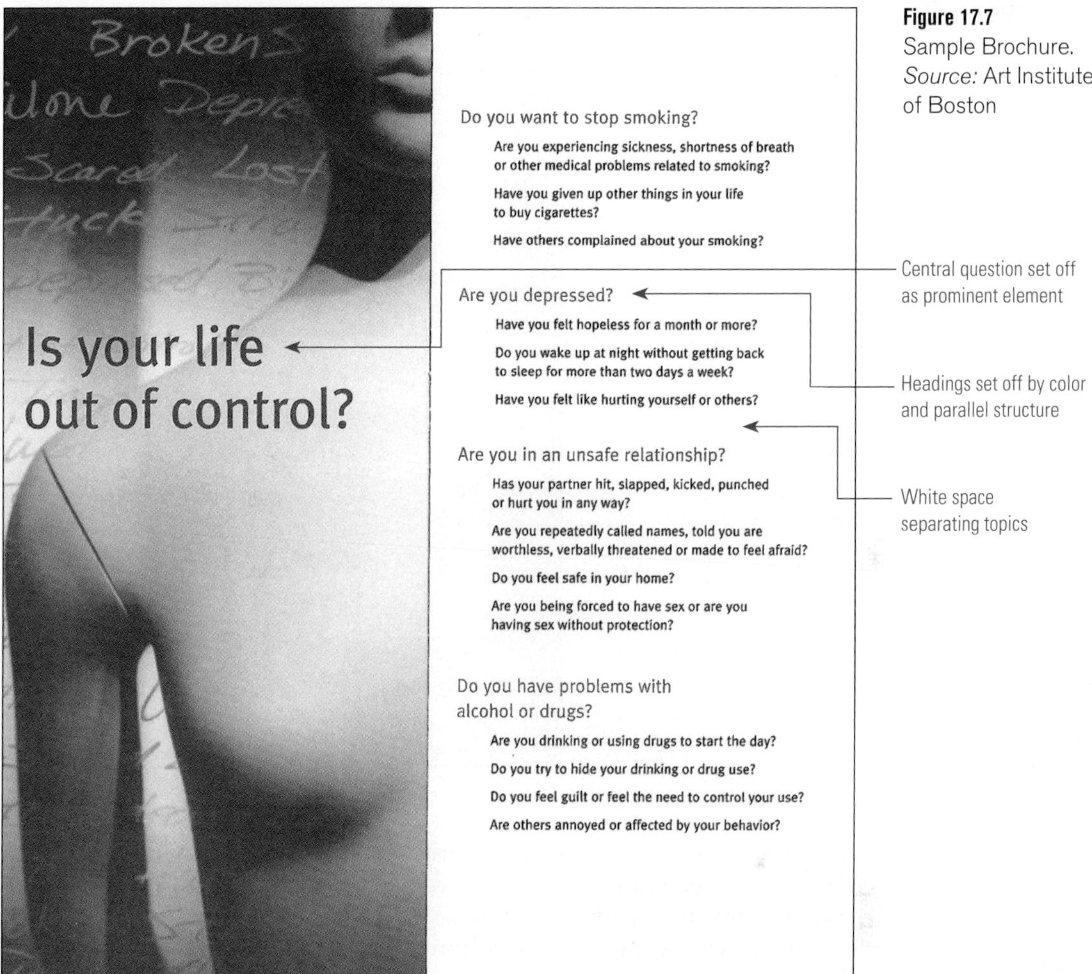

Is your life
out of control?
Do you want to stop smoking?
Are you experiencing sickness, shortness of breath or other medical problems related to smoking?
Have you given up other things in your life to buy cigarettes?
Have others complained about your smoking?
Are you depressed?
Have you felt hopeless for a month or more?
Do you wake up at night without getting back to sleep for more than two days a week?
Have you felt like hurting yourself or others?
Are you in an unsafe relationship?
Has your partner hit, slapped, kicked, punched or hurt you in any way?
Are you repeatedly called names, told you are worthless, verbally threatened or made to feel afraid?
Do you feel safe in your home?
Are you being forced to have sex or are you having sex without protection?
Do you have problems with alcohol or drugs?
Are you drinking or using drugs to start the day?
Do you try to hide your drinking or drug use?
Do you feel guilt or feel the need to control your use?
Are others annoyed or affected by your behavior?
Central question set off as prominent element
Headings set off by color and parallel structure
White space separating topics


**Figure 17.7** Sample Brochure. *Source:* Art Institute of Boston

## Format for Presentation Visuals

Effective use of space is important in visuals—such as PowerPoint or other presentation slides. Providing ample space and limiting the text on each slide helps readers absorb your major points. The slide in Figure 17.8 for recruiting service learning participants has too much text, making it hard to read and potentially distracting. In contrast, Figure 17.9 has less text and more open space, making each point easier to read. Its bullets highlight the

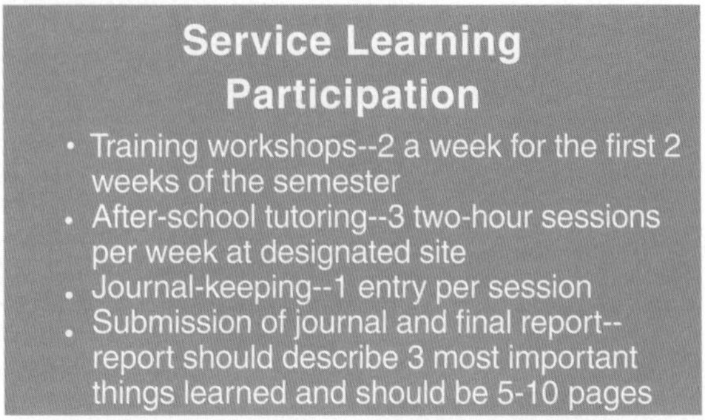

**Figure 17.8** Presentation Slide with Too Much Text and Too Little Space

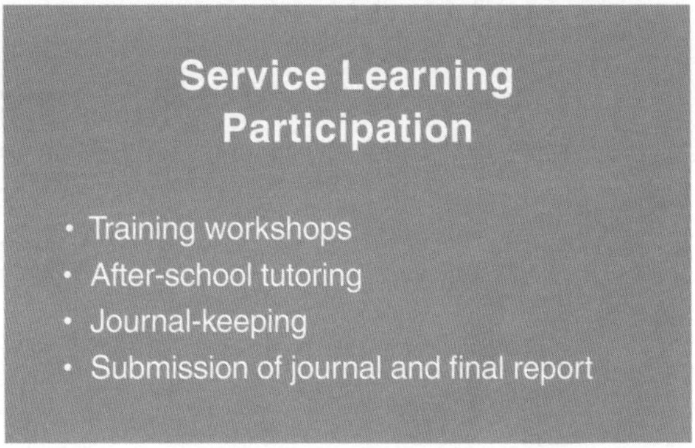

**Service Learning Participation**

- Training workshops--2 a week for the first 2 weeks of the semester
- After-school tutoring--3 two-hour sessions per week at designated site
- Journal-keeping--1 entry per session
- Submission of journal and final report--report should describe 3 most important things learned and should be 5-10 pages

**Figure 17.9** Presentation Slide with Brief Text and Effective Use of Space

**Service Learning Participation**

- Training workshops
- After-school tutoring
- Journal-keeping
- Submission of journal and final report

main points, meant only to summarize major issues and themes. The type sizes for the slides are large enough to be viewed: 44 points for the heading and 32 points for the body.

Finally, the "white space" without text in these slides is actually blue. Some public-speaking experts believe that black type on a white background can be too stark; instead, they recommend a dark blue background with yellow or white type. Others believe that black on white is fine and may be what the audience is used to. Presentation software makes it easy to experiment with these options or to use your employer's templates.

## Additional Writing Assignments

1. Use the job advertisement you located for the activity on page 361, or find one that interests you for immediate or future employment. Write your letter of application for this job, following the advice in this chapter.

For another sample letter, see p. A-19.

2. Prepare a current résumé, designed as your standard print version or tailored to a specific job. Follow the advice and format explained in this chapter.

For another sample résumé, see p. A-18.

3. Prepare your own example of a workplace document introduced in this chapter. After you have drafted, revised, and edited it, print a second copy. In its margins add notes to point out features of its format and content. Revise your document and the notes if you wish.
4. **Source Assignment.** Working individually or collaboratively with a small group, investigate the job-hunting or career advice available on campus or in your local community. Identify what you or users might want to learn about these resources (such as how to access or use them). Prepare a brief report on your findings for fellow students interested in using such resources productively.
5. **Source Assignment.** Interview a personnel manager or another person who hires people in your field of interest. Prepare by developing a brief set of questions about issues of interest to you – what kinds of jobs are typically available, how the selection process works, what background is typically required or desired, how students might prepare for employment, what tips the person would give job-seekers, or similar matters. After the interview, write an essay reporting what you have learned to other interested students. Also write a brief business letter thanking the person you interviewed.

For more about conducting an interview, see Ch. 6.

6. **Visual Assignment.** Select two or three workplace Web sites for close examination. Analyze how—and how well—each represents its corporate, small business, professional, or other workplace to visitors. Adapt the guidelines for workplace writing (pp. 352–55), and use them as criteria to evaluate the site's purpose, audience, tone, and presentation.

# PART FOUR

# A WRITER'S STRATEGIES

# 18 Strategies: A Case Study

For Erin's assignment, see Chapter 4: "Recalling a Personal Experience." For more on writing processes, see Chs. 19–23.

When Erin Schmitt enrolled in Rhetoric and Composition I, her first major college assignment was to write an essay reflecting on a personal experience. She needed to pick a specific experience that she could convey to her readers. Then she needed to reflect on its significance to show why it mattered to her. In this chapter, you can follow her writing processes as she generates ideas, develops her first draft, gathers responses from readers, revises and edits her draft, and writes a reflective letter to accompany the essay in her writing portfolio.

Erin Schmitt

Use the questions in the margin to help you develop your own essay alongside Erin.

## Generating Ideas

Erin thought back over her experiences before entering college. She had studied hard to get into college, knowing how important her high school record was for both admissions and financial aid. Although lots of students shared the stress of worrying about grades or money or both, she didn't think that she could narrow those issues to a notable experience. Then she thought about her last day at her job assisting an elderly man and the compelling recognition she had had just before she came to campus. She started mapping these recollections in the diagram on page 373.

What significant experience do you recall that might engage your readers?

When Erin finished her diagram, she felt confident that she had remembered a significant event and that she could make a compelling point about it. To fill out her ideas, she also answered the six reporter's questions.

Who: Mr. Hertli; me

What: Increased appreciation of life

When: While reading an atlas the last time I assisted Mr. Hertli

Where: Mr. Hertli's literature-crammed office/study

Why: Mr. Hertli's blindness

How: Asked to read atlas → confusion → saw child in old, blind Mr. Hertli → appreciation of life

How might you generate ideas about your recollections?

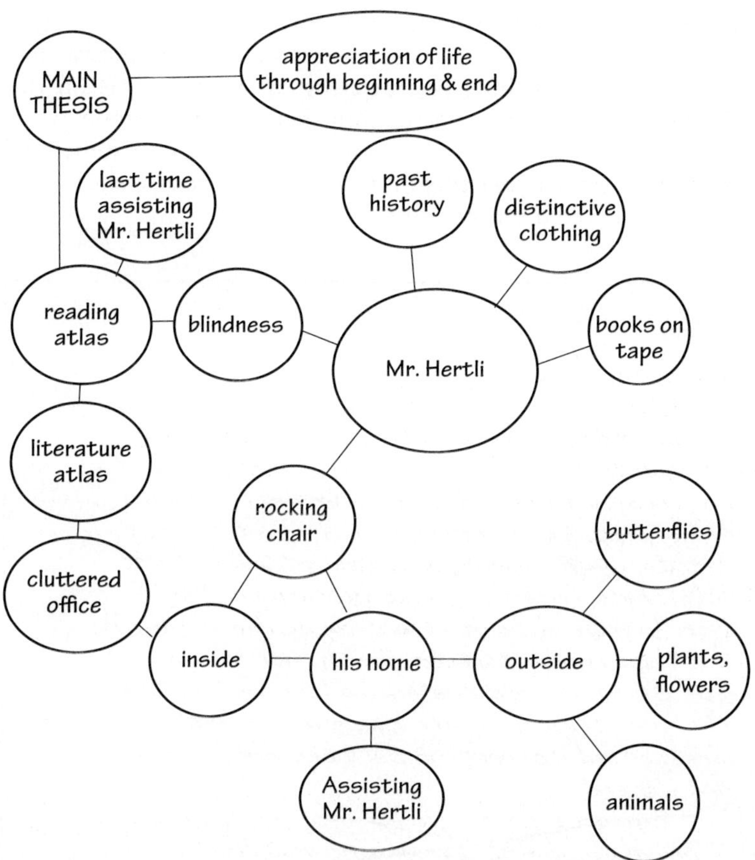


For more information and journal questions about the Part Four photograph, see the last two pages of the Appendices.

Erin was confident that she had discovered something meaningful to write about. She wanted to share her reflection about life's connections with readers. She thought that she could focus on it as a main idea or thesis to shape her essay. After working for Mr. Hertli for a long time, she could remember plenty of vivid details to bring her experience to life for readers and could see how her whole paper might fall into place.

What do you think is the importance of your experience?

## Planning, Drafting, and Developing

When Erin looked over her notes, she realized that she could easily organize her ideas in a logical sequence: first introduce the experience and its importance, next present events in chronological order as they had happened, and then return to their importance.

Assisting Mr. Hertli → Last time assisting Mr. Hertl → Reading atlas → Young and old → Appreciation of life

What organization would suit your needs?

Once Erin had a rough structure for her essay, she was ready to start developing her ideas. Between classes, she started drafting her first version by hand, following her plan but concentrating on getting ideas on the page. She crossed out false starts, including her original second paragraph. She inserted words as she thought of them and crossed some out. After all, she didn't care whether this draft was messy because she would clean it up when she keyed it on the computer.

How are you starting your draft? What process works for you?

Erin Schmitt
1st Draft

In order to fully appreciate something, to realize its value, one often must experience its beginning and its end. For example, to learn and appreciate all the material in a textbook chapter, ~~inst~~ reading and understanding must take place from the introduction to the conclusion. A book is not enjoyable if you do not read from start to finish, nor is a movie cut short before the ending is revealed. ~~The~~ My appreciation of life came in a most unexpected connection between ~~my~~ life's beginning and its end.

~~Beginning In my junior year of high school, I began to assist a man who had lost nearly all his sight to macular degeneration. Mr. Hertli~~

For Peer Response questions for Erin's assignment, see p. 72.

Erin typed her rough draft, including all her handwritten changes, to get it ready for other readers. She and her classmates were going to exchange papers during a workshop for peer response. Erin expected her classmates to ask about anything that wasn't clear and to respond to the peer response questions for the assignment. Erin also wanted their advice about her own questions:

- Is the scene I'm recalling clear? Does it come alive when you read it?
- Do I reflect enough? Should I add more about my insight?

What do you want to ask your readers?

Erin's instructor also required a conference about the draft to discuss revisions that might improve the final version. Erin expected her suggestions to concentrate on the criteria for the assignment: a clear experience with reflection about its significance for the writer. Both sets of comments—handwritten notes and highlighting from a fellow student and electronic "balloons" from her instructor—are shown next to Erin's rough draft.

## Rough Draft with Peer and Instructor Responses

Would any of the general comments about Erin's draft also apply to your draft?

Peer: You got the reflection part started right away.

1 In order to fully appreciate something, to realize its value, one often must experience its beginning and its end. For example, to learn and appreciate all the material in a textbook chapter, reading and understanding must take place from the introduction to the conclusion. A book is not enjoyable if you do not read from start to finish, nor is a movie cut short before the ending is revealed. My appreciation of life came in a most unexpected connection between life's beginning and its end.

**Instructor:** Good idea to draw readers in with analogies.

Peer: I highlighted ow you arranged the details to lead s into the house. Good progression. can really see the scene here.

2 Mr. Hertli was a brilliant old Swiss man whom I assisted every week for the last two years of my high school career. He lived 25 minutes away from my home, down a winding road surrounded by trees, grazing horses, and the occasional house. Trees arched over his steep driveway, as if bowing to all who enter, welcoming anyone with insight, help, or simply company. Mr. Hertli's house was of a very traditional build, and was surrounded by nature. Goats fed on grasses and horses galloped and played within a fenced-off grazing area. Ducks swam on a pond and dozens of sun-colored butterflies danced around bunches of tall purple flowers between which a few stepping-stones were nestled, as a walkway to the front door.

**Instructor:** Effective visual details here.

eer: I like how you d up to him. You ven got his history with the shoes!

3 Inside sat Mr. Hertli, always rocking in a chair and listening to books-on-tape in one of the various languages familiar to him. He was very tall, thin, and elderly, and wore dress slacks and a suit jacket no matter what the occasion. His leather shoes were obviously very old, and showed scuffs and wear which told stories of Switzerland, war, research, and accomplishment. Mr. Hertli also wore very dark sunglasses morning and evening to protect the mere one or two percent of his eyesight that had not yet been stolen from him by macular degeneration.

**Instructor:** Try Edit/Find to catch repetition.

eer: The details ere end on a big oint.

eer: I could see him ¶3. Now I feel like I ow him, too.

4 Mr. Hertli was an accomplished man. He had been through immigration, served the United States in war, earned various degrees, had written a book on evolution and creationism, and was fighting for his life against a terminal lung disease. He was extremely intelligent, and it was my job to read him scientific journals and books, record information and data for his next work-in-progress, manage his correspondence, fill out paperwork, dispense his medications, and do nearly all the things a blind person can not do alone.

5 One particular day, I was assisting Mr. Hertli in his office. Crimson carpeting lined the floor of the tiny literature-crammed room. Journals and books lay sprawled on every surface, and there was barely room for a computer on a desk and two chairs somewhere in all the mess. A cord around Mr. Hertli's head fed oxygen through his nose, while the other

end trailed out the door, down the steps, and into the living room where an oxygen-dispensing machine always sat, always humming. We sorted through music, storing old German and Swiss instrumental classics on a new device for the blind which stored numerous songs, audio books, and other audio literature for playback. As we waited for the media to download into the device, Mr. Hertli inquired about recent political events concerning the country of Georgia. He desired to know the geographic location of Georgia. "Read the atlas," he said, and although I had grown to understand and love his thick European accent, I sat staring at him in bafflement at his words, which he, fortunately, could not see. I reached under a desk and pushed past books about Darwin, God, evolution, and history, and found a large, blue-covered atlas, aged by years of learning, discovery, and research. Brushing the dust off, I opened the book to the index, and searched for "Georgia." I turned to the page to which the index directed me, and unsuccessfully tried to describe Georgia's relation to Turkey, Russia, and Azerbajan. "Show me," he said. Show him! How could I, for he could not see, after all, and now I had to find a way to make him see?!

**Instructor** Does everything here support your main idea? Could you be more selective to sharpen your focus?

Peer: **The quotes are good, but the whole ¶ seems long—maybe split it? Or drop some detail?**

I placed the wide atlas across his wobbly knees, in his lap, facing him. Taking his hand, I slowly directed Mr. Hertli's finger around the perimeter of each country, saying. "This is Turkey. To the east, here is Georgia." He pointed and repeated the countries back to me, and I asserted that, yes, that was Azerbajan or Russia. 6

Peer: **Spelled right?**

It was as though I were teaching a small child, who could not read, and who did not know the least about geography. And how strange it was to be feeling such a way. After all, I was helping a well-educated, cultured man, in this most elementary, basic way. In this aged man, nearing the end of his life, I saw the character of a young boy, beginning to learn a concept new to him. 7

Peer: **When I read your draft online, my software said this was a fragment. Is it? Are fragments OK in here?**

This would be the last time I helped Mr. Hertli, as I would be beginning college just a few days later. Mr. Hertli was now completely blind. Like a mother afraid to send her child to school for the first time, I was afraid to cease my assistance of this somewhat helpless man. For when I had seen this connection—the young, new child in the old, I came to realize just how valuable life itself is. 8

Peer: **I get what you're saying, but maybe explain it more? This flat statement seems too abrupt.**

**Instructor** More reflection here on the significance

Erin also received some overall comments with suggestions for revision.

? What have your readers noted or suggested for your draft?

PEER: I really think you did a good job creating the experience. You're a very descriptive writer, and I liked being able to imagine the experience—the road, the animals, the flowers by the house. I also liked how you used contrasting paragraphs—long paragraph 5 to explain the situation and then short paragraph 6 for the outcome. (But I still think 5 might be too wordy.) You got the reflection part started at the beginning, too, so I knew you were thinking about it. I just wasn't that sure about how you ended with it. My own son traces things with his hands, so I could see what you meant about Mr. Hertli, but I expected you to explain it more. Maybe you could add here to make the conclusion stronger when you revise.

INSTRUCTOR: Erin, you've selected and developed a provocative experience that changed your thinking. However, readers need more explanation and interpretation to share the intensity of your experience. If you explained its significance more fully, your conclusion would be more compelling. I'm wondering if you're trying to find that significance by synthesizing—the reading and thinking skill we discussed in class last week. You seem to be pulling together your actual experience with Mr. Hertli and your insight about the young child who grew up to be this man in order to develop a new idea that goes beyond them. Besides strengthening your concluding reflections as you revise, look also at your fine selection of details. They enrich your description, but try to make sure that all of them are forceful and relevant.

What has your instructor suggested about your draft?

## Learning by Doing Responding as a Peer

If Erin were in your class, what questions would you want to ask her? What advice for her revision would you supply in your peer response?

## Revising and Editing

What is your revision plan for your draft?

Erin met with her peers and her instructor, collecting all the comments about her draft. To help her focus on the purpose of the essay, she reread the assignment. She decided that reflecting more would strengthen her main idea, or thesis – and her instructor had already pointed out the importance of a strong thesis in college writing.

Erin concentrated first on revising her conclusion because all her readers had suggested strengthening it. Then she went back to the beginning to make other changes, responding to comments and editing details. Erin's changes are marked in the following version of her draft. The comments in the margins point out some of her revision and editing decisions.

What changes do you want to mark in your draft?

## Revised and Edited Draft

*Oops! What about a title? Just Mr. Hertli?*

1 In order to fully appreciate something, to realize its value, one often must experience its beginning and its end. For example, to learn and appreciate all the material in a textbook chapter, reading and understanding must take place from the introduct~~ion~~ *ory paragraph* to the conclusion. A book is not enjoyable ~~if you do not~~ *without reading* from start to finish, nor is a movie cut short before the ending is revealed. My appreciation of life came in a most unexpected connection between life's beginning and its end.

*Focus looks OK here.*

2 Mr. Hertli was a brilliant ~~old~~ Swiss man whom I assisted every week for the last two years of my high school career. He lived ~~25~~ *twenty-five* minutes away from my home, down a winding road, surrounded by trees, grazing horses, *goats and sheep,* and the occasional house. Trees arched over his steep driveway, as if bowing to all who enter, welcoming anyone with insight, help, or simply company. Mr. Hertli's house was of ~~a very~~ traditional build, and was surrounded by nature. Goats fed on grasses and horses galloped and played within a fenced-off grazing area. Ducks swam on a pond and dozens of sun-colored butterflies danced around bunches of tall purple flowers between which a few *worn* stepping-stones were nestled, as a walkway to the front door.

*Need to write out numbers that are a word or two*

3 Inside sat Mr. Hertli, always rocking in a chair and listening to "books-on-tape" in one of the various languages familiar to him. He was ~~very~~ tall, thin, and elderly, and wore dress slacks and a ~~suit~~ jacket no matter what the occasion. His leather shoes were obviously very old, and *they* showed scuffs and wear which told stories of Switzerland, war, research, and accomplishment. Mr. Hertli also wore ~~very~~ dark sunglasses morning and evening to protect the mere one or two percent of his eye sight that had not yet been stolen from him by macular degeneration.

*Too much repetition — plus wordy*

4 Mr. Hertli was an accomplished man. He had been through immigration, served the United States in war, earned various degrees, ~~had~~ written a book on evolution and creationism, and was *now* fighting for his life against a terminal lung disease. He was extremely intelligent, and it was my job to read him scientific journals and books, record information and data for his next work-in-progress, manage his correspondence, fill out paperwork, dispense his medications, and do nearly all the things a blind person can not do alone.

*Make this one word*

5 One particular day, I was assisting Mr. Hertli in his office. Crimson carpeting lined the floor of the tiny literature-crammed room. Journals and books lay sprawled on every surface~~, and there was~~ with barely room for a computer on a desk and two chairs somewhere in all the mess. One end of a ~~A~~ cord around Mr. Hertli's head fed oxygen through his nose, while the other end trailed out the door, down the steps, and into the living room where an oxygen-dispensing machine ~~always~~ constantly sat, ~~always~~ constantly humming. We sorted through music, storing old German and Swiss instrumental classics on a new device for the blind which ~~stored numerous songs, audio books, and other audio literature~~ saved audio files for playback. As we waited for the media to download ~~into the device~~, Mr. Hertli inquired about recent political events concerning the country of Georgia. He desired to know the geographic location of Georgia. "Read the atlas," he said, and although I had grown to understand and love his thick European accent, I sat, staring ~~at him~~ in bafflement at his words. ~~which he, fortunately, could not see.~~ I reached under a desk and pushed past books about Darwin, God, evolution, and history~~, and found~~ to find a large, blue-covered atlas, aged by years of learning~~,~~ and discovery~~, and research~~. Brushing the dust off, I opened the book to the index~~,~~ and searched for "Georgia." I turned to the page to which the index directed me~~,~~ and unsuccessfully tried to describe Georgia's relation to Turkey, Russia, and Azerba~~i~~jan. "Show me~~,~~!" he said. Show him~~!~~? How could I, for he could not see, after all, and now I ~~had~~ was to find a way to make him see~~!~~?

My goal — set the scene but drop extra words!

Too much detail here?

Check commas — end of the textbook

Luckily my reader asked about the spelling.

6 I placed the wide atlas across his wobbly knees, in his lap, facing him. Taking his fragile hand, I slowly directed Mr. Hertli's finger around the perimeter of each country, saying. "This is Turkey. To the east, here is Georgia." He pointed and repeated the countries ~~back~~ to me, and I asserted that, yes, that was indeed Azerba~~i~~jan, Armenia, or Russia.

¶ 5 set up situation — this ¶ tells what happened

7 ~~It~~ This moment felt ~~was~~ as though I were teaching a small child~~,~~ who could not read~~,~~ and who did not know the least about geography. And how strange it was to be feeling such a way. After all, I was helping a well-educated, cultured man~~,~~ in a this most elementary, basic way~~,~~! In this aged man, nearing the end of his life, I saw the character of a small ~~young~~ boy, beginning to learn a concept new to him.

Combine with ¶ 6 — event with meaning?

8 This would be the last time I helped Mr. Hertli, as I would ~~be beginning~~ begin college just a few days later. Mr. Hertli was now completely, one hundred percent blind. Like a mother afraid to send her child to kindergarten ~~school for the first time~~, I was now afraid to cease my ~~assistance of this~~ care

My big goal here is adding more reflection.

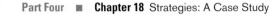

*for this seemingly* ~~somewhat~~ helpless man. For when I had seen this connection, the young, *new,* ~~new~~ *still learning* child *within an* ~~in the~~ old *man*, I came to realize just how valuable *and how unified* life itself is. *Mr. Hertli showed me how our younger selves provide deep roots for us as we get older and how our older selves still preserve our youth. Young and old, we are all somehow connected, one and the same, no one being of greater worth than the other. No matter our age, we will always have this link, through generations, and I have grown to appreciate this of life.*

I want to show how old and young connect.

How might you strengthen your essay as you revise and edit?

After Erin finished revising and editing, she spell-checked her final version and proofread it one more time. Then she submitted her final draft.

## Final Draft for Submission

For more on the MLA paper format, see A in the Quick Format Guide, p. A-1.

Erin Schmitt
Professor Hoeness-Krupsaw
ENG 101.004
19 September 2013

Mr. Hertli

1 In order to fully appreciate something, to realize its value, one often must experience its beginning and its end. For example, to learn and appreciate all the material in a textbook chapter, reading and understanding must take place from the introductory paragraph to the conclusion. A book is not enjoyable without reading from start to finish, nor is a movie cut short before the ending is revealed. My appreciation of life came in a most unexpected connection between life's beginning and its end.

2 Mr. Hertli was a brilliant Swiss man whom I assisted every week for the last two years of my high school career. He lived twenty-five minutes away from my home, down a winding road, surrounded by trees, grazing horses, goats and sheep, and the occasional house. Trees arched over his steep driveway, as if bowing to all who enter, welcoming anyone with insight, help, or simply company. Mr. Hertli's house was of traditional build and was surrounded by nature. Goats fed on grasses and horses galloped and played within a fenced-off grazing area. Ducks swam on a pond and dozens of sun-colored butterflies danced around bunches of tall purple flowers between which a few worn stepping-stones were nestled as a walkway to the front door.

3 Inside sat Mr. Hertli, always rocking in a chair and listening to "books-on-tape" in one of the various languages familiar to him. He was tall, thin, and elderly and wore dress slacks and a jacket no matter what the occasion. His leather shoes were obviously very old, and they showed scuffs and wear which told stories of Switzerland, war, research, and accomplishment. Mr. Hertli also wore dark sunglasses morning and evening to protect the mere one or two percent of his sight that had not yet been stolen from him by macular degeneration.

Mr. Hertli was an accomplished man. He had been through immigration, served the United States in war, earned various degrees, written a book on evolution and creationism, and was now fighting for his life against a terminal lung disease. He was extremely intelligent, and it was my job to read him scientific journals and books, record information and data for his next work-in-progress, manage his correspondence, fill out paperwork, dispense his medications, and do nearly all the things a blind person cannot do alone. 4

One particular day, I was assisting Mr. Hertli in his office. Crimson carpeting lined the floor of the tiny literature-crammed room. Journals and books lay sprawled on every surface with barely room for a computer on a desk and two chairs somewhere in all the mess. One end of a cord around Mr. Hertli's head fed oxygen through his nose, while the other end trailed out the door, down the steps, and into the living room where an oxygen-dispensing machine constantly sat, constantly humming. We sorted through music, storing old German and Swiss instrumental classics on a new device for the blind which saved audio files for playback. As we waited for the media to download, Mr. Hertli inquired about recent political events concerning the country of Georgia. He desired to know the geographic location of Georgia. "Read the atlas," he said, and although I had grown to understand and love his thick European accent, I sat, staring in bafflement at his words. I reached under a desk and pushed past books about Darwin, God, evolution, and history to find a large, blue-covered atlas, aged by years of learning and discovery. Brushing the dust off, I opened the book to the index and searched for "Georgia." I turned to the page to which the index directed me and unsuccessfully tried to describe Georgia's relation to Turkey, Russia, and Azerbaijan. "Show me!" he said. Show him? How could I, for he could not see, after all, and now I was to find a way to make him see? 5

Mr. Peter Hertli, at an earlier age

I placed the wide atlas across his wobbly knees, in his lap, facing him. Taking his fragile hand, I slowly directed Mr. Hertli's finger around the perimeter of each country, saying. "This is Turkey. To the east, here is Georgia." He pointed and repeated the countries to me, and I asserted that, yes, that was indeed Azerbaijan, Armenia, or Russia. This moment felt as though I were teaching a small child, one who could not read and who did not know the least about geography. And how strange it was to be feeling such a way. After all, I was helping a well-educated, cultured man in 6 this most elementary, basic way! In this aged man, nearing the end of his life, I saw the character of a small young boy, beginning to learn a concept new to him.

This would be the last time I helped Mr. Hertli, as I would begin college just a few days later. Mr. Hertli was now completely, one hundred percent blind. Like a mother afraid to send her child to kindergarten, I was now afraid to cease my care for this seemingly helpless man. For when I had seen this connection, the new, young child still learning within an old man, I came to realize just how valuable and how unified life itself is. Mr. Hertli showed me how our younger selves provide deep roots for us as we get older and how our older selves still preserve our youth. Young and old, we are all somehow connected, one and the same, no one being of greater worth than the other. No matter our age, we will always have this link, through generations, and I have grown to appreciate this of life. 7

## Reflecting as a Writer

For more about portfolios, see Ch. 16.

Erin's assignment asked her to reflect on her experience as she wrote about its significance for her. Her instructor also required a reflective letter, following the time-honored advice of writer and teacher Peter Elbow. Here Erin needed to consider her goals, strengths, remaining challenges, and responses to readers during her writing process. The letter and the essay would become part of her writer's portfolio due at the end of the term.

### Learning by Doing Writing a Reflective Letter

Select one of the following options, and write a reflective letter to your instructor.

1. Reflect on your responses to Erin's writing strategies and processes. For example, you might consider how her processes do and do not relate to yours or what you have learned from her that you might like to apply to your writing.
2. Reflect on your own first essay, as Erin did. Consider your goals, strengths, remaining challenges, and responses to readers.

## Reflective Portfolio Letter

For sample business letter formats, see pp. 361–64 and E in the Quick Format Guide, pp. A-14–A-17.

Campus Box A-456
September 19, 2013

Dr. Susanna Hoeness-Krupsaw
English Department
State University
1234 University Road
Campustown, OH 23456

Dear Dr. Hoeness-Krupsaw:

The main goal of my essay was to describe accurately and vividly the significant experience of reading to a blind, elderly man during my last two years of high school. When writing the essay I was attempting to give the reader insight to the details and scenery I experienced while visiting this man. By accurately describing the scene of most significance in great detail, I hoped to convey and emphasize that significance to the reader.

What do you want to say in a reflective letter?

The strengths I had in writing this essay were in detailing and flow. I believe my descriptions accurately put images in the mind of the reader. I began my writing process by planning with a diagram. After creating this diagram, the essay easily formed in my mind and on paper. However, if I could revise the essay further, I would focus more on word choice and strength. I would also revise and strengthen my reflections as well as my concluding paragraph. When writing, I had some difficulty in putting into words exactly what my experience made me think and feel.

The feedback I received regarding my essay was mostly positive. However, almost all feedback suggested adding more reflection at the end of my final draft. I believe this strengthened my essay overall. I would like to get a response from the reader asserting that my essay vividly conveyed images and that the importance of this event is easily understood.

I may be contacted regarding this essay at eschmitt@campus.edu or 555-5555.

Sincerely,

Erin E. Schmitt

Enc.

# 19 Strategies for Generating Ideas

For most writers, the hardest part of writing comes first—confronting a blank page. Fortunately, you can prepare for that moment by finding ideas and getting ready to write. All the tested techniques here have worked for writers—professionals and students—and some may work for you.

## Finding Ideas

When you begin to write, ideas may appear effortlessly on the paper or screen, perhaps triggered by resources around you—something you read, see, hear, discuss, or think about. (See the top half of the graphic below.) But at other times you need idea generators, strategies to try when your ideas dry up. If one strategy doesn't work for your task, try another. (See the lower half of the graphic.)

For an interactive Learning by Doing activity on Brainstorming from a Video, go to Ch. 19: **bedfordstmartins.com/bedguide**.

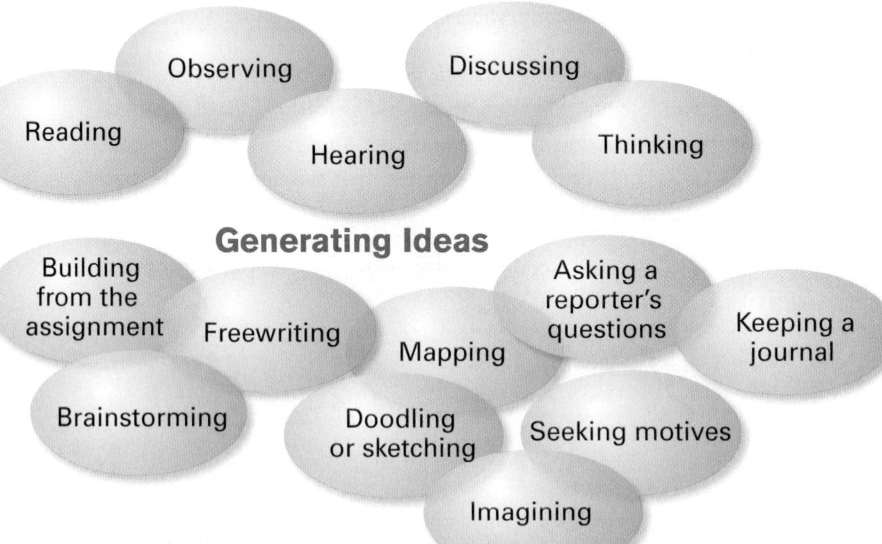

## Building from Your Assignment

Learning to write is learning what questions to ask yourself. Your assignment may trigger this process, raising some questions and answering others. For example, Ben Tran jotted notes in his book as his instructor and classmates discussed his first assignment – recalling a personal experience.

The assignment clarified what audience to address and what purpose to set. Ben's classmates asked about length, format, and due date, but Ben saw three big questions: Which experience should I pick? How did it change me? Why was it so important for me? Ben still didn't know what he'd write about, but he had figured out the questions to tackle first.

For more detail about this assignment, turn to pp. 67–68 in Ch. 4.

*event? What*
*quences?*

> Write about one specific experience that changed how you acted, thought, or felt. Use your experience as a springboard for reflection. Your purpose is not merely to tell an interesting story but to show your readers—your instructor and your classmates—the importance of that experience for you.

*readers?*
*+ prof.*

*What purpose? 2 parts!*
*Tell the story but do more — reflect & show importance.*

Sometimes assignments assume that you already know something critical – how to address a particular audience or what to include in some type of writing. When Amalia Blackhawk read her argument assignment, she jotted down questions to ask her instructor.

*ing OK?*
*y newspaper*
*f issue?*
*of what?*
*s my*
*se?*
*ading*
*s to*
*t my*
*to*
*?*

> Select a campus or local issue that matters to you, and write a letter to the editor about it. Be certain to tell readers what the issue is, why it is important, and how you propose to address it. Assume that your letter will appear in a special opinion feature that allows letters longer than the usual word-count limits.

*My classmates? The publication's readers?*

*How long is the usual letter? How long should mine be? Anything else letters like this should do?*

Try these steps as you examine an assignment:

1. *Read through the assignment once* to discover its overall direction.
2. *Read it again,* marking information about your situation as a writer. Does the assignment identify or suggest your audience, your purpose in writing, the type of paper expected, the parts typical of that kind of writing, or the format required?
3. *List the questions that the assignment raises for you.* Exactly what do you need to decide – the type of topic to pick, the focus to develop, the issues or aspects to consider, or other guidelines to follow?
4. *Finally, list any questions that the assignment doesn't answer or ask you to answer.* Ask your instructor about these questions.

### Learning by Doing — Building from Your Assignment

Select an assignment from this book, another textbook, or another class, and make notes about it. What questions does it answer? Which questions or decisions does it direct to you? What other questions might you want to ask your instructor? Then exchange assignments with a classmate; make notes about that assignment, too. With your partner, compare responses to both.

## Brainstorming

A *brainstorm* is a sudden insight or inspiration. As a writing strategy, brainstorming uses free association to stimulate a chain of ideas, often to personalize a topic and break it down into specifics. Start with a word or phrase, and spend a set period of time simply listing ideas as rapidly as possible. Write down whatever comes to mind with no editing or going back.

As a group activity, brainstorming gains from varied perspectives. At work, it can fill a specific need—finding a name for a product or an advertising slogan. In college, you can brainstorm with a few others or your entire class. Sit facing one another. Designate one person to record on paper, screen, or chalkboard whatever the others suggest. After several minutes of calling out ideas, look over the recorder's list for useful results. Online, toss out ideas during a chat or post them for all to consider.

On your own, brainstorm to define a topic, generate an example, or find a title for a finished paper. Angie Ortiz brainstormed after her instructor assigned a paper ("Demonstrate from your experience how electronic technology is changing our lives"). She wrote *electronic technology* on the page, set her alarm for fifteen minutes, and began to scribble.

> Electronic technology
> iPod, cell phone, laptop, tablet. Plus TV, cable, DVDs. Too much?!
> Always on call — at home, in car, at school. Always something playing.
> Spend so much time in electronic world — phone calls, texting, tunes. Cuts into time really hanging with friends — face-to-face time.
> Less aware of my surroundings outside of the electronic world?

When her alarm went off, Angie took a break. After returning to her list, she crossed out ideas that did not interest her and circled her final promising question. A focus began to emerge: the capacity of the electronic world to expand information but reduce awareness.

When you want to brainstorm, try this advice:

1. *Launch your thoughts with a key word or phrase.* If you need a topic, try a general term (*computer*); if you need an example for a paragraph in progress, try specifics (*financial errors computers make*).

2. *Set a time limit.* Ten minutes (or so) is enough for strenuous thinking.
3. *Rapidly list brief items.* Stick to words, phrases, or short sentences that you can quickly scan later.
4. *Don't stop.* Don't worry about spelling, repetition, or relevance. Don't judge, and don't arrange: just produce. Record whatever comes to mind, as fast as you can. If your mind goes blank, keep moving, even if you only repeat what you've just written.

When you finish, circle or check anything intriguing. Scratch out whatever looks useless or dull. Then try some conscious organizing: Are any thoughts related? Can you group them? Does the group suggest a topic?

### Learning by Doing Brainstorming

From the following list, choose a subject that interests you, that you know something about, and that you'd like to learn more about—in other words, that you might like to write on. Then brainstorm for ten minutes.

| | | |
|---|---|---|
| travel | fear | exercise |
| dieting | dreams | automobiles |
| family | technology | sports |
| advertisements | animals | education |

Now look over your list, and circle any potential paper topic. If you wish, pass around a list of three or four options, asking each classmate to check the most engaging idea.

## Freewriting

To tap your unconscious by *freewriting,* simply write sentences without stopping for about fifteen minutes. The sentences don't have to be grammatical, coherent, or stylish; just keep them flowing to unlock an idea's potential.

For Ortiz's brainstorming, see p. 386.

Generally, freewriting is most productive if it has an aim—for example, finding a topic, a purpose, or a question you want to answer. Angie Ortiz wrote her topic at the top of a page—and then explored her rough ideas.

> Electronic devices — do they isolate us? I chat all day online and by phone, but that's quick communication, not in-depth conversation. I don't really spend much time hanging with friends and getting to know what's going on with them. I love listening to my iPod on campus, but maybe I'm not as aware of my surroundings as I could be. I miss seeing things, like the new art gallery that I walk by every day. I didn't even notice the new sculpture park in front! Then, at night, I do assignments on my computer, browse the Web, and watch some cable. I'm in my own little electronic world most of the time. I love technology, but what else am I missing?

Angie's result wasn't polished prose. Still, in a short time she produced a paragraph to serve as a springboard for her essay.

If you want to try freewriting, here's what you do:

1. *Write a sentence or two at the top of your page or file*—the idea you plan to develop by freewriting.
2. *Write without stopping for at least ten minutes.* Express whatever comes to mind, even "My mind is blank," until a new thought floats up.
3. *Explore without censoring yourself.* Don't cross out false starts or grammar errors. Don't worry about connecting ideas or finding perfect words. Use your initial sentences as a rough guide, not a straitjacket. New directions may be valuable.
4. *Prepare yourself*—if you want to. While you wait for your ideas to start racing, you may want to ask yourself some questions:

   What interests you about the topic? What do you know about it that the next person doesn't? What have you read, observed, or heard about it?

   How might you feel about this topic if you were someone else (a parent, an instructor, a person from another country)?
5. *Repeat the process, looping back to expand a good idea if you wish.* Poke at the most interesting parts to see if they will further unfold:

   What does that mean? If that's true, what then? So what?

   What other examples or evidence does this statement call to mind?

   What objections might a reader raise? How might you answer them?

### Learning by Doing Freewriting

Select an idea from your current thinking or a brainstorming list. Write it at the top of a page or file, and freewrite for fifteen minutes. Share your freewriting with your classmates. If you wish, loop back to repeat this process.

## Doodling or Sketching

If you fill the margins of your notebooks with doodles, harness this artistic energy to generate ideas for writing. Elena Lopez began to sketch her collision with a teammate during a soccer tournament (Figure 19.1). She added stick figures, notes, symbols, and color as she outlined a series of events.

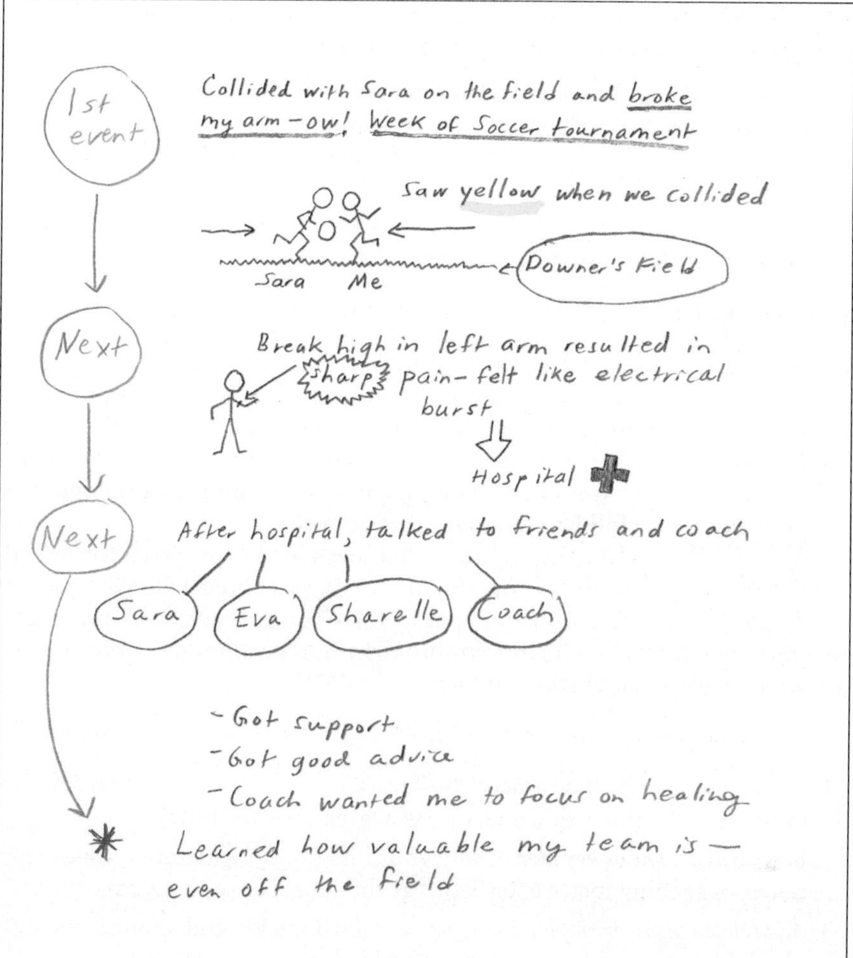


**Figure 19.1** Doodling or sketching to generate ideas

Try this advice as you develop ideas by doodling or sketching:

1. *Give your ideas room to grow.* Open a new file using a drawing program, doodle in pencil on a blank page, or sketch on a series of pages.
2. *Concentrate on your topic, but welcome new ideas.* Begin with a key visual in the center or at the top of a page. Add sketches or doodles as they occur to you to embellish, expand, define, or redirect your topic.
3. *Add icons, symbols, colors, figures, labels, notes, or questions.* Freely mix visuals and text, recording ideas without stopping to refine them.
4. *Follow up on your discoveries.* After a break, add notes to make connections, identify sequences, or convert visuals into descriptive sentences.

### Learning by Doing Doodling or Sketching

Start with a doodle or sketch that illustrates your topic. Add related events, ideas, or details to develop your topic visually. Share your material with classmates; use their observations to help you refine your direction as a writer.

## Mapping

Mapping taps your visual and spatial creativity as you position ideas on the page, in a file, or with cloud software to show their relationships or relative importance. Ideas might radiate outward from a key term in the center, drop down from a key word at the top, sprout upward from a root idea, branch out from a trunk, flow across page or screen in a chronological or causal sequence, or follow a circular, spiral, or other form.

Andrew Choi used mapping to gather ideas for his proposal for revitalizing the campus radio station (Figure 19.2). He noted ideas on colored sticky notes—blue for problems, yellow for solutions, and pink for implementation details. Then he moved the sticky notes around on a blank page, arranging them as he connected ideas.

Here are some suggestions for mapping:

1. *Allow space for your map to develop.* Open a new file, try posterboard for arranging sticky notes or cards, or use a large page for notes.
2. *Begin with a topic or key idea.* Using your imagination, memory, class notes, or reading, place a key word at the center or top of a page.
3. *Add related ideas, examples, issues, or questions.* Quickly and spontaneously place these points above, below, or beside your key word.
4. *Refine the connections.* As your map evolves, use lines, arrows, or loops to connect ideas; box or circle them to focus attention; add colors to relate points or to distinguish source materials from your own ideas.

After a break, continue mapping to probe one part more deeply, refine the structure, add detail, or build an alternate map from a different viewpoint. Also try mapping to develop graphics that present ideas in visual form.

### Learning by Doing Mapping

Start with a key word or idea that you know about. Map related ideas, using visual elements to show how they connect. Share your map with classmates, and then use their questions or comments to refine your mapping.

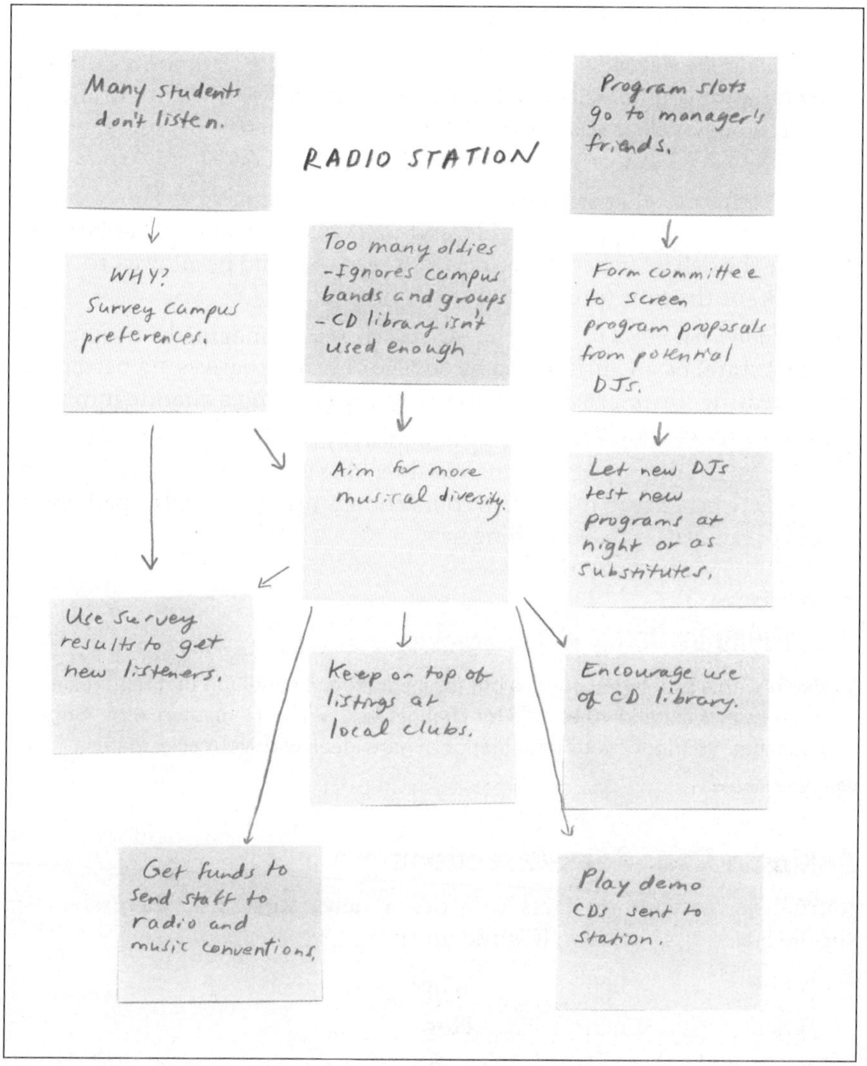

Many students don't listen.

RADIO STATION

Program slots go to manager's friends.

WHY? Survey campus preferences.

Too many oldies -Ignores campus bands and groups -CD library isn't used enough

Form committee to screen program proposals from potential DJs.

Aim for more musical diversity.

Let new DJs test new programs at night or as substitutes.

Use survey results to get new listeners.

Keep on top of listings at local clubs.

Encourage use of CD library.

Get funds to send staff to radio and music conventions.

Play demo CDs sent to station.

**Figure 19.2** Mapping to generate ideas

## Imagining

Your imagination is a valuable resource for exploring possibilities—analyzing an option, evaluating an alternative, or solving a problem—to discover surprising ideas, original examples, and unexpected relationships.

Suppose you asked, "What if the average North American lived more than a century?" No doubt many more people would be old. How would that shift affect doctors, nurses, and medical facilities? How might city planners respond? What would the change mean for shopping centers? For television programming? For leisure activities? For Social Security?

Use some of the following strategies to unleash your imagination:

1. *Speculate about changes, alternatives, and options.* What common assumption might you question or deny? What deplorable condition would you remedy? What changes in policy, practice, or attitude might avoid problems? What different paths in life might you take?
2. *Shift perspective.* Experiment with a different point of view. How would someone on the opposing side respond? A plant, an animal, a Martian? Shift the debate (whether retirees, not teens, should be allowed to drink) or the time (present to past or future).
3. *Envision what might be.* Join the others who have imagined a utopia (an ideal state) or an anti-utopia by envisioning alternatives – a better way of treating illness, electing a president, or ordering a chaotic jumble.
4. *Synthesize.* Synthesis (generating new ideas by combining previously separate ideas) is the opposite of analysis (breaking ideas down into component parts). Synthesize to make fresh connections, fusing materials – perhaps old or familiar – into something new.

### Learning by Doing Imagining

Begin with a problem that cries out for a solution, a condition that requires a remedy, or a situation that calls for change. Ask "What if?" or start with "Suppose that" to trigger your imagination. Share ideas with your classmates.

For more about analysis and synthesis, see pp. 25–27.

## Asking a Reporter's Questions

Journalists, assembling facts to write a news story, ask themselves six simple questions – the five *W*'s and an *H*:

| | | |
|---|---|---|
| Who? | Where? | Why? |
| What? | When? | How? |

In the *lead,* or opening paragraph, of a good news story, the writer tries to condense the whole story into a sentence or two, answering all six questions.

> A giant homemade fire balloon [*what*] startled residents of Costa Mesa [*where*] last night [*when*] as Ambrose Barker, 79, [*who*] zigzagged across the sky at nearly 300 miles per hour [*how*] in an attempt to set a new altitude record [*why*].

Later in the news story, the reporter will add details, using the six basic questions to generate more about what happened and why.

For your college writing, use these questions to generate details. They can help you explore the significance of a childhood experience, analyze what happened at a moment in history, or investigate a campus problem. Don't worry if some go nowhere or are repetitious. Later you'll weed out irrelevant points and keep those that look promising.

For a topic that is not based on your personal experience, you may need to do reading or interviewing to answer some of the questions. Take, for example, the topic of the assassination of President John F. Kennedy, and notice how each question can lead to further questions.

- *Who* was John F. Kennedy? What kind of person was he? What kind of president? Who was with him when he was killed? Who was nearby?
- *What* happened to Kennedy? What events led up to the assassination? What happened during it? What did the media do? What did people across the country do? What did someone who remembers this event do?
- *Where* was Kennedy assassinated – city, street, vehicle, seat? Where was he going? Where did the shots likely come from? Where did they hit him? Where did he die?
- *When* was he assassinated – day, month, year, time? When did Kennedy decide to go to this city? When – precisely – were the shots fired? When did he die? When was a suspect arrested?
- *Why* was Kennedy assassinated? What are some of the theories? What solid evidence is available? Why has this event caused controversy?
- *How* was Kennedy assassinated? How many shots were fired? Specifically what caused his death? How can we get at the truth of this event?

### Learning by Doing Asking a Reporter's Questions

Choose one of the following topics, or use one of your own:

A memorable event in history or in your life
A concert or other performance that you have attended
An accomplishment on campus or an occurrence in your city
An important speech or a proposal for change
A questionable stand someone has taken

Answer the six reporter's questions about the topic. Then write a sentence or two synthesizing the answers to the six questions. Incorporate that sentence into an introductory paragraph for an essay that you might write later.

## Seeking Motives

In much college writing, you will try to explain motives behind human behavior. In a history paper, you might consider how George Washington's conduct shaped the presidency. In a literature essay, you might analyze the motives of Hester Prynne in *The Scarlet Letter.* Because people, including characters in fiction, are so complex, this task is challenging.

For more on writing about literature, see Ch. 13.

To understand any human act, according to philosopher-critic Kenneth Burke, you can break it down into five components, a *pentad,* and ask questions about each one. Burke's pentad overlaps the reporter's questions but also can show how components of a human act affect one another, taking you deeper into motives. Suppose you are writing a political-science paper on President Lyndon Baines Johnson (LBJ), sworn in as president right after President Kennedy's assassination in 1963. A year later, he was elected to the post by a landslide. By 1968, however, he had decided not to run for a second term. You use Burke's pentad to investigate why.

1. *The act*: What was done?

   Announcing the decision to leave office without standing for reelection.

2. *The actor*: Who did it?

   President Johnson.

3. *The agency*: What means did the person use to make it happen?

   A televised address to the nation.

4. *The scene*: Where, when, and under what circumstances did it happen?

   Washington, DC, March 31, 1968. Protesters against the Vietnam War were gaining influence. The press was increasingly critical of the war. Senator Eugene McCarthy, an antiwar candidate for president, had made a strong showing against LBJ in the New Hampshire primary.

5. *The purpose or motive for acting*: What could have made the person do it?

   LBJ's motives might have included avoiding probable defeat, escaping further personal attacks, sparing his family, making it easier for his successor to pull out of the war, and easing dissent among Americans.

Next, you can pair Burke's five components and ask about the pairs:

| | | |
|---|---|---|
| actor to act | act to scene | scene to agency |
| actor to scene | act to agency | scene to purpose |
| actor to purpose | act to purpose | agency to purpose |

| | |
|---|---|
| PAIR | actor to agency |
| QUESTION | What did LBJ [actor] have to do with his televised address [agency]? |
| ANSWER | Commanding the attention of a vast audience, LBJ must have felt in control—though his ability to control the situation in Vietnam was slipping. |

Not all the paired questions will prove fruitful; some may not even apply. But one or two might reveal valuable connections and start you writing.

## Learning by Doing Seeking Motives

Choose a puzzling action—perhaps something you, a family member, or a friend has done; a decision of a political figure; something in a movie, on television, or in a book. Apply Burke's pentad to seek motives for the action.

If you wish, also pair up components. When you believe you understand the individual's motivation, write a paragraph explaining the action, and share it with classmates.

## Keeping a Journal

Journal writing richly rewards anyone who engages in it regularly. You can write anywhere or anytime: all you need is a few minutes to record an entry and the willingness to set down what you think and feel. Your journal will become a mine studded with priceless nuggets – thoughts, observations, reactions, and revelations that are yours for the taking. As you write, you can rifle your well-stocked journal for topics, insights, examples, and other material. The best type of journal is the one that's useful to *you*.

For ideas about keeping a reading journal, see p. 23.

**Reflective Journals.** When you write in your journal, put less emphasis on recording what happened, as you would in a diary, than on *reflecting* about what you do or see, hear or read, learn or believe. An entry can be a list or an outline, a paragraph or an essay, a poem or a letter you don't intend to send. Describe a person or a place, set down a conversation, or record insights into actions. Consider your pet peeves, fears, dreams, treasures, or moral dilemmas. Use your experience as a writer to nourish and inspire your writing, recording what worked, what didn't, and how you reacted to each.

**Responsive Journals.** Sometimes you *respond* to something in particular – your assigned reading, a classroom discussion, a movie, a conversation, or an observation. Faced with a long paper, you might assign *yourself* a focused response journal so you have plenty of material to use.

For more on responding to reading, see Ch. 2.

For responsive journal prompts, see the end of each selection in *A Writer's Reader*.

**Warm-Up Journals.** To prepare for an assignment, you can group ideas, scribble outlines, sketch beginnings, capture stray thoughts, record relevant material. Of course, a quick comment may turn into a draft.

**E-Journals.** Once you create a file and make entries by date or subject, you can record ideas, feelings, images, memories, and quotations. You will find it easy to copy and paste inspiring e-mail, quotations from Web pages, or images and sounds. Always identify the source of copied material so that you won't later confuse it with your original writing.

**Blogs.** Like traditional journals, "Web logs" aim for frank, honest, immediate entries. Unlike journals, they often explore a specific topic and may be available publicly on the Web or privately by invitation. Especially in an online class, you might blog about your writing or research processes.

### Learning by Doing Keeping a Journal

Keep a journal for at least a week. Each day record your thoughts, feelings, observations, and reactions. Reflect on what happens, and respond to what you read, including selections from this book or its e-Pages. Then bring your journal to class, and read aloud to your classmates the entry you like best.

## Getting Ready

Once you have generated a suitable topic and some ideas related to that topic, you are ready to get down to the job of actually writing.

### Setting Up Circumstances

If you can write only with your shoes off or with a can of soda nearby, set yourself up that way. Some writers need to hear blaring rap music; others need quiet. Create an environment that puts you in the mood for writing.

**Devote One Special Place to Writing.** Your place should have good lighting and space to spread out. It may be a desk in your room, the dining room table, or a quiet library cubicle – someplace where no one will bother you, where your mind and body will settle in, and preferably where you can leave projects and keep handy your computer and materials.

**Establish a Ritual.** Some writers find that a ritual relaxes them and helps them get started. You might open a soda, straighten your desk, turn music on (or off), and create a new file on the computer.

**Relocate.** If you're stuck, try moving from library to home or from kitchen to bedroom. Try an unfamiliar place – a restaurant, an airport, park.

**Reduce Distractions.** Most of us can't prevent interruptions, but we can reduce them. If you expect your boyfriend to call, call him before you start writing. If you have small children, write when they are asleep or at school. Turn off your phone, and concentrate hard. Let others know you are serious about writing; allow yourself to give it full attention.

**Write at Your Best Time.** Some think best early in the morning; others favor the small hours when their stern self-critic might be asleep, too. Either time can also reduce distractions from others.

**Write on a Schedule.** Writing at a predictable time of day worked marvels for English novelist Anthony Trollope, who would start at 5:30 A.M., write 2,500 words before 8:30 A.M., and then go to his job at the post office. (He wrote more than sixty books.) Even if you can't set aside the same time every day, it may help to decide, "Today from four to five, I'll write."

## Preparing Your Mind

Ideas, images, or powerful urges to write may arrive like sudden miracles. Even if you are taking a shower or heading to a movie, yield to impulse and write. Encourage such moments by opening your mind to inspiration.

**Talk about Your Writing.** Discuss ideas in person, by phone, or online with a classmate or friend, encouraging questions, comments, and suggestions. Or talk to yourself, using a voice-activated recorder, while you sit through traffic jams, walk your dog, or ride your stationary bike.

**Lay Out Your Plans.** Tell a nearby listener—your next-door neighbor, spouse, parent, friend—why you want to write this paper, what you'll put in it, how you'll lay it out. If you hear "That sounds good," you'll be encouraged. If you see a yawn, you'll still have ideas in motion.

**Keep a Notebook or Journal Handy.** Always keep some paper in your pocket or backpack or on the night table to write down good ideas that pop into your mind. Imagination may strike in the grocery checkout line, in the doctor's waiting room, or during a lull on the job.

**Read.** The step from reading to writing is a short one. Even when you're reading for fun, you're involved with words. You might hit on something for your paper. Or read purposefully: set out to read and take notes.

---

**DISCOVERY CHECKLIST**

- ☐ Is your environment organized for writing? What changes might help you reduce distractions and procrastination?
- ☐ Have you scheduled enough time to get ready to write? How might you adjust your schedule or your expectations to encourage productivity?
- ☐ Is your assignment clear? What additional questions might you want to ask about what you are expected to do?
- ☐ Have you generated enough ideas that interest you? What might help you expand, focus, or deepen your ideas?

---

### Learning by Doing Reflecting on Generating Ideas

Select one method of generating ideas that you find to be a productive or enjoyable way to begin writing. Reflect on your success using the method itself to generate ideas about why it works for you. In a pair or a team, have each person advocate for his or her preferred method, presenting its benefits, acknowledging its limitations, and trying to persuade others to give it a try.

# 20 Strategies for Stating a Thesis and Planning

Starting to write often seems a chaotic activity, but the strategies in this chapter can help create order. For most papers, you will want to consider your purpose and audience and then focus on a central point by discovering, stating, and improving a thesis. To help you arrange your material, the chapter also includes advice on grouping ideas and outlining.

## Shaping Your Topic for Your Purpose and Your Audience

For critical questions about audience and more about purpose, see p. 399. For more about both, see pp. 11–15.

For an interactive Learning by Doing activity on Analyzing a Thesis, go to Ch. 20: **bedfordstmartins.com /bedguide**.

As you work on your college papers, you may feel as if you're juggling—selecting weighty points and lively details, tossing them into the air, keeping them all moving in sequence. Busy as you are juggling, however, your performance almost always draws a crowd—your instructor, classmates, or other readers. They'll expect your attention, too, as you try to achieve your purpose—probably informing, explaining, or persuading.

Think carefully about your audience and purpose as you plan. If you want to show your classmates and instructor the importance of an event, start by deciding how much detail they need. If most of them have gotten speeding tickets, they'll need less information about that event than city commuters might. However, to achieve your purpose, you'll need to go beyond what happened to why the event mattered to you. No matter how many tickets your readers have gotten, they won't know what that experience means to you unless you share that information. They may incorrectly assume that you worried about being late to class or having to pay higher

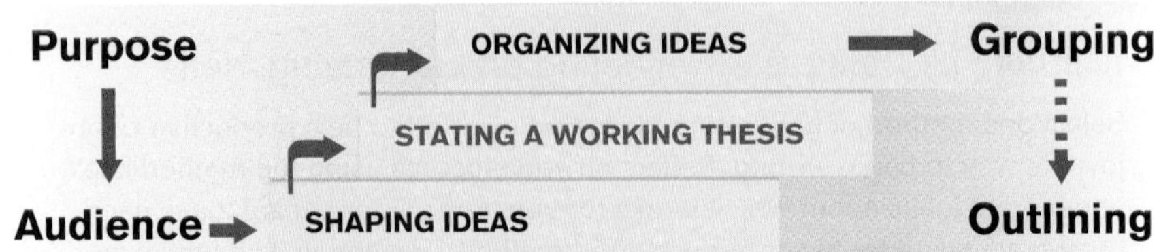

insurance rates. In fact, you had suddenly realized your narrow escape from an accident like your cousin's, a recognition that motivated you to change.

Similarly, if you want to persuade county officials to change the way absentee ballots are distributed to college students, you'll need to support your idea with reasons and evidence—drawing on state election laws and legal precedents familiar to these readers as well as experiences of student voters. You may need to show how your proposal would solve existing problems and also why it would do so better than other proposals.

Plan for your purpose and audience using questions such as these:

- *What is your general purpose?* What do you want to accomplish? Do you want readers to smile, think, or agree? To learn, accept, respect, care, change, or reply? How might your writing accomplish your aims?
- *Who are your readers?* If they are not clearly identified by your assignment or situation, what do you assume about them? What do they know or want to know? What opinions do they hold? What do they find informative or persuasive? How might you appeal to them?
- *How might you narrow and focus your ideas about the topic,* given what you know or assume about your purpose and audience? Which slant would best achieve your purpose? What points would appeal most strongly to your readers? What details would engage or persuade them?
- *What qualities of good writing have been discussed in your class,* explained in your syllabus, or identified in readings? What criteria have emerged from exchanges of drafts with classmates or comments from your instructor? How might you demonstrate these qualities to readers?

### Learning by Doing — Considering Purpose and Audience

Think back to a recent writing task—a college essay, a job application, a report or memo at work, a letter to a campus office, or some other piece. Write a brief description of your situation as a writer at that time. What was your purpose? Who—exactly—were your readers? How did you account for both as you planned? How might you have made your writing more effective?

## Stating and Using a Thesis

Most pieces of effective writing are unified around one main point. That is, all the subpoints and supporting details are relevant to that point. Generally, after you have read an essay, you can sum up the writer's main point in a sentence, even if the author has not stated it explicitly. We call this summary statement a *thesis*.

**Explicit Thesis.** Often a thesis will be explicit, plainly stated, in the selection itself. In "The Myth of the Latin Woman: I Just Met a Girl Named

María" from *The Latin Deli* (Athens: University of Georgia Press, 1993), Judith Ortiz Cofer states her thesis at the end of the first paragraph: "You can leave the Island, master the English language, and travel as far as you can, but if you are a Latina, especially one like me who so obviously belongs to Rita Moreno's gene pool, the Island travels with you." This clear statement, strategically placed, helps readers see her point.

**Implicit Thesis.** Sometimes a thesis is implicit, indirectly suggested rather than directly stated. In "The Niceness Solution," a selection from Bruce Bawer's *Beyond Queer* (New York: Free Press, 1996), Paul Varnell describes an ordinance "banning rude behavior, including rude speech," passed in Raritan, New Jersey. After discussing a 1580 code of conduct, he identifies four objections to such attempts to limit free speech. He concludes with this sentence: "Sensibly, Raritan Police Chief Joseph Sferro said he would not enforce the new ordinance." Although Varnell does not state his main point in one concise sentence, readers know that he opposes the Raritan law and any other attempts to legislate "niceness."

The purpose of most academic and workplace writing is to inform, to explain, or to convince. To achieve any of these purposes, you must make your main point crystal clear. A thesis sentence helps you clarify your idea and stay on track as you write. It also helps your readers see your point and follow your discussion. Sometimes you may want to imply your thesis, but if you state it explicitly, you ensure that readers cannot miss it.

### Learning by Doing — Identifying Theses

If you select the essays yourself, choose them from Part 2, Chs. 4–12.

Working in a small group, select and read five essays from this book (or read those your instructor has chosen). Then, individually, write out the thesis for each essay. Some thesis statements are stated outright (explicit), but others are indirect (implicit). Compare and contrast the thesis statements you identified with those your classmates found. How do you account for differences? Try to agree on a thesis statement for each essay.

Look for specific advice under headings that mention a thesis in Chs. 4–12. Watch for the red labels that identify thesis examples.

## How to Discover a Working Thesis

It's rare for a writer to develop a perfect thesis statement early in the writing process and then to write an effective essay that fits it exactly. What you should aim for is a *working thesis* — a statement that can guide you but that you will ultimately refine. Ideas for a working thesis are probably all around you.

Your topic identifies the area you want to explore. To convert a topic to a thesis, you need to add your own slant, attitude, or point. A useful thesis contains not only the key words that identify your *topic* but also the *point* you want to make or the *attitude* you intend to express.

Topic + Slant or Attitude or Point = Working Thesis

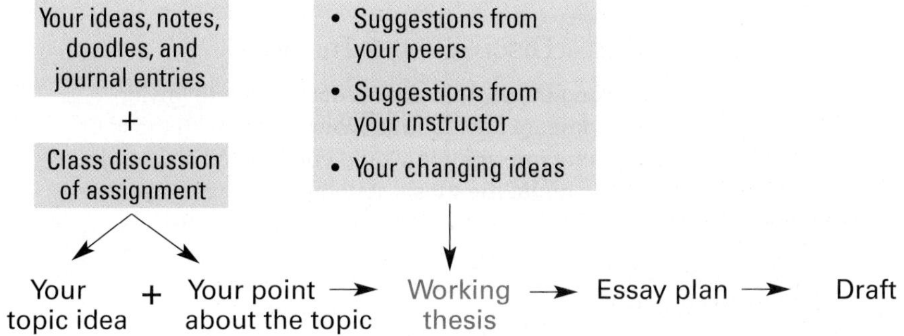


Suppose you want to identify and write about a specific societal change.

| | |
|---|---|
| TOPIC IDEA | old-fashioned formal courtesy |

Now you experiment, testing ideas to make the topic your own.

| | |
|---|---|
| TRIAL | Old-fashioned formal courtesy is a thing of the past. |

Although your trial sentence emphasizes change, it's still circular, repeating rather than advancing a workable point. It doesn't say anything new about old-fashioned formal courtesy; it simply defines *old-fashioned*. You still need to state your own slant—maybe why things have changed.

| | |
|---|---|
| TOPIC IDEA + SLANT | old-fashioned formal courtesy + its decline as gender roles have changed |
| WORKING THESIS | As the roles of men and women have changed in our society, old-fashioned formal courtesy has declined. |

With this working thesis, you could focus on how changing societal attitudes toward gender roles have caused changes in courtesy. Later, when you revise, you may refine your thesis further—perhaps restricting it to courtesy toward the elderly, toward women, or, despite stereotypes, toward men. The chart on page 403 suggests ways to develop a working thesis.

For advice about revising a thesis, see pp. 459–60.

Once you have a working thesis, be sure its point accomplishes the purpose of your assignment. Suppose your assignment asks you to compare and contrast two local newspapers' coverage of a Senate election. Ask yourself what the point of that comparison and contrast is. Simply noting a difference won't be enough to satisfy most readers.

| | |
|---|---|
| NO SPECIFIC POINT | The *Herald*'s coverage of the Senate elections was different from the *Courier*'s. |
| WORKING THESIS | The *Herald*'s coverage of the Senate elections was more thorough than the *Courier*'s. |

## Learning by Doing Discovering a Thesis

Write a sentence, a working thesis, that unifies each of the following groups of details. Then compare and contrast your theses with those of your classmates. What other information would you need to write a good paper on each topic? How might the thesis statement change as you write the paper?

1. Cigarettes are expensive.
   Cigarettes can cause fires.
   Cigarettes cause unpleasant odors.
   Cigarettes can cause health problems for smokers.
   Secondhand smoke from cigarettes can cause health problems.
2. Clinger College has a highly qualified faculty.
   Clinger College has an excellent curriculum in my field.
   Clinger College has a beautiful campus.
   Clinger College is expensive.
   Clinger College has offered me a scholarship.
3. Crisis centers report that date rape is increasing.
   Most date rape is not reported to the police.
   Often the victim of date rape is not believed.
   Sometimes the victim of date rape is blamed or blames herself.
   The effects of date rape stay with a woman for years.

## How to State a Thesis

Once you have a notion of a topic and main point, use these pointers to state or improve a thesis to guide your planning and drafting.

- *State the thesis sentence exactly.* Replace vague or general wording with concise, detailed, and down-to-earth language.

  TOO GENERAL — There are a lot of troubles with chemical wastes.

  Are you going to deal with all chemical wastes, throughout all of history, all over the world? Will you list all the troubles they can cause?

  MORE SPECIFIC — Careless dumping of leftover paint is to blame for a recent outbreak of skin rashes in Atlanta.

  For an argument, you need to take a stand on a debatable issue that would allow others to take different positions. State yours exactly.

  SPECIFIC STAND — The recent health consequences of carelessly dumping leftover paint require Atlanta officials both to regulate and to educate.

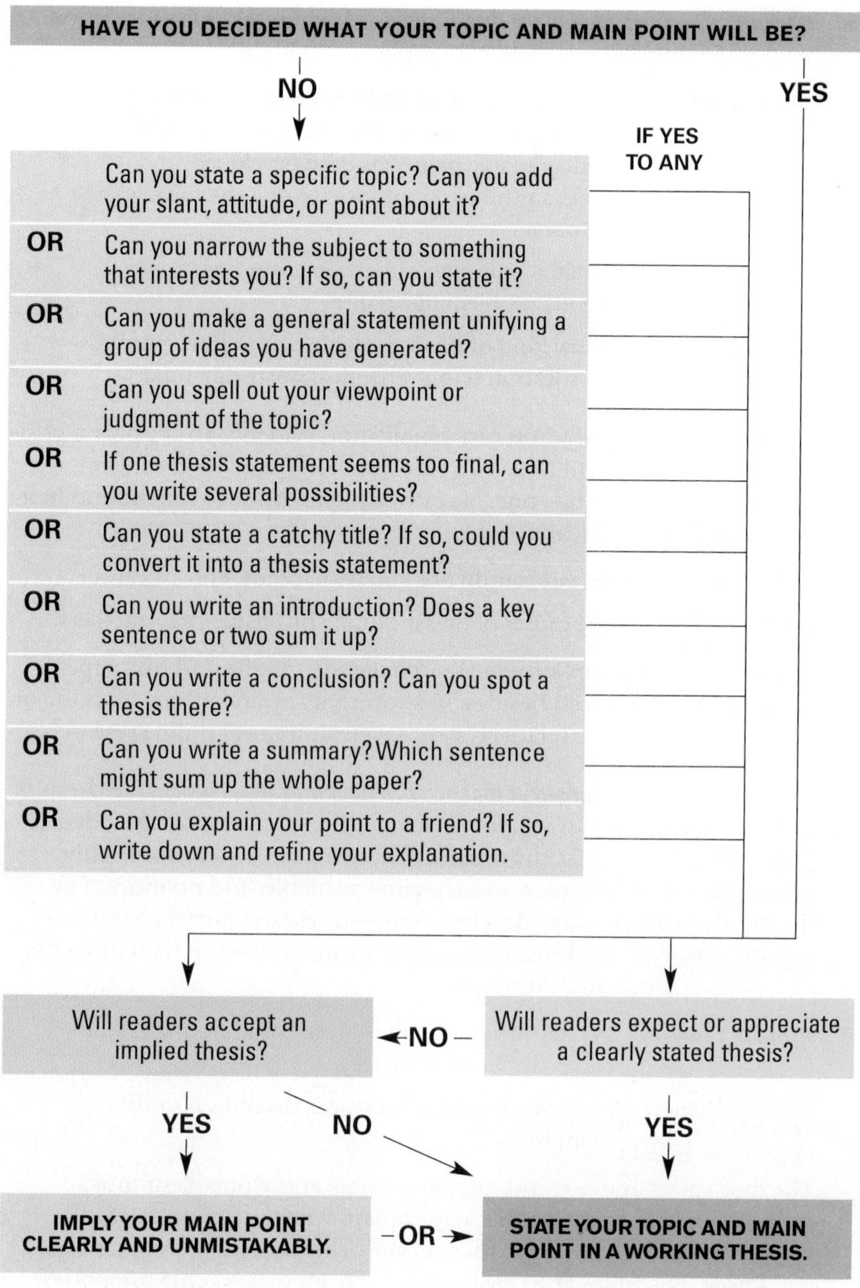
HAVE YOU DECIDED WHAT YOUR TOPIC AND MAIN POINT WILL BE?
NO
YES
IF YES TO ANY
Can you state a specific topic? Can you add your slant, attitude, or point about it?
OR Can you narrow the subject to something that interests you? If so, can you state it?
OR Can you make a general statement unifying a group of ideas you have generated?
OR Can you spell out your viewpoint or judgment of the topic?
OR If one thesis statement seems too final, can you write several possibilities?
OR Can you state a catchy title? If so, could you convert it into a thesis statement?
OR Can you write an introduction? Does a key sentence or two sum it up?
OR Can you write a conclusion? Can you spot a thesis there?
OR Can you write a summary? Which sentence might sum up the whole paper?
OR Can you explain your point to a friend? If so, write down and refine your explanation.
Will readers accept an implied thesis?
NO
Will readers expect or appreciate a clearly stated thesis?
YES
NO
YES
IMPLY YOUR MAIN POINT CLEARLY AND UNMISTAKABLY.
OR
STATE YOUR TOPIC AND MAIN POINT IN A WORKING THESIS.

- *State just one central idea in the thesis sentence.* If your paper is to focus on one point, your thesis should state only one main idea.

| | |
|---|---|
| TOO MANY IDEAS | Careless dumping of leftover paint has caused a serious problem in Atlanta, and a new kind of biodegradable paint has been developed, and it offers a promising solution to one chemical waste dilemma. |
| ONE CENTRAL IDEA | Careless dumping of leftover paint has caused a serious problem in Atlanta. |
| OR | A new kind of biodegradable paint offers a promising solution to one chemical waste dilemma. |

- *State your thesis positively.* You can usually find evidence to support a positive statement, but you'd have to rule out every possible exception in order to prove a negative one. Negative statements also may sound half-hearted and seem to lead nowhere.

| | |
|---|---|
| NEGATIVE | Researchers do not know what causes breast cancer. |
| POSITIVE | The causes of breast cancer still challenge researchers. |

  Presenting the topic positively as a "challenge" might lead to a paper about an exciting quest. Besides, to show that researchers are working on the problem would be relatively easy, given an hour of online research.

- *Limit your thesis to a statement that you can demonstrate.* A workable thesis is limited so that you can support it with sufficient convincing evidence. It should stake out just the territory that you can cover thoroughly within the length assigned and the time available, and no more. The shorter the essay, the less development your thesis should promise or require. Likewise, the longer the essay, the more development and complexity your thesis should suggest.

| | |
|---|---|
| DIFFICULT TO SHOW | For centuries, popular music has announced vital trends in Western society. |
| DIFFICULT TO SHOW | My favorite piece of music is Beethoven's Fifth Symphony. |

  The first thesis above could inform a whole encyclopedia of music; the second would require that you explain why that symphony is your favorite, contrasting it with all the other musical compositions you know. The following thesis sounds far more workable for a brief essay.

| | |
|---|---|
| POSSIBLE TO SHOW | In the past two years, a rise in the number of preteenagers has resulted in a comeback for heavy metal on the local concert scene. |

Unlike a vague statement or a broad, unrestricted claim, a limited thesis narrows and refines a topic, restricting your essay to a reasonable scope.

| | |
|---|---|
| TOO VAGUE | Native American blankets are very beautiful. |
| TOO BROAD | Native Americans have adapted to cultural shifts. |
| POSSIBLE TO SHOW | For some members of the Apache tribe, working in high-rise construction has allowed both economic stability and cultural integrity. |

If the suggestions in this chapter have helped you draft a working thesis – even an awkward or feeble one – you'll find plenty of advice about improving it in the next few pages and more later about revising it. But what if you're freezing up because your thesis simply won't take shape? First, relax. Your thesis will emerge later on – as your thinking matures and you figure out your paper's true direction, as peer readers spot the idea in your paper you're too close to see, as you talk with your instructor and suddenly grasp how to take your paper where you want it to go. In the meantime, plan and write so that you create a rich environment that will encourage your thesis to emerge.

For more on revising a thesis, see pp. 459–60.

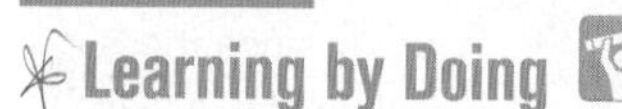

## Learning by Doing — Examining Thesis Statements

Discuss each of the following thesis sentences with your classmates. Answer these questions for each:

Is the thesis stated exactly?
Does the thesis state just one idea?
Is the thesis stated positively?
Is the thesis sufficiently limited for a short essay?
How might the thesis be improved?

1. Teenagers should not get married.
2. Cutting classes is like a disease.
3. Students have developed a variety of techniques to conceal inadequate study from their instructors.
4. Older people often imitate teenagers.
5. Violence on television can be harmful to children.
6. I don't know how to change the oil in my car.

## How to Improve a Thesis

Simply knowing what a solid working thesis *should* do may not help you improve your thesis. Whether yours is a first effort or a refined version, turn to the Take Action chart (p. 406) to help you figure out how to improve

## Take Action Building a Stronger Thesis

Ask each question at the top of the chart to consider whether your draft might need work on that issue. If so, follow the ASK—LOCATE SPECIFICS—TAKE ACTION sequence to revise.

| | Unclear Topic? | Unclear Slant? | Broad Thesis? |
|---|---|---|---|
| **1 ASK** | Could I define or state my topic more clearly? | Could I define or state my slant more clearly? | Could I limit my thesis to develop it more successfully? |
| **2 LOCATE SPECIFICS** | ■ Write out your current working thesis.<br>■ Circle the words in it that identify your topic.<br>WORKING THESIS<br>(Adaptability) is essential for World Action volunteers. [What, exactly, does the topic *adaptability* mean?] | ■ Write out your current working thesis.<br>■ Underline the words that state your slant, attitude, or point about your topic.<br>WORKING THESIS<br>Volunteering <u>is an invaluable experience</u>. [Why or in what ways is volunteering invaluable?] | ■ Write out your current working thesis.<br>■ Decide whether it establishes a task that you could accomplish given the available time and the expected length.<br>WORKING THESIS<br>Rock and roll has evolved dramatically since the 1950s. [Tracing this history in a few pages would be impossible.] |
| **3 TAKE ACTION** | ■ Rework the circled topic. State it more clearly, and specify what it means to you.<br>■ Define or identify the topic in terms of your purpose and the likely interests of your audience.<br>REVISED THESIS<br>An ability to adjust to, even thrive under, challenging circumstances is essential for World Action volunteers. | ■ Rework your underlined slant. Jot down ideas to sharpen it and express an engaging approach to your topic.<br>■ Refine it to accomplish your purpose and appeal to your audience.<br>REVISED THESIS<br>Volunteering builds practical skills while connecting volunteers more fully to their communities. | ■ Restrict your thesis to a slice of the pie, not the whole pie.<br>■ Focus on one part or element, not several. Break it apart, and pick only a chunk.<br>■ Reduce many ideas to one point, or convert a negative statement to a positive one.<br>REVISED THESIS<br>The music of the alternative-rock band Wilco continues to evolve as members experiment with vocal moods and instrumentation. |

your thesis. Skim across the top to identify questions you might ask about your working thesis. When you answer a question with "Yes" or "Maybe," move straight down the column to Locate Specifics under that question. Use the activities there to pinpoint gaps, problems, or weaknesses. Then move straight down the column to Take Action. Use the advice that suits your problem as you revise.

## How to Use a Thesis to Organize

For more on using a thesis to develop an outline, see pp. 412–15.

Often a good, clear thesis will suggest an organization for your ideas.

| | |
|---|---|
| WORKING THESIS | Despite the disadvantages of living in a downtown business district, I wouldn't live anywhere else. |
| FIRST ¶S | Disadvantages of living in the business district |
| NEXT ¶S | Advantages of living there |
| LAST ¶ | Affirmation of your preference for downtown life |

Just putting your working thesis into words can help organize you and keep you on track. A clear thesis can guide you as you select details and connect sections of the essay.

For more on key terms in college assignments, see p. 37 and pp. 336–38.

In addition, your thesis can prepare your readers for the pattern of development or sequence of ideas that you plan to present. As a writer, you look for key words (such as *compare, propose,* or *evaluate*) when you size up an assignment. Such words alert you to what's expected. When you write or revise your thesis, you can use such terms or their equivalents (such as *benefit* or *consequence* instead of *effect*) to preview for readers the likely direction of your paper. Then they, too, will know what to expect.

| | |
|---|---|
| WORKING THESIS | Expanding the campus program for energy conservation would bring welcome financial and environmental benefits. |
| FIRST ¶S | Explanation of the campus energy situation |
| NEXT ¶S | Justification of the need for the proposed expansion |
| NEXT ¶S | Financial benefits for the college and students |
| NEXT ¶S | Environmental benefits for the region and beyond |
| LAST ¶ | Concluding assertion of the value of the expansion |

As you write, however, you don't have to cling to a thesis for dear life. If further investigation changes your thinking, you can change your thesis.

| | |
|---|---|
| WORKING THESIS | Because wolves are a menace to people and farm animals, they ought to be exterminated. |
| REVISED THESIS | The wolf, a relatively peaceful animal useful in nature's scheme of things, ought to be protected. |

You can restate a thesis any time: as you write, revise, or revise again.

### Learning by Doing Using a Thesis to Preview

Each of the following thesis statements is from a student paper in a different field. With your classmates, consider how each one previews the essay to come and how you would expect the essay to be organized into sections.

1. Although the intent of inclusion is to provide the best care for all children by treating both special- and general-education students equally, some people in the field believe that the full inclusion of disabled children in mainstream classrooms may not be in the best interest of either type of student. (From "Is Inclusion the Answer?" by Sarah E. Goers)
2. With ancient Asian roots and contemporary European influences, the Japanese language has continued to change and to reflect cultural change as well. (From "Japanese: Linguistic Diversity" by Stephanie Hawkins)
3. *Manifest destiny* was an expression by leaders and politicians in the 1840s to clarify continental extension and expansion and in a sense revitalize the mission and national destiny for Americans. (From ethnic studies examination answer by Angela Mendy)
4. By comparing the *Aeneid* with *Troilus and Criseyde*, one can easily see the effects of the code of courtly love on literature. (From "The Effect of the Code of Courtly Love: A Comparison of Virgil's *Aeneid* and Chaucer's *Troilus and Criseyde*" by Cindy Keeler)
5. The effects of pollutants on the endangered Least Tern entering the Upper Newport Bay should be quantified so that necessary action can be taken to further protect and encourage the species. (From "Contaminant Residues in Least Tern [*Sterna antillarum*] Eggs Nesting in Upper Newport Bay" by Susanna Olsen)

## Organizing Your Ideas

When you organize an essay, you select an order for the parts that makes sense and shows your readers how the ideas are connected. Often your organization will not only help a reader follow your points but also reinforce your emphases by moving from beginning to end or from least to most significant, as the table on page 409 illustrates.

### Grouping Your Ideas

While exploring a topic, you will usually find a few ideas that seem to belong together—two facts on New York traffic jams, four actions of New York drivers, three problems with New York streets. But similar ideas seldom appear together in your notes because you did not discover them all at the same time. For this reason, you need to sort your ideas into groups and arrange them in sequences. Here are six ways to work:

| Organization | Movement | Typical Use | Example |
|---|---|---|---|
| Spatial | Left to right, right to left, bottom to top, top to bottom, front to back, outside to inside | ▪ Describing a place, a scene, or an environment<br>▪ Describing a person's physical appearance | Describe an ocean vista, moving from the tidepools on the rocky shore to the plastic buoys floating offshore to the sparkling water meeting the sunset sky. |
| Chronological | What happens first, second, and next, continuing until the end | ▪ Narrating an event<br>▪ Explaining steps in a procedure<br>▪ Explaining the development of an idea or a trend | Narrate the events that led up to an accident: leaving home late, stopping for an errand, checking messages while rushing along the highway, racing up to the intersection. |
| Logical | General to specific (or the reverse), least important to most, cause to effect, problem to solution | ▪ Explaining an idea<br>▪ Persuading readers to accept a stand, a proposal, or an evaluation | Analyze the effects of last year's storms by selecting four major consequences, placing the most important one last for emphasis. |

1. *Rainbow connections.* List the main points you're going to express. Highlight points that go together with the same color. When you write, follow the color code, and integrate related ideas at the same time.
2. *Emphasizing ideas.* Make a copy of your file of ideas or notes. Use your software tools to highlight, categorize, and shape your thinking by grouping or distinguishing ideas. Mark similar or related ideas in the same way; call out major points. Then move related materials into groups.

   Highlighting
   Boxing
   Showing color
   Using **bold**, *italics*, underlining

   • Adding bullets
   1. Numbering
   Changing fonts
   Varying print sizes

3. *Linking.* List major points, and then draw lines (in color if you wish) to link related ideas. Figure 20.1 illustrates a linked list for an essay on Manhattan driving. The writer has connected related points, numbered their sequence, and supplied each group with a heading. Each heading will probably inspire a topic sentence to introduce a major division of the essay. Because one point, chauffeured luxury cars, failed to relate to any other, the writer has a choice: drop it or develop it.

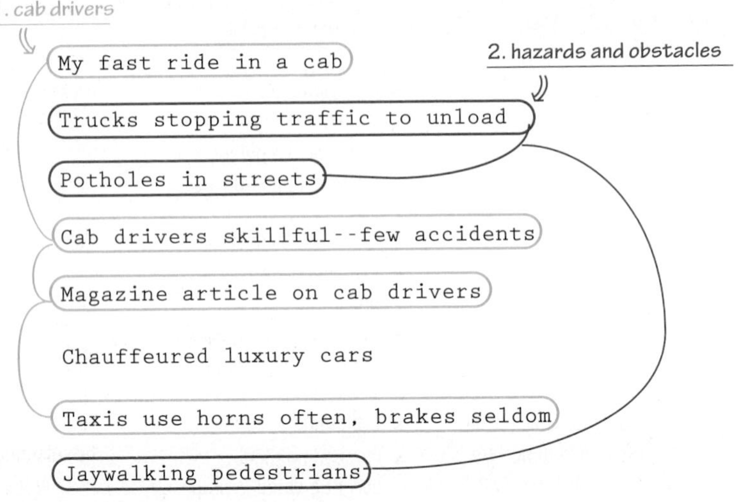


**Figure 20.1** The Linking Method for Grouping Ideas

4. *Solitaire*. Collect notes and ideas on roomy (5-by-8-inch) file cards, especially to write about literature or research. To organize, spread out the cards; arrange and rearrange them. When each idea seems to lead to the next, gather the cards into a deck in this order. As you write, deal yourself a card at a time, and turn its contents into sentences.
5. *Slide show*. Use presentation software to write your notes and ideas on "slides." When you're done, view your slides one by one or as a collection. Sort your slides into the most promising order.
6. *Clustering*. Clustering is a visual method for generating as well as grouping ideas. In the middle of a page, write your topic in a word or a phrase. Then think of the major divisions into which you might break your topic. For an essay on Manhattan drivers, your major divisions might be *types* of drivers: (1) taxi drivers, (2) bus drivers, (3) truck drivers, (4) New York drivers of private cars, and (5) out-of-town drivers of private cars. Arrange these divisions around your topic, circle them, and draw lines out from the major topic. You now have a rough plan for an essay. (See Figure 20.2.)

   Around each division, make another cluster of details you might include—examples, illustrations, facts, statistics, opinions. Circle each specific item, connect it to the appropriate type of driver, and then expand the details into a paragraph. This technique lets you know where you have enough specific information to make your paper clear and interesting—and where you don't. If one subtopic has no small circles around it (such as "Bus Drivers" in Figure 20.2), either add specifics to expand it or drop it.

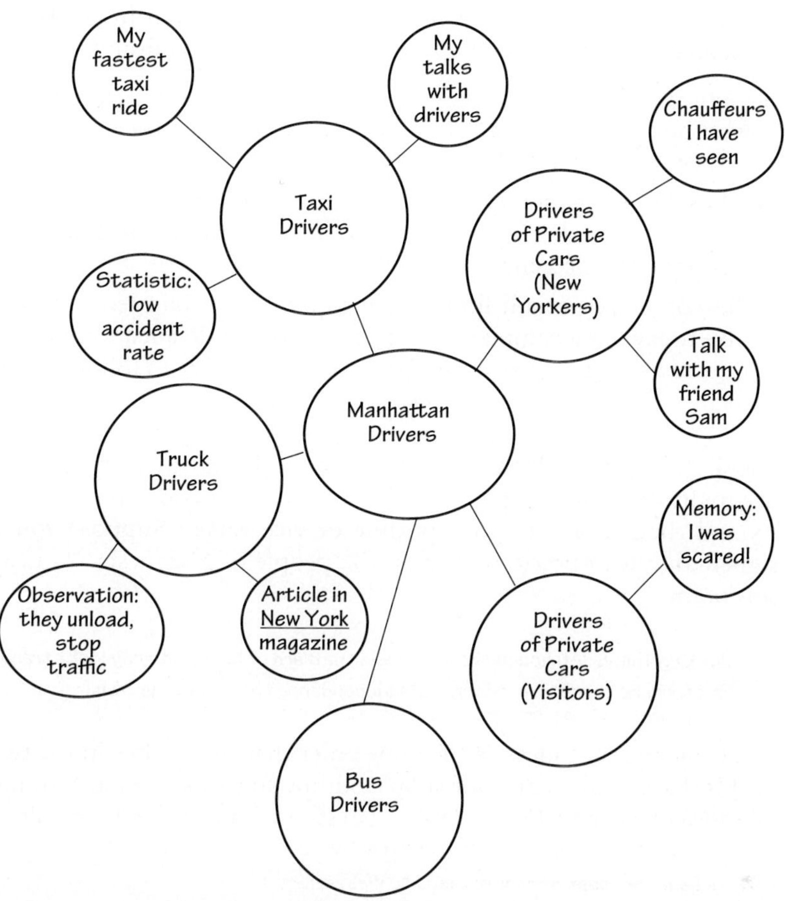


**Figure 20.2** The Clustering Method for Grouping Ideas

## Learning by Doing Clustering

Generate clusters for three of the following topics. With your classmates, discuss which one of the three would probably help you write the best paper.

| | | |
|---|---|---|
| teachers | fast food | civil rights |
| Internet sites | leisure activities | substance abuse |
| my favorite restaurants | musicians | technology |

## Outlining

A familiar way to organize is to outline. A written outline, whether brief or detailed, acts as a map that you make before a journey. It shows where to leave from, where to stop along the way, and where to arrive. If you forget where you are going or what you want to say, you can consult your outline to get back on track. When you turn in your essay, your instructor may request an outline as both a map for readers and a skeletal summary.

For more on thesis statements, see pp. 399–408.

For more on using outlining for revision, see pp. 461–62.

- Some writers like to begin with a working thesis. If it's clear, it may suggest how to develop or expand an outline, allowing the plan for the paper to grow naturally from the idea behind it.
- Others prefer to start with a loose informal outline—perhaps just a list of points to make. If readers find your papers mechanical, such an outline may free up your writing.
- Still others, especially for research papers or complicated arguments, like to lay out a complex job very carefully in a detailed formal outline. If readers find your writing disorganized and hard to follow, this more detailed plan might be especially useful.

**Thesis-Guided Outlines.** Your working thesis may identify ideas you can use to organize your paper. (If it doesn't, you may want to revise your thesis and then return to your outline or vice versa.) Suppose you are assigned an anthropology paper on the people of Melanesia. You focus on this point:

> Working Thesis: Although the Melanesian pattern of family life may look strange to Westerners, it fosters a degree of independence that rivals our own.

If you lay out your ideas in the same order that they follow in the two parts of this thesis statement, your simple outline suggests an essay that naturally falls into two parts—features that seem strange and admirable results.

1. Features that appear strange to Westerners
   - A woman supported by her brother, not her husband
   - Trial marriages common
   - Divorce from her children possible for any mother
2. Admirable results of system
   - Wives not dependent on husbands for support
   - Divorce between mates uncommon
   - Greater freedom for parents and children

When you create a thesis-guided outline, look for the key element of your working thesis. This key element can suggest both a useful question to consider and an organization, as the table on page 413 illustrates.

**Informal Outlines.** For in-class writing, brief essays, and familiar topics, a short or informal outline, also called a *scratch outline,* may serve your needs. Jot down a list of points in the order you plan to make them. Use this outline, for your eyes only, to help you get organized, stick to the point, and remember ideas under pressure. The following example outlines a short paper explaining how outdoor enthusiasts can avoid

| Sample Thesis Statement | Type of Key Element | Examples of Key Element | Question You Might Ask | Organization of Outline |
|---|---|---|---|---|
| A varied personal exercise program has four main *advantages*. | Plural word | Words such as *benefits*, *advantages*, *teenagers*, or *reasons* | What are the types, kinds, or examples of this word? | List outline headings based on the categories or cases you identify. |
| Wylie's *interpretation* of Van Gogh's last paintings unifies aesthetics and psychology. | Key word identifying an approach or vantage point | Words such as *claim*, *argument*, *position*, *interpretation*, or *point of view* | What are the parts, aspects, or elements of this approach? | List outline headings based on the components that you identify. |
| *Preparing* a pasta dinner for surprise guests can be an easy process. | Key word identifying an activity | Words such as *preparing*, *harming*, or *improving* | How is this activity accomplished, or how does it happen? | Supply a heading for each step, stage, or element that the activity involves. |
| *Although* the new wetland preserve will protect only some wildlife, it will bring several long-term benefits to the region. | One part of the sentence subordinate to another | Sentence part beginning with a qualification such as *despite*, *because*, *since*, or *although* | What does the qualification include, and what does the main statement include? | Use a major heading for the qualification and another for the main statement. |
| When Sandie Burns arrives in her wheelchair at the soccer field, other parents soon see that she is a *typical* soccer mom. | General evaluation that assigns a quality or value to someone or something | Evaluative words such as *typical*, *unusual*, *valuable*, *notable*, or other specific qualities | What examples, illustrations, or clusters of details will show this quality? | Add a heading for each extended example or each group of examples or details you want to use. |
| In spite of these tough economic times, the student senate *should* strongly recommend extended hours for the computer lab. | Claim or argument advocating a certain decision, action, or solution | Words such as *should*, *could*, *might*, *ought to*, *need to*, or *must* | Which reasons and evidence will justify this opinion? Which will counter the opinions of others who disagree with it? | Provide a heading for each major justification or defensive point; add headings for countering reasons. |

illnesses carried by unsafe drinking water. It simply lists the methods for treating potentially unsafe water that the writer plans to explain.

> Working Thesis: Campers and hikers need to ensure the safety of the water that they drink from rivers or streams.
>
> Introduction: Treatments for potentially unsafe drinking water
>
> 1. Small commercial filter
>    –Remove bacteria and protozoa including salmonella and E. coli
>    –Use brands convenient for campers and hikers
> 2. Chemicals
>    –Use bleach, chlorine, or iodine
>    –Follow general rule: 12 drops per gallon of water
> 3. Boiling
>    –Boil for 5 minutes (Red Cross) to 15 minutes (National Safety Council)
>    –Store in a clean, covered container
>
> Conclusion: Using one of three methods of treating water, campers and hikers can enjoy safe water from natural sources.

This simple outline could easily fall into a five-paragraph essay or grow to eight paragraphs – introduction, conclusion, and three pairs of paragraphs in between. You won't know how many you'll need until you write.

An informal outline can be even briefer than the preceding one. To answer an exam question or prepare a very short paper, your outline might be no more than an *outer plan* – three or four phrases jotted in a list:

> Isolation of region
> Tradition of family businesses
> Growth of electronic commuting

The process of making an informal outline can help you figure out how to develop your ideas. Say you plan a "how-to" essay analyzing the process of buying a used car, beginning with this thesis:

> Working Thesis: Despite traps that await the unwary, preparing yourself before you shop can help you find a good used car.

The key word here is *preparing*. Considering *how* the buyer should prepare before shopping for a used car, you're likely to outline several ideas:

> –Read car blogs, car magazines, and Consumer Reports.
> –Check craigslist, dealer sites, and classified ads.
> –Make phone calls to several dealers.
> –Talk to friends who have bought used cars.
> –Know what to look and listen for when you test-drive.
> –Have a mechanic check out any car before you buy it.

After some horror stories about people who got taken by car sharks, you can discuss, point by point, your advice. You can always change the sequence, add or drop an idea, or revise your thesis as you go along.

### Learning by Doing Moving from Outline to Thesis

Based on each of the following informal outlines, write a possible thesis statement expressing a possible slant, attitude, or point (even if you aren't sure that the position is entirely defensible). Compare thesis statements with classmates. What similarities and differences do you find? How do you account for these?

1. Smartphones
   Get the financial and service plans of various smartphone companies.
   Read the phone contracts as well as the promotional offers.
   Look for the time period, flexibility, and cancellation provisions.
   Check the display, keyboard, camera, apps, and other features.
2. Popular Mystery Novels
   Both Tony Hillerman and Margaret Coel have written mysteries with Native American characters and settings.
   Hillerman's novels feature members of the Navajo Tribal Police.
   Coel's novels feature a female attorney who is an Arapaho and a Jesuit priest at the reservation mission who grew up in Boston.
   Hillerman's stories take place mostly on the extensive Navajo Reservation in Arizona, New Mexico, and Utah.
   Coel's are set mostly on the large Wind River Reservation in Wyoming.
   Hillerman and Coel try to convey tribal culture accurately, although their mysteries involve different tribes.
   Both also explore similarities, differences, and conflicts between Native American cultures and the dominant culture.
3. Downtown Playspace
   Downtown Playspace has financial and volunteer support but needs more.
   Statistics show the need for a regional expansion of options for children.
   Downtown Playspace will serve visitors at the Children's Museum and local children in Head Start, preschool, and elementary schools.
   It will combine an outdoor playground with indoor technology space.
   Land and a building are available, but both require renovation.

**Formal Outlines.** A *formal outline* is an elaborate guide, built with time and care, for a long, complex paper. Because major reports, research papers, and senior theses require so much work, some professors and departments ask a writer to submit a formal outline at an early stage and to include one in the final draft. A formal outline shows how ideas relate one to another—which ones are equal and important (*coordinate*) and which are less important (*subordinate*). It clearly and logically spells out where you are going. If you outline again after writing a draft, you can use the revised outline to check your logic then as well, perhaps revealing where to revise.

When you make a full formal outline, follow these steps:

- Place your thesis statement at the beginning.
- List the major points that support and develop your thesis, labeling them with roman numerals (I, II, III).
- Break down the major points into divisions with capital letters (A, B, C), subdivide those using arabic numerals (1, 2, 3), and subdivide those using small letters (a, b, c). Continue until your outline is fully developed. If a very complex project requires further subdivision, use arabic numerals and small letters in parentheses.
- Indent each level of division in turn: the deeper the indentation, the more specific the ideas. Align like-numbered or -lettered headings under one another.
- Cast all headings in parallel grammatical form: phrases or sentences, but not both in the same outline.

For more on parallelism, see B2 (p. A-52) in the Quick Editing Guide.

For more on analysis and division, see pp. 446–53.

CAUTION: Because an outline divides or analyzes ideas, some readers and instructors disapprove of categories with only one subpoint, reasoning that you can't divide anything into one part. Let's say that your outline on earthquakes lists a 1 without a 2:

D. Probable results of an earthquake include structural damage.
   1. House foundations crack.

Logically, if you are going to discuss the *probable results* of an earthquake, you need to include more than one result:

D. Probable results of an earthquake include structural damage.
   1. House foundations crack.
   2. Road surfaces are damaged.
   3. Water mains break.

Not only have you now come up with more points, but you have also emphasized the one placed last.

A *formal topic outline* for a long paper might include several levels of ideas, as this outline for Linn Bourgeau's research paper illustrates. Such an outline can help you work out both a persuasive sequence for the parts of a paper and a logical order for any information from sources.

Crucial Choices: Who Will Save the Wetlands If Everyone Is at the Mall?

Working Thesis: Federal regulations need to foster state laws and educational requirements that will help protect the few wetlands that are left, restore as many as possible of those that have been destroyed, and take measures to improve the damage from overdevelopment.

I. Nature's ecosystem
   A. Loss of wetlands nationally
   B. Loss of wetlands in Illinois
      1. More flooding and poorer water quality
      2. Lost ability to prevent floods, clean water, and store water
   C. Need to protect humankind
II. Dramatic floods
   A. Midwestern floods in 1993 and 2011
      1. Lost wetlands in Illinois and other states
      2. Devastation in some states
   B. Cost in dollars and lives
      1. Deaths during recent flooding
      2. Costs in millions of dollars a year
   C. Flood prevention
      1. Plants and soil
      2. Floodplain overflow
III. Wetland laws
   A. Inadequately informed legislators
      1. Watersheds
      2. Interconnections in natural water systems
   B. Water purification
      1. Wetlands and water
      2. Pavement and lawns
IV. Need to save wetlands
   A. New federal laws
   B. Re-education about interconnectedness
      1. Ecology at every grade level
      2. Education for politicians, developers, and legislators
   C. Choices in schools, legislature, and people's daily lives

## Learning by Doing Responding to an Outline

Discuss the formal topic outline above with a small group or the entire class, considering the following questions:

- Would this outline be useful in organizing an essay?
- How is the organization logical? Is it easy to follow? What are other possible arrangements for the ideas?
- Is this outline sufficiently detailed for a paper? Can you spot any gaps?
- What possible pitfalls would the writer using this outline need to avoid?

A topic outline may help you work out a clear sequence of ideas but may not elaborate or connect them. Although you may not be sure how everything will fit together until you write a draft, you may find that a *formal sentence outline* clarifies what you want to say. It also moves you a step closer to drafting topic sentences and paragraphs even though you would still need to add detailed information. Notice how this sentence outline for Linn Bourgeau's research paper expands her ideas.

Crucial Choices: Who Will Save the Wetlands If Everyone Is at the Mall?

Working Thesis: Federal regulations need to foster state laws and educational requirements that will help protect the few wetlands that are left, restore as many as possible of those that have been destroyed, and take measures to improve the damage from overdevelopment.

I. Each person, as part of nature's ecosystem, chooses how to interact with nature, including wetlands.
   A. The nation has lost over half its wetlands since Columbus arrived.
   B. Illinois has lost even more by legislating and draining them away.
      1. Destroying wetlands creates more flooding and poorer water quality.
      2. The wetlands could prevent floods, clean the water supply, and store water.
   C. The wetlands need to be protected because they protect and serve humankind.

II. Floods are dramatic and visible consequences of not protecting wetlands.
   A. The midwestern floods of 1993 and 2011 were disastrous.
      1. Illinois and other states had lost their wetlands.
      2. Those states also suffered the most devastation.
   B. The cost of flooding can be tallied in dollars spent and in lives lost.
      1. Nearly thirty people died in floods between 1995 and 2011.
      2. Flooding in 2011 cost Illinois about $216 million.
   C. Preventing floods is a valuable role of wetlands.
      1. Plants and soil manage excess water.
      2. The Mississippi River floodplain was reduced from 60 days of water overflow to 12.

III. The laws misinterpret or ignore the basic understanding of wetlands.
   A. Legislators need to know that an "isolated wetland" does not exist.
      1. Water travels within an area called a watershed.
      2. The law needs to consider interconnections in water systems.
   B. Wetlands naturally purify water.
      1. Water filters and flows in wetlands.
      2. Pavement and lawns carry water over, not through, the soil.

IV. Who will save the wetlands if everyone is at the mall?
    A. Federal laws should require implementing what we know.
    B. The vital concept of interconnectedness means reeducating everyone from legislators to fourth graders.
        1. Ecology must be incorporated into the curriculum for every grade.
        2. Educating politicians, developers, and legislators is more difficult.
    C. The choices people make in their schools, legislative systems, and daily lives will determine the future of water quality and flooding.

## Learning by Doing Outlining

1. Using one of your groups of ideas from the activities in Chapter 19, construct a formal topic outline that might serve as a guide for an essay.
2. Now turn that topic outline into a formal sentence outline.
3. Discuss both outlines with your classmates and instructor, bringing up any difficulties you met. If you get better notions for organizing, change the outline.

For exercises on organizing support effectively, visit **bedfordstmartins.com/bedguide**.

## Learning by Doing Reflecting on Planning

Reflect on the purpose and audience for your current paper. Then return to the thesis, outline, or other plans you have prepared. Will your plans accomplish your purpose? Are they directed to your intended audience? Make any needed adjustments. Exchange plans with a classmate or small group, and discuss ways to continue improving them.

# 21 Strategies for Drafting

Learning to write well involves learning what key questions to ask yourself: How can I begin this draft? What should I do if I get stuck? How can I flesh out the bones of my paper? How can I end effectively? How can I keep my readers with me? In this chapter we offer advice to get you going and keep you going, drafting the first paragraph to the last.

## Making a Start Enjoyable

A playful start may get you hard at work before you know it.

- **Time Yourself.** Set your watch, alarm, or egg timer, and vow to draft a page before the buzzer sounds. Don't stop for anything. If you're writing nonsense, just push on. You can cross out later.
- **Slow to a Crawl.** If speed quotas don't work, time yourself to write with exaggerated laziness, maybe a sentence every fifteen minutes.
- **Scribble on a Scrap.** If you dread the blank paper or screen, try starting on scrap paper, the back of a list, or a small notebook page.
- **Begin Writing What You Find Most Appetizing.** Start in the middle or at the end, wherever thoughts come easily to mind. As novelist Bill Downey observes, "Writers are allowed to have their dessert first."
- **State Your Purpose.** Set forth what you want to achieve: To tell a story? To explain something? To win a reader over to your ideas?
- **Slip into a Reader's Shoes.** Put yourself in your reader's place. Start writing what you'd like to find out from the paper.
- **Nutshell It.** Summarize the paper you want to write. Condense your ideas into one small, tight paragraph. Later you can expand each sentence until the meaning is clear and all points are adequately supported.
- **Shrink Your Immediate Job.** Break the writing task into small parts, and tackle only the first, perhaps just two paragraphs.
- **Seek a Provocative Title.** Write down a dozen possible titles for your paper. If one sounds strikingly good, don't let it go to waste!

- **Record Yourself.** Talk a first draft into a recorder or your voice mail. Play it back. Then write. Even if it is hard to transcribe your spoken words, this technique may set your mind in motion.
- **Speak Up.** On your feet, before an imaginary cheering crowd, spontaneously utter a first paragraph. Then—quick!—record it or write it out.
- **Take Short Breaks.** Even if you don't feel tired, take a break every half hour or so. Get up, walk around the room, stretch, or get a drink of water. Two or three minutes should be enough to refresh your mind.

## Restarting

When you have to write a long or demanding essay that you can't finish in one sitting, you may return to it only to find yourself stalled. You crank your starter and nothing happens. Your engine seems reluctant to turn over. Try the following suggestions for getting back on the road.

For interactive Learning by Doing activities on Identifying Topic Sentences and Identifying Transitions, go to Ch. 21: **bedfordstmartins.com/bedguide**.

- **Leave Hints for How to Continue.** If you're ready to quit, jot down what might come next or the first sentence of the next section. When you return, you will face not a blank wall but rich and suggestive graffiti.
- **Pause in Midstream.** Try breaking off in midsentence or midparagraph. Just leave a sentence trailing off into space, even if you know its closing words. When you return, you can start writing again immediately.
- **Repeat.** If the next sentence refuses to appear, simply recopy the last one until that shy creature emerges on the page.
- **Reread.** When you return to work, spend a few minutes rereading what you have already written or what you have planned.
- **Switch Instruments.** Do you compose on a laptop? Try longhand. Or drop your pen to type. Write on note cards or colored paper.
- **Change Activities.** When words won't come, turn to something quite different. Run, walk your dog, cook a meal, or nap. Or reward yourself—after you reach a certain point—with a call to a friend or a game. All the while, your unconscious mind will work on your writing task.

## Paragraphing

An essay is written not in large, indigestible lumps but in *paragraphs*—small units, each more or less self-contained, each contributing some new idea in support of the essay's thesis. Writers dwell on one idea at a time, stating it, developing it, illustrating it with examples or a few facts—*showing* readers, with detailed evidence, exactly what they mean.

For more on developing ideas within paragraphs, see Ch. 22.

Paragraphs can be as short as one sentence or as long as a page. Sometimes length is governed by audience, purpose, or medium. Journalists expect newspaper readers to gobble up facts like popcorn, quickly skimming short one- or two-sentence paragraphs. College writers, in contrast, should assume their readers expect to read well-developed paragraphs.

When readers see a paragraph indentation, they interpret it as a pause, a chance for a deep breath. After that signpost, they expect you to concentrate on a new aspect of your thesis for the rest of that paragraph. This chapter gives you advice on guiding readers through your writing—using opening paragraphs to draw them in, topic sentences to focus and control body paragraphs, and concluding paragraphs to wrap up the discussion.

## Using Topic Sentences

A *topic sentence* spells out the main idea of a paragraph in the body of an essay. It guides you as you write, and it hooks your readers as they discover what to expect and how to interpret the paragraph. As the topic sentence establishes the focus of the paragraph, it also relates the paragraph to the topic and thesis of the essay as a whole. (Much of the advice on topic sentences for paragraphs also extends to thesis statements for essays.) To convert an idea to a topic sentence, add your own slant, attitude, or point.

Main Idea + Slant or Attitude or Point = Topic Sentence

For more on thesis statements, see pp. 399–408.

How do you write a good topic sentence? Make it interesting, accurate, and limited. The more pointed and lively it is, the more it will interest readers. Even a dull, vague start is enlivened once you zero in on a specific point.

| | |
|---|---|
| MAIN IDEA + SLANT | television + everything that's wrong with it |
| DULL START | There are many things wrong with television. |
| POINTED TOPIC SENTENCE | Of all the disappointing television programming, what I dislike most is melodramatic news. |
| ¶ PLAN | Illustrate the point with two or three melodramatic news stories. |

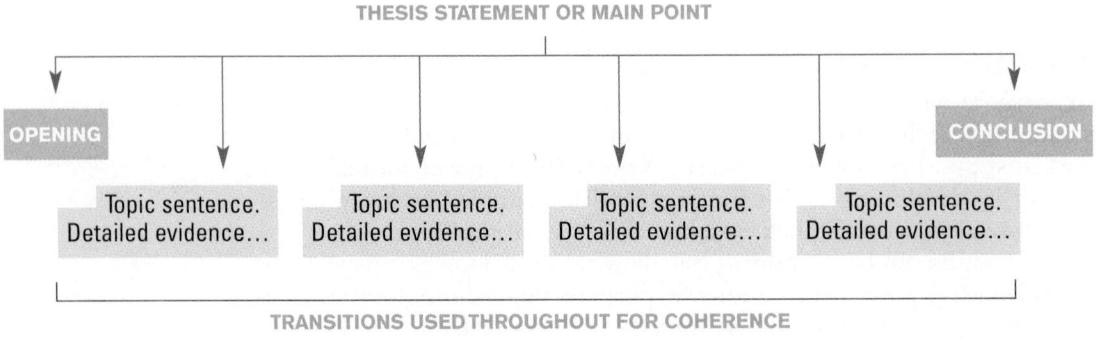

THESIS STATEMENT OR MAIN POINT

OPENING

Topic sentence. Detailed evidence...

Topic sentence. Detailed evidence...

Topic sentence. Detailed evidence...

Topic sentence. Detailed evidence...

CONCLUSION

TRANSITIONS USED THROUGHOUT FOR COHERENCE

A topic sentence also should be an accurate guide to the rest of the paragraph so that readers expect just what the paragraph delivers.

| | |
|---|---|
| INACCURATE GUIDE | All types of household emergencies can catch people off guard. [The paragraph covers steps for emergency preparedness – not the variety of emergencies.] |
| ACCURATE TOPIC SENTENCE | Although an emergency may not be a common event, emergency preparedness should be routine at home. |
| ¶ PLAN | Explain how a household can prepare for an emergency with a medical kit, a well-stocked pantry, and a communication plan. |

Finally, a topic sentence should be limited so you don't mislead or frustrate readers about what the paragraph covers.

| | |
|---|---|
| MISLEADING | Seven factors have contributed to the increasing obesity of the average American. [The paragraph discusses only one – portion size.] |
| LIMITED TOPIC SENTENCE | Portion size is a major factor that contributes to the increasing obesity of average Americans. |
| ¶ PLAN | Define healthy portion sizes, contrasting them with the large portions common in restaurants and in packaged foods. |

**Open with a Topic Sentence.** Usually the topic sentence appears first in the paragraph, followed by sentences that clarify, illustrate, and support what it says. It is typically a statement but can sometimes be a question, alerting the reader to the topic without giving away the punchline. This example from "The Virtues of the Quiet Hero," Senator John McCain's essay about "honor, faith, and service," was presented on October 17, 2005, in the "This I Believe" series on National Public Radio's *All Things Considered*. Here, as in all the following examples, we have put the topic sentence in *italics*.

> *Years later, I saw an example of honor in the most surprising of places.* As a scared American prisoner of war in Vietnam, I was tied in torture ropes by my tormentors and left alone in an empty room to suffer through the night. Later in the evening, a guard I had never spoken to entered the room and silently loosened the ropes to relieve my suffering. Just before morning, that same guard came back and retightened the ropes before his less humanitarian comrades returned. He never said a word to me. Some months later on a Christmas morning, as I stood alone in the prison courtyard, that same guard walked up to me and stood next to me for a few moments. Then with his sandal, the guard drew a cross in the dirt. We stood wordlessly there for a minute or two, venerating the cross, until the guard rubbed it out and walked away.

This paragraph moves from the general to the specific. The topic sentence clearly states at the outset what the paragraph is about. The second sentence introduces the situation McCain recalls. Then the next half-dozen sentences supply two concrete, yet concise, illustrations of his central point.

**Place a Topic Sentence near the Beginning.** Sometimes the first sentence of a paragraph acts as a transition, linking what is to come with what has gone before. Then the *second* sentence might be the topic sentence as illustrated in the following paragraph from *Tim Gunn's Fashion Bible: The Fascinating History of Everything in Your Closet* by Tim Gunn with Ada Calhoun (New York: Gallery Books, 2012, p. 190). The paragraph immediately before this one summarizes how the early history of shoe design often tried to balance competing desires for modesty, alluring beauty, and practicality. This prior paragraph begins, "Modesty got the better of the shoe industry in the seventeenth century" and concludes, "It wasn't until the late 1930s that sling-backs and open-toed heels gave us another glimpse at the toes and heels."

> Heel height has fluctuated ever since, as have platforms. One goal of a high shoe is to elevate the wearer out of the muck. Before there was pavement (asphalt didn't even appear until 1824, in Paris), streets were very muddy. People often wore one kind of shoe indoors, like a satin slipper, and another outside, perhaps with some kind of overshoe. One type of overshoe was called pattens, which were made of leather, wood, or iron, and lifted the wearer up a couple of inches or more from the sidewalk to protect the sole of the shoe from grime. Men and women wore these from the fourteenth- to the mid-nineteenth century, when street conditions started to become slightly less disgusting.

**End with a Topic Sentence.** Occasionally a writer, trying to persuade the reader to agree, piles detail on detail. Then, with a dramatic flourish, the writer *concludes* with the topic sentence, as student Heidi Kessler does.

> A fourteen-year-old writes to an advice columnist in my hometown newspaper that she has "done it" lots of times and sex is "no big deal." At the neighborhood clinic where my aunt works, a hardened sixteen-year-old requests her third abortion. A girl-child I know has two children of her own, but no husband. A college student in my dorm now finds herself sterile from a "social disease" picked up during casual sexual encounters. Multiply these examples by thousands. *It seems clear to me that women, who fought so hard for sexual freedom equal to that of men, have emerged from the battle not as joyous free spirits but as the sexual revolution's walking wounded.*

This paragraph moves from particular to general – from four examples about individuals to one large statement about American women. By the time you finish, you might be ready to accept the paragraph's conclusion.

**Imply a Topic Sentence.** It is also possible to find a perfectly unified, well-organized paragraph that has no topic sentence at all, like the following from "New York" (*Esquire* July 1960) by Gay Talese:

> Each afternoon in New York a rather seedy saxophone player, his cheeks blown out like a spinnaker, stands on the sidewalk playing "Danny Boy" in such a sad, sensitive way that he soon has half the neighborhood peeking out of windows tossing nickels, dimes, and quarters at his feet. Some of the coins roll under parked cars, but most of them are caught in his outstretched hand. The saxophone player is a street musician named Joe Gabler; for the past thirty years he has serenaded every block in New York and has sometimes been tossed as much as $100 a day in coins. He is also hit with buckets of water, empty beer cans and eggs, and chased by wild dogs. He is believed to be the last of New York's ancient street musicians.

No one sentence neatly sums up the writer's idea. Like most effective paragraphs that do not state a topic sentence, this one contains something just as good – a *topic idea.* The author doesn't wander aimlessly. He knows exactly what he wants to achieve – a description of how the famous Joe Gabler plies his trade. Because Talese keeps this purpose firmly in mind, the main point – that Gabler meets both reward and abuse – is clear to the reader as well.

## Learning by Doing Shaping Topic Sentences

In a small group, answer these questions about each topic sentence below:

> Will it catch readers' attention? Is it accurate? Is it limited? How might you develop the idea in the rest of the paragraph? Can you improve it?

1. Television commercials stereotype people.
2. Living away from home for the first time is hard.
3. It's good for a child to have a pet.
4. A flea market is a good place to buy jewelry.
5. Pollution should be controlled.
6. Everybody should recycle wastes.

## Writing an Opening

Even writers with something to say may find it hard to begin. Often they are so intent on a brilliant opening that they freeze. They forget even the essentials – set up the topic, stick to what's relevant, and establish a thesis. If you feel like a deer paralyzed by headlights, try these ways of opening:

- Start with your thesis statement, with or without a full opening paragraph. Fill in the rest later.
- Write your thesis statement – the one you planned or one you'd now like to develop – in the middle of a page. Go back to the top, and concisely add the background a reader needs to see where you're going.
- Write a long beginning for your first draft; then cut it down to the most dramatic, exciting, or interesting essentials.
- Simply set down words – any words – on paper, without trying to write an arresting opening. Rewrite later.
- Write the first paragraph last, after you know where your essay goes.
- Move your conclusion to the beginning, and write a new ending.
- Write a summary for yourself and your readers.

Your opening should intrigue readers – engaging their minds and hearts, exciting their curiosity, drawing them into the world set forth in your writing.

### DISCOVERY CHECKLIST

- ☐ What vital background might readers need?
- ☐ What general situation might help you narrow down to your point?
- ☐ What facts or statistics might make your issue compelling?
- ☐ What powerful anecdote or incident might introduce your point?
- ☐ What striking example or comparison would engage a reader?
- ☐ What question will your thesis – and your essay – answer?
- ☐ What lively quotation would set the scene for your essay?
- ☐ What assertion or claim might be the necessary prelude for your essay?
- ☐ What points should you preview to prepare a reader for what will come?
- ☐ What would compel someone to keep on reading?

**Begin with a Story.** Often a simple anecdote can capture your readers' interest and thus serve as a good beginning. Here is how Nicholas Kulish opens his essay "Guy Walks into a Bar" (*New York Times* 5 Feb. 2006):

> Recently my friend Brandon and I walked along Atlantic Avenue in Brooklyn looking for a place to watch a football game and to quench our thirst for a cold brew. I pushed open the door and we were headed for a pair of empty stools when we both stopped cold. The bar was packed with under-age patrons.

Most of us, after an anecdote, want to read on. What will the writer say next? How does the anecdote launch the essay? Here, Kulish sets the stage for his objections to parents bringing babies and toddlers to bars.

**Comment on a Topic or Position.** Sometimes a writer expands on a topic, bringing in vital details, as David Morris does to open his article "Rootlessness" (*Utne Reader* May/June 1990):

> Americans are a rootless people. Each year one in six of us changes residences; one in four changes jobs. We see nothing troubling in these statistics. For most of us, they merely reflect the restless energy that made America great. A nation of immigrants, unsurprisingly, celebrates those willing to pick up stakes and move on: the frontiersman, the cowboy, the entrepreneur, the corporate raider.

After stating his point baldly, Morris supplies statistics to support his contention and briefly explains the phenomenon. This same strategy can be used to present a controversial opinion, then back it up with examples.

**Ask a Question.** An essay can begin with a question and answer, as James H. Austin begins "Four Kinds of Chance," in *Chase, Chance, and Creativity: The Lucky Art of Novelty* (New York: Columbia UP, 1978):

> What is chance? Dictionaries define it as something fortuitous that happens unpredictably without discernible human intention. Chance is unintentional and capricious, but we needn't conclude that chance is immune from human intervention. Indeed, chance plays several distinct roles when humans react creatively with one another and with their environment.

Beginning to answer the question in the first paragraph leads readers to expect the rest of the essay to continue the answer.

**End with the Thesis Statement.** Opening paragraphs often end by stating the essay's main point. After capturing readers' attention with an anecdote, gripping details, or examples, you lead readers in exactly the direction your essay goes. In response to the question "Should Washington stem the tide of both legal and illegal immigration?" ("Symposium."

For more on thesis statements, see pp. 399–408.

*Insight on the News* 11 Mar. 2002), Daniel T. Griswold uses this strategy to begin his answer:

> Immigration always has been controversial in the United States. More than two centuries ago, Benjamin Franklin worried that too many German immigrants would swamp America's predominantly British culture. In the mid-1800s, Irish immigrants were scorned as lazy drunks, not to mention Roman Catholics. At the turn of the century a wave of "new immigrants" – Poles, Italians, Russian Jews – were believed to be too different ever to assimilate into American life. *Today the same fears are raised about immigrants from Latin America and Asia, but current critics of immigration are as wrong as their counterparts were in previous eras.*

## Writing a Conclusion

The final paragraphs of an essay linger longest for readers, as in E. B. White's "Once More to the Lake" from *One Man's Meat* (Gardiner, ME: Tilbury House, 1941). White describes his return with his young son to a vacation spot he had loved as a child. As the essay ends in an unforgettable image, he realizes the inevitable passing of generations.

> When the others went swimming my son said he was going in, too. He pulled his dripping trunks from the line where they had hung all through the shower and wrung them out. Languidly, and with no thought of going in, I watched him, his hard little body, skinny and bare, saw him wince slightly as he pulled up around his vitals the small, soggy, icy garment. As he buckled the swollen belt, suddenly my groin felt the chill of death.

White's classic ending opens with a sentence that points back to the previous paragraph as it also looks ahead. Then White leads us quickly to his final, chilling insight. And then he stops.

It's easy to say what *not* to do at the end of an essay: don't leave your readers half expecting you to go on. Don't restate all you've just said. Don't introduce a brand-new topic that leads away from your point. And don't signal that the end is near with an obvious phrase like "As I have said." For some answers to "How *do* you write an ending, then?" try this checklist.

---

**DISCOVERY CHECKLIST**

- ☐ What restatement of your thesis would give readers satisfying closure?
- ☐ What provocative implications of your thesis might answer "What now?" or "What's the significance of what I've said?"
- ☐ What snappy quotation or statement would wrap up your point?
- ☐ What closing facts or statistics might confirm the merit of your point?

- ☐ What final anecdote, incident, or example might round out your ideas?
- ☐ What question has your essay answered?
- ☐ What assertion or claim might you want to restate?
- ☐ What summary might help a reader pull together what you've said?
- ☐ What would make a reader sorry to finish such a satisfying essay?

**End with a Quotation.** An apt quotation can neatly round out an essay, as literary critic Malcolm Cowley shows in *The View from Eighty* (New York: Viking, 1980), his discussion of the pitfalls and compensations of old age.

For more on punctuating quotations, see C3 (pp. A-55–A-56) in the Quick Editing Guide.

> "Eighty years old!" the great Catholic poet Paul Claudel wrote in his journal. "No eyes left, no ears, no teeth, no legs, no wind! And when all is said and done, how astonishingly well one does without them!"

**State or Restate Your Thesis.** In a sharp criticism of American schools, humorist Russell Baker in "School vs. Education" ends by stating his main point, that schools do not educate.

> Afterward, the former student's destiny fulfilled, his life rich with Oriental carpets, rare porcelain, and full bank accounts, he may one day find himself with the leisure and the inclination to open a book with a curious mind, and start to become educated.

**End with a Brief Emphatic Sentence.** For an essay that traces causes or effects, evaluates, or argues, a pointed concluding thought can reinforce your main idea. If you use Twitter, sending messages limited to 140 characters, apply those skills in a paragraph. Stick to academic language, but craft a concise, pointed sentence, maybe with a twist. In "Don't Mess with Mother" (*Newsweek* 19 Sept. 2005), Anna Quindlen ends her essay about the environmental challenges of post-Katrina New Orleans this way:

> New Orleans will be rebuilt, but rebuilt how? In the heedless, grasping fashion in which so much of this country has been built over the past fifty years, which has led to a continuous loop of floods, fires and filth in the air and water? Or could the new New Orleans be the first city of a new era, in which the demands of development and commerce are carefully balanced against the good of the land and, in the long run, the good of its people? We have been crummy stewards of the Earth, with a sense of knee-jerk entitlement that tells us there is always more where this came from.
>
> There isn't.

**Stop When the Story Is Over.** Even a quiet ending can be effective, as long as it signals clearly that the essay is finished. Journalist Martin Gansberg simply stops when the story is over in his true account of the fatal stabbing of a young woman, Kitty Genovese, in full view of residents of a Queens, New York, apartment house. The residents, unwilling to become involved, did nothing to interfere. Here is the last paragraph of "Thirty-eight Who Saw Murder Didn't Call Police" (*New York Times* 17 Mar. 1964):

> It was 4:25 A.M. when the ambulance arrived to take the body of Miss Genovese. It drove off. "Then," a solemn police detective said, "the people came out."

## Learning by Doing Opening and Concluding

Openings and conclusions frame an essay, contributing to the unity of the whole. The opening sets up the topic and main idea; the conclusion reaffirms the thesis and rounds off the ideas. Discuss the following with your classmates.

1. Here are two possible opening paragraphs from a student essay on the importance of teaching children how to swim.
   - A. Humans inhabit a world made up of over 70 percent water. In addition to these great bodies of water, we have built millions of swimming pools for sports and leisure activities. At one time or another most people will be faced with either the danger of drowning or the challenge of aquatic recreation. For these reasons, it is essential that we learn to swim. Being a competitive swimmer and a swimming instructor, I fully realize the importance of knowing how to swim.
   - B. Four-year-old Carl, curious like most children, last spring ventured out onto his pool patio. He fell into the pool and, not knowing how to swim, helplessly sank to the bottom. Minutes later his uncle found the child and brought him to the surface. Because Carl had no pulse, his uncle administered CPR until the paramedics arrived. Eventually the child was revived. During his stay in the hospital, his mother signed him up for beginning swimming classes. Carl was a lucky one. Unlike thousands of other children and adults, he got a second chance.

   1. Which introduction is more effective? Why?
   2. What would the body of this essay consist of? What kinds of evidence would be included?
   3. Write a suitable conclusion for this essay.
2. If you were to read each of the following introductions from professional essays, would you want to read the entire essay? Why?
   - A. During my ninth hour underground, as I scrambled up a slanting tunnel through the powdered gypsum, Rick Bridges turned to me and said, "You know, this whole area was just discovered Tuesday." (David Roberts, "Caving Comes into Its Golden Age: A New Mexico Marvel," *Smithsonian* Nov. 1988: 52)

B. From the batting average on the back of a George Brett baseball card to the interest rate fluctuations that determine whether the economy grows or stagnates, Americans are fascinated by statistics. (Stephen E. Nordlinger, "By the Numbers," *St. Petersburg Times* 6 Nov. 1988: 11)

C. "What does it look like under there?"

It was always this question back then, always the same pattern of hello and what's your name, what happened to your eye and what's under there. (Natalie Kusz, "Waiting for a Glass Eye," *Road Song* [New York: Farrar, 1990], rpt. in *Harper's* Nov. 1990)

3. How effective are these introductions and conclusions from student essays? Could they be improved? If so, how? If they are satisfactory, explain why. What would be a catchy yet informative title for each essay?

A. Recently a friend down from New York astonished me with stories of several people infected—some with AIDS—by stepping on needles washed up on the New Jersey beaches. This is just one incident of pollution, a devastating problem in our society today. Pollution is increasing in our world because of greed, apathy, and Congress's inability to control this problem. . . .

Wouldn't it be nice to have a pollution-free world without medical wastes floating in the water and washing up on our beaches? Without cars and power plants spewing greenhouse gases? With every corporation abiding by the laws set by Congress? In the future we can have a pollution-free world, but it is going to take the cooperation of everyone, including Congress, to ensure our survival on this Planet Earth.

B. The divorce rate rose 700 percent in the last century and continues to rise. More than one out of every two couples who are married end up divorcing. Over one million children a year are affected by divorce in the family. From these statistics it is clear that one of the greatest problems concerning the family today is divorce and the adverse effects it has on our society. . . .

Divorce causes problems that change people for life. The number of divorces will continue to exceed the 700 percent figure unless married couples learn to communicate, to accept their mates unconditionally, and to sacrificially give of themselves.

4. Using a topic that you generated in Chapter 19, write at least three different introductions with conclusions. Ask classmates which is most effective.

## Adding Cues and Connections

Effective writing proceeds in some sensible order, each sentence following naturally from the one before it. Yet even well-organized prose can be hard to read unless it is *coherent* and smoothly integrates its elements. Readers need cues and connections—devices to tie together words in a sentence, sentences in a paragraph, paragraphs in an essay.

**Add Transitional Words and Sentences.** Many words and phrases specify connections between or within sentences and paragraphs. In fact, you use transitions every day as cues or signals to help others follow your train of thought. For example, you might say to a friend, "Well, *on the one hand,* a second job would help me save money for tuition. *On the other hand,* I'd have less time to study." But some writers rush through, omitting links between thoughts or mistakenly assuming that connections they see will automatically be clear to readers. Often just a word, phrase, or sentence of transition inserted in the right place transforms a disconnected passage into a coherent one. In the chart on page 433, *transitional markers* are grouped by purpose or the kind of relation or connection they establish.

Occasionally a whole sentence serves as a transition. The opening of one paragraph may hark back to the last one while revealing a new or narrower direction. The next excerpt came from "Preservation Basics: Why Preserve Film?" a Web page of the National Film Preservation Foundation (NFPF) at filmpreservation.org. The first paragraph introduces the organization's mission; the next two each open with transitional sentences (italics ours) that introduce major challenges to that mission.

> Since Thomas Edison's invention of the kinetoscope in 1893, Americans have traveled the world using motion pictures to tell stories, document traditions, and capture current events. Their work stands as the collective memory of the first century witnessed by the moving image. By saving and sharing these motion pictures, we can illuminate our common heritage with a power and immediacy unique to film.
>
> *Preservationists are working against the clock.* Made on perishable plastic, film decays within years if not properly stored.
>
> *Already the losses are high.* The Library of Congress has documented that fewer than 20 percent of U.S. feature films from the 1920s survive in complete form in American archives; of the American features produced before 1950, only half still exist. For shorts, documentaries, and independently produced works, we have no way of knowing how much has been lost.

The first paragraph establishes the value of "saving and sharing" the American film legacy. The next two paragraphs use key words related to preservation and its absence (*perishable, decays, losses, lost*) to clarify that what follows builds on what has gone before. Each also opens with a short, dramatic transition to one of the major problems: time and existing loss.

**Supply Transition Paragraphs.** Transitions may be even longer than sentences. In a long and complicated essay, moving clearly from one idea to the next will sometimes require a short paragraph of transition.

| Common Transitions | |
|---|---|
| TO MARK TIME | then, soon, first, second, next, recently, the following day, in a little while, meanwhile, after, later, in the past, finally |
| TO MARK PLACE OR DIRECTION | in the distance, close by, near, far away, above, below, to the right, on the other side, opposite, to the west, next door |
| TO SUMMARIZE OR RESTATE | in other words, to put it another way, in brief, in simpler terms, on the whole, in fact, in a word, to sum up, in short, in conclusion, to conclude, therefore |
| TO RELATE CAUSE AND EFFECT OR RESULT | therefore, accordingly, hence, thus, for, so, consequently, as a result, because of, due to, eventually, inevitably |
| TO ADD OR AMPLIFY OR LIST | and, also, too, besides, as well, moreover, in addition, furthermore, in effect, second, in the second place, again, next |
| TO COMPARE | similarly, likewise, in like manner, in the same way |
| TO CONCEDE | whereas, on the other hand, with that in mind, still, and yet, even so, in spite of, despite, at least, of course, no doubt, even though |
| TO CONTRAST | on the other hand, but, or, however, unlike, nevertheless, on the contrary, conversely, in contrast, instead, counter to |
| TO INDICATE PURPOSE | to this end, for this purpose, with this aim |
| TO EXPRESS CONDITION | although, though |
| TO GIVE EXAMPLES OR SPECIFY | for example, for instance, in this case, in particular, to illustrate |
| TO QUALIFY | for the most part, by and large, with few exceptions, mainly, in most cases, generally, some, sometimes, typically, frequently, rarely |
| TO EMPHASIZE | it is true, truly, indeed, of course, to be sure, obviously, without doubt, evidently, clearly, understandably |

> So far, the physical and psychological effects of driving nonstop for hundreds of miles seem clear. The next consideration is why drivers do this. What causes people to become addicted to their steering wheels?

Use a transition paragraph only when you sense that your readers might get lost if you don't patiently lead them by the hand. If your essay is short, one question or statement beginning a new paragraph will be enough.

A transition paragraph also can help you move between one branch of argument and your main trunk or between a digression and your main direction. In this excerpt from *The Film Preservation Guide: The Basics for Archives, Libraries, and Museums* (San Francisco: NFPF, 2004; http://www.filmpreservation.org/userfiles/image/PDFs/fpg_3.pdf), the writer introduces the importance of inspecting film and devotes the next paragraph to a digression – referring readers to an inspection sheet in the appendix.

> Inspection is the single most important way to date a film, identify its technical characteristics, and detect damage and decay. Much can be learned by examining your film carefully, from start to finish.
>
> A standardized inspection work sheet (see appendix B) lists things to check and helps organize notes. This type of written report is the foundation for future preservation actions. Collecting the information during inspection will help you make informed decisions and enable you to document any changes in film condition over time.
>
> Signs of decay and damage may vary across the length of the film. . . .

The second paragraph acts as a transition, guiding readers to specialized information in the appendix and then drawing them back to the overall purpose of inspection: assessing the extent of damage to a film.

**Select Repetition.** Another way to clarify the relationship between two sentences, paragraphs, or ideas is to repeat a key word or phrase. Such purposeful repetition almost guarantees that readers will understand how all the parts of a passage fit together. Note the word *anger* in the following paragraph (italics ours) from *Of Woman Born* (New York: Norton, 1976), poet Adrienne Rich's exploration of her relationship with her mother.

> And I know there must be deep reservoirs of *anger* in her; every mother has known overwhelming, unacceptable *anger* at her children. When I think of the conditions under which my mother became a mother, the impossible expectations, my father's distaste for pregnant women, his hatred of all that he could not control, my *anger* at her dissolves into grief and *anger* for her, and then dissolves back again into *anger* at her: the ancient, unpurged *anger* of the child.

**Strengthen Pronouns.** Because they always refer back to nouns or other pronouns, pronouns serve as transitions by making readers refer back as well. Note how certain pronouns (in italics) hold together the following paragraph from "Misunderstood Michelle" by columnist Ellen Goodman in *At Large* (New York: Summit Books, 1981):

> I have two friends who moved in together many years ago. *He* looked upon this step as a trial marriage. *She* looked upon it as, well, moving in together. *He* was sure that in a matter of time, after *they* had built up trust and confidence, *she* would agree that marriage was the next logical step. *She,* on the other hand, was thrilled that here at last was a man *who* would never push *her* back to the altar.

The paragraph uses other transitions, too: time markers (*many years ago, in a matter of time, after*), *on the other hand* to show a contrast, and repetition of words related to marriage (*trial marriage, marriage, the altar*). All serve the main purpose of transitions—keeping readers on track.

### Learning by Doing Identifying Transitions

Go over one of the papers you have already written for this course, and circle all the transitional devices you can detect. Then exchange papers with a classmate. Can you find additional transitions in the other's paper? Or would you recommend transitions where there aren't any?

### Learning by Doing Reflecting on Drafting

Think about how you wrote your last successful draft. What did you do? How did you shape your paragraphs? How did you manage transitions to guide readers? What was your secret for success? Write out drafting directions for yourself—ready for your next assignment. Compare directions with a classmate or small group, and exchange any useful advice.

# 22 Strategies for Developing

For an interactive Learning by Doing activity on Editing Sentences, go to Ch. 22: **bedfordstmartins.com/bedguide**.

For lists of essays using various methods of development, turn to the Rhetorical Contents following the full table of contents.

How can you spice up your general ideas with the stuff of real life? How can you tug your readers deeper and deeper into your essays until they say, "I see just what you mean"? Well-developed essays have such power because they back up general points with evidence that comes alive for readers. This chapter covers nine indispensable methods of development—giving examples, providing details, defining, reasoning inductively and deductively, analyzing a subject, analyzing a process, dividing and classifying, comparing and contrasting, and identifying causes and effects. A strong essay almost always requires a combination of strategies.

Whenever you develop or revise a piece of writing, you face a challenge: How do you figure out what to do? Sometimes you may suspect that you've wandered into the buffet line at the Writer's Grill. You watch others load their plates, but still you hesitate. What will taste best? How much will fit on your plate? What will create a memorable experience? For you as a writer, the answers to such questions are individual, depending on your situation, the clarity of your main idea or thesis, and the state of your draft.

## DISCOVERY CHECKLIST

### Purpose

- ☐ Does your assignment recommend specific methods of development?
- ☐ Which methods might be most useful to explain, inform, or persuade?
- ☐ What type of development might best achieve your specific purpose?

### Audience

- ☐ Which strategies would best clarify your topic for readers?
- ☐ Which would best demonstrate your thesis to your readers?
- ☐ What kinds of evidence will your specific readers prefer? Which strategies might develop this evidence most effectively?

### Thesis

- ☐ What development does your thesis promise or imply that you will supply?
- ☐ What sequence of development strategies would best support your thesis?

### Essay Development

- ☐ Has a reader or peer editor pointed out any ideas in your draft that need fuller, more effective, or more logical development?
- ☐ Where might your readers have trouble following or understanding without more or better development?

### Paragraph Development

- ☐ Should any paragraphs with one or two sentences be developed more fully?
- ☐ Should any long paragraphs with generalizations, repetition, and wordy phrasing be developed differently so that they are richer and deeper?

---

## Giving Examples

An example – the word comes from the Latin *exemplum,* "one thing chosen from among many" – is a typical instance that illustrates a whole type or kind. Giving examples to support a generalization is probably the most often used means of development. This example, from *In Search of Excellence* (New York: Harper and Row, 1982) by Thomas J. Peters and Robert H. Waterman Jr., explains the success of America's top corporations:

> Although he's not a company, our favorite illustration of closeness to the customer is car salesman Joe Girard. He sold more new cars and trucks, each year, for eleven years running, than any other human being. In fact, in a typical year, Joe sold more than twice as many units as whoever was in second place. In explaining his secret of success, Joe said: "I sent out over thirteen thousand cards every month."
>
> Why start with Joe? Because his magic is the magic of IBM and many of the rest of the excellent companies. It is simply service, overpowering service, especially after-sales service. Joe noted, "There's one thing that I do that a lot of salesmen don't, and that's believe the sale really begins *after* the sale – not before. . . . The customer ain't out the door, and my son has made up a thank-you note." Joe would intercede personally, a year later, with the service manager on behalf of his customer. Meanwhile he would keep the communications flowing.

Notice how Peters and Waterman focus on the specific, Joe Girard. They don't write *corporation employees* or even *car salespeople.* Instead, they zero in on one particular man to make the point come alive.

| | |
|---|---|
| Joe Girard | Level 4: Specific Example |
| car salespeople | Level 3: Even More Specific Group |
| corporation employees | Level 2: More Specific Group |
| America's top corporations | Level 1: General Group or Category |

This ladder of abstraction moves from the general—America's top corporations—to a specific person—Joe Girard. The specific example of Joe Girard makes closeness to the customer *concrete* to readers: he is someone readers can relate to. To check the level of specificity in a paragraph or an outline, draw a ladder of abstraction for it. Do the same to restrict a broad subject to a topic for a short essay. If you haven't climbed to the fourth or fifth level, you are probably too general and need to add specifics.

An example doesn't have to be a specific individual. Sometimes you can create a picture of something unfamiliar or give an abstraction a personality. In this paragraph from *Prisoners of Silence: Breaking the Bonds of Adult Illiteracy in the United States* (New York: Continuum, 1980), Jonathan Kozol makes real the plight of illiterate people in our health care system:

> Illiterates live, in more than literal ways, an uninsured existence. They cannot understand the written details on a health insurance form. They cannot read waivers that they sign preceding surgical procedures. Several women I have known in Boston have entered a slum hospital with the intention of obtaining a tubal ligation and have emerged a few days later after having been subjected to a hysterectomy. Unaware of their rights, incognizant of jargon, intimidated by the unfamiliar air of fear and atmosphere of ether that so many of us find oppressive in the confines even of the most attractive and expensive medical facilities, they have signed their names to documents they could not read and which nobody, in the hectic situation that prevails so often in those overcrowded hospitals that serve the urban poor, had ever bothered to explain.

An example isn't a trivial doodad you add to a paragraph for decoration; it is what holds your readers' attention and makes an idea concrete and tangible. To give plenty of examples is one of the writer's chief tasks, and you can generate more at any point in the writing process. Begin with your experience, even with an unfamiliar topic, or try conversing with others, reading, digging in the library, or browsing on the Web.

For ways to generate ideas, see Ch. 19.

### DISCOVERY CHECKLIST

- ☐ Are your examples relevant to your main idea or thesis?
- ☐ Are your examples the best ones you can think of? Will readers find them strong and appropriate?
- ☐ Are your examples truly specific? Or do they just repeat generalities?

☐ From each paragraph, can you draw a ladder of abstraction to at least the fourth level?

## Learning by Doing Giving Examples

To help you get in the habit of thinking specifically, fill in a ladder of abstraction for five of the following general subjects. Then share your ladders with classmates, and compare and contrast your specifics with theirs.

Examples:

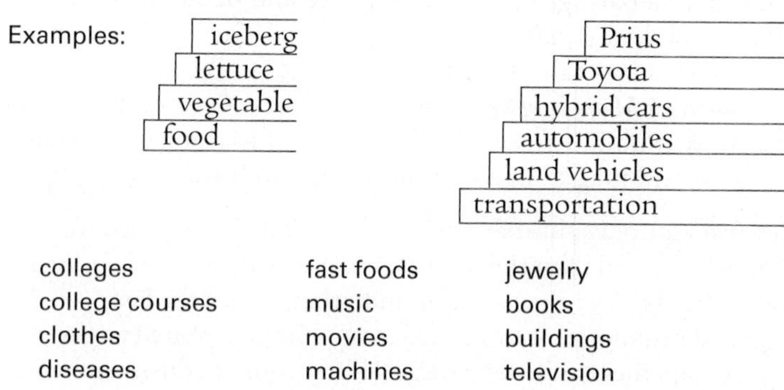


| | | |
|---|---|---|
| colleges | fast foods | jewelry |
| college courses | music | books |
| clothes | movies | buildings |
| diseases | machines | television |

# Providing Details

A *detail* is any specific, concrete piece of information—a fact, a bit of the historical record, your own observation. Details make scenes and images more realistic and vivid for readers. They also back up generalizations, convincing readers that the writer can make broad assertions with authority.

Mary Harris "Mother" Jones told the story of her life as a labor organizer in *The Autobiography of Mother Jones* (1925; Chicago: Kerr, 1980). She lends conviction to her generalization about a nineteenth-century coal miner's lot with ample evidence from her own experience and observations.

> Mining at its best is wretched work, and the life and surroundings of the miner are hard and ugly. His work is down in the black depths of the earth. He works alone in a drift. There can be little friendly companionship as there is in the factory; as there is among men who build bridges and houses, working together in groups. The work is dirty. Coal dust grinds itself into the skin, never to be removed. The miner must stoop as he works in the drift. He becomes bent like a gnome.
>
> His work is utterly fatiguing. Muscles and bones ache. His lungs breathe coal dust and the strange, damp air of places that are never filled with sunlight. His house is a poor makeshift and there is little to encourage him to make it attractive. The company owns the ground it stands on, and the miner feels the precariousness of his hold. Around

> his house is mud and slush. Great mounds of culm [the refuse left after coal is screened], black and sullen, surround him. His children are perpetually grimy from playing on the culm mounds. The wife struggles with dirt, with inadequate water supply, with small wages, with overcrowded shacks.

Although Mother Jones, not a learned writer, relies on short, simple sentences, her writing is clear and powerful because of the specific details she uses. Her opening states two generalizations: (1) "Mining . . . is wretched work," and (2) the miner's "life and surroundings" are "hard and ugly." She supports these with a barrage of factual evidence and detail, including well-chosen verbs: "Coal dust *grinds* itself into the skin." The result is a moving, convincingly detailed portrait of the miner and his family.

In *Lipstick Jihad: A Memoir of Growing Up Iranian in America and American in Iran* (New York: Public Affairs, 2005), Azadeh Moaveni uses details to evoke the "drama and magic" of a childhood visit to Iran.

> To my five-year-old suburban American sensibilities, exposed to nothing more mystical than the Smurfs, Iran was suffused with drama and magic. After Friday lunch at my grandfather's, once the last plates of sliced cantaloupe were cleared away, everyone retired to the bedrooms to nap. Inevitably there was a willing aunt or cousin on hand to scratch my back as I fell asleep. Unused to the siesta ritual, I woke up after half an hour to find the bed I was sharing with my cousin swathed in a tower of creamy gauze that stretched high up to the ceiling. "Wake up," I nudged him, "we're surrounded!" "It's for the mosquitoes, khareh, ass, go back to sleep." To me it was like a fairy tale, and I peered through the netting to the living room, to the table heaped with plump dates and the dense, aromatic baklava we would nibble on later with tea. The day before I had helped my grandmother, Razi joon, make ash-e gooshvareh, "earring stew"; we made hoops out of the fresh pasta, and dropped them into the vat of simmering herbs and lamb. Here even the ordinary had charm, even the names of stews.

For more on transitions, see pp. 431–35.

To guide readers through her details, Moaveni uses transitions—chronological (*After Friday lunch*, *after half an hour*, *The day before*), spatial (*through the netting to the living room*), and thematic (*To me it was like a fairy tale*).

Quite different from Moaveni's personal, descriptive details are Guy Garcia's objective facts in "Influencing America" (*Time* 13 Aug. 2005). Garcia heaps up statistical details to substantiate his claim that Hispanics are "helping to define" mainstream America even though they face "prejudice and enormous social and economic hurdles."

> Nearly a quarter of all Latinos live in poverty; the high school drop out rate for Latino youths between the ages of sixteen and nineteen is 21 percent—more than triple that of non-Hispanic whites. Neo-nativists like Pat Buchanan and Samuel Huntington still argue that the "tsunami" of non-English speakers from Latin America will destroy everything that

America stands for. Never mind that most Hispanics are religious, family-centric, enterprising, and patriotic. In the *Time* poll, 72 percent said they considered moral issues such as abortion and issues of faith important or very important. This year the government announced that undocumented workers were pouring billions into Social Security and Medicare for benefits that they would never be allowed to claim. Of the 27,000 troops serving in the U.S. armed forces who are not U.S. citizens, a large percentage are from Mexico and the rest of Latin America.

Providing details is a simple yet effective way to develop ideas. All it takes is close attention and precise wording to communicate details to readers. What would they see, hear, smell, or feel on the scene? Would a bit of reading or research turn up just the right fact or statistic? Effective details must have a specific purpose: to make your images more evocative or your point more convincing as they support—in some way—your main idea.

For more on observing a scene, see Ch. 5.

**DISCOVERY CHECKLIST**

- ☐ Do all your details support your point of view, main idea, or thesis?
- ☐ Do you have details of sights? Sounds? Tastes? Touch? Smells?
- ☐ Have you added enough details to make your writing clear and interesting?
- ☐ Have you arranged your details in an order that is easy to follow?

### Learning by Doing Providing Details

With classmates or alone, brainstorm specific details on one of the following topics. Include details that appeal to all five senses. Group related details, and write a paragraph or two using them. Begin by stating a main idea that conveys an engaging impression of your topic (not "My grandmother's house was in Topeka, Kansas" but "My grandmother's house was my childhood haven").

For more on brainstorming, see pp. 386–87.

| | | |
|---|---|---|
| the things in my room | a memorable event | my job |
| my grandmother's home | an unusual person | a classroom |
| a haunted house | my favorite pet | the cafeteria |
| a favorite possession | a hospital room | an incident |

## Defining

*Define* means "to set bounds to." You define a thing, word, or concept by describing it to distinguish it from all similar things. If people don't agree on the meaning of a word or an idea, they can't share knowledge about it. Scientists take special care to define their terms precisely. In "A Chemist's

Definition of pH" from *The Condensed Chemical Dictionary* (New York: Reinhold, 1981), Gessner G. Hawley begins with a brief definition:

> pH is a value taken to represent the acidity or alkalinity of an aqueous solution; it is defined as the logarithm of the reciprocal of the hydrogen-ion concentration of a solution:
>
> $$pH = 1n \frac{1}{[H^+]}$$

If you use a word in a special sense or invent a word, you have to explain it or your readers will be lost. In "The Futile Pursuit of Happiness" (*New York Times* 7 Sept. 2003), Jon Gertner reports on "affective forecasting," an intriguing area of study by economists and psychologists such as Professors Daniel Gilbert and Tim Wilson. They are exploring what people expect will bring them happiness and how their expectations pan out. Not surprisingly, their new area of study has generated new terms.

> Gilbert and his collaborator Tim Wilson call the gap between what we predict and what we ultimately experience the *impact bias*—*impact* meaning the errors we make in estimating both the intensity and duration of our emotions and *bias* our tendency to err. The phrase characterizes how we experience the dimming excitement over not just a BMW but also over any object or event that we presume will make us happy. Would a 20 percent raise or winning the lottery result in a contented life? You may predict it will, but almost surely it won't turn out that way. And a new plasma television? You may have high hopes, but the impact bias suggests that it will almost certainly be less cool, and in a shorter time, than you imagine. Worse, Gilbert has noted that these mistakes of expectation can lead directly to mistakes in choosing what we think will give us pleasure. He calls this *miswanting*.

You might define an unfamiliar word to save readers a trip to the dictionary or a familiar but often misunderstood concept—such as *guerrilla, liberal,* or *minimum wage*—to clarify the meaning you intend. The more complex or ambiguous the idea, thing, movement, phenomenon, or organization, the longer the definition you will need to clarify the term for your readers.

### DISCOVERY CHECKLIST

- ☐ Have you used definitions to help your readers understand the subject matter, not to show off your knowledge?
- ☐ Have you tailored your definition to the needs of your audience?
- ☐ Is your definition specific, clear, and accurate?
- ☐ Would your definition benefit from an example or from details?

### Learning by Doing Developing an Extended Definition

Write an extended definition (a paragraph or so) of a word listed below. Begin with a one-sentence definition of the word. Then, instead of turning to a dictionary or textbook, expand and clarify your ideas using strategies in this chapter—examples, details, induction or deduction, analysis, division, classification, comparison, contrast. You may also use *negation* (explaining what something is by stating what it is not). Share your definition with classmates.

| | | | |
|---|---|---|---|
| education | abuse | exercise | literacy |
| privacy | jazz | dieting | success |
| taboo | hip-hop | gossip | fear |
| prejudice | flu | security | gender |

## Reasoning Inductively and Deductively

A typical paragraph is likely to rely on both generalizations and particulars. A *generalization* is a broad statement that establishes a point, viewpoint, or conclusion. A *particular* is an instance, a detail, or an example—specific evidence that a general statement is reasonable. Your particulars support your generalizations; compelling instances, details, and examples back up your broader point. Likewise, your generalizations pull together your particulars, identifying patterns or connections that relate individual cases.

For more on reasoning, see Chs. 3 and 9.

For more on the statement-support pattern, see A2 (pp. A-22–A-24) in the Quick Research Guide.

To link particulars and generalizations, you can use an inductive or deductive process. An *inductive process* begins with the particulars—a convincing number of instances, examples, tests, or experiments. Together, these particulars substantiate a larger generalization. In this way a number of long-term studies of weight loss can lead to a consensus about the benefits of walking, eating vegetables, or some other variable. Less formal inductive reasoning is common as people *infer* or conclude that particulars do or do not support a generalization. If your sister ate strawberries three times and got a rash each time, she might infer that she is allergic to them. Induction breaks down when the particulars are too weak or too few to support a generalization: not enough weight-loss studies have comparable results or not enough clear instances occur when strawberries—and nothing else—trigger a reaction.

For more on induction and deduction, see Ch. 3.

A *deductive process* begins with a generalization and applies it to another case. When your sister says no to a piece of strawberry pie, she does so because, based on her assumptions, she *deduces* that it, too, will trigger a rash. Deduction breaks down when the initial generalization is flawed or when a particular case doesn't fit the generalization. Suppose that each time your sister ate strawberries she drizzled them with lemon juice, the real culprit. Or suppose that the various weight-loss studies defined low-fat food so differently that no one could determine how their findings might be related.

Once you have reached your conclusions—either by using particulars to support generalizations or by applying reliable generalizations to other particulars—you need to decide how to present your reasoning to readers. Do you want them to follow your process, perhaps examining many cases before reaching a conclusion about them? Or do you want them to learn your conclusion first and then review the evidence? Because academic audiences tend to expect conclusions first, many writers begin essays with thesis statements and paragraphs with topic sentences. On the other hand, if your readers are likely to reject an unexpected thesis initially, you may need to show them the evidence first and then lead them gently to your point.

In "The Good Heart" (*Newsweek* 3 Oct. 2005), Anne Underwood opens with a paragraph organized inductively: she describes a particular situation that helps substantiate a broad, even surprising, generalization.

> You can call it the Northridge Effect, after the powerful earthquake that struck near Los Angeles at 4:30 on a January morning in 1994. Within an hour, and for the rest of the day, medics responding to people crushed or trapped inside buildings faced a second wave of deaths from heart attacks among people who had survived the tremor unscathed. In the months that followed, researchers at two universities examined coroners' records from Los Angeles County and found an astonishing jump in cardiovascular deaths, from 15.6 on an average day to 51 on the day of the quake itself. Most of these people turned out to have a history of coronary disease or risk factors such as high blood pressure. But those who died were not involved in rescue efforts or trying to dig themselves out of the rubble. Why did they die? In the understated language of the *New England Journal of Medicine,* "emotional stress may precipitate cardiac events in people who are predisposed to such events." To put it simply, they were scared to death.

Underwood reviews the impact on heart attack patients of various factors such as anxiety, depression, and childhood trauma. Then, in the next passage, she states and supports a generalization about effects of common stresses in adult life, citing the results of an inductive study. In the second paragraph, she deductively applies the generalization to a particular case.

> And if stress in childhood can lead to heart disease, what about current stressors—longer work hours, threats of layoffs, collapsing pension funds? A study last year in the *Lancet* examined more than 11,000 heart-attack sufferers from 52 countries and found that in the year before their heart attacks, patients had been under significantly more strains—from work, family, financial troubles, depression, and other causes—than some 13,000 healthy control subjects. "Each of these factors individually was associated with increased risk," says Dr. Salim Yusuf, professor of medicine at Canada's McMaster University and senior investigator on the study. "Together, they accounted for 30 percent of overall heart-attack risk."

But people respond differently to high-pressure work situations. The key to whether it produces a coronary seems to be whether you have a sense of control over life, or live at the mercy of circumstances and superiors.

That was the experience of John O'Connell, a Rockford, Illinois, laboratory manager who suffered his first heart attack in 1996, at the age of 56. In the two years before, his mother and two of his children had suffered serious illnesses, and his job had been changed in a reorganization. "My life seemed completely out of control," he says. "I had no idea where I would end up." He ended up on a gurney with a clot blocking his left anterior descending artery – the classic "widowmaker." Two months later he had triple bypass surgery. A second heart attack when he was 58 left his cardiologist shaking his head. There's nothing more we can do for you, doctors told him.

## DISCOVERY CHECKLIST

- ☐ Do your generalizations follow logically from your particulars? Can you substantiate what and how much you claim?
- ☐ Are your particulars typical, numerous, and relevant enough to support your generalizations? Are your particulars substantial enough to warrant the conclusion you have drawn?
- ☐ Are both your generalizations and your particulars presented clearly? Have you identified your assumptions for your readers?
- ☐ How do you expect your reasoning patterns to affect readers? What are your reasons for opening with generalizations or reserving them until the end?
- ☐ Is your reasoning in an explanation clear and logical? Is your reasoning in an argument rigorous enough to withstand scrutiny? Have you avoided generalizing too broadly or illogically connecting generalizations and particulars?

## Learning by Doing Reasoning Inductively and Deductively

Skim a recent magazine for an article that explores a health, environmental, or economic issue. Read the article, looking for paragraphs organized inductively and deductively. Why do you think the writer chose one pattern or the other in the various sections of the article? How well do those patterns work from a reader's point of view? Sum up your conclusions.

## Analyzing a Subject

When you *analyze* a subject, you divide it into its parts and then examine one part at a time. If you have taken any chemistry, you probably analyzed water: you separated it into hydrogen and oxygen, its two elements. You've heard many a commentator or blogger analyze the news, telling us what made up an event – who participated, where it occurred, what happened. Analyzing a news event may produce results less certain and clear-cut than analyzing a chemical compound, but the principle is similar – to take something apart for the purpose of understanding it better.

For more on division and classification, see pp. 450–53. For more on process analysis, see pp. 448–50. For more on cause and effect, see pp. 455–57.

Analysis helps readers grasp something complex: they can more readily take it in as a series of bites than one gulp. For this reason, college textbooks do a lot of analyzing: an economics book divides a labor union into its component parts, an anatomy text divides the hand into its bones, muscles, and ligaments. In your papers, you might analyze and explain to readers anything from a contemporary subculture (What social groups make up the homeless population of Los Angeles?) to an ecosystem (What animals, plants, and minerals coexist in a rain forest?). Analysis is so useful that you can apply it in many situations: breaking down the components of a subject to classify them, separating the stages in a process to see how it works, or identifying the possible results of an event to project consequences.

In *Cultural Anthropology: A Perspective on the Human Condition* (St. Paul: West, 1987), Emily A. Schultz and Robert H. Lavenda briefly but effectively demonstrate by analysis how a metaphor like "the Lord is my shepherd" makes a difficult concept ("the Lord") easy to understand.

> The first part of a metaphor, the metaphorical subject, indicates the domain of experience that needs to be clarified (e.g., "the Lord"). The second part of a metaphor, the metaphorical predicate, suggests a domain of experience which is familiar (e.g., sheep-herding) and which may help us understand what "the Lord" is all about.

In much the same way, Lillian Tsu, a government major at Cornell University, uses analysis in her essay "A Woman in the White House" to identify major difficulties faced by female politicians in the United States.

> Although traditionally paternalistic societies like the Philippines and Pakistan and socially conservative states like Great Britain have elected female leaders, particular characteristics of the United States' own electoral system have complicated efforts to elect a female president. Despite social modernization and the progress of the women's movement, the voters of the United States have lagged far behind those of other nations in their willingness to trust in the leadership of a female executive. While the women's movement succeeded in changing Americans' attitudes as to what roles are socially acceptable for women, female candidates have faced a more difficult task in U.S. elections than their male counterparts have. Three factors have

been responsible for this situation—political socialization, lack of experience, and open discrimination.

Next, Tsu treats these three factors in turn, beginning each section with a transition that emphasizes the difficulties faced: "One obstacle," "A second obstacle," "A third obstacle." The opening list and the transitions direct readers through a complicated essay, moving from the explanation of the three factors to the final section on implications.

When you plan an analysis, you might label slices in a pielike circle or arrange subdivisions in a list running from smallest to largest or least to most important. Make sure your analysis has a purpose—that it will show something about your subject or tell your readers something they didn't know before. For example, to show the ethnic composition of New York City, you might divide the city geographically into neighborhoods—Harlem, Spanish Harlem, Yorkville, Chinatown, Little Italy. To explain New York's social classes, however, you might start with homeless people and work up to the wealthy elite. The way you slice your subject into pieces depends in part on the point you want to make about it—and the point you end up making depends in part on how you've sliced it up. You may also find that you have a stronger point to make—that New York City's social hierarchy is oppressive and unstable, for example.

How can you help readers follow your analysis? Some writers begin by identifying the subdivisions into which they will slice the subject ("The federal government has three branches"). If you name or label each part you mention, define your terms, and clarify with examples, you will also distinguish each part from the others. Finally, transitions, leading readers from one part to the next, help make your essay readable.

For more on transitions, see pp. 431–35.

**DISCOVERY CHECKLIST**

- ☐ Exactly what will you try to achieve in your analysis?
- ☐ How does your analysis support your main idea or thesis?
- ☐ How will you break your subject into parts?
- ☐ How can you make each part clear to your readers?
- ☐ What definitions, details, and examples would help clarify each part?
- ☐ What transitions would clarify your movement from part to part?

## Learning by Doing Analyzing a Subject

Analyze one of the following subjects by making a list of its basic parts or elements. Then use your list as the basis for a paragraph or short essay explaining each part. Be sure to identify the purpose or point of your analysis. Compare your analysis with those of others in your class who chose the same subject.

| | |
|---|---|
| a college | a choir, orchestra, or other musical group |
| a news source | a computer or other technological device |
| a reality TV show | a basketball, baseball, hockey, or other team |
| effective teaching | a family, tribe, clan, or neighborhood |
| a healthy lifestyle | leadership, heroism, or service |

## Analyzing a Process

Analyzing a process means telling step-by-step how something is, was, or could be done. You can analyze an action or a phenomenon – how a skyscraper is built, how a revolution begins, how sunspots form. You can also explain large, long-ago events that you couldn't possibly have witnessed or complex technical processes that you couldn't personally duplicate. In "The Case for Cloning" (*Time* 9 Feb. 1998), Madeleine Nash's *informative* process analysis sets forth how the process of cloning cells happens.

> Cloning individual human cells . . . is another matter. Biologists are already talking about harnessing for medical purposes the technique that produced the sheep called Dolly. They might, for example, obtain healthy cells from a patient with leukemia or a burn victim and then transfer the nucleus of each cell into an unfertilized egg from which the nucleus has been removed. Coddled in culture dishes, these embryonic clones – each genetically identical to the patient from which the nuclei came – would begin to divide. The cells would not have to grow into a fetus, however. The addition of powerful growth factors could ensure that the clones develop only into specialized cells and tissue. For the leukemia patient, for example, the cloned cells could provide an infusion of fresh bone marrow, and for the burn victim, grafts of brand-new skin. Unlike cells from an unrelated donor, these cloned cells would incur no danger of rejection; patients would be spared the need to take powerful drugs to suppress the immune system.

In contrast, the *directive*, or "how-to," process analysis tells readers how to do something (how to box, invest for retirement, clean a painting) or how to make something (how to draw a map, blaze a trail, fix chili). Especially on Web sites, directions may consist of simple step-by-step lists with quick advice for browsers. In essays and articles, however, the basics may be supplemented with advice, encouragement, or relevant experience. In "How to Catch More Trout" (*Outdoor Life* May 2006), Joe Brooks identifies the critical stages in the process in his first paragraph:

> Every move you make in trout fishing counts for or against you. The way you approach a pool, how you retrieve, how you strike, how you play the fish, how you land him – all are important factors. If you plan your tactics according to the demands of each situation, you'll catch a lot more trout over a season.

Then Brooks introduces the first stage:

> The first thing you should do is stand by the pool and study it awhile before you fish. Locate the trout that are rising consistently. Choose one (the lowest in the pool, preferably), and work on him. If you rush right in and start casting, you'll probably put down several fish that you haven't seen. And you can scare still more fish by false-casting all over the place. A dozen fish you might have caught with a more careful approach may see the line and go down before you even drop the fly on the surface.

He continues with stages and advice until he reaches the last step:

> The safest way to land a fish is to beach it. If no low bank is handy, you can fight a fish until he is tired and then pull his head against a bank or an up-jutting rock and pick him up. Hold him gently. The tighter your grip, the more likely he is to spurt from your fingers, break your leader tippet, and escape. Even if you intend to put him back, you want to feel that he is really yours – a trout you have cast and caught and released because you planned it that way.

Brooks skillfully addresses his audience – readers of *Outdoor Life,* people who probably already know how to fish and hunt. As his title indicates, Brooks isn't explaining how to catch trout but how to catch *more* trout. For this reason, he skips topics for beginners (such as how to cast) and instead urges readers to try more sophisticated tactics to increase their catch.

Process analysis can also turn to humor, as in this paragraph from "How to Heal a Broken Heart (in One Day)" by student Lindsey Schendel.

> To begin your first day of mourning, you will wake up at 11 a.m., thus banishing any feelings of fatigue. Forget eating a healthy breakfast; toast two waffles, and plaster them with chocolate syrup instead of maple. Then make sure you have a room of serenity so you may cry in peace. It is important that you go through the necessary phases of denial and depression. Call up a friend or family member while you are still in your serious, somber mood. Explain to that person the hardships you are facing and how you don't know if you can go on. Immediately afterwards, turn on any empowering music, get up, and dance.

Like more serious process directions, this paragraph includes steps or stages (sleeping late, eating breakfast, crying and calling, getting up and dancing).

They are arranged in chronological order with transitions marking the movement from one to the other (*To begin*, *then*, *while*, *immediately afterwards*).

For more on transitions, see pp. 431–35.

Process analyses are wonderful ways to show readers the inside workings of events or systems, but they can be difficult to follow. Divide the process into logical steps or stages, and put the steps in chronological order. Add details or examples wherever your description might be ambiguous; use transitions to mark the end of one step and the beginning of the next.

**DISCOVERY CHECKLIST**

- ☐ Do you thoroughly understand the process you are analyzing?
- ☐ Do you have a good reason to analyze a process at this point in your writing? How does your analysis support your main idea or thesis?
- ☐ Have you broken the process into logical and useful steps? Have you adjusted your explanation of the steps for your audience?
- ☐ Is the order in which you present these steps the best one possible?
- ☐ Have you used transitions to guide readers from one step to the next?

### Learning by Doing Analyzing a Process

Analyze one of the following processes or procedures in a paragraph or short essay. Then share your process analysis with classmates. Can they follow your analysis easily? Do they spot anything you left out?

| | |
|---|---|
| registering for college classes | hunting for a job |
| studying for a test | buying a used car |
| having the flu (or another illness) | moving |

## Dividing and Classifying

For more on analyzing a subject, see pp. 446–48.

To divide is to break something down, identifying or analyzing its components. It's far easier to take in a subject, especially a complex one, a piece at a time. The thing divided may be as concrete as a medical center (which you might divide into specialty units) or as abstract as a knowledge of art (which you might divide into sculpture, painting, drawing, and other forms). To classify is to make sense of a potentially bewildering array of things—works of literature, this year's movies—by sorting them into categories (*types* or *classes*) that you can deal with one at a time. Literature is customarily arranged by genre—novels, stories, poems, plays. Movies might be sorted by audience (children, teenagers, mature adults). Dividing and classifying are like two sides of the same coin. In theory, any broad subject can be *divided* into components, which can then be *classified* into categories. In practice, it's often difficult to tell where division stops and classification begins.

In his college textbook *Wildlife Management* (San Francisco: Freeman, 1978), Robert H. Giles Jr. uses division to simplify an especially large, abstract subject: the management of forest wildlife in America. To explain which environmentalists assume which duties, Giles divides forest wildlife management into six levels or areas of concern, arranged roughly from large to small, all neatly presented in fewer than two hundred words.

> There are six scales of forest wildlife management: (1) national, (2) regional, (3) state or industrial, (4) county or parish, (5) intra-state region, management unit, or watershed, and (6) forest. Each is different. At the national and regional levels, management includes decisions on timber harvest quotas, grazing policy in forested lands, official stance on forest taxation bills, cutting policy relative to threatened and endangered species, management coordination of migratory species, and research fund allocation. At the state or industrial level, decision types include land acquisition, sale, or trade; season setting; and permit systems and fees. At the county level, plans are made, seasons set, and special fees levied. At the intra-state level, decisions include what seasons to recommend, what stances to take on bills not affecting local conditions, the sequence in which to attempt land acquisition, and the placement of facilities. At the forest level, decisions may include some of those of the larger management unit but typically are those of maintenance schedules, planting stock, cutting rotations, personnel employment and supervision, road closures, equipment use, practices to be attempted or used, and boundaries to be marked.

In a textbook lesson on how babies develop from *Human Development* (New York: Freeman, 1984), Kurt W. Fischer and Arlyne Lazerson describe a research project that classified babies into three types by temperament.

> The researchers also found that certain of these temperamental qualities tended to occur together. These clusters of characteristics generally fell into three types — the easy baby, the difficult baby, and the baby who was slow to warm up. The *easy infant* has regular patterns of eating and sleeping, readily approaches new objects and people, adapts easily to changes in the environment, generally reacts with low or moderate intensity, and typically is in a cheerful mood. The *difficult infant* usually shows irregular patterns of eating and sleeping, withdraws from new objects or people, adapts slowly to changes, reacts with great intensity, and is frequently cranky. The *slow-to-warm-up infant* typically has a low activity level, tends to withdraw when presented with an unfamiliar object, reacts with a low level of intensity, and adapts slowly

to changes in the environment. Fortunately for parents, most healthy infants—40 percent or more—have an easy temperament. Only about 10 percent have a difficult temperament, and about 15 percent are slow to warm up. The remaining 35 percent do not easily fit one of the three types but show some other pattern.

When you divide and classify, your point is to make order out of a complex or overwhelming jumble.

- Make sure the components and categories you identify are sensible, given your purpose, and follow the same principle of classification or analysis for all categories. For example, to discuss campus relations, it makes sense to divide the school population into *instructors, students,* and *support staff;* it would make less sense to divide it into *people from the South, people from other states,* and *people from overseas.*
- Try to group apples with apples, not with oranges, so that all the components or categories are roughly equivalent. For example, if you're classifying television shows and you've come up with *reality shows, dramas, talk shows, children's shows, news,* and *cartoons,* then you've got a problem: the last category is probably part of *children's shows.*
- Check that your final system is easy for readers to understand. Most people can handle only about seven things at once. If you've got more than five or six components or categories, try to combine or eliminate some.

**DISCOVERY CHECKLIST**

- ☐ How does your division or classification support your main idea or thesis?
- ☐ Do you use the most logical principle to divide or classify for your purpose?
- ☐ Do you stick to one principle throughout?
- ☐ Have you identified components or categories that are comparable?
- ☐ Have you arranged your components or categories in the best order?
- ☐ Have you given specific examples for each component or category?
- ☐ Have you made a complex subject more accessible to your readers?

## Learning by Doing Dividing and Classifying

For more on brainstorming, see pp. 386–87.

Brainstorm on one or two of the following subjects to come up with as many components as you can. With classmates, create one large list by combining items for each subject. Working together, classify the items on the largest list into logical categories. Add or change components or categories as needed.

| | | | |
|---|---|---|---|
| students | customers | sports | families |
| teachers | Web sites | vacations | drivers |

## Comparing and Contrasting

Set a pair of subjects side by side to compare and contrast them. When you compare, you point out similarities; when you contrast, you discuss differences. You can use two basic methods of organization for comparison and contrast – the opposing pattern and the alternating pattern – as illustrated for a comparison and contrast of two brothers.

For sample essays and advice on writing a comparison and contrast essay, see Ch. 7.

| OPPOSING PATTERN, SUBJECT BY SUBJECT | ALTERNATING PATTERN, POINT BY POINT |
|---|---|
| Subject A: Jim | Point 1: Appearance |
| Point 1: Appearance | Subject A: Jim |
| Point 2: Personality | Subject B: Jack |
| Point 3: Interests | Point 2: Personality |
| Subject B: Jack | Subject A: Jim |
| Point 1: Appearance | Subject B: Jack |
| Point 2: Personality | Point 3: Interests |
| Point 3: Interests | Subject A: Jim |
| | Subject B: Jack |

You need a reason to compare and contrast – a final evaluation, perhaps a decision about which thing is better or another purpose. For example, compare Jack and Jim to do more than point out lanky or curly hair. Use their differences to highlight their powerful bond as brothers or their similarities to support a generalization about a family strength.

Both patterns open Chapter One of *Rousseau's Dog* by David Edmonds and John Eidinow (New York: HarperCollins, 2006). The book tells the story of the bitterness that grew between David Hume and Jean-Jacques Rousseau, two very different eighteenth-century philosophers.

> On the evening of January 10, 1766, the weather in the English Channel was foul – stormy, wet, and cold. That night, after being held in harbor by unfavorable winds, a packet boat beat its way, rolling and plunging, from Calais to Dover. Among the passengers were two men who had met for the first time some three weeks earlier in Paris, a British diplomat and a Swiss refugee. The refugee was accompanied by his beloved dog, Sultan, small and brown with a curly tail. The diplomat stayed below, tormented by seasickness. The refugee remained on deck all night; the frozen sailors marveled at his hardiness.

Alternating pattern

Significance

If the ship had foundered, she would have carried to the bottom of the Channel two of the most influential thinkers of the eighteenth century.

Opposing pattern

Subject A

The diplomat was David Hume. His contributions to philosophy on induction, causation, necessity, personal identity, morality, and theism are of such enduring importance that his name belongs in the league of the most elite philosophers, the league that would also include Plato, Aristotle, Descartes, Kant, and Wittgenstein. A contemporary and friend of Adam Smith's, he paved the way to modern economics; he also modernized historiography.

Subject B

The refugee was Jean-Jacques Rousseau. His intellectual range and achievements were equally staggering. He made epochal contributions to political theory, literature, and education. His autobiography, *The Confessions,* was a stunningly original work, one that has spawned countless successors but still sets the standard for a narrative of self-revelation and artistic development. *Émile,* his educational tract, transformed the debate about the upbringing of children and was instrumental in altering our perceptions of childhood. *On the Social Contract,* his most significant political publication, has been cited as an inspiration for generations of revolutionaries. More fundamentally, Rousseau altered the way we view ourselves, our emotions, and our relationship to society and to the natural world.

As the first chapter continues comparing and contrasting, the difference between the temperaments of the two men—and the potential for deep conflict—grows increasingly clear to readers.

## DISCOVERY CHECKLIST

- ☐ Is your reason for comparing and contrasting unmistakably clear? Does it support or develop your main idea or thesis?
- ☐ Have you chosen to write about the *major* similarities and differences?
- ☐ Have you compared or contrasted like things? Have you discussed the same categories or features for each item?
- ☐ Have you selected points of comparison and supporting details that will intrigue, enlighten, and persuade your audience?
- ☐ Have you used the best possible arrangement, given your subject and the point you're trying to make?
- ☐ If you are making a judgment, have you treated both subjects fairly?
- ☐ Have you avoided moving mechanically from "On the one hand" to "On the other hand"?

### Learning by Doing Comparing and Contrasting

Write a paragraph or two in which you compare and contrast the subjects in one of the following pairs. Exchange drafts with classmates for response, using questions from the Discovery Checklist.

baseball and football (or two other sports or activities)
living in an apartment (or dorm) and living in a house
two cities, communities, or neighborhoods you are familiar with
two musicians, artists, or performers
communicating by two methods
watching a sports event on television and in person

## Identifying Causes and Effects

For sample essays and advice on writing a cause and effect essay, see Ch. 8.

From the time we are children, we ask why. Why can't I go out and play? Why is the sky blue? Why did my goldfish die? Seeking causes and effects continues into adulthood, so it's a common method of development. To explain causal relationships successfully, think about the subject critically, gather evidence, draw judicious conclusions, and clarify relationships.

In the following paragraph from "What Pop Lyrics Say to Us Today" (*New York Times* 24 Feb. 1985), Robert Palmer speculates on the causes that led young people to turn to rock music for inspiration as well as the effects of their expectations on the musicians of the time.

> By the late '60s, the peace and civil rights movements were beginning to splinter. The assassinations of the Kennedys and Martin Luther King had robbed a generation of its heroes, the Vietnam War was escalating despite the protests, and at home, violence was on the rise. Young people turned to rock, expecting it to ask the right questions and come up with answers, hoping that the music's most visionary artists could somehow make sense of things. But rock's most influential artists—Bob Dylan, the Beatles, the Rolling Stones—were finding that serving as the conscience of a generation exacted a heavy toll. Mr. Dylan, for one, felt the pressures becoming unbearable, and wrote about his predicament in songs like "All Along the Watchtower."

Instead of focusing on causes *or* effects, often writers trace a *chain* of cause-and-effect relationships, as Charles C. Mann and Mark L. Plummer do in "The Butterfly Problem" (*Atlantic Monthly* Jan. 1992).

> More generally, the web of species around us helps generate soil, regulate freshwater supplies, dispose of waste, and maintain the quality of the atmosphere. Pillaging nature to the point where it

cannot perform these functions is dangerously foolish. Simple self-protection is thus a second motive for preserving biodiversity. When DDT was sprayed in Borneo, the biologists Paul and Anne Ehrlich relate in their book *Extinction* (1981), it killed all the houseflies. The gecko lizards that preyed on the flies ate their pesticide-filled corpses and died. House cats consumed the dying lizards; they died too. Rats descended on the villages, bringing bubonic plague. Incredibly, the housefly in this case was part of an intricate system that controlled human disease. To make up for its absence, the government was forced to parachute cats into the area.

---

**DISCOVERY CHECKLIST**

- ☐ Do you clearly tie your use of cause and effect to your main idea or thesis?
- ☐ Have you identified actual causes? Have you supplied persuasive evidence to support them?
- ☐ Have you identified actual effects, or are they conjecture? If conjecture, are they logical possibilities? What persuasive evidence supports them?
- ☐ Have you judiciously drawn conclusions about causes and effects? Have you avoided faulty thinking and logical fallacies?
- ☐ Have you presented your points clearly and logically so that your readers can follow them easily?
- ☐ Have you considered other causes or effects, immediate or long-term, that readers might find relevant?

For more on faulty thinking and logical fallacies, see pp. 51–52 and pp. 180–81.

---

## Learning by Doing Identifying Causes and Effects

1. Identify some of the *causes* of *five* of the following. Then discuss possible causes with your classmates.

   failing an exam / an automobile accident / poor/good health / stage fright / losing/winning a game / getting/losing a job / stress / going to college / getting a scholarship

| | | |
|---|---|---|
| failing an exam | stage fright | stress |
| an automobile accident | losing/winning a game | going to college |
| poor/good health | getting/losing a job | getting a scholarship |

2. Identify some of the *effects* of *five* of the following. Then discuss possible effects with your classmates.

| | | |
|---|---|---|
| an insult | dieting | winning the lottery |
| a compliment | speeding | traveling to another country |
| learning to read | divorce | drinking while driving |

3. Identify some of the *causes and effects* of *one* of the following, doing a little research as needed. How might you use the chain of causes and effects in an essay? Discuss your findings with your classmates.

   the online shopping boom
   the attacks of September 11, 2001
   the discovery of atomic energy
   a major U.S. Supreme Court decision
   recycling
   a gay marriage court case
   the uses of solar energy
   global climate change
   racial tension

## Learning by Doing Reflecting on Developing

Think back to the methods of development that you have used in recent papers. How do you generally develop your papers? What new approaches have you tried or might you try? How do you decide which method to use and where? How do you know when you have developed a section effectively, so that a reader would find it clear and compelling? Working with a classmate or small group, explain your best method, pointing out its advantages and disadvantages.

# 23 Strategies for Revising and Editing

Good writing is rewriting. In this chapter we provide strategies for revising and editing—ways to rethink muddy ideas and emphasize important ones, to rephrase obscure passages and restructure garbled sentences. Our advice applies not only to rewriting whole essays but also to rewriting, editing, and proofreading sentences and paragraphs.

## Re-viewing and Revising

*Revision* means "seeing again"—discovering again, conceiving again, shaping again. It may occur at any and all stages of the writing process, and most writers do a lot of it. *Macro revising* is making large, global, or fundamental changes that affect the overall direction or impact of writing—its

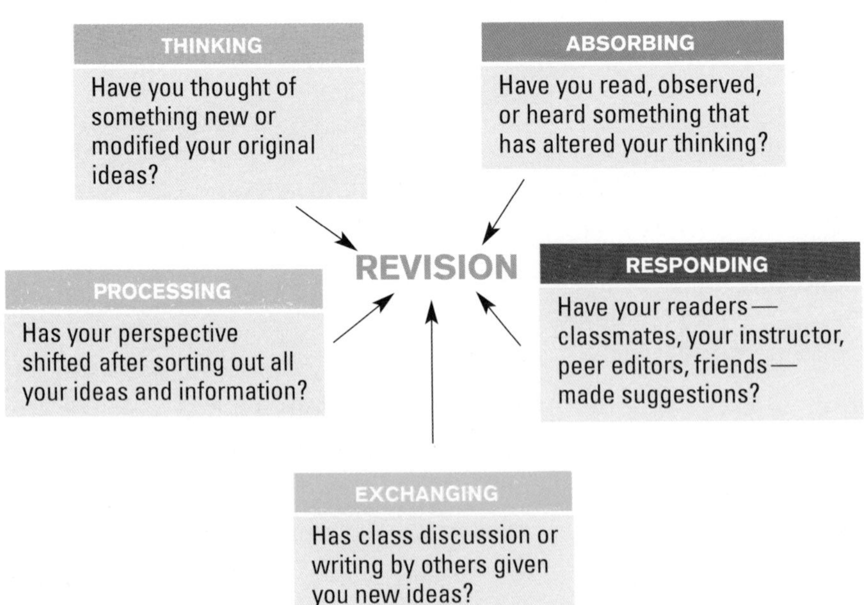

THINKING
Have you thought of something new or modified your original ideas?
ABSORBING
Have you read, observed, or heard something that has altered your thinking?
REVISION
PROCESSING
Has your perspective shifted after sorting out all your ideas and information?
RESPONDING
Have your readers—classmates, your instructor, peer editors, friends—made suggestions?
EXCHANGING
Has class discussion or writing by others given you new ideas?

purpose, organization, or audience. Its companion is *micro revising,* paying attention to sentences, words, punctuation, and grammar—including ways to create emphasis and eliminate wordiness.

**MACRO REVISING** ⇄ **MICRO REVISING**

MACRO REVISING

- **PURPOSE:** Have you refined what you want to accomplish?
- **THESIS:** Could you state your main point more accurately?
- **AUDIENCE:** Should you address your readers differently?
- **STRUCTURE:** Should you reorganize any part of your writing?
- **SUPPORT:** Do you need to add, drop, or rework your support?

MICRO REVISING

- **EMPHASIS:** Can you position your ideas more effectively?
- **CONCISENESS:** Can you spot extra words that you might cut?
- **CLARITY:** Can you make any sentences and words clearer?

## Revising for Purpose and Thesis

When you revise for purpose, you make sure that your writing accomplishes what you want it to do. If your goal is to create an interesting profile of a person, have you done so? If you want to persuade your readers to take a certain course of action, have you succeeded? When your project has evolved or your assignment grown clearer to you, the purpose of your final essay may differ from your purpose when you began. To revise for purpose, try to step back and see your writing as other readers will.

Concentrate on what's actually in your paper, not what you assume is there. Create a thesis sentence (if you haven't), or revise your working thesis statement (if you've developed one). Reconsider how it is worded:

For more on stating and improving a working thesis, see pp. 399–408.

- Is it stated exactly in concise yet detailed language?
- Is it focused on only one main idea?
- Is it stated positively rather than negatively?
- Is it limited to a demonstrable statement?

Then consider how accurately your thesis now represents your main idea:

- Does each part of your essay directly relate to your thesis?
- Does each part of your essay develop and support your thesis?
- Does your essay deliver everything your thesis promises?

If you find unrelated or contradictory passages, you have several options: revise the thesis, revise the essay, or revise both.

If your idea has deepened, your topic become more complex, or your essay developed along new lines, refine or expand your thesis accordingly.

| | |
|---|---|
| WORKING THESIS | The *Herald*'s coverage of the Senate elections was more thorough than the *Courier*'s. |
| REVISED THESIS | The *Herald*'s coverage of the Senate elections was less timely but more thorough and more impartial than the *Courier*'s. |
| WORKING THESIS | As the roles of men and women have changed in our society, old-fashioned formal courtesy has declined. |
| REVISED THESIS | As the roles of men and women have changed in our society, old-fashioned formal courtesy has declined not only toward women but also toward men. |

### REVISION CHECKLIST

- ☐ Do you know exactly what you want your essay to accomplish? Can you put it in one sentence: "In this paper I want to . . ."?
- ☐ Is your thesis stated outright in the essay? If not, have you provided clues so that your readers will know precisely what it is?
- ☐ Does every part of the essay work to achieve the same goal?
- ☐ Have you tried to do too much? Does your coverage seem too thin? If so, how might you reduce the scope of your thesis and essay?
- ☐ Does your essay say all that needs to be said? Is everything—ideas, connections, supporting evidence—on paper, not just in your head?
- ☐ In writing the essay, have you changed your mind, rethought your assumptions, made a discovery? Does anything now need to be recast?
- ☐ Have you developed enough evidence? Is it clear and convincing?

## Revising for Audience

What works with one audience can fall flat with another. Your organization, selection of details, word choice, and tone all affect your particular readers. Visualize one of them poring over the essay, reacting to what you have written. What expressions do you see on that reader's face? Where does he or she have trouble understanding? Where have you hit the mark?

**REVISION CHECKLIST**

- ☐ Who will read this essay?
- ☐ Will your readers think you have told them something worth knowing?
- ☐ Are there any places where readers might fall asleep? If so, can you shorten, delete, or liven up such passages?
- ☐ Does the opening of the essay mislead your readers by promising something that the essay never delivers?
- ☐ Do you unfold each idea in enough detail to make it clear and interesting?
- ☐ Have you anticipated questions your audience might ask?
- ☐ Where might readers raise objections? How might you answer them?
- ☐ Have you used any specialized or technical language that your readers might not understand? If so, have you worked in brief definitions?
- ☐ What is your attitude toward your audience? Are you chummy, angry, superior, apologetic, preachy? Should you revise to improve your attitude?

## Revising for Structure and Support

When you revise for structure and support, you make sure that the order of your ideas, your selection of supporting material, and its arrangement are as effective as possible. You may have all the ingredients of a successful essay—but they may be a confusing mess.

In a well-structured essay, each paragraph, sentence, and phrase serves a clear function. Are your opening and closing paragraphs relevant, concise, and interesting? Is everything in each paragraph on the same topic? Are all ideas adequately developed? Are the paragraphs arranged in the best possible order? Finally, do you lead readers from one idea to the next with clear and painless transitions?

For more on paragraphs, topic sentences, and transitions, see Ch. 21.

An outline can help you discover what you've succeeded in getting on paper. Find the topic sentence of each paragraph in your draft (or create one, if necessary), and list them in order. Label the sentences *I., II., A., B.,* and so on, to show the logical relationships of ideas. Do the same with the supporting details under each topic sentence, labeling them also with letters and numbers and indenting appropriately. Now look at the outline. Does it make sense on its own, without the essay to explain it? Would a different order or arrangement be more effective? Do any sections look thin and need more evidence? Are the connections between parts on paper, not just in your head? Maybe too many ideas are jammed into too few paragraphs. Maybe

For more on using outlining for planning, see pp. 411–19.

you need more specific details and examples—or stronger ones. Strengthen the outline and then rewrite to follow it.

### REVISION CHECKLIST

- ☐ Does your introduction set up the whole essay? Does it both grab readers' attention and hint at what is to follow?
- ☐ Does the essay fulfill all that you promise in your opening?
- ☐ Would any later passage make a better beginning?
- ☐ Is your thesis clear early in the essay? If explicit, is it positioned prominently?
- ☐ Do the paragraph breaks seem logical?
- ☐ Is the main idea of each paragraph clear? Is it stated in a topic sentence?
- ☐ Is the main idea of each paragraph fully developed? Where might you need more or better evidence? Should you omit or move any stray bits?
- ☐ Is each detail or piece of evidence relevant to the topic sentence of the paragraph and the main point of the essay?
- ☐ Would any paragraphs make more sense in a different order?
- ☐ Does everything follow clearly? Does one point smoothly lead to the next? Would transitions help make the connections clearer?
- ☐ Does the conclusion follow logically or seem tacked on?

### Learning by Doing Tackling Macro Revision

Select a draft that would benefit from revision. Then, based on your sense of its greatest need, choose one of the revision checklists to guide a first revision. Let the draft sit for a while. Then work with one of the remaining checklists.

## Working with a Peer Editor

There's no substitute for having someone else read your draft. Whether you are writing for an audience of classmates or for a different group (the town council or readers of *Time*), having a classmate go over your essay is a worthwhile revision strategy. To gain all you can as a writer from a peer review, you need to play an active part:

- Ask your reader questions. (See page 463 for ideas.) Or bring a "Dear Editor" letter or memo, written ahead, to your meeting.

## Questions for a Peer Editor

### First Questions for a Peer Editor

What is your first reaction to this paper?

What is this writer trying to tell you?

What are this paper's greatest strengths?

Does it have any major weaknesses?

What one change would most improve the paper?

### Questions on Meaning

Do you understand everything? Is the draft missing any information that you need to know?

Does this paper tell you anything you didn't know before?

Is the writer trying to cover too much territory? Too little?

Does any point need to be more fully explained or illustrated?

When you come to the end, has the paper delivered what it promised?

Could this paper use a down-to-the-ground revision?

### Questions on Organization

Has the writer begun in a way that grabs your interest and quickly draws you into the paper's main idea? Or can you find a better beginning at some later point?

Does the paper have one main idea, or does it juggle more than one?

Would the main idea stand out better if anything were removed or added?

Might the ideas in the paper be more effectively arranged? Do any ideas belong together that now seem too far apart?

Can you follow the ideas easily? Are transitions needed? If so, where?

Does the writer keep to one point of view—one angle of seeing?

Does the ending seem deliberate, as if the writer meant to conclude, not just run out of gas? How might the writer strengthen the conclusion?

### Questions on Writing Strategies

Do you feel that this paper addresses you personally?

Do you dislike or object to any statement the writer makes or any wording the writer uses? Is the problem word choice, tone, or inadequate support to convince you? Should the writer keep or change this part?

Does the draft contain anything that distracts you or seems unnecessary?

Do you get bored at any point? How might the writer keep you reading?

Is the language of this paper too lofty and abstract? If so, where does the writer need to come down to earth and get specific?

Do you understand all the words used? Do any specialized words need clearer definitions?

- Be open to new ideas—for focus, organization, or details.
- Use what's helpful, but trust yourself as the writer.

Be a helpful peer editor: offer honest, intelligent feedback, not judgment.

- Look at the big picture: purpose, focus, thesis, clarity, coherence, organization, support.
- When you spot strengths or weaknesses, be specific: note examples.
- Answer the writer's questions, and also use the questions supplied throughout this book to concentrate on essentials, not details.

See specific checklists in the "Revising and Editing" sections in Chs. 4 to 12.

## Meeting with Your Instructor

Prepare for your conference on a draft as you prepare for a peer review. Reread your paper; then write out your questions, concerns, or current revision plans. Whether you are meeting face-to-face, online, or by audio or video phone, arrive on time. Even if you feel shy or anxious, remember that you are working with an experienced reader who wants to help you improve your writing.

- If you already have received comments from your instructor, ask about anything you can't read, don't understand, or can't figure out how to do.
- If you are unsure about comments from peers, get your instructor's view.
- If you have a revision plan, ask for suggestions or priorities.
- If more questions arise after your conference, especially about comments on a draft returned there, follow up with a call, e-mail message, question after class, or second conference (as your instructor prefers).

## Decoding Your Instructor's Comments

Many instructors favor two kinds of comments:

- Summary comments—sentences on your first or last page—that may compliment strengths, identify recurring issues, acknowledge changes between drafts, make broad suggestions, or end with a grade
- Specific comments—brief notes or questions added in the margins—that typically pinpoint issues in the text

Although brief comments may seem like cryptic code or shorthand, they usually rely on key words to note common, recurring problems that probably are discussed in class and related to course criteria. They also may act as reminders, identifying issues that your instructor expects you to look up in your book and solve. A simple analysis—tallying up the repeated comments in one paper or several—can quickly help you set priorities for revision and editing. Some sample comments follow with translations, but turn to your instructor if you need a specific explanation.

| | |
|---|---|
| COMMENTS ON PURPOSE | Thesis? Vague Broad Clarify What's your point? So? So what? |
| POSSIBLE TRANSLATION | You need to state your thesis more clearly and directly so that a reader knows what matters. Concentrate on rewording so that your main idea is plain. |
| COMMENTS ON ORGANIZATION | Hard to follow Logic? Sequence? Add transitions? Jumpy |
| POSSIBLE TRANSLATION | You need to organize more logically so your paper is easy for a reader to follow without jumping from point to point. Add transitions or other cues to guide a reader. |
| COMMENTS ON SENTENCES AND WORDS | Unclear Clarify Awk Repetition Too informal |
| POSSIBLE TRANSLATION | You need to make your sentence or your wording easier to read and clearer. Rework awkward passages, reduce repetition, and stick to academic language. |
| COMMENTS ON EVIDENCE | Specify Focus Narrow down Develop more Seems thin |
| POSSIBLE TRANSLATION | You need to provide more concrete evidence or explain the relevance or nature of your evidence more clearly. Check that you support each main point with plenty of pertinent and compelling evidence. |
| COMMENTS ON SOURCES | Likely opponents? Source? Add quotation marks? Too many quotes Summarize? Synthesize? Launch source? |
| POSSIBLE TRANSLATION | You need to add sources that represent views other than your own. You include wording or ideas that sound like a source, not like you, so your quotation marks or citation might be missing. Instead of tossing in quotations, use your critical thinking skills to sum up ideas, relate them to each other, and introduce them more effectively. |
| COMMENTS ON CITATIONS | Cite? Author? Page? MLA? APA? |
| POSSIBLE TRANSLATION | Add missing source citations in your text and use the expected academic format to present them. |
| COMMENTS ON FINAL LIST OF SOURCES | MLA? APA? Comma? Period? Cap? Space? |
| POSSIBLE TRANSLATION | Your entries do not follow the expected format. Check the model entries in this book. Look for the presence, absence, or placement of the specific detail noted. |

## Revising for Emphasis, Conciseness, and Clarity

After you've revised for the large issues in your draft—purpose, thesis, audience, structure, and support—you're ready to turn your attention to micro revising. Now is the time to look at your language, to emphasize what matters most, and to communicate it concisely and clearly.

### Stressing What Counts

An effective writer decides what matters most and shines a bright light on it using the most emphatic positions in an essay, a paragraph, or a sentence—the beginning and the end.

**Stating It First.** In an essay, you might start with what matters most. For an economics paper on import quotas (such as the number of foreign cars allowed into a country), student Donna Waite summed up her conclusion.

> Although an import quota has many effects, both for the nation imposing the quota and for the nation whose industries must suffer from it, I believe that the most important effect is generally felt at home. A native industry gains a chance to thrive in a marketplace of lessened competition.

To take a stand or make a proposal, you might open with your position.

> Our state's antiquated system of justices of the peace is inefficient.

> The United States should orbit a human observer around Mars.

In a single sentence, as in an essay, you can stress things at the start. Consider the following unemphatic sentence:

> When Congress debates the Hall-Hayes Act removing existing protections for endangered species, as now seems likely to occur on May 12, it will be a considerable misfortune if this bill should pass, since the extinction of many rare birds and animals would certainly result.

The debate and its probable timing consume the start of the sentence. Here's a better use of this emphatic position:

> The extinction of many rare birds and animals would certainly follow passage of the Hall-Hayes Act.

Now the writer stresses what he most fears—the dire consequences of the act. (A later sentence might add the date and his opinion about passage.)

**Stating It Last.** To place an idea last can throw weight on it. Emphatic order, proceeding from least important to most, is dramatic: it builds up and up. In a paper on import quotas, however, a dramatic buildup might look contrived. Still, in an essay on how city parks lure visitors to the city, the thesis sentence – summing up the point of the essay – might stand at the very end: "For the urban core, improved parks could bring about a new era of prosperity." Giving evidence first and leading up to the thesis at the end is particularly effective in editorials and informal persuasive essays.

A sentence that uses climactic order, suspending its point until the end, is a *periodic* sentence as novelist Julian Green illustrates.

> Amid chaos of illusions into which we are cast headlong, there is one thing that stands out as true, and that is – love.

## Cutting and Whittling

Like pea pickers who throw out dirt and pebbles, good writers remove needless words that clog their prose. One of the chief joys of revising is to watch 200 paunchy words shrink to a svelte 150. To see how saving words helps, let's look at some strategies for reducing wordiness.

**Cut the Fanfare.** Why bother to announce that you're going to say something? Cut the fanfare. We aren't, by the way, attacking the usefulness of transitions that lead readers along.

For more on transitions, see pp. 431–35.

WORDY As far as getting ready for winter is concerned, I put antifreeze in my car.

REVISED To get ready for winter, I put antifreeze in my car.

WORDY The point should be made that . . .
Let me make it perfectly clear that . . .
In this paper I intend to . . .
In conclusion I would like to say that . . .

**Use Strong Verbs.** Forms of the verb *be* (*am, is, are, was, were*) followed by a noun or an adjective can make a statement wordy, as can *There is* or *There are*. Such weak verbs can almost always be replaced by active verbs.

WORDY The Akron game was a disappointment to the fans.

REVISED The Akron game disappointed the fans.

WORDY There are many people who dislike flying.

REVISED Many people dislike flying.

**Use Relative Pronouns with Caution.** When a clause begins with a relative pronoun (*who, which, that*), you often can whittle it to a phrase.

WORDY Venus, which is the second planet of the solar system, is called the evening star.

REVISED Venus, the second planet of the solar system, is called the evening star.

**Cut Out Deadwood.** The more you revise, the more shortcuts you'll discover. Phrases such as *on the subject of, in regard to, in terms of,* and *as far as . . . is concerned* often simply fill space. Try reading the sentences below without the words in *italics.*

Howell spoke for the sophomores, and Janet *also spoke* for the seniors.

He is *something of* a clown but *sort of the* lovable *type.*

As a major in *the field of* economics, I plan to concentrate on *the area of* international banking.

*The decision as to* whether *or not* to go is up to you.

**Cut Descriptors.** Adjectives and adverbs are often dispensable.

| | |
|---|---|
| WORDY | Johnson's extremely significant research led to highly important major discoveries. |
| REVISED | Johnson's research led to major discoveries. |

**Be Short, Not Long.** While a long word may convey a shade of meaning that a shorter synonym doesn't, in general favor short words over long ones. Instead of *the remainder,* write *the rest;* instead of *activate, start* or *begin;* instead of *adequate* or *sufficient, enough.* Look for the right word—one that wraps an idea in a smaller package.

| | |
|---|---|
| WORDY | Andy has a left fist that has a lot of power in it. |
| REVISED | Andy has a potent left. |

By the way, it pays to read. From reading, you absorb words like *potent* and set them to work for you.

## Keeping It Clear

Recall what you want to achieve—clear, direct communication with your readers using specific, unambiguous words arranged in logical order.

| | |
|---|---|
| WORDY | He is more or less a pretty outstanding person in regard to good looks. |
| REVISED | He is strikingly handsome. |

Read your draft with fresh eyes. Return, after a break, to passages that have been a struggle; heal any battle scars by focusing on clarity.

| | |
|---|---|
| UNCLEAR | Thus, after a lot of thought, it should be approved by the board even though the federal funding for all the cow-tagging may not be approved yet because it has wide support from local cattle ranchers. |
| CLEAR | In anticipation of federal funding, the Livestock Board should approve the cow-tagging proposal widely supported by local cattle ranchers. |

### MICRO REVISION CHECKLIST

- ☐ Have you positioned what counts at the beginning or the end?
- ☐ Are you direct, straightforward, and clear?
- ☐ Do you announce an idea before you utter it? If so, consider chopping out the announcement.
- ☐ Can you substitute an active verb where you use a form of *be* (*is, was, were*)?
- ☐ Can you recast any sentence that begins *There is* or *There are*?
- ☐ Can you reduce to a phrase any clause beginning with *which, who,* or *that*?
- ☐ Have you added deadwood or too many adjectives and adverbs?
- ☐ Do you see any long words where short words would do?
- ☐ Have you kept your writing clear, direct, and forceful?

## Learning by Doing Tackling Micro Revision

Think over the revisions you've already made and the advice you've received from peers or other readers. Is your paper more likely to seem bland (because it lacks emphasis), wordy (because it needs a good trimming), or foggy (because it needs to be more direct and logical)? Focus on one issue: adding emphasis, cutting extra words, or expressing ideas clearly.

For his composition class, Daniel Matthews was assigned a paper using a few sources. He was to write about an "urban legend," a widely accepted and emotionally appealing—but untrue—tale about events. The following selection from his paper, "The Truth about 'Taps,'" introduces his topic, briefly explaining the legend and the true story about it. The first draft illustrates macro revisions (highlighted in the margin) and micro revisions (marked in the text); the clear and concise final version follows.

FIRST DRAFT

*Anyone who has ever*
~~As you know, whenever you have~~ attended the funeral services for a fallen veteran of the United States of America~~, you have~~ *has* stood fast as a lone bugler filled the air with the mournful ~~and sullenly appropriate~~ last tribute to a defender of the ~~United States of America~~ *nation*. ~~As most of us know, t~~*T*he name of the bugle call is "Taps," and the ~~story~~ *legend* behind its origin ~~is one that is~~ *has* gain~~ing a~~*ed* popularity ~~of its own~~ as it

*Avoid "you" in case readers have not shared this experience.*

Rework paragraph to summarize legend when first mentioned.

INSERT: According to this story, Union Captain Robert Ellicombe discovered that a Confederate casualty was, in fact, his son, a music student in the South. The father found "Taps" in his son's pocket, and the tune was first played at a military burial as his son was laid to rest (Coulter).

Group all the discussion of the versions in one place.

Divide long sentence to keep it clear.

Strengthen paragraph conclusion by sticking to its focus.

has

is more and more frequently being circulated in this time of war and terror. Although it is clear that this tale of the origin of a beautiful ode to a fallen warrior is heartfelt and full of purposeful intent, it is an "urban legend." As such, i It fails to provide due justice to the memories of the men responsible for the true origin of "Taps."

General Daniel Butterfield is the true originator of the bugle call "Taps," formerly known as "Lights Out." Butterfield served as a general in the Union army during the Civil War and was awarded the Medal of Honor for actions during that time. One of his most endearing claims to fame is the bugle call "Taps," which he composed at Harrison's Landing in 1862 (Warner 167). The bugle call "Taps" originates from another call named "Lights Out"; this call was used by the Army to signal the end of the day. Butterfield, wanting a new and original call unique to his command, summoned bugler Oliver Willcox Norton to his tent one night. and R rather than compose an altogether new tune, he instead modified the notes to the call "Lights Out" (US Military District of Washington). Shortly thereafter Then this call could be heard being used up and down the Union lines as the other commanders who had heard the call liked it and adapted it for their own use. This call, the modified version of "Lights Out" is also and itself in a way a derivative of the British bugle call "Tattoo," a "Tattoo" which is very similar in both sound and purpose to "Lights Out," (Villanueva). notes this as well in his paper "24 Notes That Tap Deep Emotion."

REVISED DRAFT

Anyone who has ever attended the funeral services for a fallen veteran of the United States of America has stood fast as a lone bugler filled the air with a mournful last tribute to a defender of the nation. The name of the bugle call is "Taps," and the legend behind its origin has gained popularity as it has circulated in this time of war and terror. According to this story, Union Captain Robert Ellicombe discovered that a Confederate casualty was, in fact, his son, a music student in the South. The father found "Taps" in his son's pocket, and the tune was first played at a military burial as his son was laid to rest (Coulter). Although this tale of a beautiful ode to a fallen warrior is heartfelt, it is an "urban legend." As such, it fails to provide due justice to the memories of the men responsible for the true origin of "Taps."

General Daniel Butterfield is the true originator of the bugle call "Taps." Butterfield served in the Union army during the Civil War and was awarded the Medal of Honor for actions during that time. One of his most endearing claims to fame is the bugle call "Taps," which he composed at Harrison's Landing in 1862 (Warner 167). "Taps" originates from another call named "Lights Out," used by the army to signal the end of the day and itself a derivative of "Tattoo," a British bugle call similar in both sound and purpose (Villanueva). Butterfield, wanting a new and original call unique to his command, summoned bugler Oliver Willcox Norton to his tent one night. Rather than compose an altogether new tune, he instead modified the notes to the call "Lights Out" (US Military District of Washington). Shortly thereafter this call could be heard up and down the Union lines as other commanders heard the call and adapted it for their own use.

## Editing and Proofreading

Editing means correcting and refining grammar, punctuation, and mechanics. Proofreading means taking a final look to check correctness and to catch spelling or word-processing errors. Don't edit and proofread too soon. As you draft, don't fret over spelling an unfamiliar word; it may be revised out in a later version. Wait until you have revised to refine and correct. In college, good editing and proofreading can make the difference between a C and an A. On the job, it may help you get promoted. Readers, teachers, and bosses like careful writers who take time to edit and proofread.

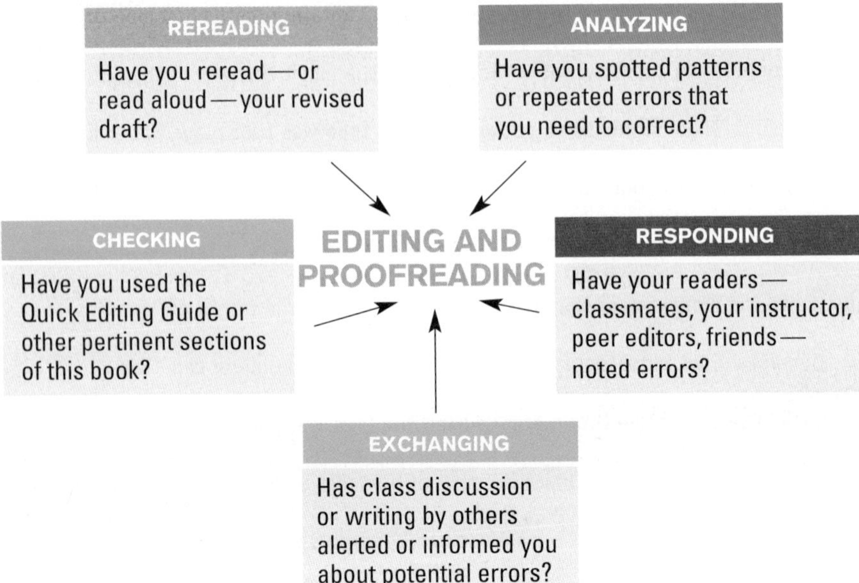


## Editing

As you edit, whenever you question whether a word or construction is correct, consult a good reference handbook. Learn the grammar conventions you don't understand so you can spot and eliminate problems in your own writing. Practice until you easily recognize major errors such as fragments and comma splices. Ask for assistance from a peer editor or a tutor in the writing center if your campus has one.

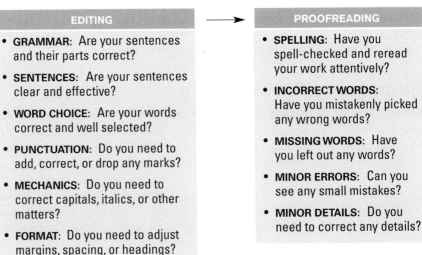

**EDITING** →

- **GRAMMAR:** Are your sentences and their parts correct?
- **SENTENCES:** Are your sentences clear and effective?
- **WORD CHOICE:** Are your words correct and well selected?
- **PUNCTUATION:** Do you need to add, correct, or drop any marks?
- **MECHANICS:** Do you need to correct capitals, italics, or other matters?
- **FORMAT:** Do you need to adjust margins, spacing, or headings?

**PROOFREADING**

- **SPELLING:** Have you spell-checked and reread your work attentively?
- **INCORRECT WORDS:** Have you mistakenly picked any wrong words?
- **MISSING WORDS:** Have you left out any words?
- **MINOR ERRORS:** Can you see any small mistakes?
- **MINOR DETAILS:** Do you need to correct any details?

Use the "Quick Editing Guide" (beginning on p. A-39) to review grammar, style, punctuation, and mechanics problems typically found in college writing. Look for definitions, examples, and a checklist to help you tackle each one. Here is an editing checklist for these problems:

---

**EDITING CHECKLIST**

**Common and Serious Problems in College Writing**

The following cross-references refer to the Quick Editing Guide section at the back of this book.

| *Grammar Problems* | *Section Number* |
|---|---|
| ☐ Have you avoided writing sentence fragments? | A1 |
| ☐ Have you avoided writing comma splices or fused sentences? | A2 |
| ☐ Have you used the correct form for all verbs in the past tense? | A3 |
| ☐ Do all verbs agree with their subjects? | A4 |
| ☐ Have you used the correct case for all pronouns? | A5 |
| ☐ Do all pronouns agree with their antecedents? | A6 |
| ☐ Have you used adjectives and adverbs correctly? | A7 |
| *Sentence Problems* | |
| ☐ Does each modifier clearly modify the appropriate sentence element? | B1 |
| ☐ Have you used parallel structure where necessary? | B2 |
| *Punctuation Problems* | |
| ☐ Have you used commas correctly? | C1 |
| ☐ Have you used apostrophes correctly? | C2 |
| ☐ Have you punctuated quotations correctly? | C3 |
| *Mechanics Problems* | |
| ☐ Have you used capital letters correctly? | D1 |
| ☐ Have you spelled all words correctly? | D2 |

---

For help documenting any sources in your paper, turn to sections D6 and E1–E2 in the Quick Research Guide (pp. A-31–A-38).

## Proofreading

*All* writers make mistakes as they put ideas on paper. Because the mind works faster than the pencil (or the computer), a moment's break in concentration—when someone talks or your phone rings—can lead to

errors. Making such mistakes isn't bad—you simply need to take the time to find and correct them.

- Let a paper sit several days, overnight, or at least a few hours before proofreading so that you allow time to gain perspective.
- Budget enough time to proofread thoroughly. For a long essay or complex research paper with a list of sources, schedule several sessions.
- Ask someone else to read your paper and tell you if it is free of errors. But take pride in your own work. *Don't* let someone else do it for you.
- Use a dictionary or a spell-checker, but remember that a spell-checker recognizes only correct spelling, not correct choices.
- Keep a list of your habitual errors, especially those your instructor has already pointed out. Double-check for these errors (such as leaving off *-s* or *-ed* endings or putting in unnecessary commas).

Proofreading does take patience but is a skill you can develop. For instance, when you simply glance at the spelling of *environment,* you may miss the second *n*. When you read normally, you usually see only the shells of words—the first and last letters. You fix your eyes on the print only three or four times per line or less. When you proofread, try to look at the letters in each word and the punctuation marks between words. Slow down and concentrate.

### PROOFREADING CHECKLIST

- ☐ Have you read your draft very slowly, looking at every word and letter? Have you tried to see what is actually written, not what you think is there?
- ☐ Have you read your paper aloud so you can see and hear mistakes?
- ☐ Have you read the essay backward so that you look at each word instead of getting caught up in the flow of ideas?
- ☐ Have you read your essay several times, focusing each time on a specific area of difficulty? (For example, read once for spelling, once for punctuation, and once for a problem that recurs in your writing.)

For editing exercises, visit Exercise Central in Re:Writing at **bedfordstmartins .com/bedguide**.

## Learning by Doing Editing and Proofreading

1. Read the following passage carefully. Assume that the organization of the paragraph is satisfactory, but find and correct fifteen errors in sentence structure, grammar, spelling, punctuation, and capitalization. After you have corrected the passage, discuss with your classmates the changes you have made and your reasons for making those changes.

   Robert Frost, one of the most poplar American poets. He was born in San Francisco in 1874, and died in Boston in 1963. His family moved to new

England when his father died in 1885. There he completed highschool and attended colledge but never graduate. Poverty and problems filled his life. He worked in a woll mill, on a newspaper, and at varous odd jobs. Because of ill health he settled on a farm and began to teach school to support his wife and children. Throughout his life he dedicated himself to writing poetry, by 1915 he was in demand for public readings and speaking engagements. He was awarded the Pulitzer Prize for poetry four times—in 1924, 1931, 1937, and 1943. The popularity of his poetry rests in his use of common themes and images. everyone can relate to his universal poems, such as "Birches" and "Stopping by Woods on a Snowy Evening." Students read his poetry in school from seventh grade through graduate school, so almost everyone recognize lines from his best-loved poems. America is proud of it's son, the homespun poet Robert Frost.

2. Select a passage, from this textbook or elsewhere, that is about one hundred words long. Type up the passage, intentionally adding ten errors in grammar, spelling, punctuation, or capitalization. Swap passages with a classmate; proofread, then check each other's work against the originals. Share your proofreading strategies.

## Learning by Doing Reflecting on Revising and Editing

Think back on your process for finishing your last paper. In what ways did you revise that paper well, working on both macro and micro changes? How might you plan to revise your next paper? In what ways did you edit your last paper well? How might you plan to edit your next paper? Working with a classmate or small group, share your successful approaches face-to-face or online.

# 24 Strategies for Future Writing

Your college writing course is designed to help you read, write, think, and rewrite. When that course ends, your writing days are not over. Instead, you move on to other courses and other writing assignments. In those future situations, whether or not the assignments and criteria are presented like those in a composition course, you still need to read, write, think, and rewrite. The assumption—and the hope—is that your experience in your writing class will equip you to write successfully in your future courses and eventually in your workplace, career, or community. To do so, you will want to transfer your learning and apply it in new situations.

For an interactive Learning by Doing activity on Researching Genre, go to Ch. 24: **bedfordstmartins.com/bedguide**.

## Transferring Knowledge

How to apply what you have learned may seem puzzling, even mysterious. For example, in your next class, would you struggle to answer a pop quiz question on two creatures, two events, or two theories? Or would you recall what you already have learned about organizing comparison and contrast? In your nursing or teaching clinical program, would you struggle every day to manage patients or maintain classroom order? Or would you apply your experience proposing a solution to your own on-site problems?

You've probably experienced both frustration, when a new situation challenges your experience, and exhilaration, when old skills and past practice make something new seem easy. Maybe your background or confidence makes the difference—or maybe the content area, skill, or kind of knowledge to be transferred does. Either way, how to transfer learning from one situation to another—and how to do so effectively—often seems a puzzle. To help you solve that puzzle when you need to write different types of papers in different situations, this chapter covers three key questions you might ask:

- What do they want?
- What is it?
- How do I write it?

### Learning by Doing — Reflecting on How to Transfer Knowledge

Reflect for a few minutes about how you have transferred learning in the past. How have you tackled a new task and figured out how to succeed? How have you successfully handled new academic situations—different teaching styles, schools of thought, types of assignments, or levels of expectation? Jot down a few notes about your strategies for success. If possible, share them with classmates.

## What Do They Want?

When you face a challenging or high-stakes writing assignment, your first question is likely to be, What do they want? Your instructor or your work supervisor may—or may not—provide explicit directions about your task. Either way, your first step is to gather information about the assignment.

**ASSIGNMENT CHECKLIST**

- ☐ Do you have a written assignment distributed in class, posted online, provided in your syllabus, or included in your job description?
- ☐ Have you taken notes on verbal advice or directions? Have you thoughtfully read advice posted online by your instructor?
- ☐ Does your assignment identify or imply a purpose and an audience?
- ☐ Does it specify the approach, activity, method, or product?
- ☐ Does it require a standard format, perhaps based on a style guide, a sample lab report, headings in a journal article, an evaluation form, past annual reports at work, or some other model?
- ☐ Does it use key words that you recognize from your writing class or other situations? For instance, does it ask you to explain effects, evaluate, or summarize, drawing on skills you have used recently?
- ☐ What criteria will be used to assess the success of your writing task?

### Analyzing Expectations

When a challenging writing assignment comes from the instructor in a class where you need to succeed, or from the boss you have to satisfy, shift your attention from yourself to your audience. Whether you feel confident, puzzled, or anxious, focus on what is expected. Apply your experience decoding past assignments to analyzing current ones. Do the same with your experience identifying a writing purpose and audience. Try writing notes on or about your assignment to help you tease out all the available clues about how to succeed.

*Starting point = problem + solution*

*Need to check grant format*

*Propose solution — I've done that!*

*Purpose + Audience*

*Good — list of required sections*

Once you have defined both a problem and a solution that you wish to propose, write your paper as a grant proposal designed to persuade a funding agency to support your proposal. Be sure to include a statement of the problem, a needs assessment, and a specific proposal.

## Connecting Expectations and Assessments

Expectations may be most clearly expressed in assessment criteria. What are the standards for performance or outcomes in your course or workplace? How will your paper or project be judged? If you will be graded or assigned points based on the presence, absence, or quality of specific features or components, these are also part of "what they want."

> You can be awarded a maximum of 25 points for each of these four features: (1) a clear and compelling introduction to your proposal, (2) a well-researched review of relevant literature, (3) a clear explanation of the theoretical framework for examining the problem, and (4) a clear description and justification of the methods proposed for your study.

Try turning your requirements or assessment criteria into a checklist or self-assessment questions for yourself. For example, you might convert the criteria in the previous example to these four questions:

1. Do I have a clear and compelling introduction to my proposal?
2. Have I included a well-researched review of relevant literature?
3. Do I clearly explain my theoretical framework for examining the problem?
4. Do I clearly describe and justify the methods for my study?

If you worry about forgetting or skipping over the assessment details, try breaking out each expectation as a separate question:

> Do I have an introduction? Is it clear? Is it compelling?

### Learning by Doing Decoding an Assignment

In a group or individually, select an assignment from another class. First identify its stated expectations. Write out what you think it asks you to do and how you might draw on your existing knowledge to do this. If grading criteria are available, turn them into questions that you could ask yourself while working on the assignment. If possible, exchange ideas with classmates to refine your analyses.

## What Is It?

Once you have figured out "what they want," your next challenge is to determine "what it is." As you read and write in a particular field, you may recognize common strategies or approaches. For example, historians frequently use cause-and-effect analysis, natural scientists rely on classification, nurses value accurate description, and specialists in many fields use comparison and contrast to examine cases, techniques, or theories. In addition, many assignments—such as lab reports, proposals, or reviews—require a genre, or type, of writing defined by specific characteristics and assumptions. Identifying assumptions and genre features will help you to tackle each kind of writing more successfully.

### Uncovering Assumptions

In advanced classes, expectations of the field or discipline are likely to underlie those of your instructor. Here, your ingenuity is engaged not in the creation of an analytical approach or a method of investigation but in its application to your particular text, project, or research question. For example, your literature essay will probably rely on a close reading of a novel, poem, or play and take an accepted approach to analyzing the work's characters, images, or other components. Your essay is unlikely to use headings such as Method, Results, or Discussion. However, those divisions are likely essentials for your psychology report on your field study. Such expectations about approach, method, organization, or format reflect the assumptions shared by scholars and researchers in a particular field—their deep agreements, for instance, that a literary study typically relies on textual analysis or that a psychology study typically follows certain research procedures.

When a field or approach is new to you, you won't know if your instructor and others in the field already share established ideas about how a paper should develop. How can you find out what is assumed? First, use your experience as a college writer to check your assignment for clues—such as references, maybe without explanation, to a certain type of paper.

Using textual evidence, write an (essay) to analyze the novel's attention to

*Maybe quotations? Repeated images? Characters? Setting? Narrator?* — textual evidence
*OK / Thesis? / Evidence?* — essay
*Break into elements? Identify components?* — analyze

problems of social justice.

*Relevance for society? Cultural commentary?*

Prepare a (review of the literature) on your topic, covering advances

*What's that? What's in it? Find sources?? Summarize? Or synthesize too?* — review of the literature
*New studies? New findings? New theories?* — advances

during the last decade.

*Last ten years? Background OK?*

Also consider the readings assigned in the course or field. For example, many journal articles in psychology, sociology, or education open with an abstract, summing up the reading. Should you add an abstract to your paper? Those same articles may have section headings with identical or similar wording. Should your paper use the same headings? Ask your instructor which features of assigned readings are expected in your paper.

By definition, assumptions and conventions (generally accepted ideas about ways to proceed) are taken for granted within a field. That's why your instructor may assume that once you enroll in a course you already share a certain set of assumptions, even though you may assume those views are what you need to learn. That's also why two researchers—for instance, an art historian and a chemist—could both investigate how to intensify color in a painting but hold different ideas about what's of interest. One might study techniques for applying paint while the other might analyze formulas for mixing paint. Likewise, the engineers at your job probably view products differently than the marketing team does.

Whenever you enter a class, field, or situation that may operate on assumptions new to you, you need to notice what is preferred:

- kinds of studies, analyses, or topics
- research procedures, accepted methods, stages of analysis, or patterns of organization

- methods of argument or explanation
- kinds and quantities of evidence
- use of technical vocabulary, authorial voice, transitions to show shifts, description or explanation, or other features

Then ask what sections, approaches, or features need to be included in your writing. Consider the unstated expectations or criteria that your writing situation – or the situation posed in your assignment – may imply.

## Analyzing Genre Models

When you choose a novel or a film, you probably know right away the type that you prefer, whether a romance, police drama, or action-packed war story. However, you may find all academic genres simply difficult – not different – until you gain experience with them and learn to spot their features. If you want to find samples of a particular written genre, your best resources may be examples such as these:

- assigned, posted, or textbook-supplied readings
- sample essays, projects, or other student work discussed in class
- published, professional models such as recommended journal articles, research studies, creative works, or Web sites

As you examine academic models, bring your experience reading and writing past assignments to your new task. The more experience you gain with a specific genre – whether a review of the literature or a lab report or a literary analysis – the easier and more familiar that form will be. Soon you, too, will absorb its assumptions and conventions. Use the following questions to help you notice which features are shared by all (and seem mandatory) and which appear in some (and seem variable or optional).

For some sets of examples that you might analyze with this checklist, see the poems on p. 219, 287–88; the short stories on p. 260 and 283; the letters on pp. 360, 363, and 383; or the newspaper opinion column on p. 53.

---

**GENRE CHECKLIST**

**Parts of the Text**

- ☐ How does the text begin – with a title, an abstract (or summary), an opening paragraph on the topic, a description, a problem, or another feature?
- ☐ What are its sections? Do they appear in a predictable sequence? Are they labeled with headings, act and scene numbers, or other markers?
- ☐ Does it have preliminaries (title page, table of contents, list of figures)?
- ☐ Does it include closing materials (list of sources, appendix)?

### Development

- ☐ How are paragraphs typically developed? Do they begin with topic sentences or work up to the main point? Do they tend to contain one example or several? Are they all about the same length or varied?
- ☐ How are sentences typically developed? Are they similar or varied in terms of length, structure, and opening wording? Do they often begin with transitions? Do they use active voice (*X did it*) or passive (*it was done by X*)? Do they use first person (*I, we*) or third (*he, she, it, they*)?
- ☐ What tone, style, vocabulary, and level of formality does the text use? Does it assume readers know certain terms or technical expressions, or does it define them?
- ☐ What types of assertions, claims, evidence, turns of the argument, or sources does it use?
- ☐ Are sources cited following MLA, APA, or another academic style?
- ☐ Do other features appear to be conventional or typical?

### Presentation

- ☐ What does the text look like on a page? Is it mostly formal text with one-inch margins, a 12-point type font, and a running header? Or does it have uneven lines or variable placement of text (as in a letter, poem, or play)?
- ☐ Does the text include diagrams or figures, tables with numerical results, graphs, photographs of places or events, sketches of creatures or objects studied, or other visuals? How are these labeled and credited (if necessary)?
- ☐ How is the final list of sources indented and spaced on the page?

---

After you analyze several models, compare your observations with the requirements in your assignment. When you find a match, you'll have both directions and an example or pattern. When in doubt, always follow your assignment; ask your instructor to clarify any confusing alternatives.

## Learning by Doing Analyzing a Genre Model

Working individually or in a group, select one or more genre models for analysis. Use the Genre Checklist to help you analyze each sample and identify its characteristic features. If you are working in a group, share your analyses. If you wish, write directions for yourself or for someone else, explaining how to write a particular genre, or type, of paper.

## How Do I Write It?

You don't need to start from scratch when you face something new. Begin with what you know to prepare for what you don't know. When you face a difficult, unfamiliar, or downright mysterious assignment, apply or adapt your past writing processes and experience to that challenge.

- Underline or annotate your assignment to identify requirements.
- Add notes to yourself, especially to distinguish what you know how to do and what you don't.
- Sort your models to find examples of unfamiliar features or sections.
- Return to the processes used in your writing class so that you generate ideas and plan instead of simply jumping into drafting.
- Turn to the campus writing center, your class study group, or your friends to identify a peer reader who can respond to your draft.
- Get a second opinion from another reader if useful.
- Meet with your instructor, or submit your draft for a preliminary reading (if possible). Use your instructor's advice, especially about the big issues, to help you look critically at your own work.
- Revise first to conform to the unfamiliar assignment. Use your analysis of it to generate your own self-assessment questions.
- Revise again to improve format, organization, clarity, or other matters.
- Edit to improve conventions and genre features as well as to correct errors.

### Learning by Doing Reflecting on New Assignments

Reflect on your writing experience. When you face a new assignment, how do you get started? What are your most reliable strategies? What adjustments have you made or are you making as a college writer? When you face a challenging assignment, how would you apply what you already know and do as a writer?

# Learning from Another Writer: A Multigenre History Assignment

When Benjamin Reitz enrolled in the class, "United States Society and Thought before 1860," he analyzed the following multigenre term paper assignment that Professor Laird included in the course packet.

**Professor Laird** **Term Paper Assignment**

## Historical Analysis and Argument

*Explains approach to history*

The ways people have lived and their beliefs and goals and expectations have been the most important ingredients of history. Everything else happens within the contexts of how and why people conduct their lives the way they do. In turn, people's ideas are profoundly related to the conditions of their lives.

*Two choices — situation and person*

*Show person's point of view*

For this paper, therefore, select an ideological position, a set of behaviors, or a social institution that existed in what is now the United States sometime between 1600 and 1860. Then explore the lives and beliefs of a person or group of persons who supported that position, activity, or institution. Select an ordinary individual, someone who is *not* well known, or create a character who is a composite of people who were involved in a major historical shift or event.

*1st part reports research*

*2nd part shows person — can choose genre*

*Purpose — analyze & argue*

Your paper will have two parts. One will detail the results of your research, explaining whose position you are taking and the historical situation in which that position was significant in political, business, or domestic matters. It will set the historical context for the second part, which will make a persuasive argument for the position you have selected based on the person you have chosen. The form that your second part takes is up to you. You may simply write an essay, or you may attempt to persuade your audience through a letter, a sermon, diary entries, or a dialogue. Remember that the purpose of this paper is to analyze and to argue from your adopted perspective, showing your understanding of the historical circumstances.

*Also need bib — 3rd part*

Length: 10 to 12 pages in addition to a bibliography at the end that lists the primary and secondary sources, including books and articles that you consulted to help you understand your character's life and beliefs.

This assignment offers students an opportunity to gain an enriched understanding of a moment in history. It requires three different sections—a report on research, a presentation of an individual, and a bibliography. It requires various types of writing (as varied as an essay, a letter, a diary, or a sermon), various critical activities (such as analysis, argument, and persuasion), and various kinds of sources (primary and secondary). Following are brief selections from Benjamin Reitz's paper, illustrating some of the different types of writing that the assignment required.

**Benjamin Reitz** **Selections from Student Term Paper**

## Historical Situation

Andrew Jackson, a nearly infamous character in the history of the presidency, has been something of an enigma for many biographers and historians. They have come to acknowledge that Jackson was the architect of many policies that led to what, by modern standards, would be considered human rights violations, not the least of which would be his Indian Removal Act of 1830. The question of Jackson's basic character, however, becomes more difficult to speak to directly when one objectively considers his stand against central banking. Certain commentators on Jackson's famous "War on the Bank" of the 1830s have approached the event with extreme bias. They have either totally condemned him or lauded him for his earnest attack on the Second Bank of the United States, and they have likely developed their assessment of his actions on the basis, however subconsciously, of their own views on central banking, which remains a hot-button issue to this day. . . . 1

In order to gain a new perspective, it will be necessary to appeal to a fictional character, Mr. Atticus Amhurst, antebellum financier from Gettysburg, Pennsylvania. Amhurst is clearly convinced of the necessity of central banking in order to establish a means by which the many different paper notes from banks across the State of Pennsylvania, and across the nation at large, could be gathered into one form and universally redeemed. He also carries strong opinions about competition between American and foreign creditors in international money markets and believes that a central bank is the only way to establish a foundation for the further satisfaction of American interests in those markets. Amhurst, eminently practical when it comes to money, does have an idealistic side, which is obvious as he gives his opinions about Jackson's character, a character which he knows well and tends to romanticize as he reminisces. 2

Letter from Atticus Amhurst, Fictional Financier

*To Lieutenant William J. Cooper of Martin's Ferry, Ohio, April 2, 1844*

My Dear, Dear Mr. Cooper,

Were I not nearly so old and forgetful, I would write a book about General Jackson. Today, as I was sifting through some old newspapers, more keepsakes now than anything with a ready utility, I came across some editorials from about 15 years ago during that dreadful business between Old Hickory and the Bank. I remember being incensed in those times as I read some of the intolerable libels against our old fine commander, and I find I have little patience for reading them through even 3 now. Equally striking to me then, but even more so these days, was the ignorance of Jacksonians who, knowing neither the man nor his mind, but merely sympathizing with his cause, shamefully slandered the Second Bank of the United States, that institution which, for a time, promised to make our nation the envy of the modern world of finance. . . . [Amhurst continues, reviewing his newspaper clippings from the 1830s.]

Your good friend and brother-in-arms,
Atticus D. Amhurst

### Questions to Start You Thinking

Meaning

1. What thesis or main idea does Reitz try to convey in his paper?
2. What is the function of the fictional letter writer in this paper?

Writing Strategies

3. For the sections of Reitz's term paper briefly illustrated here, mark or list notable features that you think are typical of its genre, or type, of writing.
4. Aside from including the required sections in his paper, what writing techniques does Reitz use to try to keep a reader's interest?

## Learning from Another Writer: A Philosophy of Teaching Portfolio

Maria Thompson was required to compile an extensive professional portfolio, completing her work for her Linguistically Diverse Education Program in the School of Education and Human Development. Her portfolio included discussions of five content areas, a list of references, and appendices with artifacts, teaching plans, and materials designed to demonstrate that she met the required standards for teachers.

**Maria Thompson** — **Selections from Student Portfolio**

### Philosophy as Autobiography

In many ways I live the American dream, but I was not always so fortunate. Prior to acquiring an American last name, I was a typical mid-twentieth-century first-generation immigrant — struggling and poor. Predictably, breaking the chains of poverty proved very difficult. Luckily, through a strong network of social support from family and friends, an extraordinary degree of perseverance, an ability to set goals, and a realistic acceptance of weakness coupled with an attitude of building on strengths, I took control of my life and became the first in my family to achieve my long-term educational goals. Needless to say, the journey toward academic success has been a long and arduous process. . . .

## Pedagogical Approach

. . . In conclusion, I believe that language acquisition is a gradual process. Yet in our current push for standardization and high-stakes testing for measuring achievement, educators are required to bridge the gap between native and non-native speakers at a fast pace. This push means I must work diligently to draw upon researched "best practices" to make content comprehensible and language acquisition attainable.

## Questions to Start You Thinking

### Meaning

1. What main idea does Thompson try to convey in the first selection where she introduces her portfolio?
2. What main idea does she try to convey in the second selection?

### Writing Strategies

3. In what ways does Thompson's approach and style differ in the two selections? How do these differences support the purposes of the two selections?
4. What writing techniques does Thompson use to try to keep a reader's interest?

### Learning by Doing Reflecting on Resources for the Future

Look back at the preceding selections from the two student writers. What approaches or skills might they have drawn from their writing classes? In your own case, which of your current writing strengths might you use in other settings in the future? Which areas might you want to strengthen right now for the future?

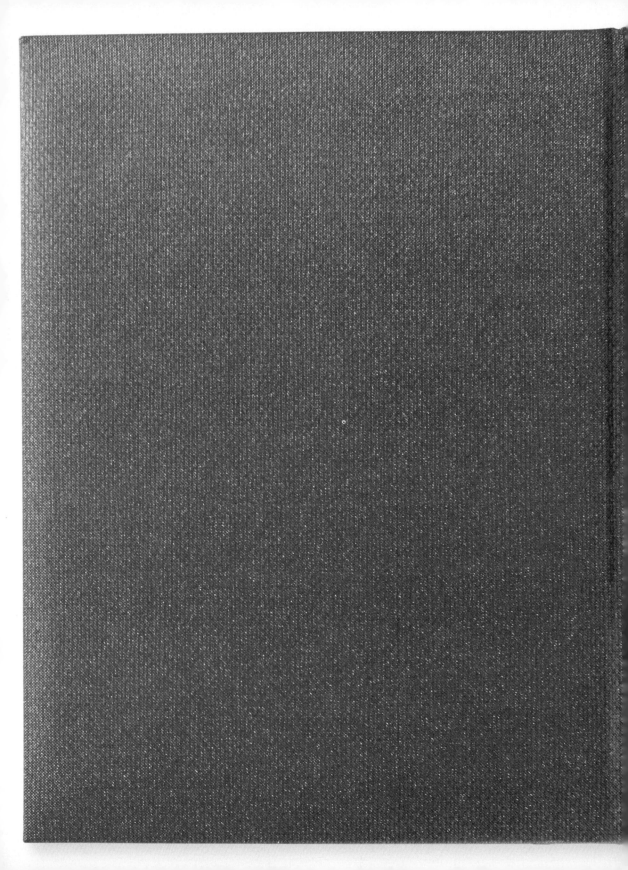

# A WRITER'S READER

# A Writer's Reader Contents

# Introduction: Reading to Write

A *Writer's Reader* is a collection of forty professional essays and multimedia readings. We hope, first of all, that you will read these pieces simply for the sake of reading—enjoying and responding to their ideas. Second, we hope that you will actively study these essays as solid examples of the situations and strategies explored in *A Writer's Guide.* The authors represented in this reader have faced the same problems and choices you do when you write. You can learn from studying their decisions, structures, and techniques. Finally, we hope that you will find the content of the essays intriguing—and along with the questions posed after each one, a source of ideas to write about.

Each chapter in *A Writer's Reader* concentrates on a broad theme—families, men and women, popular culture, life in a digital age, and the challenge of living well. Some essays focus on the inner world of personal experience and opinion. Others turn to the outer world with information and persuasion. In each chapter, the last two print selections explore the same subject, illustrating how different writers use different strategies to address similar issues. In addition, two online-only selections can be accessed at **bedfordstmartins.com/bedguide**.

Each chapter in the reader begins with an image, a visual activity, and a Web search activity to stimulate your thinking and writing. Each selection is preceded by biographical information, placing the author—and the piece itself—in a cultural and informational context. Next a reading note, As You Read, suggests a way to consider the selection. Following each reading are five Questions to Start You Thinking that consistently cover meaning, writing strategies, critical thinking, vocabulary, and connections with other selections in *A Writer's Reader.* Each paired essay is also followed by a question that asks you about a link between the essays. Next come a couple of journal prompts designed to get your writing juices flowing. Finally, two possible assignments make specific suggestions for writing. The first is directed toward your inner world, asking you to draw generally on your personal experience and your understanding of the essay. The second is outer directed, asking you to look outside yourself and write an evaluative or argumentative paper that may require further reading or research.

For more on journal writing, see pp. 395–96.

# 25 Families

## Responding to an Image

Carefully examine this family photograph, making thorough notes about the clothing, positions, facial expressions, posture, race, relationships, and other attributes of the people. Also, note the surroundings. What might these attributes and surroundings indicate about the occasion and about family roles and traditions? Does this family portrait remind you of any others you have seen?

## Web Search

Search the Library of Congress online archive called American Memory at memory.loc.gov by entering a subject related to your family's traditions or history, such as a place where your ancestors or family have lived, an industry a relative has worked in, or a historical event or natural disaster that affected your family. Locate and study a specific photograph or document on this subject. Imagine that your family has a direct connection to the photo or document you have found. Write an imaginary narrative about one or more members of your family based on your finding.

## Terrell Jermaine Starr

### How My Illiterate Grandmother Raised an Educated Black Man

Terrell Jermaine Starr works as an associate editor at *NewsOne*, an online journal featuring national and world news geared toward an African American audience. His *NewsOne* articles include opinion pieces on the films of Tyler Perry and Spike Lee as well as reports on the African American community, such as "Teen Sings the Bullies Away" and "More Than Half of Black Girls Are Sexually Assaulted." Starr completed an MS in journalism, served in the Peace Corps from 2003 to 2005, and was awarded a Fulbright scholarship for journalism in 2009. In this essay, first published in *NewsOne* in January 2012, Starr explains his grandmother's positive effects on him.

**AS YOU READ:** Identify the ways in which Starr's grandmother encouraged him to pursue an education.

From as early as 10 years old, I awoke to my grandmother tapping the ceiling directly underneath my bed with a wooden broomstick at 7 o'clock each morning during the school week. I rolled from underneath my covers, bathed, then made my way downstairs to the kitchen, where she would have a bowl of grits, a side of bacon, and a glass of orange juice ready for me on our kitchen countertop. 1

Ever-watching the clock, she would make sure I finished breakfast in time to be out of the house at half-past seven, so I would make it to school on time. Before I left, my grandmother would often ask me if I had completed any homework assignments teachers had given the day before. I was a good student, so I almost always said, yes. But even if I didn't do my homework, she would have no way of knowing. 2

My grandmother, Inez Starr, could neither read nor write. In fact, she could barely write her own name, and I often had to handle any important business affairs on her behalf. Still, I never met a woman who cared more about education than she did. She, as some of my family members recall, put books in my hands as early as 3 years old. Never mind the fact that neither she nor I could read the words on the pages. 3

Her "Rell" (as she affectionately nicknamed me) was going to learn how to read—even if she couldn't. "There is always a way to do what you *want* to do," was a constant refrain of hers. And no matter how violent and rough my West Side neighborhood in Detroit was, she never allowed me to make excuses when I got in trouble. I was a good kid for the most part, but temptation was hard to ignore sometimes. 4

At 13, one of my more rebellious years, I favored hanging out with some of the more mischievous young men in the neighborhood rather than coming straight home from school. My grandmother was elderly and couldn't run after me on the streets, I figured. I could do *what* I wanted and come home *when* I wanted. One day, after hanging out in the streets, I arrived home only to see a police car drive up in front of our house moments later. 5

"Those streets are no good," the officer told me. "They'll get you killed." My grandmother had threatened to call the police to get me in line before, but I didn't believe her. That was the last time I tested her word. 6

One day we were watching scholars on some talk show intellectualize, ad nauseam,° about how violence and sexual images on television can make young people act out negatively in real life. She was not convinced. Worried that these scholars may have won my support, she stared directly into my eyes and, in her ungrammatical profundity,° delivered her own, more succinct° perspective: "You can go on out here and do something stupid if you want to," she said. "But the police ain't go come here and put handcuffs on that TV; they coming to arrest yo' Black *ss!" 7

In my grandmother's eyes, there was no such thing as "external influences." I had full control of my actions, and if I got into trouble, there always was some way I could have avoided it. The best way to stay out of trouble was to avoid it at all costs. 8

Sometimes my grandmother's loving guardianship went too far. One time I spotted a girl I knew from school walking past my house. (Let's call her "Sharmaine.") She didn't know the neighborhood well and asked me if I could walk her to a store several blocks away. When I told my grandmother I was going to escort Sharmaine to the store and would return in less than 30 minutes, she balked, responding, "No, you ain't." 9

Shocked at the thought that my grandmother would not allow me to walk Sharmaine to a destination less than three blocks away, I pleaded with her not to take away my manhood. My grandmother didn't relent an inch. So, sullen-faced, I returned to my front porch to deliver the news that she would have to make her way to the store on her own. 10

"What?" Sharmaine said. "You joking?" 11

"Nope," I replied. Sharmaine then burst out laughing and walked away, leaving me on my porch steps embarrassed out of my skin. I was 17 years old. 12

**ad nauseam:** To an excessive degree. **profundity:** Deep thought. **succinct:** To the point.

My grandmother's logic behind why she wouldn't allow me to be the gentleman of the ghetto: "That girl may try to set you up and get you robbed by some dopeboy friend," she said. "Who are her parents? Have I met her? Why she come all the way over here from where she lives? I don't trust her." 13

My grandmother may have been a little too cautious in this case, but given how rough my neighborhood was and how many of my friends had become fathers before finishing high school (if they finished at all), I think she did the right thing, in hindsight. 14

We need more parents like my grandmother. Parents who love their children so much, they are willing to make them uncomfortable in order to make them successful. And like my grandmother, love to the extreme to ensure their children do not slip into the unassuming pitfalls of incarceration and teenage pregnancy that negate a successful life trajectory.° 15

Now some people may think my views or the approach taken by my grandmother is, and I am sorry for using dirty language, conservative. But it was this "conservative" upbringing that allowed me to grow into the college-educated and, for lack of a better word, liberal-thinking 31-year-old reporter I am today. 16

My old broom-tapping grandmother is gone now. She died right after I finished high school. But when I wake up each morning in my Bronx apartment to prepare for work, I still hear that broom-tapping sound that woke me up more than 15 years earlier. 17

She may not have been able to read, but she taught me to cook a mean pot roast! I make my own food now. As a life-long domestic maid, she taught me what knowledge she had. And I continued to hear her omnipresent tapping during my four years of undergrad at Philander Smith College and three years of graduate school at the University of Illinois. Even in death, my grandmother "tapped" me through three degrees. And now she is tapping me toward a promising writing career. 18

All of this from a woman who wouldn't be able to read this ode° I wrote in her honor. My grandmother is a testament to how a parent with few resources and little education can produce a productive human being, and it started with a broomstick and a simple caring "tap." 19

**trajectory:** Path.  **ode:** Poem.

## Questions to Start You Thinking

1. **Considering Meaning:** Starr argues that more parents should be willing to make their children "uncomfortable in order to make them successful" (paragraph 15). Why is it helpful, or even necessary, for young people to feel uncomfortable? How can that feeling contribute to later success?
2. **Identifying Writing Strategies:** In the first two paragraphs Starr describes a scene from his childhood. What details make the scene come alive for you as a reader? How does this description support his conclusions about the role of family in his education?

3. **Reading Critically:** In paragraph 16, Starr emphasizes the contrast between his grandmother's lack of education and the value she places on her grandson's schooling. What does this contrast signify about the author's education? Why is it important to the message of this essay?
4. **Expanding Vocabulary:** Starr describes his upbringing with what he fears might be taken as a dirty word: *conservative* (paragraph 16). How would you define *conservative* in general? According to Starr, what exactly was conservative about his upbringing?
5. **Making Connections:** Compare Inez Starr's opinion about violence in the media (paragraph 7) with the arguments of Gerard Jones in "Violent Media Is Good for Kids" (pp. 565–69). Explain the differences in their opinions, and identify any common ground.

## Journal Prompts

1. Starr writes about an incident with a girl that embarrassed him as a teenager but that he saw differently "in hindsight" (paragraph 14). What episode from your life do you see differently in hindsight? Why has your opinion changed over time?
2. Write about a family member or friend who profoundly influenced your life. What incidents illustrate that influence? How is your life different for having known this person?

## Suggestions for Writing

1. Recall an event or situation from your early school days in a personal essay. What do you remember about the feeling of going to school or doing your homework? What people are important to your recollection?
2. Interview a parent, guardian, friend, or teacher about his or her goals for your education. How did that person try to foster your studies? How was that approach informed by his or her schooling or life experience?

## Sandra Cisneros

# Only Daughter

Sandra Cisneros is an accomplished author, well regarded since the publication of her first novel, *The House on Mango Street* (1984), and her short story collection, *Woman Hollering Creek and Other Stories* (1991). She has been praised for her literary experimentation and her keen eye for cultural connections and economic struggles. Her work has earned her several awards, including a National Endowment for the Arts Fellowship, and her Macondo Foundation provides socially conscious writing workshops for writers. The following essay, detailing Cisneros's relationship with her father, was first published in 1990 in *Glamour* magazine.

**AS YOU READ:** In what ways does Cisneros's father treat her differently in a family full of boys?

Once, several years ago, when I was just starting out my writing career, I was asked to write my own contributor's note for an anthology I was part of. I wrote: "I am the only daughter in a family of six sons. *That* explains everything." 1

Well, I've thought about that ever since, and yes, it explains a lot to me, but for the reader's sake I should have written: "I am the only daughter in a *Mexican* family of six sons." Or even: "I am the only daughter of a Mexican father and a Mexican-American mother." Or: "I am the only daughter of a working-class family of nine." All of these had everything to do with who I am today. 2

I was/am the only daughter and *only* a daughter. Being an only daughter in a family of six sons forced me by circumstance to spend a lot of time by myself because my brothers felt it beneath them to play with a *girl* in public. But that aloneness, that loneliness, was good for a would-be writer—it allowed me time to think and think, to imagine, to read and prepare myself. 3

Being only a daughter for my father meant my destiny would lead me to become someone's wife. That's what he believed. But when I was in the fifth grade and shared my plans for college with him, I was sure he understood. I remember my father saying, "*Que bueno, mi'ja*, that's good." That meant a lot to me, especially since my brothers thought the idea hilarious. What I didn't realize was that my father thought college was good for girls—good for finding a husband. After four years of college and two more in graduate school, and still no husband, my father shakes his head even now and says I wasted all that education. 4

In retrospect,° I'm lucky my father believed daughters were meant for husbands. It meant it didn't matter if I majored in something silly like English. After all, I'd find a nice professional eventually, right? This allowed me the liberty to putter about embroidering my little poems and stories without my father interrupting with so much as a "What's that you're writing?" 5

But the truth is, I wanted him to interrupt. I wanted my father to understand what it was I was scribbling, to introduce me as "My only daughter, the writer." Not as "This is only my daughter. She teaches." *Es maestra*—teacher. Not even *profesora*. 6

In a sense, everything I have ever written has been for him, to win his approval even though I know my father can't read English words, even though my father's only reading includes the brown-ink *Esto* sports magazines from Mexico City and the bloody *¡Alarma!* magazines that feature yet another sighting of *La Virgen de Guadalupe*° on a tortilla or a wife's revenge on her philandering° husband by bashing his skull in with a *molcajete* (a 7

**retrospect:** Considering the past. ***La Virgen de Guadalupe*:** The Lady of Guadalupe, a Mexican icon of the Virgin Mary. **philandering:** Cheating.

kitchen mortar made of volcanic rock). Or the *fotonovelas,* the little picture paperbacks with tragedy and trauma erupting from the character's mouths in bubbles.

My father represents, then, the public majority. A public who is uninterested in reading, and yet one whom I am writing about and for, and privately trying to woo. 8

When we were growing up in Chicago, we moved a lot because of my father. He suffered bouts of nostalgia. Then we'd have to let go of our flat, store the furniture with mother's relatives, load the station wagon with baggage and bologna sandwiches, and head south. To Mexico City. 9

We came back, of course. To yet another Chicago flat, another Chicago neighborhood, another Catholic school. Each time, my father would seek out the parish priest in order to get a tuition break, and complain or boast: "I have seven sons." 10

He meant *siete hijos*, seven children, but he translated it as "sons." "I have seven sons." To anyone who would listen. The Sears Roebuck employee who sold us the washing machine. The short-order cook where my father ate his ham-and-eggs breakfasts. "I have seven sons." As if he deserved a medal from the state. 11

My papa. He didn't mean anything by that mistranslation, I'm sure. But somehow I could feel myself being erased. I'd tug my father's sleeve and whisper: "Not seven sons. Six! and *one daughter*." 12

When my oldest brother graduated from medical school, he fulfilled my father's dream that we study hard and use this – our heads, instead of this – our hands. Even now my father's hands are thick and yellow, stubbed by a history of hammer and nails and twine and coils and springs. "Use this," my father said, tapping his head, "and not this," showing us those hands. He always looked tired when he said it. 13

Wasn't college an investment? And hadn't I spent all those years in college? And if I didn't marry, what was it all for? Why would anyone go to college and then choose to be poor? Especially someone who had always been poor. 14

Last year, after ten years of writing professionally, the financial rewards started to trickle in. My second National Endowment for the Arts Fellowship. A guest professorship at the University of California, Berkeley. My book, which sold to a major New York publishing house. 15

At Christmas, I flew home to Chicago. The house was throbbing, same as always; hot *tamales* and sweet *tamales* hissing in my mother's pressure cooker, and everybody – my mother, six brothers, wives, babies, aunts, cousins – talking too loud and at the same time, like in a Fellini° film, because that's just how we are. 16

I went upstairs to my father's room. One of my stories had just been translated into Spanish and published in an anthology of Chicano° writing, 17

**Fellini:** Federico Fellini (1920–1993), an influential Italian filmmaker. **Chicano:** Mexican American.

and I wanted to show it to him. Ever since he recovered from a stroke two years ago, my father likes to spend his leisure hours horizontally. And that's how I found him, watching a Pedro Infante° movie on Galavisión° and eating rice pudding.

There was a glass filmed with milk on the bedside table. There were several vials of pills and balled Kleenex. And on the floor, one black sock and a plastic urinal that I didn't want to look at but looked at anyway. Pedro Infante was about to burst into song, and my father was laughing. 18

I'm not sure if it was because my story was translated into Spanish, or because it was published in Mexico, or perhaps because the story dealt with Tepeyac°, the *colonia*° my father was raised in and the house he grew up in, but at any rate, my father punched the mute button on his remote control and read my story. 19

I sat on the bed next to my father and waited. He read it very slowly. As if he were reading each line over and over. He laughed at all the right places and read lines he liked out loud. He pointed and asked questions: "Is this So-and-so?" "Yes," I said. He kept reading. 20

When he was finally finished, after what seemed like hours, my father looked up and asked: "Where can we get more copies of this for the relatives?" 21

Of all the wonderful things that happened to me last year, that was the most wonderful. 22

**Pedro Infante:** José Pedro Infante Cruz (1917–1957), a famous Mexican actor and singer. **Galavisión:** A Mexican television network. **Tepeyac:** A borough north of Mexico City. ***colonia*:** Spanish for "colony."

## Questions to Start You Thinking

1. **Considering Meaning:** Cisneros clarifies her situation as an only daughter by supplying some context about her ethnicity, family, and class status. Why are these important aspects of her biography? What do they explain about her?
2. **Identifying Writing Strategies:** How does Cisneros create a picture of her father in this essay? Which descriptions help you to understand what he is like? Why do you think Cisneros chooses these particular details to recount to readers?
3. **Reading Critically:** Cisneros writes that she is "the only daughter and *only* a daughter" (paragraph 3). Why does she make this distinction? How does she explain each sense of *only* as a characteristic of her situation in the family?
4. **Expanding Vocabulary:** Studying English instead of another major, Cisneros was free to spend time "embroidering" (paragraph 5) her writ-

ing. What does *embroidering* mean in this context? How does this word contribute to Cisneros's comments on gender?

5. **Making Connections:** Both Cisneros and Terrell Jermaine Starr ("How My Illiterate Grandmother Raised an Educated Black Man," pp. 493–96) describe how families with little inclination or even ability to read can produce children determined to become writers. Contrast these two portraits of family life to consider how, in each case, childhood experience and family expectations contributed to the education of the writer.

### Journal Prompts

1. If you wrote a biographical note about yourself like the one Cisneros is asked to supply for an anthology (paragraph 1), how would you identify yourself? What detail "explains everything" about you?
2. The "most wonderful" recognition for Cisneros comes when her father reads and enjoys her story (paragraph 22), and she carefully describes the room where this exchange occurred. Describe a similar moment in your life, including both events and setting.

### Suggestions for Writing

1. Cisneros's father urged his children to find work that used their heads instead of their hands (paragraph 13). Recall a time when you heard a favorite saying from an influential person in your life. Reflect on why these words of wisdom were so important to that person or to you.
2. Compare and contrast the father's and the daughter's attitudes toward a college education as a product of their roles in society. Do they disagree because they are of different generations, of different genders, or for other reasons?

## Anna Quindlen

## Evan's Two Moms

Anna Quindlen was born in Philadelphia and graduated from Barnard College in 1974. She worked until 1994 for the *New York Times*, writing the "About New York" column and then two syndicated columns: "Life in the 30s," which drew on her experiences with her family and neighborhood, and "Public and Private," which explored political issues. She was a contributing editor and columnist for *Newsweek* from 2000 to 2009. Quindlen won the Pulitzer Prize for Commentary in 1992, and many of her columns have been collected in the books *Living Out Loud* (1986), *Thinking Out Loud* (1993), and *Loud and Clear* (2005). Quindlen also has written seven novels—most recently, *Every Last One* (2011) and *Lots of Candles, Plenty of Cake* (2012)—as well as the advice books *A Short Guide to a Happy Life* (2000) and *Being Perfect* (2005). In "Evan's Two Moms," written in 1992, Quindlen emphatically argues that gay marriages should be legalized.

**AS YOU READ:** Identify the main points Quindlen uses to support her position.

Evan has two moms. This is no big thing. Evan has always had two moms—in his school file, on his emergency forms, with his friends. "Ooooh, Evan, you're lucky," they sometimes say. "You have two moms." It sounds like a sitcom, but until last week it was emotional truth without legal bulwark.° That was when a judge in New York approved the adoption of a six-year-old boy by his biological mother's lesbian partner. Evan. Evan's mom. Evan's other mom. A kid, a psychologist, a pediatrician. A family. 1

The matter of Evan's two moms is one in a series of events over the last year that lead to certain conclusions. A Minnesota appeals court granted guardianship of a woman left a quadriplegic in a car accident to her lesbian lover, the culmination of a seven-year battle in which the injured woman's parents did everything possible to negate the partnership between the two. A lawyer in Georgia had her job offer withdrawn after the state attorney general found out that she and her lesbian lover were planning a marriage ceremony; she's brought suit. The computer company Lotus announced that the gay partners of employees would be eligible for the same benefits as spouses. 2

Add to these public events the private struggles, the couples who go from lawyer to lawyer to approximate legal protections their straight counterparts take for granted, the AIDS survivors who find themselves shut out of their partners' dying days by biological family members and shut out of their apartments by leases with a single name on the dotted line, and one solution is obvious. 3

Gay marriage is a radical notion for straight people and a conservative notion for gay ones. After years of being sledgehammered by society, some gay men and lesbian women are deeply suspicious of participating in an institution that seems to have "straight world" written all over it. 4

But the rads of twenty years ago, straight and gay alike, have other things on their minds today. Family is one, and the linchpin of family has commonly been a loving commitment between two adults. When same-sex couples set out to make that commitment, they discover that they are at a disadvantage: No joint tax returns. No health insurance coverage for an uninsured partner. No survivor's benefits from Social Security. None of the automatic rights, privileges, and responsibilities society attaches to a marriage contract. In Madison, Wisconsin, a couple who applied at the Y with their kids for a family membership were turned down because both were women. It's one of those small things that can make you feel small. 5

Some took marriage statutes that refer to "two persons" at their word and applied for a license. The results were court decisions that quoted the Bible and embraced circular argument: marriage is by definition the union of a man and a woman because that is how we've defined it. 6

**bulwark:** Strong support.

No religion should be forced to marry anyone in violation of its tenets,° although ironically it is now only in religious ceremonies that gay people can marry, performed by clergy who find the blessing of two who love each other no sin. But there is no secular° reason that we should take a patchwork approach of corporate, governmental, and legal steps to guarantee what can be done simply, economically, conclusively, and inclusively with the words "I do." 7

"Fran and I chose to get married for the same reasons that any two people do," said the lawyer who was fired in Georgia. "We fell in love; we wanted to spend our lives together." Pretty simple. 8

Consider the case of *Loving v. Virginia*, aptly named. At the time, sixteen states had laws that barred interracial marriage, relying on natural law, that amorphous° grab bag for justifying prejudice. Sounding a little like God throwing Adam and Eve out of paradise, the trial judge suspended the one-year sentence of Richard Loving, who was white, and his wife, Mildred, who was black, provided they got out of the State of Virginia. 9

In 1967 the Supreme Court found such laws to be unconstitutional. Only twenty-five years ago and it was a crime for a black woman to marry a white man. Perhaps twenty-five years from now we will find it just as incredible that two people of the same sex were not entitled to legally commit themselves to each other. Love and commitment are rare enough; it seems absurd to thwart them in any guise. 10

**tenets:** Principles. **secular:** Relating to nonreligious matters. **amorphous:** Having no specific shape.

## Questions to Start You Thinking

1. **Considering meaning:** According to Quindlen, what is unjust about not allowing gay men and lesbians to marry *legally*?
2. **Identifying Writing Strategies:** Quindlen ends her essay with a comparison of gay marriage and interracial marriage (paragraphs 9 and 10). How does she use this comparison to support her argument? Do you think it is a valid comparison? Why or why not?
3. **Reading Critically:** What kinds of appeals does Quindlen use in her essay? How are they appropriate or inappropriate for addressing her opponents' arguments? (See pp. 44–45) for an explanation of kinds of appeals.)
4. **Expanding Vocabulary:** Define *marriage* as Quindlen would define it. How does her definition of the term differ from the one in the dictionary?
5. **Making Connections:** What privileges of the majority culture are gay families and immigrant families (Tan, "Mother Tongue," pp. 506–12) sometimes denied?

## Journal Prompts

1. In your opinion, is the dictionary definition of *marriage* adequate? If so, defend it against attack. If not, how do you think it should be revised?
2. Imagine that you have the power to design and create the perfect parents. What would they be like? What criteria would they have to meet to live up to your vision of ideal parents?

## Suggestions for Writing

1. Describe the most unconventional family you know. How is this family different from other families? How is it the same?
2. In your opinion, would two parents of the same gender help or hurt a child's development? Write an essay comparing and contrasting the possible benefits and disadvantages of this type of family. Use specific examples – hypothetical or gathered from your own observation or reading – to illustrate your argument.

For a student paper that uses "Evan's Two Moms" to support a position, see pp. 227–29.

## Dagoberto Gilb

### Mi Mommy

Dagoberto Gilb grew up in Los Angeles and in El Paso but now lives in Austin, Texas. He has been a professor and is the executive director of Centro Victoria: Center for Mexican American Literature and Culture at the University of Houston–Victoria. After earning his BA and MA in philosophy and religious studies from the University of California, Santa Barbara, Gilb worked for many years on high-rise building projects as a member of the United Brotherhood of Carpenters and Joiners. As an essayist and award-winning fiction writer, he is revered for his distinctive Southwestern Chicano voice, humanistic perspective, and clear, direct style. His most recent collection of short stories is *Before the End, After the Beginning* (2011), influenced by his 2009 stroke. He also edited the acclaimed *Hecho en Tejas: An Anthology of Texas Mexican Literature* (2006). The following selection comes from his 2003 nonfiction collection *Gritos: Essays.*

**AS YOU READ:** Identify how Gilb contrasts expectation and actuality to present his mother.

On a Tuesday morning, just before dawn, I jerked myself out of a dream. It was so strong I turned on a light and wrote it down. In the dream, a voice was talking to me, asking me if I wanted to talk to my mom. Why wouldn't I? Because we never did anymore, hadn't really talked in decades. When we did, there was nothing but strain and mutual disapproval, and for several consecutive years, there was nothing at all. I'd moved far away, to El Paso. The voice, not my mom's, was asking me questions from my mom, and I'd started responding to the dream, to the voice, and straight to my mom. It was in the form of an interview, her questions and my answers. I answered the voice, yes, I always loved her. I loved my mommy so much. She had to know I didn't care about whatever was bad that had come between us, that I would re- 1 member only how much I loved her. I was always so proud of her. I said I thought she was the best mommy, the most beautiful woman. I loved her so much. I said I understood everything she'd gone through. Of course I didn't think only about the past, our troubles. Of course I forgave her, and I told her I wanted her to forgive me, too. And then I was overcome by a sob that wasn't in my dream but in my physical body and my mouth and my eyes.

Two days later, her husband called me. He was calm and positive. My mom, he said, had been taken to the hospital Tuesday. She was found unconscious. There was a problem with her liver. She was in intensive care, but he was convinced she'd be fine, she'd be home soon. He just thought I should know. I thought this sounded much more serious, so I called the hospital and got a nurse and asked bluntly. She said I was right, it usually was only a matter of time, it could be at any moment, though it could also take days or weeks. I asked about the liver, whether it was the usual reason a liver goes. The nurse asked, Well, was she always the life of the party? I got a plane ticket. I remembered a visit the year earlier, finding an empty vodka bottle—plastic, the cheapest brand you could buy—in the corner of the bedroom I was sleeping in, where she kept a mountain of purses and shoes and wallets. I'd found another bottle, most of it gone, behind a closet door that she left open. 2

I rented a car and went to the hospital. She was bloated, her hair a tussle—this woman who never missed a hairdresser's appointment—an unappealing white gown tied around her. Tubes needled into her hand and arm, a clear mask was over her mouth and nose. When she saw me, her eyes opened. She had no voice. I talked. Years had passed, she knew little about my life. She knew that I did construction work, thought it was all I did, ever, didn't know anything about the other life I led, the one as a writer. I never told her. I was afraid that she would only be his wife, not my mom, and she wouldn't care in the appropriate way. Or that she would be too relieved, and that all those other years I'd been struggling, when she didn't seem to care, when she disapproved of me, even thought I deserved whatever misery befell me, would be forgotten. I didn't want to give that up so easily. These were the reasons I had told her nothing. But I knew my mom would be proud. I knew she would be so happy for me. I told her that not only was I a writer, but I had one book published and another one just out. I had won prizes. I had been going to New York City and Washington, D.C. I'd gone there more than once, and I never paid. Her eyes smiled so big. I knew she would like this the most. She always wanted to travel the world. Can you believe they were even giving me money? I asked her. She *was* proud of me, and she was as surprised as I was about it. And then I told her why I had to come. I told her about the dream I'd had two nights before, on the first night she'd spent in the hospital. My mom's eyes stopped moving. I said, I talked to you, you were talking to me, we were talking. She nodded, and her whole weakened body squirmed while she was nodding! I wouldn't believe this story if I'd heard it. It was such a telenovela° deathbed scene, mother and son, both weeping about a 3

**telenovela:** A type of dramatic and romantic television serial, popular in Latin America.

psychic conversation routed hundreds of miles through the smog and traffic and over the mountains and across three deserts, from one dream to another, so that we wouldn't miss telling each other for the last time before she died. She was as stunned as me, as happy as me. You know? She kept nodding, looking at me, crying. Oh, Mom, I said.

## Questions to Start You Thinking

1. **Considering Meaning:** What picture emerges of Gilb's mother and her strengths and weaknesses? How does Gilb make peace with her and bring their relationship to a better place?
2. **Identifying Writing Strategies:** What is the effect of the long, last paragraph? In what ways does it bring Gilb's account to a conclusion?
3. **Reading Critically:** This essay shows someone who forgives and reconnects, even while remembering the many factors that caused the painful estrangement. Trace the theme of forgiveness and reconciliation as it is developed in this essay. What makes reconciliation possible? How do mother and son both let down their guard?
4. **Expanding Vocabulary:** In paragraph 3, Gilb writes that his mother's hair was "a tussle." What does *tussle* mean in this context? What does this detail say about his mother and about what is happening?
5. **Making Connections:** Gilb's essay explores his relationship with a parent and reveals his desire to be a writer. Compare and contrast his approach to those two matters with that of Sandra Cisneros in "Only Daughter" (pp. 496–500).

## Journal Prompts

1. In paragraph 2, Gilb recalls visiting his mother the year before she went to the hospital, a memory that reveals something about why he had been keeping his distance. Write an account of a visit you have made or experienced, positive or negative. Include details about what you saw or did that reflect on your relationship with the person visiting or visited.
2. Gilb has called his essays "fool stories," simple tales that contain a moral about how a person can gain wisdom. Do you think Gilb's description applies to this selection? Why or why not?

## Suggestions for Writing

1. Based on your observations or experiences with parents or guardians, write an essay supporting your own thesis about how their strengths can sometimes be drawbacks or their weaknesses can be strengths.
2. Gilb and his mother put aside their differences and connect on a deeper level; they *talk*, even when the mother can barely talk anymore. Write an

essay in which you analyze the importance of conversation, even when it is difficult. To deepen your analysis, draw on outside sources about communication, such as other essays in this chapter or one of Deborah Tannen's essays (see p. 543 and e-Pages) or books.

## Amy Tan

## Mother Tongue

Amy Tan was born in 1952 in Oakland, California, a few years after her parents immigrated to the United States from China. After receiving a BA and then an MA in linguistics, Tan worked as a specialist in language development before becoming a freelance business writer in 1981. Tan's first short story (1985) became the basis for her first novel, *The Joy Luck Club* (1990), which was a phenomenal bestseller and was made into a movie. Tan's second novel, *The Kitchen God's Wife* (1991), was equally popular. Besides her novels, she has written a book of autobiographical essays, a forty-three-page "bookette" (*Rules for Virgins*, 2011), children's books, and the libretto for an opera based on her novel *The Bonesetter's Daughter* (2001). Her work has been translated into thirty-five languages. Throughout her work run themes of family relationships, loyalty, and ways of reconciling past and present. "Mother Tongue" first appeared in *Threepenny Review* in 1990. In this essay, Tan explores the effect of her mother's "broken" English — the language Tan grew up with — on her life and writing.

**AS YOU READ:** Identify the difficulties Tan says exist for a child growing up in a family that speaks nonstandard English.

I am not a scholar of English or literature. I cannot give you much more than personal opinions on the English language and its variations in this country or others. 1

I am a writer. And by that definition, I am someone who has always loved language. I am fascinated by language in daily life. I spend a great deal of my time thinking about the power of language — the way it can evoke an emotion, a visual image, a complex idea, or a simple truth. Language is the tool of my trade. And I use them all — all the Englishes I grew up with. 2

Recently, I was made keenly aware of the different Englishes I do use. I was giving a talk to a large group of people, the same talk I had already given to half a dozen other groups. The nature of the talk was about my writing, my life, and my book, *The Joy Luck Club*. The talk was going along well enough, until I remembered one major difference that made the whole talk sound wrong. My mother was in the room. And it was perhaps the first time she had heard me give a lengthy speech, using the kind of English I have never used with her. I was saying things like, "The intersection of memory upon imagination" and "There is an aspect of my fiction that relates to thus-and-thus" — a speech filled with carefully wrought° grammatical phrases, burdened, it suddenly seemed to me, with nominalized° forms, past perfect tenses, conditional phrases, all the forms of Standard English that I had 3

**wrought:** Crafted. **nominalized:** Made into a noun from a verb.

learned in school and through books, the forms of English I did not use at home with my mother.

Just last week, I was walking down the street with my mother, and I again found myself conscious of the English I was using, and the English I do use with her. We were talking about the price of new and used furniture and I heard myself saying this: "Not waste money that way." My husband was with us as well, and he didn't notice any switch in my English. And then I realized why. It's because over the twenty years we've been together I've often used that same kind of English with him, and sometimes he even uses it with me. It has become our language of intimacy, a different sort of English that relates to family talk, the language I grew up with. 4

So you'll have some idea of what this family talk I heard sounds like, I'll quote what my mother said during a recent conversation which I videotaped and then transcribed.° During this conversation, my mother was talking about a political gangster in Shanghai who had the same last name as her family's, Du, and how the gangster in his early years wanted to be adopted by her family, which was rich by comparison. Later, the gangster became more powerful, far richer than my mother's family, and one day showed up at my mother's wedding to pay his respects. Here's what she said in part: 5

"Du Yusong having business like fruit stand. Like off the street kind. He is like Du Zong—but not Tsung-ming Island people. The local people call putong, the river east side, he belong to that side local people. That man want to ask Du Zong father take him in like become own family. Du Zong father wasn't look down on him, but didn't take seriously, until that man big like become a mafia. Now important person, very hard to inviting him. Chinese way, came only to show respect, don't stay for dinner. Respect for making big celebration, he shows up. Mean gives lots of respect. Chinese custom. Chinese social life that way. If too important won't have to stay too long. He come to my wedding. I didn't see, I heard it. I gone to boy's side, they have YMCA dinner. Chinese age I was nineteen." 6

You should know that my mother's expressive command of English belies° how much she actually understands. She reads the *Forbes* report, listens to *Wall Street Week,* converses daily with her stockbroker, reads all of Shirley MacLaine's books with ease—all kinds of things I can't begin to understand. Yet some of my friends tell me they understand fifty percent of what my mother says. Some say they understand eighty to ninety percent. Some say they understand none of it, as if she were speaking pure Chinese. But to me, my mother's English is perfectly clear, perfectly natural. It's my mother tongue. Her language, as I hear it, is vivid, direct, full of observation and imagery. That was the language that helped shape the way I saw things, expressed things, made sense of the world. 7

Lately, I've been giving more thought to the kind of English my mother speaks. Like others, I have described it to people as "broken" or "fractured" 8

**transcribed:** Made a written copy of what was said. **belies:** Contradicts; creates a misleading impression.

English. But I wince when I say that. It has always bothered me that I can think of no way to describe it other than "broken," as if it were damaged and needed to be fixed, as if it lacked a certain wholeness and soundness. I've heard other terms used, "limited English," for example. But they seem just as bad, as if everything is limited, including people's perceptions of the limited English speaker.

I know this for a fact, because when I was growing up, my mother's "limited" English limited *my* perception of her. I was ashamed of her English. I believed that her English reflected the quality of what she had to say. That is, because she expressed them imperfectly her thoughts were imperfect. And I had plenty of empirical evidence to support me: the fact that people in department stores, at banks, and at restaurants did not take her seriously, did not give her good service, pretended not to understand her, or even acted as if they did not hear her. 9

My mother has long realized the limitations of her English as well. When I was fifteen, she used to have me call people on the phone to pretend I was she. In this guise, I was forced to ask for information or even to complain and yell at people who had been rude to her. One time it was a call to her stockbroker in New York. She had cashed out her small portfolio and it just so happened we were going to go to New York the next week, our very first trip outside California. I had to get on the phone and say in an adolescent voice that was not very convincing, "This is Mrs. Tan." 10

And my mother was standing in the back whispering loudly, "Why he don't send me check, already two weeks late. So mad he lie to me, losing me money." 11

And then I said in perfect English, "Yes, I'm getting rather concerned. You had agreed to send the check two weeks ago, but it hasn't arrived." 12

Then she began to talk more loudly. "What he want, I come to New York tell him front of his boss, you cheating me?" And I was trying to calm her down, make her be quiet, while telling the stockbroker, "I can't tolerate any more excuses. If I don't receive the check immediately, I am going to have to speak to your manager when I'm in New York next week." And sure enough, the following week there we were in front of this astonished stockbroker, and I was sitting there red-faced and quiet, and my mother, the real Mrs. Tan, was shouting at his boss in her impeccable broken English. 13

We used a similar routine just five days ago, for a situation that was far less humorous. My mother had gone to the hospital for an appointment, to find out about a benign brain tumor a CAT scan had revealed a month ago. She said she had spoken very good English, her best English, no mistakes. Still, she said, the hospital did not apologize when they said they had lost the CAT scan and she had come for nothing. She said they did not seem to have any sympathy when she told them she was anxious to know the exact diagnosis, since her husband and son had both died of brain tumors. She said they would not give her any more information until the next time and she would have to make another appointment for that. So she said she would not leave until the doctor called her daughter. She wouldn't budge. And when the 14 doctor finally called her daughter, me, who spoke in perfect English—lo and behold—we had assurances the CAT scan would be found, promises that a conference call on Monday would be held, and apologies for any suffering my mother had gone through for a most regrettable mistake.

I think my mother's English almost had an effect on limiting my possibilities in life as well. Sociologists and linguists probably will tell you that a person's developing language skills are more influenced by peers. But I think that the language spoken in the family, especially in immigrant families which are more insular,° plays a large role in shaping the language of the child. And I believe that it affected my results on achievement tests, IQ tests, and the SAT. While my English skills were never judged as poor, compared to math, English could not be considered my strong suit. In grade school I did moderately well, getting perhaps B's, sometimes B-pluses, in English and scoring perhaps in the sixtieth or seventieth percentile on achievement tests. But those scores were not good enough to override the opinion that my true abilities lay in math and science, because in those areas I achieved A's and scored in the ninetieth percentile or higher. 15

This was understandable. Math is precise; there is only one correct answer. Whereas, for me at least, the answers on English tests were always a judgment call, a matter of opinion and personal experience. Those tests were constructed around items like fill-in-the-blank sentence completion, such as, "Even though Tom was _____ , Mary thought he was _____ ." And the correct answer always seemed to be the most bland combinations of thoughts, for example, "Even though Tom was shy, Mary thought he was charming," with the grammatical structure "even though" limiting the correct answer to some sort of semantic° opposites, so you wouldn't get answers like, "Even though Tom was foolish, Mary thought he was ridiculous." Well, according to my mother, there were very few limitations as to what Tom could have been and what Mary might have thought of him. So I never did well on tests like that. 16

The same was true with word analogies, pairs of words in which you were supposed to find some sort of logical, semantic relationship—for example, "*Sunset* is to *nightfall* as _____ is to _____ ." And here you would be presented with a list of four possible pairs, one of which showed the same kind of relationship: *red* is to *stoplight, bus* is to *arrival, chills* is to *fever, yawn* is to *boring.* Well, I could never think that way. I knew what the tests were asking, but I could not block out of my mind the images already created by the first pair, "*sunset* is to *nightfall*"—and I would see a burst of colors against a darkening sky, the moon rising, the lowering of a curtain of stars. And all the other pairs of words—*red, bus, stoplight, boring*—just threw up a mass of confusing images, making it impossible for me to sort out something as logical as saying: "A sunset precedes nightfall" is the same as "a chill precedes a fever." The only way I would have gotten that answer right would have been to imagine 17

**insular:** Detached or isolated; keeping to oneself. **semantic:** Relating to the meaning of language.

an associative situation, for example, my being disobedient and staying out past sunset, catching a chill at night, which turns into feverish pneumonia as punishment, which indeed did happen to me.

I have been thinking about all this lately, about my mother's English, about achievement tests. Because lately I've been asked, as a writer, why there are not more Asian Americans enrolled in creative writing programs. Why do so many Chinese students go into engineering? Well, these are broad sociological questions I can't begin to answer. But I have noticed in surveys—in fact, just last week—that Asian students, as a whole, always do significantly better on math achievement tests than in English. And this makes me think that there are other Asian American students whose English spoken in the home might also be described as "broken" or "limited." And perhaps they also have teachers who are steering them away from writing and into math and science, which is what happened to me. 18

Fortunately, I happen to be rebellious in nature and enjoy the challenge of disproving assumptions made about me. I became an English major my first year in college, after being enrolled as pre-med. I started writing nonfiction as a freelancer the week after I was told by my former boss that writing was my worst skill and I should hone my talents toward account management. 19

But it wasn't until 1985 that I finally began to write fiction. And at first I wrote using what I thought to be wittily crafted sentences, sentences that would finally prove I had mastery over the English language. Here's an example from the first draft of a story that later made its way into *The Joy Luck Club,* but without this line: "That was my mental quandary in its nascent° state." A terrible line, which I can barely pronounce. 20

Fortunately, for reasons I won't get into today, I later decided I should envision a reader for the stories I would write. And the reader I decided upon was my mother, because these were stories about mothers. So with this reader in mind—and in fact she did read my early drafts—I began to write stories using all the Englishes I grew up with: the English I spoke to my mother, which for lack of a better term might be described as "simple"; the English she used with me, which for lack of a better term might be described as "broken"; my translation of her Chinese, which could certainly be described as "watered down"; and what I imagined to be her translation of her Chinese if she could speak in perfect English, her internal language, and for that I sought to preserve the essence, but neither an English nor a Chinese structure. I wanted to capture what language ability tests can never reveal: her intent, her passion, her imagery, the rhythms of her speech, and the nature of her thoughts. 21

Apart from what any critic had to say about my writing, I knew I had succeeded where it counted when my mother finished reading my book and gave me her verdict: "So easy to read." 22

**nascent:** Beginning; only partly formed.

## Questions to Start You Thinking

1. **Considering Meaning:** What are the Englishes that Tan grew up with? What other Englishes has she used in her life? What does each English have that gives it an advantage over the other Englishes in certain situations?
2. **Identifying Writing Strategies:** What examples does Tan use to analyze the various Englishes she uses? How has Tan been able to synthesize her Englishes successfully into her present style of writing fiction?
3. **Reading Critically:** Although Tan explains that she writes using "all the Englishes" she has known throughout her life (paragraph 21), she doesn't do that in this essay. What are the differences between the English Tan uses in this essay and the kinds she says she uses in her fiction? How does the language she uses here fit the purpose of her essay?
4. **Expanding Vocabulary:** In paragraph 9, Tan writes that she had "plenty of empirical evidence" that her mother's "limited" English meant that her mother's thoughts were "imperfect" as well. Define *empirical.* What does Tan's use of this word tell us about her present attitude toward the way she judged her mother when she was growing up?
5. **Making Connections:** Compare and contrast Tan's cultural clash with her mother to that of Anjula Razdan with hers in "What's Love Got to Do With It?" (pp. 523–28).

## Link to the Paired Essay

Tan and Richard Rodriguez ("Public and Private Language," pp. 512–17) recount learning English as they grew up in homes where English was a second language. In what way did they face similar experiences and obstacles? How did learning English affect their self-image and influence their relationship with their family?

## Journal Prompts

1. Describe one of the Englishes you use to communicate. When do you use it, and when do you avoid using it?
2. In what ways are you a "translator," if not of language, then of current trends and fashions, for your parents or other members of your family?

## Suggestions for Writing

1. In a personal essay explain an important event in your family's history, using your family's various Englishes or other languages.
2. Take note of and, if possible, transcribe a conversation you have had with a parent or other family member, with a teacher, and with a close

friend. Write an essay comparing and contrasting the "languages" of the three conversations. How do the languages differ? How do you account for these differences? What might happen if someone used "teacher language" to talk to a friend or "friend language" in a class discussion or paper?

## Richard Rodriguez

### Public and Private Language

Richard Rodriguez, the son of Spanish-speaking Mexican American parents, was born in 1944 and grew up in San Francisco, where he currently lives. He earned a BA at Stanford University and graduate degrees in English from Columbia University and the University of California at Berkeley. A writer, lecturer, and editor for the Pacific News Service, Rodriguez has served as a contributing editor for *Harper's Magazine, U.S. News & World Report,* and the Sunday Opinion section of the *Los Angeles Times.* He also regularly contributes to PBS's *NewsHour.* His books, which often draw on autobiography to explore race and ethnicity in American society, include *Hunger of Memory* (1982), from which the following selection is drawn; *Days of Obligation: An Argument with My Mexican Father* (1992); and *Brown: The Last Discovery of America* (2002). In "Public and Private Language," he recounts the origin of his complex views of bilingual education.

**AS YOU READ:** Discover the ways in which learning English changed Rodriguez's life and his relationship with his family.

Supporters of bilingual education today imply that students like me miss a great deal by not being taught in their family's language. What they seem not to recognize is that, as a socially disadvantaged child, I considered Spanish to be a private language. What I needed to learn in school was that I had the right—and the obligation—to speak the public language of *los gringos.*° The odd truth is that my first-grade classmates could have become bilingual, in the conventional sense of that word, more easily than I. Had they been taught (as upper-middle-class children are often taught early) a second language like Spanish or French, they could have regarded it simply as that: another public language. In my case such bilingualism could not have been so quickly achieved. What I did not believe was that I could speak a single public language. 1

Without question, it would have pleased me to hear my teachers address me in Spanish when I entered the classroom. I would have felt much less afraid. I would have trusted them and responded with ease. But I would have delayed—for how long postponed?—having to learn the language of public society. I would have evaded—and for how long could I have afforded to delay?—learning the great lesson of school, that I had a public identity. 2

***los gringos:*** Spanish for "foreigners," often used as a derogatory term for English-speaking Americans.

Fortunately, my teachers were unsentimental about their responsibility. What they understood was that I needed to speak a public language. So their voices would search me out, asking me questions. Each time I'd hear them, I'd look up in surprise to see a nun's face frowning at me. I'd mumble, not really meaning to answer. The nun would persist, "Richard, stand up. Don't look at the floor. Speak up. Speak to the entire class, not just to me!" but I couldn't believe that the English language was mine to use. (In part, I did not want to believe it.) I continued to mumble. I resisted the teacher's demands. (Did I somehow suspect that once I learned public language my pleasing family life would be changed?) Silent, waiting for the bell to sound, I remained dazed, diffident,° afraid. 3

Because I wrongly imagined that English was intrinsically° a public language and Spanish an intrinsically private one, I easily noticed the difference between classroom language and the language of home. At school, words were directed to a general audience of listeners. ("Boys and girls. . . .") Words were meaningfully ordered. And the point was not self-expression alone but to make oneself understood by many others. The teacher quizzed: "Boys and girls, why do we use that word in this sentence? Could we think of a better word to use there? Would the sentence change its meaning if the words were differently arranged? And wasn't there a better way of saying much the same thing?" (I couldn't say. I wouldn't try to say.) 4

Three months. Five. Half a year passed. Unsmiling, ever watchful, my teachers noted my silence. They began to connect my behavior with the difficult progress my older sister and brother were making. Until one Saturday morning three nuns arrived at the house to talk to our parents. Stiffly, they sat on the blue living room sofa. From the doorway of another room, spying the visitors, I noted the incongruity° – the clash of two worlds, the faces and voices of school intruding upon the familiar setting of home. I overheard one voice gently wondering, "Do your children speak only Spanish at home, Mrs. Rodriguez?" While another voice added, "That Richard especially seems so timid and shy." 5

*That Rich-heard!* 6

With great tact the visitors continued, "Is it possible for you and your husband to encourage your children to practice their English when they are home?" Of course, my parents complied. What would they not do for their children's well-being? And how could they have questioned the Church's authority which those women represented? In an instant, they agreed to give up the language (the sounds) that had revealed and accentuated our family's closeness. The moment after the visitors left, the change was observed. "*Ahora,*° speak to us *en inglés,*"° my father and mother united to tell us. 7

At first, it seemed a kind of game. After dinner each night, the family gathered to practice "our" English. (It was still then *inglés,* a language foreign to us, so we felt drawn as strangers to it.) Laughing, we would try to define words we could not pronounce. We played with strange English sounds, 8

**diffident:** Shy. **intrinsically:** Essentially; inherently. **incongruity:** Lack of harmony or appropriateness. ***Ahora:*** Spanish for "now." ***en inglés:*** Spanish for "in English."

often overanglicizing our pronunciations. And we filled the smiling gaps of our sentences with familiar Spanish sounds. But that was cheating, somebody shouted. Everyone laughed. In school, meanwhile, like my brother and sister, I was required to attend a daily tutoring session. I needed a full year of special attention. I also needed my teachers to keep my attention from straying in class by calling out, *Rich-heard*—their English voices slowly prying loose my ties to my other name, its three notes, *Ri-car-do.* Most of all I needed to hear my mother and father speak to me in a moment of seriousness in broken—suddenly heartbreaking—English. The scene was inevitable: one Saturday morning I entered the kitchen where my parents were talking in Spanish. I did not realize that they were talking in Spanish however until, at the moment they saw me, I heard their voices change to speak English. Those *gringo* sounds they uttered startled me. Pushed me away. In that moment of trivial misunderstanding and profound insight, I felt my throat twisted by unsounded grief. I turned quickly and left the room. But I had no place to escape to with Spanish. (The spell was broken.) My brother and sisters were speaking English in another part of the house.

Again and again in the days following, increasingly angry, I was obliged to hear my mother and father: "Speak to us *en inglés.*" (*Speak.*) Only then did I determine to learn classroom English. Weeks after, it happened: one day in school I had my hand raised to volunteer an answer. I spoke out in a loud voice. And I did not think it remarkable when the entire class understood. That day, I moved very far from the disadvantaged child I had been only days earlier. The belief, that calming assurance that I belonged in public, had at last taken hold. 9

Shortly after, I stopped hearing the high and loud sounds of *los gringos.* A more and more confident speaker of English, I didn't trouble to listen to *how* strangers sounded, speaking to me. And there simply were too many English-speaking people in my day for me to hear American accents anymore. Conversations quickened. Listening to persons whose voices sounded eccentrically pitched, I usually noted their sounds for an initial few seconds before I concentrated on *what* they were saying. Conversations became content-full. Transparent. Hearing someone's *tone* of voice—angry or questioning or sarcastic or happy or sad—I didn't distinguish it from the words it expressed. Sound and word were thus tightly wedded. At the end of a day, I was often bemused, always relieved, to realize how "silent," though crowded with words, my day in public had been. (This public silence measured and quickened the change in my life.) 10

At last, seven years old, I came to believe what had been technically true since my birth: I was an American citizen. 11

But the special feeling of closeness at home was diminished by then. Gone was the desperate, urgent, intense feeling of being at home; rare was the experience of feeling myself individualized by family intimates. We remained a loving family, but one greatly changed. No longer so close; no longer bound tight by the pleasing and troubling knowledge of our public separateness. Neither my older brother nor sister rushed home after school 12 anymore. Nor did I. When I arrived home there would often be neighborhood kids in the house. Or the house would be empty of sounds.

Following the dramatic Americanization of their children, even my parents grew more publicly confident. Especially my mother. She learned the names of all the people on our block. And she decided we needed to have a telephone installed in the house. My father continued to use the word *gringo*. But it was no longer charged with the old bitterness or distrust. (Stripped of any emotional content, the word simply became a name for those Americans not of Hispanic descent.) Hearing him, sometimes, I wasn't sure if he was pronouncing the Spanish word *gringo* or saying gringo in English. 13

Matching the silence I started hearing in public was a new quiet at home. The family's quiet was partly due to the fact that, as we children learned more and more English, we shared fewer and fewer words with our parents. Sentences needed to be spoken slowly when a child addressed his mother or father. (Often the parent wouldn't understand.) The child would need to repeat himself. (Still the parent misunderstood.) The young voice, frustrated, would end up saying, "Never mind"—the subject was closed. Dinners would be noisy with the clinking of knives and forks against dishes. My mother would smile softly between her remarks; my father at the other end of the table would chew and chew at his food, while he stared over the heads of his children. 14

My *mother!* My *father!* After English became my primary language, I no longer knew what words to use in addressing my parents. The old Spanish words (those tender accents of sound) I had used earlier—*mamá* and *papá*—I couldn't use anymore. They would have been all-too-painful reminders of how much had changed in my life. On the other hand, the words I heard neighborhood kids call *their* parents seemed equally unsatisfactory. *Mother* and *Father; Ma, Papa, Pa, Dad, Pop* (how I hated the all-American sound of that last word especially)—all these terms I felt were unsuitable, not really terms of address for *my* parents. As a result, I never used them at home. Whenever I'd speak to my parents, I would try to get their attention with eye contact alone. In public conversations, I'd refer to "my parents" or "my mother and father." 15

My mother and father, for their part, responded differently, as their children spoke to them less and less. My mother grew restless, seemed troubled and anxious at the scarcity of words exchanged in the house. It was she who would question me about my day when I came home from school. She smiled at the small talk. She pried at the edges of my sentences to get me to say something more. (What?) She'd join conversations she overheard, but her intrusions often stopped her children's talking. By contrast, my father seemed reconciled to the new quiet. Though his English improved somewhat, he retired into silence. At dinner he spoke very little. One night his children and even his wife helplessly giggled at his garbled English pronunciation of the Catholic Grace before Meals. Thereafter he made his wife recite the prayer at the start of each meal, even on formal occasions, when there were guests in the house. Hers became the public voice of the family. On 16 official business, it was she, not my father, one would usually hear on the phone or in stores, talking to strangers. His children grew so accustomed to his silence that, years later, they would speak routinely of his shyness. (My mother would often try to explain: both his parents died when he was eight. He was raised by an uncle who treated him like little more than a menial servant. He was never encouraged to speak. He grew up alone. A man of few words.) But my father was not shy, I realized, when I'd watch him speaking Spanish with relatives. Using Spanish, he was quickly effusive.° Especially when talking with other men, his voice would spark, flicker, flare alive with sounds. In Spanish, he expressed ideas and feelings he rarely revealed in English. With firm Spanish sounds, he conveyed confidence and authority English would never allow him.

The silence at home, however, was finally more than a literal silence. 17
Fewer words passed between parent and child, but more profound was the silence that resulted from my inattention to sounds. At about the time I no longer bothered to listen with care to the sounds of English in public, I grew careless about listening to the sounds family members made when they spoke. Most of the time I heard someone speaking at home and didn't distinguish his sounds from the words people uttered in public. I didn't even pay much attention to my parents' accented and ungrammatical speech. At least not at home. Only when I was with them in public would I grow alert to their accents. Though, even then, their sounds caused me less and less concern. For I was increasingly confident of my own public identity.

Today I hear bilingual educators say that children lose a degree of "indi- 18
viduality" by becoming assimilated into public society. (Bilingual schooling was popularized in the seventies, that decade when middle-class ethnics began to resist the process of assimilation – the American melting pot.) But the bilingualists simplistically scorn the value and necessity of assimilation. They do not seem to realize that there are *two* ways a person is individualized. So they do not realize that while one suffers a diminished sense of *private* individuality by becoming assimilated into public society, such assimilation makes possible the achievement of *public* individuality.

**effusive:** Talkative; unreserved.

## Questions to Start You Thinking

1. **Considering Meaning:** What created the new "silence" in the Rodriguez household? Explain why.
2. **Identifying Writing Strategies:** How does Rodriguez use comparison and contrast to convey his experience learning English?
3. **Reading Critically:** How does Rodriguez use dialogue to make the experience he recalls more vivid for his readers? Is this strategy effective in helping him achieve his purpose? Why, or why not?

4. **Expanding Vocabulary:** Rodriguez uses the terms *private* and *public*. What do these words mean when used as adjectives to describe "language" and "identity"?

5. **Making Connections:** Rodriguez's parents changed the language spoken at home because they placed a high value on their children's educational success. Does this sacrifice relate to the types of parenting decisions described in Terrell Jermaine Starr's "How My Illiterate Grandmother Raised an Educated Black Man" (pp. 493–96)? Why or why not?

### Link to the Paired Essay

Both Rodriguez and Amy Tan ("Mother Tongue," pp. 506–12) grew up in homes in which English was spoken as a second language. Compare and contrast how each writer's mastery of English affected his or her parents.

### Journal Prompts

1. Recall a time when your public identity was at odds with your private self.
2. Has an accomplishment that you are proud of ever had a negative effect on another aspect of your life or on other people around you?

### Suggestions for Writing

1. If you speak a second language, write an essay recalling your experience learning it. What were some of your struggles? Can you relate to Rodriguez's experience? How do you use that language today? If you do not know a second language, write an essay in which you analyze possible benefits of learning one. What language would you like to learn? Why?
2. According to Rodriguez, "Supporters of bilingual education today imply that students like me miss a great deal by not being taught in their family's language" (paragraph 1). Rodriguez counters this assumption by showing how his immersion in English allowed him to develop a public identity that ultimately led to his success. At the same time, however, his English-only immersion hurt his family life. Write an essay in which you take a stand on the complex topic of bilingual education, using further reading and research to support your position about how it does or does not benefit students.

**e StrategyOne Editors** **Infographic**

## Once a Mother, Always a Mother

According to a national survey conducted by StrategyOne, a global marketing research firm, the role of the grandmother in contemporary American culture has expanded greatly to encompass many duties traditionally reserved for mothers. To view an infographic presenting this survey's findings, go to Chapter 25: **bedfordstmartins.com/bedguide**.

Many of today's grandmothers find themselves playing a major role in their grandchildren's upbringing.

## GOOD/Column Five Editors — Infographic

## Paternity Leave around the World

In the United States, most fathers of new babies are not able to take paid time off to be with their infant son or daughter and to help as the family adjusts to the baby's arrival. The United States is one of the few industrialized countries without a paternity leave policy that encourages or requires dads to spend time at home after the birth of their children. Instead, fathers in the U.S. must use vacation time or, under the Family and Medical Leave Act of 1993, take unpaid leave. To examine an infographic that explores this topic, go to Chapter 25: **bedfordstmartins.com/bedguide**.

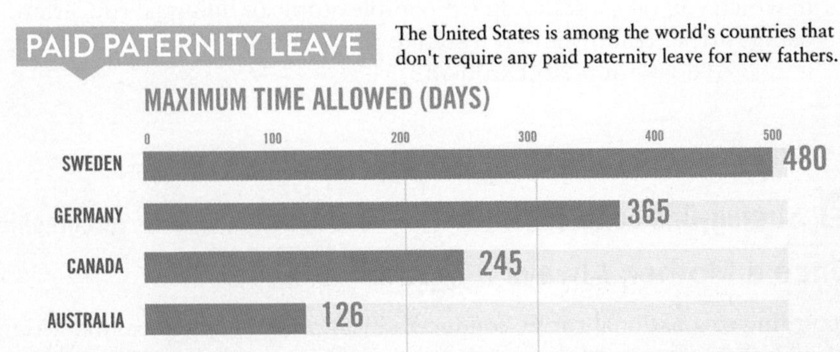


Sweden leads the world in terms of paid time off for new fathers, allowing them to take up to 480 days of leave.

# Men and Women

# 26

## Responding to an Image

When asked about this image, photographer Andrew Bear commented, "Men and women move together into the unknown, whether as friends, colleagues, couples, companions, or whatever. At any moment, we can be finding, making, or losing our way. Or be out for a pleasure stroll." Examine this photograph and compare the two main figures. What is different and the same about them? What mood do you see expressed in the photograph? If you were to add dialogue to this photograph, what might the man and woman be saying or thinking?

## Web Search

Use a search engine to find one Web source or publication marketed for women and one marketed for men. Read a few pages of each, and compare and contrast the content. How are they similar? How are they different? Do you think they stereotype women and men? How, and for what reasons?

## Brent Staples

## Black Men and Public Space

Brent Staples was born in 1951 in Chester, Pennsylvania, and earned a PhD in psychology from the University of Chicago. He wrote for the *Chicago Sun-Times* and *Down Beat* magazine before joining the *New York Times* in 1985, where he moved from metropolitan news to the *New York Times Book Review.* Since 1990, Staples has been a member of the *Times* editorial board, writing regular columns on politics and culture. His work also has appeared in such magazines as *New York Woman, Ms.,* and *Harper's,* and he is the author of the memoir *Parallel Time: Growing Up in Black and White* (1994), winner of the Anisfield Wolff Book Award. In the following essay, published in a slightly different version in *Ms.* magazine in September 1986, Staples considers how his presence affects other pedestrians at night.

**AS YOU READ:** Identify why other pedestrians respond to Staples with anxiety.

My first victim was a woman—white, well dressed, probably in her late twenties. I came upon her late one evening on a deserted street in Hyde Park, a relatively affluent neighborhood in an otherwise mean, impoverished section of Chicago. As I swung onto the avenue behind her, there seemed to be a discreet, uninflammatory distance between us. Not so. She cast back a worried glance. To her, the youngish black man—a broad six feet two inches with a beard and billowing hair, both hands shoved into the pockets of a bulky military jacket—seemed menacingly close. After a few more quick glimpses, she picked up her pace and was soon running in earnest. Within seconds, she disappeared into a cross street. 1

That was more than a decade ago. I was twenty-one years old, a graduate student newly arrived at the University of Chicago. It was in the echo of that terrified woman's footfalls that I first began to know the unwieldy inheritance I'd come into—the ability to alter public space in ugly ways. It was clear that she thought herself the quarry of a mugger, a rapist, or worse. Suffering a bout of insomnia, however, I was stalking sleep, not defenseless wayfarers. As a softy who is scarcely able to take a knife to a raw chicken—let alone hold one to a person's throat—I was surprised, embarrassed, and dismayed all at once. Her flight made me feel like an accomplice in tyranny. It also made it clear that I was indistinguishable from the muggers who occasionally seeped into the area from the surrounding ghetto. The first encounter, and those that followed, signified that a vast, unnerving gulf lay between nighttime pedestrians—particularly women—and me. And I soon gathered that being 2 perceived as dangerous is a hazard in itself. I only needed to turn a corner into a dicey situation, or crowd some frightened, armed person in a foyer somewhere, or make an errant move after being pulled over by a policeman. Where fear and weapons meet—and they often do in urban America—there is always the possibility of death.

In that first year, my first away from my hometown, I was to become thoroughly familiar with the language of fear. At dark, shadowy intersections, I could cross in front of a car stopped at a traffic light and elicit the *thunk, thunk, thunk, thunk* of the driver—black, white, male, or female—hammering down the door locks. On less traveled streets after dark, I grew accustomed to but never comfortable with people crossing to the other side of the street rather than pass me. Then there were the standard unpleasantries with policemen, doormen, bouncers, cabdrivers, and others whose business it is to screen out troublesome individuals *before* there is any nastiness. 3

I moved to New York nearly two years ago and I have remained an avid night walker. In central Manhattan, the near-constant crowd cover minimizes tense one-on-one street encounters. Elsewhere—in SoHo, for example, where sidewalks are narrow and tightly spaced buildings shut out the sky—things can get very taut indeed. 4

After dark, on the warrenlike° streets of Brooklyn where I live, I often see women who fear the worst from me. They seem to have set their faces on neutral, and with their purse straps strung across their chests bandolier-style, they forge ahead as though bracing themselves against being tackled. I understand, of course, that the danger they perceive is not a hallucination. Women are particularly vulnerable to street violence, and young black males are drastically overrepresented among the perpetrators of that violence. Yet these truths are no solace against the kind of alienation that comes of being ever the suspect, a fearsome entity with whom pedestrians avoid making eye contact. 5

It is not altogether clear to me how I reached the ripe old age of twenty-two without being conscious of the lethality nighttime pedestrians attributed to me. Perhaps it was because in Chester, Pennsylvania, the small, angry industrial town where I came of age in the 1960s, I was scarcely noticeable against a backdrop of gang warfare, street knifings, and murders. I grew up one of the good boys, had perhaps a half-dozen fistfights. In retrospect, my shyness of combat has clear sources. 6

As a boy, I saw countless tough guys locked away; I have since buried several, too. They were babies, really—a teenage cousin, a brother of twenty-two, a childhood friend in his mid-twenties—all gone down in episodes of bravado played out in the streets. I came to doubt the virtues of intimidation early on. I chose, perhaps unconsciously, to remain a shadow—timid, but a survivor. 7

The fearsomeness mistakenly attributed to me in public places often has a perilous flavor. The most frightening of these confusions occurred in the late 1970s and early 1980s, when I worked as a journalist in Chicago. One 8

**warrenlike:** Like a maze.

day, rushing into the office of a magazine I was writing for with a deadline story in hand, I was mistaken for a burglar. The office manager called security and, with an ad hoc° posse, pursued me through the labyrinthine halls, nearly to my editor's door. I had no way of proving who I was. I could only move briskly toward the company of someone who knew me.

Another time I was on assignment for a local paper and killing time before an interview. I entered a jewelry store on the city's affluent Near North Side. The proprietor excused herself and returned with an enormous red Doberman pinscher straining at the end of a leash. She stood, the dog extended toward me, silent to my questions, her eyes bulging nearly out of her head. I took a cursory look around, nodded, and bade her good night. 9

Relatively speaking, however, I never fared as badly as another black male journalist. He went to nearby Waukegan, Illinois, a couple of summers ago to work on a story about a murderer who was born there. Mistaking the reporter for the killer, police officers hauled him from his car at gunpoint and but for his press credentials would probably have tried to book him. Such episodes are not uncommon. Black men trade tales like this all the time. 10

Over the years, I learned to smother the rage I felt at so often being taken for a criminal. Not to do so would surely have led to madness. I now take precautions to make myself less threatening. I move about with care, particularly late in the evening. I give a wide berth° to nervous people on subway platforms during the wee hours, particularly when I have exchanged business clothes for jeans. If I happen to be entering a building behind some people who appear skittish, I may walk by, letting them clear the lobby before I return, so as not to seem to be following them. I have been calm and extremely congenial on those rare occasions when I've been pulled over by the police. 11

And on late-evening constitutionals I employ what has proved to be an excellent tension-reducing measure: I whistle melodies from Beethoven and Vivaldi and the more popular classical composers. Even steely New Yorkers hunching toward nighttime destinations seem to relax, and occasionally they even join in the tune. Virtually everybody seems to sense that a mugger wouldn't be warbling bright, sunny selections from Vivaldi's *Four Seasons.* It is my equivalent of the cowbell that hikers wear when they know they are in bear country. 12

## Questions to Start You Thinking

1. **Considering Meaning:** What misconceptions do people have about Staples because he is a young black man? What does he feel causes such misconceptions?
2. **Identifying Writing Strategies:** At the end of the essay, how does Staples use comparison to explain his behavior?

**ad hoc:** Spur of the moment. **berth:** Space.

3. **Reading Critically:** What kinds of appeals – emotional, logical, ethical – does Staples use? Are his appeals appropriate for the purpose of his essay? Why, or why not? (For an explanation of kinds of appeals, see pp. 44–45.)
4. **Expanding Vocabulary:** Define *affluent, uninflammatory* (paragraph 1), *unwieldy, quarry, errant* (paragraph 2), *bandolier, solace* (paragraph 5), *lethality* (paragraph 6), *bravado* (paragraph 7), and *labyrinthine* (paragraph 8). Why do you think Staples uses such formal language in this essay?
5. **Making Connections:** How might Julie Zeilinger's assertions about how society views masculinity in "Guys Suffer from Oppressive Gender Roles Too" (pp. 538–42) help to explain the way Staples is perceived in public?

## Journal Prompts

1. Are stereotypes ever useful? Why, or why not?
2. Have you or someone you know ever been wrongfully stereotyped or prejudged? How did you feel? How did you react?

## Suggestions for Writing

1. Staples describes his feelings about being the object of racial fear. Have you or someone you know ever been the object of that fear or other misconceptions based on prejudice or stereotyping? Write a short personal essay discussing the causes and effects of the experience. What preconceptions were involved? How did you or your acquaintance respond?
2. What do you think causes the stereotype of African American men that Staples is addressing? Write an essay that analyzes this stereotype, drawing on several outside sources to support your analysis.

## Anjula Razdan

## What's Love Got to Do with It?

**Anjula Razdan** is a senior editor for *Experience Life* and formerly the *Utne Reader,* where she wrote on topics ranging from international politics to pop culture. The daughter of Indian immigrants whose marriage was arranged, Razdan grew up in Illinois and earned her BA and MA in English from the University of Chicago. In this selection, which appeared in the *Utne Reader* in 2003, Razdan asks her readers to consider whether arranging marriages might more effectively create lasting relationships than choosing mates based on romantic attraction. To explore this question, she draws on her own experiences and observations as well as the testimony of experts.

**AS YOU READ:** Look for Razdan's account of both the benefits and the drawbacks of arranged marriages.

One of the greatest pleasures of my teen years was sitting down with a bag of cinnamon Red Hots and a new LaVyrle Spencer romance, immersing myself in another tale of star-crossed lovers drawn together by the heart's mysterious alchemy.° My mother didn't get it. "Why are you reading that?" she would ask, her voice tinged with both amusement and horror. Everything in her background told her that romance was a waste of time. 1

Born and raised in Illinois by parents who emigrated from India thirty-five years ago, I am the product of an arranged marriage, and yet I grew up under the spell of Western romantic love—first comes love, *then* comes marriage—which both puzzled and dismayed my parents. Their relationship was set up over tea and samosas° by their grandfathers, and they were already engaged when they went on their first date, a chaperoned trip to the movies. My mom and dad still barely knew each other on their wedding day—and they certainly hadn't fallen in love. Yet both were confident that their shared values, beliefs, and family background would form a strong bond that, over time, would develop into love. 2

"But, what could they possibly know of *real love*?" I would ask myself petulantly° after each standoff with my parents over whether or not I could date in high school (I couldn't) and whether I would allow them to arrange my marriage (I wouldn't). The very idea of an arranged marriage offended my ideas of both love and liberty—to me, the act of choosing whom to love represented the very essence of freedom. To take away that choice seemed like an attack not just on my autonomy as a person, but on democracy itself. 3

And, yet, even in the supposedly liberated West, the notion of choosing your mate is a relatively recent one. Until the nineteenth century, writes historian E. J. Graff in *What Is Marriage For? The Strange Social History of Our Most Intimate Institution* (Boston: Beacon Press, 1999), arranged marriages were quite common in Europe as a way of forging alliances, ensuring inheritances, and stitching together the social, political, and religious needs of a community. Love had nothing to do with it. 4

Fast forward a couple hundred years to twenty-first-century America, and you see a modern, progressive society where people are free to choose their mates, for the most part, based on love instead of social or economic gain. But for many people, a quiet voice from within wonders: Are we really better off? Who hasn't at some point in their life—at the end of an ill-fated relationship or midway through dinner with the third "date-from-hell" this month—longed for a matchmaker to find the right partner? No hassles. No effort. No personal ads or blind dates. 5

The point of the Western romantic ideal is to live "happily ever after," yet nearly half of all marriages in this country end in divorce, and the number of never-married adults grows each year. Boundless choice notwithstanding, 6

**alchemy:** A medieval predecessor of chemistry that aimed to turn base metals into gold. **samosas:** Small, fried Indian pastries filled with seasoned vegetables or meat. **petulantly:** Irritably.

what does it mean when the marital success rate is the statistical equivalent of a coin toss?

"People don't really know how to choose a long-term partner," offers Dr. Alvin Cooper, the director of the San Jose Marital Services and Sexuality Centre and a staff psychologist at Stanford University. "The major reasons that people find and get involved with somebody else are proximity and physical attraction. And both of these factors are terrible predictors of long-term happiness in a relationship." 7

At the moment we pick a mate, Cooper says, we are often blinded by passion and therefore virtually incapable of making a sound decision. 8

*Psychology Today* editor Robert Epstein agrees. "[It's] like getting drunk and marrying someone in Las Vegas," he quips. A former director of the Cambridge Center for Behavioral Studies, Epstein holds a decidedly unromantic view of courtship and love. Indeed, he argues it is our myths of "love at first sight" and "a knight in a shining Porsche" that get so many of us into trouble. When the heat of passion wears off—and it always does, he says—you can be left with virtually nothing "except lawyer's bills." 9

Epstein points out that many arranged marriages result in an enduring love because they promote compatibility and rational deliberation ahead of passionate impulse. Epstein himself is undertaking a bold step to prove his theory that love can be learned. He wrote an editorial in *Psychology Today* last year seeking women to participate in the experiment with him. He proposed to choose one of the "applicants," and together they would attempt to fall in love—consciously and deliberately. After receiving more than 1,000 responses, none of which seemed right, Epstein yielded just a little to impulse, asking Gabriela, an intriguing Venezuelan woman he met on a plane, to join him in the project. After an understandable bout of cold feet, she eventually agreed. 10

In a "love contract" the two signed on Valentine's Day this year to seal the deal, Epstein stipulates that he and Gabriela must undergo intensive counseling to learn how to communicate effectively and participate in a variety of exercises designed to foster mutual love. To help oversee and guide the project, Epstein has even formed an advisory board made up of high-profile relationship experts, most notably Dr. John Gray, who wrote the best-selling *Men Are from Mars, Women Are from Venus.* If the experiment pans out, the two will have learned to love each other within a year's time. 11

It may strike some as anathema° to be so premeditated about the process of falling in love, but to hear Epstein tell it, most unions fail exactly because they aren't intentional enough; they're based on a roll of the dice and a determination to stake everything on love. What this means, Epstein says, is that most people lack basic relationship skills, and, as a result, most relationships lack emotional and psychological intimacy. 12

A divorced father of four, Epstein himself married for passion—"just like I was told to do by the fairy tales and by the movies"—but eventually came to 13

**anathema:** An abomination; blasphemy.

regret it. "I had the experience that so many people have now," he says, "which is basically looking at your partner and going, 'Who are you?'" Although Epstein acknowledges the non-Western tradition of arranged marriage is a complex, somewhat flawed institution, he thinks we can "distill key elements of [it] to help us learn how to create a new, more stable institution in the West."

Judging from the phenomenon of reality-TV shows like *Married by America* and *Meet My Folks* and the recent increase in the number of professional matchmakers, the idea of arranging marriages (even if in nontraditional ways) seems to be taking hold in this country—perhaps nowhere more powerfully than in cyberspace. Online dating services attracted some twenty million people last year (roughly one-fifth of all singles—and growing), who used sites like Match.com and Yahoo Personals to hook up with potentially compatible partners. Web sites' search engines play the role of patriarchal grandfathers, searching for good matches based on any number of criteria that you select. 14

Cooper, the Stanford psychologist and author of *Sex and the Internet: A Guidebook for Clinicians* (Brunner-Routledge, 2002)—and an expert in the field of online sexuality—says that because online interaction tends to downplay proximity, physical attraction, and face-to-face interaction, people are more likely to take risks and disclose significant things about themselves. The result is that they attain a higher level of psychological and emotional intimacy than if they dated right away or hopped in the sack. Indeed, online dating represents a return to what University of Chicago Humanities Professor Amy Kass calls the "distanced nearness" of old-style courtship, an intimate and protected (cyber)space that encourages self-revelation while maintaining personal boundaries. 15

And whether looking for a fellow scientist, someone else who's HIV-positive, or a B-movie film buff, an online dater has a much higher likelihood of finding "the one" due to the computer's capacity to sort through thousands of potential mates. "That's what computers are all about—efficiency and sorting," says Cooper, who believes that online dating has the potential to lower the nation's 50 percent divorce rate. There is no magic or "chemistry" involved in love, Cooper insists. "It's specific, operationalizable factors." 16

Love's mystery solved by "operationalizable factors"! Why does that sound a little less than inspiring? Sure, for many people the Internet can efficiently facilitate love and help to nudge fate along. But, for the diehard romantic who trusts in surprise, coincidence, and fate, the cyber-solution to love lacks heart. "To the romantic," observes English writer Blake Morrison in *The Guardian,* "every marriage is an arranged marriage—arranged by fate, that is, which gives us no choice." 17

More than a century ago, Emily Dickinson mocked those who would dissect birds to find the mechanics of song: 18

*Split the Lark—and you'll find the Music—*
*Bulb after Bulb, in Silver rolled—*
*Scantily dealt to the Summer Morning*
*Saved for your Ear when Lutes be old.*

*Loose the Flood—you shall find it patent—*
*Gush after Gush, reserved for you—*
*Scarlet Experiment! Skeptic Thomas!*
*Now, do you doubt that your Bird was true?*

In other words, writes Deborah Blum in her book, *Sex on the Brain* (Penguin, 1997), "kill the bird and [you] silence the melody." For some, nurturing the ideal of romantic love may be more important than the goal of love itself. Making a more conscious choice in mating may help partners handle the complex personal ties and obligations of marriage; but romantic love, infused as it is with myth and projection and doomed passion, is a way to live *outside* of life's obligations, outside of time itself—if only for a brief, bright moment. Choosing love by rational means might not be worth it for those souls who'd rather roll the dice and risk the possibility of ending up with nothing but tragic nobility and the bittersweet tang of regret. 19

In the end, who really wants to examine love too closely? I'd rather curl up with a LaVyrle Spencer novel or dream up the French movie version of my life than live in a world where the mechanics of love—and its giddy, mysterious buzz—are laid bare. After all, to actually unravel love's mystery is, perhaps, to miss the point of it all. 20

## Questions to Start You Thinking

1. **Considering Meaning:** According to the experts whom Razdan quotes, why is cyberspace an ideal venue for facilitating relationships?
2. **Identifying Writing Strategies:** How does Razdan use cause and effect to explain the high divorce rate in the United States?
3. **Reading Critically:** What type of evidence does Razdan use to explore whether arranged marriages are more successful than relationships based on romantic attraction? Do you find the evidence relevant, credible, and sufficient? Why, or why not? What other type of evidence might she have used?
4. **Expanding Vocabulary:** In commenting on her parents' arranged marriage, Razdan asks in paragraph 3, "But, what could they possibly know of *real love*?" How do you define *real love*? Do you think that Razdan would agree with your definition?
5. **Making Connections:** Citing an expert on online sexuality, Razdan writes in paragraph 15 that people who have relationships on the Internet

are "more likely to take risks and disclose significant things about themselves." As a result, "they attain a higher level of psychological and emotional intimacy than if they dated right away." Would Sherry Turkle ("How Computers Change the Way We Think," p. 595 and e-Pages) agree? How might she respond?

### Journal Prompts

1. Write a brief personal ad for a mate, using the writing style associated with personals. Keep in mind that the words you choose and the way you organize your ad reveal something about your personality.
2. One of the experts whom Razdan quotes mentions the myth of "love at first sight" (paragraph 9). Write about a time when you fell in love at first sight or present your opinion on whether such a thing exists.

### Suggestions for Writing

1. Write an essay that uses your personal experiences and observations to develop a specific idea presented in Razdan's essay. For example, you might recall your own "date-from-hell" (paragraph 5), a friend's experience with an online dating service, or a matchmaker friend's success rate. Use your experiences and observations to support your own point about current dating practices or about "relationship skills" needed for a successful marriage.
2. Drawing examples from this reading and your own observations, write an essay arguing for or against arranged marriages. You might also do some research to find additional support for your argument.

## William Deresiewicz

## A Man. A Woman. Just Friends?

William Deresiewicz has taught at Columbia and Yale and has written several books on literary and popular culture topics, including *A Jane Austen Education: How Six Novels Taught Me about Love, Friendship, and the Things That Really Matter* (2011). His critical essays have appeared in the *Nation*, the *American Scholar*, the *London Review of Books*, and the *New York Times*. Nominated for the National Magazine Awards in 2008, 2009, and 2011, he won the National Book Critics Circle's Excellence in Reviewing citation in 2013. In the following article, first published in the *New York Times* in April 2012, Deresiewicz explores the nature of friendship between men and women.

**AS YOU READ:** Identify the social and political changes that Deresiewicz traces.

Can men and women be friends? We have been asking ourselves that question for a long time, and the answer is usually no. The movie 1

"When Harry Met Sally . . ." provides the locus classicus. The problem, Harry famously explains, is that "the sex part always gets in the way." Heterosexual people of the opposite sex may claim to be just friends, the message goes, but count on it – wink, wink, nudge, nudge – something more's going on. Popular culture enforces the notion relentlessly. In movie after movie, show after show, the narrative arc is the same. What starts as friendship (Ross and Rachel, Monica and Chandler) ends up in bed.

There's a history here, and it's a surprisingly political one. Friendship between the sexes was more or less unknown in traditional society. Men and women occupied different spheres, and women were regarded as inferior in any case. A few epistolary friendships° between monastics,° a few relationships in literary and court circles, but beyond that, cross-sex friendship was as unthinkable in Western society as it still is in many cultures. 2

Then came feminism – specifically, Mary Wollstonecraft, the mother of feminism, in the late 18th century. Wollstonecraft was actually wary of platonic relationships, which could lead too easily, she thought, to mischief. (She had a child out of wedlock herself.) But she did believe that friendship, "the most sublime of all affections," should be the mainspring of marriage. 3

In the 1890s, when feminism emerged from the drawing rooms and genteel° committees to become a mass, radical movement (the term "feminism" itself was coined in 1895), friendship reappeared as a political demand. This was the time of the "New Woman," portrayed in fiction and endlessly debated in the press. 4

The New Woman was intelligent, well read, strong-willed, idealistic, unconventional and outspoken. For her, relationships with men, whether or not they involved sex, had to involve mental companionship, freedom of choice, equality and mutual respect. They had, in short, to be friendships. Just as suffrage° represented feminism's vision of the political future, friendship represented its vision of the personal future, the central term of a renegotiated sexual contract. 5

Easier said than done, of course. But the notion of friendship as the root of romantic relationships started to seep into the culture. The terms "boyfriend" and "girlfriend" also began to appear in the 1890s. We take the words for granted now, but think of what they imply, and what a new idea it was: that romantic partners share more than erotic passion, that companionship and equality are part of the relationship. A boyfriend is a friend, as well as a lover. As for husband and wife, Wollstonecraft's ideal has long since become a cliché. Who doesn't think of their spouse – or claim to think of them, or want to think of them – as their best friend? 6

So friendship now is part of what we mean by love. Still, that doesn't get us to platonic relationships. For that we needed yet another wave of feminism, the one that started in the 1960s. Friendship wasn't part of the demand this time, but the things that were demanded – equal rights and 7

**epistolary friendships:** Friendships carried out by letter; pen pals. **monastics:** Monks or nuns. **genteel:** Upper class. **suffrage:** The right to vote.

opportunities in every sphere—created the conditions for it. Only once the sexes mixed on equal and familiar terms at school, at work and in the social spaces in between—only once it was normal and even boring to see a member of the opposite sex at the next desk—could platonic friendships become an ordinary part of life. And that's exactly what has happened.

Friendships with members of the opposite sex have been an important part of my life since I went to high school in the late 1970s, and I hardly think I'm alone. Consult your own experience, but as I look around, I don't see that platonic friendships are actually rare at all or worthy of a lot of winks and nudges. Which is why you don't much hear the term anymore. Platonic friendships now are simply friendships. But doesn't the sex thing get in the way? At times, no doubt. It's harder for the young, of course—all those hormones, and so many of your peers are unattached. In fact, one of the most common solutions to Harry's quandary° is to have sex and then remain friends. If the sex thing gets in the way, the answer often seems to be to just get it out of the way. But it doesn't always get in the way. Maybe you're not attracted to each other. Maybe you know it would never work out, so it's not worth screwing up your friendship. Maybe that's just not what it's about. 8

So if it's common now for men and women to be friends, why do we so rarely see it in popular culture? Partly, it's a narrative problem. Friendship isn't courtship. It doesn't have a beginning, a middle and an end. Stories about friendships of any kind are relatively rare, especially given what a huge place the relationships have in our lives. And of course, they're not sexy. Put a man and a woman together in a movie or a novel, and we expect the sparks to fly. Yet it isn't just a narrative problem, or a Hollywood problem. 9

We have trouble, in our culture, with any love that isn't based on sex or blood. We understand romantic relationships, and we understand family, and that's about all we seem to understand. We have trouble with mentorship, the asymmetric° love of master and apprentice, professor and student, guide and guided; we have trouble with comradeship, the bond that comes from shared intense work; and we have trouble with friendship, at least of the intimate kind. When we imagine those relationships, we seem to have to sexualize them. Close friendships between members of the same sex, after all, are also suspect. Even Oprah has had to defend her relationship with Gayle King, and as for men and men, forget about it. 10

I cannot think of another area of our lives in which there is so great a gap between what we do and what our culture says we do. But maybe things are beginning to change. Younger people, having grown up with the gay-rights movement and in many cases gone to colleges with co-ed dormitories, are open to a wider range of emotional possibility. Friendship between the sexes may no longer be a political issue, but it is an issue of liberation: the freedom to love whom you want, in the way that you want. Maybe it's time that we all took it out of the closet. 11

**quandary:** Problem. **asymmetric:** Uneven.

## Questions to Start You Thinking

1. **Considering Meaning:** How does Deresiewicz challenge the idea that men and women can't be friends because "the sex part always gets in the way" (paragraph 1)?
2. **Identifying Writing Strategies:** In order to examine intimate friendships, Deresiewicz turns to the very public world of politics. How does Deresiewicz connect large historical and political changes with friendships between individuals?
3. **Reading Critically:** Why does Deresiewicz turn to the history of feminism to investigate how friendship has changed? Why is the changing role of women particularly important to his argument?
4. **Expanding Vocabulary:** What constitutes a *platonic* friendship (paragraph 3)? Look up the origin of this word and then consider how it is used today. Why are some, including Mary Wollstonecraft, skeptical about *platonic* relationships?
5. **Making Connections:** Deresiewicz sees increasing numbers of women in college as one factor that has changed their lives and their friendships with men. How does his perspective relate to Cisneros's "Only Daughter" (pp. 496–500) or Tan's "Mother Tongue" (pp. 506–12) in terms of what a college education can mean for a woman?

## Journal Prompts

1. Deresiewicz uses the show *Friends* as one example of a narrative in which men and women who begin as friends end up in romantic relationships. What other examples from popular culture can you think of? Why do you think these stories appeal to readers or viewers? Can you think of examples of male-female friendship in popular media that follow a different path?
2. List the most important qualities you look for in a friendship. Then consider whether your ideal friendship could be fulfilled equally by a person of either gender. Why or why not?

## Suggestions for Writing

1. Evaluate Deresiewicz's historical argument for rethinking male-female friendships. What does he think the past tells us about the rarity of these relationships? How persuasive is his case that things have changed significantly between the sexes?
2. Respond to this essay by taking a stand on the central question: Can men and women be friends? You might use personal experience, analysis of examples from popular culture, research into interpersonal relationships, or other evidence to support your points—but be as specific as possible in describing the kinds of bonds you think people of opposite genders can maintain.

## Judy Brady

# I Want a Wife

**Judy Brady** was born in 1937 in San Francisco, where she now makes her home. A graduate of the University of Iowa, Brady has contributed to various publications, including the *Women's Review of Books* and *Greenpeace* magazine, and has traveled to Cuba to study class relationships and education. She edited the book *1 in 3: Women with Cancer Confront an Epidemic* (1991), drawing on her own struggle with the disease, and she continues to write and speak about cancer and its possible environmental causes. In the following piece, reprinted frequently since it appeared in *Ms.* magazine in December 1971, Brady considers the role of the American housewife. While she has said that she is "not a 'writer,'" this essay shows Brady to be a satirist adept at taking a stand and provoking attention.

**AS YOU READ:** Ask yourself why Brady says she wants a wife rather than a husband.

I belong to that classification of people known as wives. I am A Wife. And, not altogether incidentally, I am a mother. 1

Not too long ago a male friend of mine appeared on the scene fresh from a recent divorce. He had one child, who is, of course, with his ex-wife. He is looking for another wife. As I thought about him while I was ironing one evening, it suddenly occurred to me that I, too, would like to have a wife. Why do I want a wife? 2

I would like to go back to school so that I can become economically independent, support myself, and, if need be, support those dependent upon me. I want a wife who will work and send me to school. And while I am going to school I want a wife to take care of my children. I want a wife to keep track of the children's doctor and dentist appointments. And to keep track of mine, too. I want a wife to make sure my children eat properly and are kept clean. I want a wife who will wash the children's clothes and keep them mended. I want a wife who is a good nurturant° attendant to my children, who arranges for their schooling, makes sure that they have an adequate social life with their peers, takes them to the park, the zoo, etc. I want a wife who takes care of the children when they are sick, a wife who arranges to be around when the children need special care, because, of course, I cannot miss classes at school. My wife must arrange to lose time at work and not lose the job. It may mean a small cut in my wife's income from time to time, but I guess I can tolerate that. Needless to say, my wife will arrange and pay for the care of the children while my wife is working. 3

I want a wife who will take care of *my* physical needs. I want a wife who will keep my house clean. A wife who will pick up after my children, a wife who will pick up after me. I want a wife who will keep my clothes clean, ironed, mended, replaced when need be, and who will see to it that my personal things are kept in their proper place so that I can find what I need the minute I need it. I want a wife who cooks the meals, a wife who is a *good* 4

**nurturant:** Kind, loving, caring.

cook. I want a wife who will plan the menus, do the necessary grocery shopping, prepare the meals, serve them pleasantly, and then do the cleaning up while I do my studying. I want a wife who will care for me when I am sick and sympathize with my pain and loss of time from school. I want a wife to go along when our family takes a vacation so that someone can continue to care for me and my children when I need a rest and change of scene.

I want a wife who will not bother me with rambling complaints about a wife's duties. But I want a wife who will listen to me when I feel the need to explain a rather difficult point I have come across in my course of studies. 5

I want a wife who will take care of the details of my social life. When my wife and I are invited out by my friends, I want a wife who will take care of the babysitting arrangements. When I meet people at school that I like and want to entertain, I want a wife who will have the house clean, will prepare a special meal, serve it to me and my friends, and not interrupt when I talk about things that interest me and my friends. I want a wife who will have arranged that the children are fed and ready for bed before my guests arrive so that the children do not bother us. I want a wife who takes care of the needs of my guests so that they feel comfortable, who makes sure that they have an ashtray, that they are passed the hors d'oeuvres, that they are offered a second helping of the food, that their wine glasses are replenished when necessary, that their coffee is served to them as they like it. And I want a wife who knows that sometimes I need a night out by myself. 6

I want a wife who is sensitive to my sexual needs, a wife who makes love passionately and eagerly when I feel like it, a wife who makes sure that I am satisfied. And, of course, I want a wife who will not demand sexual attention when I am not in the mood for it. I want a wife who assumes the complete responsibility for birth control, because I do not want more children. I want a wife who will remain sexually faithful to me so that I do not have to clutter up my intellectual life with jealousies. And I want a wife who understands that *my* sexual needs may entail more than strict adherence to monogamy. I must, after all, be able to relate to people as fully as possible. 7

If, by chance, I find another person more suitable as a wife than the wife I already have, I want the liberty to replace my present wife with another one. Naturally, I will expect a fresh, new life; my wife will take the children and be solely responsible for them so that I am left free. 8

When I am through with school and have a job, I want my wife to quit working and remain at home so that my wife can more fully and completely take care of a wife's duties. 9

My God, who *wouldn't* want a wife? 10

## Questions to Start You Thinking

1. **Considering Meaning:** How does Brady define the traditional role of the wife? Does she think that a wife should perform all of the duties she outlines? How can you tell?

2. **Identifying Writing Strategies:** How does Brady use observation to support her stand? What other approaches does she use?
3. **Reading Critically:** What is the tone or attitude of this essay? How does Brady establish it? Considering that she was writing for a predominantly female – and feminist – audience, do you think Brady's tone is appropriate?
4. **Expanding Vocabulary:** Why does Brady use such simple language in this essay? What is the effect of her use of such phrases as *of course* (paragraph 2), *Needless to say* (paragraph 3), and *Naturally* (paragraph 8)?
5. **Making Connections:** Both Brady and Julie Zeilinger in "Guys Suffer from Oppressive Gender Roles Too" (pp. 538–42) use humor to discuss gender stereotypes. Evaluate their use of humor. Whose is more effective? Why?

## Journal Prompts

1. Exert your wishful thinking – describe your ideal mate.
2. Begin with a stereotype of a husband, wife, boyfriend, girlfriend, father, or mother, and write a satirical description of that stereotype.

## Suggestions for Writing

1. In a short personal essay, explain what you want or expect in a wife, husband, or life partner. Do your hopes and expectations differ from social and cultural norms? If so, in what way(s)? How has your parents' relationship shaped your attitudes and ideals?
2. How has the role of a wife changed since this essay was written? Write an essay comparing and contrasting the twenty-first century wife with the kind of wife Judy Brady claims she wants.

## Robert Jensen

## The High Cost of Manliness

Robert Jensen was born in 1958 and grew up in Fargo, North Dakota. After earning a BA in social studies and secondary education from Moorhead State University and graduate degrees in journalism, Jensen started his career as a newspaper journalist. Now a professor of journalism at the University of Texas at Austin, he teaches courses on media law, ethics, and politics and also regularly contributes to a variety of publications. His recent books include *The Heart of Whiteness: Confronting Race, Racism, and White Privilege* (2005), *Getting Off: Pornography and the End of Masculinity* (2007), and *All My Bones Shake: Seeking a Progressive Path to the Prophetic Voice* (2009). He also coproduced the documentary film *Abe Osheroff: One Foot in the Grave, the Other Still Dancing* (2008). In the following essay, which first appeared on *Alternet.org* in

September 2006, Jensen calls for abandoning the prevailing definition of masculinity, arguing that it is "toxic" to both men and women.

**AS YOU READ:** Identify what Jensen sees as the dominant conception of masculinity in contemporary culture. What does he think of this conception?

It's hard to be a man; hard to live up to the demands that come with the dominant conception of masculinity, of the tough guy. 1

So, guys, I have an idea—maybe it's time we stop trying. Maybe this masculinity thing is a bad deal, not just for women but for us. 2

We need to get rid of the whole idea of masculinity. It's time to abandon the claim that there are certain psychological or social traits that inherently come with being biologically male. If we can get past that, we have a chance to create a better world for men and women. 3

The dominant conception of masculinity in U.S. culture is easily summarized: men are assumed to be naturally competitive and aggressive, and being a real man is therefore marked by the struggle for control, conquest, and domination. A man looks at the world, sees what he wants, and takes it. Men who don't measure up are wimps, sissies, fags, girls. The worst insult one man can hurl at another—whether it's boys on the playground or CEOs in the boardroom—is the accusation that a man is like a woman. Although the culture acknowledges that men can in some situations have traits traditionally associated with women (caring, compassion, tenderness), in the end it is men's strength-expressed-as-toughness that defines us and must trump any femalelike softness. Those aspects of masculinity must prevail for a man to be a "real man." 4

That's not to suggest, of course, that every man adopts that view of masculinity. But it is endorsed in key institutions and activities—most notably in business, the military, and athletics—and is reinforced through the mass media. It is particularly expressed in the way men—straight and gay alike—talk about sexuality and act sexually. And our culture's male heroes reflect those characteristics: they most often are men who take charge rather than seek consensus, seize power rather than look for ways to share it, and are willing to be violent to achieve their goals. 5

That view of masculinity is dangerous for women. It leads men to seek to control "their" women and define their own pleasure in that control, which leads to epidemic levels of rape and battery. But this view of masculinity is toxic for men as well. 6

If masculinity is defined as conquest, it means that men will always struggle with each other for dominance. In a system premised on hierarchy° and power, there can be only one king of the hill. Every other man must in some way be subordinated to the king, and the king has to always be nervous about who is coming up that hill to get him. A friend who once worked on Wall Street—one of the preeminent° sites of masculine competition—described coming to work as like walking into a knife fight when all the good 7

**hierarchy:** A grouping based on relative rank. **preeminent:** Most important.

spots along the wall were taken. Masculinity like this is life lived as endless competition and threat.

No one man created this system, and perhaps none of us, if given a choice, would choose it. But we live our lives in that system, and it deforms men, narrowing our emotional range and depth. It keeps us from the rich connections with others—not just with women and children, but other men—that make life meaningful but require vulnerability. 8

This doesn't mean that the negative consequences of this toxic masculinity are equally dangerous for men and women. As feminists have long pointed out, there's a big difference between women dealing with the possibility of being raped, beaten, and killed by the men in their lives and men not being able to cry. But we can see that the short-term material gains that men get are not adequate compensation for what we men give up in the long haul—which is to surrender part of our humanity to the project of dominance. 9

Of course there are obvious physical differences between men and women—average body size, hormones, reproductive organs. There may be other differences rooted in our biology that we don't yet understand. Yet it's also true that men and women are more similar than we are different, and that given the pernicious° effects of centuries of patriarchy° and its relentless devaluing of things female, we should be skeptical of the perceived differences. 10

What we know is simple: in any human population, there is wide individual variation. While there's no doubt that a large part of our behavior is rooted in our DNA, there's also no doubt that our genetic endowment is highly influenced by culture. Beyond that, it's difficult to say much with any certainty. It's true that only women can bear children and breast-feed. That fact likely has some bearing on aspects of men's and women's personalities. But we don't know much about what the effect is, and given the limits of our tools to understand human behavior, it's possible we may never know much. 11

At the moment, the culture seems obsessed with gender differences, in the context of a recurring intellectual fad (called "evolutionary psychology" this time around, and "sociobiology" in a previous incarnation) that wants to explain all complex behaviors as simple evolutionary adaptations—if a pattern of human behavior exists, it must be because it's adaptive in some ways. In the long run, that's true by definition. But in the short term it's hardly a convincing argument to say, "Look at how men and women behave so differently; it must be because men and women are fundamentally different" when a political system has been creating differences between men and women. 12

From there, the argument that we need to scrap masculinity is fairly simple. To illustrate it, remember back to right after 9/11. A number of commentators argued that criticisms of masculinity should be rethought. Cannot we now see—recognizing that male firefighters raced into burning buildings, risking and sometimes sacrificing their lives to save others—that masculinity can encompass a kind of strength that is rooted in caring and 13

**pernicious:** Destructive. **patriarchy:** Social organization in which the father is supreme; male control of most of the power in a society.

sacrifice? Of course men often exhibit such strength, just as do women. So, the obvious question arises: What makes these distinctly masculine characteristics? Are they not simply human characteristics?

We identify masculine tendencies toward competition, domination, and violence because we see patterns of differential behavior; men are more prone to such behavior in our culture. We can go on to observe and analyze the ways in which men are socialized to behave in those ways, toward the goal of changing those destructive behaviors. That analysis is different than saying that admirable human qualities present in both men and women are somehow primarily the domain of one gender. To assign them to a gender is misguided and demeaning to the gender that is then assumed not to possess them to the same degree. Once we start saying "strength and courage are masculine traits," it leads to the conclusion that woman are not as strong or courageous. 14

Of course, if we are going to jettison° masculinity, we have to scrap femininity along with it. We have to stop trying to define what men and women are going to be in the world based on extrapolations° from physical sex differences. That doesn't mean we ignore those differences when they matter, but we have to stop assuming they matter everywhere. 15

I don't think the planet can long survive if the current conception of masculinity endures. We face political and ecological challenges that can't be met with this old model of what it means to be a man. At the more intimate level, the stakes are just as high. For those of us who are biologically male, we have a simple choice: we men can settle for being men, or we can strive to be human beings. 16

## Questions to Start You Thinking

1. **Considering Meaning:** What does Jensen see as the negative consequences of the commonly held idea of masculinity?
2. **Identifying Writing Strategies:** Where in the essay does Jensen use comparison and contrast in writing about men and women? What is his point in doing so?
3. **Reading Critically:** In paragraph 5, Jensen admits that not all men conceive of masculinity in terms of competition and aggression. Do you think he goes on to provide enough evidence to support his claim that this view of masculinity is dominant in U.S. culture? Why, or why not?
4. **Expanding Vocabulary:** In paragraph 12, Jensen refers to the current obsession with gender differences in the United States taking shape as a "recurring intellectual fad." What does he mean by this phrase? What does it add to his argument?
5. **Making Connections:** According to Jensen, "toxic masculinity" (paragraph 9) results from a "political system" that creates "differences between men and women" (paragraph 12). Do you think Brent Staples

**jettison:** Throw out. **extrapolations:** Predictions.

("Black Men and Public Space," pp. 520–23) would agree? How are views of black men shaped—or even created—by society? How does the category of race complicate Jensen's analysis?

## Link to the Paired Essay

To consider the definition of masculinity suggested by the character of James Bond, turn to the images on p. 545.

In paragraph 4, Jensen summarizes the "dominant conception of masculinity in U.S. culture." Would Zeilinger ("Guys Suffer from Oppressive Gender Roles Too," pp. 538–42) agree with his definition of masculinity? Consider where their definitions overlap and whether they differ on any points.

## Journal Prompts

1. Do you agree, as Jensen puts it, that the "worst insult one man can hurl at another . . . is the accusation that a man is like a woman" (paragraph 4)? What do you think about insults that liken a woman to a man?
2. In the essay's final paragraph, Jensen writes that he doesn't think "the planet can long survive if the current conception of masculinity endures." How do you respond to this statement?

## Suggestions for Writing

1. Jensen writes in paragraph 13 about the idea of strength. In an essay, discuss how you define *human strength,* considering the physical, the intellectual, and the emotional.
2. Jensen acknowledges that gender differences are in some part determined by biological factors. However, he is more concerned about the influence of social conditioning. Write an essay analyzing how a particular social force does or does not contribute to stereotypes of masculinity and femininity. For example, you might consider the influence of some aspect of popular culture, education, sports, or children's toys. Use examples from your experience as well as other evidence to support your point.

## Julie Zeilinger

## Guys Suffer from Oppressive Gender Roles Too

Julie Zeilinger writes blogs and articles on women's issues. She founded *The F Bomb*, a critically acclaimed feminist blog that focuses on women's rights, and has published articles in the *Huffington Post, Feminist.com*, and *Skirt Magazine*. In 2012, her book *A Little F'd Up: Why Feminism is Not a Dirty Word* was published. That same year, she was honored in *More Magazine*'s feature, "What the New Feminists Look Like." In the following selection, Zeilinger insists that men should be allowed to express their emotions.

**AS YOU READ:** How does Zeilinger contrast internal pressures and external expectations?

Guys are supposed to be rocks, inside and out. They are supposed to be defined more by their muscles and brute force than by any complex or unique personality trait. Ideally, they should physically be so steely and impervious° that they could plausibly be cast in a Transformers film . . . as an actual alien Transformer. If we were to look inside these ideal men, we'd find a tangled mess of barbed wire encapsulating° a ravenous° lion decapitating a tiny bunny. There would probably be a camouflage color scheme thrown in there too. Guys *certainly* aren't allowed to let the world see that they do in fact have emotions. No, they throw those feelings to the feral° beast within. 1

But here's the problem: Guys *do* have emotions. Guys live an external reality that is in complete contradiction with their internal reality. So what can guys do when they experience real honest-to-god feelings? Well, for those who try to adhere° to these masculinity standards to their utmost ability, they have to disconnect. They must detach themselves from their emotions. And it's not just emotions like "sad" or "ecstatic." It's emotions like "empathy" and "sympathy," which, when you think about it, is pretty damn scary. So guys can either detach and live a life numb to a true range of human emotion, or live in a state of contradiction. Not the greatest options. 2

The woes of men don't end there. Oh no. On top of embodying° various types of metals inside and out, guys must also be "successful." But the definition of male success is quite elusive.° It doesn't necessarily mean having a great, loving family and friends who care about you. It's probably not about becoming an abstract painter, or being the type of passionate, energetic high school teacher who inspires a group of jaded and self-defeating inner-city kids to want more for themselves via the power of the pen and self-expression. No. In order to be successful, guys must be cunning.° They must get ahead of others in order to obtain success, which is usually defined by two things: money and power. In fact, though I kind of hate to use the word "winning" (Charlie Sheen connotations abound), it has become kind of synonymous with "masculinity." 3

Men feel as much competition and pressure as women do. They have to be strong. They must conceal their emotions. They need to obtain wealth and power. But while we ladies generally deal with this pressure internally, forcing ourselves to get excellent grades and taking out our issues on our bodies, guys are far more external in their expression of the same pressures and competition. 4

Why do guys like violent video games so much? Why do they feel the need to physically fight (or at least threaten to), even over the stupidest stuff, in a way girls rarely do? Why do they put younger guys through ridiculous 5

**impervious:** Not vulnerable. **encapsulating:** Surrounding. **ravenous:** Very hungry. **feral:** Wild. **adhere:** Stick to. **embodying:** Physically representing. **elusive:** Hard to pin down. **cunning:** Crafty or tricky.

hazing, which ranges from gross and uncomfortable (I've heard of senior athletes forcing underclassmen players to eat ten Big Macs in less than ten minutes) to the seriously violent and dangerous (being beaten with two-by-fours)? Better yet, why do they subject themselves to such degrading° abuse at all?

Guys engage in violent activities (whether simulated or real) as a way to release the pressure, but also, circuitously,° as a way to prove their masculinity—as a way to make that competition with other guys an actuality. Guys strictly monitor each other to sniff out and point out "weaknesses" in other guys, which gives them some illusion of feeling stronger and more masculine. 6

I've always suspected that's why guys love telling jokes about women and gay guys. Even if a guy swears up and down he's not sexist or homophobic, by telling these jokes he is, at the very least, reminding the world he's a straight dude—clearly not the alternatives, which he so disdains.° 7

And what about guys who dare to take on qualities that could be considered feminine? Like, for instance, guys who care about their appearance, who wear tight clothes, or who are just generally considered "effeminate"? Well, those men are threats. For guys clinging to masculinity standards for dear life, who use those guidelines as a complete roadmap for how to exist in the world, they're terrifying. For some guys, it's a seriously deep terror rooted in the threat of losing their own identity. They see other guys rejecting what has been prescribed of them based on their gender, and they're terrified of the consequences of doing the same. Because if they were to really examine themselves, if they were to reject the masculinity standards that shape their entire identity and personality, then they might just find that they never actually had an identity to begin with. And really, what's scarier than that? 8

But forget the implications for jerks who give any guy who refuses to live up to masculinity standards a hard time. Let's consider how this actually affects the guys who reject traditional masculinity standards. Specifically, let's consider gay men. I asked a young gay friend of mine about his experience, and he had some pretty eloquent things to say. 9

"Being a gay man has instilled a sense of displacement, no matter where I may be, or who I'm with," he said. As a man, he explained, he feels the pressure to meet masculinity standards—which he (and other gay men) may manifest° by engaging in and promoting promiscuity. But he also feels a kinship with women, as he understands what it's like to be marginalized.° "Being a gay man [means] trying to overcome both male and female stigmas," he said. "Gay men and feminists have similar ambitions, but it's hard, because gay men are ultimately men, so they have to strive to promote a sense of masculinity that works for them *and* goes hand-in-hand with the feminist doctrine° of personal pride and worth." 10

**degrading:** Humiliating or dehumanizing. **circuitously:** Indirectly. **disdains:** Regards as inferior. **manifest:** Exhibit. **marginalized:** Pushed to the edges of society. **doctrine:** System of beliefs.

And that's how a gay man feels in the context of an overall peaceful and unbothered state. That's not even considering what happens when bullying, violent hate crimes, and homophobia at large get thrown into the mix. 11

In this society, adhering to the standards imposed by masculinity means never developing your true identity, never taking the opportunity to find out who you really are. Expressing feelings and exploring interests—including things that aren't strictly "manly"—are part of being human. But if you want to be the stereotypical man, you have to forget about those things. Just like we girls have to forget about enjoying food and having interests outside of shopping and boys. 12

Sometimes when I look around and see all of my peers, guys and girls alike, desperately trying to live up to their prescribed gender roles, often at the expense of their own well-being, I feel like I'm crazy. I wonder, *Am I the only one who didn't get the memo? Should I be more preoccupied with how many calories are in my food than the fact that it's buttery and delicious and my stomach is so happy it's as if there is a wild conga line proceeding through it? Should I be spending more time trying to get a boyfriend? Is that what life is about?* 13

And I'm sure there are guys who wonder these things too. Who look around and see how they're expected to put as many hours into ESPN and the weight room as they do into basic functions like sleeping and eating, all so that they can talk the talk and walk the walk. *Is this really it?* they must think. *Is this all we're supposed to care about? Things like sex, sports, and food? Of all the things available to us in this world, even if those things are great, are these the* only *things we're able to come away with?* 14

## Questions to Start You Thinking

1. **Considering Meaning:** Zeilinger considers many ways in which gender standards can be harmful. What positive effects would men see if they could escape from these expectations? What could men do in a world without rigid gender roles?
2. **Identifying Writing Strategies:** Zeilinger uses humor to point out the excesses of gender roles for men. Where do you think her humor is most effective? What truths about masculinity does she reveal in her exaggerated description of "manly" men?
3. **Reading Critically:** The title of this selection implies a response to another argument or a received opinion. Summarize the assumption about gender roles to which Zeilinger responds. What points in the essay refer to this assumption?
4. **Expanding Vocabulary:** Zeilinger describes her disappointment when she sees her peers struggling with their "prescribed gender roles"

(paragraph 13). What does it mean for something to be *prescribed*? How does this word apply to gender norms?

5. **Making Connections:** Both Zeilinger and Anjula Razdan – in "What's Love Got to Do with It?" (pp. 523–28) – attempt to debunk a cultural myth. Zeilinger challenges gender roles while Razdan questions the idea of love at first sight and reevaluates the reasons for arranged marriage. Does either admit any value in the cultural myth she questions? If so, what does she think is worth saving in that myth?

## Link to the Paired Essay

In the paired essay, Robert Jensen ("The High Cost of Manliness," pp. 534–38) makes an argument similar to Zeilinger's about the harm that comes from rigid notions of masculinity, but he makes his case from a man's point of view. How does the gender of the author affect each essay? How does Zeilinger's perspective differ from Jensen's?

## Journal Prompts

1. Zeilinger suggests that the definition of success that goes along with traditional ideas about masculinity is hollow or even destructive. Do you agree with her? How would you define success? In what ways does the kind of success you want for yourself match or defy what society values?
2. According to Zeilinger, men reinforce gender roles by pointing out "weaknesses" in other men (paragraph 6). This phenomenon may also be true for women who hold each other to feminine roles. Have you ever been on either end (or both ends) of this dynamic – being held by others to gender standards or helping to enforce them on your peers? Why do you think men and women play along with these roles?

## Suggestions for Writing

1. Zeilinger identifies masculinity standards as the cause of many problems for young men. Write an essay analyzing her claims about how rigid masculine roles affect men or how stereotypes change the way men feel and act. Do you agree with her assessment of the effects?
2. The argument of this essay is largely based on the author's personal observations of her peers. To what extent does more formal research about gender support her points? Find an article or a study that examines how gender roles affect young men or women, and write about how it supports (or challenges) Zeilinger's position.

## e Deborah Tannen

Text

# Who Does the Talking Here?

Deborah Tannen teaches linguistics at Georgetown University and has been awarded five honorary doctorates for her work in this field. Her many articles and books on the politics of language include her bestseller *You Just Don't Understand: Women and Men in Conversation* (2001), which has been translated into thirty-one languages. Her book *The Argument Culture: Stopping America's War of Words* (1999) earned the Common Ground Book Award, and *I Only Say This Because I Love You: Talking to Your Parents, Partner, Sibs, and Kids When You're All Adults* (2002) received a Books for a Better Life Award. This article, first published in the *Washington Post* in 2007, examines the stereotype that women talk more than men. To read this essay, go to Chapter 26: **bedfordstmartins.com/bedguide**.

Tannen argues that men talk more at work while women talk more at home.

## Jed Conklin

Visual Essay

# Boxing Beauties

Jed Conklin, a freelance photographer since 2007, has done work around the world, including Morocco, Iraq, and China. Back in the United States, he completed an extensive project commemorating the 1988 Yellowstone fires. His work has been recognized in competitions including Pictures of the Year International and the National Press Photographers Association's Best of Photojournalism. In his photo essay "Boxing Beauties," Conklin captures the excitement and intensity of the U.S. women's Olympic Team Trials, where three women secured spots to fight in the inaugural women's boxing competition at the 2012 London Olympic Games. To view the photo essay, go to Chapter 26: **bedfordstmartins.com/bedguide**.

Boxer Virginia Fuchs listens to the National Anthem before her match.

# Popular Culture 27

## Responding to an Image

In 1953, British naval intelligence officer Ian Fleming wrote a spy novel featuring a character named James Bond, or Agent 007. From the first Bond movie in 1962 (*Dr. No*) to the twenty-third in 2012 (*Skyfall*), the franchise has been an enduring part of popular culture. Above are Sean Connery in *Goldfinger* (1964), Roger Moore in *Live and Let Die* (1973), Daniel Craig in *Quantum of Solace* (2008), and Pierce Brosnan in *Goldeneye* (1995). Why do you think the series has lasted? What is Bond's appeal to men? To women? Pop-culture products sometimes provide alternative worlds and escapes from the ordinary. How does Bond's world fit or deviate from that pattern?

## Web Search

Visit the Movie Poster Database at movieposterdb.com, a site that archives movie posters by year and country. Use the site's filter to find U.S. posters from the current year for a movie that interests you. Then view U.S. movie posters from the past, perhaps from the year when you were born. Look for a movie from a similar genre (for example, a second movie about war or another romantic comedy), and study its posters. Compare and contrast two posters, current and past. How do their visual and written components differ? What techniques or appeals do the advertisers use to sell the movies? What does each poster reveal about the culture of its era or about its intended audience? Write an essay using specific details from the posters to support your thesis or main idea about the pair.

## Mike Haynie

## As Attitudes Shift on PTSD, Media Slow to Remove Stigma

Mike Haynie, U.S. Air Force veteran and Barnes Professor of Entrepreneurship at the Whitman School of Management, serves as the executive director at Syracuse University's Institute for Veterans and Military Families. He also writes articles such as "How to Incentivize Military Service" for *At War: Notes from the Front Lines*, a *New York Times* blog. In the following article, first published on July 2, 2012, in the *New York Times*, Haynie argues that the media plays a key role in determining how our culture perceives veterans with post-traumatic stress disorder.

**AS YOU READ:** How does Haynie support his claim that the media has failed to present an accurate portrait of veterans?

In 1999, President Bill Clinton convened the first White House Summit on Mental Health. The aim of the conference and the public campaign that followed was, in part, to educate the media on the moral and ethical imperative° related to dispelling the stigma associated with mental illness. In a radio address to announce the conference, Mr. Clinton said, "Mental illness is nothing to be ashamed of, but stigma and bias shame us all." 1

In recent years, the Department of Defense has made unprecedented progress toward eliminating the stigma associated with post-traumatic stress disorder° and other mental health issues affecting service members. This cultural shift within the military is a sea change,° as more and more of our service members are seeking and receiving the support they need and deserve 2

**imperative:** Direction or command. **post-traumatic stress disorder:** Also known as PTSD, a condition that could occur after a traumatic experience, which involves depression, anxiety, or other disturbances. **sea change:** Transformation.

from a grateful nation. In the face of that progress, it's unfortunate that some in the media continue to perpetuate a stigma linking military service to mental illness and violence.

This is seen in news articles throughout the country, with some referring to veterans as "ticking time bombs." By describing vets as "time bombs" who are highly trained in "guerrilla warfare," media outlets prove far too careless with regard to providing societal context for isolated acts of violence committed by people who sometimes happen to be veterans. 3

Reporting has been biased toward paper-selling sensationalism° that perpetuates the stigma of a dangerous combat veteran akin to Rambo, invading our neighborhoods and homes. Consider the media coverage of the case of Itzcoatl Ocampo, who has been charged with the murders of several homeless men in California. Some news outlets went as far as to identify him as a former Marine before even mentioning his name. Others were sure to immediately identify him as an Iraq war veteran, and then described how the victims were tracked in a meticulous° manner, blatantly attempting to portray Mr. Ocampo as if he believed he was still on mission. Mr. Ocampo has even been called an "Iraq war veteran" and a "monster" in the same paragraph, connecting the two. 4

If the charges against Mr. Ocampo are proved true, it's very likely he is a monster and a terrible threat—no different from a serial killer who is not a veteran. However, the unfortunate reality is that the message that far too many Americans take away from stories crafted in this way is a stigma that paints all veterans with the same brush, and the color of the paint is disturbing and dangerous. 5

Most unfortunate, and misleading, are the links these reporters imply between military service, mental health and an increased propensity° for extreme violence. In 2008, the *New York Times* published a series of articles focused on "veterans of the wars in Iraq and Afghanistan who have committed killings, or been charged with them, after coming home." The *Times* found "121 cases in which veterans of Iraq and Afghanistan committed a killing, or were charged with one, after their return from war." At the time those articles were published, the population of post-9/11 veterans was about 750,000, an offender rate of 16 homicides per 100,000 veterans. 6

Data from the Department of Justice indicates that the homicide offender rate in the civilian population during that same period varied between 25 and 28 homicides per 100,000 young American males—implying that veterans might actually be less likely than their non-veteran, age-group peers to commit a violent homicide. 7

Also not supported by facts is the link often implied by the media between combat stress and crime in general. A recent study published in the *British Medical Journal* indicates that veterans with combat trauma are no more likely than other people to end up in prison. Further, data from state 8

**sensationalism:** The use of information that will create emotional reaction. **meticulous:** Careful. **propensity:** Inclination.

and federal prisons highlights that the number of incarcerated veterans has at worst remained unchanged, and in many states declined, throughout the past decade of war.

For better or worse, the media will play a large and important role in shaping the cultural narrative that defines this generation of veterans. Unfortunately, that narrative has been a story of extremes to date. At one extreme, it's the story of the veteran as the superhero—unstoppable and iconic.° At the other extreme, it's a narrative that frames the veterans as "broken," whose life course will be defined by post-traumatic stress, domestic violence, suicide, unemployment and homelessness. The result is a caricature° of the American veteran as someone who exclusively represents one of these extremes. 9

The reality is 99 percent of veterans do not represent either extreme. Instead we live our lives in the middle of this continuum. We are teachers, plumbers, doctors, pilots and bus drivers. We're your neighbors. On behalf of this 99 percent, I appeal to the media to keep that in mind while shaping the public narrative that the entire community of veterans will ultimately inherit. 10

## Questions to Start You Thinking

1. **Considering Meaning:** What does Haynie think media outlets should do to improve the fairness and accuracy of reports on veterans?
2. **Identifying Writing Strategies:** How does Haynie use statistics to clarify the picture of U.S. veterans?
3. **Reading Critically:** How does the coverage of Itzcoatl Ocampo's case reveal larger trends in the media? What details of the reporting does Haynie find most telling? Why?
4. **Expanding Vocabulary:** Haynie uses the word *stigma* throughout this essay in describing coverage of veterans. Define *stigma*, and consider why Haynie is concerned with the harm it does to former service members.
5. **Making Connections:** Haynie discusses how media outlets focus on violent behaviors while Gerard Jones ("Violent Media Is Good for Kids," pp. 565–69) analyzes how media can help manage violent tendencies. How does nonfiction media, like journalism, treat violence differently than fictional media, like comic books and movies?

## Journal Prompts

1. In what other cases does the media represent a type of person in terms of extremes? How do these extremes appear in news or other media accounts? Why would it be more useful to see people who exist, as Haynie says, "in the middle of this continuum" (paragraph 10)?

**iconic:** Above reproach; symbolic. **caricature:** Exaggeration or distortion.

2. Well over a decade has passed since President Clinton called for a more nuanced understanding of mental illness. How would you describe current attitudes toward mental illness – either in regard to violent behavior or more generally? In what ways have American attitudes changed?

## Suggestions for Writing

1. One of Haynie's criticisms is that the media implies an inaccurate cause-and-effect relationship between military service and violence. Write an essay analyzing another false cause and effect that concerns you, explaining your more complex view of the relationship.
2. Review media coverage of a recent episode of violence – for example, a school shooting or other attack like that in the movie theater in Colorado. Analyze how these accounts link violence with mental illness. What assumptions do they make about the mental state of those who perpetrate violence?

## Kate Dailey and Abby Ellin

## America's War on the Overweight

Kate Dailey graduated from Pennsylvania State University and Columbia University's Graduate School of Journalism. She is currently the health and lifestyle editor for *Newsweek* and also runs *Newsweek*'s blog "The Human Condition." Abby Ellin has graduate degrees in creative writing from Emerson College and in international relations from Johns Hopkins. Her work has appeared in publications such as the *New York Times, Time,* the *Village Voice, Marie Claire, Glamour,* the *Daily Beast,* and the *Boston Phoenix.* She is also the author of *Teenage Waistland: A Former Fat Kid Weighs In on Living Large, Losing Weight and How Parents Can (and Can't) Help.* In this *Newsweek* essay, Dailey and Ellin grapple with the complicated issues surrounding weight and health in modern America.

**AS YOU READ:** According to the authors, why do so many people have a fat bias?

Practically the minute President Obama announced Regina M. Benjamin, a zaftig° doctor who also has an M.B.A. and is the recipient of a MacArthur "genius grant," as a nominee for the post of Surgeon General, the criticism started. 1

The attacks were vicious – Michael Karolchyk, owner of a Denver "anti-gym," told Fox News' Neil Cavuto, "Obesity is the No. 1 issue facing our country in terms of health and wellness, and she has shown not that she was born this way, not that she woke up one day and was obese. She has shown through being lazy, and making poor food choices, that she's obese." 2

**zaftig:** Full-bodied.

"This is totally disgusting to have someone so big to be advocating health," wrote one YouTube commenter. 3

The anger about Benjamin wasn't the only example of vitriol° hurled at the overweight. Cintra Wilson, style columnist for the *New York Times,* recently wrote a column so disdainful of JCPenney's plus-size mannequins that the *Times'* ombudsman° later wrote that he could read "a virtual sneer" coming through her prose. A *Newsweek* post about *Glamour's* recent plus-size model (in fact, a normal-sized woman with a bit of a belly roll) had several commenters lashing out at the positive reaction the model was receiving. "This model issue is being used as a smoke screen to justify [a] self-destructive lifestyle that cost[s] me more money in health care costs," one wrote. Health guru MeMe Roth has made a career out of bashing fat—she called size 12 *American Idol* Jordin Sparks a "bad role model" on national television, and derided size 2 Jennifer Love Hewitt for having cellulite. (That Roth is considered something of an extremist doesn't stop the media attention.) Virtually any news article about weight that is posted online garners a slew of comments from readers expressing disgust that people let their weight get so out of control. The specific target may change, but the words stay the same: Self-destructive. Disgusting. Disgraceful. Shameful. While the debate rages on about obesity and the best ways to deal with it, the attitudes Americans have toward those with extra pounds are only getting nastier. Just why do Americans hate fat people so much? 4

Fat bias is nothing new. "Public outrage at other people's obesity has a lot to do with America from the turn of the 20th century to about World War I," says Deborah Levine, assistant professor of health policy and management at Providence College. The rise of fat hatred is often seen as connected to the changing American workplace; in the early 20th century, companies began to offer snacks to employees, white-collar jobs became more prominent, and fewer people exercised. As thinness became rarer, says Peter N. Stearns, author of *Fat History: Bodies and Beauty in the Modern West* and professor of history at George Mason University, it was more prized, and conversely, fatness was more maligned. 5

At the same time, people also paid a lot of attention to President Taft's girth; while Taft was large, he wasn't all that much heavier than earlier presidents. Newspapers questioned how his weight would affect diplomacy and solicited the funniest "fat Taft" joke. "This [period] is also when you get ready-to-wear clothing," says Levine. "For the first time, [people were] buying clothes in a certain size, and that encourages a comparison amongst other people." Actuarial tables° began to connect weight and shorter lifespan, and cookbooks published around World War I targeted the overweight. "There was that idea that people who were overweight were hoarding resources needed for the war effort," Levine says. She adds that early concerns were that overweight American men would not be able to compete globally, participate in international business, or win wars. 6

**vitriol:** Abusive and bitter thought or expression. **ombudsman:** A person who investigates problems or complaints and attempts to resolve them. **actuarial tables:** Calculations and statistics used by insurance companies to determine life expectancy of their policyholders.

Fatness has always been seen as a slight on the American character. Ours is a nation that values hard work and discipline, and it's hard for us to accept that weight could be not just a struggle of will, even when the bulk of the research—and often our own personal experience—shows that the factors leading to weight gain are much more than just simple gluttony. "There's this general perception that weight can be controlled if you have enough willpower, that it's just about calories in and calories out," says Dr. Glen Gaesser, professor of exercise and wellness at Arizona State University and author of *Big Fat Lies: The Truth About Your Weight and Your Health,* and that perception leads the nonfat to believe that the overweight are not just unhealthy, but weak and lazy. Even though research suggests that there is a genetic propensity for obesity, and even though some obese people are technically healthier than their skinnier counterparts, the perception remains "[that] it's a failure to control ourselves. It violates everything we have learned about self-control from a very young age," says Gaesser. 7

In a country that still prides itself on its Puritanical ideals, the fat self is the "bad self," the epitome° of greed, gluttony, and sloth. "There's a widespread belief that fat is controllable," says Linda Bacon, author of *Health at Every Size: The Surprising Truth About Your Weight.* "So then it's unlike a disability where you can have compassion; now you can blame the individual and attribute all kinds of mean qualities to them. Then consider the thinner people that are always watching what they eat carefully—fat people are symbols of what they can become if they weren't so virtuous." 8

But considering that the U.S. has already become a size XL nation—66 percent of adults over 20 are considered overweight or obese, according to the Centers for Disease Control—why does the stigma,° and the anger, remain? 9

Call it a case of self-loathing. "A lot of people struggle themselves with their weight, and the same people that tend to get very angry at themselves for not being able to manage their weight are more likely to be biased against the obese," says Marlene Schwartz, director of the Rudd Center for Food Policy and Obesity at Yale University. "I think that some of this is that anger is confusion between the anger that we have at ourselves and projecting that out onto other people." Her research indicates that younger women, who are under the most pressure to be thin and who are also the most likely to be self-critical, are the most likely to feel negatively toward fat people. 10

As many women's magazines' cover lines note, losing the last five pounds can be a challenge. So why don't we have more compassion for people struggling to lose the first 50, 60, or 100? Some of it has to do with the psychological phenomenon known as the fundamental attribution error, a basic belief that whatever problems befall us personally are the result of difficult circumstances, while the same problems in other people are the result of their bad 11

**epitome:** Perfect example. **stigma:** A mark of infamy or disgrace.

choices. Miss a goal at work? It's because the vendor was unreliable, and because your manager isn't giving you enough support, and because the power outage last week cut into premium sales time. That jerk next to you? He blew his quota because he's a bad planner, and because he spent too much time taking personal calls.

The same can be true of weight: "From working with so many people struggling with their weight, I've seen it many times," says Andrew Geier, a postdoctoral fellow in the psychology department at Yale University. "They believe they're overweight due to a myriad of circumstances: as soon as my son goes to college, I'll have time to cook healthier meals; when my husband's shifts change at work, I can get to the gym sooner. . . ." But other people? They're overweight because they don't have the discipline to do the hard work and take off the weight, and that lack of discipline is an affront to our own hard work. (Never mind that weight loss is incredibly difficult to attain: Geier notes that even the most rigorous behavioral programs result in at most about a 12.5 percent decrease in weight, which would take a 350-pound man to a slimmer, but not svelte,° 306 pounds.) 12

But why do the rest of us care so much? What is it about fat people that makes us so mad? As it turns out, we kind of like it. "People actually enjoy feeling angry," says Ryan Martin, associate professor of psychology at the University of Wisconsin, Green Bay, who cites studies done on people's emotions. "It makes them feel powerful, it makes them feel greater control, and they appreciate it for that reason." And with fat people designated as acceptable targets of rage—and with the prevalence of fat people in our lives, both in the malls and on the news—it's easy to find a target for some soul-clearing, ego-boosting ranting. 13

And it may be that, like those World War I–era cookbook writers, we feel that obese people are robbing us of resources, whether it's space in a row of airline seats or our hard-earned tax dollars. Think of health care: when President Obama made reforming health care a priority, it led to an increased focus on obesity as a contributor to health-care costs. A recent article in *Health Affairs,* a public-policy journal, reported that obesity costs $147 billion a year, mainly in insurance premiums and taxes. At the same time, obesity-related diseases such as type 2 diabetes have spiked, and, while diabetes can be treated, treatment is expensive. So the overweight, some people argue, are costing all of us money while refusing to alter the behavior that has put them in their predicament in the first place (i.e., overeating and not exercising). 14

The reality is much more complicated. It's a fallacy to conflate the unhealthy action—overeating and not exercising—with the unhealthy appearance, says Schwartz: some overweight people run marathons; eat only organic, vegetarian fare; and have clean bills of health. Even so, yelling at the overweight to put down the doughnut is far from productive. "People are less likely to seek out healthy behaviors when they're criticized by friends, family, 15

**svelte:** Gracefully slender.

doctors, and others," says Schwartz. "If people tell you that you're disgusting or a slob enough times, you soon start to believe it." In fact, fat outrage might actually make health-care costs higher. In a study published in the 2005 issue of the *Journal of Health Politics, Policy and Law,* Abigail Saguy and Brian Riley found that many overweight people decide not to get help for medical conditions that are more treatable and more risky than obesity because they don't want to deal with their doctor's harassment about their weight. (For instance, a study from the University of North Carolina found that obese women are less likely to receive cervical exams than their thinner counterparts, in part because they worry about being embarrassed or belittled by the doctor because of their weight.)

The bubbling rage against fat people in America has put researchers like Levine in a difficult position. On the one hand, she says, she wants to ensure that obesity is taken seriously as a medical problem, and pointing out the costs associated with obesity-related illnesses helps illustrate the severity of the situation. On the other hand, she says, doing so could increase the animosity people have toward the overweight, many of whom may already live healthy lives or may be working hard to make healthier choices. 16

"The idea is to fight obesity and not obese people," she says, and then pauses. "But it's very hard for many people to disentangle the two." 17

### Questions to Start You Thinking

1. **Considering Meaning:** What is "the fundamental attribution error" (paragraph 11)? Why is it significant for understanding negative attitudes toward overweight people?
2. **Identifying Writing Strategies:** The first four paragraphs of the article provide specific examples of "fat bias." How do they fit into the overall structure of the essay? Why do you think Dailey and Ellin chose these examples?
3. **Reading Critically:** The authors claim that "fat bias is nothing new" (paragraph 5). How effectively do they support this claim? How well do they connect contemporary "fat bias" with a longer historical tradition?
4. **Expanding Vocabulary:** According to one expert, "It's a fallacy to conflate the unhealthy action – overeating and not exercising – with the unhealthy appearance" (paragraph 15). What is a *fallacy*?
5. **Making Connections:** Dailey and Ellin acknowledge that the United States "has already become a size XL nation – 66 percent of adults over 20 are considered overweight or obese" (paragraph 9). They agree with health experts about the "severity of the situation" (paragraph 16). How might Juliet Schor ("The Creation of Discontent," pp. 611–15) interpret this weight problem?

## Journal Prompts

1. Do you agree that Americans believe in hard work, self-discipline, and willpower (paragraph 7) and expect such efforts to prevent weight gain? Explore why you agree, do not agree, or want to qualify this assertion.
2. According to the article, younger women are most pressured about weight, but that pressure seems to cross many demographic lines. Have you ever felt pressure to lose weight? Was it difficult or easy to do so? Did your experience give you any insight about weight, weight loss, or fat bias?

## Suggestions for Writing

1. According to one source in the article, people like being angry because that emotion boosts their sense of power (paragraph 13). Do you agree with this? Write a personal essay exploring why or how people experience anger.
2. Dailey and Ellin describe American hostility toward overweight people as a "bubbling rage" (paragraph 16), examining examples of "fat bias," its history in America, and its psychological origins. Investigate American culture through magazines, movies, music, books, television shows, or politics for evidence to support your own thesis in an essay about attitudes toward fatness and thinness.

## Katha Pollitt

### *The Hunger Games*' Feral Feminism

Katha Pollitt writes on social and political topics, including women's rights, racism, and poverty. Her works include *Reasonable Creatures: Essays on Women and Feminism* (1994) and *Subject to Debate: Sense and Dissents on Women, Politics and Culture* (2001). She currently writes a column for the "Books and the Arts" section of the *Nation*. In the following article, published on the *Nation's* Web site on April 3, 2012, Pollitt reviews the film version of the novel *The Hunger Games*.

**AS YOU READ:** In what ways does Katniss Everdeen follow or break female stereotypes?

As a mad fan of Suzanne Collins's book *The Hunger Games*, I was totally pysched for the film. Secretly, though, I was prepared to be disappointed, because how often does Hollywood do justice to a book you love? The movie does oversimplify a bit, but then, for a book that reads like crack on paper, *The Hunger Games* is a complicated story, with many layers and lots of sharply drawn characters. While it has lost the first-person voice of its scrappy heroine, Katniss Everdeen, it's amazing how much of the book the movie gets right. 1

There are many ways to analyze *The Hunger Games*. You can see it as a savage satire of late capitalism: in a dystopian° future version of North America called Panem, the 1 percent rule through brute force, starvation, technological wizardry and constant surveillance. The Games exemplify these methods: as punishment for a past rebellion, each of the twelve districts of Panem must sacrifice two teenagers, a boy and a girl, to come to the Capitol (*sic*)° and compete in a televised ritual of murder and survivalism until only one is left. Tea Partiers° can imagine an allegory° of oppressive Washington, and traditionalists can revel in the ancient trope° of the moral superiority of the countryside: the district people are poor and downtrodden and wear Depression-style clothes but they live in families, sing folk songs and have a strong sense of community. In the Capitol, which has the dated-futuristic look of a fascist° Oz, the lifestyle is somewhere between the late Roman Empire, the court of Louis XVI and the Cirque du Soleil. You can also read the book as an indictment° of reality television, in which a bored and cynical audience amuses itself watching desperate people destroy themselves, and the movie plays this angle for all it's worth. When the unctuous° Games host Caesar Flickerman (Stanley Tucci, in a startling blue wig) interviews the teens about to be murdered as if they were trying out for *American Idol*, you start to wonder when we'll see Perez Hilton° chatting up death row prisoners on *Entertainment Tonight* ("Any last words for your family?"). 2

The element that is the most striking to me, though, is Katniss, portrayed in the film by the splendid Jennifer Lawrence. Katniss has qualities usually given to boys: a hunter who's kept her mother and sister from starving since she was 11, she's intrepid° and tough, better at killing rabbits than expressing her feelings, a skilled bargainer in the black market for meat. No teenage vegetarian she! At the same time, she's feminine: never aggressive or swaggering, tenderhearted and protective of the defenseless—when her little sister Prim's name is chosen for the Games, Katniss volunteers to take her place; during the games she risks death to protect the lovable girlchild Rue (Amandla Stenberg). Not to get too literary about this most popular of popular fiction, you can see Katniss as a version of the goddess Artemis, protectress of the young and huntress with a silver bow and arrows like the ones Katniss carries in the Games. Like the famously virginal goddess, Katniss is an independent spirit: she is not about her looks, her clothes, her weight, her popularity, gossip, drama or boys. The great Stuart Klawans° made a rare slip writing in these pages that Katniss is a typical young-adult heroine, "greatly worried" about whether "guy number one" likes her and what "guy number two might think about that." The whole 3

**dystopian:** Referring to an unpleasant or oppressive imaginary society. ***sic*:** A word that shows an error in the original material; here, Pollitt thinks *Capitol* should be spelled *capital*. **Tea Partiers:** A conservative group that became popular in 2009. **allegory:** A story or image whose characters and actions symbolize ideas. **trope:** Common theme or expression that plays on a word's meaning. **fascist:** Governed by a dictatorial, nationalist political regime. **indictment:** Condemnation. **unctuous:** Overly flattering in a distasteful way. **Perez Hilton:** An online gossip columnist. **intrepid:** Fearless. **Stuart Klawans:** A film critic for the *Nation*.

plot turns on Katniss being so romantically uninterested in Peeta, her fellow District 12 Games contestant, she doesn't realize he's in love with her. When she's not convinced he's trying to kill her, she believes he's pretending to be smitten with her to gain sympathy (and help) from the invisible TV audience. She rescues him several times anyway. As for "guy number two" back home, the devastatingly handsome Gale (Liam Hemsworth), Katniss only fleetingly thinks there might be more than friendship there. Mostly she is just trying to survive without becoming a horrible person.

Katniss is a rare thing in pop fiction: a complex female character with courage, brains and a quest of her own. She's Jo March° as coal miner's daughter in hunting boots, the opposite of Bella, the famously drippy, love-obsessed heroine of the *Twilight* books—and unlike clever and self-possessed Hermione of the *Harry Potter* series, she's the lead, not a sidekick. We're worlds away from the vicious-little-rich-girls of *Gossip Girl* and its many knockoffs, where everything revolves around looks, clothes, consumerism, social status and sexual competition. 4

She is a rare thing in real-life girl culture, too, where the latest news is of Dara-Lynn Weiss's *Vogue* article—and book deal—recounting the rigid diet regimen she forced on her 7-year-old daughter. (At least Amy Chua browbeat her daughters to read books and play musical instruments!) What does it say about us that so many mocked the slender Lawrence's Katniss as too "big"? It's true that in the book, Katniss is underfed, like almost everyone in the districts, but in the movie none of the other Games contestants are skinny either, and they all look fit and healthy, even tiny Rue, who in the book has never even had a whole bird leg to herself. Besides, the anorectic cookie-cutter young actresses favored by Hollywood don't have the acting chops for this role. Lawrence, who played another hardscrabble heroine in *Winter's Bone*, brings to life the hidden tenderness that is one key to Katniss's character. 5

The other key is Katniss's moral centeredness. Unlike most of the contestants, she kills only in self-defense. Life as a celebrity—winners are feted° and made rich for life—repels her. When she thinks about fairness and justice, she's thinking about social class and political power, not about who gets to be prom queen. What would she make of the racist response of some fans to the casting of black actors as Rue and another beloved character, Thresh? I suspect she'd be as contemptuous of them as she is of the hyperprivileged darlings of the Capitol. 6

## Questions to Start You Thinking

1. **Considering Meaning:** Pollitt professes to being a "mad fan" of both the book, *The Hunger Games*, and the movie adapted from it (paragraph 1). What does she admire about the heroine, Katniss? Why?

**Jo March:** The heroine in *Little Women*. **feted:** Honored.

2. **Identifying Writing Strategies:** In paragraph 2, Pollitt mentions several ways to analyze the *Hunger Games* film. Summarize these approaches, and then consider why she includes them in this essay. What do they suggest about the audience for popular fiction and films?
3. **Reading Critically:** Different viewers might take away different political messages from this movie. What does Pollitt tell us about how one film—or one work of literature—can suggest such different interpretations?
4. **Expanding Vocabulary:** The lead character, Katniss, reacts against "hyperprivileged" (paragraph 6) characters in *The Hunger Games*. What does the prefix *hyper-* add to the world *privileged*? How does this compound word describe the culture of the fictional world of Panem?
5. **Making Connections:** Katniss is a strong heroine in part because she has "qualities usually given to boys," yet she is also "feminine" (paragraph 3). Consider Pollitt's comments about how Katniss combines characteristics typically associated with men or women in light of Julie Zeilinger's discussion of limitations in male and female roles ("Guys Suffer from Oppressive Gender Roles Too," pp. 538–42). To what extent would Zeilinger admire Katniss? Would her reasons be similar to Pollitt's or different?

## Journal Prompts

1. In paragraph 4, Pollitt compares Katniss with other heroines in popular culture, from *Little Women* to *Gossip Girl*. Write about a heroine you think compares either favorably or unfavorably to the kind of character Pollitt describes. What are her most important qualities? What do they tell us about the values of the book or film that introduces her to us?
2. Pollitt describes the capital of Panem as "a fascist Oz" (paragraph 2). If you were the production designer for a movie like this, how would you create the look of a frightening future? What would your dystopian world look like? How would your vision convey present worries about the future?

## Suggestions for Writing

1. Pollitt argues that *The Hunger Games* makes readers and viewers consider what reality television might look like when taken to extremes. Taking into account your own responses to reality programs, do you think she is being an alarmist about this form of television entertainment, or is there something worrisome in reality shows? Write an essay that takes a stand on this question—either arguing for the redeeming features of reality TV or supporting Pollitt's reservations about it.
2. Choose a film adaptation of a short story or book, and evaluate changes the filmmakers made to the original story. Why do these changes make the film more or less satisfying than the book?

## James McBride

# Full Circle

James McBride is a Distinguished Writer in Residence at New York University as well as a successful author and musician. McBride has worked as a staff writer for the *Washington Post*, *People Magazine*, and the *Boston Globe* and has had articles published in *Essence*, *Rolling Stone*, and the *New York Times*. His novel *The Color of Water* (2004) appeared on the *New York Times* bestseller list for over two years. His compositions for musical theater have earned him the Stephen Sondheim Award and the Richard Rodgers Foundation Horizon Award. In this selection from "Hip-Hop Planet," first published in *National Geographic* in April 2007, McBride traces the cultural roots of hip-hop music.

**AS YOU READ:** Identify the relationship between hip-hop and African culture.

You breathe in and breathe out a few times and you are there. Eight hours and a wake-up shake on the flight from New York, and you are on the tarmac in Dakar, Senegal. Welcome to Africa. The assignment: Find the roots of hip-hop. The music goes full circle. The music comes home to Africa. That whole bit. Instead it was the old reporter's joke: You go out to cover a story and the story covers you. The stench of poverty in my nostrils was so strong it pulled me to earth like a hundred-pound ring in my nose. Dakar's Sandaga market is full of "local color"—unless you live there. It was packed and filthy, stalls full of new merchandise surrounded by shattered pieces of life everywhere, broken pipes, bicycle handlebars, fruit flies, soda bottles, beggars, dogs, cell phones. A teenage beggar, his body malformed by polio, crawled by on hands and feet, like a spider. He said, "Hey brother, help me." When I looked into his eyes, they were a bottomless ocean. 1

The Hotel Teranga is a fortress, packed behind a concrete wall where beggars gather at the front gate. The French tourists march past them, the women in high heels and stonewashed jeans. They sidle° through downtown Dakar like royalty, haggling in the market, swimming in the hotel pool with their children, a scene that resembles Birmingham, Alabama, in the 1950s—the blacks serving, the whites partying. Five hundred yards (460 meters) away, Africans eat off the sidewalk and sell peanuts for a pittance.° There is a restlessness, a deep sense of something gone wrong in the air. 2

The French can't smell it, even though they've had a mouthful back home. A good amount of the torching of Paris suburbs in October 2005 was courtesy of the children of immigrants from former French African colonies, exhausted from being bottled up in housing projects for generations with no job prospects. They telegraphed the punch in their music—France is the second largest hip-hop market in the world—but the message was ignored. Around the globe, rap music has become a universal expression of outrage, its macho pose borrowed from commercial hip-hop in the U.S. 3

**sidle:** Moving sideways to edge forward. **pittance:** Very little money.

In Dakar, where every kid is a microphone and turntable away from squalor,° and American rapper Tupac Shakur's° picture hangs in market stalls of folks who don't understand English, rap is king. There are hundreds of rap groups in Senegal today. French television crews troop in and out of Dakar's nightclubs filming the kora harp lute and tama talking drum° with regularity. But beneath the drumming and the dance lessons and the jingling sound of tourist change, there is a quiet rage, a desperate fury among the Senegalese, some of whom seem to bear an intense dislike of their former colonial rulers. "We know all about French history," says Abdou Ba, a Senegalese producer and musician. "We know about their kings, their castles, their art, their music. We know everything about them. But they don't know much about us." 4

Assane N'Diaye, 19, loves hip-hop music. Before he left his Senegalese village to work as a DJ in Dakar, he was a fisherman, just like his father, like his father's father before him. Tall, lean, with a muscular build and a handsome chocolate face, Assane became a popular DJ, but the equipment he used was borrowed, and when his friend took it back, success eluded him. He has returned home to Toubab Dialaw, about 25 miles (40 kilometers) south of Dakar, a village marked by a huge boulder, perhaps 40 feet (12 meters) high, facing the Atlantic Ocean. 5

About a century and a half ago, a local ruler led a group of people fleeing slave traders to this place. He was told by a white trader to come here, to Toubab Dialaw. When he arrived, the slavers followed. A battle ensued. The ruler fought bravely but was killed. The villagers buried him by the sea and marked his grave with a small stone, and over the years it is said to have sprouted like a tree planted by God. It became a huge, arching boulder that stares out to sea, protecting the village behind it. When the fishermen went deep out to sea, the boulder was like a lighthouse that marked the way home. The Great Rock of Toubab Dialaw is said to hold a magic spirit, a spirit that Assane N'Diaye believes in. 6

In the shadow of the Great Rock, Assane has built a small restaurant, Chez Las, decorated with hundreds of seashells. It is where he lives his hip-hop dream. At night, he and his brother and cousin stand by the Great Rock and face the sea. They meditate. They pray. Then they write rap lyrics that are worlds away from the bling-bling culture° of today's commercial hip-hoppers. They write about their lives as village fishermen, the scarcity of catch forcing them to fish in deeper and deeper waters, the hardship of fishing for 8, 10, 14 days at a time in an open pirogue° in rainy season, the high fee they pay to rent the boat, and the paltry price their catches fetch on the market. They write about the humiliation of poverty, watching their town sprout up around them with rich Dakarians and richer French. And they write about the relatives who leave in the morning and never return, surrendered to the sea, sharks, and God. 7

**squalor:** Filthy conditions. **Tupac Shakur:** (1971–1996) An influential American rapper in the early to mid 1990s. **kora harp lute and tama talking drum:** Traditional African instruments. **bling-bling culture:** Culture based on flashy consumerism. **pirogue:** A small, flat-bottomed boat used for fishing.

The dream, of course, is to make a record. They have their own demo, their own logo, and their own name, Salam T. D. (for Toubab Dialaw). But rap music represents a deeper dream: a better life. "We want money to help our parents," Assane says over dinner. "We watch our mothers boil water to cook and have nothing to put in the pot." 8

He fingers his food lightly. "Rap doesn't belong to American culture," he says. "It belongs here. It has always existed here, because of our pain and our hardships and our suffering." 9

On this cool evening in a restaurant above their village, these young men, clad in baseball caps and T-shirts, appear no different from their African-American counterparts, with one exception. After a dinner of chicken and rice, Assane says something in Wolof to the others. Silently and without ceremony, they take every bit of the leftover dinner – the half-eaten bread, rice, pieces of chicken, the chicken bones – and dump them into a plastic bag to give to the children in the village. They silently rise from the table and proceed outside. The last I see of them, their regal figures are outlined in the dim light of the doorway, heading out to the darkened village, holding on to that bag as though it held money. 10

## Questions to Start You Thinking

1. **Considering Meaning:** McBride quotes musician Abdou Ba saying that Senegalese people know a great deal about French history and culture but that the French "don't know much about us" (paragraph 4). How does this sentiment apply to the music that McBride travels to Senegal to investigate? What do the Senegalese learn from listening to American hip-hop? What might Europeans or Americans miss in listening to Senegalese music?
2. **Identifying Writing Strategies:** How does McBride vividly depict the Senegalese people and the French tourists in their land? In what ways do these descriptions highlight the contrast – and anticipate the conflict – between the two groups?
3. **Reading Critically:** Analyze the Great Rock (paragraph 6) as a symbol in Assane N'Diaye's life. What role does it play in the music he creates?
4. **Expanding Vocabulary:** What does McBride mean when he says hip-hop music *telegraphed* the unrest among immigrants in the Paris suburbs (paragraph 3)? Define *telegraph* when used as a verb, and then consider how it describes the appearance of young people's frustration in music.
5. **Making Connections:** Gerard Jones ("Violent Media Is Good for Kids," pp. 565–69) describes children using popular culture to release their feelings of anger and powerlessness. In what ways does the music McBride describes serve similar purposes? Explore any similarities you see.

## Journal Prompts

1. Why might Tupac Shakur be a model for Senegalese youth? Do you think these young people see something different from what Americans see in him? Or is his appeal similar around the world? Why?
2. What do you think is uniquely American about hip-hop or rap music? What is universal? Why do you think hip-hop has become so popular around the world?

## Suggestions for Writing

1. At the beginning of this excerpt, McBride describes traveling from a familiar place to a very foreign one. Recall a trip – whether distant like McBride's or closer to home – in which you felt as if you encountered an entirely new place. What was it like to be an outsider in this place?
2. Compare and contrast the subjects of Assane N'Diaye's music with the subjects of American hip-hop. How does the content of the music reflect cultural differences or different aspirations in life?

## Stephen King

## Why We Crave Horror Movies

Stephen King was born in 1947 in Portland, Maine, and attended the University of Maine at Orono. He now lives in Bangor, Maine, where he writes his best-selling horror novels, many of which have been made into popular movies. The prolific King is also the author of screenplays, teleplays, short fiction, essays, e-books, novels under the pseudonym Richard Bachman, and *On Writing: A Memoir of the Craft* (2000). His well-known horror novels include *Carrie* (1974), *Firestarter* (1980), *Pet Sematary* (1983), *Misery* (1987), *The Green Mile* (1996), and *Hearts in Atlantis* (1999). His recent books include the final installments of his epic fantasy series *The Dark Tower,* the short story collaboration with his son Joe Hill called *In the Tall Grass* (2012), and the novels *Doctor Sleep* and *Joyland* (2013). Since 2003, King has also written a regular column on pop culture for *Entertainment Weekly.* In the following essay, first published in *Playboy* in December 1981, King draws on his extensive experience with horror to explain the human craving to be frightened.

**AS YOU READ:** Identify the needs that King says horror movies fulfill for viewers.

I think that we're all mentally ill; those of us outside the asylums only hide it a little better – and maybe not all that much better, after all. We've all known people who talk to themselves, people who sometimes squinch their faces into horrible grimaces when they believe no one is watching, people who have some hysterical fear – of snakes, the dark, the tight place, the long drop . . . and, of course, those final worms and grubs that are waiting so patiently underground. 1

When we pay our four or five bucks and seat ourselves at tenth-row center in a theater showing a horror movie, we are daring the nightmare. 2

Why? Some of the reasons are simple and obvious. To show that we can, that we are not afraid, that we can ride this roller coaster. Which is not to say that a really good horror movie may not surprise a scream out of us at some point, the way we may scream when the roller coaster twists through a complete 360 or plows through a lake at the bottom of the drop. And horror movies, like roller coasters, have always been the special province° of the young; by the time one turns forty or fifty, one's appetite for double twists or 360-degree loops may be considerably depleted. 3

We also go to reestablish our feelings of essential normality; the horror movie is innately conservative, even reactionary. Freda Jackson as the horrible melting woman in *Die, Monster, Die!* confirms for us that no matter how far we may be removed from the beauty of a Robert Redford or a Diana Ross, we are still light-years from true ugliness. 4

And we go to have fun. 5

Ah, but this is where the ground starts to slope away, isn't it? Because this is a very peculiar sort of fun indeed. The fun comes from seeing others menaced—sometimes killed. One critic suggested that if pro football has become the voyeur's° version of combat, then the horror film has become the modern version of the public lynching. 6

It is true that the mythic, "fairy-tale" horror film intends to take away the shades of gray.... It urges us to put away our more civilized and adult penchant° for analysis and to become children again, seeing things in pure blacks and whites. It may be that horror movies provide psychic relief on this level because this invitation to lapse into simplicity, irrationality, and even outright madness is extended so rarely. We are told we may allow our emotions a free rein . . . or no rein at all. 7

If we are all insane, then sanity becomes a matter of degree. If your insanity leads you to carve up women like Jack the Ripper or the Cleveland Torso Murderer, we clap you away in the funny farm (but neither of those two amateur-night surgeons was ever caught, heh-heh-heh); if, on the other hand, your insanity leads you only to talk to yourself when you're under stress or to pick your nose on your morning bus, then you are left alone to go about your business . . . though it is doubtful that you will ever be invited to the best parties. 8

The potential lyncher is in almost all of us (excluding saints, past and present; but then, most saints have been crazy in their own ways), and every now and then, he has to be let loose to scream and roll around in the grass. Our emotions and our fears form their own body, and we recognize that it demands its own exercise to maintain proper muscle tone. Certain of these emotional muscles are accepted—even exalted—in civilized society; they are, of course, the emotions that tend to maintain the status quo° of civilization 9

**province:** Sphere; area of interest. **voyeur:** One who takes inordinate pleasure in the act of watching. **penchant:** Strong inclination. **status quo:** Existing state of affairs.

itself. Love, friendship, loyalty, kindness—these are all the emotions that we applaud, emotions that have been immortalized in the couplets of Hallmark cards and in the verses (I don't dare call it poetry) of Leonard Nimoy.

When we exhibit these emotions, society showers us with positive rein- 10
forcement; we learn this even before we get out of diapers. When, as children, we hug our rotten little puke of a sister and give her a kiss, all the aunts and uncles smile and twit and cry, "Isn't he the sweetest little thing?" Such coveted treats as chocolate-covered graham crackers often follow. But if we deliberately slam the rotten little puke of a sister's fingers in the door, sanctions follow—angry remonstrance° from parents, aunts, and uncles; instead of a chocolate-covered graham cracker, a spanking.

But anticivilization emotions don't go away, and they demand periodic 11
exercise. We have such "sick" jokes as "What's the difference between a truckload of bowling balls and a truckload of dead babies?" (You can't unload the truckload of bowling balls with a pitchfork . . . a joke, by the way, that I heard originally from a ten-year-old.) Such a joke may surprise a laugh or a grin out of us even as we recoil, a possibility that confirms the thesis: if we share a brotherhood of man, then we also share an insanity of man. None of which is intended as a defense of either the sick joke or insanity but merely as an explanation of [how] the best horror films, like the best fairy tales, manage to be reactionary, anarchistic, and revolutionary all at the same time.

The mythic horror movie, like the sick joke, has a dirty job to do. It deliber- 12
ately appeals to all that is worst in us. It is morbidity unchained, our most base instincts let free, our nastiest fantasies realized . . . and it all happens, fittingly enough, in the dark. For those reasons, good liberals often shy away from horror films. For myself, I like to see the most aggressive of them—*Dawn of the Dead,* for instance—as lifting a trapdoor in the civilized forebrain and throwing a basket of raw meat to the hungry alligators swimming around in that subterranean river beneath.

Why bother? Because it keeps them from getting out, man, it keeps them 13
down there and me up here. It was Lennon and McCartney who said that all you need is love, and I would agree with that.

As long as you keep the gators fed. 14

## Questions to Start You Thinking

1. **Considering Meaning:** What does King mean when he says that "we're all mentally ill" (paragraph 1)? Is this a serious statement? Why, or why not?
2. **Identifying Writing Strategies:** How does King use analysis, breaking a complex topic into parts, to support his argument?

**remonstrance:** Objection.

3. **Reading Critically:** Why do you think King uses the inclusive pronoun *we* so frequently throughout his essay? What effect does the use of this pronoun have on your response to his argument?
4. **Expanding Vocabulary:** Define *innately* (paragraph 4). What does King mean when he says horror movies are "innately conservative"? Does he contradict himself when he says they are also "reactionary, anarchistic, and revolutionary" (paragraph 11)? Why, or why not?
5. **Making Connections:** In "Black Men and Public Space" (pp. 520–23), Brent Staples writes about the reflexive fear and anxiety he arouses in people when walking at night. How might King's view of human nature help explain the reactions to Staples?

## Link to the Paired Essay

King claims that "by the time one turns forty or fifty" (paragraph 3) the desire for the thrills provided by horror movies, like those offered by roller coasters, might be diminished. Why does King believe this is true? How might Gerard Jones ("Violent Media Is Good for Kids," pp. 565–69), who focuses on the fantasy lives of children, explain such changes as people age?

## Journal Prompts

1. What is your response to "sick" jokes? Why?
2. Recall a movie that exercised your "anticivilization emotions" (paragraph 11). Describe your state of mind before, during, and after the movie.

## Suggestions for Writing

1. What genre of movie do you prefer to watch, and why? What cravings does this type of movie satisfy?
2. Do you agree that "the horror film has become the modern version of the public lynching" (paragraph 6)? Write an argument in which you defend or refute this suggestion, citing examples from King's essay and from your own moviegoing experience to support your position.

## Gerard Jones

### Violent Media Is Good for Kids

Gerard Jones began his career as a writer for *National Lampoon* magazine in 1983. He later wrote comic books for Marvel Comics and other publishers for several years, working on the *Green Lantern, Justice League*, and *Batman* series, among others. His books include *Killing Monsters: Why Children Need Fantasy, Superheroes, and Make-Believe Violence* (2002) and *Men of Tomorrow: Geeks, Gangsters, and the Birth of the Comic Book* (2004). In the following article, which first appeared in *Mother Jones* in 2000, Jones argues that engaging in fantasy violence can have a positive effect on children.

**AS YOU READ:** Identify the ways in which Jones supports his argument.

1 At 13 I was alone and afraid. Taught by my well-meaning, progressive, English-teacher parents that violence was wrong, that rage was something to be overcome and cooperation was always better than conflict, I suffocated my deepest fears and desires under a nice-boy persona. Placed in a small, experimental school that was wrong for me, afraid to join my peers in their bumptious° rush into adolescent boyhood, I withdrew into passivity and loneliness. My parents, not trusting the violent world of the 1960s, built a wall between me and the crudest elements of American pop culture.

2 Then the Incredible Hulk smashed through it.

3 One of my mother's students convinced her that Marvel Comics, despite their apparent juvenility and violence, were in fact devoted to lofty messages of pacifism° and tolerance. My mother borrowed some, thinking they'd be good for me. And so they were. But not because they preached lofty messages of benevolence.° They were good for me because they were juvenile. And violent.

4 The character who caught me, and freed me, was the Hulk: overgendered and undersocialized, half-naked and half-witted, raging against a frightened world that misunderstood and persecuted him. Suddenly I had a fantasy self to carry my stifled rage and buried desire for power. I had a fantasy self who was a self: unafraid of his desires and the world's disapproval, unhesitating and effective in action. "Puny boy follow Hulk!" roared my fantasy self, and I followed.

5 I followed him to new friends—other sensitive geeks chasing their own inner brutes—and I followed him to the arrogant, self-exposing, self-assertive, superheroic decision to become a writer. Eventually, I left him behind, followed more sophisticated heroes, and finally my own lead along a twisting path to a career and an identity. In my 30s, I found myself writing action movies and comic books. I wrote some Hulk stories, and met the geek-geniuses who created him. I saw my own creations turned into action figures, cartoons, and computer games. I talked to the kids who read my stories. Across generations, genders, and ethnicities I kept seeing the same story: people pulling themselves out of emotional traps by immersing themselves in violent stories. People integrating the scariest, most fervently denied fragments

**bumptious:** Annoyingly conceited. **pacifism:** Peacefulness. **benevolence:** Goodwill.

of their psyches into fuller senses of selfhood through fantasies of superhuman combat and destruction.

I have watched my son living the same story—transforming himself into a bloodthirsty dinosaur to embolden° himself for the plunge into preschool, a Power Ranger to muscle through a social competition in kindergarten. In the first grade, his friends started climbing a tree at school. But he was afraid: of falling, of the centipedes crawling on the trunk, of sharp branches, of his friends' derision.° I took my cue from his own fantasies and read him old Tarzan comics, rich in combat and bright with flashing knives. For two weeks he lived in them. Then he put them aside. And he climbed the tree. 6

But all the while, especially in the wake of the recent burst of school shootings, I heard pop psychologists insisting that violent stories are harmful to kids, heard teachers begging parents to keep their kids away from "junk culture," heard a guilt-stricken friend with a son who loved Pokémon lament, "I've turned into the bad mom who lets her kid eat sugary cereal and watch cartoons!" 7

That's when I started the research. 8

"Fear, greed, power-hunger, rage: these are aspects of our selves that we try not to experience in our lives but often want, even need, to experience vicariously° through stories of others," writes Melanie Moore, Ph.D., a psychologist who works with urban teens. "Children need violent entertainment in order to explore the inescapable feelings that they've been taught to deny, and to reintegrate those feelings into a more whole, more complex, more resilient° selfhood." 9

Moore consults to public schools and local governments, and is also raising a daughter. For the past three years she and I have been studying the ways in which children use violent stories to meet their emotional and developmental needs—and the ways in which adults can help them use those stories healthily. With her help I developed Power Play, a program for helping young people improve their self-knowledge and sense of potency° through heroic, combative storytelling. 10

We've found that every aspect of even the trashiest pop-culture story can have its own developmental function. Pretending to have superhuman powers helps children conquer the feelings of powerlessness that inevitably come with being so young and small. The dual-identity concept at the heart of many superhero stories helps kids negotiate the conflicts between the inner self and the public self as they work through the early stages of socialization. Identification with a rebellious, even destructive, hero helps children learn to push back against a modern culture that cultivates fear and teaches dependency. 11

At its most fundamental level, what we call "creative violence"—head-bonking cartoons, bloody video games, playground karate, toy guns—gives children a tool to master their rage. Children will feel rage. Even the sweetest and most civilized of them, even those whose parents read the better class of literary magazines, will feel rage. The world is uncontrollable and incompre- 12

**embolden:** Encourage. **derision:** Ridicule. **vicariously:** Experienced secondhand through the experiences of someone else. **resilient:** Able to bounce back. **potency:** Power.

hensible; mastering it is a terrifying, enraging task. Rage can be an energizing emotion, a shot of courage to push us to resist greater threats, take more control, than we ever thought we could. But rage is also the emotion our culture distrusts the most. Most of us are taught early on to fear our own. Through immersion in imaginary combat and identification with a violent protagonist,° children engage the rage they've stifled, come to fear it less, and become more capable of utilizing it against life's challenges.

I knew one little girl who went around exploding with fantasies so violent 13 that other moms would draw her mother aside to whisper, "I think you should know something about Emily. . . ." Her parents were separating, and she was small, an only child, a tomboy at an age when her classmates were dividing sharply along gender lines. On the playground she acted out "*Sailor Moon*"° fights, and in the classroom she wrote stories about people being stabbed with knives. The more adults tried to control her stories, the more she acted out the roles of her angry heroes: breaking rules, testing limits, roaring threats.

Then her mother and I started helping her tell her stories. She wrote 14 them, performed them, drew them like comics: sometimes bloody, sometimes tender, always blending the images of pop culture with her own most private fantasies. She came out of it just as fiery and strong, but more self-controlled and socially competent: a leader among her peers, the one student in her class who could truly pull boys and girls together.

I worked with an older girl, a middle-class "nice-girl," who held herself to- 15 gether through a chaotic family situation and a tumultuous adolescence with gangsta rap. In the mythologized street violence of Ice T,° the rage and strutting of his music and lyrics, she found a theater of the mind in which she could be powerful, ruthless, invulnerable. She avoided the heavy drug use that sank many of her peers, and flowered in college as a writer and political activist.

I'm not going to argue that violent entertainment is harmless. I think it has 16 helped inspire some people to real-life violence. I am going to argue that it's helped hundreds of people for every one it's hurt, and that it can help far more if we learn to use it well. I am going to argue that our fear of "youth violence" isn't well-founded on reality, and that the fear can do more harm than the reality. We act as though our highest priority is to prevent our children from growing up into murderous thugs—but modern kids are far more likely to grow up too passive, too distrustful of themselves, too easily manipulated.

We send the message to our children in a hundred ways that their craving 17 for imaginary gun battles and symbolic killings is wrong, or at least dangerous. Even when we don't call for censorship or forbid "*Mortal Kombat*,"° we moan to other parents within our kids' earshot the "awful violence" in the entertainment they love. We tell our kids that it isn't nice to playfight, or we steer them from some monstrous action figure to a *pro-social doll*. Even in the most progressive households, where we make such a point of letting children feel what

**protagonist:** A leading character. ***Sailor Moon*:** A Japanese comic book and cartoon that centers around a magical female warrior. **Ice T:** A rapper from the 1980s and 1990s whose raps included violent lyrics; he went on to star in *Law & Order: Special Victims Unit*. ***Mortal Kombat*:** A fighting video game known for its violent imagery and gore.

they feel, we rush to substitute an enlightened discussion for the raw material of rageful fantasy. In the process, we risk confusing them about their natural aggression in the same way the Victorians confused their children about their sexuality. When we try to protect our children from their own feelings and fantasies, we shelter them not against violence but against power and selfhood.

## Questions to Start You Thinking

1. **Considering Meaning:** Jones argues against the common assumption that young people should be shielded from violence. How does he make his case that this assumption may be harmful to children?
2. **Identifying Writing Strategies:** Jones uses two one-sentence paragraphs (2 and 8) in his essay. What is the function of each of these? Why do you think Jones chose not to develop either paragraph in the usual manner?
3. **Reading Critically:** How convincing is Jones's explanation of how adults can help children to use violent fantasies in a healthy way? What does his program of "creative violence" (paragraph 12) involve?
4. **Expanding Vocabulary:** Jones describes himself identifying with *superhuman* elements in comic books. What does it mean to be *superhuman*? How does the dream of being *superhuman* contribute to his development?
5. **Making Connections:** How similar are the impulses Jones describes as socially unacceptable to the ideals of masculinity Robert Jensen argues we should do away with in "The High Cost of Manliness" (pp. 534–38)? Compare the two authors' ideas about aggression, anger, and other potentially destructive feelings.

## Link to the Paired Essay

Both Jones and Stephen King in "Why We Crave Horror Movies" (pp. 561–64) assume that, by their nature, humans will have feelings that run counter to the way they have been socialized. Which emotions does each author focus on? How do they think people can manage these feelings?

## Journal Prompts

1. Jones describes his son turning to stories of violent characters at crucial moments in his life. Has identifying with a person or a character from popular culture helped you through similar transitions? Who, real or fictional, has helped you gain confidence and meet challenges? Why?
2. Where would you draw the line between "creative violence" (paragraph 12) and representations that could harm children? Are there any stories, characters, or images that should be off limits to young audiences? Why or why not?

### Suggestions for Writing

1. Compare and contrast Jones's attitude toward violence with that of his parents. What assumptions about humans underlie each of their positions? Which do you think is more valid?
2. Jones recalls hearing another parent equate letting her child watch cartoons with giving him unhealthy food (paragraph 7). Read a few parenting articles or blogs about media exposure for children. Then write an essay that takes a stand on this question – is violence in the media an intellectual equivalent to junk food, or does it help to nourish the mind, as Jones claims?

## e Chuck Klosterman

Text

## My Zombie, Myself: Why Modern Life Feels Rather Undead

Chuck Klosterman has written the bestsellers *Sex, Drugs, and Cocoa Puffs: A Low Culture Manifesto* (2003) and *The Visible Man* (2011). His first book, *Fargo Rock City: A Heavy Metal Odyssey in North Dakota* (2001), won the 2002 ASCAP Deems Taylor Award. Besides his articles for *GQ*, *Esquire*, *Spin*, the *Washington Post*, the *Guardian*, and *ESPN the Magazine*, he currently writes the "Ethicist" column for the *New York Times Magazine*. In the following article written for the *New York Times* in December 2010, Klosterman examines the current popularity of zombies in our culture. To read this essay, go to Chapter 27: **bedfordstmartins.com/bedguide**.

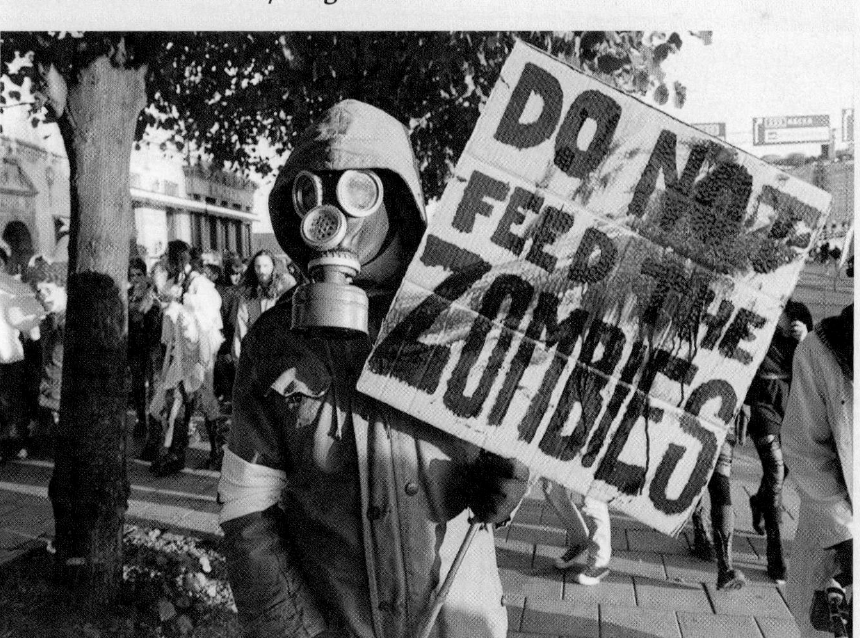


Chuck Klosterman posits, "A lot of modern life is like slaughtering zombies."

## Brad Shoup

Multimodal Essay

# "Harlem Shake" vs. History: Is the YouTube Novelty Hits Era That Novel?

Every so often a song or dance – or a music video showing a song *and* a dance – catches fire in the popular culture, and all of a sudden it is seen and heard *a lot*. Most people assume that YouTube is behind any such craze and that the Web is the only way that fads can spread quickly and widely.

Brad Shoup is a writer in Austin, Texas, and frequent contributor to *Stereogum* and other music blogs and Web sites. He looks in particular at Baauer's "Harlem Shake" and sees the novelty dance craze as a phenomenon with deep roots. To read his article and watch a related video, go to Chapter 27: **bedfordstmartins.com/bedguide**.

Baauer

# Digital Living

# 28

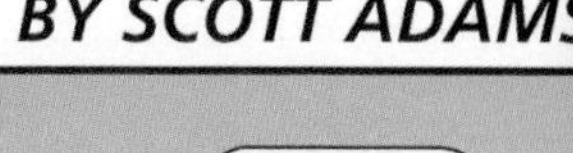

### Responding to an Image

Read this comic strip frame by frame, and summarize its basic story. Overall, what is the comic strip poking fun at? How does it combine text and visual images to comment on the difficulty of keeping up with technological change? What roles do ego and competition play in today's digital living?

### Web Search

Think of a topic of great personal interest to you – a hobby, a political or social issue, a subject of study, something you know a lot about. Then look for varied Web sites devoted to this topic, especially social-networking pages, chat rooms, blogs, and other interactive sites where individuals come together to share their views on the topic. As you browse through such

sites, think about the communities the Web creates. How do people relate to one another online? What do they learn from one another, and where do they fail to connect? Ultimately, do you think of the Internet as a unifying force – bringing together people who would not normally come into contact? Or do you view the Internet as an isolating force – allowing people to remain anonymous and to avoid direct human contact?

## Emily Yoffe

### Seeking

Emily Yoffe was born in 1955 in Newton, Massachusetts. She regularly contributes to NPR as well as the *New York Times,* the *Washington Post,* and *O Magazine.* She also writes for *Slate's* advice column, "Dear Prudence." For her regular column in *Slate* magazine, "Human Guinea Pig," she has tried undergoing hypnosis, being a telephone psychic, and even entering the Mrs. America pageant, as well as other activities suggested by her readers. Her book *What the Dog Did: Tales from a Formerly Reluctant Dog Owner* (2005) was named Book of the Year by Dogwise.com. Here Yoffe discusses how and why we can become so addicted to new media technologies.

**AS YOU READ:** How does Yoffe characterize users of the Internet and other electronic devices?

Seeking. You can't stop doing it. Sometimes it feels as if the basic drives for food, sex, and sleep have been overridden by a new need for endless nuggets of electronic information. We are so insatiably° curious that we gather data even if it gets us in trouble. Google searches are becoming a cause of mistrials as jurors, after hearing testimony, ignore judges' instructions and go look up facts for themselves. We search for information we don't even care about. . . . 1

We actually resemble nothing so much as those legendary lab rats that endlessly pressed a lever to give themselves a little electrical jolt to the brain. While we tap, tap away at our search engines, it appears we are stimulating the same system in our brains that scientists accidentally discovered more than 50 years ago when probing rat skulls. 2

In 1954, psychologist James Olds and his team were working in a laboratory at McGill University, studying how rats learned. They would stick an electrode in a rat's brain and, whenever the rat went to a particular corner of its cage, would give it a small shock and note the reaction. One day they unknowingly inserted the probe in the wrong place, and when Olds tested the rat it kept returning over and over to the corner where it received the shock. He eventually discovered that if the probe was put in the brain's lateral hypothalamus and the rats were allowed to press a lever and stimulate their own electrodes, they would press until they collapsed. 3

**insatiably:** Without being capable of satisfaction.

Olds, and everyone else, assumed he'd found the brain's pleasure center (some scientists still think so). Later experiments done on humans confirmed that people will neglect almost everything—their personal hygiene, their family commitments—in order to keep getting that buzz. But to Washington State University neuroscientist Jaak Panksepp, the supposed pleasure center didn't look very much like it was producing pleasure. . . . The rats were in a constant state of sniffing and foraging. . . . 4

It is an emotional state Panksepp tried many names for: *curiosity*, *interest*, *foraging*,° *anticipation*, *craving*, *expectancy*. He finally settled on *seeking*. Panksepp has spent decades mapping the emotional systems of the brain he believes are shared by all mammals, and he says, "Seeking is the granddaddy of the systems." It is the mammalian motivational engine that each day gets us out of the bed, or den, or hole to venture forth into the world. It's why, as animal scientist Temple Grandin writes in *Animals Make Us Human*, experiments show that animals in captivity would prefer to have to search for their food than to have it delivered to them. 5

For humans, this desire to search is not just about fulfilling our *physical* needs. Panksepp says that humans can get just as excited about abstract rewards as tangible ones. He says that when we get thrilled about the world of ideas, about making intellectual connections, about divining meaning, it is the seeking circuits that are firing. 6

The juice that fuels the seeking system is the neurotransmitter dopamine. The dopamine circuits "promote states of eagerness and directed purpose," Panksepp writes. It's a state humans love to be in. So good does it feel that we seek out activities, or substances, that keep this system aroused—cocaine and amphetamines, drugs of stimulation, are particularly effective at stirring it. 7

Ever find yourself sitting down at the computer just for a second to find out what other movie you saw that actress in, only to look up and realize the search has led to an hour of Googling? Thank dopamine. Our internal sense of time is believed to be controlled by the dopamine system. People with hyperactivity disorder have a shortage of dopamine in their brains, which a recent study suggests may be at the root of the problem. For them even small stretches of time seem to drag. An article by Nicholas Carr in the *Atlantic* last year, "Is Google Making Us Stupid?" speculates that our constant Internet scrolling is remodeling our brains to make it nearly impossible for us to give sustained attention to a long piece of writing. Like the lab rats, we keep hitting "enter" to get our next fix. 8

University of Michigan professor of psychology Kent Berridge has spent more than two decades figuring out how the brain experiences pleasure. Like Panksepp, he, too, has come to the conclusion that what James Olds's rats were stimulating was not their reward center. In a series of experiments, he and other researchers have been able to tease apart that the mammalian brain has separate systems for what Berridge calls *wanting* and *liking*. 9

**foraging:** Searching.

*Wanting* is Berridge's equivalent for Panksepp's seeking system. It is the *liking* system that Berridge believes is the brain's reward center. When we experience pleasure, it is our own opioid system, rather than our dopamine system, that is being stimulated. This is why the opiate drugs induce a kind of blissful stupor so different from the animating effect of cocaine and amphetamines. Wanting and liking are complementary. The former catalyzes us to action; the latter brings us to a satisfied pause. Seeking needs to be turned off, if even for a little while, so that the system does not run in an endless loop. . . . 10

But our brains are designed to more easily be stimulated than satisfied. "The brain seems to be more stingy with mechanisms for pleasure than for desire," Berridge has said. This makes evolutionary sense. Creatures that lack motivation, that find it easy to slip into oblivious rapture, are likely to lead short (if happy) lives. So nature imbued° us with an unquenchable° drive to discover, to explore. . . . We find ourselves letting one Google search lead to another, while often feeling the information is not vital and knowing we should stop. "As long as you sit there, the consumption renews the appetite," he explains. 11

Actually all our electronic communication devices — e-mail, Facebook feeds, texts, Twitter — are feeding the same drive as our searches. Since we're restless, easily bored creatures, our gadgets give us in abundance qualities the seeking/wanting system finds particularly exciting. Novelty is one. Panksepp says the dopamine system is activated by finding something unexpected or by the anticipation of something new. If the rewards come unpredictably — as e-mail, texts, updates do — we get even more carried away. . . . 12

Berridge says the "ding" announcing a new e-mail or the vibration that signals the arrival of a text message serves as a reward cue for us. And when we respond, we get a little piece of news (Twitter, anyone?), making us want more. These information nuggets may be as uniquely potent for humans as a Froot Loop to a rat. When you give a rat a minuscule dose of sugar, it engenders "a panting appetite," Berridge says — a powerful and not necessarily pleasant state. 13

If humans are seeking machines, we've now created the perfect machines to allow us to seek endlessly. This perhaps should make us cautious. In *Animals in Translation,* Temple Grandin writes of driving two indoor cats crazy by flicking a laser pointer around the room. They wouldn't stop stalking and pouncing on this ungraspable dot of light — their dopamine system pumping. She writes that no wild cat would indulge in such useless behavior: "A cat wants to *catch* the mouse, not chase it in circles forever." She says "mindless chasing" makes an animal less likely to meet its real needs "because it short-circuits intelligent stalking behavior." As we chase after flickering bits of information, it's a salutary° warning. 14

**imbued:** Filled. **unquenchable:** Unable to be satisfied or suppressed. **salutary:** Healthy.

## Questions to Start You Thinking

1. **Considering Meaning:** Why does Yoffe maintain that we should be "cautious" (paragraph 14) about technologies like the Internet?
2. **Identifying Writing Strategies:** Where in the essay does Yoffe use comparison and contrast? How does this method of development support her thesis?
3. **Reading Critically:** Who is Yoffe's audience? How can you tell? How might that audience affect the style and content of the essay?
4. **Expanding Vocabulary:** Yoffe presents Panksepp's claim that "humans can get just as excited about abstract rewards as tangible ones" (paragraph 6). What do the words *abstract* and *tangible* mean in this context? How does this distinction further the writer's point?
5. **Making Connections:** In "The Creation of Discontent" (pp. 611–15), Juliet Schor argues that consumer desire ends up creating permanent discontent among consumers. What insight does "Seeking" provide about Schor's claim?

## Journal Prompts

1. Do you agree with Yoffe that we need to be "cautious" (paragraph 14) about technologies like the Internet? Are you generally wary of new technology? Why, or why not?
2. Write about seeking in your own life, giving specific instances of the process or its effects.

## Suggestions for Writing

1. In paragraphs 9–11, Yoffe cites brain research suggesting that we like desiring things more than we enjoy obtaining or achieving them. Using personal experience and observation, write an essay that agrees or disagrees with this assertion.
2. Read further about research on seeking, or analyze popular Web sites, advertisements, magazines, or other materials that seem to rely on seeking. Write an essay using these sources to support your own thesis about the nature or implications of seeking.

## Nicholas A. Christakis and James H. Fowler

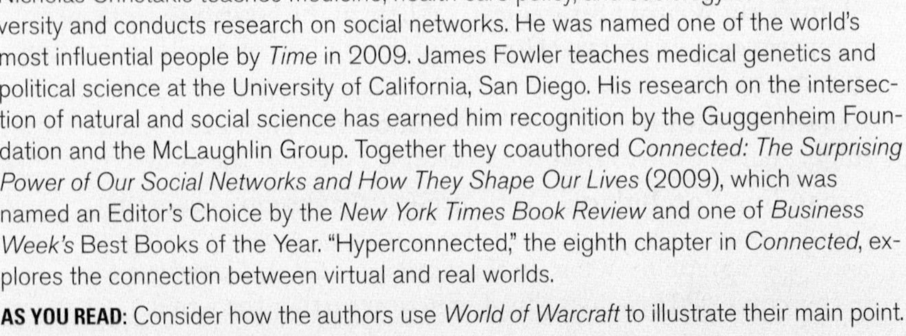

### Hyperconnected

Nicholas Christakis teaches medicine, health care policy, and sociology at Harvard University and conducts research on social networks. He was named one of the world's most influential people by *Time* in 2009. James Fowler teaches medical genetics and political science at the University of California, San Diego. His research on the intersection of natural and social science has earned him recognition by the Guggenheim Foundation and the McLaughlin Group. Together they coauthored *Connected: The Surprising Power of Our Social Networks and How They Shape Our Lives* (2009), which was named an Editor's Choice by the *New York Times Book Review* and one of *Business Week's* Best Books of the Year. "Hyperconnected," the eighth chapter in *Connected*, explores the connection between virtual and real worlds.

**AS YOU READ:** Consider how the authors use *World of Warcraft* to illustrate their main point.

Every month, eleven million people around the globe play a game on the 1
Internet known as World of Warcraft. It is a "massively multiplayer game" involving so many players that if it were its own country, it would be larger than Greece, Belgium, Sweden, and nearly 150 other nations. In this game, people adopt an online persona, known as an avatar, who inhabits a virtual world and interacts with other players in the game. This avatar has a vivid three-dimensional appearance that is customizable, and it acquires possessions, powers, and even pets over the course of play, which can last many months. Within this game, people form friendships, have sustained interactions as groups, communicate using instant messaging, collaborate to achieve shared goals, engage in economic transactions, and fight one another in complex battles. The avatars live in different realms of the virtual world, and when they "die" during combat or other activities, they are automatically returned to their homes, whereupon they happily come back to life and resume play.

Sometimes, however, things run amok. On September 13, 2005, the game 2
developers opened up a new area for advanced players, one inhabited by a massive, powerful winged serpent called Hakkar. Hakkar was equipped with a number of weapons and capabilities, among which was a contagious disease called "corrupted blood" that he could spread to his enemies. When one of his adversaries was infected, other nearby opponents also became infected. To the strong players who had banded together to fight Hakkar, this infection was intended to be a minor hindrance° that made combat more challenging. Once Hakkar was dead, players could leave the area and the contagion would stop.

The programmers at World of Warcraft thought this was a pretty neat 3
trick to challenge their players. But the players responded to the contagion in an unanticipated way. Rather than continuing the fight against Hakkar until they died of corrupted blood, some players used a teleport capability to

**hindrance:** Impediment.

transport themselves to another area of the game. As a result, the infection spread widely throughout the entire virtual world, not just among the players confronting Hakkar. What was intended to be a minor inconvenience to powerful players in a localized area—something like a cold in a healthy adult living in a small town—instead inadvertently became a worldwide epidemic in the game, rapidly killing hundreds of thousands of weaker players.

As players returned to their virtual homes, they spread the infection far and wide, including to the densely populated capital cities. In addition, through another programming glitch, the infection was permitted to spread to virtual pets. While the pets were immune and did not die, they served as reservoirs for the pathogen° and became a source of immediate reinfection after their owners came back to life or were otherwise cured of the disease. 4

The programmers scrambled to figure out what was happening as the pandemic° raged. Initially, they had no idea why vast numbers of players were suddenly dying. They eventually imposed quarantine measures, isolating infected players from uninfected areas. But this effort failed because players refused to be quarantined, and in any case it was not possible to restrict their movement to the extent required. Ultimately, the programmers resorted to a strategy that doctors and public health officials contending with a real global pandemic do not have: they pulled the plug on the whole world. After the epidemic° of corrupted blood had raged unstopped for a week, they rebooted the servers, and the epidemic came to an abrupt and complete halt. 5

### *Virtual World, Real Behaviors*

These curious events affected literally millions of players, but they also captured the imaginations of people in academia. Microbiologists, mathematicians, psychologists, and epidemiologists° were fascinated by the epidemic unleashed by Hakkar. Though the germ and the victims in this outbreak were virtual, the behaviors of the avatars were entirely realistic—so much so that scholars have studied them as indicators of how people might respond to a bioterror attack or the recurrence of a real-world pandemic like influenza. 6

Some characters in the game had healing powers, and they attempted (largely without success) to cure those afflicted with corrupted blood. They acted altruistically,° often rushing to the center of the outbreaks to try to help, and they typically died as a result. Unfortunately, their selfless behavior actually worsened the epidemic in two ways: the healers often became vectors° of the infection, and the patients they "cured" remained carriers and went on to infect more people than they otherwise would have if they had simply died. Other characters in the game, lacking the altruism or sense of 7

**pathogen:** Infectious germ. **pandemic:** A worldwide disease outbreak. **epidemic:** A disease that affects many people. **epidemiologists:** People who study the cause, distribution, and control of disease. **altruistically:** Motivated by helping others. **vectors:** Carriers of disease.

duty of the healers, fearfully fled infected cities to save themselves but wound up spreading the disease farther. Still others, driven by curiosity or thrill seeking, rushed to the outbreak sites to see what was going on or to see what an infection looked like (victims collapsed in pools of blood). Still others behaved in a sociopathic fashion, deliberately exposing themselves to infection and then quickly transporting themselves to the land of their enemies, or even to their own homeland, to spread the epidemic and cause as many deaths as possible.

Amazingly, a detailed study of the corrupted blood outbreak was published in *Lancet Infectious Diseases*, a medical journal usually devoted to covering the biology and treatment of real-world pathogens.[1] The primary motivation for the study was to see if the virtual world could be used to model real-world behaviors during epidemics. The authors noted that if future virtual epidemics were designed and presented so as to seamlessly integrate within an online game, a reasonable analogue° to real-world reactions to epidemics might be studied and even manipulated. 8

For thousands of years, social interactions were built solely on face-to-face communication. But technology changed this with the invention of ways of broadcasting information (church bells, signal fires, books, bullhorns, radio, television) and ways of communicating person-to-person at a distance (letters, telegrams, phone calls). Today, in addition to the impressive prospect of inhabiting virtual online worlds, we engage in other forms of communication and interaction that have already become plebeian° even though they are actually quite remarkable: we text, Twitter, e-mail, blog, instant-message, Google, YouTube, and Facebook one another using technology that did not exist just a few years ago. Even so, there are some things that technology does not change. 9

The invention of each new method of communication has contributed to a debate stretching back centuries about how technology affects community. Pessimists have expressed the concern that new ways of communicating might weaken traditional ways of relating, leading people to turn away from a full range of in-person interactions with others that, in bygone eras, were necessary and normal parts of life. Optimists argue that such technologies merely augment, extend, and supplement the conventional ways people form connections. 10

In the case of the Internet in particular, proponents argue that relationships that emerge online can be unfettered° by geography and even, perhaps, by awkward constraints attributable to shyness or discrimination. Internet proponents have also seen a benefit to the kind of anonymous and large-scale interactions that are much harder to arrange in the real world. Instead of having personal ties to a small number of people, we have more tenuous° ties to 11

**analogue:** Similar, comparable, or corresponding structure. **plebeian:** Commonplace. **unfettered:** Unrestricted. **tenuous:** Flimsy.

[1]E. T. Lofgren and N. H. Fefferman, "The Untapped Potential of Virtual Game Worlds to Shed Light on Real World Epidemics," *Lancet Infectious Diseases* 7 (2007): 625–29.

hundreds or thousands. Instead of simply knowing who our friends are, and perhaps our friends' friends, we can peer beyond our social horizons and even see graphical depictions of our place in a vast worldwide social network.

Yet, new technologies—whether massively multiplayer online games such as World of Warcraft or Second Life; social-network Web sites such as Facebook or Myspace; collective information sites like YouTube, Wikipedia, or eBay; or dating sites like Match.com or eHarmony—just realize our ancient propensity to connect to other humans, albeit with electrons flowing through cyberspace rather than conversation drifting through air. While the social networks formed online may be abstract, large, complex, and supermodern, they also reflect universal and fundamental human tendencies that emerged in our prehistoric past when we told stories to one another around campfires in the African savanna. Even astonishing advances in communication technology like the printing press, the telephone, and the Internet do not take us away from this past; they draw us closer to it. 12

## Questions to Start You Thinking

1. **Considering Meaning:** Why does the World of Warcraft epidemic capture the interest of doctors and scientists? What might a virtual disease reveal about the real world?

2. **Identifying Writing Strategies:** In the concluding paragraph, the authors picture prehistoric humans telling stories around a campfire (paragraph 12). What point do they make with this image? What is the relationship between this kind of storytelling and high-tech online gaming?

3. **Reading Critically:** Christakis and Fowler summarize the positions of both optimists and pessimists on the effect of new technologies on community (paragraph 10). Do you think these authors are closer to the view that technology is helpful, or do they fear the harm it can cause? What evidence in their essay supports your view?

4. **Expanding Vocabulary:** In the first paragraph of "Hyperconnected," the authors explain how World of Warcraft works. Why is having an *avatar* essential to the game? What is an *avatar*, and what kinds of things can it do?

5. **Making Connections:** Both Gerard Jones ("Violent Media Is Good for Kids," pp. 565–69) and Stephen King ("Why We Crave Horror Movies," pp. 561–64) argue that depictions of violence give people ways to manage their own antisocial feelings. When players in World of Warcraft respond to the epidemic, might they also act in ways that do or do not reflect their real-world behavior? Use examples and points from the readings to support your view.

## Journal Prompts

1. In the case of the World of Warcraft epidemic, the designers solved an apparently unsolvable problem by rebooting the game. The authors point out that starting over is not an option in the real world, but what if it were? What global problem would you like to reboot? How would you try to prevent it from happening again?
2. Why do people immerse themselves in virtual worlds? What is the appeal of role-playing games like World of Warcraft? If you have played this or similar games, use your knowledge of them to explore these questions. If not, try out an immersive game, and write about the experience as a newcomer to virtual worlds.

## Suggestions for Writing

1. The authors note how the World of Warcraft players responded to the contagion in a range of ways, expected and surprising. Write an essay comparing these responses with human behavior in a crisis or analyzing their effects in the virtual world. How do you think you would act in a similar situation?
2. The World of Warcraft epidemic inspired a study in an actual medical journal to examine whether virtual worlds could model real-world reactions. Find out how your community or a field that interests you has used simulations to prepare for problems. How would you use an online world to test human behavior? Write a proposal for a simulation that would help to research a problem and attempt to find a solution.

## David Gelernter

## Computers Cannot Teach Children Basic Skills

David Gelernter, a professor of computer science at Yale, earned his undergraduate degree from Yale University in classical Hebrew literature and his PhD in computer science from the State University of New York at Stony Brook. His books, articles, and theories on technology have been highly influential. He is a contributing editor at the *Weekly Standard*, chief scientist at Mirror Worlds Technologies, and also a painter and an art critic. In 1993, he lost part of his right hand and the sight in one eye after opening a mail bomb sent by Theodore Kaczynski, the "Unabomber" terrorist opposed to the advancement of technology, who targeted prominent professors and business executives. Gelernter chronicled his recovery in the memoir *Drawing Life: Surviving the Unabomber* (1997). His many other books include *Americanism: The Fourth Great Western Religion* (2007) and *America-Lite: How Imperial Academia Dismantled Our Culture (and Ushered In the Obamacrats)* (2012). In "Computers Cannot Teach Children Basic Skills," first published in the *New Republic* in 1994, Gelernter challenges the widely held view that computers are always a "godsend" in the classroom.

**AS YOU READ:** Identify the solution Gelernter proposes for using computers effectively in the classroom.

Over the last decade an estimated $2 billion has been spent on more than 2 million computers for America's classrooms. That's not surprising. We constantly hear from Washington that the schools are in trouble and that computers are a godsend. Within the education establishment, in poor as well as rich schools, the machines are awaited with nearly religious awe. An inner-city principal bragged to a teacher friend of mine recently that his school "has a computer in every classroom . . . despite being in a bad neighborhood!" 1

### *Computers Teach Some Things Well*

Computers should be in the schools. They have the potential to accomplish great things. With the right software, they could help make science tangible or teach neglected topics like art and music. They could help students form a concrete idea of society by displaying on-screen a version of the city in which they live—a picture that tracks real life moment by moment. 2

In practice, however, computers make our worst educational nightmares come true. While we bemoan the decline of literacy, computers discount words in favor of pictures and pictures in favor of video. While we fret about the decreasing cogency° of public debate, computers dismiss linear argument and promote fast, shallow romps across the information landscape. While we worry about basic skills, we allow into the classroom software that will do a student's arithmetic or correct his spelling. 3

### *Computers Lower Reading Skills*

Take multimedia. The idea of multimedia is to combine text, sound, and pictures in a single package that you browse on-screen. You don't just *read* Shakespeare; you watch actors performing, listen to songs, view Elizabethan buildings. What's wrong with that? By offering children candy-coated books, multimedia is guaranteed to sour them on unsweetened reading. It makes the printed page look even more boring than it used to look. Sure, books will be available in the classroom, too—but they'll have all the appeal of a dusty piano to a teen who has a Walkman handy. 4

So what if the little nippers don't read? If they're watching Olivier° instead, what do they lose? The text, the written word along with all of its attendant pleasures. Besides, a book is more portable than a computer, has a higher-resolution display, can be written on and dog-eared, and is comparatively dirt cheap. 5

**cogency:** Logic, persuasiveness. **Olivier:** Laurence Olivier, a British actor noted for his Shakespearean performances.

Hypermedia, multimedia's comrade in the struggle for a brave new classroom,° is just as troubling. It's a way of presenting documents on-screen without imposing a linear start-to-finish order. Disembodied paragraphs are linked by theme; after reading one about the First World War, for example, you might be able to choose another about the technology of battleships, or the life of Woodrow Wilson, or hemlines in the '20s. This is another cute idea that is good in minor ways and terrible in major ones. Teaching children to understand the orderly unfolding of a plot or a logical argument is a crucial part of education. Authors don't merely agglomerate° paragraphs; they work hard to make the narrative read a certain way, prove a particular point. To turn a book or a document into hypertext is to invite readers to ignore exactly what counts—the story. 6

The real problem, again, is the accentuation° of already bad habits. Dynamiting documents into disjointed paragraphs is one more expression of the sorry fact that sustained argument is not our style. If you're a newspaper or magazine editor and your readership is dwindling, what's the solution? Shorter pieces. If you're a politician and you want to get elected, what do you need? Tasty sound bites. Logical presentation be damned. 7

Another software species, "allow me" programs, is not much better. These programs correct spelling and, by applying canned grammatical and stylistic rules, fix prose. In terms of promoting basic skills, though, they have all the virtues of a pocket calculator. 8

In Kentucky, as the *Wall Street Journal* reported, students in grades K–3 are mixed together regardless of age in a relaxed environment. It works great, the *Journal* says. Yes, scores on computation tests have dropped 10 percent at one school, but not to worry: "Drilling addition and subtraction in an age of calculators is a waste of time," the principal reassures us. Meanwhile, a Japanese educator informs University of Wisconsin mathematician Richard Akey that in his country, "calculators are not used in elementary or junior high school because the primary emphasis is on helping students develop their mental abilities." No wonder Japanese kids blow the pants off American kids in math. Do we really think "drilling addition and subtraction in an age of calculators is a waste of time"? If we do, then "drilling reading in an age of multimedia is a waste of time" can't be far behind. 9

Prose-correcting programs are also a little ghoulish, like asking a computer for tips on improving your personality. On the other hand, I ran this viewpoint through a spell checker, so how can I ban the use of such programs in schools? Because to misspell is human; to have no idea of correct spelling is to be semiliterate. 10

### *Conditions on the Use of Computers*

There's no denying that computers have the potential to perform inspiring feats in the classroom. If we are ever to see that potential realized, however, we ought to agree on three conditions. First, there should be a completely 11

**brave new classroom:** Reference to the Aldous Huxley novel *Brave New World,* in which technology makes life happy but empty. **agglomerate:** Jumble together. **accentuation:** Emphasizing or intensifying.

new crop of children's software. Most of today's offerings show no imagination. There are hundreds of similar reading and geography and arithmetic programs, but almost nothing on electricity or physics or architecture. Also, they abuse the technical capacities of new media to glitz up old forms instead of creating new ones. Why not build a time-travel program that gives kids a feel for how history is structured by zooming you backward? A spectrum program that lets users twirl a frequency knob to see what happens?

Second, computers should be used only during recess or relaxation periods. Treat them as fillips,° not as surrogate teachers. When I was in school in the '60s, we all loved educational films. When we saw a movie in class, everybody won: teachers didn't have to teach, and pupils didn't have to learn. I suspect that classroom computers are popular today for the same reasons. 12

Most important, educators should learn what parents and most teachers already know: you cannot teach a child anything unless you look him in the face. We should not forget what computers are. Like books—better in some ways, worse in others—they are devices that help children mobilize their own resources and learn for themselves. The computer's potential to do good is modestly greater than a book's in some areas. Its potential to do harm is vastly greater, across the board. 13

## Questions to Start You Thinking

1. **Considering Meaning:** What are the primary shortcomings Gelernter believes computers have as educational tools?
2. **Identifying Writing Strategies:** Where in the essay does Gelernter propose his solution as to how computers should be used in the classroom? Do you find this placement effective? Why, or why not?
3. **Reading Critically:** In several places in the essay, Gelernter compares computers with books. Review what he has to say about computers and books. Do you think he makes an effective argument here? Why, or why not?
4. **Expanding Vocabulary:** Define *bemoan, literacy, fret, linear,* and *romps* (paragraph 3). Then, in your own words, summarize Gelernter's point in paragraph 3. What does his word choice suggest about his intended audience?
5. **Making Connections:** What might Gelernter say about Clive Thompson's "The New Literacy" (pp. 584–87)? Which writer is more persuasive, and why?

## Journal Prompts

1. What kind of learning have you done on computers? How effective do you find such learning?

**fillips:** Things that are added for excitement but are not essential.

2. In his final paragraph, Gelernter claims "you cannot teach a child anything unless you look him in the face." What does he mean? Do you agree?

## Suggestions for Writing

1. To what extent do you agree or disagree with Gelernter? Write an essay in which you take a stand about the value of classroom computers. Focus on the basic skills of reading, writing, and math, but feel free to consider computers as teaching tools in other areas, too.
2. Gelernter wrote this essay in 1994. Do some research on how the classroom use of computers has changed since then. For example, what kinds of educational software have been developed? How much time does the average student spend on a classroom computer? Are computers used to teach basic skills? Write an essay, using your findings to support your position about how Gelernter would feel about the use of classroom computers today.

## Clive Thompson

## The New Literacy

Clive Thompson is a science and technology writer for the *New York Times Magazine*, *WIRED*, and *New York Magazine*, the video-game columnist for *Slate*, and a finance columnist for *Details*. He has received the National Magazine Award in Canada twice, and in 2002–2003 was the Knight Science Journalism fellow at MIT. His commentary can be heard on NPR, CNN, and the Canadian Broadcasting Corporation. He also keeps a blog, "Collision Detection," which "collects bits of offbeat research . . . and musings thereon." Here, Thompson discusses some counterintuitive research by Professor Andrea Lunsford on literacy in the digital age.

**AS YOU READ:** What did the Stanford Study of Writing discover about student writing?

For a student response to this essay, see pp. 30–31.

As the school year begins, be ready to hear pundits° fretting once again about how kids today can't write—and technology is to blame. Facebook encourages narcissistic° blabbering, video and PowerPoint have replaced carefully crafted essays, and texting has dehydrated language into "bleak, bald, sad shorthand" (as University College of London English professor John Sutherland has moaned). An age of illiteracy is at hand, right? 1

Andrea Lunsford isn't so sure. Lunsford is a professor of writing and rhetoric at Stanford University, where she has organized a mammoth project called the Stanford Study of Writing to scrutinize° college students' prose. 2

**pundits:** Critics and commentators. **narcissistic:** Self-centered. **scrutinize:** Examine carefully.

From 2001 to 2006, she collected 14,672 student writing samples—everything from in-class assignments, formal essays, and journal entries to emails, blog posts, and chat sessions. Her conclusions are stirring.

"I think we're in the midst of a literacy revolution the likes of which we haven't seen since Greek civilization," she says. For Lunsford, technology isn't killing our ability to write. It's reviving it—and pushing our literacy in bold new directions. 3

The first thing she found is that young people today write far more than any generation before them. That's because so much socializing takes place online, and it almost always involves text. Of all the writing that the Stanford students did, a stunning 38 percent of it took place out of the classroom—life writing, as Lunsford calls it. Those Twitter updates and lists of 25 things about yourself add up. 4

It's almost hard to remember how big a paradigm shift this is. Before the Internet came along, most Americans never wrote anything, ever, that wasn't a school assignment. Unless they got a job that required producing text (like in law, advertising, or media), they'd leave school and virtually never construct a paragraph again. 5

But is this explosion of prose good, on a technical level? Yes. Lunsford's team found that the students were remarkably adept at what rhetoricians call *kairos*—assessing their audience and adapting their tone and technique to best get their point across. The modern world of online writing, particularly in chat and on discussion threads, is conversational and public, which makes it closer to the Greek tradition of argument than the asynchronous° letter and essay writing of 50 years ago. 6

The fact that students today almost always write for an audience (something virtually no one in my generation did) gives them a different sense of what constitutes good writing. In interviews, they defined good prose as something that had an effect on the world. For them, writing is about persuading and organizing and debating, even if it's over something as quotidian° as what movie to go see. The Stanford students were almost always less enthusiastic about their in-class writing because it had no audience but the professor: It didn't serve any purpose other than to get them a grade. As for those texting short-forms and smileys defiling° *serious* academic writing? Another myth. When Lunsford examined the work of first-year students, she didn't find a single example of texting speak in an academic paper. 7

Of course, good teaching is always going to be crucial, as is the mastering of formal academic prose. But it's also becoming clear that online media are pushing literacy into cool directions. The brevity of texting and status updating teaches young people to deploy haiku°-like concision.° At the same time, the proliferation° of new forms of online pop-cultural exegesis°—from 8

**asynchronous:** Not occurring at the same time. **quotidian:** Ordinary, commonplace. **defiling:** Making dirty; corrupting. **haiku:** Japanese form of poetry having three unrhymed lines of five, seven, and five syllables. **concision:** The quality of being brief; brevity. **proliferation:** Rapid increase. **exegesis:** Explanation or analysis.

sprawling TV-show recaps to 15,000-word videogame walkthroughs—has given them a chance to write enormously long and complex pieces of prose, often while working collaboratively with others.

We think of writing as either good or bad. What today's young people know is that knowing who you're writing for and why you're writing might be the most crucial factor of all. 9

## Questions to Start You Thinking

1. **Considering Meaning:** According to the author, what is the effect of the Internet on writing?
2. **Identifying Writing Strategies:** Where does Thompson use comparison and contrast? How does it support his argument?
3. **Reading Critically:** Who seems to be the intended audience for this essay? What is the writer's purpose? How well do you think he achieves it?
4. **Expanding Vocabulary:** In paragraph 5, Thompson writes, "It's almost hard to remember how big a paradigm shift this is." What is a *paradigm shift*? Why is this concept important to Thompson's larger purpose?
5. **Making Connections:** According to Thompson, the Internet and other new media forms are stimulating literacy. How might Sherry Turkle ("How Computers Change the Way We Think," p. 595 and e-Pages) respond to Thompson's article? What would she make of this "paradigm shift"?

## Journal Prompts

1. Thompson claims that people are writing more than ever as they socialize online (paragraph 4). Consider your own time spent writing online, texting, or tweeting. Has this time and involvement made you a better writer? Why, or why not?
2. According to Thompson, students surveyed in the Stanford Study of Writing "defined good prose as something that had an effect on the world" (paragraph 7). Do you agree with this definition? Can you think of a better one? What examples come to mind?

## Suggestions for Writing

1. Drawing on your own experience and observations, write an essay in which you explore the cause-and-effect relationship, positive or negative, between the use of the Internet (or another new media form) and its consequences for writing.

2. In his opening sentence, Thompson anticipates commentary blaming technology for educational gaps or failures, just as video games, television, radio, and even early novels have been criticized over the years as negative influences. Investigate one or several historical examples of people worrying about the bad effects of a new technology. Then, write an essay that examines those concerns and their validity, in retrospect.

## Elizabeth Stone

## Grief in the Age of Facebook

Elizabeth Stone teaches English and media studies at Fordham University. Her critically acclaimed nonfiction work, *A Boy I Once Knew: What a Teacher Learned from Her Student*, was published in 2002. In 2004 she followed that book with *Black Sheep and Kissing Cousins: How Our Family Stories Shape Us*. In the following article, first published in the *Chronicle Review* on March 5, 2010, Stone recalls the death of one of her students and examines how that death was subsequently mourned on Facebook.

**AS YOU READ:** What questions does the author raise about this form of grieving?

On July 17 last year, one of my most promising students died. Her name was Casey Feldman, and she was crossing a street in a New Jersey resort town on her way to work when a van went barreling through a stop sign. Her death was a terrible loss for everyone who knew her. Smart and dogged,° whimsical and kind, Casey was the news editor of *The Observer*, the campus paper I advise, and she was going places. She was a finalist for a national college reporting award and had just been chosen for a prestigious television internship for the fall, a fact she conveyed to me in a midnight text message, entirely consistent with her all-news-all-the-time mind-set. Two days later her life ended. 1

I found out about Casey's death the old-fashioned way: in a phone conversation with Kelsey, the layout editor and Casey's roommate. She'd left a neutral-sounding voice mail the night before, asking me to call her when I got her message, adding, "It's OK if it's late." I didn't retrieve the message till midnight, so I called the next morning, realizing only later what an extraordinary effort she had made to keep her voice calm. But my students almost never make phone calls if they can help it, so Kelsey's message alone should have raised my antenna. She blogs, she tweets, she texts, and she pings. But voice mail? No. 2

Paradoxically it was Kelsey's understanding of the viral nature of her generation's communication preferences that sent her rushing to the phone, and not just to call boomers° like me. She didn't want anyone to learn of Casey's 3

**dogged:** Hard-working; determined. **boomers:** Baby boomers, the generation born directly after World War II.

death through Facebook. It was summer, and their friends were scattered, but Kelsey knew that if even one of Casey's 801 Facebook friends posted the news, it would immediately spread.

So as Kelsey and her roommates made calls through the night, they monitored Facebook. Within an hour of Casey's death, the first mourner posted her respects on Casey's Facebook wall, a post that any of Casey's friends could have seen. By the next morning, Kelsey, in New Jersey, had reached *The Observer*'s editor in chief in Virginia, and by that evening, the two had reached fellow editors in California, Missouri, Massachusetts, Texas, and elsewhere—and somehow none of them already knew. 4

In the months that followed, I've seen how markedly technology has influenced the conventions of grieving among my students, offering them solace but also uncertainty. The day after Casey's death, several editorial-board members changed their individual Facebook profile pictures. Where there had been photos of Brent, of Kelsey, of Kate, now there were photos of Casey and Brent, Casey and Kelsey, Casey and Kate. 5

Now that Casey was gone, she was virtually everywhere. I asked one of my students why she'd changed her profile photo. "It was spontaneous," she said. "Once one person did it, we all joined in." Another student, who had friends at Virginia Tech when, in 2007, a gunman killed 32 people, said that's when she first saw the practice of posting Facebook profile photos of oneself with the person being mourned. 6

Within several days of Casey's death, a Facebook group was created called "In Loving Memory of Casey Feldman," which ran parallel to the wake and funeral planned by Casey's family. Dozens wrote on that group's wall, but Casey's own wall was the more natural gathering place, where the comments were more colloquial and addressed to her: "casey im speechless for words right now," wrote one friend. "I cant believe that just yest i txted you and now your gone . . . i miss you soo much rest in peace." 7

Though we all live atomized° lives, memorial services let us know the dead with more dimension than we may have known them during their lifetimes. In the responses of her friends, I was struck by how much I hadn't known about Casey—her equestrian skill, her love of animals, her interest in photography, her acting talent, her penchant° for creating her own slang ("Don't be a cow"), and her curiosity—so intense that her friends affectionately called her a "stalker." 8

This new, uncharted form of grieving raises new questions. Traditional mourning is governed by conventions. But in the age of Facebook, with selfhood publicly represented via comments and uploaded photos, was it OK for her friends to display joy or exuberance online? Some weren't sure. Six weeks after Casey's death, one student who had posted a shot of herself with Casey wondered aloud when it was all right to post a different photo. Was there a right time? There were no conventions to help her. And would she be judged if she removed her mourning photo before most others did? 9

**atomized:** Small; separate. **penchant:** Inclination.

As it turns out, Facebook has a "memorializing" policy in regard to the pages of those who have died. That policy came into being in 2005, when a good friend and co-worker of Max Kelly, a Facebook employee, was killed in a bicycle accident. As Kelly wrote in a Facebook blog post last October, "The question soon came up: What do we do about his Facebook profile? We had never really thought about this before in such a personal way. How do you deal with an interaction with someone who is no longer able to log on? When someone leaves us, they don't leave our memories or our social network. To reflect that reality, we created the idea of "memorialized" profiles as a place where people can save and share their memories of those who've passed." 10

Casey's Facebook page is now memorialized. Her own postings and lists of interests have been removed, and the page is visible only to her Facebook friends. (I thank Kelsey Butler for making it possible for me to gain access to it.) Eight months after her death, her friends are still posting on her wall, not to "share the memories" but to write to her, acknowledging her absence but maintaining their ties to her—exactly the stance that contemporary grief theorists recommend. To me, that seems preferable to Freud's prescription, in "Mourning and Melancholia," that we should detach from the dead. Quite a few of Casey's friends wished her a merry Christmas, and on the 17th of every month so far, the postings spike. Some share dreams they've had about her, or post a detail of interest. "I had juice box wine recently," wrote one. "I thought of you the whole time :( Miss you girl!" From another: "i miss you. the new lady gaga cd came out, and if i had one wish in the world it would be that you could be singing (more like screaming) along with me in my passenger seat like old times." 11

It was against the natural order for Casey to die at 21, and her death still reverberates° among her roommates and fellow editors. I was privileged to know Casey, and though I knew her deeply in certain ways, I wonder—I'm not sure, but I wonder—if I should have known her better. I do know, however, that she would have done a terrific trend piece on "Grief in the Age of Facebook." 12

## Questions to Start You Thinking

1. **Considering Meaning:** Stone argues that, in the face of grief, technology gives people "solace but also uncertainty" (paragraph 5). How do Casey's friends find consolation in Facebook? What kinds of uncertainty do they face?
2. **Identifying Writing Strategies:** Stone includes in her essay quotes from Casey's Facebook page, written in lowercase with text-messaging abbreviations. How do these quotes convey the feeling of the memorial-

**reverberates:** Echoes or repeats.

ized Facebook page? What is the effect of the contrast between these casual bits of writing and Stone's more formal essay?

3. **Reading Critically:** How does Stone show that her students and their friends have a different relationship to digital media than she does? How does her relative unfamiliarity with Facebook affect this discussion of how people use technology to mourn a loss?
4. **Expanding Vocabulary:** Stone observes that Casey's friend Kelsey responded *paradoxically* (paragraph 3). What is a *paradox*? How do Kelsey's phone calls to those who knew Casey fit the definition?
5. **Making Connections:** Read Stone's account of the messages to Casey posted on her memorialized page alongside the conclusion (paragraphs 9–12) of "Hyperconnected" (pp. 576–80). In what ways does a memorialized Facebook page weaken or strengthen community?

## Link to the Paired Essay

Both "Grief in the Age of Facebook" and Copeland's "Is Facebook Making Us Sad?" (pp. 591–95) pay particular attention to college students and the impact of social media on their emotional lives. What do you see as the nature and the extent of the generational divide between people who have grown up with Facebook and those for whom it is a new technology? In what ways does Facebook bridge or boost that divide?

## Journal Prompts

1. As Stone points out, the creators of Facebook only realized after the fact that their site could become a place to mourn people (paragraph 10). Have you used Facebook to acknowledge a loss? If so, how? How else do you or your friends use Facebook in ways that the creators might not have anticipated? What do such uses say about digital media?
2. Stone's essay brings up an old question about how we should deal with death: should we cultivate an ongoing relationship with the loved one's memory, as Casey's friends do on Facebook, or should we, as Freud recommends, "detach" from people we have lost (paragraph 11)? Think about someone you have lost – either through death or other circumstances, like a move – and reflect on how you coped.

## Suggestions for Writing

1. At the end of "Grief in the Age of Facebook," Stone imagines Casey writing a "trend piece" of the same title (paragraph 12). Write an essay considering Stone's closing, why she ends on this note, how this conclusion affects you as a reader, or how Casey's approach to this topic might differ from her professor's.

2. Stone says that she learned new things about Casey by looking at her Facebook page (paragraph 8). Do you think that people can gain a deeper understanding of someone from his or her online presence? Write an essay that takes a stand, presenting your own position, supporting Stone's point, or arguing that Facebook is not a good way to get to know someone. Use other technology examples, if you wish, as well as your own experience, observation, or research.

**Libby Copeland**

## Is Facebook Making Us Sad?

Libby Copeland, a New York–based freelance journalist, regularly writes on a wide range of topics for *Slate*, an online magazine that features articles on politics, business, technology, and the arts. Before joining *Slate*, Copeland worked for eleven years as a staff writer for the *Washington Post*. Her other publications include articles for *New York Magazine*, the *Wall Street Journal*, and *Cosmopolitan*. In 2009, she won the Feature Specialty Reporting award presented by the American Association of Sunday and Feature Editors. In the following article, published in *Slate*, Copeland reports what researchers have concluded about the effects of social networking.

**AS YOU READ:** Identify how the researchers cited in this article support the claim that a link exists between social networking and loneliness.

There are countless ways to make yourself feel lousy. Here's one more, according to research out of Stanford: Assume you're alone in your unhappiness. "Misery Has More Company Than People Think," a paper in the January [2011] issue of *Personality and Social Psychology Bulletin*, draws on a series of studies examining how college students evaluate moods, both their own and those of their peers. Led by Alex Jordan, who at the time was a Ph.D. student in Stanford's psychology department, the researchers found that their subjects consistently underestimated how dejected° others were—and likely wound up feeling more dejected as a result. Jordan got the idea for the inquiry after observing his friends' reactions to Facebook: He noticed that they seemed to feel particularly crummy about themselves after logging onto the site and scrolling through others' attractive photos, accomplished bios, and chipper status updates. "They were convinced that everyone else was leading a perfect life," he told me. 1

The human habit of overestimating other people's happiness is nothing new, of course. Jordan points to a quote by Montesquieu:° "If we only wanted to be happy it would be easy; but we want to be happier than other people, which is almost always difficult, since we think them happier than 2

**dejected:** Depressed or downhearted. **Montesquieu:** (1689–1755); a French philosopher during the Enlightenment era.

they are." But social networking may be making this tendency worse. Jordan's research doesn't look at Facebook explicitly, but if his conclusions are correct, it follows that the site would have a special power to make us sadder and lonelier. By showcasing the most witty, joyful, bullet-pointed versions of people's lives, and inviting constant comparisons in which we tend to see ourselves as the losers, Facebook appears to exploit an Achilles' heel of human nature. And women – an especially unhappy bunch of late – may be especially vulnerable to keeping up with what they imagine is the happiness of the Joneses.°

In one of the Stanford studies, Jordan and his fellow researchers asked 80 freshmen to report whether they or their peers had recently experienced various negative and positive emotional events. Time and again, the subjects underestimated how many negative experiences ("had a distressing fight," "felt sad because they missed people") their peers were having. They also overestimated how much fun ("going out with friends," "attending parties") these same peers were having. In another study, the researchers found a sample of 140 Stanford students unable to accurately gauge others' happiness even when they were evaluating the moods of people they were close to – friends, roommates and people they were dating. And in a third study, the researchers found that the more students underestimated others' negative emotions, the more they tended to report feeling lonely and brooding over their own miseries. This is correlation,° not causation,° mind you; it could be that those subjects who started out feeling worse imagined that everyone else was getting along just fine, not the other way around. But the notion that feeling alone in your day-to-day suffering might increase that suffering certainly makes intuitive sense. 3

As does the idea that Facebook might aggravate this tendency. Facebook is, after all, characterized by the very public curation° of one's assets in the form of friends, photos, biographical data, accomplishments, pithy° observations, even the books we say we like. Look, we have baked beautiful cookies. We are playing with a new puppy. We are smiling in pictures (or, if we are moody, we are artfully moody.) Blandness will not do, and with some exceptions, sad stuff doesn't make the cut, either. The site's very design – the presence of a "Like" button, without a corresponding "Hate" button – reinforces a kind of upbeat spin doctoring. (No one will "Like" your update that the new puppy died, but they may "Like" your report that the little guy was brave up until the end.) 4

Any parent who has posted photos and videos of her child on Facebook is keenly aware of the resulting disconnect from reality, the way chronicling parenthood this way creates a story line of delightfully misspoken words, 5

**happiness of the Joneses:** A play on the saying "keeping up with the Joneses," which refers to the competitive tendency to attempt the same standard of living as those around you. **correlation:** A relationship between two or more things. **causation:** A cause-and-effect relationship. **curation:** Intentional organization, as for a collection. **pithy:** Meaningful.

adorably worn hats, dancing, blown kisses. Tearful falls and tantrums are rarely recorded, nor are the stretches of pure, mind-blowing tedium.° We protect ourselves, and our kids, this way; happiness is impersonal in a way that pain is not. But in the process, we wind up contributing to the illusion that kids are all joy, no effort.

Facebook is "like being in a play. You make a character," one teenager tells 6
MIT professor Sherry Turkle in her new book on technology, *Alone Together*. Turkle writes about the exhaustion felt by teenagers as they constantly tweak their Facebook profiles for maximum cool. She calls this "presentation anxiety," and suggests that the site's element of constant performance makes people feel alienated from themselves. (The book's broader theory is that technology, despite its promises of social connectivity, actually makes us lonelier by preventing true intimacy.)

Facebook oneupsmanship may have particular implications for women. 7
As Meghan O'Rourke has noted here in *Slate*, women's happiness has been at an all-time low in recent years. O'Rourke and two University of Pennsylvania economists who have studied the male-female happiness gap argue that women's collective discontent may be due to too much choice and second-guessing—unforeseen fallout, they speculate, of the way our roles have evolved over the last half-century. As the economists put it, "The increased opportunity to succeed in many dimensions may have led to an increased likelihood in believing that one's life is not measuring up."

If you're already inclined to compare your own decisions to those of other 8
women and to find yours wanting, believing that others are happier with their choices than they actually are is likely to increase your own sense of inadequacy. And women may be particularly susceptible to the Facebook illusion. For one thing, the site is inhabited by more women than men, and women users tend to be more active on the site, as Forbes has reported. According to a recent study out of the University of Texas at Austin, while men are more likely to use the site to share items related to the news or current events, women tend to use it to engage in personal communication (posting photos, sharing content "related to friends and family"). This may make it especially hard for women to avoid comparisons that make them miserable. (Last fall, for example, the *Washington Post* ran a piece about the difficulties of infertile women in shielding themselves from the Facebook crowings° of pregnant friends.)

Jordan, who is now a postdoctoral fellow studying social psychology at 9
Dartmouth's Tuck School of Business, suggests we might do well to consider Facebook profiles as something akin to the airbrushed photos on the covers of women's magazines. No, you will never have those thighs, because nobody has those thighs. You will never be as consistently happy as your Facebook friends, because nobody is that happy. So remember Montesquieu, and, if you're feeling particularly down, use Facebook for its most exalted purpose: finding fat exes.

**tedium:** Boredom. **crowings:** Joyful noises.

## Questions to Start You Thinking

1. **Considering Meaning:** Why is the problem Copeland describes particularly difficult for women? What factors make women especially susceptible to the illusion of perfect happiness that others present on Facebook?
2. **Identifying Writing Strategies:** Copeland turns to a variety of writers and researchers to support her views about the negative effects of Facebook. What kinds of evidence and expertise does she rely on? What makes her experts credible?
3. **Reading Critically:** Copeland points out that the relationship between underestimating negative or overestimating positive experiences of others and feeling sad about one's own circumstances is "correlation, not causation" (paragraph 3). How does she make the case that Facebook causes people to feel worse?
4. **Expanding Vocabulary:** Copeland cites the function of the "Like" button as an indication that Facebook encourages *spin doctoring* (paragraph 4). What does it mean to *spin doctor* one's profile, and why do people do it?
5. **Making Connections:** In "Hyperconnected" (pp. 576–80), Christakis and Fowler describe a disease spreading through the virtual world of an online game. Does Copeland's essay support the idea that Facebook contributes to a real-world epidemic? Is sadness a contagion especially easily spread by social networks?

## Link to the Paired Essay

While Elizabeth Stone ("Grief in the Age of Facebook," pp. 587–91) describes young people mourning their friend online, Copeland argues that Facebook actually makes users feel worse about themselves. Can the observations of both writers be accurate? How can digital media be both a place to express sadness and also a source of sadness?

## Journal Prompts

1. Do you present a happier version of yourself online than you would face to face? If so, do you purposefully craft this rosier picture of your life, or is the rosier picture a product of the way social networks are designed? To what extent does your online persona represent your emotional life?
2. When she considers why people craft a happier persona online, Copeland suggests that "happiness is impersonal in a way that pain is not" (paragraph 5). Do privacy issues affect these questions of happiness and sadness online? What have you decided is suitable for public view online, and where do you draw the line at what is too personal?

## Suggestions for Writing

1. Write an essay exploring the longstanding human tendency to overestimate others' happiness. Why do you think people are more likely to believe others are happy? How have your own experiences illustrated or defied this tendency?
2. One of the students interviewed by Sherry Turkle (below and e-Pages) compares Facebook to a play in which users are constantly performing (paragraph 6). Recall your experience with social networking, and use it to develop the idea of social networking as playacting – or propose another analogy for this kind of online interaction. If you wish, analyze postings or sites of others to expand your supporting evidence.

## e Sherry Turkle Text

## How Computers Change the Way We Think

Sherry Turkle, nicknamed "Cybershrink," is a clinical psychologist and a professor of sociology at the Massachusetts Institute of Technology. She also founded and directs the MIT Initiative on Technology and Self, a research center devoted to "the social and psychological dimensions of technological change." In her essay, first published in the *Chronicle of Higher Education* in 2004, Turkle explores how technologies such as online chat, PowerPoint, word processors, and simulation games are radically affecting our "habits of mind." To read the article, go to Chapter 28: **bedfordstmartins.com/bedguide**.

Philip Rosedale, creator of the virtual world Second Life, stands in front of a computer projection of his original avatar.

## Off Book Editors

Video

# Generative Art – Computers, Data, and Humanity

Off Book is a Web series from PBS that chronicles the intersection of art, culture, and the Internet. In this episode, three innovative creators discuss how they push the boundaries of art and design by allowing computers to make key decisions about their creations. To see these fascinating projects and hear their creators talk about them, go to Chapter 28: **bedfordstmartins.com/bedguide**.

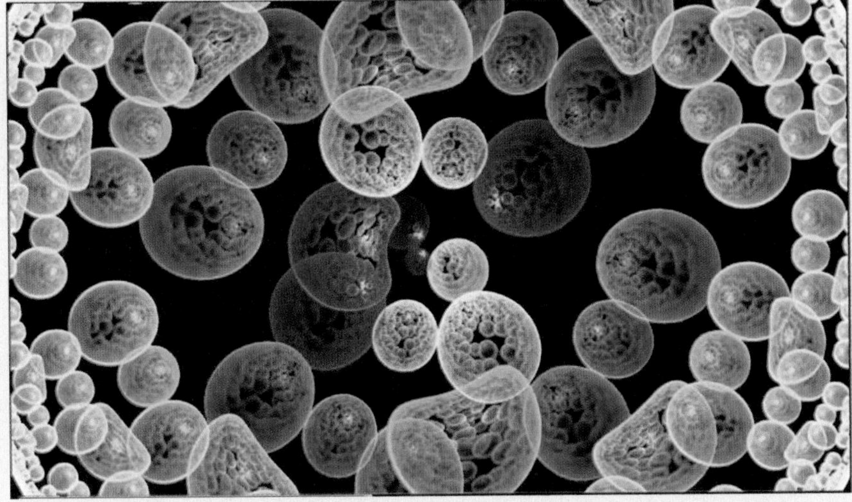

A frame from Scott Draves's "Electric Sheep," a screensaver that evolves based on audience input.

# Explorations on Living Well

# 29

### Responding to an Image

Look carefully at one of these four photographs. What time of day do you imagine the photograph was taken? Where are the people, and what are they doing? What relationships and emotions does the image suggest? Write about what the photograph seems to be saying about one or more possible elements of a happy life or a life well lived. If the photograph reminds you of your own experiences, either similar or dissimilar, bring those recollections into your written response to the photograph.

## Web Search

American and global economic and social changes during recent years have challenged many people to examine their assumptions about what it means to live well. The surveys and polls conducted by the Pew Research Center for the People and the Press report on public opinions and beliefs at people-press.org. Likewise, the United States Census Bureau site, census.gov, supplies local, regional, and national data about American values and preferences, as suggested by employment, education, and other life factors. Finally, the *This I Believe* series on National Public Radio archives personal statements on living at thisibelieve.org. Explore these or other sites that investigate possible definitions of a life well lived. What method of addressing this question do you find most compelling? Why?

## Jhumpa Lahiri

### Rice

Jhumpa Lahiri won the 2000 Pulitzer Prize for Fiction for her short story collection *Interpreter of Maladies* (1999). She also gained acclaim for her novel *The Namesake* (2003), which was adapted into a popular film. Her writing, often autobiographically inspired, explores issues of assimilation experienced by Indian immigrants in America. President Barack Obama recently appointed her to the President's Committee on the Arts and Humanities. In the following article, first published on November 23, 2009, in the *New Yorker*, Lahiri focuses on the significance of the meal that her father prepared for special occasions.

**AS YOU READ:** Consider why this meal is so important to the author's father.

My father, seventy-eight, is a methodical man. For thirty-nine years, he has had the same job, cataloguing books for a university library. He drinks two glasses of water first thing in the morning, walks for an hour every day, and devotes almost as much time, before bed, to flossing his teeth. "Winging it" is not a term that comes to mind in describing my father. When he's driving to new places, he does not enjoy getting lost. 1

In the kitchen, too, he walks a deliberate line, counting out the raisins that go into his oatmeal (fifteen) and never boiling even a drop more water than required for tea. It is my father who knows how many cups of rice are necessary to feed four, or forty, or a hundred and forty people. He has a reputation for *andaj*—the Bengali° word for "estimate"—accurately gauging quantities that tend to baffle other cooks. An oracle° of rice, if you will. 2

But there is another rice that my father is more famous for. This is not the white rice, boiled like pasta and then drained in a colander, that most Bengalis 3

**Bengali:** An ethnic group from the historic Bengal region, located in eastern India and Bangladesh. **oracle:** A prophet.

eat for dinner. This other rice is pulao, a baked, buttery, sophisticated indulgence, Persian in origin, served at festive occasions. I have often watched him make it. It involves sautéing grains of basmati in butter, along with cinnamon sticks, cloves, bay leaves, and cardamom pods. In go halved cashews and raisins (unlike the oatmeal raisins, these must be golden, not black). Ginger, pulverized into a paste, is incorporated, along with salt and sugar, nutmeg and mace, saffron threads if they're available, ground turmeric if not. A certain amount of water is added, and the rice simmers until most of the water evaporates. Then it is spread out in a baking tray. (My father prefers disposable aluminum ones, which he recycled long before recycling laws were passed.) More water is flicked on top with his fingers, in the ritual and cryptic manner of Catholic priests. Then the tray, covered with foil, goes into the oven, until the rice is cooked through and not a single grain sticks to another.

Despite having a superficial knowledge of the ingredients and the technique, I have no idea how to make my father's pulao, nor would I ever dare attempt it. The recipe is his own, and has never been recorded. There has never been an unsuccessful batch, yet no batch is ever identical to any other. It is a dish that has become an extension of himself, that he has perfected, and to which he has earned the copyright. A dish that will die with him when he dies. 4

In 1968, when I was seven months old, my father made pulao for the first time. We lived in London, in Finsbury Park, where my parents shared the kitchen, up a steep set of stairs in the attic of the house, with another Bengali couple. The occasion was my *annaprasan*, a rite of passage in which Bengali children are given solid food for the first time; it is known colloquially as a *bhath*, which happens to be the Bengali word for "cooked rice." In the oven of a stove no more than twenty inches wide, my father baked pulao for about thirty-five people. Since then, he has made pulao for the *annaprasans* of his friends' children, for birthday parties and anniversaries, for bridal and baby showers, for wedding receptions, and for my sister's Ph.D. party. For a few decades, after we moved to the United States, his pulao fed crowds of up to four hundred people, at events organized by Prabasi, a Bengali cultural institution in New England, and he found himself at institutional venues—schools and churches and community centers—working with industrial ovens and stoves. This has never unnerved him. He could probably rig up a system to make pulao out of a hot-dog cart, were someone to ask. 5

There are times when certain ingredients are missing, when he must use almonds instead of cashews, when the raisins in a friend's cupboard are the wrong color. He makes it anyway, with exacting standards but a sanguine° hand. 6

When my son and daughter were infants, and we celebrated their *annaprasans*, we hired a caterer, but my father made the pulao, preparing it at home in Rhode Island and transporting it in the trunk of his car to Brooklyn. The occasion, both times, was held at the Society for Ethical Culture, in 7

**sanguine:** Cheerful or confident.

Park Slope. In 2002, for my son's first taste of rice, my father warmed the trays on the premises, in the giant oven in the basement. But by 2005, when it was my daughter's turn, the representative on duty would not permit my father to use the oven, telling him that he was not a licensed cook. My father transferred the pulao from his aluminum trays into glass baking dishes, and microwaved, batch by batch, rice that fed almost a hundred people. When I asked my father to describe that experience, he expressed no frustration. "It was fine," he said. "It was a big microwave."

## Questions to Start You Thinking

1. **Considering Meaning:** How is the rice Lahiri writes about in this essay an extension of her father? How does she connect the attributes of the signature dish and the characteristics of the man?
2. **Identifying Writing Strategies:** Lahiri describes how her father makes his famous pulao, but her recipe is not precise enough to reproduce her father's magic. What do these detailed instructions convey to the reader? What do they leave out?
3. **Reading Critically:** Lahiri shows the importance of rice to Bengali culture. List the different appearances of rice in this essay. Analyze its role in the life of Lahiri's family.
4. **Expanding Vocabulary:** Why is the writer's knowledge of the process of making pulao "superficial" (paragraph 4). Define *superficial*, and discuss how it characterizes Lahiri's relationship to her father's particular skill.
5. **Making Connections:** Consider how "Rice" and Amy Tan's "Mother Tongue" (pp. 506–12) reflect the experiences of children of immigrants. How do these writers experience the customs of a country that they do not call home but that shaped their parents' lives?

## Journal Prompts

1. Using Lahiri's first paragraph as a model, write a brief portrait of a parent or other family member. Choose details carefully to convey as much as possible about the person in a short space.
2. What skill defines you? Is there some knowledge you have that would be difficult to transfer? Write about a task you have perfected, and consider how this ability reflects your personality.

## Suggestions for Writing

1. Recall an experience in which food played an important role for you. Describe a dish or meal that is particularly memorable, and reflect on what makes it stand out in your mind. Why do you think food takes central stage at important moments in your life?

2. Analyze how "Rice" functions as a work of praise. Though she does not say directly that this is a function of her essay, Lahiri does communicate a great deal about what she admires in her father. What does her discussion of his cooking imply about him? Why does he deserve praise? What criteria has she used to evaluate his admirable qualities?

## William Zinsser

### The Right to Fail

William Zinsser was born in New York City in 1922. With a BA from Princeton University, he became a feature writer for the *New York Herald Tribune* and later the drama and film critic. Although he has covered subjects ranging from American landmarks to jazz in his many books and magazine articles, he is probably best known for his classic guides to writing: *On Writing Well* (1976), *Inventing the Truth* (1987), *Writing to Learn* (1988), *Writing about Your Life* (2004), and *Writing Places* (2010). Zinsser has taught at Yale University, the New School, and the Columbia University Graduate School of Journalism. In "The Right to Fail," an excerpt from *The Lunacy Boom* (1970), Zinsser makes the case that failure is an important aspect of human experience.

**AS YOU READ:** Identify the benefits of failure that Zinsser presents.

I like "dropout" as an addition to the American language because it's brief and it's clear. What I don't like is that we use it almost entirely as a dirty word. 1

We only apply it to people under twenty-one. Yet an adult who spends his days and nights watching mindless TV programs is more of a dropout than an eighteen-year-old who quits college, with its frequently mindless courses, to become, say, a VISTA volunteer. For the young, dropping out is often a way of dropping in. 2

To hold this opinion, however, is little short of treason in America. A boy or girl who leaves college is branded a failure—and the right to fail is one of the few freedoms that this country does not grant its citizens. The American dream is a dream of "getting ahead," painted in strokes of gold wherever we look. Our advertisements and TV commercials are a hymn to material success, our magazine articles a toast to people who made it to the top. Smoke the right cigarette or drive the right car—so the ads imply—and girls will be swooning into your deodorized arms or caressing your expensive lapels. Happiness goes to the man who has the sweet smell of achievement. He is our national idol, and everybody else is our national fink.° 3

I want to put in a word for the fink, especially the teen-age fink, because if we give him time to get through his finkdom—if we release him from the pressure of attaining certain goals by a certain age—he has a good chance of 4

**fink:** Tattletale or other contemptible person.

becoming our national idol, a Jefferson° or a Thoreau,° a Buckminster Fuller° or an Adlai Stevenson,° a man with a mind of his own. We need mavericks° and dissenters and dreamers far more than we need junior vice presidents, but we paralyze them by insisting that every step be a step up to the next rung of the ladder. Yet in the fluid years of youth, the only way for boys and girls to find their proper road is often to take a hundred side trips, poking out in different directions, faltering, drawing back, and starting again.

"But what if we fail?" they ask, whispering the dreadful word across the Generation Gap to their parents, who are back home at the Establishment, nursing their "middle-class values" and cultivating their "goal-oriented society." The parents whisper back: "Don't!" 5

What they should say is "Don't be afraid to fail!" Failure isn't fatal. Countless people have had a bout with it and come out stronger as a result. Many have even come out famous. History is strewn with eminent dropouts, "loners" who followed their own trail, not worrying about its odd twists and turns because they had faith in their own sense of direction. To read their biographies is always exhilarating, not only because they beat the system, but because their system was better than the one that they beat. 6

Luckily, such rebels still turn up often enough to prove that individualism, though badly threatened, is not extinct. Much has been written, for instance, about the fitful scholastic career of Thomas P. F. Hoving, New York's former Parks Commissioner and now director of the Metropolitan Museum of Art. Hoving was a dropout's dropout, entering and leaving schools as if they were motels, often at the request of the management. Still, he must have learned something during those unorthodox years, for he dropped in again at the top of his profession. 7

His case reminds me of another boyhood—that of Holden Caulfield in J. D. Salinger's *The Catcher in the Rye*, the most popular literary hero of the postwar period. There is nothing accidental about the grip that this dropout continues to hold on the affections of an entire American generation. Nobody else, real or invented, has made such an engaging shambles of our "goal-oriented society," so gratified our secret belief that the "phonies" are in power and the good guys up the creek. Whether Holden has also reached the top of his chosen field today is one of those speculations that delight fanciers of good fiction. I speculate that he has. Holden Caulfield, incidentally, is now thirty-six. 8

I'm not urging everyone to go out and fail just for the sheer therapy of it, or to quit college just to coddle° some vague discontent. Obviously it's better to succeed than to flop, and in general a long education is more helpful than 9

**Jefferson:** Thomas Jefferson (1743–1826), the third president of the United States and the main author of the Declaration of Independence. **Thoreau:** Henry David Thoreau (1817–1862), an American writer and naturalist. **Buckminster Fuller:** American inventor, architect, and engineer (1895–1983) who dropped out of Harvard to work on solving global resource and environmental problems. **Adlai Stevenson:** American politician (1900–1965) who was greatly admired for championing liberal causes but badly lost two presidential elections. **mavericks:** Nonconformists. **coddle:** Indulge; satisfy.

a short one. (Thanks to my own education, for example, I can tell George Eliot from T. S. Eliot. I can handle the pluperfect tense in French, and I know that Caesar beat the Helvetii because he had enough frumentum.°) I only mean that failure isn't bad in itself, or success automatically good.

Fred Zinnemann, who has directed some of Hollywood's most honored 10
movies, was asked by a reporter, when *A Man for All Seasons* won every prize, about his previous film *Behold a Pale Horse,* which was a box-office disaster. "I don't feel any obligation to be successful," Zinnemann replied. "Success can be dangerous—you feel you know it all. I've learned a great deal from my failures." A similar point was made by Richard Brooks about his ambitious money loser, *Lord Jim.* Recalling the three years of his life that went into it, talking almost with elation about the troubles that befell his unit in Cambodia, Brooks told me that he learned more about his craft from this considerable failure than from his many earlier hits.

It's a point, of course, that applies throughout the arts. Writers, play- 11
wrights, painters, and composers work in the expectation of periodic defeat, but they wouldn't keep going back into the arena if they thought it was the end of the world. It isn't the end of the world. For an artist—and perhaps for anybody—it is the only way to grow.

Today's younger generation seems to know that this is true, seems willing 12
to take the risks in life that artists take in art. "Society," needless to say, still has the upper hand—it sets the goals and condemns as a failure everybody who won't play. But the dropouts and the hippies are not as afraid of failure as their parents and grandparents. This could mean, as their elders might say, that they are just plumb lazy, secure in the comforts of an affluent state. It could also mean, however, that they just don't buy the old standards of success and are rapidly writing new ones.

Recently it was announced, for instance, that more than two hundred 13
thousand Americans have inquired about service in VISTA (the domestic Peace Corps) and that, according to a Gallup survey, "more than three million American college students would serve VISTA in some capacity if given the opportunity." This is hardly the road to riches or to an executive suite. Yet I have met many of these young volunteers, and they are not pining for traditional success. On the contrary, they appear more fulfilled than the average vice president with a swimming pool.

Who is to say, then, if there is any right path to the top, or even to say 14
what the top consists of? Obviously the colleges don't have more than a partial answer—otherwise the young would not be so disaffected with an education that they consider vapid.° Obviously business does not have the answer—otherwise the young would not be so scornful of its call to be an organization man.

The fact is, nobody has the answer, and the dawning awareness of this 15
fact seems to me one of the best things happening in America today. Success

**frumentum:** Latin word for corn or grain. **vapid:** Dull.

and failure are again becoming individual visions, as they were when the country was younger, not rigid categories. Maybe we are learning again to cherish this right of every person to succeed on his own terms and to fail as often as necessary along the way.

## Questions to Start You Thinking

1. **Considering Meaning:** What does Zinsser mean when he says that "dropping out is often a way of dropping in" (paragraph 2)? Why is this especially true for young adults?
2. **Identifying Writing Strategies:** Identify some of the concrete examples that Zinsser uses to illustrate his points. Are his examples extensive and varied enough to be convincing? Why, or why not?
3. **Reading Critically:** Zinsser is savvy enough to admit that his position is "little short of treason in America" (paragraph 3). Where else does he acknowledge that his advice might seem outlandish? How does he counter the opposition?
4. **Expanding Vocabulary:** In paragraph 3, Zinsser writes, "Our advertisements and TV commercials are a hymn to material success." Define *hymn*. What does the word suggest about the American attitude toward material success? How does Zinsser feel about the American dream?
5. **Making Connections:** Zinsser says in paragraph 13 that the volunteers he has met seemed "more fulfilled than the average vice president." Using Gareth Cook's essay "Getting It All Done" (pp. 605–07) as evidence, explain why Zinsser's statement could be true.

## Journal Prompts

1. What is your definition of the "American dream" (paragraph 3)?
2. Who would you like to share Zinsser's essay with in order to open up that person's mind about failure? Why?

## Suggestions for Writing

1. In paragraph 10, Zinsser offers the following quote from a movie director: "Success can be dangerous—you feel you know it all. I've learned a great deal from my failures." Write an essay in which you recall a personal experience that illustrates this statement.
2. Originally written in 1970, Zinsser's essay includes some examples that may not be familiar to you. Write an essay that supports and updates Zinsser's position by drawing on more current examples from history, literature, sports, current events, or popular culture. Imagine a specific audience for your essay (perhaps a sibling, a friend, or a high school class). Be sure your examples will have an impact on those readers.

## Gareth Cook

## Getting It All Done

Gareth Cook is currently a columnist for the *Boston Globe*, writing a variety of science-based articles. He also edits *Mind Matters*, a blog for *Scientific American*. His piece for *WIRED* magazine, "Untangling the Mystery of the Inca," was included in *Best American Science Writing* in 2008. In the following April 2012 article in the *Boston Globe*, Cook offers a coping strategy for those who feel that there is not enough time in the day to get everything done.

**AS YOU READ:** Identify Cook's solution to the problem of getting everything done.

1 America has a time problem. About half of us tell pollsters that we don't have enough time to do what we want. Another survey found that most people would prefer two more weeks of vacation than two more weeks of pay. And every new "labor-saving" technology — e-mail, smartphones — seems to make things worse, not better.

2 Books for the time-starved and productivity-challenged would fill a small library. Beyond the books, there are the seminars, videos, apps, and "methods" (like "Getting Things Done")° — which feature books, videos, seminars and apps. Yet for all the advice that has been offered, I doubt anyone has come up with the bit of wisdom on offer from a professor at Harvard Business School: Spend more time doing things for other people.

3 This is, of course, absurd. How could taking on another task possibly help? The answer has to do with the important distinction between time — that thing that can be measured with atomic clocks, that marches on, merciless — and subjective time, our experience of the flow of events. And this is why the advice, the product of recent scientific study, is both unexpected and wise. "It is not so much how much time you have," says Harvard Business School's Michael Norton, "as how you feel about what you can get done in the time that you do have."

4 Norton, working with Cassie Mogilner at the University of Pennsylvania and Zoe Chance at Yale, arrived at this conclusion through a series of investigations into our perception of time. Students were asked to either give time away (writing an encouraging note to a gravely ill child) or waste time (counting instances of the letter "e" in a Latin text). Afterwards, the letter writers felt that they had more time, according to a survey.

5 But maybe, the researchers reasoned, doing the time-wasting task was simply unpleasant, and this bad mood made people feel they had less time. So they did another experiment, asking students on a Saturday morning to do something they hadn't planned to, either for themselves or for someone else. They found that the people who did a good turn for another felt like they had more time.

**Getting Things Done:** A program designed to teach clients to be more productive.

Finally, they did an experiment that got right to the heart of the matter. They told a class that at the end of a lab session they would be helping at-risk students from a local high school by editing an essay they were working on. When the time came, half were given the essays to work on, and the other half of the class was told that there were no more essays to work on, and they could leave early. Here, then, the researchers were comparing the effect of doing something for someone else, and having a sudden, unexpected windfall of time. As they report in the journal *Psychological Science*, the people who helped with the essays said that they felt they had more time to take care of their work than the people who'd been given free time. 6

Allow this strange fact to sink in: The best solution for not having enough time is not being given more time. It turns out that people are extraordinarily bad at estimating how much time a task will take to complete; this is known in psychology as "the planning fallacy." 7

"One of the things that can happen when you are overbooked or overstressed is that even the tiniest thing that comes up can feel insurmountable,"° says Norton. "We have all had the experience of getting that one more e-mail and feeling like, 'O, I am doomed.'" 8

The planning fallacy means that we have a poor sense of how much effort it will take to complete that to-do list we carry around with us. And this, in turn, means that the stress we all feel—How can I get it all done?—is only loosely connected to reality. Norton argues that doing something for someone else provides a tremendous boost in our confidence that we can get things done. It makes us feel in control of our lives—effective. The future feels more open. 9

There is certainly an upper limit to this effect, a point at which the hours of helping others become an additional stress. And, clearly, improving one's time-management skills is bound to help. Yet the research solves a central paradox:° Americans feel daunting time pressures, and yet, by any historical measure, they have a tremendous amount of leisure time. We are all busy, yes. But we also labor under potent illusions, and isn't it a wondrous thing we can help ourselves see through them by lending a hand to someone else? 10

## Questions to Start You Thinking

1. **Considering Meaning:** Cook reviews research that suggests we do not need more time to *feel* like we have more time. What, instead, would help Americans to feel less rushed? How does the research ask us to reevaluate our time management?

**insurmountable:** Impossible to conquer. **paradox:** Something that seems to contradict itself.

2. **Identifying Writing Strategies:** Cook calls Michael Norton's findings "absurd" before going on to explain them (paragraph 3). Why does Cook make this statement? How does his initial skepticism affect you as a reader?
3. **Reading Critically:** Which of the experiments that Cook cites do you find most persuasive? Why? What does this research show about our perceptions of time?
4. **Expanding Vocabulary:** What is a *fallacy* (paragraph 7)? How does that word describe the way people plan, or fail to plan, their time?
5. **Making Connections:** Like Cook, Libby Copeland ("Is Facebook Making Us Sad?" pp. 591–95) considers how subjective perception can have a greater impact on feelings than what is true. Why does the way we see the world play such an important role in our emotional lives? Explain how you think each author would answer this question.

## Journal Prompts

1. Does your experience support the distinction Cook draws between clock time and "subjective time" (paragraph 3)? Under what circumstances or in what situations is the difference between these two kinds of time most apparent? Why do you think this is the case?
2. Keep a careful log of how you use your time for a few days. Are you surprised by how you spend your hours or by how much leisure time you have? What have you learned from keeping track of your time in this way?

## Suggestions for Writing

1. Propose a solution for time-strapped college students based on the findings reported in this essay. How could you and your classmates implement a program that helps others and enhances, rather than reduces, the time you spend on your studies?
2. Interview a friend, instructor, or coworker about how he or she uses time-saving technology, such as e-mail, texting, or Skype. In what ways does the technology actually save time? How does it place new demands on one's schedule? Overall, is the technology worth it? Write an essay reporting the focus of the interview.

## Mihaly Csikszentmihalyi

## Happiness Revisited

Mihaly Csikszentmihalyi (pronounced MEE-hy CHEEK-sent-ma-HY-ee) is a researcher and psychology professor at Claremont Graduate University, where he runs the Quality of Life Research Center. His research on happiness and creativity led to his theory on "flow," a positive psychology concept that involves a person's total immersion in an activity to the point of full focus and the resulting enjoyment. Csikszentmihalyi has written widely on the theory, which has been applied to a variety of different disciplines. "Happiness Revisited" is a chapter from one of his most successful works, *Flow: The Psychology of Optimal Experience* (1990).

**AS YOU READ:** Identify the ways that Csikszentmihalyi maintains we can experience happiness.

Twenty-three hundred years ago Aristotle° concluded that, more than anything else, men and women seek happiness. While happiness itself is sought for its own sake, every other goal—health, beauty, money, or power—is valued only because we expect that it will make us happy. Much has changed since Aristotle's time. Our understanding of the worlds of stars and of atoms has expanded beyond belief. The gods of the Greeks were like helpless children compared to humankind today and the powers we now wield. And yet on this most important issue very little has changed in the intervening centuries. We do not understand what happiness is any better than Aristotle did, and as for learning how to attain that blessed condition, one could argue that we have made no progress at all. 1

Despite the fact that we are now healthier and grow to be older, despite the fact that even the least affluent among us are surrounded by material luxuries undreamed of even a few decades ago (there were few bathrooms in the palace of the Sun King,° chairs were rare even in the richest medieval houses, and no Roman emperor could turn on a TV set when he was bored), and regardless of all the stupendous scientific knowledge we can summon at will, people often end up feeling that their lives have been wasted, that instead of being filled with happiness their years were spent in anxiety and boredom. 2

Is this because it is the destiny of mankind to remain unfulfilled, each person always wanting more than he or she can have? Or is the pervasive° malaise° that often sours even our most precious moments the result of our seeking happiness in the wrong places? . . . 3

Happiness is not something that happens. It is not the result of good fortune or random chance. It is not something money can buy or power command. It does not depend on outside events, but rather, on how we interpret them. Happiness, in fact, is a condition that must be prepared for, culti- 4

**Aristotle:** An ancient Greek philosopher (427 BCE–347 BCE), who studied under Plato. **Sun King:** Louis XIV (1638–1715), who ruled as king of France for seventy-two years. **pervasive:** Something widely spread. **malaise:** A general feeling of anxiety or depression with no identifiable source.

vated,° and defended privately by each person. People who learn to control inner experience will be able to determine the quality of their lives, which is as close as any of us can come to being happy.

5 Yet we cannot reach happiness by consciously searching for it. "Ask yourself whether you are happy," said John Stuart Mill,° "and you cease to be so." It is by being fully involved with every detail of our lives, whether good or bad, that we find happiness, not by trying to look for it directly. Viktor Frankl, the Austrian psychologist, summarized it beautifully in the preface to his book *Man's Search for Meaning*: "Don't aim at success—the more you aim at it and make it a target, the more you are going to miss it. For success, like happiness, cannot be pursued; it must ensue°. . . as the unintended side effect of one's personal dedication to a cause greater that oneself."

6 So how can we reach this elusive goal that cannot be attained by a direct route? My studies of the past quarter century have convinced me that there is a way. It is a circuitous path that begins with achieving control over the contents of our consciousness.

7 Our perceptions about our lives are the outcome of many forces that shape experience, each having an impact on whether we feel good or bad. Most of these forces are outside our control. There is not much we can do about our look, our temperament, or our constitution. We cannot decide—at least so far—how tall we will grow, how smart we will get. We can choose neither parents nor time of birth, and it is not in your power or mine to decide whether there will be a war or a depression. The instructions contained in our genes, the pull of gravity, the pollen in the air, the historical period into which we are born—these and innumerable other conditions determine what we see, how we feel, what we do. It is not surprising that we should believe that our fate is primarily ordained by outside agencies.

8 Yet we have all experienced times when, instead of being buffeted° by anonymous forces, we do feel in control of our actions, masters of our own fate. On the rare occasions that it happens, we feel a sense of exhilaration, a deep sense of enjoyment that is long cherished and that becomes a landmark in memory for what life should be like.

9 This is what we mean by "optimal experience." It is what the sailor holding a tight course feels when the wind whips through her hair, when the boat lunges through the waves like a colt—sails, hull, wind, and sea humming a harmony that vibrates in the sailor's veins. It is what a painter feels when the colors on the canvas begin to set up a magnetic tension with each other, and a new *thing*, a living form, takes shape in front of the astonished creator. Or it is the feeling a father has when his child for the first time responds to his smile. Such events do not occur only when the external conditions are favorable, however: people who have survived concentration camps or who have lived through near-fatal physical dangers often recall that in the midst of

**cultivated:** Grown in a controlled, intentional manner. **John Stuart Mill:** A British philosopher (1806–1873). **ensue:** Result. **buffeted:** Knocked around.

their ordeal they experienced extraordinarily rich epiphanies° in response to such simple events as hearing the song of a bird in the forest, completing a hard task, or sharing a crust of bread with a friend.

Contrary to what we usually believe, moments like these, the best moments in our lives, are not the passive, receptive, relaxing times—although such experiences can also be enjoyable, if we have worked hard to attain them. The best moments usually occur when a person's body or mind is stretched to its limits in a voluntary effort to accomplish something difficult and worthwhile. Optimal experience is thus something that we *make* happen. For a child, it could be placing with trembling fingers the last block on a tower she has built, higher than any she has built so far; for a swimmer, it could be trying to beat his own record; for a violinist, mastering an intricate° musical passage. For each person there are thousands of opportunities, challenges to expand ourselves. 10

Such experiences are not necessarily pleasant at the time they occur. The swimmer's muscles might have ached during his most memorable race, his lungs might have felt like exploding, and he might have been dizzy with fatigue—yet these could have been the best moments of his life. Getting control of life is never easy, and sometimes it can be definitely painful. But in the long run optimal experiences add up to a sense of mastery—or, perhaps better, a sense of *participation* in determining the content of life—that comes as close to what is usually meant by happiness as anything else we can conceivably imagine. 11

## Questions to Start You Thinking

1. **Considering Meaning:** Csikszentmihalyi says people achieve happiness "not by trying to look for it directly" (paragraph 5). What does he suggest someone can do instead of striving for it?
2. **Identifying Writing Strategies:** Paragraph two is one long sentence. Examine the structure and the parts that make up the sentence. What effect does the sentence have on a reader?
3. **Reading Critically:** Csikszentmihalyi points out that while the world has changed radically since Aristotle's time, our understanding of happiness has not progressed much. Why is this the case? How does Csikszentmihalyi think people should change their mindset?
4. **Expanding Vocabulary:** Look up the definition of *circuitous*. Why does Csikszentmihalyi think a "circuitous path" is more likely to lead to happiness than a "direct route" (paragraph 6)?
5. **Making Connections:** What does this article's suggestion about how to achieve happiness through "optimal experience" (paragraphs 9–11)

**epiphanies:** Sudden, joyous feelings of understanding. **intricate:** Complex.

have in common with "Getting It All Done" (pp. 605–07), Gareth Cook's investigation into how people can feel like they have more time?

### Journal Prompts

1. Csikszentmihalyi defines happiness in terms of how we achieve it. How would you describe the way happiness feels? What exactly is this state that humans try so hard to achieve?
2. Csikszentmihalyi takes some cues from a group of philosophers called the Stoics, who suggested that humans stop worrying about things they cannot control. What would he say about what humans *can* control? What do you think people can control in life?

### Suggestions for Writing

1. Does Csikszentmihalyi have a hopeful view of happiness? Write an essay in which you take a stand on whether this view of happiness is positive or pessimistic.
2. Interview someone you know about his or her "optimal experience" (paragraph 9). Would he or she agree that these moments offer the greatest happiness in life? Write an essay about the interview, clearly focusing on the dominant impression you want to convey to readers.

## Juliet Schor

## The Creation of Discontent

Juliet Schor, a professor of sociology at Boston College, currently is studying trends in environmental sustainability, consumerism, and the relationship between work and family. She is a cofounder of South End Press, the Center for Popular Economics, and the Center for a New American Dream. Schor is a Guggenheim Fellowship recipient, and her awards have included the George Orwell Award for Distinguished Contributions to Honesty and Clarity in Public Language from the National Council of Teachers of English. Her books include *The Overspent American: Why We Want What We Don't Need* (1998), *Do Americans Shop Too Much?* (2000), *Born to Buy: The Commercialized Child and the New Consumer Culture* (2004), *Plenitude: The New Economics of True Wealth* (2010), and *The Overworked American: The Unexpected Decline of Leisure* (1992), from which this reading is taken. Here, Schor examines Americans' increasing material wealth and questions the assumption that it leads to greater fulfillment.

**AS YOU READ:** How does Schor connect material prosperity and unhappiness?

*I never knew how poor I was until I had a little money.*
—a banker

1 There is no doubt that the growth of consumption has yielded major improvements in the quality of life. Running water, washing machines, and electrical appliances eliminated arduous, often backbreaking labor. Especially for the poor women who not only did their own housework, but often someone else's as well, the transformation of the home has been profoundly liberating. Other products have also enhanced the quality of life. The compact disc raises the enjoyment of the music lover; the high-performance engine makes the car buff happy; and the fashion plate loves to wear a designer suit.

2 But when we add up all the items we consume, and consider the overall impact, rather than each in isolation, the picture gets murkier. The farther we get from the onerous° physical conditions of the past, the more ambiguous° are the effects of additional commodities. The less "necessary" and more "luxurious" the item, the more difficult it is automatically to assume that consumer purchases yield intrinsic value.

3 In an era when the connections between perpetual growth and environmental deterioration are becoming more apparent, with the quality of public life declining in many areas (public safety, decline of community, failing education system), shouldn't we at least step back and re-examine our commitment to ever-greater quantities of consumer goods? Do Americans need high-definition television, increasingly exotic vacations, and climate control in their autos? How about hundred-dollar inflatable sneakers, fifty-dollar wrinkle cream, or the ever-present (but rarely used) stationary bicycle? A growing fraction of homes are now equipped with jacuzzis (or steam showers) and satellite receivers. Once we take the broader view, can we still be so sure that all these things are really making us better off?

4 We do know that the increasing consumption of the last forty years has not made us happier. The percentage of the population who reported being "very happy" peaked in 1957, according to two national polls. By the last years these polls were taken (1970 and 1978), the level of "very happy" had not recovered, in spite of the rapid growth in consumption during the 1960s and 1970s. Similar polls taken since then indicate no revival of happiness.[1]

5 Despite the fact that possessions are not creating happiness, we are still riding the consumer merry-go-round. In fact, for some Americans the quest for material goods became more intense in the last decade: according to the pollster Louis Harris, "by the mid-1980s, the American people were far more oriented toward economic growth and materialism than before. Most significant, young people were leading the charge back to material values" (148).

**onerous:** Heavy, oppressive. **ambiguous:** Unclear; having several possible meanings.

1. A number of polls ask identical questions, yet give different levels of happiness. For example, the General Social Survey polls yield consistently higher results than the Survey Research Center or the National Opinion Research Corporation. SRC and NORC polls end in the 1970s; the GSS poll continues through the 1980s. The conclusion that "very happy" has not recovered is based on the GSS poll, which begins in 1972 and is the only poll still being taken during the 1980s. The GSS peaks in 1973 and does not recover throughout the 1980s. See Niemi, 290.

Materialism has not only failed to make us happy. It has also bred its own form of discontent—even among the affluent.° Newspaper and magazine articles chronicle the dissatisfaction. One couple earning $115,000 tallied up their necessary expenses of $100,000 a year and complained that "something's gone terribly wrong with being 'rich'" (Hewitt). An unmarried Hollywood executive earning $72,000 worried about bouncing checks: "I have so much paid for by the studio—my car, my insurance, and virtually all food and entertainment—and I'm *still* broke." Urbanites° have it especially hard. As one New York City inhabitant explained, "It's incredible, but you just can't live in this city on a hundred thousand dollars a year" (Tobias 24). According to the *New York Times,* the fast lane is not all it's cracked up to be, and Wall Streeters are "Feeling Poor on $600,000 a Year." "When the Joneses they are keeping up with are the Basses . . . $10 million in liquid capital° is not rich" (Kroeger). 6

Whatever we think of these malcontents°—whether we find them funny, pathetic, or reprehensible°—we must acknowledge that these feelings are not confined to those in the income stratosphere. Many who make far less have similar laments. Douglas and Maureen Obey earn $56,000 a year—an income that exceeds that of roughly 70 percent of the population (Mishel 25). Yet they complain that they are stretched to the breaking point. Douglas works two jobs "to try to keep it all together. . . . I feel I make a fairly good income that should afford a comfortable life style, but somehow it doesn't. . . . [I'm] in hock° up to my eyeballs." The Obeys own their home, two cars, a second rental property, and a backyard pool (Coakley 1). 7

Complaints about life style have been particularly loud among the baby-boom generation. One writer explained a state of mind shared by many in her generation: she was convinced she would not achieve the comfortable middle-class life style enjoyed by her parents (four-bedroom house, two-car garage, private schools for the children, and cashmere blankets at the bottom of the beds): "I thought bitterly of my downward mobility . . . and [had] constant conversations with myself about wanting . . . a new couch, a weekend cottage, a bigger house on a quieter street" (Butler 34). Eventually she realized that more money was not the answer. Her needs were satisfied. As she acknowledged: "Discontent was cheating me of the life I *had*" (37). 8

## Works Cited

Butler, Katy. "The Great Boomer Bust." *Mother Jones* June 1989: 32–38. Print.

Coakley, Tom. "One Couple's Lament Captures Anti-tax Mood." *Boston Globe* 2 Feb. 1990: 1. Print.

Harris, Louis. *Inside America.* New York: Vintage, 1987. Print.

Hewitt, Paul S. "Something's Gone Terribly Wrong with Being 'Rich.'" *Los Angeles Herald Tribune* 7 Jan. 1989. Print.

The sources for Schor's study are presented in MLA style.

**affluent:** Wealthy. **urbanites:** People who live in cities. **liquid capital:** Cash, or assets that can be easily converted into cash. **malcontents:** People who are never satisfied. **reprehensible:** Deserving of criticism or blame. **hock:** Debt.

Kroeger, Brooke. "Feeling Poor on $600,000 a Year." *New York Times* 26 Apr. 1987. Print.

Mishel, Lawrence, and David Frankel. *The State of Working America.* Armonk, NY: M. E. Sharpe, 1991. Print.

Niemi, Richard G., John Mueller, and Tom W. Smith. *Trends in Public Opinion: A Compendium of Survey Data.* New York: Greenwood, 1989. Print.

Tobias, Andrew. "Getting by on $100,000 a Year." *Esquire* 23 May 1978: 24. Print.

## Questions to Start You Thinking

1. **Considering Meaning:** How does increasing consumption and materialism also increase discontent, according to Schor?
2. **Identifying Writing Strategies:** Schor begins this essay with a quotation from an anonymous banker. How does this quotation function as an introduction to her essay?
3. **Reading Critically:** What is the purpose of Schor's first paragraph? What point is she making? Why is it necessary?
4. **Expanding Vocabulary:** Schor notes that it is increasingly unclear whether the items people buy have any "intrinsic value" (paragraph 2). What does it mean for something to have intrinsic value? Why is "intrinsic value" important to Schor's argument about consumption and happiness?
5. **Making Connections:** Schor and Mihaly Csikszentmihalyi ("Happiness Revisited," pp. 608–11) argue that money cannot buy happiness. Contrast the nature of their arguments. For example, how does Schor structure her argument differently than Csikszentmihalyi structures his? How do they employ sources differently?

## Link to the Paired Essay

To analyze two appeals to magazine readers, based on different assumptions about life, turn to p. 14.

In paragraph 3, Schor asks a series of rhetorical questions such as, "Do Americans need high-definition television, increasingly exotic vacations, and climate control in their autos? How about hundred-dollar inflatable sneakers, fifty-dollar wrinkle cream, or the ever-present (but rarely used) stationary bicycle?" How might Llewellyn H. Rockwell Jr. ("In Defense of Consumerism," pp. 615–20) react to these questions? How do you think he would respond to other aspects of Schor's essay? Which writer do you find more persuasive, and why?

## Journal Prompts

1. Schor argues that the differences between "necessary" and "luxurious" consumer purchases have become blurred (paragraph 2). Have you ever

bought something that you felt was a necessity, but that others might view as a luxury, or vice versa? What made you decide that the item was a luxury or a necessity?

2. In 1986, a newspaper writer coined the term *retail therapy*, which is the practice of buying things in order to change your mood or state of mind, not because you need a particular product. Have you ever engaged in "retail therapy"? Did you find it helpful or harmful?

## Suggestions for Writing

1. Schor writes about a woman who worries that she will never have as comfortable a lifestyle as her parents had when she was growing up (paragraph 8). Do you expect to lead a better or worse lifestyle than your parents? What elements of their lifestyle would you like to experience? What elements would you prefer not to include in your own life?
2. Schor cites a pollster who asserts that, by the mid-1980s, increased materialism was primarily being driven by young people (paragraph 5). Is that still the case today? Based on your experience and observation of today's culture and on some research about current economics, write an essay discussing what segment of society drives consumer spending.

## Llewellyn H. Rockwell Jr.

## In Defense of Consumerism

Llewellyn H. Rockwell Jr. was born in 1944 in Boston, Massachusetts. He received his degree in English from Tufts University. He is an American political commentator and chairman and CEO of the libertarian Ludwig von Mises Institute. From 1978 to 1982, he was Ron Paul's congressional chief of staff. His work includes *The Left, The Right, & The State* (2009); *Speaking of Liberty,* an anthology of editorials and speeches; and the *Journal of Libertarian Studies,* which he publishes with the Ludwig von Mises Institute. His work also appears in *Conservative Digest.* He maintains a Web site, LewRockwell.com, where he blogs, records podcasts, and reprints articles with a libertarian perspective. In this essay, written for the Ludwig von Mises Institute, Rockwell offers a spirited defense of consumption and free-market capitalism.

**AS YOU READ:** How does Rockwell defend consumerism?

I'm beginning to think that the epithet° "consumerism" is just another word for freedom in the marketplace. 1

It's true that the market is delivering goods, services, and technological advances by leaps, day after day. People claim that they are so inundated° with techno advances that they don't want any more. Say no to the latest gizmo! 2

**epithet:** Characterization; insult. **inundated:** Flooded.

But we really don't mean it. No one wants to be denied Web access, and we want it faster and better with more variety. We want to download songs, movies, and treatises on every subject. No amount of information is too much when it is something specific we seek. 3

And that's not all. 4

We want better heating and cooling in our homes and businesses. We want more varieties of food, wine, cleaning products, toothpaste, and razors. We want access to a full range of styles in our home furnishing. If something is broken, we want the materials made available to repair it. We want fresh flowers, fresh fish, fresh bread, and new cars with more features. We want overnight delivery, good tech support, and the newest fashions from all over the world. 5

The libraries are going online, as is the world's art. Commerce has made the shift. New worlds are opening to us by the day. We find that phone calls are free. We can link with anyone in the world through instant messaging, and email has become the medium that makes all communication possible. We are abandoning our tube-televisions and landline telephones – staples of 20th-century life – for far superior modes of information technology. 6

We want speed. We want wireless. We want access. And improvements. Clean and filtered water must flow from our refrigerators. We want energy drinks, sports drinks, bubbly drinks, juicy drinks, and underground spring water from Fiji. We want homes. We want safety and security. We want service. We want choice. 7

We are getting all these things. And how? Through that incredible production and distribution machine called the market economy, which is really nothing but billions of people cooperating and innovating to make better lives for themselves. There's no dog-eat-dog. Competition is really nothing but entrepreneurs and capitalists falling over themselves in a quest to win the hearts and minds of the consuming public. 8

Sure, it's easy to look at all this and shout: ghastly consumerism! But if by "consume" we mean to purchase products and services with our own money in order to improve the human condition, who can't help but plead guilty? 9

The whole history of ideas about society has been spent trying to come up with some system that serves the common man rather than just the elites, the rulers, and the powerful. When the market economy, and its capitalistic structure, came into being, that institution was finally discovered. With the advent of economic science, we came to understand how this could be. We began to see how it is that billions of unplanned economic choices could conspire to create a beautiful global system of production and distribution that served everyone. And how do the intellectuals respond to this? By denouncing it as providing too much to too many. 10

But are people buying superfluous° things that they can do without? Certainly. But who is to say for sure what is a need as versus a mere want? A 11

**superfluous:** Unnecessary.

dictator who knows all? How can we know that his desires will accord with my needs and yours? In any case, in a market economy, wants and needs are linked, so that one person's necessities are met precisely because other people's wants are met.

Here is an example. 12

If my grandchild is desperately sick, I want to get her to a doctor. The 13 urgent-care clinic is open late, as is the drug store next door, and thank goodness. I'm in and out, and I have the medicine and materials necessary to restore her to health. No one would say that this is a superficial demand.

But it can only stay open late because its offices are nestled in a strip mall 14 where the rents are low and the access is high. The real estate is shared by candy stores, sports shops selling scuba gear, a billiard hall, and a store that specializes in party favors—all stores selling "superficial" things. All pay rent. The developer who made the mall wouldn't have built the place were it not for these less urgent needs.

The same is true for the furniture and equipment and labor used in the 15 urgent-care clinic. They are less expensive and more accessible than they otherwise would be due to the persistence of non-essential consumer demands. The computers they use are up-to-date and fast precisely because technicians and entrepreneurs have innovated to meet the demands of gamers, gamblers, and people who use the Web to do things they shouldn't.

The same point can be made about "luxury goods" and bleeding-edge 16 technologies. The rich acquire them and use them until the bugs are gone, the imitators are aroused, capitalists seek out cheaper suppliers, and eventually prices tumble and the same technology hits the mass market. Moreover, it is the rich who donate to charity, the arts, and to religion. They provide the capital necessary for investment. If you think through any service or good that is widely considered to be a need, you will find that it employs products, technologies, and services that were first created to meet superficial demands.

Maybe you think quality of life is no big deal. Does it really matter 17 whether people have access to vast grocery stores, drug stores, subdivisions, and technology? Part of the answer has to do with natural rights: people should be free to choose and buy as they see fit. But another argument is buried in data we don't often think about.

Consider life expectancy in the age of consumerism. Women in 1900 typi- 18 cally died at 48 years old, and men at 46. Today? Women live to 80, and men to 77. This is due to better diet, less dangerous jobs, improved sanitation and hygiene, improved access to health care, and the entire range of factors that contribute to what we call our standard of living. Just since 1950, the infant mortality rate has fallen by 77 percent. Population is rising exponentially as a result.

It's easy to look at these figures that suggest that we could have achieved 19 the same thing with a central plan for health, while avoiding all this disgusting consumerism that goes along with it. But such a central plan was tried in socialist countries, and their results showed precisely the opposite in mortality statistics. While the Soviets decried our persistent poverty amidst rampant consumerism, our poverty was being beaten back and our longevity was increasing, in large part because of the consumerism for which we were being reviled.°

Nowadays we are being told that consumption is aesthetically displeasing, and that we should strive to get back to nature, stop driving here and there, make a compost pile, raise our own vegetables, unplug our computers, and eat nuts off trees. This longing for the primitive is nothing but an attempt to cast a pleasing gloss on the inevitable effects of socialist policies. They are telling us to love poverty and hate plenty. 20

But the beauty of the market economy is that it gives everyone a choice. For those people who prefer outhouses to indoor plumbing, pulling their teeth to dentistry, and eating nuts from trees rather than buying a can of Planters at Wal-Mart, they too have the right to choose that way of life. But don't let them say that they are against "consumerism." To live at all requires that we buy and sell. To be against commerce is to attack life itself. 21

## Questions to Start You Thinking

1. **Considering Meaning:** According to Rockwell, why is superfluous spending (paragraph 11) and "rampant consumerism" (paragraph 19) a good thing?
2. **Identifying Writing Strategies:** Why does Rockwell write much of the essay in the first person plural (using *we*)? What effect does it have?
3. **Reading Critically:** Other than including statistics on life expectancy in paragraph 18, Rockwell cites no sources, no supporting evidence, and no one who opposes his point of view. How does this choice affect the effectiveness of his essay? What does it suggest about his audience? What sources might he have included to support his argument?
4. **Expanding Vocabulary:** Rockwell writes, "Nowadays we are being told that consumption is aesthetically displeasing . . ." (paragraph 20). What does *aesthetically displeasing* mean? Why would people describe consumption in this way?
5. **Making Connections:** Rockwell describes consumers as wanting variety and access. How might the behavior described in Emily Yoffe's "Seeking" (pp. 572–75) feed into consumer motivations? Use evidence from both selections to support your thesis.

## Link to the Paired Essay

Rockwell states that "to be against commerce is to attack life itself" (paragraph 21). How might Juliet Schor ("The Creation of Discontent," pp. 611–15) respond to Rockwell's conception of "life," as stated here?

**reviled:** Verbally attacked.

## Journal Prompts

1. Rockwell argues that we may say that we do not want more goods or technological advancements, but "we really don't mean it" (paragraph 3). Do you have any hesitations or mixed emotions about consumption or new technologies in the marketplace?
2. According to Rockwell, freedom of individual consumption "has to do with natural rights" (paragraph 17). What is a "natural right"? Do you consider freedom of choice as a consumer a "natural right"? How do your rights as a consumer and your rights as a citizen differ?

## Suggestions for Writing

1. Write an essay that articulates your own view of consumption and consumer culture. Do you see it as an unqualified good, as Rockwell does? Do you take a more skeptical view, along the lines of Juliet Schor?
2. Rockwell disparages those who believe that people should live closer to nature – making compost, growing vegetables, reducing driving, and so forth – because he sees a more primitive lifestyle as one of "the inevitable effects of socialist policies" (paragraph 20). Write an essay agreeing or disagreeing with him, using evidence from popular culture, contemporary politics, or recent history to support or refute his claim.
3. Eric Weiner, the author of the popular book *The Geography of Bliss: One Grump's Search for the Happiest Places in the World* (2008), found that social scientists have been studying the question of what makes people happy, looking for broad patterns. He summarizes their research findings in this way:

    > Extroverts are happier than introverts; optimists are happier than pessimists; married people are happier than singles, though people with children are no happier than childless couples; Republicans are happier than Democrats; people who attend religious services are happier than those who do not; people with college degrees are happier than those without, though people with advanced degrees are less happy than those with just a BA; people with an active sex life are happier than those without; women and men are equally happy, though women have a wider emotional range; having an affair will make you happy but will not compensate for the massive loss of happiness that you will incur when your spouse finds out and leaves you; people are least happy when they're commuting to work; busy people are happier than those with too little to do; wealthy people are happier than poor ones, but only slightly.
    >
    > – *The Geography of Bliss,* New York: Twelve, 2008, p. 14.

    These findings suggest, as do the essays of Schor and Rockwell, that the factors contributing to "a good life" are often varied, interconnected, and complicated, with no one formula that works for all.

Drawing on your own experience, write an essay on what happiness means for you. What are the essential factors for happiness from your perspective, including both obvious factors and less obvious ones. In your essay, quote from Schor's "The Creation of Discontent," Rockwell's "In Defense of Consumerism," and Weiner's excerpt, tying your own experience with the general points these writers express.

4. Rainbows are a natural phenomenon, caused by optics and weather. They cannot be touched nor reached. They are caused when the sun's white light is separated into its various component wavelengths (which we perceive as colors) by water drops suspended in the Earth's atmosphere. The droplets act as prisms. The sun's white light rays are bent as they enter the drops, and the degree to which they are bent depends on their wavelengths. The different colors of light emerge from the droplets and merge together again to form a big, bright, multilayered, white circular disk in the sky. Although the disk appears as white or clear light, the rainbow is visible at the disk's edge, where the different colors remain distinct. With its longer wavelength, red appears on the outside of the arc, and violet, with its shorter wavelength, on the inside. Compare this elusive naturally occurring phenomenon with man-made objects that can be purchased and possessed. In your essay, make reference to Schor's critique of consumer culture or Rockwell's defense of it or both. Why do you think that rainbows symbolize peace, diversity, new beginnings, good luck, potential wealth, harmony, and a happy future?

## Sarah Adams — Audio and Text

### Be Cool to the Pizza Dude

Sarah Adams grew up in Wisconsin and is now a professor of English at Olympic Community College in Seattle, Washington. Adams's essay, "Be Cool to the Pizza Dude," was one of the first listener-submitted pieces read on National Public Radio's *This I Believe* series. In this piece, Adams discusses her personal philosophy of life, through the lens of pizza delivery. To hear and read Adams's argument, go to Chapter 29: **bedfordstmartins.com/bedguide**.

## Brent Foster — Video

### Highway Angel

Brent Foster began his career as an award-winning photojournalist and cinematographer with an internship in photojournalism during his freshman year of high school. As part of his job, he has traveled to more than fifteen countries, covering everything from London fashion shows to the untenable living conditions in Jharkhand, India. In "Highway Angel," which was produced by the *Los Angeles Times*, Foster followed Thomas Weller as he traveled the highways looking to help stranded motorists. To watch the video, go to Chapter 29: **bedfordstmartins.com/bedguide**.

Weller cruises the San Diego highways helping strangers for free.

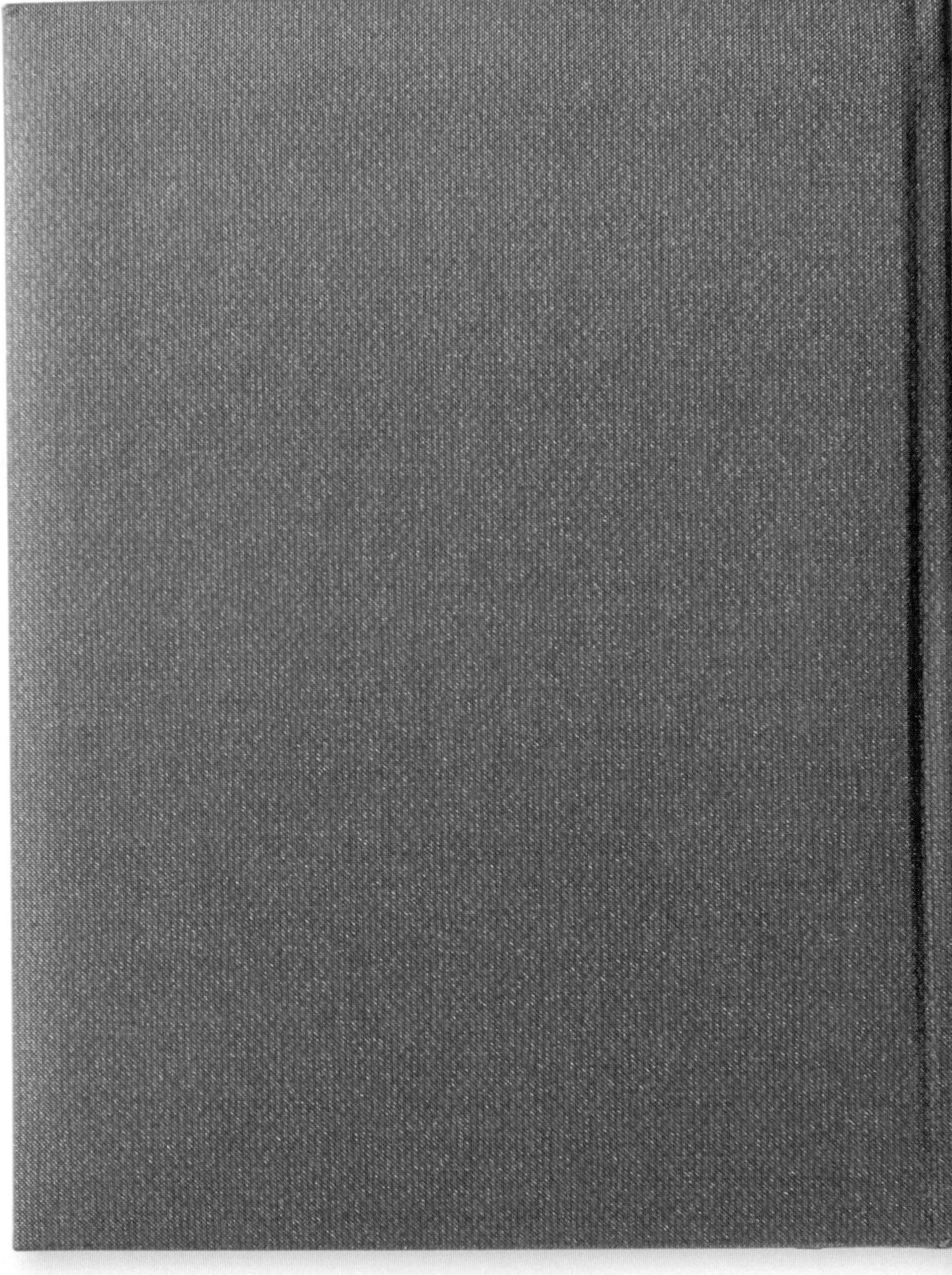

# A WRITER'S RESEARCH MANUAL

# A Writer's Research Manual Contents

# Introduction: The Nature of Research

Does cell phone use cause brain tumors?

What steps can law enforcement take to help prevent stalking?

How does fan violence affect sporting events?

Is it true that about a million children in the United States are homeless?

Why is cyberbullying so widespread?

You may ask questions like these, discuss them with friends, or read about them. If so, you are conducting informal research to satisfy your curiosity. Just as *revision* means "seeing again," so *research* means "seeking or hunting again"—reconsidering information to revise and deepen what you know.

In your day-to-day life, you conduct practical research as you solve problems and make decisions. You may want to buy a digital camera, consider an innovative medical procedure, or plan a vacation. To become better informed, you may talk with friends, search the Internet, request product information, compare prices, read articles, and check advertising. You pull together and weigh as much information as you can, preparing yourself to make a well-informed decision based on the available evidence. At work you may do the same—conduct research by gathering information, pulling it together, and using it to make decisions about feasibility, marketing, or best practices.

When one of your college professors assigns a research paper due in a month or two, you won't be expected to discover the secrets of the human brain or to solve the problem of world hunger. On the other hand, research isn't merely pasting together information and opinions from others. Instead, the excitement lies in using research to draw conclusions and arrive at your own fresh view.

The key is to start your investigation as professional researchers do—with a research question that you truly want to learn more about. Like a detective, you will need to plan your work but remain flexible, backtracking or jumping ahead or going sideways if you meet an obstacle. Whenever you use research to come to a conclusion based on facts and expert opinions—whether in your personal life, for a college class, or on the job—this research manual will provide you with effective, efficient strategies and procedures.

# 30 Planning Your Research Project

Conducting research is a lifelong skill, valuable in college, at work, and in your personal life. Yet this skill is increasingly complex. You must actively engage, inquire, search, access, evaluate, integrate, and synthesize information from moving, not fixed, targets. Electronic databases are fluid, sources may change, and details may shift over time.

As a result, a research project requires information literacy – the capacity to handle information – as well as critical reading and thinking as you join the academic exchange. The graphic on page 627 identifies major stages in a typical research process, moving from the exploration of a topic to the evaluation, analysis, and synthesis that eventually evolve into a final paper with well-integrated sources.

## Why Planning a Research Project Matters

### In a College Course

- You plan ahead to finish – on time and on target – the research project assigned in your writing class.
- You apply your planning experience to your capstone research project for your major.

### In the Workplace

- You organize your work group to investigate a potential client base, using available demographic data.

### In Your Community

- You arrange the needs assessment necessary to justify a new recreation center.

When have you planned a research project? In what situations do you expect to do so again?

## THE RESEARCH PROCESS

***Engage: Explore a topic that intrigues you, following your assignment (see pp. 628–30).***

***Inquire: State your research question (see pp. 630–33).***

***Organize: Manage your project (see pp. 634–37).***

- Plan a method of recording information.
- Organize a research archive, and create a schedule.

***Investigate: Work with your sources (see Ch. 31).***

- Start a working bibliography, and draw the details from sources.
- Quote, paraphrase, and summarize to capture information in your notes (see pp. 651–54).

***Search: Seek and evaluate reliable sources that might help to answer your question (see Chs. 32 and 33).***

- Use the Internet, library catalog, databases, and reference materials.
- Develop search strategies for print and electronic resources.
- Interview, observe, or conduct other field research.
- Analyze and evaluate the reliability and relevance of each source.

***Synthesize: Integrate reliable information and evidence to support your answer to your research question.***

- Use sources ethically to avoid plagiarism (see Chs. 31 and 34).
- Quote, paraphrase, summarize, and synthesize to capture and integrate source materials in your paper (see Chs. 31 and 34).
- Clarify the thesis that answers your question, and support it as you write your paper (see Ch. 35).
- Cite and list your sources (see pp. 642–49 and Ch. 36 or 37).

# Beginning Your Inquiry

A research paper is often the most engaging and complex assignment in a course. This chapter will help you plan and manage your project by developing the skills and tools you will need to accomplish even the most formidable research task.

## The Assignment: Writing from Sources

Find a topic that intrigues you, and develop a focused research question about it. After conducting whatever research is necessary, synthesize the information you assemble to develop your own reasonable answer to the research question. Then write a paper, persuasively using a variety of source material to convey your conclusions.

Because your final paper answers your research question, you are writing for a reason, not just stacking up facts. Reading and digesting the ideas of others is just the first step. You'll also analyze, evaluate, and synthesize, thinking critically to achieve your purpose. Answering your question will probably require you to return to writing situations you addressed earlier—perhaps comparing, taking a stand, evaluating, or supporting a position. You also may turn to field methods such as observing or interviewing.

For advice on scheduling your research project, see pp. 636–37.

Aim to persuade your audience to consider, respect, accept, or act on the answer to your question. If possible, use this project to benefit your college, employer, local community, or campus cause. Having a real audience will help you select what to include or exclude as you write your paper.

For Additional Writing Assignments, see p. 706.

### Learning by Doing Reflecting on Research

Reflect on your past research experience. Have you written a research paper in the past? Do you feel confident that you can handle a college research assignment? Or does even the word *research* make you feel anxious? Sum up your past experience. Then list the skills you have already developed in this class that might help you begin your current research project.

# Asking a Research Question

What assistance most effectively helps members of the military return to civilian life after a stressful tour of duty?

How accurately do standardized tests measure learning?

What can be done to aid hungry children in your community?

To define a narrow research question, start with your interests and research goals. Choose a territory—a research topic that stimulates your curiosity. If you need ideas, listen to the academic exchanges around you.

Perhaps the reading, writing, or discussion in your geography course alerts you to global environmental threats. Then target your research, maybe narrowing "global threats to forests" to "farming practices that threaten rain forests."

**DISCOVERY CHECKLIST**

- ☐ What experience can you recall that raises intriguing questions or creates unusual associations in your mind?
- ☐ What have you observed recently – at school or work, online, or on television today – that you could more thoroughly investigate?
- ☐ What new perspectives on issues or events have friends, classmates, instructors, commentators, bloggers, or others offered?
- ☐ What have you read or heard about lately that you would like to pursue?
- ☐ What problem would you like to solve?

## Exploring Your Territory

Like explorers in new territory, research writers first take a broad look at promising viewpoints, changes, and trends. Then they zero in on a small area.

**Go Online.** You may start out by searching for your topic; *families*, for instance, turned up about 739 million Google entries. In our search, the first two came from Wikipedia, the collaborative online encyclopedia which may orient you to key words and subtopics. (Be cautious, however. Because users can edit entries on this site, instructors may or may not consider it reliable for deeper research.) Next came organizations with *families* in their names – nonprofit, government, religious, for-profit groups, all jumbled together. Similarly, Google Scholar's first item covered plant (not human) families, while Google Groups led to more personal family interests. A vast Internet search can produce many sources but little focus.

For more on electronic searches, see Ch. 32.

**Browse the Library.** For more focused, academic sources, visit your campus library or its Web site. The library probably subscribes to many general databases (such as Academic Search Premier, Academic OneFile, and Gale Virtual Reference), as well as field-specific resources. Ask a reference librarian (electronically or in person) where to start investigating a topic.

**Talk with Experts.** If you're curious about America's fascination with cars, meet with a professor, such as a sociologist or a journalist, who specializes in the area. Talk with friends who are passionate about their cars. Or go to an auto show, observing and talking with people who attend.

For more on interviewing, see p. 674 and Ch. 6.

For more on purpose and audience, see pp. 11–15 and 398–99.

**Revisit Your Purpose and Audience.** Refine your purpose and your audience analysis in light of your discoveries thus far. Consider what goal you'd like your research to accomplish—whether in your personal life, for a college class, or on the job.

| | |
|---|---|
| Satisfy curiosity | Analyze a situation |
| Take a new perspective | Substantiate a conclusion |
| Make a decision | Support a position |
| Solve a problem | Advocate for change |

Suppose your survey of campus programs leads you to a proposal by the International Students Office for matching first-year students with host families during holidays. You wonder what such programs cost, how they work, what they offer students and host families. At first, you think that your purpose is to persuade the community to participate. Then you see that the real challenge is to gain the activity director's support.

## Turning a Topic into a Question

As you explore, move from broad to specific by asking more precise questions. Ask exactly what you want to learn; your task will leap into focus.

| | |
|---|---|
| BROAD OVERVIEW | Family structures |
| TOPIC | Blended families |
| SPECIFIC QUESTION | How do blended families today differ from those a century ago? |
| BROAD OVERVIEW | Contemporary architecture |
| TOPIC | Landscape architecture |
| SPECIFIC QUESTION | In what ways have the principles of landscape architecture shaped the city's green design? |

For more on generating ideas, see Ch. 19.

**Generate Ideas.** Freewrite, map, or brainstorm, and then select a question that appears promising. Your instructor may have suggestions, but you will probably be more motivated investigating a question you choose.

**Size Up Your Question.** If your question is too broad, you'll be swamped with information. If it has been overdone, you'll struggle to sound fresh. Focus to find a workable research question:

- Is it interesting to you? Will your discoveries interest your readers?
- Is it debatable? Does it allow for a range of opinions? Will you be able to support your own view rather than explain what's generally known and accepted?

- Is it narrow enough for a productive investigation in the few weeks you have? Would a background search supply the vocabulary you need to stick to a single focus?

| | |
|---|---|
| BROAD QUESTION | How is the climate of the earth changing? |
| NARROWER QUESTION | How will El Niño affect climate changes in California during the next decade? |
| BROAD QUESTION | Who are the world's best living storytellers? |
| NARROWER QUESTION | How is Irish step dancing a form of storytelling? |
| BROAD QUESTION | Why are people homeless? |
| NARROWER QUESTION | What housing programs succeed in our region? |

Although you should restrict your topic, a question can be too narrow or too insignificant. If so, it may be difficult to find relevant sources.

| | |
|---|---|
| TOO NARROW | How did John F. Kennedy's maternal grandfather influence the decisions JFK made during his first month as president? |

A question may also be so narrow that it's uninteresting. Avoid questions that can be answered with a simple yes or no or with a few statistics.

| | |
|---|---|
| TOO NARROW | Are there more black students or white students in the entering class this year? |
| BETTER | How does the racial or ethnic diversity of students affect campus relations at our school? |

Shape a question that leads you into the heart of a lively controversy. The best research questions ask about issues and problems that others take seriously and debate, matters of real interest to you and your readers.

**Hone Your Question.** Make your question specific and simple: identify one thing to find out, not several. The very phrasing of a well-crafted question can suggest keywords – and useful synonyms – for searches.

| | |
|---|---|
| QUESTION | What has caused a shortage of affordable housing in northeastern cities? |
| POSSIBLE SEARCH TERMS | Housing shortage, affordable urban housing |

**Refine Your Question.** Until you start your research, you can't know how fruitful your first question will be. At least it establishes a starting point. If it doesn't lead you to definite facts or reliable opinions, if it doesn't start you thinking critically, reword it or throw it out and ask a new question.

RESEARCH CHECKLIST

**Questioning Your Question**

- ☐ Does your question probe an issue that engages you personally?
- ☐ Is its scope appropriate—neither huge nor puny? Will you be able to answer it given the time and length limits for your paper?
- ☐ Can you find both current and background information about it?
- ☐ Have you worded your question concretely and specifically, so that it states exactly what you are looking for?

## Learning by Doing Polling Your Peers

On a blank page, list your three most interesting ideas with a brief description of each topic's research potential. Working with a small group or whole class, pass your page to the person next to you. On the page you receive, mark a check by the idea that you find most intriguing. Repeat this process until everyone has responded to each page, and your page returns to you. Taking into account the group's check marks, turn one topic into a research question, and then outline your tentative approach to it. Decide whether you've found the question you want to explore. Repeat the process if the group wants more response.

For more on stating and using a thesis, see pp. 399–408.

**Predict an Answer in a Working Thesis.** Some writers find a project easier to tackle if they have in mind not only a question but also a possible answer, even a working thesis. However, be flexible, ready to change either answer or question as your research progresses.

| | |
|---|---|
| RESEARCH QUESTION | How does a nutritious lunch benefit students? |
| WORKING THESIS | Nutritious school lunches can improve students' classroom performance. |

**Use Your Working Thesis to Guide Your Research.** You probably will revise or replace your working thesis before you finish, but it can guide you now.

- Identify terms to define and subtopics or components to explore.
- List or informally outline points you might develop.
- Note opposing views, alternatives, or solutions likely to emerge.

This early exploration will help you pursue the sources and information you need but avoid any wild goose chase that might distract you.

However, if all you find is support for what you already think, your working thesis may be too dominant. You may be simply defending your

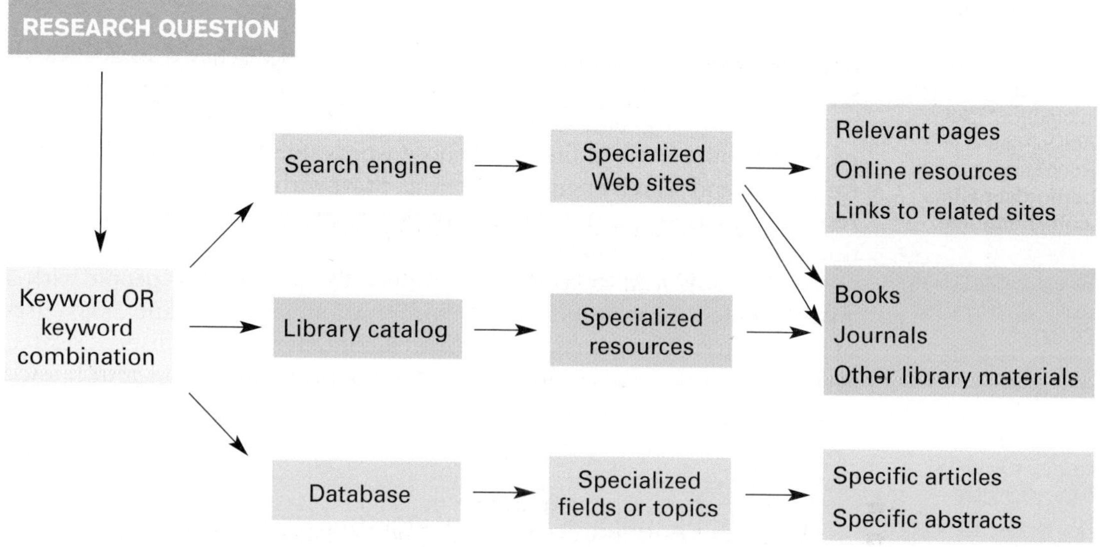


view, not conducting true research. For this reason, some writers delay stating a thesis until they've done substantial research or even begun drafting.

## Surveying Your Resources

Test whether your question is likely to lead to an ample research paper with a fast search at the library site. You'll need enough ideas, opinions, facts, statistics, and expert testimony to address your question. If you turn up a skimpy list, change search terms. For hundreds of sources, refine your question. Aim for a question that is the focus of a dozen or twenty available sources. If you need help, talk to a reference librarian.

Also decide which types of sources to target. Some questions require a wide range, others a narrower range, restricted by date or discipline.

- Opinions on controversies? Turn to newspaper editorials, opinion columns, issue-oriented sites, and partisan groups for diverse views.
- News and analysis? Look for stories from newsmagazines, newspapers, news services, and public broadcasting.
- Statistics and facts? Try census or other government data, library databases, annual fact books, and almanacs.
- Professional or workforce information? Turn to reports and surveys with academic, government, and corporate sponsors to reduce bias.
- Research-based analysis? Try scholarly or well-researched nonfiction, government reports, specialized references, and academic databases.
- Original records or images? Check archives, online historical records, and materials held by institutions such as the Library of Congress.

To review the types of evidence, see pp. 44–45.

e For an interactive Learning by Doing activity on Narrowing Online Research, go to Ch. 30: **bedfordstmartins .com/bedguide**.

## Using Keywords and Links

For practice using keywords, go to the interactive "Take Action" charts in Re:Writing at **bedfordstmartins .com/bedguide**.

*Keywords* are terms or phrases that identify topics discussed in a research source. When you enter keywords into an electronic search engine (whether in a library catalog, database, or Web site), the engine returns to you a list of all the sources it can find with those words. Finding the best keywords for a topic and search engine is essential. Start with the main terms in your research question. Record the keywords you try, noting whether they produce too few or too many results.

For Internet and library search strategies, see Ch. 32.

As keywords lead to Web sites compiled by specialists or people with a shared interest, browse through the information, resources, and *links* — lists of related sites. These links, in turn, often contain their own lists of related Web pages. Follow these connections systematically to expand your knowledge rapidly, but avoid only supporting a preconceived notion.

For advice on creating a working bibliography, see pp. 640–41.

### Learning by Doing Proposing Your Project

Assemble and review your research materials — topic ideas, research question, any working thesis, notes on resources and keywords, and anything else you've planned or gathered. Then write a short informal proposal that sums up what you want to discover and how you plan to proceed. In a small group, present your proposals, and exchange ideas about how to continue your inquiry.

## Managing Your Project

No matter what your question or where you plan to look for material, you will want to keep track of where you've been and where you need to go.

### Recording Information

Plan ahead to produce what you need: relevant evidence from reliable sources to develop and support your answer to your research question. Avoid two extremes — collecting everything or counting only on memory.

For advice on working with sources, see Ch. 31; for advice on integrating sources, see Ch. 34.

**Use Time-Honored Methods for Depth.** Selective copying (photocopying or saving to a file) helps you accumulate material, but copying whatever you find wastes time. Instead, take notes, annotate, highlight, quote, paraphrase, and summarize — all time-honored methods for absorbing, evaluating, and selecting information from a source. Such methods help you identify potentially useful materials and, later, integrate them smoothly into your paper.

**Innovate for Efficiency.** Develop efficient techniques such as these:

- Write a summary on the first page of a printout or photocopy.
- Add a paraphrase in the margin next to a key section of a printout.

- Identify a lively or concrete quotation with a highlighter.
- E-mail information from a library database to yourself so that it is easy to move into an electronic folder or file.
- Bookmark useful Web sites; save productive searches and results to a folder.
- Record key quotations in a computer file so that you can easily reorganize them. (Note source details, including database name, access date, URL, and any page number.)
- Summarize sources on sticky notes or cards so that you can quickly rearrange them in various orders on your wall, desk, or bed.
- Use a concept mapping program or poster board to sketch a "storyboard" for the main "events" that you want to cover in your paper.

Many researchers use word-processing files with clearly separate entries, 4″ × 6″ card format, or color coding; some stick to traditional note cards (with one note on each). Both are more flexible than notebook pages. When the time comes to organize, it's easy to reshuffle cards, print electronic notes, or sort them into a logical order.

**Read as a Skeptical Critic.** Distinguish what's significant for answering your research question and what's only slightly related. If you wish, add your own ratings (*, +, !! or – , ??) at the top or in the margin.

For more on critical reading, see Ch. 2.

**Take Accurate and Thorough Notes.** Read the entire article or section of a book before beginning to take notes. Then decide what—and how much—to record so you dig out the useful nuggets without distorting the meaning. Double-check all statistics and lists. Record enough notes and citations that, once they're written, you are independent of the source.

## Starting a Research Archive

Organize your information from sources by creating a research archive. An *archive* is a place where information is systematically stored for later use. Clearly distinguish sources you save from your own notes. Use highlighting and other markers to make key passages easy to find in any format.

**Save Computer Files.** Save Web pages, e-mails, posts to newsgroups and lists, transcripts of chats, and database records to a drive or other storage device. Note URLs or search paths, dates of access, and similar details. Give each file a descriptive name so that you can find the information quickly later on. You can also organize the files in different electronic folders or directories, clearly named. Back up all electronic records.

**Save Favorites and Bookmarks.** Save the locations of Web sites in your browser so that you can easily return to your *favorites* or *bookmarks*. Annotate and organize them into folders.

**Save Search Results.** If a database or Internet search is productive, note where you searched and what keywords you used. Then you can easily repeat the search later, print out the results, or save them to a file.

**File Paper Copies.** If you prefer a paper format, photocopy book passages and articles, print out electronic sources (noting the database and date of access), and keep field material. File these using a separate folder for each source, labeled with title or subject and author. Attach sticky notes to mark key passages, or highlight them. Be sure the author (or title) and page number appear on each page so you can credit your source.

---

RESEARCH CHECKLIST

**Getting Organized**

- ☐ Have you identified and stated an intriguing research question?
- ☐ What has your quick survey of library and online sources revealed? Can you find enough information – but not too much – to answer your question?
- ☐ Which types of sources might be best for beginning your research?
- ☐ Have you created a realistic schedule based on your deadlines? Have you allowed plenty of time for research while meeting other commitments?
- ☐ Have you tested your method of recording research information? Will it be easy to keep up? Will it help you compile useful and accurate information?
- ☐ Have you begun organizing your research archive – opening files, setting up electronic folders, or buying file folders for paper copies?

---

### Learning by Doing Interviewing a Researcher

Pair up with a classmate, and interview each other as researchers. Ask about your classmate's interest in the topic, research question, investigative approach, and project concerns. After your classmate has interviewed you, write out any advice for yourself as a researcher.

## Creating a Schedule

If your instructor doesn't assign a series of deadlines, set your own. Use campus time-management software, if available. Count on a research paper taking longer than you expect. If you procrastinate and try to toss it together in an all-night siege, you will not be satisfied with the result. Instead, start with a clear-cut schedule that breaks your project into a series of small tasks.

SAMPLE SCHEDULE

- *Week One:* If you are not assigned a topic, start thinking about your interests. Explore by searching through your library or on the Internet. Look for any time-saving library resource guide. Record where you searched and which terms you used to avoid duplication.
- *Week Two:* Narrow your topic to a workable research question. Get a librarian's advice on searches and resources. Survey available resources, start your working bibliography, and organize your research archive. Annotate possible sources when useful.
- *Week Three:* Begin your research in earnest. Locate and evaluate your most promising sources. Take notes, and build your archive.
- *Week Four:* Continue narrowing your research, identifying sources, evaluating them as you go along, and taking efficient notes.
- *Week Five:* State your working thesis, and begin planning or outlining your paper. Update your bibliography and archive, arranging sources in the order in which you might use them. Target any information gaps.
- *Week Six:* Refine your thesis statement. Start your first draft, noting each place where you draw on your sources.
- *Week Seven:* Complete your first draft. Begin thinking about ways to revise and improve it. Seek feedback from a peer editor.
- *Week Eight:* Revise and edit your draft. Check that you have correctly presented and credited all quotations, paraphrases, and summaries from your sources. Proofread the entire paper, checking for any errors.

Each week you can make up a more detailed schedule, identifying tasks by the day or by the type to increase your efficiency.

DAILY SCHEDULE

Monday – finish catalog search

Tuesday – start article indexes

Thursday – read e-mails and printouts from databases

Sunday night – organize files and add notes

ACTIVITY SCHEDULE

library search – LexisNexis?

Web search – government sites

reading – new printouts and e-mails from databases

writing – revised research question – thesis?

## Learning by Doing Planning Your Personal Schedule

In accord with your instructor's guidelines and deadlines, plan your research schedule so you'll be motivated and organized. Identify tasks, define specific checkpoints, plan to meet all deadlines, and allow extra time for unexpected problems. Align your schedule with your class, work, family, or other time commitments so that it helps you reserve the many hours that your project will require. Discuss your plans with classmates, making realistic adjustments as needed.

## Planning Collaborative Research

Research groups, in class or at work, require cooperative effort but can produce deeper and more creative outcomes than one individual could achieve. If your project is collaborative, you will need to make agreements with others and meet your commitments. Your team might consolidate all its work or share the research but produce separate papers or presentations. With your instructor's approval, divide up the tasks so that all members are responsible for their own portions. Then agree on your due dates and group meetings.

SAMPLE SCHEDULE FOR A GROUP PROJECT

- *Week One:* Meet to get acquainted and to select someone to act as an organizer, e-mailing or texting to make sure things progress as planned. Individually explore options for a project topic.
- *Week Two:* Meet again to select a topic, narrow it, and develop a research question that your instructor approves.
- *Week Three:* Meet to assign tasks and report progress. Individually survey resources, contribute entries and annotations to a collaborative working bibliography, and gather material for the group's research archive. (Check for campus or library access to citation management tools.)
- *Weeks Four and Five:* Continue to find, read, evaluate, and record notes.
- *Week Six:* Meet to evaluate the sources and information gathered; decide how to address what is missing or weak. Draft a working thesis and outline for presenting what everyone has learned.
- *Week Seven:* Individually draft assigned sections. Swap drafts, read them over, and respond with suggestions.
- *Week Eight:* Work together to consolidate the revised draft and agree on final changes. Appoint one member to prepare a polished copy and one or two others to act as final editors and proofreaders.

# Working with Sources 31

As you turn to sources, gather complete information.

- First, in a source entry, record the details that identify each source so you can find it and eventually credit it correctly in your paper. Assemble these entries in a working bibliography.
- Second, in source notes, capture information of value to your inquiry as quotations, paraphrases, or summaries ready for use in your paper.
- Finally, if required or useful to you as a researcher, combine a source entry with a summary to build an annotated bibliography.

## Why Working with Sources Matters

### In a College Course

- You read case studies, theories, industry projections, and much more for your economics class, so you need to capture information efficiently.
- You combine what you learn from clinic observations with information about your own child's diagnosis to direct your paper to an audience of parents.

### In the Workplace

- You use company sales data, but you want to develop an annotated list of industry and government sources to expand available statistics.

### In Your Community

- You agree to write a brief history of your campus social group, presenting the old records accurately but not offending potential contributors on alumni day.

? When have you quoted, paraphrased, summarized, or credited sources? In what situations do you expect to do so again?

## Drawing the Details from Your Sources

For more examples, see Ch. 36 on MLA style, Ch. 37 on APA style, and the Quick Research Guide, p. A-20.

The Source Navigators on pages 642–49 show how to find the details needed to identify several types of sources you are likely to use. Each source is keyed to a menu to show where you might look for the details you need to record in a source entry, ready to be copied from a working bibliography to the list of sources ending the paper. Each entry also is accompanied by sample source notes.

The sample source entries show two common academic styles: MLA (Modern Language Association) and APA (American Psychological Association). Because MLA and APA entries differ, stick to the style your instructor expects. However, both require much the same information, as do academic styles for other fields. The chart on page 650 summarizes what you'll need to record, both the basics—details nearly always required to identify each type of source—and common additions or likely complications. When in doubt, record more than you're likely to need so you won't have to return to a source later on.

## Starting a Working Bibliography

Your working bibliography is a detailed and evolving list of articles, books, Web sites, and other resources that may contribute to your research. It guides your research by recording the sources you plan to consult and adding notes about those you do examine. Each entry in your working bibliography eventually needs to follow the format your instructor expects, generally either MLA or APA style.

**Choose a Method.** Pick the method you can use most efficiently.

- Note cards, recording one source per card
- Small notebook, writing on one side of the page
- Word-processor file
- Citation management software or other database

**Keep Careful Records.** The more carefully you record possible sources, the more time you'll save later when you list the works you actually used and cited. At that point, you'll be grateful to find all the necessary titles, authors, dates, page numbers, and other details at your fingertips—and you'll avoid a frantic, last-minute database search or library trip.

When you start a bibliographic entry for a source, your information may be incomplete: "Find bionic ears article—maybe last year in science magazine." Start with whatever clues you can gather—keywords, partial titles, authors, relevant publications, rough dates. Once you locate the source, you can fill in the detail. Eventually each entry should include everything you need to find the source as well as to prepare the list of sources at the end of your paper.

As your working bibliography develops, your circumstances may favor different methods of recording information. For example, when you find that science magazine with the article on bionic ears, you may read a printed copy or print the full text from a database. Either way, you can easily take notes using your usual method: on paper or in an electronic file. For field research, you might simply start with the name of a possible contact: "Dr. Edward Denu – cardiologist – interview about drug treatments." Should you interview Dr. Denu or someone from his staff about medication for heart patients, you might record the conversation (with that person's permission) or jot notes in a handheld electronic storage tool as you talk, later adding the information to your notes.

For a table on types of information to record, see p. 650.

### Learning by Doing Teaming Up for Source "Warm-Ups"

Working with a partner or team, do some source citation warm-ups, just as you might do push-ups or run a lap before a game or meet. Using this book, write a sentence that mentions a chapter, a reading, or the book as a whole. Use samples from the Source Navigators (pp. 642–49) or the Quick Research Guide (pp. A-20–A-38) to help you figure out how to identify that item in the list of sources at the end of your paper. Then add a sentence and a reference for a second source, such as a related reading, an e-Page, or a complementary Web page. Work together to cross-check and improve all your source references.

e For an interactive Learning by Doing activity on Practicing with Online Sources, go to Ch. 31: **bedfordstmartins.com/bedguide**.

## Capturing Information in Your Notes

Read critically to decide what each source offers. If you cannot understand a source that requires specialized background, don't take notes or use it in your paper. On the other hand, if a source seems accurate, logical, and relevant, consider exactly how you want to record it in your notes.

For more examples of capturing information from sources, see pp. 236–43, pp. 690–95, and D in the Quick Research Guide, pp. A-28–A-31.

**Identify What's from Where.** Clearly identify the author of the source, a brief title if needed, and the page number (or other location) where a reader could find the information. These details connect each source note to your corresponding bibliography entry. Adding a keyword at the top of each note will help you cluster related material in your paper.

## Source Navigator

### Article in a Print Magazine

**Record this information in your notes about each source:**

1. The complete name of the author
2. The title and any subtitle of the article
3. The title and any subtitle of the magazine
4. The full date of the issue
5. The article's page numbers
6. The periodical's volume number and issue number if available (for APA), sometimes found on title or contents page
7. The medium of publication (for MLA)

CITIES

SCIENTIFIC AMERICAN

6 Volume 305, Number 3

**Cynthia Rosenzweig** is a senior research scientist at the NASA Goddard Institute for Space Studies and at Columbia University's Earth Institute.

2 All Climate Is Local

Mayors are often better equipped than presidents to cut greenhouse gases

1 *By Cynthia Rosenzweig*

FOR YEARS SCIENTISTS HAVE URGED national leaders to tackle climate change, based on the assumption that prevention efforts would require the coordinated actions of entire nations to be effective. But as anyone who has watched the past 15 years of international climate negotiations can attest, most countries are still reluctant to take meaningful steps to lower their production of greenhouse gases, much less address issues such as how to help developing countries protect themselves from the extreme effects of climate change. Frustrated by the ongoing diplomatic stalemate, a number of urban leaders have decided to take mat- severe. Most of the world's major metropolises were originally built on rivers or coastlines and are therefore subject to flooding from rising seas and instances of heavier rainfall.

Many civic leaders point to Hurricane Katrina and the devastation it visited on New Orleans in 2005 as their moment of awakening. They saw how the multiple failures of an aging and inadequate infrastructure, plus indifferent planning, sharply increased the death toll of a catastrophe that had long been predicted. Indeed, two major alliances of city mayors to combat climate change formed within months after Hurricane Katrina's landfall. The organization now known as the C40 Cities Climate Leadership Group launched in London in October

5 70 Scientific American, September 2011

*Photograph by Dan Saelinger*

3 4

**Create a source entry out of the information you collect:**

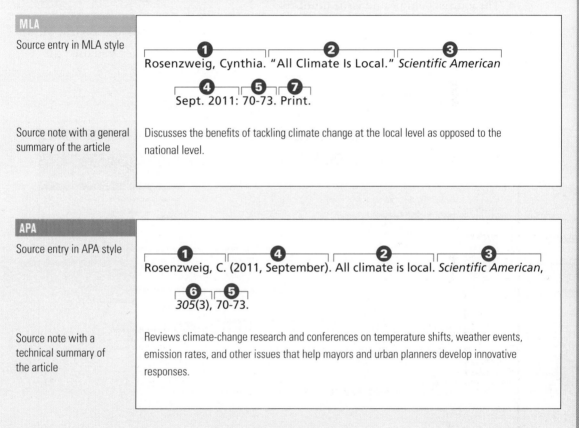

Source entry in MLA style

1
2
3
Rosenzweig, Cynthia. "All Climate Is Local." *Scientific American*
4
5
7
Sept. 2011: 70-73. Print.


Source note with a general summary of the article

Discusses the benefits of tackling climate change at the local level as opposed to the national level.

APA

Source entry in APA style

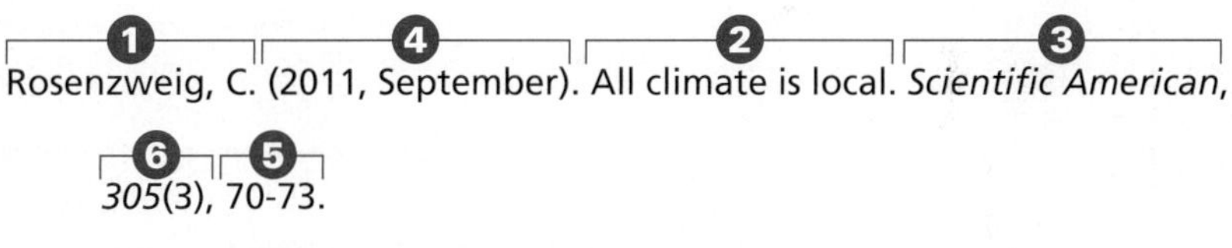

1
4
2
3
Rosenzweig, C. (2011, September). All climate is local. *Scientific American*,
6
5
*305*(3), 70-73.


Source note with a technical summary of the article

Reviews climate-change research and conferences on temperature shifts, weather events, emission rates, and other issues that help mayors and urban planners develop innovative responses.

# Source Navigator

## Article in a Scholarly Journal from a Database

**Record this information in your notes about each source:**

1 The complete name of the author(s)

2 The title and any subtitle of the article

3 The title and any subtitle of the journal

4 The journal volume and issue numbers

5 The year of the issue

6 The printed article's original page numbers if available

7 The name of the database, subscriber service, or library service (for MLA)

8 DOI (digital object identifier) if available or URL for journal's home page (for APA)

9 The medium of publication (for MLA)

10 The access date when you used the source (for MLA)

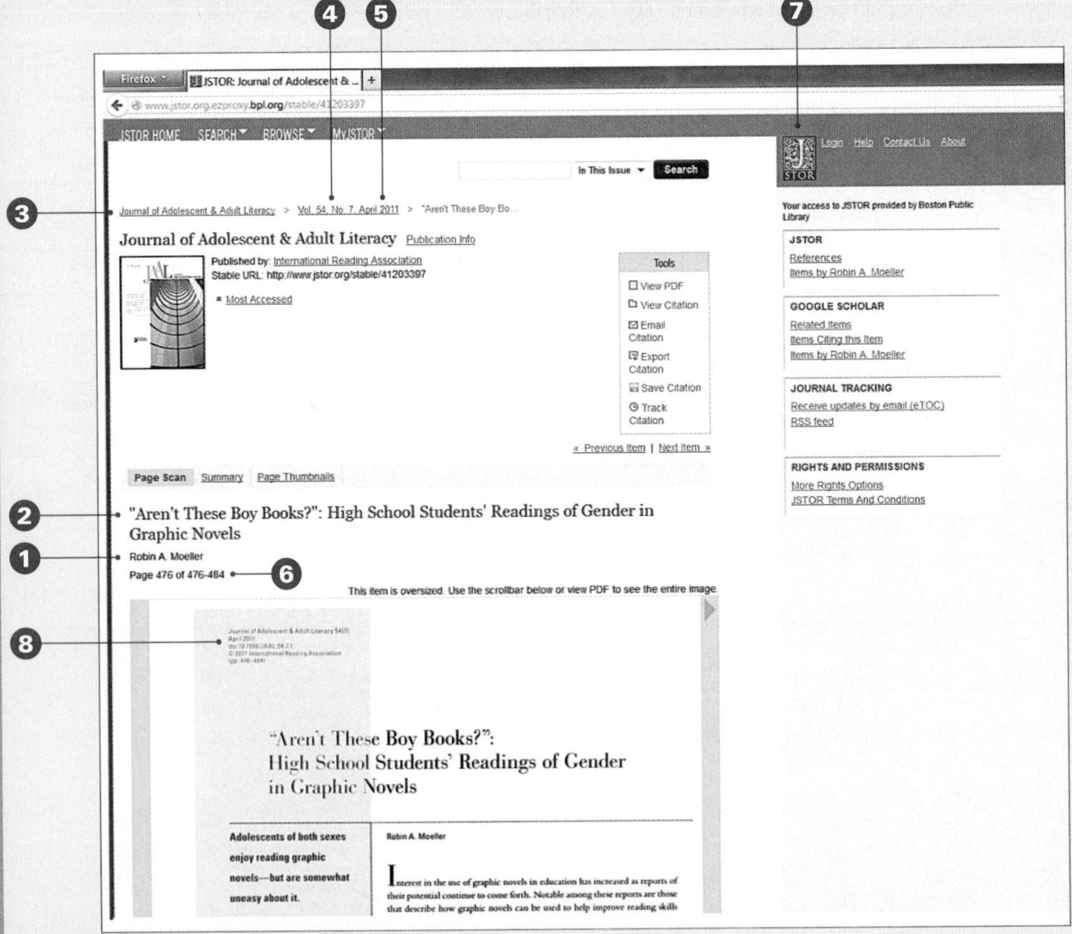

**Create a source entry out of the information you collect:**

**MLA**

Source entry in MLA style, e-mailed from database and recorded in a computer file

(1) (2) (3) (4) (5) (6) (7) (9) (10)

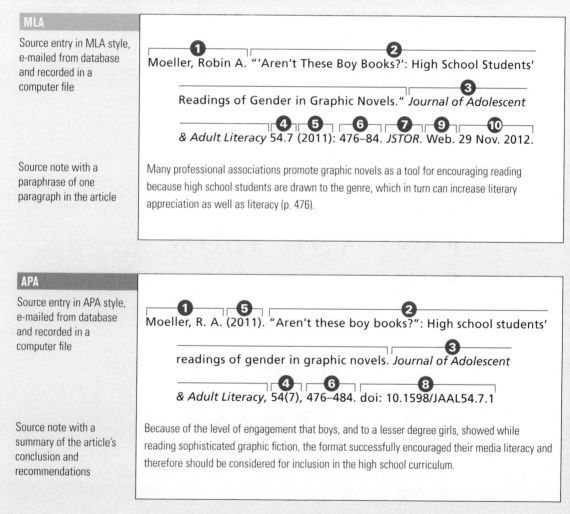

Moeller, Robin A. "'Aren't These Boy Books?': High School Students' Readings of Gender in Graphic Novels." *Journal of Adolescent & Adult Literacy* 54.7 (2011): 476–84. *JSTOR*. Web. 29 Nov. 2012.

Source note with a paraphrase of one paragraph in the article

Many professional associations promote graphic novels as a tool for encouraging reading because high school students are drawn to the genre, which in turn can increase literary appreciation as well as literacy (p. 476).

**APA**

Source entry in APA style, e-mailed from database and recorded in a computer file

(1) (5) (2) (3) (4) (6) (8)

Moeller, R. A. (2011). "Aren't these boy books?": High school students' readings of gender in graphic novels. *Journal of Adolescent & Adult Literacy*, 54(7), 476–484. doi: 10.1598/JAAL54.7.1

Source note with a summary of the article's conclusion and recommendations

Because of the level of engagement that boys, and to a lesser degree girls, showed while reading sophisticated graphic fiction, the format successfully encouraged their media literacy and therefore should be considered for inclusion in the high school curriculum.

## Source Navigator

### Book

**Record this information in your notes about each source:**

1. The complete name of the author
2. The title and any subtitle of the book
3. The place of publication, using the first city listed, and the state (for APA)
4. The name of the publisher, in short form
5. The latest date of publication (from the front or back of the title page)
6. The medium of publication (for MLA)
7. The call number or library location (for your future use)
8. Keyword or author (for your filing system)

2 THINKING,
FAST AND SLOW
1 DANIEL
KAHNEMAN
4 FARRAR, STRAUS AND GIROUX / NEW YORK 3



Front of title page

Back of title page

**Create a source entry out of the information you collect:**

**MLA**

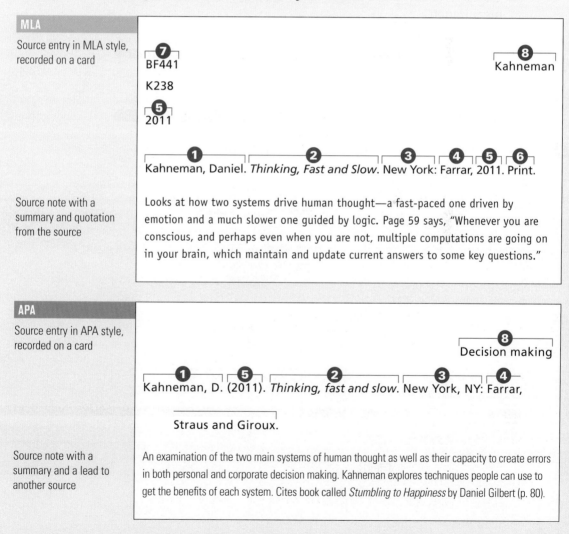

Source entry in MLA style, recorded on a card

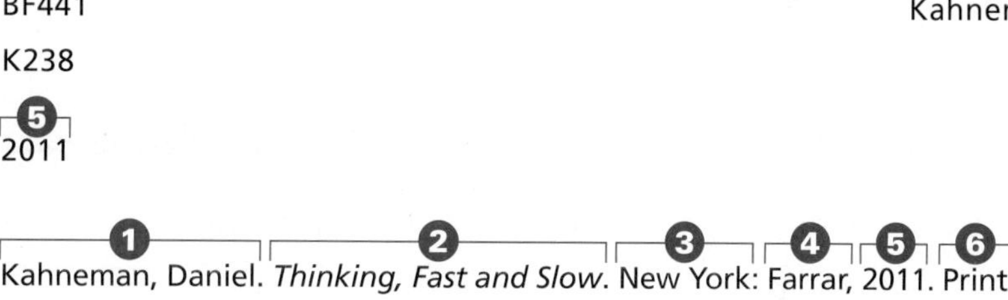


Source note with a summary and quotation from the source

Looks at how two systems drive human thought—a fast-paced one driven by emotion and a much slower one guided by logic. Page 59 says, "Whenever you are conscious, and perhaps even when you are not, multiple computations are going on in your brain, which maintain and update current answers to some key questions."

**APA**

Source entry in APA style, recorded on a card

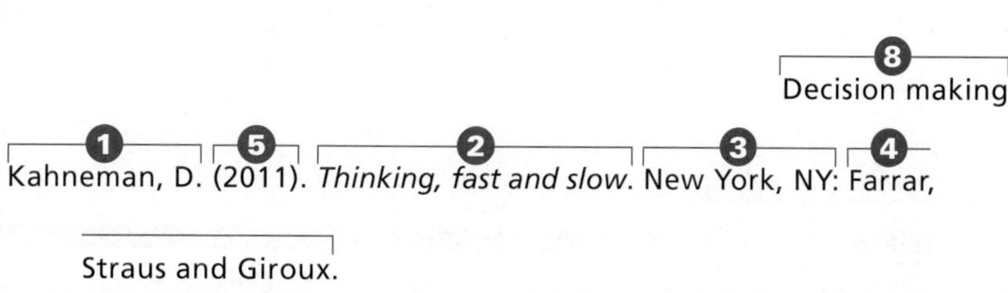

8
Decision making
1 5 2 3 4
Kahneman, D. (2011). *Thinking, fast and slow*. New York, NY: Farrar,
Straus and Giroux.


Source note with a summary and a lead to another source

An examination of the two main systems of human thought as well as their capacity to create errors in both personal and corporate decision making. Kahneman explores techniques people can use to get the benefits of each system. Cites book called *Stumbling to Happiness* by Daniel Gilbert (p. 80).

# Source Navigator

## Page from a Web Site

**Record this information in your notes about each source:**

1. The complete name of the author, if available, often from the beginning or end of the page
2. The title of the page
3. The name of the site
4. The name of any sponsoring organization
5. The date of the last update
6. The medium of publication (for MLA)
7. The access date when you used the source
8. The Internet address (URL) (for APA)

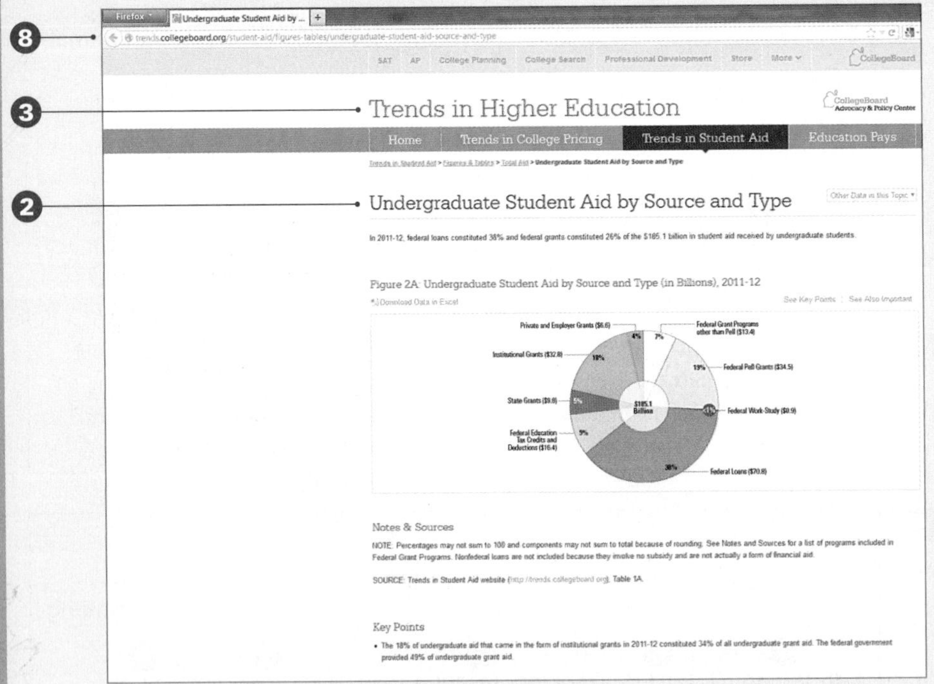

8
3
2
Firefox
Undergraduate Student Aid by ...
trends.collegeboard.org/student-aid/figures-tables/undergraduate-student-aid-source-and-type
SAT
AP
College Planning
College Search
Professional Development
Store
More
CollegeBoard
Trends in Higher Education
CollegeBoard Advocacy & Policy Center
Home
Trends in College Pricing
Trends in Student Aid
Education Pays
Undergraduate Student Aid by Source and Type
In 2011-12, federal loans constituted 38% and federal grants constituted 26% of the $185.1 billion in student aid received by undergraduate students.
Figure 2A: Undergraduate Student Aid by Source and Type (in Billions), 2011-12
Notes & Sources
NOTE: Percentages may not sum to 100 and components may not sum to total because of rounding. See Notes and Sources for a list of programs included in Federal Grant Programs. Nonfederal loans are not included because they involve no subsidy and are not actually a form of financial aid.
SOURCE: Trends in Student Aid website (http://trends.collegeboard.org), Table 1A.
Key Points
The 18% of undergraduate aid that came in the form of institutional grants in 2011-12 constituted 34% of all undergraduate grant aid. The federal government provided 49% of undergraduate grant aid.


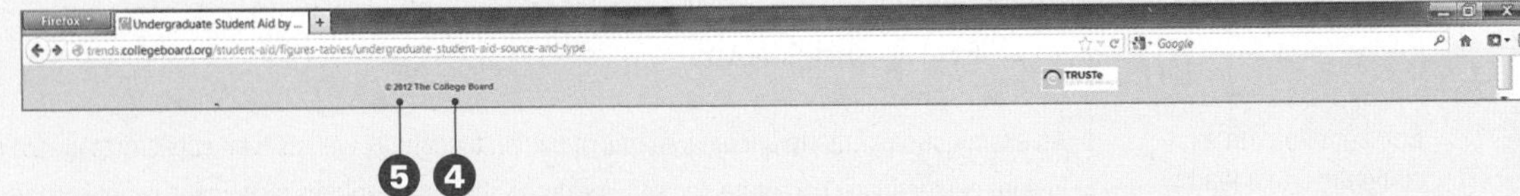

**Create a source entry out of the information you collect:**

MLA

Source entry in MLA style, recorded in a computer file

"Undergraduate Student Aid by Source and Type." *Trends in Higher Education.* College Board, 2012. Web. 29 Nov. 2012.

Source note summarizes topic of pie chart

Chart breaks down the types of financial aid undergraduate students received in 2011–2012 as well as the sources from which the aid came.

APA

Source entry in APA style, recorded in a computer file

College Board. (2012). *Trends in Higher Education.* Retrieved from http://trends.collegeboard.org/student-aid/figures-tables/undergraduate-student-aid-source-and-type

[Access dates are not required for sources whose content is not expected to change.]

Source note records specifics from table; retrieval URL simplifies return to source.

Federal work-study funds accounted for less than 1% of the financial aid distributed to undergraduate students in 2011–2012. See figure 2A: Undergraduate Student Aid by Source and Type.

## Types of Information to Record

| | The Basics | Common Additions |
|---|---|---|
| **Names** | ▪ Complete name of the author, as supplied in the source, unless not identified | ▪ Names of coauthors, in the order listed in the source<br>▪ Names of any editor, compiler, translator, or contributor |
| **Titles** | ▪ Title and any subtitle of an article, Web page, or posting (in quotation marks for MLA)<br>▪ Title and any subtitle of a journal, magazine, newspaper, book, or Web site (italicized) | ▪ Title of a journal special issue<br>▪ Title of a series of books or pamphlets and any item number |
| **Publication Details for Periodicals** | ▪ Volume and issue numbers for a journal (and a magazine for APA)<br>▪ DOI (digital object identifier) article number (for APA)<br>▪ Section number or letter for a newspaper | ▪ Any edition of a newspaper (for MLA) |
| **Publication Details for Books** | ▪ City of publication, using the first city listed (for MLA) with state or country (for APA)<br>▪ Name of the publisher | ▪ Edition number (4th) or description (revised)<br>▪ Volume number and total volumes, if more than one<br>▪ Names and locations of copublishers<br>▪ Publisher's imprint (for MLA) |
| **Publication Details for Electronic Sources** | ▪ Name (italicized) of the database, subscriber service, or library service (for MLA)<br>▪ Name of any site sponsor or publisher | ▪ Details of any original or alternate print publication<br>▪ Document numbers |
| **Dates** | ▪ Year of publication, full date (periodical), or date of creation or last update (electronic source)<br>▪ Your access date for an electronic source as printed or written on your hard copy (for MLA) or only for documents that change (for APA) | ▪ Original date of publication for a literary work or classic |
| **Location of Information** | ▪ Article's opening and concluding page numbers and any page for citing exact location of material in source | ▪ Paragraph, screen, chapter, or section numbers if supplied or section names, as in electronic sources |
| **Location of Source** | ▪ Internet address (URL, or uniform resource locator) for a hard-to-find source or, for APA, publication or publisher home page if no DOI | ▪ Call number, library area, or electronic address (to simplify your future use) |
| **Medium of Publication** | ▪ Medium of publication or reception such as Web, Print, CD, Film (for MLA) or of material reviewed (Motion picture, Book) or type of source (Computer software) (for APA) | |

Also identify which ideas are yours and which are your source's. For example, you might mark your source notes with these labels:

*"...":* quotation marks to set off all the exact words of the source

*para:* your paraphrase, restatement, or translation of a passage from the source into your own words and sentences

*sum:* your overall summary of the source's main point

*paste:* your cut-and-paste, quoting a passage moved electronically

*JN (your initials) or [ ]:* your own ideas, connections, or reactions

A system like this helps you develop your ideas, distinguish them from your paraphrase or cut-and-paste, and avoid accidental plagiarism, using another writer's words or ideas without appropriate credit.

**Decide What You Need.** When it comes time to draft your paper, you will incorporate your source material in three basic ways:

- *Quoting*: transcribing the author's exact words directly from the source
- *Paraphrasing*: fully rewording the author's ideas in your own words
- *Summarizing*: reducing the author's main point to essentials

Your notes, too, should use these three forms. Weighing each source carefully and guessing how you might use it—even as you are reading—is part of the dynamic process of research.

## Quoting

If you intend to use a direct quotation, capture it carefully, copying by hand or pasting electronically. Reproduce the words, spelling, order, and punctuation exactly, even if they're unusual. Put quotation marks around the material in your notes so you'll remember that it's a direct quotation.

RECORDING A GOOD QUOTATION

1. Quote sparingly, selecting only strong passages that might add support and authority to your assertions.
2. Mark the beginning and the ending with quotation marks.
3. Carefully write out or copy and paste each quotation. Check your copy—word by word—for accuracy. Check capitals and punctuation.
4. Record the page number where the quotation appears in the source. If it falls on two pages, note both; mark where the page turns.

Sometimes it doesn't pay to copy a long quotation word for word. If you take out one or more irrelevant words, indicate the omission with an ellipsis mark (. . .). If you need to add wording, especially so that a selection makes sense, enclose your addition in brackets [like this].

## Sample Quotations, Paraphrase, and Summary (MLA Style)

### Passage from Original Source

Obesity is a major issue because (1) vast numbers of people are affected; (2) the prevalence is growing; (3) rates are increasing in children; (4) the medical, psychological, and social effects are severe; (5) the behaviors that cause it (poor diet and inactivity) are themselves major contributors to ill health; and (6) treatment is expensive, rarely effective, and impractical to use on a large scale.

Biology and environment conspire to promote obesity. Biology is an enabling factor, but the obesity epidemic, and the consequent human tragedy, is a function of the worsening food and physical activity environment. Governments and societies have come to this conclusion very late. There is much catching up to do.

### Sample Quotations from Second Paragraph

Although human biology has contributed to the pudgy American society, everyone now faces the powerful challenge of a "worsening food and physical activity environment" (Brownell and Horgen 51). As Brownell and Horgen conclude, "There is much catching up to do" (51).

### Sample Paraphrase of First Paragraph

The current concern with increasing American weight has developed for half a dozen reasons, according to Brownell and Horgen. They attribute the shift in awareness to the number of obese people and the increase in this number, especially among youngsters. In addition, excess weight carries harsh consequences for individual physical and mental health and for society's welfare. Lack of exercise and unhealthy food choices worsen the health consequences, especially because there's no cheap and easy cure for the effects of eating too much and exercising too little (51).

### Sample Paraphrase Mixed with Quotation

Lack of exercise and unhealthy food choices worsen the health consequences, especially because they remain "major contributors to ill health" (Brownell and Horgen 51).

### Sample Summary

After outlining six reasons why obesity is a critical issue, Brownell and Horgen urge Americans to eat less and become more active (51).

### Sample Summary Mixed with Quotation

After outlining six reasons why obesity is a critical issue, Brownell and Horgen urge Americans to remedy "the worsening food and physical activity environment" (51).

### Works Cited Entry (MLA Style)

Brownell, Kelly D., and Katherine Battle Horgen. *Food Fight: The Inside Story of the Food Industry, America's Obesity Crisis, and What We Can Do about It.* Chicago: Contemporary-McGraw, 2004. Print.

## Paraphrasing

When paraphrasing, express an author's ideas, fairly and accurately, in your own words and sentences. Avoid judging, interpreting, or merely echoing the original. A good paraphrase may retain the organization, emphasis, and details of the original, so it may not be much shorter. Even so, paraphrasing is useful to walk your readers through the points made in the original.

For more on quotations and ellipsis marks, see C3 in the Quick Editing Guide, beginning on p. A-39, or handbook sections 25 and 27e–f.

| | |
|---|---|
| ORIGINAL | "In staging an ancient Greek tragedy today, most directors do not mask the actors." |
| TOO CLOSE TO THE ORIGINAL | Most directors, in staging an ancient Greek play today, do not mask the actors. |
| A GOOD PARAPHRASE | Few contemporary directors of Greek tragedy insist that their actors wear masks. |

WRITING A GOOD PARAPHRASE

1. Read the entire passage through several times.
2. Divide the passage into its most important ideas or points, either in your mind or by highlighting or annotating the passage.
3. Look away from the original, and restate the first idea in your own words. Sum up the support for this idea. Review the section if necessary.
4. Go on to the next idea, and do the same. Continue in this way.
5. Go back and reread the original passage one more time, making sure you've conveyed its ideas faithfully without repeating its words or sentence structure. Revise your paraphrase if necessary.

## Summarizing

Sometimes a paraphrase uses up too much space or disrupts the flow of your own ideas. Instead, you simply want to capture the main ideas of a source "in a nutshell." A summary can save space, distilling detailed text into one or two succinct sentences in your own words. Be careful as you reduce a long passage not to distort the original meaning or emphasis.

WRITING A GOOD SUMMARY

1. Read the original passage several times.
2. Without looking back, recall and state its central point.
3. Reread the original passage one more time, making sure you've conveyed its ideas faithfully. Revise your summary if necessary.

## Mixing Methods

Sometimes you paraphrase for precision or summarize for brevity but want to include notable wording from your source. In this situation, add quotation marks to identify what is directly quoted. Whatever your method, identify your source, and note the page where the quotation or paraphrase originates.

For practice quoting, paraphrasing, and summarizing, go to the interactive "Take Action" charts in Re:Writing at **bedfordstmartins.com/bedguide**.

### RESEARCH CHECKLIST

**Taking Notes with Quotations, Paraphrases, and Summaries**

- ☐ For each source note, have you identified the source (by the author's last name or a keyword from the title) and the exact page? Have you added a keyword heading to each note to help you group ideas?
- ☐ Have you added a companion entry to your bibliography for each new source?
- ☐ Have you remained true to the meaning of the original source?
- ☐ Have you quoted sparingly – selecting striking, short passages?
- ☐ Have you quoted exactly? Do you use quotation marks around significant words, phrases, and passages from the original sources? Do you use ellipsis marks or brackets to show where any words are omitted or added?
- ☐ Are most notes in your own words – paraphrasing or summarizing?
- ☐ Have you avoided paraphrasing too close to the source?

For practice incorporating sources, go to the interactive "Take Action" charts in Re:Writing at **bedfordstmartins.com/bedguide**.

## Learning by Doing Capturing Information from Sources

Identify a substantial paragraph or passage from a source you might use for your research paper or from a reading in this book (selected by you, your small group, or your instructor). Study this passage until you understand it thoroughly. Then use it as you respond to the following activities.

1. Quoting
   Identify one notable quotation from the passage you selected. Write a brief paragraph justifying your selection, explaining why you find it notable and why you might want to use it in a paper. Share your paragraph with classmates. In what ways were your reasons for selection similar or different?
2. Paraphrasing
   Write a paraphrase of your passage. Use your own language to capture what it says without parroting its words or sentence patterns. Share your paraphrase with classmates. What are its strengths and weaknesses? Where might you want to freshen the language?
3. Summarizing
   In one or two sentences, summarize the passage you selected. Capture its essence in your own words. Share your summary with classmates. What are its strengths and weaknesses? Where might you want to simplify or clarify?
4. Reflecting and Exchanging
   After completing 1, 2, and 3 above, decide which method of working with a passage proved most challenging. Write out specific tips for yourself about how to make that task easier, faster, and more successful. Compare your tips with those of your classmates so that you all gain fresh ideas about how to quote, paraphrase, and summarize.

## Developing an Annotated Bibliography

An annotated bibliography is a list of your sources – read to date or credited in your final paper – that includes a short summary or annotation for each entry. This common assignment quickly informs a reader about the direction of your research. It also shows your mastery of two major research skills: identifying a source and writing a summary.

To develop an annotated bibliography, find out which format you are expected to use to identify sources and what your annotations should do – summarize only, add evaluation, or meet a special requirement (such as interpretation). A summary is a brief, neutral explanation in your own words of the source's thesis or main points. In contrast, an evaluation is a judgment of the source's accuracy, reliability, or relevance.

**Summary with Source Identification and Proposed Use.** Several drafts of Schyler Martin's annotated bibliography were due as he identified possible sources for his MLA-style essay, "Does Education Improve Social Ills in Native American Communities?" He identified each source as primary (a firsthand or eyewitness account) or secondary (a secondhand analysis based on primary material), summarized it, and described how he expected it to support his position.

For more on the MLA and APA formats, see Chs. 36 and 37.

Loew, Patty. *Indian Nations of Wisconsin: Histories of Endurance and Renewal.* Madison: Wisconsin Historical Society Press, 2001. Print.

Secondary source. Professor Loew, a member of the Ojibwe tribe, presents Wisconsin history from a Native point of view. I will be using Loew's interviews to support my claims of education changing lives.

Wildcat, Daniel R. "Practical Professional Indigenous Education." *Power and Place: Indian Education in America*. Comp. Vine Deloria, Jr., and Daniel R. Wildcat. Golden: Fulcrum, 2001. 113-21. Print.

Secondary source. This book compares and contrasts the "Western" idea of education with Native American beliefs, showing where the "holes" are in today's educational policies. I will use Wildcat's chapter to demonstrate the argument of education only being useful when it is applied.

For her history paper, Shari O'Malley summed up relevance:

Goodman, Phil. "Patriotic Femininity: Women's Morals and Men's Morale During the Second World War." *Gender & History* 10.2 (1998): 278-93. Print.

Goodman examines British attitudes about women replacing men in the workplace and related wartime issues.

**Summary with Evaluation.** As Stephanie Hawkins worked on the annotated bibliography for her APA-style paper "Japanese: Linguistic Diversity," she wanted to show her critical thinking. Besides summarizing her sources, she evaluated their contributions, relationships, or usefulness to her study.

Abe, H. N. (1995). From stereotype to context: The study of Japanese women's speech. *Feminist Studies, 21*(3), 647-671.

Abe discusses the roots of Japanese women's language, beginning in ancient Japan and continuing into modern times. I was able to use this peer-reviewed article to expand on the format of women's language and the consequences of its use.

Kristof, N. (1995, September 24). On language: Too polite for words. *New York Times Magazine,* pp. SM22-SM23.

Kristof, a regular columnist for the *New York Times Magazine,* briefly describes the use of honorifics as an outlet for sarcasm and insults. Although the article discusses cultures other than Japanese, it provides insight into the polite vulgarity of the Japanese language.

**Summary with Interpretation.** Often an annotated bibliography includes unfamiliar materials, and your readers can benefit from extra explanation, background, or context. Examples include primary sources, interviews, oral histories, music, images, artistic works, texts from other times or cultures, or translations. In such cases, you may want to summarize the source and also interpret it for your readers, as this MLA-style entry and annotation illustrates.

Virginia Slims Lights. Advertisement. *Family Circle.* 26 Dec. 1985: 34–35. Print.

This advertisement for cigarettes, one of five in this issue of a popular women's magazine, illustrates how advertisers appealed to women smokers during this era. The ad's heading, "Introducing the LONGEST Slims of all," runs across two pages with a long-legged woman smoker lying on her side, also stretched across both pages. She is dressed not in alluring evening wear but in a blue-flowered sweater and woolly gold slacks. Both her attire and her wholesome look suit the issue's date and holiday features which include read-aloud stories, cookie recipes, and holiday decorating. Her head is thrown back and she smiles, holding her cigarette, which apparently promises enjoyment and relaxation at a busy time of the year for the magazine's readers.

## Learning by Doing Writing an Annotation

Select one of your sources (or a reading from this book), and write a few sentences to describe what the source covers and why it is relevant to your project. If your instructor has specified a particular approach, tailor your annotation to follow those directions. Exchange annotation drafts with a classmate or small group, and discuss ways to clarify contents or relevance.

# Finding Sources

# 32

Although research begins with an intriguing question or issue, it quickly becomes a fast-paced hunt, moving among electronic, print, and human resources. Time is always limited, so you need efficient search strategies to help you find substantial, relevant sources. Should you begin your search for sources on the Internet? Or should you first log onto the campus library site?

Many instructors advocate beginning your research through the campus library. They are confident that you will be able to identify and access reliable information there, especially "peer-reviewed" or "refereed" articles—those whose scholarship and research methods have been assessed by experts in the field before being accepted for publication. Because college papers are built through an academic exchange, you need to rely on high-quality sources and strive to draw solid, well-grounded conclusions for your audience.

However, instructors also know that most of us spend a lot of time on the Internet, so you—and they—can easily browse for ideas or run a quick search for key terms. For news-oriented topics or opinions on trending social issues, you also can find up-to-the-minute, though not necessarily reliable, information. Where you begin your research may depend on your experience and the nature of your topic. Even if you start looking for a topic on the Web, turn to your campus library for focus and depth.

## Why Finding Sources Matters

### In a College Course

- You need to support your paper for the most demanding professor in the entire nursing school, so you know that means more than Google and Wikipedia.
- Your annotated bibliography is a third of your grade in history, so you need to find books and articles by reliable historians as well as original documents from the time period.

For more on the Academic Exchange, see pp. 236 and 238–39.

### In the Workplace

- You want to organize objectives for the next decade, using available projections for your profession.

### In Your Community

- You organize focus groups for a community grant proposal, identifying sources to inform participants.

? When have you needed to find specific types of sources? In what situations do you expect to do so again?

---

## Searching the Internet

The Internet contains an ever-growing number of resources that vary greatly in quality and purpose. A quick search may turn up intriguing topic ideas or slants, but it also will turn up thousands—maybe millions—of Web pages of uncertain relevance. These pages are far more likely to be motivated by the desire to sell something, to promote an opinion, to socialize, or to attract you to an advertising platform than to meet your academic research needs. They also will not necessarily be grouped by academic field or be designed to meet any academic standards. And even if you believe that a Web search with millions of returns has located everything that exists, it will not include the thousands of private, corporate, or government sites from the "deep" or "hidden" Web that requires passwords, limits access, or simply has not yet been indexed. The sheer bulk of this information makes searching for relevant research materials both too easy and too difficult, but a few basic principles can help.

For a checklist for finding recommended sources, see B1 in the Quick Research Guide on p. A-25.

### Finding Recommended Internet Resources

For more on campus library resources, see pp. 662–74.

For more on evaluating sources, see Ch. 33.

Go first to online resources recommended by your instructor, department, or library. Their recommendations save search time, avoid random sites, and can take you directly to respected resources prepared by experts (scholars or librarians) for academic researchers (like you). Your college library, on campus or online, will offer many more resources such as these.

- Research Web sites sponsored by another library, academic institution, or consortium such as ipl2, the Internet Public Library at ipl.org, the Michigan eLibrary at mel.org, InfoMine at infomine.ucr.edu, or the authoritative World Wide Web Virtual Library at vlib.org
- Self-help guides or Internet databases organized by area (social sciences or business), topic (literary analysis), or type of information, such as the extensive Auraria Library *Statistics and Facts* guide at guides.auraria.edu/statistics
- Other research centers or major libraries with their own collections of links, such as the Library of Congress online catalog at catalog2.loc.gov or its "Newspaper & Current Periodical Reading Room" at loc.gov/rr/news
- Specialty search engines for government materials and agencies at FedWorld.ntis.gov and usa.gov

- Specialty search engines for specific materials such as Google Images at images.google.com, including the *Life* magazine photo archive, or Creative Commons at search.creativecommons.org
- Collections of sources such as those gathered in the New York University LibGuides at nyu.libguides.com
- Collections of e-books, including reference books and literary texts now out of copyright, such as Bartleby.com at bartleby.com/ and Project Gutenberg at gutenberg.org
- Web databases with "unrestricted access" (not online subscription services restricted to campus users) as varied as the United Nations databases at un.org/en/databases, the extensive health resources of MedlinePlus at nlm.nih.gov/medlineplus, and controversies at ProCon.org
- Community resources or organizations, often useful for local research and service learning reports

## Selecting Search Engines

Unlike a library, the Internet has no handy catalog, and search engines are not objective searchers. Each has its own system of locating material, categorizing it, and establishing the sequence for reporting results. One search site, patterned on a library index, might be selective. Another might separate advertising from search results, while a third pops up "sponsors" that pay advertising fees first, even though sites listed later might be better matches.

The best search engine is one you select and learn to use well. If you have a favorite, check its search practices. As you work out a combination of search terms relevant to your research question, think of your wording as a zoom lens. Tinker with it to search as narrowly as possible, finding relevant sites but avoiding endless options. Then try the identical search with another search engine to compare the results.

---

**RESEARCH CHECKLIST**

**Comparing Search Engine Results**

- ☐ What does the search engine's home page suggest its typical users want—academic information, business news, sports, shopping, or music?
- ☐ What does the search engine gather or index—information from and about a Web page (Google), each word on a Web page (Yahoo!), academic sources (Google Scholar), a collection of other search engines (Metacrawler), or returns compared for several engines (TurboScout)?
- ☐ What can you learn from a search engine's About, Search Tips, or Help?
- ☐ How does the advanced search work? Does it improve your results?
- ☐ Does the search engine take questions (Ask, Wolfram Alpha), categorize by source type (text, images, news), or group by topic (About)?

- ☐ How well does the search engine target your query—the words that define your specific search?
- ☐ How can you distinguish results (responses to your query), sponsors (advertisers who pay for priority placement), and other ads by placement, color, or other markers?

For an interactive Learning by Doing activity on Comparing Google and Database Searches, go to Ch. 32: **bedfordstmartins .com/bedguide**.

### Learning by Doing Comparing Web Searches

Working with some classmates, agree on the topic and terms for a test search. (Or agree to test terms each of you selects.) Have everyone conduct the same search using different search engines, and then compare the results. Use the checklist above to suggest features for comparison. If possible, sit together, using your tablets, laptops, or campus computers so that you can easily see, compare, and evaluate the search engine results. Report your conclusions to the class.

## Conducting Advanced Electronic Searches

Search engines contain millions of records on Web sites, much as a database or library catalog contains records on books, periodicals, or other materials found in a library. Generally, search engines can be searched by broad categories such as *education* or *health* or by more specific keywords.

For sample keyword searches, see p. 661 and p. 667.

**Limit the Search.** When you limit your search to keywords and broad categories, you may be overwhelmed with information. For example, Figure 32.1 illustrates a keyword search for sources on *foster care* on Google that produced more than 200 million entries. A keyword search may be ideal for a highly specialized term or topic, such as training for distance runners. For a more general topic—such as *foster care*—limit your search to find more relevant results. As Figure 32.2 shows, an advanced search produced fewer sources on one aspect of foster care—placing teenagers.

**Select Limitations for Advanced Searches.** Google and Metacrawler, for example, allow you to limit searches to all, exactly, any, or none of the words you enter. Look for directions for limitations such as these:

- a phrase such as "elementary school safety," requested as a unit (exactly these words) or enclosed in quotation marks to mark it as a unit
- a specific language (human or computer) such as English or Spanish
- a specific format or type of software such as a PDF file
- a date range (before, after, or between creation, revision, or indexing)

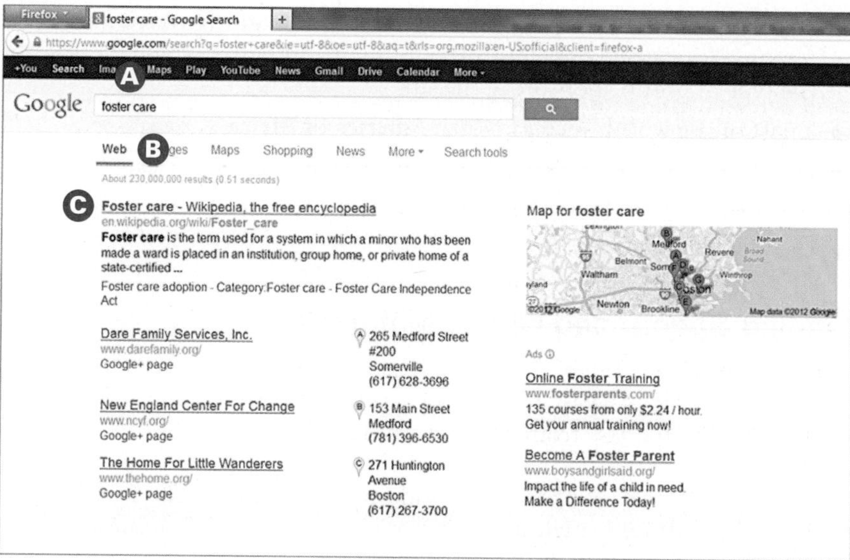


**Figure 32.1** Results of a keyword search for *foster care* using Google, reporting more than 200 million entries

**A.** Search terms
**B.** Total number of entries located
**C.** Highlighted search terms found in entries

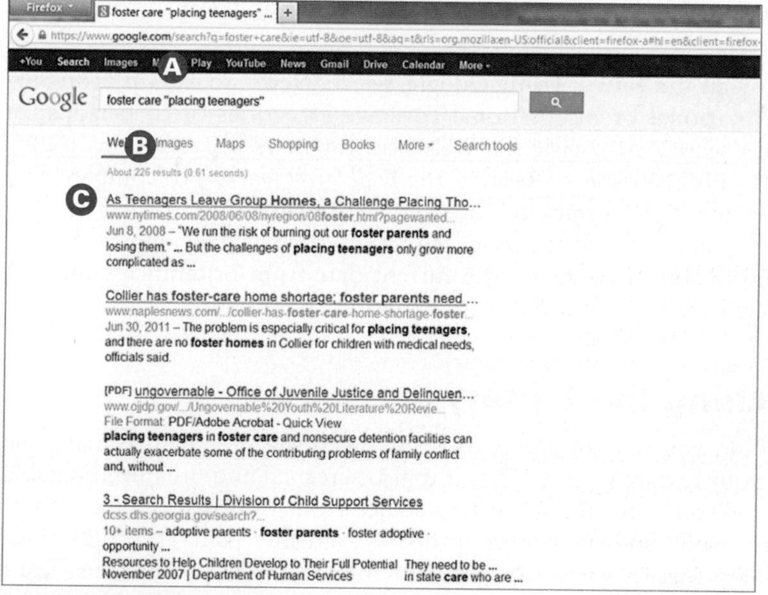


**Figure 32.2** Advanced search results on *foster care + "placing teenagers"* using Google, reporting 226 entries

**A.** Search terms
**B.** Total number of entries located
**C.** Highlighted search terms found in entries

- a domain such as .edu (educational institution), .gov (government), .org (organization), or .com (commercial site or company), which indicates the type of group sponsoring the site
- a part of the world, such as North America or Africa
- the location (such as the title, the URL, or the text) of the search term
- the audio or visual media enhancements
- the file size

## Finding Specialized Online Materials

You can locate a variety of material online, ranging from e-zines (electronic magazines) to blogs (Web logs) to conversations among people. Be careful to distinguish expertise from opinion and speculation.

**Look for Electronic Publications.** Wide public access to the Internet has given individuals and small interest groups an economical publication option. Evaluate and use such texts cautiously.

**Browse the Blogs.** Globe of Blogs at globeofblogs.com provides access to the personal, political, and topical commentaries of individuals around the globe. Google features blog searches by topic at google.com/blogsearch. You may want to use RSS (often expanded as "Real Simple Syndication") software to alert you to breaking news or to sample blogging on a current topic.

**Keep Up with the News.** Using Google, select "News" to call up "Top Stories" and national or international coverage categories or to personalize your news search. Also visit the Web sites for news organizations (NBC, BBC, NPR, PBS Newshour, Reuters, the *Wall Street Journal*) to compare coverage and depth or to track recent stories. RSS feeds and mailing lists are available for news as well as specialized topics, such as daily quotes, biographies, and historical events on the current date from Britannica Online at http://newsletters.britannica.com/toolbox.

# Searching the Library

What would you pay for access to a 24/7 Web site designed to make the most of your research time? What if it also screened and organized reliable sources for you—and tossed in free advice from information specialists? Whatever your budget, you've probably already paid—through your tuition—for these services. To get your money's worth, simply use your student ID to access your college library, online or on campus.

Visit the library home page for an overview of resources such as these:

- the online catalog for finding the library's own books, journals, newspapers, and materials you can read or check out on campus

- databases (with subscription fees paid) for electronic access to scholarly or specialized citations, abstracts, articles, and other resources
- access to the resources of the state, region, or nation through Interlibrary Loan (ILL), a regional consortium, or a trip to a nearby library
- links for finding specialized campus libraries, archives, or collections
- pages, tutorials, and tours for advice on using the library productively

To introduce you to the campus library, your instructor may arrange a class orientation. If not, visit the library Web site and campus facility yourself.

RESEARCH CHECKLIST

**Accessing Library Resources**

- ☐ What services, materials, and information does the home page present?
- ☐ How do you gain online access to the library from your own computer? What should you do if you have trouble logging in?
- ☐ How can you get live help from library staff: by drop-in visit, appointment, phone, e-mail, text message, chat, or other technology?
- ☐ What resources – such as the library catalog and databases – can you search in the library, on campus, or off campus?
- ☐ How can you identify databases useful for your project? What tutorials from the library or database provider show how to use them efficiently?
- ☐ How are print books, journals, magazines, or newspapers organized?
- ☐ How do you find resources such as government documents, maps, legal records, statistics, videos, images, recordings, or local historical archives?
- ☐ Where can you study individually or meet with a group in the library?
- ☐ What links or no-fee access to reliable Web sites, search engines such as Google Scholar, or academic style guides does the library provide?
- ☐ What other services – copying, printing, computer access – are available at your library?

For links to free reliable research resources, go to Re:Writing at **bedfordstmartins .com/bedguide**.

## Learning by Doing: Reflecting on Your Library Orientation Session

After visiting the library for your class orientation, list the most useful things you have learned – such as directions for access, advice about off-campus use, ways to get search advice, specific resources for your likely project or major, types of materials new to you, the name of a reference librarian, or helpful tricks for doing faster research. Then list your current questions about your own research project, and figure out where to start looking for the best and fastest answers.

**Target Your Search.** Your campus library may surprise you with its sophisticated technology and easy access to an overwhelming array of resources. Identify and hunt for what you want to find.

- Do you need a mixture of sources? Use the catalog to find specialized books or journals, databases to identify individual articles, reference books to look up definitions or overviews, or government sites or indexes to find reports. If your library offers WorldCat Local or a mega search system, you can search all types of resources at one time.
- Do you need current or historical information? Look for articles in periodicals (regularly published newspapers, magazines, and journals) for news of the day, week, or year – now or in the past. Turn to scholarly books for well-seasoned discussions.

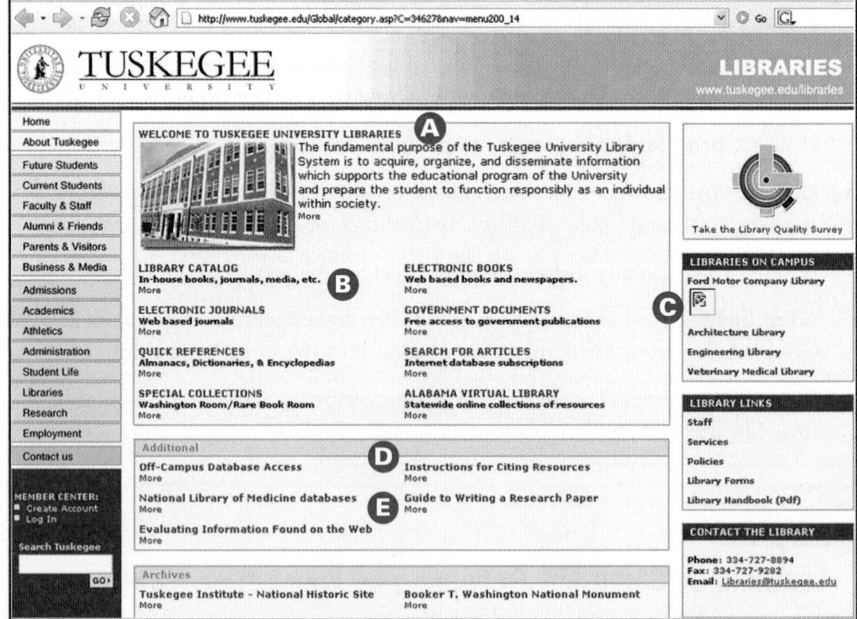


**Figure 32.3** Sample home page from the Tuskegee University Libraries

**A.** Overview of libraries and their purpose
**B.** Access to library holdings and resources
**C.** Information on specific campus libraries
**D.** Off-campus access
**E.** Other research resources

- Does your instructor require articles from peer-reviewed or refereed journals? Use *Ulrich's Periodicals Directory* or databases to screen for journals that rely on expert reviewers to assess articles considered for publication.
- Do you need opinions about current issues? Search databases for newspapers or magazines that carry opinion pieces, issue-oriented or investigative articles, or contrasting regional, national, or international views.
- Do you need the facts? Check state or federal agencies or nonprofit groups for statistics about people such as those in your zip code, including education, employment, or health.

For practice using keywords, visit Re:Writing at **bedfordstmartins.com/bedguide**.

**Search the Library Catalog Creatively.** Electronic catalogs may allow many search options, as the chart below illustrates. Consult a librarian or follow the prompts to find out which searches your catalog allows.

| Type of Search | Explanation | Examples | Search Tips |
|---|---|---|---|
| Keyword | Terms that identify topics discussed in the source, including works by or about an author, but may generate long lists of relevant and irrelevant sources | ▪ workplace mental health<br>▪ geriatric home health care<br>▪ Creole cookbook<br>▪ Jane Austen novels | Use a cluster of keywords to avoid broad terms (whale, nursing) or to reduce irrelevant topics using the same terms (people of color, color graphics) |
| Subject | Terms assigned by library catalogers, often following the Library of Congress Subject Headings (LCSH) | ▪ motion pictures (not films)<br>▪ developing countries (not Third World)<br>▪ cooking (not cookbooks) | Consult the online LCSH or note the linked subject headings with search results to find the exact phrasing used |
| Author | Name of individual, organization, or group, leading to list of print (and possibly online) works by author (or editor) | ▪ Hawthorne, Nathaniel<br>▪ Colorado School of Mines<br>▪ North Atlantic Treaty Organization | Begin as directed with an individual's last name or first; for a group, first use a keyword search to identify its exact name |
| Title | Name of book, pamphlet, journal, magazine, newspaper, video, CD, or other material | ▪ *Peace and Conflict Studies*<br>▪ *Los Angeles Times*<br>▪ *Nursing Outlook* | Look for a separate search option for titles of periodicals (journals, newspapers, magazines) |
| Identification Numbers | Library or consortium call numbers, publisher or government publication numbers | ▪ MJ BASI, local call number for recordings by Count Basie | Use the call number of a useful source to find related items online or shelved nearby |
| Dates | Publication or other dates used to search (or limit searches) for current or historical materials | ▪ Elizabeth 1558 (when she became queen of England)<br>▪ science teaching 2013 | Add dates to keyword or other searches to limit the topics or time of publication |

### Learning by Doing Brainstorming for Search Terms

Start with a class topic or your rough ideas for a research question. Working with a classmate or small group, brainstorm in class or online for keywords or synonyms that might be useful search terms for each person's topic. Test your terms by searching several places — the library catalog, a subject-area database, a newspaper database, a reliable consumer Web page, a relevant government agency, or other library resources. Compare search results in terms of type, quantity, quality, and relevance of sources. Note which terms work best in which situations. Then refine your search terms — add limitations, change key words, narrow the ideas, and so forth. Search again, trying to increase the relevance of what you find.

**Sort Your Search Results.** When your search produces a list of possible sources, click on the most promising items to learn more about them. See Figure 32.4 for a sample keyword search and Figure 32.5 for the online record for one source. Besides the call number or shelf location, the record will identify the author, title, place of publication, date, and often the book's contents, length, scope, and search terms that may help focus your search. Use these clues to help you select options wisely.

**Sample the Field.** Many libraries supply Library Guides or lists of well-regarded starting points for research within a field. These valuable shortcuts help you quickly find a cluster of useful resources. The chart on page 668 supplies only a small sampling of the specialized indexes, dictionaries, encyclopedias, handbooks, yearbooks, and other resources available.

**Browse the Shelves.** A call number, like a building's address, tells where a book "resides." College libraries generally use the Library of Congress system with letters and numbers rather than the numerical Dewey Decimal system, but both systems group items by subject. With a call number from an online record, follow the library map and section signs to the shelf with a promising book. Once there, browse through its intriguing neighbors, which will treat the same subject.

**Use the Resources.** Your campus library can help you become a more efficient and productive student. Try its wide variety of resources, advice, and tools: e-books, audio books, podcasts, videos, tutorials, workshops, citation managers, source organizers, and apps for academic tasks (note takers, time managers, project schedules, group organizers, file hosting services).

## Searching Library Databases

To practice using databases, visit the Bedford Research Room Web site at **bedfordstmartins .com/researchroom**.

Databases gather information. Your library may subscribe to dozens or hundreds to give you easy access to current, screened resources, including hard-to-find fee-based Web sources. Check the library site for its database

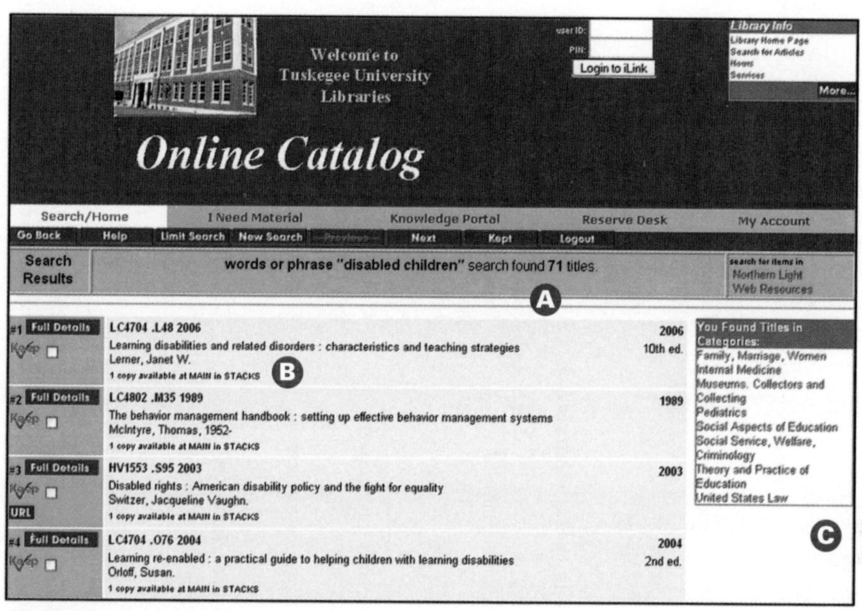


**Figure 32.4** General results of a keyword search on "disabled children" using an online library catalog

**A.** Number of search results

**B.** Results screen (linked to full entries) with call numbers, titles, authors, and availability

**C.** Topic areas where results were found

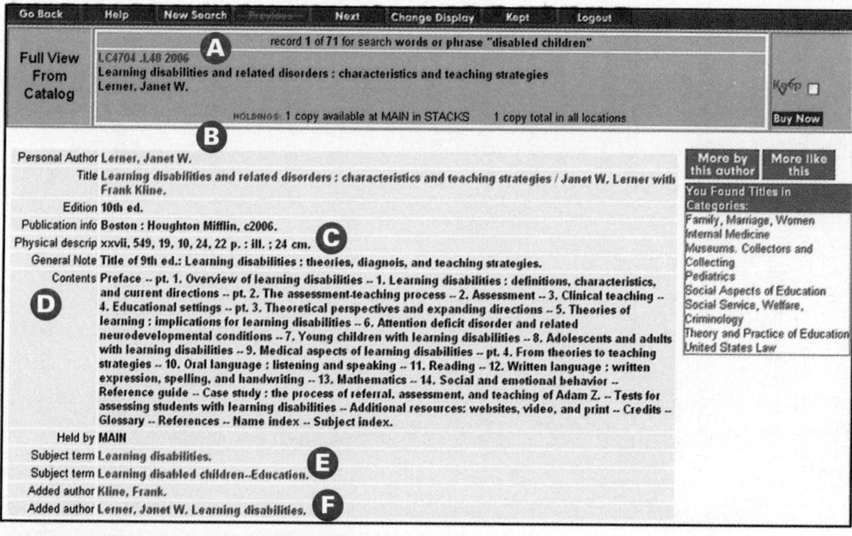


**Figure 32.5** Specific record selected from keyword search results

**A.** Call number, title, and author

**B.** Availability and location

**C.** Number of pages, illustrations, and height of book

**D.** Contents by part and chapter

**E.** Alternate subject heading (often hyperlinked)

**F.** Additional author

| Field | Specialized Indexes | Reference Works | Government Resources | Internet Resources |
|---|---|---|---|---|
| **Humanities** | *Essay and General Literature Index; JSTOR* | *The Humanities: A Selective Guide to Information Sources* | EDSITEment at edsitement.neh.gov | Voice of the Shuttle at vos.ucsb.edu |
| **Film and Theater** | *Film & Television Literature Index*<br>*Films on Demand* | *McGraw-Hill Encyclopedia of World Drama* | Smithsonian Archives Center: Film, Video, and Audio Collections at amhistory.si.edu /archives/d-4.htm | Performing Arts links at tla-online.org/links/libraries.html |
| **History** | *Historical Abstracts*<br>*America: History and Life* | *Dictionary of Concepts in History* | The Library of Congress: American Memory at memory.loc.gov/ammem/index .html | WWW Virtual Library: History Central Catalogue at vlib.iue.it/history/index.html |
| **Literature** | *MLA International Bibliography* | *Encyclopedia of the Novel* | National Endowment for the Humanities at neh.gov | American Studies Journals at theasa.net/journals |
| **Social Sciences** | *Social Sciences Citation Index* | *International Encyclopedia of the Social and Behavioral Sciences* | Fedstats at fedstats.gov | Intute: Social Sciences at intute.ac.uk/socialsciences/ |
| **Education** | *Education Abstracts* | *International Encyclopedia of Education* | National Center for Education Statistics at nces.ed.gov | ERIC: Education Resources Information Center at eric.ed.gov |
| **Political Science** | *Worldwide Political Science Abstracts* | *State Legislative Sourcebook: A Resource Guide to Legislative Information in the 50 States* | Fedworld at fedworld.ntis.gov/ | Political Resources on the Net at politicalresources.net<br>National Security Archive at gwu.edu/~nsarchiv |
| **Women's Studies** | *Women's Studies International* | *Women in World History: A Biographical Encyclopedia* | U.S. Department of Labor Women's Bureau at dol.gov/wb/ | Institute for Women's Policy Research at iwpr.org/index.cfm |
| **Science and Technology** | *General Science Abstracts*<br>*Web of Science* | *McGraw-Hill Encyclopedia of Science and Technology* | National Science Foundation at nsf.gov | EurekAlert! at eurekalert.org |
| **Earth Sciences** | *Bibliography and Index of Geology* | *Facts on File Dictionary of Earth Science* | USGS (U.S. Geological Survey): Science for a Changing World at usgs.gov | Center for International Earth Science Information Network at ciesin.org |
| **Environmental Studies** | *Environmental Abstracts* | *Encyclopedia of Environmental Science* | EPA: U.S. Environmental Protection Agency at epa.gov | EnviroLink at envirolink.org |
| **Life Sciences** | *Biological Abstracts* | *Encyclopedia of Human Biology* | National Agricultural Library at nal.usda.gov | CAPHIS Top 100 List at caphis.mlanet.org/consumer |

descriptions and lists by topic or field. A librarian can help match your research question to the databases likely to provide what you need.

- **General databases** with citations, abstracts, or full-text articles from many fields: Academic Search Premier, General OneFile, LexisNexis, OmniFile Full Text
- **General-interest databases** with news and culture of the time: Reader's Guide Full-Text or Retrospective (popular periodicals); New York Times Historical, America's Newspapers, LexisNexis (news)
- **Specialized databases by type of material:** JSTOR, Project Muse, Sage (scholarly journals); Biological Abstracts (summaries of sources); WorldCat (books), American Periodical Series Online (digitized magazines from 1741 to 1900)
- **Specialized databases by field:** MedlinePlus, ScienceDirect, GreenFILE (biology, medicine, health); ABI/Inform (business), AGRICOLA (agriculture)
- **Issue-oriented databases:** PAIS International (public affairs), CQ Researcher (featured issues), Opposing Viewpoints in Context (debatable topics)
- **Reference databases:** Gale Virtual Reference Library, Oxford Reference, Credo Reference

For specific information, select a database that covers the exact field, scholarly level, type of source, or time period that you need. Databases identify sources only in publications they analyze and only for dates they cover. Take tricky problems to a librarian who may suggest a different database or older print or CD-ROM indexes for historical research.

**Keywords.** Start your search with the keywords in your research question:

| | | |
|---|---|---|
| college costs | campus budgets | wetlands |

If your first search produces too many sources, narrow your terms:

| | | |
|---|---|---|
| college tuition increases | state campus budget cuts | Illinois wetlands and Great Midwestern Flood |

Or add specifics, such as an author, title, or date.

**Advanced Searches.** Fill in the database's advanced search screen to restrict by date or other options, or try common search options. For example, a database might allow wildcard or truncation symbols to find all forms of a term, often * for multiple or ? for individual characters:

| | |
|---|---|
| child* | children, childcare, childhood |
| Colorad* | Colorado, Coloradan, Coloradans |

A database also might allow Boolean searches that combine or rule out terms:

| | |
|---|---|
| AND (narrows: all terms must appear in a result) | Colorado and River |
| OR (expands: any one of the terms must appear) | Colorado or River |
| NOT (rules out: one term must not appear) | Colorado not River |

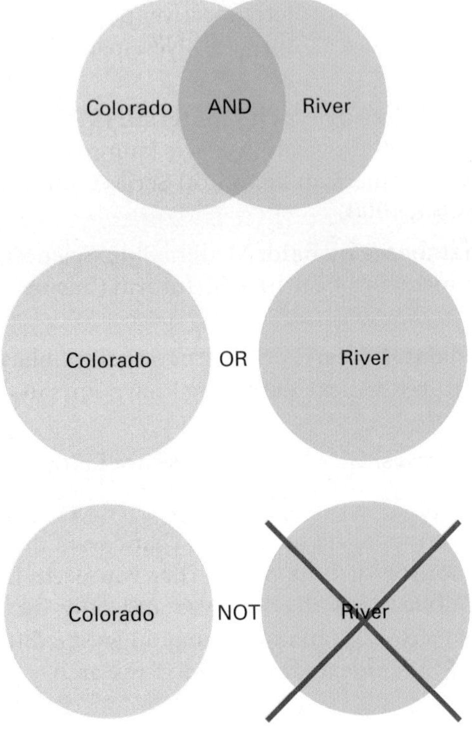


**Search Returns.** Your search calls up a list of records or entries that include your search terms. Click on one of these for specifics about the item (title, author, publication information, date, other details) and possibly a description or summary (often called an abstract) or a link to the full text of the item. When you find a useful item, read, take notes, print, save, or e-mail the citation or article to yourself, as your system allows. If the database supplies only an abstract, read it to decide whether you need to track down the full article elsewhere.

---

RESEARCH CHECKLIST

**Selecting Periodical Articles from a Database**

☐ What does the periodical title suggest about its audience, interest area, and popular or scholarly orientation? How likely are its articles to supply what you need?

- ☐ Have the periodical articles been peer-reviewed (evaluated by other scholars prior to acceptance for publication), edited and fact-checked by journalists, or accepted for publication based on popular appeal?
- ☐ Does the title or description of the article suggest that it will answer your research question? Or does the entry sound intriguing but irrelevant?
- ☐ Does the date of the article fit your need for current, contemporary, eyewitness, or classic material?
- ☐ Does the length of the article suggest that it is a short review, a concise overview, or an exhaustive discussion? How much detail will you need?
- ☐ Does the database offer the full text of the article in direct-scan pdf or re-formatted html? If not, is the periodical likely to be available from another database, its Web site, or your library's shelves?

## Learning by Doing Comparing Databases

Work with others interested in a particular subject or field. Pick at least three databases in that area. For each, investigate what type of response it provides (source references, abstracts, summaries, full-text articles), which dates it covers, how extensive its collection might be, and how you can most successfully use it. Report back to your group or to the entire class.

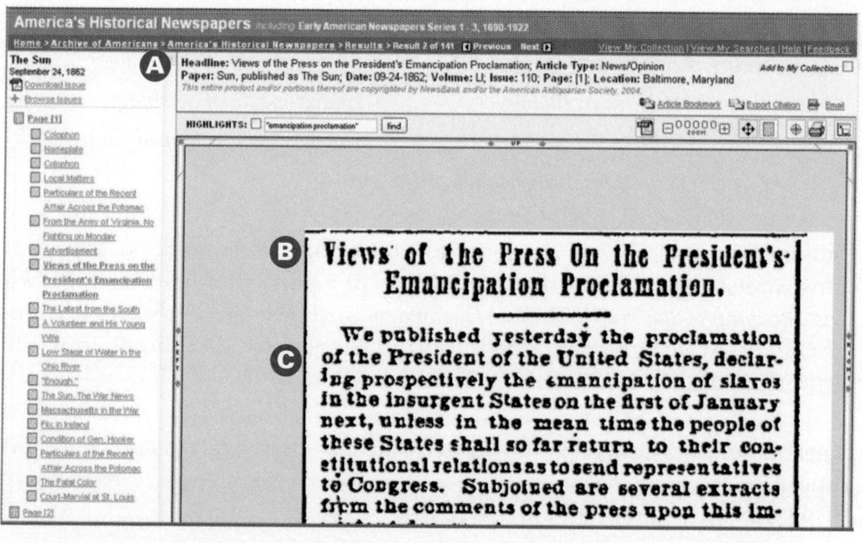


**Figure 32.6** Search result from *America's Historical Newspapers*

A. Publication name, date, volume number, page number
B. Article title (and author, if available)
C. Text of article

## Learning by Doing Comparing Google and Database Searches

Work in pairs or a small group, using your tablets or laptops in class or online. Agree on a few search terms relevant for topics that interest you individually or collectively. Search for each term twice – first using Google and then using your library's general academic database. Compare and contrast the results based on quantity, relevance, usefulness, status (as peer-reviewed or refereed academic sources), or other criteria. If you wish, expand your comparisons to include Google Scholar, a different Internet search engine, a library database for a specific field, or other options.

# Using Specialized Library Resources

Many other library resources are available to you beyond what you can access from your library's home page. If you need help locating or using materials, consult a librarian.

**Encyclopedias.** Multivolume general references, such as the *New Encyclopaedia Britannica* and *Encyclopedia Americana,* can help you survey a topic. Specialized encyclopedias cover a field in much greater depth. You can also conduct "reverse research" – reading a useful encyclopedia or other reference entry first to inform you and then to follow its bibliography to reliable sources.

*Dictionary of American History*
*Encyclopedia of Human Biology*
*Gale Encyclopedia of Science*
*New Grove Dictionary of Music and Musicians*
*Encyclopedia of Psychology*
*Encyclopedia of Sociology*
*Encyclopedia of World Cultures*

**Dictionaries.** Specialized dictionaries cover foreign languages, abbreviations, and slang as well as the terminology of a particular field, as in *Black's Law Dictionary, Stedman's Medical Dictionary,* or the *Oxford Dictionary of Natural History.* After you read a definition in a specialty dictionary, look for terms that might narrow your database searches.

**Handbooks and Companions.** Concise articles survey terms and topics on a specific subject.

*Bloomsbury Guide to Women's Literature*
*Dictionary of the Vietnam War*

**Government Documents.** The U.S. government, the most prolific publisher in the world, makes an increasing number of documents available for all citizens on the Web, along with indexes like these:

- *Monthly Catalog of United States Government Publications,* which is the most complete index to federal documents available
- *CIS Index,* which specializes in congressional documents with a handy legislative history index
- *Congressional Record Index,* which indexes daily reports on Congress

The government also compiles valuable statistics:

- *Statistical Abstract of the United States*, which may be the most useful single compilation of statistics, with hundreds of tables relating to population, social issues, economics, and so on
- *census.gov*, which collects an extraordinary amount of statistical data and releases much of it on the Web

**Atlases.** For a geographical angle, use maps of countries and regions as well as history, natural resources, ethnic groups, and other topics.

**Biographical Sources.** Directories list basic information about prominent people. Tools such as *Biography Index* and the *Biography and Genealogy Master Index* locate resources like *American Men and Women of Science, The Dictionary of American Biography, The Dictionary of Literary Biography, The Dictionary of National Biography, Who's Who in Politics,* and *Who's Who in the United States.*

**Bibliographies.** A bibliography lists a wide variety of sources on a specific subject, research others have already done. Every time you find a good book or article, look at the sources the author draws on; some of these may be useful to you and can lead to sources that you wouldn't otherwise find. For example, *The Essential Shakespeare: An Annotated Bibliography of Major Modern Studies* lists the best books and articles published on each of Shakespeare's works, a wonderful shortcut when you're looking for worthwhile criticism. If you're lucky, adding the word *bibliography* to a subject or keyword search on your topic will turn up a similarly helpful list of sources with annotations.

**Special Materials.** Your library is likely to have other collections of materials, especially on regional or specialized topics, but you may need to ask what's available. For example, firsthand diaries, letters, speeches, and interviews are increasingly available in searchable databases. Your library also may collect pamphlets and reports distributed by companies, trade groups, and professional organizations.

---

RESEARCH CHECKLIST

**Managing Your Project**

- ☐ Are you on schedule? Do you need to adjust your timetable to give yourself more or less time for any of the stages?
- ☐ Are you using your research question to stay on track and avoid digressions?

☐ Are you keeping your materials up-to-date – listing new sources in your working bibliography and storing new material in your archives?

☐ Do you have a clear idea of where you are in the research process?

## Finding Sources in the Field

The goal of field research is the same as that of library and Internet research – to gather the information you need to answer your research question and then to marshal persuasive evidence to support your conclusions. When you interview, observe, or ask questions of people, you generate your own first-hand (or primary) evidence. Almost any paper will be enriched by authentic and persuasive field sources, and you'll almost certainly learn more by going into the field. Before you begin, find out from your instructor whether you need institutional approval for research involving other people ("human subjects approval" from your IRB, Institutional Review Board).

### Interviewing

For more on interviewing, see Ch. 6.

Interviews – conversations with a purpose – may be your main source of field material. Whenever possible, interview an expert in the field or, if you are researching a group, someone representative or typical. Prepare carefully.

TIPS FOR INTERVIEWING

- Be sure your prospect is willing to be quoted in writing.
- Make an appointment for a day when the person will have enough time – an hour if possible – to have a thorough talk with you.
- Arrive promptly, with carefully thought-out questions to ask.
- Come ready to take notes, including key points, quotations, and descriptive detail. If you also want to record, ask permission.
- Really listen. Let the person open up.
- Be flexible, and allow the interview to move in unanticipated directions.
- If a question draws no response, don't persist; go on to the next one.
- At the end of the interview, thank your interviewee, and arrange for an opportunity to clarify comments and confirm direct quotations.
- Make additional notes right after the interview to preserve anything you didn't have time to record during the interview.

If you can't talk in person, try a telephone or online interview. Make an appointment for a convenient time, write out questions before you dial, and take notes. Federal regulations, by the way, forbid recording a phone interview without notifying the person talking that you are doing so.

## Observing

An observation may provide essential information about a setting such as a workplace or a school. If so, make an appointment and, on arrival, identify yourself and your purpose. Some receptionists will insist on identification; ask your instructor for a statement on college letterhead declaring that you are a student doing field research.

For more on observing, see Ch. 5.

TIPS FOR OBSERVING

- Establish a clear purpose—exactly what you want to observe and why.
- Take notes so that you don't skip important details in your paper.
- Record facts, telling details, and sensory impressions. Notice the features of the place, the actions or relationships of the people who are there, or whatever relates to the purpose of your observation.
- Consider using a still or video camera if you have the equipment and can operate it without being distracted from the scene. Photographs can illustrate your paper and help you recall and interpret details while you write. If you are in a private place, get written permission from the owner (or other authority) and any people you film or photograph.
- Pause, look around, fill in missing details, and check the accuracy of your notes before you leave the observation site.
- Thank the person who arranged your observation so you will be welcome again if you need to return to fill gaps or test new ideas.

## Using Questionnaires

Questionnaires gather the responses of a number of people to a fixed set of questions. Professional researchers carefully design their questions and randomly select representative people to respond in order to reach reliable answers. Because your survey will not be that extensive, avoid generalizing about your findings. It's one thing to say that "many of the students" who filled out a questionnaire hadn't read a newspaper in the past month; it's another to claim that this is true of 72 percent of the students at your school—especially when your questionnaires went only to those at the gym on Friday, and most of them just threw out the forms.

A more reliable way to treat questionnaires is as group interviews: assume that you collect typical views, use them to build your overall knowledge, and cull the responses for compelling details or quotations. Use a questionnaire to concentrate on what a group thinks as a whole or when an interview to cover all your questions is impractical. (See Figure 32.7 for a sample questionnaire.)

TIPS FOR USING A QUESTIONNAIRE

- Ask yourself what you want to discover with your questionnaire. Then thoughtfully invent questions to fulfill that purpose.

QUESTIONNAIRE

Thank you for completing this questionnaire. All information you supply will be kept strictly confidential.

1. What is your age? ____
2. What is your gender? ____
3. What is your class?
   ____ Freshman  ____ Sophomore  ____ Junior  ____ Senior
4. How old were you when you first began using the Internet? ____
5. How do you currently access the Internet? Indicate which of the following statements is true for you.
   ____ With my own computer  ____ With computers at the library or campus lab
   ____ With my laptop or tablet  ____ Someone I live with has a computer
   ____ Other (please specify): ____________
6. Approximately how many hours a week do you use the Internet? ____
7. What is your primary reason for using the Internet?
   ____ Personal  ____ School-related  ____ Work-related
8. Check all of the ways in which you use the Internet.
   ____ E-mailing
   ____ Visiting social networking sites or chatting
   ____ Recreational Web surfing
   ____ Recreational media use (listening to music, watching videos, playing games)
   ____ Taking an online course
   ____ Conducting optional research for a class
   ____ Conducting mandatory research for a class
   ____ Conducting personal research (such as planning travel, evaluating products)
   ____ Searching for a job or an internship
   ____ Posting résumés or job applications
   ____ Managing financial accounts
   ____ Maintaining a Web site or blog
   Other: ____________
9. For which activities above do you use the Internet most? ____________
10. On a scale of 1 to 5, rate how comfortable you are using the Internet.
   (not very comfortable) 1 2 3 4 5 (very comfortable)
11. Do you feel that you could benefit from further instruction in using the Internet?
   ____ Yes  ____ No  ____ Maybe

**Figure 32.7** Questionnaire asking college students about Internet use

- State your questions clearly, and supply simple directions for easy responses. Test your questionnaire on classmates or friends before you distribute it to the group you want to study.
- Ask questions that call for checking options, marking yes or no, circling a number on a five-point scale, or writing a few words so responses are easy to tally. Try to ask for one piece of information per question.
- If you wish to consider differences based on age, gender, or other variables, include some demographic questions.
- Write unbiased questions that solicit factual responses. Do not ask, "How religious are you?" Instead ask, "What is your religious affiliation?" and "How often do you attend religious services?" Then you could report actual numbers and draw logical inferences about respondents.
- When appropriate, ask open-ended questions that call for short written responses. Although qualitative responses are more difficult to tally than quantitative, the answers may supply worthwhile quotations or suggest important issues or factors.
- Try to distribute questionnaires at a set location or event, and collect them as they are completed. If necessary, have them returned to your campus mailbox or another secure location. The more immediate and convenient the return, the higher your return rate is likely to be.
- Use a blank questionnaire or make an answer grid to mark and add up the answers for each question. Total the responses so you can report that a certain percentage selected a specific answer.
- For fill-in or short answers, type each answer into a computer file. (Code each questionnaire with a number, and note it if you might want to return to the individual questionnaire.) You can rearrange the answers in the file, looking for logical groups, categories, or patterns that accurately reflect the responses and enrich your analysis.

## Corresponding

Does a person with views you need live too far away to interview? Do you need information from a group such as the American Red Cross or an elected official? Check your library or the Internet for directories of campus alumni, professionals, businesses, government agencies, or special-interest groups that might supply expert information. Visit a group's Web site for an e-mail option for your request, a correspondence address, a FAQ page (that answers frequently asked questions), or files of brochures.

For advice on writing e-mail messages, see p. 355, and business letters, see pp. 361–64.

TIPS FOR CORRESPONDING

- Plan ahead, and allow plenty of time for responses to your requests.
- Make your message short and polite. Identify yourself, and explain your request. List any questions. Thank your correspondent.
- Enclose a stamped, self-addressed envelope with a letter. Include your e-mail address in your message.

## Attending Public and Online Events

College organizations bring interesting speakers to campus. Check the campus schedule of events and the newspaper. In addition, professionals and special-interest groups convene for regional or national conferences. A lecture or conference can be a source of fresh ideas and an excellent introduction to the language of a discipline.

TIPS FOR ATTENDING EVENTS

- Take notes on the lectures, usually given by experts in the field who supply firsthand opinions or research findings.
- Ask questions from the audience or talk informally with a speaker later.
- Record who attended the event, how the audience reacted, or other background details that could prove useful in writing your paper.
- Depending on the gathering, a speaker might distribute the paper or presentation slides or be willing to send you a copy. Conferences often publish their proceedings—usually a set of the lectures delivered—but publication takes months. Try the library for past proceedings.

If you join an online discussion, you can observe, ask a question, or save or print the transcript for your records.

## Reconsidering Your Field Sources

Each type of field research can raise particular questions. For example, when you observe an event or a setting, are people aware of being observed? If so, have they changed their behavior? Is your random sampling of people truly representative? Have you questioned everyone in a group thoroughly enough?

In addition, consider the credibility and consistency of your particular field sources. Did your source seem biased or prejudiced? If so, is this viewpoint so strong that you have to discount some of the source's information? Did your source provide evidence to support or corroborate claims? Have you compared different people's opinions, accounts, or evidence? Is any evidence hearsay—one person telling you the thoughts of another or recounting actions that he or she hasn't witnessed? If so, can you check the information with another source or a different type of evidence? Did your source seem to respond consistently, seriously, and honestly? Has time possibly distorted memories of past events? Adjust your conclusions based on your field research in accord with your answers to such questions.

# Evaluating Sources 33

After you locate and collect information, you need to think critically and evaluate – in other words, judge – your sources.

For more on critical reading and thinking, see Chs. 2–3.

- Which of your sources are reliable?
- Which of these sources are relevant to your topic?
- What evidence from these sources is most useful for your paper?

## Why Evaluating Sources Matters

### In a College Course

- You have found half a dozen sources about your topic, but they wildly disagree; you have to decide what to do next.
- You found a Web site without any author, a testimonial by a TV star you dimly remember, and a boring article by a professor, but you don't know which one to believe.

### In the Workplace

- You have to prepare a recommendation for a client after deciding what data and field reports to provide.

### In Your Community

- You disagree with the mayor's decision to ban urban gardening, so you want to find current, substantial information that will change her mind.

? When have you decided which sources to use and which to skip? In what situations do you expect to evaluate sources again?

## Evaluating Library and Internet Sources

Not every source you locate will be equally reliable or equally useful. Sites recommended by your library have been screened by professionals, but each has its own point of view or approach, often a necessary bias to restrict its focus. Sources from the Web require special care. Like other firsthand materials, postings, blogs, and sites reflect the biases, interests, or information gaps of their writers or sponsors. Commercial and organizational sites may supply useful material, but they provide only what supports their goals—selling their products, serving their clients, enlisting new members, or persuading others to accept their activities or views. See Figure 33.1 for a sample evaluation of a Web site that provides both informative and persuasive materials.

How can you simplify evaluation? Begin with your selection of sources. Suppose you draw information from an article in a print or online peer-reviewed journal. The evaluation of that article actually began when the journal editors first read it and then asked expert reviewers to evaluate whether it merited publication. Similarly, a serious book from a major publishing company or university press probably has been submitted to knowledgeable reviewers. Such reviewers may be asked to assess whether the book or article seems well reasoned, logically presented, and competently researched. However, they can't decide if the work is pertinent to your research question or contains evidence useful for your paper.

How do you know what evidence is best? Do what experienced researchers do—ask key questions. Use the time-tested journalist's questions—who, what, when, where, why, how—to evaluate each of your sources.

---

RESEARCH CHECKLIST

**Evaluating Sources**

*Who?*

For advice on evaluating field sources, see p. 678.

- ☐ Who is the author of the source? What are the author's credentials and profession? What might be the author's point of view?
- ☐ Who is the intended audience of the source? Experts in the field? Professionals? General readers? People with a special interest? In what ways does the source's tone or evidence appeal to this audience?
- ☐ Who is the publisher of the source or the sponsor of the site? Is it a corporation, a scholarly organization, a professional association, a government agency, or an issue-oriented group? Have you heard of this publisher or sponsor before? Is it well regarded? Does it seem reputable and responsible? Is it considered academic or popular?
- ☐ Who has reviewed the source prior to publication? Only the author? Peer reviewers who are experts in the area? An editorial staff?

*What?*

- ☐ What is the purpose of the publication or Web site? Is it to sell a product or service? To entertain? To supply information? To publish new research? To shape opinion about an issue or a cause?
- ☐ What bias or point of view might affect the reliability of the source?

- ☐ What kind of information does the source supply? Is it a primary source (a firsthand account) or a secondary source (an analysis of primary material)? If it is a secondary source, does it rely on sound evidence from primary sources?
- ☐ What evidence does the source present? Does it seem accurate and trustworthy? Is it sufficient and relevant given what you know? Does its argument or analysis seem logical and complete, or does it leave questions unanswered? Does it identify and list its sources or supply active links?

*When?*

- ☐ When was the source published or created? Is its information current?
- ☐ When was it last revised or updated? Is its information up-to-date?

*Where?*

- ☐ Where did you find the source? Is it available through your campus library's site? Is it on a Web site that popped up in a general search?
- ☐ Where has the source been recommended? On an instructor's syllabus or Web page? On a library list? In another reliable source? During a conference with an instructor or a librarian?

*Why?*

- ☐ Why should you use this source rather than others?
- ☐ Why is its information directly relevant to your research question?

*How?*

- ☐ How does the selection of evidence in the source reflect the interests and expertise of its author, publisher or sponsor, and intended audience? How might you need to qualify its use in your paper?
- ☐ How would its information add to your paper? How would it help answer your research question and provide evidence to persuade your readers?

### Learning by Doing Evaluating Your Sources

Select a source that you expect to be useful for your paper. Using the preceding checklist, jot down notes as you examine the source for reliability and relevance. Working with a classmate or group, present your evaluations to each other. Then discuss strategies for dealing with the strengths and limitations of the sources you have evaluated. (Use the next sections to help you deepen your evaluation.)

e For an interactive Learning by Doing activity on Evaluating Online Sources, go to Ch. 33: **bedfordstmartins.com/bedguide**.

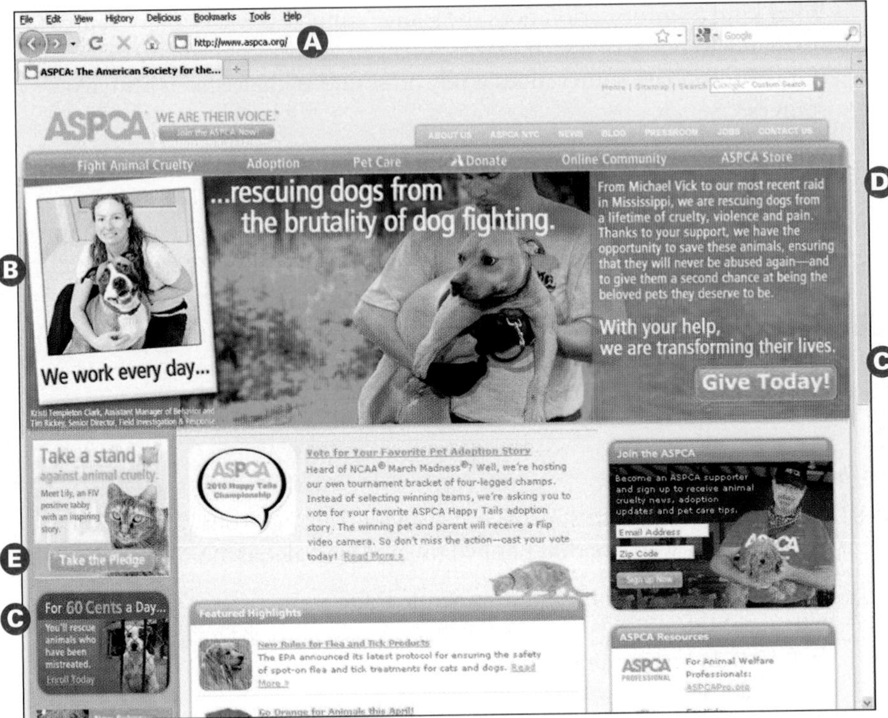


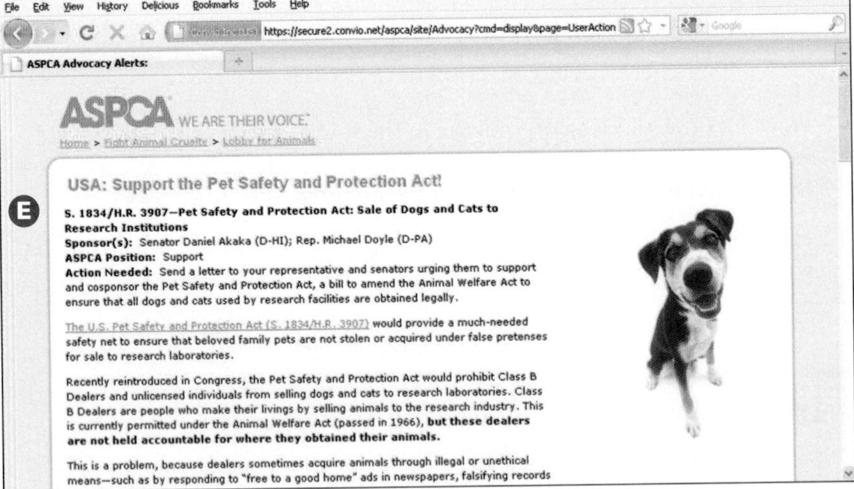


**Figure 33.1** Evaluating the purpose, audience, and bias of a Web site offering informative and persuasive materials

A. Identifies group as organization (.org), not school (.edu) or company (.com)
B. Uses engaging animal graphics
C. Appeals for support
D. Explains purpose of group and provides toolbar link to contact information
E. Links to information and recommends action about issues that concern animal lovers

## Who Is the Author?

Learn about each author's credentials, affiliations, and reputation so that any author who shapes or supports your ideas is reliable and trustworthy.

**Print Credentials.** Check for the author's background in any preface, introduction, or concluding note in an article or a book. National newsmagazines (for example, *The Economist* or *Time*) usually identify experts before or next to their contributions. However, most of their articles are written by reporters who try to substantiate facts and cover multiple views, perhaps compiling regional contributions. In contrast, some other magazines select facts to mirror editorial opinions.

**Internet Credentials.** For a Web site, look for a hyperlinked author's name leading to other articles, a link to author information, or an e-mail address so you could contact the author about his or her background. If your source is a posting to a newsgroup or a mailing list, deduce what you can from the writer's e-mail address and any signature file. Try a Web search for the person's name, looking for associated sites or links to or from the author's site. If you can't find out about the author, treat the information as background for you, not as evidence in your paper.

**Field Credentials.** For field research, you may be able to select your sources. Consider their backgrounds, credentials, and biases. To investigate safety standards for infant car seats, a personal interview with a local pediatrician will probably produce different information than an interview with a sales representative.

**Reputation.** A good measure of someone's expertise is the regard of other experts. Do others cite the work of your source's author? Does your instructor or a campus expert recognize or recommend the author? Is the author listed in a biographical database? Does a search for the author on Google Scholar produce other sources that cite the author?

**Material with No Author Identified.** If no author is given, try to identify the sponsor, publisher, or editor. On a Web site, check the home page or search for a disclaimer, contact information, or an "About This Site" page. If a print source doesn't list an author, consider the publication: Is the article in a respected newspaper like the *Wall Street Journal* or a supermarket tabloid? Is the source a news story, an opinion piece, or an ad? Is the brochure published by a leader in its field?

## Who Else Is Involved?

**Intended Audience.** A source written for authorities in a field is likely to assume that readers already have plenty of background. Such sources typically skip overviews and tailor their details for experts. In contrast, sources for general audiences usually define terms and supply background. Instead of beginning your paper on HIV treatments with an article in a well-known medical journal for physicians that discusses the most favorable chemical composition for a protease inhibitor drug, turn first to a source that defines *protease inhibitor* and explains how it helps HIV patients.

**Publisher or Sponsor.** The person, organization, agency, or corporation that prints or sponsors a source also may shape its content. Like authors, publishers often hold a point of view. Critically question what might motivate a publisher. Is a Web site created for commercial (.com) purposes, such as selling a product or service? Is it sponsored by an organization devoted to a cause (.org, as in Figure 33.1) or a government agency (.gov)? Is it the work of an individual with strong opinions but little expertise? Is a newsgroup or list limited to a particular interest? Is a publisher noted for works in a specific field or with a political agenda? Does a periodical have a predictable point of view? A faith-based publication will take a different view than a newsmagazine, just as a conservative publication will differ from a liberal one. For a Web site sponsor, look for a mission statement or an "About" page. Consult a librarian if you need help with these difficult questions.

For an example showing how a URL identifies a publisher, see A on p. 682.

**Reviewers before Publication.** Consider whether a publisher has an editorial staff, an expert editor, or an advisory board of experts. Does it rely on peer reviewers to critique articles or books under consideration? Does it expect research to meet professional standards? Does it outline such standards in its advice for prospective authors or its description of its mission? Does a sponsor have a solid reputation as a professional organization?

## What Is the Purpose?

A library reference book serves a different purpose from a newspaper editorial, a magazine ad, or a Web site that promotes a service. To understand the purpose or intention of a source, ask critical questions: Is its purpose to explain or inform? To report new research? To persuade? To add a viewpoint? To sell a product? Does the source acknowledge its purpose in its preface, mission statement, or "About Us" or FAQ (Frequently Asked Questions) page?

**Bias.** A *bias* is a preference for a particular side of an issue. Because most authors and publishers have opinions on their topics, there's little point in asking whether they are biased. Instead, ask how that viewpoint affects the presentation of information and opinion. What are the author's or sponsor's allegiances? Does the source treat one side of an issue more favorably than another? Is that bias hidden or stated? A strong bias does not invalidate a source. However, if you spot such bias early, you can look for other viewpoints to avoid lopsided analyses.

**Primary or Secondary Information.** A *primary source* is a firsthand account written by an eyewitness or a participant. It contains raw data and immediate impressions. A *secondary source* is an analysis of information in one or more primary sources. Primary sources for investigating the Korean War might include diaries or letters written by military personnel, accounts of civilian witnesses, articles by journalists on the scene, and official military reports. If a historian used those accounts as evidence in a study of military strategy or if a peace activist used them in a book on consequences of warfare for civilians, the resulting works would be secondary sources.

Most research papers benefit from both primary and secondary sources. If you repeatedly cite a fact or an authority quoted in someone else's analysis, try to go to the primary source. After all, a bombing raid that spared 70 percent of a village also leveled 30 percent of it. The original research (published as a primary source) can help you learn where facts end and interpretation begins.

## When Was the Source Published?

In most fields, new information and discoveries appear every year, so a source needs to be up-to-date or at least still timely. New information may appear first in Web postings, media broadcasts, newspapers, and eventually magazines, though such sources may not allow time to consider information thoughtfully. Later, as material is more fully examined, it may appear in scholarly articles and books. For this reason, older materials can supply a valuable historical, theoretical, or analytical focus.

## Where Did You Find the Source?

Is it recommended by your instructor? Is it in the library's collection? When instructors or academic units direct you to sources, you benefit from both their subject-matter and teaching expertise. On the other hand, when you find a Web source while randomly browsing or pick up a magazine at the dentist's office, you'll need to do all the source evaluation yourself. Begin by asking where the source got its information.

## Why Would You Use This Source?

Why use one source rather than another? Is its information useful for your purposes? Would its strong quotations or hard facts be effective? Does it tackle the topic in a relevant way? For one paper, you might appropriately rely on a popular magazine; for another, you might need the scholarly findings on which the magazine relied. Look for the best sources for your purpose, asking not only "Will this do?" but also "Would something else be better?"

For more on selecting sources, see section B in the Quick Research Guide, pp. A-24–A-26.

For more on testing evidence, see pp. 40–44.

## How Would This Source Contribute to Your Paper?

The evidence in a source—its ideas, facts, and expert or other opinions—can tell you about its reliability and usefulness for your project. Is its evidence complete, up-to-date, and carefully assembled? Is there enough convincing evidence to support its claims? Does visual material enhance the source, not distract from its argument or information? Does the source identify its own sources in citations and a bibliography? Even a highly reliable source needs to be relevant to your research question and your ideas about how to answer that question. An interesting fact or opinion could be just that—interesting. Instead, you need facts, expert opinions, information, and quotations that relate directly to your purpose and audience.

### Learning by Doing  Adding Useful Sources

Writers often use common organizational patterns to review a group of solid sources. For example, you might arrange sources chronologically to trace history or development, compare and contrast sources to present alternatives, or trace cause and effect through several sources. Examine the contributions of your current sources to your argument. Do you need to complete a chronology with an established view or a current one? Do you need to fill out a comparison or a causal analysis? Add relevant sources as needed for balance or depth.

For more on using time order, see Ch. 4; for more on comparison and contrast, see Ch. 7; for more on cause and effect, see Ch. 8.

## Reconsidering Purpose and Thesis

Once you have gathered and evaluated a reasonable collection of sources, it's time to step back and consider them as a group.

- Have you found enough relevant and credible sources to satisfy the requirements of your assignment? Have you found enough to suggest sound answers to your research question?
- Are your sources thought provoking? Can you tell what is generally accepted, controversial, or possibly unreliable? Have your sources enlightened you while substantiating, refining, or changing your ideas?
- Are your sources varied? Have they helped you achieve a reasonably complete view of your topic, including other perspectives, approaches, alternatives, or interpretations? Have they deepened your understanding and helped you reach well-reasoned, balanced conclusions?
- Are your sources appropriate? Do they answer your question with evidence your readers will find persuasive? Do they have the range and depth necessary to achieve your purpose and satisfy your readers?

Use these questions to check in with yourself. Make sure that you have a clear direction for your research—whether it's the same direction you started with or a completely new one. Perhaps you are ready to answer your research question, refine your thesis, and begin a draft that pulls together your ideas and those of your sources. On the other hand, you may want to find other sources to support or challenge your assumptions, to counter strong evidence against your position, or to pursue a tantalizing new direction.

# Integrating Sources

# 34

Your paper should project your own voice and showcase your ideas—your thesis and main points about your research question. It also should marshal compelling support, using the evidence that you have quoted, paraphrased, and summarized from sources. Add this support responsibly, identifying both the sources and the ideas or exact words captured from them.

For more on using sources in your writing, see Ch. 12 and D1–D6 in the Quick Research Guide, pp. A-28–A-31.

## Why Integrating Sources Matters

**In a College Course**

- You have read and read for your sociology paper, but now you need to fit your sources into your paper very efficiently so you finish on time.
- You need to integrate your class projects and reading log into your capstone portfolio to complete the final requirement for your credential.

**In the Workplace**

- You must synthesize materials from three rival departments in a collaborative report.

**In Your Community**

- You know that parents exchange information about autism, but the school board wants academic sources to identify best practices for teachers.

? When have you integrated a jumble of sources? In what situations do you expect to do so again?

## Using Sources Ethically

The complex, lively process of research is enriched by the exchange of ideas. However, discussions of research ethics sometimes reduce that topic to one issue: plagiarism. Plagiarism is viewed especially seriously in college because it shows a deep disrespect for the work of the academic world—investigating, evaluating, analyzing, interpreting, and synthesizing ideas. And it may have

| Plagiarism Problem | Remedy |
|---|---|
| You have dawdled. Someone tells you about a site that sells papers, but you know this is wrong. Plus their topics don't sound like your assignment, and you need to hand in drafts and an annotated bibliography, too. | Don't buy the paper. Ask your instructor for more time, even with a penalty. Cancel your social life for the week, and hunt for recommended sources. Be proud that you showed integrity and didn't risk your college career. |
| You've fully investigated a serious research question about a problem affecting your family, but now you're mixing up what you've quoted, summed up, and thought up yourself. You're afraid your disorganization will look like plagiarism. | Stop and get organized. Link every note or file to its source with the author's last name (or brief title) and page number. Treat unidentified leftover notes as background. Don't add what you can't credit. |
| You found a great book in the library but had only a minute to record the basics. Later you found these notes:<br>InDfCult, HUP, Cambridge, Carol Padden, Tom Humphries, 5<br>122 For Df voice/technol = issue<br>Relates to cult def | Go back to the library, and get help finding the book. Spell out clear information about *Inside Deaf Culture* by Carol Padden and Tom Humphries, published in Cambridge, MA, by Harvard University Press in 2005. Turn back to p. 122. Decide what to do: quote (exact words with quotation marks) or paraphrase (your own words, not "parroting"). |
| You've never read a book with hard words like *transmogrify* and *heuristic*. You can't restate them because you don't understand them. You're afraid your instructor will think you're a cheater who just copied, not an embarrassed student who can't read well enough. | Don't use a source you can't understand. Look for others shelved nearby or listed under the same keywords. If the source is required, reread and sum up each passage in turn to master it. Spend time improving your reading using campus or community support services. |
| You're struggling to start writing. Finally you're creating sentences, then pasting in notes. You suddenly wonder how you'll figure out where to add your source citations. What if you didn't identify a few sources or add the page numbers for quotations? | Backtrack fast. Add notes (color, brackets, or comments) to mark exactly where you need to add a source citation later. For yourself, note the basics—author and page. Add quotation marks for words directly from the source at the moment you integrate them. |
| In your home country, you and your friends worked together to state the answer the teacher expected. Everyone handed it in, so nobody was left out. Here your teacher wants different papers, and you are afraid yours will be wrong. | Different cultures have different expectations. Research papers here often are explorations, not right answers. Think about ideas of classmates or sources, but write down your own well-reasoned thoughts. Get advice from the ESL or writing center. |

serious consequences—failing a paper, failing a course, or being dismissed from the institution.

Plagiarists intentionally present someone else's work as their own—whether they dishonestly submit as their own a paper purchased from the Web, pretend that passages copied from an article are their own writing, present the ideas of others without identifying their sources, or paste in someone else's graphics without acknowledgment or permission.

Although college writers may not intend to plagiarize, most campus policies look at the outcome, not the intent. Working carefully with sources and treating ideas and expressions of others respectfully can build the skills necessary to avoid mistakes. Educating yourself about the standards of your campus, instructor, and profession also can protect you from ethical errors with heavy consequences. The chart on page 688 illustrates how to avoid or remedy common situations that can generate problems.

Careful researchers acknowledge intellectual obligations and responsibilities, showing respect for all engaged in the academic exchange:

- researchers whose studies provide a sturdy foundation
- readers curious about discoveries, reasons, and evidence
- themselves as they gain experience with credible research practices

### RESEARCH CHECKLIST
### Learning How to Conduct Research Ethically

- ☐ Have you accepted the responsibility of reviewing your campus standards for ethical academic conduct? Have you checked your syllabus for any explanation about how those standards apply in your course?
- ☐ If you feel ill prepared for doing research, have you sought help from your instructor or staff at the library, writing center, or computer lab?
- ☐ Are you regularly recording source entries in your working bibliography?
- ☐ Are you carefully distinguishing your own ideas from those of your sources when you record notes or gather material for your research archive? Have you tried putting source notes in one column on a page and your thoughts in a second column?
- ☐ Are you sticking to your research schedule to avoid a deadline crisis?
- ☐ Have you analyzed your paper-writing habits to identify any, such as procrastination, that might create ethical problems for you? How do you plan to change such habits to avoid problems?
- ☐ Have you used this book to practice and improve research skills (such as quoting, paraphrasing, or summarizing)?
- ☐ Have you found the chapter in this book that explains the documentation style you'll use in your paper? If not, find it now.
- ☐ Have you identified and followed campus procedures for conducting field research involving other people?
- ☐ Have you recorded contact information so that you can request permission to include any visual materials from sources in your paper?

☐ If your research is part of a group project, have you honored your agreements, meeting your obligations in a timely manner?

☐ Have you asked your instructor's advice about any other ethical issues that have arisen during your research project?

## Capturing, Launching, and Citing Evidence

For more on stating a thesis, see pp. 399–408.

Sources alone do not make for an effective research paper. Instead, the ideas, explanations, and details from your sources need to be integrated—combined and mixed—with your own thoughts and conclusions about the question you have investigated. Together they eventually form a unified whole that conveys your perspective and the evidence that logically supports it. To make sure that your voice isn't drowned out by your sources, keep your research question and working thesis—maybe still evolving—in front of you as you integrate information. On the other hand, identify and credit your sources appropriately, treating them with the respect they deserve.

Once you have recorded a source note, you may be tempted to include it in your paper at all costs. Resist. Include only material that answers your research question and supports your thesis. A note dragged in by force always sticks out like a pig in the belly of a boa constrictor.

For more about how to quote, paraphrase, and summarize, see pp. 236–43 and 651–54.

When material does fit, consider how to incorporate it effectively and ethically. Quoting reproduces an author's exact words. Paraphrasing restates an author's ideas in your own words and sentences. Summarizing extracts the essence of an author's meaning. You also need to launch captured material by introducing it to readers and to cite it by crediting its source.

### Quoting and Paraphrasing Accurately

To illustrate the art of capturing source material, let's first look at a passage from historian Barbara W. Tuchman. In *A Distant Mirror: The Calamitous Fourteenth Century* (New York: Knopf, 1978), Tuchman sets forth the effects of the famous plague known as the Black Death. In her foreword, she admits that any historian dealing with the Middle Ages faces difficulties. For one, large gaps exist in the records. Here is her original wording:

| Capture | Launch | Cite |
|---|---|---|
| ▪ Quote<br>▪ Paraphrase<br>▪ Summarize<br>▪ Synthesize | ▪ Identify authority<br>▪ Provide credentials for credibility<br>▪ Usher in the source<br>▪ Connect support to your points | ▪ Credit the source in your draft<br>▪ Link the citation to your final list of sources<br>▪ Specify the location of the material used |

ORIGINAL

A greater hazard, built into the very nature of recorded history, is overload of the negative: the disproportionate survival of the bad side — of evil, misery, contention, and harm. In history this is exactly the same as in the daily newspaper. The normal does not make news. History is made by the documents that survive, and these lean heavily on crisis and calamity, crime and misbehavior, because such things are the subject matter of the documentary process — of lawsuits, treaties, moralists' denunciations, literary satire, papal Bulls. No Pope ever issued a Bull to approve of something. Negative overload can be seen at work in the religious reformer Nicolas de Clamanges, who, in denouncing unfit and worldly prelates in 1401, said that in his anxiety for reform he would not discuss the good clerics because "they do not count beside the perverse men."

Disaster is rarely as pervasive as it seems from recorded accounts. The fact of being on the record makes it appear continuous and ubiquitous whereas it is more likely to have been sporadic both in time and place. Besides, persistence of the normal is usually greater than the effect of disturbance, as we know from our own times. After absorbing the news of today, one expects to face a world consisting entirely of strikes, crimes, power failures, broken water mains, stalled trains, school shutdowns, muggers, drug addicts, neo-Nazis, and rapists. The fact is that one can come home in the evening — on a lucky day — without having encountered more than one or two of these phenomena.

For an interactive Learning by Doing activity on Quoting and Paraphrasing Accurately, go to Ch. 34: **bedfordstmartins .com/bedguide**.

Although you might highlight this passage as you read it, it is too long to include in your paper. Quoting it directly would let your source overshadow your own voice. Instead, you might quote a striking line or so and paraphrase the rest by restating the details in your own words. Here, the writer puts Tuchman's ideas into other words but retains her major points and credits her ideas.

PARAPHRASE WITH QUOTATION

Tuchman points out that historians find some distortion of the truth hard to avoid, for more documentation exists for crimes, suffering, and calamities than for the events of ordinary life. As a result, history may overemphasize the negative. The author reminds us that we are familiar with this process in our news coverage, which treats bad news as more interesting than good news. If we believed that news stories told all the truth, we would feel threatened at all times by technical failures, crime, and violence—but we are threatened only some of the time, and normal life goes on. The good, dull, ordinary parts of our lives do not make the front page, and the praiseworthy tend to be ignored. "No Pope," says Tuchman, "ever issued a Bull to approve of something." But in truth, social upheaval did not prevail as widely as we might think from the surviving documents of medieval life (xviii).

In this reasonably complete paraphrase, about half as long as the original, most of Tuchman's points are spelled out. The writer doesn't interpret or evaluate Tuchman's ideas—she only passes them on. Paraphrasing helps her emphasize ideas important to her research. It also makes readers more aware of them as support for her thesis than quoting the passage would. The writer has directly quoted Tuchman's remark about papal Bulls because it would be hard to improve on that short, memorable statement.

Often you paraphrase to emphasize one point. This passage comes from Evelyn Underhill's classic study *Mysticism* (New York: Doubleday, 1990):

> ORIGINAL
>
> In the evidence given during the process for St. Teresa's beatification, Maria de San Francisco of Medina, one of her early nuns, stated that on entering the saint's cell whilst she was writing this same "Interior Castle" she found her [St. Teresa] so absorbed in contemplation as to be unaware of the external world. "If we made a noise close to her," said another, Maria del Nacimiento, "she neither ceased to write nor complained of being disturbed." Both these nuns, and also Ana de la Encarnacion, prioress of Granada, affirmed that she wrote with immense speed, never stopping to erase or to correct, being anxious, as she said, to write what the Lord had given her before she forgot it.

Suppose that the names of the witnesses do not matter to a researcher who wishes to emphasize, in fewer words, the renowned mystic's writing habits. That writer might paraphrase the passage (and quote it in part) like this:

> PARAPHRASE WITH QUOTATION
>
> Underhill has recalled the testimony of those who saw St. Teresa at work on *The Interior Castle*. Oblivious to noise, the celebrated mystic appeared to write in a state of complete absorption, driving her pen "with immense speed, never stopping to erase or to correct, being anxious, as she said, to write what the Lord had given her before she forgot it" (242).

## Summarizing Concisely

For Tuchman's original passage, see p. 691.

To illustrate how summarizing can serve you, this example sums up the passage from Tuchman:

> SUMMARY
>
> Tuchman reminds us that history lays stress on misery and misdeeds because these negative events attracted notice in their time and so were reported in writing; just as in news stories today, bad news predominates. But we should remember that suffering and social upheaval didn't prevail everywhere all the time (xviii).

This summary merely abstracts from the original. Not everything is preserved—not Tuchman's thought about papal Bulls, not examples such as neo-Nazis. But the gist—the summary of the main idea—echoes Tuchman faithfully.

Before you write a summary, an effective way to sense the gist of a passage is to pare away examples, details, modifiers, and nonessentials. Here is the quotation from Tuchman as one student marked it up on a photocopy, crossing out elements she decided to omit from her summary.

> ~~A greater hazard,~~ built into the ~~very~~ nature of recorded history, is ~~overload of the negative:~~ the disproportionate survival of the bad side—~~of evil, misery, contention, and harm. In history~~ this is exactly the same as in the daily newspaper. ~~The normal does not make news. History is made by the~~ documents that survive, ~~and these~~ lean heavily on crisis and calamity, crime and misbehavior, because such things are the subject matter of the documentary process~~—of lawsuits, treaties, moralists' denunciations, literary satire, papal Bulls. No Pope ever issued a Bull to approve of something. Negative overload can be seen at work in the religious reformer Nicolas de Clamanges, who, in denouncing unfit and worldly prelates in 1401, said that in his anxiety for reform he would not discuss the good clerics because "they do not count beside the perverse men."~~
>
> Disaster is rarely as pervasive as it seems from recorded accounts. ~~The fact of being on the record makes it appear continuous and ubiquitous whereas~~ it is more likely to have been sporadic both in time and place. Besides, persistence of the normal is usually greater than the effect of disturbance, as we know from our own times. ~~After absorbing the news of today, one expects to face a world consisting entirely of strikes, crimes, power failures, broken water mains, stalled trains, school shutdowns, muggers, drug addicts, neo Nazis, and rapists. The fact is that one can come home in the evening—on a lucky day—without having encountered more than one or two of these phenomena.~~

Rewording what was left, she wrote the following condensed version:

SUMMARY

History, like a morning newspaper, reports more bad than good. Why? Because the documents that have come down to us tend to deal with upheavals and disturbances, which are seldom as extensive and long-lasting as history books might lead us to believe (Tuchman xviii).

In writing her summary, the student could not simply omit the words she had deleted. The result would have been less readable and still long. She knew she couldn't use Tuchman's very words: that would

For more on avoiding plagiarism and using accepted methods of adding source material, see Ch. 12 and D1 in the Quick Research Guide, pp. A-28–A-29.

be plagiarism. To make a compact, honest summary that would fit smoothly into her paper, she had to condense the passage into her own words.

## Avoiding Plagiarism

Never lift another writer's words or ideas without giving that writer due credit and transforming them into words of your own. If you do use words or ideas without giving credit, you are plagiarizing. When you honestly summarize and paraphrase, clearly show that the ideas are the originator's, here Tuchman or Underhill. In contrast, the next examples are unacceptable paraphrases of Tuchman's passage that use, without thanks, her ideas and even her very words. Finding such gross borrowings in a paper, an instructor might hear the ringing of a burglar alarm. The first example lifts both thoughts and words, underlined here with the lines in the original noted in the margin.

For Tuchman's original passage, see p. 691.

PLAGIARIZED THOUGHTS AND WORDS

Sometimes it's difficult for historians to learn the truth about the everyday lives of people from past societies because of the disproportionate survival of the bad side of things. Historical documents, like today's newspapers, tend to lean rather heavily on crisis, crime, and misbehavior. Reading the newspaper could lead one to expect a world consisting entirely of strikes, crimes, power failures, muggers, drug addicts, and rapists. In fact, though, disaster is rarely so pervasive as recorded accounts can make it seem.

Quoted from line 2
Close to lines 5–6
Close to line 19
Lists from lines 19–21
Close to ¶ 2 opening

For more on managing a research project, see Ch. 30.

This writer did not understand the passage well enough to put Tuchman's ideas in his or her own words. If you allow enough time to read, think, and write, you are likely to handle sources more effectively than those who procrastinate or rush through their research. The next example is a more subtle theft, lifting thoughts but not words.

PLAGIARIZED THOUGHTS

It's not always easy to determine the truth about the everyday lives of people from past societies because bad news gets recorded a lot more frequently than good news does. Historical documents, like today's news channels, tend to pick up on malice and disaster and ignore flat normality. If I were to base my opinion of the world on what is on the news, I would expect death and destruction around me all the time. Actually, I rarely come up against true disaster.

By using the first-person pronoun *I,* this student suggests that Tuchman's ideas are his own. That is just as dishonest as quoting without using quotation marks, as reprehensible as not citing the source of ideas.

The next example fails to make clear which ideas belong to the writer and which to Tuchman.

PLAGIARIZED WITH FAULTY CREDIT

Barbara Tuchman explains that it can be difficult for historians to learn about the everyday lives of people who lived long ago because historical documents tend to record only bad news. Today's news is like that, too: disaster, malice, and confusion take up a lot more room than happiness and serenity. Just as the ins and outs of our everyday lives go unreported, we can suspect that upheavals do not play as important a part in the making of history as they seem to.

For a tutorial on avoiding plagiarism, go to the interactive "Take Action" charts in Re:Writing at **bedfordstmartins.com/bedguide**.

After rightly attributing ideas in the first sentence to Tuchman, the writer makes a comparison to today's world in sentence 2. In sentence 3, she returns to Tuchman's ideas without giving Tuchman credit. The placement of sentence 3 suggests that this last idea is the student's, not Tuchman's.

As you write, use ideas and words from your sources carefully, and credit those sources. Supply introductory and transitional comments to launch and attribute quotations, paraphrases, and summaries to the original source ("As Tuchman observes . . ."). Rely on quotation marks and other punctuation to show exactly which words come from your sources.

For more on working with sources, see Chs. 12 and 31 as well as the Quick Research Guide, beginning on p. A-20. For more on quotation marks, ellipses, and brackets, see C3 in the Quick Editing Guide, p. A-55.

RESEARCH CHECKLIST

**Avoiding Plagiarism**

- ☐ Have you identified the author of material you quote, paraphrase, or summarize? Have you credited the originator of facts and ideas you use?
- ☐ Have you clearly shown where another writer's ideas stop and yours begin?
- ☐ Have you checked each paraphrase or summary against the original for accuracy? Do you use your own words? Do you avoid words and sentences close to those in the original? Do you avoid distorting the original meaning?
- ☐ Have you checked each quotation against the original for accuracy? Have you used quotation marks for both passages and significant words taken directly from your source? Have you noted the page in the original?
- ☐ Have you used an ellipsis mark (. . .) to show your omissions from the original? Have you used brackets ([ ]) to indicate your changes or additions in a quotation? Have you avoided distorting the original meaning?

## Launching Source Material

You need to write a launch statement to identify the source of each detail and each idea—whether a quotation, summary, or paraphrase. Whenever possible, help readers see why you have selected particular sources, why you find their evidence pertinent, or how they support your conclusions. Select the verb that conveys to readers each source's contribution: says, claims, agrees, challenges, argues, discusses, interprets, describes, and so forth. Use

For more on the format for source citations in the text, see D6 in the Quick Research Guide, p. A-31.

your launch statements to show not only that you have read your sources but also that you have absorbed and applied what they say about your research question. Try the following strategies to strengthen launch statements.

- Name the author in the sentence that introduces the source:

  As Wood explains, the goal of American education continues to fluctuate between gaining knowledge and applying it (58).

- Add the author's name in the middle of the source material:

  In *Romeo and Juliet,* "That which we call a rose," Shakespeare claims, "By any other word would smell as sweet" (2.2.43–44).

- Note the professional title or affiliation of someone you've interviewed to add authority and increase the credibility of your source:

  According to Jan Lewis, a tax attorney at Sands and Gonzales, . . .

  Briefly noting relevant background or experience can do the same:

  Recalling her tour of duty in Iraq, Sergeant Nelson noted . . .

- Identify information from your own field research:

  When interviewed about the campus disaster plan, Natalie Chan, Director of Campus Services, confirmed . . .

- Name the author only in the source citation in parentheses if you want to keep your focus on the topic:

  A second march on Washington followed the first (Whitlock 83).

- Explain for the reader why you have selected and included the material:

  As Serrano's three-year investigation of tragic border incidents shows, the current policies carry high financial and human costs.

- Interpret what you see as the point or relevance of the material:

  Stein focuses on stem-cell research, but his discussion of potential ethical implications (18) also applies to other medical research.

- Relate the source clearly to the thesis or point it supports:

  Although Robinson analyzes workplace interactions, her conclusions (289–92) suggest the need to look at the issues in schools as well.

- Compare or contrast the point of view or evidence of two sources:

  While Desmond emphasizes the European economic disputes, Lewis turns to the social stresses that also set the stage for World War II.

Adding transitional expressions to guide readers can strengthen your launch statements by relating one source to another (*in addition, in contrast, more recently, in a more favorable view*) or particular evidence to your line of reasoning (*next, furthermore, in addition, despite, on the other hand*). However, transitions alone are not enough. Your analysis and your original thought need to introduce and follow from source information.

## Take Action Integrating and Synthesizing Sources

Ask each question at the top of the chart to consider whether your draft might need work on that issue. If so, follow the ASK—LOCATE SPECIFICS—TAKE ACTION sequence to revise.

| | Weak Group of Sources? | Unclear Connections? | No New Ideas? |
|---|---|---|---|
| **1 ASK** | Do I need to reexamine the group of sources that I plan to synthesize? | Do I need to relate my sources more deeply and clearly to each other? | Do I need to deepen my synthesis so it goes beyond my sources to my own ideas? |
| **2 LOCATE SPECIFICS** | ■ List the sources you're synthesizing.<br>■ Write out principles you have used (or could use) to select and group them—chronology to show change over time, theme to show aspects of a topic, comparison to show similarities, or another system.<br>■ Eliminate any fudging about your sources: pin down your guesses; summarize or paraphrase quotes; specify rather than generalize. | ■ For each source, review your notes so you can sum up its focus.<br>■ Highlight connective statements or transitions already used in your draft to link the sources.<br>■ Mark any jumps from source to source without transitions.<br>■ Read your draft out loud to yourself, marking any weak or incomplete synthesis of sources.<br>■ Ask a peer to mark any unclear passages. | ■ Schedule several blocks of time so that you can concentrate on your intellectual task.<br>■ Mark a check by any part of your synthesis that reads like a grocery list (bread, eggs, milk or Smith, Jones, Chu).<br>■ Star each spot where you repeat the source's point without relating it to your point or adding your interpretation. |
| **3 TAKE ACTION** | ■ Write down how each source develops your principles.<br>■ Redefine your principles or your ideas about what each source shows, as needed.<br>■ Revise your group: drop or add sources; move some if they don't fit well. If a source fits at several places, pick the best spot or fill a gap. | ■ If a connection is missing, review the focus for the source; add a statement to connect it to the source before or after it.<br>■ Brainstorm or jot notes to refine, restate, or expand connections.<br>■ Use your notes to deepen connections as you refine your synthesis. | ■ Generate ideas to build a cache of notes about how you want to relate your sources to your ideas and what they collectively suggest. Be creative; let your original ideas emerge.<br>■ For each check or star, use your own voice and ideas to fill gaps, deepen connections, or state relationships. |

## Learning by Doing Connecting Your Sources

For more on connections and transitions, see pp. 431–35.

Work on a chunk of your draft that pulls together multiple sources. In your file or on a printout, highlight each connection that you have stated in that passage. Look for transitional words, transitional sentences, repeated key words or synonyms, and significant pronouns that refer back to key words or terms. (Use one highlighting color for all these types of transitions, or use a separate color for each common type.) Now look for any gaps in your transitions — sections without any highlighting where you need to connect ideas. Also look for too much highlighting, places where you might thin out wordy transitions that obscure your point.

## Citing Each Source Clearly

For examples of citations, see Ch. 36 for MLA or Ch. 37 for APA.

Often your launch statement does double duty: naming a source as well as introducing the quotation, paraphrase, or summary from it. Naming, or citing, each source both credits it and helps locate it at the end of your paper in the list of sources called Works Cited (MLA) or References (APA). There you provide full publication information so that readers could find your original sources if they wished.

To make this connection clear, identify each source by mentioning the author (or the title if no author is identified) as you add information from the source to your paper. (In APA style, also add the date.) You can emphasize this identification by including it in your launch statement, or you can tuck it into parentheses after the information. Then, supply the specific location of any quotation or paraphrase (usually the page number in the original) so that a reader could easily turn to the exact material you have used. Check your text citations against your concluding list of sources to be sure that the two correspond.

## Learning by Doing Launching and Citing Your Sources

Work on a section of your draft that mentions several sources. In your file or on a printout, highlight each launch statement. First check each highlighted passage to be sure that you have named the author or source and stated the page number for a quotation or paraphrase. (Also add the date in APA style.) Next check each passage to be sure that you have clearly conveyed to a reader the value or contribution of each source — what it adds to your understanding, how it supports your conclusion, or why you have included it. Exchange drafts with a classmate to benefit from a second opinion.

## Synthesizing Ideas and Sources

Regardless of how you launch sources, you need to figure out how to integrate and synthesize them effectively. Use the Take Action chart (p. 697) for this purpose. Skim across the top to identify questions you might ask about your draft. When you answer a question with "Yes" or "Maybe," move straight down the column to Locate Specifics under that question. Use the activities there to identify gaps or weaknesses. Then move straight down to Take Action. Use the advice that suits your problem as you revise.

Integrating source notes into your paper generally requires positioning materials in a sequence, fitting them in place, and then reworking and interpreting them to convert them into effective evidence that advances your case. Synthesizing sources and evidence weaves them into a unified whole.

For more on synthesizing, see pp. 246–47. To Take Action on synthesizing, see chart on p. 697.

Build your synthesis on critical reading and thinking: pulling together what you read and think, relating ideas and information, and drawing conclusions that go beyond those of your separate sources. If you have a sure sense of your paper's direction, you may find this synthesis fairly easy. On the other hand, if your research question or working thesis has changed or you have unearthed persuasive information at odds with your original direction, consider these questions:

- Taken as a whole, what does all this information mean?
- What does it actually tell you about the answer to your research question?
- What's the most important thing you've learned?
- What's the most important thing you can tell your readers?

### Learning by Doing — Synthesizing Your Sources

Working with a classmate or small group, exchange sections of your drafts where you want or need to pull ideas together. Explain to your peers what you are trying to say or do in that section. Then ask them for ideas about how to synthesize more clearly and forcefully in your draft.

# 35 Writing Your Research Paper

You may have your own tried-and-true system of moving from research notes to a rough draft. If so, stick to your own system. On the other hand, if you are worried about how to pull together your paper, try some suggestions here as you plan, draft, revise, and edit.

## Why Writing a Research Paper Matters

**In a College Course**

- You have read everything for your hardest class, but your grade rides on the final paper you submit.
- You gave an excellent oral presentation about life in your region during the 1940s, but you still have to write up the formal research paper.

**In the Workplace**

- You have gathered all the background assembled by your team, but now you have to pull it together in a report for your demanding boss.

**In Your Community**

- Your term chairing the citizen committee is ending, so you need to present a final report about types of complaints, criteria for resolution, and recommendations to the board.

? When have you written a research project? In what situations do you expect to do so again?

## Planning and Drafting

You began gathering material from library, Internet, and field sources with a question in mind. By now, if your research has been thorough and fruitful, you know your answer. The moment has come to weave together the material you have gathered. We can vouch for two time-proven methods.

**The Thesis Method.** Decide what your research has led you to believe. Sum up what it all means in a sentence. That sentence is your thesis, the one main idea your paper will demonstrate. Then plan and draft. Include other points of view, but focus on what supports your thesis and makes it clear.

For advice on stating and using a thesis, see pp. 399–408.

**The Answer Method.** You may prefer to plunge in and start writing without stating any thesis at all. If so, recall your original research question. Start writing with the purpose of answering it, lining up evidence as you go and discovering what you want to say as you write. (With this method, allow more time for revising than with the thesis method.)

For more on research questions, see pp. 628–32.

## Using Your Sources to Support Your Ideas

Moving from nuggets of information to a smooth, persuasive analysis or argument is the most challenging part of the research process. Though every writer's habits of mind are different, you'll probably cycle through four basic activities: interpreting your sources, refining your thesis, organizing your ideas, and forming a draft.

For more on evidence, see pp. 40–44, 170–74, and section A in the Quick Research Guide, pp. A-21–A-24.

**Interpret Your Sources.** On their own, your source notes are only pieces of information. They need your interpretation to transform them into effective evidence. What does each mean in the context of your paper? Is it strong enough to bear the weight of your claim? Do you need more evidence to shore up an interesting but ambiguous fact? Keep your sources in their supporting role and your voice in the lead. Alternate statements and support to sustain this balance.

**Refine Your Thesis.** Your thesis clearly, precisely states the point you want to make. It helps you decide what to say and how to say it. When it is clear to your readers, it prepares them for your scope and general message.

If you've used a working thesis to guide your research, sharpen and refine it before drafting, even if you change it later. Explicitly stating it in your opening is only one option. Sometimes you can craft your opening so that readers know exactly what your thesis is even though you only imply it. (Check this option with your instructor if you're unsure about it.) Make your thesis precise and concrete; don't claim more than you can show. If your paper is argumentative – you take a stand, propose a solution, or evaluate something – make your stand, solution, or appraisal clear.

| | |
|---|---|
| TOPIC | Americans' attitudes toward sports |
| RESEARCH QUESTION | Is America obsessed with sports? |
| THESIS | The national obsession with sports must end. |

**Organize Your Ideas.** It isn't enough for your paper to describe your research steps or to string data together in chronological order. Instead, you need to report the significance of what you found out. If you began with a clear research question, select and organize your evidence to answer it. But don't be afraid to reorganize around a new question.

For more on organizing, drafting, and developing ideas, see Chs. 20–22.

If your material resists taking shape, arrange your source notes or archive in an order that makes sense. Then this sequence becomes a plan to follow as you write. Or write out an informal or formal outline, perhaps using your software's outline tool. If you lack source notes for a certain section, reconsider your plan, or seek other sources to fill the gap.

For more on outlining, see pp. 411–19.

**Begin to Draft.** An outline is only a skeleton until you flesh it out with details. Use yours as a working plan, but change the subdivisions or sequence if you discover a better way as you draft. Even if everything isn't in perfect order, get something down on paper. Start at the beginning or wherever you feel most comfortable. Try also to connect the parts of your paper. For example, summarizing the previous section will refresh readers' memories, especially in a long paper.

## Launching and Citing Your Sources as You Draft

Citing your sources as you draft saves time when you put your paper into final form. And it prevents unintentional plagiarism. Right after every idea, fact, quotation, paraphrase, or summary captured from your reading or field research, refer your readers to the exact source of your material. In MLA style, name the author, and give the page of the source. (In APA style, add the date.) If you quote a field source, name the speaker, if possible.

When you add a quotation to your draft, copy and paste the passage from your note file, setting it off with quotation marks. Or just tape a note card into a handwritten or printed draft. If your draft looks messy, who cares? Then shape the words to launch or introduce the source to show why you have quoted it or what authority it lends to your paper.

If no transition occurs to you as you place a quotation or borrowed idea in your draft, don't sit around waiting for one. A series of slapped-in summaries and quotations makes rough reading, but you can add connective tissue later. Highlight these spots so it is easy to return to them.

For more on launching source material, see pp. 245–46, 250, 695–98, and D6 in the Quick Research Guide, p. A-31.

## Beginning and Ending

Perhaps you will think of a good beginning and conclusion only after you have written the body of your paper. The head and tail of your paper might simply make clear your answer to your initial question. But that is not the only way to begin and end a research paper.

**Build to Your Finish.** You might start out slowly with a clear account of an event to draw your readers into the paper. You could then build up to a strong finish, saving your strongest argument for the end—after you have presented the evidence to support your thesis. Suppose your paper argues that American children are harmed by the national obsession with sports:

- Begin with a real event so you and a reader are on the same footing.
- Explore that event's implications to prepare your reader for your view.
- State your thesis: "The national obsession with sports must end."
- Present each assertion, and support it with evidence captured from well-chosen sources, moving to your strongest argument.
- Then end with a rousing call to action, stopping the sports mania.

For more strategies for opening and concluding, see pp. 426–30.

For more on transitions, see pp. 431–35.

**Sum Up the Findings of Others.** Another way to begin a research paper is to summarize the work of other scholars. One research biologist, Edgar F. Warner, has reduced this time-tested opening to a formula.

> First, in one or two paragraphs, you review everything that has been said about your topic, naming the most prominent earlier commentators. Next you declare why all of them are wrong. Then you set forth your own claim, and you spend the rest of your paper supporting it.

That pattern may seem cut and dried, but it is useful because it places your research and ideas into a historical and conceptual framework. If you browse in specialized journals, you may be surprised to see how many articles begin this way. Of course, one or two other writers may be enough to argue with. For example, a student writing on the American poet Charles Olson starts her research paper by disputing two views of him.

To Cid Corman, Charles Olson of Gloucester, Massachusetts, is "the one dynamic and original epic poet twentieth-century America has produced" (116). To Allen Tate, Olson is "a loquacious charlatan" (McFinnery 92). The truth lies between these two extremes, nearer to Corman's view.

Whether or not you fully stated your view at the beginning, you will certainly need to make it clear in your closing paragraph. A suggestion: before writing the last lines of your paper, read over what you have written. Then, without referring to your paper, try to put your view into writing.

e For an interactive Learning by Doing activity on Practicing Beginnings, go to Ch. 35: **bedfordstmartins.com/bedguide**.

## Learning by Doing: Focusing Your Point

After you finish your working draft, take a short break. Then sit down, and quickly write out a short summary or abstract of your paper, stating your main points and conclusions. Exchange and discuss your summaries with a classmate or small group, concentrating on ways to clarify each paper's thesis, purpose, and main points for readers.

## Revising and Editing

For advice on integrating sources and avoiding plagiarism, see Ch. 34.

Looking over your draft, you may find your essay changing. Don't be afraid to develop a whole new interpretation, shift the organization, strengthen your evidence, drop a section, or add a new one.

For more revising and editing strategies, see Ch. 23.

For more on using your own voice, see pp. 247–48.

### REVISION CHECKLIST

- ☐ Have you said something original, not just heaped up statements by others? Does your voice interpret and unify so your ideas dominate, not your sources?
- ☐ Is your thesis (main idea) clear? Do all your points support your main idea? Does all your evidence support your points?
- ☐ Does each new idea follow from the one before it? Can you see any stronger arrangement? Have you used transitions to connect the parts?
- ☐ Do you need more—or better—evidence to back up any point? If so, where might you find it?
- ☐ Are the words that you quote truly memorable? Are your paraphrases and summaries accurate and clear? Have you launched everything?
- ☐ Is the source of every quotation, fact, or idea unmistakably clear?

### Learning by Doing Meeting Expectations

Before you decide that your paper is finished, return to your instructor's directions—any assignment packet, assessment criteria, or advice about problems. Also take a final look at any comments about earlier drafts. Remedy anything you have overlooked. Follow any specific directions about format, organization, or presentation. Pay attention to what's expected so that you benefit from your hard work.

After you have revised your research paper, edit and proofread it. Carefully check the grammar, word choice, punctuation, and mechanics—and then correct any problems. Check your documentation, too—how you identify sources and how you list the works you have cited.

## Peer Response Writing Your Research Paper

Have a classmate or friend read your draft and suggest how you might make your paper more informative, tightly reasoned, and interesting. Ask your peer editor to answer questions such as these about writing from sources:

For general questions for a peer editor, see p. 463.

- What is your overall reaction to this paper?
- What is the research question? Does the writer answer that question?
- How effective is the opening? Does it draw you into the paper?
- How effective is the conclusion? Does it merely restate the introduction? Is it too abrupt or too hurried?
- Is the organization logical and easy to follow? Are there any places where the essay is hard to follow?
- Do you know which ideas are from the writer and which from sources?
- Does the writer need all the quotations he or she has used?
- Do you have any questions about the writer's evidence or the conclusions drawn from the evidence? Point out any areas where the writer has not fully backed up his or her conclusions.
- If this paper were yours, what is the one thing you would be sure to work on before handing it in?

### EDITING CHECKLIST

- ☐ Have you used commas correctly, especially in complicated sentences that quote or refer to sources? C1
- ☐ Have you punctuated quotations correctly? C3
- ☐ Have you used capital letters correctly, especially in titles of sources? D1
- ☐ Have you used correct manuscript form? D3
- ☐ Have you used correct documentation style?

For more help, find the relevant checklist sections in the Quick Editing Guide on p. A-39. Turn also to the Quick Format Guide, beginning on p. A-1.

For more on documentation, see Ch. 36 (MLA), Ch. 37 (APA), or the Quick Research Guide, beginning on p. A-20.

## Documenting Sources

A research paper calls on you to follow special rules for documenting your sources—citing them as you write and listing them at the end of your paper. In humanities courses and the social sciences, most writers follow

the style of the Modern Language Association (MLA) or the American Psychological Association (APA). Your instructor will probably suggest which style to follow; if you are not told, use MLA. The first time you prepare a research paper in either style, you'll need extra time to look up exactly what to do in each situation. (See Ch. 36 or 37.)

### Learning by Doing Presenting Your Findings

For more about oral presentations, see pp. 347–49.

If you are expected to present your research findings to classmates or at a campus event, you may need to develop an oral presentation, a poster showing the answer to your question, or an online summary. Review your instructor's directions and any relevant advice in this book. View your presentation as a separate project; allow enough time to develop it effectively.

## Additional Writing Assignments

Using library, Internet, and field sources, write a research paper on one of the following topics or another that your instructor approves. Proceed as if you had chosen to work on the main assignment described on page 628.

1. Investigate career opportunities, workplace changes, or trends for work that interests you. Include data from interviews with people in the field.
2. Compare student achievement in schools with different characteristics—for example, those with limited or extensive technology access or those with low and high numbers of students who move in and out.
3. Study the growth of working online from home or another advance that has changed the relationship between work and home.
4. Write a portrait of life in your town or neighborhood as it was in the past, using sources such as local library archives, photographs or other visual evidence, articles in the local newspaper, and interviews with longtime residents or a local historian.
5. Write a short history of your immediate family, drawing on interviews, photographs, scrapbooks, old letters, and any other available sources.
6. Study the reasons students today give for going to college. Gather information from interviews or surveys of a variety of students at your college.
7. Investigate a current trend you have noticed on television or online, collecting evidence by observing programs, commercials, sites, or pages.
8. Write a survey of recent films of a certain kind (such as horror movies, martial arts films, comedies, or love stories). Support your generalizations with evidence from your film watching.

# MLA Style for Documenting Sources 36



The *MLA Handbook for Writers of Research Papers,* Seventh Edition (New York: MLA, 2009), supplies extensive recommendations for crediting sources. If you want more advice than that given here, you can purchase a copy of the *MLA Handbook* or consult a copy through your college library. For MLA updates, visit mla.org/handbook_faq.

MLA style is often used in the humanities, including composition, literature, and foreign languages. Although other disciplines follow other style guides, MLA style can help you get used to scholarly practice. MLA style uses a two-part system to credit sources.

For a brief overview of MLA style, see E1–E2 in the Quick Research Guide, pp. A-20–A-38. Turn also to the Quick Format Guide beginning on p. A-1.

- Briefly cite or identify the source in your text, usually by noting the author's last name in your discussion or in parentheses right after you supply the information from the source. In most cases, complete the in-text citation with the page number in the source.
- Then use the author's name to begin a full description of the source in your concluding alphabetical list, called "Works Cited." For each entry there, look up the sample for that type of source. Follow its pattern for details, format, punctuation, and spacing. Check all similar entries for consistency, too.

For advice about using APA style, see Ch. 37.

To review how to find details about sources, turn to the Source Navigators on pp. 642–49.

Credit your source every time you quote, paraphrase, or sum up someone else's ideas. The only general exception is "common knowledge," uncontested information that readers in a field know and accept. Examples might include dates, facts about events, and popular expressions such as proverbs. Identify your source any time your readers would—or might—wonder about it, especially if you are unsure what they consider controversial.

Use the Take Action chart (p. 710) to figure out how to improve the MLA style in your draft. Skim across the top to identify questions you might ask about your draft. When you answer a question with "Yes" or

## Citing and Listing Sources in MLA Style

Skim the following directory to find sample entries to guide you as you cite and list your sources. Notice that the examples are organized according to questions you might ask and that comparable print and electronic sources are grouped together. See pages 726–34 for a sample paper that illustrates MLA style.

### CITING SOURCES IN MLA STYLE

**Who Wrote It?**



**What Type of Source Is It?**



**How Are You Capturing the Source Material?**



### LISTING SOURCES IN MLA STYLE

**Who Wrote It?**



**What Type of Source Is It?**

ARTICLE IN A PRINTED OR AN ELECTRONIC PERIODICAL



PRINTED OR ELECTRONIC BOOK



PART OF A PRINTED OR AN ELECTRONIC BOOK

## Citing and Listing Sources in MLA Style (*continued*)



"Maybe," move straight down the column to Locate Specifics under that question. Use those activities to identify problems. Then move straight down to Take Action. Use the advice that suits your draft as you revise.

## Citing Sources in MLA Style

The core of an MLA citation is the author of the source. That person's last name links your use of the source in your paper with its full description in your list of works cited. The most common addition to this name is a specific location, usually a page number, identifying where the material appears in the original source: (Valero 231). This basic form applies whatever the type of source—article, book, or Web page.

As you check your MLA style, keep in mind these three questions:

- Who wrote it?
- What type of source is it?
- How are you capturing the source material?

## Take Action Citing and Listing Sources in MLA Style

Ask each question at the top of the chart to consider whether your draft might need work on that issue. If so, follow the ASK—LOCATE SPECIFICS—TAKE ACTION sequence to revise.

| | Different Citations in Your Text and Your List? | Incorrect Author Formats? | Incorrect Source Title Formats? |
|---|---|---|---|
| **1 ASK** | Do any of my text citations differ from my Works Cited entries—or vice versa? | Have I inconsistently or incorrectly presented any of the authors in my list of works cited? | Have I inconsistently or incorrectly presented any source titles in my list of works cited? |
| **2 LOCATE SPECIFICS** | ■ Circle any material from a source that is not identified.<br>■ Add a ✓ by each text citation that matches a Works Cited entry.<br>■ Add a ✓ by each Works Cited entry that matches a text citation.<br>■ Circle any source not checked in both places. | ■ Read only the author part of each entry.<br>■ Circle any spot where you need to check the arrangement of first and last names.<br>■ Circle any spot where you need to check spelling or punctuation.<br>■ Mark any entries out of alphabetical order.<br>■ Circle any repeated problems. | ■ Read only the title part of each entry, checking the format of each article, journal, book, Web site, or other title.<br>■ Circle any entry that you need to correct or look up by type, especially complications (such as an anthology) or tricky details (such as a newspaper section).<br>■ Circle any repeated problems. |
| **3 TAKE ACTION** | ■ Correct each of your circled items by adding what's missing.<br>■ Drop from your Works Cited any source not cited in your draft. (Or add it to your draft if it belongs there.)<br>■ Confirm that names of authors are spelled the same in both places so that the citation and list entry match. | ■ Look up and correct all circled items.<br>■ Correct spelling or punctuation errors, such as a missing comma after the first name of the first of several authors.<br>■ Conclude each author section with a period.<br>■ Rearrange entries alphabetically as needed.<br>■ If you find patterns—repetition of an error—check all entries only for that problem and correct it. | ■ Look up and correct all circled items.<br>■ Use quotation marks for an article or posting title; use italics for a book, journal, or site title.<br>■ Correct the capitalization, spelling, or punctuation.<br>■ End each title with a period before the final quotation mark or after italics.<br>■ If you find patterns—repetition of an error—check all entries only for that problem and correct it. |

## Who Wrote It?

### Individual Author Not Named in Sentence

Place the author's last name in parentheses, right after the source information, to keep readers focused on the sequence and content of your sentences.

One approach to the complex politics of Puerto Rican statehood is to return to the island's colonial history (Negrón-Muntaner 3).

Author with page

### Individual Author Named in Sentence

Name the author in your sentence, perhaps with credentials or experience, to capitalize on the persuasive value of the author's "expert" status.

The analysis of filmmaker and scholar Frances Negrón-Muntaner connects Puerto Rican history and politics with cultural influences (xvii).

Author

Page

### Two or Three Authors

Include each author's last name either in your sentence or in parentheses.

Ferriter and Toibin note Irish historical objectivity about the famine (5).

Irish historians tend to report the famine dispassionately (Ferriter and Toibin 5).

### Four Authors or More

Name all the authors, or follow the first with "et al." (Latin abbreviation for "and others"). Identify the source the same way in your list of works cited.

See the listing on p. 716.

Between 1870 and 1900, cities grew at an astonishing rate (Roark et al. 671).

### Organization Author

If a source is sponsored by a corporation, a professional society, or another group, name the sponsor as the author if no one else is specified.

Each year, the Kids Count program (Annie E. Casey Foundation) alerts children's advocates about the status of children in their state.

### Author of an Essay from a Reader or Collection

Suppose you consulted Amy Tan's essay "Mother Tongue" in a collection edited by Wendy Martin. You'd cite Tan as the author, not Martin, and begin your Works Cited entry with Tan's name.

See the listing on p. 721.

Tan explains the "Englishes" of her childhood and family (32).

#### Unidentified Author

For a source with an unknown author, supply the complete title in your sentence or the first main word or two of the title in parentheses.

Use quotation marks in MLA style for titles of articles. Use italics, not underlining, for titles of books, periodicals, and Web sites. For more style conventions, see p. 716.

Due to download codes and vinyl's beauty, album sales are up ("Back to Black" 1).

#### Same Author with Multiple Works

If you are citing several of an author's works, the author's name alone won't identify which one you mean. Add the title, or identify it with a few key words. For example, you would cite two books by Bill McKibben, *Deep Economy* and *Eaarth: Making a Life on a Tough New Planet*, as follows.

McKibben cites advocates of consistent economic expansion (*Deep Economy* 10) yet calls growth "the one big habit we finally must break" (*Eaarth* 48).

#### Different Authors of Multiple Works

Separate more than one source in parentheses with a semicolon. For easy reading, favor shorter, separate references, not long strings of sources.

Ray Charles and Quincy Jones worked together for many years and maintained a strong friendship throughout Charles's life (Jones 58-59; Lydon 386).

## What Type of Source Is It?

Because naming the author is the core of a citation, the basic form applies to any type of source. Even so, a few types of sources may present complications.

#### Multivolume Work

Add both volume and page numbers, with a colon between.

Malthus has long been credited with this conservative shift in population theory (Durant and Durant 11: 400-03).

Volume number

#### Indirect Source

If possible, find the original source. If you can't access it, add "qtd. in" to show that the material was "quoted in" the source you cite.

Author of original source

Author of source you used

Zill says that, psychologically, children in stepfamilies, even those living in a two-parent household, most resemble children in single-parent families (qtd. in Derber 119).

#### Visual Material

When you include a visual, help your reader connect it to your text. In your discussion, identify the artist or the artwork, and refer to its figure number.

For advice about permission to use visuals, see B1 in the Quick Format Guide, pp. A-8–A-9.

Johnson's 1870 painting *Life in the South* is a sentimental depiction of African Americans after the Civil War (see fig. 1).

Below the visual, supply a figure number and title, including the source.

Fig. 1. Eastman Johnson, *Life in the South,* High Museum of Art, Atlanta.

## How Are You Capturing the Source Material?

How you capture source material—in your words or in a short or long quotation—affects how you credit it. Always set off the source's words using quotation marks or the indented form for a long "block" quotation.

If material, quoted or not, comes from a specific place in a source, add a page number or other location, such as the section number supplied in an electronic source or the chapter or line in a literary work. No page number is needed for general material (an overall theme or concept) or a source without page numbers (a Web site, film, recording, performance).

For more on capturing and integrating source materials, see pp. 236–43, pp. 651–54, and Ch. 34.

For a sample block quotation, see p. 714.

For sample quotations from literature, see pp. 714–15.

#### Overall Summary or Important Idea

Terrill's *Malcolm X: Inventing Radical Judgment* takes a fresh look at the rhetorical power and strategies of Malcolm X's speeches.

#### Specific Summary or Paraphrase

One analysis of Malcolm X's 1964 speech "The Ballot or the Bullet" concludes that it exhorts listeners to the radical action of changing vantage point (Terrill 129-31).

If you paraphrase or summarize a one-page article, no page number is needed because it will appear in your list of works cited.

Vacuum-tube audio equipment is making a comeback, with aficionados praising the warmth and glow from the tubes, as well as the sound (Patton).

#### Blended Paraphrase and Quotation

When your words are blended with those of your source, clearly distinguish the two. Use quotation marks to set apart the words of your source.

To avoid generalizing about "people-with-dementia" (Pearce xxii), the author simply uses names.

**Brief Quotation with Formal Launch Statement**

Vecsey states his claim for baseball: "No other sport has this endurance" (6).

**Brief Quotation Integrated in Sentence**

"No other sport" (6), according to Vecsey's *Baseball: A History of America's Favorite Game*, requires players to tolerate double or triple headers.

Double and triple headers require more stamina than any "other sport" (Vecsey 6).

Only baseball, according to Vecsey, "has this endurance" (6).

**Long Quotation**

When a quotation is longer than four typed lines, double-space and indent the entire quotation one inch instead of using quotation marks. If it is one paragraph or less, begin its first line without extra paragraph indentation. Use ellipsis marks (. . .) to show any omission from the middle.

Colon follows complete sentence

Cynthia Griffin Wolff comments on Emily Dickinson's incisive use of language:

No quotation marks

Indent 1"

> Language, of course, was a far subtler weapon than a hammer. Dickinson's verbal maneuvers would increasingly reveal immense skill in avoiding a frontal attack; she preferred the silent knife of irony to the strident battering of loud complaint. . . . Scarcely submissive, she had acquired the cool calculation of an assassin. (170-71)

No period after page(s)

**Quotation from the Bible**

Instead of the page, note the version, book, chapter, and verse numbers.

Once again, the author alludes to the same passage: "What He has seen and heard, of that He testifies" (*New American Bible,* John 3.32).

**Quotation from a Novel or Short Story**

First note the page number in your own copy. If possible, add the section or chapter where the passage could be found in any edition.

In *A Tale of Two Cities,* Dickens describes Stryver as "shouldering himself (morally and physically) into companies and conversations" (110; bk. 2, ch. 4).

**Quotation from a Play**

For a verse play, list the act, scene, and line numbers, divided by periods.

Love, Iago says, "is merely a lust of the blood and a permission of the will" (*Oth.* 1.3.326).

**Quotation from a Poem**

Add a slash to show where a new line begins. Use "line" or "lines" in the first reference but only numbers in subsequent references, as in these examples from William Wordsworth's "The World Is Too Much with Us." The first reference:

"The world is too much with us; late and soon, / Getting and spending, we lay waste our powers" (lines 1-2).

Slash between lines

The next reference:

"Or hear old Triton blow his wreathed horn" (14).

Line number

Separate part and line numbers by a period, without the word "line."

In "Ode: Intimations of Immortality," Wordsworth ponders the truths of human existence, "Which we are toiling all our lives to find, / In darkness lost, the darkness of the grave" (8.116-17).

**RESEARCH CHECKLIST**

**Citing Sources in MLA Style**

- ☐ Have you double-checked to be sure that you have acknowledged all material from a source?
- ☐ Have you placed your citation right after your quotation, paraphrase, summary, or other reference to the source?
- ☐ Have you identified the author of each source in your text or in parentheses?
- ☐ Have you used the first few words of the title to cite a work without an identified author?
- ☐ Have you noted a page number or other location when needed and available?
- ☐ Have you added necessary extras, whether volume numbers or poetry lines?
- ☐ Have you checked your final draft to be sure that every source cited in your text also appears in your list of works cited?

## Listing Sources in MLA Style

At the end of your paper, list the sources from which you have actually cited material. Center the title "Works Cited" at the top of a new, double-spaced page. Alphabetize entries by authors' last names or, for works with no author, by title. When an entry exceeds one line, indent the following lines one-half inch. (Use your software menu – Format-Paragraph-Indentation – to set this special "hanging" indentation.)

For a sample Works Cited page, see pp. 733–34 and p. A-3 in the Quick Format Guide.

Listing sources correctly depends on following patterns and paying attention to details such as capitalization and punctuation. The basic MLA pattern places a period after each of an entry's main parts such as author, title, publication details, and medium. MLA style simplifies many details:

- Abbreviate months and scholarly terms.
- List only the first city, and no state, to locate a publisher.
- List only the first name (without initials) of a publishing company.
- Drop "Inc.," "Co.," and "Press" from the company name, and abbreviate "University Press" as "UP."
- Use the most recent copyright date for a book.
- Add the medium of publication, reception, or delivery such as Print, Web, Television, Radio, CD, DVD, Film, Performance, Lecture.
- Omit the URL (uniform resource locator), or Internet address, unless the source would otherwise be hard to find or your assignment requests it.

Keep in mind these two key questions, which are used to organize the sample entries that follow:

Who wrote it?

What type of source is it?

As you prepare your own entries, begin with the author: first things first. The various author formats apply no matter what your source. Then, from the following examples, select the format for the rest of the entry depending on the type of work you have used—article, book, Web page, or other material. Match your entry to the example, supplying the same information in the same order with the same punctuation and other features.

## Who Wrote It?

### Individual Author

Hazzard, Shirley. *The Great Fire.* New York: Farrar, 2003. Print.

Medium

### Two or Three Authors

Name the authors in the order in which they are listed on the title page.

Last name first to alphabetize

Steil, Benn, and Manuel Hinds. *Money, Markets, and Sovereignty.* New Haven: Yale UP, 2009. Print.

Regular name order

### Four Authors or More

Name all the authors, or follow the name of the first author with the abbreviation "et al." (Latin for "and others"). Identify the source in the same way you cite it in the text.

See the citation on p. 711.

Roark, James L., et al. *The American Promise.* 5th ed. Boston: Bedford, 2012. Print.

#### Same Author with Multiple Works

Arrange the author's works alphabetically by title. Use the author's name for the first entry only; for the rest, replace the name with three hyphens.

Gould, Stephen Jay. *Dinosaur in a Haystack: Reflections in Natural History*. Cambridge: Belnap-Harvard UP, 2011. PDF file.

---. *Punctuated Equilibrium*. Cambridge: Belnap-Harvard UP, 2007. Print.

#### Organization Author

Name the organization as author without its opening "the," "a," or "an."

Canadian Standards Association. *Manufactured Homes*. Mississauga: Canadian Standards Assn., 2009. Print.

Author

Organization may repeat as publisher

#### Author and Editor

If your paper focuses on the work or its author, cite the author first.

Marx, Karl, and Frederick Engels. *The Communist Manifesto*. 1848. Ed. John E. Toews. Boston: Bedford, 1999. Print.

If your paper focuses on the editor or the edition used, cite the editor first.

Toews, John E., ed. *The Communist Manifesto*. By Karl Marx and Frederick Engels. 1848. Boston: Bedford, 1999. Print.

#### Author and Translator

Homer. *The Odyssey*. Trans. Robert Fagles. New York: Penguin, 1996. Print.

If your paper focuses on the translation, cite the translator first.

Fagles, Robert, trans. *The Odyssey*. By Homer. New York: Penguin, 1996. Print.

#### Unidentified Author

"2012 Cars: Safety." *Consumer Reports* Apr. 2012: 72–76. Print.

## What Type of Source Is It?

Once you have found the author format that fits, look for the type of source that matches. Mix and match the patterns illustrated as needed. For example, a two-volume printed book in its second edition might send you to several examples until you have covered all of its elements.

## Article in a Printed or an Electronic Periodical

### Article from a Printed Journal

Provide the volume number, issue number, year, page numbers, and medium for all journals.

McHaney, Pearl Amelia. "Eudora Welty (1909-2001)." *South Atlantic Review* 66.4 (2001): 134-36. Print.

Volume — Issue — Pages

### Article from an Online Journal

Supply the information that you would for a print article, using "n. pag." if the article lacks page numbers; end with the medium and your access date.

Purdy, James P., and Joyce R. Walker. "Digital Breadcrumbs: Case Studies of Online Research." *Kairos* 11.2 (2007): n. pag. Web. 29 May 2012. — Access date from your printout or notes

### Article Accessed Online through a Library or Subscription Database

To see how to create the listing for a journal article from a database, turn to pp. 644–45.

If you find a source through a library database or a subscription service, include the name of the service, the medium, and your access date.

Vanacore, Andrew. "Free TV Could Get Its Curtain Call." *Boston Globe* 30 Dec. 2009: B1. *Newsbank: America's Newspapers*. Web. 1 Mar. 2013.

### Article from a Printed Magazine

To see how to create the listing for a magazine article, turn to pp. 642–43.

Give the month and year of the issue, or its specific date.

Jenkins, Lee. "He's Gotta Play Hurt." *Sports Illustrated* 26 Oct. 2009: 42-43. Print.

If the article's pages are not consecutive, add a + after its initial page.

"Reinventing College." *Time* 29 Oct. 2012: 31+. Print.

### Article from an Online Magazine

Fallows, James. "Busy and Busier." *TheAtlantic.com*. Atlantic Monthly Group, Nov. 2012. Web. 23 Nov. 2012.

### Article from a Printed Newspaper

If the newspaper has different editions, indicate after the date the one where the article can be found. For example: natl. ed. If the pages for the article are not consecutive, add a + after its initial page.

Ostrow, Joanne. "Saturated." *Denver Post* 11 Nov. 2012: E2+. Print.

#### Article from an Online Newspaper

Cave, Damien. "Long Border, Endless Struggle." *New York Times.* New York Times, 3 Mar 2013, late ed. Web. 10 Mar. 2013.

#### Editorial from a Printed Periodical

McGrath, Neal. "Concussion Care for Student-Athletes." Editorial. *Boston Globe* 30 Dec. 2009, Opinion sec.: 17. Print.

#### Editorial from an Online Periodical

Duncan, Arne. "Investing in Students, Not the Banks." Editorial. *Washington Post.* Washington Post, 26 Feb. 2010. Web. 1 Mar. 2013.

#### Letter to the Editor

Ryan, Beth. Letter. *Smithsonian* Sept. 2012: 12. Print.

#### Review

Include the words "Rev. of" before the title of the work reviewed.

Coukell, Allan. "The Cell That Wouldn't Die." Rev. of *Culturing Life: How Cells Became Technologies,* by Hannah Landecker. *Discover* Feb. 2007: 68. Print.

### Printed or Electronic Book

#### Printed Book

Wrangham, Richard W. *Catching Fire: How Cooking Made Us Human.* New York: Basic, 2009. Print.

To see how to create the listing for a book, turn to pp. 646–47.

#### Online Book

For an online book, supply what you would for a printed book. Then add the name of the site, the medium, and your access date.

Wharton, Edith. *The Age of Innocence.* New York: Appleton, 1920. N. pag. *Bartleby.com: Great Books Online.* Web. 23 Nov. 2012.

#### E-book

Quammen, David. *Spillover: Animal Infections and the Next Pandemic.* New York: Norton, 2012. Nook file.

#### Multivolume Work

To cite the full work, include the number of volumes ("vols.") after the title.

*Who Built America? Working People and the Nation's Economy, Politics, Culture, and Society*. 2 vols. New York: Worth, 2000. Print.

To cite only one volume, give its number after the title. If you wish, you then can add the total number of volumes after the date.

*Who Built America? Working People and the Nation's Economy, Politics, Culture, and Society*. Vol. 1. New York: Worth, 2000. Print. 2 vols.

#### Revised Edition

Volti, Rudi. *Society and Technological Change*. 6th ed. New York: Worth, 2010. Print.

#### Book Published in a Series

After the title, add the series name as it appears on the title page, followed by any series number.

Smith, Philip E., II, ed. *Approaches to Teaching the Works of Oscar Wilde*. New York: MLA, 2008. Print. Approaches to Teaching World Lit. 103.

#### Book with Copublishers

If a book has more than one publisher, list them in the order on the title page, separated by a semicolon. (If the publisher uses an imprint name for a line of books, identify both with the imprint first: AltaMira-Rowman.)

*Presidential Campaign Posters*. Washington: Library of Congress; Philadelphia: Quirk, 2012. Print.

#### Book without Publisher, Date, or Page Numbers

Provide what's available. Bracket information gained outside the source. Use "c." ("around," from the Latin *circa*) to indicate an inexact date: c. 1995. Show doubt with a question mark: [1972?]. For an unknown date, use "n.d." (no date). Use "n.p." for no publisher or no place, or simply leave out the publisher's name if the work is pre-1900: New York, 1882. If pages are not numbered, use "n. pag." (no pagination).

Rosholt, Malcolm. *Days of the Ching Pao: A Photographic Record of the Flying Tigers-14th Air Force in China in World War II*. N.p.: n.p., 1978. Print.

## Part of a Printed or an Electronic Book

Give the author of the part first. Add the editor of the book after its title and the page numbers of the selection after the publication information. For an online book, add the site and your access date.

### Selection from a Printed Book

Searle, John. "Can Computers Think?" *Analytic Philosophy: An Anthology*. 2nd ed. Ed. A. P. Martinich and David Sosa. Malden: Blackwell, 2011. 277-83. Print.

### Selection from an Online Book

Webster, Augusta. "Not Love." *A Book of Rhyme*. London, 1881. *Victorian Women Writers Project*. Web. 8 Mar. 2013.

### Selection from an E-book

For a PDF, cite the fixed page numbers. For other files, cite divisions (ch. 4) or the whole work but not the file's own location system.

Acey, Joy. "Keys." *The Poetry Friday Anthology*. Ed. Sylvia Vardell and Janet Wong. Princeton: Pomelo, 2012. Kindle file.

### Preface, Introduction, Foreword, or Afterword

Harjo, Joy. Introduction. *The Secret Powers of Naming*. By Sara Littlecrow-Russell. Tucson: U of Arizona P, 2006. ix-xi. Print.

### Essay, Short Story, or Poem from an Edited Collection

Cash, Johnny. "Folsom Prison Blues." *Good Poems, American Places*. Ed. Garrison Keillor. New York: Viking-Penguin, 2011. 24. Print.

### Two or More Works from the Same Edited Collection

If you list more than one selection from an anthology, prepare and refer to an entry for the collection (instead of repeating it for each selection).

Cisneros, Sandra. "Only Daughter." Martin 10-13.

Martin, Wendy, ed. *The Beacon Book of Essays by Contemporary American Women*. Boston: Beacon, 1996. Print.

Tan, Amy. "Mother Tongue." Martin 32-37.

See the citation on p. 711.

#### Article from a Printed Reference Work

No editor, publisher, or place of publication is needed for well-known references such as *Webster's, World Book Encyclopedia,* or *Encyclopaedia Britannica.* No volume and page numbers are needed when a reference book is organized alphabetically. If an article's author is identified by initials, check the book's list of contributors, which should supply the full name.

Raymer, John D., and Margarita Nieto. "Octavio Paz." *Notable Latino Writers.* Pasadena: Salem, 2006. Print.

#### Article from an Online Reference Work

"'Hansel and Gretel' by the Brothers Grimm." *Encyclopedia Mythica.* 2004. Web. 1 Mar. 2013.

### Other Printed or Electronic Document

#### Printed Government Document

Generally, the "author" will be the government and the agency, separated by periods. If the document identifies an author or editor, give that name before the title or after it, if you give the agency as author.

United States. Census Bureau. *Statistical Abstract of the United States, 2012: The National Data Book.* 131st ed. Washington: GPO, 2011. Print.

#### Online Government Document

United States. National Institutes of Health. "Your Microbes and You." *NIH News in Health.* NIH, Nov. 2012. Web. 23 Nov. 2012.

#### Online Document

First identify the document; then supply the details about its electronic location.

Carter, Jimmy. "Inaugural Address of Jimmy Carter." 20 Jan. 1977. *The Avalon Project.* Yale Law School, 2008. Web. 10 Mar. 2013.

#### Pamphlet

Campus Recreation at Auraria. *Drop-in Schedule: Spring 2012.* Denver: Campus Recreation at Auraria, 2012. Print.

#### Doctoral Dissertation or Master's Thesis

If the study is unpublished, place the title in quotation marks; if published, italicize the title. Follow the title with "Diss." (for a dissertation) or with a master's abbreviation (such as "MA thesis").

Allen, Cleo Joffrion. "Foreign News Coverage in Selected U.S. Newspapers 1927-1997: A Content Analysis." Diss. Louisiana State U, 2005. Print.

## Internet or Electronic Source

Helping a reader find the material you cited and listed can be difficult with Internet materials. Web sites exist only electronically and may change. When new forms (such as blogs) rapidly develop, adapt the formats as needed.

### Personal Web Page

If no title is available, include an identification such as "Home page."

Tannen, Deborah. Home page. Georgetown U and Deborah Tannen, 2009. Web. 10 Mar. 2013.

See the directory on pp. 708–09 for entries for other electronic sources, including books and articles.

### Organization Web Page

"Library Statistics." *American Library Association*. Amer. Lib. Assn., 2012. Web. 23 Nov. 2012.

### Home Page for a Campus Department or Course

*CSUN Department of Communication Studies*. CSUN, n.d. Web. 26 Feb. 2012.

### Blog or Blog Entry

To cite a blog entry, give the title of the entry in quotation marks. If it lacks a title, use a label such as "Blog comment." If there is no apparent sponsor, use "N.p." for no publisher.

To see how to create the listing for a Web page, turn to pp. 648–49.

Knight, Christopher. "The Watts Towers' Perpetual State of Crisis." *Culture Monster.* Los Angeles Times, 28 May 2010. Web. 29 May 2010.

Wray, William. Blog comment. *Culture Monster.* Los Angeles Times, 28 May 2010. Web. 29 May 2010.

### Publication on CD-ROM

Woodward, Bob. *The Price of Politics*. New York: Simon Audio, 2012. CD-ROM.

## Visual or Audio Source

### Advertisement

Feeding America. Advertisement. *Time* 21 Dec. 2009: 59. Print.

### Comic or Cartoon

Supply the cartoonist's name and identification as a comic strip or cartoon.

Adams, Scott. "Dilbert." Comic strip. *Denver Post* 9 Mar. 2013: 7C. Print.

### Photograph

Supply the place (museum or gallery and city) where the photograph is housed. If you are citing it from a publication, identify that source.

Stieglitz, Alfred. *Self Portrait*. J. Paul Getty Museum, Los Angeles. *Stieglitz: A Beginning Light*. By Katherine Hoffman. New Haven: Yale UP, 2004. 251. Print.

Strand, Paul. *Fifth Avenue, New York*. 1915. Photograph. Museum of Modern Art, New York.

For a family or personal photograph, identify who took it and when.

*Black Forest*. Personal photograph by author. 6 Aug. 2013. JPEG file.

### Work of Art

Botticelli, Sandro. *The Birth of Venus*. 1482-86. Tempera on canvas. Uffizi Gallery, Florence.

### Audiotape or Recording

Begin with the name of the artist, composer, speaker, writer, or other contributor, based on your interest in the recording. Include the medium, such as "Audiocassette," "CD," or "LP."

Byrne, Gabriel. *The James Joyce Collection*. Dove Audio, 1996. Audiocassette.

### Program on Television or Radio

"Newton Divided." *Frontline*. PBS. WGBH, Boston, 19 Feb. 2013. Television.

"Can Detroit Be Saved?" *Weekend Edition*. Natl. Public Radio. KCFR, Denver, 2 Mar. 2013. Radio.

### Film

Start with the title, unless you wish to emphasize the work of a person connected with the film.

*True Grit*. Dir. Ethan Coen and Joel Coen. Perf. Jeff Bridges and Hailee Steinfeld. Paramount, 2010. Film.

Coen, Ethan, and Joel Coen, dir. *True Grit*. Paramount, 2010. Film.

### Live Performance

*Sense and Sensibility: The Musical*. Lyrics by Jeffrey Haddow. Dir. Marcia Milgram Dodge. Denver Center Theatre Company, Denver. 5 Apr. 2013. Performance.

## Conversation or Field Artifact

### Personal, Telephone, or E-mail Interview

Indicate how you conducted the interview: in person, by telephone, or by e-mail.

Boyd, Dierdre. Personal interview. 5 Feb. 2013.

### Broadcast Interview

Begin with the person interviewed; if you wish, you may also add the interviewer (Interview by X) or the URL to locate a podcast.

Schatz, Amy. "Net Neutrality: Who's in Charge of the Internet?" Interview by Terry Gross. *Fresh Air.* Natl. Public Radio. KCFR, Denver. 25 May 2010. Radio.

### Published Interview

Marshall, Chan. Interview. *Spin*. Dec. 2006: 72-75. Print.

### Speech or Lecture

Wexel, Beth. Fall Convocation. Craig Hall, Wilton College. 28 Aug. 2013. Address.

### Personal Letter

Use "MS" for handwritten manuscript or "TS" for typescript or printout.

Finch, Katherine. Letter to the author. 1 Oct. 2013. TS.

### E-mail

Moore, Jack. Message to the author. 11 Aug. 2013. E-mail.

### Online Posting

Use the subject line as the title; label as "Online posting" if it has no title.

Robinson, Meena. "Mansfield Park." *PBS Discussions*. PBS, 28 Jan. 2008. Web. 18 May 2008.

Cite a posting to a discussion group as you would an e-mail message.

Walsh, Karen. "Responsible Use of Technology." Message to the education technology discussion list. 28 May 2009. E-mail.

RESEARCH CHECKLIST

**Listing Sources in MLA Style**

- ☐ Have you begun each entry with the right pattern for the author's name?
- ☐ Have you figured out what type of source you have used? Have you followed the sample pattern for that type as exactly as possible?
- ☐ Have you used quotation marks and italics correctly for titles?
- ☐ Have you used the conventional punctuation – periods, commas, colons, parentheses – in your entry?
- ☐ Have you accurately recorded the name of the author, title, and publisher?
- ☐ Have you checked the accuracy of numbers for pages, volumes, and dates?
- ☐ Have you identified the medium of publication, reception, or delivery?
- ☐ Have you checked any entry from a citation management system as carefully as your own entries?
- ☐ Have you arranged your entries in alphabetical order?
- ☐ Have you checked your final list against your text citations so that every source appears in both places?
- ☐ Have you double-spaced your list, just like the rest of your paper? Have you allowed an inch margin on all sides?
- ☐ Have you begun the first line of each entry at the left margin? Have you indented each additional line one-half inch?

For a list of labels, see p. 716.

## A Sample MLA Research Paper

For more on MLA paper format, see the Quick Format Guide, p. A-1.

In her paper "Meet Me in the Middle: The Student, the State, and the School," Candace Rardon investigates the rising costs of a college education and how schools have responded to the problem. Besides incorporating many features of effective research papers, this paper also illustrates the conventions for citing and listing sources in MLA style. No cover page is needed for an MLA paper. Because an outline was required by the instructor, it precedes the paper. Although this sample paper is presented for easy reading in a textbook, your paper should use the type style and size that MLA suggests: Times New Roman font, 12-point size. Set one-inch margins on all four sides, double-space all the lines, and turn off automatic hyphenation. Use your software's Help feature or visit the campus computer lab for help setting up this format for your file.

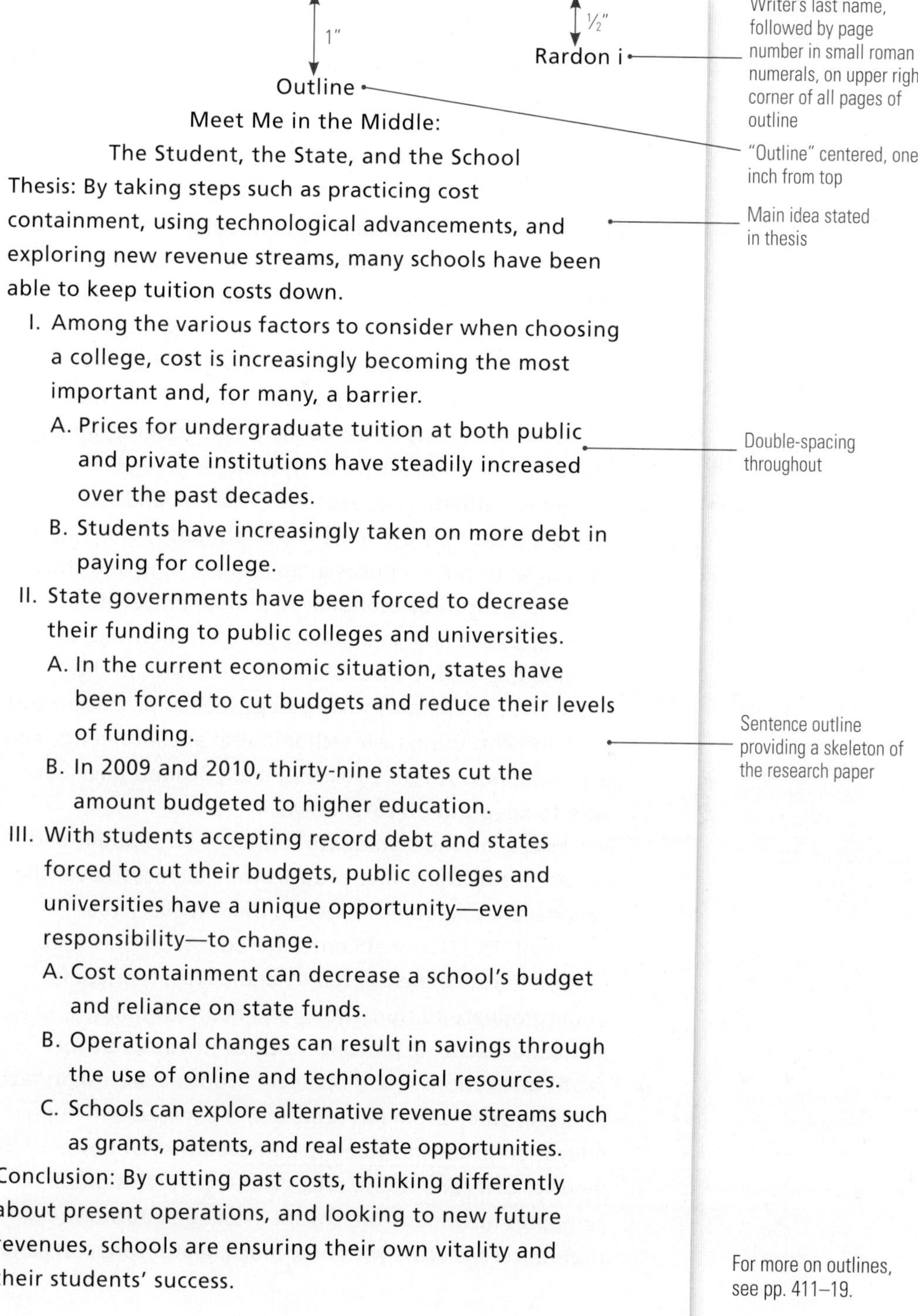
1"
½"
Rardon i
Outline
Meet Me in the Middle:
The Student, the State, and the School
Thesis: By taking steps such as practicing cost containment, using technological advancements, and exploring new revenue streams, many schools have been able to keep tuition costs down.
I. Among the various factors to consider when choosing a college, cost is increasingly becoming the most important and, for many, a barrier.
A. Prices for undergraduate tuition at both public and private institutions have steadily increased over the past decades.
B. Students have increasingly taken on more debt in paying for college.
II. State governments have been forced to decrease their funding to public colleges and universities.
A. In the current economic situation, states have been forced to cut budgets and reduce their levels of funding.
B. In 2009 and 2010, thirty-nine states cut the amount budgeted to higher education.
III. With students accepting record debt and states forced to cut their budgets, public colleges and universities have a unique opportunity—even responsibility—to change.
A. Cost containment can decrease a school's budget and reliance on state funds.
B. Operational changes can result in savings through the use of online and technological resources.
C. Schools can explore alternative revenue streams such as grants, patents, and real estate opportunities.
Conclusion: By cutting past costs, thinking differently about present operations, and looking to new future revenues, schools are ensuring their own vitality and their students' success.

Writer's last name, followed by page number in small roman numerals, on upper right corner of all pages of outline

"Outline" centered, one inch from top

Main idea stated in thesis

Double-spacing throughout

Sentence outline providing a skeleton of the research paper

For more on outlines, see pp. 411–19.

Writer's last name and page number ½" from top of page

½"

1"

Rardon 1

Writer's name

Instructor's name

Course

Date

Title, centered

Candace Rardon

Professor Snyder

English Composition I

10 May 2012

Meet Me in the Middle:

The Student, the State, and the School

½" indent

Opening with current events to spark interest

Double-spacing throughout

1"

1"

For more on beginning a research paper, see pp. 702–03.

Comments on current situation

Thesis previews development and central argument

For more on a thesis for a research paper, see p. 701.

Paragraph establishes background for the paper's general topic

No page number available in online source

Figure cited in text

Dramatic campus demonstrations, fasts, and even take-overs continue, especially in California (Altavena), as college costs keep rising (Walker). Images of student protesters convey a sober picture of the current state of college tuition costs in the country. For students, among the factors to consider when choosing a college—academics, athletics, student life, location, and so on—cost is increasingly the most important and, for many, a barrier. With tuition prices at an all-time high and state funding reduced by economic recession, universities themselves are now in a unique position to bridge the funding gap and to meet students and states in the middle of the crisis. By taking steps such as practicing cost containment, using new technological advancements, and exploring new revenue streams, many schools have been able to keep tuition costs down.

Prices for undergraduate tuition at both public and private institutions have progressively increased over the past decades and now "exceed inflation every year" (Hayden). The National Center for Education Statistics reports that "Between 2000-01 and 2010-11, prices for undergraduate tuition, room, and board at public institutions rose 42 percent" and "at private, not-for-profit institutions rose 31 percent" (United States). In fact, as CreditUnions.com has reported, the increase in higher education prices has steadily outpaced that of both medical costs and house prices (see fig. 1). This graph compares how much the cost of a college education has risen in recent years with how much health care costs and

1"

Rardon 2

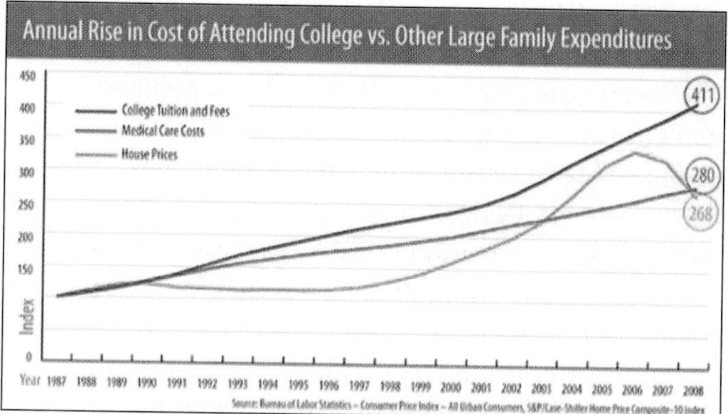


Fig. 1. Annual Rise in Cost of Attending College. Source: Bureau of Labor Statistics, Consumer Price Index, and All Urban Consumers, Standard & Poor/Case-Schiller Home Price Composite-10 Index (Hoffman).

Figure labeled in caption; source information provided

Source presents and credits findings of another study

house prices have gone up over the same period. While the cost of all three has gone up, the expense of college has increased the most.

As the graph shows, the prices of tuition, medical care, and houses are plotted against both time and the Consumer Price Index. Computed by the Department of Labor's Bureau of Labor Statistics, the Consumer Price Index is a calculation generally used to measure inflation over a period of time, based on how the prices of common goods and services change. From 1989 to 2008, the price of higher education has consistently risen more than the prices of medical care and houses, a burden that often falls on the student.

Key term is defined

Trends in student borrowing point to a crisis in the amount of debt that students and families have to shoulder to afford an education. *Trends in Student Aid 2012,* a College Board report, states that in 2010-11, only 43% of students who graduated with a bachelor's degree from a public four-year institution did so without

Only one citation needed for material in sequence in a paragraph and clearly from the same source

Facts and statistics support main point

For an explanation of statistics as evidence, see pp. 41–42.

Page numbers provided for quotations

Original quote from another source

Paper continues to lay out background of argument

Rardon 3

education debt (Baum and Payea). The rest graduated with debt averaging $23,800. Despite a recent 4% drop in borrowing, the first in two decades, these numbers demonstrate the rising financial burden placed on college students. Many continue "making decisions and trade-offs among schools, living arrangements, work, and finances" (Bozick 278). Economist Richard Vedder has summed up the situation: "What we have now is an unsustainable trend" (qtd. in Sandler 199).

Due to the economic recession, states have been forced to cut their budgets and reduce their funding to higher education. The Center on Budget and Policy Priorities reports that in 2009 and 2010, thirty-nine states decreased their budgets for higher education, leading to "reductions in faculty and staff in addition to tuition increases" (Johnson, Oliff, and Williams 6). Like California, the state of Florida was forced to raise tuition by 15% in 2009-10. The tuition increases that result from a lack of state funds have become a nationwide threat.

Transition from background to central argument

First way to avoid raising tuition is explained

Specific examples provide evidence for point

For more on integrating sources, see Ch. 34.

With students accepting record debt and states forced to cut their budgets, public colleges and universities have a unique opportunity—even responsibility—to change. Instead of raising tuition to make up for lost state funds, many schools have begun to cut costs. Through cost containment, schools can decrease their operating budgets and their reliance on state funds. In an article for *Time*, Sophia Yan outlines reductions on more than twenty campuses. For instance, Harvard University saved $900,000 by cutting hot breakfasts during the week in the dining halls. Western Washington University saved $485,000 by cutting its football team, and Whittier College saved $50,000 by cutting first-year orientation by a day. On the theory that "every little bit helps," schools are finding ways to save money.

Rardon 4

Going beyond cutbacks in services, schools have also considered operational changes that will result in even more savings. The Delta Project on Postsecondary Education Costs, Productivity, and Accountability, a nonprofit group that analyzes college costs and spending trends, recommends ways to increase productivity:

> Make investments in course redesign and other curricula changes that will make for a more cost-effective curriculum. . . . This includes redesigning large undergraduate courses, creating cost-effective developmental education modules that can be delivered statewide; and redesigning the general education curriculum to enhance community college transfer. (4)

1″

Other suggestions include making buildings more energy efficient and creating work opportunities for jobless students as interns or research assistants (4). Such changes can lead to substantial savings and help schools across the country.

Another alternative to raising tuition is for schools to embrace technological advances. As Kamenetz observes, "Whether hybrid classes, social networks, tutoring programs, games, or open content, technology provides speed skates for students and teachers, not crutches." Specific models have come from the National Center for Academic Transformation, a nonprofit organization that uses information technology to raise student performance and lower costs. Its six course redesign models vary in the amount of in-class instruction replaced by technology (Natl. Center, "Six Models" 1). When the University of Alabama adopted the emporium model for Intermediate Algebra and replaced lectures with an online learning resource center (3), the redesign increased student success, met individual needs, and saved 30% of costs (Natl. Center, "Program"). Of course, such course redesign cannot always be applied across the curriculum, but schools giving serious

Point from last paragraph used for transition to new point

Launch statement refers to organization as author

Direct quotation longer than four lines set off from text without quotation marks, followed by page number in parentheses

Transition leads to second way to avoid raising tuition

Quotation and source clearly identified but pages are not numbered in source

Short title added to distinguish two sources by the same author

Basic models are explained before giving a specific example

Statistics support claims

Rardon 5

thought to current technology can transform the classroom, saving money and helping students.

Third way to avoid raising tuition is introduced

Finally, schools can supplement income from student tuition by considering additional sources of revenue. *Business Week* writer Francesca Di Meglio reports that many schools already look to grants, patents, real estate, and popular graduate courses to "protect [their] bottom line from fiscal and demographic trends that are making the college business more challenging." As early as the 1950s, three Indiana University researchers patented Crest toothpaste, and its returns went on to fund an on-campus dental research institute. Similarly, in 2004 Emmanuel College in Boston allowed Merck, a large pharmaceuticals company, to build a research facility on an acre of land with a 75-year lease for $50 million. Di Meglio's examples show how schools can tap into these alternative income streams and reduce some of the pressure on tuition.

Launch statement names publication and author

Brackets identify words added to original text

Paraphrase of original source

Final sentence in paragraph connects examples from source with overall argument

For more on concluding a research paper, see pp. 702–03.

Rising tuition costs, growing student borrowing, and shrinking government funding have endangered widespread access to a college education. As President Obama himself said in the 2010 State of the Union Address, "in the United States of America, no one should go broke because they chose to go to college. . . . it's time for colleges and universities to get serious about cutting their own costs—because they, too, have a responsibility to help solve this problem." In an era of economic strain, schools can embrace this chance to think creatively about the way they operate. By cutting costs where they spent money in the past, thinking differently about how they operate in the present, and looking to new ways of bringing in revenue in the future, schools can ensure their own vitality and their students' success. When public colleges and universities take such steps to ensure that a college education is available to everyone, meeting students and states in the middle with innovative ideas, students can stop protesting and start welcoming in an era of increased college access.

Ellipses show where words are omitted

Conclusion emphasizes critical points in argument

Conclusion returns to events in opening

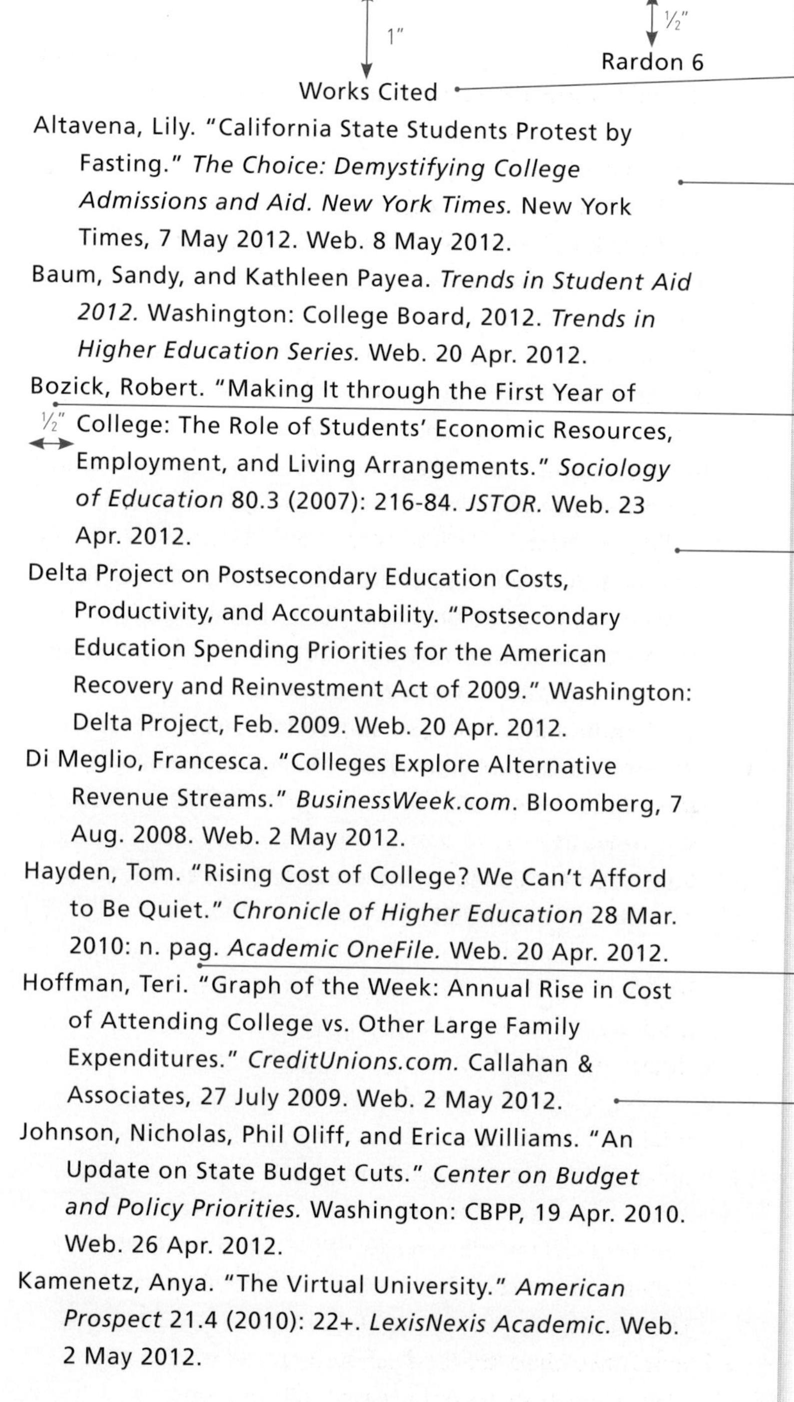

1"

½"

Rardon 6

Works Cited

Altavena, Lily. "California State Students Protest by Fasting." *The Choice: Demystifying College Admissions and Aid. New York Times.* New York Times, 7 May 2012. Web. 8 May 2012.

Baum, Sandy, and Kathleen Payea. *Trends in Student Aid 2012.* Washington: College Board, 2012. *Trends in Higher Education Series.* Web. 20 Apr. 2012.

Bozick, Robert. "Making It through the First Year of College: The Role of Students' Economic Resources, Employment, and Living Arrangements." *Sociology of Education* 80.3 (2007): 216-84. *JSTOR.* Web. 23 Apr. 2012.

Delta Project on Postsecondary Education Costs, Productivity, and Accountability. "Postsecondary Education Spending Priorities for the American Recovery and Reinvestment Act of 2009." Washington: Delta Project, Feb. 2009. Web. 20 Apr. 2012.

Di Meglio, Francesca. "Colleges Explore Alternative Revenue Streams." *BusinessWeek.com.* Bloomberg, 7 Aug. 2008. Web. 2 May 2012.

Hayden, Tom. "Rising Cost of College? We Can't Afford to Be Quiet." *Chronicle of Higher Education* 28 Mar. 2010: n. pag. *Academic OneFile.* Web. 20 Apr. 2012.

Hoffman, Teri. "Graph of the Week: Annual Rise in Cost of Attending College vs. Other Large Family Expenditures." *CreditUnions.com.* Callahan & Associates, 27 July 2009. Web. 2 May 2012.

Johnson, Nicholas, Phil Oliff, and Erica Williams. "An Update on State Budget Cuts." *Center on Budget and Policy Priorities.* Washington: CBPP, 19 Apr. 2010. Web. 26 Apr. 2012.

Kamenetz, Anya. "The Virtual University." *American Prospect* 21.4 (2010): 22+. *LexisNexis Academic.* Web. 2 May 2012.

½"

List of works cited on a separate page

List alphabetized by names of authors or by titles (when no author is named); names match source citations in text

First line of entry at left margin, additional lines indented ½"

All lines double spaced, within and between entries

Appropriate abbreviations used if no information given for publisher or date

No URLs for accessible Internet sources unless required by instructor

Rardon 7

Three hyphens replace repeating exact name from previous entry

National Center for Academic Transformation. "Program in Course Redesign: The University of Alabama." *The National Center for Academic Transformation.* NCAT, 2005. Web. 2 May 2012.

---. "Six Models for Course Redesign." *The National Center for Academic Transformation.* NCAT, 2008. Web. 2 May 2012.

Obama, Barack. "Remarks by the President in State of the Union Address." United States Capitol, Washington. 27 Jan. 2010. Address.

Sandler, Corey. *Cut College Costs Now! Surefire Ways to Save Thousands of Dollars.* Avon: Adams Media, 2006. Print.

United States. Dept. of Education. National Center for Education Statistics. "Fast Facts: Tuition Costs of Colleges and Universities." 2012. *Digest of Education Statistics,* 2011. Web. 26 Apr. 2012.

Walker, Brianne. "UC, CSU Tuition Increases: The Causes and Consequences." *Neon Tommy: Annenberg Digital News.* USC Annenberg, 13 Dec. 2011. Web. 20 Apr. 2012.

Yan, Sophia. "Colleges Find Creative Ways to Cut Back." *Time* 21 Sept. 2009: 81. Print.

# APA Style for Documenting Sources 37



The American Psychological Association (APA) details the style most commonly used in the social sciences in its *Publication Manual,* Sixth Edition (Washington, D.C.: APA, 2010). For advice and updates, visit apastyle.apa.org, purchase the manual, or use a library copy.

For a brief overview of APA style, see E1–E2 in the Quick Research Guide, pp. A-32–A-38.

APA style uses a two-part system to credit sources.

- Briefly cite or identify the author and date of the source in your text, either by mentioning them in your discussion or by noting them in parentheses right after you refer to the information drawn from the source. In many cases, you also supply the page number or other location in the original source.
- Lead from this brief identification, through the author's name, to a full description of the source in your concluding list, called "References."

Turn also to the Quick Format Guide beginning on p. A-1.

Use the Take Action chart (p. 738) to help you figure out how to improve the APA style in your draft. Skim across the top to identify questions you might ask about your draft. When you answer a question with "Yes" or "Maybe," move straight down the column to Locate Specifics under that question. Use these activities to identify problems. Then move straight down to Take Action. Use the advice that suits your draft as you revise.

To review how to find details about sources, turn to the Source Navigators on pp. 642–49.

## Citing Sources in APA Style

The core of an APA citation is the author of the source. That person's last name links your use of the source in your paper with its full description in your list of references. Next comes the source's date, which often tells readers its current or classic status. Include both each time you cite the source in parentheses, but don't repeat the date if you simply refer to the source again unless a reader might mix up sources under discussion.

## Citing and Listing Sources in APA Style

Skim the following directory to find sample entries to guide you as you cite and list your sources. Notice that the examples are organized according to questions you might ask and that comparable print and electronic sources are grouped together. See pages 751–59 for a sample paper that illustrates APA style.

### CITING SOURCES IN APA STYLE



### LISTING SOURCES IN APA STYLE

## Citing and Listing Sources in APA Style (*continued*)



A common addition is a specific location, such as a page number (using "p." for "page" or "pp." for "pages"), that tells where the material appears in the original source. Unless the source lacks page numbers or other locators, this information is required for quotations and recommended for paraphrases and key concepts. When you supply these elements in parentheses, separate them with commas: (Westin, 2013, p. 48). This basic form applies whatever the type of source—article, book, or Web page.

As you check your APA style, keep in mind these three questions:

- Who wrote it?
- What type of source is it?
- How are you capturing the source material?

## Who Wrote It?

**Individual Author Not Named in Sentence**

Finding lying without other pathologies is unlikely (Healy, 2008, p. 11).

**Individual Author Named in Sentence**

As Healy (2008) notes, other pathologies typically accompany lying (p. 11).

## Take Action Citing and Listing Sources in APA Style

Ask each question at the top of the chart to consider whether your draft might need work on that issue. If so, follow the ASK—LOCATE—TAKE ACTION sequence to revise.

| | Different Citations in Your Text and Your List? | Incorrect Author Formats? | Incorrect Source Title Formats? |
|---|---|---|---|
| **1 ASK** | Do any of my text citations differ from my References entries — or vice versa? | Have I inconsistently or incorrectly presented any of the authors in my list of references? | Have I inconsistently or incorrectly presented any source titles in my list of references? |
| **2 LOCATE SPECIFICS** | ■ Circle any material from a source not identified.<br>■ Add a √ by each text citation that matches a References entry.<br>■ Add a √ by each References entry that matches a text citation.<br>■ Circle any source not checked in both places. | ■ Read only the author part of each entry.<br>■ Circle any spot where you need to check the sequence of initials and last names or the alphabetical order of entries.<br>■ Circle any spot where you need to check spelling or punctuation.<br>■ Circle any repeated problems. | ■ Read only the title part of each entry.<br>■ Circle any title that you need to correct or look up by type.<br>■ Circle any title where you are unsure about capitals, italics, or quotation marks.<br>■ Circle any repeated problems. |
| **3 TAKE ACTION** | ■ Correct each of your circled items by adding what's missing.<br>■ Drop from your References list any source not cited in your draft. (Or add it to your draft if it belongs there.)<br>■ Confirm that names of authors are spelled the same in both places so that the text citation and the list entry match. | ■ Look up and correct all circled items.<br>■ Correct spelling or punctuation errors, such as missing periods after an author's initials, a missing space between them, or "and" instead of & between co-authors' names.<br>■ Rearrange entries alphabetically as needed.<br>■ If you find patterns—repetition of an error—check all entries only for that problem. Correct it each time you spot it. | ■ Look up and correct all circled items.<br>■ Omit quotation marks with an article title; use italics for a book, journal, or site title.<br>■ Correct spelling, punctuation, and capitals (first word and proper nouns for books or articles; main words for journals).<br>■ End titles with a period unless volume, issue, or page numbers follow.<br>■ If you find patterns—repetition of an error—check all entries only for that problem and correct it. |

#### Two Authors

List the last names of coauthors in the order in which they appear in the source. Join the names with "and" if you mention them in your text and with an ampersand (&) if the citation is in parentheses.

Legal professionals may fear that psychologists' testimony will unfairly influence juries (Fulero & Wrightsman, 2009, p. 18).

In *Forensic Psychology*, Fulero and Wrightsman (2009) note that attorneys remain wary of influential testimony by psychologists (p. 18).

#### Three Authors or More

For three to five authors, include all the last names in your first reference. In any later references, follow only the first author with "et al." (for "and others") in the text or in parentheses. For six authors or more, simply follow the first author with "et al." for all citations.

Learning disabilities occur with each other, with emotional or attention disorders, or with social deficits (Fletcher, Lyon, Fuchs, & Barnes, 2006, p. 9). Thus Fletcher et al. characterize this likelihood as "co-morbidity" (p. 9).

#### Organization Author

Nutrition is critical for cancer patients who may have specific dietary needs (American Cancer Society, 2003, p. 7).

#### Author of an Essay from a Reader or Collection

Cite the essay author; list the collection editor later with your references.

Studies have yet to investigate why campus fraternity houses are more likely venues for rape than other college gathering places (Martin & Hummer, 2003).

See the listing on p. 748.

#### Unidentified Author

Identify the source with its title in your text or the first few words in parentheses so it is easy to locate in your alphabetical list of references.

Parents need to monitor their child's online activities ("Social Networking," 2012).

#### Same Author with Multiple Works

Three significant trends in parent-school relations evolved (Grimley, 2007) after the original multistate study (Grimley, 1987).

#### Different Authors with Multiple Works

Within a single citation, list the authors of multiple works in alphabetical order (as in your reference list). Separate the works with semicolons.

Several studies examined attributes of smokers and cessation programs (Kottke et al., 1988; Osler & Prescott, 1998; Perz, DiClemente, & Carbonari, 1996).

## What Type of Source Is It?

Naming the author is the core of a citation, regardless of the type of source used. Even so, a few types may present complications.

#### Indirect Source

If possible, locate and cite the original source. Otherwise, begin your citation with "as cited in" and name your source.

According to Claude Fischer, the belief in individualism favors "the individual over the group or institution" (as cited in Hansen, 2005, p. 5).

#### Government or Organization Document

If no specific author is identified, treat the sponsor as the author. Give its full name in your first citation. If the name is complicated or commonly shortened, you may add an abbreviation in brackets.

The *2005 National Gang Threat Assessment* (National Alliance of Gang Investigators Associations [NAGIA], 2005, pp. vii-viii) identified specific regional trends.

In later citations, use just the abbreviation and the date: (NAGIA, 2005)

#### Source without a Date

When the date is unknown, use "n.d." ("no date").

Interval training encourages rotation between high-intensity spurts and "active recovery, which is typically a less-intense form of the original activity" (*Interval Training,* n.d., para. 2).

#### A Classic

If the original date is unknown, use "n.d." ("no date"). If it is known, show it with your edition's date: (Burton, 1621/1977). For ancient texts, use the year of the translation: (Homer, trans. 1990). For a quotation from a classic, identify lines, sections, or other standard divisions that locate a passage in any edition. For biblical references, specify the version in your initial citation. Classics—ancient or religious—need not be listed as references.

Many cultures affirm the importance of religious covenant in accounts as varied as the biblical "Behold, I make a covenant" in Exodus 34:10 (King James Version) and *The Iliad* (Homer, trans. 1990), which opens with the cause of the Trojan War, "all because Agamemnon spurned Apollo's priest" (Book 1, line 12).

#### Visual Material

To refer to your own figure or table, mention its number in your sentence: "As Figure 2 shows, . . ." Clearly cite a visual from a source.

Teenagers who play video games with a high degree of violence are more likely to show aggressive behavior (Anderson & Bushman, 2001, Table 1).

To include or adapt a source's table or visual, you may need to request permission from the author or copyright holder. Many sources—from scholarly journals to Web sites—state their permissions policy in the issue or on the site. (Ask your instructor's advice if you are unsure how to proceed.) Credit the material in a "From" or "Adapted from" note below it.

#### Personal Communication

Personal communications—such as face-to-face or telephone interviews, letters, memos, and e-mail—are not included in the reference list because your readers would not be able to find and use such sources. Simply name your source and the date of the communication in your paper.

J. T. Moore (personal communication, October 10, 2012) has made specific suggestions for stimulating the local economy.

## How Are You Capturing the Source Material?

The way that you have captured source material—whether in your own words or in a quotation—affects how you present and credit it. Always identify words taken directly from a source by using quotation marks or the indented form for a long "block" quotation. Specify the location of quoted words. If you present in your own words material from a specific place in your source, APA also recommends that you add the location. A citation, but no location, is needed for general information, such as your summary of an overall finding.

For more on capturing and integrating source material, see pp. 236–43, 651–54, and Ch. 34.

To identify the location of material in a source, supply the page number. For an unpaginated source, especially online, give the paragraph number it supplies (para. 3). Otherwise, give the section name (or a short version), and identify the paragraph within the section (Methods section, para. 2). If appropriate, identify other parts: Chapter 5, Figure 2, Table 3.

The next few examples illustrate how Emily Lavery varied her presentation of sources in her paper "A New Time: Female Education and Teachers in Western Territories" about education during the mid-1800s.

#### Overall Summary or Important Idea

Horace Mann and other educational reformers began the Common School Movement, advocating for public primary schools (Nasaw, 1979, p. 30). The movement was revolutionary for education and marked the first attempt to create public school systems, across the United States and all its territories, in order to educate the youth.

#### Blended Paraphrase and Quotation

According to Hoffman (2003), Mann's movement sought to develop the "informal rural schools supported by parents" (p. 30) and establish a state-sponsored school system.

#### Brief Quotation Integrated in Sentence

Jennifer Madigan (2009) defined a dame school as a "school influenced by the English model of home instruction for small groups of children" (p. 11).

#### Long Quotation

If you quote forty words or more, indent the quotation one-half inch and double-space it instead of using quotation marks. After it, add your citation with no additional period, including whatever information you have not already mentioned in your launch statement.

Emma Willard and Catharine Beecher fought for female educational opportunities, such as a more inclusive curriculum and higher educational opportunities. In 1848, Elizabeth Cady Stanton published the "Declaration of Sentiments" at the Seneca Falls Convention to address and rectify the wrongs done to women, including this resolution:

> That the speedy success of our cause depends upon the zealous and untiring efforts of both men and women, for the overthrow of the monopoly of the pulpit, and for securing to woman an equal participation with men in the various trades, professions, and commerce. (p. 73)

---

**RESEARCH CHECKLIST**

**Citing Sources in APA Style**

- ☐ Have you double-checked to be sure that you have acknowledged all material from a source?
- ☐ Does your citation fall right after a quotation or reference to a source?

- ☐ Have you identified the author of each source in your text or in parentheses?
- ☐ Have you used the first few words of the title to cite a work without an identified author?
- ☐ Have you noted the date (or added "n.d." for "no date") for each source?
- ☐ Have you added a page number or other location whenever needed?
- ☐ Have you checked your final draft to be sure that every source cited in your text also appears in your list of references?

## Listing Sources in APA Style

List your sources at the end of your paper. Title a new page with "References" centered. Double-space your list, and organize it alphabetically by authors' last names (or by titles for works without an identified author). Arrange several works by the same author by date, moving from earliest to most recent. If an author has two works published in the same year, arrange these alphabetically, and add a letter after each date (2009a, 2009b) so the date in your text citation leads to the correct entry.

For a sample reference page, see p. 759 or p. A-6 in the Quick Format Guide.

Format each entry with a "hanging indent" so that subsequent lines are indented one-half inch (about five to seven spaces), just as a paragraph is. (Use the menu in your software—Format-Paragraph-Indentation—to set up this hanging or special indentation.) Include only sources that you actually cite in your paper unless your instructor requests otherwise.

APA style simplifies the following details:

- Supply only initials (with a space between them) for an author's first and middle names.
- Use an ampersand (& as in a citation in parentheses), not "and" (as you would write in your paper), before the name of the last of several authors.
- Spell out names of months, but abbreviate terms common in academic writing (such as "p.m.," "Vol." for "Volume," or "No." for "Number").
- Capitalize only the first word, proper names, and the first word after a colon in the title of a book, article, or Web site. Capitalize all main words in the title of a journal or other periodical.
- Do not use quotation marks or italics for an article title in your reference list (but use quotation marks if you mention it in your text).
- Italicize a Web site, book, or periodical title (and its volume number).
- List only the first of several cities where a publisher has offices, and add the abbreviated state (unless a university's name identifies it). For locations abroad, spell both city and country.
- Shorten the name of a publisher, but include "Press" and "Books."

- Use "Author" instead of the publisher's name if the two are the same.
- For an article, give volume, issue (if each begins with page 1), and any digital object identifier (DOI), a unique number that identifies it with a permanent link. If no DOI is available for an online article, supply the URL for the journal or publisher home page, even if you used a database.
- Include an access date only for online sources that might change.
- Omit a final period after the URL.

Keep in mind these two key questions, which are used to organize the sample entries that follow:

Who wrote it?

What type of source is it?

As you prepare your own entries, begin with the author. The various author formats apply whatever your source – article, book, Web page, or other material. Then, from the following examples, select the format for the rest of the entry, depending on the type of source you have used. Follow its pattern in your entry, supplying the same information in the same order with the same punctuation and other features.

## Who Wrote It?

### Individual Author

O'Reilly, B. (2006). *Culture warrior.* New York, NY: Broadway Books.

### Two Authors

Boggs, C., & Pollard, T. (2007). *The Hollywood war machine: U.S. militarism and popular culture.* Boulder, CO: Paradigm.

### Three Authors or More

Provide names for three to six authors; for more than six, simply use "et al." ("and others") instead of adding more names.

Schiller, B., Hill, C., & Wall, S. (2012). *The economy today.* New York, NY: McGraw-Hill.

### Same Author with Multiple Works

Arrange the titles by date, the earliest first. If some share the same date, arrange them alphabetically, and letter them after the date.

Space initials

Gould, S. J. (1996). *Full house: The spread of excellence from Plato to Darwin.* New York, NY: Harmony.

Follow with periods

Gould, S. J. (2003a). *The hedgehog, the fox, and the magister's pox: Mending the gap between science and the humanities.* New York, NY: Harmony.

Gould, S. J. (2003b). *Triumph and tragedy in Mudville: A lifelong passion for baseball.* New York, NY: Norton.

#### Organization Author

American Lung Association. (2012). *New standards bring cleaner air to you.* Washington, DC: Author.

#### Author of Edited Work

Roach, M., & Folger, T. (Eds.). (2011). *The best American science and nature writing.* New York, NY: Houghton Mifflin Harcourt.

#### Author and Translator

Ishinomori, S. (1988). *Japan Inc.: Introduction to Japanese economics* (B. Scheiner, Trans.). Berkeley: University of California Press. (Original work published 1986)

#### Unidentified Author

Environment awareness: No child left inside. (2007, February 10). *The Economist, 382,* 32-33.

## What Type of Source Is It?

Once you have found the author format that fits, look for the type of source that matches. Mix and match the patterns illustrated as needed. For example, the revised edition of an edited collection of articles might send you to several examples until you have identified all of its elements.

### Article in a Printed or an Electronic Periodical

#### Article from a Journal Paginated by Volume

If the pages for the year's volume are numbered consecutively, no issue number is needed. Italicize the volume number as well as the journal title.

Barker, T. (2009). Hong Kong film, Hollywood and the new global cinema: No film is an island. *Asian Journal of Social Science, 37,* 970-971. doi:10.1163/156848409X12526657425668 — No period added

#### Article from a Journal Paginated by Issue

If each issue begins with page 1, add the issue number in parentheses, without italics, leaving no space after the volume number.

Kissam, E. (2005). The fulcrum for immigrant civic engagement. *Journal of Latino-Latin American Studies, 1*(4), 191-205.

If you want to list a special issue about a topic, rather than singling out an article, begin with the issue editor or, if none, with the issue title.

Latinos in rural America [Special issue]. (2005). *Journal of Latino-Latin American Studies, 1*(4).

#### Article from a Journal with a DOI

Give volume, issue (if needed), and digital object identifier (DOI) numbers.

Het, S., & Wolf, O. T. (2007). Mood changes in response to psychosocial stress in healthy young women: Effects of pretreatment with cortisol. *Behavioral Neuroscience, 121*(1), 11-20. doi:10.1037/0735-7044.121.1.11

#### Article from a Journal without a DOI

If an article you found online has no DOI, add the journal's home page URL.

Doherty, S. D., & Rosen, T. (2006). Shark skin laceration. *Dermatology Online Journal, 12*(6), 6. Retrieved from http://dermatology.cdlib.org

To see how to create the listing for a journal article from a database, turn to pp. 644–45.

#### Article Accessed through a Library or Subscription Database

Supply any DOI, or search for and identify the home page for the journal. Name the database only for a source otherwise hard to find.

Nicol, S. (2012). Volunteering and young people. *Youth Studies Australia, 31*(3), 3-4. Retrieved from http://www.acys.info/ysa

No period added

#### Abstract for an Article

If you use only the abstract, cite it, not the full article. Add "Abstract" in brackets after the title, or use it to begin the retrieval line.

Chion, M. (2010). No man's France. *Studies in French Cinema 10*(3), 251-256. Abstract retrieved from Academic Search Premier Database.

To see how to create the listing for a magazine article, turn to pp. 642–43.

#### Article from a Printed Magazine

Stewart, D. C. (2012, May). Airport 2052. *Discover, 33,* 44-49.

#### Article from an Online Magazine

Levine, B. E. (2012, October 30). Does TV actually brainwash Americans? *Salon.com.* Retrieved from http://www.salon.com

#### Article from a Newsletter

Responding to historic flooding in Thailand. (2011, December). *Pacific Disaster Center: PDC in Print, 6*(4), 1.

#### Article from a Printed Newspaper

Broadwater, L. (2012, November 8). City awards new traffic-camera contract. *The Baltimore Sun*, p. A6.

#### Article from an Online Newspaper

Davidson, A. (2012, November 20). Skills don't pay the bills. *The New York Times.* Retrieved from http://www.nytimes.com

#### Editorial

Rushed primaries. [Editorial]. (2007, March 19). *The Nation, 284,* 3.

#### Letter to the Editor

Lardner, G. (2007, March 19). Impeach, impeach, impeach [Letter to the editor]. *The Nation, 284,* 24.

#### Review

Wertheim, M. (2012, October 23). Science strange and dangerous [Review of the book *The pseudoscience wars*]. *The Wall Street Journal,* p. A15.

### Printed or Electronic Book

#### Printed Book

Zelden, C. L. (2009). *The Supreme Court and elections.* Washington, DC: CQ Press.

To see how to create a listing for a book, turn to pp. 646–47.

#### Online Book

Oblinger, D. G., & Oblinger, J. L. (Eds.). (2005). *Educating the Net generation.* Retrieved from http://www.educause.edu/educatingthenetgen/

#### E-book

Goldemberg, J. (2012). *Energy: What everyone needs to know*. Retrieved from http://www.barnesandnoble.com/w/energy-jose-goldemberg/1110866917

#### Multivolume Work

Fink, G. (Ed.). (2007). *Encyclopedia of stress* (Vols. 1-4). San Diego, CA: Academic Press.

#### Revised Edition

Conrad, P., & Leiter, V. (2013). *The sociology of health and illness: Critical perspectives* (9th ed.). New York, NY: Worth.

#### Book without a Date

Reade, T. (n.d.). *American Originals.* Wichita, KS: Midtown Press.

## Part of a Printed or an Electronic Book

### Selection from a Printed Book

See the citation on p. 739.

Martin, P. Y., & Hummer, R. A. (2003). Fraternities and rape on campus. In M. Silberman (Ed.), *Violence and society: A reader* (pp. 215-222). Upper Saddle River, NJ: Prentice Hall.

### Selection from an Online Book

Brown, M. (2005). Learning spaces. In D. G. Oblinger & J. L. Oblinger (Eds.), *Educating the Net generation* (chap. 12). Retrieved from http://www.educause .edu/educatingthenetgen/

Divide URL before puncturation

### Selection from an E-book

Ikeda, Y. (2001). Names. In The Quakebook Community (Ed.), *2:46: Aftershocks: Stories from the Japan earthquake*. Retrieved from http://www.amazon.com /Aftershocks-Stories-Japan-Earthquake-ebook/

### Preface, Introduction, Foreword, or Afterword

Napier, M. (2011). Foreword. In M. Hicks, *Chicago comedy: A fairly serious history* (pp. 9-10). Charleston, SC: History Press.

### Article from a Reference Work

Norman, C. E. (2003). Religion and food. In *Encyclopedia of food and culture* (Vol. 3, pp. 171-176). New York, NY: Charles Scribner's Sons.

## Printed or Electronic Report or Other Document

Many research reports and similar documents are collaborative products, prepared under the auspices of government, academic, or other organizational sponsors. Start with the agency name if no specific author is identified. In parentheses, add any report number assigned by the agency right after the title. Add the publisher (unless it is also the author) before the URL.

### Printed Government Document

U.S. Bureau of the Census. (2009). *Statistical abstract of the United States: The national data book: 2010.* (129th ed.) (NTIS Order Number: PB2010-965801). Washington, DC: U.S. Government Printing Office.

### Online Government Document

U.S. Federal Trade Commission. (2010). *Medical identity theft.* Retrieved from http://www.consumer.ftc.gov/articles/0171-medical-identity-theft

#### Research Report

Liu, J., Allspach, J. R., Feigenbaum, M., Oh, H.-J., & Burton, N. (2004). *A study of fatigue effects from the new SAT* (RR-04-46). Princeton, NJ: Educational Testing Service.

#### Online Research Report

National Institute on Drug Abuse. (2012). *Inhalant abuse* (NIH Publication No. 10-3818). Retrieved from http://www.drugabuse.gov/sites/default/files/rrinhalants.pdf

#### Online Research Report from a Database

Ross, D. B., & Driscoll, R. (2006). *Test anxiety: Age appropriate interventions.* Retrieved from ERIC database. (ED493897)

#### Report from an Academic Institution

Henderson, S., & Heinonen, O. (2012). *Nuclear Iran: A glossary of terms.* Cambridge, MA: Harvard Kennedy School, Belfer Center for Science and International Affairs.

#### Pamphlet

Label the source in brackets as a brochure.

U.S. Department of Veterans Affairs. (2012). *Federal benefits for veterans, dependents, and survivors* [Brochure]. Washington, DC: Author.

#### Doctoral Dissertation

Richter, P. (2004). *Improving nursing in the age of managed care* (Unpublished doctoral dissertation). University of Wisconsin, Madison.

### Internet or Electronic Source

To help a reader find the same material you used, identify a specific document and give its URL.

See the directory on pp. 736–37 for entries for other electronic sources, including books and articles.

For any updates on online formats, visit the APA Web site at apastyle.apa.org.

#### Section or Page from an Online Document

Detweiler, L. (1993). What is the future of privacy on the Internet? In *Identity, privacy, and anonymity on the Internet* (sec. 2.12). Retrieved from http://cyber.eserver.org/identity.txt

#### Document from a Campus Web Site

Identify the university and sponsoring program or department (if applicable) before giving the URL for the specific page or document.

To see how to create the listing for a Web page, turn to pp. 648–49.

Allin, C. (2012). *Common sense for college students: How to do better than you thought possible.* Retrieved from Cornell College, Department of Politics Web site: http://www.cornellcollege.edu/politics/resources-students/policies/common-sense-cwa.shtml

#### Computer Software

Microsoft Office 2010 [Computer software]. Redmond, WA: Microsoft.

### Visual or Audio Source

#### Audiotape or Recording

Atandi Anyona, A., & Koons, R. (Writers). (2012). *Singing against apartheid: An audio essay* [Audio essay]. Retrieved from http://ethnomusicologyreview.ucla.edu/content/singing-against-apartheid-audio-essay

#### Program on Television or Radio

Tibbon, T., & Locke, J. (Director/Producer). (2012). Hurricane Sandy: Inside the megastorm [Television series episode]. In C. Schmidt & J. Cort (Executive producer), *Nova.* Boston, MA: WGBH.

#### Film

George, T., & Kitman Ho, A. (Producers). (2004). *Hotel Rwanda* [Motion picture]. United States: United Artists/Lions Gate.

### Conversation or Field Artifact

#### Personal Interview

See the citation on p. 741.

Omit a personal interview from your reference list because it is not accessible to readers. Instead, mention it in your paper as a personal communication.

#### E-mail or Electronic Posting

See the citation on p. 741.

Cite inaccessible, nonpublic messages as personal communications. Otherwise, supply author, date, title, a description such as [Web log post], and a "Retrieved from" line with the URL.

---

**RESEARCH CHECKLIST**

#### Listing Sources in APA Style

- ☐ Have you started each entry with the appropriate pattern for the author's name? Have you left spaces between the initials for each name?
- ☐ Have you used "&" (not "and") to add the last coauthor's name?
- ☐ Have you included the date in each entry?

- ☐ Have you followed the sample pattern for the type of source used?
- ☐ Have you used capitals and italics correctly for the titles in your entries?
- ☐ Have you included the conventional punctuation – periods, commas, colons, parentheses – in your entry?
- ☐ Have you accurately recorded names of the author, title, and publisher?
- ☐ Have you checked the accuracy of dates, pages, and other numbers?
- ☐ Have you correctly typed or pasted in the DOI or URL of an electronic source? Have you split a long URL before a punctuation mark? Have you ended without adding a final period after a DOI or URL?
- ☐ Have you arranged your entries in alphabetical order?
- ☐ Have you checked your final list of references against your text citations so that every source appears in both places?
- ☐ Have you double-spaced your reference list, like the rest of your paper? Have you allowed an inch margin on all sides?
- ☐ Have you begun the first line of each entry at the left margin? Have you used your software to indent each additional line one-half inch (or five to seven spaces)?
- ☐ Have you checked any entry from a citation management system as carefully as your own entries?

## A Sample APA Research Paper

In "Sex Offender Lists: A Never-Ending Punishment," Jenny Lidington explores the intention of the sex offender registry and its many functional problems. Her scholarly approach is designed to help readers grasp the complexities of a difficult societal issue that often generates strong feelings. Notice how thoughtfully she tackles the topic: defining terms, making distinctions, reviewing history, tracing consequences, distinguishing differences, and establishing the basis for her questions. Her paper illustrates APA paper format and the APA conventions for citing and listing sources. Although this sample paper is presented for easy reading in a textbook, your paper should use the type style and size that APA suggests: Times New Roman font, 12-point size. Set one-inch margins on all four sides, double-space all the lines, and turn off automatic hyphenation. Use your software's Help feature or visit the campus computer lab for help setting up this format for your file.

For more on APA format, see the Quick Format Guide, p. A-1.

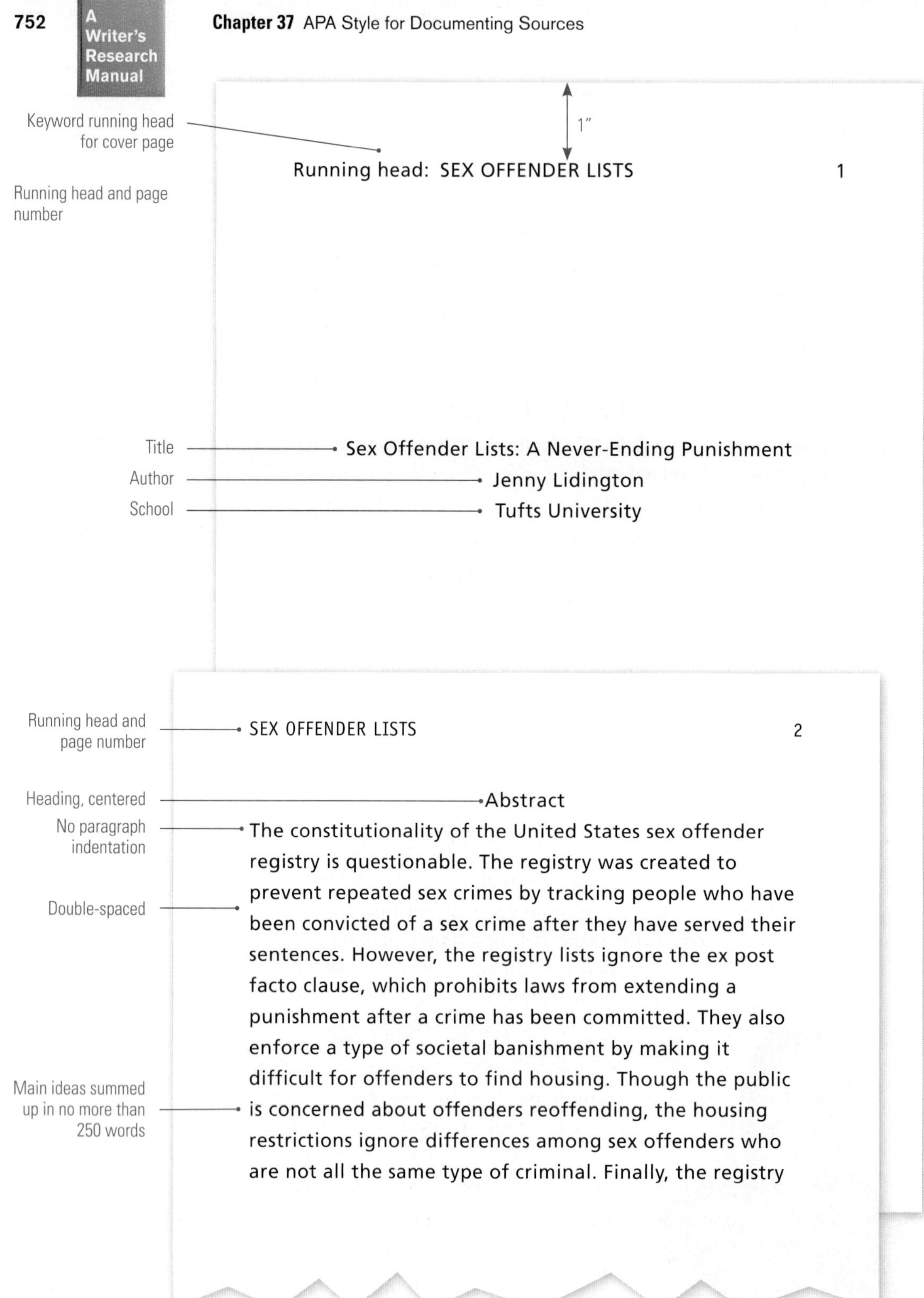
Keyword running head for cover page
1"
Running head and page number
Running head: SEX OFFENDER LISTS
1
Title
Sex Offender Lists: A Never-Ending Punishment
Author
Jenny Lidington
School
Tufts University
Running head and page number
SEX OFFENDER LISTS
2
Heading, centered
Abstract
No paragraph indentation
The constitutionality of the United States sex offender registry is questionable. The registry was created to prevent repeated sex crimes by tracking people who have been convicted of a sex crime after they have served their sentences. However, the registry lists ignore the ex post facto clause, which prohibits laws from extending a punishment after a crime has been committed. They also enforce a type of societal banishment by making it difficult for offenders to find housing. Though the public is concerned about offenders reoffending, the housing restrictions ignore differences among sex offenders who are not all the same type of criminal. Finally, the registry
Double-spaced
Main ideas summed up in no more than 250 words

½"

SEX OFFENDER LISTS 1" 3

Sex Offender Lists: A Never-Ending Punishment

Title centered

½" indent (or 5 spaces)

Whether someone is 18 years old having consensual sex with his 17-year-old high school sweetheart or 40 years old preying on young children, both are considered sexual predators in the eyes of the law. In both cases, jail time and registration as a sex offender are the penalties for those caught and convicted. No real distinction is made over the severity of the crime when one is labeled a sex offender, even though the extent of the sexual misconduct can vary tremendously. All those deemed sex offenders are required to register their addresses with local police or be rearrested; the police then release this information to the general public. Although the sex offender lists were created with the honorable intention of raising awareness of dangerous citizens in communities, they ultimately inflict unwarranted punishment on offenders in the interest of protecting potential victims. Not only are these lists unconstitutional, but the public's misunderstanding and misuse of the provided information can lead to unintended and sometimes heinous consequences.

Double-spaced throughout

1" 1"

**History of Sex Offender Registration**

First-level heading, bold and centered (second-level heading is bold, at left margin)

The earliest form of sex offender registration was implemented over 50 years ago in California and slowly spread to a handful of states. The early registries were primarily used to create a database, accessible only to local authorities for reference when sex crimes occurred, of the whereabouts of potentially dangerous citizens. However, with these registries came a "sex crime panic," strongly enhanced by media coverage of more extreme sex crimes (Thomas, 2011, p. 37). During this panic, the public began to push heavily for more stringent legislation.

Background presented in chronological order

Specific pages noted

The tipping point came with the case of a young Minnesota boy named Jacob Wetterling. On October 22,

1"

1989, Jacob was bicycling with his brother and a friend when a masked gunman intercepted them and kidnapped Jacob. Though Jacob and his attacker were never found, it is believed that Jacob was sexually assaulted and murdered. In light of this tragedy, the Jacob Wetterling Act was established in 1994, requiring states to create and maintain sex offender registries. Notably, the information on the registries was accessible only to appropriate authorities. While this policy had monumental implications, it did not satisfy the public as communities wanted access to records of sex offenders' residences (Thomas, 2011, p. 42).

Figures (not words) used for pages, dates, ages, and numbers with more than one digit

On July 29, 1994, another horrific and highly publicized incident occurred, which substantiated the argument for public notification and would significantly impact sex offenders' quality of life. Megan Kanka, a 7-year-old girl from New Jersey, was raped and murdered by her neighbor, Jesse Timmenequas. Jesse, unbeknownst to the community, was a repeat sex offender. This event spurred legislators to create the registry reforms the public desired by passing Megan's Law. This legislation amended the Jacob Wetterling Act by requiring community notification of nearby sex offenders' residences. Along with publishing the registration information, other methods of notification were encouraged. Louisiana, for example, required sex offenders "to post signs at their homes declaring their status as sex offenders" (Thomas, 2011, p. 45).

**Constitutional Questions about Sex Offender Registries**

Overlooking the rights of perpetrators of abominable crimes can be easy; however, the constitutionality of sex offender registration is entirely questionable. Whatever the crime, the rights of the convicted should be upheld. Because the registration process occurs after an offender is released from incarceration, these lists fail to comply with the ex post facto clause, which prohibits the creation of laws that add punishments after a crime has been committed. These lists have been taken to court on grounds of retrospection, though rulings have not favored the offenders (Pattis, 2011), and also on grounds of due process, as offenders have no opportunity to argue against community notification.

A third constitutional issue is whether the residential restrictions imposed by the lists constitute banishment, an illegal form of punishment under the constitution. In many states, sex offenders are not allowed within a few blocks of schools, daycare centers, or playgrounds. Particularly in communities with many facilities, acceptable livable areas for registered offenders may be limited or nonexistent. "I never realized how many schools and parks there were until I had to stay away from them," a registered sex offender conceded in Levenson and Cotter's 2005 survey (as cited in Thomas, 2011, p. 129). Essentially, these restrictions, intended to make given areas safer, create potentially dangerous sex-offender communities. This was the case in Broward County, Florida, where 95 registered sex offenders lived within a five-block tract (Thomas, 2011, p. 129). Those who cannot find housing or afford available housing are left homeless though commonly banished from homeless shelters and hostels, too (Thomas, 2011, p. 129).

Multiple authors joined by *and* in text

Additional source cited in source where it was mentioned

**Public Misconceptions**

Those who argue that sex offender registries are constitutional often maintain that the lists are not punitive and provide the public with vital information that can prevent future sex crimes. Even those who admit that the lists may infringe upon offenders' rights argue that any minor violations are outweighed by the contribution to public safety. This argument might be the case if the critically flawed information in sex offender lists was not subject to public misinterpretation. One shortcoming is a lack of specificity: A person who urinated in public is on the same list as one who repeatedly raped young children. In California, one of each 375 adults is registered as a sex offender, a testament to this loose definition of sex crimes (Leon, 2011, p. 119). Although offenders are ranked on a scale of one to three (the worst) in terms of likelihood of reoffending, people tend to ignore these distinctions. As a police officer stated for the *Seattle Times*, "People look at them in a bucket. They say 'Any kind of sex offender is a sex offender, and always will be a sex offender'" (Farley, 2011, para. 13).

Paragraph number supplied for online article without numbered pages

Another flaw lies in the accuracy of the rankings. Most crimes require a post-incarceration evaluation to determine whether the criminal is still a threat to society, but sex offenders have no follow-up. When they are released from prison, their names go into a sex offender registry, no matter how much time has passed since the crime. The "threat level" classification represents the level at the time of the crime, not the offender's current risk level. Therapy sessions both during and after prison could result in the offender no longer posing a threat to the community. Studies show that within three years of being released from prison, only 5.3 percent of sex offenders are rearrested for another sex crime (Smith, 2003; U.S. Department of Justice, 2003, p. 1), which further suggests that the sex offender lists are extremely questionable.

In addition, due to the potentially inaccurate classifications, offenders may be assigned inappropriate punishments for their given crime. For example, many sex offenders whose crimes were not against children (or who may be children themselves) are given the same living restrictions as child rapists. The man imprisoned for having sex with his girlfriend days before she was legally old enough to give consent does not pose enough risk to restrict him from living near playgrounds and schools. Although some states such as New Jersey and Washington are working to assess risks more accurately, they are the exceptions (Leon, 2011, pp. 141–142).

**Consequences of a Lack of Privacy**

These major flaws in the sex offender registry system can have counterproductive and tragic effects. When sex offenders must register, their personal information is not given on a need-to-know basis; it is blazoned across the community where they live. Their names, photographs, license plate numbers, and home and work addresses are posted online for the world to view. They may struggle to find housing, to avoid public disapproval or embarrassing exposure of their pasts, and to pass background checks necessary to find work. Because these offenders are often shunned by the adult world, they may seek companionship with children, which potentially tempts some to offend again. With their faces plastered on local bulletin boards or e-mail alerts, offenders can grow increasingly aggravated, which also may lead them to new crimes (Chen, 2009).

This lack of privacy also makes offenders vulnerable to public vigilantes who can inflict harsh punishments. According to a Los Angeles County study by Gallo et al.,

> A number of judges felt that although the avowed purpose of the registration statute is to facilitate the process of law enforcement by providing a list of suspects . . . the information obtained under section 290 is subject to some abuse—either through police harassment or by indiscriminate revelation to unauthorized persons. (as cited in Leon, 2011, pp. 68–69)

Long quotation (40 words or longer) indented ½″ without quotation marks

Tragically, public harassment can lead to suicides and murders of registered sex offenders, as was the case for 24-year-old William Elliot. At age 20, Elliot was sentenced to four months in jail for having sex with his girlfriend who was two weeks away from turning 16 (the legal age of consent in Maine). Four years later, a young man named Stephen Marshall found Elliot's residential information on an online sex-offender database. Marshall used this information to stalk Elliot and shoot him to death in his own home (Ahuja, 2006). This incident is a horrific example of the unintended effects of public misinterpretation of sex offender lists, but it also calls into question whether these lists can be considered nonpunitive.

**Violations of Rights of Citizens**

Perceived as monsters, fiends, and psychopaths, sex offenders are not easily seen as victims; however, as American citizens, they have the same right to life, liberty, and the pursuit of happiness as anyone else. Although the sex registry laws were created with the best of intentions, they violate these constitutional rights and can have gruesome unintended consequences. Most importantly, they are not especially effective.

Many people believe that the typical sex crime is child rape when in reality most sex crimes are much more benign. The dramatic cases encourage regulation that far exceeds what is necessary for most offenders, placing those who have urinated publicly in the same category as pedophiles (Bonnar-Kidd, 2010, p. 416). However, the sex-crime taboos make it difficult for the public to override emotionally charged ideas of the misconduct that the lists represent and then to see the critical flaws in the current registry system. If these lists are to continue to exist, they should no longer serve as dehumanizing blacklists for the public to use at its own discretion.

SEX OFFENDER LISTS 9

References

Ahuja, G. (2006, April 18). Sex offender registries: Putting lives at risk? ABC News. Retrieved from http://abcnews.go.com

Bonnar-Kidd, K. K. (2010). Sexual offender laws and prevention of sexual violence or recidivism. *American Journal of Public Health*, 100, 412-419. doi: 10.2105/AJPH.2008.153254

Chen, S. (2009, February 19). After prison, few places for sex offenders to live. *The Wall Street Journal*. Retrieved from http://wsj.com

Farley, J. (2011, January 1). Sex-offender rankings: Is there room for gray areas? *The Seattle Times*. Retrieved from http://seattletimes.com

Leon, C. S. (2011). *Sex fiends, perverts, and pedophiles: Understanding sex crime policy in America*. New York, NY: New York University Press.

Pattis, N. (2011, February 7). Time to revisit ex post facto clause for sex offenders [Web log post]. Retrieved from http://www.pattisblog.com/index.php?article=Time_To_Revisit_Ex_Post_Facto_Clause_For_Sex_Offenders_2983

Smith, S. (2003, November 16). Five percent of sex offenders rearrested for another sex crime. [Press release]. Retrieved from U.S. Department of Justice, Office of Justice Programs, Bureau of Justice Statistics website: http://bjs.ojp.usdoj.gov/content/pub/press/rsorp94pr.cfm

Thomas, T. (2011). *The registration and monitoring of sex offenders: A comparative study*. New York, NY: Routledge.

U.S. Department of Justice, Office of Justice Programs, Bureau of Justice Statistics. (2003). *Recidivism of sex offenders released from prison in 1994* (NCJ 198281). Retrieved from http://bjs.ojp.usdoj.gov/content/pub/pdf/rsorp94.pdf

Page numbering continues

Heading, centered

First line of entry at left margin, additional lines indented ½"

List alphabetized by names of authors

All author names begin with last name

No period after URL

First word in title and after colon and all proper nouns capitalized

For more sample student research papers, visit **bedfordstmartins.com/bedguide** and go to Re:Writing.

# A WRITER'S HANDBOOK

# A Writer's Handbook Contents

# Introduction: Grammar, or The Way Words Work

Every speaker of English, even a child, commands a grammatical system of tremendous complexity. Take the sentence "A bear is occupying a phone booth while a tourist impatiently waits in line." In theory, there are nineteen billion different ways to state the idea in that sentence.[1] (Another is "A tourist fumes while he waits for a bear to finish yakking on a pay phone.") How do we understand this unique sentence? For we do understand it, though we have never heard it before – not in those same words, in that same order.

To begin with, we recognize familiar words and their meanings. Just as significantly, we recognize grammatical structures. We know that the sentence contains a familiar pattern of **syntax,** or word order, that helps it make sense to us. Ordinarily we aren't even conscious of such an order, but to notice it, all we need to do is rearrange the words of our sentence:

> Phone a impatiently line in waits tourist bear a occupying is a booth while.

The result is nonsense: it defies English grammar. The would-be sentence doesn't follow familiar patterns or meet our expectations of order.

Hundreds of times a day, with wonderful efficiency, we perform tasks of understanding and constructing complex sentences. Isn't it possible to write well without contemplating grammar at all? Yes. If your innate sense of grammar is reliable, you can write clearly and logically and forcefully without knowing a predicate nominative from a handsaw. Most successful writers, though, have practiced for many years to gain this sense. When you doubt a word or a construction, a handbook can clear up your confusion and restore your confidence – just as a dictionary can help your spelling.

The grammatical conventions in this handbook are not mechanical rules but accepted ways in which skilled writers put words together to convey meaning clearly. The college writer can learn by following their example, just as an athlete, artist, or mechanic can learn by watching professionals.

## Learning by Doing — Asking What You Need to Know

Based on your sense of how English works, identify a few spots in your draft that don't sound right to you. Working with a classmate or small group, present your passages to each other. Exchange responses about what to look up and how to improve correctness and clarity.

[1]Richard Ohmann, "Grammar and Meaning," *American Heritage Dictionary* (Boston: Houghton, 1979), pp. xxxi–xxxii.

# 38 Grammatical Sentences



**sentence:** A word group that includes both a subject and a predicate and can stand alone

## 1 | Sentence Fragments

Unlike a complete sentence, a **fragment** is partial or incomplete. It may lack a subject (naming someone or something), a predicate (making an assertion about the subject), or both. A fragment also may otherwise fail to express a complete thought. Unless you add what's missing or reword what's incomplete, a fragment cannot stand alone as a sentence. Even so, we all use fragments in everyday speech, where their context and delivery make them understandable and therefore acceptable.

That bicycle over there.

Good job.

Not if I can help it.

In writing, fragments like these fail to communicate complete, coherent ideas. Notice how much more effective they are as complete sentences.

I'd like to buy that bicycle over there.

You did a good job sanding the floor.

Nobody will steal my seat if I can help it.

Some writers use fragments on purpose. Advertisers are fond of short, emphatic fragments that command attention, like quick jabs to the head.

For seafood lovers. Every Tuesday night. All you can eat.

Those who text-message or tweet compress what they write because time and space are limited. They rely on the recipient to fill in the gaps.

Thru with lab. CU @ 8. Pizza?

In college writing, though, it is good practice to express your ideas in complete sentences. Besides, complete sentences usually convey more information than fragments—a big advantage in essay writing.

## 1a If a fragment is a phrase, link it to a nearby sentence, or make it a complete sentence.

You have two choices for revising a fragment if it is a phrase: (1) link it to an adjoining sentence, using punctuation such as a comma or a colon, or (2) add a missing subject or verb to make it a complete sentence.

For more on editing for fragments, see A1 in the Quick Editing Guide, pp. A-40–A-41.

FRAGMENT Malcolm has two goals. *Wealth and power.*

SENTENCE Malcolm has two goals: wealth and power. [The phrase *Wealth and power* has no verb; a colon links it to *goals.*]

FRAGMENT Al ends his stories as he mixes his martinis. *With a twist.*

SENTENCE Al ends his stories as he mixes his martinis, with a twist. [The prepositional phrase *With a twist* has no subject or verb; a comma links it to the main clause.]

FRAGMENT *To stamp out the union.* That was the bosses' plan.

SENTENCE To stamp out the union was the bosses' plan. [The infinitive phrase *To stamp out the union* has no main verb or subject; it becomes the sentence subject.]

FRAGMENT The students taking the final exam in the auditorium.

SENTENCE The students were taking the final exam in the auditorium. [The helping verb *were* completes the verb and makes a sentence.]

**phrase:** Two or more related words that work together but may lack a subject (*will walk*), a verb (*my uncle*), or both (*to the attic*)

**subject:** The part of a sentence that names something—a person, an object, an idea, a situation—about which the verb in the predicate makes an assertion: The *king* lives.

**verb:** A word that shows action (The cow *jumped* over the moon) or a state of being (The cow *is* brown)

## 1b If a fragment is a subordinate clause, link it to a nearby sentence, or drop the subordinating conjunction.

Some fragments are missing neither subject nor verb. Instead, they are subordinate clauses, unable to express complete thoughts unless linked with main clauses. When you find a subordinating conjunction at the start or in the middle of a word group, that word group may be a subordinate clause. You can (1) combine the fragment with a main clause (a complete sentence)

**subordinating conjunction:** A word (such as *because, although, if, when*) used to make one clause dependent on, or subordinate to, another: *Unless* you have a key, we are locked out. (See 14d–14f.)

nearby, or (2) make the subordinate clause into a complete sentence by dropping the subordinating conjunction.

FRAGMENT The new law will help create jobs. *If it passes.*

SENTENCE The new law will help create jobs, if it passes.

FRAGMENT *Because Jay is an avid skier.* He loves winter in the mountains.

SENTENCE Because Jay is an avid skier, he loves winter in the mountains.

SENTENCE Jay is an avid skier. He loves winter in the mountains.

## 1c If a fragment has a participle but no other verb, change the participle to a main verb, or link the fragment to a nearby sentence.

A present participle (the *-ing* form of the verb) can serve as the main verb in a sentence only with a form of *be* ("Sally *is working* harder than usual"). A participle alone, used as a main verb, results in a fragment.

FRAGMENT Jon was used to the pressure of deadlines. *Having worked the night shift at the daily newspaper.*

One solution is to combine the fragment with an adjoining sentence.

SENTENCE Jon was used to the pressure of deadlines, having worked the night shift at the daily newspaper.

A second solution is to choose another form of the verb.

SENTENCE Jon was used to the pressure of deadlines. He *had worked* the night shift at the daily newspaper.

## 1d If a fragment is part of a compound predicate, add it to the sentence with the subject and the rest of the predicate.

**compound predicate:** A predicate consisting of two or more verbs linked by a conjunction: My sister *stopped and stared.*

For punctuation advice, see 14a.

FRAGMENT In spite of a pulled muscle, Jeremy ran the race. *And won.*

A fragment such as *And won* sounds satisfyingly punchy, but it lacks a subject. Create a sentence by linking the two verbs in the compound predicate.

SENTENCE In spite of a pulled muscle, Jeremy *ran* the race *and won.*

To emphasize the second verb, add punctuation and another subject.

SENTENCE In spite of a pulled muscle, Jeremy ran the race—and *he* won.

## ESL Guidelines: Using Participles, Gerunds, and Infinitives

A **verbal** is a form of a verb that cannot function as the main verb in a sentence but can function as an adjective, an adverb, or a noun.

**Using participles**

When used as an adjective, the present (***-ing***) form expresses cause, and the past (***-ed*** and ***-d***) forms express effect or result.

The movie was *terrifying to the children.*
[The movie caused terror.]

The children were *terrified by the movie.*
[The movie resulted in terrified children.]

**Using verbs with gerunds and infinitives**

Some verbs are followed by gerunds (verb + *-ing,* functioning as a noun), others by infinitives (*to* + base verb), and still others by either.

- Verbs that are followed by gerunds

  *appreciate, avoid, consider, deny, discuss, enjoy, finish, imagine, keep, miss, practice, recall,* and *suggest,* among others

  My family enjoys *going* to the beach.

- Verbs that are followed by infinitives

  *agree, decide, expect, pretend, refuse,* and *want,* among others

  My mother decided *to eat* dinner at the Salad Shop.

- Verbs that can be followed by either a gerund or an infinitive

  *continue, like, love, hate, remember, forget, start,* and *stop,* among others

  I like going to the museum, but Nadine likes *to go* to the movies.

*NOTE:* Some verbs, such as *stop, remember,* and *forget,* have significantly different meanings when followed by a gerund or by an infinitive.

I stopped *smoking.* [I do not smoke anymore.]

I stopped *to smoke.* [I stopped so that I could smoke.]

- *Used to* (meaning "did in the past") is followed by the basic form of the verb. *Be used to* or *get used to* (meaning "be or become accustomed to") is followed by a gerund.

  I *used to live* in Rio, but now I live in Ohio. [I lived in Rio in the past.]

  I *am used to living* in Ohio. [I am accustomed to living in Ohio.]

  I *got used to living* in Ohio. [I became accustomed to living in Ohio.]

For practice, visit **bedfordstmartins .com/bedguide**.

## Exercise 1–1 ▪ Eliminating Fragments

For more practice, visit **bedfordstmartins.com/bedguide**.

Eliminate any fragments in the following examples. Some sentences may be correct. Possible revisions for the lettered sentences appear at the end of the handbook. Example:

Bryan hates parsnips. And loathes squash.

Bryan hates parsnips *and* loathes squash.

a. Michael had a beautiful Southern accent. Having lived many years in Georgia.
b. Pat and Chris are determined to marry each other. Even if their families do not approve.
c. Jack seemed well qualified for a career in the air force. Except for his tendency to get airsick.
d. Lisa advocated sleeping no more than four hours a night. Until she started nodding off through her classes.
e. They met. They talked. They fought. They reached agreement.

1. Being the first person in his family ever to attend college. Alex is determined to succeed.
2. Does our society rob children of their childhood? By making them aware too soon of adult ills?
3. Richard III supposedly had the young princes murdered. No one has ever found out what really happened to them.
4. For democracy to function, two elements are crucial. An educated populace and a collective belief in people's ability to chart their own course.
5. You must take his stories as others do. With a grain of salt.

## Exercise 1–2 ▪ Eliminating Fragments

Rewrite the following paragraph, eliminating all fragments. Explain why you made each change. Example:

Many people exercise to change their body image. And may become obsessed with their looks. [The second word group is a fragment because it has no subject.]

Many people exercise to change their body image *and* may become obsessed with their looks. [This revised sentence links the fragment to the rest of the sentence.]

Some people assume that only women are overly concerned with body image. However, men often share this concern. While women tend to exercise vigorously to stay slender, men usually lift weights to "bulk up." Because of their desire to look masculine. Both are trying to achieve the "ideal" body form. The muscular male and the slim female. Sometimes working out begins to interfere with other aspects of life. Such as sleeping, eating regularly, or going to school or work. These are warning signs. Of too much emphasis on physical appearance. Preoccupation with body image may turn a healthy lifestyle into an unhealthy obsession. Many people believe that looking attractive will bring them happiness. Unfortunately, when they become compulsive. Beautiful people are not always happy.

## 2 | Comma Splices and Fused Sentences

Splice two ropes, and you join them into one. Splice two main clauses by putting only a comma between them, however, and you get a faulty construction called a **comma splice.** Here are two perfectly good main clauses, each separate, each able to stand on its own as a sentence:

> The detective wriggled on his belly toward the campfire. The drunken smugglers didn't notice him.

Splicing those sentences with a comma makes for difficult reading.

COMMA SPLICE — The detective wriggled on his belly toward the campfire, the drunken smugglers didn't notice him.

Even more confusing than a comma splice is a **fused sentence:** two main clauses joined without any punctuation.

FUSED SENTENCE — The detective wriggled on his belly toward the campfire the drunken smugglers didn't notice him.

**main clause:** A group of words that has both a subject and a verb and can stand alone as a complete sentence: *My friends play softball.*

For more on editing for comma splices and fused sentences, see A2 in the Quick Editing Guide, pp. A-41–A-42.

### Sentence Parts at a Glance

The **subject (S)** identifies some person, place, thing, situation, or idea.

The **predicate (P)** includes a verb (expressing action or state of being) and makes an assertion about the subject.

An **object (O)** is the target or recipient of the action described by the verb.

A **complement (C)** renames or describes a subject or object.

The *campus* (S) *center is* (P) *beautiful* (C). The new *sculpture* (S) *draws* (P) *crowds* (O).

Lacking clues from the writer, a reader cannot tell where to pause. To understand the sentence, he or she must halt and reread.

The next two pages show five easy ways to eliminate both comma splices and fused sentences, also called **run-ons.** Your choice depends on the length and complexity of your main clauses and the effect you desire.

## 2a Write separate complete sentences to correct a comma splice or a fused sentence.

COMMA SPLICE — Freud has been called an enemy of sexual repression, the truth is that he is not a friend of free love.

FUSED SENTENCE — Freud has been called an enemy of sexual repression the truth is that he is not a friend of free love.

Neither sentence yields its meaning without a struggle. To point readers in the right direction, separate the clauses.

**sentence:** A word group that includes both a subject and a predicate and can stand alone

SENTENCE — Freud has been called an enemy of sexual repression. The truth is that he is not a friend of free love.

## 2b Use a comma and a coordinating conjunction to correct a comma splice or a fused sentence.

If both clauses are of roughly equal weight, you can use a comma to link them—as long as you add a coordinating conjunction after the comma.

**coordinating conjunction:** A one-syllable linking word (*and, but, for, or, nor, so, yet*) that joins elements with equal or near-equal importance: Jack *and* Jill, sink *or* swim

COMMA SPLICE — Hurricane winds hit ninety miles an hour, they tore the roof from every house on Paradise Drive.

SENTENCE — Hurricane winds hit ninety miles an hour, *and* they tore the roof from every house on Paradise Drive.

## 2c Use a semicolon or a colon to correct a comma splice or a fused sentence.

For advice on coordination, see 14a–14c.

A semicolon can connect two closely related thoughts, emphasizing each one.

COMMA SPLICE — Hurricane winds hit ninety miles an hour, they tore the roof from every house on Paradise Drive.

SENTENCE — Hurricane winds hit ninety miles an hour; they tore the roof from every house on Paradise Drive.

If the second thought illustrates or explains the first, add it with a colon.

SENTENCE — The hurricane caused extensive damage: it tore the roof from every house on Paradise Drive.

The only punctuation powerful enough to link two main clauses single-handedly is a semicolon, a colon, or a period. A lone comma won't do the job except in the case of joining certain very short, similar main clauses.

Jill runs by day, Tom walks by night.

I came, I saw, I conquered.

Commas are not required with short, similar clauses; you can stick with semicolons to join all main clauses, short or long.

Jill runs by day; Tom walks by night.

I came; I saw; I conquered.

## 2d Use subordination to correct a comma splice or a fused sentence.

If one main clause is more important than the other or you want to give it more importance, make the less important one subordinate, which throws weight on the main clause. In effect, you show your reader how one idea relates to another: you decide which matters more.

**main clause:** A group of words that has both a subject and a verb and can stand alone as a complete sentence: *My friends play softball.*

FUSED SENTENCE Hurricane winds hit ninety miles an hour they tore the roof from every house on Paradise Drive.

SENTENCE *When hurricane winds hit ninety miles an hour,* they tore the roof from every house on Paradise Drive.

SENTENCE Hurricane winds, *which tore the roof from every house on Paradise Drive,* hit ninety miles an hour.

For advice on subordination, see 14d–14f. For a list of subordinating words, see p. 827.

## 2e Use a conjunctive adverb with a semicolon and a comma to correct a comma splice or a fused sentence.

If you want to cram more than one clause into a sentence, you may join two clauses with a **conjunctive adverb.** Conjunctive adverbs show relationships such as addition (*also, besides*), comparison (*likewise, similarly*), contrast (*instead, however*), emphasis (*namely, certainly*), cause and effect (*thus, therefore*), or time (*finally, subsequently*). These transitional words and phrases can be a useful way of linking clauses – but only with the right punctuation.

COMMA SPLICE Freud has been called an enemy of sexual repression, however the truth is that he is not a friend of free love.

A writer might consider a comma plus the conjunctive adverb *however* enough to combine the two main clauses, but that glue won't hold. Stronger binding – the semicolon along with a comma – is required.

For a list of conjunctive adverbs, see p. 827.

SENTENCE Freud has been called an enemy of sexual repression; however, the truth is that he is not a friend of free love.

## Exercise 2–1 ▪ Revising Comma Splices and Fused Sentences

For more practice, visit **bedfordstmartins .com/bedguide**.

In the following examples, correct each comma splice or fused sentence in two ways, and decide which way works better. Be creative: don't correct all the same way. Some may be correct as written. Possible revisions for the lettered sentences appear at the end of the handbook. Example:

The castle looked eerie from a distance, it filled us with nameless fear.

The castle looked eerie from a *distance;* it filled us with nameless fear.

*Or*

The castle, *which looked eerie from a distance,* filled us with nameless fear.

a. We followed the scientist down a flight of wet stone steps at last he stopped before a huge oak door.
b. Dr. Frankenstein selected a heavy key, he twisted it in the lock.
c. The huge door gave a groan it swung open on a dimly lighted laboratory.
d. Before us on a dissecting table lay a form with closed eyes to behold it sent a quick chill down my spine.
e. The scientist strode to the table, he lifted a white-gloved hand.

1. Dr. Frankenstein flung a switch, blue streamers of static electricity crackled about the table, the creature gave a grunt and opened smoldering eyes.
2. "I've won!" exclaimed the scientist in triumph he circled the room doing a demented Irish reel.
3. The creature's right hand strained, the heavy steel manacle imprisoning his wrist began to creak.
4. Like a staple wrenched from a document, the manacle yielded.
5. The creature sat upright and tugged at the shackles binding his ankles, Frankenstein uttered a piercing scream.

## Exercise 2–2 ▪ Revising Comma Splices and Fused Sentences

Revise the following passage, using subordination, a conjunctive adverb, a semicolon, or a colon to correct each comma splice or fused sentence. You may also write separate complete sentences. Some sentences may be correct. Example:

English can be difficult to learn, it is full of expressions that don't mean what they literally say.

English can be difficult to learn *because* it is full of expressions that don't mean what they literally say.

Have you ever wondered why you drive on parkways and park on driveways, that's about as logical as your nose running while your feet smell! When you think about it, these phrases don't make sense yet we tend to accept them without thinking about what they literally mean we simply take their intended meanings for granted. Think, however, how confusing they are for a person who is just learning the language. If, for example, you have just learned the verb *park,* you would logically assume that a parkway is where you should park your car, of course when most people see a parkway or a driveway they realize that braking on a parkway would be hazardous, while speeding through a driveway will not take them very far. However, our language is full of idiomatic expressions that may be difficult for a person from another language background to understand. Fortunately, there are plenty of questions to keep us *all* confused, such as why Americans commonly refer to going to work as "punching the clock."

# 3 | Verbs

Most verbs are called **action verbs** because they show action (*swim, eat, sleep*). Some are called **linking verbs** (*is, become, seem, feel*) because they show a state of being by linking the subject of a sentence with a word that renames or describes it. A few verbs accompany a main verb to add information about its action; they are called **helping** or **auxiliary verbs** (*have, must, can*).

For help editing verbs, see A3 in the Quick Editing Guide, pp. A-42–A-44.

## Verb Forms

### 3a Use a linking verb to connect the subject of a sentence with a subject complement.

A linking verb (LV) shows what the subject of a sentence *is* or is *like.* The verb creates a sort of equation, either positive or negative, between the subject and its complement (SC)—a noun, a pronoun, or an adjective.

**subject complement:** A noun, an adjective, or a group of words that follows a linking verb and renames or describes the subject: This plum tastes *ripe.*

LV SC
Julia will *make* a good *doctor.* [Noun]

LV SC
Jorge *is* not the *one.* [Pronoun]

LV SC
London weather *seems foggy.* [Adjective]

A verb may be a linking verb in some sentences and not in others. If you focus on what the verb means, you can usually tell how it is functioning.

I often *grow* sleepy after lunch.
[Linking verb + subject complement *sleepy*]

**transitive verb:** An action verb that must have an object to complete its meaning: Alan *hit* the ball.

I often *grow* tomatoes in my garden.
[Transitive verb + direct object *tomatoes*]

### Common Linking Verbs at a Glance

Some linking verbs tell what a noun is, was, or will be.

*be, become, remain:* I *remain* optimistic.

*grow:* The sky is *growing* dark.

*make:* One plus two *makes* three.

*prove:* His warning *proved* accurate.

*turn:* The weather *turned* cold.

Some linking verbs tell what a noun might be.

*appear, seem, look:* The child *looks* cold.

Most verbs of the senses can operate as linking verbs.

*feel, smell, sound, taste:* The smoothie *tastes* sweet.

## 3b Use helping verbs to add information about the main verb.

Adding a **helping** or **auxiliary verb** to a simple verb (*go, shoot, be*) allows you to express a wide variety of tenses and moods (*am going, did shoot, would have been*). (See 3g–3l and 3n–3p.) The parts of this combination, called a **verb phrase,** need not appear together but may be separated by other words.

I probably *am going* to France this summer.

You *should* not *have shot* that pigeon.

This change *may* well *have been contemplated* before the election.

### Helping Verbs at a Glance

Of the twenty-three helping verbs, fourteen can also act as main verbs that identify the central action.

be, is, am, are, was, were, being, been

do, does, did

have, has, had

The other nine act only as helping verbs, never as main verbs. As **modals,** they show actions that are possible, doubtful, necessary, required, and so on.

can, could, should, would, may, might, must, shall, will

## 3c Use the correct principal parts of the verb.

The **principal parts** are the forms the verb can take – alone or with helping verbs – to indicate the full range of times when an action or a state of being does, did, or will occur. Verbs have three principal parts.

For the principal parts of many irregular verbs, see **bedfordstmartins.com/bedguide**.

- The **infinitive** is the simple, base, or dictionary form of the verb (*go, sing, laugh*), often preceded by *to* (*to go, to sing, to laugh*).
- The **past tense** signals completed action (*went, sang, laughed*).
- The **past participle** is combined with helping verbs to indicate action at various past or future times (*have gone, had sung, will have laughed*). With forms of *be,* it makes the passive voice. (See 3m.)

All verbs also have a present participle, the *-ing* form of the verb (*going, singing, laughing*). This form is used to make the progressive tenses. (See 3k and 3l.) It also can modify nouns and pronouns ("the *leaking* bottle") or, as a gerund, function as a noun ("*Sleeping all day* pleases me").

## 3d Use *-d* or *-ed* to form the past tense and past participle of regular verbs.

Most verbs in English are **regular verbs:** they form the past tense and past participle in a standard, predictable way. Regular verbs that end in *-e* add *-d* to the infinitive; those that do not end in *-e* add *-ed.*

| INFINITIVE | PAST TENSE | PAST PARTICIPLE |
|---|---|---|
| (to) smile | smiled | smiled |
| (to) act | acted | acted |

## 3e Use the correct forms for the past tense and past participle of irregular verbs.

At least two hundred **irregular verbs** form the past tense and past participle in some way other than adding *-d* or *-ed*: *go, went, gone.* Most irregular verbs, familiar to native English speakers, pose no problem.

For the forms of *be* and *have,* see A4 in the Quick Editing Guide, pp. A-44–A-45.

## 3f Use the correct forms of *lie* and *lay* and *sit* and *set.*

Try taking two easy steps to eliminate confusion between *lie* and *lay.*

- Learn the principal parts and present participles of both (see p. 776).
- Remember that *lie,* in all its forms, is intransitive and never takes a direct object: "The island *lies* due east." *Lay* is transitive, so its forms always require an object to answer "Lay what?": "*Lay* that pistol down."

The same distinction exists between *sit* and *set.* Usually, *sit* is intransitive: "He *sits* on the stairs." *Set* almost always takes an object: "He *sets* the

**intransitive verb:** A verb that is complete in itself and needs no object: The surgeon *paused.*
**transitive verb:** An action verb that must have an object to complete its meaning: Alan *hit* the ball.

## Forms of *Lie* and *Lay*, *Sit* and *Set*

**lie, lay, lain, lying:** recline

| PRESENT TENSE | | PAST TENSE | |
|---|---|---|---|
| I lie | we lie | I lay | we lay |
| you lie | you lie | you lay | you lay |
| he/she/it lies | they lie | he/she/it lay | they lay |

PAST PARTICIPLE
lain (We have *lain* in the sun long enough.)

PRESENT PARTICIPLE
lying (At ten o'clock he was still *lying* in bed.)

**lay, laid, laid, laying:** put in place, deposit

| PRESENT TENSE | | PAST TENSE | |
|---|---|---|---|
| I lay | we lay | I laid | we laid |
| you lay | you lay | you laid | you laid |
| he/she/it lays | they lay | he/she/it laid | they laid |

PAST PARTICIPLE
laid (Having *laid* his clothes on the bed, Mark jumped in the shower.)

PRESENT PARTICIPLE
laying (*Laying* her cards on the table, Lola cried, "Gin!")

**sit, sat, sat, sitting:** be seated

| PRESENT TENSE | | PAST TENSE | |
|---|---|---|---|
| I sit | we sit | I sat | we sat |
| you sit | you sit | you sat | you sat |
| he/she/it sits | they sit | he/she/it sat | they sat |

PAST PARTICIPLE
sat (I have *sat* here long enough.)

PRESENT PARTICIPLE
sitting (Why are you *sitting* on that rickety bench?)

**set, set, set, setting:** place

| PRESENT TENSE | | PAST TENSE | |
|---|---|---|---|
| I set | we set | I set | we set |
| you set | you set | you set | you set |
| he/she/it sets | they set | he/she/it set | they set |

PAST PARTICIPLE
set (Paul has *set* the table for eight.)

PRESENT PARTICIPLE
setting (Chanh-Duy has been *setting* traps for the mice.)

bottle on the counter." Note a few easily memorized exceptions: The sun *sets.* A hen *sets.* Gelatin *sets.* You *sit* the canter in a horse show.

## Exercise 3–1 ▪ Using Irregular Verb Forms

Underline each incorrectly used irregular verb in the following sentences; substitute the verb's correct form. Some sentences may be correct. Answers for the lettered sentences appear at the end of the handbook. Example:

For more practice, visit **bedfordstmartins.com/bedguide**.

We have already drove eight hundred miles from campus.

We have already *driven* eight hundred miles from campus.

a. Benjamin wrote all the music, and his sister sung all the songs.
b. After she had eaten her bagel, she drank a cup of coffee with milk.
c. When the bell rung, darkness had already fell.
d. Voters have chose some new senators, who won't take office until January.
e. Carol threw the ball into the water, and the dog swum after it.

1. He brought along two of the fish they had caught the day before.
2. By the time the sun set, the birds had all went away.
3. Teachers had spoke to his parents long before he stole the bicycle.
4. While the cat laid on the bed, the mouse ran beneath the door.
5. For the past three days the wind has blew hard from the south, but now the clouds have began to drift in.

## Tenses

The **simple tenses** indicate whether the verb's action took place in the past, takes place in the present, or will take place in the future. The **perfect tenses** narrow the timing further, specifying that the action was or will be completed by the time of some other action. The **progressive tenses** add precision, indicating that the action did, does, or will continue.

For advice on consistent verb tense, see 9a.

### 3g Use the simple present tense for actions that take place once, repeatedly, or continuously in the present.

The simple present tense is the infinitive form of a regular verb plus *-s* or *-es* for the third-person singular (used with *a singular noun* or *he, she,* or *it*).

| | |
|---|---|
| I like, I watch | we like, we watch |
| you like, you watch | you like, you watch |
| he/she/it likes, he/she/it watches | they like, they watch |

## ESL Guidelines Selection of Verbs to Show the Past, Present, and Future

| TIME OF ACTION OR STATE + ITS DURATION OR TIME RELATIONSHIP | PAST TIME Yesterday, some time ago, long ago | PRESENT TIME Right now, today, or at this moment | FUTURE TIME Tomorrow, soon, or at some expected or possible moment |
|---|---|---|---|
| Action or state occurs once | The team *lost* the game last week. (past tense) | Everyone *is* now on the field. (present tense) | The bus *will leave* at noon on Friday. (future tense) The bus *leaves* after lunch. (present tense) |
| Action or state occurs repeatedly | The team *won* every home game. (past tense) | The team *wins* when everyone *concentrates* on the game. (present tense) | The bus *will leave* at noon on Fridays. (future tense) The bus *leaves* at noon on Fridays. (present tense) |
| Action or state occurs continuously | The players *followed* the coach's directions. (past tense) | The coach always *encourages* the players. (present tense) | The bus *will leave* at noon from now on. (future tense) The bus always *leaves* at noon. (present tense) |
| Action or state is a general or timeless fact | | Coaching *is* a challenging job. (present tense) | |
| Action or state completed before the time of another action | The players *had practiced* for only two weeks in August before their games began. (past perfect tense) | The team *has played* every week this fall. (present perfect tense) | The team *will have played* at six other campuses before the season ends. (future perfect tense) |
| Action or state begun in the past but still going on | | The players *have practiced* every day. (present perfect tense) | |

### Verb Tenses at a Glance

NOTE: The examples show first person only.

SIMPLE TENSES

| *Present* | *Past* | *Future* |
|---|---|---|
| I cook | I cooked | I will cook |
| I see | I saw | I will see |

PERFECT TENSES

| *Present perfect* | *Past perfect* | *Future perfect* |
|---|---|---|
| I have cooked | I had cooked | I will have cooked |
| I have seen | I had seen | I will have seen |

PROGRESSIVE TENSES

| *Present progressive* | *Past progressive* | *Future progressive* |
|---|---|---|
| I am cooking | I was cooking | I will be cooking |
| I am seeing | I was seeing | I will be seeing |
| *Present perfect progressive* | *Past perfect progressive* | *Future perfect progressive* |
| I have been cooking | I had been cooking | I will have been cooking |
| I have been seeing | I had been seeing | I will have been seeing |

Some irregular verbs, such as *go,* form their simple present tense following the same rules as regular verbs (*go/goes*). Other irregular verbs, such as *be* and *have,* are special cases for which you should learn the correct forms.

| | |
|---|---|
| I am, I have | we are, we have |
| you are, you have | you are, you have |
| he/she/it is, he/she/it has | they are, they have |

You can use the simple present tense for an action happening right now ("I *welcome* this news"), happening repeatedly in the present ("Judy *goes* to church every Sunday"), or ongoing in the present ("Wesley *likes* ice cream"). In some cases, if you want to ask a question, intensify the action, or form a negative, use the helping verb *do* or *does* before the main verb.

I *do think* you should take the job. I *don't think* it will be difficult.

*Does* Christos *want* it? *Do* you *want* it? *Doesn't* anyone *want* it?

You can use the simple present for future action: "Football *starts* Wednesday." With *before, after,* or *when,* use it to express a future meaning: "When the team bus *arrives,* the players will board." Use it also for a general or timeless truth, even if the rest of the sentence is in a different tense:

Columbus proved in 1492 that the world *is* round.

Mr. Hammond will argue that people *are* basically good.

## 3h Use the simple past tense for actions already completed.

Regular verbs form the past tense by adding *-d* or *-ed* to the infinitive; the past tense of irregular verbs must be memorized. Use the past tense for an action at a specific past time, stated or implied.

Jack *enjoyed* the party. [Regular verb]

Akira *went* home early. [Irregular verb]

Though speakers may not pronounce the *-d* or *-ed* ending, standard written English requires that you add it to regular past tense verbs.

| | |
|---|---|
| NONSTANDARD | I *use* to wear weird clothes when I was a child. |
| STANDARD | I *used* to wear weird clothes when I was a child. |

In the past tense, you can use the helping verb *did* (past tense of *do*) to ask a question or intensify the action. Use *did* (or *didn't*) with the infinitive form of the main verb for both regular and irregular verbs.

| | | |
|---|---|---|
| I went. | I did go. | Why did I go? |
| You saw. | You did see. | What did you see? |
| She ran. | She did run. | Where did she run? |

## 3i Use the simple future tense for actions that are expected to happen but have not happened yet.

Although the present tense can indicate future action ("We *go* on vacation next Monday"), most actions that have not yet taken place are expressed in the simple future tense, including promises and predictions.

George *will arrive* in time for dinner.

*Will* you please *show* him where to park?

To form the simple future tense, add *will* to the infinitive form of the verb.

| | |
|---|---|
| I will go | we will go |
| you will go | you will go |
| he/she/it will go | they will go |

You can also use *shall* to inject a tone of determination ("We *shall overcome*!") or in polite questions ("*Shall* we dance?").

## 3j Use the perfect tenses for actions completed at the time of another action.

The perfect tenses consist of a form of *have* plus the past participle (*-ed* or *-en* form). The tense of *have* indicates the tense of the whole verb phrase.

## ESL Guidelines Negatives

You can make a sentence negative by using ***not*** or another negative adverb such as *seldom, rarely, never, hardly, hardly ever,* or *almost never.*

- With ***not:*** subject + helping verb + ***not*** + main verb

  Gina did *not* go to the concert.

  They will *not* call again.

- For questions: helping verb + *n't* (contraction for *not*) + subject + main verb

  *Didn't* [for *Did not*] Gina go to the concert?

  *Won't* [for *Will not*] they call again?

- With a negative adverb: subject + negative adverb + main verb *or* subject + helping verb + negative adverb + main verb

  My son *seldom* watches TV.

  Danh may *never* see them again.

- With a negative adverb at the beginning of a clause: negative adverb + helping verb + subject + verb

  *Not only* does Emma struggle with tennis, but she also struggles with golf.

  *Never* before have I been so happy.

*NOTE:* Do not pile up several negatives for intensity or emphasis in a sentence. Readers may consider double negatives (*not never, not hardly, wouldn't not*) sloppy repetition or assume that two negatives cancel each other out.

FAULTY The students did *not never* arrive late.

CORRECT The students did *not* ever arrive late.

CORRECT The students *never* arrived late.

For practice, visit **bedfordstmartins.com/bedguide**.

The action of a **present perfect** verb was completed before the sentence is uttered. Its helping verb is in the present tense: *have* or *has.*

I *have* never *been* to Spain, but I *have been* to Mexico.

*Have* you *seen* Mr. Grimaldi? Mr. Grimaldi *has gone* home.

You can use the present perfect tense for an action completed before some other action: "I *have washed* my hands of the whole affair, but I am watching from a distance." With *for* or *since,* it shows an action begun in the past and still going on: "Max *has worked* in this office for years."

The action of a **past perfect** verb was completed before some other action in the past. Its helping verb is in the past tense: *had.*

The concert *had ended* by the time we found a parking space.

Until I met her, I *had* not *pictured* Jenna as a redhead.

*Had* you *wanted* to clean the house before your parents arrived?

In informal writing, the simple past may be used when the relationship between actions is made clear by *when, before, after,* or *until.*

Observers *saw* the plane catch fire before it landed.

The action of a **future perfect** verb will be completed by some point (specified or implied) in the future. Its helping verb is in the future tense: *will have.*

The builders *will have finished* the house by June.

When you get the new dime, *will* you *have collected* every coin you want?

The store *will* not *have closed* by the time we get there.

## 3k Use the simple progressive tenses for actions in progress.

The progressive tenses consist of a form of *be* plus the present participle (the *-ing* form). The tense of *be* determines the tense of the whole verb phrase.

The **present progressive** expresses an action that began in the past and is taking place now. Its helping verb is in the present tense: *am, is,* or *are.*

I *am thinking* of a word that starts with *R.*

*Is* Stefan *babysitting* while Marie *is visiting* her sister?

You can express future action with the present progressive of *go* plus an infinitive phrase or with other words that make the time clear.

*Are* you *going to sign up* for the CPR class? Jeff *is taking* it Monday.

Use the present tense, not the present progressive, when verbs express being or emotion (*seem, be, belong, need*) rather than action.

I *guess* that the library is open. I *like* to study there.

The **past progressive** expresses an action that took place continuously at some time in the past, whether or not that action is still going on. Its helping verb is in the past tense: *was* or *were.*

The old men *were sitting* on the porch when we passed.

Lucy *was planning* to take the weekend off.

The **future progressive** expresses an action that will take place continuously at some time in the future. Its helping verb is in the future tense: *will be.* It also can use a form of *be* with *going to be.*

They *will be answering* the phones while she is gone.

She *is going to be flying* to Rome.

*Will* we *be dining* out every night on our vacation?

### 3l Use the perfect progressive tenses for continuing actions that began earlier.

The **present perfect progressive** indicates an action that started in the past and is continuing in the present. Form it by adding the present perfect of *be* (*has been, have been*) to the present participle (*-ing* form) of the main verb. Often *for* or *since* are used with this tense.

Fred *has been complaining* about his neighbor since the wild parties began.

*Have* you *been reading* Uma's postcards from England?

The **past perfect progressive** expresses a continuing action that was completed before another past action. Form it by adding the past perfect of *be* (*had been*) to the present participle of the main verb.

By the time Khalid finally arrived, I *had been waiting* for half an hour.

The **future perfect progressive** expresses an action that is expected to continue into the future for a specific time and then end before or continue beyond another future action. Form it by adding *will have been* to the present participle of the main verb.

They *will have been driving* for three days by the time they get to Oregon.

By fall Joanne *will have been attending* school longer than anyone else I know.

## Exercise 3–2 ▪ Identifying Verb Tenses

For more practice, visit **bedfordstmartins.com/bedguide**.

Underline each verb or verb phrase, and identify its tense in the following sentences. Answers for the lettered sentences appear at the end of the handbook. Example:

John is living in Hinsdale, but he prefers Joliet.

John is living [present progressive] in Hinsdale, but he prefers [simple present] Joliet.

a. He has been living like a hunted animal ever since he hacked into the university computer lab in order to change all of his grades.

b. I have never appeared on a reality television show, and I will never appear on one unless my family gets selected.

c. James had been at the party for only fifteen minutes when his host suddenly pitched the caterer into the swimming pool.

d. As of next month, I will have been studying karate for six years, and I will be taking the test for my orange belt in July.

e. The dachshund was running at its fastest speed, but the squirrel strolled toward the tree without fear.

1. As of May 1, Ira and Sandy will have been going together for a year.
2. She will be working in her study if you need her.
3. Have you been hoping that Carlos will come to your party?
4. I know that he will not yet have returned from Chicago.
5. His parents had been expecting him home any day until they heard that he was still waiting for the bus.

## Voice

Intelligent students read challenging books.

Challenging books are read by intelligent students.

These two statements convey similar information, but their emphasis is different. In the first sentence, the subject (*students*) performs the verb's action (*read*); in the second sentence, the subject (*books*) receives the verb's action (*are read*). One sentence states its idea directly, the other indirectly. We say that the first sentence is in the **active voice** and the second is in the **passive voice.**

### 3m Use the active voice rather than the passive voice.

Verbs in the **active voice** consist of principal parts and helping verbs. Verbs in the **passive voice** consist of the past participle (*-ed* or *-en* form) preceded by a form of *be* ("you *are given,*" "I *was given,*" "she *will be given*"). Most writers prefer the active to the passive voice because it is clearer and simpler, requires fewer words, and identifies the actor and the action more explicitly.

ACTIVE VOICE *Sergeants give* orders. *Privates obey* them.

Normally the subject of a sentence is the focus of readers' attention. If that subject does not perform the verb's action but instead receives the action, readers may wonder: What did the writer mean to emphasize?

PASSIVE VOICE *Orders are given* by sergeants. *They are obeyed* by privates.

Other writers misuse the passive voice to try to lend pomp to a humble truth (or would-be truth). For example, "Slight technical difficulties are being experienced" may replace "The airplane needs repairs." Some even use the passive voice deliberately to obscure the truth.

You do not need to drop the passive voice entirely from your writing. Sometimes the performer of a verb's action is irrelevant, as in a lab report, which emphasizes the research, not the researcher. Sometimes the performer is understood: "Automobiles are built in Detroit." (Of course they are built *by people.*) Other times the performer is unknown and simply omitted: "Many fortunes were lost in the stock market crash of 1929." It's a good idea, though, to substitute the active voice for the passive unless you have a good reason for using the passive.

### Exercise 3-3 ▪ Using Active and Passive Voice Verbs

For more practice, visit **bedfordstmartins.com/bedguide**.

Revise the following passage, changing the passive voice to the active voice in each sentence, unless you can justify keeping the passive. Example:

> The Galápagos Islands were reached by many species of animals in ancient times.
>
> Many species of animals *reached* the Galápagos Islands in ancient times.

The unique creatures of the Galápagos Islands have been studied by many scientists. The islands were explored by Charles Darwin in 1835. His observations led to the theory of evolution, which he explained in *On the Origin of Species.* Thirteen species of finches on the islands were discovered by Darwin, all descended from a common stock; even today this variety of species can be seen by visitors to the islands. Each island species has evolved by adapting to local conditions. A twig is used by the woodpecker finch to probe trees for grubs. Algae on the ocean floor are fed on by the marine iguana. Salt water can be drunk by the Galápagos cormorant, thanks to a salt-extracting gland. Because of the tameness of these animals, they can be studied by visitors at close range.

## Mood

Another characteristic of every verb is its **mood.** The **indicative** mood is most common. The **imperative** and **subjunctive** moods add valuable versatility.

### 3n Use the indicative mood to state a fact, to ask a question, or to express an opinion.

FACT Danika *left* home two months ago.

QUESTION *Will* she *find* happiness as a belly dancer?

OPINION I *think* not.

## 3o Use the imperative mood to make a request or to give a command or direction.

The understood but usually unstated subject of a verb in the imperative mood is *you*. The verb's form is the base form or infinitive.

REQUEST Please *be* there before noon. [*You* please be there. . . .]

COMMAND *Hurry!* [*You* hurry!]

DIRECTION *Drive* east on State Street. [*You* drive east. . . .]

## 3p Use the subjunctive mood to express a wish, requirement, suggestion, or condition contrary to fact.

The subjunctive mood is used in a subordinate clause to suggest uncertainty: the action expressed by the verb may or may not actually take place as specified. In any clause opening with *that* and expressing a requirement, the verb is in the subjunctive mood and takes the base or infinitive form.

For practice, visit **bedfordstmartins.com/bedguide**.

### ESL Guidelines Conditionals

**Conditional sentences** usually contain an ***if*** clause, which states the condition, and a result clause.

- When the condition is true or possibly true in the present or future, use the present tense in the ***if*** clause and the present or future tense in the result clause. The future tense is not used in the ***if*** clause.

  If Jane *prepares* her essay early, she usually *writes* very well.

  If Maria *saves* enough money, she *will buy* a car.

- When the condition is not true in the present, for most verbs use the past tense in the ***if*** clause; for the verb ***be,*** use ***were.*** Use ***would, could,*** or ***might*** + infinitive form in the result clause.

  If Carlos *had* a computer, he *would need* a monitor, too.

  If Claudia *were* here, she *could do* it herself.

- When the condition was not true in the past, use the past perfect tense in the ***if*** clause. If the possible result was in the past, use ***would have, could have,*** or ***might have*** + past participle (***-ed*** or ***-en*** form) in the result clause. If the possible result is in the present, use ***would, could,*** or ***might*** + infinitive form in the result clause.

  If Claudia *had saved* enough money, she *could have bought* a car. [Result in the past]

  If Annie *had finished* law school, she *might* be a successful lawyer now. [Result in the present]

Professor Vogt requires that every student *complete* the essay promptly.

She asked that we *be* on time for all meetings.

When you use the subjunctive mood to describe a condition that is contrary to fact, use *were* if the verb is *be*; for other verbs, use the simple past tense. Wishes, whether present or past, follow the same rules.

If I *were* rich, I would be happy.

If I *had* a million dollars, I would be happy.

Elissa wishes that Ted *were* more goal oriented.

Elissa wished that Ted *knew* what he wanted to do.

For a condition contrary to fact in the past, use the past perfect tense.

If I *had been* awake, I would have seen the meteor showers.

If Jessie *had known* you were coming, she would have cleaned her room.

Although use of the subjunctive has grown scarcer over the years, it still sounds crude to write "If I *was* you. . . ." If you ever feel that the subjunctive makes a sentence sound stilted, rewrite it with an infinitive phrase.

Professor Vogt requires every student *to complete* the essay promptly.

**infinitive:** The base form of a verb, often preceded by *to* (*to go, to play*)

## Exercise 3–4 ▪ Using the Correct Mood of Verbs

For more practice, visit **bedfordstmartins.com/bedguide**.

Find and correct any errors in mood in the following sentences. Identify the mood of the incorrect verb as well as its correct replacement. Some sentences may be correct. Answers for the lettered sentences appear at the end of the handbook. Example:

The law requires that each person files a tax return by April 15.

The law requires that each person *file* a tax return by April 15.
[Incorrect: *files,* indicative; correct: *file,* subjunctive]

a. Dr. Belanger recommended that Juan flosses his teeth every day.
b. If I was you, I would have done the same thing.
c. Tradition demands that Daegun shows respect for his elders.
d. Please attends the training lesson if you plan to skydive later today.

1. If she was slightly older, she could stay home by herself.
2. If they have waited a little longer, they would have seen some amazing things.
3. Emilia's contract stipulates that she works on Saturdays.
4. If James invested in the company ten years ago, he would have made a lot of money.

# 4 | Subject-Verb Agreement

For more on editing for subject-verb agreement, see A4 in the Quick Editing Guide, pp. A-44–A-45.

What does it mean for a subject and a verb to agree? Practically speaking, it means that their forms match: plural subjects take plural verbs, third-person subjects take third-person verbs, and so forth. When your subjects and verbs agree, you prevent a mismatch that could distract readers.

**subject:** The part of a sentence that names something—a person, an object, an idea, a situation—about which the predicate makes an assertion: The *king* lives.
**verb:** A word that shows action (The cow *jumped* over the moon) or a state of being (The cow *is* brown)

## 4a A verb agrees with its subject in person and number.

Subject and verb agree in person (first, second, or third):

*I write* my papers on my laptop. [Subject and verb in first person]

*Eamon writes* his papers in the lab. [Subject and verb in third person]

Subject and verb agree in number (singular or plural):

*Grace has enjoyed* college. [Subject and verb singular]

*She and Jim have enjoyed* their vacation. [Subject and verb plural]

The present tense of most verbs is the infinitive form, with no added ending except in the third-person singular. (See 3g–3l.)

| | |
|---|---|
| I enjoy | we enjoy |
| you enjoy | you enjoy |
| he/she/it enjoys | they enjoy |

Forms of the verb *be* vary.

| | |
|---|---|
| I am | we are |
| you are | you are |
| he/she/it is | they are |

## 4b A verb agrees with its subject, not with any words that intervene.

My *favorite* of O. Henry's short stories *is* "The Gift of the Magi."

*Home sales,* once driving the economy, *have fallen* during recent years.

**prepositional phrase:** The preposition and its object (a noun or pronoun), plus any modifiers: *in the bar, under a rickety table*

A singular subject linked to another noun or pronoun by a prepositional phrase beginning with wording such as *along with, as well as,* or *in addition to* remains a singular subject and takes a singular verb.

My cousin *James* as well as his wife and son *plans* to vote for Levine.

## 4c Subjects joined by *and* usually take a plural verb.

In most cases, a compound subject takes a plural verb.

*"Howl" and "Gerontion" are* Barry's favorite poems.

*Sugar, salt, and fat* adversely *affect* people's health.

However, phrases like *each boy and girl* or *every dog and cat* consider subjects individually, as "each one" or "every one," and use a singular verb.

*Each man and woman* in the room *has* a different story to tell.

Use a singular verb for two singular subjects that form or are one thing.

*Lime juice and soda quenches* your thirst.

**compound subject:** A subject consisting of two or more nouns or pronouns linked by *and: Scott and Liz* drove home.

## 4d With subjects joined by *or* or *nor*, the verb agrees with the part of the subject nearest to it.

Either they or *Max is* guilty.

Subjects containing *not . . . but* follow this rule also.

Not we but *George knows* the whole story.

You can remedy awkward constructions by rephrasing.

Either they are guilty or Max is.

We do not know the whole story, but George does.

## 4e Most collective nouns take singular verbs.

When a collective noun refers to a group of people acting as one, use a singular verb.

The *jury finds* the defendant guilty.

When the members of the group act individually, use a plural verb.

The *jury do* not yet *agree* on a verdict.

If you feel that using a plural verb results in an awkward sentence, reword the subject so that it refers to members of the group individually.

The *jurors do* not yet *agree* on a verdict.

**collective noun:** A singular noun that represents a group of people or items, such as *committee, family, jury, trio*

For more on agreement with collective nouns, see 7e.

## 4f Most indefinite pronouns take a third-person singular verb.

The indefinite pronouns *each, one, either, neither, anyone, anybody, anything, everyone, everybody, everything, no one, nobody, nothing, someone, somebody,* and *something* are considered singular and take a third-person singular verb.

*Someone is bothering* me.

Even when one of these subjects is followed by a phrase containing a noun or pronoun of a different person or number, use a singular verb.

*Each* of you *is* here to stay.

*One* of the pandas *seems* dangerously ill.

For a list of indefinite pronouns, see A6 in the Quick Editing Guide, pp. A-46–A-48.

## 4g The indefinite pronouns *all, any,* and *some* use a singular or plural verb, depending on their meaning.

I have no explanation. *Is any* needed?

*Any* of the changes considered critical *have* been made already.

*All is* lost.

*All* of the bananas *are gone.*

*Some* of the blame *is* mine.

*Some* of us *are* Democrats.

For more on agreement with indefinite pronouns, see 7d.

*None*—like *all, any,* and *some*—takes a singular or a plural verb, depending on the sense in which the pronoun is used.

*None* of you *is* exempt.

*None* of his wives *were* blond.

## 4h In a subordinate clause with a relative pronoun as the subject, the verb agrees with the antecedent.

For more information on subordination, see 14d–14f.

**relative pronoun:** A pronoun (*who, which, that, what, whom, whomever, whose*) that opens a subordinate clause, modifying a noun or pronoun in another clause: The gift *that* I received is very practical.

To determine the person and number of the verb in a subordinate clause whose subject is *who, which,* or *that,* look back at the word to which the pronoun refers. This word, known as an antecedent, is usually (but not always) the noun closest to the relative pronoun.

I have a roommate *who studies* day and night.
[The antecedent of *who* is the third-person singular noun *roommate.* Therefore, the verb in the subordinate clause is third-person singular, *studies.*]

I bought one of the new cars *that have* defective brakes.
[The antecedent of *that* is *cars,* so the verb is third-person plural, *have.*]

This is the only one of the mayor's new ideas *that has* any worth.
[Here *one,* not *ideas,* is the antecedent of *that.* Thus, the verb in the subordinate clause is third-person singular, *has,* not *have.*]

## 4i A verb agrees with its subject even when the subject follows the verb.

Introductory expressions such as *there* or *here* change the ordinary order so that the subject follows the verb. Remember that verbs agree with subjects and that *here* and *there* are never subjects.

Here *is* a *riddle* for you.

There *are* forty *people* in my law class.

Under the bridge *were* a broken-down *boat and* a worn *tire.*

## 4j A linking verb agrees with its subject, not its subject complement.

When a form of the verb *be* links two or more nouns, the subject is the noun before the linking verb. Nouns that follow the linking verb are subject complements. Make the verb agree with the subject of the sentence, not the subject complement.

*Jim is* a gentleman and a scholar.

Amy's *parents are* her most enthusiastic audience.

## 4k When the subject is a title, use a singular verb.

In sixth grade, *Harry Potter and the Sorcerer's Stone was* my favorite book.

*"People"* sung by Barbra Streisand *is* my aunt's favorite song.

## 4l Singular nouns that end in *-s* take singular verbs.

Some nouns look plural even though they refer to a singular subject: *measles, logistics, mathematics, electronics.* Such nouns take singular verbs.

The *news is* that *economics has become* one of the most popular majors.

**linking verb:** A verb (*is, become, seem, feel*) that shows a state of being by linking the sentence subject with a word that renames or describes the subject: The sky *is* blue. (See 3a.)

**subject complement:** A noun, an adjective, or a group of words that follows a linking verb and renames or describes the subject: This plum tastes *ripe.* (See 3a.)

## Exercise 4–1 ▪ Making Subjects and Verbs Agree

Find and correct any subject-verb agreement errors in the following sentences. Some sentences may be correct. Answers for the lettered sentences appear at the end of the handbook. Example:

Addressing the audience tonight is the nominees for club president.

Addressing the audience tonight *are* the nominees for club president.

a. For many college graduates, the process of looking for jobs are often long and stressful.

b. Not too long ago, searching the classifieds and inquiring in person was the primary methods of job hunting.

c. Today, however, everyone also seem to use the Internet to search for openings or to e-mail their résumés.

d. My classmates and my cousin sends most résumés over the Internet because it costs less than mailing them.

e. All of the résumés arrives quickly when they are sent electronically.

For more practice, visit **bedfordstmartins .com/bedguide**.

1. There are many people who thinks that interviewing is the most stressful part of the job search.
2. Sometimes only one person conducts an interview, while other times a whole committee conduct it.

3. Either the interviewer or the committee usually begin by asking simple questions about your background.
4. Making eye contact, dressing professionally, and appearing confident is some of the qualities an interviewer may consider important.
5. After an interview, most people sends a thank-you letter to the person who conducted it.

For advice on editing pronoun case, see A5 in the Quick Editing Guide, pp. A-45–A-46.

## 5 | Pronoun Case

The first-person pronoun can be *I, me, my, mine, we, us, our,* or *ours.* Which form do you pick? It depends on what job you want the pronoun to do.

Depending on a pronoun's function in a sentence, we say that it is in the **subjective case,** the **objective case,** or the **possessive case.** Some pronouns change form when they change case, and some do not. The personal pronouns *I, he, she, we,* and *they* and the relative pronoun *who* have different forms in the subjective, objective, and possessive cases. Other pronouns, such as *you* and *it,* have only two forms: the plain case (which serves as both subjective and objective) and the possessive case.

We can pin the labels *subjective, objective,* and *possessive* on nouns as well as on pronouns. Like the pronouns *you* and *it,* nouns shift from plain form only in the possessive (*teacher's* pet, *Jonas's* poodle, her *parents'* home).

When you are not sure which case to choose, beware of falling back on a reflexive pronoun (*myself, himself*). Instead of writing, "Return the form to John or *myself*" or "John and *myself* are in charge," replace the reflexive pronoun: "Return the form to John or *me*"; "John and *I* are in charge."

### 5a Use the subjective case for the subject of a sentence or clause.

Jed and *I* ate the granola.

*Who* cares?

Maya recalled that *she* played baseball.

Election officials are the people *who* count.

**subject:** The part of a sentence that names something—a person, an object, an idea, a situation—about which the predicate makes an assertion: The *king* lives.

A pronoun serving as the subject for a verb is subjective even when the verb isn't written but is only implied:

Jed is hungrier than *I* [am].

Don't be fooled by a pronoun that appears immediately after a verb, looking as if it were a direct object but functioning as the subject of a clause. The pronoun's case is determined by its role, not by its position.

The judge didn't believe *I* hadn't been the driver.

We were happy to interview *whoever* was running. [Subject of *was running*]

## 5b Use the subjective case for a subject complement.

When a pronoun functions as a subject complement, it plays essentially the same role as the subject and its case is subjective.

The phantom graffiti artist couldn't have been *he*. It was *I*.

## 5c Use the subjective case for an appositive to a subject or subject complement.

A pronoun in apposition to a subject or subject complement is like an identical twin to the noun it stands beside. It has the same meaning and case.

The class *officers*—Ravi and *she*—announced a senior breakfast.

## 5d Use the objective case for a direct object, an indirect object, the object of a preposition, or a subject of an infinitive.

The custard pies hit *him* and *me*. [Direct object]

Mona threw *us* towels. [Indirect object]

Mona threw towels to *him* and *us*. [Object of a preposition]

We always expect *him* to win. [Subject of an infinitive]

## 5e Use the objective case for an appositive to a direct or indirect object or the object of a preposition.

Mona helped us *all*—Mrs. Van Dumont, *him*, and *me*.
[*Him* and *me* are in apposition to the direct object *us*.]

Bob gave his favorite *students*, Tom and *her*, an approving nod.
[*Her* is in apposition to the indirect object *students*.]

Yelling, the team ran after *us*—Mona, *him*, and *me*.
[*Him* and *me* are in apposition to *us*, the object of the preposition *after*.]

## 5f Use the possessive case to show ownership.

Possessive pronouns can function as adjectives or as nouns. *My, your, his, her, its, our,* and *their* function as adjectives by modifying nouns or pronouns.

*My* new bike is having *its* first road test today.

The possessive pronoun *its* does not contain an apostrophe. *It's* with an apostrophe is a contraction for *it is*, as in "*It's* a beautiful day for bike riding."

The possessive pronouns *mine, yours, his, hers, ours,* and *theirs* can discharge the whole range of noun duties, serving as subjects, subject complements, direct objects, indirect objects, or objects of prepositions.

*Yours* is the last vote we need. [Subject]

This day is *ours*. [Subject complement]

**subject complement:** A noun, an adjective, or a group of words that follows a linking verb (*is, become, feel, seem,* or another verb that shows a state of being) and that renames or describes the subject: This plum tastes *ripe*. (See 3a.)
**appositive:** A word or group of words that adds information by identifying a subject or object in a different way: my dog *Rover,* Hal's brother *Fred*
**direct object:** The target of a verb that completes the action performed by the subject or asserted about the subject: I met *the sheriff.*
**indirect object:** A person or thing affected by the subject's action, usually the recipient of the direct object, through the action indicated by a verb such as *bring, get, offer, promise, sell, show, tell,* and *write:* Charlene asked *you* a question.
**object of a preposition:** The noun or pronoun that follows the preposition (such as *in, on, at, of, from*) that connects it to the rest of the sentence: She opened the door to the *garage.*
**infinitive:** The base form of a verb, often preceded by *to: to go, to play*

Don't take your car; take *mine.* [Direct object]

If we're honoring requests, give *hers* top priority. [Indirect object]

Give her request priority over *theirs.* [Object of a preposition]

For a chart of possessive personal pronouns, see C2 in the Quick Editing Guide, p. A-54.

## 5g Use the possessive case to modify a gerund.

A possessive pronoun (or possessive noun) is the appropriate escort for a gerund. As a noun, a gerund requires an adjective for a modifier.

**gerund:** A form of a verb, ending in *-ing,* that functions as a noun: Lacey likes *playing* in the steel band.

Mary is tired of *his griping.* [The possessive pronoun *his* modifies the gerund *griping.*]

I can stand *their being* late every day but not *his drinking* on the job. [The possessive pronoun *their* modifies the gerund *being*; the possessive pronoun *his* modifies the gerund *drinking.*]

However, editing possessives can be confusing because two different verb forms both end in *-ing*: gerunds that act as nouns and present participles that act as adjectives. If you are not sure whether to use a possessive for a gerund or an objective pronoun with a word ending in *-ing,* look closely at your sentence. Which word—the pronoun or the *-ing* word—is the object of your main verb? That word functions as a noun; the other word modifies it.

**present participle:** A form of a verb ending in *-ing* that cannot function alone as a main verb but can act as an adjective: *Leading* the pack, Michael crossed the finish line.

Mr. Phipps remembered *them* smoking in the boys' room. [Mr. Phipps remembers *them,* those naughty students. *Them* is the object of the verb, so *smoking* is a participle modifying *them.*]

Mr. Phipps remembered *their* smoking in the boys' room. [Mr. Phipps remembers *smoking,* that nasty habit. The gerund *smoking* is the object of the verb, and the possessive pronoun *their* modifies it.]

In everyday speech, rules about pronoun case apply less rigidly. Someone who correctly says, "To whom are you referring?" is likely to sound pretentious. Say, if you like, "It's *me,*" but in formal situations write "It is *I.*" Say, if you wish, "*Who* did he ask to the party?" but write "*Whom* did he ask?"

## Exercise 5-1 ▪ Using Pronouns Correctly

For more practice, visit **bedfordstmartins.com/bedguide**.

Replace any pronouns used incorrectly in the following sentences. Explain why each was incorrect. (Consider all these examples as written—not spoken—English, so apply the rules strictly.) Some sentences may be correct. Answers for the lettered sentences appear at the end of the handbook. Example:

That is her, the new university president, at the podium.

That is *she,* the new university president, at the podium. [*She* is a subject complement.]

a. I didn't appreciate you laughing at her and I.
b. Lee and me would be delighted to serenade whomever will listen.
c. The managers and us servers are highly trustworthy.
d. The neighbors were driven berserk by him singing.
e. Jerry and myself regard you and she as the very people who we wish to meet.

1. Have you guessed the identity of the person of who I am speaking?
2. It was him asking about the clock that started me suspecting him.
3. They—Jerry and her—are the troublemakers.
4. Mrs. Van Dumont awarded the prize to Mona and I.
5. The counterattack was launched by Dusty and myself.

# 6 | Pronoun Reference

The main use of pronouns is to refer in a brief, convenient form to some **antecedent** that has already been named. A pronoun usually has a noun or another pronoun as its antecedent. Often the antecedent is the subject or object of the same clause in which the pronoun appears.

> Josie hit the *ball* after *its* first bounce.
>
> Smashing into *Greg,* the ball knocked off *his* glasses.

The antecedent also can appear in a different clause or even a different sentence from the pronoun.

> *Josie* hit the *ball* when *it* bounced back to *her.*
>
> The *ball* smashed into *Greg. It* knocked off *his* glasses.

A pronoun as well as a noun can be an antecedent.

> My *dog* hid in the closet when *she* had *her* puppies. [*Dog* is the antecedent of *she*; *she* is the antecedent of *her.*]

## 6a Name the pronoun's antecedent: don't just imply it.

When editing, be sure you have identified clearly the antecedent of each pronoun. A writer who leaves a key idea unsaid is likely to confuse readers.

**antecedent:** The word to which a pronoun refers: *Lyn* plays golf, and *she* putts well.

> VAGUE Ted wanted a Norwegian canoe because he'd heard that *they* produce the lightest canoes afloat.

What noun or pronoun does *they* refer to? Not to *Norwegian,* which is an adjective. We may guess that this writer has in mind Norwegian canoe

For more on choosing *that* or *which*, see 21e.

For practice, visit **bedfordstmartins .com/bedguide**.

**ESL Guidelines** Adjective Clauses and Relative Pronouns

Be sure to use relative pronouns (*who, whose, which, that*) correctly in sentences with adjective clauses. Use *who,* not *which,* for a person. Select *that* to introduce necessary information that defines or specifies; reserve *which* for additional, but not defining, information.

- Do not omit the relative pronoun when it is the subject within the adjective clause.

INCORRECT The woman *gave us directions to the museum* told us not to miss the Picasso exhibit.

CORRECT The woman *who gave us directions to the museum* told us not to miss the Picasso exhibit.
[*Who* is the subject of the adjective clause.]

- In speech and informal writing, you can imply (not state) a relative pronoun when it is the object of a verb or preposition within the adjective clause. In formal writing, you should use the relative pronoun.

FORMAL Jamal forgot to return the book *that I gave him.*
[*That* is the object of *gave.*]

INFORMAL Jamal forgot to return the book *I gave him.*
[The relative pronoun *that* is implied.]

FORMAL This is the box *in which we found the jewelry.*
[*Which* is the object of the preposition *in.*]

INFORMAL This is the box *we found the jewelry in.*
[The relative pronoun *which* is implied.]

*NOTE:* When the relative pronoun is omitted, the preposition moves to the end of the sentence but must not be left out.

- *Whose* is the only possessive form of a relative pronoun. It is used with persons, animals, and things.

INCORRECT I bought a chair *that its* legs were wobbly.

CORRECT I bought a chair *whose* legs were wobbly.

*NOTE:* When in doubt about a pronoun, you can rephrase the sentence: I bought a chair *with wobbly legs.*

builders, but no such noun has been mentioned. To make the sentence work, the writer must supply an antecedent for *they.*

CLEAR Ted wanted a Norwegian canoe because he'd heard that Norway produces [*or* Norwegians produce] the lightest canoes afloat.

Watch out for possessive nouns. They won't work as antecedents.

VAGUE On William's canoe, *he* painted a skull and bones.

CLEAR On his canoe, William painted a skull and bones.

VAGUE In Hemingway's story, he describes the powerful sea.

CLEAR In the story, Hemingway describes the powerful sea.

## 6b Give the pronoun *it, this, that,* or *which* a clear antecedent.

**antecedent:** The word to which a pronoun refers: *Lyn* plays golf, and *she* putts well.

Vagueness arises, thick as fog, whenever *it, this, that,* or *which* points to something a writer assumes is said but indeed isn't. Often the best way out of the fog is to substitute a specific noun or expression for the pronoun.

VAGUE I was an only child, and *it* was hard.

CLEAR I was an only child, and my solitary life was hard.

VAGUE Judy could not get along with her younger brother. *This* is the reason she wanted to get her own apartment.

CLEAR Because Judy could not get along with her younger brother, she wanted to get her own apartment.

## 6c Make the pronoun's antecedent clear.

Confusion strikes if a pronoun points in two or more directions. When more than one antecedent is possible, the reader wonders which the writer means.

CONFUSING Hanwei shouted to Kenny to take off his burning sweater.

Whose sweater does *his* mean – Kenny's or Hanwei's? Simply changing a pronoun won't clear up the confusion. The writer needs to revise enough to move the two possible antecedents out of each other's way.

CLEAR "Kenny!" shouted Hanwei. "Your sweater's on fire! Take it off!"

CLEAR Flames were shooting from Kenny's sweater. Hanwei shouted to Kenny to take it off.

CLEAR Hanwei realized that his sweater was on fire and shouted to Kenny for help.

## 6d Place the pronoun close to its antecedent to keep the relationship clear.

Watch out for distractions that slip in between noun and pronoun. If your sentence contains two or more nouns that look like antecedents to a pronoun, your readers may become bewildered.

CONFUSING Harper steered his dinghy alongside the cabin cruiser that the drug smugglers had left anchored under an overhanging willow in the tiny harbor and eased it to a stop.

**antecedent:** The word to which a pronoun refers: *Lyn* plays golf, and *she* putts well.

What did Harper ease to a stop? By the time readers reach the end of the sentence, they are likely to have forgotten. To avoid confusion, keep the pronoun and its antecedent reasonably close together.

CLEAR Harper steered his dinghy into the tiny harbor and eased it to a stop alongside the cabin cruiser that the drug smugglers had left anchored under an overhanging willow.

Never force your readers to stop and think, "What does that pronoun stand for?" You, the writer, have to do this thinking for them.

## Exercise 6–1 ▪ Making Pronoun Reference Clear

For more practice, visit **bedfordstmartins.com/bedguide**.

Revise each sentence or group of sentences so that any pronoun needing an antecedent clearly points to one. Possible revisions for the lettered sentences appear at the end of the handbook. Example:

I took the money out of the wallet and threw it in the trash.

I took the money out of the wallet and threw *the wallet* in the trash.

a. I could see the moon and the faint shadow of the tree as it began to rise.

b. Katrina spent the summer in Paris and traveled throughout Europe, which broadened her awareness of cultural differences.

c. Most managers want employees to work as many hours as possible. They never consider the work they need to do at home.

d. I worked twelve hours a day and never got enough sleep, but it was worth it.

e. Kevin asked Mike to meet him for lunch but forgot that he had class at that time.

1. Bill's prank frightened Josh and made him wonder why he had done it.
2. Korean students study up to twenty subjects a year, including algebra, calculus, and engineering. Because they are required, they must study them year after year.
3. Pedro Martinez signed a baseball for Chad that he had used in a game.
4. When the bottle hit the windshield, it shattered.
5. My friends believe they are more mature than many of their peers because of the discipline enforced at their school. However, it can also lead to problems.

# 7 | Pronoun-Antecedent Agreement

A pronoun's job is to fill in for a noun, much as an actor's double fills in for the actor. Pronouns are a short, convenient way to avoid repeating the noun.

The sheriff drew a six-shooter; he fired twice.

In this action-packed sentence, first comes a noun (*sheriff*) and then a pronoun (*he*) that refers back to it. *Sheriff* is the antecedent of *he*. Just as verbs need to agree with their subjects, pronouns need to agree with the nouns they stand for without shifting number, person, or gender in midsentence.

For more on editing for pronoun-antecedent agreement, see A6 in the Quick Editing Guide, pp. A-46–A-48.

## 7a Pronouns agree with their antecedents in person and number.

A pronoun matches its antecedent in person (first, second, or third) and in number (singular or plural), even when intervening words separate the pronoun and its antecedent.

FAULTY All *campers* should bring *your* knapsacks.

Here, noun and pronoun disagree in person: third person *campers*; second person *your*.

FAULTY Every *camper* should bring *their* knapsack.

Here, noun and pronoun disagree in number: singular *camper*; plural *their*.

REVISED All *campers* should bring *their* knapsacks.

REVISED Every *camper* should bring *his or her* knapsack. (See also 7f.)

## 7b Most antecedents joined by *and* require a plural pronoun.

A **compound subject** is plural; use a plural pronoun to refer to it.

**compound subject:** A subject consisting of two or more nouns or pronouns linked by *and*: *Scott and Liz* drove home.

*George,* who has been here before, *and Jenn,* who hasn't, need *their* maps.

If the nouns in a compound subject refer to the same person or thing, they make up a singular antecedent. Use a singular pronoun too.

The *owner and founder* of this company carries *his* laptop everywhere.

## 7c A pronoun agrees with the closest part of an antecedent joined by *or* or *nor*.

If your subject is two or more nouns (or a combination of nouns and pronouns) connected by *or* or *nor*, look closely at the subject's parts. Are they all singular? If so, your pronoun should be singular.

Neither *Joy nor Jean* remembered *her* book last week.

If *Sam, Arthur, or Dieter* shows up, tell *him* I'm looking for *him*.

If the part of the subject closest to the pronoun is plural, the pronoun should be plural.

Neither *Joy nor her sisters* rode *their* bikes today.

If you see *Sam, Arthur, or their friends,* tell *them* I'm looking for *them.*

## 7d An antecedent that is a singular indefinite pronoun takes a singular pronoun.

For a list of indefinite pronouns, see A6 in the Quick Editing Guide, pp. A-46–A-48. For more on agreement with indefinite pronouns, see 4f and 7f.

Most indefinite pronouns (such as *everyone* and *anybody*) are singular in meaning, so the pronouns that refer to them are also singular.

*Either* of the boys can do it, as long as *he's* on time.

Warn *anybody* who's still in *her* swimsuit that a shirt is required for dinner.

An indefinite pronoun that is plural (*both, many*) takes a plural pronoun.

Tell *both* the guests I will see *them* soon.

## 7e Most collective nouns used as antecedents require singular pronouns.

When the members of a group (such as a committee, family, jury, or trio) act as a unit, use a singular pronoun to refer to them.

The *cast* for the play will be posted as soon as the director chooses *it.*

For more on agreement with collective nouns, see 4e.

When the group members act individually, use a plural pronoun.

The *cast* will go *their* separate ways when summer ends.

## 7f A pronoun agrees with its antecedent in gender.

If *one of your parents* brings you to camp, invite *him* for lunch.

For more on bias-free language, see 18.

While technically correct (the singular *he* refers to the singular *one*), this sentence overlooks the fact that some parents are male, some female.

If *one of your parents* brings you to camp, invite *him or her* for lunch.

If your *parents* bring you to camp, invite *them* for lunch.

---

## Exercise 7–1 ▪ Making Pronouns and Antecedents Agree

For more practice, visit **bedfordstmartins.com/bedguide**.

If any nouns and pronouns disagree in number, person, or gender in the following sentences, substitute pronouns that agree with the nouns. If you prefer, strengthen any sentence by rewriting it. Some sentences may be correct. Possible revisions for the lettered sentences appear at the end of the handbook. Example:

A cat expects people to feed them often.

A *cat* expects people to feed *it* often. *Or*

*Cats* expect people to feed *them* often.

a. Many architects find work their greatest pleasure.
b. Neither Melissa nor James has received their application form yet.
c. He is the kind of man who gets their fun out of just sipping one's beer and watching his Saturday games on TV.
d. Many a mother has mourned the loss of their child.
e. When one enjoys one's work, it's easy to spend all your spare time thinking about it.

1. All students are urged to complete your registration on time.
2. When a baby doesn't know their own mother, they may have been born with some kind of vision deficiency.
3. Each member of the sorority has to make her own bed.
4. If you don't like the songs the choir sings, don't join them.
5. Young people should know how to protect oneself against AIDS.

# 8 | Adjectives and Adverbs

An adjective's job is to provide information about the person, place, object, or idea named by the noun or pronoun.

Karen bought a *small red* car.

The radios *on sale* are an *excellent* value.

For advice on nouns and articles, see pp. 804–05.

For more on editing adjectives and adverbs, see A7 in the Quick Editing Guide, pp. A-48–A-49.

### Adjectives and Adverbs at a Glance

ADJECTIVES
1. Typically answer the question Which? or What kind?
2. Modify nouns or pronouns

ADVERBS
3. Answer the question How? When? Where? or sometimes Why?
4. Modify verbs, adjectives, and other adverbs

An adverb describes a verb, adjective, or other adverb.

Karen bought her car *quickly.*

The phones arrived *yesterday*; we put them *in the electronics department.*

## 8a Use an adverb, not an adjective, to modify a verb, adjective, or another adverb.

FAULTY Karen bought her car *quick.*

FAULTY It's *awful* hot today.

Though an informal speaker might get away with these sentences, a writer cannot. *Quick* and *awful* are adjectives, so they can modify only nouns or pronouns. Adverbs are needed to modify the verb *bought* and the adjective *hot.*

EDITED Karen bought her car *quickly.*

EDITED It's *awfully* hot today.

## 8b Use an adjective, not an adverb, as a subject complement or an object complement.

**subject complement:** A noun, an adjective, or a group of words that follows a linking verb (*is, become, feel, seem,* or another verb that shows a state of being) and renames or describes the subject: This plum tastes *ripe.* (See 3a.)

**object complement:** A noun, an adjective, or a group of words that renames or describes a direct object: The judges rated Hugo *the best skater.*

If we write, "Her old car looked awful," the adjective *awful* is a **subject complement**: it follows a linking verb and modifies the subject, *car.* An **object complement** completes the description of a direct object and can be an adjective or a noun, but never an adverb.

Early to bed and early to rise makes a man *healthy, wealthy,* and *wise.*
[Adjectives modifying the direct object *man*]

When you are not sure whether you're dealing with an object complement or an adverb, look closely at the word's role in the sentence. If it modifies a noun, it is an object complement and should be an adjective.

The coach called the referee *stupid* and *blind.*
[*Stupid* and *blind* are adjectives modifying the direct object *referee.*]

If it modifies a verb, you want an adverb instead.

In fact, the ref had called the play *correctly.*
[*Correctly* is an adverb modifying the verb *called.*]

## 8c Use *good* as an adjective and *well* as an adverb.

This sandwich tastes *good.* [The adjective *good* is a subject complement following the linking verb *tastes* and modifying the noun *sandwich.*]

Al's skin healed *well* after surgery.
[The adverb *well* modifies the verb *healed.*]

## ESL Guidelines Cumulative Adjectives

**Cumulative adjectives** are two or more adjectives used directly before a noun and not separated by commas or the word *and.*

She is an *attractive older French* woman.

His *expressive large brown* eyes moved me.

Cumulative adjectives usually follow a specific order of placement before a noun. Use this list as a guide, but keep in mind that the order can vary.

1. Articles or determiners
   *a, an, the, some, this, these, his, my, two, several*
2. Evaluative adjectives
   *beautiful, wonderful, hardworking, distasteful*
3. Size or dimension
   *big, small, huge, obese, petite, six-foot*
4. Length or shape
   *long, short, round, square, oblong, oval*
5. Age
   *old, young, new, fresh, ancient*
6. Color
   *red, pink, aquamarine, orange*
7. Nation or place of origin
   *American, Japanese, European, Bostonian, Floridian*
8. Religion
   *Protestant, Muslim, Hindu, Buddhist, Catholic, Jewish*
9. Matter or substance
   *wood, gold, cotton, plastic, pine, metal*
10. Noun used as an adjective
    *car* (as in *car mechanic*), *computer* (as in *computer software*)

For advice on using commas with adjectives, see 21d.

For practice, visit **bedfordstmartins .com/bedguide**.

Only if the verb is a linking verb can you safely follow it with *good.* Other kinds of verbs need adverbs, not subject complements.

FAULTY After a bad start, the game ended *good.*

EDITED After a bad start, the game ended *well.*

Complications arise when we write or speak about health. It is perfectly correct to say *I feel good,* using the adjective *good* as a subject complement after the linking verb *feel.* However, generations of confusion have nudged the

**linking verb:** A verb (*is, become, seem, feel*) that shows a state of being by linking the sentence subject with a word that renames or describes the subject: The sky *is* blue. (See 3a.)

For practice, visit **bedfordstmartins.com/bedguide**.

## ESL Guidelines Count and Noncount Nouns and Articles

### Count Nouns and Articles

Nouns referring to items that can be counted are called **count** (or **countable**) nouns. Count nouns can be made plural.

*table, chair, egg* two *tables,* several *chairs,* a dozen *eggs*

Singular count nouns must be preceded by a **determiner.** The class of words called determiners includes **articles** (*a, an, the*), **possessives** (*John's, your, his, my,* and so on), **demonstratives** (*this, that, these, those*), **numbers** (*three, the third,* and so on), and **indefinite quantity words** (*no, some, many,* and so on).

*a* dog, *the* football, *one* reason, *the* first page, *no* chance

### Noncount Nouns and Articles

Nouns referring to items that cannot be counted are called **noncount** (or **uncountable**) nouns. Noncount nouns cannot be made plural.

INCORRECT I need to learn more *grammars.*

CORRECT I need to learn more *grammar.*

- Common categories of noncount nouns include types of **food** (*cheese, meat, bread*), **solids** (*dirt, salt, chalk*), **liquids** (*milk, juice, gasoline*), **gases** (*methane, hydrogen, air*), and **abstract ideas,** including emotions (*democracy, gravity, love*).
- Another category of noncount nouns is **mass** nouns, which usually represent a large group of countable nouns (*furniture, mail, clothing*).
- The only way to count noncountable nouns is to use a countable noun with them, usually to indicate a quantity or a container.

  one *piece* of furniture, two *quarts* of water, an *example* of jealousy
- Noncount nouns, such as *advice,* are never preceded by an indefinite article; they are often preceded by *some.*

  INCORRECT She gave us *a* good advice.

  CORRECT She gave us good advice.

  CORRECT She gave us *some* good advice.
- When noncount nouns are *general* in meaning, no article is required, but when the context makes them specific (usually in a phrase or a clause after the noun), the definite article is used.

  GENERAL Good continues to fight *evil.*

  SPECIFIC The *evil* that humans do lives after them.

**count noun:** A noun with both singular and plural forms that refers to an item that can be counted: *apple, apples*

**noncount noun:** A noun that cannot be made plural because it refers to an item that cannot be counted: *cheese, salt, air*

## ESL Guidelines Definite and Indefinite Articles

**The Definite Article (*the*)**

- Use *the* with a specific count or noncount noun mentioned before or familiar to both the writer and the reader.

  She got a huge box in the mail. *The* box contained oranges from Florida. [*The* is used the second time the noun (*box*) is mentioned.]

  Did you feed *the* baby? [Both reader and writer know which baby.]

- Use *the* before specific count or noncount nouns when the reader is given enough information to identify what is being referred to.

  *The* furniture in my apartment is old and faded. [Specific furniture]

- Use *the* before a singular count noun to state a generality.

  *The* dog has been a companion for centuries. [*The dog* refers to all dogs.]

- Use *the* before some geographical names.

  *Collective Nations:* the United States, the United Kingdom

  *Groups of Islands:* the Bahamas, the Canary Islands

  *Large Bodies of Water* (except lakes): the Atlantic Ocean, the Dead Sea, the Monongahela River, the Gulf of Mexico

  *Mountain Ranges:* the Rockies, the Himalayas

- Use *the* or another determiner when plural count nouns name a definite or specific group; use no article when they name a general group.

  Hal is feeding *the horses* in the barn, and he has already fed *his cows*.

  *Horses* don't eat meat, and neither do *cows*.

**The Indefinite Article (*a, an*)**

- Use *a* or *an* with a nonspecific, singular count noun when it is not known to the reader or to the writer.

  Jay has *an* antique car.
  [The car's identity is unknown to the reader.]

  I saw *a* dog in my backyard this morning.
  [The dog's identity is unknown to the writer.]

- Use *a* or *an* when the noun is first used; use *the* when it is repeated.

  I saw *a* car that I would love to buy. *The* car was red with tan seats.

- Use *some* or no article with general noncount or plural nouns.

| | |
|---|---|
| INCORRECT | I am going to buy *a* furniture for my apartment. |
| CORRECT | I am going to buy *some* furniture for my apartment. |
| CORRECT | I am going to buy furniture for my apartment. |

**indefinite article:** An article (*a* or *an*) that indicates any one of many possible items: I will make *a* cake or *an* apple pie.

**definite article:** An article (*the*) that indicates one particular item: I ordered *the* spaghetti, not *the* lasagna.

adverb *well* into the adjective category, too. A nurse may speak of "a well baby"; greeting cards urge patients to "get well"—meaning, "become healthy." Just as *healthy* is an adjective here, so is *well.*

When someone asks, "How do you feel?" you can duck the issue with "Fine!" Otherwise, in speech *good* or *well* is acceptable; in writing, use *good.*

## 8d Form comparatives and superlatives of most adjectives and adverbs with *-er* and *-est* or *more* and *most.*

Comparatives and superlatives are forms that describe one thing in relation to another. Put most adjectives into comparative form (for two things) by adding *-er* and into superlative form (for three or more) by adding *-est.*

> The budget deficit is *larger* than the trade deficit.
>
> This year's trade deficit is the *largest* ever.

We usually form the comparative and superlative of potentially cumbersome long adjectives with *more* and *most* rather than with *-er* and *-est.*

> The lake is *more beautiful* than I'd imagined.
>
> The shoreline is the *most beautiful* in the region.

For short adverbs that do not end in *-ly,* usually add *-er* and *-est.* With all others, use *more* and *most.* (Also see 8f.)

> The trade deficit grows *fastest* and *most uncontrollably* when exports fall.

For negative comparisons, use *less* and *least* for adjectives and adverbs.

> Michael's speech was *less dramatic* than Louie's.
>
> Paulette spoke *less dramatically* than Michael.

For a chart of comparative forms of irregular adjectives and adverbs, see A7 in the Quick Editing Guide, p. A-48.

Use irregular adjectives and adverbs (such as *bad* and *badly*) with care.

> Tom's golf game is *bad,* but no *worse* than George's.
>
> Tom plays golf *badly,* but no *worse* than George does.

## 8e Omit *more* and *most* with an adjective or adverb that is already comparative or superlative.

Some words become comparative or superlative when we tack on *-er* or *-est.* Others, such as *top, favorite,* and *unique,* mark whatever they modify as one of a kind. Neither category requires further assistance to make its point. To say "a *more worse* fate" or "my *most favorite* movie" is redundant.

FAULTY Lisa is *more uniquely* qualified for the job than any other candidate.

EDITED Lisa is *better* qualified for the job than any other candidate.

EDITED Lisa is *uniquely* qualified for the job.

## 8f Use the comparative form of an adjective or adverb to compare two people or things, the superlative form to compare more than two.

No matter how wonderful something is, we can call it the *best* only when we compare it with more than one other thing. Any comparison between two things uses the comparative form (*better*), not the superlative (*best*).

FAULTY Chocolate and vanilla are both good, but I like chocolate *best.*

EDITED Chocolate and vanilla are both good, but I like chocolate *better.*

### Exercise 8–1 ▪ Using Adjectives and Adverbs Correctly

For more practice, visit **bedfordstmartins.com/bedguide**.

Find and correct any incorrect adjectives and adverbs in the following sentences. Some sentences may be correct. Answers for the lettered sentences appear at the end of the handbook. Example:

The deal worked out good for both of us.
The deal worked out *well* for both of us.

a. Credit-card debt is becoming increasing common among students.
b. Students often lack the necessary experience to use their credit cards wisely.
c. Some students charge many items on different cards and make only the lower payments possible each month.
d. Unfortunately, when juggling multiple credit cards, many students lose sight of how rapid the debt is accumulating.
e. It is a well idea to charge only as much as you can pay in full each month.

1. A popular trend in television today is voyeurism, or the act of secret watching people as they go about their daily lives.
2. In the late 1990s, the popularity of MTV's *The Real World* sparked increasingly interest in this concept.
3. Music videos and commercials also began to incorporate voyeuristic elements, although, of the two, videos used the technique most frequently.
4. With the millennium came a flood of new "reality" programs, all trying to capitalize more distinctively on the current trend.
5. On the program *Survivor*, contestants are filmed living in challenging settings with limited supplies, while viewers at home watch breathless to see how the contestants will behave.

# 9 | Shifts

Just as you can change position to view a scene from different vantage points, in your writing you can change the time or perspective. However, shifting tense or point of view unconsciously or unnecessarily within a passage creates ambiguity and confusion for readers.

## 9a Maintain consistency in verb tense.

**tense:** The time when the action of a verb did, does, or will occur

In a passage or an essay, use the same verb tense unless the time changes.

| | |
|---|---|
| INCONSISTENT | The driver *yelled* at us to get off the bus, so I *ask* him why, and he *tells* me it *is* none of my business. |
| CONSISTENT PRESENT | The driver *yells* at us to get off the bus, so I *ask* him why, and he *tells* me it *is* none of my business. |
| CONSISTENT PAST | The driver *yelled* at us to get off the bus, so I *asked* him why, and he *told* me it *was* none of my business. |

## 9b If the time changes, change the verb tense.

To write about events in the past, use past tense verbs. To write about events in the present, use present tense verbs. If the time shifts, change tense.

> I *do* not *like* the new television programs this year. The comedies *are* too realistic to be amusing, the adventure shows *don't have* much action, and the law enforcement dramas *drag* on and on. Last year the programs *were* different. The sitcoms *were* hilarious, the adventure shows *were* action packed, and the dramas *were* fast paced. I *prefer* last year's reruns to this year's shows.

The time and the verb tense change appropriately from present (*do like, are, don't have, drag*) to past (*were, were, were, were*) back to present (*prefer*), contrasting this year's *present* with last year's *past* programming.

NOTE: When writing about literature, the accepted practice is to use present tense verbs to summarize what happens in a story, poem, or play. When discussing other aspects of a work, use present tense for present time, past tense for past, and future tense for future.

> Steinbeck *wrote* "The Chrysanthemums" in 1937. [Past tense for past time]
>
> In "The Chrysanthemums," Steinbeck *describes* the Salinas Valley as "a closed pot" cut off from the world by fog. [Present tense for story summary]

## 9c Maintain consistency in the voice of verbs.

For more on using active and passive voice, see 3m.

Shifting unnecessarily from active to passive voice may confuse readers.

| | |
|---|---|
| INCONSISTENT | My roommates and I *sit* up late many nights talking about our problems. Grades, teachers, jobs, money, and dates *are discussed* at length. |

CONSISTENT — My roommates and I *sit* up late many nights talking about our problems. We *discuss* grades, teachers, jobs, money, and dates at length.

## 9d Maintain consistency in person.

Person indicates your perspective as a writer. First person (*I, we*) establishes a personal, informal relationship with readers as does second person (*you*), which brings readers into the writing. Third person (*he, she, it, they*) is more formal and objective. In a formal scientific report, second person is seldom appropriate, and first, if used, might be reserved for reporting procedures. In a personal essay, using *he, she,* or *one* to refer to yourself would sound stilted. Choose the person appropriate for your purpose, and stick to it.

For more on pronoun forms, see 5 and also A5 in the Quick Editing Guide, pp. A-45–A-46.

INCONSISTENT — College *students* need transportation, but *you* need a job to pay for the insurance and the gasoline.

CONSISTENT — College *students* need transportation, but *they* need jobs to pay for the insurance and the gasoline.

INCONSISTENT — *Anyone* can go skydiving if *you* have the guts.

CONSISTENT — *Anyone* can go skydiving if *he or she* has the guts.

CONSISTENT — *You* can go skydiving if *you* have the guts.

## 9e Maintain consistency in the mood of verbs.

Avoid shifts in mood, usually from indicative to imperative.

For examples of the three moods of verbs, see 3n–3p.

INCONSISTENT — Counselors *advised* students to register early. Also *pay* tuition on time. [Shift from indicative to imperative]

CONSISTENT — Counselors *advised* students to register early. They also *advised* them to pay their tuition on time. [Both indicative]

## 9f Maintain consistency in level of language.

To impress readers, writers sometimes inflate their language or slip into slang. The level of language should fit your purpose and audience throughout an essay. For a personal essay, use informal language.

INCONSISTENT — I felt like a typical tourist. I carried an expensive digital camera with lots of icons I didn't quite know how to decode. But I was in a quandary because there was such a plethora of picturesque tableaus to record for posterity.

Instead of suddenly shifting to formal language, the writer could end simply: *But with so much beautiful scenery all around, I couldn't decide where to start.*

For an academic essay, use formal language.

INCONSISTENT Puccini's *Turandot* is set in a China of legends, riddles, and fantasy. Brimming with beautiful melodies, this opera is music drama at its most spectacular. It rules!

Cutting the last sentence avoids an unnecessary shift in formality.

## Exercise 9–1 ▪ Maintaining Grammatical Consistency

For more practice, visit **bedfordstmartins .com/bedguide**.

Revise the following sentences to eliminate shifts in verb tense, voice, mood, person, and level of language. Possible revisions for the lettered sentences appear at the end of the handbook. Example:

I needed the job at the restaurant, so I tried to tolerate the insults of my boss, but a person can take only so much.

I needed the job at the restaurant, so I tried to tolerate the insults of my boss, but *I could* take only so much.

a. Dr. Jamison is an erudite professor who cracks jokes in class.

b. The audience listened intently to the lecture, but the message was not understood.

c. Scientists can no longer evade the social, political, and ethical consequences of what they did in the laboratory.

d. To have good government, citizens must become informed on the issues. Also, be sure to vote.

e. Good writing is essential to success in many professions, especially in business, where ideas must be communicated in down-to-earth lingo.

1. Our legal system made it extremely difficult to prove a bribe. If the charges are not proven to the satisfaction of a jury or a judge, then we jump to the conclusion that the absence of a conviction demonstrates the innocence of the subject.
2. Before Morris K. Udall, Democrat from Arizona, resigns his seat in the U.S. House of Representatives, he helped preserve hundreds of acres of wilderness.
3. Anyone can learn another language if you have the time and the patience.
4. The immigration officer asked how long we planned to stay, so I show him my letter of acceptance from Tulane.
5. Archaeologists spent many months studying the site of the African city of Zimbabwe, and many artifacts were uncovered.

# Effective Sentences 39



**Learning by Doing** Focusing on Sentences

Tackle a sentence error that can undermine your credibility with academic readers — maybe fragments, comma splices, fused sentences, incorrect agreement, or shifts. Write down what you already know about how to find and fix the problem. Then look up the advice in this book's handbook, Quick Editing Guide, or Web site. Based on this research, present your own online posting or class handout with advice and examples to classmates.

## 10 | Misplaced and Dangling Modifiers

The purpose of a **modifier,** such as an adjective or adverb, is to give readers more information. To do so, the modifier must be linked clearly to whatever it is meant to modify or describe. If you wrote, "We saw a stone wall around a house on a grassy hill, beautiful and distant," your readers would have to guess what was *beautiful* and *distant:* the wall, the house, or the hill. Edit your modifiers — especially prepositional phrases and subordinate clauses — to make sure each is in the right place.

For more on editing for misplaced or dangling modifiers, see B1 in the Quick Editing Guide, p. A-49.

### 10a Keep modifiers close to what they modify.

**Misplaced modifiers** — phrases and clauses that wander away from what they modify — produce results more likely to amuse readers than to inform them. Place your modifiers as close as possible to whatever they modify.

MISPLACED She offered toys to all the children in colorful packages. [Does the phrase *in colorful packages* modify *toys* or *children*?]

CLEAR She offered toys in colorful packages to all the children.

MISPLACED We removed the dishes from the crates that got chipped. [Does the clause *that got chipped* modify *dishes* or *crates*?]

CLEAR We removed from the crates the dishes that got chipped.

## 10b Place each modifier so that it clearly modifies only one thing.

A **squinting modifier** is one that looks two ways, leaving the reader uncertain whether it modifies the word before or after it. To avoid ambiguity, place your modifier close to the word it modifies and away from another that might cause confusion.

SQUINTING The book that appealed to Amy *tremendously* bored Marcus.

CLEAR The book that *tremendously* appealed to Amy bored Marcus.

CLEAR The book that appealed to Amy bored Marcus *tremendously*.

### Exercise 10-1 ▪ Placing Modifiers

For more practice, visit **bedfordstmartins.com/bedguide**.

Revise the following sentences, which contain modifiers that are misplaced or squinting. Possible revisions for the lettered sentences appear at the end of the handbook. Example:

Patti found the cat using a flashlight in the dark.

*Using a flashlight in the dark,* Patti found the cat.

a. The bus got stuck in a ditch full of passengers.

b. He was daydreaming about fishing for trout in the middle of a meeting.

c. The boy threw the paper airplane through an open window with a smirk.

d. I reached for my sunglasses when the glare appeared from the glove compartment.

e. High above them, Sally and Glen watched the kites drift back and forth.

1. In her soup she found a fly at one of the best restaurants in town.
2. Andy learned how to build kites from the pages of an old book.
3. Alex vowed to return to the island sometime soon on the day he left it.
4. The fish was carried in a suitcase wrapped in newspaper.
5. The reporters were informed of the crimes committed by a press release.

## 10c State something in the sentence for each modifier to modify.

Generally readers assume that a modifying phrase at the start of a sentence refers to the subject of the main clause to follow. If readers encounter a modifying phrase midway through a sentence, they assume that it modifies something just before or (less often) after it.

**main clause:** A group of words that has both a subject and a verb and can stand alone as a complete sentence: *My friends play softball.*

*Feeling tired after the long hike, Jason* went to bed.

*Alicia, while sympathetic,* was not inclined to help.

Sometimes a writer slips up, allowing a modifying phrase to dangle. A **dangling modifier** is one that doesn't modify anything in its sentence.

DANGLING *Noticing a pain behind his eyes,* an aspirin seemed a good idea. [The opening doesn't modify *aspirin* or, in fact, anything.]

To correct a dangling modifier, first figure out what noun, pronoun, or noun phrase the modifier is meant to modify. Then make that word or phrase the subject of the main clause.

CLEAR *Noticing a pain behind his eyes, he* decided to take an aspirin.

Another way to correct a dangling modifier is to turn the dangler into a clause that includes the missing noun or pronoun.

DANGLING Her progress, *although talented,* has been slowed by poor work habits.

CLEAR *Although she is talented,* her progress has been slowed by poor work habits.

Sometimes rewriting will clarify what the modifier modifies.

CLEAR *Although talented,* she has been hampered by poor work habits.

## Exercise 10–2 ▪ Revising Dangling Modifiers

For more practice, visit **bedfordstmartins.com/bedguide**.

Revise any sentences that contain dangling modifiers. Some sentences may be correct. Possible revisions for the lettered sentences appear at the end of the handbook. Example:

> Angry at her poor showing, geology would never be Joan's favorite class.
>
> *Angry at her poor showing, Joan* knew that geology would never be her favorite class.

a. Unpacking the suitcase, a horrible idea occurred to me.
b. After fixing breakfast that morning, the oven might be left on at home.
c. Trying to reach my neighbor, her phone was busy.
d. Desperate to get information, my solution was to ask my mother to drive over to check the oven.
e. With enormous relief, my mother's call confirmed everything was fine.

1. After working six hours, the job was done.
2. Further information can be obtained by calling the specified number.
3. To compete in the Olympics, talent, training, and dedication are needed.
4. Pressing hard on the brakes, the car spun into a hedge.
5. Showing a lack of design experience, the architect advised the student to take her model back to the drawing board.

# 11 | Incomplete Sentences

For advice on editing fragments, see 1 and also A1 in the Quick Editing Guide, p. A-40.

A fragment fails to qualify as a sentence because it lacks a subject or a predicate (or both) or it fails to express a complete thought. However, a sentence with the essentials can still miss the mark. If it lacks a crucial word or phrase, the sentence may be *incomplete.* When you make comparisons and use elliptical constructions, be certain that you complete the thought you want to express.

## Comparisons

### 11a Make your comparisons clear by stating fully what you are comparing with what.

INCOMPLETE Roscoe loves spending time online more than Diane.

Does Roscoe prefer the company of a keyboard to the company of his friend? Or, of these two people, is Roscoe (and not Diane) the online addict? Adding a word would complete the comparison.

CLEAR Roscoe loves spending time online more than Diane *does.*

CLEAR Roscoe loves spending time online more than *with* Diane.

## 11b When you start to draw a comparison, finish it.

The unfinished comparison is a favorite of advertisers—"Our product is better!"—because it dodges the question "Better than what?" A sharp writer knows that any item must be compared *with* something else.

INCOMPLETE Scottish tweeds are warmer.

COMPLETE Scottish tweeds are warmer *than any other fabric you can buy.*

## 11c Be sure the things you compare are of the same kind.

A sentence that compares should reassure readers on two counts: the items are similar enough to compare, and the terms of comparison are clear.

INCOMPLETE The engine of a Ford truck is heavier than a Piper Cub airplane.

What is being compared? Truck engine and airplane? Or engine and engine? Because a truck engine is unlikely to outweigh a plane, we can guess the writer meant to compare engines. Readers, however, should not have to make the effort to complete a writer's thought.

CLEAR The engine of a Ford truck is heavier than *that of* a Piper Cub airplane.

CLEAR A Ford truck's engine is heavier than a *Piper Cub's.*

In this last example, parallel structure (*Ford truck's* and *Piper Cub's*) helps to make the comparison concise as well as clear.

For more on parallel structure, see 13.

## 11d To compare an item with others of its kind, use *any other.*

A comparison using *any* shows how something relates to a group without belonging to the group.

Alaska is larger than *any* country in Central America.

A comparison using *any other* shows how one member of a group relates to other members of the same group.

Death Valley is drier than *any other* place in the United States.

## Exercise 11–1 ■ Completing Comparisons

For more practice, visit **bedfordstmartins.com/bedguide**.

Revise the following sentences by adding needed words to any comparisons that are incomplete. (There may be more than one way to complete some comparisons.) Some sentences may be correct. Possible revisions for the lettered sentences appear at the end of the handbook. Example:

> I hate hot weather more than you.
>
> I hate hot weather more than you *do. Or*
>
> I hate hot weather more than *I hate* you.

a. The movie version of *The Brady Bunch* was much more ironic.
b. Taking care of a dog is often more demanding than a cat.
c. I received more free calendars in the mail for 2014 than any year.
d. The crime rate in the United States is higher than Canada.
e. Liver contains more iron than any meat.

1. Driving a sports car means more to Jake than his professors.
2. People who go to college aren't necessarily smarter, but they will always have an advantage at job interviews.
3. I don't have as much trouble getting along with Michelle as Karen.
4. A hen lays fewer eggs than a turtle.
5. Singing is closer to prayer than a meal of Chicken McNuggets.

## Elliptical Constructions

Robert Frost begins his well-known poem "Fire and Ice" with these lines:

> Some say the world will end in fire, / Some say in ice.

When Frost wrote that opening, he avoided needless repetition by implying certain words rather than stating them. The result is more concise and more effective than a complete version of the same sentence would be:

> Some say the world will end in fire, some say the world will end in ice.

This common tactic produces an **elliptical construction** – one that leaves out (for conciseness) words that are unnecessary but clearly understood by readers. Elliptical constructions can be confusing, however, if a writer gives readers too little information to fill in those missing words.

## 11e When you eliminate repetition, keep all the words essential for clarity.

An elliptical construction avoids repeating what a reader already knows, but it should omit only words that are stated elsewhere in the sentence, including prepositions. Otherwise, your reader may fill the gap incorrectly.

INCOMPLETE The train neither goes nor returns from Middletown.

Readers are likely to fill in an extra *from* after *goes.* Write instead:

COMPLETE The train neither goes *to* nor returns from Middletown.

## 11f In a compound predicate, leave out only verb forms that have already been stated.

Compound predicates are prone to incomplete constructions, especially if the verbs are in different tenses. Be sure no necessary part is missing.

**compound predicate:** A predicate consisting of two or more verbs linked by a conjunction: My sister *stopped and stared.*

INCOMPLETE Lee never has and never will vote to raise taxes.

COMPLETE Lee never has *voted* and never will vote to raise taxes.

## 11g If you mix comparisons using *as* and *than,* include both words.

To contrast two things, use the comparative form of an adjective followed by *than: better than, more than, fewer than.* To show a similarity between two things, sandwich the simple form of an adjective between *as* and *as: as good as, as many as, as few as.* Often you can combine two *than* or two *as* comparisons into an elliptical construction.

For more on comparative forms, see 8d–8f.

The White House is smaller [than] and newer than Buckingham Palace.

Some elegant homes are as large [as] and as grand as the White House.

However, merging a *than* comparison with an *as* comparison won't work.

INCOMPLETE The White House is smaller but just as beautiful as Buckingham Palace.

COMPLETE The White House is smaller *than* but just *as* beautiful *as* Buckingham Palace.

## Exercise 11–2 ▪ Completing Sentences

Revise the following sentences by adding needed words to any constructions that are incomplete. (There may be more than one way to complete some constructions.) Some sentences may be correct. Possible revi-

For more practice, visit **bedfordstmartins .com/bedguide**.

sions for the lettered sentences appear at the end of the handbook. Example:

The general should have but didn't see the perils of invasion.

The general should have *seen* but didn't see the perils of invasion.

a. Eighteenth-century China was as civilized and in many respects more sophisticated than the Western world.
b. Pembroke was never contacted, much less involved with, the election committee.
c. I haven't yet but soon will finish my research paper.
d. Ron likes his popcorn with butter, Linda with parmesan cheese.
e. George Washington always has been and will be regarded as the father of this country.

1. You have traveled to exotic Tahiti; Maureen to Asbury Park, New Jersey.
2. The mayor refuses to negotiate or even talk to the civic association.
3. Building a new sewage treatment plant would be no more costly and just as effective as modifying the existing one.
4. You'll be able to tell Jon from the rest of the team: Jon wears white Reeboks, the others black high-tops.
5. Erosion has and always will reshape the shoreline.

**phrase:** Two or more related words that work together but may lack a subject (as in *will walk*), a verb (*my uncle*), or both (*to the attic*)

**clause:** A group of related words that includes both a subject and a verb: *The sailboats raced* (independent clause) *until the sun set* (subordinate clause).

**preposition:** A transitional word (such as *in, on, at, of, from*) that leads into a phrase such as *in the bar, under a rickety table*

## 12 | Mixed Constructions and Faulty Predication

Sometimes a sentence contains all the necessary ingredients but still doesn't make sense. The problem may be a discord between two or more of its parts: phrases or clauses that don't fit together (a *mixed construction*) or a verb and its subject, object, or modifier (*faulty predication*) that don't match.

### 12a Link phrases and clauses logically.

A **mixed construction** results when a writer connects phrases or clauses (or both) that don't work together as a sentence.

MIXED In her efforts to solve the tax problem only caused the mayor additional difficulties.

The prepositional phrase *In her efforts to solve the tax problem* is a modifier; it can't act as the subject of a sentence. The writer, however, has used this phrase as a noun—the subject of the verb *caused.* To untangle this mixed construction, the writer has two choices: (1) rewrite the phrase so that it works as a noun, or (2) use the phrase as a modifier, not a subject.

REVISED Her efforts to solve the tax problem only caused the mayor additional difficulties.
[With *in* gone, *efforts* becomes the subject.]

REVISED In her efforts to solve the tax problem, the mayor created additional difficulties.
[The phrase now modifies the verb *created*.]

## ESL Guidelines Mixed Constructions, Faulty Predication, and Subject Errors

**Mixed constructions** result when phrases or clauses are joined even though they do not logically go together. Combine clauses with either a coordinating conjunction or a subordinating conjunction, never both.

INCORRECT *Although* baseball is called "the national pastime" of the United States, *but* football is probably more popular.

CORRECT *Although* baseball is called "the national pastime" of the United States, football is probably more popular.

CORRECT Baseball is called "the national pastime" of the United States, *but* football is probably more popular.

**Faulty predication** results when a verb and its subject, object, or modifier do not match. Do not use a noun as both the subject of the sentence and the object of a preposition.

INCORRECT *In my neighborhood has* several good restaurants.

CORRECT *My neighborhood has* several good restaurants.

CORRECT *In my neighborhood, there are* several good restaurants.

**Subject errors** include leaving out and repeating subjects of clauses.

- Do not omit *it* used as a subject. A subject is required in all English sentences except commands (imperatives).

  INCORRECT *Is* interesting to visit museums.

  CORRECT *It is* interesting to visit museums.

- Do not repeat the subject of a sentence with a pronoun.

  INCORRECT *My brother-in-law, he* is a successful investor.

  CORRECT *My brother-in-law* is a successful investor.

For more on coordination and subordination, see 14a–14f.

**coordinating conjunction:** A one-syllable linking word (*and, but, for, or, nor, so, yet*) that joins elements with equal or near-equal importance: Jack *and* Jill, sink *or* swim

**subordinating conjunction:** A word (such as *because, although, if, when*) used to make one clause dependent on, or subordinate to, another: *Unless* you have a key, we are locked out.

To fix a mixed construction, check your links—especially prepositions and conjunctions.

MIXED Jack, although he was picked up by the police, but was not charged.

Using both *although* and *but* gives this sentence one link too many.

REVISED Jack was picked up by the police but was not charged.

REVISED Although he was picked up by the police, Jack was not charged.

**subject:** The part of a sentence that names something—a person, an object, an idea, a situation—about which the predicate makes an assertion: The *king* lives.
**predicate:** The part of a sentence that makes an assertion about the subject involving an action (Birds *fly*), a relationship (Birds *have feathers*), or a state of being (Birds *are warm-blooded*)
**direct object:** The target of a verb that completes the action performed by or asserted about the subject: I met *the sheriff.*
**linking verb:** A verb (*is, become, seem, feel*) that shows a state of being by linking the sentence subject with a subject complement that renames or describes the subject: The sky *is* blue. (See 3a.)

For more on using active and passive voice, see 3m.

## 12b Relate the parts of a sentence logically.

**Faulty predication** refers to a skewed relationship between a verb and some other part of a sentence.

FAULTY *The temperature of water freezes* at 32 degrees Fahrenheit.

At first glance, that sentence looks all right. It contains both subject and predicate. It expresses a complete thought. What is wrong with it? The writer has mismatched the subject and verb. The sentence tells us that *temperature freezes,* when science and common sense tell us *water* freezes. The writer needs to select a subject and verb that fit each other.

REVISED *Water freezes* at 32 degrees Fahrenheit.

Faulty predication also results from a mismatched verb and direct object.

FAULTY Rising costs *diminish college* for many students.

Costs don't *diminish college.* To correct this error, the writer must change the sentence so that its direct object follows logically from its verb.

REVISED Rising costs *diminish the number of students who can attend college.*

Subtler predication errors result when a writer uses a linking verb to forge a false connection between the subject and a subject complement.

FAULTY *Industrial waste* has become *an important modern priority.*

Is it *waste* that has become a *priority*? Or is it *solving problems caused by careless disposal of industrial waste*? A writer who says all that, though, risks wordiness. Why not just replace *priority* with a closer match for *waste*?

REVISED *Industrial waste* has become a *modern menace.*

Mismatches between a verb and another part of the sentence are easier to avoid when the verb is active rather than passive.

FAULTY The idea of giving thanks for a good harvest *was not done* first by the Pilgrims.

REVISED The idea of giving thanks for a good harvest *did not originate* with the Pilgrims.

## 12c Avoid starting a definition with *when* or *where.*

A definition needs to fit grammatically with the rest of the sentence.

FAULTY Dyslexia is when you have a reading disorder.

REVISED Dyslexia is a reading disorder.

FAULTY A lay-up is where a player dribbles close to the basket and then makes a one-handed, banked shot.

REVISED To shoot a lay-up, a player dribbles in close to the basket and then makes a one-handed, banked shot.

## 12d Avoid using *the reason is because . . .*

Anytime you start an explanation with *the reason is,* what follows *is* should be a subject complement: an adjective, a noun, or a noun clause. *Because* is a conjunction; it cannot function as a noun or adjective.

FAULTY *The reason* Al hesitates *is because* no one supported him last year.

REVISED *The reason* Al hesitates *is that* no one supported him last year.

REVISED Al hesitates *because* no one supported him last year.

REVISED *The reason* Al hesitates *is simple:* no one supported him last year.

## Exercise 12–1 ▪ Correcting Mixed Constructions and Faulty Predication

Correct any mixed constructions and faulty predication you find in the following sentences. Possible revisions for the lettered sentences appear at the end of the handbook. Example:

For more practice, visit **bedfordstmartins.com/bedguide**.

The storm damaged the beach erosion.

The storm worsened the beach erosion. *Or*

The storm damaged the beach.

a. The cost of health insurance protects people from big medical bills.

b. In his determination to prevail helped him finish the race.

c. The AIDS epidemic destroys the body's immune system.

d. The temperatures are too cold for the orange trees.

e. A recession is when economic growth is small or nonexistent and unemployment increases.

1. The opening of the new shopping mall should draw out-of-town shoppers for years to come.
2. The reason the referendum was defeated was because voters are tired of paying so much in taxes.
3. In the glacier's retreat created the valley.
4. A drop in prices could put farmers out of business.
5. The researchers' main goal is cancer.

# 13 | Parallel Structure

You use **parallel structure,** or parallelism, when you create a series of words, phrases, clauses, or sentences with the same grammatical form. The pattern created by the series—its parallel structure—emphasizes the similarities or differences among the items, whether things, qualities, actions, or ideas.

> My favorite foods are roast beef, apple pie, and linguine with clams.
>
> Louise is charming, witty, intelligent, and talented.
>
> Manuel likes to swim, ride, and run.
>
> Dave likes movies that scare him and books that make him laugh.

For more on editing for parallel structure, see B2 in the Quick Editing Guide, p. A-50.

Each series is a perfect parallel construction, composed of equivalent words: nouns in the first example, then adjectives, verbs, and adjective clauses.

## 13a In a series linked by a coordinating conjunction, keep all elements in the same grammatical form.

A coordinating conjunction (*and, but, for, or, nor, so, yet*) cues your readers to expect a parallel structure. Whether your series consists of single words, phrases, or clauses, its parts should balance one another.

For more on coordination, see 14a–14c.

AWKWARD The puppies are *tiny, clumsily bumping* into each other, *and cute.*

Two elements in this series are parallel one-word adjectives (*tiny, cute*), but the third, the verb phrase *clumsily bumping,* is inconsistent.

**gerund:** A form of a verb, ending in *-ing,* that functions as a noun: Lacey likes *playing* in the steel band.
**infinitive:** The base form of a verb, often preceded by *to* (*to go, to play*)

PARALLEL The puppies are *tiny, clumsy, and cute.*

Don't mix verb forms, such as gerunds and infinitives, in a series.

AWKWARD Plan a winter vacation if you like *skiing and to skate.*

PARALLEL Plan a winter vacation if you like *skiing and skating.*

PARALLEL Plan a winter vacation if you like *to ski and to skate.*

In a series of phrases or clauses, be sure that all elements in the series are similar in form, even if they are not similar in length.

AWKWARD The fight in the bar takes place *after the two lovers have their scene together* but *before the car chase.* [The clause starting with *after* is not parallel to the phrase starting with *before.*]

PARALLEL The fight in the bar takes place *after the love scene* but *before the car chase.*

AWKWARD You can take the key, or don't forget to leave it under the mat. [The declarative clause starting with *You can* is not parallel to the imperative clause starting with *don't forget.*]

PARALLEL You can *take the key,* or you can *leave it* under the mat.

## 13b In a series linked by correlative conjunctions, keep all elements in the same grammatical form.

When you use a correlative conjunction, follow each part with a similarly structured word, phrase, or clause.

**correlative conjunction:** A pair of linking words (such as *either/or, not only/but also*) that appear separately but work together to join elements of a sentence: *Neither* his friends *nor* hers like pizza.

AWKWARD I'm looking forward *to either attending* Saturday's wrestling match *or to seeing* it on closed-circuit TV. [*To* precedes the first part (*to either*) but follows the second part (*or to*).]

PARALLEL I'm looking forward *either to attending* Saturday's wrestling match *or to seeing* it on closed-circuit TV.

AWKWARD Take my advice: try *neither to be first nor last* in the lunch line. [*To be* follows the first part but not the second part.]

PARALLEL Take my advice: try to be *neither first nor last* in the lunch line.

## 13c Make the elements in a comparison parallel in form.

A comparative word such as *than* or *as* cues the reader to expect a parallel structure. This makes logical sense: to be compared, two things must resemble each other, and parallel structure emphasizes this resemblance.

For more on comparisons, see 11a–11d and 11g.

AWKWARD Philip likes *fishing* better than *to sail.*

PARALLEL Philip likes *fishing* better than *sailing.*

PARALLEL Philip likes *to fish* better than *to sail.*

AWKWARD *Maintaining* railway lines is as important to the public transportation system as *to buy* new trains.

PARALLEL *Maintaining* railway lines is as important to the public transportation system as *buying* new trains.

## 13d Reinforce parallel structure by repeating rather than mixing lead-in words.

Parallel structures are especially useful when a sentence contains a series of clauses or phrases. For example, try to precede potentially confusing clauses with *that, who, when, where,* or some other connective, repeating the same connective every time to help readers follow them with ease.

> No one in this country needs a government *that* aids big business at the expense of farmers and workers, *that* ravages the environment in the name of progress, or *that* slashes budgets for health and education.

If the same lead-in word won't work for all elements in a series, try changing the order of the elements to minimize variation.

AWKWARD The new school building is large but not very comfortable, and expensive but unattractive.

PARALLEL The new school building is large and expensive, but uncomfortable and unattractive.

---

### Exercise 13–1 ▪ Making Sentences Parallel

For more practice, visit **bedfordstmartins .com/bedguide**.

Revise the following sentences by substituting parallel structures for awkward ones. Possible revisions for the lettered sentences appear at the end of the handbook. Example:

> In the Rio Grande Valley, the interests of conservationists, government officials, and those trying to immigrate collide.
>
> In the Rio Grande Valley, the interests of conservationists, government officials, and immigrants collide.

a. The border separating Texas and Mexico marks not only the political boundary of two countries, but it also is the last frontier for some endangered wildlife.

b. In the Rio Grande Valley, both local residents and the people who happen to be tourists enjoy visiting the national wildlife refuges.

c. The tall grasses in this valley are the home of many insects, birds, and there are abundant small mammals.

d. Two endangered wildcats, the ocelot and another called the jaguarundi, also make the Rio Grande Valley their home.

e. Many people from Central America are desperate to immigrate to the United States by either legal or by illegal means.

1. Because the land along the Rio Grande has few human inhabitants and the fact that the river is often shallow, many illegal immigrants attempt to cross the border there.

2. To capture illegal immigrants more easily, the U.S. government has cut down tall grasses, put up fences, and the number of immigration patrols has been increased.
3. For illegal immigrants, crossing the border at night makes more sense than to enter the United States in broad daylight, so the U.S. government has recently installed bright lights along the border.
4. The ocelot and the jaguarundi need darkness, hiding places, and to have some solitude if they are to survive.
5. Neither the immigration officials nor have wildlife conservationists been able to find a solution that will protect both the U.S. border and these endangered wildcats.

# 14 | Coordination and Subordination

Coordination and subordination can use conjunctions to specify relationships between ideas. Coordination connects thoughts of equal importance; subordination shows how one thought affects another.

## 14a Coordinate clauses or sentences that are related in theme and equal in importance.

The car skidded for a hundred yards. It crashed into a brick wall.

These two clauses make equally significant statements about the same subject, a car accident. Because the writer has not linked the sentences, we can only guess that the crash followed from the skid.

The car skidded for a hundred yards, and it crashed into a brick wall.

Now the sequence is clear: first the car skidded; then it crashed. That's coordination. To tighten it, reduce the clauses to a compound predicate.

The car skidded for a hundred yards and crashed into a brick wall.

Now the connection is so clear we can almost hear screeching brakes. Once you decide to coordinate two clauses, try these three ways to do it.

1. Join two main clauses with a coordinating conjunction.

UNCOORDINATED Ari does not want to be placed on your mailing list. He does not want a salesperson to call him.

COORDINATED Ari does not want to be placed on your mailing list, nor does he want a salesperson to call him.

COORDINATED Ari does not want to be placed on your mailing list or called by a salesperson.

**conjunction:** A linking word that connects words or groups of words through coordination (*and, but*) or subordination (*because, although, unless*)

**clause:** A group of related words that includes both a subject and a verb: *The sailboats raced* (independent clause) *until the sun set* (subordinate clause).

**compound predicate:** A predicate consisting of two or more verbs linked by a conjunction: My sister *stopped and stared*.

**coordinating conjunction:** A one-syllable linking word (*and, but, for, or, nor, so, yet*) that joins elements with equal or near-equal importance: Jack *and* Jill, sink *or* swim

**conjunctive adverb:** A linking word that can connect independent clauses and show a relationship between two ideas: Jen studied hard; *finally,* she passed the exam.

2. Join two main clauses with a semicolon and a conjunctive adverb. Conjunctive adverbs show relationships such as addition, comparison, contrast, emphasis, cause and effect, or time (see p. 827).

UNCOORDINATED The guerrillas did not observe the truce. They never intended to.

COORDINATED The guerrillas did not observe the truce; furthermore, they never intended to.

For more on semicolons and colons, see 22 and 23.

3. Join two main clauses with a semicolon or a colon.

UNCOORDINATED The army wants to negotiate. The guerrillas prefer to fight.

COORDINATED The army wants to negotiate; the guerrillas prefer to fight.

UNCOORDINATED The guerrillas have two advantages. They know the terrain, and the people support them.

COORDINATED The guerrillas have two advantages: they know the terrain, and the people support them.

## 14b Coordinate clauses only if they are clearly and logically related.

Whenever you hitch together two sentences, make sure they get along. Will the relationship between them be evident to your readers?

FAULTY The sportscasters were surprised by Easy Goer's failure to win the Kentucky Derby, but it rained on derby day.

Readers need enough information to see why two clauses are connected.

COORDINATED The sportscasters were surprised by Easy Goer's failure to win the Kentucky Derby; *however, he runs poorly on a muddy track,* and it rained on derby day.

Choose a coordinating conjunction, conjunctive adverb, or punctuation mark that accurately reflects this relationship.

FAULTY The sportscasters all expected Easy Goer to win the Kentucky Derby, and Sunday Silence beat him.

COORDINATED The sportscasters all expected Easy Goer to win the Kentucky Derby, *but* Sunday Silence beat him.

## 14c Coordinate clauses only if they work together to make a coherent point.

When a writer strings together several clauses in a row, often the result is excessive coordination. Packing too much information into a single sentence can make readers dizzy, unable to pick out which points really matter. Each key idea deserves its own sentence so readers see its importance.

For common types of sentences using coordination and subordination, see p. 832.

## Coordinating and Subordinating Words at a Glance

### Coordinating Conjunctions

and, but, for, nor, or, so, yet

### Correlative Conjunctions

| | | |
|---|---|---|
| as . . . as | just as . . . so | not only . . . but also |
| both . . . and | neither . . . nor | whether . . . or |
| either . . . or | not . . . but | |

### Common Conjunctive Adverbs

| | | | |
|---|---|---|---|
| accordingly | finally | likewise | otherwise |
| also | furthermore | meanwhile | similarly |
| anyway | hence | moreover | still |
| as | however | nevertheless | then |
| besides | incidentally | next | therefore |
| certainly | indeed | nonetheless | thus |
| consequently | instead | now | undoubtedly |

### Common Subordinating Conjunctions

| | | | |
|---|---|---|---|
| after | before | since | until |
| although | even though | so | when |
| as | how | so that | whenever |
| as if | if | than | where |
| as soon as | in order that | that | wherever |
| as though | once | though | while |
| because | rather than | unless | why |

### Relative Pronouns

| | | | |
|---|---|---|---|
| that, which | what | who | whom |
| whose | whatever | whoever | whomever |

EXCESSIVE Easy Goer was the Kentucky Derby favorite, and all the sportscasters expected him to win, but he runs poorly on a muddy track, and it rained on derby day, so Sunday Silence beat him.

REVISED Easy Goer was the Kentucky Derby favorite, and all the sportscasters expected him to win. However, he runs poorly on a muddy track, and it rained on derby day. Therefore, Sunday Silence beat him.

Excessive coordination may result from repeating the same conjunction.

EXCESSIVE Phil was out of the house all day, so he didn't know about the rain, so he went ahead and bet on Easy Goer, so he lost twenty bucks, so now he wants to borrow money from me.

REVISED Phil was out of the house all day, so he didn't know about the rain. He went ahead and bet on Easy Goer, and he lost twenty bucks. Now he wants to borrow money from me.

One solution to excessive coordination is subordination: making one clause dependent on another instead of giving both clauses equal weight.

For advice on subordination, see 14d.

## Exercise 14–1 ▪ Using Coordination

For more practice, visit **bedfordstmartins .com/bedguide**.

Revise the following sentences, adding coordination where appropriate and removing faulty or excessive coordination. Possible revisions for the lettered sentences appear at the end of the handbook. Example:

> The wind was rising, and leaves tossed on the trees, and the air seemed to crackle with electricity, and we knew that a thunderstorm was on the way.
>
> The wind was rising, leaves tossed on the trees, and the air seemed to crackle with electricity. We knew that a thunderstorm was on the way.

a. Professional poker players try to win money and prizes in high-stakes tournaments. They may lose thousands of dollars.

b. Poker is not an easy way to make a living. Playing professional poker is not a good way to relax.

c. A good "poker face" reveals no emotions. Communicating too much information puts a player at a disadvantage.

d. Hidden feelings may come out in unconscious movements. An expert poker player watches other players carefully.

e. Poker is different from most other casino gambling games, for it requires skill and it forces players to compete against each other, and other casino gambling pits players against the house, so they may win out of sheer luck, but skill has little to do with winning those games.

1. The rebels may take the capital in a week. They may not be able to hold it.
2. If you want to take Spanish this semester, you have only one choice. You must sign up for the 8 a.m. course.
3. Peterson's Market has raised its prices. Last week tuna fish cost $1.29 a can. Now it's up to $1.59.
4. Joe starts the morning with a cup of coffee, which wakes him up, and then at lunch he eats a chocolate bar, so that the sugar and caffeine will bring up his energy level.
5. The *Hindenburg* drifted peacefully over New York City. It exploded just before landing.

## 14d Subordinate less important ideas to more important ideas.

Subordination is extremely useful because it shows your readers the relative importance of ideas, how one follows from another or affects another. You stress what counts, thereby encouraging your readers to share your viewpoint. You can subordinate one sentence to another in any of these three ways.

For a list of subordinating words, see p. 827.

1. Turn the less important idea into a subordinate clause by introducing it with a subordinating conjunction such as *because, if,* or *when.*

Jason has a keen sense of humor. He has an obnoxious, braying laugh.

From those sentences, readers don't know what to feel about Jason. Is he likable or repellent? The writer needs to show which trait matters more.

*Although Jason has a keen sense of humor,* he has an obnoxious, braying laugh.

This revision makes Jason's sense of humor less important than his annoying hee-haw. The less important idea is stated as a subordinate clause opening with *Although*; the more important idea is stated as the main clause.

The writer could reverse the meaning by combining the other way:

*Although Jason has an obnoxious, braying laugh,* he has a keen sense of humor.

That version makes Jason sound fun to be with, despite his mannerism.

Which of Jason's traits to emphasize is up to the writer. What matters is that, in both combined versions, the writer takes a clear stand by making one sentence a main clause and the other a subordinate clause.

2. Turn the less important idea into a subordinate clause by introducing it with a relative pronoun such as *who, which,* or *that.*

Jason, *who has an obnoxious, braying laugh,* has a keen sense of humor.

Jason, *whose sense of humor is keen,* has an obnoxious, braying laugh.

3. Turn the less important idea into a phrase.

Jason, *a keen humorist,* has an obnoxious, braying laugh.

*Despite his obnoxious, braying laugh,* Jason has a keen sense of humor.

**main clause:** A group of words that has both a subject and a verb and can stand alone as a complete sentence: *My friends play softball.*

**relative pronoun:** A pronoun (*who, which, that, what, whom, whomever, whose*) that opens a subordinate clause, modifying a noun or pronoun in another clause: The gift *that* I received is very practical.

**phrase:** Two or more related words that work together but may lack a subject (as in *will walk*), a verb (*my uncle*), or both (*to the attic*)

## 14e Express the more important idea in the main clause.

Sometimes a writer accidentally subordinates a more important idea to a less important one and turns the sentence's meaning upside down.

| | |
|---|---|
| FAULTY SUBORDINATION | Although the heroism of the Allied troops on D-Day lives on in spirit, many of the World War II soldiers who invaded Normandy are dead now. |

This sentence is accurate. Does the writer, however, want to stress death over life? This is the effect of putting *are dead now* in the main clause and *lives on* in the subordinate clause. Instead, the writer can reverse the two.

REVISED Although many of the World War II soldiers who invaded Normandy are dead now, the heroism of the Allied troops on D-Day lives on in spirit.

## 14f Limit the number of subordinate clauses in a sentence.

**subordinate clause:** A group of words that contains a subject and a verb but cannot stand alone because it depends on a main clause to help it make sense: *When the snow is deep,* a truck plows our road.

Excessive subordination strings too many ideas together without helping readers pick out what matters.

EXCESSIVE SUBORDINATION Debate over the Strategic Defense Initiative (SDI), which was originally proposed as a space-based defensive shield that would protect America from enemy attack, but which critics have suggested amounts to creating a first-strike capability in space, has to some extent focused on the wrong question.

REVISED Debate over the Strategic Defense Initiative (SDI) has to some extent focused on the wrong question. The plan was originally proposed as a space-based defensive shield that would protect America from enemy attack. Critics have suggested, however, that it amounts to creating a first-strike capability in space.

### Exercise 14–2 ▪ Using Subordination

For more practice, visit **bedfordstmartins.com/bedguide**.

Revise the following sentences, adding subordination where appropriate and removing faulty or excessive subordination. Possible revisions for the lettered sentences appear at the end of the handbook. Example:

Some playwrights like to work with performing theater companies. It is helpful to hear a script read aloud by actors.

Some playwrights like to work with performing theater companies *because* it is helpful to hear a script read aloud by actors.

a. Cape Cod is a peninsula in Massachusetts. It juts into the Atlantic Ocean south of Boston. The Cape marks the northern turning point of the Gulf Stream.

b. The developer had hoped the condominiums would sell quickly. Sales were sluggish.

c. Tourists love Italy. Italy has a wonderful climate, beautiful towns and cities, and a rich history.

d. At the end of Verdi's opera *La Traviata*, Alfredo has to see his beloved Violetta again. He knows she is dying and all he can say is good-bye.

e. I usually have more fun at a concert with Rico than with Morey. Rico loves music. Morey merely tolerates it.

1. Although we occasionally hear horror stories about fruits and vegetables being unsafe to eat because they were sprayed with toxic chemicals or were grown in contaminated soil, the fact remains that, given their high nutritional value, these fresh foods are generally much better for us than processed foods.
2. English has become an international language. Its grammar is filled with exceptions to the rules.
3. Some television cartoon shows have become cult classics. This has happened years after they went off the air. Examples include *The Bullwinkle Show* and *Speed Racer*.
4. Although investors have not fully regained confidence in the stock market, stock prices have gone up.
5. Violetta gives away her money. She bids adieu to her faithful servant. After that she dies in her lover's arms.

# 15 | Sentence Variety

Most writers rely on some patterns more than others to express ideas directly and efficiently, but sometimes they combine sentence elements in unexpected ways to emphasize ideas and to surprise readers.

## 15a Normal Sentences

In a **normal sentence,** a writer puts the subject before the verb at the beginning of the main clause. This pattern is the most common in English because it expresses ideas in the most straightforward manner.

Most college *students* today *want* interesting classes.

## 15b Inverted Sentences

In an **inverted sentence,** a writer inverts or reverses the subject-verb order to emphasize an idea in the predicate.

NORMAL *My peers are uninterested* in reading.

INVERTED How *uninterested* in reading *are my peers*!

### Types of Sentences at a Glance

A **simple sentence** contains only one main clause, even with modifiers, objects, complements, and phrases in addition to its subject and verb.

MAIN CLAUSE

Even amateur stargazers can easily locate the Big Dipper in the night sky.

It may have a compound subject (*Fred and Sandy*) or a compound verb (*laughed and cried*). Sometimes its subject is unstated but clearly understood: "Run!"

A **compound sentence** consists of two or more main clauses joined by a coordinating conjunction such as *and* or *but,* by a semicolon, or by a semicolon followed by a conjunctive adverb such as *however* or *nevertheless.*

For lists of coordinating and subordinating words, see p. 827.

MAIN CLAUSE — MAIN CLAUSE

I would like to accompany you, but I can't.

MAIN CLAUSE — MAIN CLAUSE

My car broke down; therefore, I missed the first day of class.

A **complex sentence** has one main clause and one or more subordinate clauses.

MAIN CLAUSE — SUBORDINATE CLAUSE

I will be at the airport when you arrive.

The relative pronoun linking the clauses may be implied.

MAIN CLAUSE — SUBORDINATE CLAUSE

I know [that] you saw us.

A **compound-complex sentence** combines a compound sentence (two or more main clauses) and a complex sentence (at least one subordinate clause).

MAIN CLAUSE — SUBORDINATE CLAUSE — SUBORDINATE CLAUSE — MAIN CLAUSE

I'd gladly wait until you're ready; but if I do, I'll miss the boat.

## 15c Cumulative Sentences

In a **cumulative sentence,** a writer piles details at the end of a sentence to help readers visualize a scene or understand an idea.

> They came walking out in heavily brocaded yellow and black costumes, the familiar "toreador" suit, heavy with gold embroidery, cape, jacket, shirt and collar, knee breeches, pink stockings, and low pumps.
>
> —Ernest Hemingway, "Bull Fighting a Tragedy"

## 15d Periodic Sentences

The positions of emphasis in a sentence are the beginning and the end. In a **periodic sentence,** a writer suspends the main clause for a climactic ending, emphasizing an idea by withholding it until the end.

> Leaning back in his chair, shaking his head slowly back and forth, frustrated over his inability to solve the equation, Franklin scowled.

## Exercise 15–1 ▪ Increasing Sentence Variety

Revise the following passage, adding sentence variety to create interest, emphasize important ideas, and strengthen coherence.

For more practice, visit **bedfordstmartins.com/bedguide**.

> We are terrified of death. We do not think of it, and we don't speak of death. We don't mourn in public. We don't know how to console a grieving friend. In fact, we have eliminated or suppressed all the traditional rituals surrounding death.
>
> The Victorians coped with death differently. Their funerals were elaborate. The yards of black crepe around the hearse, hired professional mourners, and solemn procession leading to an ornate tomb are now only a distant memory. They wore mourning jewelry. They had a complicated dress code for the grieving process. It governed what mourners wore, and it governed how long they wore it. Many of these rituals may seem excessive or even morbid to us today. The rituals served a psychological purpose in helping the living deal with loss.

# 40 Word Choice



## 16 | Appropriateness

When you talk to people face-to-face, you can gauge their reactions to what you say. Often their responses guide your tone and your choice of words. When you write, you cannot see your readers. Instead, you must imagine yourself in their place, focusing on their responses when you revise.

Besides affecting how well you achieve your purpose as a writer, your language can affect how well you are regarded by others. When you accurately assess the tone, formality, and word choice expected in a situation, you use the power of language to enhance your position. When you misjudge, you may find that others judge you harshly. Your future employer, your teacher, your supervisor, or others with authority may or may not be aware of their power to set language expectations or of their own responses to your use of language. However, when they see you try to write and speak as they feel a situation requires, they will appreciate your effort to use language powerfully, adjusting it to your audience and situation.

### 16a Choose a tone appropriate for your topic and audience.

Like a speaker, a writer may come across as friendly or aloof, furious or merely annoyed, playful or grimly serious. This attitude is the writer's **tone,** and it strongly influences the audience's response. A tone that seems right to a reader conveys concern for the reader's reaction. For instance, readers might reject as inappropriate a humorous approach to cancer or AIDS that ignores their feelings about the disease. To convey your tone, use sentence length, level of language, and vocabulary. The key is to be aware of your readers and their expectations.

## 16b Choose a level of formality appropriate for your tone.

Considering the tone you want to convey helps you choose words that are neither too formal nor too informal. **Formal** language means the impersonal language of educated persons who consider topics seriously. Usually written, formal language is marked by relatively complex sentences and a large vocabulary. It doesn't use contractions (such as *doesn't*). In contrast, **informal** language more closely resembles ordinary conversation. It uses relatively short sentences and common words. It may include contractions, slang, and references to everyday objects and activities (cheeseburgers, T-shirts, CDs). The writer may use *I* and address the reader as *you*.

The right language for most college essays lies somewhere between formal and informal. If your topic and tone are serious (say, for a research project on terrorism), then your language may lean toward formality. If your topic is not weighty and your tone is light (say, for a humorous essay about giving your dog a bath), then your language may be informal.

### Exercise 16–1 ▪ Choosing an Appropriate Tone and Level of Formality

For more practice, visit **bedfordstmartins.com/bedguide**.

Revise the following passages to ensure that both the tone and the level of formality are appropriate for the topic and audience. Example:

> I'm sending you this letter because I want you to meet with me and give me some info about the job you do.
>
> I'm writing to inquire about the possibility of an informational interview about your profession.

1. Dear Senator Crowley:

   I think you've got to vote for the new environmental law, so I'm writing this letter. We're messing up forests and wetlands – maybe for good. Let's do something now for everybody who's born after us.

   Thanks,
   Glenn Turner

2. The United States Holocaust Memorial Museum in Washington, D.C., is a great museum dedicated to a real bad time in history. It's hard not to get bummed out by the stuff on show. Take it from me, it's an experience you won't forget.

3. Dear Elaine,

   I am so pleased that you plan on attending the homecoming dance with me on Friday. It promises to be a gala event, and I am confident that we will enjoy ourselves immensely. I understand a local group by the name of Electric Bunny will provide musical entertainment. Please call me at your earliest convenience to inform me when to pick you up.

   Sincerely, Bill

## 16c Choose common words instead of jargon.

**Jargon** is the term for the specialized vocabulary used by people in a certain field, such as music, carpentry, law, or sports. Nearly every academic, professional, and recreational field has its own jargon. To a specialist addressing other specialists, jargon is convenient and necessary. Without technical terms, after all, two surgeons could hardly discuss a patient's anatomy. To an outsider, though, such terms may be incomprehensible. To communicate with readers without confusing them, avoid unnecessary jargon.

Jargon also can include ways of using words. Some politicians and bureaucrats like to make nouns into verbs by tacking on suffixes like *-ize.*

JARGON The government intends to *privatize* federal land.

CLEAR The government intends to *sell* federal land to *private buyers.*

Although *privatize* implies merely "convert to private ownership," usually its real meaning is "sell off"—as might occur were a national park to be auctioned to developers. *Privatize* thus also can be called a *euphemism,* a pleasant term that masks an underlying different meaning (see 16d).

Similarly, technology terms such as *access, format, interface, database,* and *parameters* are useful to explain technical processes. When thoughtlessly applied to nontechnical ideas, they can obscure meaning.

JARGON A democracy needs the electorate's *input.*

CLEAR A democracy needs the electorate *to vote and to express its views to elected officials.*

Avoid needless jargon by favoring a perfectly good old word over a trendy one. Also avoid the jargon of a special discipline—say, psychology or fly-fishing—unless you are writing for readers familiar with the field's details and terms. For general readers, define any specialized terms.

### Exercise 16–2 ▪ Avoiding Jargon

For more practice, visit **bedfordstmartins.com/bedguide**.

Revise the following sentences to eliminate the jargon. If necessary, revise extensively. If you can't tell what a sentence means, decide what it might mean, and rewrite it so that its meaning is clear. Possible revisions for the lettered sentences appear at the end of the handbook. Example:

The proximity of Mr. Fitton's knife to Mr. Schering's arm produced a violation of the integrity of the skin.

Mr. Fitton's knife cut Mr. Schering's arm.

a. Everyone at Boondoggle and Gall puts in face time at the holiday gatherings to maximize networking opportunities.

b. This year, in excess of fifty nonessential employees were negatively impacted by Boondoggle and Gall's decision to downsize effective September 1.

c. The layoffs made Jensen the sole point of responsibility for telephone interface in the customer-service department.

d. The numerical quotient of Jensen's telephonic exchanges increased by a factor of three post-downsizing, yet Jensen received no additional fiscal remuneration.

e. Jensen was not on the same page with management re her compensation, so she exercised the option to terminate her relationship with Boondoggle and Gall.

1. The driver-education course prepares the student for the skills of handling a vehicle on the highway transportation system.
2. In the heart area, Mr. Pitt is a prime candidate-elect for intervention of a multiple bypass nature.
3. The deer hunter's activity of quietizing a predetermined amount of the deer populace balances the ecological infrastructure.

## 16d Use euphemisms sparingly.

**Euphemisms** are plain truths dressed attractively, sometimes hard facts stated gently. To say that someone *passed away* instead of *died* is a common euphemism—humane, perhaps, in breaking terrible news to an anxious family. In such language, an army that *retreats* makes *a strategic withdrawal,* a person who is *underweight* turns *slim,* and an acne cream treats not *pimples* but *blemishes.* Even if you aren't prone to using euphemisms, note them when you read evidence from partisan sources and spokespersons.

## 16e Avoid slang in formal writing.

Slang, when new, can be colorful ("She's not playing with a full deck"), playful ("He's wicked cute!"), and apt (*ice* for diamonds, a *stiff* for a corpse). Most slang, however, quickly seems as old and wrinkled as the Jazz Age's *twenty-three skidoo!* Your best bet is to stick to words that are usual but exact.

### Exercise 16–3 ▪ Avoiding Euphemisms and Slang

Revise the following sentences to replace euphemisms with plainer words and slang with Standard English. Possible revisions for the lettered sentences appear at the end of the handbook. Example:

For more practice, visit **bedfordstmartins.com/bedguide**.

Some dude ripped off my wallet, so I am currently experiencing a negative cash flow.

*Someone stole* my wallet, so I am now *in debt.*

a. At three hundred bucks a month, the apartment is a steal.

b. The soldiers were victims of friendly fire during a strategic withdrawal.

c. Churchill was a wicked good politician.

1. Saturday's weather forecast calls for extended periods of shower activity.
2. The caller to the talk-radio program sounded totally wigged out.
3. We anticipate a downturn in economic vitality.

# 17 | Exact Words

What if you read that a leading citizen is a *pillow of the community*? Good writing depends on knowing what words mean and how to use them precisely.

## 17a Choose words for their connotations as well as their denotations.

The **denotation** of a word is its basic meaning—its dictionary definition. *Excited, agitated,* and *exhilarated* all denote a similar state of physical and emotional arousal. The **connotations** of a word are the shades of meaning that set it apart from its synonyms. You might be *agitated* by the prospect of exams next week, but *exhilarated* by your plans for the vacation afterward. When you choose one of several options, you base your choice on connotation.

IMPRECISE Advertisers have given light beer a macho image by showing football players *sipping* the product with *enthusiasm.*

REVISED Advertisers have given light beer a macho image by showing football players *guzzling* the product with *gusto.*

## 17b Avoid clichés.

A **cliché** is a trite expression, once vivid or figurative but now worn out from too much use. When a story begins, "It was a dark and stormy night," then its author is obviously using dull, predictable words. Many a strike is settled after a *marathon bargaining session.* Fires customarily *race* and *gut.* And when everything is *terrific,* a reader will suspect that it isn't. Clichés abound when writers and speakers try hard to sound lively but don't bother to invent anything vigorous, colorful, and new.

COMMON CLICHÉS

a sneaking suspicion
above and beyond the call of duty
add insult to injury
beyond a shadow of a doubt
come hell or high water
cool as a cucumber
few and far between
hard as a rock
last but not least
little did I dream
make a long story short
stab me in the back
that's the way the ball bounces
through thick and thin
tip of the iceberg
tried and true

## 17c Use idioms in their correct form.

Every language contains **idioms,** or **idiomatic expressions:** phrases that, through long use, have become standard even though their construction may defy logic or grammar. For example, although *fender bender* may suggest the outcome of a minor collision between two cars, someone unfamiliar with that expression might struggle to connect the literal words with the idiomatic meaning. In addition, many idioms require us to choose the right preposition. We work *up* a sweat while working *out* in the gym. We argue *with* someone but *about* something, *for* or *against* it. And someone who decides to *set up* a meeting doesn't expect to be *upset.* Sometimes we must know which article to use before a noun—if any. We're occasionally in *a tight spot* but never in *a trouble.* Idioms also can involve choosing the right verb: we *seize* an opportunity, but we *catch* a plane. The dictionary can help you choose the right idiom. Look up *agree,* for instance, to find examples for using *agree to, agree with,* or *agree that.*

## Exercise 17–1 ▪ Selecting Words

For more practice, visit **bedfordstmartins.com/bedguide**.

Revise the following passage to replace inappropriate connotations, clichés, and faulty idioms. Example:

> The Mayan city of Uxmal is a common tourist attraction. The ruins have stood alone in the jungle since time immemorial.
>
> The Mayan city of Uxmal is a *popular* tourist attraction. The ruins have stood alone in the jungle since *ancient times.*

We spent the first day of our holiday in Mexico arguing around what we wanted to see on our second day. We finally agreed to a day trip out to

**preposition:** A transitional word (such as *in, on, at, of, from*) that leads into a phrase such as *in the bar, under a rickety table*

For practice, visit **bedfordstmartins .com/bedguide**.

## ESL Guidelines *In, On, At:* Prepositions of Location and Time

### Location Expressions

Elaine lives *in* Manhattan *at* a swanky address *on* Fifth Avenue.

- ***In*** means "within" or "inside of" a place, including geographical areas, such as cities, states, countries, and continents.

  I packed my books *in* my backpack and left to visit my cousins *in* Canada.

- Where ***in*** emphasizes *location* only, ***at*** is often used to refer to a place when a specific *activity* is implied: *at the store* (to shop), *at the office* (to work), *at the theater* (to see a play), and so on.

  Angelo left his bicycle *in* the bike rack while he was *at* school.

- ***On*** means "on the surface of" or "on top of" something and is used with floors of buildings and planets. It is also used to indicate a location *beside* a lake, river, ocean, or other body of water.

  The service department is *on* the fourth floor.

  We have a cabin *on* Lake Michigan.

- ***In, on,*** and ***at*** can all be used in addresses. ***In*** is used to identify a general location, such as a city or neighborhood. ***On*** is used to identify a specific street. ***At*** is used to give an exact address.

  We live *in* Boston *on* Medway Street.

  We live *at* 20 Medway Street.

- ***In*** and ***at*** can both be used with the verb *arrive.* ***In*** indicates a large place, such as a city, state, country, or continent. ***At*** indicates a smaller place, such as a specific building or address. (*To* is never used with *arrive.*)

  Alanya arrived *in* Alaska yesterday; Sanjei will arrive *at* the airport soon.

### Time Expressions

- ***In*** indicates the span of time during which something occurs or a time in the future; it is also used in the expressions *in a minute* (meaning "shortly") and *in time* (meaning "soon enough" or "without a moment to spare"). ***In*** is also used with seasons, months, and periods of the day.

  He needs to read this book *in* the next three days.
  [During the next three days]

  I'll meet you *in* the morning *in* two weeks. [Two weeks from now]

- ***On*** is used with the days of the week, with the word *weekend,* and in the expression *on time* (meaning "punctually").

  Let's have lunch *on* Friday.

- ***At*** is used in reference to a specific time on the clock as well as a specific time of the day (*at night, at dawn, at twilight*).

  We'll meet again next Monday *at* 2:15 p.m.

## ESL Guidelines *To, For:* Indirect Objects and Prepositions

These sentences mean the same thing:

I sent the president a letter.

I sent a letter to the president.

In the first sentence, *the president* is the **indirect object:** he or she receives the direct object (*a letter*), which was acted on (*sent*) by the subject of the sentence (*I*). In the second sentence, the same idea is expressed using a **prepositional phrase** beginning with *to.*

- Some verbs can use either an indirect object or the preposition *to: give, send, lend, offer, owe, pay, sell, show, teach, tell.* Some verbs can use an indirect object or the preposition *for: bake, build, buy, cook, find, get, make.*

  I paid *the travel agent* one hundred dollars.

  I paid one hundred dollars *to the travel agent.*

  Margarita cooked *her family* some chicken.

  Margarita cooked some chicken *for her family.*

- Some verbs cannot have an indirect object; they must use a preposition. The following verbs must use the preposition *to: describe, demonstrate, explain, introduce,* and *suggest.*

  INCORRECT Please explain me indirect objects.

  CORRECT Please explain indirect objects *to me.*

- The following verbs must use the preposition *for: answer* and *prepare.*

  INCORRECT He prepared me the punch.

  CORRECT He prepared the punch *for me.*

- Some verbs must have an indirect object; they cannot use a preposition. The following verbs must have an indirect object: *ask* and *cost.*

  INCORRECT Sasha asked a question to her.

  CORRECT Sasha asked *her* a question.

### Two-Word Verbs: Particles, Not Prepositions

Many two-word verbs end with a **particle,** a word that can be used as a preposition on its own but becomes part of a **phrasal verb.** Once the particle is added, the verb takes on a new idiomatic meaning that must be learned.

break up: to separate; to end a romantic relationship; to laugh

decide on: to select or to judge a person or thing

eat at: to worry or disturb a person

feel for [a person]: to sympathize with another's unhappiness

see to: to take care of a person or situation

take in [a person]: to house a person; to trick by gaining a person's trust

**indirect object:** A person or thing affected by the subject's action, usually the recipient of the direct object, through tho action indicated by a verb such as *bring, get, offer, promise, sell, show, tell,* and *write:* Charlene asked *you* a question.

some Mayan ruins. The next day we arrived on the Mayan city of Uxmal, which is as old as the hills. It really is a sight for sore eyes, smack-dab in a jungle stretching as far as the eye can see, with many buildings still covered in plants and iguanas moving quickly over the decayed buildings. The view from the top of the Soothsayer's Temple was good, although we noticed storm clouds gathering in the distance. The rain held up until we got off of the pyramid, but we drove back to the hotel in a lot of rain. After a day of sightseeing, we were so hungry that we could have eaten a horse, so we had a good meal before we turned in.

# 18 | Bias-Free Language

Thoughtful writers try to avoid harmful bias in language. They respect their readers and don't want to insult them, anger them, or impede communication. You may not be able to eliminate discrimination from society, but you can eliminate discriminatory language in your writing. Be on the lookout for words that insult or stereotype individuals or groups by gender, age, race, ethnic origin, sexual preference, or religion.

## 18a To eliminate sexist language, use alternatives that make no reference to gender.

Decades ago American feminists challenged the male bias built into the English language. Why, they asked, do we talk about *prehistoric man, manpower,* and *the brotherhood of man,* when by *man* we mean the entire human race? Why do we focus attention on the gender of an accomplished woman by calling her a *poetess* or a *lady doctor*? Why does a letter to a corporation have to begin "Gentlemen:"? On the other hand, to substitute "Everyone prefers their own customs" for "Everyone prefers *his* own customs" replaces sexism with bad grammar. Although there are no perfect solutions, sensitive writers try to minimize the sexist constraints of English.

## 18b Avoid terms that include or imply *man.*

Try substituting *human* for *man* or a word starting with *man.*

SEXIST Mankind studies man's inhumanity to man.

CLUMSY *Humankind* studies *humans'* inhumanity to *other humans.*

If the result weighs down the sentence, look for a more graceful solution.

REVISED *Human beings* study *people's* cruelty to one another.

Similarly, you need not simply replace the ending *-man* with *-person*. Instead, think about meaning and find a truly neutral synonym.

SEXIST Did you leave a note for the mailman?

REVISED Did you leave a note for the *letter carrier*?

SEXIST Ask your steward [or stewardess] for a pillow.

REVISED Ask your *flight attendant* for a pillow.

## 18c Use plural instead of singular forms.

Replace the singular with the plural (*they* and *their* for *he* and *his*).

SEXIST Today's student values his education.

REVISED Today's students value *their* education.

## 18d Where possible, omit words that denote gender.

You can make your language more bias-free by omitting pronouns and other words that needlessly indicate gender.

SEXIST There must be rapport between a stockbroker and his client, a teacher and her student, a doctor and his patient.

REVISED There must be rapport between stockbroker and *client*, teacher and *student*, doctor and *patient*.

Also treat men and women equally in terms of description or title.

SEXIST I now pronounce you man and wife.

REVISED I now pronounce you *husband* and wife.

SEXIST Please page Mr. Pease, Mr. Mankodi, and Emily Brillantes.

REVISED Please page Mr. Pease, Mr. Mankodi, and *Ms.* Brillantes.

## 18e Avoid condescending labels.

A responsible writer does not call women *chicks, babes, woman drivers,* or any other names that imply that they are not to be taken seriously. Nor should an employee ever be called a *girl* or *boy*. Avoid terms that put down individuals or groups because of age (*old goat, the grannies*), race or ethnicity (*Indian giver, Chinaman's chance*), or disability (*gimpy, handicapped*).

CONDESCENDING The girls in the office got Mr. Birt a birthday cake.

REVISED The *administrative assistants* got Mr. Birt a birthday cake.

CONDESCENDING My neighbor is just an old fogy.

REVISED My neighbor *has old-fashioned ideas.*

When describing a group, try to use the label or term that its members prefer, even if it is difficult to determine.

POSSIBLY OFFENSIVE Alice wants to study Oriental culture.

REVISED Alice wants to study *Asian* culture.

## 18f Avoid implied stereotypes.

Sometimes a stereotype is linked to a title. Aside from obvious exceptions, never assume that all the members of a group are of the same gender.

STEREOTYPE Pilots have little time to spend with their wives and children.

REVISED Pilots have little time to spend with their *families.*

Avoid stereotyping individuals or groups, negatively or positively.

STEREOTYPE Roberto isn't very good at paying his rent on time, which doesn't surprise me because he is from Mexico.

REVISED Roberto isn't very good at paying his rent on time.

STEREOTYPE I assume Ben will do very well in medical school because his parents are Jewish.

REVISED I assume Ben will do very well in medical school.

## 18g Use *Ms.* for a woman with no other known title.

*Ms.* is the preferred title of polite address for women because, like *Mr.* for men, it does not indicate marital status. Use *Miss* or *Mrs.* only if you know that the woman prefers this form. If a woman holds a doctorate, professional office, or position with a title, use that title rather than *Ms.*

| | |
|---|---|
| Ms. Jane Doe, Editor | Dear Ms. Doe: |
| Professor Jane Doe, Department of English | Dear Professor Doe: |
| Senator Jane Doe, Washington, D.C. | Dear Senator Doe: |

## Exercise 18–1 ▪ Avoiding Bias

For more practice, visit **bedfordstmartins.com/bedguide**.

Revise the following sentences to eliminate bias. Possible revisions for the lettered sentences appear at the end of the handbook. Example:

A fireman needs to check his equipment regularly.

*Firefighters* need to check *their* equipment regularly.

a. Our school's athletic program will be of interest to black applicants.
b. The new physicians include Dr. Scalia, Anna Baniski, and Dr. Morton.
c. The diligent researcher will always find the sources he seeks.

1. Simon drinks like an Irishman.
2. Like most Asian Americans, Soon Li excels at music and mathematics.
3. Dick drives a Porsche because he likes the way she handles on the road, despite the little old ladies who slow down traffic.

For strategies for cutting extra words, see Ch. 23.

## 19 | Wordiness

Conciseness takes more effort than wordiness. For clarity, simplify expressions or omit them (*area of, field of, kind of, sort of, type of, very*).

SAMPLE WINDY WORDS AND PHRASES

| WORDY | CONCISE |
|---|---|
| a period of a week | a week |
| arrive at an agreement, conclude an agreement | agree |
| at an earlier point in time | before, earlier |
| a large number of | many |
| lend assistance to | assist, aid, help |
| past experience, past history | experience, history |
| persons of the Methodist faith | Methodists |
| plan ahead for the future | plan |
| resemble in appearance | look like |
| sufficient number (or amount) of | enough |
| true facts | facts, truth |
| utilize, make use of | use |

### Exercise 19–1 ▪ Eliminating Wordiness

For more practice, visit **bedfordstmartins .com/bedguide**.

Revise the following passage to eliminate wordiness. Example:

> At this point in time, a debate pertaining to freedom of speech is raging across our campuses.
>
> A debate *about* freedom of speech is raging across our campuses.

The media in recent times have become obsessed with the conflict on campuses across the nation between freedom of speech and the attempt to protect minorities from verbal abuse. Very innocent remarks or remarks of a humorous nature, sometimes taken out of context, have got a large number of students into trouble for the violation of college speech codes.

Numerous students have become very vocal in attacking these "politically correct" speech codes and defending the right to free speech. But is the campaign against the politically correct really pertaining to freedom of speech, or is it itself a way in which to silence debate? Due to the fact that the phrase "politically correct" has become associated with liberal social causes and sensitivity to minority feelings, it now carries a very extraordinary stigma in the eyes of conservatives. To accuse someone of being politically correct is to refute their ideas before hearing their argument. The attempt to silence the opposition is a dangerous sign of our times and suggests that we are indeed in a cultural war.

## Learning by Doing Refining Your Wording

After you have read or skimmed through Chapter 40, consider which types of words you most often wrestle with. Do you have trouble regulating your tone, your attitude, and your degree of formality? Do you lapse into specialized jargon, slang, or clichés? Do you fall into biased or stereotypical wording rather than sticking to fair, neutral language? Or are you just plain wordy? Identify the problem you want to tackle, review the section about it, and plan a strategy—maybe highlighting words to reconsider, maybe applying your instructor's past suggestions in the current paper, or maybe searching for key words or passages to rephrase. After you have made improvements, exchange papers with a peer, and help each other spot any other word choice issues.

# Punctuation

41



**Learning by Doing** Tackling Punctuation Patterns

Check comments in past drafts or final papers for similar punctuation errors that suggest a pattern. Have readers questioned your use of commas? Do you guess about where to put colons? Look up the handbook guidelines for that punctuation problem, and write out useful "rules" in your own words. Present your "rules" or your remaining questions to a small group of classmates.

## 20 | End Punctuation

Three marks can signal the end of a sentence: the period, the exclamation point, and the question mark.

### 20a Use a period to end a declarative sentence, a directive, or an indirect question.

Most sentences are **declarative,** meaning that they make a statement.

> Most people on earth are malnourished.

A period, not a question mark, ends an **indirect question,** which states that a question was asked or is being asked.

> The counselor asked Marcia why she rarely gets to class on time.
>
> I wonder why Roland didn't show up.

Written as **direct questions,** those sentences require a question mark.

The counselor asked, "Marcia, why do you rarely get to class on time?"

Why, I wonder, didn't Roland show up?

## 20b Use a period after some abbreviations.

A period within a sentence shows that what precedes it has been shortened.

Dr. Robert A. Hooke's speech will be broadcast at 8:00 p.m.

For more on abbreviating names, see 28e.

The names of many organizations (YMCA, PTA), countries (USA, UK), and people (JFK, FDR) are abbreviated using all capitals without periods. Other abbreviations, such as those for designations of time, use periods. When an abbreviation ends a sentence, follow it with one period, not two.

## 20c Use a question mark to end a direct question.

How many angels can dance on the head of a pin?

For advice on punctuating indirect quotations and questions, see 25a. For examples of indirect questions, see 20a.

The question mark comes at the end of the question even if the question is part of a longer declarative sentence.

"What'll I do now?" Marjorie wailed.

It can indicate doubt about the accuracy of a number or date.

Aristophanes, born in 450(?) BC, was a master comic playwright.

Often the same purpose can be accomplished more gracefully in words:

Aristophanes, born around 450 BC, was a master comic playwright.

In formal writing, avoid using a question mark to express irony or sarcasm: *her generous (?) gift.* If your doubts are worth including, state them directly: *her meager but highly publicized gift.*

## 20d Use an exclamation point to end an interjection or an urgent command.

Rarely used in college writing, an exclamation point signals strong emotion.

We've struck an iceberg! We're sinking! I can't believe it!

It may mark an **interjection** or emphasize an urgent directive.

Oh, no! Fire! Hurry up! Help me!

**interjection:** A word or expression (*oh, alas*) that inserts an outburst of feeling at the beginning, middle, or end of a sentence

### Exercise 20–1 ▪ Using End Punctuation

If needed, correct end punctuation in the following sentences. Give reasons for any changes you make. Some sentences may be correct. Answers for the lettered sentences appear at the end of the handbook. Example:

Tom asked Cindy if she would be willing to coach him in tennis?

Tom asked Cindy if she would be willing to coach him in tennis. [Not a direct question]

For more practice, visit **bedfordstmartins .com/bedguide**.

a. The question that still troubles the community after all these years is why federal agents did not act sooner?

b. I wonder what he was thinking at the time?

c. If the suspect is convicted, will lawyers appeal the case?

1. What will Brad and Emilia do if they can't take vacations at the same time.
2. When a tree falls in a forest, but no one hears it, does it make a sound.
3. What will happen next is anyone's guess.

# 21 | Commas

Like a split-second pause in conversation, a well-placed comma helps your readers to catch your train of thought. It keeps them from stumbling over a solid block of words or drawing an inaccurate conclusion.

For more on comma usage, see C1 in the Quick Editing Guide, pp. A-53–A-54.

Lyman paints fences and bowls.

From this statement, we can deduce that Lyman is a painter who works with both a large and a small brush. But add commas and the portrait changes:

Lyman paints, fences, and bowls.

Now Lyman wields a paintbrush, a sword, and a bowling ball. What we learn about his activities depends on how the writer punctuates the sentence.

## 21a Use a comma with a coordinating conjunction to join two main clauses.

When you join main clauses with a coordinating conjunction (*and, but, for, or, nor, so, yet*), add a comma after the first clause, right before the conjunction.

**main clause:** A group of words that has both a subject and a verb and can stand alone as a complete sentence: *My friends play softball.*

**phrase:** Two or more related words that work together but may lack a subject (as in *will walk*), a verb (*my uncle*), or both (*to the attic*)

The pie whooshed through the air, but the agile Hal ducked.

If your clauses are short and parallel in form, you may omit the comma. Or you may keep the comma to throw emphasis on your second clause.

| | |
|---|---|
| Spring passed and summer came. | Spring passed, and summer came. |
| They urged but I refused. | They urged, but I refused. |

CAUTION: Don't use a comma with a coordinating conjunction that links two phrases or that links a phrase and a clause.

FAULTY The mustangs galloped, and cavorted across the plain.

EDITED The mustangs galloped and cavorted across the plain.

## 21b Use a comma after an introductory clause, phrase, or word.

**clause:** A group of related words that includes both a subject and a verb: *The sailboats raced* (independent clause) *until the sun set* (subordinate clause).

*Weeping,* Lydia stumbled down the stairs.

*Before that,* Arthur saw her reading an old love letter.

*If he knew who the writer was,* he didn't tell.

Placed after any such opening word, phrase, or subordinate clause, a comma tells your reader, "Enough preliminaries: now the main clause starts."

EXCEPTION: You need not use a comma after a single introductory word or a short phrase or clause if there is no danger of misreading.

*Sooner or later* Lydia will tell us the whole story.

### Exercise 21–1 ▪ Using Commas

For more practice, visit **bedfordstmartins.com/bedguide**.

Add any necessary commas to the following sentences, and remove any commas that do not belong. Some sentences may be correct. Answers for the lettered sentences appear at the end of the handbook. Example:

Your dog may have sharp teeth but my lawyer can bite harder.

Your dog may have sharp teeth, but my lawyer can bite harder.

a. Farmers around the world tend to rely on just a few breeds of livestock so some breeds are disappearing.
b. Older breeds of livestock are often less profitable, for they have not been genetically engineered to grow quickly.
c. For instance modern breeds of cattle usually grow larger, and produce more meat and milk than older breeds.
d. In both wild and domestic animals genetic diversity can make the animals resistant to disease, and parasites so older breeds can give scientists important information.
e. Until recently, small organic farmers were often the only ones interested in raising old-fashioned breeds but animal scientists now support this practice as well.

1. During the summer of the great soybean failure Larry paid little attention.
2. Unaware of the world he worked two jobs to earn his tuition.
3. While across the nation farmers were begging for mortgages he fed the livestock every morning.
4. Neither the mounting agricultural crisis, nor any other current events, disturbed his dinner shift at the restaurant.
5. In fact you might have called him oblivious.

## 21c Use a comma between items in a series.

When you list three or more items, whether they are nouns, verbs, adjectives, adverbs, or entire phrases or clauses, separate them with commas.

> Country ham, sweet corn, and potatoes weighted Grandma's table.
>
> Joel prefers music that shakes, rattles, and rolls.
>
> In one afternoon, we climbed the Matterhorn, voyaged beneath the sea, and flew on a rocket through space.

Notice that no comma *follows* the final item in the series.

NOTE: Some writers omit the comma *before* the final item in the series. This custom may throw off the rhythm of a sentence and, in some cases, obscure the writer's meaning. Using the comma in such a case is never wrong and is preferred in academic style; omitting it can create confusion.

> I was met at the station by my cousins, brother and sister.

Are these people a brother-and-sister pair who are the writer's cousins? Or are they a group consisting of the writer's cousins, her brother, and her sister? If they are more than two people, a comma would clear up the confusion.

> I was met at the station by my cousins, brother, and sister.

## 21d Use a comma between coordinate adjectives but not between cumulative adjectives.

Adjectives that function independently of each other, though they modify the same noun, are called **coordinate adjectives.** Set them off with commas.

> Ruth was a clear, vibrant, persuasive speaker.
>
> Life is nasty, brutish, and short.

CAUTION: Don't use a comma after the final adjective before a noun.

> FAULTY My professor was a brilliant, caring, teacher.
>
> EDITED My professor was a brilliant, caring teacher.

To check whether adjectives are coordinate, ask two questions. Can you rearrange the adjectives without distorting the meaning? (*Ruth was a persuasive, vibrant, clear speaker.*) Can you insert *and* between them? (*Life is nasty and brutish and short.*) If the answer to both is yes, the adjectives are coordinate. Removing any one of them would not greatly affect the others. Use commas between them to show that they are separate and equal.

**conjunction:** A linking word that connects words or groups of words through coordination (*and, but*) or subordination (*because, although, unless*)

NOTE: If you link coordinate adjectives with *and* or another conjunction, omit the commas except in a series (see 21c).

> New York City is huge and dirty and beautiful.

**Cumulative adjectives** work together to create a single unified picture of the noun they modify. No commas separate them.

Ruth has two small white poodles.

Who's afraid of the big bad wolf?

For more on cumulative adjectives, see p. 803.

If you remove, rearrange, or insert *and* between cumulative adjectives, the effect is distorted (*two white small poodles; the big and bad wolf*).

## Exercise 21–2 ▪ Using Commas

For more practice, visit **bedfordstmartins.com/bedguide**.

In these sentences, add any necessary commas, remove any unneeded ones, and change any incorrect punctuation. Some sentences may be correct. Answers for the lettered sentences appear at the end of the handbook. Example:

Mel has been a faithful hardworking consistent band manager.

Mel has been a faithful, hardworking, consistent band manager.

a. Mrs. Carver looks like a sweet, little, old lady, but she plays a wicked electric guitar.

b. Her bass player, her drummer and her keyboard player all live in the same retirement community.

c. They practice individually in the afternoon, rehearse together at night and play at the community's Saturday night dances.

d. The Rest Home Rebels have to rehearse quietly, and cautiously, to keep from disturbing the other residents.

e. Mrs. Carver has organized the group, scheduled their rehearsals, and acquired backup instruments.

1. When she breaks a string, she doesn't want her elderly crew to have to grab the guitar change the string and hand it back to her, before the song ends.
2. The Rest Home Rebels' favorite bands are U2, Arcade Fire and Lester Lanin and his orchestra.
3. They watch a lot of MTV because it is fast-paced colorful exciting and informative and it has more variety than soap operas.
4. Just once, Mrs. Carver wants to play in a really, huge, sold-out, arena.
5. She hopes to borrow the community's big, white, van to take herself her band and their equipment to a major, professional, recording studio.

## 21e Use commas to set off a nonrestrictive phrase or clause.

A **nonrestrictive modifier** adds a fact that, while perhaps interesting and valuable, isn't essential. You could leave it out of the sentence and still make sense. Set off the modifier with commas before and after.

> Potts Alley, *which runs north from Chestnut Street,* is too narrow for cars.
>
> At the end of the alley, *where the fair was held last May,* a getaway car waited.

**modifier:** A word (such as an adjective or adverb), phrase, or clause that provides more information about other parts of a sentence: Plays *staged by the drama class* are *always successful.*

A **restrictive modifier** is essential. Omit it and you significantly change the meaning of the modified word and the sentence. Such a modifier is called *restrictive* because it limits what it modifies: it specifies this place, person, or action and no other. Because a restrictive modifier is part of the identity of whatever it modifies, no commas set it off from the rest of the sentence.

> They picked the alley *that runs north from Chestnut Street* because it is close to the highway.
>
> Anyone *who robs my house* will be disappointed.

Leaving out the modifier in that last sentence changes the meaning from potential robbers to humankind.

NOTE: Use *that* to introduce (or to recognize) a restrictive phrase or clause. Use *which* to introduce (or to recognize) a nonrestrictive phrase or clause.

> The food *that I love best* is chocolate.
>
> Chocolate, *which I love,* is not on my diet.

## 21f Use commas to set off nonrestrictive appositives.

Like the modifiers discussed in 21e, an **appositive** can be either restrictive or nonrestrictive. If it is nonrestrictive – if the sentence still makes sense when it is omitted or changed – then set it off with commas before and after.

**appositive:** A word or group of words that adds information by identifying a subject or object in a different way: my dog *Rover,* Hal's brother *Fred*

> My third ex-husband, *Hugo,* will be glad to meet you.
>
> We are bringing dessert, *a blueberry pie,* to follow dinner.

If the appositive is restrictive – if you can't take it out or change it without changing your meaning – then include it without commas.

> Of all the men I've been married to, my ex-husband *Hugo* is the best cook.

### Exercise 21–3 ▪ Using Commas

Add any necessary commas to the following sentences, and remove any commas that do not belong. Draw your own conclusions about what the writer

For more practice, visit **bedfordstmartins.com/bedguide**.

meant to say, as needed. Some sentences may be correct. Possible revisions for the lettered sentences appear at the end of the handbook. Example:

> Jay and his wife the former Laura McCready were college sweethearts.
>
> Jay and his wife, the former Laura McCready, were college sweethearts.

a. We are bringing a dish vegetable lasagna, to the potluck supper.

b. I like to go to Central Bank, on this side of town, because this branch tends to have short lines.

c. The colony, that the English established at Roanoke disappeared mysteriously.

d. If the base commanders had checked their gun room where powder is stored, they would have found that several hundred pounds of gunpowder were missing.

e. Brazil's tropical rain forests which help produce the air we breathe all over the world, are being cut down at an alarming rate.

1. The aye-aye which is a member of the lemur family is threatened with extinction.
2. The party, a dismal occasion ended earlier than we had expected.
3. The general warned that the concessions, that the military was prepared to make, would be withdrawn if not matched by the rebels.
4. Although both of Don's children are blond, his daughter Sharon has darker hair than his son Jake.
5. Herbal tea which has no caffeine makes a better after-dinner drink than coffee.

---

## 21g Use commas to set off conjunctive adverbs.

When you drop a conjunctive adverb into the middle of a clause, set it off with commas before and after.

> Using lead paint in homes has been illegal, *however,* since 1973.
>
> Builders, *indeed,* gave it up some twenty years earlier.

**conjunctive adverb:** A linking word that can connect independent clauses and show a relationship between two ideas: Jen studied hard; *finally,* she passed the exam. (See 14a–14c.)

**parenthetical expression:** An aside to readers or a transitional expression such as *for example* or *in contrast*

## 21h Use commas to set off parenthetical expressions.

Use a pair of commas around any parenthetical expression or any aside from you to your readers.

> Home inspectors, *for this reason,* sometimes test for lead paint.
>
> Cosmic Construction never used lead paint, *or so their spokesperson says,* even when it was legal.

## 21i Use commas to set off a phrase or clause expressing contrast.

It was Rudolph, *not Dasher,* who had a red nose.

EXCEPTION: Short contrasting phrases beginning with *but* need no commas.

It was not Dasher but Rudolph who had a red nose.

## 21j Use commas to set off an absolute phrase.

The link between an absolute phrase and the rest of the sentence is a comma or two commas if the phrase falls in midsentence.

*Our worst fears drawing us together,* we huddled over the letter.

Luke, *his knife being the sharpest,* slit the envelope.

**absolute phrase:** An expression, usually a noun followed by a participle, that modifies an entire clause or sentence and can appear anywhere in the sentence: The stallion pawed the ground, *chestnut mane and tail swirling in the wind.*

### Exercise 21–4 ▪ Using Commas

Add any necessary commas to the following sentences, and change any punctuation that is incorrect. Answers for the lettered sentences appear at the end of the handbook. Example:

The officer a radar gun in his hand gauged the speed of the passing cars.

The officer, a radar gun in his hand, gauged the speed of the passing cars.

a. The university insisted however that the students were not accepted merely because of their parents' generous contributions.

b. This dispute in any case is an old one.

c. It was the young man's striking good looks not his acting ability that first attracted the Hollywood agents.

d. Gretchen learned moreover not always to accept as true what she had read in celebrity magazines.

e. The hikers most of them wearing ponchos or rain jackets headed out into the steady drizzle.

1. The lawsuit demanded furthermore that construction already under way be halted immediately.
2. It is the Supreme Court not Congress or the president that ultimately determines the legality of a law.
3. The judge complained that the case was being tried not by the court but by the media.
4. The actor kneeling recited the lines with great emotion.
5. Both sides' patience running thin workers and management carried the strike into its sixth week.

For more practice, visit **bedfordstmartins.com/bedguide**.

## 21k Use commas to set off a direct quotation from your own words.

When you briefly quote someone, distinguish the source's words from yours with commas (and, of course, quotation marks). When you insert an explanation into a quotation (such as *he said*), set that off with commas.

For advice on using punctuation marks with quotations, see 25g–25i; for advice on using quotation marks, see 25a–25d and C3 in the Quick Editing Guide, pp. A-55–A-56.

> Shakespeare wrote, "Some are born great, some achieve greatness, and some have greatness thrust upon them."
>
> "The best thing that can come with success," commented the actress Liv Ullmann, "is the knowledge that it is nothing to long for."

The comma always comes *before* the quotation marks.

EXCEPTION: Do not use a comma with a very short quotation or one introduced by *that.*

> Don't tell me "yes" if you mean "maybe."
>
> Jules said that "Nothing ventured, nothing gained" is his motto.

**linking verb:** A verb (*is, become, seem, feel*) that shows a state of being by linking the sentence subject with a word that renames or describes the subject: The sky *is* blue. (See 3a.)

Don't use a comma with any quotation run into your own sentence and read as part of it. Often such quotations are introduced by linking verbs.

> Her favorite statement at age three was "I can do it myself."
>
> Shakespeare originated the expression "my salad days, when I was green in judgment."

## 21l Use commas around *yes* and *no,* mild interjections, tag questions, and the name or title of someone directly addressed.

**interjection:** A word or expression (*oh, alas*) that inserts an outburst of feeling at the beginning, middle, or end of a sentence

| | |
|---|---|
| YES AND NO | *Yes,* I'd like a Rolls-Royce, but, *no,* I didn't order one. |
| INTERJECTION | *Well,* don't blame it on me. |
| TAG QUESTION | It would be fun to ride in a Silver Cloud, *wouldn't it?* |
| DIRECT ADDRESS | Drive us home, *James.* |

## 21m Use commas to set off dates, states, countries, and addresses.

> On June 6, 1995, Ned Shaw was born.
>
> East Rutherford, New Jersey, seemed like Paris, France, to him.
>
> His family moved to 11 Maple Street, Middletown, Ohio.

Do not add a comma between state and zip code: *Bedford, MA 01730.*

### Exercise 21-5 ▪ Using Commas

For more practice, visit **bedfordstmartins.com/bedguide.**

Add any necessary commas to the following sentences, remove any commas that do not belong, and change any punctuation that is incorrect. Some sentences may be correct. Answers for the lettered sentences appear at the end of the handbook. Example:

> When Alexander Graham Bell said "Mr. Watson come here, I want you" the telephone entered history.
>
> When Alexander Graham Bell said, "Mr. Watson, come here, I want you," the telephone entered history.

a. César Chávez was born on March 31 1927, on a farm in Yuma, Arizona.

b. Chávez, who spent years as a migrant farmworker, told other farm laborers "If you're outraged at conditions, then you can't possibly be free or happy until you devote all your time to changing them."

c. Chávez founded the United Farm Workers union and did indeed, devote all his time to changing conditions for farmworkers.

d. Robert F. Kennedy called Chávez, "one of the heroic figures of our time."

e. Chávez, who died on April 23, 1993, became the second Mexican American to receive the highest civilian honor in the United States, the Presidential Medal of Freedom.

1. Yes I was born on April 14 1988 in Bombay India.
2. Move downstage Gary, for Pete's sake or you'll run into Mrs. Clackett.
3. Vicki my precious, when you say, "great" or "terrific," look as though you mean it.
4. Perhaps you have forgotten darling that sometimes you make mistakes, too.
5. Well Dotty, it only makes sense that when you say, "Sardines!," you should go off to get the sardines.

---

## 21n Do not use a comma to separate a subject from its verb or a verb from its object.

FAULTY The athlete driving the purple Jaguar, was Jim Fuld. [Subject separated from verb]

EDITED The athlete driving the purple Jaguar was Jim Fuld.

FAULTY The governor should not have given his campaign manager, such a prestigious appointment. [Verb separated from direct object]

EDITED The governor should not have given his campaign manager such a prestigious appointment.

## 21o Do not use a comma between words or phrases joined by correlative or coordinating conjunctions.

For lists of coordinating words, see p. 827.

Do not divide a compound subject or predicate unnecessarily with a comma.

FAULTY Neither Peter Pan, nor the fairy Tinkerbell, saw the pirates sneaking toward their hideout. [Compound subject]

EDITED Neither Peter Pan nor the fairy Tinkerbell saw the pirates sneaking toward their hideout.

FAULTY The chickens clucked, and pecked, and flapped their wings. [Compound predicate]

EDITED The chickens clucked and pecked and flapped their wings.

## 21p Do not use a comma before the first or after the last item in a series.

FAULTY We had to see, my mother's doctor, my father's lawyer, and my dog's veterinarian, in one afternoon.

EDITED We had to see my mother's doctor, my father's lawyer, and my dog's veterinarian in one afternoon.

## 21q Do not use a comma to set off a restrictive word, phrase, or clause.

For an explanation of restrictive modifiers, see 21e.

A restrictive modifier is essential to the definition or identification of whatever it modifies; a nonrestrictive modifier is not.

FAULTY The fireworks, that I saw on Sunday, were the best I've ever seen.

EDITED The fireworks that I saw on Sunday were the best I've ever seen.

## 21r Do not use commas to set off indirect quotations.

For more on quoting someone's exact words, see 25a–25c.

When *that* introduces a quotation, the quotation is indirect and requires neither a comma nor quotation marks.

FAULTY He told us that, we shouldn't have done it.

EDITED He told us that we shouldn't have done it.

This sentence also could be recast as a direct quotation.

EDITED He told us, "You shouldn't have done it."

# 22 | Semicolons

A semicolon is a sort of compromise between a comma and a period: it creates a stop without ending a sentence.

## 22a Use a semicolon to join two main clauses not joined by a coordinating conjunction.

Suppose, having written one statement, you want to add another that is closely related in sense. You decide to keep them both in a single sentence.

> Shooting baskets was my brother's favorite sport; he would dunk them for hours at a time.

A semicolon is a good substitute for a period when you don't want to bring your readers to a complete stop.

> By the yard life is hard; by the inch it's a cinch.

NOTE: When you join a subordinate clause to a main one or join two statements with a coordinating conjunction, you generally need just a comma. Reserve the semicolon to emphasize a close connection or to avoid confusion when long, complex clauses include internal punctuation.

**coordinating conjunction:** A one-syllable linking word (*and, but, for, or, nor, so, yet*) that joins elements with equal or near-equal importance: Jack *and* Jill, sink *or* swim

## 22b Use a semicolon to join two main clauses that are linked by a conjunctive adverb.

You can use a conjunctive adverb to show a relationship between clauses such as addition (*besides*), comparison (*likewise, similarly*), contrast (*instead, however*), emphasis (*namely, certainly*), cause and effect (*thus*), or time (*finally*). When a second statement begins with (or includes) a conjunctive adverb, you can join it to the first with a semicolon. No matter where the conjunctive adverb appears, the semicolon is placed between the two clauses.

For punctuation with conjunctive adverbs within clauses, see 21g.

> Bert is a stand-out player; *indeed,* he's the one hope of our team.
>
> We yearned to attend the concert; tickets, *however,* were hard to come by.

## 22c Use a semicolon to separate items in a series that contain internal punctuation or that are long and complex.

The semicolon is especially useful for setting off one group of items from another. More powerful than a comma, it divides a series of series.

> The auctioneer sold clocks, watches, and cameras; freezers of steaks and tons of bean sprouts; motorcycles, cars, speedboats, canoes, and cabin cruisers; and rare coins, curious stamps, and precious stones.

### Exercise 22–1 ▪ Using Semicolons

Add any necessary semicolons to the following sentences, and change any that are incorrectly used. Some sentences may be correct.

For more practice, visit **bedfordstmartins .com/bedguide**.

Answers for the lettered sentences appear at the end of the handbook. Example:

> They spent all their money, they barely had enough to get home.
>
> They spent all their money; they barely had enough to get home.

a. By the beginning of 2014, Shirley was eager to retire, nevertheless, she agreed to stay on for two more years.

b. The committee was asked to determine the extent of violent crime among teenagers, especially those between the ages of fourteen and sixteen, to act as a liaison between the city and schools and between churches and volunteer organizations, and to draw up a plan to reduce violence, both public and private, by the end of the century.

c. The leaves on the oak trees near the lake were tinged with red, swimmers no longer ventured into the water.

d. The football team has yet to win a game, however, the season is still young.

1. Although taking the subway is slow, it is still faster than driving to work.
2. The Mariners lost all three games to Milwaukee, worse yet, two star players were injured.
3. There was nothing the firefighters could do; the building already had been consumed by flames.
4. Chess is difficult to master; but even a child can learn the basic rules.

---

# 23 | Colons

A colon introduces a further thought, one added to throw light on a first. Some writers use a capital letter to start any complete sentence that follows a colon; others prefer a lowercase letter. Whichever you choose, be consistent. A phrase that follows a colon always begins with a lowercase letter.

## 23a Use a colon between two main clauses if the second exemplifies, explains, or summarizes the first.

**main clause:** A group of words that has both a subject and a verb and can stand alone as a complete sentence: *My friends play softball.*

Like a semicolon, a colon can join two sentences into one. The chief difference is this: a semicolon says merely that two main clauses are related; a colon, like an abbreviation for *that is* or *for example,* says that the second clause gives an example or explanation of the point in the first clause.

> She tried everything: she scoured the Internet, made dozens of phone calls, wrote e-mails, even consulted a lawyer.

## 23b Use a colon to introduce a list or a series.

A colon can introduce a word, a phrase, a series, or a second main clause, sometimes strengthened by *as follows* or *the following.*

> The dance steps are as follows: forward, back, turn, and glide.

When a colon introduces a series of words or phrases, it often means *such as* or *for instance.* A list of examples after a colon need not include *and* before the last item unless all possible examples have been stated.

> On a Saturday night many kinds of people crowd our downtown area: drifters, bored senior citizens, college students out for a good time.

## 23c Use a colon to introduce an appositive.

A colon preceded by a main clause can introduce an **appositive.**

**appositive:** A word or group of words that adds information by identifying a subject or object in a different way: my dog *Rover,* Hal's brother *Fred*

> I have discovered the key to the future: robots.

## 23d Use a colon to introduce a long or comma-filled quotation.

Sometimes you can't conveniently introduce a quoted passage with a comma. Perhaps the quotation is too long or heavily punctuated, or your prefatory remarks demand a longer pause. In either case, use a colon.

> God told Adam and Eve: "Be fruitful, and multiply, and replenish the earth, and subdue it."

## 23e Use a colon when convention calls for it.

| | |
|---|---|
| AFTER A SALUTATION | Dear Professor James: |
| BIBLICAL CITATIONS | Job 9:2 [The book, chapter, verse], but Job 9.2 [MLA] |
| TITLES: SUBTITLES | *Convergences: Essays on Art and Literature* |
| SOURCE REFERENCES | Welty, Eudora. *The Eye of the Story.* New York: Random, 1978. |
| TIME OF DAY | 2:02 p.m. |

## 23f Use a colon only at the end of a main clause.

In a sentence, a colon always follows a complete sentence, never a phrase. Avoid using a colon between a verb and its object, between a preposition and its object, and before a list introduced by *such as.*

**main clause:** A group of words that has both a subject and a verb and can stand alone as a complete sentence: *My friends play softball.*

| | |
|---|---|
| FAULTY | My mother and father are: Bella and Benjamin. |
| REVISED | My mother and father are Bella and Benjamin. |

| | |
|---|---|
| FAULTY | Many great inventors have changed our lives, such as: Edison, Marconi, and Glutz. |
| REVISED | Many great inventors have changed our lives, such as Edison, Marconi, and Glutz. |
| REVISED | Many great inventors have changed our lives: Edison, Marconi, Glutz. |

## Exercise 23–1 ▪ Using Colons

For more practice, visit **bedfordstmartins.com/bedguide**.

Add, remove, or replace colons wherever appropriate in the following sentences. Where necessary, revise the sentences further to support your changes in punctuation. Some sentences may be correct. Possible revisions for the lettered sentences appear at the end of the handbook. Example:

Yum-Yum Burger has franchises in the following cities; New York, Chicago, Miami, San Francisco, and Seattle.

Yum-Yum Burger has franchises in the following cities: New York, Chicago, Miami, San Francisco, and Seattle.

a. The Continuing Education Program offers courses in: building and construction management, engineering, and design.

b. The interview ended with a test of skills, taking messages, operating the computer, typing a sample letter, and proofreading documents.

c. The sample letter began, "Dear Mr. Rasheed, Please accept our apologies for the late shipment."

1. In the case of *Bowers v. Hardwick,* the Supreme Court decided that: citizens had no right to sexual privacy.
2. He ended his speech with a quotation from Homer's *Iliad*, "Whoever obeys the gods, to him they particularly listen."
3. Professor Bligh's book is called *Management, A Networking Approach.*

# 24 | Apostrophes

For advice on editing for apostrophes, see C2 in the Quick Editing Guide, pp. A-54–A-55.

Use apostrophes for three purposes: to show possession, to indicate an omission, and to add an ending to a number, a letter, or an abbreviation.

### 24a To make a singular noun possessive, add *-'s.*

The *plumber's* wrench left grease stains on *Harry's* shirt.

Add *-'s* even when your singular noun ends with the sound of *s*.

*Felix's* roommate enjoys reading *Henry James's* novels.

### Possessive Nouns and Plural Nouns at a Glance

Both plural nouns and possessive nouns often end with *-s.*

- *Plural* means more than one (two *dogs,* six *friends*), but *possessive* means ownership (the *dogs'* biscuits, my *friends'* cars).
- If you can substitute the word *of* for the *-s'* (the biscuits *of* the dogs, the cars *of* my friends), you need the plural possessive with an apostrophe after the *-s.*
- If you cannot substitute *of,* you need the simple plural with no apostrophe (the *dogs* are well fed, my *friends* have no money for gas).

Some writers find it awkward to add *-'s* to nouns that already end in an *-s,* especially those of two syllables or more. You may, if you wish, form such a possessive by adding only an apostrophe.

The Egyptian king *Cheops'* death occurred centuries before *Socrates'.*

## 24b To make a plural noun ending in -*s* possessive, add an apostrophe.

A *stockbrokers'* meeting combines *foxes'* cunning with the noisy chaos of a *boys'* locker room.

## 24c To make a plural noun not ending in -*s* possessive, add -*'s.*

Nouns such as *men, mice, geese,* and *alumni* form the possessive case the same way as singular nouns: with *-'s.*

What effect has the *women's* movement had on *children's* literature?

## 24d To show joint possession by two people or groups, add an apostrophe or -*'s* to the second noun of the pair.

I left my *mother and father's* home with *friends and neighbors'* good wishes.

If the two members of a noun pair possess a set of things individually, add an apostrophe or *-'s* to each noun.

*Men's* and *women's* marathon records are improving steadily.

## 24e To make a compound noun possessive, add an apostrophe or -*'s* to the last word in the compound.

A compound noun consists of more than one word (*commander in chief, sons-in-law*); it may be either singular or plural.

The *commander in chief's* duties will end on July 1.

Esther does not approve of her *sons-in-law's* professions.

## 24f To make an indefinite pronoun possessive, add *-'s*.

Indefinite pronouns such as *anyone, nobody,* and *another* are usually singular; they form the possessive case with *-'s*. (See 24a.)

What caused the accident is *anybody's* guess, but it was *no one's* fault.

## 24g To indicate the possessive of a personal pronoun, use its possessive case.

**personal pronoun:** A pronoun (*I, me, you, it, he, we, them*) that stands for a noun that names a person or thing: Mark awoke slowly, but suddenly *he* bolted from the bed.

The personal pronouns are irregular; each has its own possessive form, none with an apostrophe. Resist adding an apostrophe or *-'s*.

NOTE: *Its* (no apostrophe) is always a possessive pronoun.

I retreated when the Murphys' German shepherd bared *its* fangs.

*It's* (with an apostrophe) is always a contraction of *it is*.

*It's* [It is] not our fault.

For a chart of possessive personal pronouns, see C2 in the Quick Editing Guide, p. A-54.

## 24h Use an apostrophe to indicate an omission in a contraction.

*They're* [They are] too sophisticated for me.

Pat *didn't* [did not] finish her assignment.

Americans grow up admiring the Spirit of *'76* [1776].

*It's* [It is] nearly eight *o'clock* [of the clock].

## 24i Use an apostrophe to form the plural of a letter or word mentioned as a word.

| | |
|---|---|
| LETTER | How many *n*'s are there in *Cincinnati*? |
| WORD | Try replacing all the *should*'s in that list with *could*'s. |

No apostrophes are needed for plural numbers and most abbreviations.

For advice on italicizing a letter, word, or number named as a word, see p. 884.

| | |
|---|---|
| DECADE | The 1990s differed greatly from the 1980s. |
| NUMBER | Cut out two 3s to sew on Larry's shirt. |
| ABBREVIATION | Do we need IDs at YMCAs in other towns? |

## Exercise 24-1 ▪ Using Apostrophes

Correct any errors in the use of the apostrophe in the following sentences. Some sentences may be correct. Answers for the lettered sentences appear at the end of the handbook. Example:

Youd better put on you're new shoes.

*You'd* better put on *your* new shoes.

For more practice, visit **bedfordstmartins.com/bedguide**.

a. Joe and Chucks' fathers were both in the class of 90.
b. They're going to finish their term papers as soon as the party ends.
c. It was a strange coincidence that all three womens' cars broke down after they had picked up their mother's-in-law.
d. Don't forget to dot you're *is* and cross you're *ts*.
e. Mario and Shelley's son is marrying the editor's in chief's daughter.

1. The Hendersons' never change: their always whining about Mr. Scobee farming land thats rightfully their's.
2. Its hard to join a womens' basketball team because so few of them exist.
3. I had'nt expected to hear Janice' voice again.
4. Don't give the Murphy's dog it's biscuit until it's sitting up.
5. Isnt' it the mother and fathers' job to tell kid's to mind their *ps* and *qs*?

# 25 | Quotation Marks

Quotation marks always come in pairs: one at the start and one at the finish of a quoted passage. In the United States, the double quotation mark (“) is preferred over the single one (‘) for most uses. Use quotation marks to set off quoted or highlighted words from the rest of your text.

For more on editing quotation marks, see C3 in the Quick Editing Guide, pp. A-55–A-56.

“Injustice anywhere is a threat to justice everywhere,” wrote Martin Luther King Jr.

For more on quoting, paraphrasing, and summarizing, see Ch. 12, D3–D5 in the Quick Research Guide (pp. A-29–A-30), or Chs. 31 and 34 in *A Writer's Research Manual.*

## 25a Use quotation marks around direct quotations from another writer or speaker.

Enclose someone's exact words in quotation marks.

Anwar al-Sadat reflected the Arab concept of community when he said, “A man's village is his peace of mind.”

Use an indirect quotation to credit and report someone else's idea accurately. Do not use his or her exact words or quotation marks.

For capitalization with quotation marks, see 29j.

Anwar al-Sadat asserted that a community provides a sense of well-being.

For punctuation of direct and indirect quotations, see 21r.

## 25b Use single quotation marks around a quotation inside another quotation.

Sometimes you may quote a source that quotes someone else or puts words in quotation marks. When that happens, use single quotation marks around the internal quotation (even if your source used double ones); put double quotation marks around the larger passage you are quoting.

“My favorite advice from Socrates, ‘Know thyself and fear all women,’” said Dr. Blatz, “has been getting me into trouble lately.”

## ESL Guidelines Direct and Indirect Quotations

When you quote directly, use the exact words of the original writer or speaker; set them off with double quotation marks. When you change a direct quotation into an indirect quotation (someone else's idea reported without using his or her exact words), be sure to reword the quotation. Do not repeat the original wording from a source.

- Be sure to change the punctuation and capitalization. You also may need to change the verb tense.

  DIRECT QUOTATION — Pascal said, “The assignment is on Chinua Achebe, the Nigerian writer.”

  INDIRECT QUOTATION — Pascal said that the assignment was on Chinua Achebe, the Nigerian writer.

- If the direct quotation is a question, you must change the word order in the indirect quotation.

  DIRECT QUOTATION — Jean asked, “How far is it to Boston?”

  INDIRECT QUOTATION — Jean asked how far it was to Boston.

*NOTE:* Use a period, not a question mark, with questions in indirect quotations.

- You often must change pronouns for an indirect quotation.

  DIRECT QUOTATION — Antonio said, “I think you are mistaken.”

  INDIRECT QUOTATION — Antonio said that he thought I was mistaken.

For practice, visit **bedfordstmartins .com/bedguide**.

### 25c Instead of using quotation marks, indent longer quotations.

Suppose you are writing an essay about the value of a college education. You might include a paragraph like this:

In his 2004 commencement address at the College of William & Mary, comedian Jon Stewart advised students to look beyond academic definitions of success:

> College is something you complete. Life is something you experience. So don't worry about your grade, or the results or success. Success is defined in myriad ways, and you will find it, and people will no longer be grading you, but it will come from your own internal sense of decency, which I imagine, after going through the program here, is quite strong . . . although I'm sure downloading illegal files . . . but, nah, that's a different story.

For more on the MLA and APA styles, see section E in the Quick Research Guide (pp. A-32–A-38) and Chs. 36–37.

Indenting the passage shows it is a direct quotation without adding quotation marks. In MLA style, indent quotations of five lines or more by one inch. In APA style, indent quotations of forty words or more by about one-half inch. In both, double-space the quoted lines, and cite the source.

Follow the same practice if you quote four or more lines of a poem.

Phillis Wheatley, the outstanding black poet of colonial America, often made emotional pleas in her poems:

> Attend me, Virtue, thro' my youthful years
> O leave me not to the false joys of time!
> But guide my steps to endless life and bliss.
> Greatness, or Goodness, say what I shall call thee,
> To give me an higher appellation still,
> Teach me a better strain, a nobler lay,
> Oh thou, enthron'd with Cherubs in the realms of day (15-21).

Notice that not only the source's words but her punctuation, capitalization, and line breaks are quoted exactly.

For advice on capitalization and quotations, see 29j.

## 25d In dialogue, use quotation marks around a speaker's words, and mark each change of speaker with a new paragraph.

Randolph gazed at Ellen and sighed. “What extraordinary beauty.”

“They are lovely,” she replied, staring at the roses, “aren't they?”

## 25e Use quotation marks around the titles of a speech, an article in a newspaper or magazine, a short story, a poem shorter than book length, a chapter in a book, a song, and an episode of a television or radio program.

The article “An Updike Retrospective” praises “Solitaire” as the best story in John Updike's collection *Museums and Women.*

In Chapter 5, “Expatriates,” Schwartz discusses Eliot's famous poem “The Love Song of J. Alfred Prufrock.”

For advice on italicizing or underlining titles, see 31a and the chart on p. 884.

## 25f Avoid using quotation marks to show slang, wit, or irony.

INADVISABLE By the time I finished my “chores,” my “day off” was over.

REVISED By the time I finished my chores, my day off was over.

No quotation marks are needed after *so-called* or similar words.

FAULTY The meet included many so-called “champions.”

REVISED The meet included many so-called champions.

## 25g Put commas and periods inside quotation marks.

For more on commas with quotations, see 21k.

A comma or a period is always placed before quotation marks, even if it is not part of the quotation.

We pleaded, "Keep off the grass," in hope of preserving the lawn.

The sign warned pedestrians: "Keep off the grass."

## 25h Put semicolons and colons outside quotation marks.

We said, "Keep off the grass"; they still tromped onward.

## 25i Put other punctuation inside or outside quotation marks depending on its function in the sentence.

Parentheses that are part of the quotation go inside the quotation marks. Parentheses that are your own, not part of the quotation, go outside.

We said, "Keep off the grass (unless it's artificial turf)."

They tromped onward (although we had said, "Keep off the grass").

If a question mark, exclamation point, or dash is part of the quotation, place it inside the quotation marks. Otherwise, place it after them.

Who hollered "Fire"? She hollered, "Fire!"

Don't close a sentence with two end punctuation marks, one inside and one outside the quotation marks. If the quoted passage ends with a dash, exclamation point, question mark, or period, you need not add any further end punctuation. If the quoted passage falls within a question asked by you, however, the sentence should finish with a question mark, even if that means dropping other end punctuation (*Who hollered "Fire"?*).

### Exercise 25–1 ▪ Using Quotation Marks

For more practice, visit **bedfordstmartins .com/bedguide**.

Add quotation marks wherever they are needed in the following sentences, and correct any other errors. Answers for the lettered sentences appear at the end of the handbook. Example:

Annie asked him, Do you believe in free will?

Annie asked him, "Do you believe in free will?"

a. What we still need to figure out, the police chief said, is whether the victim was acquainted with his assailant.

b. A skillful orator, Patrick Henry is credited with the comment Give me liberty or give me death.

c. I could hear the crowd chanting my name – Jones! Jones! – and that spurred me on, said Bruce Jones, the winner of the 5,000-meter race.

d. The video for the rock group Guns N' Roses' epic song November Rain is based on a short story by Del James.

e. In response to a possible asteroid strike on Earth, former astronaut Rusty Schweickart says, Every country is at risk.

1. That day at school, the kids were as "high as kites."
2. Notice, the professor told the class, Cassius's choice of imagery when he asks, Upon what meat doth this our Caesar feed, / That he is grown so great?
3. "As I was rounding the bend," Peter explained, "I failed to see the sign that said Caution: Ice.
4. John Cheever's story The Swimmer begins with the line It was one of those midsummer Sundays when everyone sits around saying, I drank too much last night.
5. Who coined the saying Love is blind?

# 26 | Dashes

A **dash** is a horizontal line used to separate parts of a sentence – a dramatic substitute for a comma, semicolon, or colon. Your software may turn a typed dash, two hyphens without any spaces, to an unbroken line.

## 26a Use a dash to indicate a sudden break in thought or shift in tone.

The dash signals that a surprise is in store: a shift in viewpoint, perhaps, or an unfinished statement.

Ivan doesn't care which team wins – he bet on both.

I didn't notice my parents' accented speech – at least not at home.

## 26b Use a dash to introduce an explanation, an illustration, or a series.

Use a dash to add an informal preparatory pause or to introduce an appositive that needs drama or contains commas.

**appositive:** A word or group of words that adds information by identifying a subject or object in a different way: my dog *Rover,* Hal's brother *Fred*

My advice to you is simple – stop complaining.

Longfellow wrote about three young sisters – grave Alice, laughing Allegra, and Edith with golden hair – in "The Children's Hour."

## 26c Use dashes to set off an emphatic aside or parenthetical expression from the rest of a sentence.

**parenthetical expression:** An aside to readers or a transitional expression such as *for example* or *in contrast*

It was as hot – and I mean *hot* – as the Fourth of July in Death Valley.

## 26d Avoid overusing dashes.

To compare dashes with commas, see 21, and with parentheses, see 27a–27b.

The dash becomes meaningless if used too often. Use it only when a comma, a colon, or parentheses don't seem strong enough.

EXCESSIVE Algy's grandmother—a sweet old lady—asked him to pick up some things at the store—milk, eggs, and cheese.

EDITED Algy's grandmother, a sweet old lady, asked him to pick up some things at the store: milk, eggs, and cheese.

### Exercise 26–1 ■ Using Dashes

For more practice, visit **bedfordstmartins.com/bedguide**.

Add, remove, or replace dashes wherever appropriate in the following sentences. Some sentences may be correct. Possible answers for the lettered sentences appear at the end of the handbook. Example:

Stanton had all the identifying marks, boating shoes, yellow slicker, sunblock, and an anchor, of a sailor.

Stanton had all the identifying marks—boating shoes, yellow slicker, sunblock, and an anchor—of a sailor.

a. I enjoy going hiking with my friend John—whom I've known for fifteen years.
b. Pedro's new boat is spectacular: a regular seagoing Ferrari.
c. The Thompsons devote their weekends to their favorite pastime, eating bags of potato chips and cookies beside the warm glow of the television.

1. The sport of fishing—or at least some people call it a sport—is boring, dirty—and tiring.
2. At that time, three states in the Sunbelt, Florida, California, and Arizona, were the fastest growing in the nation.
3. LuLu was ecstatic when she saw her grades, all A's!

# 27 | Parentheses, Brackets, and Ellipses

Parentheses (singular, *parenthesis*) work in pairs. So do brackets. Both surround bits of information to make a statement perfectly clear. An ellipsis mark is a trio of periods inserted to show that something has been cut.

## Parentheses

### 27a Use parentheses to set off interruptions that are useful but not essential.

> FDR (as people called Franklin D. Roosevelt) won four elections.
>
> He occupied the White House for so many years (1933 to mid-1945) that babies became teens without having known any other president.

The material within parentheses may be helpful, but it isn't essential. Use parentheses to add a qualification, a helpful date, or a brief explanation – words that, in conversation, you might add in a changed tone of voice.

### 27b Use parentheses around letters or numbers indicating items in a series.

> Archimedes asserted that, given (1) a lever long enough, (2) a fulcrum, and (3) a place to stand, he could move the earth.

No parentheses are needed for numbers or letters in an indented list.

---

### Exercise 27–1 ▪ Using Parentheses

For more practice, visit **bedfordstmartins.com/bedguide**.

Add, remove, or replace parentheses wherever appropriate in the following sentences. Some sentences may be correct. Possible answers for the lettered sentences appear at the end of the handbook. Example:

> The Islamic fundamentalist Ayatollah Khomeini – 1900-1989 – was a cleric and leader of Iran in the late twentieth century.
>
> The Islamic fundamentalist Ayatollah Khomeini (1900-1989) was a cleric and leader of Iran in the late twentieth century.

a. Our cafeteria serves the four basic food groups: white – milk, bread, and mashed potatoes – brown – mystery meat and gravy – green – overcooked vegetables and underwashed lettuce – and orange – squash, carrots, and tomato sauce.

b. The hijackers will release the hostages only if the government, 1, frees all political prisoners and, 2, allows the hijackers to leave the country.

c. When Phil said he works with whales (as well as other marine mammals) for the Whale Stranding Network, Lisa thought he meant that his group lures whales onto beaches.

1. The new pear-shaped bottles will hold 200 milliliters, 6.8 fluid ounces, of lotion.

2. World War I, or "The Great War," as it was once called, destroyed the old European order forever.
3. The Internet is a mine of fascinating, and sometimes useless, information.

## Brackets

Brackets, those open-ended typographical boxes, work in pairs like parentheses. Their special purpose is to mark changes in quoted material.

### 27c Use brackets to add information or to make changes within a direct quotation.

For advice on quoting, paraphrasing, and summarizing, see Ch. 12, D3–D5 in the Quick Research Guide (pp. A-29–A-30), or Chs. 31 and 34 in *A Writer's Research Manual.*

A quotation must be quoted exactly. If you add or alter a word or a phrase in a quotation from another writer, place brackets around your changes.

Suppose you are writing about James McGuire's being named chairman of the board of directors of General Motors. In your source, the actual words are these: "A radio bulletin first brought the humble professor of philosophy the astounding news." But in your paper, you want readers to know the professor's identity. So you add that information, in brackets.

> "A radio bulletin first brought the humble professor of philosophy [James McGuire] the astounding news."

Never alter a quoted statement any more than you have to. Ask yourself: Do I really need this quotation, or should I paraphrase?

### 27d Use brackets around *sic* to indicate an error in a direct quotation.

When you faithfully quote a statement that contains an error, follow the error with a bracketed *sic* (Latin for "so" or "so the writer says"). Usually you're better off paraphrasing an error-riddled passage.

> The book *Cake Wrecks* includes a photo of a cake with this message written on top in icing: Happy Thanksgiven [*sic*].

## Ellipses

### 27e Use ellipses to signal that you have omitted part of a quotation.

Occasionally you will want to quote just the parts of a passage that relate to your topic. Acknowledge your cuts with **ellipses:** three periods with a space between each one (. . .). If ellipses conclude a sentence, precede them with a period placed at the end of the sentence. Suppose you want to quote from Marie Winn's book *Children without Childhood* (New York: Penguin, 1984) but omit some of its detail. Use ellipses to show each cut:

According to Winn, children's innocence can be easily lost: "Today's nine- and ten-year-olds . . . not infrequently find themselves involved in their own parents' complicated sex lives, . . . at least as advisers, friendly commentators, and intermediaries."

## 27f Avoid using ellipses at the beginning or end of a quotation.

Even though a source continues after a quoted passage, you don't need ellipses at the end of your quotation. Nor do you need to begin a quotation with three dots. Save the ellipses for words you omit *inside* whatever you quote. If you cut more than a section or two, think about paraphrasing.

For more on quoting, paraphrasing, and summarizing, see Ch. 12, D3–D5 in the Quick Research Guide (pp. A-29–A-30), or Chs. 31 and 34 in *A Writer's Research Manual.*

## Exercise 27–2 ▪ Using Brackets and Ellipses

The following are two hypothetical passages from original essays. Each one is followed by a set of quotations. Paraphrase or adapt each quotation, using brackets and ellipses, and splice it into the essay passage.

For more practice, visit **bedfordstmartins .com/bedguide**.

1. ESSAY PASSAGE

Most people are willing to work hard for a better life. Too often, however, Americans do not realize that the desire for more possessions leads them away from the happiness they hope to find. Many people work longer and longer hours to earn more money and as a result have less time to devote to family, friends, and activities that are truly important. When larger houses, sport-utility vehicles, and wide-screen TVs fail to bring them joy, they find even more things to buy and work even harder to pay for them. This cycle can grind down the most optimistic American. The only solution is to realize how few material possessions people absolutely need to have.

QUOTATIONS

a. Only when he has ceased to need things can a man truly be his own master and so really exist. —Anwar al-Sadat

b. I like to walk amidst the beautiful things that adorn the world; but private wealth I should decline, or any sort of personal possessions, because they would take away my liberty. —George Santayana

c. To live content with small means; to seek elegance rather than luxury, and refinement rather than fashion; to be worthy, not respectable and wealthy, not rich; to study hard, think quietly, talk gently, act frankly; to listen to stars and birds, to babes and sages, with open heart; to bear all cheerfully, do all bravely, await occasions, hurry never. In a word, to let the spiritual, unbidden and unconscious, grow up through the common. This is to be my symphony.

—William Henry Channing

2. ESSAY PASSAGE

Every human life is touched by the natural world. Before the modern industrial era, most people recognized the earth as the giver and supporter of existence. Nowadays, with the power of technology, we can (if we choose) destroy many of the complex balances of nature. With such power comes responsibility. We are no longer merely nature's children, but nature's parents as well.

QUOTATIONS

a. The overwhelming importance of the atmosphere means that there are no longer any frontiers to defend against pollution, attack, or propaganda. It means, further, that only by a deep patriotic devotion to one's country can there be a hope of the kind of protection of the whole planet, which is necessary for the survival of the people of other countries. —Anthropologist Margaret Mead

b. The survival of our wildlife is a matter of grave concern to all of us in Africa. These wild creatures amid the wild places they inhabit are not only important as a source of wonder and inspiration but are an integral part of our natural resources and of our future livelihood and well-being. —Former president of Tanzania Julius Nyerere

# Mechanics

42



**Learning by Doing** Justifying Conventions

Working with a group, select a troublesome convention for using hyphens, italics, or other mechanics. Read through one section about that mark, and decode that guideline. Then try to figure out why you think this convention is expected in academic writing and how you can remember to apply it. (Feel free to make up humorous examples to help all of you more consistently follow convention.)

## 28 | Abbreviations

Abbreviations enable a writer to include necessary information in capsule form. Limit abbreviations to those common enough for readers to recognize, or add an explanation so that a reader does not wonder, "What does this mean?" Remember: when in doubt, spell it out.

### 28a Use abbreviations for some titles with proper names.

Abbreviate the following titles:

Mr. and Mrs. Hubert Collins　　Dr. Martin Luther King Jr.
Ms. Martha Reading　　St. Matthew

For advice on punctuating abbreviations, see 20b.

Write out other titles in full, including titles unfamiliar to readers of English, such as *M.* (for the French *Monsieur*) or *Sr.* (for the Spanish *Señor*).

| | |
|---|---|
| General Douglas MacArthur | Senator Dianne Feinstein |
| President Barack Obama | Professor Shirley Fixler |

Spell out most titles that appear without proper names.

FAULTY Tomás is studying to be a dr.

REVISED Tomás is studying to be a doctor.

When an abbreviated title (such as an academic degree) follows a proper name, set it off with commas. Don't add commas otherwise.

Alice Martin, CPA, is the accountant for Charlotte Cordera, PhD.

My brother has a BA in economics.

Avoid repeating forms of the same title before and after a proper name. Use either *Dr. Jane Doe* or *Jane Doe, DDS,* but not *Dr. Jane Doe, DDS.*

## 28b Use *a.m., p.m., BC, AD,* and *$* with numbers.

9:05 a.m. 3:45 p.m. 2000 BC AD 1066

In case you are curious about abbreviations pinpointing years and times, *a.m.* means *ante meridiem,* Latin for "before noon"; *p.m.* means *post meridiem,* "after noon." AD is *anno domini,* Latin for "in the year of the Lord"—that is, since the official year of Jesus' birth. BC stands for "before Christ" and BCE for "before the common era."

For exact prices that include cents and for amounts in the millions, use a dollar sign with figures (*$17.95, $10.52, $3.5 billion*). Avoid combining an abbreviation with wording that means the same: *$1 million,* not *$1 million dollars; 9:05 a.m.* or *9:05 in the morning,* not *9:05 a.m. in the morning.*

## 28c Avoid abbreviating names of months, days of the week, units of measurement, or parts of literary works.

Many abbreviations in citations should be spelled out in MLA essay style.

NAMES OF MONTHS AND DAYS OF THE WEEK

After their session on September 3 [*or* the third of September], they did not meet until Friday, December 12.

UNITS OF MEASUREMENT

It would take 10,000 pounds of concrete to build a causeway 25 feet by 58 inches.

PARTS OF LITERARY WORKS

Von Bargen's reply appears in volume 2, chapter 12, page 187.

Leona first speaks in act 1, scene 2 [*or* the second scene of act 1].

## 28d Use the full English version of most Latin abbreviations.

Follow the conventions of your citation style if you use Latin abbreviations in source citations, parentheses, and brackets. However, unless you are writing for an audience of ancient Romans, translate most Latin abbreviations into English in your text.

For the use of *sic* to identify an error, see 27d.

COMMON LATIN ABBREVIATIONS

| ABBREVIATION | LATIN | ENGLISH |
|---|---|---|
| et al. | *et alia* | and others, and the others (people) |
| etc. | *et cetera* | and so forth, and others, and the rest |
| i.e. | *id est* | that is |
| e.g. | *exempli gratia* | for example, such as |

## 28e Use abbreviations for familiar organizations, corporations, and people.

Most sets of initials that are capitalized and read as letters do not require periods between the letters (CIA, JFK, UCLA). A set of initials that is pronounced as a word is called an **acronym** (NATO, AIDS, UNICEF) and never has periods between letters.

To avoid misunderstanding, write out an organization's full name the first time you mention it, followed by its initials in parentheses. Then, in later references, you can rely on initials alone. (For very familiar initials, such as FBI or CBS, you need not give the full name.)

## 28f Avoid abbreviations for countries.

When you mention the United States or another country in your text, give its full name unless the repetition would weigh down your paragraph.

> The president will return to the United States [*not* US] on Tuesday from a trip to the United Kingdom [*not* UK].

EXCEPTION: Unlike *US* as a noun, the abbreviation, used consistently with traditional periods or without, is acceptable as an adjective: *US Senate, U.S. foreign policy*. For other countries, find an alternative: *British ambassador*. Follow your citation style when you cite or list government documents.

## Exercise 28–1 ▪ Using Abbreviations

Substitute abbreviations for words and vice versa as appropriate in the following sentences. Correct any incorrectly used abbreviations. Answers for the lettered sentences appear at the end of the handbook. Example:

For more practice, visit **bedfordstmartins.com/bedguide**.

> Please return this form no later than noon on Wed., Apr. 7.
>
> Please return this form no later than noon on *Wednesday, April 7.*

a. Prof. James has office hours on Mon. and Tues., beginning at 10:00 a.m.
b. Emotional issues, e.g., abortion and capital punishment, cannot be settled easily by compromise.
c. The red peppers are selling for three dollars and twenty-five cents a lb.

1. Hamlet's famous soliloquy comes in act three, sc. one.
2. A.I.D.S. has affected people throughout U.S. society, not just gay men and IV-drug users.
3. The end of the cold war between the U.S. and the Soviet Union complicated the role of the U.N. and drastically altered the purpose of N.A.T.O.

---

# 29 | Capital Letters

For advice and a useful chart on capitalization, see D1 in the Quick Editing Guide, p. A-56.

Use capital letters only with good reason. If you think a word will work in lowercase letters, you're probably right.

For capitalization following a colon, see 23.

## 29a Capitalize proper names and adjectives made from proper names.

Proper names designate individuals, places, organizations, institutions, brand names, and certain other distinctive things. Any proper noun can have an adjective form, also capitalized.

| | | |
|---|---|---|
| Miles Standish | University of Iowa | Australian beer |
| Belgium | a Volkswagen | a Renaissance man |
| United Nations | a Xerox copier | Shakespearean comedy |

## 29b Capitalize a title or rank before a proper name.

During her second term, Senator Wilimczyk proposed several bills.

In his lecture, Professor Jones analyzed fossil evidence.

Titles that do not come before proper names usually are not capitalized.

Ten senators voted against the research appropriation.

Jones is the department's only full professor.

EXCEPTION: The abbreviation of an academic or professional degree is always capitalized. The informal name of a degree is not capitalized.

Dora E. McLean, MD, also holds a BA in music.

Dora holds a bachelor's degree in music.

## 29c Capitalize a family relationship only when it is part of a proper name or when it substitutes for a proper name.

Do you know the song about Mother Machree?

I have invited Mother to visit next weekend.

I would like you to meet my aunt, Emily Smith.

## 29d Capitalize the names of religions, their deities, and their followers.

| | | | |
|---|---|---|---|
| Christianity | Muslims | Jehovah | Krishna |
| Islam | Methodists | Allah | the Holy Spirit |

## 29e Capitalize proper names of places, regions, and geographic features.

| | | |
|---|---|---|
| Los Angeles | the Black Hills | the Atlantic Ocean |
| Death Valley | Big Sur | the Philippines |

Do not capitalize *north, south, east,* or *west* unless it is part of a proper name (*West Virginia, South Orange*) or refers to formal geographic locations.

Drive south to Chicago and then east to Cleveland.

Jim, who has always lived in the South, likes to read about the Northeast.

A common noun such as *street, avenue, boulevard, park, lake,* or *hill* is capitalized when part of a proper name.

Meinecke Avenue Hamilton Park Lake Michigan

## 29f Capitalize days of the week, months, and holidays, but not seasons or academic terms.

During spring term, by the Monday after Passover, I have to choose between the January study plan and junior year abroad.

## 29g Capitalize historical events, periods, and documents.

| | |
|---|---|
| Black Monday | the Roaring Twenties |
| the Civil War [*but* a civil war] | Magna Carta |
| the Holocaust [*but* a holocaust] | Declaration of Independence |
| the Bronze Age | Atomic Energy Act |

## 29h Capitalize the names of schools, colleges, departments, and courses.

West School, Central High School [*but* middle school, high school]

Reed College, Arizona State University [*but* the college, a university]

Department of History [*but* history department, department office]

Feminist Perspectives in British Literature [*but* literature course]

## 29i Capitalize the first, last, and main words in titles.

When you write the title of a paper, book, article, work of art, television show, poem, or performance, capitalize the first and last words and all main words in between. Do not capitalize articles (*a, an, the*), coordinating conjunctions (*and, but, for, or, nor, so, yet*), or prepositions (such as *in, on, at, of, from*) unless they come first or last in the title or follow a colon.

For advice on using quotation marks and italics for titles, see 25e and 31a.

| | |
|---|---|
| ESSAY | "Once More to the Lake" |
| NOVEL | *Of Mice and Men* |
| VOLUME OF POETRY | *Poems after Martial* |
| POEM | "A Valediction: Of Weeping" |

## 29j Capitalize the first letter of a quoted sentence.

For advice on punctuating quotations, see 25g–25i.

Oscar Wilde wrote, "The only way to get rid of a temptation is to yield to it."

Only the first word of a quoted sentence is capitalized, even when you break the sentence with words of your own.

"The only way to get rid of a temptation," wrote Oscar Wilde, "is to yield to it."

For advice on using brackets to show changes in quotations, see 27c.

If you quote more than one sentence, start each one with a capital letter.

"Art should never try to be popular," said Wilde. "The public should try to make itself artistic."

Select a quoted passage carefully so that you can present its details accurately as it blends in with your sentence.

### Exercise 29-1 ▪ Using Capitalization

For more practice, visit **bedfordstmartins.com/bedguide**.

Correct any capitalization errors in the following sentences. Some sentences may be correct. Answers for the lettered sentences appear at the end of the handbook. Example:

"The quality of mercy," says Portia in Shakespeare's *The Merchant Of Venice*, "Is not strained."

"The quality of mercy," says Portia in Shakespeare's *The Merchant of Venice,* "is not strained."

a. At our Family Reunion, I met my Cousin Sam for the first time, as well as my father's brother George.
b. I already knew from dad that his brother had moved to Australia years ago to explore the great barrier reef.
c. When my Uncle announced that he was moving to a Continent thousands of miles Southwest of the United States, his Mother gave him a bible to take along.

1. My Aunt, Linda McCallum, lived in the San Fernando valley and received her Doctorate from one of the State Universities in California.
2. She has pursued her interest in Hispanic Studies by traveling to South America from her home in Northeastern Australia.
3. She uses her maiden name – Linda McCallum, PhD – for her nonprofit business, Hands across the Sea.

# 30 | Numbers

Unless you are writing in a scientific field or your essay relies on statistics, you'll generally want to use words (*twenty-seven*). Figures (*27*) are most appropriate in contexts where readers are used to seeing them, such as times and dates (*11:05 p.m. on March 15*).

## 30a In general, write out a number that consists of one or two words, and use figures for longer numbers.

Short names of numbers are easily read (*ten, six hundred*); longer ones take more thought (*two thousand four hundred eighty-seven*). For numbers of more than a word or two, use figures.

Two hundred fans paid twenty-five dollars apiece for that shirt.

A frog's tongue has 970,580 taste buds; a human's has six times as many.

EXCEPTION: For multiples of a million or more, use a figure plus a word.

The earth is 93 million miles from the sun.

## 30b Use figures for most addresses, dates, decimals, fractions, parts of literary works, percentages, exact prices, scores, statistics, and times.

For examples, see Figures at a Glance on p. 882.

Using figures is mainly a matter of convenience. If you think words will be easier for your readers to follow, you can always write out a number.

### Figures at a Glance

| | |
|---|---|
| ADDRESSES | 4 East 74th Street; also, One Copley Place, 5 Fifth Avenue |
| DATES | May 20, 2007; 450 BC; also, Fourth of July |
| DECIMALS | 98.6° Fahrenheit; .57 acre |
| FRACTIONS | 3½ years; 1¾ miles; half a loaf, three-fourths of voters |
| PARTS OF LITERARY WORKS | volume 2, chapter 5, page 37, act 1, scene 2 (*or* act I, scene ii) |
| PERCENTAGES | 25 percent; 99.9 percent; also, 25%, 99.9% |
| EXACT PRICES | $1.99; $200,000; also, $5 million, ten cents, a dollar |
| SCORES | a 114–111 victory; a final score of 5 to 3 |
| STATISTICS | men in the 25–30 age group; odds of 5 to 1 (*or* 5–1 odds); height 5′7″; also, three out of four doctors |
| TIMES | 2:29 p.m.; 10:15 tomorrow morning; also, half past four, three o'clock (always with a number in words) |

## 30c Use words or figures consistently for numbers in the same category throughout a passage.

For more on the plurals of figures (*6s, 1960s*), see 24i.

Switching back and forth between words and figures for numbers can be distracting to readers. Choose whichever form suits like numbers in your passage, and use that form consistently for all numbers in the same category.

> Of the 276 representatives who voted, 97 supported a 25 percent raise, while 179 supported a 30 percent raise over five years.

## 30d Write out a number that begins a sentence.

When a number starts a sentence, either write it out, move it deeper into the sentence, or reword the opening.

> Five percent of the frogs in our aquarium ate sixty-two percent of the flies.
>
> Ten thousand people packed an arena built for 8,550.

## Exercise 30–1 ▪ Using Numbers

For more practice, visit **bedfordstmartins .com/bedguide**.

Correct any inappropriate uses of numbers in the following sentences. Some sentences may be correct. Answers for the lettered sentences appear at the end of the handbook. Example:

As Feinberg notes on page 197, a delay of 3 minutes cost the researchers 5 years' worth of work.

As Feinberg notes on page 197, a delay of *three* minutes cost the researchers *five* years' worth of work.

a. A program to help save the sea otter transferred more than eighty animals to a new colony over the course of 2 years; however, all but 34 otters swam back home again.

b. 12 percent or so of the estimated fifteen billion plastic water bottles purchased annually in the United States are recycled.

c. In act two, scene nine, of Shakespeare's *The Merchant of Venice,* Portia's 2nd suitor fails to guess which of 3 caskets contains her portrait.

1. *Fourscore* means 4 times 20; a *fortnight* means 2 weeks; and a *brace* is two of anything.
2. 50 years ago, traveling from New York City to San Francisco took approximately 15 hours by plane, 50 hours by train, and almost 100 hours by car.
3. At 7 o'clock this morning the temperature was already ninety-seven degrees Fahrenheit.

# 31 | Italics

*Italic type—as in this line—slants to the right.* In handwriting, indicate italics by underlining. Slightly harder to read than perpendicular type, it is usually saved for emphasis or other special uses.

## 31a Italicize certain titles, names, and words. Use italics for the types of titles, names, and words shown on page 884.

We read the story "Araby" in James Joyce's book *Dubliners.*

The Broadway musical *My Fair Lady* was based on Shaw's play *Pygmalion.*

## 31b Use italics sparingly for emphasis.

When you absolutely *must* stress a term, use italics. In most cases, the structure of your sentence should give emphasis where emphasis is due.

He put the package *under* the mailbox, not *into* the mailbox.

People living in affluent countries may not be aware that nearly *sixteen thousand children per day* die of starvation or malnutrition.

For titles that need to be placed in quotation marks, see 25e.

## Italics at a Glance

### Titles

MAGAZINES, NEWSPAPERS, AND SCHOLARLY JOURNALS

*Newsweek* the *London Times* *Film & History*

LONG LITERARY WORKS

*The Bluest Eye* (a novel) *The Less Deceived* (a collection of poems)

FILMS

*Psycho* *Casablanca* *Avatar*

PAINTINGS AND OTHER WORKS OF ART

*Four Dancers* (a painting) *The Thinker* (a sculpture)

LONG MUSICAL WORKS

*Aïda* Handel's *Messiah*

CDS AND RECORD ALBUMS

*Crash* *The Chronic*

TELEVISION AND RADIO PROGRAMS

*Heroes* *All Things Considered*

### Other Words and Phrases

NAMES OF AIRCRAFT, SPACECRAFT, SHIPS, AND TRAINS

the *Orient Express* the *Challenger*

A WORD OR PHRASE FROM A FOREIGN LANGUAGE IF IT IS NOT IN EVERYDAY USE

Gandhi taught the principles of *satya* and *ahimsa:* truth and nonviolence.

EVERYDAY USE

I prefer provolone to mozzarella.

A LETTER, NUMBER, WORD, OR PHRASE WHEN YOU DEFINE IT OR REFER TO IT AS A WORD

The neon *5* on the door identified the club's address.

The rhythmic motion of the alimentary canal is called *peristalsis.*

What do you think *fiery* suggests in the second line?

When you give a synonym or translation — a definition of just a word or so — italicize the word and put its definition in quotation marks.

The word *orthodoxy* means "conformity."

*Trois, drei,* and *tres* are all words for "three."

EXCEPTION: The names of the Bible (King James Version, Revised Standard Version), the books of the Bible (Genesis, Matthew), and other sacred books (the Qur'an, the Rig-Veda) are not italicized.

For more practice, visit **bedfordstmartins.com/bedguide**.

## Exercise 31–1 ▪ Using Italics

Add or remove italics as needed in the following sentences. Some sentences may be correct. Answers for the lettered sentences appear at the end of the handbook. Example:

> Hiram could not *believe* that his parents had seen *the Beatles'* legendary performance at Shea Stadium.
>
> Hiram could not believe that his parents had seen the Beatles' legendary performance at Shea Stadium.

a. Does "avocado" mean "lawyer" in Spanish?

b. During this year's *First Night* celebrations, we heard Verdi's Requiem and Monteverdi's Orfeo.

c. It was fun watching the passengers on the Europa trying to dance to *Blue Moon* in the midst of a storm.

1. Jan can never remember whether Cincinnati has three n's and one t or two n's and two t's.
2. My favorite comic bit in "The Pirates of Penzance" is Major General Stanley's confusion between "orphan" and "often."
3. In Tom Stoppard's play "The Real Thing," the character Henry accuses Bach of copying a *cantata* from a popular song by *Procol Harum.*

# 32 | Hyphens

The hyphen, the transparent tape of punctuation, is used to join words and to connect parts of words.

## 32a Use hyphens in compound words that require them.

Compound words in the English language take three forms:

1. Two or more words combined into one (*crossroads, salesperson*)
2. Two or more separate words that function as one (*gas station, high school*)
3. Two or more words linked by hyphens (*sister-in-law, window-shop*)

Compounds fall into these categories more by custom than by rule. When you're not sure which way to write a compound, refer to a current collegiate dictionary. If the compound is not listed, write it as two words.

Use a hyphen in a compound word containing one or more elements beginning with a capital letter.

> Bill says that, as a *neo-Marxist* living in an *A-frame* house, it would be politically incorrect for him to wear a Mickey Mouse *T-shirt.*

Exceptions to this rule include *unchristian,* for one.

## 32b Use a hyphen in a compound adjective preceding, but not following, a noun.

> Jerome, a devotee of *twentieth-century* music, has no interest in the classic symphonies of the *eighteenth century.*

> I'd like living in an *out-of-the-way* place better if it weren't so far *out of the way.*

In a series of hyphenated adjectives with the same second word, you can omit that word (but not the hyphen) in all but the last adjective of the series.

> Julia is a lover of eighteenth-, nineteenth-, and twentieth-century music.

The adverb *well,* when coupled with an adjective, follows the same hyphenation rules as if it were an adjective.

> It is *well known* that Tony has a *well-equipped* kitchen, although his is not as *well equipped* as the hotel's.

Do *not* use a hyphen to link an adverb ending in *-ly* with an adjective.

> The sun hung like a newly minted penny in a freshly washed sky.

## 32c Use a hyphen after the prefixes *all-, ex-,* and *self-* and before the suffix *-elect.*

> Lucille's *ex-husband* is studying *self-hypnosis.*

> This *all-important* debate pits Senator Browning against the *president-elect.*

## 32d Use a hyphen in most cases if an added prefix or suffix creates a double vowel, a triple consonant, or an ambiguous pronunciation.

It is also acceptable to omit the hyphen in the case of a double *e: reeducate.*

> The contractor's *pre-estimate* did not cover any *pre-existing* flaws.

> The recreation department favors the *re-creation* of a summer program.

## 32e Use a hyphen in spelled-out fractions and compound whole numbers from twenty-one to ninety-nine.

When her sister gave Leslie's age as six and *three-quarters,* Leslie corrected her: "I'm six and *five-sixths!*"

The fifth graders learned that *forty-four* rounds down to forty while *forty-five* rounds up to fifty.

## 32f Use a hyphen to indicate inclusive numbers.

The section covering the years 1975-1980 is found on pages 20-27.

## 32g Use a hyphen to break a word between syllables at the end of a line.

Academic style guides (such as MLA and APA) prefer that you turn off your word processor's automatic hyphenation function. If you are designing a text that requires breaking a word, check your dictionary for its syllable divisions.

### Exercise 32–1 ▪ Using Hyphens

Add necessary hyphens and remove incorrectly used hyphens in the following sentences. Some sentences may be correct. Answers for the lettered sentences appear at the end of the handbook. Example:

Her exhusband works part-time as a short order cook.

Her *ex-husband* works part-time as a *short-order* cook.

a. Jimmy is a lively four year old boy, and his sister is two years old.
b. The badly damaged ship was in no condition to enter the wide-open waters beyond the bay.
c. Tracy's brother in law lives with his family in a six room apartment.

1. Heat-seeking missiles are often employed in modern air-to-air combat.
2. *The Piano* is a beautifully-crafted film with first-rate performances by Holly Hunter and Harvey Keitel.
3. Nearly three fourths of the money in the repair and maintenance account already has been spent.

For more practice, visit **bedfordstmartins.com/bedguide**.

For a list of commonly confused homonyms, see D2 in the Quick Editing Guide, pp. A-56–A-59. See also A Glossary of Troublemakers, in 34.

For more spelling information and practice, visit **bedfordstmartins .com/bedguide**.

# 33 | Spelling

English spelling so often defies the rules that many writers wonder if, indeed, there *are* rules. How, then, are you to cope? You can proofread carefully and use your spell checker. You can refer to lists of commonly misspelled words and of **homonyms,** words that sound the same, or almost the same, but are spelled differently.

You can also use several tactics to teach yourself to be a better speller.

1. *Use mnemonic devices.* To make unusual spellings stick in your memory, invent associations. Using such mnemonic devices (tricks to aid memory) may help you with whatever troublesome spelling you are determined to remember. *Weird* behaves *weirdly*. Rise ag*ain*, Brit*ain*! One *d* in *dish,* one in *radish*. Why isn't *math*ematics like *ath*letics? You write a *letter* on station*ery*. Any silly phrase or sentence will do, as long as it brings tricky spellings to mind.
2. *Keep a record of words you misspell.* Buy yourself a little notebook for entering words that invariably trip you up. Each time you proofread a paper you have written and receive one back from your instructor, write down any words you have misspelled. Then practice pronouncing, writing, and spelling them out loud until you have mastered them.
3. *Check any questionable spelling by referring to your dictionary,* your good-as-gold best friend. Use it to check words as you come up with them and to double-check them as you proofread and edit. If you are multilingual and originally learned British English, a good dictionary will distinguish American and British spellings (*color, colour; terrorize, terrorise*).
4. *Learn commonly misspelled words.* If you know that you are likely to confuse different words that sound alike, turn to the list of Commonly Confused Homonyms in the "Quick Editing Guide" (see p. A-39) and the Glossary of Troublemakers in the next section. Checkmark the words that you consider the trickiest – but don't stop there. Spend a few minutes each day going over them. Spell every troublesome word out loud; write it ten times. Do the same with any common problem words that your spell checker routinely catches, such as *nucular* for *nuclear* or *exercize* for *exercise*. Your spelling will improve rapidly.

# 34 | A Glossary of Troublemakers

**Usage** refers to the way in which writers customarily use certain words and phrases, including matters of accepted practice or convention. This glossary lists words and phrases whose usage may trouble writers. Not every possible problem is listed – only some that frequently puzzle students. Refer to this brief list when needed, and follow its cross-references to *A Writer's Handbook*.

**a, an** Use *an* only before a word beginning with a vowel sound. "*An* asp can eat *an* egg *an* hour." (Some words, such as *hour* and *honest,* open with a vowel sound even though spelled with an *h.*)

**above** Using *above* or *below* to refer back or forward in an essay is awkward and may not be accurate. Instead, try "the *preceding* argument," "in the *following* discussion," "on the *next* page."

**accept, except** *Accept* is a verb meaning "to receive willingly"; *except* is usually a preposition meaning "not including." "This childcare center *accepts* all children *except* those under two." Sometimes *except* is a verb, meaning "to exempt." "The entry fee *excepts* children under twelve."

**advice, advise** *Advice* is a noun, *advise* a verb. When someone *advises* you, you receive *advice.*

**affect, effect** Most of the time, the verb *affect* means "to act on" or "to influence." "Too much beer can *affect* your speech." *Affect* can also mean "to put on airs." "He *affected* a British accent." *Effect,* a noun, means "a result": "Too much beer has a numbing *effect.*" But *effect* is also a verb, meaning "to bring about." "Pride *effected* his downfall."

**agree to, agree with, agree on** *Agree to* means "to consent to"; *agree with,* "to be in accord." "I *agreed to* attend the lecture, but I didn't *agree with* the speaker's views." *Agree on* means "to come to or have an understanding about." "Chuck and I finally *agreed on* a compromise: the children would go to camp but not overnight."

**ain't** Don't use *ain't* in writing; it is nonstandard English for *am not, is not* (*isn't*), and *are not* (*aren't*).

**a lot** Many people mistakenly write the colloquial expression *a lot* as one word: *alot.* Use *a lot* if you must, but in writing *much* or *a large amount* is preferable. See also *lots, lots of, a lot of.*

**already, all ready** *Already* means "by now"; *all ready* means "set to go." "At last our picnic was *all ready,* but *already* it was night."

**altogether, all together** *Altogether* means "entirely." "He is *altogether* mistaken." *All together* means "in unison" or "assembled." "Now *all together* – heave!" "Inspector Trent gathered the suspects *all together* in the drawing room."

**among, between** *Between* refers to two persons or things; *among,* to more than two. "Some disagreement *between* the two countries was inevitable. Still, there was general harmony *among* the five nations represented at the conference."

**amount, number** Use *amount* to refer to quantities that cannot be counted or to bulk; use *number* to refer to countable, separate items. "The *number* of people you want to serve determines the *amount* of ice cream you'll need."

**an, a** See *a, an.*

**and/or** Usually use either *and* or *or* alone. "Tim *and* Elaine will come to the party." "Tim *or* Elaine will come to the party." For three options, write, "Tim *or* Elaine, *or both,* will come to the party, depending on whether they can find a babysitter."

**ante-, anti-** The prefix *ante-* means "preceding." *Antebellum* means "before the Civil War." *Anti-* most often means "opposing": *antidepressant.* It needs a hyphen in front of *i* (*anti-inflationary*) or in front of a capital letter (*anti-Marxist*).

**anybody, any body** When *anybody* is used as an indefinite pronoun, write it as one word: "*Anybody* in his or her right mind abhors murder." Because *anybody* is singular, do not write "Anybody in *their* right mind." (See 7d.) *Any body,* written as two words, is the adjective *any* modifying the noun *body*. "Name *any body* of water in Australia."

**anyone, any one** *Anyone* is an indefinite pronoun written as one word. "Does *anyone* want dessert?" The phrase *any one* consists of the pronoun *one* modified by the adjective *any* and is used to single out something in a group: "Pick *any one* of the pies – they're all good."

**anyplace** *Anyplace* is colloquial for *anywhere* and should not be used in formal writing.

**anyways, anywheres** These nonstandard forms of *anyway* and *anywhere* should not be used in writing.

**as** Sometimes using the subordinating conjunction *as* can make a sentence ambiguous. "*As* we were climbing the mountain, we put on heavy sweaters." Does *as* here mean "because" or "while"? Whenever using *as* would be confusing, use a more specific term instead, such as *because* or *while.*

**as, like** Use *as, as if,* or *as though* rather than *like* to introduce clauses of comparison. "Dan's compositions are tuneful, *as* [not *like*] music ought to be." "Jeffrey behaves *as if* [not *like*] he were ill." *Like,* because it is a preposition, can introduce a phrase but not a clause. "My brother looks *like* me." "Henrietta runs *like* a duck."

**as to** Usually this expression sounds stilted. Use *about* instead. "He complained *about* [not *as to*] the cockroaches."

**at** See *where at, where to.*

**bad, badly** *Bad* is an adjective; *badly* is an adverb. Following linking verbs (*be, appear, become, grow, seem, prove*) and verbs of the senses (*feel, look, smell, sound, taste*), use the adjective form. "I feel *bad* that we missed the plane." "The egg smells *bad.*" (See 8a, 8b.) The adverb form is used to modify a verb or an adjective. "The Tartans played so *badly* they lost to the last-place team, whose *badly* needed victory saved them from elimination."

**being as, being that** Instead of "*Being as* I was ignorant of the facts, I kept still," write "*Because* I was ignorant" or "*Not knowing* the facts."

**beside, besides** *Beside* is a preposition meaning "next to." "Sheldon enjoyed sitting *beside* the guest of honor." *Besides* is an adverb meaning "in addition." "*Besides,* he has a sense of humor." *Besides* is also a preposition meaning "other than." "Something *besides* shyness caused his embarrassment."

**between, among** See *among, between.*

**between you and I** The preposition *between* always takes the objective case. "Between *you* and *me* [not *I*], Joe's story sounds suspicious." "Between *us* [not *we*], what's going on between Bob and *her* [not *she*] is unfathomable." (See 5a–5f.)

**but that, but what** "I don't know *but what* [or *but that*] you're right" is a wordy, imprecise way of saying "Maybe you're right" or "I believe you're right."

**can, may** Use *can* to show ability. "Jake *can* benchpress 650 pounds." *May* involves permission. "*May* I bench-press today?" "You *may,* if you *can.*"

**capital, capitol** A *capital* is a city that is the center of government for a state or country. *Capital* can also mean "wealth." A *capitol* is a building in which legislators meet. "Who knows what the *capital* of Finland is?" "The renovated *capitol* is a popular attraction."

**center around** Say "Class discussion *centered on* [or *revolved around*] her paper." In this sense, the verb *center* means "to have one main concern"—the way a circle has a central point. (To say a discussion centers *around* anything is a murky metaphor.)

**cite, sight, site** *Cite,* a verb, means "to quote from or refer to." *Sight* as a verb means "to see or glimpse"; as a noun it means "a view, a spectacle." "When the police officer *sighted* my terrier running across the playground, she *cited* the leash laws." *Site,* a noun, means "location." "Standing and weeping at the *site* of his childhood home, he was a pitiful *sight.*"

**climatic, climactic** *Climatic,* from *climate,* refers to meteorological conditions. Saying "climatic conditions," however, is wordy—you can usually substitute "the climate": "*Climatic* conditions are [or "The *climate* is"] changing because of the hole in the ozone layer." *Climactic,* from *climax,* refers to the culmination of a progression of events. "In the *climactic* scene, the hero drives his car off the pier."

**compare, contrast** *Compare* has two main meanings. The first, "to liken or represent as similar," is followed by *to.* "She *compared* her room *to* a jail cell." The second, "to analyze for similarities and differences," is generally followed by *with.* "The speaker *compared* the American educational system *with* the Japanese system."

*Contrast* also has two main meanings. As a transitive verb, taking an object, it means "to analyze to emphasize differences" and is generally followed by *with.* "The speaker *contrasted* the social emphasis of the Japanese primary grades *with* the academic emphasis of ours." As an intransitive verb, *contrast* means "to exhibit differences when compared." "The sour taste of the milk *contrasted* sharply *with* its usual fresh flavor."

**complement, compliment** *Compliment* is a verb meaning "to praise" or a noun meaning "praise." "The professor *complimented* Sarah on her perceptiveness." *Complement* is a verb meaning "to complete or reinforce." "Jenn's experiences as an intern *complemented* what she learned in class."

**could care less** This is nonstandard English for *couldn't care less* and should not be used in writing. "The cat *couldn't* [not *could*] *care less* about which brand of cat food you buy."

**could of** *Could of* is colloquial for *could have* and should not be used in writing.

**couple of** Write "a *couple of* drinks" when you mean two. For more than two, say "a *few* [or *several*] drinks."

**criteria, criterion** *Criteria* is the plural of *criterion,* which means "a standard or requirement on which a judgment or decision is based." "The main *criteria* for this job are attention to detail and good computer skills."

**data** *Data* is a plural noun. Write "The data *are*" and "*these* data." The singular form of *data* is *datum*— rarely used because it sounds musty. Instead, use *fact, figure,* or *statistic.*

**different from, different than** *Different from* is usually the correct form to use. "How is good poetry *different from* prose?" Use *different than* when a whole clause follows. "Violin lessons with Mr. James were *different than* I had imagined."

**don't, doesn't** *Don't* is the contraction of *do not,* and *doesn't* is the contraction of *does not.* "They *don't* want to get dressed up for the ceremony." "The cat *doesn't* [not *don't*] like to be combed."

**due to** *Due* is an adjective and must modify a noun or pronoun; it can't modify a verb or an adjective. Begin a sentence with *due to* and you invite trouble: "*Due to* rain, the game was postponed." Write instead, "*Because of* rain." *Due to* works after the verb *be.* "His fall was *due to* a banana peel." There, *due* modifies the noun *fall.*

**due to the fact that** A windy expression for *because.*

**effect, affect** See *affect, effect.*

**either** Use *either* when referring to one of two things. "Both internships sound great; I'd be happy with *either.*" When referring to one of three or more things, use *any one* or *any.* "*Any one* of our four counselors will be able to help you."

**et cetera, etc.** Sharpen your writing by replacing *et cetera* (or its abbreviation, *etc.*) with exact words. Even translating the Latin expression into English ("and other things") is an improvement, as in "high-jumping, shot-putting, and other field events."

**everybody, every body** When used as an indefinite pronoun, *everybody* is one word. "Why is *everybody* on the boys' team waving his arms?" Because *everybody* is singular, it is a mistake to write, "Why is *everybody* waving *their* arms?" (See 7d.) *Every body* written as two words refers to separate, individual bodies. "After the massacre, they buried *every body* in *its* [not *their*] own grave."

**everyone, every one** Used as an indefinite pronoun, *everyone* is one word. "*Everyone* has *his or her* own ideas." Because *everyone* is singular, it is incorrect to write, "*Everyone* has *their* own ideas." (See 7d.) *Every one* written as two words refers to individual, distinct items. "I studied *every one* of the chapters."

**except, accept** See *accept, except.*

**expect** In writing, avoid the informal use of *expect* to mean "suppose, assume, or think." "I *suppose* [not *expect*] you're going on the geology field trip."

**fact that** This is a wordy expression that, nearly always, you can do without. Instead of "*The fact that* he was puny went unnoticed," write, "That he was puny went unnoticed." "Because [not *Because of the fact that*] it snowed, the game was canceled."

**farther, further** In your writing, use *farther* to refer to literal distance. "Chicago is *farther* from Nome than from New York." When you mean additional degree, time, or quantity, use *further*: "Sally's idea requires *further* discussion."

**fewer, less** *Less* refers to general quantity or bulk; *fewer* refers to separate, countable items. "Eat *less* pizza." "Salad has *fewer* calories."

**field of** In a statement such as "He took courses in *the field of* economics," omit *the field of* to save words.

**firstly** The recommended usage is *first* (and *second,* not *secondly; third,* not *thirdly;* and so on).

**former, latter** *Former* means "first of two"; *latter,* "second of two." They are an acceptable but heavy-handed pair, often obliging your reader to backtrack. Your writing generally will be clearer if you simply name again the persons or things you mean. Instead of "The *former* great artist is the master of the flowing line, while the *latter* is the master of color," write, "Picasso is the master of the flowing line, while Matisse is the master of color."

**further, farther** See *farther, further.*

**get, got** *Get* has many meanings, especially in slang and colloquial use. Some, such as the following, are not appropriate in formal writing:

To start, begin: "Let's start [not *get*] painting."

To stir the emotions: "His frequent interruptions finally started annoying [not *getting to*] me."

To harm, punish, or take revenge on: "She's going to take revenge on [not *get*] him." Or better, be even more specific: "She's going to spread rumors about him to ruin his reputation."

**good, well** To modify a verb, use the adverb *well,* not the adjective *good.* "Jan dives *well* [not *good*]." Linking verbs (*be, appear, become, grow, seem, prove*) and verbs of the senses (such as *feel, look, smell, sound, taste*) call for the adjective *good.* "The paint job looks *good.*" *Well* is an adjective used only to refer to health. "She looks *well*" means that she seems to be in good health. "She looks *good*" means her appearance is attractive. (See 8b, 8c.)

**hanged, hung** Both words are the past tense of the verb *hang. Hanged* refers to an execution. "The murderer was *hanged* at dawn." For all other situations, use *hung.* "Jim *hung* his wash on the line to dry."

**have got to** In formal writing, avoid using the phrase *have got to* to mean "have to" or "must." "I *must* [not *have got to*] phone them right away."

**he, she, he or she** Using *he* to refer to an indefinite person is considered sexist; so is using *she* with traditionally female occupations or pastimes. However, the phrase *he or she* can seem wordy and awkward. For alternatives, see 18.

**herself** See *-self, -selves.*

**himself** See *-self, -selves.*

**hopefully** *Hopefully* means "with hope." "The children turned *hopefully* toward the door, expecting Santa Claus." In writing, avoid *hopefully* when you mean "it is to be hoped" or "let us hope." "*I hope* [not *Hopefully*] the posse will arrive soon."

**if, whether** Use *whether*, not *if*, in indirect questions and to introduce alternatives. "Father asked me *whether* [not *if*] I was planning to sleep all morning." "I'm so confused I don't know *whether* [not *if*] it's day or night."

**imply, infer** *Imply* means "to suggest"; *infer* means "to draw a conclusion." "Maria *implied* that she was too busy to see Tom, but Tom *inferred* that Maria had lost interest in him."

**in, into** *In* refers to a location or condition; *into* refers to the direction of movement or change. "The hero burst *into* the room and found the heroine *in* another man's arms."

**infer, imply** See *imply, infer.*

**in regards to** Write *in regard to, regarding,* or *about.*

**inside of, outside of** As prepositions, *inside* and *outside* do not require *of.* "The students were more interested in events *outside* [not *outside of*] the building than those *inside* [not *inside of*] the classroom." In formal writing, do not use *inside of* to refer to time or *outside of* to mean "except." "I'll finish the assignment *within* [not *inside of*] two hours." "He told no one *except* [not *outside of*] a few friends."

**irregardless** *Irregardless* is a double negative. Use *regardless.*

**is because** See *reason is because, reason . . . is.*

**is when, is where** Using these expressions results in errors in predication. "Obesity *is when* a person is greatly overweight." "Biology *is where* students dissect frogs." *When* refers to a point in time, but *obesity* is not a point in time; *where* refers to a place, but *biology* is not a place. Write instead, "Obesity is the condition of extreme overweight." "Biology is a laboratory course in which students dissect frogs." (See 12c.)

**its, it's** *Its* is a possessive pronoun, never in need of an apostrophe. *It's* is a contraction of *it is.* "Every new experience has *its* bad moments. Still, *it's* exciting to explore the unknown." (See 24g.)

**it's me, it is I** Although *it's me* is widely used in speech, don't use it in formal writing. Write "It is *I,*" which is grammatically correct. The same applies to other personal pronouns. "It was *he* [not *him*] who started the mutiny." (See 5.)

**kind of, sort of, type of** When you use *kind, sort,* or *type*—singular words—make sure that the sentence construction is singular. "That *type* of show *offends* me." "Those *types* of shows *offend* me." In speech, *kind of* and *sort of* are used as qualifiers. "He is *sort of* fat." Avoid them in writing. "He is *rather* [or *somewhat* or *slightly*] fat."

**latter, former** See *former, latter.*

**lay, lie** The verb *lay,* meaning "to put or place," takes an object. "*Lay* that pistol down." *Lie,* meaning "to rest or recline," does not. "*Lie* on the bed until your headache goes away." Their principal parts are *lay, laid, laid* and *lie, lay, lain.* (See 3f.)

**less, fewer** See *fewer, less.*

**liable, likely** Use *likely* to mean "plausible" or "having the potential." "Jake is *likely* [not *liable*] to win." Save *liable* for "legally obligated" or "susceptible." "A stunt man is *liable* to injury."

**lie, lay** See *lay, lie.*

**like, as** See *as, like.*

**likely, liable** See *liable, likely.*

**literally** Don't sling *literally* around for emphasis. Because it means "strictly according to the meaning of a word (or words)," it will wreck your credibility if you are speaking figuratively. "Professor Gray *literally* flew down the hall" means that Gray traveled on wings. Save *literally* to mean that you're reporting a fact. "Chemical wastes travel on the winds, and the skies *literally* rain poison."

**loose, lose** *Loose,* an adjective, most commonly means "not fastened" or "poorly fastened." *Lose,* a verb, means "to misplace" or "to not win." "I have to be careful not to *lose* this button—it's so *loose.*"

**lots, lots of, a lot of** Use these expressions only in informal speech. In formal writing, use *many* or *much.* See also *a lot.*

**mankind** This term is considered sexist by many people. Use *humanity, humankind, the human race,* or *people* instead.

**may, can** See *can, may.*

**media, medium** *Media* is the plural of *medium* and most commonly refers to the various forms of public communication. "Some argue that, of all the *media,* television is the worst for children."

**might of** *Might of* is colloquial for *might have* and should not be used in writing.

**most** Do not use *most* when you mean "almost" or "nearly." "*Almost* [not *Most*] all of the students felt that Professor Crey should receive tenure."

**must of** *Must of* is colloquial for *must have* and should not be used in writing.

**myself** See *-self, -selves.*

**not all that** *Not all that* is colloquial for *not very;* do not use it in formal writing. "The movie was *not very* [not *not all that*] exciting."

**number, amount** See *amount, number.*

**of** See *could of, might of, must of, should of.*

**O.K., o.k., okay** In formal writing, do not use any of these expressions. *All right* and *I agree* are possible substitutes.

**one** Like a balloon, *one,* meaning "a person," tends to inflate. One *one* can lead to another. "When *one* is in college, *one* learns to make up *one's* mind for *oneself.*" Avoid this pompous usage. Whenever possible, substitute *people* or a more specific plural noun. "When *students* are in college, *they* learn to make up their minds for *themselves.*"

**ourselves** See *-self, -selves.*

**outside of, inside of** See *inside of, outside of.*

**percent, per cent, percentage** When you specify a number, write *percent* (also written *per cent*). "Nearly 40 *percent* of the listeners responded to the offer." The only time to use *percentage,* meaning "part," is with an adjective, when you mention no number. "A high *percentage* [or *a large percentage*] of listeners responded." *A large number* or *a large proportion* sounds better yet.

**phenomenon, phenomena** *Phenomena* is the plural of *phenomenon,* which means "an observable fact or occurrence." "Of the many mysterious supernatural *phenomena,* clairvoyance is the strangest *phenomenon* of all."

**precede, proceed** *Precede* means "to go before or ahead of"; *proceed* means "to go forward." "The fire drill *proceeded* smoothly; the children *preceded* the teachers onto the playground."

**principal, principle** *Principal* means "chief," whether used as an adjective or as a noun. "According to the *principal,* the school's *principal* goal will be teaching reading." Referring to money, *principal* means "capital." "Investors in high-risk companies may lose their *principal.*" *Principle,* a noun, means *rule* or *standard.* "Let's apply the *principle* of equality in hiring."

**proved, proven** Although both forms can be used as past participles, *proved* is recommended. Use *proven* as an adjective. "They had *proved* their skill in match after match." "Try this *proven* cough remedy."

**quote, quotation** *Quote* is a verb meaning "to cite, to use the words of." *Quotation* is a noun meaning "something that is quoted." "The *quotation* [not *quote*] next to her photograph fits her perfectly."

**raise, rise** *Raise,* meaning "to cause to move upward," is a transitive verb and takes an object. *Rise,* meaning "to move up (on its own)" is intransitive and does not take an object: "I *rose* from my seat and *raised* my arm."

**rarely ever** *Rarely* by itself is strong enough. "George *rarely* [not *rarely ever*] eats dinner with his family."

**real, really** *Real* is an adjective, *really* an adverb. Do not use *real* to modify a verb or another adjective, and avoid overusing either word. "*The Ambassadors* is a *really* [not *real*] fine novel." Even better: "*The Ambassadors* is a fine novel."

**reason is because, reason . . . is** *Reason . . . is* requires a clause beginning with *that.* Using *because* is nonstandard. "The *reason* I can't come *is that* [not *is because*] I have the flu." It is simpler and more direct to write, "I can't come because I have the flu." (See 12d.)

**rise** See *raise, rise.*

**-self, -selves** Don't use a pronoun ending in *-self* or *-selves* in place of *her, him, me, them, us,* or *you.* "Nobody volunteered but Jim and *me* [not *myself*]." Use the *-self* pronouns to refer back to a noun or another pronoun and to lend emphasis. "*We* did it *ourselves.*" "Sarah *herself* is a noted musician."

**set, sit** *Set,* meaning "to put or place," is a transitive verb and takes an object. *Sit,* meaning "to be seated," is intransitive and does not take an object. "We were asked to *set* our jewelry and metal objects on the counter and *sit* down." (See 3f.)

**shall, will; should, would** The helping verb *shall* formerly was used with first-person pronouns. It is still used to express determination ("We *shall* overcome") or to ask consent ("*Shall* we march?"). Otherwise, *will* is commonly used with all three persons. "I *will* enter medical school in the fall." *Should* is a helping verb that expresses obligation; *would,* a helping verb that expresses a hypothetical condition. "I *should* wash the dishes before I watch TV." "He *would* learn to speak English if you *would* give him a chance."

**she, he or she** See *he, she, he or she.*

**should of** *Should of* is colloquial for *should have* and should not be used in writing.

**sight** See *cite, sight, site.*

**since** Sometimes using *since* can make a sentence ambiguous. "*Since* the babysitter left, the children have been watching television." Does *since* here mean "because" or "from the time that"? If using *since* might be confusing, use an unambiguous term (*because, ever since*).

**sit** See *set, sit.*

**site** See *cite, sight, site.*

**sort of** See *kind of, sort of, type of.*

**stationary, stationery** *Stationary,* an adjective, means "fixed, unmoving." "The fireplace remained *stationary* though the wind blew down the house." *Stationery* is paper for letter writing. To spell it right, remember that *letter* also contains *-er.*

**suppose to** Write *supposed to.* "He was *supposed to* read a novel."

**sure** *Sure* is an adjective, *surely* an adverb. Do not use *sure* to modify a verb or another adjective. If you mean "certainly," write *certainly* or *surely* instead. "He *surely* [not *sure*] makes the Civil War come alive."

**than, then** *Than* is a conjunction used in comparisons; *then* is an adverb indicating time. "Marlene is brainier *than* her sister." "First crack six eggs; *then* beat them."

**that, where** See *where, that.*

**that, which** Which pronoun should open a clause—*that* or *which*? If the clause adds to its sentence an idea that, however interesting, could be left out, then the clause is nonrestrictive. It should begin with *which* and be separated from the rest of the sentence with commas. "The vampire, *which* hovered nearby, leaped for Sarah's throat."

If the clause is essential to your meaning, it is restrictive. It should begin with *that* and should not have commas around it. "The vampire *that* Mel brought from Transylvania leaped for Sarah's throat." The clause indicates not just any old vampire but one in particular. (See 21e.)

Don't use *which* to refer vaguely to an entire clause. Instead of "Jack was an expert drummer in high school, *which* won him a scholarship," write "Jack's skill as a drummer won him . . ." (See 6b.)

**that, who, which, whose** See *who, which, that, whose.*

**themselves** See *-self, -selves.*

**then, than** See *than, then.*

**there, their, they're** *There* is an adverb indicating place. *Their* is a possessive pronoun. *They're* is a contraction of *they are.* "After playing tennis *there* for three hours, Lamont and Laura went to change *their* clothes because *they're* going out to dinner."

**to, too, two** *To* is a preposition. *Too* is an adverb meaning "also" or "in excess." *Two* is a number. "Janet wanted to go *too,* but she was *too* sick to travel for *two* days. Instead, she went *to* bed."

**toward, towards** *Toward* is preferred in the United States, *towards* in Britain.

**try and** Use *try to.* "I'll *try to* [not *try and*] attend the opening performance of your play."

**type of** See *kind of, sort of, type of.*

**unique** Nothing can be *more, less,* or *very unique. Unique* means "one of a kind." (See 8e.)

**use to** Write *used to.* "Jeffrey *used to* have a beard, but now he is clean-shaven."

**wait for, wait on** *Wait for* means "await"; *wait on* means "to serve." "While *waiting for* his friends, George decided to *wait on* one more customer."

**well, good** See *good, well.*

**where, that** Although speakers sometimes use *where* instead of *that,* you should not do so in writing. "I heard on the news *that* [not *where*] it got hot enough to fry eggs on car hoods."

**where . . . at, where . . . to** The colloquial use of *at* or *to* after *where* is redundant. Write "*Where* were you?" not "Where were you *at*?" "I know *where* she was rushing [not *rushing to*]."

**whether** See *if, whether.*

**which, that** See *that, which.*

**who, which, that, whose** *Who* refers to people, *which* to things and ideas. "Was it Pogo *who* said, 'We have met the enemy and he is us'?" "The blouse, *which* was green, accented her dark skin." *That* refers to things but can also be used for a class of people. "The team *that* increases sales the most will get a bonus." Because *of which* can be cumbersome, use *whose* even with things. "The mountain, *whose* snowy peaks were famous the world over, was covered by fog." See also *that, which.*

**who, whom** *Who* is used as a subject, *whom* as an object. In "*Whom* do I see?" *Whom* is the object of *see.* In "*Who* goes there?" *Who* is the subject of "goes." (See also 5a.)

**who's, whose** *Who's* is a contraction of *who is* or *who has.* "*Who's* going with Phil?" *Whose* is a possessive pronoun. "Bill is a conservative politician *whose* ideas are unlikely to change."

**whose, who, which, that** See *who, which, that, whose.*

**will, shall** See *shall, will; should, would.*

**would, should** See *shall, will; should, would.*

**would of** *Would of* is colloquial for *would have* and should not be used in writing.

**you** *You,* meaning "a person," occurs often in conversation. "When *you* go to college, *you* have to work hard." In writing, use *one* or a specific, preferably plural noun. "When *students* go to college, *they* have to work hard." See *one* and 18c.

**your, you're** *Your* is a possessive pronoun; *you're* is the contraction of *you are.* "*You're* lying! It was *your* handwriting on the envelope."

**yourself, yourselves** See *-self, -selves.*

# Answers for Lettered Exercises

### EXERCISE 1–1 ▪ Eliminating Fragments, p. 768

*Suggested revisions:*

**a.** Michael had a beautiful Southern accent, having lived many years in Georgia.
**b.** Pat and Chris are determined to marry each other, even if their families do not approve.
**c.** Jack seemed well qualified for a career in the air force, except for his tendency to get airsick.
**d.** Lisa advocated sleeping no more than four hours a night until she started nodding through her classes.
**e.** Complete sentences

### EXERCISE 2–1 ▪ Revising Comma Splices and Fused Sentences, p. 772

*Suggested revisions:*

**a.** We followed the scientist down a flight of wet stone steps. At last he stopped before a huge oak door.
We followed the scientist down a flight of wet stone steps until at last he stopped before a huge oak door.
**b.** Dr. Frankenstein selected a heavy key; he twisted it in the lock.
Dr. Frankenstein selected a heavy key, which he twisted in the lock.
**c.** The huge door gave a groan; it swung open on a dimly lighted laboratory.
The huge door gave a groan and swung open on a dimly lighted laboratory.
**d.** Before us on a dissecting table lay a form with closed eyes. To behold it sent a quick chill down my spine.
Before us on a dissecting table lay a form with closed eyes; beholding it sent a quick chill down my spine.
**e.** The scientist strode to the table and lifted a white-gloved hand.
The scientist strode to the table; he lifted a white-gloved hand.

### EXERCISE 3–1 ▪ Using Irregular Verb Forms, p. 777

**a.** Benjamin wrote all the music, and his sister *sang* all the songs.
**b.** Correct
**c.** When the bell *rang,* darkness had already *fallen.*
**d.** Voters have *chosen* some new senators, who won't take office until January.
**e.** Carol threw the ball into the water, and the dog *swam* after it.

### EXERCISE 3–2 ▪ Identifying Verb Tenses, p. 783

**a.** has been living: present perfect progressive; hacked: simple past; change: simple present **b.** have never appeared: present perfect; will never appear: simple future; gets selected: simple present **c.** had been: past perfect; pitched: simple past **d.** will have been studying: future perfect progressive; will be taking: future progressive **e.** was running: past progressive; strolled: simple past

### EXERCISE 3–4 ▪ Using the Correct Mood of Verbs, p. 787

**a.** Dr. Belanger recommended that Juan *floss* his teeth every day. (Incorrect *flosses,* indicative; correct *floss,* subjunctive)
**b.** If I *were* you, I would have done the same thing. (Incorrect *was,* indicative; correct *were,* subjunctive)
**c.** Tradition demands that Daegun *show* respect for his elders. (Incorrect *shows,* indicative; correct *show,* subjunctive)
**d.** Please *attend* the training lesson if you plan to skydive later today. (Incorrect *attends,* indicative; correct *attend,* imperative)

### EXERCISE 4–1 ▪ Making Subjects and Verbs Agree, p. 791

**a.** For many college graduates, the process of looking for jobs *is* often long and stressful.
**b.** Not too long ago, searching the classifieds and inquiring in person *were* the primary methods of job hunting.
**c.** Today, however, everyone also *seems* to use the Internet to search for openings or to e-mail *his or her* résumés.
**d.** My classmates and my cousin *send* most résumés over the Internet because it costs less than mailing them.
**e.** All of the résumés *arrive* quickly when they are sent electronically.

### EXERCISE 5–1 ▪ Using Pronouns Correctly, p. 794

**a.** I didn't appreciate *your* laughing at her and *me*. (*Your* modifies the gerund *laughing; me* is an object of the preposition *at*.)
**b.** Lee and *I* would be delighted to serenade *whoever* will listen. (*I* is a subject of the verb phrase *would be delighted; whoever* is the subject of the clause *whoever will listen*.)
**c.** The managers and *we* servers are highly trustworthy. (*We* is a subject complement.)
**d.** The neighbors were driven berserk by *his* singing. (The gerund *singing* is the object of the verb *driven;* the possessive pronoun *his* modifies *singing*.) *Or*
Correct as is. (*Him* is the object of the verb *driven; singing* is a participle modifying *him*.)
**e.** Jerry and *I* regard you and *her* as the very people *whom* we wish to meet. (*I* is a subject of the verb *regard; her* is a direct object of the verb *regard; whom* is the object of the infinitive *to meet*.)

### EXERCISE 6–1 ▪ Making Pronoun Reference Clear, p. 798

*Suggested revisions:*

**a.** As the moon began to rise, I could see the faint shadow of the tree.
**b.** While she spent the summer in Paris, Katrina broadened her awareness of cultural differences by traveling throughout Europe.
**c.** Most managers want employees to work as many hours as possible. They never consider the work their employees need to do at home.
**d.** Working twelve hours a day and never getting enough sleep was worth it.
**e.** Kevin asked Mike to meet him for lunch but forgot that Mike had class at that time. *Or*
Kevin forgot that he had class at the time he asked Mike to meet him for lunch.

### EXERCISE 7–1 ▪ Making Pronouns and Antecedents Agree, p. 800

*Suggested revisions:*

**a.** Correct
**b.** Neither Melissa nor James has received an application form yet. *Or*
Melissa and James have not received their application forms yet.
**c.** He is the kind of man who gets his fun out of just sipping his beer and watching his Saturday games on TV.
**d.** Many a mother has mourned the loss of her child. *Or*
Many mothers have mourned the loss of their children.
**e.** When you enjoy your work, it's easy to spend all your spare time thinking about it. *Or*
When one enjoys one's work, it's easy to spend all one's spare time thinking about it.

### EXERCISE 8–1 ▪ Using Adjectives and Adverbs Correctly, p. 807

**a.** Change *increasing* to *increasingly*. **b.** Correct. **c.** Change *lower* to *lowest*. **d.** Change *rapid* to *rapidly*. **e.** Change *well* to *good*.

## EXERCISE 9-1 ▪ Maintaining Grammatical Consistency, p. 810

*Suggested revisions:*

**a.** Dr. Jamison is an erudite professor who tells amusing anecdotes in class. (Formal) *Or* Dr. Jamison is a funny teacher who cracks jokes in class. (Informal)
**b.** The audience listened intently to the lecture but did not understand the message.
**c.** Scientists can no longer evade the social, political, and ethical consequences of what they do in the laboratory.
**d.** To have good government, citizens must become informed on the issues. Also, they must vote.
**e.** Good writing is essential to success in many professions, especially in business, where ideas must be communicated clearly.

## EXERCISE 10-1 ▪ Placing Modifiers, p. 812

*Suggested revisions:*

**a.** The bus full of passengers got stuck in a ditch.
**b.** In the middle of a meeting, he was daydreaming about fishing for trout.
**c.** With a smirk, the boy threw the paper airplane through an open window.
**d.** When the glare appeared, I reached for my sunglasses from the glove compartment.
**e.** Sally and Glen watched the kites high above them drift back and forth.

## EXERCISE 10-2 ▪ Revising Dangling Modifiers, p. 814

*Suggested revisions:*

**a.** As I was unpacking the suitcase, a horrible idea occurred to me.
**b.** After fixing breakfast that morning, I might have left the oven on at home.
**c.** Although I tried to reach my neighbor, her phone was busy.
**d.** Desperate to get information, I asked my mother to drive over to check the oven.
**e.** I felt enormous relief when my mother's call confirmed everything was fine.

## EXERCISE 11-1 ▪ Completing Comparisons, p. 816

*Suggested revisions:*

**a.** The movie version of *The Brady Bunch* was much more ironic *than the television show.*
**b.** Taking care of a dog is often more demanding than *taking care of* a cat.
**c.** I received more free calendars in the mail for the year 2014 than *I have for* any other year.
**d.** The crime rate in the United States is higher than *it is in* Canada.
**e.** Liver contains more iron than any *other* meat.

## EXERCISE 11-2 ▪ Completing Sentences, p. 817

*Suggested revisions:*

**a.** Eighteenth-century China was as civilized *as* and in many respects more sophisticated than the Western world.
**b.** Pembroke was never contacted *by,* much less involved with, the election committee.
**c.** I haven't yet *finished* but soon will finish my research paper.
**d.** Ron likes his popcorn with butter; Linda *likes hers* with parmesan cheese.
**e.** Correct

## EXERCISE 12-1 ▪ Correcting Mixed Constructions and Faulty Predication, p. 821

*Suggested revisions:*

**a.** Health insurance protects people from big medical bills.
**b.** His determination to prevail helped him finish the race.
**c.** AIDS destroys the body's immune system.

**d.** The temperatures are too low for the orange trees.
**e.** In a recession, economic growth is small or nonexistent, and unemployment increases.

## EXERCISE 13–1 ▪ Making Sentences Parallel, p. 824

*Suggested revisions:*

**a.** The border separating Texas and Mexico marks not only the political boundary of two countries but also the last frontier for some endangered wildlife.
**b.** In the Rio Grande Valley, both local residents and tourists enjoy visiting the national wildlife refuges.
**c.** The tall grasses in this valley are the home of many insects, birds, and small mammals.
**d.** Two endangered wildcats, the ocelot and the jaguarundi, also make the Rio Grande Valley their home.
**e.** Many people from Central America are desperate to immigrate to the United States by either legal or illegal means.

## EXERCISE 14–1 ▪ Using Coordination, p. 828

*Suggested revisions:*

**a.** Professional poker players try to win money and prizes in high-stakes tournaments; however, they may lose thousands of dollars.
**b.** Poker is not an easy way to make a living, and playing professional poker is not a good way to relax.
**c.** A good "poker face" reveals no emotions, for communicating too much information puts a player at a disadvantage.
**d.** Hidden feelings may come out in unconscious movements, so an expert poker player watches other players carefully.
**e.** Poker is different from most other casino gambling games, for it requires skill and it forces players to compete against each other. Other casino gambling pits players against the house, so they may win out of sheer luck, but skill has little to do with winning those games.

## EXERCISE 14–2 ▪ Using Subordination, p. 830

*Suggested revisions:*

**a.** Cape Cod is a peninsula in Massachusetts that juts into the Atlantic Ocean south of Boston, marking the northern turning point of the Gulf Stream.
**b.** Although the developer had hoped the condominiums would sell quickly, sales were sluggish.
**c.** Tourists love Italy because it has a wonderful climate, beautiful towns and cities, and a rich history.
**d.** At the end of Verdi's opera *La Traviata,* Alfredo has to see his beloved Violetta again, even though he knows she is dying and all he can say is good-bye.
**e.** I usually have more fun at a concert with Rico than with Morey because Rico loves music while Morey merely tolerates it.

## EXERCISE 16–2 ▪ Avoiding Jargon, p. 836

*Suggested revisions:*

**a.** Everyone at Boondoggle and Gall attends holiday gatherings in order to meet and socialize with potential business partners.
**b.** This year, more than fifty employees lost their jobs after Boondoggle and Gall's decision to reduce the number of employees by September 1.
**c.** The layoffs left Jensen in charge of all telephone calls in the customer-service department.
**d.** Jensen was responsible for handling three times as many telephone calls after the layoffs, yet she did not receive any extra pay.
**e.** Jensen and her managers could not agree on a fair compensation, so she decided to quit her job at Boondoggle and Gall.

### EXERCISE 16-3 ▪ Avoiding Euphemisms and Slang, p. 837

*Suggested revisions:*

**a.** At three hundred dollars a month, the apartment is a bargain.
**b.** The soldiers were accidentally shot by members of their own troops while they were retreating.
**c.** Churchill was an excellent politician.

### EXERCISE 18-1 ▪ Avoiding Bias, p. 844

*Suggested revisions:*

**a.** Our school's athletic program will be of interest to *many* applicants.
**b.** The new physicians include Dr. Scalia, *Dr.* Baniski, and Dr. Morton.
**c.** *Diligent researchers* will always find the sources *they* seek.

### EXERCISE 20-1 ▪ Using End Punctuation, p. 848

**a.** The question that still troubles the community after all these years is why federal agents did not act sooner. [Not a direct question]
**b.** I wonder what he was thinking at the time. [Not a direct question]
**c.** Correct

### EXERCISE 21-1 ▪ Using Commas, p. 850

**a.** Farmers around the world tend to rely on just a few breeds of livestock, so some breeds are disappearing.
**b.** Correct
**c.** For instance, modern breeds of cattle usually grow larger and produce more meat and milk than older breeds.
**d.** In both wild and domestic animals, genetic diversity can make the animals resistant to disease and parasites, so older breeds can give scientists important information.
**e.** Until recently, small organic farmers were often the only ones interested in raising old-fashioned breeds, but animal scientists now support this practice as well.

### EXERCISE 21-2 ▪ Using Commas, p. 852

**a.** Mrs. Carver looks like a sweet little old lady, but she plays a wicked electric guitar.
**b.** Her bass player, her drummer, and her keyboard player all live in the same retirement community.
**c.** They practice individually in the afternoon, rehearse together at night, and play at the community's Saturday night dances.
**d.** The Rest Home Rebels have to rehearse quietly and cautiously to keep from disturbing the other residents.
**e.** Correct

### EXERCISE 21-3 ▪ Using Commas, p. 853

*Suggested revisions:*

**a.** We are bringing a dish, vegetable lasagna, to the potluck supper.
**b.** I like to go to Central Bank on this side of town because this branch tends to have short lines.
**c.** The colony that the English established at Roanoke disappeared mysteriously.
**d.** If the base commanders had checked their gun room, where powder is stored, they would have found that several hundred pounds of gunpowder were missing.
**e.** Brazil's tropical rain forests, which help produce the air we breathe all over the world, are being cut down at an alarming rate.

### EXERCISE 21-4 ▪ Using Commas, p. 855

**a.** The university insisted, however, that the students were not accepted merely because of their parents' generous contributions.
**b.** This dispute, in any case, is an old one.
**c.** It was the young man's striking good looks, not his acting ability, that first attracted the Hollywood agents.
**d.** Gretchen learned, moreover, not always to accept as true what she had read in celebrity magazines.
**e.** The hikers, most of them wearing ponchos or rain jackets, headed out into the steady drizzle.

### EXERCISE 21-5 ▪ Using Commas, p. 856

**a.** César Chávez was born on March 31, 1927, on a farm in Yuma, Arizona.
**b.** Chávez, who spent years as a migrant farmworker, told other farm laborers, "If you're outraged at conditions, then you can't possibly be free or happy until you devote all your time to changing them."
**c.** Chávez founded the United Farm Workers union and did, indeed, devote all his time to changing conditions for farmworkers.
**d.** Robert F. Kennedy called Chávez "one of the heroic figures of our time."
**e.** Correct

### EXERCISE 22-1 ▪ Using Semicolons, p. 859

**a.** By the beginning of 2014, Shirley was eager to retire; nevertheless, she agreed to stay on for two more years.
**b.** The committee was asked to determine the extent of violent crime among teenagers, especially those between the ages of fourteen and sixteen; to act as a liaison between the city and schools and between churches and volunteer organizations; and to draw up a plan to reduce violence, both public and private, by the end of the century.
**c.** The leaves on the oak trees near the lake were tinged with red; swimmers no longer ventured into the water.
**d.** The football team has yet to win a game; however, the season is still young.

### EXERCISE 23-1 ▪ Using Colons, p. 862

*Suggested revisions:*

**a.** The Continuing Education Program offers courses in building and construction management, engineering, and design.
**b.** The interview ended with a test of skills: taking messages, operating the computer, typing a sample letter, and proofreading documents.
**c.** The sample letter began, "Dear Mr. Rasheed: Please accept our apologies for the late shipment."

### EXERCISE 24-1 ▪ Using Apostrophes, p. 864

**a.** Joe's and Chuck's fathers were both in the class of '90.
**b.** Correct
**c.** It was a strange coincidence that all three women's cars broke down after they had picked up their mothers-in-law.
**d.** Don't forget to dot your *i*'s and cross your *t*'s.
**e.** Mario and Shelley's son is marrying the editor in chief's daughter.

**EXERCISE 25-1 ▪ Using Quotation Marks, p. 868**

**a.** "What we still need to figure out," the police chief said, "is whether the victim was acquainted with his assailant."
**b.** A skillful orator, Patrick Henry is credited with the phrase "Give me liberty or give me death."
**c.** "I could hear the crowd chanting my name—'Jones! Jones!'—and that spurred me on," said Bruce Jones, the winner of the 5,000-meter race.
**d.** The video for the rock group Guns and Roses' epic song "November Rain" is based on a short story by Del James.
**e.** In response to a possible asteroid strike on Earth, former astronaut Rusty Schweickart says, "Every country is at risk."

**EXERCISE 26-1 ▪ Using Dashes, p. 870**

*Suggested revisions:*

**a.** I enjoy going hiking with my friend John, whom I've known for fifteen years.
**b.** Pedro's new boat is spectacular—a regular seagoing Ferrari.
**c.** The Thompsons devote their weekends to their favorite pastime—eating bags of potato chips and cookies beside the warm glow of the television.

**EXERCISE 27-1 ▪ Using Parentheses, p. 871**

*Suggested revisions:*

**a.** Our cafeteria serves the four basic food groups: white (milk, bread, and mashed potatoes), brown (mystery meat and gravy), green (overcooked vegetables and underwashed lettuce), and orange (squash, carrots, and tomato sauce).
**b.** The hijackers will release the hostages only if the government (1) frees all political prisoners and (2) allows the hijackers to leave the country.
**c.** Correct

**EXERCISE 28-1 ▪ Using Abbreviations, p. 877**

**a.** *Professor* James has office hours on Monday and Tuesday, beginning at 10:00 a.m.
**b.** Emotional issues, *for example,* abortion and capital punishment, cannot be settled easily by compromise.
**c.** The red peppers are selling for *$3.25 a pound.*

**EXERCISE 29-1 ▪ Using Capitalization, p. 880**

**a.** At our family reunion, I met my cousin Sam for the first time, as well as my father's brother George.
**b.** I already knew from Dad that his brother had moved to Australia years ago to explore the Great Barrier Reef.
**c.** When my uncle announced that he was moving to a continent thousands of miles southwest of the United States, his mother gave him a Bible to take along.

**EXERCISE 30-1 ▪ Using Numbers, p. 882**

**a.** A program to help save the sea otter transferred more than eighty animals to a new colony over the course of *two* years; however, all but *thirty-four* otters swam back home again.
**b.** *Twelve percent* or so of the estimated *15* billion plastic water bottles purchased annually in the United States is recycled.
**c.** In act 2, scene 9, of Shakespeare's *The Merchant of Venice,* Portia's *second* suitor fails to guess which of *three* caskets contains her portrait [or act II, scene ix, as directed].

### EXERCISE 31–1 ▪ Using Italics, p. 885

**a.** Does *avocado* mean "lawyer" in Spanish?
**b.** During this year's First Night celebrations, we heard Verdi's *Requiem* and Monteverdi's *Orfeo.*
**c.** It was fun watching the passengers on the *Europa* trying to dance to "Blue Moon" in the midst of a storm.

### EXERCISE 32–1 ▪ Using Hyphens, p. 887

**a.** Jimmy is a lively four-year-old boy, and his sister is two years old.
**b.** Correct
**c.** Tracy's brother-in-law lives with his family in a six-room apartment.

APPENDIX

# Quick Format Guide



When you think about a newspaper, a specific type of publication comes to mind because the newspaper is a familiar *genre,* or form. Almost all printed newspapers share a set of defined features: a masthead, headlines, pictures with captions, graphics, and articles arranged in columns of text. Even if the details vary, you can still recognize a newspaper as a newspaper. Popular magazines, academic journals, letters of recommendation, corporate annual reports, and many other types of writing can be identified and distinguished by such features.

Readers also have expectations about how a college paper should look, sometimes including the presentation of visual material such as graphs, tables, photographs, or other illustrations, depending on the field and the assignment. How can you find out what's expected? Check your course materials. Look for directions about format, advice about common problems, requirements for a specific academic style – or all three.

## A | Following the Format for an Academic Paper

You can easily spot the appealing features of a magazine, newspaper, or Web site with bold headlines, colorful images, and creative graphics. These lively materials serve their purpose, attracting your attention and promoting the interests of the publication's owners, contributors, or sponsors. In contrast, academic papers may look plain, even downright dull. However, their aim is not to entertain you but to engage your mind.

*(continued on p. A-7)*

**MLA FIRST PAGE**

Running head with writer's last name, one space, and the page number on every page

Writer's name

Instructor's name

Course

Date

Title, centered but not in quotes or italics

½" indent or 5 spaces

Double-spaced 12-point Times New Roman font recommended

Right margin uneven with no automatic hyphenation

Thesis previews paper's development

Launch statement names publication and author

Long quotation (5 prose or 4 poetry lines or more) indented without quotation marks

Ellipses show omissions, and brackets show additions within a quotation

Page number locates information in source

Electronic sources without page numbers cited only by author or by title with organization as author

1"

½"

Williams 1

Christopher Williams

Professor Smith

Composition I

12 May 2013

Watercoolers of the Future

The traditional office environment includes many challenges such as commuting in rush-hour traffic, spending long hours in a cubicle, and missing family events due to strict work hours. These challenges are all changing, however, now that technology is altering how and where people work. With more and more freelance and home-based possibilities, a trend known as co-working has led to the development of shared workspaces. As technology changes the traditional office workspace, new co-working cooperatives are creating the watercoolers of the future, positive gathering spots where working people can meet and share ideas.

1" 1"

New technology is leading the shift away from corporate offices. In *The Future of Work,* Malone explains this move away from the physical office with four walls:

1"

> Dispersed physically but connected by technology, workers are now able . . . to make their own decisions using information gathered from many other people and places. . . . [They] gain the economic benefits of large organizations, like economies of scale and knowledge, without giving up the human benefits of small ones, like freedom, creativity, motivation, and flexibility. (4)

Working at a distance or from home can take a toll on workers, however. Loneliness and lack of social opportunities are some of the largest problems for people who do not work in a traditional office (Miller). This is where co-working comes in. Independent workers such as freelancers, people starting their own businesses, and telecommuters share office space. They often pay a monthly fee in exchange for use of the rented area and whatever it provides, such as desk space, meeting rooms,

1"

**MLA WORKS CITED**

Williams 7

Works Cited

Butler, Kiera. "Works Well with Others." *Mother Jones* Jan./Feb. 2008: 66-69. Print.

Cetron, Marvin J., and Owen Davies. "Trends Shaping Tomorrow's World: Economic and Social Trends and Their Impacts." *The Futurist* 44.3 (2010): 35-51. *Academic OneFile*. Web. 1 May 2013.

Citizen Space. "Our Philosophy." *Citizen Space*. Citizen Space, n.d. Web. 1 May 2013.

Donkin, Richard. *The Future of Work*. Hampshire: Palgrave Macmillan, 2009. Print.

Godin, Seth. "The Last Days of Cubicle Life." *Time*. Time, 14 May 2009. Web. 30 Apr. 2013.

Goetz, Kaomi. "Co-working Offers Community to Solo Workers." *National Public Radio*. Natl. Public Radio, 6 Jan. 2010. Web. 7 May 2013.

---. "For Freelancers, Landing a Workspace Gets Harder." *National Public Radio*. Natl. Public Radio, 10 Apr. 2012. Web. 7 May 2013.

Malone, Thomas W. *The Future of Work: How the New Order of Business Will Shape Your Organization, Your Management Style and Your Life*. Boston: Harvard Business, 2004. Print.

McConville, Christine. "Freelancers Bag Cheap Office Space." *Boston Herald*. Boston Herald and Herald Media, 15 Aug. 2009. Web. 30 Apr. 2013.

Miller, Kerry. "Where the Coffee Shop Meets the Cubicle." *Bloomberg Businessweek*. Bloomberg, 26 Feb. 2007. Web. 30 Apr. 2013.

1" (left margin) 1" (right margin)

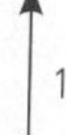


List of Works Cited on a separate page

Running head continues

List alphabetized by last names of authors or by titles (when no author is named)

First line of entry at left margin

Additional lines indented ½"

Double-spaced throughout

Three hyphens show same author continues

## APA TITLE PAGE AND ABSTRACT

Running head with short title in capital letters on left and page number on right

1"

Running head: PET HEALTH INSURANCE 1

Double-spaced 12-point Times New Roman font recommended

Title, centered

Author

School

Limitations of Pet Health Insurance

Jennifer Miller

Springfield Community College

Running head continues on following pages

PET HEALTH INSURANCE 2

Heading, centered

No paragraph indentation

Double-spaced

Main ideas summed up, usually in less than 250 words

Key words, common for journal articles, also may be expected by your instructor

Abstract

In recent years, the amount of money spent annually in the United States on veterinary care for the millions of household pets has risen into the billions of dollars. One option for owners is to buy a pet health insurance policy. Policies currently available have both advantages and disadvantages. Benefits can include coverage of increasingly complicated treatments. Drawbacks to coverage include the exclusion of pre-existing conditions and hidden fees. In the end, interest-bearing savings accounts may be a better option than policy premiums for most pet owners.

*Key words:* pet health insurance, pet ownership

**APA FIRST PAGE OF TEXT**

Running head continues

PET HEALTH INSURANCE 3

1″

½″

Title centered

½″ (or 5–7 spaces)

Limitations of Pet Health Insurance

The Humane Society of the United States (2012) reports in *U.S. Pet Ownership Statistics* that over 78 million dogs and 84 million cats are owned as household pets. However, only 3% of household pets are insured. Furthermore, in 2007, "only 850,000 pet insurance policies [were] in effect . . . according to the National Commission on Veterinary Economic Issues" (Weston, 2010). Recent studies suggest that, despite the growing availability of insurance plans for pet health care, these policies may not be the cheapest way to care for a household pet. Pet owners need to consider a number of factors before buying a policy, including the pet's age, any preexisting diseases that an insurance carrier might decide not to cover, and a policy's possible hidden fees.

1″ 1″

Launch statement names organization as author with date added in parentheses

Double-spaced throughout

Brackets show additions, and ellipses show omissions within a quotation

Electronic source without page cited only by author and date

Thesis previews paper's development

**Types of Pet Health Insurance Currently Available**

First-level heading in bold type and centered

Pet ownership is important to many people, and pets can do a great deal to improve the mental health and quality of life for their owners (McNicholas et al., 2005, p. 1252). However, paying for a pet's own health care can be stressful and expensive. Mathews (2009) reported on the costs in the *Wall Street Journal:*

Citation identifies authors, date, and location in the source (required for quotation and preferred for paraphrase)

½″

> This year, pet owners are expected to spend around $12.2 billion for veterinary care, up from $11.1 billion last year and $8.2 billion five years ago, according to the American Pet Products Association. Complex procedures widely used for people, including chemotherapy and dialysis, are now available for pets, and the potential cost of treating certain illnesses has spiked as a result. (Introduction section, para. 4)

Long quotation (40 words or more) indented without quotation marks

Section name and paragraph number locate quotation in electronic source without page numbers

Many providers currently offer plans to insure household pets. The largest of the providers is the long-standing Veterinary Pet Insurance (VPI), holding over two-thirds of the country's market (Weston, 2010). Other companies include ASPCA Pet Health Insurance, Petshealth Care Plan, and AKC Pet Healthcare Plan. All offer plans for dogs and cats, yet VPI is one of only a

Right margin uneven with no automatic hyphenation

1″

## APA REFERENCES

Running head with page numbering continues

Heading, centered

List alphabetized by last names of authors or by titles (when no author is named)

First line of entry at left margin

Additional lines indented ½″

Double-spaced throughout

No period after URL

As many as seven authors named in References

No period after DOI (digital object identifier) for article

Long URL divided before period, slash, or other punctuation mark

1″ ½″

PET HEALTH INSURANCE 12

References

Barlyn, S. (2008, March 13). Is pet health insurance worth the price? *The Wall Street Journal,* p. D2.

Busby, J. (2005). *How to afford veterinary care without mortgaging the kids.* Bemidji, MN: Busby International.

Calhoun, A. (2008, February 8). What I wouldn't do for my cat. *Salon.* Retrieved from http://www.salon.com

Darlin, D. (2006, May 13). Vet bills and the priceless pet: What's a practical owner to do? *The New York Times.* Retrieved from http://www.nytimes.com

Humane Society of the United States (2012). U.S. pet ownership statistics. Retrieved from http://www.humanesociety.org/issues/pet_overpopulation/facts/pet_ownership_statistics.html

Kenney, D. (2009). *Your guide to understanding pet health insurance.* Memphis, TN: PhiloSophia.

1″ Mathews, A. W. (2009, December 9). Polly want an insurance policy? *Wall Street Journal.* Retrieved from http://online.wsj.com 1″

McNicholas, J., Gilbey, A., Rennie, A., Ahmedzai, S., Dono, J., & Ormerod, E. (2005). Pet ownership and human health: A brief review of evidence and issues. *British Medical Journal, 331,* 1252-1254. doi:10.1136/bmj.331.7527.1252

Price, J. (2010, April 9). Should you buy pet health insurance? *Christian Science Monitor.* Retrieved from http://www.csmonitor.com

Weston, L. P. (2010, November 4). Should you buy pet insurance? *MSN Money.* Retrieved from http://money.msn.com/insurance/should-you-buy-pet-insurance-weston.aspx

1″

*(continued from p. A-1)*
The conventions—the accepted expectations—for college papers vary by field but typically support core academic values: to present ideas, reduce distractions, and integrate sources. A conventional format reassures readers that you respect the values behind the guidelines.

| Common Academic Values | Common Paper Expectations and Format |
|---|---|
| Clear presentation of ideas, information, and research findings | ■ Word-processed text on one side of a white sheet of paper, double-spaced, one-inch margins<br>■ Paper printed in crisp, black, 12-point Times New Roman type with numbered pages |
| Investigation of an intriguing issue, unanswered question, unsolved puzzle, or unexplored relationship | ■ Title and running head to clarify focus for reader<br>■ Abstract in social sciences or sciences to sum up<br>■ Opening paragraph or section to express thesis, research question, or conclusions<br>■ Closing paragraph or section to reinforce conclusions |
| Academic exchange of ideas and information, including evidence from reliable authorities and investigations | ■ Quotations from sources identified by quotation marks or block format<br>■ Paraphrase, summary, and synthesis of sources<br>■ Citation of each source in the text when mentioned<br>■ Well-organized text with transitions and cues to help readers make connections<br>■ Possibly headings to identify sections |
| Identification of evidence to allow a reader to evaluate its contribution and join the academic exchange | ■ Full information about each source in a concluding list<br>■ Specific format used for predictable, consistent arrangement of detail |

MLA (Modern Language Association) style, explained in the *MLA Handbook for Writers of Research Papers,* Seventh Edition (New York: MLA, 2009), is commonly used in the humanities. APA (American Psychological Association) style, explained in the *Publication Manual of the American Psychological Association,* Sixth Edition (Washington, D.C.: American Psychological Association, 2010), is commonly used in the social and behavioral sciences. Both MLA and APA, like other academic styles, specify how a page should look and how sources should be credited. (See pp. A-2–A-6.)

For examples showing how to cite and list sources in MLA and APA styles, see E in the Quick Research Guide, pp. A-32–A-38.

# B | Integrating and Crediting Visuals

Visuals in your text can engage readers, convey information, and reinforce your words. The MLA and APA style guides divide visuals into two groups:

- **Tables** are grids that clearly report numerical data or other information in columns (running up and down) and rows (running across).
- **Figures** include charts, graphs, diagrams, drawings, maps, photographs, or other images.

Much of the time you can create pie charts, bar graphs, or tables in your text file using your software, spreadsheet, or presentation options. Try a drawing program for making diagrams, maps, or sketches or an image editor for scanning print photographs or adding your own digital shots.

When you add visuals from other sources, you can photocopy or scan printed material, pick up online graphics, or turn to the computer lab for sophisticated advice. For a complex project, get help well ahead of your deadline, and allow plenty of time to learn new techniques.

Select or design visuals that are clear, easy to read, and informative.

- To present statistical information, use graphs, charts, or tables.
- To discuss a conflict in a certain geographical area, supply a map.
- To illustrate a reflective essay, scan an image of yourself or an event.
- To clarify stages, steps, or directions for a process, add a diagram.

## B1 Position visuals and credit any sources.

Present each visual: provide a context for it, identify its purpose, explain its meaning, and help a reader see how it supports your point. Following your style guide, identify and number it as a table or figure. Place the visual near the related text discussion so readers can easily connect the two.

Solve any layout problems in your final draft as you arrange text and visual on the page. For instance, align an image with the left margin to continue the text's forward movement. Use it to balance and support, not overshadow, text. Let the visual draw a reader's eye with an appropriate—not excessive—share of the page. To present a long table or large photograph on its own page, simply add page breaks before and after it. To include tables or figures for reference, such as your survey forms, place them in an appendix or collect them in an electronic supplement, as APA suggests.

Acknowledge visual sources as carefully as textual sources. Credit material from a source, printed or electronic, as you present the visual. Ask permission, if required, to use an image from a copyrighted source, including most printed books, articles, and other resources; credit the owner of the copyright. If you download an image from the Web, follow the site guidelines for the use of images. If you are uncertain about whether you can use an image from a source, ask your teacher's advice.

## B2 Prepare tables using MLA or APA format.

If you conduct a small survey, use the insert or table menu to create a simple table to summarize responses. Supply a label and a title or caption before the table. (Italicize its name if you are using APA style.) Double-space, add lines to separate sections, and use letters to identify any notes.

**TABLE FORMAT FOR PRESENTING YOUR SURVEY FINDINGS**

Table 1 — Label with number

Sources of Financial Support Reported by Survey Participants[a] — Title or caption; Letter keyed to note

| Type of Support | First-Year Students (n = 20) | Other Undergraduates (n = 30) |
|---|---|---|
| Scholarship or Campus Grant | 25% | 20% |
| Student Loans | 40% | 57% |
| Work Study | 20% | 7% |
| Family Support | 50% | 40% |
| Part-Time or Full-Time Job | 25% | 57% |
| Employer or Military Contribution | 10% | 17% |
| Other | 5% | 7% |

Column headings

Pair of rules or lines to enclose heading

Rule or line to mark end

a. Percentages based on the total number of respondents (n) were calculated and rounded to the nearest whole number.

Note of explanation if needed

If your results came from only a few students at one campus, you might compare them with state or national findings, as in the next sample table. When you include a table or an image from a source, credit it, and identify it as a source (MLA) or as adapted (APA) if you have modified it.

**TABLE FORMAT FOR MLA AND APA SOURCE CREDITS**

Label with number

Table 2

Title or caption

Percentages of Undergraduates Receiving Selected Types of Financial Aid, by Type of Institution, Attendance Pattern, Dependency Status, and Income Level: 2007-08

Column headings

Spanner heading (for all rows) centered

| Institution Characteristics | Any Grants | Any Student Loans | Work-Study | Veterans Benefits |
|---|---|---|---|---|
| | | Public | | |
| 2-year | 39.6 | 13.2 | 3.3 | 2.0 |
| 4-year (non-doctorate) | 52.5 | 43.4 | 7.3 | 2.4 |
| 4-year (doctorate) | 53.1 | 47.8 | 8.0 | 2.0 |

MLA source credit

Source: United States, Dept. of Educ., Inst. of Educ. Statistics, Natl. Center for Educ. Statistics; *2007-08 National Postsecondary Student Aid Study;* US Dept. of Educ., Apr. 2009; Web; 1 Dec. 2012; table 1.

The credit above follows MLA style; the credit below follows APA. At the end, add the date and name as any copyright holder requests.

APA source credit

*Note.* Adapted from U.S. Department of Education, Institute of Education Sciences, National Center for Education Statistics. 2009. *2007-08 National Postsecondary Student Aid Study* (NCES Publication No. NPSAS:08), Table 1.

## B3 Add diagrams, graphs, charts, and other figures.

Select or design figures purposefully. Consider your readers' needs as you decide which types might convey information effectively. A diagram can help readers see the sequence of steps in a process. A graph can show how different groups of people behave over time. A sketch of an old building can illustrate the style of its era. Add a clear caption or title to identify what you are illustrating as well as labels for readers to note key elements, add numerical or textual detail, and use visual elements—size, shape, direction, color—to emphasize, connect, or contrast.

- A diagram can simplify a complex process and clarify its stages. Figure A.1 shows the stages in wastewater treatment.
- A comparative line graph can show how trends change over time. Figure A.2 compares trends in food allergies over a decade, marking percentages on the vertical line and years on the horizontal line.

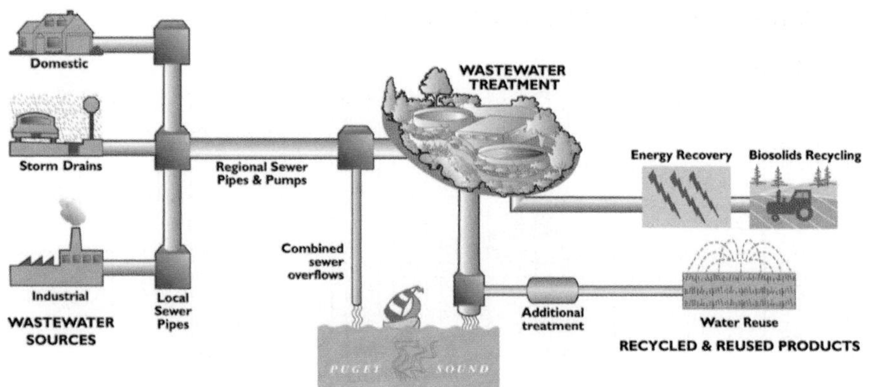


**Figure A.1** A Diagram Showing the Process of Wastewater Treatment in King County, Washington. Source: King County, Washington, Department of Natural Resources Wastewater Treatment Division

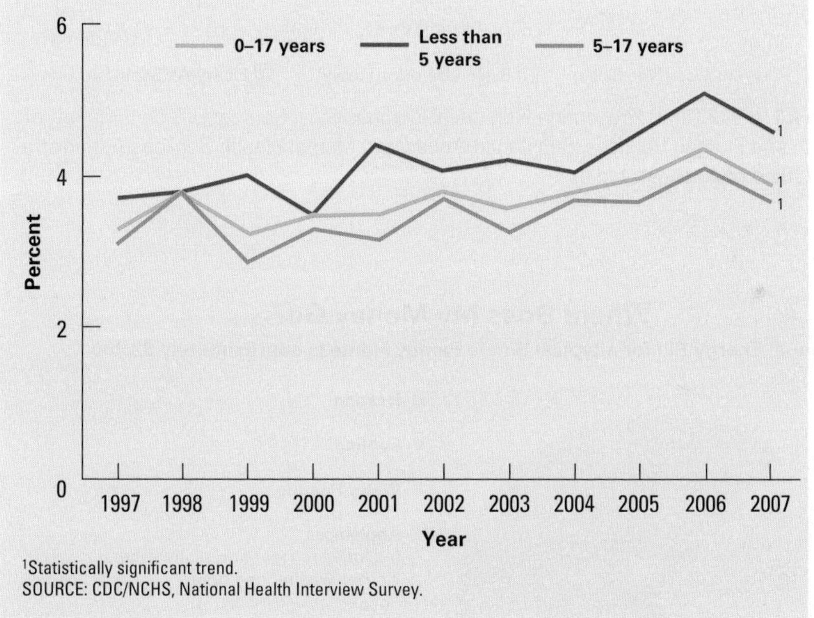


**Figure A.2** A Comparative Line Graph Showing the Percentage of Children with a Reported Food or Digestive Allergy from 1997 through 2007 by Age Group. Source: The Centers for Disease Control and Prevention

- A column or bar graph can compare relative values. Figure A.3 illustrates the relative levels of alcohol usage among different age groups.
- A pie chart can compare components with each other and the whole. Figure A.4 shows how the total energy bill (100%) for a single family home is spent on various uses.

For a tutorial on preparing effective graphs and charts, go to Re:Writing at **bedfordstmartins.com/bedguide**.

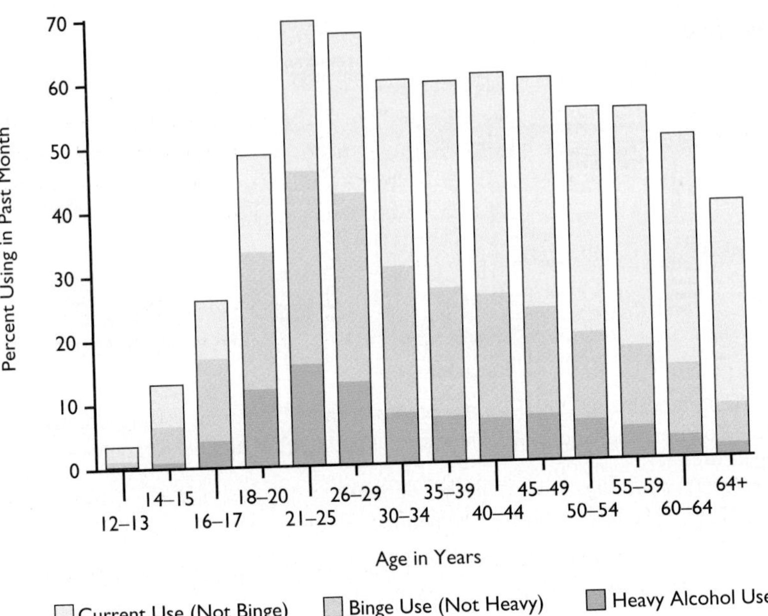


**Figure A.3** A Bar Chart Presenting Numerical Comparisons. Source: U.S. Department of Health and Human Services, Substance Abuse and Mental Health Services Administration, Office of Applied Studies

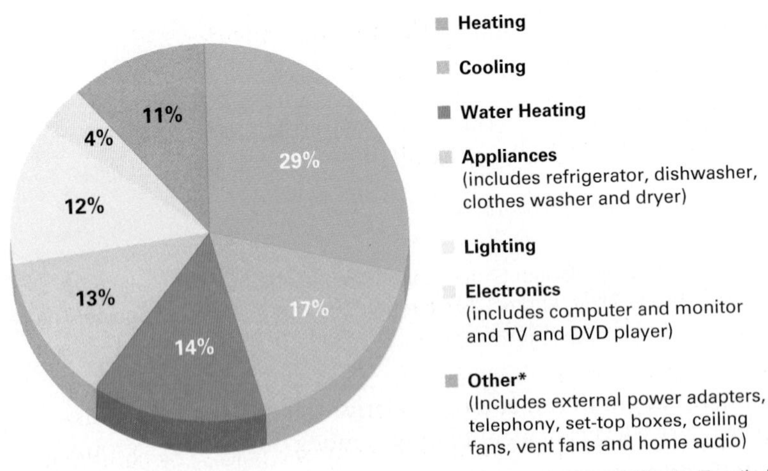


**Figure A.4** Pie Chart Showing Energy Consumption for a Typical Single Family Home in 2009. Source: ENERGYSTAR, The U.S. Environmental Protection Agency, The U.S. Department of Energy

## C | Preparing a Document Template

Unless your teacher encourages creative formatting, avoid experimenting with a college paper. Follow the assigned format and style; check your draft against your instructor's directions and against examples (such as the MLA and APA samples here). Use your software's Help function to learn how to set font, page, format, or template features such as these:

- placement of information on the first page
- margin widths for the top, bottom, and sides of the page (such as 1″)
- name of font (Times New Roman), style (regular roman, italics, or bold), and size of type (12 point)
- running head with automatic page numbering
- double spacing (without extra space between paragraphs)
- text alignment, even on the left but not on the right (left alignment, not centered text, with automatic hyphenation of words turned off)
- width of the paragraph indentation and special "hanging" indentation for your final list of sources
- any other features of the required format

A template simplifies using expected features every time you write a paper with the same specifications. If you have trouble setting features or saving the template, get help from your instructor, a classmate, the writing center, or the computer lab. Follow these steps to create your template:

1. Format your paper the way you want it to look.
2. Create a duplicate copy of your formatted file.
3. Delete all of the text discussion in the duplicate document.
4. Use the Save As feature to save the file as a document template.
5. Give the template a clear name ("Comp paper" or "MLA form").
6. To open a new file, select this template from your template folder.

## D | Solving Common Format Problems

Software programs differ, as do versions of the same software. Watch for default settings or format shifts that do not match an academic format.

- When you find unconventional features, such as extra lines between paragraphs or automatic hyphenation, reset these features.
- Use your software's Help function to look up the feature by naming it (paragraph), identifying the issue (paragraph spacing), or specifying what you want to do (troubleshoot paragraph spacing).
- Print Help screens for a complicated path or confusing directions.

Other problems can arise because academic style guides make their own assumptions about the texts their users are likely to write. For example, MLA style assumes you will write an essay, simply separate items in a list with commas, and probably limit additions to tables and illustrations. On the other hand, APA style assumes you probably need section headings, lists (numbered, bulleted, or lettered within a sentence), and appendices, especially for research materials such as sample questionnaires. In addition, your instructor might require an outline or links for online sources. Follow your instructor's advice if your paper requires formatting that the style you are using (MLA or APA) does not recognize.

Readers appreciate your consideration of their practical problems, too. A clear, neat, readable document is one that readers can readily absorb. For example, your instructor might ask you to reprint a paper if your toner cartridge is nearly empty. Clear papers in a standard format are easier on the eyes than those with faint print or unusual features. In addition, such papers have margin space for comments so they are easy to grade. If you submit an electronic file, pay attention to online formatting conventions.

# E | Designing Other Documents for Your Audience

Four key principles of document design can help you prepare effective documents in and out of the classroom: know your audience, satisfy them with the features and format they expect, consider their circumstances, and remember your purpose.

**DISCOVERY CHECKLIST**

- ☐ Who are your readers? What matters to them? How might the format of your document acknowledge their values, goals, and concerns?
- ☐ What form or genre do readers expect? Which of its features and details do they see as typical? What visual evidence would they find appropriate?
- ☐ What problems or constraints will your readers face as they read your document? How can your design help to reduce these problems?
- ☐ What is the purpose of your document? How can its format help achieve this purpose? How might it enhance your credibility as a writer?
- ☐ What is the usual format of your document? Find and analyze a sample.

## E1 Select type font, size, and face.

*Typography* refers to the appearance of letters on a page. You can change typeface or font, style from roman to bold or italics, or type size for a passage by highlighting it and clicking on the appropriate toolbar icon. Selecting Font in the Home, Format, or Page Layout menu usually leads to options such as superscript, shadows, or small capitals.

Most college papers and many other documents use Times New Roman in a 12-point size. Signs, posters, and visuals such as slides for presentations might require larger type (with a larger number for the point size). Test such materials for readability by printing samples in various type sizes and standing back from them at the distance of your intended audience. Size also varies with different typefaces because they occupy different amounts of horizontal space on the page. Figure A.5 shows the space required for the same sentence written in four different 12-point fonts.

| | |
|---|---|
| Times New Roman | An estimated 40 percent of young children have an imaginary friend. |
| Courier New | An estimated 40 percent of young children have an imaginary friend. |
| Arial | An estimated 40 percent of young children have an imaginary friend. |
| Comic Sans MS | An estimated 40 percent of young children have an imaginary friend. |

**Figure A.5** Space Occupied by Different Typefaces

Fonts also vary in design. Times New Roman and Courier New are called *serif* fonts because they have small tails, or serifs, at the ends of the letters. Arial and the more casual Comic Sans MS are *sans serif*—without serifs—and thus have solid, straight lines without tails at the tips of the letters.

Times New Roman (serif) K k P p

Arial (sans serif) K k P p

Sans serif fonts have a clean look, desirable for headlines, ads, "pull quotes" (in larger type to catch the reader's eye), and text within APA-style figures. More readable serif fonts are used for article (or "body") text. Times New Roman, the common word-processor default font preferred for MLA and APA styles, was developed for the *Times* newspaper in London. As needed, use light, slanted *italics* (for certain titles) or dark **bold** (for APA headings).

## E2 Organize effective lists.

The placement of material on a page—its layout—can make information more accessible for readers. MLA style recognizes common ways of integrating a list within a sentence: introduce the list with a colon or dash (or set it off with two dashes); separate its items with commas, or use semicolons if the items include commas. APA style adds options, preceding each item in a sentence with a letter enclosed by parentheses: (a), (b), and (c) or using display lists—set off from text—for visibility and easy reading.

One type of displayed list, the numbered list, can emphasize priorities, conclusions, or processes such as steps in research procedures, how-to advice, or instructions, as in this simple sequence for making clothes:

**NUMBERED LIST**

1. Lay out the pattern and fabric you have selected.
2. Pin the pattern to the fabric, noting the arrows and grain lines.
3. Cut out the fabric pieces, following the outline of the pattern.
4. Sew the garment together using the pattern's step-by-step instructions.

Another type of displayed list sets off a bit of information with a bullet, most commonly a small round mark (•) but sometimes a square (■), from the Home or Symbol menu. Bulleted lists are common in résumés and business documents but not necessarily in academic papers, though APA style now recognizes them. Use them to identify steps, reasons, or items when you do not wish to suggest any order of priority, as in this list of tips for saving energy.

**BULLETED LIST**

- Let your hair dry without running a hair dryer.
- Commute by public transportation.
- Turn down the thermostat by a few degrees.
- Unplug your phone charger and TV during the day.

## E3 Consider adding headings.

In a complex research report, business proposal, or Web document, headings can show readers how the document is structured, which sections are most important, and how parts are related. Headings also name sections so readers know where they are and where they are going. Headings at the same level should be consistent and look the same; headings at different levels should differ from each other and from the main text in placement and style, making the text easy to scan for key points.

For academic papers, MLA encourages writers to organize by outlining their essays but does not recommend or discuss text headings. In contrast, APA illustrates five levels of headings beginning with these two:

First-Level Heading Centered in Bold

**Second-Level Heading on the Left in Bold**

Besides looking the same, headings at the same level in your document should be brief, clear, and informative. They also should use consistent parallel phrasing. If you write a level-one heading as an *-ing* phrase, do the same for all the level-one headings that follow. Here are some examples of four common patterns for phrasing headings.

For more on parallel structure, see section B2 in the Quick Editing Guide, p. A-52.

| ***-ING* PHRASES** | **QUESTIONS** |
|---|---|
| Using the College Catalog | What Is Hepatitis C? |
| Choosing Courses | Who Is at Risk? |
| Declaring a Major | How Is Hepatitis C Treated? |
| **NOUN PHRASES** | **IMPERATIVE SENTENCES** |
| E-Commerce Benefits | Initiate Your IRA Rollover |
| E-Commerce Challenges | Balance Your Account |
| Online Shopper Profiles | Select New Investments |

Web pages—especially home pages and site guides—are designed to help readers find information quickly, within a small viewing frame. For this reason, they generally have more headings than other documents. If you design a Web page or post your course portfolio, consider what different readers might want to find. Then design your headings and content to meet their needs.

## F | Organizing a Résumé and an Application Letter

When your reader is a prospective employer, present a solid, professional job application, preferably a one-page résumé and application letter (see pp. A-18–A-19). Both should be clearly organized to show why you are a strong candidate for the position. The purpose of your résumé is to organize the details of your education and experience (usually by category and by reverse chronology) so they are easy to review. Wording matters, so use action verbs and parallel structure to convey your experience and enthusiasm. The purpose of your application letter is to highlight your qualifications and motivate the reader to interview and eventually hire you. A follow-up letter might thank your interviewer, confirm your interest, and supply anything requested. Write clearly, and use a standard format; a sloppy letter might suggest that you lack the communication skills employers value.

For more on application letters and résumés, see pp. 356–61.

Your campus career center may provide sample application letters and résumés so you can compare layout variations, evaluate their impact, and effectively design your own. To apply for a professional program, internship, or other opportunity, simply adapt your letter and résumé. For an electronic job application form, select relevant information from your résumé and embed as many key words as possible that might be used to sort or rank applications.

Splits heading with contact information

**Joseph Cauteruccio, Jr.**

65 Oakwood Ave. Apt. #105
Somerville, MA 02144
Mobile 617-555-5555
jcjr@comnet.com

Places current information first

## Experience

**Research Analyst** *June 2012 – Present*
**Industrial Economics, Incorporated** — Cambridge, MA

Develop profit estimation model, adopted as practice area standard, for petroleum bulk stations
Create and implement valuation methodology for a major privately held forestry company

**Intern, Global Treasury — Investment Management Team** *June 2011 – August 2011*
**State Street Corporation —** Boston, MA

Specifies activities

Research and analyze corporate bonds, including economic and industry analyses

## Education

**Bachelor of Arts —** Bates College, Lewiston, ME *September 2008 – May 2012*

Major: Economics
Minor: Japanese

Related courses: Calculus; Advanced Statistics and Econometrics

Uses bold type to highlight categories

## Skills & Competencies

**Statistical Packages:** SAS, STATA, R
**Programming Languages & Related:** VBA, Python, SQL, LINUX/UNIX, Scripting (KSH/BASH), DOS
**Microsoft Office:** Advanced Excel, PowerPoint
**Other:** Cloud Computing (PaaS, AWS, shell interaction, batch processing), Hadoop Ecosystem
**Languages and Music:** Conversational Japanese, Guitar, Saxophone, Banjo

Labels sections and uses dividers

## Leadership & Involvement

**Analytic Pro Bono Work (present)**
Leverage data mining skills to assist nonprofit organizations
Consult on data collection and management
Improve donation volume and donor retention

**Boston Data Science Community**
Participate actively in industry groups, Boston Predictive Analytics, Boston R Users

**Alpine Climbing (2007-present)**
Organize route finding and equipment logistics
Lead trips throughout California, Canadian Rockies, and New England

65 Oakwood Ave. Apt. #105
Somerville, MA 02144
15 May 2013

Follows standard letter format

Ross Landon
Denver Strategists
8866 Larimer Street, Suite 404
Denver, CO 80217

Addresses specific person

Dear Mr. Landon:

Josh Greenway, formerly a data analyst with Denver Strategists, recommended that I contact you about the upcoming expansion of your Marketing Analysis Group. I am looking for an opportunity to combine my college major in economics with my long-standing interest in statistics. Because your expansion promises an excellent opportunity to do so, I wish to apply for one of your openings for a data analyst.

Identifies job sought and describes interests

As my résumé indicates, my college internship with the Investment Management Team at Global Treasury introduced me to the many processes involved in industry analyses. Since graduation, I have worked as a research analyst at Industrial Economics, estimating valuation and profits for clients in diverse industries. In addition, as a pro bono consultant with Boston nonprofit organizations, I have expanded my expertise with statistics packages. For these groups, I have directed my skills to improving data mining and data management in order to help them cultivate and retain contributors more effectively.

Explains qualifications

I am now looking forward to designing and conducting more complex data mining and data analysis projects. Joining your expansion team would offer me a welcome opportunity to develop my analytic skills, expand my experience with various statistical methods, and gain sophistication working with team colleagues as well as a variety of clients. For me, data analysis is a challenging and rewarding way to combine my skills in math, statistics, and technology with the creativity data science requires. Both my education and my experience have prepared me to address a company's problems or change a client's perspective through data-based analysis.

Confirms interest

I would be happy to meet with you to learn more about your plans for the Marketing Analysis Group. Please call me at 617-555-5555, e-mail me at jcjr@comnet.com, or write to me at the address above. I appreciate your consideration and look forward to hearing from you.

Supplies contact information

Sincerely,

*Joe Cauteruccio*

Joseph Cauteruccio

Enclosure: Résumé

Includes résumé with letter

APPENDIX

# Quick Research Guide



When you begin college, you may feel uncertain about what to say and how to speak up. As you gain experience, you will join the academic exchange around you by reading, thinking, and writing with sources. You will turn to articles, books, and Web sites for evidence to support your thesis and develop your ideas, advancing knowledge through exchange.

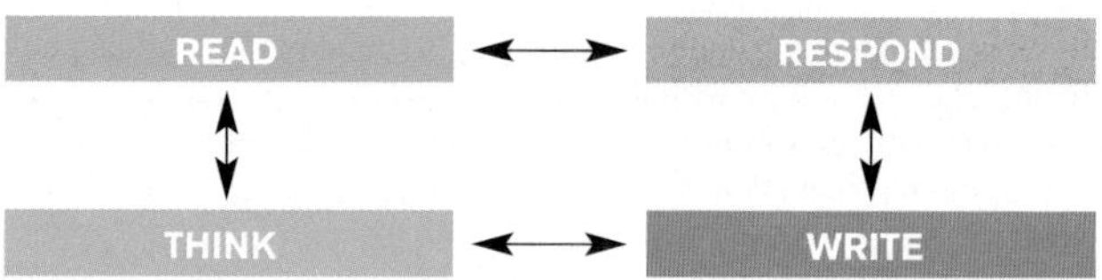


Conducting research requires time to explore, to think, and to respond. However, efficient and purposeful research can produce greater success in less time than optimistic browsing. Maybe you need more confidence or good advice fast: you've procrastinated, you're overwhelmed, or you're uncertain about how to succeed. To help you, this Quick Research Guide concentrates on five key steps.

**TURNING TO SOURCES FOR SUPPORTING EVIDENCE**

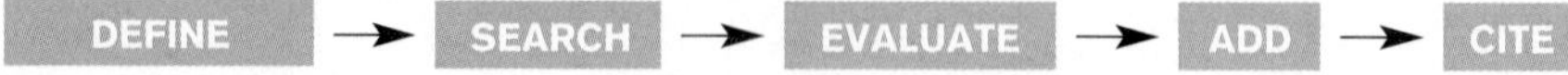

# A | Defining Your Quest

Especially when your research goals are specific and limited, you're more likely to succeed if you try to define the hunt in advance.

**PURPOSE CHECKLIST**

- ☐ What is the thesis you want to support, point you want to show, question you want to answer, or problem you want to solve?
- ☐ Does the assignment require or suggest certain types of supporting evidence, sources, or presentations of material?
- ☐ Which ideas do you want to support with good evidence?
- ☐ Which ideas might you want to check, clarify, or change?
- ☐ Which ideas or opinions of others do you want to verify or counter?
- ☐ Do you want to analyze material yourself (for example, comparing different articles or Web sites) or to find someone else's analysis?
- ☐ What kinds of evidence do you want to use — facts, statistics, or expert testimony? Do you also want to add your own firsthand observation?

For more about stating and using a thesis, see pp. 399–408.

For more about types of evidence, see pp. 40–44.

**TWO VIEWS OF SUPPORTING EVIDENCE**

| COLLEGE WRITER | COLLEGE READER |
|---|---|
| • Does it answer my question and support my thesis? | • Is it relevant to the purpose and assignment? |
| • Does it seem accurate? | • Is it reliable, given academic standards? |
| • Is it recent enough? | • Is it current, given the standards of the field? |
| • Does it add enough detail and depth? | • Is it of sufficient quantity, variety, and strength? |
| • Is it balanced enough? | • Is it typical and fair? |
| • Will it persuade my audience? | • Does the writer make a credible case? |

For evidence checklists, see pp. 43–44 and p. A-24.

## A1 Decide what supporting evidence you need.

When you want to add muscle to college papers, you need reliable resources to supply facts, statistics, and expert testimony to back up your claims. You may not need comprehensive information, but you will want to hunt—quickly and efficiently—for exactly what you do need. That evidence should satisfy you as a writer and meet the criteria of your college readers—instructors and possibly classmates. Suppose you want to propose solutions to your community's employment problem.

**WORKING THESIS**

Many residents of Aurora need more—and more innovative—higher education to improve their job skills and career alternatives.

Because you already have ideas based on your firsthand observations and the experiences of people you know, your research goals are limited. First, you want to add accurate facts and figures that will show why you believe a compelling problem exists. Next, you want to visit the Web sites of local educational institutions and possibly locate someone to interview about existing career development programs.

## A2 Decide where you need supporting evidence.

As you plan or draft, you may tuck in notes to yourself—figure that out, find this, look it up, get the numbers here. Other times, you may not know exactly what or where to add. One way to determine where you need supporting evidence is to examine your draft, sentence by sentence.

- What does each sentence claim or promise to a reader?
- Where do you provide supporting evidence to demonstrate the claim or fulfill the promise?

The answers to these questions—your statements and your supporting evidence—often fall into a common alternating pattern:

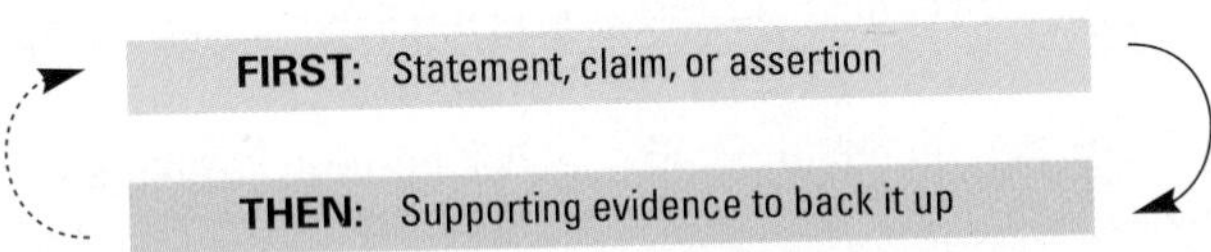
**FIRST:** Statement, claim, or assertion
**THEN:** Supporting evidence to back it up

For more about arguments based on claims of substantiation, evaluation, or policy, see pp. 167–74.

For more on inductive and deductive reasoning, see pp. 443–45.

When you spot a string of assertions without much support, you have found a place where you might need more evidence. Select reliable evidence so that it substantiates the exact statement, claim, or assertion that precedes it. Likewise, if you spot a string of examples, details, facts, quotations, or other evidence, introduce or conclude it with an interpretive statement that explains the point the evidence supports. Make sure your general statement connects and pulls together all of the particular evidence.

When Carrie Williamson introduced her cause-and-effect paper, "Rain Forest Destruction," she made a general statement and then supported it by quoting facts from a source. Then she repeated this statement-support pattern, backing up her next statement in turn. By using this pattern from the very beginning, Carrie reassured her readers that she was a trustworthy writer who would try to supply convincing evidence throughout her paper.

For the source entries from Carrie Williamson's MLA list of works cited, see pp. A-35–A-36.

The tropical rain forests are among the most biologically diverse communities in the world. According to the Rainforest Alliance, "The forests of the Neotropics are the habitat for tens of thousands of plant and wildlife species," as in "a single square mile of tropical forest in Rondonia, Brazil," which is home to "1,200 species of butterflies—twice the total number found in the United States and Canada" ("Conservation"). These amazing communities depend on each part being intact in order to function properly but are being destroyed at an alarming rate. Over several decades, even in protected areas, only 2% increased while 85% "suffered declines in surrounding forest cover" (Laurance et al. 291). Many rain forest conservationists debate the leading cause of deforestation. Regardless of which is the major cause, logging, slash-and-burn farming, and resource exploitation are destroying more of the rain forests each year.

Statement

Supporting evidence: Information and statistics about species

Statement

Supporting evidence: Facts about destruction

Statement identifying cause-and-effect debate

Statement previewing points to come

The table below shows some of the many ways this common statement-support pattern can be used to clarify and substantiate your ideas.

| First: Statement, Claim, or Assertion | Then: Supporting Evidence |
|---|---|
| Introduces a topic | Facts or statistics to justify the importance or significance of the topic |
| Describes a situation | Factual examples or illustrations to convey reality or urgency |
| Introduces an event | Accurate firsthand observations to describe an event that you have witnessed |
| Presents a problem | Expert testimony or firsthand observation to establish the necessity or urgency of a solution |
| Explains an issue | Facts and details to clarify or justify the significance of the issue |
| States your point | Facts, statistics, or examples to support your viewpoint or position |
| Prepares for evidence that follows | Facts, examples, observations, or research findings to develop your case |
| Concludes with your recommendation or evaluation | Facts, examples, or expert testimony to persuade readers to accept your conclusion |

Use the following checklist to help you decide whether—and where—you might need supporting evidence from sources.

### EVIDENCE CHECKLIST

- ☐ What does your thesis promise that you'll deliver? What additional evidence would ensure that you effectively demonstrate your thesis?
- ☐ Are your statements, claims, and assertions backed up with supporting evidence? If not, what evidence might you add?
- ☐ What evidence would most effectively persuade your readers?
- ☐ What criteria for useful evidence matter most for your assignment or your readers? What evidence would best meet these criteria?
- ☐ Which parts of your paper sound weak or incomplete to you?
- ☐ What facts or statistics would clarify your topic?
- ☐ What examples or illustrations would make the background or the current circumstances clearer and more compelling for readers?
- ☐ What does a reliable expert say about the situation your topic involves?
- ☐ What firsthand observation would add authenticity?
- ☐ Where have peers or your instructor suggested more or stronger evidence?

## B | Searching for Recommended Sources

When you need evidence, you may think first of the Internet. However, random Web sites require you to do extra work—checking what's presented as fact, looking for biases or financial motives, and searching for what's not stated rather than accepting what is. Such caution is required because anyone—expert or not—can build a Web site, write a blog entry, post an opinion, or send an e-mail. Repetition does not ensure accuracy, reliability, or integrity because the Internet has no quality controls.

On the other hand, when your college library buys books, subscribes to scholarly journals, and acquires resources, print or electronic, these publications are expected to follow accepted editorial practices. Well-regarded publishers and professional groups turn to peer reviewers—experts in the field—to assess articles or books before they are selected for publication. These quality controls bring readers material that meets academic or professional standards. When you need to search efficiently, begin with reliable sources, already screened by professionals.

## B1 Seek advice about reliable sources.

Although popular search engines can turn up sources on nearly any topic, will those sources meet your criteria and those of your readers? After all, your challenge is not simply to find any sources but to find solid sources with reliable evidence. The following shortcuts can help you find solid sources fast—ideally already screened, selected, and organized for you.

### RESOURCE CHECKLIST

- ☐ Have you talked with your instructor after class, during office hours, or by e-mail to ask for advice about resources for your topic? Have you checked the assignment, syllabus, handouts, or class Web site?
- ☐ Have your classmates recommended useful academic databases, disciplinary Web sites, or similar resources?
- ☐ Does the department offering the course have a Web site with lists of library resources or links to sites well regarded in that field?
- ☐ Does your textbook Web site provide links to additional resources?
- ☐ Which search strategies and library databases does the librarian at the reference desk recommend for your course and topic?
- ☐ Which databases or links on your library's Web site lead to government (federal, state, or local) resources or articles in journals and newspapers?
- ☐ Which resources are available through the online library catalog or in any periodicals or reference area of your campus library?

## B2 Select reliable sources that meet readers' criteria.

If you planned to investigate common Internet hoaxes for a paper about online practices, you might deliberately turn to sources that are, by definition, unreliable. However, in most cases, you want to turn right away to reliable sources. For some assignments, you might be expected to use varied sources: reports from journalists, advice from practitioners in the field, accounts of historical eyewitnesses, or opposing opinions on civic policy. For other assignments, you might be expected to turn only to scholarly sources—also identified as peer-reviewed or refereed sources—with characteristics such as these:

- in-depth investigation or interpretation of an academic topic or problem
- discussion of previous studies, which are cited in the text and listed at the end for easy reference by readers
- use of research methods accepted in a discipline or several fields

- publication by a reputable company or sponsoring organization
- acceptance for publication based on the author's credentials and reviews by experts (peer reviewers) who assess the quality of the study
- preparation for publication supervised by academic or expert editors or by authors and professional staff

Your instructors are likely to favor these quality controls. Your campus librarian can help you limit your searches to peer-reviewed journals or check the scholarly reputation of sources that you find.

## C | Evaluating Possible Sources

Like the perfect wave or the perfect day, the perfect source is hard to come by. Instead of looking for perfect sources, evaluate sources on the basis of practicality, standards, and evidence.

### C1 Evaluate sources as a practical researcher.

Your situation as a writer may determine how long or how widely you can search or how deeply you can delve into the sources you find. If you are worried about finishing on time or about juggling several assignments, you will need to search efficiently, using your own practical criteria.

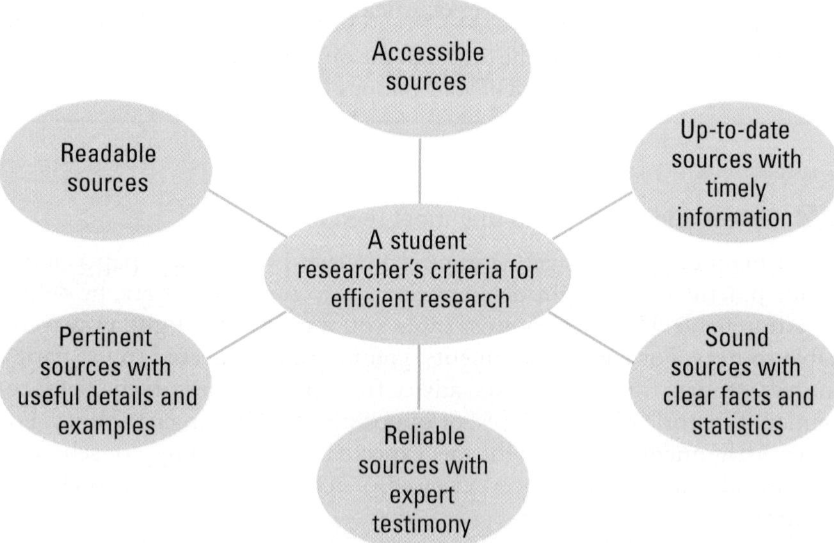


### C2 Evaluate sources as your readers would.

If you are uncertain about college requirements, start with recommended sources that are easily accessible, readable, and up-to-date. Look for sources that are chock-full of reliable facts, statistics, research findings, case studies, observations, examples, and expert testimony to persuade your readers.

| | | |
|---|---|---|
| • Where do you need to add evidence?<br>• What evidence might support your thesis?<br>• What evidence is likely to persuade a reader? | → | • Which solid sources supply what you need?<br>• Which sources meet your needs as a researcher?<br>• Which sources meet the expectations of readers? |

## C3 Evaluate sources for reliable and appropriate evidence.

When you use evidence from sources to support your points, both you and your readers are likely to hold two simple expectations:

- that your sources are reliable so you can trust their information
- that the information you select from them is appropriate for your paper

After all, how could an unreliable source successfully support your ideas? And what could unsuitable or mismatched information contribute? The difficulty, of course, is learning how to judge what is reliable and appropriate. The following checklist suggests how you can use the time-tested journalist's questions to evaluate print or electronic sources.

### EVALUATION CHECKLIST

*Who?*

- ☐ Who is the author? What are the author's credentials and experience?
- ☐ Who is the intended audience? Is it general or academic?
- ☐ Who publishes or sponsors the source? Is this publisher well regarded?
- ☐ Who has reviewed the source before publication? Only the author? Expert peer reviewers or referees? An editorial staff?

*What?*

- ☐ What is the purpose of the publication or Web site? Is it trying to sell, inform, report, or shape opinion?
- ☐ What bias or point of view might affect the reliability of the source?
- ☐ What evidence does the source present? Does the source seem trustworthy and logical? Does it identify its sources or supply active links?

*When?*

- ☐ When was the source published or created? When was it revised?
- ☐ When has it been cited by others in the field?

*Where?*

- ☐ Where did you find the source?
- ☐ Where is the source recommended? Has your library supplied it?

*Why?*

- ☐ Why would you use this source rather than others?
- ☐ Why is its information relevant to your research question?

*How?*

- ☐ How would it support your thesis and provide persuasive evidence?
- ☐ How does the source reflect its author, publisher or sponsor, and audience? How might you need to qualify its use in your paper?

For practice incorporating source material, go to the interactive "Take Action" charts in Re:Writing at **bedfordstmartins .com/bedguide**.

For examples in both MLA and APA style, see E1–E2.

For a tutorial on avoiding plagiarism, go to Re:Writing at **bedfordstmartins .com/bedguide**.

## D | Capturing, Launching, and Citing Evidence Added from Sources

Sometimes researchers concentrate so hard on hunting for reliable sources that they forget what comes next. The value of every source remains potential until you successfully capture its facts, statistics, expert testimony, examples, or other information in a form that you can incorporate into your paper. Then, you need to launch—or introduce—the information in order to identify its source or its contribution to your paper. Finally, you must accurately cite, or credit, both in the text of your paper and in a final list of sources, each source whose words or ideas you use.

### D1 Avoid plagiarism.

Allow enough time to add information from sources skillfully and correctly. Find out exactly how your instructor expects you to credit sources. Even if you do not intend to plagiarize—to use another writer's words or ideas without appropriately crediting them—a paper full of sloppy or careless shortcuts can look just like a paper deliberately copied from unacknowledged sources. Instead, borrow carefully and honestly.

Identify the source of information, any idea, summary, paraphrase, or quotation, right away, as soon as you add it to your notes. Carry that acknowledgment into your first draft and all the drafts that follow. You generally do not need to identify a source if you use what is called "common knowledge"—quotations, expressions, or information widely known and widely accepted. If you are uncertain about the need for a citation, ask your instructor, or simply provide the citation.

## D2 Read your source critically.

Before you pop outside material into your paper, read critically to evaluate its reliability and suitability. If you cannot understand a source that requires specialized background, don't use it. If its ideas, facts, claims, or viewpoint seem unusual, incorporate only what you can substantiate in unrelated sources. If its evidence seems accurate, logical, and relevant, decide exactly how you might want to add it to your paper. Carefully distinguish it from your own ideas, whether you quote, paraphrase, or summarize.

For more on critical reading, see Ch. 2. For more on evaluating evidence, see pp. 40–44. For more on logical fallacies, see pp. 51–52, and 180–81.

## D3 Quote accurately.

As you take notes, record as many quotations as you want if that process helps you master the material. When you add quotations to your paper, be selective. A quotation in itself is not necessarily effective evidence, and too many quotations will suggest that your writing is padded or lacks original thought. Quote exactly, and credit your source using the format expected.

For more on punctuating quotations and using ellipsis marks, see C3 in the Quick Editing Guide, pp. A-55–A-56.

### QUOTATION CHECKLIST

- ☐ Have you quoted only a notable passage that adds support and authority?
- ☐ Have you checked your quotation word by word, for accuracy?
- ☐ Have you marked the beginning and the ending with quotation marks?
- ☐ Have you used ellipses (. . .) to mark any spot where you have left out words in the original?
- ☐ Have you identified the source of the quotation in a launch statement (see D6) or in parentheses?
- ☐ Have you recorded in parentheses the page number where the quotation appears in the source?

## D4 Paraphrase carefully.

A paraphrase presents a passage from a source in your own words and sentences. It may include the same level of detail as the original, but it should not slip into the original wording (unless you identify those

For more about how to quote, paraphrase, and summarize, see pp. 236–43.

snippets with quotation marks). Credit the original source as you do when you quote.

### PARAPHRASE CHECKLIST

- ☐ Have you read the passage critically to be sure you understand it?
- ☐ Have you paraphrased accurately, reflecting both the main points and the supporting details in the original?
- ☐ Does your paraphrase use your own words without repeating or echoing the words or the sentence structure of the original?
- ☐ Does your paraphrase stick to the ideas of the original?
- ☐ Have you revised your paraphrase so it reads smoothly and clearly?
- ☐ Have you identified the source of the paraphrase in a launch statement (see D6) or in parentheses?
- ☐ Have you recorded in parentheses the page number where the passage appears in the source?

## D5 Summarize fairly.

A summary clearly identifies the source and reduces its ideas to their essence. Using your own words, your summary may boil a book, a chapter, an article, or a section down to a few sentences that accurately and clearly sum up the sense of the original.

### SUMMARY CHECKLIST

- ☐ Have you read critically to be sure you understand the source?
- ☐ Have you fairly stated the author's main point in your own words?
- ☐ Have you briefly stated any supporting ideas that you wish to sum up?
- ☐ Have you stuck to the overall point without bogging down in details?
- ☐ Is your summary respectful of others, even if you disagree with them?
- ☐ Have you revised your summary so it reads smoothly and clearly?
- ☐ Have you identified the source of the summary in a launch statement (see D6) or in parentheses?
- ☐ Have you recorded in parentheses the page number where any specific passage appears in the source?

## D6 Launch and cite each quotation, paraphrase, summary, and synthesis.

Weave ideas from sources into your paper so that they effectively support the point you want to make. As you integrate each idea, take three steps.

**1. Capture.** Begin with the evidence you have captured from your source. Refine this material so that it will fit smoothly into your paper. Reduce your quotation to its most memorable words, freshen the wording of your paraphrase, or tighten your summary. Synthesize by pulling together your own ideas and those of your sources to reach new insights. Position the evidence where it is needed to support your statements.

**2. Launch.** Launch, or introduce, the material captured from each source. Avoid tossing stand-alone quotations into your paper or stacking up a series of paraphrases and summaries. Instead, use your launch statement to lead smoothly into your source information. Try to draw on the authority of the source, mention the author's credentials, or connect the material to other sources or to your points. Let readers know why you have selected this evidence and what you think it adds to your paper.

> Dalton, long an advocate of "green" construction, recommends . . . (18).
>
> As a specialist in elder law, attorney Tamara Diaz suggests . . .
>
> Like Westin, regional director Neil urges that ". . ." (308). Brown, however, takes an innovative approach to local conservation practices and recommends . . . (108).
>
> Another policy analyst, arguing from principles expressed in the Bill of Rights, maintains . . . (Frank 96).
>
> While Congress pits secure borders against individual liberties, immigration analyst Smith proposes a third option that . . . (42).

For more on launch statements, see pp. 245–50.

For more on punctuating quotations, see C3 in the Quick Editing Guide, pp. A-55–A-56.

**3. Cite.** Identify each source briefly yet accurately. Follow MLA, APA, or another academic format.

- Name the author in parentheses (unless named in your launch statement).
- In APA style, add the date of the source.
- Add an exact page number to locate the original passage.
- If a source does not name its author, begin the citation with the first words of the title.
- Add a full entry for each source to a list at the end of your paper.

For examples showing how to cite and list sources in your paper, see section E.

# E | Citing and Listing Sources in MLA or APA Style

For practice citing and listing sources in MLA style, go to the interactive "Take Action" charts in Re:Writing at **bedfordstmartins .com/bedguide**.

MLA style is the format for crediting sources that is recommended by the Modern Language Association and often required in English classes. APA style, the format recommended by the American Psychological Association, is often used in social sciences, business, and some composition classes. These two styles are widely used in college papers, but your specialized courses may require other academic styles, depending on the field. Because instructors expect you to credit sources carefully, follow any directions or examples supplied, or refer to the style manual required. Although academic styles all credit sources, their details differ. Stick to the one expected.

In both the MLA and APA styles, your sources need to be identified twice in your paper: first, briefly, at the very moment you draw upon the source material and later, in full, at the end of your paper. The short reference includes the name of the author of the source (or a short form of the title if the source does not name an author), so it's easy for a reader to connect that short entry in your text with the related full entry in the final alphabetical list.

## E1 Cite and list sources in MLA style.

If you need to find formats for other types of sources, consult the current *MLA Handbook for Writers of Research Papers,* often available in the library, or check your research manual or research guide for more information.

**Cite in the text.** At the moment you add a quotation, paraphrase, or summary, identify the source. Citations generally follow a simple pattern: name the author, and note the page in the original where the material is located.

(Last Name of Author ##) (Talia 35) (Smitt and Gilbert 152–53)

Place this citation immediately after a direct quotation or paraphrase.

> When "The Lottery" begins, the reader thinks of the "great pile of stones" (Jackson 260) as children's entertainment.

If you name the author in your launch, the citation is even simpler.

> As Hunt notes, the city faced "a decade of deficits and drought" (54).

For quotations from poems, plays, or novels, supply line, act and scene, or chapter numbers rather than page numbers.

> The speaker in Robinson's poem describes Richard Cory as "richer than a king" (line 9), an attractive man who "fluttered pulses when he said,/ 'Good-morning'" (7–8).

If you use only one source, identify it as your essay begins. Then just give page or line numbers in parentheses after each quote or paraphrase.

CITATION CHECKLIST

- ☐ Have you placed your citation right after your quotation, paraphrase, or summary?
- ☐ Have you enclosed your citation with a pair of parenthesis marks?
- ☐ Have you provided the last name of the author either in your launch statement or in your citation?
- ☐ Have you used a short title for a work without an identified author?
- ☐ Have you added any available page or other location number (such as a Web paragraph, poetry line, novel chapter, or play act and scene), as numbered in the source, to identify where the material appears?

**List at the end.** For each source mentioned in the text, supply a corresponding full entry in a list called Works Cited at the end of your paper.

WORKS CITED CHECKLIST

- ☐ Have you figured out what type of source you have used? Have you followed the sample pattern for that type as exactly as possible?
- ☐ Have you used quotation marks and italics correctly for titles?
- ☐ Have you used correct punctuation—periods, commas, colons, parentheses?
- ☐ Have you checked the accuracy of numbers: pages, volumes, dates?
- ☐ Have you accurately recorded names: authors, titles, publishers?
- ☐ Have you correctly typed or copied in the address of an electronic source that a reader could not otherwise find or that your instructor requires?
- ☐ Have you correctly arranged your entries in alphabetical order?
- ☐ Have you checked your final list against your text citations so that every source appears in both places?
- ☐ Have you double-spaced your list just like your paper, without any extra space between entries?
- ☐ Have you begun the first line of each entry at the left margin and indented each additional line (the same space you would indent a paragraph)?

For format examples, see the Quick Format Guide, pp. A-2–A-3.

**Follow MLA patterns.** Use the following examples as patterns for your entries. For each type of source, supply the same information in the same order, using the same punctuation or other features.

### Book

**TEXT CITATION**

(Blyth 37)

**WORKS CITED ENTRY**

Author's name | Period | Title of book, in italics | Period | City of publication

Blyth, Mark. *Austerity: The History of a Dangerous Idea.* New York: Oxford UP, 2013. Print.

Publisher | Year of publication | Period | Medium of publication | Period

### Essay, Story, or Poem from a Book

**TEXT CITATION**

(Brady 532)

**WORKS CITED ENTRY**

See the title page of this book and the reading on pp. 532–33 to find the details needed for this entry.

Author of selection | Title of selection, in quotation marks | Original date (optional) | Title of book or anthology, in italics

Brady, Judy. "I Want a Wife." 1971. *The Bedford Guide for College Writers.* 10th ed. Ed. X. J. Kennedy, Dorothy M. Kennedy, and Marcia F. Muth. Boston: Bedford, 2014. 532-33. Print.

Authors or editors of book | City of publication | Publisher of book | Year of publication | Page numbers of the selection | Medium of publication | Period

### Online e-Pages Selection in a Book

**TEXT CITATION**

(Consumer Reports)

**WORKS CITED ENTRY**

Organization as author of selection | Title of selection | Medium of selection | Title of book, in italics

Consumer Reports. *Best Buttermilk Pancakes.* Video. *The Bedford Guide for College Writers.* 10th ed. Bedford, 2014. Web. 15 Feb. 2014.

Edition of book | Publisher | Year of publication | Medium of publication | Date of visit

### Popular Magazine Article

The author's name and the title generally appear at the beginning of an article. If the author is not identified, simply begin your entry with the title.

Typically, the magazine name, the date, and page numbers appear at the bottom of pages. Arrange the date in this order: 4 Oct. 2013.

**TEXT CITATION**

(Freedman 10)

**WORKS CITED ENTRY**

Author's name | Title of article, in quotation marks | Title of magazine, in italics

Freedman, David H. "The Happiness App." *Discover* Jan.-Feb. 2013: 10-11. Print.

Medium of publication | Date of publication | Page numbers of the article

### Scholarly Journal Article

**TEXT CITATION**

(Goodin and Rice 903)

**WORKS CITED ENTRY**

Authors' names | Title of article, in quotation marks

Goodin, Robert E., and James Mahmud Rice. "Waking Up in the Poll Booth." *Perspectives on Politics* 7.4 (2009): 901-10. Print.

Title of journal, in italics | Volume and issue numbers | Year | Colon | Page numbers of the article | Medium of publication

### Article from a Library Database

In databases, the print publication details often appear at the top of the online entry. A printout usually records this information plus your date of access. Select the paginated pdf format, or follow the first page number of the print source by a hyphen if the page range is not known.

**TEXT CITATION**

Omit the page number when it is not available online.

See p. A-23 for the text reference from Carrie Williamson's paper.

(Laurance et al. 291)

**WORKS CITED ENTRY**

Author's name | Title of article, in quotation marks | Page numbers in print version

Laurance, William F., et al. "Averting Biodiversity Collapse in Tropical Forest Protected Areas." *Nature* 489.7415 (13 Sept. 2012): 290-94. *Academic OneFile*. Web. 6 Dec. 2012.

Name of database in italics | Medium of publication | Date of visit | Title of magazine, in italics | Volume and issue numbers | Date | Colon

### Page from a Web Site

The page title and site title often appear at the top of a given page. The date when a site was posted or last updated often appears at the bottom, as does the name of the sponsor (which also may appear as a link). A printout of the page will record this information as well as the date you visited.

See p. A-23 for the text reference from Carrie Williamson's paper.

**TEXT CITATION**

A site is identified by title if it does not name an author. Page or paragraph numbers may not be available for a Web page.

According to the Rainforest Alliance, . . .

**WORKS CITED ENTRY**

No author identified — Title of page, in quotation marks — Title of site, in italics — Sponsor name

"Conservation in the Neotropics." *Rainforest-alliance.org.* Rainforest Alliance, 2012. Web. 6 Dec. 2012.

Date posted or updated — Medium of publication — Date of visit

## E2 Cite and list sources in APA style.

If you need to find formats for other types of sources, consult the current *Publication Manual of the American Psychological Association,* often available in the library, or check your research manual or research guide for more information.

**Cite in the text.** After the author's last name, add the date. Use p. (for "page") or pp. (for "pages") before the page numbers.

(Last Name of Author, Date, p. ##) (Talia, 2013, p. 35)
(Smith & Gilbert, 2012, pp. 152–153)

**List at the end.** Call your list of sources References. Include all the sources cited in your text except for personal communications and classics.

**Follow APA patterns.** Use the following examples as patterns for your entries. For each type of source, supply the same information in the same order using the same punctuation or other features.

### Book

**TEXT CITATION**

(Blyth, 2013, p. 37)

**REFERENCES ENTRY**

Blyth, M. (2013). *Austerity: The history of a dangerous idea.* New York, NY: Oxford University Press.

### Work or Section in a Book

**TEXT CITATION**

(Brady, 1971/2014, p. 532)

**REFERENCES ENTRY**

Brady, J. (2014). I want a wife. In X. J. Kennedy, D. M. Kennedy, & M. F. Muth (Eds.), *The Bedford guide for college writers* (10th ed., pp. 532-533). Boston, MA: Bedford/St. Martin's. (Original work published 1971)

Turn to the title page of this book and the reading selection on pp. 532–33 to find the details needed for this entry.

### Online e-Pages Selection in a Book

**TEXT CITATION**

(Consumer Reports, 2014)

**REFERENCES ENTRY**

Consumer Reports. (Producer). (2014). *Best buttermilk pancakes* [Video file]. In X. J. Kennedy, D. M. Kennedy, & M. F. Muth (Eds.), *The Bedford guide for college writers*, 10th ed., Retrieved from: www.bedfordstmartins.com/bedguide/epages

### Popular Magazine Article

**TEXT CITATION**

(Freedman, 2013, p. 11)

**REFERENCES ENTRY**

Freedman, D. H. (2013, January-February). The happiness app. *Discover, 34*(1), 10-11.

### Scholarly Journal Article

For a magazine or journal article, add any volume number in italics and any issue number in parentheses, without a space or italics.

**TEXT CITATION**

(Goodin & Rice, 2009, p. 903)

**REFERENCES ENTRY**

Goodin, R. E., & Rice, J. M. (2009). Waking up in the poll booth. *Perspectives on Politics, 7*, 901-910. doi:10.1017/S1537592709991873

### Article from a Library Database

**IN-TEXT CITATION**

No exact page or paragraph number may be available for an online article.

(Laurance et al., 2012, p. 291)

**REFERENCES ENTRY**

The database does not need to be named unless a reader would have trouble finding the item without the URL.

Laurance, W. F., Useche, D. C., Rendeiro, J., Kalka, M., Bradshaw, C. J. A., Sloan, S. P., Laurance, S. G., et al. (2012). Averting biodiversity collapse in tropical forest protected areas. *Nature*, *489*, 290-294. doi:10.1038/nature11318

### Page from a Web Site

**TEXT CITATION**

For APA format examples, see the Quick Format Guide, pp. A-4–A-6.

Because the Web site does not name an author, the citation identifies the site's sponsor.

According to the Rainforest Alliance (2012) . . .

**REFERENCES ENTRY**

Your access date is not needed unless the material is likely to change.

Rainforest Alliance. (2012). Conservation in the neotropics. Retrieved from: http://www.rainforest-alliance.org/adopt/conservation

## APPENDIX

# Quick Editing Guide



This Quick Editing Guide provides an overview of grammar, style, punctuation, and mechanics problems typical of college writing.

### EDITING CHECKLIST

**Common and Serious Problems in College Writing**

*Grammar Problems*

- ☐ Have you avoided writing sentence fragments? A1
- ☐ Have you avoided writing comma splices or fused sentences? A2
- ☐ Have you used the correct form for all verbs in the past tense? A3
- ☐ Do all verbs agree with their subjects? A4
- ☐ Have you used the correct case for all pronouns? A5
- ☐ Do all pronouns agree with their antecedents? A6
- ☐ Have you used adjectives and adverbs correctly? A7

*Sentence Problems*

- ☐ Does each modifier clearly modify the appropriate sentence element? B1
- ☐ Have you used parallel structure where needed? B2

*Punctuation Problems*

- ☐ Have you used commas correctly? C1
- ☐ Have you used apostrophes correctly? C2
- ☐ Have you punctuated quotations correctly? C3

*Mechanics Problems*

- ☐ Have you used capital letters correctly? D1
- ☐ Have you spelled all words correctly? D2

Editing and proofreading are needed at the end of the writing process because writers—*all* writers—find it difficult to write error-free sentences the first time they try. Once you are satisfied that you have expressed your ideas, you should make sure that each sentence and word is concise, clear, and correct. Certain common errors in Standard Written English are like red flags to careful readers: they signal that the writer is either ignorant or careless. Use the editing checklist on page A-39 to check your paper for these problems; then use the editing checklists in each section to help you correct specific errors. Concentrate on any problems likely to reappear in your writing.

For editing and proofreading strategies, see pp. 471–75.

Your grammar checker or software can help you catch some errors, but not others. Always consider the grammar checker's suggestions carefully before accepting them and continue to edit on your own.

- A grammar checker cannot always correctly identify the subject or verb in a sentence; it may question whether a sentence is complete or whether its subject and verb agree, even when the sentence is correct.
- Grammar checkers are likely to miss misplaced modifiers, faulty parallelism, possessives without apostrophes, or incorrect commas.
- Most grammar checkers do a good job of spotting problems with adjectives and adverbs, such as confusing *good* and *well.*
- Keep track of your mistakes to develop an "error hit list." Use your software's Find capacity (try the Home or Edit menu) to check for searchable problems such as instances of *each* (always singular) or *few* (always plural) to see if all the verbs agree.

# A | Editing for Common Grammar Problems

## A1 Check for any sentence fragments.

A complete sentence has a subject, has a predicate, and can stand on its own. A **sentence fragment** cannot stand on its own as a sentence because it lacks a subject, a predicate, or both, or for some other reason fails to convey a complete thought. Though common in ads and fiction, fragments are not usually effective in college writing because they do not express coherent thoughts.

To edit for fragments, check that each sentence has a subject and a verb and expresses a complete thought. To correct a fragment, complete

## At-A-Glance Guide



it by adding a missing part, dropping an unnecessary subordinating conjunction, or joining it to a nearby sentence, if that would make more sense.

| | |
|---|---|
| FRAGMENT | Roberto has two sisters. Maya and Leeza. |
| CORRECT | Roberto has two sisters, Maya and Leeza. |
| FRAGMENT | The children going to the zoo. |
| CORRECT | The children were going to the zoo. |
| CORRECT | The children going to the zoo were caught in a traffic jam. |
| FRAGMENT | Last night when we saw Viola Davis's most recent movie. |
| CORRECT | Last night we saw Viola Davis's most recent movie. |

**subject:** The part of a sentence that names something—a person, an object, an idea, a situation—about which the predicate makes an assertion: The *king* lives.

**predicate:** The part of a sentence that makes an assertion about the subject involving an action (Birds *fly*), a relationship (Birds *have feathers*), or a state of being (Birds *are warm-blooded*)

**subordinating conjunction:** A word (such as *because, although, if, when*) used to make one clause dependent on, or subordinate to, another: *Unless* you have a key, we are locked out.

### EDITING CHECKLIST
**Fragments**

- ☐ Does the sentence have both a subject and a predicate?
- ☐ If the sentence contains a subordinate clause, does it contain a clause that is a complete sentence too?
- ☐ If you find a fragment, can you link it to an adjoining sentence, eliminate its subordinating conjunction, or add any missing element?

For exercises on fragments, visit **bedfordstmartins.com/bedguide** and go to Re:Writing.

## A2 Check for any comma splices or fused sentences.

A complete sentence has a subject and a predicate and can stand on its own. When two sentences are combined as one sentence, each sentence within the larger one is called a *main clause.* However, writers need to

**main clause:** A group of words that has both a subject and a verb and can stand alone as a complete sentence: *My friends like baseball.*
**coordinating conjunction:** A one-syllable linking word (*and, but, for, or, nor, so, yet*) that joins elements with equal or near-equal importance: Jack *and* Jill, sink *or* swim
**subordinating conjunction:** A word (such as *because, although, if, when*) used to make one clause dependent on, or subordinate to, another: *Unless* you have a key, we are locked out.

follow the rules for joining main clauses to avoid serious sentence errors. A **comma splice** is two main clauses joined with only a comma. A **fused sentence** (or **run-on**) is two main clauses joined with no punctuation at all.

| | |
|---|---|
| COMMA SPLICE | I went to the shop, I bought a new coat. |
| FUSED SENTENCE | I went to the shop I bought a new coat. |

To find these errors, examine the main clauses in each sentence to make sure they are joined correctly. Correct a comma splice or fused sentence in one of these four ways, depending on which makes the best sense:

| | |
|---|---|
| ADD A PERIOD | I went to the shop. I bought a new coat. |
| ADD A COMMA AND A COORDINATING CONJUNCTION | I went to the shop, and I bought a new coat. |
| ADD A SEMICOLON | I went to the shop; I bought a new coat. |
| ADD A SUBORDINATING CONJUNCTION | I went to the shop, where I bought a new coat. |

EDITING CHECKLIST

**Comma Splices and Fused Sentences**

- ☐ Can you make each main clause a separate sentence?
- ☐ Can you link the two main clauses with a comma and a coordinating conjunction?
- ☐ Can you link the two main clauses with a semicolon or, if appropriate, a colon?
- ☐ Can you subordinate one clause to the other?

For exercises on comma splices and fused sentences, visit **bedfordstmartins.com/bedguide** and go to Re:Writing.

## A3 Check for correct past tense verb forms.

**verb:** A word that shows action (The cow *jumped* over the moon) or a state of being (The cow *is* brown)

The **form** of a verb, the way it is spelled and pronounced, can change to show its **tense**—the time when its action did, does, or will occur (in the past, present, or future). A verb about something in the present will often have a different form than a verb about something in the past.

| | |
|---|---|
| PRESENT | Right now, I *watch* only a few minutes of television each day. |
| PAST | Last month, I *watched* television shows every evening. |

**Regular verbs** are verbs whose forms follow standard rules; they form the past tense by adding *-ed* or *-d* to the present tense form:

*watch/watched* *look/looked* *hope/hoped*

Check all regular verbs in the past tense for one of these endings.

| | |
|---|---|
| FAULTY | I *ask* my brother for a loan yesterday. |
| CORRECT | I *asked* my brother for a loan yesterday. |

| | |
|---|---|
| FAULTY | Nicole *race* in the track meet last week. |
| CORRECT | Nicole *raced* in the track meet last week. |

TIP: If you say the final *-d* sound when you talk, you may find it easier to add the final *-d* or *-ed* when you write past tense regular verbs.

Because **irregular verbs** do not have standard forms, their unpredictable past tense forms must be memorized. In addition, the past tense may differ from the past participle. Check a dictionary for these forms.

**participle:** A form of a verb that cannot function alone as a main verb, including present participles ending in *-ing* (*dancing*) and past participles often ending in *-ed* or *-d* (*danced*)

| | |
|---|---|
| FAULTY | My cat *laid* on the tile floor to take her nap. |
| CORRECT | My cat *lay* on the tile floor to take her nap. |

| | |
|---|---|
| FAULTY | I *have swam* twenty laps every day this month. |
| CORRECT | I *have swum* twenty laps every day this month. |

TIP: In college papers, follow convention by using the present tense, not the past, to describe the work of an author or the events in a literary work.

| | |
|---|---|
| FAULTY | In "The Lottery," Jackson *revealed* the power of tradition. As the story *opened,* the villagers *gathered* in the square. |
| CORRECT | In "The Lottery," Jackson *reveals* the power of tradition. As the story *opens,* the villagers *gather* in the square. |

### Irregular Verbs at a Glance

| INFINITIVE (BASE) | PAST TENSE | PAST PARTICIPLE |
|---|---|---|
| begin | began | begun |
| burst | burst | burst |
| choose | chose | chosen |
| do | did | done |
| eat | ate | eaten |
| go | went | gone |
| lay | laid | laid |
| lie | lay | lain |
| speak | spoke | spoken |

For a list of the principal parts of common irregular verbs (infinitive, past tense, and past participle forms), visit **bedfordstmartins .com/bedguide** and go to Re:Writing.

For exercises on verbs, visit **bedfordstmartins .com/bedguide** and go to Re:Writing.

EDITING CHECKLIST

**Past Tense Verb Forms**

- ☐ Have you identified the main verb in the sentence?
- ☐ Is the sentence about past, present, or future? Does the verb show this time?
- ☐ Is the verb regular or irregular? Have you used its correct form?

## A4 Check for correct subject-verb agreement.

The **form** of a verb, the way it is spelled and pronounced, can change to show **number**—whether the subject is singular (one) or plural (more than one). It can also show **person**—whether the subject is *you* or *she,* for example.

**verb:** A word that shows action (The cow *jumped* over the moon) or a state of being (The cow *is* brown)

**subject:** The part of a sentence that names something—a person, an object, an idea, a situation—about which the predicate makes an assertion: The *king* lives.

| | |
|---|---|
| SINGULAR | Our instructor *grades* every paper carefully. |
| PLURAL | Most instructors *grade* tests using a standard scale. |
| SECOND PERSON | You *write* well-documented research papers. |
| THIRD PERSON | She *writes* good research papers, too. |

A verb must match (or *agree with*) its subject in terms of number and person. Regular verbs (whose forms follow a standard rule) are problems only in the present tense. There they have two forms: one that ends in *-s* or *-es* and one that does not. Only the subjects *he, she, it,* and singular nouns use the verb form that ends in *-s* or *-es.*

| | |
|---|---|
| I like | we like |
| you like | you like |
| he/she/it/Dan/the child likes | they like |

The verbs *be* and *have* are irregular, so their present tense forms must be memorized. The verb *be* is also irregular in the past tense.

**Forms of *Be* and *Have* at a Glance**

| THE PRESENT TENSE OF *BE* | | THE PAST TENSE OF *BE* | |
|---|---|---|---|
| I am | we are | I was | we were |
| you are | you are | you were | you were |
| he/she/it is | they are | he/she/it was | they were |

| THE PRESENT TENSE OF *HAVE* | | THE PAST TENSE OF *HAVE* | |
|---|---|---|---|
| I have | we have | I had | we had |
| you have | you have | you had | you had |
| he/she/it has | they have | he/she/it had | they had |

Problems in agreement often occur when the subject is hard to find, is an indefinite pronoun, or is confusing. Make sure that you include any *-s* or *-es* endings and use the correct form for irregular verbs.

| | |
|---|---|
| FAULTY | Jim *write* at least fifty e-mails a day. |
| CORRECT | Jim *writes* at least fifty e-mails a day. |
| FAULTY | The students *has* difficulty with the assignment. |
| CORRECT | The students *have* difficulty with the assignment. |
| FAULTY | Every one of the cakes *were* sold at the fundraiser. |
| CORRECT | Every one of the cakes *was* sold at the fundraiser. |

**indefinite pronoun:** A pronoun standing for an unspecified person or thing, including singular forms (*each, everyone, no one*) and plural forms (*both, few*): *Everyone* is soaking wet.

For exercises on subject-verb agreement, visit **bedfordstmartins .com/bedguide** and go to Re:Writing.

EDITING CHECKLIST

**Subject-Verb Agreement**

- ☐ Have you correctly identified the subject and the verb in the sentence?
- ☐ Is the subject singular or plural? Does the verb match?
- ☐ Have you used the correct form of the verb?

## A5 Check for correct pronoun case.

Depending on the role a pronoun plays in a sentence, it is said to be in the **subjective case, objective case,** or **possessive case.** Use the subjective case if the pronoun is the subject of a sentence, the subject of a subordinate clause, or a subject complement (after a linking verb). Use the objective case if the pronoun is a direct or indirect object of a verb or the object of a preposition. Use the possessive case to show possession.

| | |
|---|---|
| SUBJECTIVE | *I* will argue that our campus needs more parking. |
| OBJECTIVE | This issue is important to *me.* |
| POSSESSIVE | *My* argument will be quite persuasive. |

Writers often use the subjective case when they should use the objective case – sometimes trying to sound formal and correct. Instead, choose the correct form based on a pronoun's function in the sentence. If the sentence pairs a noun and a pronoun, try the sentence with the pronoun alone.

| | |
|---|---|
| FAULTY | My company gave my husband and *I* a trip to Hawaii. |
| PRONOUN ONLY | My company gave *I* a trip? |
| CORRECT | My company gave my husband and *me* a trip to Hawaii. |
| FAULTY | My uncle and *me* had different expectations. |
| PRONOUN ONLY | *Me* had different expectations? |
| CORRECT | My uncle and *I* had different expectations. |

**pronoun:** A word that stands in place of a noun (*he, him,* or *his* for *Nate*)

**subject:** The part of a sentence that names something — a person, an object, an idea, a situation — about which the predicate makes an assertion: The *king* lives.

**subject complement:** A noun, an adjective, or a group of words that follows a linking verb (*is, become, feel, seem,* or another verb that shows a state of being) and that renames or describes the subject: This plum tastes *ripe.*

**object:** The target or recipient of the action of a verb: Some geese bite *people.*

## Personal Pronoun Cases at a Glance

| SUBJECTIVE | OBJECTIVE | POSSESSIVE |
|---|---|---|
| I | me | my, mine |
| you | you | your, yours |
| he | him | his |
| she | her | hers |
| it | it | its |
| we | us | our, ours |
| they | them | their, theirs |
| who | whom | whose |

FAULTY Jack ran faster than my brother and *me.*

PRONOUN ONLY Jack ran faster than *me* ran?

CORRECT Jack ran faster than my brother and *I.*

A second common error with pronoun case involves gerunds. Whenever you need a pronoun to modify a gerund, use the possessive case.

FAULTY Our supervisor disapproves of *us* talking in the hallway.

CORRECT Our supervisor disapproves of *our* talking in the hallway.

**gerund:** A form of a verb, ending in *-ing,* that functions as a noun: Lacey likes *playing* in the steel band.

EDITING CHECKLIST

**Pronoun Case**

- ☐ Have you identified all the pronouns in the sentence?
- ☐ Does each one function as a subject, an object, or a possessive?
- ☐ Given the function of each, have you used the correct form?

For exercises on pronoun case, visit **bedfordstmartins .com/bedguide** and go to Re:Writing.

**pronoun:** A word that stands in place of a noun (*he, him,* or *his* for *Nate*)

## A6 Check for correct pronoun-antecedent agreement.

The **form** of a pronoun, the way it is spelled and pronounced, can change to show **number**—whether the subject is singular (one) or plural (more than one). It also can change to show **gender**—masculine or feminine, for example—or **person:** first (*I, we*), second (*you*), or third (*he, she, it, they*).

SINGULAR My brother took *his* coat and left.

PLURAL My brothers took *their* coats and left.

MASCULINE I talked to Steven before *he* had a chance to leave.

FEMININE I talked to Stephanie before *she* had a chance to leave.

A pronoun refers to its **antecedent**, usually a specific noun or pronoun nearby. The connection between the two must be clear so that readers know what the pronoun means in the sentence. The two need to match (or *agree*) in number and gender.

A common error is using a plural pronoun to refer to a singular antecedent. This error often crops up when the antecedent is difficult to find, is an indefinite pronoun, or is confusing for another reason. First, find the antecedent, and decide whether it is singular or plural. Then make the pronoun match its antecedent.

FAULTY Neither Luz nor Pam received approval of *their* financial aid.

CORRECT Neither Luz nor Pam received approval of *her* financial aid. [*Neither Luz nor Pam* is a compound subject joined by *nor.* Any pronoun referring to it must agree with only the nearer part of the compound: *her* agrees with *Pam,* which is singular.]

Indefinite pronouns are troublesome antecedents when they are grammatically singular but create a plural image in the writer's mind. Fortunately, most indefinite pronouns are always singular or always plural.

**indefinite pronoun:** A pronoun standing for an unspecified person or thing, including singular forms (*each, everyone, no one*) and plural forms (*both, few*): *Everyone* is soaking wet.

FAULTY Each of the boys in the club has *their* own custom laptop.

CORRECT Each of the boys in the club has *his* own custom laptop. [The word *each,* not *boys,* is the antecedent. *Each* is an indefinite pronoun and is always singular. Any pronoun referring to it must be singular as well.]

FAULTY Everyone in the meeting had *their* own cell phone.

CORRECT Everyone in the meeting had *his or her* own cell phone. [*Everyone* is an indefinite pronoun that is always singular. Any pronoun referring to it must be singular as well.]

### Indefinite Pronouns at a Glance

| ALWAYS SINGULAR | | | ALWAYS PLURAL |
|---|---|---|---|
| anybody | everyone | nothing | both |
| anyone | everything | one (of) | few |
| anything | much | somebody | many |
| each (of) | neither (of) | someone | several |
| either (of) | nobody | something | |
| everybody | no one | | |

For exercises on pronoun-antecedent agreement, visit **bedfordstmartins .com/bedguide** and go to Re:Writing.

EDITING CHECKLIST

**Pronoun-Antecedent Agreement**

- ☐ Have you identified the antecedent for each pronoun?
- ☐ Is the antecedent singular or plural? Does the pronoun match?
- ☐ Is the antecedent masculine, feminine, or neuter? Does the pronoun match?
- ☐ Is the antecedent first, second, or third person? Does the pronoun match?

**modifier:** A word (such as an adjective or adverb), phrase, or clause that provides more information about other parts of a sentence: Plays *staged by the drama class* are *always successful*.

## A7 Check for correct adjectives and adverbs.

**Adjectives** and **adverbs** describe or give information about (*modify*) other words. Many adverbs are formed by adding *-ly* to adjectives: *simple, simply; quiet, quietly.* Because adjectives and adverbs resemble one another, writers sometimes mistakenly use one instead of the other. To edit, find the word that the adjective or adverb modifies. If that word is a noun or pronoun, use an adjective (to describe which or what kind). If that word is a verb, adjective, or another adverb, use an adverb (to describe how, when, where, or why).

FAULTY Kelly ran into the house *quick.*

CORRECT Kelly ran into the house *quickly.*

FAULTY Gabriela looked *terribly* after her bout with the flu.

CORRECT Gabriela looked *terrible* after her bout with the flu.

Adjectives and adverbs with similar comparative and superlative forms can also cause trouble. Always ask whether you need an adjective or an adverb in the sentence, and then use the correct word.

FAULTY His scar healed so *good* that it was barely visible.

CORRECT His scar healed so *well* that it was barely visible.

*Good* is an adjective; it describes a noun or pronoun. *Well* is an adverb; it modifies or adds to a verb (*heal,* in this case) or an adjective.

### Irregular Adjectives and Adverbs at a Glance

| POSITIVE ADJECTIVES | COMPARATIVE ADJECTIVES | SUPERLATIVE ADJECTIVES |
|---|---|---|
| good | better | best |
| bad | worse | worst |
| little | less, littler | least, littlest |
| many, some, much | more | most |
| **POSITIVE ADVERBS** | **COMPARATIVE ADVERBS** | **SUPERLATIVE ADVERBS** |
| well | better | best |
| badly | worse | worst |
| little | less | least |

EDITING CHECKLIST
**Adjectives and Adverbs**

- ☐ Have you identified which word the adjective or adverb modifies?
- ☐ If the word modified is a noun or pronoun, have you used an adjective?
- ☐ If the word modified is a verb, adjective, or adverb, have you used an adverb?
- ☐ Have you used the correct comparative or superlative form?

For exercises on adjectives and adverbs, visit **bedfordstmartins.com/bedguide** and go to Re:Writing.

# B | Editing to Ensure Effective Sentences

## B1 Check for any misplaced or dangling modifiers.

For a sentence to be clear, the connection between a modifier and the thing it modifies must be obvious. Usually a modifier should be placed just before or just after what it modifies. If the modifier is too close to some other sentence element, it is a **misplaced modifier.** If the modifier cannot logically modify anything in the sentence, it is a **dangling modifier.** Both errors can confuse readers—and sometimes create unintentionally humorous images. As you edit, place a modifier directly before or after the word modified and clearly connect the two.

**modifier:** A word (such as an adjective or adverb), phrase, or clause that provides more information about other parts of a sentence: Plays *staged by the drama class* are *always successful.*

MISPLACED Dan found the leftovers when he visited in the refrigerator.

CORRECT Dan found the leftovers in the refrigerator when he visited.
[In the faulty sentence, *in the refrigerator* seems to modify Dan's visit. Obviously the leftovers, not Dan, are in the refrigerator.]

DANGLING Looking out the window, the clouds were beautiful.

CORRECT Looking out the window, I saw that the clouds were beautiful.

CORRECT When I looked out the window, the clouds were beautiful.
[In the faulty sentence, *Looking out the window* should modify *I*, but *I* is not in the sentence. The modifier dangles without anything logical to modify until *I* is in the sentence.]

EDITING CHECKLIST
**Misplaced and Dangling Modifiers**

- ☐ What is each modifier meant to modify? Is the modifier as close as possible to that sentence element? Is any misreading possible?
- ☐ If a modifier is misplaced, can you move it to clarify the meaning?
- ☐ What noun or pronoun is a dangling modifier meant to modify? Can you make that word or phrase the subject of the main clause? Or can you turn the dangling modifier into a clause that includes the missing noun or pronoun?

For exercises on misplaced and dangling modifiers, visit **bedfordstmartins.com/bedguide** and go to Re:Writing.

# Take Action Improving Sentence Style

Ask each question at the top of the chart to consider whether your draft might need work on that issue. If so, follow the ASK—LOCATE SPECIFICS—TAKE ACTION sequence to revise.

| | Passive Voice? | Faulty Parallelism? | Repetitive Sentence Patterns? |
|---|---|---|---|
| **1 ASK** | Have I relied on sentences in the passive voice instead of the active voice? | Have I missed opportunities to emphasize comparable ideas by stating them in comparable ways? | Do my sentences sound alike because they repeat the same opening, pattern, or length? |
| **2 LOCATE SPECIFICS** | ■ Reread your sentence. If its subject also performs the action, it is in the active voice. (Underline the performer; double underline the action.)<br>■ If the sentence subject does not perform the action, your sentence is in the passive voice. You have tucked the performer into a *by* phrase or have not identified the performer. | ■ Read your sentences, looking for lists or comparable items.<br>■ Underline items in a series to compare the ways you present them.<br>**Draft:** Observing primates can reveal how they cooperate, their tool use, and building secure nests. | ■ Add a line break at the end of every sentence in a passage so you can easily compare sentence openings, patterns, or lengths.<br>■ Use your software (or yourself) to count the words in each sentence.<br>■ Search for variations such as colons (:) and semicolons (;) to see how often you use them. |
| **3 TAKE ACTION** | ■ Consider changing passive voice to active. Make the performer of the action the sentence subject (which reduces extra words by dropping the *by* phrase).<br>**Passive:** The primate play area was arranged by the zookeeper. (9 words; emphasizes object of the action)<br>**Active:** The zookeeper arranged the primate play area. (7 words; emphasizes zookeeper who performed the action) | ■ Rework so that items in a series all follow the same grammatical pattern.<br>■ Select the common pattern based on the clarity and emphasis it adds to your sentence.<br>**Parallel:** Observing primates can reveal how they cooperate, use tools, and build secure nests. | ■ Rewrite for variety if you repeat openings (*During, Because, After, Then, And*).<br>■ Rewrite for directness if you repeat indirect openings (*There are, There is, It is*).<br>■ Rewrite to vary sentence lengths. Tuck in a few short sentences. Combine choppy sentences. Add a complicated sentence to build up to your point.<br>■ Try some colons or semicolons for variety. |

## **Take Action** Improving Sentence Clarity

Ask each question at the top of the chart to consider whether your draft might need work on that issue. If so, follow the ASK—LOCATE SPECIFICS—TAKE ACTION sequence to revise.

| | Disconnected or Scattered Ideas? | Wordy Sentences? | Any Other Improvements in Sentence Style? |
|---|---|---|---|
| **1 ASK** | Have I tossed out my ideas without weighting or relating them? | Have I used more words than needed to say what I mean? | After a final look at the sentences in my draft, should I do anything else to improve them? |
| **2 LOCATE SPECIFICS** | ■ Highlight the transitional words (*first, second, for example, however*).<br>■ Star all the sentences or sentence parts in a passage that seem to be of equal weight. | ■ Read your draft out loud. Put a check by anything that sounds long-winded, repetitive, chatty, or clichéd.<br>■ Use past papers to help you list your favorite wordy expressions (such as *a large number of* for *many*) or extra words (such as *very* or *really*). | ■ Read your draft out loud. Mark any sentences that sound incomplete, awkward, confusing, boring, or lifeless.<br>■ Ask your peer editors how you might make your sentences stronger and more stylish. |
| **3 TAKE ACTION** | ■ Review passages with little highlighting; add more transitions to relate ideas.<br>■ In your starred sentences, strengthen the structure. Introduce less significant parts with subordinating words (*because, although*). Use *and* or *but* to coordinate equal parts. | ■ At each check, rephrase with simpler or more exact words.<br>■ Search with your software for wordy expressions; replace or trim them.<br>■ Highlight a passage; use the Tools or Review menu to count its words. See how many extra words you can drop. | ■ Return to each mark to make weak sentences clear, emphatic, interesting, and lively.<br>■ Consider the useful suggestions of your peers.<br>■ Review sections A and B of this guide, and edit until your sentences express your ideas as you wish. |

## B2 Check for parallel structure.

**correlative conjunction:** A pair of linking words (such as *either/or, not only/but also*) that appear separately but work together to join elements of a sentence: *Neither* his friends *nor* hers like pizza.

A series of words, phrases, clauses, or sentences with the same grammatical form is said to be **parallel.** Using parallel form for elements that are parallel in meaning or function helps readers grasp the meaning of a sentence more easily. A lack of parallelism can distract, annoy, or even confuse readers.

To use parallelism, put nouns with nouns, verbs with verbs, and phrases with phrases. Parallelism is particularly important in a series, with correlative conjunctions, and in comparisons using *than* or *as*.

FAULTY I like to go to Estes Park for skiing, ice skating, and to meet interesting people.

CORRECT I like to go to Estes Park to ski, to ice skate, and to meet interesting people.

FAULTY The proposal is neither practical, nor is it innovative.

CORRECT The proposal is neither practical nor innovative.

FAULTY Teens need a few firm rules rather than having many flimsy ones.

CORRECT Teens need a few firm rules rather than many flimsy ones.

Edit to reinforce parallel structures by repeating articles, conjunctions, prepositions, or lead-in words as needed.

AWKWARD His dream was that he would never have to give up his routine but he would still find time to explore new frontiers.

PARALLEL His dream was that he would never have to give up his routine but *that* he would still find time to explore new frontiers.

For exercises on parallel structure, visit **bedfordstmartins.com/bedguide** and go to Re:Writing.

---

EDITING CHECKLIST

**Parallel Structure**

- ☐ Are all the elements in a series in the same grammatical form?
- ☐ Are the elements in a comparison parallel in form?
- ☐ Are the articles, conjunctions, prepositions, or lead-in words for elements repeated as needed rather than mixed or omitted?

---

Use the Take Action charts (pp. A-50 and A-51) to help you figure out how to improve your draft. Skim across the top to identify questions you might ask about the sentences in your draft. When you answer a question with “Yes” or “Maybe,” move straight down the column to Locate Specifics under that question. Use the activities there to pinpoint gaps, problems, or weaknesses. Then move straight down the column to Take Action. Use the advice that suits your problem as you revise.

# C | Editing for Common Punctuation Problems

## C1 Check for correct use of commas.

The **comma** is a punctuation mark indicating a pause. By setting some words apart from others, commas help clarify relationships. They prevent the words on a page and the ideas they represent from becoming a jumble.

1. Use a comma before a coordinating conjunction (*and, but, for, or, so, yet, nor*) joining two main clauses in a compound sentence.

   The discussion was brief, *so* the meeting was adjourned early.

2. Use a comma after an introductory word or word group unless it is short and cannot be misread.

   *After the war*, the North's economy developed rapidly.

3. Use commas to separate the items in a series of three or more items.

   The chief advantages will be *speed*, *durability*, and *longevity*.

4. Use commas to set off a modifying clause or phrase if it is nonrestrictive—if it can be taken out of the sentence without significantly changing the essential meaning of the sentence.

   Good childcare, *which is hard to find*, should be available at work.

   Good childcare *that is reliable and inexpensive* is every employee's hope.

5. Use commas to set off a nonrestrictive appositive, an expression that comes directly after a noun or pronoun and renames it.

   Sheri, my sister, has a new job as an events coordinator.

6. Use commas to set off parenthetical expressions, conjunctive adverbs, and other interrupters.

   The proposal from the mayor's commission, however, is not feasible.

**appositive:** A word or group of words that adds information about a subject or object by identifying it in a different way: Terry, *the drummer,* manages the band.

**parenthetical expression:** An aside to readers or a transitional expression such as *for example* or *in contrast*

**conjunctive adverb:** A linking word that can connect independent clauses and show a relationship between two ideas: Jen studied hard; *consequently,* she passed the exam.

---

**EDITING CHECKLIST**

**Commas**

- ☐ Have you added a comma between two main clauses joined by a coordinating conjunction?
- ☐ Have you added commas needed after introductory words or word groups?
- ☐ Have you separated items in a series with commas?
- ☐ Have you avoided commas before the first item in a series or after the last?

For exercises on commas, visit **bedfordstmartins.com/bedguide** and go to Re:Writing.

- ☐ Have you used commas before and after each nonrestrictive (nonessential) word, phrase, or clause?
- ☐ Have you avoided using commas around a restrictive word, phrase, or clause that is essential to the meaning of the sentence?
- ☐ Have you used commas to set off appositives, parenthetical expressions, conjunctive adverbs, and other interrupters?

## C2 Check for correct use of apostrophes.

An **apostrophe** is a punctuation mark that either shows possession (*Sylvia's*) or indicates that one or more letters have intentionally been left out to form a contraction (*didn't*). An apostrophe is never used to create the possessive form of a pronoun; use the possessive pronoun form instead.

FAULTY *Mikes* car was totaled in the accident.

CORRECT *Mike's* car was totaled in the accident.

FAULTY *Womens'* pay is often less than *mens'*.

CORRECT *Women's* pay is often less than *men's*.

FAULTY Che *did'nt* want to stay at home and study.

CORRECT Che *didn't* want to stay at home and study.

FAULTY The dog wagged *it's* tail happily. [it's = it is? No.]

CORRECT The dog wagged *its* tail happily.

FAULTY *Its* raining.

CORRECT *It's* raining. [it's = it is]

### Possessive Personal Pronouns at a Glance

| PERSONAL PRONOUN | POSSESSIVE CASE |
|---|---|
| I | my, mine |
| you | your, yours (*not* your's) |
| he | his |
| she | her, hers (*not* her's) |
| it | its (*not* it's) |
| we | our, ours (*not* our's) |
| they | their, theirs (*not* their's) |
| who | whose (*not* who's) |

EDITING CHECKLIST

**Apostrophes**

- ☐ Have you used an apostrophe when letters are left out in a contraction?
- ☐ Have you used an apostrophe to create the possessive form of a noun?
- ☐ Have you used the possessive case – not an apostrophe – to show that a pronoun is possessive?
- ☐ Have you used *it's* correctly (to mean *it is*)?

For exercises on apostrophes, visit **bedfordstmartins.com/bedguide** and go to Re:Writing.

## C3 Check for correct punctuation of quotations.

When you quote the exact words of a person you have interviewed or a source you have read, enclose those words in quotation marks. Notice how student Betsy Buffo presents the words of her subject in this passage from her essay "Interview with an Artist":

> Derek is straightforward when asked about how his work is received in the local community: "My work is outside the mainstream. Because it's controversial, it's not easy for me to get exposure."

She might have expressed and punctuated this passage in other ways:

> Derek says that "it's not easy" for him to find an audience.
>
> Derek struggles for recognition because his art falls "outside the mainstream."

If your source is quoting someone else (a quotation within a quotation), put your subject's words in quotation marks and the words he or she is quoting in single quotation marks. Always put commas and periods inside the quotation marks; put semicolons and colons outside. Include all necessary marks in the correct place or sequence.

> As Betsy Buffo explains, "Derek struggles for recognition because his art falls 'outside the mainstream.'"

Substitute an ellipsis mark (. . .) – three spaced dots – for any words you have omitted from the middle of a direct quotation. If you are following MLA style, you may place the ellipses inside brackets ([. . .]) when necessary to avoid confusing your ellipsis marks with those of the original writer. If the ellipses come at the end of a sentence, add another period to conclude the sentence. You don't need an ellipsis mark to show the beginning or ending of a quotation that is clearly incomplete.

In this selection from "Overworked!" student Melissa Lamberth identifies quotations and an omission. (She cites Joe Robinson's essay from the reader in her *Bedford Guide*):

In his essay "Four Weeks Vacation," Robinson writes, "The health implications of sleep-deprived motorists weaving their way to the office . . . are self-evident" (481).

For more about quotations from sources, see D3 in the Quick Research Guide, p. A-29.

EDITING CHECKLIST

**Punctuation with Quotations**

- ☐ Are the exact words quoted from your source enclosed in quotation marks?
- ☐ Are commas and periods placed inside closing quotation marks?
- ☐ Are colons and semicolons placed outside closing quotation marks?
- ☐ Do ellipses show where you omit words from the middle of a quote?

For exercises on using and punctuating quotation marks, visit **bedfordstmartins .com/bedguide** and go to Re:Writing.

# D | Editing for Common Mechanics Problems

## D1 Check for correct use of capital letters.

Capital letters begin a new sentence; names of specific people, nationalities, places, dates, and things (proper nouns); and main words in titles.

FAULTY During my Sophomore year in College, I took World Literature, Biology, American History, Psychology, and French – courses required for a Humanities Major.

CORRECT During my sophomore year in college, I took world literature, biology, American history, psychology, and French – courses required for a humanities major.

EDITING CHECKLIST

**Capitalization**

- ☐ Have you used a capital letter at the beginning of each complete sentence, including sentences that are quoted?
- ☐ Have you used capital letters for proper nouns and pronouns?
- ☐ Have you avoided using capital letters for emphasis?
- ☐ Have you used a capital letter for the first, last, and main words in a title? (Main words exclude prepositions, coordinating conjunctions, and articles.)

For exercises on using capital letters, visit **bedfordstmartins .com/bedguide** and go to Re:Writing.

**preposition:** A transitional word (such as *in, on, at, of, from*) that leads into a phrase

**coordinating conjunction:** A one-syllable linking word (*and, but, for, or, nor, so, yet*) that joins elements with equal or near-equal importance

**article:** The word *a, an,* or *the*

## D2 Check spelling.

Misspelled words are difficult to spot in your own writing. You usually see what you think you wrote. Spell checkers offer a handy alternative to the dictionary, but you need to know their limitations. A spell checker compares the words in your text with the words in its dictionary, and it highlights words that do not appear there, including most proper nouns. Spell checkers will not highlight words misspelled as different words, such as *except* for *accept, to* for *too,* or *own* for *won.*

For a list of commonly confused words, see p. A-58.

## Capitalization at a Glance

THE FIRST LETTER OF A SENTENCE, INCLUDING A QUOTED SENTENCE

She called out, "Come in! The water's warm."

PROPER NAMES AND ADJECTIVES MADE FROM THEM

| | | |
|---|---|---|
| Smithsonian Institution | a Freudian reading | Marie Curie |

RANK OR TITLE BEFORE A PROPER NAME

| | | |
|---|---|---|
| Ms. Olson | Professor Santocolon | Dr. Frost |

FAMILY RELATIONSHIP ONLY WHEN IT SUBSTITUTES FOR OR IS PART OF A PROPER NAME

| | |
|---|---|
| Grandma Jones | Father Time |

RELIGIONS, THEIR FOLLOWERS, AND DEITIES

| | | |
|---|---|---|
| Islam | Orthodox Jew | Buddha |

PLACES, REGIONS, GEOGRAPHIC FEATURES, AND NATIONALITIES

| | | |
|---|---|---|
| Palo Alto | the Berkshire Mountains | Egyptians |

DAYS OF THE WEEK, MONTHS, AND HOLIDAYS

| | | |
|---|---|---|
| Wednesday | July | Labor Day |

HISTORICAL EVENTS, PERIODS, AND DOCUMENTS

| | | |
|---|---|---|
| the Boston Tea Party | the Middle Ages | the Constitution |

SCHOOLS, COLLEGES, UNIVERSITIES, AND SPECIFIC COURSES

| | |
|---|---|
| Temple University | Introduction to Clinical Psychology |

FIRST, LAST, AND MAIN WORDS IN TITLES OF PAPERS, BOOKS, ARTICLES, WORKS OF ART, TELEVISION SHOWS, POEMS, AND PERFORMANCES

*The Decline and Fall of the Roman Empire* "The Lottery"

EDITING CHECKLIST

### Spelling

- ☐ Have you checked for the words you habitually misspell?
- ☐ Have you checked for commonly confused or misspelled words?
- ☐ Have you checked a dictionary for any words you are unsure about?
- ☐ Have you run your spell checker? Have you read your paper carefully for errors that it would miss such as a stray letter?

For a list of commonly misspelled words and spelling exercises, visit **bedfordstmartins.com/bedguide** and go to Re:Writing.

**COMMONLY CONFUSED HOMONYMS**

**accept** (v., receive willingly); **except** (prep., other than)

*Mimi could* *accept* all of Lefty's gifts *except* his ring.

**affect** (v., influence); **effect** (n., result)

If the new rules *affect* us, what will be their *effect*?

**capital** (adj., uppercase; n., seat of government); **capitol** (n., government building)

The *Capitol* building in our nation's *capital* is spelled with a *capital* C.

**cite** (v., refer to); **sight** (n., vision or tourist attraction); **site** (n., place)

Did you *cite* Aunt Peg as your authority on which *sites* feature the most interesting *sights*?

**complement** (v., complete; n., counterpart); **compliment** (v. or n., praise)

For Lee to say that Sheila's beauty *complements* her intelligence may or may not be a *compliment.*

**desert** (v., abandon; n., hot, dry region); **dessert** (n., end-of-meal sweet)

Don't *desert* us by leaving for the *desert* before *dessert.*

**elicit** (v., bring out); **illicit** (adj., illegal)

By going undercover, Sonny should *elicit* some offers of *illicit* drugs.

**led** (v., past tense of *lead*); **lead** (n., a metal)

Gil's heart was heavy as *lead* when he *led* the mourners to the grave.

**principal** (n. or adj., chief); **principle** (n., rule or standard)

The *principal* problem is convincing the media that the high school *principal* is a person of high *principles.*

**stationary** (adj., motionless); **stationery** (n., writing paper)

Hubert's *stationery* shop stood *stationary* until a flood swept it away.

**their** (pron., belonging to them); **there** (adv., in that place); **they're** (contraction of *they are*)

Sue said *they're* going over *there* to visit *their* aunt.

**to** (prep., toward); **too** (adv., also or excessively); **two** (n. or adj., numeral: one more than one)

Let's not take *two* cars *to* town – that's *too* many unless Hal comes *too.*

**who's** (contraction of *who is*); **whose** (pron., belonging to whom)

*Who's* going to tell me *whose* dog this is?

**your** (pron., belonging to you); **you're** (contraction of *you are*)

*You're* not getting *your* own way this time!

Acknowledgments *(continued from p. iv)*

Adams, Sarah. "Be Cool to the Pizza Dude." Copyright © 2005 by Sarah Adams. From the book *This I Believe: The Personal Philosophies of Remarkable Men and Women* edited by Jay Allison and Dan Gediman. Copyright © 2006 by This I Believe, Inc. Reprinted by arrangement with Henry Holt and Company, LLC.

Baker, Russell. "The Art of Eating Spaghetti." Reprinted by permission of Don Congdon Associates, Inc. © 1982 by Russell Baker.

Bertoni, Timothy J. and Patrick D. Nolan. Excerpt from "Dead Men Do Tell Tales." Reprinted by permission of *Sociation Today*.

Brady, Judy. "I Want a Wife." Copyright © 1971 by Judy Brady. Reprinted with the permission of the author.

Brooks, David. "The Opportunity Gap." From *The New York Times*, July 9, 2012 © 2012 *The New York Times*. All rights reserved. Used by permission and protected by the Copyright Laws of the United States. The printing, copying, redistribution, or retransmission of this Content without express written permission is prohibited.

Christakis, Nicholas A. and James H. Fowler. "Hyperconnected." From *Connected* by Nicholas A. Christakis MD, PhD, James Fowler PhD. Copyright © 2009 by James H. Fowler & Nicholas Christakis. By permission of Little, Brown and Company. All rights reserved.

Cisneros, Sandra. "Only Daughter." Copyright © 1990 by Sandra Cisneros. First published in *Glamour*, November 1990. By permission of Susan Bergholz Literary Services, New York, NY and Lamy, NM. All rights reserved.

Cook, Gareth. "Getting It All Done." From *The Boston Globe*, April 1, 2012 © 2012 Boston Globe. All rights reserved. Used by permission and protected by the Copyright Laws of the United States. The printing, copying, redistribution, or retransmission of this Content without express written permission is prohibited.

Copeland, Libby. "Is Facebook Making Us Sad?" From *Slate*. © 2011, The Slate Group. All rights reserved. Used by permission and protected by the Copyright Laws of the United States. The printing, copying, redistribution, or retransmission of the Material without express written permission is prohibited.

Csikszentmihalyi, Mihaly. Excerpt from pp. 1–4 from *Flow: The Psychology of Optimal Experience* by Mihaly Csikszentmihalyi. Copyright © 1990 by Mihaly Csikszentmihalyi. Reprinted by permission of HarperCollins Publishers.

Dailey, Kate and Abby Ellin. "America's War on the Overweight." From *Newsweek*, August 25, 2009. © 2009, The Newsweek/Daily Beast Company LLC. All rights reserved. Used by permission and protected by the Copyright Laws of the United States. The printing, copying, redistribution, or retransmission of the Material without express written permission is prohibited.

Deresziewicz, William. "A Man. A Woman. Just Friends?" From *The New York Times*, April 8, 2012. © 2012, *The New York Times*. All rights reserved. Used by permission and protected by the Copyright Laws of the United States. The printing, copying, redistribution, or retransmission of this Content without express written permission is prohibited.

Edmonds, David and John Eidinow. Excerpt from "Fear and Flight" (pp. 1–4: about 1,000 words) from *Rousseau's Dog: Two Great Thinkers at War in the Age of Enlightenment* by David Edmonds and John Eidinow. Copyright © 2006, 2007 by David Edmonds and John Eidinow. Reprinted by permission of HarperCollins Publishers and David Higham.

Gelernter, David. "Computers Cannot Teach Children Basic Skills" from *The New Republic*. Copyright © 1994. Reprinted with the permission of the publisher.

Gilb, Dagoberto. "Mi Mommy" from *Gritos*. Copyright © 2003 by Dagoberto Gilb. Used by permission of Grove/Atlantic, Inc. Any third party use of this material, outside of this publication, is prohibited.

Halpern, Jake. Excerpt from *Fame Junkies: The Hidden Truths Behind America's Favorite Addiction* by Jake Halpern. Copyright © 2007 by Jake Halpern. Reprinted by permission of Houghton Mifflin Harcourt Publishing Company. All rights reserved.

Harjo, Suzan Shown. "Last Rites for Indian Dead." First published in the *Los Angeles Times*, September 16, 1989. Copyright © 1989 by Suzan Shown Harjo. Reprinted with the permission of the author.

Haynie, Mike. "As Attitudes Shift on PTSD, Media Slow to Remove Stigma." From *The New York Times*, July 2, 2012. © 2012, *The New York Times*. All rights reserved. Used by permission and protected by the Copyright Laws of the United States. The printing, copying, redistribution, or retransmission of this Content without express written permission is prohibited.

Jackson, Shirley. "The Lottery" from *The Lottery* by Shirley Jackson. Copyright © 1948, 1949 by Shirley Jackson. Copyright renewed 1976, 1977 by Laurence Hyman, Barry Hyman, Mrs. Sarah Webster, and Mrs. Joanne Schnurer. Reprinted by permission of Farrar, Straus and Giroux, LLC.

Jensen, Robert. "The High Cost of Manliness." Reprinted by permission of the author.

Jones, Gerard. "Violent Media Is Good For Kids." © 2000, Foundation for National Progress. Reprint courtesy of *Mother Jones* magazine.

King, Stephen. "Why We Crave Horror Movies." Reprinted With Permission. © Stephen King. All rights reserved. Originally appeared in *Playboy*, 1982.

Klosterman, Chuck. "My Zombie, Myself." From *The New York Times*, December 5, 2010. © 2010, *The New York Times*. All rights reserved. Used by permission and protected by the Copyright Laws of the United States. The printing, copying, redistribution, or retransmission of this Content without express written permission is prohibited.

Lahiri, Jhumpa. "Rice." Copyright © 2009 by Jhumpa Lahiri.

Liu, Eric. "The Chinatown Idea," from *The Accidental Asian: Notes of a Native Speaker* by Eric Liu. Copyright © 1998 by Eric Liu. Used by permission of Random House, Inc. Any third party use of this material, outside of this publication, is prohibited. Interested parties must apply directly to Random House, Inc. for permission.

Manjoo, Farhad. "You Will Want Google Goggles." From *MIT Technology Review* magazine or technologyreview.com. © MIT Technology Review, Inc. Reprinted with Permission.

McBride, James. "Full Circle." Reprinted by permission of *National Geographic*.

McCain, John. Excerpt from "The Virtues of the Quiet Hero." Copyright © 2005 by John McCain. From the book *This I Believe: The Personal Philosophies of Remarkable Men and Women*, edited by Jay Allison and Dan Gediman. Copyright © 2006 by This I Believe, Inc. Reprinted by arrangement with Henry Holt and Company, LLC.

Pfeffer, Jeffrey. "Lay Off the Layoffs." From *Newsweek*, February 4, 2010. © 2010, The Newsweek/Daily Beast Company LLC. All rights reserved. Used by permission and protected by the Copyright Laws of the United States. The printing, copying, redistribution, or retransmission of the Material without express written permission is prohibited.

Pollitt, Katha. "Hunger Games' Feral Feminism." Reprinted by permission of the author.

Quindlen, Anna. "Evan's Two Moms." From *The New York Times*, February 5, 1992. Copyright © 1992, *The New York Times*. All rights reserved. Used by permission and protected by the Copyright Laws of the United States. The printing, copying, redistribution, or retransmission of this Content without express written permission is prohibited.

Razdan, Anjula. "What's Love Got to Do with It?" Reprinted from *Utne Reader* (May-June 2003). Copyright © 2003 by Ogden Publications. www.utne.com.

Rideau, Wilbert. "Why Prisons Don't Work" from *Time* (March 21, 1994). Copyright ©1994 by Wilbert Rideau. Reprinted with the permission of the author, c/o The Permissions Company, Inc., www.permissionscompany.com.

Rockwell, Llewellyn H. "In Defense of Consumerism." Reprinted by permission of the author.

Rodriguez, Richard. "Public and Private Language." *Hunger of Memory* by Richard Rodriguez. Copyright © 1982 by Richard Rodriguez. Reprinted by permission of Georges Borchardt, Inc., on behalf of the author.

Rothkopf, David. "A Proposal to Draft America's Elderly." Reprinted by permission of the author.

Saletan, William. Excerpt from "Please Do Not Feed the Humans" from *Slate*. © September 2, 2006, The Slate Group. All rights reserved. Used by permission and protected by the Copyright Laws of the United States.

Schor, Juliet. "The Creation of Discontent." Copyright © 1992 by Juliet B. Schor. Reprinted by permission of Basic Books, a member of the Perseus Books Group.

Shermer, Michael. "The Science of Righteousness." Reproduced with permission. Copyright © 2012, *Scientific American*, a division of Nature America, Inc. All rights reserved.

Shoup, Brad. "'Harlem Shake' vs. History: Is the YouTube Novelty Hits Era That Novel?" Reprinted by permission of Atlantic Media Company.

Staples, Brent. "Black Men and Public Space." First published in *Ms.* Magazine, September 1986. Copyright © 1986 by Brent Staples. Reprinted with the permission of the author.

Starr, Terrell Jermaine. "How My Illiterate Grandmother Raised an Educated Black Man." Terrell Jermaine Starr, Editor, NewsOne.com, An Interactive One, LLC Website.

Stone, Elizabeth. "Grief in the Age of Facebook." Reprinted by permission of the author.

Tan, Amy. "Mother Tongue." Copyright © 1990 by Amy Tan. First appeared in *The Threepenny Review*. Reprinted by permission of the author and the Sandra Dijkstra Literary Agency.

Tannen, Deborah. "Who Does the Talking Here?" *The Washington Post*, July 15, 2007. Copyright by Deborah Tannen. Adapted from *You Just Don't Understand: Women and Men in Conversation*, HarperCollins. Reprinted with Permission.

Tennis, Cary. "Why am I Obsessed with Celebrity Gossip?" This article first appeared in Salon.com, at http://www.salon.com. An online version remains in the Salon archives. Reprinted with permission.

Thompson, Clive. "New Literacy." Copyright © 2009 by Clive Thompson. Reprinted with the permission of the author.

Tobias, Scott. Review of *The Hunger Games*. Reprinted with permission of THE AV CLUB. Copyright © 2013 by ONION, INC. www.avclub.com.

Turkle, Sherry. "How Computers Change the Way We Think." Reprinted by permission of the author.

Underwood, Anne. Excerpts from "The Good Heart." From *Newsweek*, October 2, 2005. © 2005, The Newsweek/Daily Beast Company LLC. All rights reserved. Used by permission and protected by the Copyright Laws of the United States. The printing, copying, redistribution, or retransmission of the Material without express written permission is prohibited.

White, E. B. Excerpt from "Once More to the Lake" from *One Man's Meat*, text copyright © 1941, 1944 by E. B. White. Copyright renewed. Reprinted by permission of Tilbury House, Publishers, Gardiner, Maine, and International Creative Management. All rights reserved.

Yoffe, Emily. "Seeking" from *Slate*, © August 12, 2009, The Slate Group. All rights reserved. Used by permission and protected by the Copyright Laws of the United States. The printing, copying, redistribution, or retransmission of the Material without express written permission is prohibited.

Zeilinger, Julie. "Guys Suffer from Gender Roles Too." From *A Little F'd Up: Why Feminism Is Not a Dirty Word* by Julie Zeilinger. Reproduced with permission of Publishers Group West in a book/e-book via Copyright Clearance Center.

Zinsser, William K. "The Right to Fail." Copyright © 1969, 1970 by William K. Zinsser. Reprinted by permission of the author.

*Art Credits (in order of appearance):*

Pages 4–5: Fountain and bathers. David L. Ryan/*The Boston Globe* via Getty Images.

Page 14: *works & conversation* photo: R. Whittaker.

Page 18: Hansel & Gretel. Private Collection/©Look and Learn/Bridgeman Art Library.

Page 32: Michael Shermer. Photo by David Patton.

Page 34: Heat maps of Web pages from eye-tracking studies. Copyright Nielsen Norman Group. All rights reserved.

Page 42: Candy bar. iStockphoto.

Page 53: David Rothkopf. Photo by Christopher Leaman.

Pages 56–57: Rowboats tied to dock. David L. Ryan/*The Boston Globe* via Getty Images.

Page 58: Photo collage of recalled experiences. Clockwise from top left: Michael Schwarz/The Image Works; Mario Tama/Getty Images; Lawrence Migdale/Science Source; D. Miller/Classicstock/Aurora Photos.

Page 60: Russell Baker. Yvonne Hemsey/Getty Images.

Page 61: Lady Macbeth. Tristram Kenton/Lebrecht/The Image Works.

Page 69: Soccer goalie. Robert Llewellyn/Aurora Photos.

Page 75: Group of women sharing dinner. Veer/Corbis Photography.

Page 76: Hikers in silhouette. © Andrew Dillon Bustin.

Page 76: Times Square crowd. Photo by Bojune Kwon, from The Neurosis in the City.

Page 77: Concert crowd and airport. © Andrew Dillon Bustin.

Page 78: Baseball player making catch. Jared Wickenham/Getty Images.

Page 80: Eric Liu. Photo by Alan Alabastro.

Page 82: Market in New York City's Chinatown. Dorling Kindersley/Getty Images.

Page 86: The *Titanic* 1912. © The Mariners' Museum/Corbis.

Page 87: Emergency room. David Joel/Getty Images.

Page 89: Elvis impersonators. Chris Jackson/Getty Images.

Page 95: View from bicycle. Robert van Waarden/Getty Images.

Page 96: Server at party. Doug Mills/*The New York Times*/Redux Pictures.

Page 96: Climbers on Mt. Rushmore. Kevin Steele/Aurora Photos.

Page 97: Photo collage of famous people. Clockwise from top left: AP Photo/ PRNewsFoto/U.S.-India Business Council; John Shearer/ Invision/AP; EPA/Anindito Mukherjee/Landov; © Deborah Feingold/Corbis.

Page 99: Farhad Manjoo. Photo by Helen Bailey.

Page 100: Google goggles. Matthew Sumner/Getty Images.

Page 100: Google goggles view. AP Photo/Google.

Page 105: Still of visors from ASU video. The State Press, Arizona State University.

Page 107: Frost/Nixon interview. AP Photo/Ray Stubblebine.

Page 115: Census interview in desert landscape. Reuters/STR/Landov.

Page 115: FEMA worker interviewing flood victim. FEMA/Getty Image.

Page 115: Job interviews. AP Photo/*The State*, Gerry Melendez.

Page 116: Couple at Woodstock, 1969. © Burk Uzzle, Laurence Miller Gallery.

Page 116: Couple at Woodstock, 2009. *N.Y. Daily News*.

Page 118: David Brooks. Brendan Smialowski/Getty Images.

Page 122: Karate. helenved/Shutterstock.com.

Page 122: Kung fu. © IMAGEMORE Co., Ltd./Alamy.

Page 124: Hurricane Katrina aftermath. Mario Tama/Getty Images. Caption: NG Staff/*National Geographic* Stock.

Pages 134–35: Families with a week's worth of food. © Peter Menzel/menzelphoto.com.

Page 136: Rusted boats in the Aral Sea. Photo by Neil Banas.

Page 136: Satellite photo of Aral Sea. NASA Earth Observatory.

Page 138: Jeffrey Pfeffer. Courtesy of Jeffrey Pfeffer.

Page 144: Detail from drunk-driving infographic. Provided by TotalDui.com.

Page 147: Series showing car and crane falling into water. Nicholas Griffin.

Page 154: Chart showing manufacturing job openings. U. S. Department of Labor: Bureau of Labor Statistics.

Page 154: Map showing manufacturing job openings. © WANTED Analytics.

Page 155: Closed factory. Photo by Kirk Crippens.

Page 155: Ford assembly plant. AP Photo/Paul Sancya.

Page 156: Protestors. © Alex Milan Tracy/Demotix/Corbis.

Page 158: Suzan Shown Harjo. AP Photo/Manuel Balce Ceneta.

Page 159: Native Americans returning ancestral remains. AP Photo/*The Albuquerque Journal*, Eddie Moore.

Page 164: Dirty Water campaign. Casanova-Pendrill.

Page 165: Joan of Arc. Imagno/Getty Images.

Page 183: Boy in hospital. Suzanne Kreiter/*The Boston Globe* via Getty Images.

Page 183: Family reading. Nicole Bengiveno/*The New York Times*/Redux Pictures.

Page 184: Cell phone tower disguised as tree. © Robert Voit.

Page 185: FEMA PSA. FEMA Ready Campaign.

Page 187: Wilbert Rideau. Courtesy of Wilbert Rideau.

Page 192: Still from "texting while walking" video showing Malik Perry. Photo by Casey Neistat.

Page 193: Living wall. © Nano Calvo/VW Pics/ZUMApress.com.

Page 197: "Don't Mess With Texas" anti-littering sign. AP Photo/Donna McWilliam.

Page 199: Agriculture student. Jack Dykinga/USDA.

Page 202: Traffic congestion. Bloomberg/Getty Images.

Page 203: Graffiti on train car. Photo © Martha Cooper.

Page 203: Student with heavy backpack. Heather Stone/KRT/Newscom.

Page 204: Judging giant pumpkins. Justin Sullivan/Getty Images.

Page 206: Scott Tobias. Courtesy of Scott Tobias.

Page 207: Map of Panem. *The Panem Companion*, Smart Pop Books, 2012. © V. Arrow.

Page 211: Still from *Consumer Reports* pancakes video. "Best Buttermilk Pancakes" Copyright 2012 Consumers Union of U.S., Inc. Yonkers, NY 10703-1057, a nonprofit organization. Reprinted with permission from ConsumerReports.org for educational purposes only. www.ConsumerReports.org.

Page 212: George Gershwin. Hulton Archive/Getty Images.

Page 213: Still from *The Cabinet of Dr. Caligari*. Photofest.

Page 220: Photo of church at Auvers-sur-Oise. Pierre-Franck Colombier/Getty Images.

Page 220: *The Church at Auvers-sur-Oise* by Vincent van Gogh. Buyenlarge/Getty Images.

Page 221: Sony office, 1999. © TWPhoto/Corbis.

Page 221: Google Campus, 2012. Bloomberg via Getty Images.

Page 222: Photo collage of source usage. Clockwise from top left: Scott Bauer/USDA; © Mika/Corbis; © Journal-Courier/Steve Warmowski/The Image Works; Jeff Greenberg/The Image Works.

Page 224: Jake Halpern. Courtesy of Jake Halpern.

Page 230: Red carpet at Academy Awards. Anna Donovan/Getty Images.

Page 237: Mojave Desert. iStockphoto.

Page 253: Contestant in child beauty pageant. Konstantin Zavrazhin/Getty Images.

Page 254: No Swearing sign. Patrick Strattner/Getty Images.

Page 254: Shark Warning sign. © Andrew Dillon Bustin.

Page 255: Gamblers in Las Vegas. Bloomberg/Getty Images.

Pages 256–57: Trains. David L. Ryan/*The Boston Globe* via Getty Images.

Page 260: Shirley Jackson. AP Photo.

Page 283: Kate Chopin. The Granger Collection, New York.

Page 291: Public-service announcement with one prominent element. This image has been reproduced with permission from the American Psychological Association and the Advertising Council. Copyright © 2005 by the American Psychological Association. Retrieved from http://actagainstviolence.apa.org/materials/psa/ADCA04B0113-Driver.pdf. No further reproduction or distribution is permitted without written permission from the American Psychological Association.

Page 292: Batman at a donut shop. Photograph by Ian Pool.

Page 296: Volkswagen advertisement. Used with permission of Volkswagen Group of America, Inc.

Page 297: Chevrolet advertisement. Everett Collection.

Page 298: "Stairway" type design. Instructor Hyunmee Kim, Samsung Art and Design Institute.

Page 299: Type as cultural cliché. From *Publication Design*, 3/e, by Roy Paul Nelson, © 1983 McGraw-Hill Education.

Page 299: Type that contributes to meaning. © Andrew Dillon Bustin.

Page 301: Photograph conveying a mood. AP Photo/*The Advocate-Messenger*, Ben Kleppinger.

Page 302: Photograph with missing element. Courtesy of Americans for National Parks.

Page 303: Public-service advertisement showing wordplay. D. Reed Monroe.

Page 303: Billboard showing wordplay. Bill Aron/PhotoEdit.

Page 304: Poster conveying a theme. The Ad Council.

Pages 311–13: Autism photo series. Shannon Kintner/*The Daily Texan*.

Page 322: Still from video tutorial. The Writing Center at Portland State University.

Page 349: City from above. Creatas/Jupiter Images.

Page 349: Apartment buildings. Jeff Greenberg/The Image Works.

Page 349: Map of New York City, 1807. The Granger Collection, New York.

Page 350: Frank Deford. George Bridges/KRT/Newscom.

Page 350: Junior Seau. UPI/Terry Schmitt/Landov.

Page 367: Brochure design showing prominent elements. Studio InFlux/The Art Institute of Boston at Lesley University: Jenny Barrett, ManChingCheng, Lisa Goode, and Yehudit Massouda-Winiarz.

Page 370–71: Flooded baseball fields. David L. Ryan/*The Boston Globe* via Getty Images.

Page 372: Erin Schmitt. Courtesy of Erin Schmitt.

Page 381: Peter Hertli. Courtesy of Alice Hertli.

Page 492: Native American family. M. Williams Woodbridge/*National Geographic*/ Getty Images.

Page 493: Terrell Jermaine Starr. Courtesy of Terrell Jermaine Starr.

Page 496: Sandra Cisneros. Ulf Andersen/Getty Images.

Page 500: Anna Quindlen. AP Photo/Evan Agostini.

Page 503: Dagoberto Gilb. © Marion Ettlinger/Corbis.

Page 506: Amy Tan. Will Ragozzino/Getty Images.

Page 512: Richard Rodriguez. © Roger Ressmeyer/Corbis.

Page 518: Detail from "Once a Mother, Always a Mother" infographic. Edelman Berland.

Page 518: Detail from "Paternity Leave around the World" infographic. Originally appeared on *www.GOOD.is* on June 7, 2012. Reprinted with permission from GOOD.

Page 519: Man and woman on bridge. © Andrew Dillon Bustin.

Page 520: Brent Staples. Fred R. Conrad/*The New York Times*/ Redux.

Page 528: William Deresiewicz. Photo by Aleeza Nussbaum.

Page 532: Judy Brady. Courtesy of Judy Brady.

Page 534: Robert Jensen. Courtesy of Robert Jensen.

Page 538: Julie Zeilinger. Photo courtesy of Eric Mull.

Page 543: Deborah Tannen. George Bridges/KRT/Newscom.

Page 543: Man and woman talking. Lilly Roadstones/Getty Images.

Page 544: Jed Conklin. Courtesy of Jed Conklin.

Page 544: Boxer Virginia Fuchs. Courtesy of Jed Conklin.

Page 545: Sean Connery. Photos 12/Alamy

Page 545: Roger Moore. Photononstop/SuperStock.

Page 545: Daniel Craig. AF archive/Alamy.

Page 545: Pierce Brosnan. Photos 12/Alamy

Page 546: Mike Haynie. Courtesy of J. Michael Haynie.

Page 549: Kate Dailey. Courtesy of Kate Dailey.

Page 549: Abby Ellin. Courtesy of Abby Ellin.

Page 554: Katha Pollitt. © Christina Pabst.

Page 558: James McBride. Albert E. Rodriquez/Getty Images.

Page 561: Stephen King. AFP/Getty Images.

Page 569: Chuck Klosterman. Essdras M. Suarez/*The Boston Globe* via Getty Images.

Page 569: Do not feed the zombies. Christian Aslund/Getty Images.

Page 570: Baauer. ZUMA Press, Inc./Alamy.

Page 571: DILBERT. DILBERT © 2012 Scott Adams. Used by permission of UNIVERSAL UCLICK. All rights reserved.

Page 572: Emily Yoffe. Photo by Christopher Leaman.

Page 576: Nicholas A. Christakis. Pat Greenhouse/*The Boston Globe* via Getty Images.

Page 576: James H. Fowler. Photo by Kent Horner.

Page 580: David Gelernter. Andreas Rentz/Getty Images.

Page 587: Elizabeth Stone. Courtesy of Elizabeth Stone.

Page 591: Libby Copeland. Photo by Danylo Berko.

Page 595: Sherry Turkle. Pat Greenhouse/*The Boston Globe* via Getty Images.

Page 595: Man in front of avatar. MCT via Getty Images.

Page 596: Frame from "Electric Sheep" screensaver. Kornhaber Brown and PBS Digital Studios.

Page 597: Photo collage of ways to live well. Clockwise from top left: Jose Luis Pelaez Inc./Getty Images; *Palm Beach Post*/ZUMAPRESS.com; Lynette Peizer/Alamy; © Carlos Gonzalez/*Star Tribune*/ ZUMA Press.

Page 598: Jhumpa Lahiri. Gary Gershoff/WireImage/Getty Images.

Page 601: William Zinsser. Time & Life Pictures/Getty Images.

Page 605: Gareth Cook. Photo by Mike Swartz.

Page 611: Juliet Schor. Photo by Gary Gilbert.

Page 615: Llewellyn H. Rockwell Jr. Courtesy of Llewellyn H. Rockwell Jr. and the Ludwig von Mises Institute.

Page 620: Rainbow. © Andrew Dillon Bustin.

Page 621: Sarah Adams. © Nubar Alexanian.

Page 621: Brent Foster. Courtesy of Brent Foster Photography.

Page 621: Thomas Weller's rescue truck. Brent Foster/www.brentfostercinema.com.

Page 642: Facsimile for Source Navigator: From "All Climate Is Local" by Cynthia Rosenzweig in *Scientific American*. Reproduced with permission. Copyright © 2011 *Scientific American*, a division of Nature America, Inc. All rights reserved.

Page 644: Facsimile for Source Navigator: "'Aren't These Boy Books?': High School Students' Readings of Gender in Graphic Novels," by Robin A. Moeller, from *Journal of Adolescent & Adult Literacy*, ©2011 International Reading Association. Reproduced with permission of Wiley Inc. Reprinted Courtesy of JSTOR.

Page 646: Facsimile for Source Navigator: Title page from *Thinking, Fast and Slow* by Daniel Kahneman, Copyright © 2011 by Farrar, Straus and Giroux, LLC. Reprinted by permission of Farrar, Straus and Giroux, LLC..

Page 648: Facsimile for Source Navigator: Source: *Trends in Student Aid*. Copyright © 2012. The College Board. www.collegeboard.org. Reproduced with permission.

Page 661: Results of a keyword search and an advanced search using Google. Google and the Google logo are registered trademarks of Google Inc., used with permission.

Pages 664 and 667: Sample home page and online catalog search results from Tuskegee University Libraries. Tuskegee University Libraries, Archives and Legacy Museum.

Page 671: Search result from *America's Historical Newspapers*. Readex, a division of NewsBank Inc.

Page 682: Screenshots from The American Society for the Prevention of Cruelty to Animals Web site. Copyright © 2012. The American Society for the Prevention of Cruelty to Animals (ASPCA). All Rights Reserved.

Page 729: Line graph comparing rise in higher education costs with medical and housing costs. Callahan & Associates (www.creditunions.com).

Page A-11: Diagram of wastewater treatment. King County, Department of Natural Resources, Wastewater Treatment Division.

Page A-11: Line graph showing percentage of children with food or digestive allergies. The Centers for Disease Control and Prevention.

Page A-12: Bar graph presenting numerical comparisons. U. S. Department of Health and Human Services, Substance Abuse and Mental Health Services Administration, Office of Applied Studies.

Page A-12: Pie chart showing energy consumption of typical single family home. ENERGYSTAR, The U.S. Environmental Protection Agency, The U.S. Department of Energy.

# ABOUT THE PHOTOGRAPHS THAT OPEN PARTS 1–4

## A Series of Aerial Photographs by David L. Ryan

A long-time staff photographer at the *Boston Globe*, David L. Ryan is well known for his distinctive aerial photography. His witty and moving images often show familiar scenes from fresh perspectives and reveal beautiful patterns hidden among commonplace, everyday realities. Like a writer, he keeps his audience close in his thoughts as he works, with the goal of sharing his curiosity, knowledge, and enthusiasm with those who see his images. As he puts it, "I've been in Boston all my life. I've gone around here by boat, helicopter, plane, train, bicycle, and walking. I want to make people say, '*How did you get that*?'" In another parallel with writing, he finds an open-minded, "learning by doing" approach to be beneficial: "I'm still experimenting with it," he says of his work. "Everything is an experiment."

**Part 1: Fountain and bathers (pages 4–5)**
It's obvious that a photographer must choose a point of view. He or she must literally choose a place to stand and an angle from which to view a scene. So must a writer.

In this image, what effects are created by the photographer's chosen point of view? What effect does his elevated perspective have on how the scene appears? What is gained and lost by photographing from this distance? What observations do you think the photographer is making about what he is seeing?

**Part 2: Rowboats tied to dock (pages 56–57)**
If you were to take something you have written and rewrite it from an entirely different point of view, the two versions would likely have different meanings and might accomplish different purposes. You convey meaning and purpose, in part, through your choice of perspective. Similarly, for a photographer, a change in perspective can create a feeling of strangeness, make a point, or offer a commentary. From the air things might look like something else for a second.

In this image, what point or points do you think the photographer is making? Is his focus the season, sport, recreation, equipment, place, person, state of mind, or some other subject? How does his point of view help to convey that meaning?

**Part 3: Trains (pages 256–57)**

Before a photographer takes a picture, he or she has to decide how much of the scene to include. Will the image be a close-up of a face or an aerial view? Does the image give the viewer specific information about a specific individual or show more general patterns? Writers, too, must make decisions about how much of a topic or a discussion to include and how to define the boundaries of a topic.

What does this photograph include? What does it leave out? What can you tell about the people — either as individuals or as groups — shown in this photo? What does the image communicate that might be less apparent from ordinary photographs taken of people at ground level? How does the image find interest and import in the routine?

**Part 4: Flooded baseball fields (pages 370–71)**

Photographers and writers are both alert to rhythms and correspondences as well as to patterns and meanings below the surface. Writers can express rhythm by selecting their words, by controlling the length of sentences and paragraphs, and by creating a structure that helps the reader follow an unfolding essay. Ryan makes his work compelling by conveying a sense of rhythm through geometry.

What is the mood of this photograph? What does this image of flooded fields say to you, the viewer? How does it balance ordinary and extraordinary elements against each other?

# INDEX

# A GUIDE TO THE HANDBOOK

# CORRECTION SYMBOLS

Many instructors use these abbreviations and symbols to mark errors in student papers. Refer to this chart to find out what they mean.

| Abbreviation or Symbol | Meaning | For more information in Handbook | For more information in Quick Editing Guide |
|---|---|---|---|
| *abbr* | abbreviation | 28 (p. 875) | |
| *adj* | misuse of adjective | 8 (p. 801) | A7 (p. A-48) |
| *adv* | misuse of adverb | 8 (p. 801) | A7 (p. A-48) |
| *agr* | faulty agreement | 4 (p. 788), 7 (p. 799) | A4 (p. A-44), A6 (p. A-46) |
| *awk* | awkward | | |
| *cap* | capital letter | 29 (p. 878) | |
| *case* | error in case | 5 (p. 792) | A5 (p. A-45) |
| *coord* | faulty coordination | 14a–c (p. 825) | |
| *cs* | comma splice | 2 (p. 769) | A2 (p. A-41) |
| *dm* | dangling modifier | 10c (p. 813) | B1 (p. A-49) |
| *f* | format (see Quick Format Guide) | | |
| *frag* | fragment | 1 (p. 764) | A1 (p. A-40) |
| *fs* | fused sentence | 2 (p. 769) | A2 (p. A-41) |
| *gl* or *gloss* | see Glossary of Troublemakers | 34 (p. 888) | A (p. A-40) |
| *hyph* | error in use of hyphen | 32 (p. 885) | |
| *inc* | incomplete construction | 11 (p. 814) | |
| *irreg* | error in irregular verb | 3e–f (p. 775) | A3 (p. A-42) |
| *ital* | italics | 31 (p. 883) | |
| *lc* | use lowercase letter | 29 (p. 878) | D1 (p. A-56) |
| *mixed* | mixed construction | 12 (p. 818) | |
| *mm* | misplaced modifier | 10a–b (p. 811) | B1 (p. A-49) |
| *mood* | error in mood | 3n–p, 9e (pp. 785, 809) | |
| *num* | error in the use of numbers | 30 (p. 881) | |
| *p* | error in punctuation | 20–27 (p. 847) | C (p. A-53) |
| *pass* | ineffective passive voice | 3m (p. 784) | |
| *ref* | error in pronoun reference | 6 (p. 795) | A6 (p. A-46) |
| *rep* | careless repetition | 19 (p. 845) | |
| *rev* | revise | (See Ch. 23) | |
| *run-on* | comma splice or fused sentence | 2 (p. 769) | A2 (p. A-41) |
| *sp* | misspelled word | 33 (p. 888) | D2 (p. A-56) |
| *sub* | faulty subordination | 14d–f (p. 829) | |
| *t* or *tense* | error in verb tense | 3g–l, 9a–b (pp. 777, 808) | A3 (p. A-42) |
| *v* | voice | 3m, 9c (pp. 784, 808) | |
| *vb* | error in verb form | 3a–f (p. 773) | A3 (p. A-42) |
| *wc* | word choice | 16–19 (p. 834) | |
| *w* | wordy | 19 (p. 845) | |
| — ( ) [ ] . . . | dash, parentheses, brackets, ellipses | 26–27 (pp. 869, 870) | |
| // | faulty parallelism | 13 (p. 822) | B2 (p. A-52) |
| x | obvious error | | |

# PROOFREADING SYMBOLS

Use these standard proofreading marks when making minor corrections in your final draft. If extensive revision is necessary, type or print out a clean copy.

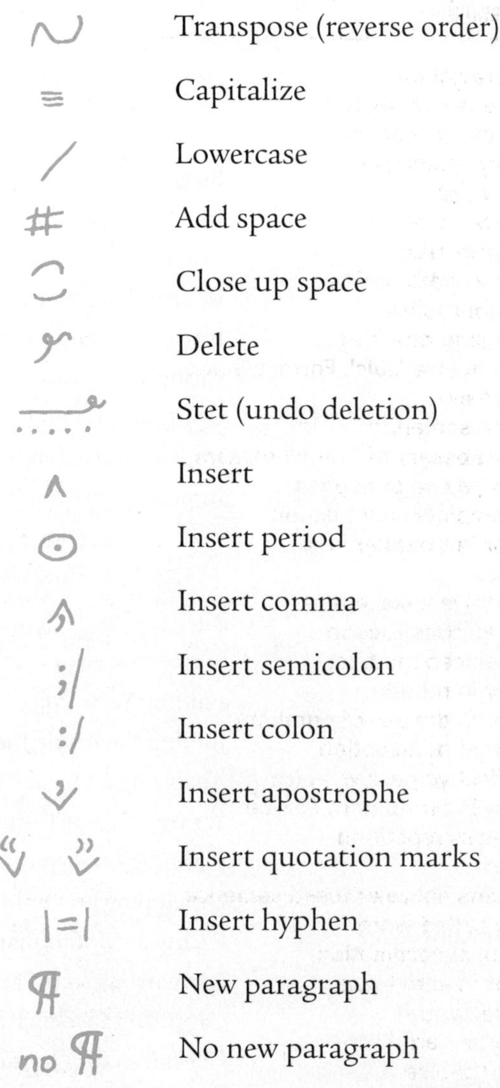


**Add your instructor's own abbreviations below:**

# Active Learning and Transferable Skills

## Learning by Doing

### A Selected List of Activities

**From** ***A Writer's Guide***



**From** ***A Writer's Research Manual***



## Take Action

### Self-Assessment Flowcharts for Improving Your Writing



## Resources for Building Transferable Skills